Central America in the Nineteenth and Twentieth Centuries
an annotated bibliography

Reference
Publications
in
Latin American
Studies

William V. Jackson,
Editor

Central America in the
Nineteenth and Twentieth Centuries
an annotated bibliography

KENNETH J. GRIEB

G.K. HALL &CO.
70 LINCOLN STREET, BOSTON, MASS.

Library of Congress Cataloging-in-Publication Data

Grieb, Kenneth J.
  Central America in the nineteenth and twentieth centuries.

  (Reference publications in Latin American studies)
  Includes index.
  1. Central America—Bibliography.   I. Title.
II. Series.
Z1437.G74   1988   [F1428]   016.9728   87-28240
ISBN 0-8161-8130-6

This publication is printed on permanent/durable acid-free paper
MANUFACTURED IN THE UNITED STATES OF AMERICA

For my parents

Contents

The Author   viii
Preface   ix
Acknowledgments   xiii
Abbreviations and Acronyms   xv
Location Symbols   xvii

General Central America   1
Belize   101
Costa Rica   119
El Salvador   223
Guatemala   261
Honduras   397
Nicaragua   443

Author Index   511
Subject Index   537

The Author

Kenneth J. Grieb is John McNaughton Rosebush Professor of history and international studies, coordinator of international studies, and director of the Interdisciplinary Center at the University of Wisconsin-Oshkosh. He received his B.A. and M.A. degrees from the University of Buffalo (now the State University of New York at Buffalo) and his Ph.D. from Indiana University.

Dr. Grieb is the author of The United States and Huerta (University of Nebraska Press, 1969), The Latin American Policy of Warren G. Harding (Texas Christian University Press, 1st printing, 1976, 2d printing, 1977), and Guatemalan Caudillo: The Regime of Jorge Ubico, Guatemala--1931-1944 (Ohio University Press, 1979); co-author of Essays on Miguel Angel Asturias (University of Wisconsin-Milwaukee, 1973) and Latin American Government Leaders (Arizona State University Press, 1st edition, 1970, 2d edition, 1975); and editor-in-chief of the Research Guide to Central America and the Caribbean (University of Wisconsin Press, 1985). He is also the author of numerous articles and book reviews that have appeared in a wide range of professional journals, and has contributed articles relating to Latin America and diplomatic history to several volumes, handbooks, and encyclopedias. Grieb has also presented papers to numerous professional conferences.

His service to professional organizations includes two terms as chairman and one as executive secretary of the Caribe-Centro America Committee of the Conference on Latin American History; terms as President of the Midwest Association for Latin American Studies and the North Central Council of Latin Americanists; and membership on the Constitution Committee of Sigma Iota Rho, the International Studies Honor Society. He currently serves as a member of the board of editors of The Americas and The Historian.

Preface

PURPOSE

This volume is intended to facilitate research about and knowledge of Central America and its nations by providing a broad but selective guide to books dealing with Central America since independence. Although it encompasses a broad range of disciplines and subjects, the primary focus is on the social sciences. It spans existing publications dealing with Central America and its nations, including the local and international, the scholarly, polemical and whimsical, and the systematic and broad. The extent of such literature certainly remains terra incognita to scholars in many fields. The purpose of this guide is to aid researchers interested in the region by identifying works that deal with a broad range of themes, by providing sufficient information about them to enable the user to assess their utility in research, and by indicating libraries where they are available. Its comprehensiveness should facilitate direct investigation of the Central American nations and peoples as well as enhance the role of the isthmus in comparative and general studies by providing a key to the existing secondary literature, scholarly studies, memoirs, observations, travelogues, official publications, and other monographic resources.

As in any such work, selectivity was necessary owing to the vast array of publications and the limits of available space. Although this guide takes a comprehensive approach, it was still impossible to include everything.

SCOPE

The Central American definition of the region is employed. This guide therefore focuses on the five core countries, Guatemala, Honduras, El Salvador, Nicaragua, and Costa Rica. The inclusion of Belize but not of Panama reflects the viewpoint of residents in the area; their outlook stems from the fact that Panama was not part of the Captaincy General of Central America during Colonial days and its evolution after independence differed from that of the five core countries of the isthmus. Each of these six nations is represented by a country section. While works dealing exclusively with Panama are consequently outside the scope of this guide, items dealing with the controversy regarding potential canal locations can be found within the Nicaragua section, since they affected that nation. The coverage extends from the era of the independence movement, generally beginning in 1810, to the present. Works with imprints through 1980 are included.

This bibliography lists only books of more than twelve pages in length issued in typeset form in bound volumes, primarily by trade and scholarly publishers, that deal exclusively or principally with Central America or one or more of its countries. Books that deal only partly with the region, such as the memoirs of diplomats who have served there, are included only if they focus on the isthmus or devote a large proportion of their pages to its countries. Space precluded listing works with only a single chapter or brief portions dealing with the area, even though this decision excludes certain items of significance to some social-science researchers. Items mimeographed, photo offset from typescript, microfilmed, or reproduced by any other informal means are excluded, except in rare instances when they provide vital data unobtainable in monographic form.

Journals, periodicals, articles, and items that are serial in nature are excluded. (This includes the annual reports of the various government bodies and presidents.) Theses and dissertations are included only if subsequently published by a trade or scholarly press. Congressional hearings and debates, volumes dealing with personal legal issues, and Corona Funebre-type works are excluded. Other special commemorative volumes appear only if they contain substantial scholarly studies or material likely to be of use to scholars. Standard primary-school textbooks from the Central American nations and popular tour guides are not listed unless deemed to contain sufficiently detailed information to be of interest to a broader audience, such as historians. Texts prepared for higher education that deal specifically with the region are listed.

In the legal realm, only codifications of laws or indexes to them are included; individual laws and annual compilations are omitted. Treaties, constitutions, contracts, agreements, and diplomatic documents are treated similarly, that is, items published singly are not included but compilations, indexes, or studies of such items are listed. For example, compilations of all the treaties of a given nation or volumes collecting diplomatic notes or documents appear, while items limited to individual treaties or notes do not. Exceptions are made for single items only when they involve questions that became major political issues or affected a dispute covered in broader works that are listed. There are listings for collections of constitutions for each nation, but not of individual constitutions.

While this bibliography contains citations from many fields, its principal focus is the social sciences, particularly the political, social, and economic evolution of the nations and the region. Scientific works are included only if pertinent to economic development or social and political issues (e.g., studies dealing with resources, climate, agricultural production, and the impact of earthquakes or volcanic eruptions). Excluded are those examining general geological structure or detailing specific information about particular volcanes, along with agricultural "how to do it" books designed to aid farming or to promote particular or potential crops. Travelogues are entered if they deal principally or exclusively with the region; this includes works providing observations both on flora and fauna and on society and/or politics, with annotations distinguishing between them. Limitations of space precluded listing scientific studies on individual plant or animal forms such as orchids, grasses, amphibians, or insects found in the region.

Literary works required distillation through the selection criteria listed above, given the vast number of publications in this field. Selection was based primarily on content rather than literary merit; listings consist of items available in book form with political and social content. Hence only literary works set in and dealing with the isthmus or the individual countries and focusing on their problems, development, history, political life and social situation since independence appear in this guide, and annotations for novels are more extensive than for poetry or other forms, reflecting the fact that they deal with these issues in greater depth. While poetry is a major literary form in the isthmus, only a small portion of it fits these criteria, and the annotations focus only on subject matter. Short stories, another major form in the region, are represented more fully. Works dealing with folklore, local lifestyles, or regional traditions were considered to have social and political content and are included, but patriotic exhortations are omitted. As in the case of the social sciences, items dealing only partly or briefly with the region were excluded. Publications by major authors from the region dealing with general themes or with other parts of the world are beyond the scope of this guide. Anthologies are included only if they encompass works dealing with social themes or provide historically significant literary background about the writers. Literary analyses are represented only if they deal with the themes of works whose content results in their inclusion. Those focusing on literary values, styles, and European influences on the writers are omitted. While these criteria mean that purely literary criticism and some forms of literature are beyond the scope of the present guide, literary scholars will find numerous entries useful to them. Only comprehensive studies of the significance and origins of national anthems and symbols are included, with patriotic or literary works dealing with them omitted. Volumes detailing such items as postage stamps and coins are treated similarly, that is, only comprehensive scholarly works are included in limited numbers, with collector's guides generally omitted. Studies of folk music are included, while compilations of song lyrics are not, unless accompanied by scholarly analyses.

METHODOLOGY AND COLLECTIONS COVERED

This bibliography is based on the collections of the four major research libraries with the largest holdings dealing with Central America--two in the United States and two in the isthmus. To be sure, entries also reflect extensive bibliographic searches through all existing guides for Latin America and those dealing with the countries of the region, as well as review of the bibliographies in existing social-science monographs dealing with Central America. The volume is intended, however, to emphasize the holdings of the four major repositories. Hence works found in these collections contain library symbols for each of these four depositories if they are present in their collections. The institutions and their symbols are the Library of Congress in Washington (DLC), the Tulane University Library in New Orleans (LNHT), the National Library of Guatemala in Guatemala City (Biblioteca Nacional de Guatemala) (BNG), and the National Library of Costa Rica in San José (Biblioteca Nacional de Costa Rica) (BNCR). The Library of Congress presents a special situation because it also contains the Luís Dobles Segreda Collection, which, although purchased many years ago, remains an uncataloged separate group within the library. This bibliography consequently provides researchers their first access to that collection, as it was surveyed in its entirety to select appropriate items fitting the criteria indicated. The citations from this group contain a different symbol, DLC-LDS. Because the collection consists of bound volumes, with items in random order, most of the references contain a volume number, which would be necessary to locate a specific item. A single volume is indicated even if the group contains multiple editions.

The editor visited each of these four institutions to work with their Central American holdings volume by volume rather than relying on their card catalogs. The National Library of Guatemala (Biblioteca Nacional de Guatemala) and the National Library of Costa Rica (Biblioteca Nacional de Costa Rica) were surveyed during 1977, and the Library of Congress (including the Luís Dobles Segreda Collection) and the Tulane University Library in 1978. Items published after those dates through the 1980 cutoff date have been verified in individual collections, but not necessarily in all of them.

It is hoped that by indicating the presence of copies of works cited in all four institutions, this guide will provide researchers with access to these works at the major depository closest to them. Of course, the user should remember that, despite its size, this bibliography is inevitably selective, in accordance with the criteria indicated above.

Entries for items not found in one of the four libraries usually indicate a single library symbol, identifying one location in a United States institution--wherever possible one of the principal libraries for Latin American research. Entries with no location symbols are not listed in the National Union Catalog (or are listed without a library code), and were consulted in private collections. A few items appear without annotation, representing either volumes whose titles were sufficiently descriptive, recent issues that appeared in the final stages of the preparation of this work, or items not seen by the editor (which however are verified, either through the National Union Catalog or through at least two listings from researchers who have handled the works). Such items are kept to a minimum. Of course, location symbols were not available for some recently published works not yet cataloged or entered in the National Union Catalog; they are listed because their existence can be confirmed, even if their location cannot. It is probable that most such works will eventually appear in the four principal libraries employed.

ARRANGEMENT

There are separate sections for each of the six nations covered, plus a General Central America section. Each has its own numbering sequence.

Volumes dealing with a single country are in the section for that country, while those dealing with the region as a whole are in the General section. Works dealing with two or more countries normally appear in the General section unless they focus principally on one nation, with minor references to others--in that case they are filed in the section dealing with the principal nation they treat. Similarly works referring to other areas or themes outside Central America but dealing only partially with a single Central American nation will be found under that nation.

Boundary disputes between Central American nations and issues involving more than one isthmian country, such as wars, are filed in the General section, save in the case of the Guatemala-Belize issue, which is filed in the Belize section. Items relating to the William Walker episode, the Mosquito Coast, and the canal location question are filed under Nicaragua, unless they deal principally with the involvement of another isthmian nation in that event or question. Studies of the independence movement in general are found in the General file unless limited to actions in a single state.

The works are filed alphabetically by author within sections. Whenever possible, they are listed under the author's full compound surname, as in general Spanish and Latin American practice, rather than under shortened names. Hence full first names are used rather than initials, as well as double surnames rather than single or partial last names, even when these are not listed on the title page or are not used in cataloging in the United States or in the National Union Catalog. Thus Roberto Luís López Gómez will be found under "López Gómez, Roberto Luís," as in proper Latin American usage. Even if the author shortens his name to Roberto

López G. or Roberto López, he will be listed under full compound surname if available, to differentiate authors with similar names from each other. In cases where listings in the National Union Catalog sometimes employ Gómez, his maternal name, the author index contains a cross-reference.

Wherever possible, volumes are filed under personal author or editor rather than corporate author. Hence a study issued by the Banco Central of Honduras but actually edited or written by Manuel Tosco is listed under Tosco, not the bank. Similarly, items sponsored by government ministries are often listed under the minister's name if signed by him, rather than under the ministry. The author index provides cross-references.

Items issued by government agencies that show the agency as author, in the absence of an identifiable individual, are listed under the heading "(Country), Gov't of," which in turn is alphabetized at the end of authors using the country name. Hence nongovernmental organizations appear together, before governmental agencies as authors, meaning that "Guatemala, Sociedad de Abogados," preceeds "Guatemala, Gov't of." Within "(Country), Gov't of," cabinet ministries are filed as "Ministerio," even if they call themselves Secretarias, to file all items from a single entity in one place in spite of name changes reflecting governmental turnovers. The ministries are alphabetized with (Country), Gov't of, Ministerio de . . .," by Spanish title of the office if that is the nation's language. Wherever possible entries are placed under the ministries rather than sub-units, just as entries for other agencies are placed under the agency rather than subentity. For example, a university is used in most cases as the author or publisher rather than an institute within the university. Presidential press offices pose a special problem since several of the countries employ public information offices within the Presidential Secretariat, and these offices seem to be more susceptible to name changes than other entities. Hence all are filed together under "(Country), Gov't of, Presidencia, Secretaría de Información," regardless of title changes. Within each author items are arranged alphabetically by title in accordance with standard filing and cataloging rules.

While compound surnames have been employed in accordance with traditional Latin American usage, some concessions to common Yankee usage were necessary. The nation of El Salvador is alphabetized under E as is common in English, rather than under S as would be its correct usage in its native Spanish. In addition, items beginning with Ch are alphabetized in the Cs as in English usage, rather than as a separate letter of the alphabet as in Spanish, which would have placed them at the end of the other Cs. Latin American users will need to keep these aspects in mind.

FORM OF USAGE

Each entry consists of author (with pseudonym where appropriate); title; number of volumes (if a series); imprint information including city, publisher, and date when available; list of supplementary information such as notes or index where appropriate; an annotation; and a location symbol.

All entries are based on the original edition, using that title and providing full imprint information for that edition to the extent available. Imprint data are also provided for the latest known edition, with title variances noted in the annotation. Items reissued frequently list the latest edition or the notation "Many editions." Editions in other languages are also indicated, by title and with the same imprint information when available. English translations are provided only for titles in non-West European languages. Languages not using the Latin alphabet are presented only in transliterated form. Entries indicate numbers of pages and information on indexes, maps, illustrations, tables, and scholarly apparatus such as notes and bibliographies as completely as possible. The number of pages is provided for items of three volumes or less when available, but is omitted for more extensive multivolume works. This format should provide scholars using this guide with detailed information regarding the volume, its origin, and its availability.

ANNOTATIONS

The annotations are designed to indicate the content, focus, degree of scholarship, and type of approach of the work, as well as any variations from its title. The scope of the coverage, the time period involved, the purpose of the book, and its importance are emphasized, subject to availability and within space limitations for annotation. While viewpoints and approaches are identified, the purpose is to indicate content rather than to provide criticism. The presence of scholarly apparatus and citations and the basis of the work are indicated, with the time and location of the research, fieldwork, or travel provided where pertinent. Background regarding the author and his or her involvement in the episode under discussion are included where appropriate. As indicated earlier, within literary works the focus is on subject matter, not style. Of course, the degree to which such information can be provided varies with the book and its degree of focus or clarity. In a short annotation it is obviously difficult or impossible to explain a work dealing with a broad range of themes.

INDEXES

This guide contains both author and subject indexes to assist users. The Author Index gathers works by the same author that are listed in the various sections of the bibliography. It also serves to identify pseudonyms, with cross-references to the author's real name; all entries are listed under real name whenever it is known. Listings by institution also serve to identify works published under corporate auspices that are listed under the personal author's name, via cross-references.

The Subject Index will be most useful to researchers tracing a topic for comparative purposes, though it can also assist individuals in identifying works pertinent to a topic within a single country. This index contains entries both by topic and by topic within individual countries. Entries include both specific and general subjects. Hence an individual tracing a particular political party will find useful titles under the party's name and under the appropriate country, as well as under "Political Parties." Within the country entry, the subheading "Politics" identifies works relating to the politics of a particular era. Entries can also be located under the name of the individual leaders of the party, since individuals who are subjects of studies are included in the Subject Index. A researcher interested in social classes might also find useful items under "Indians," "Peasants," "Land Tenure," and "Immigration," among others.

Sections with a large number of entries in each nation, such as "Agriculture," "Politics," or "Society," are subdivided by time period into three subsections within each century, "Early" (years 00-30), "Middle" (years 30-70) and "Late" (years 70-99). Items indexed under the individual countries are cross-referenced in the general name listing, referring the user to the country sections.

Acknowledgments

Naturally in a project of this size, the compiler has received valuable assistance from many individuals during the course of gathering the information, locating the publications, and preparing the final product for publication. While the number of such individuals is far to many to allow mention of them all in this short list, I want to express appreciation to key individuals and institutions.

Given the nature of this work, special thanks go to the staffs of the four key collections utilized. I am especially grateful to Dr. William E. Carter, chief of the Hispanic Division of the Library of Congress and his entire staff, notably John Hébert, assistant chief, Georgette M. Dorn, and Everett Larsen, all of whom devoted considerable time to facilitating the efforts of the editor and offering suggestions at early stages of this project; to Dr. Thomas Niehaus, director of the Latin American Library of the Howard Tilton Library of Tulane University and his entire staff; to Señora Eva Evans V. de Sagastume, director of the Biblioteca Nacional de Guatemala and her entire staff; and to Señora Carmen Quirós Saborío, director of the Biblioteca Nacional de Costa Rica and her entire staff. Don Rigoberto Bran Azmitia, director of the Hemeroteca Nacional de Guatemala and Lic. Manuel Rubio Sánchez of the Sociedad de Geografía e Historia de Guatemala provided valuable assistance. The staff of the Forrest R. Polk Library at the University of Wisconsin-Oshkosh, particularly the Interlibrary Loan Division helped in first locating and then securing a seemingly endless list of scarce items. The final product benefitted from the suggestions of Dr. William V. Jackson of the University of Texas at Austin, and those of Janice Meagher and Karin Kiewra of G.K. Hall and Co.

The editor prepared the entries and annotations. Throughout this project, a group of highly capable student research assistants, typists, and proofreaders assisted him; they played a key role in compiling the information resulting from the research, and in preparing the final manuscript. While they are too numerous to list individually, the editor wishes to acknowledge here their valuable assistance.

Abbreviations and Acronyms

A.C.   América Central
AUFS   American Universities Field Service
C.A.   Central America
CEDAL   Congreso Centroamericano de Historia
         Demográfica, Económica y Social
CELADE   Centro Latinoamericano de Demografía
CEPAL   Comisión Económica para América Latina
         (of the United Nations)
CIDOC   Centro de Documentación (Cuernavaca,
         México)
CSUCA   Consejo Superior Universitaria
         Centroamericana
ECLA   Economic Commission on Latin America (Of the
         United Nations)
EDUCA   Editorial de la Universidad de Centro
         América
ESAPAC   Escuela Superior de Administración Pública
         de América Central (San José)
FSLN   Frenta Sandinista de Liberación Nacional
         (Nicaragua)
GPO   U.S. Government Printing Office
h.   hijo (junior)
HMSO   His (Her) Majesty's Stationary Office (Great
         Britain)
Hnos.   Hermanos
ILO   International Labor Organization
Lic.   Licenciado
MARI   Middle American Research Institute (Tulane
         University)
MLN   Movimiento de Liberación Nacional
         (Guatemala)
OAS   Organization of American States
ODECA   Organización de Estados Centro Americanos
         (Organization of Central American States)
OEA   Organización de Estados Americanos
         (Organization of American Studies)
OIT   Oficina Internacional del Trabajo
ONU   Organización des Naciones Unidas
ORIT   Organización Regional Internacional de
         Trabajadores
PAIGH   Pan American Institute of Geography and
         History
PAU   Pan American Union
PLN   Partido de Liberación Nacional (Costa Rica)
PRELAC   Programa Regional del Empleo para América
         Latina y el Caribe
ROCAP   Regional Organization for Central America
         and Panama (of the U.S. Agency for
         International Development)
SIECA   Secretario Permanente del Tratado General de
         Integración Economica Centroamericana

UCA   Universidad de Centro América José Simeon
         Cañas (San Salvador)
UFCO   United Fruit Company
UNAM   Universidad Nacional Autonoma de México
UNECLA   United Nations Economic Commission on Latin
         America
UNESCO   United Nations Educational Scientific and
         Cultural Organization

Location Symbols

AAP	Auburn University, Auburn
AzU	University of Arizona, Tucson
BNCR	Biblioteca Nacional de Costa Rica
BNG	Biblioteca Nacional de Guatemala
CLL	Los Angeles County Law Library, Los Angeles
CLU	University of California, Los Angeles
CoU	University of Colorado, Boulder
CSmH	Henry E. Huntington Library, San Marino
CSt	Stanford University Libraries, Stanford
Cst-H	Stanford University Libraries, Stanford – Hoover Institution on War, Revolution and Peace
CtY	Yale University, New Haven
CtY-D	Yale University, New Haven – Divinity School
CtY-L	Yale University, New Haven – Law Library
CU	University of California, Berkeley
CU-B	University of California, Berkeley – Bancroft Library
CU-BANC	University of California, Berkeley – Bancroft Library
DBRE	Bureau of Railway Economics. Library of the Association of American Railroads, Washington
DLC	Library of Congress, Washington
DLC-LDS	Luís Dobles Segreda Collection, Library of Congress, Washington
DNAL	U.S. National Agricultural Library, Washington
DNW	U.S. National War College Library, Fort McNair
DPU	Pan American Union Library, Washington
DS	U.S. Department of State Library, Washington
DWHO-PSB	World Health Organization, Pan American Sanitary Bureau Library, Washington, D.C.
FMU	University of Miami, Coral Gables
FU	University of Florida, Gainesville
IaAS	Iowa State University, Ames
IaU	University of Iowa, Iowa City
ICarbS	Southern Illinois University, Carbondale
ICJ	John Crerar Library, Chicago
ICN	Newberry Library, Chicago
ICU	University of Chicago, Chicago
IEdS	Southern Illinois University, Edwardsville
InU	Indiana University, Bloomington
IU	University of Illinois, Urbana
KU	University of Kansas, Lawrence
LNHT	Tulane University Library, New Orleans
LTC-WU	Land Tenure Center, University of Wisconsin, Madison
LU	Louisiana State University, Baton Rouge
MH	Harvard University, Cambridge
MH-L	Harvard University – Law School Library, Cambridge
MiU	University of Michigan, Ann Arbor
MiUL	University of Michigan – Law Library, Ann Arbor
MnU	University of Minnesota, Minneapolis
MoSW	Washington University, St. Louis
MU	University of Massachusetts, Amherst
MWelC	Wellesley College, Wellesley
NBuU	State University of New York at Buffalo
NcD	Duke University, Durham
NcGU	University of North Carolina, Greensboro
NcU	University of North Carolina, Chapel Hill
NhD	Dartmouth College, Hanover
NIC	Cornell University, Ithaca
NjP	Princeton University, Princeton
NjPT	Princeton Theological Seminary, Princeton
NN	New York Public Library
NNC	Columbia University, New York
NNCU-G	City University of New York, Graduate Center
NNH	Hispanic Society of America, New York
NNUN	United Nations Library, New York
OCl	Cleveland Public Library
OU	Ohio State University, Columbus
PHi	Historical Society of Pennsylvania, Philadelphia
PPAN	Academy of Natural Sciences, Philadelphia
PPC	College of Physicians of Philadelphia
PPG	German Society of Pennsylvania, Philadelphia
PPiU	University of Pittsburgh, Pittsburgh
PSt	Pennsylvania State University, University Park
PUMU	University of Pennsylvania – University Museum
RPB	Brown University, Providence
ScU	University of South Carolina, Columbia
TNJ	Joint University Libraries (now Vanderbilt University Library), Nashville
TU	University of Tennessee, Knoxville
TxFTC	Texas Christian University, Forth Worth
TxHU	University of Houston, Houston
TxLT	Texas Tech University, Lubbock
TxU	University of Texas, Austin
ViU	University of Virginia, Charlottesville
VtU	University of Vermont and State Agricultural College, Burlington
WaU	University of Washington, Seattle
WU	University of Wisconsin, Madison

General Central America

1 Abd-al-Majīd, Muhammad Fayīd. <u>Amrīkā al-Wustā</u> [Central America]. Cairo: Dār al-Nahdah al-Misrīyah, 1967. 207 pp.

2 Adams, Frederick Upham. <u>Conquest of the Tropics: The Story of the Creative Enterprises Conducted by the United Fruit Company</u>. Garden City, N.Y.: Doubleday, 1914. xii, 368 pp. Index, illus., maps. Reprint. New York: Arno Press, 1976, xii, 368 pp. Index, illus.
    A sympathetic account of the beginnings of the banana culture and the early days of the United Fruit Company, based on information furnished by the company and written in a chatty, tour-book style. Contains chapters on Costa Rica and Guatemala, the latter including El Salvador, as well as on other Latin American countries and accounts of general aspects. Lavishly illustrated, with numerous maps of the region, countries, and cities. The author lauds the company, hailing the commercialization of the tropical regions of the globe as the next step in the advance of civilization and calling for increased efforts by Yankees to exploit the commercial possibilities of Latin America for fun and profit. DLC LNHT BNCR

3 Adams, Richard Newbold. <u>Cultural Surveys of Panama-Nicaragua-Guatemala-El Salvador-Honduras</u>. Washington, D.C.: Pan American Sanitary Bureau, 1957. iii, 669 pp. Biblio., maps, tables. Latest ed. Detroit: Blaine Ethridge, 1976. iii, 669 pp. Biblio., illus.
    An important collection of anthropological research papers that describes the rural culture of each individual nation, based on surveys by teams of trained anthropologists of thirty to fifty different communities in each, conducted during the 1950s. The emphasis is on distinguishing between the Indian and ladino culture in the rural areas. Descriptions of numerous aspects of life such as the household, family, agriculture, and the local social structure are included. DLC LNHT

4 Adams, Richard Newbold, et al. <u>Community Culture and National Change</u>. New Orleans: Tulane University Press, 1972. 275 pp. Biblio., notes, illus., map, tables.

Five anthropological papers by various authors dealing with culture and culture change in Indian communities, three focusing on Guatemala, one on Costa Rica, and one on Yucatan. Each was written separately and deals with a different community, based on secondary sources and field research, providing illustrations, statistics, and graphs. The focus is on description of the principal aspects of the life of each community, accenting changes in the 1945-66 period. DLC

5 Águilar, Arturo. <u>Hombres de la independencia de Nicaragua y Costa Rica</u>. León: Tipografía la Patria, 1940. 248 pp. Biblio., illus.
    Essays about the role of eighteen individuals in the independence of Central America and of Nicaragua, focusing on individuals of Nicaraguan origin rather than the more generally known isthmian heroes, and dealing with the period of the 1820s. The essays vary in size from two to fifty pages, and also in quality, some containing extensive quotations, others narrative, and some being merely in <u>Vita</u> form. All are based on secondary works or published documents. DLC

6 Aguirre, José Ignacio. <u>La fiera vertical</u>. Mexico: n.p., 1947. 212 pp. Illus. 2d ed. Mazatenango, Guatemala: Tipografía Byron Zadik, 1964. 204 pp.
    A description, in novelistic form, of conditions in Guatemala and Honduras as observed by the author, criticizing the Yankee influence, calling for a unified Latin American effort at reform and rejection of Yankee dominance. The volume includes the author's thesis, dealing with international law as the basis for Latin American action against the Northern colossus. Includes some descriptive passages regarding the various zones of Honduras and Guatemala. DLC LNHT BNG

7 Alemán, Hugo Gilberto. <u>La mano de obra en Centroamérica</u>. San Salvador: ODECA, 1970. vi, 243 pp. Illus., tables.
    An ODECA-sponsored study that seeks to compile statistics regarding the region's labor situation and project future needs and problems and that deals with each country and

(Alemán, Hugo Gilberto)

the region as a whole, though with the analysis focused on the region. Includes figures regarding population growth, density, age and sex distribution, employment, social security programs, other relevant government agencies, etc. The need for long-range planning to meet expanding population growth is emphasized, with proposals for education, service needs, and economic expansion. DLC LNHT BNCR

8   _____. Trabajadores y condiciones de trabajo en Centroamérica. San Salvador: ODECA, 1971. 111 pp.

A general summary of current labor conditions throughout the isthmus, focusing on contemporary problems. Based on the author's earlier and more extensive volume. DLC

9   Alemán, Vicente. Fechas de sangre. San Salvador: Editorial Nosotros, 1946. 15 pp.

A series of poems acclaiming the heroics of the various clashes of the contemporary Central American revolutions, with a separate piece for each of the dates on which the events occurred. The emphasis is on emotion rather than narration, with country, city, and day, but not year, specified. DPU

10   Alemán Bolaños, Gustavo. Centro y Sud-América. Santiago: Imprenta Universitaria, 1915. 96 pp.

Originally published in El Mercurio of Santiago and other unidentified newspapers in Buenos Aires and Rio de Janeiro, these articles by a well-known scholar-journalist deal with relations between Central and South America and place isthmian questions within their hemispheric context. He favors isthmian union, and advocates more attention to the isthmus by the ABC countries. DLC BNCR

11   _____. Espectacular viaje de Gato Félix y Ratoncito Pérez a través de la América Central. Guatemala: Sánchez & de Guise, 1950. 96 pp. Illus.

A tour of Central America, in allegory form, using as protagonists the Walt Disney characters Felix the Cat and Mickey Mouse. The author recounts their experiences in short-story form, explaining the various characteristics of the region and its peoples and customs through the observations of the characters. DLC

12   _____. Lo que aprendieron el buen Gato Félix y el inteligente Ratoncito Pérez. Guatemala: Sánchez & de Guise, 1930. 39 pp. Illus. 7th ed. Guatemala: Sánchez & de Guise, 1950. 30 pp.

A reader designed for young children in the primary grades, using the cartoon characters to teach basic civics, morals, and hygiene, with some drawings, but relying mainly on the written text. DLC

13   _____. La serena inquietud: memorias. Guatemala: Sánchez & de Guise, 1926. 109 pp.

A memoir of the travels of this well-known Nicaraguan journalist, written between 1910 and 1922. Covers visits to several of the isthmian nations and to other parts of Latin America and the United States. Though memoirs, they are exceptionally brief for so prolific a writer; they contain only a broad outline of his experiences, focusing on his career as a journalist and his political observations about the nations visited. DLC BNG

14   Alfaro, Olmedo. El peligro Antillano en la América Central: la defensa de la raza. Panamá: Imprenta Nacional, 1924. 18 pp.

A pamphlet warning about the threat posed by the continued immigration of black people from the islands into Panama. Notes that the Panamanian labor movement has protested that blacks are usurping jobs from local residents and threatening the "right of the existence of the Panamanian people." Offers statistics from other countries regarding the rapid reproduction rate of blacks, stating that it is time all Central America awoke to this threat, which will spread to the other states. Illustrates the fact that the prevailing racial prejudices of the era were present in the isthmus and not confined merely to Gringos. DLC

15   Alfaro, Ricardo Joaquín. Costa Rica y Panamá: en defensa de los que quieren paz y amistad. Panamá: Imprenta Nacional, 1927. 13 pp.

A defense of the Panamanian claims regarding the validity of the White award in the boundary dispute, contending that the Costa Rican position on the White award is inconsistent with its stance toward the Loubet ruling. Emphasizes the necessity of a legal settlement to prevent conflict. DLC-LDS-394

16   _____. Límites entre Panamá y Costa Rica. Panamá: Tipografía "El Istmo," 1913. viii, 112 pp.

A study regarding the Panama-Costa Rica boundary dispute, prepared by the attorney of the Panamanian legation in Washington as part of the Panamanian case for the arbitration. Defends the Panamanian claims and traces their historical antecedents. DLC BNCR

17   Allwood Paredes, Juan. Consideraciones acerca de una política centroamericana en salud pública. San Salvador: Impresora La Unión, 1969. 68 pp.

A summary of the author's Los recursos de la salud pública en Centro América. DPU

18   _____. Los recursos de la salud pública en Centro América. San Salvador: Imprenta La Unión, 1968. 162 pp. Biblio., notes, illus., maps, tables. 2d ed. San Salvador: ODECA, 1969. 162 pp. Biblio., notes, illus., maps, tables.

An ODECA-sponsored study that compiles data and statistics about the state of health, health-care facilities, and the population in each of the nations. Projects needs for the 1970s, makes proposals, and provides cost estimates through 1980. Includes figures on population trends, doctors, nurses, aides, hospitals and other health-care facilities, international aid, and costs for each of the nations and the region as a whole. DLC LNHT

19 Alonso, Isidro, and Gines Garrido. La iglesia en América Central y el Caribé: estructuras eclesiásticas. Bogotá: Federación Internacional de los Institutos Católicas de Investigaciones Sociales, 1962. 282 pp. Illus., maps.
      A summary and compilation of data about the current church structure in the region, containing chapters on each of the isthmian and several island nations and providing statistics and summaries of clerical and diocesan organization, clerical function, distribution, age, national origin, and trends within the church and the clergy. Offers a good deal of useful and scarce data, though without information allowing historical comparison to note changes or trends. DLC LNHT

20 Alvarado, José Antonio. Continuación de las observaciones sobre el comercio de Centro América. Guatemala: Imprenta Nueva, 1833. 29 pp.
      A continuation of the following item.

21 _____. Observaciones sobre el comercio de Centroamérica: en general todo comercio exterior no puede convenir a una nación que carece de capitales, y cuya agricultura y fábricas están decaídas por falta de capitales. Guatemala: Imprenta Nueva, 1833. 33 pp.
      A discussion of the commercial and development possibilities of the region, contending that despite its resources it lacks capital, an important ingredient, and that Europe is interested only in large-scale trade, not small-scale exchanges. Consequently, it advocates greater development efforts, principally through encouraging immigration, although it expresses skepticism about the prospects for development in the meantime. The author, a priest, bases his comments on the theories of the economist Juan Bautista Say, whose works are quoted extensively throughout the text. DLC

22 Alvarado, Miguel Antonio, ed. Asuntos de Centro América: reprodución de documentos. Guatemala: Ministerio de Educación Pública, 1969. 147 pp.
      A reproduction of a portion of the Memoria de relaciones exteriores, justicia, comercio, e agricultura of 1877, written by Anselmo H. Rivas, recounting the events of the turbulent 1870s that led to the treaties of 1876 involving Guatemala, El Salvador, and Nicaragua. Includes the text of the accords and appropriate background communications. DLC LNHT BNG

23 Alvarado, Néstor Enrique. El gran rebelde: vida y obra de Francisco Morazán. Tegucigalpa: Universidad Nacional Autónoma de Honduras, 1967. 68 pp.
      Part of a series of "perfiles heroicos," this work fits that title in its treatment of Morazán, though in the process it provides an effective overview of the independence era, albeit within the prevailing nationalistic stereotypes. DLC

24 Alvarado García, Ernesto. La obra progresista del general Francisco Morazán. Tegucigalpa: Ministerio de Educación Pública, 1960. 36 pp.
      A brief pamphlet that stresses the policies of Morazán while he held power and laudes his foresight and the beneficial results of his efforts to stamp out Colonial remnants and open the country to growth. DLC LNHT

25 Alvaro Menéndez, Leal [Alvaro Menen Desleal, pseud.]. Ciudad, casa de todos: contribución al estudio del fenómeno urbano, plan general (proyecto) para las ciudades capitales de América Central. San Salvador: Ministerio de Educación, 1968. 93 pp. Illus. 2d ed. San Salvador: Ministerio de Educación, 1970. 93 pp. Illus.
      DLC

26 _____. Revolución en el país que edificó un castillo de hadas y otros cuentos maravillosos. San José: EDUCA, 1971. 95 pp.
      A series of satirical short stories. The principal one, dealing with a fictitious and confused revolution in a small agricultural country in Central America, lampoons dictatorship by means of the story of a regime that regressed to medieval customs. DLC BNCR

27 Amador, Alberto. Memoria de la cuestión de límites entre México y Guatemala y de los trabajos ejecutados en la frontera de ambos países por la Comisión Mexicana de Reconocimiento de dicha frontera, primero, y después, por la Comisión Mexicana de Límites para el trazo de la línea divisoria entre ambas repúblicas. Mexico: Ministerio de Relaciones Exteriores, 1931. 683 pp. Illus., maps, tables.
      A detailed account of the case from the Mexican viewpoint, tracing the numerous efforts to solve it, the treaties and commissions involved, and detailing the attempts to mark the frontier, with extensive excerpts from appropriate documents. DLC

28 Amaya Amador, Ramón. Los brujos de Ilamatepeque. Tegucigalpa: Editorial Paulino Valladares, 1958. 218 pp.
      One of many novels of this communist militant, as ever adopting the viewpoint of the oppressed peasant, calling for class warfare, and denouncing the capitalist imperialists as exploiters; vividly portrays the state of the peasants and draws on his own experience as well as on ideology. DLC

29 Amaya Leclair, Manuel, et al. Hacia la integración física de Centro América: principales proyectos para 1969-1973. Managua: Banco Centroamericano de Integración Económica, 1969. 138 pp. Maps.
      A publication of the Banco Centroamericano de Integración Económica, detailing its plan to provide loans for an effort to link transportation facilities in the various isthmian

nations, thereby promoting what it calls "physical integration" to assist regional trade and the Common Market. DPU

30 Anderson, Chandler P. Costa Rica-Panama Arbitration: Synopsis of Case and Argument for Costa Rica in Reply. Washington, D.C.: Gibson Brothers, 1914. 49 pp.
The Costa Rican reply to the Panamanian case, prepared by a noted Yankee jurist who represented that nation in the proceedings that eventually led to the White decision upholding the Loubet award. DLC

31 _____. Nicaragua-Honduras Boundary Mediation. n.p., 1920. 217 pp.
An analysis of the question by a Yankee diplomat and international lawyer who served as consul for Nicaragua in the proceedings. DLC

32 Anderson Morúa, Luís. Los Estados Unidos y las ocupaciones británicos en Centro América. Havana: Talleres Tipográficos de Cansa y Cía, 1940. 60 pp. Notes.
The United States and British Occupancy in Central America. Guatemala: N.p., 1943.
A study by a noted Costa Rican international lawyer and jurist of the Anglo-American disputes regarding Central America during the nineteenth century. He credits the Yankees with making a "colossal effort" to oust the British from the isthmus, but notes that they were primarily concerned about potential canal routes. He concludes that the 1863 Anglo-Guatemalan treaty regarding Belize was a violation of the Monroe Doctrine, the keystone of Yankee policy, because it ceded to England territory over which it did not have a previous legal title, and therefore that the 1863 accord is null and void. DLC

33 _____. El gobierno de facto. San José: Imprenta Lehmann, 1925. 78 pp. 2d ed. San José: Editorial Costa Rica, 1950. 44 pp. Illus.
A legal study examining a question of considerable concern to Central America, though dealing with it in terms of legal theory rather than specific cases. He concludes that states do not lose their rights merely because of a coup, and hence that de facto governments must be dealt with. DLC-LDS-338

34 _____. El laudo Loubet: contribución al estudio de la cuestión de límites entre Costa Rica y Panamá. San José: Imprenta Alsina, 1911. 96 pp. Notes, maps.
A study of the Costa Rican-Panamanian boundary dispute and the arbitration decision by French president Loubet, supporting the decision. Prepared as part of the Costa Rican case in the new arbitration resulting from the Panamanian objections to the Loubet award. DLC-LDS-173 BNCR

35 _____. Límites entre Honduras y Nicaragua: validez y fuerza obligatoria del laudo de S.M. el rey de España. San José: Imprenta

Borrasé, 1938. 2d ed. Tegucigalpa: Tipografía Nacional, 1957. 190 pp.
A study supporting the Honduran contention that the 1906 ruling of the king of Spain, acting as arbitor under the Bonilla-Gámez Treaty, was fully in compliance with the accord and therefore had definitively settled the dispute, making subsequent Nicaraguan claims invalid. The title varies slightly in the second edition. DLC DLC-LDS-881 LNHT

36 Apstein, Theodore, Ben F. Carruthers, and Ellen Gut. The Universities of Costa Rica, El Salvador, Guatemala, Honduras, Nicaragua, and Panama. Washington, D.C.: PAU, 1947. x, 186 pp. Tables.
Discusses each of the national universities separately, providing basic data regarding calendar, organization, programs, costs, admission requirements, grading systems, libraries, etc., as well as a brief description of the programs of each faculty. Nicaragua is the only country for which information regarding more than the National University is provided. BNCR

37 Araya Pochet, Carlos. Centroamérica y los prolegómenos de la guerra nacional de 1856. San José: Universidad de Costa Rica, 1968. 24 pp. Biblio., notes.
A brief essay, based on appropriate secondary sources, that analyzes the Central American milieu prior to the Yankee interventions, emphasizing the church-state struggle, and the class structure and social stratification of the society as typical of all of Latin America. The author concludes that the opportunities offered by the resulting instability to the great powers, which were then seeking markets as well as raw materials, made Central America a tempting site for intervention. BNCR

38 Arbingast, Stanley A., et al. Atlas of Central America. Austin: University of Texas Press, 1979. 65 pp. Maps, tables.
A collection of fourteen-by-eleven-inch color maps of each of the isthmian states, with basic information. For each republic there are maps showing physical features, population density, agricultural zones, mineral resources, transportation facilities, and economic activity. Surprisingly, there are no maps showing the internal provinces as such, though the provincial boundaries are indicated on many maps showing other features. A valuable collection of accurate, up-to-date maps. DLC LNHT

39 Arce, Manuel A., ed. Modelo de curriculum. Guatemala: Ministerio de Educación Pública, 1964. 127 pp. Illus.
A model curriculum for the primary schools of Central America, prepared under the auspices of the Alliance for Progress, the Regional Organization for Central America and Panama, and the Organization of Central American States. BNG

40 Arce, Manuel A., and Donald A. Lemke. An Experiment in Regionalism: The Central American Textbook Project. Milwaukee: University of Wisconsin--Milwaukee, 1970. 43 pp. Notes, tables.

A summary of the efforts to coordinate the production of a common grade-school textbook for use throughout the region, involving contributions by teachers from the various nations. Explains the project and its problems, and draws lessons from it as a case study for future joint efforts. LNHT

41 Arce, Manuel José. Breves indicaciones sobre la reorganización de Centro América escritas por José Manuel Arce en la ciudad de San Salvador. San Salvador: Dutriz Hermanos, 1846. 80 pp.

One of the leaders of Central American independence presents his thoughts regarding the situation of the Federation of Central America in view of the threat of its splitting into separate republics. Advocates a new constitutional convention to reorganize the government to save the Federation by eliminating present causes for dispute and expanding the role of the separate state governments within the scope of the Federation. DLC BNCR

42 _____. Memoria de la conducta pública y administrativa de Manuel José Arce, durante el período de su presidencia: escrita en defensa de las calumnias que contra su persona han vertido los mismos que rebelaron contra el gobierno y la nación de Centro América. Mexico: Imprenta de Galvan, 1830. Latest ed. San Salvador: n.p., 1959. 140 pp.

An official account of the actions of his regime, written to counter various charges made by opponents. Stresses his programs and plans and the benefits to the nation. NN

43 _____. Memoria del general Manuel José Arce, primer presidente de Centro América; comentada por Modesto Barrios; breves indicaciones sobre la reorganización de Centro América y documentos inéditos relacionados con la incorporación de la provincia de Sonsonate al estado de El Salvador. San Salvador: Tipografía La Luz, 1903. 330 pp. Latest ed. San Salvador: Ministerio de Cultura, 1959. 314 pp. Notes, illus.

The memoirs of the first president of Central America and independence leader, defending and explaining his actions during the turbulent years from 1811 to 1828. Originally published in Mexico in 1830, the volume has passed through many editions, reflecting its importance for the region; several have various explanatory notes appended. It contains a collection of documents, correspondence, and decrees from the era, Arce's proposals for the political reorganization of the isthmus, and documentation regarding the annexation of the province of Sonsonate by El Salvador. Includes items CA41-42 plus additional material. DLC LNHT BNCR

44 Ardón, Victor M. La educación agropecuaria en Centro América. Guatemala: Universidad de San Carlos, 1964. 95 pp. Map, tables.

A survey of education in the realm of agriculture and cattle ranching, including appropriate tables. Covers the isthmus in general, with specific chapters for each of the five republics. Includes recommendations, arising from a joint effort by the University of San Carlos and Michigan State University under the auspices of AID, for meeting future needs. BNG

45 _____. La educación industrial en Centro América. Guatemala: Imprenta Hispania, 1965. 103 pp. Biblio., maps, tables.

A survey of contemporary industrial and vocational education in the five republics, with appropriate classification by types and subfields, and tables comparing the availability of such instruction. The study recommends expansion of this field, better organization through national commissions, fixed national curricula, and increased regional coordination and cooperation. LNHT BNG BNCR

46 Ardón F., José Enrique. Monseñor y Josefina. Guatemala: Tipografía Nacional, 1972. 199 pp.

An historical novel set in independence times and dealing with the lives of the various political figures during the Mexican intervention and the struggle for independence. DLC BNG

47 Argüello, Santiago. La fraternidad universal y el centroamericanismo. Guatemala: Tipografía Nacional, 1934. 31 pp.

One of the unionist leader's many calls for the unification of the isthmus, this one citing the modern trends of universal ties among nations to contend that the moment is propitious and that Central American federation would be compatible with the larger world ideal. He emphasizes that this will be a gradual process, one that will need much advance preparation to promote a broader Central American consciousness among the youth. He hails the efforts of the regime of General Jorge Ubico at the 1934 Central American Conference and Ubico's concept of a union of people, not of governments, to be achieved through increasing contacts and cooperation among the populace of the various states. LNHT BNG

48 _____. Mi mensaje a la juventud, y otras orientaciones. Mexico: Editorial Herrero, 1928. 262 pp. 2d ed. Guatemala: Tipografía Nacional, 1935. 320 pp.

A well-known Nicaraguan intellectual and unionist leader offers a message intended for the future, indicating the principal preoccupations he sees ahead for Central America. Among the diverse themes are the importance of culture, the threat of Yankee imperialism, legal studies, feminism, the relation between state and church, and historical studies. The emphasis is on the virtues of isthmian union.

In the preface to the second edition the
author comments that Yankee imperialism has
become a less serious problem due to the Good
Neighbor Policy. DLC-LDS-426 LNHT BNG BNCR

49 Arias de Blois, Jorge. La población de
Centroamérica y sus perspectivas. Guatemala:
Universidad de San Carlos, 1966. 59 pp.
Tables.
     The rector of the University of San Carlos
provides an overview of Central America's
population, classifying it by age, literacy,
and civil status. He discusses population
growth since 1940 and the factors that account
for its expansion, such as the declining death
rate. After considering other factors, such
as the birth rate, he discusses the potential
implications for the area of future population
expansion and its impact on economic development and the need for social services, though
refraining from specific projections. DLC
LNHT BNG

50 d'Arlach, H. de T. Souvenirs de l'Amérique
Centrale. Paris: Charpentier Libraire, 1850.
168 pp.
     The memoirs of a French consul in Central
America, providing his view of the events of
the immediate post-independence period. While
the commentary reflects his scant grounding in
local history and the European viewpoint characteristic of that era, his account of the
local factors enabling the rise of the regime
of Rafael Carrera is illuminating, indicating
that the author was an effective observer.
DLC

51 Armijo Lozano, Modesto. Por la senda del
istmo. León: Editorial Universitaria, 1970.
204 pp.
     A collection of short essays dealing with
various themes, both historical and contemporary and with significant individuals in Central American history, written over a period
of more than fifty years by a Nicaraguan educator, professor, and sometime government
official who is a partisan of union. DLC

52 Arredondo, Alberto, and Alfredo Costales
Samaniego. La realidad social de
Centroamérica. Mexico: B. Costa-Amic, 1965.
108 pp. Illus., tables, appendix.
     A pro-unionist description, written by a
Cuban economist and an Ecuadorian rural-
sociologist, of current Central American
conditions that focuses on the state of the
rural peasants and landholding in the rural
areas and calls for changes in the landholding
pattern and for an effort to improve the lives
of the poor. Includes an appendix of documents and current statistics indicating the
economic situation of the various nations.
DLC LNHT

53 Arriola, Jorge Luís, ed. Hacia la integración
educacional de Centro América. Guatemala:
Tipografía Nacional, 1959. 376 pp,.
     The recommendations and resolutions of the
initial series of isthmian educational seminars, with one for each of the various levels

and types, held and published under the sponsorship of the Organization of Central American States. They recommend more uniform
curricula and closer cooperation among the
five nations, elaborating various programs for
promoting this effort. BNG

54 Arthur, Henry B., James P. Houck, and George
L. Beckford. Tropical Agribusiness Structures
and Adjustments--Bananas. Boston: Harvard
Business School, 1968. xi, 210 pp. Index,
biblio., illus., maps, tables.
     Part of a series of studies focusing on the
production and marketing of commodities, this
volume provides an overview and statistical
survey of the banana industry. Provides copious data regarding production, demand, international movement, and other factors,
covering the years 1947-63. Presents numerous
tables and graphs. Includes considerable
information about the major banana companies
and their rivalry, indicating the degree to
which production is based on marketing efforts
in the United States and illustrating the
major production problems and the means
adopted to deal with them. DLC LNHT

55 Asta-Buruaga y Cienfuegos, Francisco Solano.
Repúblicas de Centro-América o idea de su
historia y de su estado actual. Santiago:
Imprenta del Ferrocarril, 1857. 116 pp.
Maps. Latest ed. San José: Talleres
Gutenberg, 1929.
     A brief folio describing the impressions of
a Chilean geographer during a visit to Central
America in 1857. The emphasis is on physical
description and statistics for each of the
isthmian nations. The author visited the
isthmus as a diplomat, and reflects the concern of the South American nations regarding
the Walker intervention in Nicaragua; he came
bearing a proposed pact of Latin American
union, signed by Chile, Ecuador, and Peru, to
jointly protect the independence of the
Hispanic American nations against outside
threats. The second edition bears the shorter
title Repúblicas de Centro América. LNHT

56 Asturias, Miguel Ángel. Latino América y
otros ensayos. Madrid: Guadiana de
Publicaciones, 1968. 87 pp. 2d ed. Madrid:
Guadiana de Publicaciones, 1970. 122 pp.
     A collection of essays primarily on polit-
ical themes, overtly reflecting the denunciation of dictatorship and Yankee dominance
which is evident in many of the author's
novels. Includes comments on a wide range of
subjects such as the need for reform, the
future of Guatemala, and a cry for increased
unity and cooperation among the Latin American
nations. The volume also reprints an inter-
view with Guillermo Medina in which Asturias
comments on his work and on the themes of his
novels. DLC BNCR

57 Aube, Théophile (Hyacinthe Laurent
Théophile Aube). Notes sur le Centre-
Amérique: Vancouver et la Colombie Anglaise.
Paris: Berger-Levrault & Cie., 1877. 59 pp.

A résumé of basic information regarding Costa Rica, Nicaragua, El Salvador, and Belize, prepared by a French naval captain for the Ministry of the Navy. Places particular emphasis on commerce, transport, and economic factors. DLC

58 Aubrun, Charles V. L'Amérique Centrale. Paris: Presses Universitaires de France, 1952. 126 pp. Biblio., illus., maps. 4th ed. Paris: Presses Universitaires de France, 1974. 126 pp. Biblio., illus., maps.

An overview providing a brief historical sketch of each nation and discussion of some general aspects. Intended to be an introduction for the general reader. DLC

59 Avilés, Orontes. Las programas de salud pública de Centroamérica y Panamá, 1961-1970, y las metas señaladas en la carta de Punta del Este. San Salvador: ODECA, 1971. 80 pp. Tables.

A brief summary of the health programs of the Central American nations during the years in question, through the compilation of the health statistics reflecting their actions. LNHT

60 Aycinena, Juan José de [Un Centro-Americano, pseud.]. Reflecciones sobre la necesidad de una reforma política en Centroamérica: escritas por un centroamericano. San Salvador: Imprenta del Estado, 1833. 24 pp.

A commentary on the problems of the Central American Federation, comparing it to that of the United States. Notes that in North America the federalist movement preserved the power of the states, while in Central America all power was vested in the federal government; contends that this requires reconsideration. LNHT

61 Babson, Roger Ward. A Central American Journey. Yonkers, N.Y.: World Book Co., 1920. ix, 219 pp. Index, Illus., maps. 3d ed. Yonkers, N.Y.: World Book Co., 1926. 219 pp. Index, illus., maps.

A businessman and former member of the U.S. Central American Commission draws upon his professional experience and travel in the isthmus in this novel for young people. It is designed to provide basic information about the region, heighten interest in it, and emphasize its commercial possibilities to future generations. The novel describes the experiences of a Yankee businessman who has moved his family to Guatemala to set up an office of his firm, and in the form of anecdotes, sympathetically presents the local social customs and culture. It also indicates the author's conviction that the isthmus will be important to the future commerce and hence economic growth of the United States. DLC

62 Baily, John. Central America: Describing each of the States of Guatemala, Honduras, Salvador, Nicaragua, and Costa Rica; Their Natural Features, Products, Population, and Remarkable Capacity for Colonization. London:

Trelawney Saunders, 1850. xii, 164 pp. Illus.
Die Staaten Zentral-Amerika's, Guatemala, Salvador, Honduras, Nicaragua, und Costa Rica. Berlin: Besser, 1851. viii, 200 pp. Maps.

The author, a British naval officer with lengthy residence in Guatemala, offers a description of each of the isthmian nations, with considerable detail regarding geographic features and economies, making liberal use of statistics. He advocates a British presence in the isthmus. DLC LNHT

63 Banco Centroamericano de Integración Económica. Investment Opportunities in the Central American Common Market. Tegucigalpa: Published by the Bank, 1965. 65 pp. Tables. 3d ed. Tegucigalpa: Published by the Bank, 1971.

A general description of the region, the market, and its financial incentives and facilities for investors, designed to interest foreign companies in the region. DLC LNHT

64 _____. Un mercado de capitales centroamericano: dos estudios. Mexico: Centro de Estudios Monetarios Latinoamericanos, 1967. 221 pp. Tables.

Two separate studies examining the prospects and difficulties of organizing a regional financial structure to complement the Common Market, detailing the advantages and examining the differences between the existing structures in each of the nations and summarizing their financial institutions. Concludes that such an effort is desirable and recommends the formation of commissions for its study. Includes extensive statistics about the present state of credit in the region. DLC LNHT

65 Bancroft, Hubert Howe. History of Central America. Many editions. 3 vols. San Francisco: A.L. Bancroft, 1882-87. Illus., maps.

A classic and detailed history dating from the nineteenth century, by one of the early Yankee scholars of the isthmus. Draws heavily on contemporary secondary works and available documentation. Exhaustive in detail, but reflects the biases inherent in the condescending Yankee attitudes characteristic of the global era of imperialism. The first two volumes deal with the Colonial era, and the third with the post-independence years. DLC LNHT BNCR

66 Bank of London & Montreal, Ltd. The Central American Common Market. London: Waterlow, 1967. 67 pp. Biblio., illus.

A brief description of the Common Market, designed to provide an introduction for the British reader or investor. Includes a history of the integration movement and basic data about the market and its potential. MoSW

67 Barrantes Ferrero, Mario. La frontera entre Costa Rica y Panamá. San José: Instituto Geográfico de Costa Rica, 1959. 18 pp. Illus., maps.

An illustrated physical description of the Costa Rican-Panamanian frontier, with photos of the boundary commission and the markers placed on the frontier. DLC LNHT BNCR

68 Barrientos, Alfonso Enrique. El desertor. Guatemala: Círculo Literario de Guatemala, 1961. 358 pp.
    A novel, set in Central America, that follows the career of a young man who enters the military academy during a military regime. Ridicules the military, its practices, and its political role and emphasizes its brutality. DLC LNHT BNG

69 Barrios Castro, Carlos. Labor americana: evolución de sus ideales. San José: Imprenta Lehmann, 1926. 34 pp. Illus.
    A discussion of the unionist ideal and other noble aspirations that the author feels characterize Central America, with expressions of hope for their future attainment. The initial essay hails the efforts of Costa Rican president José María Castro Madriz, who headed the nation in 1867, on behalf of these ideals. DLC-LDS-351 BNCR

70 Batista y Pereyna, Eugenio. Ni imperialismo yankee ni comunismo. San José: Editorial Aurora Social, n.d. 110 pp. 2d ed. San José: Editorial Aurora Social, 1955. 244 pp.
    A call for Latin America to reject both superpowers and define its own future through cooperation among its nations. Engages in lengthy criticism of both systems, sometimes by reprinting resolutions of various groups or speeches. LNHT BNCR

71 Batres, Luís. La cuestión de unión centro-americana. San José: Imprenta Nacional, 1881. 96 pp. Index.
    A pro-unionist tract by a Guatemalan in exile in Costa Rica. Discusses the failures and limits of previous attempts, emphasizing the importance of and need for federation and offering specific suggestions for the form of government. The work stresses the importance of the sovereignty of the federal government and condemns state sovereignty, offering a full plan of governmental organization that emphasizes the need for a strong executive and a balance of .powers. It contends that efforts to promote union by military force are doomed to failure and advocates a cautious course of peaceful persuasion, thus implicitly opposing the plans of Guatemalan general Justo Rufino Barrios and reflecting both the official Costa Rican position of the regime of Tomás Guardia and the author's role in the Carrera administration, which was overthrown by the Guatemalan Liberal revolution. DLC DLC-LDS-67 BNCR

72 Batson, Alfred. Vagabond's Paradise. Boston: Little Brown, 1931. 281 pp. Illus.
    A picturesque narrative of the adventures of two would-be soldiers of fortune who journeyed overland from Nicaragua through Honduras, Guatemala, and Mexico, to return to the United States when "de-commissioned" from the Nicaraguan Liberal Army by U.S. Marines launching the intervention. DLC

73 Battelle Memorial Institute, Columbus Laboratories. Projections of Supply and Demand for Selected Agricultural Products in Central America through 1980. Jerusalem: Foreign Agricultural Service, 1969. xxi, 261 pp. Biblio., notes, maps, tables.
    A compilation of statistics, mainly from the 1950s and 1960s, though some sequences extend further, covering the production of all major agricultural products, as well as gross domestic product, population, salaries, and budget categories, with projections for 1970 and 1980. Includes information on the formulas used in the projections. This report was originally prepared for the U.S. Department of Agriculture. FU

74 Baudez, Claude F. Amérique Centrale. Geneva, Paris, and Munich: Nagel, 1970. 256 pp. Biblio., illus.
    Central America. London: Barrie & Jenkins, 1970. 255 pp. Index, biblio., illus., maps.
    América Central. Madrid: Juventud, 1976. 260 pp.
    DLC LNHT

75 Beals, Carlton. Banana Gold. Philadelphia and London: Lippincott, 1932. 367 pp. Index, illus. Latest ed. New York: Arno Press, 1970. 367 pp. Index, illus.
    A well-known reporter and travel-book author's account of his experiences in Central America, written in exposé fashion condemning the role of the United Fruit Company, the United States, local officials, and virtually everything else, including the jungle and the tropical heat. Reflects the Yankee attitudes characteristic of the era, yet also details personal episodes that do show some of the customs and problems through the eyes of a practiced observer. Includes an account of his visit to Sandino's guerrillas and comments supporting their efforts. DLC LNHT

76 Bello Codecido, Emilio. El arbitraje y la equidad: puntos de derecho internacional expuestos por el autor, como miembro del Tribunal Especial de Límites, que funcionó en Washington a virtud del tratado de arbitraje celebrado por las repúblicas de Guatemala y Honduras, el 16 de julio de 1930. Santiago: Imprenta El Imparcial, 1939. 87 pp. Maps.
    A legalistic analysis of the Guatemala-Honduras Boundary Tribunal and its powers and duties in settling the dispute, based on the treaty and the legal precedents. Includes the text of the treaty and statements by the parties, though not their presentations to the tribunal. DLC

77 Belly, Félix. L'isthme américain: note d'un premier voyage, 1858, précédé d'une biographie de l'auteur par Ch. Potvin. Brussels: Weissenbruch, 1889. 161 pp. Maps.

78 Beltrán y Rózpide, Ricardo. La Mosquitia: algunas notas documentadas para escribir la historia territorial de Centro América.

Madrid: Patronato de Huerfonos de Administración Militar, 1910. 27 pp. Latest ed. Tegucigalpa: Talleres Tipográficos Nacionales, 1937. 12 pp.

A review of the possession of the territory, primarily dealing with the Colonial era, and contending that it was part of Honduras. The discussion of the nineteenth century is brief. DLC

79 Beneš, Vlastislav, et al. Střední Amerika [Central America]. Prague: Institut Zahraničního Obchodu ČTK, 1974. 297 pp. Biblio., maps, tables.

A country-by-country survey of Central America designed to provide current data, with chapters for each nation on history, culture, politics, economics, finance, and Czech trade, including discussion of potential. The volume is designed for the informed general reader and seeks to encourage Czechoslovakian interest in the region and in possible trade. DLC

80 Beresford, Marcus [Marc Brandel, pseud.]. The Rod and the Staff. New York and London: Harper, 1947. 254 pp.

A novel set in a fictitious Central American nation, about passion, oppression of the peasants by a corrupt government, an Indian rebellion, the thirst for justice, and the futility of these efforts. DLC

81 Bermúdez, Alejandro. Lucha de razas: esfuerzos que se necesitan para defender la nuestra. San José: Imprenta Alsina, 1912. 31 pp. 2d ed. Mexico: Tipografía Económica, 1912.

A speech by a member of the Central American Unionist party, warning against the Yankee threat and calling for unity to repel it. Alludes to the necessity of the unity of all of Latin America. DLC DLC-LDS-95 BNCR

82 Bermúdez Meza, Antonio. Límites definitivos entre Honduras y Nicaragua. Tegucigalpa: Talleres Tipográficas Nacionales, 1938. 112 pp. Maps. 2d ed. Tegucigalpa: Talleres Tipográficas Nacionales, 1938. 112 pp. Maps.

A critical study of the Bonilla-Gámez Treaty of 1894, which provided for arbitration of the dispute. Published under the auspices of the Honduran Ministry of Foreign Relations. Contends that in accord with its terms, the 1906 ruling of the king of Spain ended the dispute and that since all was done in accordance with the treaty there could no longer be any question about the boundary, hence implying that subsequent Nicaraguan claims were invalid. Includes the full text of the treaty, the reports of the technical commissions, the ruling of the king of Spain, and all relevant documentation. DLC

83 Bert Zdeněk, and Arnost Tauber. Pod sopkami Střední Ameriky [Under volcanoes of Central America]. Prague: SNPL, 1959. 192 pp.

84 Beteta, José Antonio. Morazán y la Federación. Guatemala: Imprenta de Silva, 1887. 118 pp.

An enthusiastic summary hailing Morazán's efforts to unify the isthmus through the Federation. BNG

85 Bitter, Wilhelm Frederich. Die wirtschaftliche Eroberung Mittelamerikas durch den Bananen-Trust: Organisation und imperialistische Bedeutung der United Fruit Company. Hamburg: Verlag George Westermann, 1921. 145 pp. Biblio., maps, tables. 2d ed. Darmstadt: Wissenschaftliche Buchgesellschaft, 1971. 145 pp. Biblio., maps.

A detailed study providing the European view of the banana trusts. Focusing on the United Fruit Company, it treats them in an anti-imperialistic vein and contends that the use of such international trusts is part of Yankee policy designed to secure economic control of Latin America in pursuance of the Monroe Doctrine and to exclude European competition, enabling the United States to dominate the region and utilize its resources. It details the methods of control of the various aspects of the industry and the operations of the trust, considering operations throughout the Caribbean but focusing principally on Central America. DLC LNHT

86 Blaney, Henry Robertson. The Golden-Caribbean: A Winter Visit to the Republics of Colombia, Costa Rica, Spanish Honduras, Belize, and the Spanish Main via Boston and New Orleans. Boston: Lee & Shepard, 1900. viii, 116 pp. Illus.

A travelogue mixing discussion of conditions and accommodations, description, and narration of the legends recounted to the author to explain the sights he saw. The descriptions are impressionistic and reflect a lack of knowledge of the area as well as Yankee prejudices. DLC LNHT

87 Bobadilla, José Ángel, et al. Programa regional de carreteras centroamericanas. 3 vols. Guatemala: n.p., 1963. Biblio., maps, tables. Regional Program of Central American Highways. 3 vols. Tegucigalpa: n.p., 1963. Biblio., maps, tables.

A transportation plan prepared by the Banco Central de Integración Económica, with specific details on the existing highways in the 1960s and plans for linking them, prepared as part of its effort to promote such linkage to facilitate trade. BNG

88 Bodenheimer Jonas, Susanne, et al. La inversión extranjera en Centroamérica. San José: EDUCA, 1974. 362 pp. Biblio., notes, illus., tables. 3d ed. San José: EDUCA, 1976. 362 pp. Biblio., notes, illus., tables.

A collection of articles condemning Yankee investment and its imperialistic implications, employing a dependency analysis in dealing with disparate questions. Statistical tables in the appendix cover the years 1955 to 1969. Effectively summarizes the dependency viewpoint and its application to Central America.

The second edition sometimes lists Rafael
Menjivar as the editor.   DLC LNHT BNCR

89   Boesch, Hans Heinrich. Zentralamerika. Bern:
Kümmerly & Frey, 1951. 103 pp. Illus., maps.
La tierra del Quetzal: Zentralamerika heute.
Bern: Kümmerly & Frey, 1952. 262 pp.
Illus., maps.
     A general introduction for the German
reader by a Swiss geographer, which treats the
isthmus as a whole. The focus is on agriculture, land use, climate, and economy but includes an ethnographic chapter on the Indians
and a chapter on the Colonial period. Well
illustrated with helpful maps. The initial
edition was extremely brief, written to fit a
series format aimed at providing background
for tourists, while the expanded second edition, though still aimed at the general
reader, offers much fuller geographic and
economic data.   DLC

90   Bologna, Alfredo Bruno. Conflicto Honduras-El
Salvador: análisis sociológico de las
relaciones internacionales. Buenos Aires:
Editorial Tierra Nueva, 1977. 161 pp. Notes,
tables.
     A compilation of descriptive data from
published sources about Central America in
general and the two specific nations involved
in the 1969 conflict in particular, arranged
by topic to allow comparison, with a brief
summary of some of the effects of the conflict
on the unification movement and the various
diplomatic efforts to restore normality in the
region.   LNHT

91   Bonilla, Policarpo. Labor on Behalf of the
Autonomy of Central America. New Orleans:
American Printing Company, 1913. 16 pp.
     Reflecting the unionist views of this well-
known Honduran political leader, this pamphlet
condemns the Nicaraguan canal arrangements
with the United States, contending that all
the Central American states should be involved
in the talks because of the importance of the
issue and the rights of the other states to
portions of the canal route involving the Bay
of Fonseca and the San Juan River.   DLC

92   _____. Límites entre Honduras y Nicaragua:
mediación del gobierno de Estados Unidos;
alegatos, pruebas y dictámenes presentados por
Honduras ante el mediador, demostrando la
validez y justicia del laudo pronunciado por
el rey de España, que puso término a la
cuestión, 1920-1921. New York: De Laisne &
Carranza, 1921. vii, 382 pp. Maps.
     The complete documentation of the Honduran
case.   DLC LNHT

93   _____. La Unión de Centro América. New York:
De Laisne & Carranza, 1921. 20 pp.
     A pro-unionist address to a unionist club
in New York in 1921 at Columbia University,
which nevertheless includes discussion of the
limitations and problems of the Federalist
Pact of that year, calling for caution and
remedies. Includes a brief survey of the
unionist movement and a list of pros and cons

of federation; it is clear that this ex-
president of Honduras is sympathetic to the
idea but seeks to protect the interests of his
nation.   DLC

94   Bonilla Baldares, Abelardo. En los caminos de
la unidad centroamericana. San José: EDUCA,
1973. 110 pp.
     A Costa Rican essayist's pro-unionist tract
contending that the most effective route to
unification is through culture. Asserts that
the important precondition is for education to
stress traits common throughout the isthmus,
for history to emphasize the common experiences, and for literature to propagate the
idea of a single country and region.   LNHT
BNCR

95   Bonilla Ruano, José María. Acontecimiento
bibliográfico (en torno de la obra "La unión
de Centroamérica" del licenciado Alberto
Herrarte). Guatemala: Ministerio de
Educación Pública, 1956. 110 pp.
     A series of articles, originally published
in El Imparcial of Guatemala City, commenting
on and hailing Herrarte's book; by a fellow
unionist who seeks to draw greater attention
to the book.   DLC

96   Borda, Francisco de P. Dos libros sobre
límites por don Manuel M. de Peralta. Bogotá:
Tipografía La Luz, 1894. 100 pp. Notes.
     A Colombian jurist's counterattack on the
volumes by Peralta, the Costa Rican envoy to
Colombia who defended the Costa Rican claims.
Originally written as a series of newspaper
articles published in El Telegrama of Bogota,
Borda's vitriolic attack criticized all the
arguments, the documents, and even what he
considers the terrible writing style of
Peralta, characterizing his studies as frauds.
BNCR

97   _____. Límites de Colombia con Costa Rica:
memoria redactada de orden del gobierno de
Colombia. Bogotá: Imprenta La Luz, 1896.
lxii, 549 pp. Index, notes.
     An extensive study supporting the Colombian
claims regarding the frontier between Panama,
then a province of Colombia, and Costa Rica.
Focuses on Colonial times and meticulously
defines, with extensive documentary excerpts,
the jurisdictional boundaries of this era.
There are also some references to the independence era.   DLC BNCR

98   Boyle, Frederick. A Ride across a Continent:
A Personal Narrative of Wanderings through
Nicaragua and Costa Rica. 2 vols. London:
Richard Bentley, 1868. xxviii, 299; vii, 297
pp. Illus.
     An experienced travel-book author's account
of his adventures in Nicaragua and Central
America during an expedition undertaken to
find a supposed lost tribe. The tribe remained lost, but numerous adventures were
experienced and recorded during the expedition. Emphasizes description of Indians and
archeological finds, but includes physical

description of the area, its tropical vegetation and jungle animals, as well as travel conditions, accounts of individuals met, and some discussion of history as related to the author. DLC LNHT

99 Buell, Raymond Leslie. <u>The</u> <u>Central</u> <u>Americas</u>. New York: Foreign Policy Association, 1931. 31 pp. Maps.
   A brief summary of the author's optimistic impressions during a tour of the region in 1931. His comments focus on political developments, foreign enterprise, and the international position of the republics. DLC

100 Bülow, Alexander (Freiherr) von. <u>Auswanderung</u> <u>und</u> <u>Kolonisation</u> <u>im</u> <u>Interesse</u> <u>des</u> <u>deutschen</u> <u>Handels</u>. Berlin and Posen: E.S. Mittler, 1849. 404 pp. Notes, maps, tables.
   A history of German colonization throughout the world, with detailed accounts of the trade between Germany and the various nations it settled. Includes information about the colonies and about the respective national economies, with just over 100 pages devoted to Central America. The data focus on the 1840s, and the volume is clearly designed to encourage increased German interest in trade with and emigration to these nations. DLC

101 Bumgartner, Louis E. <u>José</u> <u>del</u> <u>Valle</u> <u>of</u> <u>Central</u> <u>America</u>. Durham, N.C.: Duke University Press, 1963. 302 pp. Index, biblio., notes, illus., tables.
   Based on documents from Guatemala and Mexico, as well as published works, this volume adds a great deal to what is known of this leader of the isthmian independence movement. Del Valle emerges as an ambitious politician and creole leader who had reservations about independence, and was a partisan of annexation to Mexico when independence became inevitable. His thinking and governmental service as a member of the plural executive and his role in drafting the constitutions are carefully detailed, emphasizing the broader world outlook that distinguished him from his contemporaries. DLC LNHT BNG

102 Business International Corporation, New York. <u>The</u> <u>Central</u> <u>American</u> <u>Common</u> <u>Market</u>: <u>Profits</u> <u>and</u> <u>Problems</u> <u>in</u> <u>an</u> <u>Integrating</u> <u>Economy</u>. New York: Business International, 1969. 67 pp. Maps, tables, appendixes.
   Basic facts about the Common Market, designed to explain the opportunities, facilities, and prospects for the private sector and small businessman, and to encourage and facilitate activity by such firms in the isthmus. The positive aspects and potential are stressed, and the analysis seeks openly to provide the private-sector viewpoint. DLC LNHT

103 Bustamante y Sirvén, Antonio Sánchez de. <u>Controversia</u> <u>de</u> <u>límites</u> <u>entre</u> <u>Panamá</u> <u>y</u> <u>Costa</u> <u>Rica</u>: <u>dictamen</u> <u>emitido</u> <u>por</u> <u>el</u> Dr. Antonio Sánchez de Bustamante y <u>Sirvén</u>. Panamá: Imprenta Nacional, 1921. 20 pp. <u>Panama-Costa</u> <u>Rica</u> <u>Boundary</u> <u>Controversy</u>: <u>Opinion</u> <u>Given</u> <u>by</u>. . . . Panamá: Imprenta Nacional, 1921. 21 pp.
   An analysis by a Cuban jurist supporting the contentions of Panama against the validity of the White award. DLC

104 Byam, George. <u>Wild</u> <u>Life</u> <u>in</u> <u>the</u> <u>Interior</u> <u>of</u> <u>Central</u> <u>America</u>. London: John W. Parker, 1849. viii, 253 pp. <u>Wildes</u> <u>Leben</u> <u>im</u> <u>Innern</u> <u>von</u> <u>Zentral-Amerika</u>. Dresden: n.p., 1852.
   The memoirs of the adventures of an Englishman in Nicaragua in the 1840s, stressing his experiences in what he calls a "very strange land" among "wild animals of the human species." Includes physical setting, individuals met, and all manner of incidents; written colorfully but with a condescending eye that regards the local inhabitants as peculiar and uncivilized. DLC LNHT

105 Cagliero, Giovanni (Juan). <u>Bodas</u> <u>de</u> <u>plata</u> <u>episcopales</u> <u>del</u> <u>Exmo.</u> <u>y</u> <u>reverendísimo</u> <u>monseñor</u> <u>doctor</u> <u>don</u> <u>Juan</u> <u>Cagliero,</u> <u>arzobispo</u> <u>titular</u> <u>de</u> <u>Sebaste</u> <u>y</u> <u>delegado</u> <u>apostólico</u> <u>en</u> <u>Centro-</u> <u>América</u>. San José: Tipografía Nacional, 1910. 100 pp. Illus.
   A collection of commentaries, speeches, and writings of the apostolic delegate to Central America from 1908 to 1910, including commentaries on religious and political themes relating to the entire isthmus but focusing on Costa Rica, where he had his residence. DLC-LDS-106

106 Cajina Uriarte, José León. <u>Cinco</u> <u>nicaragüenses</u> <u>en</u> <u>la</u> <u>América</u> <u>Central</u>. Managua: Editorial Nuevos Horizontes, 1945. 158 pp.
   A rambling account of travels and experiences in the various countries of Central America, mixing comment on disparate themes such as the postwar settlements of both world wars and the Good Neighbor Policy. Also reprints newspaper editorials. DLC LNHT

107 Calderón, José Tomás. <u>El</u> <u>ejército</u> <u>federal</u> <u>de</u> <u>la</u> <u>República</u> <u>de</u> <u>Centroamérica,</u> <u>1921</u>. San Salvador: Imprenta Nacional, 1922. 348 pp. Maps, tables.
   A detailed account of the organization and campaigns of the army of Francisco Morazán, covering its composition and the sources of recruits as well as the battles. DLC

108 Camacho, Daniel, et al. <u>El</u> <u>fracaso</u> <u>social</u> <u>de</u> <u>la</u> <u>integración</u> <u>centroamericana:</u> <u>capital,</u> <u>tecnología,</u> <u>empleo</u>. San José: EDUCA, 1979. 373 pp. Biblio., tables.
   A work by several members of the faculty of the University of Costa Rica, consisting of studies of various aspects of the impact of the Central American Common Market on the region, and including essays on employment change in each of the region's six nations. The authors contend that the Common Market has favored the rich, contributed to dependency, benefited the multinational corporations, and failed to create significant numbers of jobs, concluding that the creation of jobs is the key aspect affecting the local societies, and

hence that the market and its current policies
have had an adverse impact. DLC

109 Camejo Farfán, Hugo. La unión centro-
     americana. Guatemala: Tipografía Nacional,
     1949. 25 pp. Illus.
        An address made to the Cuban Society of
     International law in 1949, briefly tracing
     attempts to unify the isthmus, hailing the
     concept, and acclaiming the leadership of Juan
     José Arévalo in seeking to renew efforts to
     achieve the long sought ideal. LNHT

110 Canales Salazar, Félix. Controversia
     fronteriza con El Salvador: conferencia
     dictada en el paraninfo de la Universidad
     Nacional Autónoma de Honduras. Tegucigalpa:
     Universidad Nacional Autónoma de Honduras,
     1968. 40 pp. Maps. 2d ed. Tegucigalpa:
     Academía de Geografía e Historia de Honduras,
     1968. 40 pp. Maps.
        A Honduran version of the boundary dispute
     with El Salvador and the migration crisis
     involved, written prior to the outbreak of
     hostilities in 1969. Includes a brief summary
     of the controversy and a recitation of the
     Honduran legal arguments. The elements of the
     title are rearranged slightly in the second
     edition. LNHT

111 _____. Derechos territoriales de Honduras.
     Tegucigalpa: Secretaría de Fomento, 1957.
     Pages unnumbered. Maps, tables.
        A statement in behalf of the committee of
     the Honduran Society of Engineers and Archi-
     tects. Supports the ruling of the king of
     Spain in 1906 regarding the boundary with
     Nicaragua with maps, tables regarding settle-
     ment in the region, and numerous excerpts from
     the various documents, rulings, and the press,
     while denigrating the Nicaraguan claims. Pro-
     vides an overview from the 1894 accord through
     the mediations of 1918 and 1937, followed by
     legal arguments. DLC

112 _____. Derechos territoriales de Honduras y
     derechos adventicios de Nicaragua confirmados
     en el mapa oficial de Nicaragua de 1859:
     desde el Río de San Juan hasta el Río Perlas,
     en el Atlántico. Tegucigalpa: Asociación de
     Estudiantes de la Ingeniería, 1953. 24 pp.
     Maps.
        A statement of the Honduran claims against
     Nicaragua based on the finding of a
     nineteenth-century map that supports the
     Honduran contentions. LNHT

113 Carbajo, Deodato. Medio siglo de servicio a
     Centroamérica de la provincia franciscana de
     Cartagena. 2 vols. Guatemala: Tipografía
     Nacional, 1974. 454, 382 pp. Illus.
        A history of the Franciscan order in Cen-
     tral America from 1922 through 1972, tracing
     the activities of the members from the prov-
     ince of Cartagena, Spain, in the isthmus.
     Volume 1 gives a general history of the order
     and provides specific information about each
     location at which it works; volume 2 discusses
     the leaders of the group, its regulations, and
     various specific programs. BNG

114 Cardenal, Ernesto, ed. The Gospel in
     Solentiname. 4 vols. Maryknoll, N.Y.:
     Orbis, 1978-84. 288, 272, 320, 288 pp.
        Essays based on tape-recorded conversations
     by the author with villagers in a remote inte-
     rior town in his native Nicaragua, discussing
     the meaning of the Gospel to them. Designed
     to show the perspective of common peasants
     untrained in theology and how they interpret
     the readings the priest presents to them. DLC

115 Cardoso, Ciro Flamarion Santana, and Héctor
     Pérez Brignoli. Centroamérica y la economía
     occidental, 1520-1930. San José: Universidad
     de Costa Rica, 1977. xiii, 382 pp. Biblio.,
     illus., maps, tables.
        An economic survey of the region, intended
     as a university text. Covers the years from
     discovery through 1930, with the major empha-
     sis on the Colonial years and the nineteenth
     century. Provides a broad outline of the
     stages of development, the introduction of new
     crops, and foreign investment, focusing on the
     region's linkage to the world economy and
     hence on external influences. LNHT

116 Carías, Marco Virgilio, et al. Análisis del
     conflicto entre Honduras y El Salvador.
     Tegucigalpa: Universidad Nacional Autónoma de
     Honduras, 1969. viii, 82 pp. Index, biblio.,
     tables, appendixes. 2d ed. Tegucigalpa:
     Universidad Nacional Autónoma de Honduras,
     1970. 118 pp. Index, biblio., tables,
     appendixes.
        A brief analysis of the conflict from the
     Honduran viewpoint, published only three
     months after the war, under the auspices of
     the Faculty of Economics of the National
     Autonomous University of Honduras. The study
     characterizes the conflict as a Salvadoran
     invasion of Honduras contrived by the Salva-
     doran oligarchy to prevent a social revolution
     by distracting the peasants with patriotic
     rhetoric in response to Honduran resistance to
     the Salvadoran efforts to dominate Honduras
     commercially. Identifies the basic factors as
     population growth in El Salvador, the class
     structure, capitalism, and Yankee imperialism,
     which is alleged to be promoting dependency
     through the Central American Common Market and
     assisting the Salvadoran bourgeoisie. The
     latter argument links the Honduran rationale
     regarding the conflict with its opposition to
     the Common Market. Includes extensive quota-
     tions from official statements, a chronology
     of the events, and statistical tables. In the
     first edition the cover title and the title
     page are different; the title-page wording is
     cited here. DLC

117 Carías, Marco Virgilio, Daniel Slutzky, et al.
     La guerra inútil: análisis socioeconómico del
     conflicto entre Honduras y El Salvador. San
     José: EDUCA, 1971. 338 pp.
        A combined effort by the professors at the
     national universities of Honduras and El
     Salvador, this volume seeks to overcome the
     heritage of the 1969 war by blaming it on the
     Yankee capitalists and their imperialistic
     machinations, adopting a dependency analysis

of the crisis. The book contains three separate studies, the first being a reprint of Carías's previous volume about the conflict. The other two essays are a study of Salvadoran migration into Honduras emphasizing the class conflict that promotes it, and an economic study contending that the new manufacturing sectors in El Salvador seek to expand "horizontally" by selling their industrial products to other countries rather than "vertically" by producing the goods needed by the lower classes in their nation. Although there are only two names on the title page, each of the studies has several contributors. LNHT

118 Carías Reyes, Marcos, ed. <u>Álbum morazánico</u> (<u>homenaje del gobierno que preside el Dr. y Gral. don Tiburcio Carías Andino</u>). Tegucigalpa: Talleres Tipográficas Nacionales, 1942. 285 pp.
A collection of letters and documents by Morazán, along with excerpts from several studies of Morazán. The major item is from the biography by Eduardo Martínez Lopez. DLC BNCR

119 Carnero Checa, Genaro. <u>El águila rampante: el imperialismo yanqui sobre América Latina</u>. Mexico: Ediciones Semanario Peruano, 1956. 366 pp. Biblio.
A denunciation of the dominance of Yankee financial and business enterprises and their monopoly control of Latin America, contending that they dominate all fields, control nations, and retard indigenous economic development. The focus is on the contemporary era, with chapters dealing with each of the isthmian nations. DLC BNCR

120 Carpenter, Frank George. <u>Lands of the Caribbean</u>. Garden City, N.Y.: Doubleday Page, 1925. xiv, 309 pp. Index, illus.
An experienced travelogue writer's account of a trip through the region, with extensive description of its cities and means of transportation, including accounts of the author's observations and the people he met. About half the book deals with Central America. DLC LNHT

121 Carpenter, Rhys. <u>The Land Beyond Mexico</u>. Boston: R.G. Badger, 1920. 181 pp. Illus.
A descriptive account of the muleback travels of an archeologist through the remote backlands of Guatemala, El Salvador, and northern Honduras. This work focuses on the areas he passed through rather than the archeological zones, and provides a vivid and detailed description, through a keen eye, of the people and conditions he found, as well as of the terrain. His observations provide considerable insights about life and social conditions in the backlands. DLC

122 Carter, Dorothy Sharp. <u>The Enchanted Orchard and Other Folktales of Central America</u>. New York: Harcourt Brace Jovanovich, 1973. 126 pp. Illus.
A series of children's folktales collected by the author during a residence in the

isthmus and translated in an effort to bring them to the attention of Yankee children. Includes Indian tales, stories dealing with animals common to the region, and legends. There is no rationale for this grouping and no discussion of whether it is typical. Neither is there any analysis. DLC

123 <u>Cartografía de la América Central</u>. Guatemala: Tipografía Nacional, 1929. cxxv, 125 pp.
A collection of historical maps covering the various phases of Central American development from discovery to the date of printing. BNG

124 Castañeda de Machado, Elvia. <u>Valle en la génesis del panamericanismo</u>. Tegucigalpa: Ministerio de Cultura, 1977. 129 pp. Biblio.
The author argues that Valle thought about the ideal of uniting the former Spanish colonies under a single republic just as Bolívar did, and deserves credit for conceiving Pan-Americanism. Includes references to other commentators about Valle's life and some excerpts from his letters to indicate his references to the ideal, along with some discussion of later Pan-American meetings that she seeks to show fulfill Valle's ideals. LNHT

125 Castillo, Carlos M. <u>Growth and Integration in Central America</u>. New York: Praeger, 1965. x, 188 pp. Biblio., maps. <u>Estado del programa de integración económica Centroamérica</u>. Guatemala: Universidad de San Carlos, 1967.
An overview of Central American economic history since independence and a commentary on the potential impact of the Common Market. The author, a staff member of the ECLA, emphasizes the problems of an economy oriented to agricultural export, stressing the concentration of land ownership and the inability of the local economy to respond to pressures for change and to the increase in population. He sees the Common Market as capable of creating a large enough market to enable use of the ECLA strategy of import substitution, which would lead to industrial growth, economic expansion, and social change. DLC

126 Castillo Ricas, Donald. <u>Acumulación de capital y empresas transnacionales: en Centroamérica</u>. Mexico: Siglo XXI, 1980. 277 pp.

127 Castrillo, Salvador. <u>Alegato sobre la cuestión pendiente entre Nicaragua y Honduras acerca de la línea divisoria de los terrenos comprendidos en la región de la Costa Atlántica y documentos en que se apoya el alegato</u>. Managua: Tipografía Mercantil, 1902. 171 pp. Appendixes.
The Nicaraguan attorney's statement of the case in one of the numerous boundary commissions on this question, prior to the ruling by the king of Spain. Accompanied by supporting documents. DLC

128 Castrillo Zeledón, Mario. El régimen de libre
comercio en Centro América. San José: EDUCA,
1970. 335 pp. Notes, tables.
    An examination of the Central American
Common Market, its development, and its effect
on regional commerce, written by an official
of SIECA who uses both the history of the
movement and economic theories regarding integration to evaluate the various measures designed to promote regional free trade. The
various special titles and provisions of the
agreements and the subregional arrangements
within the isthmus are all examined separately
and systematically. The chapters include
quotation of the accords, discussion of the
results, comparison to theory and other existing accords, and analysis. The impact of the
market on consumption, exports and imports,
transportation, unions, and trade within the
isthmus is also considered. The account is
favorable to the unionist movement and emphasizes the need to develop a unique system
suitable to the region and to developing countries rather than following other examples.
DLC LNHT BNG

129 Castro Lujan, V.M. Unificación de la
identidad personal en los cinco estados
centroamericanos. San Salvador: Imprenta
Nacional, 1955. 35 pp.
    A statement in support of the ODECA pro-
posal for a common cédula de identidad in the
five republics, commenting on the practices of
the various states and the advantages of the
proposal. BNG BNCR

130 Castro Ramírez, Manuel. Cinco años en la
Corte de Justicia Centroamericana. San José:
Imprenta Lehmann, 1918. 184 pp.
    An "insider's view" of the Central American
Court of Justice from its creation in the
Washington Treaties of 1907 through 1914,
written by a Salvadoran jurist who served on
it. Despite the author's vantage point, the
volume is basically a description of the
various cases and rulings that draws upon
official documents but does not shed much
light on the court's internal deliberations.
DLC DLC-LDS-388 BNCR

131 _____. Manuel José Arce, prócer de la
independencia y primer presidente de Centro
América (1787-1847). San Salvador: Editorial
Ahora, 1947. 94 pp.
    A brief summary of Arce's career, hailing
his role in the independence movement. DLC

132 Castro Ramírez, Manuel, Reyes Arrieta Rossi,
and Enrique Córdova. Límites entre Honduras y
Nicaragua: el laudo de Su Majestad Alfonso
XIII frente al derecho internacional.
Tegucigalpa: Ministerio de Relaciones
Exteriores, 1937. 38 pp.
    A study by three prominent Salvadoran ju-
rists, including two former foreign ministers
and the head of the lawyer's association,
prepared for the Honduran Foreign Ministry.
Supports the Honduran stand that the arbitral
decision is fully valid, cites the legal

precedents, and refutes the Nicaraguan contentions. DLC

133 Castro Ramírez, Manuel, et al. Genecidio en
Centroamérica. San Salvador: Imprenta
Nacional, 1969. 20 pp.
    A study by five Salvadoran jurists repeat-
ing the Salvadoran charges against Honduras,
published as part of the propaganda related to
the 1969 war. LNHT

134 Cauca Prada, Antonio. Pedro Molina: patricio
centroamericano. Guatemala: Ministerio de
Educación Pública, 1978. 193 pp. Biblio.,
illus.
    A Colombian diplomat and scholar's biogra-
phy of one of the leaders of Central American
independence, based on extensive research in
documents in the Archivo General de
Centroamérica and appropriate published works.
Provides a complete biography, but understandably focuses heavily on Molina's diplomatic career and service as one of the
representatives of the Central American
Federation to the Panama Congress called by
Simon Bolívar. DLC BNG

135 CEDAL. América Central: evolución y
capacitación de recursos humanos (educación de
adultos). San José: CEDAL, 1974. 126 pp.
    An evaluation and description of the adult-
education programs of each of the six republics, with a series of recommendations for
their expansion and improvement, urging
greater cooperation among them. BNCR

136 _____. Centro de Estudios Democráticos de
América Latina: historia, finalidad y
estructura. San José: CEDAL, n.d. 55 pp.
Illus.
    A description of CEDAL, its facilities and
personnel, as well as its links with the
Friedrich Ebert Foundation of West Germany.
Includes lists of the conferences it sponsored
from 1968 through 1972, and of its publications. BNCR

137 _____. Problemas de organización y formación
de partidos social democráticas en México y
América Central. San José: CEDAL, 1976.
Pages not consecutively numbered.
    A series of reports by the various parties,
including those from Mexico and one from
Guatemala (Frente Unido de la Revolución) and
the PLN of Costa Rica, followed by an overall
essay focusing on Costa Rica by Luís Alberto
Monge. BNCR

138 C.E.I. Técnica agropecuaria S.R.L. 2 vols.
San José: n.p., 1970. 220, 181 pp. Biblio.,
tables.
    A detailed study of the Central American
internal markets and production possibilities
for beef, milk, dairy products, pork, chicken,
and eggs, with elaborate statistics for the
1960s and projections for the 1970s. Indicates the potential expansion of these industries in view of the growth of the population
and dietary changes. Argues that a considerable and largely untapped domestic market

exists within the isthmus itself, exclusive of the export field. Present imports and exports of these foods are traced, and a survey of areas of potential production is included. BNCR

139 Central America, Presidents. Reunión de los presidentes de Centroamérica, San Salvador. N.p.: SIECA, 1968. 47 pp.

140 Central America: A Bibliography. Los Angeles: California State University, Latin American Studies Center, 1979. 112 pp.
A brief preliminary bibliographical listing encompassing books and articles, arranged alphabetically by country, without annotation, focusing on works published in the years 1965-75. The sections are short, with only four to five pages per country, and there are some variances in the data provided. Selection criteria within the years indicated are not stated.

141 Central American Conference (1889). Documentos relativos a la unión de Centro-América. Guatemala: Tipografía La Unión, 1889. 137 pp.
A collection of letters and telegrams, all dated 1889, relating to the San Salvador Conference of 1889 and the resulting unionist attempt. The minutes of the conference and the resulting treaties are included. Published in each of the countries under various titles. This is the most complete edition. DLC

142 _____ (1906). Conferencia de paz centro-americana celebrada en San José de Costa Rica, del 15 al 25 de septiembre de 1906. San José: Tipografía Nacional, 1906. 70 pp.
DLC DLC-LDS-102 BNCR

143 _____ (1907). Documentos relativos a la conferencia de paz centroamericana: tratados y convenciones concluídos por los delegados de las cinco repúblicas de Centro América a la conferencia de paz celebrada en Washington, D.C., el 20 de diciembre de 1907; comunicaciones relativas a la ejecución de esos actos internacionales. San Salvador: Tipografía "La Unión," 1908. 52 pp.
DLC BNCR

144 _____. The Central American Peace Conference at Washington, September, November and December 1907: Minutes, Supplementary Documents, and Treaties Signed December 20, 1907. Washington, D.C.: GPO, 1907. 166, 26, 17, 50 pp.
The agreements signed at the 1907 Washington Conference among the Central American states, with the documents and minutes of the sessions. DLC LNHT BNCR

145 _____. Tratados general de paz y amistad celebrados en Washington, el día 20 de diciembre de 1907, por los respectivos plenipotenciarios de los gobiernos de Costa Rica, Guatemala, Honduras, Nicaragua, y El Salvador, y aprobado por el Congreso Nacional con fecha 25 de diciembre de 1908. San José: Tipografía Nacional, 1908. 66 pp.
See item CA 144. DLC

146 _____ (1910). Segunda Conferencia Centro-americano (actas de las sesiones, convenciones firmadas). San Salvador: Imprenta Nacional, 1910. 36 pp.
The minutes of the sessions and treaties signed at the Second Central American Conference which met in 1910 in San Salvador. DLC BNCR

147 _____ (1911). Tercera Conferencia Centro-Americana, 1911. Guatemala: Editorial Aguirre Velasquez, 1911. 47 pp.
The minutes of the sessions and agreements reached by the Third Central American Conference, which met in Guatemala City in 1911. DLC DLC-LDS-800 BNCR

148 _____ (1913). Quinta Conferencia Centro-americana. San José: Imprenta Lehmann, 1913. 76 pp.
The preliminaries, communications, minutes, and agreements at the Fifth Central American Conference in San José during 1913, which was not one of the meetings most noted for its results. DLC BNCR

149 _____ (1914). Sexta Conferencia Centro-americana. Tegucigalpa: Tipografía Nacional, 1914. 74 pp.
The minutes of the sessions and accords of the Sixth Central American Conference, which met in Tegucigalpa during 1914. DLC LNHT BNCR

150 _____ (1921). Conferencia de plenipotenciarios centroamericanos celebrados en San José de Costa Rica del 4 de diciembre de 1920 al 19 de enero de 1921. San José: Imprenta Nacional, 1921. 156 pp.
The accords signed at the Conference, including the pact forming the Central American Federation and creating the International Office for Central America, along with portions of the exchanges that preceeded the conference. Published in each country with varying titles. DLC DLC-LDS-800 LNHT BNCR

151 _____ (1923). Central American Conference: Washington, Dec. 4, 1922-Feb. 7, 1923: Proceedings. Washington, D.C.: n.p., n.d. 404 pp.
Contains the invitation, the Tacoma agreement, the minutes of the sessions, and the treaties and protocols adopted. DLC

152 _____. The Conference on Central American Affairs held in Washington, D.C. from December 4, 1922 to February 7, 1923. Washington, D.C.: American Association for International Conciliation, 1923, 106 pp. Maps. DLC

153 _____. Conference on Central American Affairs. Washington, D.C.: GPO, 1922. DLC

(Central American Conference)

154 _____. Tratados general de paz y amistad y
convenciones celebrados en Washington el 7 de
febrero 1923 por los respectivos
plenipotenciarios de los gobiernos de Costa
Rica, Guatemala, Honduras, Nicaragua y El
Salvador y aprobados por el Congreso
Constitucional de Costa Rica con fecha 24 de
noviembre de 1924. San José: Imprenta
Nacional, 1924. 78 pp.
    Published in each country with varying
titles, each containing the treaties and its
own ratification. DLC BNCR

155 _____ (1934). Documentación relativa a los
tratados centroamericanos firmados en
Guatemala el 12 de abril de 1934. San José:
Imprenta Nacional, 1934. 43 pp.
    Contains the correspondence relative to
setting the date, the various draft proposals
submitted by the separate governments, and the
final accord, along with a brief introduction
by the minister of foreign relations. DLC

156 Central American Court of Justice.
Comunicaciones cruzadas entre la Corte Suprema
de Justicia Centro-Americana y el gobierno de
El Salvador con motivo del reciente conflicto
hondureño. San Salvador: Imprenta La
República, 1908. 104 pp.
    The official exchanges in which El Salvador
pledged to refrain from interference in the
political disturbances in Honduras and declared its loyalty to the 1907 Washington
Treaty. DLC

157 _____. Opinions Given by Seven American
Jurists Regarding the Litigation between
Guatemala and Honduras Pending before the
Court of Justice of Central America;
Dictamenes emitidos por siete jurisconsultos
americanos acerca del litigio entre Guatemala
y Honduras pendiente ante la Corte de Justicia
Centro-Americana. Washington, D.C.: Published by the Guatemalan Special Mission to
the U.S.A., 1908. 80 pp.
    A series of legal opinions, apparently
solicited by the Guatemalan mission from prominent Yankee jurists, all supporting the
Guatemalan stand and rejecting the Honduran
complaint of 1908 against Guatemala and El
Salvador, which was filed under the provisions
of the 1907 Washington Treaty. The arguments
are technical and involve the types of evidence submitted and the procedures that were
necessary prior to invoking the court, rather
than dealing with the facts of the episode.
Opinions offered by William I. Penfield,
Marion Butler, Josiah M. Vale, Joseph H.
Choate, William M. Ivins, and Hopkins and
Hopkins are printed in both Spanish and English in parallel columns. DLC DLC-LDS-690

158 _____. Sentencia en el juicio promovido por
la República de Honduras contra las repúblicas
de El Salvador y Guatemala. San José:
Imprenta Alsina, 1908. 183 pp.
    The court's ruling, rejecting the Honduran
charges that both Guatemala and El Salvador
had aided a revolution in Honduras in 1907,

with most of the rulings on the various
charges being by a vote of four to one. DLC
DLC-LDS-797 BNCR

159 Unos Centroamericanos. Soconusco: territorio
de Centro-América ocupado militarmente [sic]
de orden del gobierno mexicano. Guatemala:
Imprenta la Paz, 1842. 12 pp.
    A brief tract charging that Mexico violated
a treaty in occupying Soconusco, which it
claims was done in response to the desires of
the citizens of that district, noting that the
territory was in dispute and had been considered neutral since 1823. The Mexicans
claim it as part of Chiapas, while the Guatemalans contend that it was a separate district
that did not participate in the decision to
adhere to Mexico by the larger entity. The
entire case of the Central American claim is
rehearsed with patriotic rhetoric. LNHT

160 Chamberlain, Robert Stoner. Francisco
Morazán: Champion of Central American Federation. Coral Gables, Fla.: University of
Miami Press, 1950. 58 pp.
    A brief overview of the career of one of
the leaders of Central American independence,
based on secondary sources, though without a
bibliography, focusing particularly on his
efforts to unify the isthmus through federation. DLC

161 Chamorro, Diego Manuel. La controversia
territorial entre Nicaragua y Honduras:
análisis del manifesto de la Sociedad de
Abogados de Honduras a los pueblos del
continente y a sus entidades jurídicas.
Managua: Talleres Tipográficos Nacionales,
1938. 42 pp.
    A brief and legalistic analysis of the
boundary dispute stating the Nicaraguan case
and replying to a publication of the Honduran
lawyers' association, which it charges is
false. Chamorro reviews the issue of Colonial
jurisdiction, repeats the contention that the
king of Spain exceeded his powers in his 1906
arbitral ruling, and contends that Nicaragua
never accepted his ruling, hence rendering it
invalid. DLC

162 _____. Mediación del honorable secretario de
estado de los Estados Unidos en la
controversia de límites entre la República de
Nicaragua y la República de Honduras, 1920-
1921, Washington. 3 vols. Washington, D.C.:
Gibson Brothers, 1920. 214, 274, 129 pp.
Maps.
    The complete Nicaraguan case including its
reply to the Honduran case, as presented to
the 1920 arbitration by the United States,
with all documentation, annexes, maps, etc.
DLC LNHT BNCR

163 _____. La posición jurídica de Nicaragua y de
Honduras ante el laudo del rey de España.
Managua: Talleres Nacionales, 1937. 15 pp.
    The Nicaraguan case arguing that the king
of Spain exceeded his powers under the arbitral agreement and hence that his action has

no validity, reserving and reiterating Nicaraguan claims. CU-B

164 Chamorro Zelaya, Pedro Joaquín. *Defensa y refutación, contra la obra del Lic. Rómulo E. Durón titulada; "Límites de Nicaragua, rectificaciones al Dr. Pedro Joaquín Chamorro."* Managua: Editorial La Prensa, 1940. xvii, 336 pp. Illus., maps.

Part of the legal arguments involved in the Honduras-Nicaragua boundary question, this work was written as a reply to Durón's reply to Chamorro's earlier work, *Límites de Nicaragua*, which was part of the official Nicaraguan case to the arbitor. The citations deal with the jurisdiction during Colonial days and their implications for the present, abounding in legal terminology and interpretation. DLC LNHT

165 _____. *Historia de la Federación de la América Central, 1823-1840*. Madrid: Ediciones Cultura Hispánica, 1951. 644 pp. Biblio., notes, appendixes.

A detailed history of the Federation and its fall, from a Conservative and nationalistic perspective, based on and quoting heavily from published documentation and the memoirs of participants. The emphasis is on the political aspects, seeking consciously to downplay the military actions, though these are also included. The volume includes an introductory chapter on conditions in Central America at the time of independence, and also considers foreign affairs and external threats. The author is critical of the role of Morazán in supporting the formation of the sixth state of Los Altos, which he contends contributed to the demise of the Federation. Includes over 100 pages of reproduced documentation. DLC LNHT BNCR

166 _____. *Límites de Nicaragua: su formación histórico-geográficia durante la conquista y el período colonial, 1502-1821*. San José: Imprenta Lehmann, 1938. 127 pp. Illus., maps. 2d ed. Managua: Editorial La Prensa, 1941. 121 pp. Maps.

A review of the development of the province of Nicaragua during the Colonial era, tracing its history and that of its neighbor Honduras, seeking to justify the Nicaraguan claims in the boundary question through Colonial jurisdiction. DLC DLC-LDS-895 LNHT

167 Cheron, Luís. *América Central: nuevo punto de apertura del istmo americano*. San José: Imprenta de la República, 1850. 23 pp.

A brief description of Nicaragua and Costa Rica and a discussion of potential canal routes through the area, by a longtime resident of the region. DLC BNCR

168 Childs, James Bennett. *The Memorias of the Republics of Central America and of the Antilles*. Washington, D.C.: GPO, 1932. v, 170 pp.

A listing for each nation, by Ministry, of the memorias published, by year, from independence through 1928-29, containing full bibliographic citations, identification of the minister, and in some cases a brief indication of contents. Includes the changes in the ministry's organization and names. DLC LNHT

169 Chinchilla Águilar, Ernesto. *Compendio de historia moderna de Centroamérica*. Guatemala: Unión Tipográfica, 1972. 175 pp. Biblio.

A basic outline history of Central America, with a chapter dealing with each of the five countries, Panama, and Belize, from independence to the 1970s. The Federation period receives the most detailed treatment along with Guatemala. Based on appropriate secondary works. LNHT BNG

170 _____. *Historia de Centroamérica*. 3 vols. Guatemala: Ministerio de Educación Pública, 1974-77. 213, 551, 545 pp. Biblio., illus.

A three-volume series by a well-known Guatemalan historian, presenting an overview of the development of the isthmus. The initial volume deals with the pre-Columbian era, and the second with the Colonial period. The post-independence period is treated only in the second half of the final volume, which includes a brief account of the independence era, and a 100-page account of the 1838-1974 period, including commentaries on the economic and literary currents of the nineteenth and twentieth centuries. DLC BNG

171 Chumakova, Marina L'vovna. *Organizatsiia Central'noamerikanskikh Gosudarstv* [The Organization of Central American States]. Moscow: Izdetel'stvo, Mezhdunarodnye Otnosheniia, 1970. 127 pp. Biblio., tables. 2d ed. Moscow: Science Publishers, 1972. 171 pp. Biblio., notes, tables.

A Soviet political scientist's view of ODECA and the Common Market, which are depicted as structures designed to enable continued Yankee economic domination and political control. DLC

172 Churchill, Anthony, et al. *Road User Charges in Central America*. Baltimore: Johns Hopkins University Press, 1972. xii, 176 pp. Biblio., illus., tables.

A study of the highway system and the method of charging users to recover costs, providing considerable statistics regarding the transportation system and the economy, as well as discussion of the various types of charge systems possible and their relative advantages. The study argues for higher charges in more heavily used urban areas, to enable lower fees in the rural areas to encourage development. DLC

173 Cifuentes Díaz, Carlos. *La marihuana en Centroamérica*. San Salvador: ODECA, 1970. 118 pp. Biblio., illus., tables.

A brief survey of marihuana use in the region, combining information from teachers, social agencies, the police, etc., to provide some indications of its prevalence, and concluding that it is a problem in the region, particularly among the young. Recommends strong governmental action, through the creation of special task forces and educational campaigns to deal with the situation. All the data is current, focusing on 1967-69, though there clearly are limitations in the data gathering, sampling, and the tabulations. DLC LNHT

174 Cleveland, Grover. <u>Laudo pronunciado por el Exmo. Grover Cleveland, en las cuestiones sometidas a su decisión por las repúblicas de Costa Rica y Nicaragua</u>. Washington, D.C.: Legation of Costa Rica, 1888. 32 pp.

Cleveland's ruling in the Costa Rican-Nicaraguan boundary arbitration. The decision was actually written by George L. Rives, subsecretary of state, and was issued in 1888, supporting the boundary treaty of 1858 and granting Costa Rica the right to navigate the San Juan River except by warships, and defining the precise location of the frontier. DLC BNCR

175 Cline, William R., and Enrique Delgado, eds. <u>Economic Integration in Central America</u>. Washington, D.C.: Brookings Institution, 1978. xxvi, 712 pp. Notes, tables, appendixes.

A monumental quantitative study of the Common Market, financed by ROCAP and USIA and sponsored by the Brookings Institution and the Secretariat of Economic Integration of Central America, analyzing the experience, effects, benefits, and problems of the market in topical studies. Items considered include employment, income distribution, agricultural development, prices and purchasing power, industrial advantage within the market, and others, with extensive statistical data and computer analysis. The appendixes contain models for analyzing and predicting the changes in the Central American economy. Contends that the economic benefits to the member countries of the Common Market have been large and significant, but that regional imbalances exist particularly in the case of Honduras, that internal distribution of the benefits in each of the nations is also a problem, and that the major barriers to the future of the market are political rather than economic. Concludes that common markets on a regional scale can be beneficial in developing third-world areas and are a feasible policy alternative in such areas. DLC LNHT

176 Club Estudiantil Unionista Francisco Morazán de Tegucigalpa. <u>Los abuelos de mármol</u>. Tegucigalpa: Tipografía Nacional, 1917. 45 pp. Illus.

A unionist pamphlet, including some speeches at a rally by various individuals involved in the unionist movement, extolling the virtues of such an effort. DLC

177 Cochrane, James D. <u>The Politics of Regional Integration: The Central American Case</u>. New Orleans: Tulane University Press, 1969. vii, 225 pp. Index, biblio., notes, tables.

A study of the political factors involved in the Central American Common Market, including consideration of the background, description of the process and institutions, and

assessment of the impact. Emphasizes the uniqueness of the Central American effort and its differentiation from European developments, noting the isolation of the isthmus from international politics and the ideal of federalism. Cautions that the effort indicates that such programs are beneficial to development but must be unique to each region, with no readily transferable formula. DLC

178 Coello, Augusto C. <u>El tratado de 1843 con los indios moscos (refutación a don Diego Manuel Chamorro)</u>. Tegucigalpa: Tipografía Nacional, 1923. 82 pp. 2d ed. Tegucigalpa: Talleres Tipográficos Nacionales, 1938. 36 pp.

A response to a statement by the Nicaraguan official in the latter's case presented to the arbitor during the 1920 proceedings referring to the frontier question in the Mosquito Coast region. Coello challenges the ruling of the king of Spain in 1906 on the basis of accords signed in 1845, citing numerous documents from 1845-50 regarding the pacts and the role of the British. DLC LNHT BNCR

179 Cohen Orantes, Isaac. <u>Regional Integration in Central America</u>. Lexington, Mass.: Heath, 1973. xiii, 126 pp. Index, biblio., notes.

A general account of the integration process from 1950 through 1968 and an analysis based on international relations theory, based on the published reports of the various entities. Concludes that the Market attained minimal success because of the external support and the cautious approach that assured that the cost, both monetary and political, to the member governments was low, while the import substitution model proposed by the ECLA assured rapid results in some sectors; but while this approach enabled building the institutions, it made the integration movement the prisoner of the governments that created it, preventing drastic innovation or political integration. DLC LNHT

180 Colvin, Gerard. <u>The Lands and Peoples of Central America: Guatemala, El Salvador, Costa Rica, Honduras, Nicaragua, Panama, British Honduras</u>. London: Adam & Charles Black; New York: Macmillan, 1961. 96 pp. Illus., maps.

An illustrated descriptive volume, focusing on the contemporary era and written for the general reader in England. DLC LNHT BNCR

181 Comité Unionista Centroamericana. <u>¡La comedia é finitta!</u> New York: Carlos López Press, 1922. 18 pp.

A kaleidoscopic account of the 1921 political manipulations in Central America attendant to the unionist movement, calling for support of the Federation as a means of alleviating the confusing political situation and improving conditions of the entire isthmus. LNHT

182 Committee for Economic Development. <u>Economic Development of Central America; Desarrollo económico de Centroamérica</u>. New York:

Published by the Committee, 1964. 123 pp. Tables.

A bilingual overview of the Central American economic scene by a business study group, suggesting specific policies for further development. Advocates greater planning, more government involvement, expansion of trade, and a greater emphasis on integration. Provides ample statistics for the years 1955 through 1962, with tables covering prices and quantities of major products, U.S. assistance, financial institutions, education, price indices, and many more items, all arranged by country. DLC LNHT

183 Confederación de Trabajadores CentroAmericanos (CTCA-ORIT). La participación sindical en los procesos de desarrollo social e integración económica centroamericana. Tegucigalpa: CTCA, 1971. 70 pp. Biblio., tables.

A statement of principles by the union, indicating its support for regional integration and using this discussion to indicate its social goals and organizational aspirations. DLC

184 Conferencia Regional Centroamericana de la Sociedad Internacional para el Desarrollo (SID). Aspectos sociales y políticos de la integración centroamericana. Guatemala: Ministerio de Educación Pública, 1970. 549 pp.

A collection of thirty-three papers dealing with various questions related to integration and the impact of integration on all aspects of society, considering the economy, political scene, social services, population, education, and similar aspects. DLC

185 Conferencia sobre la Familia, la Infancia, y la Juventud de Centroamerica y Panamá. Las sociedades centroamericanas actuales: análisis y sugerencias para la planificación de sus desarrollos tomando en cuenta la formación de sus nuevas generaciones. Guatemala: Ministerio de Educación Pública, 1972. 317 pp. Tables.

An overview of Central American society and its principal characteristics, as well as a discussion of the impact and potential impact of integration on society in the region; enunciates a program of social development for the 1960s, advocating income taxes, labor legislation, agrarian reform, health, nutritional and educational programs, and family service and family planning efforts. BNG

186 Congreso Centroamericano de Economistas, Contadores Públicos y Auditores. Compendio de los estudios técnicos presentados al Segundo Congreso Centroamericano de Economistas, Contadores Públicos, y Auditores. San Salvador: Instituto Salvadoreño de Fomento Industrial, 1965. 456 pp. Biblio., tables.

While aimed at accountants and focusing on legal aspects, this collection contains several statistical studies on various themes such as development, economy, and integration, that provide data to scholars in many fields,

while also discussing the methods of accounting and record keeping involved. DLC

187 Congreso Centroamericano de Estudiantes de Derecho sobre Integración Política del Istmo. Integración política de Centroamérica. Guatemala: Imprenta Iberia, 1966. 151 pp.

The papers presented at the conference conducted in 1966, extolling the future of the Common Market and the goal of unionism and citing the Market as a step toward political union. DLC LNHT

188 Constandse, Anton L. Mexico en Midden-Amerika: erflanden van maja's en azteken. Meppel, The Netherlands: J.A. Boom, 1957. 223 pp. Biblio., illus., maps.

A general geographical account presenting basic information and brief historical summaries of Mexico and the Central American nations, focusing primarily on present problems and prospects, with essays on revolution, communism, contemporary regimes, and dictators. About half the volume deals with Central America. DLC LNHT

189 Contreras, Agustín. Centroamérica vista por un mexicano. Mexico: Imprenta Moderna, 1951. 146 pp. Index.

A brief, general chronicle of observations during a trip through the five republics and Panama, with comments about southern Mexico. DLC LNHT BNCR

190 Contreras, Ricardo. Cuatro artículos sobre el reciente conflicto centroamericano. Guatemala: n.p., 1903. 27 pp.

A collection of newspaper articles reproducing the charges and countercharges involving Guatemala, El Salvador, and Nicaragua, alleging support for exile groups and containing mutual accusations of reputed invasion plans. The focus is on Guatemalan suspicions of Salvadoran President Tomás Regalado and Nicaraguan President José Santos Zelaya. BNG

191 Coronado Aguilar, Manuel. Influencia de España en Centro América. Guatemala: Sánchez & De Guise, 1943. 113 pp.

An analysis of Spanish influences, inevitably focusing principally on the Colonial era, but with chapters tracing the various aspects of this influence topically, considering such questions as philosophy, religion, literature, fine arts, and social customs to the modern era. Includes a chapter supporting union and backing the Guatemalan claims to Belize, as well as advocating increased ties between Spain and its former colonies during the then current wartime era. DLC

192 Corpeño, José Dolores. Patria. San Salvador: Imprenta Nacional, 1914. 77 pp.

An emotional series of chapters written in the rhetoric of addresses (which some of them originally were) calling for the union of the isthmus, and stating that although the centennial of the independence movement is significant, it should serve as a point of departure

(Corpeño, José Dolores)
for a new unionist effort, as true independence has not been attained as long as the
isthmus is divided. DLC BNCR

193 _____. Un prócer inmortal de 1811: ofrenda
cívica. San José: Imprenta María Viuda de
Lines, 1922. 58 pp.
A brief essay extolling the role of José
Matías Delgado in the Central American independence movement, and citing his thoughts and
writings on various subjects to demonstrate
his vision of the future. DLC DLC-LDS-328

194 Costa Rica, Sociedad de Geografía e Historia.
Dictamen sobre la cuestión de límites entre
las repúblicas de Costa Rica y de Panamá. San
José: Imprenta Trejos, 1942. 111 pp.
A republication of two studies, by international lawyers Segismundo Moret y
Prendergast and Vicente Santamaria de Paredes,
prepared at the behest of the Costa Rican
government and submitted as part of its case,
supporting the Costa Rican contention in the
arbitration by the United States that followed
the Panamanian challenge to the Loubet award.
The statements support the legality of the
award and hence the Costa Rican position.
BNCR

195 Costa Rica, Gov't of. Ministerio de
Relaciones Exteriores. Correspondencia
relativa á los asuntos entre Nicaragua i
Costa-Rica. Managua: Imprenta Nacional,
1872. 24 pp.
A series of exchanges regarding transportation rights on the San Juan River, citing the
previous boundary rulings as the basis, and
detailing the stands of the two nations. The
official letters of the respective foreign
ministers are reproduced in full, without
comment. DLC

196 _____. _____. Costa Rica-Panama Arbitration:
Answer of Costa Rica to the Argument of
Panama. Washington, D.C.: Gibson Brothers,
1914. 312 pp.
See item CA691. DLC LNHT BNCR

197 _____. _____. Costa Rica-Panama Arbitration:
Argument of Costa Rica. Washington, D.C.:
Gibson Brothers, 1913. 632 pp. Maps.
The Costa Rican case in the proceedings
that led to the White award regarding the
Panamanian frontier with Costa Rica. Includes
the basic briefs, the numerous supplemental
documents submitted in support of them, and
the opinions of international jurists retained
by the Costa Rican government. DLC LNHT
BNCR

198 _____. _____. Costa Rica-Panama Arbitration:
Diagrams Annexed to the Argument of Costa
Rica. Washington, D.C.: Gibson Brothers,
1913. pages unnumbered.
See preceding item. DLC LNHT BNCR

199 _____. _____. Costa Rica-Panama Arbitration:
Maps Annexed to the Answer of Costa Rica to

the Argument of Panama. Washington, D.C.:
Gibson Brothers, 1914.
See item CA197. DLC LNHT BNCR

200 _____. _____. Documentos relativos a la
controversia de límites con la República de
Panamá. San José: Tipografía Nacional, 1909.
113 pp.
A collection of exchanges regarding the
boundary question, including the Loubet award,
the notes regarding its rejection by Panama,
and the resulting legal expositions by both
governments. DLC DLC-LDS-48 BNCR

201 _____. _____. Documentos relativos a los
asuntos entre Costa Rica y Nicaragua. San
José: Imprenta Nacional, 1872. 45 pp.
The exchanges of 1872 regarding the boundary dispute, with both nations restating their
positions. DLC DLC-LDS LNHT BNCR

202 _____. _____. Documentos relativos al
conflicto de jurisdicción territorial con la
República de Panamá y sus antecedentes. San
José: Imprenta Nacional 1921. 252 pp.
A collection of documents relating to the
Panamanian-Costa Rican boundary controversy,
including the 1825 treaty between the Federation of Central America and Colombia, the
arbitrations with Colombia, the various arbitrations with Panama, and the final disposition through the forceful actions of the
Harding administration, when a frontier conflict broke out. Includes texts of the treaties and arbitral rulings, and the various
notes exchanged between the governments. DLC
DLC-LDS BNCR

203 _____. _____. Exposición presentada por la
Comisión de Límites de Costa Rica al ingeniero
árbitro honorable E.F. Alexander el día 30
junio de 1897. San José: Tipografía
Nacional, 1897. 44 pp.
Exposition Submitted by the Costa Rican Boundary Commission to Hon. E.P. Alexander, Engineer, Arbitrator, Presented on 30th June,
1897. San José: Tipografía Nacional, 1897.
31 pp.
The Costa Rican case in the arbitration of
the boundary with Nicaragua, following the
disputes and frontier crisis of 1897. DLC
BNCR

204 _____. _____. Límites, Costa Rica y Panamá.
San José: Imprenta Nacional, 1938. 39 pp.
Maps.
A summary of the Costa Rican position by
the foreign minister. DLC BNCR

205 _____. _____. Recopilación de documentos
oficiales referentes á las cuestiones
pendientes entre el gobierno de la República
de Costa Rica y la dieta de la República Mayor
de Centro América, con motivo de los
incidentes promovidos por el gobierno de
Nicaragua. San José: Tipografía Nacional,
1897. 50 pp.
A series of exchanges between Costa Rica
and Nicaragua regarding the boundary dispute
caused by frontier incidents, reflecting the

(Costa Rica, Gov't of)
passions and containing charges and counter-charges. DLC DLC-LDS-45 BNCR

206 _____. _____. Reply to the Argument of the Nicaraguan Boundary Commission brought before the Hon. E.P. Alexander, Engineer Arbitrator. Filed on Behalf of the Costa Rican Commission. San José: Tipografía Nacional, 1897. 46 pp.
The Costa Rican reply denouncing the Nicaraguan argument regarding jurisdiction over the San Juan River. DLC DLC-LDS-635

207 Costales Samaniego, Alfredo. Diccionario de modismos y regionalismos centroamericanos. San José: Universidad de Costa Rica, n.d. 83 pp.
An alphabetically arranged list of almost 800 entries, with definitions. DLC BNCR

208 Coto Romero, Rafael. Visión de Centro América, complejos interamericanos. San Salvador: Tipografía "La Unión," 1946. 150 pp.
A series of essays, written during the author's travels throughout the isthmus, emphasizing a denunciation of Yankee influence and intervention in Central America, with pro-unionist appeals. DLC

209 Covell, Frank E. The Awakening of Central America. Minneapolis: Press of Commercial Legal Printing, Co., 1917. 24 pp. Illus., maps.
A general survey designed to call American attention to the region, with extensive photos. DLC

210 Crane, John. Francisco Morazán: The National Hero of Honduras. Washington, D.C.: Monumental Press, 1942. 23 pp. Illus.
A brief and profusely illustrated pamphlet, outlining Morazán's role in the independence movement, published under the sponsorship of the Honduran government and its legation in the United States, commemorating the anniversary of Morazán's death. It emphasizes background material and general information about the Republic of Honduras and its lineage, as well as about the subject. DLC

211 Crespi, Panchita. Wings over Central America. New York: Scribners, 1947. 169 pp. Illus.
A travelogue, by a resident of Costa Rica, that touches all of the isthmian republics. The focus is on people and economy, and hence the descriptions emphasize customs, culture, and the way of life in considerable detail, along with background notes and local legends. DLC LNHT BNCR

212 Crowther, Samuel. The Romance and Rise of the American Tropics. Garden City, N.Y.: Doubleday, Doran, 1929. xvii, 390 pp. Index, illus., maps. Latest ed. New York: Arno Press, 1976. x, vii, 390 pp. Illus.
A general survey of the Caribbean and Central America that emphasizes the struggle for survival of humans in the tropics and details recent progress. The author traveled in the region, and his impressions are reflected here, but in a series of topical chapters rather than in a travelogue. He emphasizes recent developments and hails the beneficial results of Yankee investment, particularly by the United Fruit Company, as an improvement in the life of the region, mirroring the Yankee stereotypes of the day. He also stresses economic interdependence. DLC LNHT

213 Cruz, Ernesto. Derecho, desarrollo e integración regional en Centro América: análisis y evaluación. San Salvador: ODECA, 1967. 116 pp.
A study of the implications of the Common Market for law and the legal profession, focusing particularly on the educational system and the implications for practicing attorneys, advocating greater cooperation among the region's law schools and more focus on regional law. MH

214 Cruz, Fernando, and Lorenzo Montúfar y Rivera Maestre. La verdad histórica acerca del tratado de límites entre Guatemala y México. Guatemala: Tipografía "La Unión," 1888. 48 pp.
A brief summary of the Guatemalan documentation supporting its claims, contending that full publication of the documents would require too large a volume, but providing an overview of the items cited by the government. DPU

215 Cruz, Ramón Ernesto. En defensa de la soberría hondureña. Tegucigalpa: Imprenta La Democracia, 1961. 49 pp.

216 _____. Problemas territoriales centroamericanos: derechos de Honduras. Tegucigalpa: Imprenta La República, 1967. 55 pp.
A brief summary of the Salvadoran-Honduran boundary dispute and a restatement of the Honduran case, consisting of a speech delivered to the Honduran Society of Geography and History in 1966 by one of the nation's leading lawyers and political figures, and a supporting series of articles by him dealing with various aspects of the pending questions. DLC LNHT

217 CSUCA. Eficiencia del sistema educativo primario en Centroamérica y escolaridad, que produce. San José: Proyecto de Recursos Humanos en América Central, 1963. 12 pp. Tables, appendixes.
A collection of statistical information about education, literacy, and educational facilities in Central America, published as the initial work in an intended series to focus on the educational status and needs of the region. DPU

218 _____. Encuesta sobre demanda de personal calificado en Centroamérica. San José: CSUCA, 1966. xv, 234 pp. Tables.
A survey and statistical study of the demand throughout Central America for educated and trained personnel, particularly in management positions; includes consideration of future needs and the educational levels of

(CSUCA)

present executives, encompassing such factors as age, training, fields, etc. The total number of specialists in each of numerous fields is given for each country, with separate profiles of each nation indicating the age distribution of present personnel with training in each field. DLC LNHT BNCR

219 _____. Estudio de los recursos humanos en Centroamérica. 7 vols. San José: Universidad de Costa Rica, 1967. Illus., tables.

A monumental multivolume statistical study of population in each of the Central American nations, using census, fertility, and economic data. Principally a collection of statistical tables, with current (1963) data and projections into the 1970s of the population and employment situation in the region, by country, tracing the trends in each nation and projecting the needs in the principal occupational fields, particularly for trained personnel in various realms, hence demonstrating the shortages that presently exist, the educational efforts needed to train people for the future, and the numbers of jobs needed to absorb the population. The text is designed only to supplement and explain the statistical tables. Includes general volumes for the entire isthmus and separate ones for each of the five republics. DLC LNHT

220 _____. Los estudios generales en Centroamérica. San José: Universidad de Costa Rica, 1963. 402 pp.

The proceedings of a conference called in part at the suggestion of the UNESCO educational technical mission, to examine general studies in Central American Universities and consider future directions in the Liberal Arts. Includes reports on the current situation in the various schools and a discussion of the future objectives of such general broadfield requirements and their role in the universities and their development. DLC

221 _____. Plan para la integración regional de la educación superior centroamericana. San José: CSUCA, 1963. 41 pp.

A series of proposed accords among the Central American Universities, approved by CSUCA in 1961, and designed to promote cooperation and exchange among them. The accords emphasize student and professor exchanges, the mutual recognition of credits and degrees, cooperative investigation, and the formation of general studies components to move away from domination by professional schools and facilitate the movement of students at the basic levels. DLC BNCR

222 Cuadra Chamorro, Pedro Joaquín. La nacionalidad centroamericana y la guerra del 63. Managua: Talleres Gráficos de La Prensa, 1952. 139 pp.

An account of the war resulting from the efforts of Gerardo Barrios to forcibly unite the isthmus, analyzing the positions of El Salvador, Guatemala, and Costa Rica regarding the diplomatic conferences and mediation efforts, as well as the various personal

alliances involved in the maneuvering. Includes copious quotations from correspondence, proclamations, and some Barrios correspondence in the Cuadra family archives regarding mediation attempts, as well as the full texts of the basic pacts of these years. DLC

223 Cunningham, Eugene. Gypsying through Central America. London: Fisher Unwin, 1922. 259 pp. Illus., maps. Reprint. New York: E.P. Dutton, 1922. 259 pp.

A travelogue emphasizing description of physical features and people and detailing transportation difficulties. The stress is on the hinterlands, with ample discussion of customs, people, appearances, and life-styles, though mirroring the Yankee-European viewpoint and suspicions. Covers all five of the nations. DLC LNHT

224 Cuzán, Alfred G. A Tale of Two Sites: Political Structure and Policy Performance in Costa Rica and El Salvador. Austin: University of Texas Press, 1977. 12 pp. Notes.

A brief survey of decisions involving the location of major local projects, the Cerron Grande Dam in El Salvador and a garbage dump in San José; stresses the different decision-making patterns that allowed local participation and advance discussion of objections in Costa Rica, but was exclusively a decision of the national government in El Salvador, with no provision for local participation or advance objection. DLC

225 Dane, Hendrik. Die wirtschaften Beziehungen Deutschlands zu Mexiko und Mittelamerika im 19 Jahrhundert. Cologne and Vienna: Bohlau-Verlag, 1971. 265 pp. Index, biblio., notes, tables, appendixes.

A survey of German trade with Mexico and Central America from 1821 to 1870, drawn from secondary sources and research in the archives of Germany and all the countries involved, with extensive statistical compilations. While trade with Mexico existed from independence, Central America became a factor in German commerce only in the 1840s, and only Guatemala and Costa Rica achieved importance for Germany, though there was also considerable interest in Nicaragua due to the canal question. The role of particular nations often depended on chance, such as the role of C.F.R. Klee, who settled in Guatemala. The author notes that Central American trade was more extensive than German records indicate, as much was carried in Danish ships. DLC

226 Dardón, Andrés [Un Centro-Americano, pseud.]. La cuestión de límites entre México y Guatemala. Mexico: Imprenta de Ignacio Escalante, 1875. 150 pp. 2d ed. Guatemala: Ministerio de Educación Pública, 1964. 232 pp. Maps.

An impassioned defense of the Guatemalan position, designed to answer the Mexican press. Though focusing on the dispute from 1874 to the date of publication, the volume traces the boundary question from the days of independence. Originally published under a pseudonym, it was the work of Dardón. The second edition, by the Foreign Ministry, appends a series of Guatemalan newspaper articles from 1895, covering the years since Dardón's volume and restating the Guatemalan case with equal passion. It uses the title Límites entre Guatemala y México. DLC BNG

227 Davis, Richard Harding. Three Gringos in Venezuela and Central America. New York: Harper & Brothers, 1896. xi, 282 pp. Illus., maps. 2d ed. New York: Harper & Brothers, 1903. xi, 282 pp. Illus., maps.
A travelogue describing the experiences of three Yankees on safari in Honduras, Panama, and Venezuela, including stops in British Honduras and Guatemala, during the 1890s. Narration and description predominate, with emphasis on the rigors of travel in remote regions, jungles, and the strangeness of conditions in a remote land. Includes descriptions of the people and places they saw, commentary on the state of the military or government, and observations regarding the economy. DLC LNHT

228 Dengo, Gabriel. Estructura geológica, historia tectónica y morfología de América Central. Mexico and Buenos Aires: Centro Regional de Ayuda Técnica (AID), 1968-73. 50 pp. Biblio., illus., maps.
A Costa Rican geographer's analysis of the geological formations and soil types of Central America, their origins and development, and their relationship to the Caribbean. DLC BNG BNCR

229 Diario de Costa Rica (San José). Reportajes y opiniones tomados de "Diario de Costa Rica" acerca del asunto de límites con la República de Panamá. San José: Imprenta Nacional, 1938. 34 pp. Maps.
The president's official statement, followed by commentaries by various prominent lawyers, diplomats, and political figures in the nation, all supporting the national position based on the White arbitral decision. DLC-LDS-861 LNHT

230 Díaz, Francisco. Francisco Morazán: tragedia en verso hecha por el famoso poeta salvadoreño Francisco Díaz de los acontecimientos que tuvieron lugar en Costa Rica y dieron fin el 16 de septiembre del año de 1842. Tegucigalpa: La Prensa Popular, 1892. 76 pp. 2d ed. Managua: Librería Española, 1894. 122 pp.
A poetic play acclaiming Morazán and detailing the final tragic days of his life when he unsuccessfully sought to put down a Costa Rican effort to withdraw from the Federation, only to be defeated, captured, and shot during September 1842. LNHT

231 Díaz, Víctor Miguel. Conmociones terrestres en la América Central, 1469-1930. Guatemala: Tipografía "El Santuario," 1931. 268 pp.
A collection of reports regarding earthquakes in Central America from 1469 to 1930, drawn from the contemporary press, memoirs, and Colonial chronicles. The quakes are listed by date, with very brief accounts, indicating the area affected, damage, casualties, etc. DLC LNHT BNG

232 Díaz Chávez, Filander. La independencia de Centro América: dilatado proceso histórico de la liberación nacional. Tegucigalpa: Federación de Estudiantes Universitarios, 1973. 145 pp. Biblio., notes.
More concerned with the present than with history, treating the independence era as a struggle for liberation from feudalism by leaders who fought for an ideal not yet realized; seeks to employ history to justify the present revolutionary aspirations among the intellectual youth. Most of the volume deals with the independence era, seeking to portray its leaders as real politicians akin to those of today, and to focus on what it considers their broader ideals for the isthmus. It then jumps to the present, denouncing Yankee imperialism, dictatorship, and the Common Market, and calling for a continuation of the revolutionary struggle. DLC LNHT

233 _____. La revolución morazanista: génesis; desarrollo y aniquilamiento; su importancia histórica. Tegucigalpa: Editorial Paulino Valladares, 1965. 170 pp. Notes.
A review of the independence era, focusing on Morazán, viewing him as a combative politician confronting the feudalism of the Spanish system; draws from previously published works, particularly the writings of Rodrigo Facio, who is cited and quoted extensively. Morazán's efforts are compared to those of the current generation who struggle for liberation from oppression. LNHT

234 Díaz Ordaz, Gustavo. Amistad: diálogos con Guatemala, El Salvador, Honduras, Nicaragua, Costa Rica y Panamá. Mexico: Presidencia de la República, 1966. 430 pp. Illus.
A lavishly illustrated compilation of the speeches and exchanges attendant to the visit of the Mexican president to all the Central American republics in January of 1966. DLC

235 Documentos relativos a las cuestiones con Inglaterra por parte de Nicaragua, Honduras y San Salvador. Guatemala: Imprenta de la Paz, 1850. 15 pp.
A brief pamphlet containing exchanges with England regarding the British occupation of the Mosquito Coast. DLC LNHT

236 Documentos relativos al Dr. y presbítero José Simeón Cañas y Villacorta, libertador de los esclavos de Centro América. San Salvador: Ministerio de Educación, 1966. 91 pp. Illus.
A collection of documents and scholarly commentaries relating to the priest who led the movement to abolish slavery in Central America, took part in the independence movement, and served as the rector of the University of San Carlos. Includes documents from the late Colonial and early independence era, and brief excerpts from subsequent scholarship about him to the date of publication. DLC

237 Dollfus, Auguste, and E. de Mont-Serrat. Voyage géologique dans les républiques de Guatemala et de Salvador. Paris: Imprimerie Impériale, 1868. liv, ix, 539 pp. Biblio., illus., maps, tables.

A detailed study based on secondary literature and a trip through the region by two French geologists in 1866. Includes description of physical and climatic features observed in El Salvador and Guatemala, followed by topical considerations of climate, volcanoes, earthquakes, and other similar physical features throughout the isthmus, with extensive charts, tables, maps, and drawings. The title listed is on the cover and title page, but the spine employs the title Mission scientifique au Mexico et dans l'Amérique Centrale. DLC LNHT

238 Domville-Fife, Charles William. Guatemala and the States of Central America. London: Francis Griffiths, 1913. 310 pp. Illus., maps.

A British author's survey of the region, for the general European reader, designed to call attention to its development and economic prospects. Part of a series dealing with Latin America, it recounts history as seen through British eyes, reflecting British attitudes, emphasizing the present situations of the nations and their emergence from "happy-go-luckydom" and "a long sleep," viewing the rise of strongmen as a hopeful sign that stability will come out of chaos. Description in travelogue form and historical narration are combined, along with discussion of economic development. Slightly more than half the volume deals with Guatemala, and another third with Nicaragua, with the remaining nations receiving only cursory summaries. LNHT

239 Dozier, Craig Lanier. Indigenous Tropical Agriculture in Central America: Land Use, Systems, and Problems. Washington, D.C.: National Academy of Sciences, 1958. 134 pp. Illus., maps.

A geographer's general description of the region's agricultural and land-use patterns, treated by geographical zone, based on an observational trip in 1957. Includes climatic and geographical data, commentary on the social implications of the forms of cultivation employed, and extensive illustrations. The author contends that little more than observation is possible due to what he considers the absence of basic geographical studies of the region. DLC LNHT

240 Ducoff, Louis Joseph. Human Resources of Central America, Panama, and Mexico, 1950-1980, in Relation to Some Aspects of Economic Development. Mexico: ECLA, 1960. viii, 155 pp. Notes, maps, tables.

A detailed analysis of population trends, with particular attention to age and sex distribution and their implications for development, covering the 1950s and projecting the trends to 1980. The focus is on developmental prospects and potential problems. DLC LNHT

241 Dueñas Van Severén, Ricardo [Justo Nonualco, pseud.]. Biografía del general Francisco Morazán. San Salvador: Ministerio de Educación, 1961. 443 pp. Biblio., illus.

Awarded a prize in competition in the isthmus, this detailed but sympathetic work is among the better of the standard pro-Morazán accounts of the role of this leader of Central American independence. It is based principally on secondary works and includes full accounts of the various events of Morazán's career, along with quotations from proclamations and other contemporary broadsides. DLC LNHT

242 Durham, William H. Scarcity and Survival in Central America: Ecological Origins of the Soccer War. Stanford, Calif.: Stanford University Press, 1979. xvii, 209 pp. Index, biblio., illus., tables, appendixes.

An anthropological study based on surveys and data gathered in two municipalities and extensive statistical analysis, contending that the 1969 war was a result not of population density, but of the concentration of land ownership and declining availability of land for the lower classes. The author argues that the problem in Honduras was not a conflict between Salvadoran and Honduran peasants for land but rather a result of the expansion of commercial agriculture, which diminished the peasants' access to land, creating social tensions similar to those in El Salvador despite the differing population densities. DLC LNHT

243 Durón, Jorge Fidel. Últimos días de Francisco Morazán. Tegucigalpa: Talleres Tipográficos Nacionales, 1942. 49 pp. 2d ed. Tegucigalpa: Talleres Tipográficos Nacionales, 1952. 50 pp.

The script of a semifictional radio drama recounting Morazán's last days and his heroic role, in the manner of an historical novel. DLC LNHT

244 Durón y Gamero, Rómulo Ernesto. Don Joaquín Rivera y su tiempo. Tegucigalpa: Ministerio de Educación Pública, 1965. 177 pp. Biblio.

A sympathetic biography by a prolific writer and scholar detailing the role of Rivera, a deputy from the Honduran department of Yoro to the Federation Congress, who supported Morazán and with him attempted to defend the Federation and continue the principle of Union. The study includes quotations from official documents and correspondence, all from published memorias and other previously published studies of this era. DLC LNHT

245 _____. Límites de Nicaragua: rectificaciones al doctor Diego Manuel Chamorro. Tegucigalpa: Talleres Tipográficos Nacionales, 1938. 107 pp. Maps.

A reply to Chamorro's work of the same title, regarding the boundary and the arbitral decision of 1906. Chamorro enunciated a Nicaraguan uti possidentis at the time of independence on the basis of Colonial jurisdictions. Durón replies that the province of

(Durón y Gamero, Rómulo Ernesto)
Veragua or Cartago existed only briefly and hence granted no rights to Nicaragua, and counters with arguments regarding the jurisdiction of the bishoprics and other provinces. DLC LNHT

246 _____. Nicaragua ante el laudo del rey de España. Tegucigalpa: Talleres Tipográficos Nacionales, 1938. 52 pp. Maps.
A brief statement of the Honduran position in the boundary dispute, contending that the problem is that Nicaragua refuses to accept the ruling of the king of Spain in 1906 and summarizing the Honduran position that this ruling ended the dispute. This statement is clearly designed for the general reader and not for the tribunal, and is far more succinct than the technical arguments, providing an overview rather than details of the basis of the dispute. DLC

247 ECLA. Estudio sobre la posible incorporación de Panamá al Mercado Común Centroamericano. Panamá: Ministerio de Hacienda y Tesoro, 1962. 2d ed. New York: U.N., 1962. 101 pp.
Despite its title, this volume focuses on the implications of market membership for Panama rather than on the potential benefits of Panamanian participation for the Market, its functioning, and institutions. DLC

248 _____. Estudio sobre pesas y medidas en los paises centroamericanos. Guatemala: Banco de Guatemala (for the U.N. Program of Technical Assistance), 1958. 227 pp. Tables. 2d ed. Mexico: ECLA, 1959. 227 pp. Tables.
A detailed survey by the United Nations Technical Assistance Program of the system of weights and measures used in Central America and each of the five republics, with recommendations for legislation guaranteeing the operation of the system and standardizing the forms in the region in accordance with world trends. The study notes that the region uses a profusion of different systems, combining elements from Spain, England, and the United States, and that no national standards bureaus exist; it recommends the establishment of such bureaus and a uniform decimal system. BNG

249 _____. Evaluación de la integración económica en Centroamérica. New York: U.N., 1966. 295 pp. Notes, tables, appendix.
A summary of the progress of the Central American Common Market and a description of the various instruments created by the movement to integrate the region economically, with an extensive documentary appendix. Compiled by an official United Nations body, it emphasizes the progress to date and the benefits from the effort. DPU

250 _____. La integración económica de Centroamérica. Mexico: ECLA, 1956. 64 pp. Tables.
A brief description of the Central American integration efforts, with an economic analysis of the region and its prospects, using statistics for the 1945-54 era. Includes tables, graphs, and projections of future markets for virtually all current agricultural products, as well as analysis of industrial and agricultural products now imported that might be provided by local production. DLC LNHT BNCR

251 _____. La política tributaria y el desarrollo económico en Centroamérica. New York: U.N., 1956. 141 pp. Notes, tables, appendixes.
A descriptive survey of the development-expenditure policies and tax patterns of each of the five Central American nations, providing an account of their policies and major changes in them, with statistical data regarding the impact of the policies, covering the period from 1939 to the mid-1950s. Some of the statistical tables are selective, using three-to-five-year intervals. WU

252 _____. Possibilities of Integrated Industrial Development in Central America. New York: U.N., 1964. ix, 54 pp. Illus., maps, tables.
A study of the possibilities for the development of several industries in the region, concluding that manufacturing has lagged in the area and that the promotion of basic industry is one of its greatest needs and will be a key element in its future economic development. Industries studied include steel, petroleum, rayon, glass, chemicals, tubes, and several others. DLC LNHT

253 _____. Reactivación del Mercado Común Centroamericano. Santiago: U.N., 1976. vii, 145 pp.
This official study of the UNECLA, made at the request of the Central American governments, was designed to suggest options for future negotiations regarding the development of the Common Market. It offers a brief survey of the market to date and specific recommendations in areas such as industry, transport, tourism, agriculture, finance, energy, water resources, etc., and includes the resolutions passed at the tenth meeting of the Committee for Central American Cooperation. DLC

254 _____. Tenencia de la tierra y desarrollo rural en Centroamérica. San José: EDUCA, 1976. 199 pp. Biblio., tables.
A descriptive study undertaken by several international organizations headed by the U.N. Economic Commission for Latin America. Focuses on demonstrating current conditions rather than enunciating recommendations, simply letting the facts speak for themselves. The study offers current data as well as figures covering the years 1950-62, seeking to demonstrate the concentration of land, the substandard living conditions of the poor, and the limited growth in food production. Concludes that these factors render land reform programs essential, citing the potential social and economic impact, and emphasizing the need for proper planning, provision of financing and technical services, and creation of responsible agencies with sufficient means and power. DLC LNHT

(ECLA)
255 _____. El transporte en el Istmo Centroamericano: informe de la Misión Técnica
designada por la secretaría de la Comisión
Económica para América Latina y la
Administración de Asistencia Técnica con la
colaboración de la Organización de la Aviación
Civil Internacional e informe sobre el
seminario de transporte, celebrado en San
José, Costa Rica, del 9 al 20 de junio de
1953. Mexico: U.N., 1953. 244 pp. Maps,
tables.
     A descriptive survey of existing isthmian
transportation facilities, with extensive statistics and maps, as well as recommendations
for future expansion and projections of needs.
DLC LNHT

256 Econometrica Ltda. Granos básicos en
Centroamérica. San José: Econometrica,
1970. Pages not consecutively numbered.
Biblio., maps, tables.
     A discussion of production of basic food-
stuffs in the isthmus, considering corn, rice,
and black beans during the 1960s. Includes
data regarding areas of production, size of
production, and markets. BNCR

257 Ehkdosis Diethnous Emboriku Ehpēmeh-lētēriou.
Ehthnikēs Ehlēnikēs Ehpitropēs [International
Chamber of Commerce. Greek National Commit-
tee]. E Dēmokratia tou Panama keh eh Horeh
tēs Kentrēkēs Amerikēs apo Ekonomēkēs Apopseos
[Panama and the nations of Central America].
Athens: n.p., 1962. 22 pp.

258 Elliott, Lilian Elivyn. Central America: New
Paths in Ancient Lands. London: Methuen,
1924. xii, 280 pp. Index, illus., maps. 2d
ed. New York: Dodd, Mead, 1925. xi, 280 pp.
Index, illus., maps.
Mittelamerika: Neues Leben auf alten
Kulturen. Leipzig: n.p., 1926.
     A travelogue-style account based on a num-
ber of trips through the region and written as
a composite. The emphasis is on description
of both physical features and people, with
considerable attention to life-styles and
customs. These are accompanied by explanatory
comments and brief historical notes to provide
a comprehensive view of the region during the
early years of the century. DLC

259 El Salvador-Guatemala Joint Boundary Commission. Informe de la comisión mixta de límites
relativo al trazo de la frontera entre
Guatemala y El Salvador. Guatemala:
Tipografía Nacional, 1942. 523 pp. Illus.,
tables.
     The documents of the boundary commission
that reported in 1940 and marked the frontier
in accordance with an agreement signed in the
1930s and completed during that decade. DLC
LNHT

260 El Salvador, Gov't of. Ministerio de Defensa.
La barbarie hondureña y los derechos humanos:
proceso de una agresión. San Salvador:
Imprenta Nacional, 1969. 111 pp. Illus.,
maps.

A collection of Salvadoran press reports
repeating the charges of genocide made against
Honduras, recounting the searches of all captured cities by Salvadoran authorities, with
catalogs of alleged abuses noted and the testimony of Salvadorans from the captured areas
of Honduras as to the oppression against them.
LNHT

261 _____. Ministerio de Economía. Integración
económica centroamericana. San Salvador:
Imprenta Nacional, 1968. iii, 73 pp.
     A general review and outline of the inte-
gration process. DLC

262 _____. _____. El programa de integración
económica de Centroamérica. San Salvador:
Editorial Ahora, 1958. 82 pp. Biblio.,
tables.
     A general description of the integration
movement, its progress, and the institutions
it has spawned. DLC

263 _____. Ministerio de Relaciones Exteriores.
Convenio de Chingo: documentos y comentarios
relativos a las cuestiones entre Guatemala y
El Salvador, publicados en aquella capital,
adicionados con los últimos documentos
relativos a la conclusión de la guerra,
incluso la falsificación del Convenio de
Chingo. San Salvador: Imprenta Nacional,
1876. 38 pp.

264 _____. _____. Correspondencia y texto de los
convenios celebrados con ocasión de la reunión
de ministros de relaciones exteriores de El
Salvador, Guatemala y Honduras, que tuvo lugar
en la ciudad de San Salvador, del 23 al 28 de
mayo de 1927. San Salvador: Imprenta
Nacional, 1927. 27 pp.
     The exchanges that led to the meeting of
the foreign ministers of Guatemala, El
Salvador, and Honduras in 1927, the text of
their agreement, and the subsequent correspondence and ratifications. In an effort to
promote joint action against external threats,
the three agreed to mutual consultation regarding policy toward nations outside Central
America. DLC

265 _____. _____. Libro Blanco: El Salvador y
su diferendo con Honduras, nuestra lucha por
los derechos humanos. San Salvador: Imprenta
Nacional, 1970. 239 pp. Index, illus., maps.
     The official Salvadoran version of its
dispute with Honduras, contending that
Honduras practiced genocide and discriminated
against Salvadorans. Most of the volume consists of excerpts from official communications
and studies seeking to illustrate the contention that Honduras provoked the crisis and was
the aggressor. DLC

266 _____. _____. Libro Rosado: contiene la
actuación de la cancillería salvadoreña
relacionada con los acontecimientos políticos
de la República de Costa Rica. San Salvador:
Imprenta Nacional, 1919. 68 pp.
     A statement of the Salvadoran position
regarding the 1919 Costa Rican coup by
Federico Tinoco, accompanied by a collection

(El Salvador, Gov't of)
of documents from the foreign ministry representing the Salvadoran government's exchanges
with the Tinoco regime. The Salvadorans
attempted to mediate between the Costa Rican
regime and the other Central American governments that followed the Yankee lead in refusing recognition. DLC

267 ____. ____. Libro Rosado: contiene la
actuación de la cancillería salvadoreña
relativo al negociado de unión
centroamericana. San Salvador: Imprenta
Nacional, 1921. 299 pp.
The complete documentation regarding the
Salvadoran participation in the 1920 San José
Conference and its unification attempt. Contains the report of the Salvadoran delegation,
the pacts of the conference, and the various
exchanges that preceded and followed the
meeting, as the Federation was carried forward, including the Salvadoran adhesion to the
document. DLC LNHT

268 ____. ____. El tratado general de paz y
amistad suscrito por las repúblicas de Centro
América en Washington el 7 de febrero de 1923,
y el proceso de su denuncia por el gobierno de
El Salvador: algunas opiniones al respecto.
San Salvador: Imprenta Nacional, 1933.
106 pp.
An official publication designed to justify
the Salvadoran action in denouncing the treaties, contending that it had become evident
(with the application of the treaty sanctions
to the then-incumbent Salvadoran government of
General Maximiliano Hernández Martínez) that
the treaties not only failed to solve the
problems of the isthmus, but added to them by
interfering with the expression of the free
will of the populace. Predictably, it hails
the Costa Rican government for also denouncing
the treaties. The official notice is contained herein, along with many letters and
declarations, all by Salvadorans and Costa
Ricans, including many prominent figures in
both countries, expressing approval of the
government's action and criticizing the treaties. DLC DLC-LDS-751

269 ____. ____. Tratados centroamericanos de
libre comercio suscritos por El Salvador,
Honduras, Nicaragua, Guatemala, Costa Rica.
San Salvador: Imprenta Nacional, 1953.
123 pp.
The texts of isthmian trade treaties, covering those from 1918 to 1953 and showing the
efforts to promote regional economic inter-
change. DLC

270 ____. Presidencia, Secretaría de Información
y Relaciones Públicas. Nuestra patria
centroamericana. San Salvador: Imprenta
Nacional, 1969. 199 pp. Illus.
A collection of documents relating to Central American independence encompassing most
of the major documents, combined with excerpts
from historical accounts and brief biographical sketches of the era's leading figures,
illustrated with their photos and the scores
of patriotic songs. Also included are a group

of speeches by scholars and government officials that commemorate the events. DLC

271 ____. ____. La verdad sobre el conflicto
bélico entre El Salvador y Honduras. San
Salvador: Imprenta Nacional, 1969. 15 pp.
A brief propaganda statement of the
Salvadoran position and its view of the
causes of the 1969 war, charging that Honduras
was at fault and that Salvador was fighting
for human rights because Honduras had
oppressed Salvadoran settlers in Honduras.
The folio also alleges that Honduran political
instability and machinations contributed to
the situation. DLC LNHT

272 Emery-Waterhouse, Frances. Banana Paradise.
New York: Stephen-Paul, 1947. 260 pp.
Illus., maps.
The memoirs of the wife of a banana grower,
recounting her many adventures throughout the
isthmus and in the process providing some
description of life-styles and physical settings, but principally focusing on the life in
the banana zone. DLC LNHT

273 La Época (Tegucigalpa). La voz de los
nicaragüenses: divulgaciones de La Época.
Tegucigalpa: Talleres Tipográficos
Nacionales, 1937. 21 pp.
Responding to the furor caused by the publication of Nicaraguan postage stamps showing
territory claimed by Honduras as part of
Nicaragua and by the Nicaraguan rejection of
the arbitral decision of the king of Spain,
this volume consists of a collection of excerpts from Nicaraguan statements in diplomatic documents and related exchanges,
designed to demonstrate that Nicaragua did
indeed accept the decision initially and had
in fact committed itself to do so in advance,
and hence that the Nicaraguan reservations
were an effort to raise the issue again. DLC

274 Ermolaev, Vasilii Ivanovich. Natsional'no-
osvoboditel'noe i rabochee dvizhenie v
stranakh latinskoi Ameriki posle Vtoroi
Mirovoi voiny: lektsi [National liberation
and workers movements in Latin American countries after the Second World War; Lessons].
Moscow: Vysshaia Partiinaia Shkola pri TsK
KPSS, 1958. 98 pp.
A Marxist survey tracing the crystallizing
of the class struggle in Latin America into
anti-imperialist fronts in various countries,
including Guatemala, El Salvador, and
Honduras. DLC

275 ESAPAC. Características del personal ocupado
en el sector público de Centroamérica. San
José: ESAPAC, 1967. 40 pp. Tables.
A collection of statistical information
about the individuals employed in public-
service jobs in Central America, drawn from
the data accumulated by CSUCA during its survey Recursos humanos, detailing by country the
numbers of individuals at the various levels
and types of posts and their professional
training and educational background. LNHT

(ESAPAC)

276 _____. Catálogo de la biblioteca. San José: ESAPAC, 1960. 124 pp. Index.

An unannotated list of the library, arranged by subject with cross-index for authors. Contains title, author, city, publisher, and date but no other information. The library of this institution was focused on general subjects and particularly general public administration volumes and texts, with little that relates to Central America specifically, save for the studies of ODECA and CEPAL. BNCR

277 _____. Diagnóstico y macroanálisis administrativos del sector público del Istmo Centroamericano. San José: ESAPAC, 1964. 65 pp. Tables, appendix.

An analysis of the situation and state of public administration in Central America, which not surprisingly calls for greater professionalization, better organization, and greater cooperation both within the various sectors of each government and within the isthmus as a whole. Contains an appendix describing the organization of ODECA, which it clearly sees as a prospective vehicle for promoting cooperation and the establishment of more uniform systems throughout the region. BNCR

278 _____. Las empresas públicas del Istmo Centroamericano. San José: ESAPAC, 1966. 74 pp. Tables.

A brief overview of the existing public enterprises and state-owned industries in Central America, including public services, providing an historical sketch and describing their administrative organization and economic and financial condition, as well as their relations with private entities in the economy. The focus is on the descriptive, with a question-and-answer format employed to facilitate the use of this folio as a guidebook by managers. DLC LNHT BNCR

279 _____. Estudio comparativo de sistemas tributarios de los paises centroamericanos. San José: ESAPAC, 1966. 31 pp. Tables.

A collection of statistics, in tabular form to enable comparison between the various Central American nations, covering the years 1960-64 and providing data about national finance, income, taxation, budgets, and expenditures. LNHT BNCR

280 _____. Informe del seminario sobre discrepancias en las estadísticas de comercio exterior de los países del Istmo Centroamericano. San José: ESAPAC, 1966. 214 pp.

The report of a conference studying the reasons for and problems caused by the different methods of keeping statistics regarding foreign commerce in the member nations of the Central American Common Market, with proposals for the regulation of reporting to facilitate the operation of the market. BNCR

281 _____. Los instrumentos del Mercado Común Centroamericano. San José: ESAPAC, 1965. 142 pp.

Summaries of the various treaties and accords establishing the Central American Common Market, with brief statements of the various terms and procedures. Designed to provide an outline and guide for potential users. LNHT BNCR

282 Escamilla, Miguel. Compendio de historia de Centro-América. San Salvador: Imprenta Nacional, 1895. ix, 141 pp.

A general survey covering the Colonial and modern eras through the end of the nineteenth century. DLC

283 Escobar Galindo, David. Una grieta en el agua. San José: Ministerio de Cultura, 1972. 68 pp.

A novel about the kidnapping of a wealthy individual by a revolutionary group, emphasizing the neurosis and guilt feelings of the group's leader and presenting a critical view of the impetus for such allegedly politically motivated violence. DLC

284 Escobar P., Alfredo. Arancel aduanero centroamericano. San José: ESAPAC, 1955. 87 pp.

A compilation of basic data regarding customs regulations in Central America, designed for the use of the school's students. BNCR

285 Escoto León, Claudio. Leyes de reforma agraria en América Central. Bogotá: Instituto Interamericana de Ciencias Agrícolas, 1965. 65 pp.

A summary of the agrarian-reform laws of each of the five nations, as they were then in force. DPU

286 Esguerre, Manuel. La Costa Mosquitia y el Archipiélago de San Andrés y Providencia: demonstración del derecho de domino de Colombia sobre esos territorios y refutación de los folletos de la cancillería nicaragüense [sic], de junio de 1925. San José: Imprenta María Viuda de Lines, 1925. 84 pp.

The Colombian minister in Costa Rica responds to the Nicaraguan contentions, tracing the development of the region and claims to it through a chronology, with documentary excerpts, seeking to demonstrate the primacy of the Colombian claim to the islands and tracing it to Colonial jurisdictions. DLC-LDS-347

287 Espinosa, Luís. Independencia de la Provincia de las Chiapas [sic] y su unión a México. Mexico: Imprenta Victoria, 1918. 68 pp. Notes, illus.

A brief summary of the independence era in Chiapas, detailing the state's activities and its shift from Guatemala to Mexico, with extensive quotations from the acts and declarations of the era, arguing that the state proclaimed its independence and joined Mexico prior to the Guatemalan independence movement. Prepared by a deputy in the Mexican Congress from Chiapas as a means of reminding Mexicans that the state joined that nation voluntarily, because of neglect by the Guatemalan Colonial

authorities, and in response to a promise for
more benefits to the region, which he contends
have not been forthcoming. DLC LNHT

288 Espinoza, Francisco. La Organización de los
Estados Centroamericanos y la carta de San
Salvador. San Salvador: Ministerio de
Relaciones Exteriores, 1953. 40 pp. Illus.
     The text of the "Charter of San Salvador" of
1950, pledging cooperation between the Central
American nations, with the texts of the offi-
cial addresses and a brief introduction. LNHT

289 Esser, Klaus, et al. Hochschulentwicklung und
Integration in Zentralamerika am Beispiel
regionaler Ausbildungs und Forschungzentren.
Berlin: Institut für Entwicklungs Politik,
1974. 176 pp. Notes, tables.
     A comparative study of high schools in the
five isthmian nations, encompassing curriculum, organization, and training of teachers,
with appropriate statistics and analysis of
the similarities and differences and comment
on the basis for cooperation and the impact of
the integration movement. DLC

290 Estado político de Guatemala ocurrencias de
aquel país, derrota del General Morazán.
Mexico: Ignacio Cumplido, 1840. 17 pp.
     A brief and relatively balanced account of
the Carrera-Morazán confrontation regarding
union or separatism and the battlefield results, drawn from contemporary isthmian newspapers. The account seems to favor Carrera,
but points out the pros and cons of both sides
as well as the claims and the criticisms of
each. DLC

291 Etchison, Don L. The United States and Militarism in Central America. New York:
Praeger, 1975. xii, 150 pp. Index, biblio.
     Originally a master's thesis based on pub-
lished sources and the Yankee press, this
volume focuses on the years 1960-74 and traces
United States military aid during those years,
charging that it was a major factor in promoting militarism in the isthmus. The focus is
narrow, with little background or consideration of the historical role of the military in
the isthmus prior to these years, which coin-
cide with the height of the aid program. DLC
LNHT

292 Facio Brenes, Rodrigo. La Federación de
Centroamérica: sus antecedentes, su vida y su
disolución. San José: ESAPAC, 1960. 80 pp.
     A study of the idea of federation in Cen-
tral America, emphasizing its origins during
the Colonial era and tracing the initial effort after independence, with commentary on
the legal and philosophical basis of the concept. By a well-known Costa Rican scholar and
political leader, who extols the ideal but
notes the difficulties. DLC

293 _____. Trayectoria y crisis de la Federación
Centroamericana. San José: Imprenta
Nacional, 1949. 138 pp. Index, notes.
     Two essays on the Federation of Central
America of the independence era, the first

narrating its rise and fall, and the second
defending the Costa Rican role in its collapse, arguing that the problem was Morazán's
actions rather than Costa Rican opposition to
Federation. DLC LNHT BNCR

294 Fagan, Stuart I. Central American Economic
Integration: The Politics of Unequal Benefits. Los Angeles and Berkeley: University
of California Press, 1970. xiv, 81 pp.
Biblio., notes, tables.
     An analysis of the operation of the Common
Market and its resolution of problems, seeking
to discover why what the author calls this
"alien system" borrowed from the European
Common Market worked in a third-world area
where it theoretically should have failed.
Concludes that the nations relied on a free-
market system, emphasized industrialization,
and increasingly politicized the CACOM. The
regional balance-of-payments problems and
trade imbalances that favored the more developed states as against Honduras and Nicaragua
are cited as the cause of the principal problems, and the disputes between Salvador and
Honduras as the weak link. DLC LNHT

295 Falla, Salvador. Carta al señor presidente de
la república, general Lázaro Chacón, sobre la
cuestión de límites entre Guatemala y
Honduras, 1928. Guatemala: Tipografía
Nacional, 1928. 23 pp.
     A collection of documents from the Colonial
period supporting the Guatemalan position in
the boundary dispute with Honduras. BNG

296 Fernández, Guido, et al. Seminario sobre el
Mercado Común Centroamericano. San José:
Asociación Nacional de Fomento Económico,
1968. 60 pp.
     A brief review of the proposals for the
Common Market, then in the process of formation, from the point of view of the businessmen, in the form of the proceedings of a
round-table discussion on 29-31 July 1968
involving Guido Fernández, José Miguel Alfaro,
Eduardo Lizano, and Miguel Barzuna, and providing a full transcription of the exchanges.
Its recommendations stress the necessity of
providing free movement of the means of production, including resources, capital, and
labor, as well as of products, and of eliminating obstacles to trade such as the dual
exchange rate in Costa Rica and the high cargo
air fares between the countries. DLC LNHT

297 Fernández Bonilla, León, ed. Documentos
relativos a los movimientos de independencia
en el Reino de Guatemala. San Salvador:
Ministerio de Instrucción Pública, 1929. xi,
121 pp.
     A collection of documents from the Archivo
General de las Indias consisting of twelve
letters to and from Spanish government officials in the isthmus during the years 1810 to
1816 and reporting on pro-independence activities in El Salvador and Nicaragua. Most were
previously unpublished. Includes letters from
the captain general and the bishop, as well as

various proclamations by local juntas. DLC
DLC-LDS-432 BNCR

298   Fernández Cruz, Soledad. <u>Morazanida:</u>
<u>espíritu de América</u>. San Pedro Sula:
Imprenta La Independencia, 1942. 36 pp.
Illus.
      An essay hailing Morazán and his efforts to
unify the isthmus. LNHT

299   Fernández Guardia, Ricardo, ed. <u>Documentos</u>
<u>históricos posteriores a la independencia</u>.
San José: Imprenta María Viuda de Lines,
1923. 774 pp. Tables.
      A collection of documents regarding the
independence era, beginning in the late
Colonial years and extending through 1832.
Includes the various acts relating to independence and the activities of specific
cities, as well as relations with the Federation of Central America. DLC

300   Fernández Shaw, Felix Guillermo. <u>La</u>
<u>integración de Centroamérica</u>. Madrid:
Cultura Hispánica, 1965. 1086 pp. Index,
biblio., notes, illus., tables.
      A massive tome reproducing all the relevant
documents, including tariff schedules, with
some linking narration, tracing the period of
the formation of the Common Market and its
organizations. Contains information on everything from organization charts to uniform road
signs. DLC LNHT

301   _____. <u>Panamá y sus relaciones centro-</u>
<u>americanas</u>. Madrid: Cultura Hispánica, 1964.
329 pp. Index, biblio., notes.
      An account by a Spanish diplomat tracing
Panamanian relations with Central America
during the period since 1948, focusing particularly on its links to the Common Market
and economic integration movement, noting the
contrast with earlier Panamanian stances.
About half the volume consists of a compilation of official exchanges, statements, and
trade statistics. Includes consideration of
cultural and political linkages. DLC LNHT

302   Ferro, Carlos A. <u>Las banderas</u>
<u>centroamericanas: su inspiración en el</u>
<u>pabellón argentino</u>. San José: Editorial
Centroamericana, 1970. 186 pp. Biblio.,
appendixes.
      In an effort to promote friendship for his
nation the Argentine ambassador in Honduras
prepared this historical study of the origins
of the Central American flags. Beginning with
the fact that they all use the color blue,
like the Argentine flag, he developed the
thesis that the Central American flags were
inspired by an early Argentine flag, also blue
and white, flown by the frigate <u>La Argentina</u>
sent by Buenos Aires to aid Central American
independence. DLC BNCR

303   _____. <u>San Martín y Morazán</u>. Tegucigalpa:
Editorial Nuevo Continente, 1971. 254 pp.
Illus., appendix.
      A study comparing the lives, actions, and
ideals of the two liberators, citing the

parallels between them and emphasizing the
similarity of their goals for Latin America as
a whole and the parallel nature of their objectives for their respective regions. Includes an extensive appendix of documents and
proclamations issued by both. DLC

304   _____. <u>Vida de Luís Aury</u>. Buenos Aires:
Editorial Cuatro Poder, 1976. 269 pp.
Biblio., appendixes.
      A biography of an Argentine pirate who
devoted his efforts to aiding the Latin
American independence movements, and fought
throughout the hemisphere, including in Central America. The major portion of the volume
is devoted to a detailed account of his campaigns in the isthmus. A documentary appendix
contains correspondence from the period.
Based on published documents and appropriate
secondary works. DLC

305   Fiallos Gil, Mariano, Alfonso Trejos, and José
Enrique Silva. <u>El proceso cultural</u>
<u>centroamericano</u>. San Salvador: Editorial
Universitaria, 1964. 162 pp.
      The proceedings of a September 1963 con-
ference on contemporary history held at the
University of El Salvador, with papers dealing
with the elements of Central American culture,
their common linkages, uniqueness, and emergence. Includes summaries of the discussion
that followed the papers. José Enrique Silva
argues for the contribution of the university
to the national culture, noting the importance
of autonomy and unbiased judgments, while
Alfonso Trejos and Mariano Fiallos Gil trace a
wide range of cultural traits, including Indian and Spanish elements as well as intellectual and philosophical trends, with extensive
discussion of the writings of Central American
literary figures. LNHT

306   Fiat Delegación para la América Latina.
<u>Mercado Común Centroamericano: síntesis</u>
<u>económica y financiera</u>. Buenos Aires:
Talleres Gráficos La Técnica Impresora, 1968.
327 pp. Illus., maps, tables.
      A brief description, with extensive tables
of statistics and multicolor graphs, of the
economic and financial development of Central
America since 1950, dealing separately with
each industry and nation, considering all
aspects of the economy, including industry,
agriculture, transport, energy, finance, and
foreign trade. LNHT

307   Figeac, José Flores. <u>Crisoles</u>. 2 vols. San
Salvador: Talleres Gráficos Cisneros, 1946-
48. 260, 304 pp. Illus.
      A series of historical essays, originally
published in various isthmian newspapers,
dealing with miscellaneous themes but consisting mainly of vignettes about the region's
principal political figures, reprinted here
with accompanying letters and exchanges. They
span the entire period of Central American
history through the nineteenth century, and
contain a strong liberal and anticlerical
bias. Though unfootnoted, the articles

include quotations and textual citations to published works and documents. DLC

308 Filio, Carlos. <u>Tierras de Centroamérica</u>. Mexico: Ediciones Coli, 1946. 154 pp. Illus.

A journalist's commentary and travelogue of a trip through the four northern nations of the isthmus, combining physical description with impressions of the presidents, their governments, and the political characteristics of each nation, and criticizing the dictators of the early 1940s. NN

309 Filísola, Vicente. <u>La cooperación de México en la independencia de Centro América</u>. 2 vols. Mexico: Imprenta del Gobierno del Estado, 1824. 132, 140 pp. 2d ed. Mexico: Librería de la Viuda de Ch. Bouret, 1911. 327, 340 pp. Index, illus.

A collection of correspondence and manifestos comprising the record of Filísola's illfated efforts to annex Central America to Mexico during the independence era, compiled during his military expedition to that area on behalf of the Iturbide Empire. Includes all his public proclamations, several polemical statements, and his archive of correspondence and letters, including exchanges with all the leading citizens of the day, with the local governing bodies, and some of his exchanges with Iturbide. There is an index but no table of contents. A portion of the volume, containing political polemics with Barrundia, was published in 1824 in Puebla, Mexico. DLC

310 _____. <u>Manifiesto de general Filísola sobre su expedición a Guatemala: ó refutación de lo dicho por los ciudadanos Molina, Barrundia, Gálvez, Mayorga y Arce</u>. Mexico: Imprenta del Gobierno Nacional, 1824. 20 pp.

Filísola's reply to the proclamations and charges of the Central American independence movement leaders, defending his actions in Central America and citing his honor and good intentions, while charging that these attacks distort the facts. DLC

311 First National City Bank, Foreign Information Service. <u>The Central American Common Market</u>. New York: First National City Bank, 1964. 30 pp. Illus., tables.

A brief survey of the current state of the national economies of the member nations, with statistics from the 1950s and 1960s, extolling the future growth prospects and the potential of the region and the Common Market, published on the occasion of the opening of the bank's first office in the isthmus. TxU

312 _____. <u>The Central American Common Market: A Progress Report on . . . .</u> New York: First National City Bank, 1967. 17 pp. NIC

313 Flores Ochoa, Santiago. <u>El retorno de Caín</u>. Buenos Aires: Schmidel, 1970. 149 pp. Maps.

A Honduran diplomat's defense of his nation's position in the 1969 war with Salvador, focusing on the diplomatic efforts and the propaganda conflict, in which he alleges that the Salvadorans succeeded in affecting world opinion with unfounded charges. The volume recounts the accusations and provides counterevidence, contending that the attack on Honduras was unprovoked, rejecting allegations of genocide, and arguing that Salvador was the aggressor both on the battlefield and in the press. He hails the role of the OAS, and also comments on Argentine press coverage of the episode, reflecting the fact that he served in Buenos Aires at the time. DLC LNHT

314 Fonseca, Pedro S. <u>Economía centroamericana</u>. San Salvador: Imprenta Funes y Ungo, 1935. 77 pp.

Analysis of the Central American economy during the late 1920s and early 1930s, with the emphasis on natural resources and commercial balances, though there are chapters on climate, population, regional and international commerce, tourism, finance, and transportation, all describing the current situation and looking to future possibilities. The author was director general of statistics of El Salvador. DLC BNG

315 Foote, Mrs. Henry Grant. <u>Recollections of Central America and the West Coast of Africa</u>. London: T.C. Newby, 1869. 221 pp.

The widow of a British consular representative provides her recollections of her residence in and travel through various locations during the 1850s and 1860s. Among the points of residence are Greytown, Nicaragua and San Salvador, which of course entailed a trip across Nicaragua. The emphasis is on description, though it includes accounts of people and conversations, snatches of history as told to the author, and an account of the 1854 earthquake in San Salvador. The initial 152 pages deal with Central America, and the rest with Africa. DLC

316 Forero, Juan F. <u>Nuevos estados emancipados economicamente con precidencia de sistemas entronizados, libres de la influencia capitalista, para ocupar el remanente de brazos, saldo del maquinismo: colonias-escuelas agrícolas</u>. San José: Imprenta Borrasé, 193-? 19 pp.

A detailed proposal for rural settlement-schools under military control to absorb the unemployed population, on the model of the Yankee CCC (though this is not mentioned), but for the additional purpose of training a new type of citizen for a cooperative agricultural life outside the capitalist system. DLC-LDS-833

317 Forss, Elis. <u>Mañanaland</u>. Stockholm: Albert Bonniers Forlag, 1937. 220 pp. Illus.

A travelogue with emphasis on adventure and life in the jungles and mountains, but containing observations on the economy and people. Includes Colombia and the Central American republics save for El Salvador. DLC

318 Foster, Harry la Tourette. <u>A Gringo in Mañana-Land</u>. New York: Dodd, Mead, 1924.

xi, 357 pp. Illus. 2d. ed. New York: Dodd, Mead, 1925. xi, 357 pp.

A memoir of the author's travels during the 1920s, with half devoted to Mexico and the rest to all of Central America. His focus is on the people he met, with discussion of customs, narration of adventures, and descriptions, as well as details of the cities visited and the means of travel. He is sympathetic to the local people and their customs, though still clearly regarding the region as exotic. Provides an indication of the state of the region, its people, and its capitals during that era. DLC

319 Fox, Robert W., and Jerrold W. Huguet. Population and Urban Trends in Central America and Panama. Washington, D.C.: Inter-American Development Bank, 1977. vii, 224 pp. Biblio., illus., tables.

A survey of population trends in the isthmus, sponsored by the bank and based on data from the five republics in 1975 and 1976. The focus is on identifying population-growth trends and spatial-distribution changes within each of the nations and in the isthmus as a whole, with projections to the year 2000 to facilitate planning and show the results of the current trends. Includes some historical statistics to the beginning of the century for comparative purposes. DLC

320 Franck, Harry Alverson. Tramping through Mexico, Guatemala, and Honduras. New York: Appleton-Century, 1916. 378 pp. Illus., maps.

An experienced travel-book author's account covering day-to-day experiences during his trip through Mexico, Guatemala, and Honduras. He describes people and places as well as physical setting, and complains about bad roads and poor lodging and facilities, yet sympathizes with the peasants and people he meets. DLC

321 Franck, Harry Alverson, and Herbert C. Lanks. The Pan American Highway from the Río Grande to the Canal Zone. New York: Appleton-Century, 1940. 249 pp. Index, illus., maps.

A profusely illustrated travelogue describing the authors' trip down the Pan American Highway through Mexico and Central America to the Canal Zone, with details on each of the countries. The focus is the highway, its condition and facilities, but descriptions of terrain and all stopping points as well as people are included. The authors are observant and experienced travel-book writers who catch the flavor of the cities and nations they visit even though the data is limited and the focus is on description. DLC

322 Frias y Soto, Hilarion. Cuestión de límites entre México y Guatemala. Mexico: Tipografía de Filomeno Mata, 1883. 40 pp. Illus., maps.

A brief statement of the Mexican position and a review of the 1881 accord, followed by an essay on the career of Mexican Foreign Minister Ignacio Mariscal. DLC

323 Friedman, Burton Dean. La administración pública de la educación en Centro América. Guatemala: Imprenta Universitaria, 1963. 35 pp.
The Public Administration of Education in Central America. East Lansing: Michigan State University Press, 1964. 28 pp.

A commentary regarding the administration of education in the isthmus and future needs, stemming from the first Central American conference on the preparation of teachers for middle grades. LNHT BNG

324 Fröbel, Karl Ferdinand Julius. Seven Years' Travel in Central America, Northern Mexico, and the Far West of the United States. London: Richard Bentley, 1859. xxiv, 587 pp. Illus.
Siete años de viaje. Managua: Banco de América, 1978. xix, 382 pp. Index, illus.

The first 200 pages of this descriptive account deal with Central America, more than three fourths of them focusing on Nicaragua. The author also visited Honduras and Belize. He describes in detail all his activities (including conversations and illnesses) with a particular eye for physical description. DLC LNHT

325 Fuentes Mohr, Alberto. La creación de un mercado común: apuntes históricos sobre la experiencia de Centroamérica. Buenos Aires: Instituto Para la Integración de América Latina, 1973. xi, 270 pp. Biblio.

A participant's account of the formation of the Common Market, focusing on the historical antecedents and preliminary steps and terminating with the conclusion of the formative process. The focus is on the years 1951 through 1963, with a detailed account of the various separate accords that drew the nations together and created the parts of the Common Market. The chapters are essentially narrative, with quotations from CEPAL documents and government publications, as well as from public declarations of the participants. DLC LNHT

326 Gaimusho Keizaikyoku Raten Amerikaka. Atarashii Shijô Chûbei to Keizaitôgô [Central America and its integration]. Tokyo: n.p., 1964. 109 pp.

An analysis of the formation of the Central American Common Market and its potential.

327 _____. Chûbei Kyôdô Shijô no Subete [All about the Central American Common Market]. Tokyo: n.p., 1967. 37 pp.

A brief summary of the Central American Common Market and its functioning.

328 Galindo, Juan. On Central America. London: Royal Geographic Society, n.d. [1836]. 17 pp.

A general description for the Royal Geographic Society in London, in 1832, providing basic data for the European general reader. DLC

329 Galinier, Hector. L'Amérique Centrale, son présent, son avenir, ou considérations

générales sur cette importante et fertile
région au point de vue du développement, du
commerce et de l'industrie française.
Carcassonne: Labau, 1871. 108 pp. Maps,
tables.
    DLC

330 Gallardo, Ricardo, ed. Las constituciones de
la República Federal de Centro-América. 2
vols. Madrid: Instituto de Estudios
Políticos, 1958. xxxi, 1397 pp. Biblio.,
notes, illus.
    A study of the antecedents to independence
and the influences of the Cortés of Cádiz on
Central America, followed by the complete
texts of the declarations of independence, the
constitution of the Federation of Central
America, and various federalist constitutions
from 1824 through 1921, with analytical commentaries comparing them with their antecedents. Includes the documents and treaties
creating ODECA and the Common Market, the
Washington Treaties of 1907 and 1923, and
commentaries regarding unionism and Pan-
Americanism. DLC LNHT

331 Gamboa Alvarado, Emma, and Félix Hernández
Andrino. Formación de profesores de educación
media. Guatemala: Imprenta Universitaria,
1963. 27 pp. Tables.
    Curriculum recommendations, based on the
first Central American Conference on the preparation of teachers for the middle grades.
BNG

332 Gámez, José Dolores. Límites históricas entre
las repúblicas de Nicaragua y Honduras.
Managua: n.p., 1900. lxxxii, 641 pp.
    A collection of documents regarding the
Nicaragua-Honduras border dispute, ranging
from the 1500s to the 1890s, including diplomatic correspondence and royal edicts, with an
extensive introduction in which the author, a
Nicaraguan historian, supports the stand of
his country. DLC

333 ____. Reminiscencias históricas de la tierra
centroamericana. Vol. 1, La independencia de
Centro América: historia patria (El Imperio).
San Salvador: Diario de El Salvador, 1913.
268 pp. Notes.
    A narrative of the independence period,
ending with the declaration of independence,
including extensive excerpts from the documents and tracts of the period, drawn principally from published sources. Includes
accounts of the unsuccessful 1814 effort and
chapters summarizing the independence activities of each of the major cities of the isthmus, including the capitals of the later
states and other important urban centers such
as León and Granada. The majority of the
volume focuses on 1812-14. DLC LNHT

334 Gamio de Alba, Ana Margarita. La mujer
indígena de Centro América: sumaria
recopilación acerca de sus condiciones de
vida. Mexico: Ediciones Especiales del
Instituto Indigenista Interamericano, 1957.
90 pp. Biblio., notes, illus.

A description of the conditions of life of
women among the various Indian groups of Central America, drawn from a survey of existing
anthropological literature. Designed to summarize the available data in handy form to
complement new fieldwork being undertaken by
the Instituto Indigenista Interamericano; prepared under their sponsorship. DPU

335 Gann, Thomas William Francis. In an Unknown
Land. New York: Scribner's 1924. 263 pp.
Index, illus., maps. Reprint. Freeport,
N.Y.: Books for Libraries Press, 1971. 263
pp. Illus., maps.
    Memoirs of an expedition from Belize into
the jungles of Guatemala, Belize, and the
Yucatan, which located several previously
unknown Mayan cities. Provides details of the
trips and the discoveries, but emphasizes
colorful narration of the joys of jungle
travel and living, with vivid description of
the surroundings, the author's adventures, and
his observations of the people and places he
visited. Provides as much information about
contemporary customs and living conditions as
about the archeological discoveries, though
all are observed through the author's biases
and with an air of condescension. DLC LNHT

336 ____. Maya Cities: A Record of Exploration
and Adventure in Middle America. London:
Duckworth; New York: Scribner's 1928. 256
pp. Maps.
    Follows the pattern of the author's other
volumes, detailing his explorations throughout
Belize, Guatemala, and the Yucatan from his
base in Belize City, narrating the travels,
experiences, and sights, as well as the
archeological finds.

337 ____. Mystery Cities: Exploration and Adventure in Lubaantun. New York: Scribner's;
London: Duckworth, 1925. 252 pp. Index,
illus.
    Colorful and vivid memoir of jungle adven-
tures, which, though written about an expedition to a Maya archeological site and
containing some information about the
explorations there, emphasizes adventure,
travel, and the difficulties of working and
living in the jungle. Conveys author's impressions of the people and places he visited,
which on this trip included British Honduras
and Guatemala. LNHT

338 García, Miguel Ángel. Estudio histórico del
procer, don José Francisco Barrundia. San
Salvador: Imprenta Nacional, 1917. 18 pp.
Illus.
    A brief and sympathetic sketch of
Barrundia's role in the independence era,
written as part of the commemoration of the
anniversary of independence. DLC LNHT

339 ____. Gral. don Manuel José Arce: homenaje
en el primer centenario de su fallecimiento;
recopilación de documentos para el estudio de
su vida y su obra. 3 vols. San Salvador:
Imprenta Nacional, 1944-45. Illus.

(García, Miguel Ángel)

Though technically part of the <u>Diccionario histórico enciclopédico de la República de El Salvador</u> series (see item ES186), these three volumes all deal with Arce and consist principally of reproductions of documents spanning the years 1823–46, with emphasis on the 1823–32 period and particular emphasis on Arce. Explanatory notes and biographies of Arce are included. DLC LNHT

340 _____, ed. <u>Procesos por infidencia contra los próceres salvadoreños de la independencia de Centroamérica, desde 1811 hasta 1818</u>. San Salvador: Imprenta Nacional, 1940. 533 pp. Illus.

Published as part of the author's continuing series, the <u>Diccionario histórico</u>, this volume consists of the documentary records of the trials of suspected independence advocates in San Salvador conducted under orders of the captain general between 1811 and 1818 in an effort to stamp out the independence movement. Most of the well-known figures who later lead the effort are included. DLC LNHT

341 García L., Graciela. <u>Corrientes históricas y dictaduras en Centro América</u>. Mexico: Impresora Periodística y Comercial, 1948. 40 pp.

A semi-Marxist tract contending that history is made by social classes, not by individuals. Extols the recent revolutions in El Salvador and Guatemala, exhorting the working classes to support the bourgeois democratic revolutions as the first step that would at least destroy feudalism in the region and bring about land reform, citing this as a necessary preliminary step to better days; attacks the dictatorships still surviving in Honduras and Nicaragua. LNHT

342 García Laguardia, Jorge Mario. <u>Orígines de la democracia constitucional en Centro América</u>. San José: EDUCA, 1971. 351 pp. Biblio., illus., tables.

A discussion of the Colonial origins of democracy in Central America, focusing on the influence of foreign books and travelers, on the participation of Central America in the Constitution of Cádiz and on the influence of that document in the isthmus, which the author feels was a key item in the move toward independence and democratic government. DLC LNHT BNG BNCR

343 García Peláez, Francisco de Paula. <u>Vindicación del sistema federal centroamericano</u>. San Salvador: Imprenta del Gobierno, 1825. 38 pp.

A commentary on the Federation of the independence era, by a priest who participated in the independence efforts and later became archbishop of Guatemala.

344 Gay-Calbó, Enrique. <u>La América indefensa: la intromisión norteamericana en Centroamérica</u>. Havana: Imprenta de Rambla, Bouza y Cía, 1925. 118 pp.

An anti-Yankee tract that attacks the imperialist forces and details their actions in Nicaragua and throughout Central America, contending the Yankees have prevented the unification of Central America. Cites the destruction of the Central American Court of Justice through the Bryan-Chamorro Treaty and alleged support of regimes that resisted unionism. The author, a Cuban lawyer who is clearly pro-unionist as well as anti-imperialist, calls for a more unified Latin American stand against the northern menace. DLC LNHT

345 Gehlert Mata, Carlos, and Carlos Orellana. <u>Salud pública y crecimiento demográfico en Centro América</u>. Guatemala: Instituto Centro Americano de Población y Familia, 1968. 73 pp. Tables.

A collection of statistics and comments thereon regarding population and health data from the five nations and Panama, spanning the years 1950 through 1965, though with the precise years covered varying from chart to chart. Includes graphs, tables, and statistics covering such themes as life expectancy, birth and death rates, population, health facilities, and doctors in the region. DLC

346 Geisert, Harold L. <u>Population Problems in Mexico and Central America</u>. Washington, D.C.: George Washington University Press, 1959. 48 pp. Tables.

Population projections noting that Mexico and Central America are among the areas of the world with the highest growth rates, stressing especially fast rates in Costa Rica and El Salvador. The projections are larger than those of the U.N. study. DLC

347 Giesecke, Helmut. <u>Zentralamerika und sein gemeinsamer Markt</u>. Hamburg: Ubersee-Verlag, 1964. 115 pp. Maps, appendixes.

An optimistic review of the Central American Common Market and its prospects, citing it as an integrationist movement that is working, though considering problems as well as accomplishments. DLC LNHT

348 Gómez Carrillo, Agustín. <u>Compendio de historia de la América Central: Obra premiada por la Academia de Honduras en . . . 1890; ampliada después con noticias inéditas hasta hoy, sobre el régimen colonial, y con importantes datos sobre la parte moderna respecto a las cinco secciones centroamericana</u>. Many editions. Barcelona: López Robert, Impresores, 1916. 311 pp.

An overview of Central American history, focusing on the Colonial era but including consideration of the independence era, and briefly covering the nineteenth century through 1890 with emphasis on the Walker intervention. The volume is unionist in viewpoint, and argues that the situation is propitious at the end of the century. DLC BNG

349 _____. <u>Estudio histórico sobre la América Central</u>. San Salvador: Tipografía La

(Gómez Carrillo, Agustín)
Concordia, 1884. 194 pp. 3d ed. Madrid:
Imprenta de Hernando, 1886. 225 pp.

A survey devoted to basic data. Includes
Indian cultures, conquest, and the Colonial
and modern periods, though the period since
independence consists mainly of lists of governors and the focus is on the Colonial era,
as the author believes that consideration of
the "contemporary" years would mar his objec-
tivity. DLC DLC-LDS-730 LNHT

350 _____. Historia de la América Central: desde
el descubrimiento del país por los españoles
(1502) hasta su independencia de España
(1821); precedida de una "Noticia histórica"
relativa a las naciones que habitaban la
América Central a la llegada de los españoles;
obra continuada bajo la administración del
señor general don José María Reyena Barrios y
en virtud de encargo oficial. 3 vols.
Guatemala: Tipografía de El Progreso,
1879-1905. 320, 351, 381 pp. Latest ed.
Barcelona: López Robert y Cía, 1916.

A general but detailed survey of Central
American history, by one of the region's best-
known novelists and writers, undertaken by
presidential appointment as a continuation of
the series begun by José Milla y Vidaurre.
Milla dealt only with the Colonial era, in two
volumes; Gómez Carrillo's three volumes begin
with independence, covering the Federation and
the nineteenth century through the Liberal
Reforms. BNG

351 _____. Instrucción pedagógica centro-américa.
San Salvador: Tipografía La Concordia, 1883.
126 pp.

A manual for primary-school teachers that
provides a discussion of preferred curricula,
methodology, and attitudes to be promoted in
the schools, as well as admonitions regarding
conditions in the classroom and the proper
attitudes to be maintained by the teachers.
IU

352 Gómez Naranjo, Pedro Alejandro. Faro de cinco
luces: perfiles de Centro América.
Bucaramanga Colombia: Imprenta del
Departmento, 1950. 190 pp.

A series of short miscellaneous essays by a
Colombian diplomat and journalist, written
under the inspiration of or during his trips
to Central America, originally prepared for
the newspaper El Tiempo of Bogotá. They treat
diverse themes, ranging from descriptions to
literature. Despite the title, the book deals
mostly with themes relating to Guatemala and
Nicaragua, with the other three countries
relegated to only a few pages. DLC

353 González, Nancie L. Solien. Black Carib
Household Structure: A Study of Migration and
Modernization. Seattle: University of
Washington Press, 1969. xxiii, 163 pp.
Index, biblio., illus., maps, tables.

An anthropological analysis of black Carib
households and their basic societal patterns,
focusing on Livingston, Guatemala, but based
also on field research in Honduras and Belize

during 1956-57. The author emphasizes what
she calls the "consanguineal household" rather
than the family as the societal unit, noting
that its members are not necessarily related.
This is characterized as an adaptation to the
social situation, since nuclear families increase when employment opportunities expand,
allowing males to support their offspring.
Includes descriptive material regarding Carib
society, kinship, and domestic life, with
comparison to other cultures. DLC

354 Gonzalez Dubon, Cristina Idalia. Bibliografía
analítica sobre la integración económica
centroamericana. Guatemala: Universidad de
San Carlos, 1970. 368 pp. Index.

A detailed, topically arranged list emphasizing items published in the isthmus and
particularly the reports and studies of the
official agencies, which often are issued only
in mimeographed form in limited numbers. The
majority of citations is of official reports
and periodical articles. Many include the
table of contents or a short annotation. The
index is quite limited, rendering it necessary
to search for items in the various topical
sections. DLC LNHT

355 González Galván, Manuel. De Guatemala a
Nicaragua: diario del viaje de un estudiante
de arte. Mexico: UNAM, 1968. 145 pp.
Illus.

A series of commentaries by a Mexican art
professor regarding his travels through
Guatemala, El Salvador, Nicaragua, and
Honduras during 1958. His observations
include descriptions and analyses of the
architecture of the public buildings and monuments that constitute his focus, accompanied
by photos and drawings of the edifices. His
drawings identifying the various images and
parts of the cathedral retableaus and altars
are particularly detailed. Comparative discussion and analysis based on the author's
knowledge of the theories and history of architecture and art are employed. DLC LNHT

356 González Sibrián, José Luís. Las 100 horas;
la guerra de legítima defensa de la República
de El Salvador. San Salvador: Tipografía
Offset Central, 1973. 404 pp. Biblio.,
illus., maps.

A statement of the Salvadoran position in
its war with Honduras in 1969, providing a
detailed account of the military campaigns,
with excellent maps. Includes discussions of
the diplomatic phase and foreign reactions,
but the emphasis is on the military action.
Excerpts from press reports and statements
supporting Salvadoran charges against Honduras
are also included. DLC LNHT

357 González Víquez, Cleto. Apuntes sobre
geografía histórica de Costa Rica. San José:
Imprenta Alsina, 1906. 100 pp. Notes.

A discussion of the Costa Rican claims in
the boundary dispute with Colombia regarding
the location of what is now the frontier with
Panama. Includes geographic and historical
data ranging from Colonial times to the nineteenth century, regarding jurisdiction,

communications, and economy in the region. Seeks to demonstrate Panama's linkages with Costa Rica; provides geographic data seeking to identify it as a logical part of Costa Rica. DLC-LDS-23 LNHT BNCR

358 Gramajo, José Ramón. <u>Fuentes históricas</u>. Mazatenango, Guatemala: Torres Hermanos, 1946. 180 pp.

A disparate collection of essays and letters dealing with various historical events in Central America and Guatemala, ranging from independence to 1944, arranged capriciously. A considerable portion of the work deals with the life of Juan Leets, and many of the letters reproduced are from his correspondence with various historical figures. The book is pro-unionist. BNG

359 _____. <u>María novela histórica centro-americana</u>. Mazatenango, Guatemala: Torres Hermanos, 1936. 149 pp. 2d ed. San Salvador: Tipografía Excelsior, 1936. 183 pp.

A novel of politics and love set in the 1898-1920 era, including in its plot travels by the principal figures throughout Central America, which provide opportunities for wide-ranging comment about the entire region and its situation. Includes commentary on the class structure, dictatorship, corruption, the role of the Yankees, agricultural development, and the similarities in the region. The author clearly sympathizes with the civilian politicians and with democracy. All the leading political figures of the region during this era pass through these pages. DLC LNHT

360 Grases G., José. <u>Sismicidad de la región asociada a la cadena volcánica centroamericana del Cuaternario</u>. Caracas: Universidad Central de Venezuela, 1975. 106 pp. Biblio., tables.

An exhaustive compilation of seismic observations and data regarding volcanic activity since 1915, with detailed charts, tables, maps, and mathematical calculations, as well as extensive data from observations. Includes a detailed tectonic history of the region, and criticism of previous works examining this phenomenon and their use of observation data. DLC

361 Great Britain, Gov't of. <u>Correspondence Respecting Central America, 1856-1860, Presented to Both Houses of Parliament by Command of Her Majesty</u>. London: HMSO, 1860. xiv, 329 pp.

The continuing exchanges between Great Britain and the United States regarding jurisdiction over the Mosquito Territory, including the Dallas-Calderon Agreement and the subsequent discussions, in which both sides remained adamant about their positions. Cites precedents justifying British views. LNHT

362 _____. <u>Correspondence with the United States, Respecting Central America, Presented to Both Houses of Parliament</u>. London: Harrison, 1856. xii, 303 pp.

Exchanges covering the years 1849 through 1856 including the Clayton-Bulwer Treaty and the subsequent disputes about the Mosquito Territory and its relation to the accord. LNHT

363 Gropp, Arthur E. <u>Guide to Libraries and Archives in Central America and the West Indies, Panama, Bermuda, and British Guiana</u>. New Orleans: MARI, 1941. xv, 721 pp. Biblio., illus., maps.

A listing, by country, and within countries by city, of the libraries and archives of the region, as of 1941. Includes all school and public libraries, listing location, librarian, size of collection, classification system, and specialization and type of holdings, as well as physical details such as hours of service, and any restrictions or conditions of use. In some cases even floor plans and the size of budget are provided. A pioneer effort to compile a useful listing of the resources available, though it serves more as a guide to institutions than to the resources within them. DLC LNHT

364 Grubb, Kenneth George. <u>Religion in Central America</u>. London: World Dominion Press, 1937. 147 pp. Index, notes, illus., maps, tables, appendixes.

Basic data about the nations of the region, with a description of the various Protestant missionary activities. Includes discussion of the contemporary situation, the origins of the various missions, and statistical data regarding each mission and converts in each nation. DLC

365 Guardiola Cubas, Esteban. <u>General Francisco Morazán: baceto biográfico escrito con motivo del primer centenario de la muerte de aquel preclaro republicano</u>. Tegucigalpa: Talleres Tipográficos Nacionales, 1943. 22 pp.

A brief summary extolling Morazán's role in the independence of the isthmus and the Federation attempt. DPU

366 Guardiola Cubas, Esteban, and Ramón E. Cruz. <u>Réplica a la impugnación del manifiesto de la Sociedad de Abogados de Honduras por los licenciados Esteban Guardiola y Ramón E. Cruz, individuos de número de la Sociedad de Abogados de Honduras</u>. Tegucigalpa: Talleres Tipográficos Nacionales, 1938. 23 pp.

A continuation of the polemics and exchanges regarding the boundary dispute between Honduras and Nicaragua, in this case replying to a piece by Diego Manuel Chamorro entitled <u>La controversia territorial entre Nicaragua y Honduras</u>, rejecting his arguments as invalid and inappropriate and sustaining the Honduran case. DLC LNHT

367 Guardiola Cubas, Esteban, and Félix Salgado. <u>Impugnación al folleto que, con el título de "Jurisdicción territorial atlántica de la República de Nicaragua, civil, política y eclesiástica," ha publicado . . . Ramón Ignacio Matus</u>. Tegucigalpa: Talleres Tipográficos Nacionales, 1938. 123 pp.

A detailed and sarcastic reply to the publication in question, which the authors contend libels the Honduran government, dealing with its contentions chapter by chapter, with an appended series of supporting documents. DLC LNHT

368 Guatemala-Honduras Joint Boundary Commission. Acta de la Comisión Técnica Mixta de Límites de Honduras y Guatemala. Tegucigalpa: Ministerio de Relaciones Exteriores, 1932. 470 pp.

The proceedings and decisions of the commission charged with determining the precise location of the line in accordance with the arbitral decision.

369 _____. Anexo: actas de la Comisión Mixta de Límites de Honduras y Guatemala reunida en 1908, 1909, 1910 y 1916. Tegucigalpa: Ministerio de Relaciones Exteriores, 1918. 471 pp.

370 _____. Cartografía de la América Central: publicaciónes de la Comisión de Límites. Guatemala: Tipografía Nacional, 1929. 125 pp. Maps.

A collection and study of maps relating to the frontier question. DLC LNHT

371 _____. Explanatory Notes on Geographical Names. Washington, D.C.: n.p., 1932. 42 pp.

A gazetteer of places along the disputed frontier, prepared by the Guatemalan representatives in support of their case. DLC

372 _____. Informe detallado de la Comisión Técnica de demarcación de la frontera entre Guatemala y Honduras rendido a los gobiernos de Guatemala y Honduras y al presidente del tribunal de arbitraje, de conformidad con el artículo IX de la convención adicional al tratado de arbitraje respectivo, celebrada en Washington, D.C., E.U. de A., el 16 de julio de 1930. Washington, D.C.: W.F. Roberts, 1937. xii, 476 pp. Maps.

The official report of the surveying commission that actually marked the frontier in accordance with the arbitral award, detailing its work and the location of the line. The commission consisted of both Guatemalan and Honduran engineers, and was chaired by a Yankee, Sidney H. Birdseye. BNG

373 _____. Límites entre Guatemala y Honduras: estudio económico de la zona fronteriza hecho en 1919, por una comisión del Departamento de Agricultura de los EE. UU. Guatemala: Tipografía Nacional, 1928. 36 pp.

374 _____. Límites entre Guatemala y Honduras. Publicaciones de la Comisión de Límites. 23 Vols. Guatemala: Tipografía Nacional, 1928-32.

The collected volumes combining all cases and documentation involved. DLC LNHT

375 _____. Opinion and Award: tribunal especial de límites entre Guatemala y Honduras: opinión y laudo. Washington, D.C.: n.p., 1933. 98 pp. Maps.
Opinión y laudo: límites entre Guatemala y Honduras. Tegucigalpa: Secretaría de Relaciones Exteriores, 1933. 99 pp.

The ruling of the arbitral commission setting the frontier after years of dispute, ruling largely in favor of the Guatemalan claims. DLC BNG

376 Guatemala-Mexico Joint Boundary Commission. Difficulties between Mexico and Guatemala: Proposed Mediation of the United States; Some Official Documents. New York: n.p., 1882. 60 pp.
Proyecto de arbitramento entre Guatemala y México. New York: Imprenta "Las Novedades," 1882.

A collection of exchanges and documents regarding a proposed U.S. mediation between Guatemala and Mexico, during 1881, when Secretary of State James G. Blaine sought unsuccessfully to promote such an effort. Includes the U.S. proposal and the resulting exchanges with Mexico, which provided summaries of its version of earlier efforts at solution, and previous publications about the controversy. DLC

377 Guatemala, Gov't of. Consejo Nacional de Planificación Económica. Recopilación de los convenios, protocolos y acuerdos celebrados entre los cinco paises del istmo, relativos a la integración centroamericana. Guatemala: Tipografía Nacional, 1969. 396 pp. Index, tables, appendixes.

A collection of appropriate documents relative to Central American cooperation and economic integration, beginning with the Washington Treaties of 1923 and continuing through the 1960 agreements. BNG

378 _____. Ministerio de Relaciones Exteriores. The Boundary Dispute between Guatemala and Honduras. Guatemala: Tipografía Nacional, 1928. 63 pp. Maps.

A summary of the Guatemalan case. DLC

379 _____. _____. The Boundary Dispute between Guatemala and Honduras, Published by the Boundary Commission of Guatemala. Guatemala: Tipografía Nacional, 1929. 40 pp.

A summary of the Guatemalan position. DLC

380 _____. _____. Defensa del gobierno de Guatemala ante la Corte de Justicia Centro-Americana de Cartago en el asunto de Honduras. Washington, D.C.: Bryon S. Adams, 1908. 124 pp.
Brief in Behalf of the Government of Guatemala before the Central American Court of Justice in Reply to the Charges Made by the Government of Honduras. New Orleans: J.G. Hauser, 1908. 146 pp.

The Guatemalan defense against the Honduran charges, contending that Guatemala took all proper precautions and was not involved in the Honduran uprising of 1907. DLC LNHT BNCR

381 _____. _____. El esfuerzo de Guatemala para canalizar el Río Motagua y el domino

(Guatemala, Gov't of)

indisputado que el mismo ha ejercito desde el siglo XVIII, 1928. Guatemala: Tipografía Nacional, 1928. 40 pp.
Boundaries between Guatemala and Honduras: Guatemala's Effort to Canalize the Motagua River and the Undisputed Jurisdiction that She Has Exercised over Its Valley since the XVIII Century. 1929. Guatemala: Tipografía Nacional, 1929. 36 pp. Illus., maps.
Yet another brief official statement of the Guatemalan claim in its dispute with Honduras, emphasizing its Colonial title. DLC

382 ____. ____. Límites con México. Guatemala: Imprenta "La Unión," 1896. 57 pp. Maps.
A restatement of the Guatemalan claims, charging that Mexico has violated the 1882 accord between the nations setting the boundary, and seeking redress. DLC

383 ____. ____. Límites entre Guatemala y Honduras: algunos documentos presentados en las conferencias de Cuyamel. Guatemala: Tipografía Nacional, 1928. 32 pp.
LNHT BNG

384 ____. ____. Límites entre Guatemala y Honduras: documentos relacionados con el mediación del Departamento de Estado de los Estados Unidos en 1918, 1919, 1928. 2 vols. Guatemala: Tipografía Nacional, 1928-29. 304 pp.
LNHT BNG

385 ____. ____. Límites entre Guatemala y Honduras: la prensa de Guatemala y la cuestión de límites con Honduras. Guatemala: Tipografía La Libertad, 1932. 248 pp. Illus.
Reprints three series of articles and editorials from Nuestro Diario and El Imparcial of Guatemala City, stating the Guatemalan case in the controversy. They contend that this is the most important border dispute in Latin America, and that if Honduras won it would effectively leave Guatemala without a coastline on the Caribbean, depriving it of its trade outlet to the rest of the world, not to mention its vital railroad and port and the investment involved. Hence, they argue, the survival of the nation is at stake. All examine the technicalities at length, asserting the justness of the Guatemalan claim. DLC LNHT

386 ____. ____. Memoria sobre la cuestión de límites entre Guatemala y México: presentada al señor ministro de relaciones exteriores; por el jefe de la comisión guatemalteca. Many editions. Guatemala: Tipografía Nacional, 1900. 325 pp. Tables. Latest ed. 2 vols. Guatemala: Tipografía Nacional, 1964. 350, 232 pp. Tables.
A detailed statement of the Guatemalan claims. DLC LNHT

387 Guatemala; República de Guatemala; El Salvador; República de El Salvador; Honduras; República de Honduras: Külkereskedelmi útmutató [The republics of Guatemala, El Salvador, Honduras: guide to foreign trade]. Budapest: Közgazdasági és Jogi Kk., 1957. 137 pp.

388 Unos Guatemaltecos. Centro América y la Inglaterra. Guatemala: Imprenta de la Paz, 1843. 22 pp.
Part of the political polemics associated with the collapse of the Federation, this brief pamphlet replies to statements in Salvadoran broadsides and newspapers, discussing the Federation's collapse, the role of Guatemala, the alleged involvement of the British, and alleged Guatemalan-British cooperation, providing the Guatemalan viewpoint. DLC

389 Guerrero Castillo, Julián N., and Lola Soriano de Guerrero. 100 biografías centroamericanas. 2 vols. Managua: Imprenta Artes Gráficos & Imprenta Nacional, 1971-74. 252, 408 pp.
The title refers to the intention of the series (which was appearing irregularly) that consists of biographies of significant figures in Central American history. To date two volumes have appeared, each containing several biographies of varying lengths. The subjects range from Colonial times to the twentieth century, and are arranged neither in chronological nor in alphabetical order, rendering it difficult to identify the intended contents of the series or the selection criteria. The biographies are of unpredictable length, and offer basic data with copious quotations from existing secondary works that are cited in the text. DLC

390 Guevara Fallas, Manuel. Los instrumentos del Mercado Común Centroamericano. San José: ICAP, 1965. viii, 142 pp.
An analysis of the accords involved in the Central American Common Market, written by one of its officials and designed as a manual for use by the customs officials of the various nations. It includes summaries and analysis of the meaning of the various accords, as well as the full texts. FU

391 Guier Esquivel, Fernando. La función presidencial en Centroamérica. San José: Editorial Costa Rica, 1973. 140 pp. Biblio.
A discussion of the presidency and its role in the Central American nations, contrasting the theory with the reality and criticizing the excessive power and dominance of the office. Includes analysis of the presidential system and its theory as drawn from Europe and the United States, the Central American autocratic tradition drawn from Spain and the Indian cultures, and the resulting reality in which separation of powers is a fiction and politics revolves around personalities. The author contends that most revolutions are really struggles among individuals for control of the presidency, regardless of the rhetoric. DLC LNHT

392 Guier Saenz, Enrique. El general Morazán. San José: Imprenta Atenea, 1963. 162 pp.
A sympathetic biography that is nonetheless somewhat more balanced than the standard hymns

of praise, for while the author considers Morazán a hero, he views him as neither a saint nor a devil, but rather as a "man of action" who came to represent the ideal of unionism. Includes quotations from secondary works and documents, which are identified in the text but without specific citations. The author is a Costa Rican judge, and this volume constituted his initial foray outside the field of law. DLC LNHT BNCR

393 Guillén, Flavio. Un fraile prócer y una fábula poema: estudio acerca de Fray Matías de Córdova. Guatemala: Tipografía Nacional, 1932. 262 pp. Illus. 2d ed. Guatemala: Ministerio de Educación Pública, 1966. 262 pp. Illus.
    The initial portion of this volume offers a study of the life of Father Matías de Córdova and his role in the Central American independence movement and as an educator in the region. The second part contains a poem by Matías de Córdova regarding the fable of the lion, and a series of critical commentaries hailing it. DLC LNHT BNCR

394 Gutiérrez, Rodrigo, and Fernando Rath, eds. Población y recursos en Centro América: el desafío del siglo XX. San José: Universidad de Costa Rica, 1969. xiv, 354 pp. Biblio., illus., maps.
    The papers presented at a conference examining the population growth of recent decades, focusing on the services needed and discussing the implications for the future. DLC

395 Gutiérrez Gutiérrez, Carlos José. La Corte de Justicia Centroamericana. San Salvador: ODECA, 1957. 61 pp. Biblio., illus. 2d ed. San José: Editorial Juricentro, 1978. 161 pp.
    Originally a thesis, this work, published by ODECA to promote Central American union, provides a brief overview of the work of the Central American Court of Justice in the years immediately preceding World War I, summarizing the various cases that came before it, the contentions of the respective governments, and the rulings. LNHT BNCR

396 Gutiérrez Pimentel, Rodolfo. Alcohol y alcoholismo en Centroamérica. San Salvador: ODECA, 1970. 110 pp. Biblio., illus., tables.
    A general profile of the dimensions of alcoholism in the isthmus, based on official reports and interviews with health officials. Includes statistics regarding alcohol consumption in the isthmus for the mid-1960s showing the greatest per capita level in Panama and Nicaragua. DLC

397 Guzmán, Horacio. The Case of the Republic of Nicaragua, Submitted to His Excellency Hon. Grover Cleveland, President of the United States, Arbitrator under the Treaty of Guatemala of December 24, 1886. Washington, D.C.: Gibson Brothers, 1888. 39 pp.
    The Nicaraguan argument in the arbitration conducted in 1886 by U.S. president Grover Cleveland of the Nicaraguan-Costa Rican boundary dispute. DLC DLC-LDS-697 BNCR

398 Guzmán, Mauricio. La federación colegiada de las repúblicas de Centroamérica. San Salvador: Ministerio de Cultura, 1957. 138 pp.
    A unionist tract arguing that the economic union is doomed to failure without political federation and proposing an outline for a formal union, including a collegial executive, which the author offers as a basis for a new effort. Followed by a commentary on the plan by longtime unionist leader Salvador Mendieta and several speeches and commentaries by Mendieta, advocating union. DLC LNHT

399 Guzmán, Virgilio A. El vestido en Centroamérica. San Salvador: ODECA, 1968. 85 pp. Biblio., tables.
    A description of the clothing-use patterns in the isthmus, based on a survey of 768 families in the six nations, including both urban and rural samples. Includes current description of consumption patterns and projections to 1980, based on expressed needs, current situation, and population projections, seeking to demonstrate the needs and industrial potential in the region. DLC

400 Haines, Peter G. La educación comercial en Centro América. Guatemala: Universidad de San Carlos, 1964. 126 pp. Tables.
    A description of commercial education in the isthmus, considering all five republics, with recommendations for its improvement. The report was compiled by a Michigan State University professor as part of a cooperative program with the University of San Carlos. He stresses the need for business education to aid national development, notes the dearth of facilities, and advocates its expansion and programs to improve its quality. BNG

401 Hale, John. Six Months' Residence and Travels in Central America, etc. New York: W. Borrodaile, 1826. 32 pp.
    A Yankee of Irish extraction provides his impressions during an extensive tour of Central America in 1825, offering one of the earliest descriptions of the region, and furnishing an outsider's view of the state of the area during the independence struggle. The account is written in memoir form but is rich in description and data. CtY

402 Halle, Louis Joseph. Transcaribbean: A Travel Book of Guatemala, El Salvador, British Honduras. New York: Longmans, Green, 1936. 311 pp. Illus.
    A chatty account by a U.S. Army officer, tracing his adventures and observations while sailing along the Caribbean coast. Reflects a sharp eye for detail, attitudes, and social customs in descriptions of everyday activities as well as of the topography and transportation facilities. DLC LNHT

403 Hancock, Ralph. The Rainbow Republics, Central America. New York: Coward-McCann, 1947. xii, 305 pp. Index, maps.

Designed as a guide to and encouragement of travel, this volume approaches the area topically, with country sections under each topic, combining ample context and historical background with specific information. In this sense it varies from the typical travel guide or travelogue. Its chapters include historical and geographical background, cultural comments, data regarding capitals and significant villages (combining description with historical data and entomological descriptions of the origins of their names), the arts, and economics, as well as detailed information regarding places to stay and things to see, food, holidays, etc. DLC LNHT

404 Hansen, Roger D. Central America: Regional Integration and Economic Development. Washington, D.C.: National Planning Association, 1967. xvi, 102 pp. Notes, tables.
A brief but clear summation of the benefits and problems of the Common Market, which the author feels has accomplished a great deal and created considerable opportunities for the future. States that the early stage was run by technocrats and that political problems are bringing the era of technocrats to an end, requiring more political cooperation in the future. He concludes that the effort has successfully integrated the five separate economies to a considerable extent. DLC LNHT

405 Hanzelka, Jiří, and Miroslav Zikmund. Mezi dvema Oceany [Between two oceans]. Prague: n.p., n.d. 315 pp.
Mittelamerika; Zwischen zwei Ozeanen. Berlin: Verlag Volk & Welt, 1959. 393 pp. Index, biblio., illus.
A travel account, covering the entire isthmus, written in the 1950s. DLC

406 Harris, Garrard. Central America as an Export Field. Washington, D.C.: GPO, 1916. 229 pp. Biblio., illus., maps, tables.
A survey prepared under the auspices of the U.S. Department of Commerce designed to encourage American trade with and investment in Central America. Includes descriptions and data of current situations, as well as recommendations for particularly promising fields and products. Though part of a general series of such volumes for the world, few were issued for Central America, and the coverage is unusually comprehensive, with considerable data and statistics about the state of the economy at this time. DLC

407 Helbig, Karl Martin. Indioland am Karibischen Meer: Zentralamerikanische. Leipzig: Brockhaus Verlag, 1961. 322 pp. Illus., maps.
A descriptive travelogue of the author's trips in Mexico, Guatemala, Honduras, El Salvador, and Cuba, focusing on the Indians but also including accounts of physical setting and of current conditions with references to the United Fruit Company. DLC

408 _____. Von Mexico bis zur Mosquitia. Leipzig: Brockhaus Verlag, 1958. 151 pp. Illus., maps.

A modern travelogue covering Mexico, Guatemala, Honduras, Salvador, and Nicaragua, with a large color photo portfolio. The emphasis is on the economic prospects of the region, with extensive geographical description of resources, land, and terrain, focusing particularly on the remote Mosquito area of the Caribbean coast. DLC

409 _____. Die Wirtschaft Zentralamerikas: kartografisch dargestellt und erlautert. Hamburg: Ubersee Verlag, 1966. 127 pp. Biblio., illus., maps.
An analysis and description of the Central American economy, focusing on products and exports, as well as prospects and climatic factors. Each agricultural crop and type of industry is discussed individually. DLC LNHT

410 Helfritz, Hans. Mexiko und Mittelamerika. Berlin: Safari-Verlag, 1954. 737 pp. Biblio., illus, maps.
Though based on the author's observations, this volume differs from the standard travelogue in that it is written by an experienced travel-book author who focuses on particular themes and hence groups his chapters by subject. He emphasizes agriculture, crops, and archeology, though his agricultural essays combine observation with investigation, employing both economic and social information, utilizing themes such as the contrasts between the coastal regions and the capitals. Includes photos of cities and rural areas as well as of tourist attractions. More than half the volume deals with Central America, covering the five nations and Belize. DLC LNHT

411 _____. Zentralamerika; Die Länderbrucke im Karibischen Raum. Berlin: Safari-Verlag, 1963. 439 pp. Biblio., illus, maps.
A travelogue, with extensive historical background, encompassing the five republics, plus brief chapters on Cuba and Belize. Includes careful geographical descriptions and current economic data, as well as discussion of the culture and the state of the Indians of the region. DLC

412 Helms, Mary W. Middle America: A Culture History of Heartlands and Frontiers. Englewood Cliffs, N.J.: Prentice-Hall, 1975. xiv, 367 pp. Biblio., illus., maps.
An anthropological overview of the social trends of the isthmus from the beginning of time to the present, emphasizing the effects of changing political and economic structures on people's lives. The focus is on the pre-independence era, with about a third of the volume dealing with the modern era. Mexico receives the bulk of attention, though Central America receives more emphasis in the modern era than in the earlier period. DLC

413 Helms, Mary W., and Franklin O. Loveland, eds. Frontier Adaptations in Lower Central America. Philadelphia: Institute for the Study of Human Issues, 1976. 178 pp. Index, biblio., illus., maps, tables.

A series of papers originally presented at the 1974 meeting of the Southern Anthropological Society dealing with land use and its effect on the communities and various ethnic groups in the region. Encompasses the pre-Columbian, Colonial, and modern eras. DLC LNHT

414 Hereford, Karl Thomas. <u>Plan de gastos públicos para la educación en Centro América</u>. Guatemala: Imprenta Universitaria, 1964. 56 pp. Illus., tables.
A discussion of the costs of education; projects current cost per student into the 1970s; considers population figures; provides a projection of needed facilities and their costs. DLC LNHT BNG

415 Hernandez, Daniel. <u>Límites de Honduras y Guatemala</u>. San Salvador: Diario de El Salvador, 1928. 44 pp.
A series of commentaries by a Salvadoran journalist, originally published in the <u>Diario del Occidente</u> in 1928, supporting the Honduran claims. Includes quotations from the accords and documents. LNHT

416 Hernández Mendez, Jorge Hegberto. <u>Geopolítica</u>. Guatemala: Editorial del Ejército, 1959. 92 pp. Biblio., maps, appendixes. 2d ed. Tegucigalpa: Fuerzas Armadas de Honduras, 1960. 92 pp. Biblio., maps, appendixes.
A brief introduction to the geopolitics of the Caribbean zone, treated as a whole, emphasizing natural resources, military frontiers, and political problems. Designed for use by the armed forces in their basic courses. The author held the rank of colonel in the Guatemalan Army and served as Guatemalan military attaché in Honduras. The edition published in Honduras is headed <u>Curso de aplicación para oficiales superiores</u>. DLC BNG

417 Herrarte, Alberto, ed. <u>Documentos de la Unión Centroamericana</u>. Guatemala: Ministerio de Educación Pública, 1957. 378 pp.
A well-known unionist scholar serving as secretario general adjunto of ODECA collected the documents he judged the most important of the unionist movement in this officially sponsored work supported by ODECA. It includes the various constitutions of the repeated attempts at federation, the communiqués of pertinent conferences, and various broadsides calling for union, beginning with the independence movement and concluding with the ODECA charter. DLC LNHT BNG BNCR

418 Herrarte, Alberto. <u>El federalismo en Centroamérica</u>. Guatemala: Ministerio de Educación Pública, 1972. 181 pp. Appendixes.
An overview of the unionist movement from independence through ODECA, by a leading unionist. He summarizes the various efforts and, writing with the conviction that union is the best course, emphasizes the factors favoring union and the potential benefits. Attributes the failure of previous efforts to personal ambitions and the influence of the

various militaries, advocating continuing effort, concluding that the Common Market is a step in the right direction and that the difficulties of the Honduran-Salvadoran conflict can be successfully surmounted. The appendixes include documents from the various unionist efforts. DLC LNHT

419 _____. <u>Panamá en la integración centroamericana</u>. Guatemala: Ministerio de Educación Pública, 1961. 83 pp.
A leading integrationist discusses the important question of the role of Panama, which is not normally considered part of Central America by the other five republics because of its different Colonial background. Herrarte contends that geographic proximity mitigates in favor of Panamanian participation in the Central American integration movement, emphasizing that despite the differing pasts there are many historical links. DLC LNHT BNG

420 _____. <u>La unión de centroamérica: tragedia y esperanza; ensayo político-social sobre la realidad de Centroamérica</u>. Guatemala: Ministerio de Educación Pública, 1955. 581 pp. Index, maps, appendixes. 2d ed. Guatemala: Ministerio de Educación Pública, 1964. 428 pp.
A major treatise by a leading unionist surveying the history and economy of the isthmus, contending that only union offers any prospect for the improvement of its lifestyle. The region is treated as a whole, emphasizing the common elements, with references to reasons for unification, its advantages, and sympathetic references to previous efforts, whose failure is viewed as a disaster for all and attributed to imperfect methods. The author contends that these methods should not obscure the desirability of the goal, and offers theoretical comments on the preferred basis for modern unification and the benefits anticipated. DLC LNHT BNG BNCR

421 Herrera Cáceres, H. Roberto. <u>El diferendo hondureño-salvadoreño: su evolución y perspectivas</u>. Tegucigalpa: Universidad Nacional Autónoma de Honduras, 1976. 215 pp.
A legal analysis of the conflict and its origins, by a Honduran jurist supporting his country's outlook but recognizing the long-term issues and legal basis of both parties. DLC

422 Un Hijo Del Salvador y Ciudadaño de Centro América. <u>Escrito que demuestra y persuade la medida que unicamente conviene tomar para establecer facilmente un gobierno nacional que de ser a Centro-América</u>. San Salvador: Imprenta del Estado, 1845. 17 pp.
A pro-unionist tract lamenting the demise of the Federation, and proposing a constitution for a new attempt to unify the isthmus, together with arguments proclaiming the benefits of such a movement. DLC

423 Hilton, Ronald, ed. <u>Who's Who in Latin America</u>. Part 2, <u>Central America and Panama</u>.

Stanford, Calif.: Stanford University Press; London: Oxford University Press, 1945. 103 pp. 2d ed. Stanford, Calif.: Stanford University Press, 1947.

Modeled on the Who's Who format, this volume offers the usual biographical sketches of individuals prominent in the mid 1940s, though the selection process is somewhat uneven. Entries are arranged alphabetically within each country. DLC

424 Holbik, Karel, and Philip L. Swan. Trade and Industrialization in the Central American Common Market: The First Decade. Austin: University of Texas Press, 1972. xiii, 67 pp. Biblio., notes, tables.

A brief study of the Common Market, concluding that its initial efforts to increase intraregional trade were very successful, but that the limited size of the market and the restrictions on the potential numbers of plants as well as political balancing restrict the future prospects for industrialization in the region despite the market and its success to date. Adds that the re-entrance of Honduras into the market is essential to its success. DLC

425 Honduras, Sociedad de Abogados de. Manifiesto de la Sociedad de Abogados de Honduras a los pueblos del Continente Americano y a sus entidades jurídicas con motivo del incidente provocado por el gobierno de Nicaragua con sus pretensiones sobre el territorio de Honduras, 3 de octubre de 1937. Tegucigalpa: Tipografía Ariston, 1937. 119 pp.

A legal brief defending the Honduran claims, arguing that the 1906 arbitration was fully correct and that therefore it had terminated the issue despite Nicaraguan challenges, and that the territory was legally Honduran by virtue of this ruling, with no room left for dispute. Includes a review of the arbitration and the respective cases, as well as selected documents relating to the 1906 proceeding; denigrating the Nicaraguan claims. DLC LNHT

426 Honduras, Gov't of. Agresión salvadoreña contra la República de Honduras. Tegucigalpa: Talleres Tipográficos Nacionales, 1969. 26 pp. Illus., maps.

A propaganda piece denouncing the Salvadoran actions in the 1969 war and branding Salvador the aggressor, with numerous photos of death and destruction. Includes a speech by Honduran President Oswaldo López Arellano and excerpts from a report by the OAS detailing abuses by the Salvadoran troops occupying Honduran territory during the conflict. DLC LNHT

427 _____. Ministerio de Instrucción Pública. Compendio de la vida de Francisco Morazán: el más grande de los Centroamericanos. Tegucigalpa: Tipografía Nacional, 1930. 36 pp.

A compilation of articles and speeches by various individuals hailing Morazán and his contributions to the region and his efforts to unify the isthmus. DLC LNHT BNCR

428 _____. Ministerio de Relaciones Exteriores. Actas de las Conferencias de Paz en Puerto Cortés, a bordo del vapor de guerra Americano Tacoma del 21 de febrero al 15 de marzo de 1911. Tegucigalpa: Tipografía Nacional, 1911. 65 pp.

The official accords of the Tacoma Conference and minutes of the sessions at which the United States mediated a dispute that threatened to lead to war in the isthmus.

429 _____. _____. Algunos documentos importantes sobre los límites entre Honduras y Nicaragua. Tegucigalpa: Ministerio de Relaciones Exteriores, 1938. 349 pp. 2d ed. New York: n.p., 1938. 295 pp.

A collection of decrees and laws pertaining to the disputed territory, mainly from the nineteenth century, designed to demonstrate that Honduras had exercised effective jurisdiction over the region throughout the period in question. Compiled by the government and reprinted without comment, save for excerpts from presidential and ministerial messages referring to the region. The documents consist principally of concessions for mining and petroleum exploration, and regulations relating specifically to this region. DLC

430 _____. _____. Algunos documentos sobre la soberanía y posesión ejercidos por Honduras en el territorio de la Mosquitia que la disputa Nicaragua, 1894-1937. 3 vols. Tegucigalpa: Tipografía Nacional, 1938. 110, 112, 216 pp.

A collection of all the pertinent treaties and conventions, with ratifications and exchanges relating to the dispute, covering the years 1869 through 1900, reprinted in full without commentary. The absence of an index or table of contents limits the utility of the volume. DLC LNHT

431 _____. _____. Boundary Question between the Republic of Guatemala and the Republic of Honduras under Mediation of the Honorable Secretary of State of the United States of America: Brief on Behalf of Honduras. New York: Evening Post, 1918. vii, 168 pp.

The Honduran argument, as presented by its counsel, with annexes supporting Honduran claims. DLC LNHT

432 _____. _____. Boundary Question between the Republic of Guatemala and the Republic of Honduras under Mediation of the Honorable Secretary of State of the United States of America: Reply on Behalf of Honduras. New York: Evening Post, 1920. ii, 108 pp.

The Honduran reply to the Guatemalan case. DLC LNHT

433 _____. _____. Cuestión de límites entre Honduras y Guatemala, ventilados ante el gobierno de mediador los Estados Unidos de América, 1918-1919. New York: Imprenta M.D. Danon, 1918. xviii, 255 pp. 2d ed.

(Honduras, Gov't of)
Tegucigalpa: Ministerio de Relaciones
Exteriores, 1919. 387 pp. Illus.
DLC

434 _____. _____. Demanda entablada ante la
Corte de Justicia Centro-Americana, por el
gobierno de Honduras contra el gobierno de la
República de Guatemala. Guatemala:
Tipografía de Arturo Siguere, 1908. 177,
175 pp.
A complaint filed by the Honduran government alleging that the Guatemalan government
aided a revolution against the Honduran regime
in April 1907, with supporting documents. The
texts are printed in both Spanish and English.
DLC DLC-LDS-706 BNG BNCR

435 _____. _____. Demanda entablada por el
gobierno de Honduras contra el gobierno de la
República de El Salvador y contestación
definitiva dada por éste ante La Corte de
Justicia Centroamericana. San Salvador:
Imprenta Melendez, 1908. 184 pp.
The Honduran charges that the Salvadoran
government aided a revolt in Honduras during
1907, and the Salvadoran government's denial.
DLC LNHT BNCR

436 _____. _____. Documentos referentes a los
límites entre Honduras y Nicaragua.
Tegucigalpa: Tipografía Nacional, 1904.
361 pp.
A collection of nineteenth-century exchanges regarding the question, with Colonial
documents on which the dispute is based, tracing it through the boundary agreement of 1894.
LNHT

437 _____. _____. Fronteras de Honduras:
límites con Guatemala. 3 vols. Tegucigalpa:
Tipografía Nacional, 1929-33.
A continuing series that was part of the
arbitration case, with at least eight parts
and supplemental documents. DLC LNHT

438 _____. _____. Honduras y Nicaragua: resumen
de los alegatos y pruebas presentados a Su
Majestad el rey don Alfonso XIII, árbitro en
la cuestión de límites pendiente entre ambas
repúblicas. Madrid: Tipográfico de Fortanet,
1906. 43 pp.
Resumen de los alegatos y pruebas presentados
por Honduras y Nicaragua ante S.M. el rey de
España, Alfonso XIII, como árbitro único en el
juicio que puso fin a la controversia de
límites entre ambos países. Tegucigalpa:
Tipografía Nacional, 1956. 21 pp. Illus.,
maps.
A series of excerpts and summaries of the
pertinent portions of the alegatos and replies
of both nations, condensing the heart of their
arguments into a very brief overview. DLC
LNHT

439 _____. _____. Laudo pronunciado por Su
Majestad el rey de España en la cuestión de
límites entre las repúblicas de Honduras y
Nicaragua: precedido de una reseña del acto
de su entrega oficial de las alocuciones
pronunciadas en él y del decreto no. 18

expedido por el poder ejectivo. Tegucigalpa:
Tipografía Nacional, 1907. 31 pp. 2d ed.
Tegucigalpa: Talleres Tipográficos
Nacionales, 1937. 15 pp.
The official ruling of the king of Spain in
1906, in favor of the Honduran claim, which
later was disputed by Nicaragua on technical
grounds and itself became a source of prolonged controversy. DLC

440 _____. _____. Límites entre Honduras y
Guatemala: publicación del Ministerio de
Relaciones Exteriores de Honduras.
Tegucigalpa: Tipografía Nacional, 1928.
112 pp.
A summary of the Honduran case. DLC

441 _____. _____. Límites entre Honduras y
Nicaragua: alegato presentado a Su Majestad
Católica el rey de España en calidad de
árbitro por los representantes de la República
de Honduras. Madrid: Tipográfico de
Fortanet, 1905. 240 pp. Maps. 2d ed. New
York: n.p., 1938. 254 pp. Maps.
The Honduran reply to the Nicaraguan case
during the 1904-6 proceedings that led to the
ruling of 1906 that favored Honduras but was
later disputed by Nicaragua. DLC LNHT

442 _____. _____. Límites entre Honduras y
Nicaragua: incidente suscitado por Nicaragua.
Tegucigalpa: Tipografía Nacional, 1912. iv,
174 pp. Maps. 2d ed. Tegucigalpa: Talleres
Tipográficos Nacionales, 1938. iv, 155 pp.
Maps.
A series of exchanges between the governments of Honduras and Nicaragua during 1911-12
regarding the validity of the 1906 decision by
the king of Spain, which Honduras contends is
the first time Nicaragua challenged the ruling. The notes are reprinted in full, with
supplemental documents from the arbitration.
DLC LNHT

443 _____. _____. Límites y arbitraje entre
Honduras y Nicaragua. Tegucigalpa:
Ministerio de Relaciones Exteriores, 1938.
824 pp. Maps, appendixes.
The complete case of Honduras, including
documents, maps, annexes, and replies to the
Nicaraguan case.

444 Huck, Eugene R., and Edward H. Moseley, eds.
Militarists, Merchants, and Missionaries: The
United States Expansion in Middle America.
University: University of Alabama Press,
1970. ix, 172 pp. Biblio., index, notes,
appendixes.
A collection of miscellaneous articles
designed as a festschrift; contains three
articles on Central America, one dealing with
the 1783 Anglo-Spanish dispute about Belize
and the Bay Islands, one on the Protestant
missionary efforts in Guatemala in the late
nineteenth and early twentieth centuries, and
a third dealing with Panama. DLC

445 Humboldt, Alexander von. Ober den
Tegenwoordigen Toestand Van den Vrijen Staat
Centro-Amerika of Guatemala. Hamburg: n.p.,
1826. 76 pp.

A detailed description of the situation in
Central America by the noted German geographer
and traveler. Includes physical descriptions,
a discussion of the newly formed Federation of
Central America and its constituent states
providing basic information such as a listing
of their provinces, and a brief account of the
independence movement. DLC

446 Huxley, Aldous Leonard. Beyond the Mexique
Bay. London: Chatto & Windus; New York:
Harper, 1934. 295 pp. Index, illus.
Reprint. Westport, Conn.: Greenwood, 1975.
295 pp.
   Observations and comments by an accomplished British writer during a Caribbean
voyage. The book includes the islands,
Mexico, Belize, Guatemala, and Honduras. The
author was a good observer and writes in vivid
prose, though replete with the European outlook and prejudices of the day. DLC LNHT

447 _____. Prácticas religiosas en Mesoamérica.
Guatemala: Ministerio de Educación Pública,
1965. 37 pp. Illus.
   A translation of a work that originally
appeared as an article in English in the Geographic Magazine in 1935, reporting the auth-
or's observations regarding the survival of
traces of pre-Colonial Indian cults and their
practices. The material was collected during
his investigations for his volume Beyond the
Mexique Bay, and serves to supplement that
work. DLC BNG

448 Iaroshevskii, Boris Gfimovich. Zelenoe
chudóvishehe [The green monster]. Moscow:
Izdatelstvo Politicheskoj Literatury, 1967.
69 pp.
   DLC

449 Iglesias, Francisco María de, ed. Documentos
relativos a la independencia. 3 vols. San
José: Tipografía Nacional, 1899-1902. vi,
300, 416, 340 pp.
   A collection of documents from the independence era focusing on the years 1821
through 1824, compiling the minutes of the
various city and governmental councils that
exercised authority and reflecting their
debates regarding independence and the initial
actions of the nation. DLC DLC-LDS-31 BNCR

450 Iglesias, Francisco María de. Pro patria:
una memoria y un discurso . . . 15 de
septiembre de 1898. San José: Tipografía
Nacional, 1898. 27 pp.
   A brief historical essay regarding some of
the problems of the original Central American
Federation, followed by a speech delivered by
the author in 1888 to one of the isthmian
conferences discussing unification. Both are
quite general and brief. DLC BNCR

451 _____. Pro patria: una reseña y un episodio
histórico y algunos documentos sobre unión
centroamericana, 15 de septiembre 1900. San
José: Tipografía Nacional, 1900. iii, 98 pp.
   A series of letters and proposals by the
author for the unification of Central America,
dating from the 1860s when he served as Costa

Rican foreign minister. They include his
letters to the various conferences discussing
union, ranging from general polemics to detailed proposals, as well as retrospective
references. All are pro-unionist, but condemn
the efforts of Gerardo Barrios of El Salvador
to impose union by force. DLC DLC-LDS-25
LNHT BNCR

452 _____. Réplica al folleto comprobaciones
históricas. San José: Imprenta de Alfredo
Greñas, 1900. 31 pp.
   A reply to the Comprobaciones históricas of
Rafael Montúfar, contesting his statements
regarding various events of the 1850s and the
religious struggles in the isthmus that formed
part of the Liberal-Conservative confrontation, and replying to Montúfar's charges that
Yglesias was "an agent of the Jesuits" in
opposing the Liberal reforms. DLC-LDS-368
LNHT BNCR

453 Inoati, Andras. The Central American Common
Market: An Example of Integration between
Developing Countries. Budapest: Hungarian
Academy of Sciences, 1971. x, 113 pp.
Biblio., notes, tables.
   Published as part of the institute's Studies on Developing Countries series, this volume is a sympathetic view of the Common
Market, hailing its accomplishments and
contending that it succeeded despite difficulties because each of the members was too
small to develop significantly alone. Contends that integration was brought about by
the main interest group, the landowners, but
has spawned a new group, the capitalist-
industrialists, who have superceded the landowners; hence, the integration movement has
outgrown its creators. Predicts that the
movement will continue to prosper. The
English is somewhat uneven. DLC LNHT

454 Instituto Centroamericano de Administración
Pública. Las empresas públicas del Istmo
Centroamericano. San José: Instituto
Centroamericano de Administración Pública,
1966. 74 pp.
   One of the initial efforts of the Inter-
American School of Public Affairs, this volume
surveys the independent public institutions of
the various Central American countries, providing an overview of their creation and functioning. The emphasis is inevitably on Costa
Rica, which has the largest number of such
autonomous agencies, and the choice of topic
undoubtedly reflected the location of the
center in that country. The authors are experts from many American nations, and most are
clearly sympathetic to this type of institution, seeing autonomous public service agencies as a means of dealing with the region's
social problems and providing stability of
planning and administration by insulating such
agencies from the tumultuous local politics,
and hence promoting the development of a cadre
of professional administrators dedicated
solely to their programs. DLC BNCR

455 _____. Necesidades de personal del sector
público de Centro América: 1974. San José:

44

(Instituto Centroamericano de Administración Pública)
Instituto Centroamericano de Administración Pública, 1969. 117 pp. Tables.
An estimate of the present and future needs for trained professional administrators to work in the government public agencies in the isthmus, with tables demonstrating the need and discussion of the necessity of establishing adequate training facilities. BNCR

456 _____. Recursos humanos: el sector público y su situación actual en Centro América. San José: Instituto Centroamericano de Administración Pública, 1968. 170 pp. Tables.
A discussion of the public sector and its role in the use of labor and of the occupational patterns of the Central American nations, replete with extensive statistics about manpower, training, types of jobs, expansion, etc., designed to trace the situation of the governments and the effects of their employment actions on the nations. Includes budgetary statistics, focusing on 1960–66. DLC BNCR

457 Instituto Centroamericano de Investigación y Tecnología Industrial. Trabajos técnicos. Guatemala: Instituto Centroamericano de Investigación y Tecnología Industrial, 1969. 88 pp. Biblio., illus., maps, tables.
Seventeen papers dealing with a broad range of geological issues affecting the region, representing the fruits of a conference in Guatemala City during 1966. DLC

458 Instituto Universitario Centroamericano de Investigaciones Sociales y Económicas. Encuestas socioeconómicas en zonas agrícolas seleccionadas de los países centroamericanos: resultados y análisis. San José: Universidad de Costa Rica, 1964. 148 pp. Maps, tables.
A study of economic change in selected sample sectors of Central America conducted during 1960–62 under the auspices of various international agencies. Describes the characteristics of the small producers in each region, discussing such factors as access to land and capital, types of crops, sources of labor, income, efficiency, etc. The sample zones in each country are discussed separately. BNCR

459 Inter-American Institute of International Legal Studies. Derecho comunitario centroamericano: ensayo de sistematización. San José: Imprenta Trejos, 1968. 460 pp.
Designed for law school students, this compilation of laws and case studies focuses on the legal aspects of the economic integration movement, detailing the common isthmian practices and the consequences of the various accords, contrasting them with domestic law in the various states, and showing the consequences for internal law. DLC

460 _____. Instrumentos relativos a la integración económica en América Latina. Washington, D.C.: Published by the Institute, 1964. xiii, 346 pp. Biblio.

Instruments Relating to the Economic Integration of Latin America. Dobbs Ferry, N.Y.: Oceana Publications, 1968. ix, 452 pp. Biblio.
A collection of the treaties involved in the Central American Common Market and the Latin American Free Trade Association, providing the full texts, grouped according to subject but offered without comment. DLC

461 Intercontinental Railway Commission. Report of the Transactions of the Commission and of the Surveys and Explorations of Its Engineers in Central and South America, 1891–1898. 3 vols. Washington, D.C.: Intercontinental Railway Commission, 1895–98. Index, illus., maps, tables.
An elaborate and detailed survey of potential intercontinental railroad routes, encompassing Central America and northern South America, based on fieldwork in 1891–93. Costa Rica is split between volumes 1 and 2, while the rest of Central America appears in volume 1. Includes detailed geographical and geological reporting of the region, as well as recommendations regarding potential railroad routes in the area, with extensive photos. DLC BNCR

462 International Court of Justice. Case Concerning the Arbitral Award Made by the King of Spain on 23 December 1906 (Honduras v. Nicaragua): General List No. 39, Judgment of 18 December 1960. Leyden: A.W. Sijthoff, 1960. v, 930 pp.
The official ruling of the International Court of Justice sustaining the validity of the 1906 arbitral decision by the king of Spain and rejecting the Nicaraguan objections to that decision, contending on legal grounds that the arbitor acted within his powers, and hence that his decision in favor of Honduras was legally valid. DLC

463 Ireland, Gordon. Boundaries, Possessions, and Conflicts in Central and North America and the Caribbean. Cambridge, Mass.: Harvard University Press, 1938. 345 pp. Index, notes maps, tables, appendixes. Reprint. New York: Octagon, 1971. xv, 432 pp. Index, notes, maps, tables, appendixes.
A series of concise summaries of the existing disputes and their course to the date of publication, listed by country, followed by discussion of the then-current state of treaty relations of each of the countries with all Latin American states. The boundary-conflict summaries comprising the initial 300 pages, based on published treaties, documents, and secondary works, are designed as overviews for the layman or for the specialist not familiar with the specific episodes. They include quotations from the treaties and exchanges, and appropriate maps. DLC LNHT

464 Istituto Italo-Latino Americano. Struttúra di bàse en Centroamérica per la promozióne del le esportazióni a mercàti di paési tèrzi. Rome: Istituto Italo-Latino Americano, 1975. 18 pp. Tables.

A brief summary of contemporary resources and transportation facilities in Central America, and its export potential. DLC

465 Istituto Nazionale per il Commèrcia Estèrno. Centro América: sintési unitaria politico-económica. Rome: Published by the Institute, 1963. 123 pp. Maps, tables, graphs.

A detailed summary of the current economic situation of the isthmus, emphasizing trade and commerce, with excellent maps and statistics. DLC

466 Jérez Alvarado, Rafael. En defensa de la soberanía e integridad territorial de Honduras. Tegucigalpa: Tipografía Nacional, 1957. 95 pp. Illus., maps.

A history of the boundary dispute between Honduras and Nicaragua, sustaining the Honduran position defending the 1906 decision by the king of Spain and charging that Nicaraguan occupation of the town of Mocoron during 1957 violated the ruling and thus constituted aggression against Honduras. The Nicaraguan rejection of the decision is regarded as invalid by the author. DLC

467 Jiménez, Eddy E. La guerra no fué de fútbol: mención ensayo. Havana: Casa de las Américas, 1974. 164 pp. Biblio., notes, illus.

An account of the 1969 war, denouncing the name and emphasizing more serious causes such as hunger, land, and poverty, attributing the problems to the actions of foreign imperialistic powers and companies and the maldistribution of income. While noting the consequences of the war, which hurt the interests of the imperialists by upsetting the Common Market, the volume contends that the prestige of the armies and the pretext for the acquisition of new weapons will enhance the means of repression in the hands of the upper classes. The criticism leveled at El Salvador is more severe than that directed at Honduras. DLC LNHT

468 Jiménez Castro, Wilburg. Educación y adiestramiento en el Istmo Centroamericano. San José: Central American School of Public Administration, 1963. 31 pp.

A brief statement of the need for education and training in the field of public administration, which is vital to the entire isthmus if it is to deal effectively with its social and economic problems. DLC

469 Jiménez Solís, José Jorge. Francisco Morazán: su vida y su obra. Guatemala: Tipografía Nacional, 1952. 265 pp. Biblio., illus.

An uncritical and laudatory but detailed biography of one of the leaders of Central American independence recounting his efforts to promote the union of the isthmus. The volume focuses on his career as president of the Federation of Central America and the military campaigns undertaken in his efforts to preserve the unity of the isthmus, viewing his efforts favorably and hailing the ideal of union. Includes numerous and unfootnoted

quotations from documents and secondary works. DLC BNG BNCR

470 Jones Vargas, Fernando. Estudio bibliográfico sobre la sociología rural en Centroamérica. San José: Universidad de Costa Rica, 1964. 40 pp.

A brief and limited list that covers books, articles, and particularly locally produced theses for all five of the nations, with brief annotations, which leaves little space for each. The most useful aspect is the coverage of local theses. DLC

471 Jordan, William F. Central American Indians and the Bible. New York: Fleming H. Revell, 1926. 91 pp. Index, illus., maps.

A longtime missionary and staff member of the American Bible Society describes some of his experiences in Guatemala, El Salvador, and Panama, emphasizing the need for missionary work in Indian America, which he dubs "the greatest stretch of unevangelized territory in the world." His emphasis is on the role of missionaries and the Bible in changing the life-style and attitudes of the "heathens," and the wonders worked by the Lord's word. The book is both a memoir and an exhortation to recruits for the missions. DLC LNHT

472 Joy, Charles Rhind. Young People of Mexico and Central America. New York: Duell, Sloan & Pearce, 1962. 152 pp. Maps.

Part of a series that seeks to provide basic social-studies information to a junior high school audience, this volume takes the form of telling the stories of young people from other countries and narrating their lives in the first person. It includes brief summaries of basic material about the countries and the region, its geography and history. Contains a section on each of the isthmian republics, as well as on Mexico and Panama. DLC

473 Juárez Muñoz, J. Fernando. Nuestros límites con Honduras: aspecto básico de la cuestión. Guatemala: Tipografía "El Santuario," 1928. 18 pp.

A succinct statement of the Guatemalan case. LNHT

474 Juncadella G., Salvador. La organización de sucursales en el Mercado Común Centroamericano y Panamá. San José: Empresa Fertilizantes de Centro América, 1969. 63 pp. 2d ed. San José: Imprenta Lehmann, 1970. 95 pp.

A summary of the legislation regarding the formation of branches of foreign businesses in the six republics, with complete information on the procedures and forms necessary, designed to serve as a handbook for firms interested in entering the region. DLC LNHT

475 Kaigai Keizai Kyoryoku Kikin Chosabu. Chûnanbei 6 Kakoku no Keizai Kaihatsu [Economic development plans in the six Central American countries]. Tokyo: n.p., 1965. 94 pp. Illus., maps.
DLC

476 Kalijarvi, Thorsten Waino Valentine. Central America: Land of Lords and Lizards. Princeton, N.J.: Van Nostrand, 1962. 128 pp. Index, biblio., maps.
A brief synopsis, as part of a "search-light" series, designed as an introduction to the area for the layman. Although it appears in a geographical series, its author, a former United States ambassador to El Salvador, focuses primarily on history in overview and on the communist threat, arguing for greater Yankee attention to and involvement in the area, contending that geography determined its isolation, since it is remote from normal world-travel routes. DLC LNHT

477 Kapp, Kit S. Central America: Early Maps up to 1860. North Bend, Ohio: K.S. Kapp, 1974. 64 pp. Index, illus., maps.
A bibliography of maps of Central America and its nations, arranged by author, with dimensions, a list of editions and publishing data, and location codings to the principal depositories in the U.S. and the Canal Zone. Includes citations of published versions and some sample illustrations. DLC

478 Karen, Ruth. The Land and the People of Central America. Philadelphia: Lippincott, 1965. 160 pp. Index, illus., maps. 2d ed. Philadelphia: Lippincott, 1972. 159 pp. Index, illus., maps.
A lavishly illustrated, chatty, travelogue account, mainly descriptive, but including opinionated historical résumés. The emphasis is on the contemporary, though there are discussions of the Indian cultures and Colonial era. DLC

479 Karnes, Thomas L. The Failure of Union: Central America, 1824-1975. Chapel Hill: University of North Carolina Press, 1961. xii, 277 pp. Index, biblio., notes, illus., maps. 2d ed. Tempe: Arizona State University Press, 1976. x, 283 pp. Index, biblio., notes, maps.
A survey of the more than twenty-five efforts to unify the isthmus from the initial Federation at the time of independence through the Washington Conference of 1923, based on newspapers, secondary works, and available documents. The coverage for the years after 1923 is far more general, though the initial edition did contain a final chapter spanning the years through 1960 and the later edition has a very brief section bringing the account to 1975. Focuses on the interplay of regional and local political forces and the reasons for the failure of the many unification efforts; considers the permanence of the ideal, its advocates, and the local nationalism, suspicions, and rivalries that mitigate against the dream. DLC LNHT

480 _____. Tropical Enterprise: The Standard Fruit and Steamship Company in Latin America. Baton Rouge: Louisiana State University Press, 1978. xv, 332 pp. Index, biblio., notes, illus., maps.
A carefully researched company history, based on the corporate archives and extensive interviews with officials of the company, tracing the development of the firm from its foundation by four immigrants through its emergence as a major banana supplier to its merger with one of the larger corporations of the nation. Indicates the tremendous effort of the international banana companies to promote the development of the industry in the face of great difficulties and at considerable expense, providing a different perspective on their impact in the region. DLC LNHT

481 Kelam, T.P. Strany TSentral'noi Ameriki [The countries of Central America]. Tallinn, U.S.S.R.: Estonskoe gosudarstvennoe izdatel'stvo, 1960. 43 pp.

482 Kennedy, Paul Patrick. The Middle Beat: A Correspondent's View of Mexico, Guatemala, and El Salvador. New York: Teachers College Press, 1971. xix, 235 pp. Index, illus., maps.
A journalistic view of the region by the New York Times reporter who covered it from 1954 through 1965, offering a combination of memoirs and portions of his reports for those years. About a third of the volume deals with Guatemala and El Salvador, the rest with Mexico. The treatment is episodic, but it includes descriptions, impressions of, and interviews with many of the outstanding figures of that era, along with anecdotes drawn from personal experience to illustrate the social situation and journalistic reports of some of the era's principal events. DLC

483 Kepner, Charles David, Jr. Social Aspects of the Banana Industry. New York: Columbia University Press, 1936. 230 pp. Index, biblio., notes, maps. 2d ed. New York: AMS Press, 1967. 230 pp. Maps.
Though conducted as part of the same study that led to the author's earlier anti-imperialistic denunciation of the company, this is the academic portion, submitted as a doctoral dissertation at the University of Chicago, and hence is more balanced despite the retention of the critical tone. The author focuses on living conditions, considering land ownership, labor conditions, health facilities, wages and benefits conflicts, labor organization, and company profits and costs. He notes that despite the problems, banana-plantation wages exceed those on domestically owned coffee estates and that the company health programs deserve praise. But he maintains that the company is seeking to control production and manipulate it to maintain prices, contends that social programs could go well beyond the present ones, notes the implications of land ownership and foreign domination, and proposes that the company engage in social experimentation to parallel its scientific efforts in order to contribute to the success of democracy in the region. DLC

484 Kepner, Charles David, Jr., and Jay Henry Soothill. The Banana Empire: A Case Study of Economic Imperialism. New York: Vanguard Press, 1935. xiii, 392 pp. Index, biblio., notes, illus., maps. Reprint. New York: Russell & Russell, 1967. 392 pp. Index, biblio., notes, illus., maps.
El imperio del banano: las compañías bananeras contra la soberanía de las naciones del Caribe. Many editions in several countries. Mexico: Ediciones del Caribe, 1937. 385 pp. Index, biblio., notes, illus., maps. Latest ed. Havana: Imprenta Nacional de Cuba, 1961. 207 pp.
   A well-known and pioneering account of the United Fruit Company, originally written as part of an anti-imperialist series whose volumes sought to apply muckraking techniques to the operations of American corporations and the government abroad. Soothill is a former employee of UFCO, and Kepner is a student of international affairs. Clearly designed as an indictment of the company, providing an effective chronicle of the company's abuses, but should be read in conjunction with other works that show the other side and place the behavior in the context of the business practices that prevailed at the time. This is the volume on which Guatemalan author Miguel Ángel Asturias drew in writing his well known "banana trilogy." DLC LNHT BNG BNCR

485 Key, Helmer. Kaffe, socker och bananer: en resa till Cuba och Guatemala. Stockholm: A. Bonniers Forlag, 1928. 336 pp. Biblio., notes, illus., maps, tables.
Kaffee, Zucker und Bananen: eine Reise nach Cuba und Guatemala. Munich: Drei Masken Verlag, 1929. x, 360 pp. Biblio., notes, illus., maps, tables.
   A Swedish traveler's impressions, focusing on economic aspects and agriculture, with about 100 pages devoted to Cuba and Guatemala separately, and a final portion dealing with Swedes prominent throughout the Western hemisphere and plantations in which Swedes have investments, including two large units on the Pacific coast of Guatemala. Lavishly illustrated, showing a variety of crops, houses, typical scenes, and virtually every Swedish resident or representative in both countries. DLC

486 Koebel, William Henry. Central America. New York: Scribner's, 1914. 382 pp., Illus., maps. 4th ed. London: T. Fisher Unwin, 1925. 382 pp. Illus., maps.
   Intended as a general survey, approximately half the pages are devoted to an historical account that ends with the regime of Rafael Carrera. The remaining portion of the volume consists of a description of contemporary Central America, country by country, which constitutes the only coverage of the era since the mid-nineteenth century. There are also several chapters on British interests in the isthmus. The author emphasizes the backwardness and instability of the area's past, and hence the importance of foreign interests in bringing development and stability, which he

sees as a cause for optimism. The later editions bear the title Central America: Guatemala, Nicaragua, Costa Rica, Honduras, Panama, and Salvador. DLC

487 Korea. Embassy in Mexico. Chungmi Kongdong: Sijang Yŏn'gu [A study of the Central American Free Trade Association]. Seoul: Oemubu, 1965. 91 pp.
   A summary of the Central American unification movement and the emergence of the Common Market, seeking to encourage Korean trade with the Common Market countries.

488 Krehm, William. Democracias y tiranías en el Caribe. Mexico: Unión Democrática Centroamericana, 1949. 303 pp. 2d ed. Buenos Aires; Editorial Parnaso, 1957.
   A Time correspondent's account of Central America in the 1940s, dealing principally with the revolutions of 1944, but including background regarding the countries and their regimes, and criticism of United States policy. The correspondent is clearly antidictatorial, and hence prorevolutionary in his interpretations. The Somoza regime is one of the primary targets. DLC LNHT

489 Kuhlenkamp-Schenck, E. Die Volksdichte von Mittelamerika. Bonn and Leipzig: Kurt Schroeder, 1923. 67 pp. Biblio., notes, illus., maps, tables.
   A brief compilation of physical, climatic, and population data, mainly in descriptive form, though with some maps and tables. DLC

490 Kumamoto Daigaku. Chûnanbei Jijô Kenkyûjo [Fishing industries of Central and South America]. Kumamoto: Chûnambei ni Okeru Gyogyô Jigyô, 1965.

491 Laycayo Fernández, Eliseo. El peligro visible: la política norteamericana en la América Latina y las Antillas. Santa Tecla: Imprenta La Tecleña, 1929. 76 pp. Illus. 2d ed. Managua: n.p., 1933. 87 pp. Illus.
   A collection of articles denouncing the Yankee peril in the Caribbean-Central American region, most of them general, but including several dealing with Sandino, extolling his resistance to the Yankees. The items were originally published in the Diario del Pueblo of Santa Ana, El Salvador, during the mid-1920s. DLC

492 Lamarre, Clovis, and Charles Wiener. L'Amérique Centrale et Méridionale et l'exposition de 1878. Paris: Librairie Ch. Delagrave, 1878. 1v, 316 pp. Index, illus., maps.
   Part of a general series about the exposition, this volume provides brief historical sketches of each of the countries, followed by descriptions of their displays at the fair. DLC LNHT

493 Lamb, Dean Ivan. The Incurable Filibuster: Adventures of Colonel Dean Ivan Lamb. New York: Farrar & Rinehart, 1934. 298 pp. Illus. London: Hutchinson, 1934. 287 pp.

A rambling tale of adventure by a soldier of fortune that covers many Latin American nations, including Nicaragua, Guatemala, and Costa Rica in the early twentieth century. The emphasis is on drama and adventure, and the time periods of political events are not always clear. DLC

494 Lambert de Sainte-Croix, Alexandre. Onze mois au Mexique et au Centre-Amérique. Paris: E. Plon, Nourrit & Cie, 1897. viii, 292 pp. Maps.
A travelogue in journal form describing the author's observations during a trip through Mexico and Central America, including all the countries. About half the volume deals with Central America, with the principal focus on Guatemala. The emphasis is on travel, facilities, and brief descriptions of the physical setting and people met that provide some indication of travel and living conditions, as well as of the author's European viewpoint. DLC LNHT

495 Landarech, Alfonso María. Estudios literarios: capítulos de literatura centroamericana. San Salvador: Ministerio de Cultura, 1959. 282 pp. Notes.
A series of critical essays that the author offers as a contribution to a literary history and analysis of the region, saying that no single work can cover the entire field. The writer, a Spanish Jesuit who has lived and taught in El Salvador for most of his career, includes several general thematic chapters dealing with subjects such as costumbrismo and short stories in El Salvador, and a brief account of journalism in El Salvador, though most of the volume consists of a series of essays on individual significant writers, combining excerpts from their works with brief critical essays on each of their principal writings. DLC LNHT

496 Landenberger, Emil. Durch Zentral-Amerika: Erinnerungen an Costa Rica, Nicaragua, Honduras, Salvador, Guatemala. Stuttgart: Gustav Hopf, Verlag, 1922. 304 pp.
A travel account emphasizing physical descriptions, particularly of the cities, and including background information. DLC LNHT

497 Lansing, Marion Florence. Liberators and Heroes of Mexico and Central America. Boston: Page, 1941. xviii, 299 pp. Index, biblio., illus. Reprint. Freeport, N.Y.: Books for Libraries Press, 1971. 299 pp. Biblio., illus.
A collection of brief but vividly written biographical sketches of fourteen independence leaders, designed for the general reader and drawn from existing knowledge. Includes most of the leading figures of Central American independence. DLC

498 Lardé y Larín, Jorge. El grito de la merced, 5 de noviembre de 1811. San Salvador: Ministerio de Cultura, 1960. 132 pp. Illus.
An analysis of the independence movement contending that the Grito by Father Delgado is the true starting point of the Salvadoran independence movement, comparing its significance to the Mexican Grito de Dolores. Concludes that the Grito de Delgado should be celebrated as independence day in Central America along with the traditional September 1821 date, as they are both of equal significance. DLC LNHT

499 ____. Isidro Menéndez. San Salvador: Ministerio de Cultura, 1958. 213 pp. Illus.
A brief sketch of the life of a priest who served El Salvador, Costa Rica, and the Federation during the early nineteenth century, assisting in the independence movement and the foundation of the various states, and particularly stimulating the systematic codification of legislation and the establishment of uniform law codes. Traces his career, quoting extensively from his addresses and from commentaries about him in secondary literature. DLC LNHT

500 ____. José Simeón Cañas. San Salvador: Ministerio de Cultura, 1956. 117 pp. Illus.
A laudatory biography of Cañas, whom the author characterizes as "the immaculate figure," designed to acquaint the youth with his magnificent example. Includes liberal excerpts from documents. DLC LNHT

501 Larraínzar, Manuel. Chiapas y Soconusco con motivo de la cuestión de límites entre México y Guatemala. Mexico: Imprenta del Gobierno, 1875. 154 pp. Notes. 2d ed. Mexico: Imprenta de I. Escalante, 1882. viii, 148 pp.
A defense of the Mexican claims, written as yet another response to the work by Andres Dardón, with extensive documentary excerpts designed to support the Mexican claim, tracing the question back to Colonial times and recounting the process by which the areas decided to affiliate with Mexico at independence. DLC LNHT

502 ____. Noticia histórica de Soconusco y su incorporación a la República Mexicana. Mexico: Imprenta de J.M. Lara, 1843. viii, 194 pp. Notes, tables.
A defense of the Mexican actions, seeking to demonstrate that the initiative in the separation of Soconusco and Chiapas from Central America during the turbulent independence era lay with the local inhabitants and that the Mexican effort to annex the region was a response to the petitions of the local citizens. Includes a brief summary of the Colonial era and detailed accounts of the events of the independence period, portraying the Guatemalans as the aggressors in the region. DLC

503 Láscaris Comneno, Constantino. Historia de las ideas en Centroamérica. San José: EDUCA, 1970. 485 pp. Biblio., notes.
This volume emphasizes the writers and scholars of Central America as examples of the intellectual currents therein, focusing mainly on the Colonial era but encompassing the first half of the nineteenth century. It criticizes

the repressive aspects of Spanish government and the church during the Colonial era, and the problems of dictatorship and church-state relations in the independence era, being self-described as "belligerent." The nineteenth century portions, however, consist of a series of brief essays about each of the leading writers, providing a summary of outlook and classification encompassing no more than a few paragraphs, often followed by a list of the subject's publications. Based on extensive use of secondary works and particularly the publications of the individuals under discussion. DLC LNHT BNCR

504 Lavine, Harold. *Central America*. New York: Time-Life Books, 1964. 160 pp. Index, biblio., illus., maps. 2d ed. New York: Time Incorporated, 1968. 159 pp. Index, illus., maps, appendixes. *América Central*. Mexico: Editorial Life, 1966. Illus.
    A profusely illustrated general introduction to the contemporary situation. Most valuable for its many photos. DLC

505 Lehmann, Walter. *Zentral-Amerika: Die Sprachen Zentral-Amerikas in ihren Beziehungen zueinander sowie zu Süd-Amerika und Mexiko.* Berlin: Dietrich Reimer, 1920. 1090 pp. Biblio., maps.
    A linguistic survey of the languages, idioms, and dialects of the Indians of Central America, with comparisons to those of Mexico and South America, including consideration of their geographical distribution, their origins, and definitions of terms. The focus is on dialects and languages in use during the initial decades of the twentieth century. DLC DLC-LDS-385

506 Leíva Quirós, Elias. *Por nuestras fronteras naturales: ecos de una campaña patriótica para impedir que Costa Rica ceda a Panamá territorios en la Costa Atlántica.* San José: Imprenta Gutenberg, 1935. 58 pp.
    A series of essays originally published in the press during the 1930s objecting to a boundary settlement and urging the Costa Rican government not to cede any territory to Panama. DLC-LDS-813 BNCR

507 Leíva Vivas, Rafael. *Valle: precursor del sistema interamericano.* Tegucigalpa: Offset Sectin, 1977. 41 pp. Notes, illus.
    A Honduran diplomat's summary of Valle's thought and role in the independence movement, contending that his ideas extended beyond Central America to the unification of all the former Spanish colonies, and hence that he deserves credit for the idea of Pan-Americanism along with Bolívar. The approach is highly laudatory of Valle. LNHT

508 León, F. de. *Unión centroamericana: datos para la historia de Centro-América relativos a los trabajos sobre unión de las repúblicas del istmo y sus efectos.* Guatemala: Tipografía La Independencia, 1912. 106 pp.

A discussion of various unionist efforts from 1885 through 1912, reproducing appropriate correspondence. The focus is the 1885 effort of Justo Rufino Barrios and the resulting exchanges between Barrios and the presidents of the other isthmian republics, with subsequent correspondence among the participants after Barrios's death also included. DLC BNG

509 Leonov, Nikolai Sergeevich. *Nekotorye problemy politicheskoi istorii TSentral'noi Ameriki XX Stoletiia* [Some problems in the political history of Central America in the twentieth century]. Moscow: Izdatel'stvo Nauka, 1972. 253 pp.
    A Marxist interpretation devoted principally to condemning Yankee imperialism, the international bourgeoisie, and Yankee capitalist corporations, which are blamed for all the problems of Central America. The focus is on the U.S. interventions in Nicaragua in the 1920s and in Guatemala in the 1950s, as well as on the United Fruit Company. DLC

510 _____. *Ocherki novoi i noveishei istorii stran TSentral'noi Ameriki* [Monographs on the contemporary and the current history of the countries of Central America]. Moscow: Izdatel'stvo "Mysl." 236 pp.
    DLC

511 Lever, Edward A. *Central America: The Land of the Quiches and Chontales.* New Orleans: E.A. Brandao, 1885. 293 pp.
    The foreign editor of the *New Orleans Times-Democrat*, who has traveled extensively in Central America, provides a descriptive account, seeking to fill what he considers a void in the literature attributable to the lack of writing on this area since J. Lloyd Stephens's work first called attention to it. Lever places particular emphasis on trade, exhorting the businessmen and merchants of New Orleans to seek to dominate the isthmian trade as a means of seizing an opportunity to contribute to the city's growth. He praises the new era of stability and progress brought to the isthmus by Justo Rufino Barrios, which he concludes has overcome the region's previous chaotic situation, and offers the prospect of a new era of prosperity and development with increasingly valuable trade that can benefit his home city. DLC LNHT

512 Leytón Rodríguez, Rubén. *Morazán.* Tegucigalpa: Imprenta Bulnes, 1953. 198 pp. Biblio. 2d ed. Tegucigalpa: Imprenta Bulnes, 1954. 184 pp. Biblio.
    An avowed pro-unionist scholar offers his views on Morazán, emphasizing his efforts to promote unification of the isthmus and lauding his principles. The author describes the book as his "homage" to Morazán, and liberally intersperses his own views with those of the hero. In addition to a brief biography, he comments extensively about the era and also about the relevance of Morazán to later and present unionist attempts. DLC LNHT

(Leytón Rodríguez, Rubén)
513 _____. Valle: padre del panamericanismo.
Guatemala: Ediciones Rubén Leytón Prado,
1955. 218 pp. Biblio.
Focusing on a neglected aspect of Valle,
namely, on his thoughts regarding cooperation
among the former Spanish colonies, the author
contends that Valle enunciated the basic ideas
of Pan-Americanism before Bolívar, and hence
that Guatemala is the real birthplace of the
concept and Valle the greatest thinker of his
age. The first portion of the volume is a
discussion of Pan-Americanism and its origins
in general, reflecting the author's views more
than Valle's. The book abounds with excerpts
from publications and statements by a variety
of individuals, without citations. The main
portion consists of selected short excerpts
from Valle's writings. DLC LNHT BNG

514 Liano, Andres, ed. Integración centroamericana: ley de incentivos fiscales para el
área centroamericana. Guatemala: J. de
Liano, 1969. 49 pp. Tables.
A collection of excerpts from and summaries
of the pertinent legislation relating to the
formation of the Common Market and its economic preferences and regulations, designed
for businessmen who need a quick guide to the
opportunities involved. LNHT

515 Liga de la Defensa Nacional Centro-Americana.
Labor hondureña por la autonomía de Centro-
América. Comayagüela: Imprenta El Sol, 1914.
368 pp. Illus.
A compilation of formal acts, public statements, and newspaper accounts opposing the
United States protectorate over Nicaragua and
attacking Yankee imperialism as a threat to
all Central America. DLC LNHT

516 Lindo, Hugo. La integración centroamericana
ante el derecho internacional. 2 vols. San
Salvador: Ministerio de Educación, 1971.
263, 290 pp. Biblio., notes, tables,
appendixes.
A legal study analyzing in detail each of
the parts of the various accords that brought
about the Common Market, examining the legal
precedents involved in the region and its
nations, and citing the unionist movement and
the previous efforts at federation. Concludes
that the present documents are limited by a
lack of policy orientation and clear definition and calls for a stronger effort designed
to promote integration through political as
well as economic methods. The discussion of
legal precedents does demonstrate the linkage
of the current efforts to those of the past
and shows the potential advantages to be drawn
from previous attempts. LNHT

517 Lizano Fait, Eduardo. La crisis del proceso
de integración de Centroamérica. San José:
Universidad de Costa Rica, 1968. 35 pp.
Notes.
A brief summary of the differences that
have surfaced among the various Central American nations regarding ideological and methodological objectives, and the differing

interpretations of the integration pacts.
BNCR

518 _____, ed. La integración económica centroamericana. San José: Universidad de Costa
Rica, 1972. 99 pp. Notes. 2d ed. Mexico:
Fondo de Cultura Económica, 1975. 438 pp.
Index, notes, tables.
A collection of articles dealing with the
origins of the Common Market and its economic
and legal aspects, written by participants in
and well-known scholars of the market. The
topics range widely, and among them are imports, fiscal organization, agriculture, the
evolution of Central American law, and the
operation of the institutions that comprise
the market. DLC LNHT

519 Lizano Fait, Eduardo. El Mercado Común y la
distribución del ingreso. San José: EDUCA,
1970. 175 pp. Index, notes, illus., tables.
An examination of the trends and potential
implications of the Common Market for internal
distribution of wealth and income within the
region. Concludes that an increase in regional trade will hurt the working class,
since it will raise prices faster than salaries and promote economic expansion that will
discourage loans to workers or peasants who
wish to buy land by diverting funds to more
profitable industrial and large-scale agricultural ventures. Examining trends within the
market, the author contends that a program of
balanced growth will be essential to assure
the continued participation of all the nations, just as in the domestic sphere a policy
favoring better income distribution will promote support by the various elements of the
population. DLC LNHT

520 Lizano Fait, Eduardo, and Raúl Hess Estrada.
Teoría y práctica de la integración económica
con especial referencia al caso de Centro
América. San José: Universidad de Costa
Rica, 1968. 88 pp. Biblio.
A series of conference presentations that
focus on the integration movement in Central
America and examine it in the light of general
integration theory. DLC

521 Lockley, Lawrence C. A Guide to Market Data
in Central America. Tegucigalpa: Central
American Bank for Economic Integration, 1964.
161 pp. Index, biblio., tables.
Características del mercado centroamericano.
Tegucigalpa: Banco Centroamericano de
Integración Económica, 1964. 163 pp. Index,
biblio., tables.
A description of the present resources and
market and labor conditions, with particular
emphasis on exports and imports, designed to
identify the markets for prospective investors
or present producers, indicating what can be
marketed in the region and where. Contains
detailed statistics and numerous tables indicating the current and recent situation
throughout the region. DLC LNHT BNCR

522 Lockwood, Belva A. The Central American Peace
Congress and an International Arbitration

Court for Five Central American Republics.
Washington, D.C.: n.p., 1908. 15 pp.
   A brief paper presented to the International Peace Conference in London that
discusses the newly formed court and the
Washington Conference of 1907, and provides
specifics regarding the accords. DLC

523   Long, William Rodney. Railways of Central
America and the West Indies. 2 vols.
Washington, D.C.: GPO, 1925-27. xvi, 376 pp.
Illus., maps, tables.
   A compilation of data on the state of
transportation in the area in 1925 by an
employee of the U.S. Department of Commerce.
About half the volume deals with Central
America. Includes brief accounts of railroad
development, focusing on providing exhaustive
current data about track, facilities, rolling
stock, revenues, tonnage, capacity, and current operation. DLC LNHT

524   López, Francisco Marcos. Centro América
esparcida. Guatemala: Imprenta Hispania,
1958. 58 pp. Illus.
   A unionist tract extolling the virtues of
unification and citing the historical precedents to and advantages of cooperation, particularly the common Hispanic heritage, the
latter undoubtedly reflecting the fact that
the author is a Spaniard. DLC LNHT BNG

525   _____. Metas centroamericanas: ideas
generales sobre el acercamiento centroamericano. Guatemala: Imprenta Excelsior,
195-? 16 pp.
   A brief discussion of the advantages of
Central American unification, expressing support for ODECA. DLC LNHT

526   López Barahona, Sotero. Exposición y alegato
que presenta el abogado por Honduras al
tribunal de arbitraje centroamericano, sobre
los sucesos ocurridos en la frontera
hondureña-nicaragüense, con motivo de la
invasión a Honduras. . . . San Salvador:
n.p., 1907. 68 pp.
   DLC BNCR

527   López Jiménez, Ramón. Esbozo biográfico del
prócer don Juan Vicente Villacorta. San
Salvador: Ministerio de Educación, 1964. 79
pp. Illus.
   A sympathetic biography of one of the leaders of Salvadoran independence, who later
served on the Executive Council of the Central
American Federation, headed the province of El
Salvador, fought against the Mexican annexation, and served as emissary to Rome in an
effort to win support for the revolution. The
author hails Villacorta as a dedicated public
servant who always had the best interests of
his country and its people in mind. Includes
documentary excerpts. DLC LNHT

528   _____. José Cecilio del Valle: fouché de
Centro América. Guatemala: Ministerio de
Educación Pública, 1968. 406 pp. Illus.,
appendixes.

   A sympathetic political biography of Valle,
focusing on his role in the independence of
the isthmus, his opposition to the attempted
Mexican annexation, and on the formation and
operation of the Central American Federation.
Contains extensive reproductions of pertinent
documents and decrees and of Valle's correspondence (with no indication of the location
of these sources), as well as excerpts from
previous biographies. DLC LNHT BNG

529   _____. José Matías Delgado y de León: su
personalidad, su obra y su destino; ensayo
histórico. San Salvador: Ministerio de
Educación, 1962. 301 pp. Index, biblio.
   A study of Delgado's independence efforts,
focusing on the years 1821-28 and emphasizing
his role in the actual independence movement,
the government of the area, the formation of
the Federation, and his opposition to Mexican
annexation efforts. The author emphasizes
Delgado's political and religious role, characterizing him as a statesman rather than a
philosopher or a warrior. Based on secondary
works. DLC LNHT

530   _____. José Simeón Cañas: su obra, su
verdadera personalidad y su destino. San
Salvador: Ministerio de Educación, 1970. 562
pp. Biblio., notes, illus.
   A detailed account of Cañas's career, this
work was awarded a prize at the commemoration
of the anniversary of the death of Cañas.
Based on extensive research in published and
archival sources, with liberal excerpts from
the pertinent documentation. The book details
Cañas's activities, but also encompasses the
history of slavery in the world. DLC LNHT

531   López Jiménez, Ramón, and Rafael Díaz.
Biografía de José Simeón Cañas. San Salvador:
Imprenta Nacional, 1968. 173 pp. Illus.
   An account of Cañas's career, including
copious quotation and reproduction of pertinent documents detailing his interaction with
his contemporaries. DLC LNHT

532   López Pineda, Julián. El general Morazán:
ensayo biográfico. Tegucigalpa: Tipografía
Ariston, 1944. 156 pp.
   A sympathetic view of Morazán's efforts to
unify the isthmus, quoting liberally from
documents, though without footnotes. DLC

533   Lovo Castelar, Luís. La Guardia Nacional en
campaña: relatos y crónicas de Honduras. San
Salvador: Editorial Lea, 1971. 185 pp.
Maps, tables.
   An account of the Guard's combats during
the 1969 war with Honduras, which the author,
an officer of the Guard and former director of
the Salvadoran Military Academy, characterizes
as a "punative expedition." His emphasis is
on the successful employment of tactics
learned. Includes a complete list of all
Guard personnel and maps of the battles in
which it participated, as well as various
summaries of the campaigns and comments from
the diaries of participants. DLC LNHT

534 Luján Muñoz, Jorge. La independencia y la anexión de Centroamérica a México. Guatemala: Editorial Universitaria, 1975. 93 pp.
A series of interpretative essays by a Guatemalan historian, emphasizing independence as a long-term process reflecting societal conditions and susceptible to diverse interpretations and definitions. The articles were previously published in various scholarly journals in Latin America and reflect extensive research in secondary sources, published documents, and memoirs from the era. LNHT BNG

535 Mac Armour, Roberto A. Plan de invasión salvadoreña. La Ceiba: Imprenta Renovación, 1971. 31 pp.
A discussion of Salvadoran army tactics in the 1969 war, denouncing the Salvadoran actions as indicating an advance plan by that nation, which the author feels demonstrates that the conflict was premeditated.

536 McCall, Louis A. Regional Integration: A Comparison of European and Central American Dynamics. Beverly Hills and London: Sage Publications, 1976. 77 pp. Biblio., notes, illus., tables.
An effort to develop a theory of integration providing general postulates applicable to all such movements, with few specifics regarding either Central American or European integration efforts. DLC

537 McCamant, John F. Development Assistance in Central America. New York: Praeger, 1968. xvi, 351 pp. Biblio., notes, tables.
A survey of the impact of development assistance from the United States during the late 1950s and 1960s, concluding that it promoted the development of the region. The author contends that the private sector is ahead of the public sector in development in the region and consequently that foreign assistance serves to prod the governments to action and facilitate faster action when coupled with the private sector. DLC LNHT

538 McCann, Thomas P. An American Company: The Tragedy of United Fruit. New York: Crown, 1976. 244 pp. Index, illus.
An episodic insider's exposé by a former executive of the United Fruit Company, detailing its "dirty tricks" and supporting many of the accusations against it with circumstantial evidence and accounts of related actions, revealing much of the behind-the-scenes maneuvering and corporate rivalries. The focus is on the years 1952-71 when the author worked for the company and was active in its machinations and in disguising them as its public relations director. DLC LNHT

539 McClellan, Albert. Rainbow South. Nashville: Broadman Press, 1952. 131 pp. Illus., maps, tables.
A Southern Baptist missionary and journalist who devotes his life to propaganda for the church provides this account of a three-week swing through Central America to visit and report on the Baptist missions in Guatemala and Costa Rica. His account stresses the work of the few missionaries there, hailing their dedication, and portrays the region as one with serious problems, a lack of services, and misguided religious views in need of evangelization. Includes some general information and description of conditions in rural areas. DLC

540 McClelland, Donald H. The Central American Common Market: Economic Policies, Economic Growth, and Choices for the Future. New York: Praeger, 1972. xiii, 243 pp. Biblio., tables.
A detailed analysis of the impact of the Common Market, with statistics and analysis regarding trends in GNP, industries, regional trade, investment, balance of payments, and many other economic factors. DLC LNHT

541 McVicker, Roy H. Central America: Some Observations on Its Common Market, Binational Centers, and Housing Programs. Washington, D.C.: GPO, 1966. vii, 33 pp. Tables, appendixes.
A brief and very general statement by a Congressman reporting his observations on a rapid fact-finding mission, basically emphasizing agreement with current U.S. policy and supporting a larger role for private enterprise. DLC

542 Magliano, Roberto. Interessi italiani nella America Centrale. Rome: Tipografía Delle Mantellate, 1889. 192 pp.
The Italian minister to Central America describes Italian trade with and colonization attempts in the isthmus, clearly seeking to promote such activities and to make his countrymen aware of the opportunities in the isthmus. His account indicates that the Italian colony was then the largest European colony in the isthmus, and that it was concentrated principally in Costa Rica, Guatemala, and El Salvador, though present in each of the five republics. DLC

543 Maldonado Koerdell, Manuel. Bibliografía geológica y paleontológica de America Céntral. Mexico: PAIGH, 1958. 288 pp. Index. 2d ed. Guatemala: Instituto Geográfico Nacional, 1966. 81 pp. Index.
Geological and Paleontological Bibliography of Central America. Mexico: PAIGH, 1958. 288 pp. Index.
A comprehensive listing encompassing journal articles and volumes, arranged by author, without annotation. The introduction provides a brief history of the geological exploration of Central America. Citings are quite complete and include Central American, United States, and European publications. DLC BNG

544 Malugani, María Dolores, and Alfredo Alvear, eds. Tesis de la Escuela para Graduados: 1948-1968; resúmenes. Turrialba: Instituto Interamericano de Ciencias Agrícolas, 1969. ii, 234 pp. Index.
A listing of theses, with abstracts, arranged alphabetically by author within

topical chapters, with an author index. DLC
LNHT

545 Marañón Richi, Luís. Centroamérica paso a
paso. Madrid: Editorial Prensa Española,
1968. 301 pp.
    A travelogue, focusing on the capitals,
consisting of extremely brief descriptions and
reactions, based on the author's sojourn in
the isthmus and Mexico. DLC LNHT

546 Markman, Sidney David. Colonial Central
America: A Bibliography. Tempe: Arizona
State University Press, 1977. xii, 345 pp.
Index.
    Despite its title, this volume encompasses
the modern as well as the Colonial period,
though focusing on the latter, with some 2,200
entries that include books, periodical articles, and some documents. Annotations are
usually limited to one or two lines. Some
items are location-coded for the Library of
Congress and Duke University, but the abbreviations used are not the standard ones and
the listing does not include all items at
these depositories dealing with Central America. The focus is on art and architecture,
and the basis of selection is not clear, with
the listings consequently somewhat capricious.
Documents involved come only from the Archivo
General de Centro América in Guatemala City.
DLC LNHT

547 Marr, Friedrich Wilhelm Adolf. Reise nach
Central Amerika. 2 vols. Hamburg: O.
Meissner, 1863. 322, 276 pp. 2d ed.
Hamburg: n.p., 1870.
Viaje a América Central. 2 vols. Hamburg:
n.p., 1863.
    A description of the author's travels in
Central America (including stops in the United
States and Mexico) during the 1850s. DLC
DLC-LDS-383 LNHT

548 Martín Carranza, Ernesto, ed. Anales de la
Corte de Justicia Centroamericana. San José:
Imprenta Alsina, 1911. 424 pp.

549 Martín Carranza, Ernesto. La labor del
pacifismo y la Corte de Justicia Centroamericana: conferencias dadas en el ateneo de
Costa Rica. San José: Tipografía Alsina,
1908. 64 pp.
    Analysis of the court and its relation to
Central American aspirations and cooperation,
originally presented as a paper. Includes
considerable discussion of war and peace and
national power in general, focusing on the
possibilities of arms limitation, with only
about half the volume detailing the court and
its operation. DLC DLC-LDS-23 BNCR

550 _____. Palabras dichas: discursos y
conferencias. San José: Imprenta Nueva,
1913. 130 pp. Illus. 2d ed. San José:
Imprenta Gutenberg, 1930. 226 pp. Notes,
tables.
    A collection of speeches on various sub-
jects, most dealing with significant historic

events or historical figures of Central America, but ranging widely. Includes essays
dealing with Lorenzo Montúfar and Santiago
Argüello, as well as comments on Spain,
Guatemala, Nicaragua, Costa Rican democracy,
etc. The second edition is entitled Discursos
y conferencias. DLC DLC-LDS-145 BNCR

551 Martínez, Miguel. Cuestión entre México y
Guatemala. Mexico: Imprenta de Ignacio
Escalante, 1882. viii, 279 pp. Appendixes.
    A nationalistic call for a strong Mexican
stand in the dispute, recounting the polemics
and official exchanges then taking place and
condemning the Guatemalans as "enemies" and
troublemakers. Originally published as a
series of articles in the Mexican newspaper La
Voz de México, it recounts the events of the
independence era, rehearsing the Mexican arguments that the districts of Chiapas and
Soconusco freely chose to join Mexico in full
exercise of their rights, and that Guatemala
has nothing to say about the matter. DLC

552 Martínez, Sebastián. Francisco Morazán frente
a la historia. Tegucigalpa: Imprenta
Calderón, 1968. 45 pp. Illus.
    A very brief sketch of the principal por-
tions of Morazán's life and political career,
including poems and hymns in his honor,
acclaiming his efforts to unify the region.
Includes an attack on Clemente Marroquín
Rojas's volume, refuting his criticism of
Morazán and reiterating the traditional interpretation critical of Carrera and favorable to
Morazán. DLC

553 Martínez Aybar, Juan Vicente. Correspondencia
de los presidentes y otros personajes de
Centro América relativa a la revolución
centroamericana de 1876 y otros
acontecimientos políticos de 1877 y 1878.
Sonsonate: Imprenta La Luz, 1895. 676 pp.

554 Martínez López, Eduardo. Al margen de Centro
América: miscelánea escotufística.
Tegucigalpa: Tipografía Nacional, 1931. 216
pp. Illus.
    A collection of miscellaneous essays com-
prising the author's writings during his travels in the isthmus outside his native
Honduras. The brief essays concern historical
topics and figures, as well as narrations of
miscellaneous incidents. DLC LNHT

555 _____. Biografía del general Francisco
Morazán. Tegucigalpa: Tipografía Nacional,
1899. xxiv, 409 pp. Illus. 4th ed. San
Pedro Sula: Ministerio de Educación Pública,
1968. 429 pp.
    A detailed and sympathetic biography of
what the author calls "the most glorious figure of modern Central America." Quotes copiously from historical documents from the
Honduran Archives, though without footnotes.
The original edition of 1899, was designed to
restore this hero to his proper glory. Includes a series of laudatory decrees and orations commemorating Morazán's contributions

(Martínez López, Eduardo)
and dedicating various monuments to him, with appropriate photos. DLC LNHT

556 _____. Honduras y Guatemala límites: ¡Alerta Hondureños! Tegucigalpa: Imprenta El Sol, 1928. 124 pp. Illus., maps.
A summary of the boundary dispute from the Honduran perspective, including quotations from the Colonial decrees and the arguments in the dispute. DLC LNHT

557 Martínez Suarez, Francisco. Vida de José Matías Delgado. San Salvador: Tipografía La Unión, 1911. 94 pp. 2d ed. San Salvador: Imprenta Nacional, 1917. 87 pp. Illus.
An account of Matías Delgado's role in the independence movement, lauding his efforts and quoting liberally from contemporary documents and public pronouncements. DLC

558 Martz, Mary Jeanne Reid. The Central American Soccer War: Historical Patterns and Internal Dynamics of OAS Settlement Procedures. Athens: Ohio University Center for International Studies, 1978. 113 pp. Biblio.
A brief account of the crisis, focusing on settlement efforts and casting the events in the context of OAS practice and experience. Includes consideration of the nature of the underlying dispute and the long-range problems that must be dealt with in any real solution to the basic elements. DLC LNHT

559 Marure, Alejandro. Bosquejo histórico de las revoluciones de Centro-América, desde 1811 hasta 1834. Many editions. 2 vols. Guatemala: Imprenta de la Nueva Academia de Estudios, 1837. Index, illus. Latest ed. Guatemala: Ministerio de Educación Pública, 1960. 3 vols. 704 pp. Notes, illus., appendixes.
A history of the Central American independence movements from 1811 through 1828, focusing on Guatemala and its role in the Federation and on the episode of Los Altos, written by a well-known Guatemalan Liberal scholar and political figure. Appendix contains documents. The interpretation is Liberal, a fact that resulted in the suppression of the second volume and the failure to complete the series, hence its termination in 1828 despite its title. Yet while Liberal, Marure still sought to refute the extreme interpretations of Montúfar y Coronado's Memorias. DLC LNHT BNG

560 _____. Eferménides de los hechos notables acaecidos en la República de Centro-América desde el año 1821 hasta él de 1842: seguidas de varios catálogos de los presidentes de la república, jefes de los estados, etc. Many editions. Guatemala: Imprenta de la Paz, 1844. 79 pp. Latest ed. Guatemala: Ministerio de Educación Pública, 1956. 157 pp. Illus.
A well-known Guatemalan historian provides a day-by-day listing of events, covering the years 1821 through 1842, indicating the course of the independence movement and the

subsequent Federation. The listings are cryptic, merely stating the event without details or comment. The latter portion of the volume contains chronological tables of the heads of government in Colonial and independence times. DLC LNHT BNG BNCR

561 Masferrer de Miranda, Teresa. Viendo pasar la vida. Guatemala: Talleres Gutenberg, 1960. 113 pp.
This small volume by the sister of a well-known Salvadoran social reformer contains a series of brief disparate commentaries on numerous social problems in Guatemala, Salvador, and Central America. BNG

562 Mata Gavidia, José. Anotaciones de historia patria centro-americana. Guatemala: Cultural Centroamericana, 1953. 432 pp. Biblio., illus., maps. Latest ed. Guatemala: Editorial Universitaria, 1969. 402 pp.
A general history, with frequent quotations in the text reflecting research in published works and documents, written from an avowedly unionist and patriotic viewpoint and designed to familiarize Central Americans with the principal points of their history. Nearly two-thirds of the volume deals with the pre-independence period, and only forty pages are devoted to the post-1920 era. In the modern period the focus is on the most important governments, particularly those of Guatemala, with brief chapters outlining the other republics, and some topical considerations of cultural factors in general. DLC LNHT

563 _____. Lo auténtico y lo circunstanciado en la independencia de Centro América. Guatemala: Centro Italo-Guatemalteca, 1953. 34 pp. Notes.
A brief discourse, previously published in the Revista de la Universidad de San Carlos, discussing the causes of the independence movement, and differentiating between the internal or authentic causes and the external or circumstantial factors. The author contends that the region was approaching an intellectual maturity and social condition that rendered it ripe for independence, and that the circumstantial events merely affected the timing. LNHT

564 Matamoros, Luís. Costa Rica-Panama Arbitration: Report Submitted to the Representative of Costa Rica. Washington, D.C.: Gibson, 1913. vii, 151 pp. Illus.
The report of the Costa Rican government's consulting engineer, defining the precise lines claimed by that nation in its dispute with Panama. BNCR

565 Matus, Ramón Ignacio. La cuestión hondureño-nicaragüense: estudio crítico-jurídico sobre las nulidades del laudo del rey de España de 23 de diciembre de 1926, respecto a límites entre Nicaragua y Honduras. Managua: Tipografía Nacional, 1927. 430 pp.
A Nicaraguan priest's study of the boundary dispute, arguing the Nicaraguan case with vehemence and contending that Honduras, in

(Matus, Ramón Ignacio)
rejecting consideration by the Yankee arbitration of the validity of the decision of the
king of Spain, has in effect nullified this
new arbitration effort. Proposes that the
National Congress therefore withdraw from the
arbitration and create a permanent Department
of Límites in the Ministry of Foreign Relations dedicated solely to preparing studies
and arguments regarding this question and to
continuing the dispute. Includes a detailed
restatement of the Nicaraguan position and
refutation of the Honduran arguments before
the Spanish king. DLC

566   _____. Jurisdicción territorial atlántica de
la República de Nicaragua, civil, política y
eclesiástica, desde las bocas del desaguadero
o Río San Juan del Norte, hasta la medianería
de las aguas navegables del Río Grande o
Aguán, hacia el poniente del Cabo Camarón, en
su colindencia con la República de Honduras.
Managua: Talleres Nacionales, 1938. 186 pp.
     A polemical statement of the Nicaraguan
case in the border dispute with Honduras,
challenging the entire Honduran position somewhat more boldly than the official government
statements. Written by a priest but published
with official sanction, which provoked an
equally violent reply from Guardiola and
Salgado. The focus is the issue of Colonial
jurisdictions and the meaning of the accord
that led to the 1906 arbitration by the
Spanish king. DLC LNHT

567   May, Charles Paul. Central America: Lands
Seeking Unity. Camden, N.J.: Thomas Nelson,
1966. 224 pp. Index, biblio., illus., maps.
     A general account, part of a series de-
signed to introduce teenaged Yankees to other
countries of the world. Emphasizes people and
economics, based primarily on the author's
observations in the area. Includes brief
historical summaries. DLC

568   May, Jacques M., and Donna L. McLellan. The
Ecology of Malnutrition in Mexico and Central
America. New York: Hafner, 1972. xiii, 395
pp. Index, biblio., illus., maps, tables.
     A survey of the current nutritional situa-
tion in each nation, including consideration
of geography, food production, diets, and
nutritional diseases, detailing the characteristics of production, the shortages, the
distribution problems, and the differences
between rural and urban problems. Each nation
is treated in a separate section with no comparisons. DLC LNHT

569   May, Stacy, and Galo Plaza Lasso. La United
Fruit Company en América Latina. Washington,
D.C.: National Planning Association, 1958.
xv, 291 pp. Illus., maps, tables.
The United Fruit Company in Latin America.
Washington, D.C.: National Planning Associa-
tion, 1958. xv, 263 pp. Illus. 2d ed. New
York: Arno Press, 1976. xv, 262 pp. Illus.
     An examination of the United Fruit Company
by a well-known economist and a Latin American

government official who later served as secretary general of the Organization of American
States. The study focuses on the 1950s and
concentrates on the positive side of the company's operations, emphasizing its economic
impact on its host nations and its contributions to their development, growth, and employment, concluding that the company's
reputation is undeserved and ignores the
benefits it brings. The volume thus provides
a counterpoint to many of the criticisms of
the company and some context regarding the
banana trade and production factors. DLC
LNHT BNG

570   Mayora, Eduardo, ed. La prensa de Guatemala y
la cuestión de límites con Honduras.
Guatemala: Tipografía La Libertad, 1932. 248
pp. Illus.
     A collection of articles from the
Guatemalan press that appeared during the
course of the arbitration of the boundary
dispute with Honduras, which naturally hail
the Guatemalan stand and defend the nation's
claims. BNG

571   Mayorga, Juan de Dios. Exposición sobre el
derecho que tiene la Provincia de Chiapa [sic]
para pronunciar libremente su voluntad, y el
que tiene Goatemala [sic] para ser
independiente. . . . Mexico: Imprenta de
Tomás Lorrain, 1823. 60 pp.
     A Guatemalan protest against the Mexican
annexation of Chiapas, contending that it was
accomplished by force and requesting that the
area have the right to choose its destiny
freely. Rehearses the independence maneuverings and hails Mexican acceptance of the
Guatemalan decision to separate from Mexico,
while calling for the same consideration for
Chiapas. Reprints several petitions from
ayuntamientos in Chiapas alleging Mexican
coercion in the decision regarding annexation.
DLC LNHT

572   Maza, Emilio. La Corte de Justicia Centroamericana: comentarios. San Salvador:
ODECA, 1966. 89 pp. Tables.
     A proposal for the establishment of a new
Central American court to supplement the
existing ODECA structure and the Common
Market, with a draft treaty and an explanation
of the proposed powers of the court, its limitations, and the needs it would address. LNHT

573   Mejía, Medardo. Los diezmos de Olancho. 2
vols. Tegucigalpa: Revista Ariel, 1965-71.
138, 118 pp.
     Two of an intended trilogy of plays deal-
ing with the civil wars following the collapse of
the nineteenth-century Federation, when the
church vs. Liberal confrontation was the dominant item in the isthmus, designed to present
the era in popular form. DLC

574   Mejía Nieto, Arturo. Morazán: presidente de
la desaparecida República Centroamericana.
Buenos Aires: Editorial Nova, 1947. 215 pp.
Biblio., illus.

A sympathetic account of Morazán's career, seeking to make him better known to present generations and South American audiences in honor of the centennial of his death. The author notes that Morazán belongs to the generation of hemispheric liberators, but not in the sense of the South American leaders, as he did not need to lead an armed rebellion against Spain. Rather, his significance lies in his personification of the ideal of unionism, his efforts to sustain it, and the fact that he was the region's first Liberal, bringing reforms to the isthmus that predated similar legislation in South America. Based on existing secondary works about Morazán and the era. DLC LNHT BNCR

575 Meléndez Chaverri, Carlos. El presbítero y doctor José Matías Delgado en la forja de la nacionalidad centroamericana: ensayo histórico. San Salvador: Ministerio de Educación, 1962. 357 pp. Biblio., notes, illus., maps.
A study of one of the leaders of the independence movement, focusing on the years 1811-32, by a well-known historian of that era. Includes background data setting the context, based on research in secondary sources and appropriate documents. DLC LNHT BNCR

576 _____, ed. Próceres de la independencia centroamericana. San José: EDUCA, 1971. 394 pp. Notes, illus.
A collection of biographical essays, each by a different scholar, detailing the contributions of eight leading figures of Central American Independence. The essays range from thirty-five to eighty pages each, and deal with Arce, Aycinena, Barrundia, Córdova, Delgado, de Larreynaga, Molina, and Valle. DLC LNHT BNG BNCR

577 _____. Textos fundamentales de la independencia centroamericana. San José: EDUCA, 1971. 424 pp. Biblio.
A collection of documents including communications describing conditions in the isthmus during the early years of the nineteenth century, items relating to intellectual developments and the antecedents of independence, the principal documents of the independence movement in the various localities, and declarations relating to the Mexican incursion. Some come from published works, and others from archives. DLC LNHT BNG BNCR

578 Membreño, Alberto. Límites entre Honduras y Nicaragua: alegato presentado a Su Majestad Católica el rey de España en calidad de árbitro. Madrid: Tipográfico de Idamor Moreno, 1905. 254 pp. Maps. 2d ed. Tegucigalpa: Imprenta Calderón, 1938. 255 pp.
The original Honduran case in the 1904 proceedings that led to the 1906 ruling by the king. DLC LNHT

579 Membreño, María B. de. ¿Porqué fuimos a la guerra . . . ? San Salvador: Editores La Nación, 1969. Pages unnumbered. Illus.
A passionate account of the Salvadoran version of the 1969 conflict with Honduras, with extensive photos of the armed forces and refugees. Emphasizes Honduran atrocities against Salvadoran settlers, the heroism of the Salvadoran armed forces, and the popular solidarity with the government, contending that Salvador was victorious in the conflict. Also contains many presidential messages and proclamations, and some diplomatic exchanges. Concludes with a useful chronology of the conflict, though like the rest of the volume it reflects the Salvadoran viewpoint and the passion of the Salvadoran press. DLC LNHT

580 Mencos Franco, Agustín. Rasgos biográficos de Francisco Morazán: apuntes para la historia de Centroamérica. Guatemala: Tipografía El Comercio, 1893. ii, 224 pp. 4th ed. Guatemala: Imprenta La República, 1906. 254 pp. Index.
Originally a series of articles, written at various times for newspapers seeking to debunk the image of Morazán, in response to the celebration of his centennial and the resulting glorification. Criticizing Morazán's ambition and characterizing him as a dictator, the author contends that José Cecilio del Valle deserved most of the credit for the Federation, characterizing Morazán as a "mediocre" politician, an "absolute nulity." DLC-LDS-635 BNG

581 Méndez I., Jorge. Organizaciones de fachada del comunismo internacional. Mexico: Ediciones Occidentales, n.d. [195?]. 101 pp.
A denunciation of communist infiltration efforts and front organizations, reflecting the disputes and polemics of the 1950s, written in exposé fashion. BNG

582 Mendieta, Salvador. Alrededor del problema unionista Centro-América. 2 vols. Barcelona: Tipografía Maucci, 1934. 577, 462 pp. 2d ed. Madrid: Tipografía Maucci, 1935. 583, 462 pp.
The first volume of this series by the founder and leader of the Unionist party focuses on Nicaraguan politics during the 1920s, in which the author was involved, viewing local affairs in the context of the unionist efforts. Includes a series of letters between the author and various individuals during this period. The second volume analyzes the history of the unionist movement, seeking to demonstrate that the aspiration is part of the Central American tradition. The discussion is not chronological but rather jumps about, covering the era from the Panama Congress of Bolívar to 1898, reproducing documents and communications from the Unionist party. DLC BNG

583 _____. Conferencia dada por el jefe del Partido Unionista Centroamericana ante la convención seccional del mismo, el 31 de

(Mendieta, Salvador)

octubre de 1910 en Managua. Managua: Tipografía Moderna, 1911. 47 pp.

A defense of the Unionist party, contending that it is a separate movement rather than a part of liberalism, and thus, although it opposes the Conservatives, it stands alone and is not involved in the political coups of the isthmus. DLC

584   ____. Cuentos caciquistas centroamericanos. Managua: Tipografía Moderna, 1911. xiv, 223 pp.

A collection of short stories and essays written over a period of many years and dealing with various political problems in Central America, combining portrayal in fiction of the problems of dictatorship and democracy and their operation with papers referring to real individuals and governments from the 1895-1910 era. Not surprisingly, this unionist views the local dictators as shortsighted and seeking to preserve their own power. DLC

585   ____. La enfermedad de Centro-América. 3 vols. Madrid: Tipografía Maucci, 1934-36. 444, 386, 678 pp.

The unionist leader's discussion of what he considers the "disease" of separatism that prevents the unification of the isthmus. Volume 1 provides a "description of the subject and the symptoms of the disease," consisting principally of a descriptive geography and an historical account of the unionist efforts from 1920 through 1934. The second volume, "diagnosis and origins of the disease," includes a detailed analysis of the reasons for the failure of the efforts, considering geography, institutions, Colonial heritage, the church, caciquismo, and the politics of the independence era, with the emphasis on the Colonial setting and heritage. The final volume contains the author's prescribed treatment which, of course, is union, which will provide the means of solving all the area's problems. The arguments for federation and its potential effects are all enumerated, along with a proposed constitution and organizational scheme for the new isthmian state. The initial portion of volume 1 was published in 1910, with the rest added in the 1930s with the other two volumes. DLC LNHT BNG

586   ____. La nacionalidad y el Partido Unionista Centroamericano. San José: Imprenta Alsina, 1905. 98 pp.

Another unionist tract, contending that the ideal persists and that the separate countries reflect the rivalries, personal conflicts, and transportation problems of the region, and that the states are separatist rather than nationalist. Inevitably, he sees his party as a means of overcoming this localism and reconstituting the Federation. BNCR

587   ____. Páginas de unión. Nicaragua: Tipografía de J.C. Gurdián, n.d. [1903]. 310 pp.

Yet another account of the need for union, cataloguing the various efforts, from the prolific pen of a tireless propagandist for the ideal. DLC

588   ____. El problema unionista de centroamérica y los gobiernos locales. Quezaltenango: F. Ocheita, n.d. [1930]. 180 pp.

A series of commentaries regarding the various unionist attempts by the Nicaraguan unionist leader and longtime head of the Unionist Party, terminating with his speech to the 1921 unionist Constituent Assembly. He emphasizes the advantages of union, hails the heroes who promoted it, and berates the shortsighted opponents who frustrated previous efforts. DLC LNHT BNG

589   ____. Tratado de educación cívica centroamericano. Managua: Tipografía "Progreso," 1916. 2d ed. Managua: Talleres Nacionales, 1964. 172 pp.

A grade-school text, constituting the official statement of the Juventud Centro-Americana movement. Written by one of the leading Nicaraguan unionists, it emphasizes the common experiences among the five republics and the desirability of union. DLC LNHT BNG

590   Mendoza, Juan Manuel. Salvador Mendieta. Guatemala: Sánchez & de Guise, 1930. 185 pp.

A friendly biography of the Nicaraguan unionist leader, written by an avowed unionist, hailing his career as a politician, polemicist, and propagandist for the unionist ideal through the 1920s, concluding that his efforts have kept the ideal of union alive throughout the isthmus. DLC BNG

591   ____. Semblanzas y artículos. Guatemala: Tipografía Nacional, 1902. xix, 162 pp. Illus.

A collection of articles written for the press, including descriptions of all the leading political figures of late nineteenth-century Central America and many of its intellectual figures, followed by articles on a number of then current topics such as unionism. All are dated, though the original paper in which they appeared is not indicated. They vary from brief commentaries that are largely impressionistic to longer, more analytical pieces. LNHT

592   El Mensajero de Centro América. Cuestionario entre Guatemala y Méjico. Guatemala: Tipografía Moderna, 1895. 88 pp. Maps. The Questions between Mexico and Guatemala. Guatemala: n.p., 1895. 46 pp. Maps.

A collection of articles originally published by the Guatemalan newspaper El Mensajero de Centro América, with no author indicated, analyzing the Mexican-Guatemalan border disputes and commenting on the 1895 treaty that marked the boundary. Defends the Guatemalan position while criticizing the government for signing the accord, which relinquished the Guatemalan claims to Chiapas and Soconusco, establishing the present frontier. The articles are highly critical of the

Mexican refusal to accept arbitration by the United States as proposed by Guatemala, and consider the present accord an imposition by Mexico. DLC LNHT BNG

593 Merin, Boris Moiseevich. TSentral'naĩa Amerika: Problemy sotsialnopoliticheskogo razvitiia [Central America: the problems of sociopolitical development]. Moscow: Izdatel'stvo "Nauka," 1973. 158 pp. Biblio., notes, tables.
DLC

594 Merlos, Salvador R. América Latina ante el peligro. San José: Imprenta Nueva de Gerardo Matamoros, 1914. 419 pp. Illus.
A denunciation of Yankee imperialism in Central America and particularly in Nicaragua, detailing the armed actions and condemning Woodrow Wilson's recognition policy as merely a new form, citing his actions in Mexico. Calls for Central American unity to repel the Yankee threat. DLC DLC-LDS-144 BNCR

595 ____. Centro-América en el conflicto. San Salvador: Talleres Gráficos Cisneros, 1942. 23 pp.
A brief, general discussion of the impact of World War II on the region, reflecting the oratory and passion of the era.

596 ____. Hacia la unión: política centro-americana. San Salvador: Tipografía Vanguardia, n.d. [1920]. viii, 96 pp.
A unionist tract hailing the efforts of 1920 and the Unionist Party. DLC

597 Mexico, Gov't of. Congreso. Cámara de Diputados. Incorporación de Chiapas á México: discursos leídos en la velada que se verificó en la Cámara de Diputados, en celebración de LXXVIII aniversario de la federación de Chiapas a la República de México. Mexico: Tipografía de la Oficina Impresora de Estampillas, 1902. 42 pp.
The patriotic addresses and celebrations conducted by the Chamber of Deputies, extolling the decision of Chiapas to become part of Mexico at independence, hailing its right to do so, and seeking to identify the state with Mexico more effectively, with little mention of the boundary dispute that resulted. LNHT

598 ____. Ministerio de Relaciones Exteriores. Cuestión de límites entre México y Guatemala: nota y memorandum que dirigió el señor ministro de Guatemala al gobierno de México y contestación dada por el ministro de relaciones exteriores de la República. Mexico: Imprenta del Gobierno, 1875. 104 pp.
An 1874 exchange between Juan Ramón Uriarte, the Guatemalan envoy, and Mexican Foreign Minister José María Lafragua regarding the boundary question. The Guatemalan note, which is quite short, reiterates earlier proposals for negotiations and/or arbitration, noting that Guatemala, in accordance with earlier stances, recognized the annexation of Chiapas to Mexico but disputes title to the

Soconusco district. The lengthy Mexican response, which comprises most of the volume, recounts at length the Mexican claims, with full documentation, and offers a counterproposal to mark the boundary according to the Mexican claim. DLC LNHT

599 ____. ____. Límites con México: correspondencia oficial con motivo de "Invasiones de Guatemala en territorio mexicano" con antecedentes y el arreglo final. Mexico: Imprenta del Gobierno, 1895. 246 pp. Maps.
A statement of the Mexican case in the ongoing dispute, including official exchanges and the year's charges and countercharges regarding alleged efforts to occupy the disputed areas.

600 Middle American Information Bureau. Middle America and the United States: Proceedings of the One Day Institute, April 12, 1943. New York: Middle American Information Bureau, 1943. 101 pp.
A series of brief papers delivered to a conference, designed to encourage investment and extolling the trade potential of the region. DLC

601 Mitchell, Willard H. CSUCA: A Regional Strategy for Higher Education in Central America. Princeton, N.J.: Princeton University Press, 1966. 2d ed. Lawrence: University of Kansas Press, 1967. 66 pp. Biblio., notes.
A brief summary of the programs of the regional organization that promotes cooperation among the Central American universities, summarizing its creation and functioning and noting the various viewpoints regarding its future role and purposes. The author emphasizes that the organization is pursuing a moderate course, advocating a continuation of this policy of serving clearly identified needs rather than seeking to promote change. DLC LNHT

602 Molina, Cayteano Antonio. Opusculo para la historia de la revolución de Centro-América: escrito por . . . enviado del supremo gobierno del Salvador cerca del de Guatemala en defensa de su gobierno y en contestación a los folletos del comisionado de Honduras, Ldo. señor Felipe Jáuregui. Guatemala: Imprenta La Paz, 1845. 36 pp.
Part of an exchange of polemics and pamphlets among the various governments during the collapse of the Federation, this is a defense of the Salvadoran position against that of the Federal government in Honduras. Some correspondence is appended. DLC

603 Molina, Felipe. Costa Rica y Nueva Granada: examen de la cuestión de límites, que hay pendiente entre los dos repúblicas mencionadas, y testimonios de los títulos antiguos de Costa-Rica. Washington, D.C.: R.A. Waters, 1852. 50 pp. Maps.
Costa Rica and New Granada: An Inquiry into the Question of Boundaries, Which Is Pending between the Two Republics Aforesaid (With a

(Molina, Felipe)
    <u>Map</u> <u>for</u> <u>the</u> <u>Better</u> <u>Understanding</u> <u>of</u> <u>the</u> <u>Sub-</u>
<u>ject,</u> <u>and</u> <u>Documentary</u> <u>Evidence</u> <u>in</u> <u>Support</u> <u>of</u>
<u>the</u> <u>Ancient</u> <u>Titles</u> <u>of</u> <u>Costa</u> <u>Rica</u> <u>to</u> <u>Which</u> <u>an</u>
<u>Appendix</u> <u>Has</u> <u>Been</u> <u>Added</u> <u>Containing</u> <u>a</u> <u>Brief</u>
<u>Account</u> <u>of</u> <u>the</u> <u>Question</u> <u>between</u> <u>Costa</u> <u>Rica</u> <u>and</u>
<u>Nicaragua</u>). Washington, D.C.: R.A. Waters,
1853. 54 pp. Maps.
    A brief summary of the Costa Rican posi-
tion, defending its claims. The English version contains a preface arguing that Costa
Rica would be happy to facilitate an interoceanic canal through its territory, and contending that the case of Costa Rica is not
understood in the U.S. Also notes the degree
to which the boundary question was exacerbated
by conflicting concessions to different foreign companies for colonization and canal
construction, an aspect omitted from the official exchanges. DLC

604   ____. <u>Mémoire</u> <u>sur</u> <u>les</u> <u>questions</u> <u>de</u> <u>límites</u>
<u>entre</u> <u>la</u> <u>República</u> <u>de</u> <u>Costa</u> <u>Rica</u> <u>et</u> <u>l'état</u> <u>de</u>
<u>Nicaragua</u>. Paris: Schiller, 1850. 40 pp.
<u>Memoir</u> <u>on</u> <u>the</u> <u>Boundary</u> <u>Question</u> <u>Pending</u> <u>be-</u>
<u>tween</u> <u>the</u> <u>Republic</u> <u>of</u> <u>Costa</u> <u>Rica</u> <u>and</u> <u>the</u> <u>State</u>
<u>of</u> <u>Nicaragua</u>. Washington, D.C.: Gideon,
1851. 40 pp. Maps.
<u>Memoria</u> <u>sobre</u> <u>las</u> <u>cuestiones</u> <u>de</u> <u>límites</u> <u>que</u> <u>se</u>
<u>versan</u> <u>entre</u> <u>la</u> <u>República</u> <u>de</u> <u>Costa</u> <u>Rica,</u> <u>y</u> <u>el</u>
<u>estado</u> <u>de</u> <u>Nicaragua</u>. Madrid: Imprenta de la
Viuda de Calero, 1850. 47 pp. Maps.
    An account by the Costa Rican envoy, giving
his country's perspective regarding the boundary question with Nicaragua resulting from the
collapse of the Federation of Central America.
Includes his assessment of the failure of the
Federation and what he considers its demonstrated inability to function effectively.
DLC DLC-LDS-180 LNHT BNCR

605 Molina, Pedro. <u>Escritos</u> <u>del</u> <u>doctor</u> <u>Pedro</u>
<u>Molina</u> <u>conteniendo</u> <u>la</u> <u>reproducción</u> <u>íntegra</u> <u>de</u>
<u>los</u> <u>escritos</u> <u>del</u> <u>primer</u> <u>semestre</u> <u>del</u> <u>periódico</u>
<u>"El Editor Constitucional"</u> <u>y</u> <u>"El Genio de la</u>
<u>Libertad"</u> . . . <u>Guatemala</u>. 3 vols.
Guatemala: Ministerio de Educación Pública,
1954. 342, 592, 895 pp. 2d ed. Guatemala:
Ministerio de Educación Pública, 1969. 343,
240, 294 pp.
    A reprinting of one of the first unionist
political periodicals in Guatemala, <u>El Editor</u>
<u>Constitucional</u>, which was the newspaper of
Pedro Molina, issued in honor of the centennial of the independence movement. It provides discussions of isthmian problems during
the early years of independence, covering the
years 1820 and 1821, from the viewpoint of a
Liberal Guatemala City unionist. DLC LNHT
BNG

606 Molina Chocano, Guillermo. <u>Integración</u>
<u>centroamericana</u> <u>e</u> <u>dominación</u> <u>internacional:</u>
<u>un</u> <u>ensayo</u> <u>de</u> <u>interpretación</u> <u>sociológica</u>. San
José: EDUCA, 1971. 95 pp. Biblio., notes,
tables.
    A sociological study based on the depend-
ency theory. Follows the standard dependency
line that the Common Market facilitates the
penetration of foreign firms and investment,
which are best able to exploit the larger

regional market and hence are the primary
beneficiaries of economic integration. DLC
LNHT BNCR

607 Moncada, José María. <u>Cosas</u> <u>de</u> <u>Centro</u> <u>América:</u>
<u>memorias</u> <u>de</u> <u>un</u> <u>testigo</u> <u>ocular</u> <u>de</u> <u>los</u> <u>sucesos</u>.
Madrid: Imprenta de Fortanet, 1908. 311 pp.
    An account of the 1890 to 1906 period,
condemning the activities of Zelaya and praising those of Estrada Cabrera in Guatemala.
The account portrays Zelaya as an ambitious
intriguer who intervened in neighboring countries and was the cause of all the disturbances of the peace in the isthmus, and
Estrada Cabrera as an innocent victim, governing constitutionally and responding only
when attacked. The book is based on the
author's role in politics during this era,
offering his viewpoint written from exile.
DLC LNHT

608   ____. <u>Nicaragua</u> <u>y</u> <u>Honduras:</u> <u>su</u> <u>antigua</u>
<u>cuestión</u> <u>de</u> <u>límites</u>. Managua: Talleres
Gráficos Pérez, 1937. 15 pp.
    Another statement of the Nicaraguan case
regarding the technicalities surrounding the
1906 ruling by the king of Spain, arguing that
it was invalid because of procedures and because it exceeded the scope imposed by the
governing accord. DLC

609   ____. <u>Social</u> <u>and</u> <u>Political</u> <u>Influence</u> <u>of</u> <u>the</u>
<u>United</u> <u>States</u> <u>in</u> <u>Central</u> <u>America</u>. New York:
Gahan, 1911. 50 pp.
    A denunciation of Yankee intervention in
the isthmus, written in the manner of an
appeal to the American people, proposing a
joint conference, an end to monopoly, an
International Court of Arbitration for the
Americas, and other steps to enable cooperation for the development of the region without
direct intervention. Cites the declarations
of President Taft as indicating that the
Yankees might be receptive to these ideas.
DLC LNHT

610 Moncarz, Raúl. <u>Moneda</u> <u>y</u> <u>banca</u> <u>en</u> <u>América</u>
<u>Central</u>. Tegucigalpa: Escuela Bancaria
Superior Centroamericana, 1978. xvi, 291 pp.
Index, biblio., tables.
    A text on banking and financial practice in
contemporary Central America, analyzing the
prevailing practices and legal background.
DLC

611 Monteforte Toledo, Mario, et al. <u>Centro-</u>
<u>américa:</u> <u>subdesarrollo</u> <u>y</u> <u>dependencia</u>. 2
vols. Mexico: UNAM, 1972. 438 pp. Maps,
tables.
    A monumental dependency analysis of the
region, focusing on its sociological, political, and economic characteristics in the
present era, though including some discussion
of its antecedents. Includes extensive statistics and consideration of all aspects of
the society and economy, with chapters devoted
to such themes as the military, the laborers,
the guerrillas, political parties, population,
economic integration, agriculture, and industry. All include the usual critiques of the
local oligarchy and landowners, as well as

denunciation of the Yankee imperialists who are held responsible for many of the problems, the familiar attacks on foreign enterprises and particularly the United Fruit Company, and commentary regarding the limits of capitalist economic thinking. An effective summary of these viewpoints and their bases. DLC LNHT

612 Montiero, Palmyra V.M. A Catalogue of Latin American Flat Maps, 1926-1964. 2 vols. Austin: University of Texas Press, 1967. xvi, 395 pp. Index, appendixes.

A listing of maps published within these dates, with publication information, data on size, and a description of content. The first volume covers Mexico, Central America, and the West Indies, including sections for each of the Central American nations, as well as a general section of maps dealing with the entire isthmus. About 150 pages of the volume are devoted to Central America. Within each section maps are arranged by type and title. While addresses of publishing agencies are appended, there is no indication of depositories containing the maps. Geological maps and city plans are excluded. DLC

613 Montes, Arturo Humberito. Morazán y la Federación Centroamericana. Mexico: Libro Mex Editores, 1958. 381 pp. Biblio., illus.

A detailed biography of Morazán, following his entire life to the fall of the Federation. Based on secondary works, with copious quotation from existing studies and the documents used in them. The volume is pro-unionist and pro-Morazán, condemning those who opposed the Federation as "factionalists" and hailing Morazán as the "maximum hero" of Honduras. The author is a Honduran journalist. The final chapters deal with the various monuments to Morazán in each of the countries and various acts of homage to him. DLC LNHT BNCR

614 Montes, Luís. Bananas: The Fruit Empire of Wall Street. New York: International Pamphlets, 1933. 23 pp. Illus., maps.

A Communist party attack on the United Fruit Company reflecting the unrest in the plantation areas during the 1930s where the party controlled several of the banana-workers' unions. NN

615 Montessus de Ballore, Fernand J.B. Comte de. Tremblements de terre et éruptions volcaniques au Centre Amérique depuis la conquête espagnole jusqu'à nos jours. Dijon: Imprimerie Eugène Jobard, 1888. 293 pp. Biblio., illus., maps, tables. Tremblores y erupciones volcánicas en Centro-América. San Salvador: Imprenta F. Sagrini, 1884. 246 pp. Index, biblio., illus.

After a brief introduction discussing the causes and characteristics of earthquakes and volcanic eruptions, the main portion of the volume presents a chronological list of 772 such events in Central America from 1469 to 1886, drawn from various secondary accounts. For each the listing provides a date, location, and description, as well as an indication of damage. DLC LNHT

616 Montúfar, Rafael. El folleto de don Fernando Cruz sobre la cuestión de límites entre Guatemala y México. Guatemala: Tipografía La Unión, 1888. 27 pp.

A brief pamphlet endorsing the arguments of Cruz in the recent publication, La verdad histórica.

617 _____. Por la unión: vindicación del congreso Liberal de Tegucigalpa. Guatemala: Sánchez & de Guise, 1920. 63 pp.

A defense of the work of the Liberal congress of Tegucigalpa of 1920, written by its president. Recounts its reasoning, endorses its unionist efforts, and reiterates its stand in opposition to the Bryan-Chamorro Treaty, which became one of the stumbling blocks to the subsequent efforts at union. BNG

618 Montúfar y Coronado, Manuel. Memorias para la historia de la revolución de Centro-América. Jalapa, Guatemala: Impreso por Aburto y Blanco, 1832. xxxii, 257 pp. Latest ed. Guatemala: Ministerio de Educación Pública, 1963. 187 pp.

A leading Conservative politician's view of the period of the independence movement from 1821 to 1831, written from exile and in prison. Also known as the Memorias de Jalapa. Montúfar was prominent in the era, rising to the position of vice-president of Guatemala before falling into disfavor. He spent the years of his nation's early Liberal governments in exile, returning during the Conservative regime of Rafael Carrera. Includes supporting documents. DLC LNHT BNG BNCR

619 _____. Recuerdos y anecdótas. Guatemala: n.p., 1837. 73 pp.

An appendix to his previously published Memorias para la historia de la revolución.

620 Montúfar y Rivera Maestre, Lorenzo. Apuntamientos sobre economía política. Guatemala: Tipografía La Unión, 1887. 312 pp.

A general economic treatise or text, treating broad themes with examples from many nations. DLC-LDS-706

621 _____. El general Francisco Morazán: artículos publicados en 1892 y 1893 con motivo de la conmemoración del primer aniversario de aquel héroe por el doctor.... Guatemala: Tipografía Americana, 1896. 229 pp. Illus. 3d ed. San José: EDUCA, 1970. 174 pp.

Originally published as a series of articles in various newspapers during 1892 and 1893 in connection with the celebration of the centennial of Morazán's birth, the comments in this volume defend Morazán, refuting what the author considers biased and politically motivated attacks by contemporaries, localists, and Conservatives. The volume seeks to restore Morazán to what the author regards as his rightful place, not just as a leader of Central American independence, but as a hero of the continental independence movement. It links Morazán and his unionist ideals to the then-incumbent regime of Justo Rufino Barrios

(Montúfar y Rivera Maestre, Lorenzo)
and the Liberal party. The comments mirror
the author's well-known liberalism, his unionist sentiments, and his ties to the Barrios
regime. DLC LNHT BNG BNCR

622 _____. Nociones de derecho de gentes y leyes
de la guerra para los ejércitos centroamericanos. Guatemala: Tipografía Nacional,
1893. 294 pp.
    A general summary of the key legal points
involved in diplomatic rights and the laws of
war, designed as a text for the military to
instruct its officers in the legalities they
must observe during conflicts. DLC LNHT

623 _____. Reseña histórica de Centro-América. 7
vols. Guatemala: Tipografía El Progreso,
1877-87.
    A history of the nineteenth-century
Liberal-Conservative conflict from 1828 to
1860, covering the Federation but focusing on
the author's native Guatemala, by a well-known
Liberal scholar and politician who was active
in the Guatemalan Liberal governments of the
latter portion of that century. A classic
work despite its Liberal bias, replete with
many details and extensive reproductions of
the full text of documents and pamphlets. DLC
DLC-LDS-586 LNHT BNG BNCR

624 Moore, John Bassett. Costa Rica-Panama Arbitration: Memorandum on uti possidentis.
Rosslyn, Va.: Commonwealth, 1913. 51 pp.
Notes.
    A noted Yankee international lawyer and
State Department official's commentary on the
principle invoked by Colombia and Panama in
their arbitral cases regarding the frontier
with Costa Rica, explaining the origins and
definition of this legal doctrine, concluding
that the Colombian case in the Loubet award
proceedings went well beyond the principle and
hence invoked it without justification. Contends that the 1825 treaty between the Central
American Federation and Colombia had little
bearing on the question because of its vague-
ness, adding that it certainly did not support
the Colombian-Panamanian contention. DLC
LNHT BNCR

625 _____. En defensa de la validez y fuerza
obligatoria del laudo del rey de España.
Tegucigalpa: Tipografía Ariston, 1957.
190 pp.
    A series of studies by the former counselor
of the State Department, in his capacity as
attorney for Honduras before the 1920 mediation of the boundary dispute with Nicaragua,
defending the legality of the arbitral ruling
by the king of Spain in 1906, arguing that the
king acted within his powers and that the
award is valid. Cites appropriate legal
precedents and provides a detailed analysis of
the accord that led to the arbitration and a
review of its procedures. Published by the
Honduran Ministry of Foreign Relations.
Moore's name does not appear on the title page
of the volume, but rather as the author of
each of its separate studies. DLC

626 Mora Velardo, Eduardo. Centro América en la
integración económica latinoamericana. San
José: Ediciones Revolución, 1969. 78 pp.
Tables.
    A socialist interpretation of the origins
and process of Latin American economic integration, contending that it is necessary to
enable development in the face of opposition
from the imperialists and to fortify the region for the confrontation with imperialism,
identifying factors that it feels promote and
retard the process, with the blame for the
latter falling on capitalism and imperialism.
Includes economic statistics for Central America, though they cover varying periods and the
selection criteria is not always clear. BNCR

627 Morales Molina, Manuel. El Salvador: un
pueblo que se rebela; conflicto de julio de
1969. 2 vols. San Salvador: Tipografía
Central, 1973. 644, 580 pp. Biblio., illus.,
maps.
    A massive collection of material recounting
Salvador's version of the 1969 war with
Honduras, compiled by a Salvadoran army
colonel. It consists principally of reproductions of newspaper articles and official
declarations, though it also incorporates the
author's comments regarding what he considers
the long-range and immediate causes of the
war. He lists the usual charges of genocide,
but adds such far-ranging items as allegations
that the United Fruit Company supported
Honduras and Honduran expansionist ambitions.
Volume 1 also contains information regarding
internal conditions in both countries on the
eve of the war, principally official statements and press comments. A major portion of
volume 2 consists of the author's daily log of
military operations during the conflict. Despite the title there is little reference to
rebellion. The bibliography consists principally of works on strategy, tactics, and European wars. DLC LNHT

628 Morazán, Francisco. Memorias del benemérito
general Francisco Morazán, antiguo presidente
de la República de Centro-América, escritas
por él mismo en David, Nueva Granada, en 1840.
Many editions. Latest ed. Tegucigalpa:
Tipografía Ariston, 1971. 72 pp.
    A passionate defense of Morazán's actions;
includes a declaration of Liberal principles
and denunciations of Carrera and the separatist movement. Written from exile after the
collapse of the Federation. The various items
have been reprinted many times, often combined
with other commentary, under various titles.
DLC LNHT

629 _____. Testamento y memorias del general
Francisco Morazán: discursos y artículos
relativos al héroe. Tegucigalpa: Talleres
Tipográficos Nacionales, 1942. 60 pp. Illus.
    Published on the centennial of the death of
Morazán, this volume reprints his will and
memoirs, along with a series of addresses and
articles extolling him as a hero. All have
been published before. DLC LNHT

630 Morazán, Miguel. Biografía y epopeya del general Francisco Morazán: homenaje en el primer centenario de su muerte, fusilado en Costa Rica. Tegucigalpa: Tipografía Ariston, 1942. 85 pp.

A lyrical poem to Morazán, recounting his life. Preceded by a brief outline sketch of his significant posts and accomplishments. Published as part of the celebration of the Morazán centennial. DLC

631 Moreno, José Vicente. Las Naciones Unidas en el ámbito centroamericano. San Salvador: Ministerio de Educación, 1970. 206 pp. Biblio., illus., appendixes.

Intended as a school text, this work seeks to summarize the United Nations and its various organs while emphasizing their projects in Central America and seeking to link the national programs of the isthmus to the international organization and its purposes, thereby making it relevant to the residents of the isthmus. The organization provides an overview of the various U.N.-sponsored projects in the isthmus. DLC

632 Moreno, Laudelino. Historia de las relaciones interstatuales de Centroamérica. Madrid: Compañía Ibero-Americana de Publicaciones, 1928. 507 pp. Biblio., maps.

A discussion of the unionist movement from independence through the 1920s, viewing the efforts favorably and emphasizing the advantages of union while analyzing the reasons for the failure of previous attempts. Despite the title, this volume deals principally with unionist efforts and issues of significance for the entire isthmus, such as filibustering, Yankee intervention, and the Washington conferences, rather than with relations among the various Central American states. Contains only brief narrations of the interim periods to link the major episodes. DLC

633 _____. Independencia de la Capitanía General de Guatemala: memoria. . . . Madrid: Talleres Poligráficos, 1927. 24 pp.

A brief narrative of the principal events of the independence period, arranged chronologically and covering the entire isthmus. Based on data in the Archivo General de Indias. MH

634 Moret y Prendergast, Segismundo, and Vicente Santamaría de Paredes. Dictamen sobre la cuestión de límites entre las repúblicas de Costa Rica y Panamá, examinada con arreglo al derecho colonial español. San José: Ministerio de Educación Pública, 1911. 2d ed. San José: Trejos Hermanos, 1942. 111 pp. Costa Rica-Panama Arbitration: Opinion Concerning the Question of Boundaries between the Republics of Costa Rica and Panama: Examined with Respect to the Spanish Law and Given at the Request of the Government of Costa Rica. Washington, D.C.: Gibson Brothers, 1913. 194 pp.

Two Spanish jurists provide an opinion supporting the Costa Rican claim. DLC-LDS-134

635 Morgan Guaranty Trust Company. The Central American Common Market. New York: Morgan Guaranty Trust, 1964. ii, 35 pp. Maps, tables.

A brief summary of the present state of the Common Market, designed for potential investors. Concludes with guarded optimism that despite its difficulties the region appears stable and industrialization is increasing, and hence that investment offers good prospects for American firms. Contains a general description of the region's present economy and accompanying statistics. LNHT

636 Mörne, Hakan. Den Förgyllda Fattigdomen: en resa i Centralamerika. Stockholm: Wahlstrom & Widstrand, 1949. 388 pp. Illus. 2d ed. Stockholm: Lindqvist, 1956. 239 pp. Caribbean Symphony. London: Elek Books, 1955. 206 pp. Illus. Vulkaner och bananer: en resa i Centroamerika. Helsinki: H. Schildt, 1956. 239 pp. Illus.

A travel account by a Swedish voyager. Concentrates on descriptions of physical settings and his adventures, especially transportation difficulties. Also contains some comments regarding the social setting, and background notes regarding the situations he encountered. The emphasis is on Nicaragua and Costa Rica, though there are also chapters dealing with sea voyages, Venezuela, and Panama. DLC

637 Morrill, Gulian Lansing. Rotten Republics: A Tropical Tramp in Central America. Chicago: M.A. Donahue, 1916. 302 pp. Illus.

A travelogue in journal style, by an experienced travel-book author and Minneapolis cleric, written in picturesque language, detailing the author's adventures and observations in pejorative terminology that reveals at least as much about the author's biases as about the areas he visited. Provides a critical, detailed account of the seamy side of all his stops. Includes illustrations, usually focusing on the disarray of the local facilities, and invariably showing the author in a suitcoat, even in the tropics. He states that the volume is designed to "tell the truth" about the area, which he calls "a land of dirt, disease, destitution, darkness, dilapidation, despots, delay, debt, deviltry, and degeneracy." DLC LNHT

638 Mory, Warren H., Jr. Salvador Mendieta: escritor y apóstol de la unión centroamericana. Birmingham: Birmingham Southern College, 1971. 135 pp. Biblio., notes.

A brief review of the writings of the unionist leader, including consideration of his short stories and literary works, as well as of his political and unionist propaganda. Emphasizes his literary talents and his humanism, which the author says are often ignored due to the focus on his political commentaries, while hailing his unionist ideals. DLC LNHT

639 Moser, Don, et al. <u>Central American Jungles:</u>
<u>The American Wilderness.</u> New York: Time-Life
Books, 1975. 184 pp. Index, biblio., illus.
     A wide-eyed description of the jungle por-
tions of the region, viewing them as the last
unexplored frontier and hence a source of
wonder and adventure. Contains detailed descriptions and photographs that do capture the
aura of the jungle, though the dramatic treatment could serve to perpetuate Yankee stereotypes about the region. DLC

640 Müllerried, Friedrich Karl Gustav.
<u>Investigaciones y exploraciones geográfico-</u>
<u>geológicas en la porción nor-oeste de la</u>
<u>América Central.</u> Mexico: PAIGH, 1939. 52
pp. Illus., maps.
     A study, sponsored by the institute, pro-
viding a summary of basic data on the Central
American region, focusing on the volcanoes and
the northern zone of mountains in southern
Mexico, Guatemala, Salvador, and northern
Honduras. Seeks to update existing material,
and is based on fieldwork conducted in 1937
and 1938. DLC

641 Munro, Dana Gardner. <u>The Five Republics of</u>
<u>Central America: Their Political and Economic</u>
<u>Development and Their Relations with the</u>
<u>United States.</u> New York: Oxford University
Press, 1918. xvi, 332 pp. Index, biblio.,
notes, maps. Reprint. New York: Russell &
Russell, 1967. xvi, 332 pp. Index, biblio.,
notes, maps.
     Although now dated, this volume by a former
State Department official was the most useful
commentary of its era and still serves to
demonstrate the viewpoint of the early twentieth century and the issues considered important then. It provides a survey of the
isthmus focusing on the late nineteenth and
early twentieth century and emphasizing economic growth and United States influence. The
summary of the contemporary state of these
nations reflects the outlook of the era and
some Yankee biases, but also the knowledge of
a diplomat experienced in the region who has
access to official information and familiarity
with the literature dealing with it. DLC
LNHT

642 _____. <u>Intervention and Dollar Diplomacy in</u>
<u>the Caribbean, 1900-1921.</u> Princeton, N.J.:
Princeton University Press, 1964. ix, 553 pp.
Index, biblio., notes, maps.
     An insider's view of the evolution of U.S.
policy in the region, written as a kind of
scholarly memoir by an official active in its
conception and execution. Includes discussions of the significance of the canal and its
effect on Yankee policy in the region, the
various interventions in Nicaragua, the nonrecognition policy applied to the isthmus, and
the Washington conferences. Particularly illuminating on the making of U.S. policy and
its rationale. DLC LNHT

643 _____. <u>The United States and the Caribbean</u>
<u>Area.</u> Boston: World Peace Foundation, 1934.
322 pp. Index, biblio., notes. Reprint. New

York: Johnson Reprint Corp., 1966. 316 pp.
Index, biblio., notes.
     This volume covers the era from the turn of
the century to 1934. Includes chapters on
Panama and Nicaragua, and a general account of
Central America. Focuses on Yankee involvement and objectives, but demonstrates the
interaction between the Yankees and the local
governments as well as the impact of U.S.
actions and influence. There is considerable
discussion of economic cooperation, the Yankee
concern for the canal, and the Yankee desire
for stability in the region; also contains
accounts of the Washington conferences and
mediation that sought to calm the local
conflicts. DLC LNHT

644 _____. <u>The United States and the Caribbean</u>
<u>Republics, 1921-1933.</u> Princeton, N.J.:
Princeton University Press, 1974. x, 394 pp.
Index, notes.
     A scholarly memoir by a former State De-
partment official with a solid knowledge of
the area, written from the Department's perspective and drawing almost exclusively on
personal recollections and official documents.
The comments reflect his involvement in the
making of these policies, and provide an excellent account of the rationale behind U.S.
actions and the factors involved, as well as
of the State Department's objectives in and
view of the region. Most of the work focuses
on the years 1921-26, with the intervention in
Nicaragua receiving extensive consideration.
About 100 pages are devoted to Central America, though the general portions also have
implications for U.S. policy in the isthmus,
and the author emphasizes the transition from
the overt military intervention of the Wilson
years to the more subtle political efforts of
the Good Neighbor Policy. DLC LNHT

645 Naraváez López, Carlos. <u>Objeciones a la</u>
<u>instancia hondurense ante el Tribunal de La</u>
<u>Haya.</u> Managua: n.p., 1959. 67 pp. Biblio.,
illus.
     A series of brief essays summarizing the
Nicaraguan contention that the king of Spain
exceeded his powers under the agreement that
governed his arbitration, and hence that his
1906 decision was invalid. Presents the
Nicaraguan arguments made before the International Court and discusses the legal disputes. Includes a bibliography on the
question. DLC

646 Navarrete, Sarbelio. <u>La verdadera fecha de</u>
<u>nuestra independencia, 15 de septiembre de</u>
<u>1821.</u> San Salvador: Ministerio de
Instrucción Pública, 1930. 135 pp.
     Originally a series of newspaper articles
in the <u>Diario Latino</u>, these essays were prepared in reply to the studies of Jorge Lardé y
Larín, published in <u>El Salvadoreño</u>, contending
that the 1821 effort did not really win independence, and arguing for use of a later date
after the rejection of the Mexican annexation
effort. Navarrete defends the validity of the
traditional date, though noting that it was
provisional, contending that 1821 marked the

separation from Spain and hence was the starting point of all subsequent efforts that eventually led to definitive independence for
Central America and then for El Salvador. DLC

647 Netherlands, Gov't of. Economische
Voorlichtingsdienst. Central Amerika. The
Hague: n.p., 1967. 77 pp. Tables.
     A general review of the present economic
development of the region. Presents statistics. DLC

648 Nicaragua, Gov't of. Ministerio de Relaciones
Exteriores. Alegato de la comisión
nicaragüense contestando la exposición de la
comisión de Costa Rica sobre límites. San
José: Tipografía Nacional, 1897. 69 pp.
     The counterarguments of Nicaragua in the
boundary arbitration with Costa Rica. DLC-
LDS-45 BNCR

649 _____. _____. Correspondencia entre los
gabinetes de Nicaragua i Costa Rica sobre la
reclamación entablada por hechos abusivos
perpetrados en territorio de esta república
por fuerzas costarricenses. Managua:
Imprenta Nacional, 1875. 17 pp.
     The Nicaraguan note protesting a minor
border intrusion, dated 12 November 1874.
DLC-LDS-98

650 _____. _____. La cuestión de límites
territoriales entre las repúblicas de
Nicaragua i Costa Rica: observaciones a la
nota del señor ministro doctor don Lorenzo
Montúfar dirijida al señor ministro de
relaciones exteriores del gobierno de
Nicaragua en 22 de julio del presente año.
Managua: Imprenta de El Centro-Americano,
1872. 26 pp.
     Another exchange regarding the frontier
question, with this reply from Nicaragua repudiating all the contentions of the Costa Rican
note. Involves the usual arguments about the
locations of rivers and Colonial jurisdictions. DLC

651 _____. _____. Documentos relativos a las
últimas negociaciones entre Nicaragua i Costa
Rica sobre límites territoriales y canal
interoceánico. Managua: Imprenta Nacional,
1872. 47 pp.
     Exchanges between the two governments in
1872 relating to navigation of the San Juan
River and the boundary question, during the
efforts to reach agreement on these matters.
Includes draft protocols proposed by
Nicaragua. DLC-LDS-739

652 _____. _____. Estado actual de la cuestión
de límites entre Nicaragua y Colombia.
Managua: Tipografía Progreso, 1925. 27 pp.
     A restatement of the Nicaraguan case
against Colombia in the dispute regarding the
Caribbean islands. Includes a description of
the exchanges between the governments. DLC

653 _____. _____. Exposición sobre la cuestión
de límites entre Nicaragua y Honduras y
protocolo de arreglo suscrito el 21 de enero

de 1931. Managua: Imprenta Nacional, 1931.
23 pp. Tegucigalpa: Talleres Tipográficos
Nacionales, 1938, 21 pp.
     The Nicaraguan Foreign Ministry's summary
of the question, the 1894 accord, and the
negotiations that led to the 1931 protocol for
United States arbitration, with the protocol
appended. DLC

654 _____. _____. Exposición sobre límites,
presentada al árbitro señor general E.P.
Alexander por la comisión nicaragüense, 14 de
junio de 1897. San José: Tipografía
Nacional, 1897. 31 pp.
     The Nicaraguan arguments in the boundary
arbitration involving the frontier with Costa
Rica. DLC DLC-LDS-45

655 _____. _____. El litigio de fronteras entre
Nicaragua y Honduras en la Corte Internacional
de Justicia de la Haya. Managua: n.p., 1960.
518 pp. Maps.
     The full case and documentation submitted
by Nicaragua to the International Court of
Justice protesting that body's 1960 ruling in
favor of Honduras in the boundary dispute
between the nations. Seeks to reopen the case
by disputing the legal interpretations involved, thereby demonstrating the enduring
quality of the dispute and the resistance to
any form of settlement, including judicial
action. DLC

656 _____. _____. Memorándum explicativo de la
controversia entre Nicaragua y Colombia sobre
el dominio de las Islas de San Andrés; Memorandum Explanatory [sic] of the Controversy
between Nicaragua and Colombia on the Dominion
of San Andres Islands. Managua: Tipografía
Alemana, 1924. 95 pp.
     A bilingual explanation of the Nicaraguan
case in the dispute involving several small
islands and reefs in the Caribbean. NN

657 _____. _____. Nicaragua y Colombia; últimas
comunicaciones sobre la cuestión mosquita
entre el ministerio de relaciones exteriores y
la legación de Colombia. Managua: Tipografía
Progreso, 1925. xv, 156 pp.
     A series of exchanges involving the title
to the San Andres Islands. Nicaragua's claim
that they are part of the Mosquito Territory
is disputed by Colombia, which contends that
Nicaraguan claims are restricted to the main-
land. States the full case of each nation,
with historical citations to Colonial days.
DLC

658 _____. _____. Nota de la cancillería de
Nicaragua a la de Costa Rica, con motivo del
atentado contra el señor presidente de
Nicaragua, general Anastasio Somoza. Managua:
Ministerio de Relaciones Exteriores, 1954.
159 pp. Illus.
     A formal complaint by Nicaragua charging
that the attempted revolution and assassination of Somoza was organized in and by Costa
Rica. Complete with annexed confessions and
photos showing that the guns employed bore the
seal of Costa Rica and the imprint that they

(Nicaragua, Gov't of)
were the property of the Costa Rican government, and that the boxes of arms bore the trademark of a Costa Rican firm. BNCR

659 _____. _____. Situatión jurídica del Río San Juan. Managua: Impresa Editorial "San Enrique," 1954. 48 pp. Maps.
A reprinting of the various documents involved in the lengthy border disputes, including the treaties, the arbitral rulings, and the engineering studies. Contends that Nicaragua has exclusive control and sovereignty over the river but that Costa Rica has navigation rights only, rather than control or sovereignty, despite the fact that the river forms the boundary between the two states. DLC

660 _____. _____. Statement and Reply and Documents Annexed Presented by the Nicaraguan Commission to the Arbitrator, General E.P. Alexander on the Boundary Questions between Nicaragua and Costa Rica. Washington, D.C.: n.p., 1897. 148 pp.
Exposición y alegato y documentos anexos presentados por la comisión nicaragüense al árbitro, señor general E.P. Alexander sobre la cuestión de límites entre Nicaragua y Costa Rica. Managua: n.p., 1897. 148 pp.
The Nicaraguan case in the arbitration of the question of jurisdiction over the Río San Juan, including the Nicaraguan reply to the Costa Rican case. In English and Spanish in parallel columns, though the English translation leaves something to be desired. Contains the texts of the pertinent accords, including the Matus-Pacheco Convention of 1896, the ruling of President Cleveland in 1888, and the 1858 Treaty. DLC LNHT

661 _____. _____. El tratado de límites firmado entre Nicaragua y Costa Rica el 15 de abril de 1858, sometido al juicio arbitral de S.E. el señor presidente de los Estados Unidos, 1887. Washington, D.C.: Imprenta de Tomás McGill, 1887. 90 pp. Maps.
The Nicaraguan case in the arbitration regarding the dispute over the Treaty's terms, focusing on the precise location of the frontier and the navigation of the San Juan River. DLC BNCR

662 Nicholas, Francis Child. Around the Caribbean and across Panama. Boston and New York: Caldwell, 1903. xxii, 373 pp. Illus., maps. 3d ed. Boston and New York: Caldwell, 1909. xxii, 373 pp. Illus., maps.
An account of the author's travels in the isthmus and the Caribbean. Despite the title, most of the volume details his adventures in Honduras, Nicaragua, Costa Rica, and Panama. The emphasis is on adventure, anecdotes, and descriptions, with discussion of prospective canal routes also included. The 1909 edition reversed the title, appearing as Across Panama and around the Caribbean, reflecting an expansion of the section on Panama. DLC LNHT

663 Nuestra patria centroamericana. San Salvador: Imprenta Nacional, 1968. 199 pp. Illus.

A patriotic collection of documents and sketches of the heroes of independence in Central America, covering each of the republics. DLC

664 Nugent, Jeffrey B. Economic Integration in Central America. Baltimore: Johns Hopkins University Press, 1974. xvi, 209 pp. Index, biblio.
An empirical analysis of the Common Market, employing and testing various models and forms of analysis to examine its impact on its member nations and its future potential. The author is concerned with common markets in general and views the Central American one as a model for use in testing; hence, he employs general analysis and seeks to place his conclusions in universal terms applicable outside the region, with some comparison with findings on the European Common Market, concluding that the market impact has been greater in Central America than in the European case. DLC

665 Nuhn, H., P. Krieg, and W. Schlick. Zentralamerika: Karten zur Bevölkerung und Wirtschaftsstruktur. Hamburg: Universität Hamburg, 1975. xv, 180 pp. Biblio., maps, tables.
A collection of geographical articles providing detailed statistics, tables, and information regarding the economy, land use, development, and transport, with an excellent set of maps. Most of the articles have bibliographies, with citations in the text. DLC

666 Núñez Monge, Francisco María. Interpretación histórica del momento morazánico, 1821-1842. San José: Diario de Costa Rica, 1942. 42 pp. Illus.
A brief essay criticizing Morazán and his actions during the years of the Federation of Central America. Contends that his policy was inconsistent and argues that he acted as a Liberal in the northern republics but as a Conservative in the southern states, installing a Conservative as head of Costa Rica. The author also contends that Morazán made many "errors" in his policy in Costa Rica, which contributed to that nation's withdrawal from the Federation, and generally defends the Costa Rican position. BNCR

667 Nye, Joseph S. Central American Regional Integration. New York: Carnegie Endowment for International Peace, 1967. 66 pp. Notes, maps, tables.
A special issue of the journal International Concilliation devoted entirely to this theme, providing a summary of the present state of the Common Market and its background, with analysis of its problems and future prospects and assessment of its activities to date. While noting the limits as well as the accomplishments of the Common Market, the study is cautiously optimistic about prospects for continued expansion of the integration effort. DLC

668 OAS. Documentos relativos a la situación entre Costa Rica y Nicaragua, del 11 de

(OAS)

diciembre de 1948 al 28 de enero de 1949. Washington, D.C.: PAU, 1949. 225 pp.

A collection of exchanges referring to the crisis resulting from Nicaraguan assistance to the government forces in the 1948 revolution in Costa Rica. DPU

669 _____. Documentos relativos a la situación entre Costa Rica y Nicaragua. Suplemento: 17 de febrero al 15 de junio de 1949. Washington, D.C.: PAU, 1949. 170 pp.

A continuation of the previous work, reflecting continued border incidents between the mutually suspicious regimes. DPU

670 _____. El régimen de las inversiones privadas en el Mercado Común Centroamericano y en la Asociación Latinoamericana de Libre Comercio. Washington, D.C.: PAU, 1964. 528 pp.

A summary of current investment regulations and practices of the two integration movements. MH-L

671 _____. Sectoral Study of Transnational Enterprises in Latin America: The Banana Industry. Washington, D.C.: OAS; 1975. ii, 63 pp. Notes, tables, appendixes.

A collection of statistics about the banana industry, focusing on the 1960s and early 1970s but including some earlier data. Provides information about prices, markets, role in the national economies, and similar factors. Brief discussion of the important characteristics of the industry, including the high initial investment and extensive marketing capability required, which explain the role of the companies. Emphasizes the mutual benefits to company and host country. DLC

672 _____. La vivienda de interés social en América Latina: Istmo Centroamericano: Guatemala, El Salvador, Honduras, Nicaragua, Costa Rica, Panamá. Washington, D.C.: PAU, 1956. 122 pp. Illus. 2d ed. Washington, D.C.: PAU, 1957. 122 pp. Illus.

A compilation of data regarding current housing and future needs. Notes progress in construction efforts, comments on the national programs, details future needs, and makes recommendations. DLC

673 ODECA. Arancel de aduanas centroamericana. San Salvador: ODECA, n.d. Pages not consecutively numbered. Tables.

A compilation of current customs regulations of each of the five Central American states, along with the texts of agreements for their modification signed as part of the integration movement. Contains tabular lists of duties and requirements. BNCR

674 _____. Hacia la integración educacional de Centro América. Guatemala: Tipografía Nacional, 1959. 376 pp.

The reports and recommendations of five seminars sponsored by ODECA to enable educators throughout the region to examine the prospects and problems of a more unified educational system throughout the isthmus. FU

675 _____. Integración económica de Centro América. Guatemala: Ministerio de Educación Pública, 1957. 383 pp.

The speeches, papers, commentaries, and discussions of the first seminar on economic integration held in 1957, sponsored by ODECA, at which scholars from throughout the isthmus met to examine the potential and progress to date. Provides considerable economic data about the current state of the region, as well as details regarding plans and actions for the Common Market. DLC LNHT

676 _____. Una organización regional en marcha: ODECA. San Salvador: ODECA, 1967. 67 pp. Illus., tables.

A brief history of the Organization of Central American States, with emphasis on its organs, operation, objectives, and plans. Quotes liberally from the treaties. BNCR

677 _____. Reuniones y conferencias de ministros de relaciones exteriores de Centro América, 1951-1967. San Salvador: ODECA, 1968. 265 pp.

Reproduces the communications and agreements of the various meeetings. DLC

678 Oficina Internacional Centro-Americana. Monografía de las cinco repúblicas de Centro-América. Guatemala: Sánchez & de Guise, 1915. 46 pp. Illus.

General descriptive information designed to encourage tourism, trade, and investment. Extensive illustrations. DLC

679 Ohara, Yoshinori, ed. Chûbei Kyôdo Shijô [Central American Common Market]. Tokyo: Ajia Keizai Kenkyûjo, 1967. viii, 229 pp. Notes.

DLC

680 Organización del Tratado General de Integración Económica Centroamericana. Centroamérica y su mercado común. Guatemala: SIECA, 1964. 72 pp. Biblio., maps, tables.

A tabulation of the moves toward economic unification, and a description of the market to date and its accomplishments, with appropriate maps and tables. BNG

681 Ørsted, Anders Sandøe. L'Amérique Centrale: récherches sur sa flora et sa géographie physique; résultats d'un voyage dans les états de Costa Rica et de Nicaragua, exécutée pendant les années 1846-1848. Copenhagen: Imprimerie de Blanco Luno, 1863. 18 pp. Illus., maps. América Central: investigaciones sobre su flora y su geografía física; resultados de un viaje por los estados de Costa Rica y de Nicaragua efectuado durante los años de 1846-1848. Copenhagen: Livraison, 1863. Illus., maps.

A prominent Danish geographer's partial account of his observations during a visit to Costa Rica and Nicaragua in 1846-48, with maps and rich description of the physical characteristics, flora, and fauna. He traveled extensively in both countries and was an effective observer, compiling data regarding the major population centers and the volcanoes, as well as climates and landforms. DLC

682 Ortez Colindres, Enrique. <u>Integración política de Centroamérica</u>. San José: EDUCA, 1975. 396 pp. Biblio., notes, appendix.

A Honduran scholar who served as president of the Banco Centroamericano de Integración Económica offers a well-researched and clearly written history of the Federation of Central America. It is written in a pro-unionist vein but presents an analysis of the federation's problems. Concludes with a detailed examination of the most recent efforts and the state of unionist programs, particularly ODECA and the Common Market. A documentary appendix contains copies of the Federation's basic agreements and treaties. LNHT BNG BNCR

683 _____. <u>La República Federal de Centro América a la luz del derecho internacional público</u>. San Salvador: ODECA, 1963. 305 pp. Biblio., notes.

Originally a doctoral thesis at the University of Paris, this work examines the early attempts at union and the Central American Federation of postindependence days, concluding with a call for further efforts and arguing that the isthmus should be unified and that a federal system would be the most effective method. The author later served in the Honduran diplomatic corps and in the secretariat of the Organization of Central American States. DLC LNHT

684 Ortiz, Santiago. <u>Primera aplicación del Tratado Interamericano de Asistencia Recíproca: situación surgida entre Costa Rica y Nicaragua en diciembre de 1948</u>. Washington, D.C.: PAU, 1949. 53 pp.

A summary of the OAS role in mediating the dispute between Nicaragua and Costa Rica in 1948. TxU

685 Ortiz Urruela, Manuel. <u>La Inglaterra y los Estados Unidos en Centro-América</u>. Paris: Imprenta de Gustavo Gratiot, 1856. 15 pp.

A very brief discussion of the period from independence to the mid-nineteenth century. DLC

686 Padilla, José Augusto. <u>Límites entre Honduras y Nicaragua: el laudo de S.M. el rey de España don Alfonso XIII, que dirimió la controversia de límites entre Honduras y Nicaragua; no es contradictorio ni ofrece dudas para su ejecución; estudio técnico</u>. Tegucigalpa: Tipografía Ariston, 1938. 16 pp. Maps.

An expert's technical study of the 1906 ruling, prepared for the Honduran Foreign Ministry. Disputes the Nicaraguan contention that the ruling is not clear and hence is unenforceable; provides the Honduran interpretation of the award and its implications for the location of the frontier. DLC LNHT

687 Palmer, Bradley Webster. <u>The American Banana Company</u>. Boston: George H. Ellis, 1907. xxix, 331 pp. Maps.

An account of the enterprises of Herbert L. McConnell along the Costa Rica-Panama frontier, his problems with the border dispute, and its effects on his efforts to launch a banana company at the turn of the century. Includes his letters, the contracts, and particularly his complaints to the State Department regarding the problems the dispute caused his business. There is little narration. The letters do provide some insight into the dispute and the effect of the coming of the banana business to the region on the confrontation between the governments. DLC BNCR

688 Palmer, Frederick. <u>Central America and Its Problems: An Account of a Journey from the Río Grande to Panama with Introductory Chapters on Mexico and Her Relations to Her Neighbors</u>. London: T. Werner Lavrie; New York: Moffat, Yard, 1910. xiv, 347 pp. Biblio., maps. 3d ed. New York: Moffat, Yard, 1913. 347 pp. Index, biblio., illus., maps.

A journalistic view of contemporary Central America by a <u>Chicago Tribune</u> reporter with some experience in Latin America, who reflects a practiced eye, a knack for description, and the prevailing Yankee stereotypes of the era. Includes vivid descriptions of life in the various nations and particularly of the governments of Manuel Estrada Cabrera in Guatemala and José Santos Zelaya in Nicaragua, both of which are viewed critically. DLC LNHT

689 Panama, Gov't of. Ministerio de Relaciones Exteriores. <u>Arbitration before the Honorable Edward D. White, Chief Justice of the Supreme Court of the United States of the Differences between the Republic of Panama and the Republic of Costa Rica: Additional Documents Submitted on Behalf of the Republic of Panama</u>. Washington, D.C.: Legation of Panama, 1914. 44 pp.
DLC BNCR

690 _____. _____. <u>Arbitration before the Honorable Edward D. White, Chief Justice of the Supreme Court of the United States of the Differences between the Republic of Panama and the Republic of Costa Rica: Answer on Behalf of the Republic of Panama to the Argument Submitted on Behalf of the Republic of Costa Rica</u>. Washington, D.C.: n.p., n.d. [1914]. 72 pp. Notes.
DLC BNCR

691 _____. _____. <u>Arbitration before the Honorable Edward D. White, Chief Justice of the Supreme Court of the United States of the Differences between the Republic of Panama and the Republic of Costa Rica: Statement on Behalf of the Republic of Panama</u>. Washington, D.C.: n.p., n.d. [1914]. 41 pp. Map, appendixes.

The official statement of the Panamanian case, notable in contrast to that of Costa Rica for its brevity. The authors were Minister Eusebio A. Morales and legal consuls William Nelson Cromwell and Edward Bruce Hill. DLC BNCR

(Panama, Gov't of)

692 ____. ____. Controversia de límites entre Panamá y Costa Rica: repuesta de Panamá a los Estados Unidos. 2 vols. Panama: Imprenta Nacional, 1921. 374, 490 pp. Illus.

The Panamanian case in the arbitration that led to the White award, with the attendant documents, exchanges, and letters, most signed by Belisario Porras, the Panamanian representative in the arbitration. The initial volume contains the Panamanian case and its reservations after the award, while the second volume contains exchanges attendant to the border conflict of 1921, contending that Costa Rica was at fault and quoting many letters, statements, petitions, and newspaper editorials designed to evoke Panamanian nationalism and establish national solidarity behind the government's stance. DLC DLC-LDS-738

693 ____. ____. Panama-Costa Rica Boundary Controversy: Panama's Reply to the United States. Panama: National Printer, 1921. 18 pp.

The Panamanian note of 18 March 1921 in reply to the U.S. stand regarding the boundary question, rejecting the Yankee stance in support of the White and Loubet awards and restating Panama's case. DLC DLC-LDS-738

694 Pan American Union, Division of Philosophy and Letters. Diccionario de la literatura latinoamericana: América Central. Washington, D.C.: PAU, 1958. 292 pp.

The Central American volume of a Pan American Union series that encompasses all of Latin America. Like the others, it combines brief biographies, anthologies of critical commentaries, and bibliographies that cover works by and about each author. An initial section deals with authors from historical eras; the major portion focuses on the current generation of writers. DLC

695 Parada, Alfredo. El proceso de la agresividad hondureña. San Salvador: Editorial Ahora, 1974. viii, 71 pp. Index.

A narration of the disputes betweeen Salvador and Honduras, tracing them throughout the 1960s, and contending that the war was predictable and that Honduras was at fault for constantly assuming stronger and stronger positions. DLC LNHT

696 Pardo Gallardo, José Joaquín. Catálogo de los manuscritos existentes en la Colección Latino Americana de la biblioteca de la Universidad de Texas relativos a la historia de Centro América. Guatemala: Editorial Piedra Santa, 1958. ii, 45 pp. Index.

A listing of manuscripts pertinent to the region, which are principally Colonial, but do include some items from the independence era and the early nineteenth century. Includes an alphabetical listing by author within offices of the government that constitute the source of the documents, with indexes and descriptions of the contents of the items. DLC

697 Paredes, Victoriano de Diego. The Coast of Mosquito and the Boundary Question between New Granada and Costa Rica; La Costa de los Mosquitos y la cuestión de límites entre Nueva Granada y Costa Rica. New York: N. Muller, 1855. 124 pp. Maps.

The chargé d'affaires of New Granada in the U.S. provides a summary of the question, in English and Spanish, on facing pages numbered separately, defending the claims of his nation and contending that even the British recognized the sovereignty of New Granada, and hence that British occupation did not alter the juridical status of that nation's claim. DLC

698 Parker, Franklin Dallas. The Central American Republics. London and New York: Oxford University Press, 1964. x, 348 pp. Index, biblio., notes, maps.

A concise historical survey of Central America, from its discovery through the date of publication, based on secondary sources. Each of the five republics is treated separately with forty to sixty pages outlining the general contours of their development. Encompasses political, economic, and social trends. DLC LNHT

699 ____. José Cecilio del Valle and the Establishment of the Central American Confederation. Tegucigalpa: Talleres Tipográficos Nacionales, 1954. 85 pp. Biblio., notes.

Originally a master's thesis, this brief work summarizes the independence movement in Central America and the efforts of Valle, emphasizing the internal antecedents as against the external influences and drawing on secondary sources. DLC

700 ____, ed. Travels in Central America, 1821-1840. Gainesville: University of Florida Press, 1970. xiv, 340 pp. Index, biblio., notes, maps.

An anthology of selections from the works of ten travelers, including Yankees and Europeans, who visited Central America from the Colonial era through the mid-nineteenth century. Collects their observations in topical chapters to allow comparison of their commentaries on people, politics, agriculture, commerce, transportation, education, recreation, the arts, religion, and other themes, with linking comments and explanations by the editor. DLC LNHT

701 Partido Nacional de Honduras. Agresión. Tegucigalpa: Partido Nacional de Honduras, 1969. Pages unnumbered. Illus., maps.

A collection of press articles and statements regarding the 1969 conflict with El Salvador, with an extensive collection of photos showing the damage caused by the combat. Charges the Salvadorans with barbarism, looting, and other misdeeds. DLC

702 Pasos Arana, Manuel, and Emilio Álvarez. El laudo de Su Majestad Alfonso XIII frente al derecho internacional. San José: Imprenta La Tribuna, 1938. 36 pp.

Two Nicaraguan lawyers seek to refute the royal ruling that favored Honduras and to

reestablish the Nicaraguan claims to the disputed region. Includes some of the correspondence relating to the original ruling. DLC
LNHT BNCR

703 Paz Barnica, Edgardo. Reestructuración
institucional de la integración centroamericana. Tegucigalpa: Editorial Nuevo
Continente, 1972. xiv, 534 pp. Biblio.,
illus.
    A legal analysis of the institutions of the
Common Market, tracing their history, accomplishments, and problems, suggesting institutional changes and reorganizations to deal
with the difficulties to promote the operation
and development of the market. DLC LNHT

704 Peck, Anne Merriman. The Pageant of Middle
American History. New York and London:
Longmans Green, 1947. x, 496 pp. Index,
biblio., illus., maps. Reprint. New York:
McKay, 1963. x, 496 pp. Index, biblio.,
illus., maps.
    A survey of Mexico and Central America,
which is far more detailed than the standard
general work but still far from a textbook,
based mainly on general studies and travel
accounts reflecting existing Yankee stereotypes. DLC LNHT

705 Pector, Désiré. Régions isthmiques de
l'Amérique tropicale: études ou notes
descriptives, économiques, historiques,
sociales et scientifiques, sur les
républiques: du Mexique, du Guatémala, du
Salvador. Paris: Société d'Éditions
Géographiques, Maritimes, & Coloniales, 1925.
x, 236 pp. Biblio., maps, tables.
    A longtime consul general of Honduras,
Nicaragua, and El Salvador in Paris provides a
general introduction to the region for the
French reader. It emphasizes economics, production, financing, and contacts with the
outside world, and also includes brief geographical descriptions and outline historical
surveys. Contains numerous statistics relating to economics. DLC LNHT

706 _____. Les richesses de l'Amérique Centrale:
Guatémala, Honduras, Salvador, Nicaragua,
Costa Rica. Paris: E. Guilmoto, 1908. xiv,
363 pp. Maps. 2d ed. Paris: E. Guilmoto,
1910.
    A general survey of resources and geo-
graphic description, designed to call the
commercial possibilities of the region to the
attention of the French audience. The focus
is on resources, economic development, financial status, and agricultural production, with
the latter occupying the largest portion of
the space. Includes figures regarding foreign
trade as well as current production. Discusses future prospects in glowing terms. DLC

707 Peña, José María S. Viajes por la costa del
Pacífico: de San Salvador a Costa Rica. San
Salvador: Talleres Gráficos Cisneros, 1909.
67 pp.
    A travelogue, with description centering on
transport and economic factors, intended as

the start of a series designed to emphasize
sailing factors and trade possibilities. DLC

708 Peralta, Manuel María de. Atlas histórico-
geográfico de la República de Costa Rica,
Veragua y Costa de Mosquitos, para servir al
arbitraje de la cuestión de límites entre
Costa Rica y Colombia. Brussels: Instituto
Nacional de Geografía, 1890. Maps.
    A collection of maps designed to support
the Costa Rican claims in its boundary dispute
with Colombia. DLC

709 _____, ed. Costa Rica, Nicaragua y Panamá en
el siglo XVI: su historia y su límites según
los documentos del Archivo de Sevilla, del
Simancas, etc. Madrid and Paris: M. Murillo,
1883. xxiii, 832 pp. Maps. 2d ed.
Brussels: Imprenta de Ad. Mertens, 1887.
    One of several compilations of Spanish
Colonial documents relative to the boundaries
of Costa Rica, assembled by the indefatigable
Costa Rican envoy in Europe who represented
his nation in many of the boundary arbitrations. Designed to support the Costa Rican
position in its disputes with Colombia and
Nicaragua. DLC LNHT

710 _____. Costa Rica y Colombia de 1573 a 1881:
su jurisdicción y sus límites territoriales
según los documentos inéditos del Archivo de
Indias de Sevilla y otras autoridades. Madrid
and Paris: M. Murillo & Ernst Leroux, 1886.
vii, 408 pp. Index, maps, tables.
    See item CA709. DLC LNHT

711 _____. Costa Rica y la Costa de Mosquitos:
documentos para la historia de la jurisdicción
territorial de Costa Rica y Colombia;
publicados por don Manuel M. de Peralta,
enviado extraordinario y ministro
plenipotenciario de Costa Rica. Paris:
Legación de Costa Rica, 1898. iii, 566 pp.
    This work demonstrates that the jurisdic-
tion of the Colonial province of Cartago did
include the Mosquito Coast, giving Costa Rica
a claim as its successor. See item CA709.
DLC LNHT

712 Peralta, Manuel María de. Historia de la
jurisdicción territorial de la República de
Costa Rica, 1502-1880. Madrid: D. Manuel
Ginés Hernández, 1891. 240 pp.
Exposé des droits territoriaux de la
República de Costa-Rica soumis à S.E.M. le
président de la République Française, arbitre
de la question des límites entre Costa-Rica et
Colombie. Paris: Imprimerie Lahure, 1898.
374 pp.
    Adds citations to the rights of Costa
Rica's predecessor province of Cartago, as
well as portions of the dukedom of Veragua.
See item CA709. DLC DLC-LDS-22 LNHT

713 _____. Juridiction territoriale de la
République de Costa Rica: Réplique à l'exposé
de la République de Colombie, soumis à S.E.M.
le président de la République Française,
arbitre de la question de limites entre Costa-

(Peralta, Manuel María de)
Rica et Colombie. Paris: Imprimerie Lahure, 1899. 58 pp.
The Costa Rican counterarguments regarding the proceeding that led to the Loubet award. DLC DLC-LDS-347

714 _____. Juridiction territoriale de la République de Costa Rica: Titres et documents justificantifs soumis à S.E.M. le président de la République Française, arbitre de la question de limites entre Costa-Rica et Colombie. Paris: Imprimerie Lahure, 1899. 516 pp.
The basic Costa Rican case and the documents. DLC LNHT BNCR

715 _____. Límites de Costa-Rica y Colombia: nuevos documentos para la historia de su jurisdicción territorial, con notas, comentarios y un examen de la cartografía de Costa-Rica y Veragua. Madrid: Manuel Ginés Hernández, 1890. xii, 778 pp. Index, maps. La géographie historique et les droits territoriaux de Costa-Rica. Paris: Imprimerie Lahure, 1900. 385 pp. Index, maps.
See item CA714. DLC DLC-LDS-56 LNHT BNCR

716 _____. El Río de San Juan de Nicaragua: derechos de sus ribereños; las repúblicas de Costa Rica y Nicaragua, según los documentos históricos. Madrid: M. Murillo, 1882. 28 pp.
Argues that both Nicaragua and Costa Rica possess navigational rights on the river and that this is a precedent from the Colonial era. Because this brief pamphlet was published at the same time and on the same press as the author's larger Costa Rica y Colombia de 1573-1881 and is bound into the same volume, it is often overlooked by searchers. DLC LNHT

717 Pereira, Ricardo S. Documentos sobre límites de los Estados Unidos de Colombia, copiados de los originales que se encuentran en el Archivo de Indias de Sevilla. 1st ser., Límites entre el antiguo Virreinato de la Nueva Granada y las capitanías generales de Venezuela y Guatemala. Bogotá: C. Roldan & Tamayo, 1883. xvi, 168 pp. Biblio., maps.
A compilation of Colonial documents detailing the boundaries of Colombia, prepared by a Columbian envoy to the arbitration hearings in response to the publications of the Costa Rican envoy, Manuel María de Peralta. Demonstrates that the same depositories could yield documents supporting the Colombian claims. DLC

718 Pereira Pinto, Juan Carlos. El Mercado Común Centroamericano. Buenos Aires: Editorial El Coloquio, 1969. 30 pp. Maps, tables.
Basic data for the general reader, viewing the market sympathetically. Includes some statistical tables of current data. DLC

719 Pereyra, Carlos. Historia de la América Española. Vol. 5, Los países Antillanos y la

América Central. Mexico: Editoria Nacional, 1959. 428 pp. Notes, illus., maps.
A volume (from an eight-volume work) that serves as a general history of the entire region, focusing mainly on the Colonial era but also encompassing the nineteenth century and the early years of the twentieth century. Includes commentaries on the Yankee interventions and role in the region. About one fourth of the volume relates to Central America since independence. CU

720 Pérez, Rafael. La Compañía de Jesús en Colombia y Centro-América despúes de su restauración. 3 vols. Valladolid: Lin de Gaviria, 1896-98. 453, 439, 678 pp.
A detailed account of Jesuit activities in the region during the mid-nineteenth century by a member of the order, covering the years 1851-71. Provides narratives of each post and church and their activities, considered in five-year segments by country, based on the order's archives. Includes consideration of their disputes with the local governments that led to their reexpulsion from the region by 1880. DLC BNCR

721 Pérez Cadalso, Eliseo. La Dieta de Chinandega y sus proyecciones político-jurídicas: tesis de incorporación como miembro activo del Ateneo de El Salvador. San Salvador: Imprenta Ateneo, 1959. 39 pp.
A brief address summarizing the actions of the convention that formally declared Central America independent from Mexico as well as Spain after the collapse of the Iturbide Empire, and established the Federation of Central America. Includes a list of the delegates, summary of the debates, the Constitution, and the official actions of the convention. LNHT

722 _____. Valle, apóstol de América. Tegucigalpa: Imprenta Calderón, 1952. 185 pp. Latest ed. Tegucigalpa: Imprenta Calderón, 1968. 244 pp. Biblio.
A sympathetic account of Valle's role in the independence of Central America. Includes lengthy quotations from his writings and correspondence, apparently taken from previously published collections of his papers and publications. DLC LNHT

723 Pérez Valle, Eduardo. Un laudo con dos incógnitas: Hara y la Isla de San Pío. Managua: Ediciones de Public Service, 1961. 119 pp. Illus., maps.
Originally a series of articles in La Prensa of Managua, this commentary reexamines the Cabo de Gracias a Dios region of the border, commenting on the ruling in November 1960 by the International Court of Justice in the Hague endorsing the arbitral decision of the king of Spain in 1906 in favor of the Honduran claim to the area but giving the island of San Pío to Nicaragua. Designed to familiarize Nicaraguans with the island and the region, it offers a detailed study of its settlement and use as a port, as well as of the various existing maps of the region and

the changes in the channels due to erosion and the action of the rivers. DLC LNHT

724 Pérez Zeledón, Pedro. Informe sobre la cuestión de validez del tratado de límites de Costa Rica y Nicaragua y puntos accesorios sometidos al arbitraje del señor presidente de los Estados Unidos de América: presentado en nombre del gobierno de Costa Rica. Washington, D.C.: Gibson Brothers, 1887. xi, 291 pp.
Argument on the Question of the Validity of the Treaty of Limits between Costa Rica and Nicaragua and Other Supplementary Points Connected with It Submitted to the Arbitration of the President of the United States of America, Filed on Behalf of the Government of Costa Rica. Washington, D.C.: Gibson Brothers, 1887. xi, 310 pp.
The Costa Rican position, recapitulating the Colonial jurisdictions over the San Juan River and recounting the annexation of Nicoya province by Costa Rica. Reproduces the various documents and argues that the 1858 treaty is fully valid and must be enforced. DLC DLC-LDS LNHT BNCR

725 _____. Réplica al alegato de Nicaragua en la cuestión sobre validez ó nulidad del tratado de límites de 15 de abril de 1858 que ha de decidir como árbitro el señor presidente de los Estados Unidos de América: presentada en nombre del gobierno de Costa Rica. Washington, D.C.: Gibson Brothers, 1887. ix, 207 pp.
Reply to the Argument of Nicaragua on the Question of the Validity or Nullity of the Treaty of Limits of April 15, 1858, to be Decided by the President of the United States of America, as Arbitrator, Filed on Behalf of the Government of Costa Rica. Washington, D.C.: Gibson Brothers, 1887. ix, 210 pp.
DLC

726 Périgny, Maurice C. de. Les cinq républiques de l'Amérique Centrale. Paris: Pierre Roger & Cie, 1911. vi, 259 pp. Illus., maps. 3d ed. Paris: Pierre Roger & Cie, 1919. 259 pp.
A former French diplomat provides an account aimed at the general reader, as part of the "Les pays modernes" series, with emphasis on economics and finances. The author is critical of the role of the United States and seeks to encourage more European interest in the region, although this latter point is not overtly evident. Provides a brief geographical description and historical overview with a firsthand description of the present situation and appearance of the principal cities and transportation facilities, including discussion of the principal crops and economic aspects, shipping connections to Europe, tariffs, etc. DLC LNHT

727 Peterwerth, Reinhard. Das Vertragswerk des Zentralamerikanischen Gemeinsamen Marktes. Berlin: Colloquim Verlag, 1973. 134 pp. Index, biblio., notes.

A description and discussion of the Common Market and its effects in Central America based on the published documents and existing secondary works, focusing on industrialization, trade, developmental prospects, and the legal framework, and cautioning that the market is not a cure-all for the region's problems. DLC

728 Picado Michalski, Teodoro, and Ricardo Fournier Quirós, eds. Unión centroamericana: resultado de una encuesta. San José: Imprenta Minerva, 1921. 86 pp.
A collection of excerpts from writings, speeches, and letters by various Costa Rican political and intellectual figures, some with citations and dates, designed to indicate the evolution of the concept of union in Costa Rica. DLC-LDS BNCR

729 Pincus, Joseph. Analysis of the General Treaty of Economic Integration (Signed at Managua, Nicaragua, on December 13, 1960). Washington, D.C.: International Cooperation Administration, 1961. 15 pp.
Despite the title, the pamphlet consists mainly of a paraphrase of the treaty.

730 _____. The Central American Common Market. Washington, D.C.: ROCAP, 1962. 231 pp. Notes, tables, appendixes.
El Mercado Común Centroamericano. Mexico: ROCAP, 1963. 84 pp. Notes, tables, appendixes.
A sympathetic review of the integration efforts, the formation of the Common Market, and its potential. Presents extensive statistics and a historical review of the region's economy. The appendixes contain the treaties and agreements. DLC LNHT

731 Pineda M., Leónidas. Ensayo biográfico de Francisco Morazán. Tegucigalpa: Tipografía Ariston, 1944. 55 pp.
A brief biography focusing on Morazán's political contributions and extolling his virtues, while criticizing Carrera. DLC

732 Pineda Madrid, Pedro. José Cecilio del Valle y la economía política. Tegucigalpa: Universidad Nacional Autónoma de Honduras, 1960. 20 pp.
A brief discussion of the economic thinking of this Central American independence leader, seeking to demonstrate that he saw far ahead of his time and anticipated many of the present developments, such as a social security system. Offers quotations from his writings, usually of a single paragraph, in support. LNHT

733 Poincaré, Raymond, ed. Différend au sujet de limites entre la Colombie et la Costa-Rica: résumé chronologique des titres territoriaux de la République de Colombie. Paris: Imprimerie Réunies, 1899. 160 pp.
A chronological table tracing the jurisdictional changes in the disputed region through the Colonial era and nineteenth century, with single-paragraph descriptions of the events,

(Poincaré, Raymond, ed.)
followed by documentary excerpts. All support
the Colombian claims contending that the region belonged to cities and provinces in the
isthmus of Panama that reported to New
Granada, and that the British recognized this
residual jurisdiction. Compiled as part of
the Colombian case in the proceedings that led
to the Loubet award. DLC

734 ____. Différend de limites entre la Colombie
et la Costa-Rica: arbitrage de Son
Excellence, le président de la République
Française; consultations et mémoires présentés
par la Colombie. Paris: Imprimerie Réunies,
1900. Pages not consecutively numbered.
A collection of opinions from various European jurists, written in support of the Colombian claims and submitted as part of that
nation's case, with a conclusion by Poincaré.
DLC

735 ____. Différend entre la Colombie et la
Costa Rica: arbitrage de Son Excellence, le
président de la République Française:
deuxième mémoire. Paris: Imprimerie
Motteroz, 1899. 106 pp.
Cuestión de límites entre Colombia y Costa
Rica: arbitraje de S.E. el Sr. presidente de
la República Francesa: segunda memoria
presentada en nombre de la República de
Colombia. Sevilla: Imprenta de Izquierdo,
1899. viii, 114 pp.
A French attorney's argument supporting the
Colombian case in the boundary arbitration
with Costa Rica. Although the title identifies it as the second memorandum, no others
were located. DLC DLC-LDS-658 BNCR

736 Poliakov, Mikhail Il'ich. TSentral'na
Amerika: o nekotorykh problemakh
mezhdunarodnykh otnoshenii v basseine
Karibskogo moria [Central America: some
problems relating to international contacts in
the Caribbean area]. Moscow: Znanie, 1964.
30 pp.
MH

737 Pollan, Arthur Aclair. The United Fruit Company and Middle America. New York: Middle
American Information Bureau, 1944. 27 pp.
La United Fruit Company y la región americana
que comprende a México, la América Central y
las Antillas. San Pedro Sula: Editorial
Nacional, 1944. 20 pp.
An address by the executive vice-president
of the United Fruit Company detailing the
company's accomplishments and future plans.
DLC LNHT

738 Porras, Belisario. Boundary between Panama
and Costa Rica: Argument upon the Jurisdiction and Power of the Arbitrator Submitted to
the Honorable Chief Justice of the United
States of America, by Belisario Porras. . . .
Washington, D.C.: n.p., n.d. [1914]. 33 pp.
A synopsis of the Panamanian government's
stand. See following item. DLC BNCR

739 ____. Límites entre Panamá y Costa Rica,
jurisdicción y poderes del árbitro, primera
exposición. Washington, D.C.: Press of B.S.
Adams, 1911. 129 pp.
The full Panamanian argument, quoting the
various accords to contend that the arbitor
exceeded his powers and that he was restricted
by the agreements to defining the line in
accordance with the Loubet awards. This was
the basis of Panama's rejection of the resulting White award. DLC

740 Porter, William Sydney [O. Henry, pseud.]. Of
Cabbages and Kings. New York: Doubleday,
Page, 1904. 312 pp. Reprint. New York:
Penguin, 1946. 184 pp.
A picturesque novel about dictatorship,
intrigue, and corruption in Central America,
emphasizing the problems of dictatorship and
the greediness of the local Yankees, and exhibiting the then-prevailing attitudes and
stereotypes of Yankees and Europeans toward
the region. DLC

741 Portocarrero, José D. ¡Grito de alarma!:
Mister Taft y las repúblicas convulsivas. San
José: Imprenta Alsina, 1912. 24 pp.
A warning against Yankee interventionism
(particularly in Nicaragua, but with what the
author considers implications for all of Cen-
tral America) detailing the maneuvers of the
Northern Colossus. DLC-LDS-104 BNCR

742 Pozuelo A., José. Por la patria y por el
amigo: testimonio relativo a los hechos que
culminaron con el definitivo y feliz arreglo
del problema fronterizo entre Costa Rica y
Panamá. San José: Imprenta La Tribuna, 1943.
27 pp. Illus., maps.
An account of the meeting between Costa
Rican president Rafael Angel Calderón Guardia
and Panamanian president Arnulfo Arias Madrid
that led to the definitive settlement of the
long-standing boundary disputes between the
two nations, though in fact the lines had been
established earlier but had been accepted by
Panama only under protest. DLC BNCR

743 Prem, Marcial. Memorándum sobre nuestra
antigua cuestión de límites con Honduras.
Guatemala: Imprenta Alvarado Fajardo, 1926.
29 pp. Maps.
A brief analysis of the Guatemala-Honduras
boundary question, sustaining the Guatemalan
claims and criticizing the Honduran contentions. DLC LNHT

744 La Prensa (Managua). Divulgaciones de "La
Prensa." 4 vols. Managua: Tipografía La
Prensa, 1937. Maps.
A series of pamphlets reprinting editorials
from this paper supporting the Nicaraguan
stand in the boundary dispute with Honduras,
dealing with various aspects of the controversy, including the Royal Cedulas, the history of the question, and the various Colonial
jurisdictions, while responding to arguments
by the Honduran press, particularly El
Cronista. Pagination varies. DLC

745 Putnam, George Palmer. The Southland of North America. New York: Putnam's, 1913. xiv, 425 pp. Biblio., illus., maps.
  An account of the author's travels through the isthmus during 1912. Conversations and observations on social life and customs are interspersed with physical description, though mirroring Yankee prejudices. DLC LNHT

746 Quiñónes, Alfredo. Proyecto de unión centroamericana. Guatemala: Tipografía Nacional, 1920. 18 pp.
  A unionist tract publicizing the proposals for the 1920 federation effort, written by a unionist who served as the Guatemalan representative to the conclave.

747 Ramírez, Marco Antonio. Los alimentos en Centroamérica. San Salvador: ODECA, 1968. iv, 124 pp. Illus., tables.
  A study of Central American dietary composition and food production, with projections for both to 1980, designed to facilitate planning and demonstrate future needs. DLC

748 Ramírez Brown, Gerónimo. La hora actual: síntesis de la cuestión de límites entre Nicaragua y Honduras, circular dirigida a los jefes políticos de la república el 12 de octubre de 1937. Managua: Talleres Nacionales, 1937. 18 pp.
  A brief summary of the Nicaraguan claims. DLC

749 Ramírez Peña, Abraham. Conferencias centroamericanas: 1909-1914, seguido de un apéndice que comprende los últimos tratados y convenciones celebrados por El Salvador, con datos sobre la vigencia internacional de ellos. San Salvador: Imprenta Nacional, 1916. 305 pp. Appendixes.
  A compendium of documents from the various isthmian conferences attempting to promote union during these years. Consists principally of the accords signed, reglamentos of the conclaves, and relevant correspondence, with brief introductions. DLC LNHT

750 _____. Por la paz de Centro América. San Salvador: Centro Editorial Meléndez, 1910. 199 pp. Index.
  A unionist tract emphasizing the prospects of the 1907 Washington Conference and the formation of the Central American Court for bringing a new era of peace and cooperation to the region. Includes excerpts from the agreements and the official pronouncements regarding them, as well as the author's general commentary on the importance of peace and regional cooperation. ICU

751 Ramírez y Fernández Fontecha, Antonio Abad. Por la justicia y por la verdad: el arbitraje entre Honduras y Nicaragua. Tegucigalpa: Tipografía Nacional, 1908. 236 pp. Maps. 2d ed. Tegucigalpa: Ministerio de Relaciones Exteriores; New York: n.p., 1938. 236 pp. Notes, maps, appendixes.
  A statement defending the 1906 decision by the king of Spain, written by the Honduran

lawyer in the proceedings and addressed to the Nicaraguan Ministry of Foreign Relations, repeating the Honduran arguments and contending that Nicaragua had initially accepted the ruling. Includes various maps and documents supporting the Honduran claims. DLC LNHT

752 Ramsett, David E. Regional Industrial Development in Central America: A Case Study of the Integration Industries Scheme. New York: Praeger, 1969. xvi, 133 pp. Biblio., notes, maps, tables, appendixes.
  A detailed study of the integration industries scheme whereby certain industries received regional designation and special tax privileges. Provides full explanation of the origin and intention, the legislation and agreements involved, and its operation. Identifies the principal problem as the political decision to insist that the industries be equally distributed among the member nations, which eventually halted the program as the potential investors preferred the more developed and populated countries, which offered closer proximity to suppliers and market. DLC LNHT

753 Rath, Ferdinand. América Central: tendencias pasadas y perspectivas de su población. San José: Centro Latinoamericano de Demografía, 1970. 33 pp. Biblio., notes, tables.
  A brief overview of population trends from 1920 to 1965, with appropriate tables and comparative comments about the countries. Current data is broken into subcategories, with implications for the future discussed. DLC LNHT

754 Refutación de las hechas al C. Matías Romero por el gobierno de Guatemala. Mexico: Imprenta de C. Ramiro y Ponce de León, 1876. 377 pp.
  Part of the propaganda involved in the boundary dispute, this volume replies to a speech by Justo Rufino Barrios. Presents extensive documentation supporting the Mexican claim. DLC

755 Regalado Dueñas, Miguel. El hipotético presidente de Centro América. San Salvador: Tipografía Santa Anita, 1974. 68 pp.
  A theoretical essay promoting the unionist ideal and offering a semifictional proposed program of the means by which a hypothetical future democratic caudillo could unite the isthmus under a strong presidential system by seeking the support of the masses in a time of crisis. Details the steps and methods that would need to be employed to achieve unity without conflict. LNHT

756 _____. La realidad política centroamericana como crítica proyectiva. Guatemala: n.p., 1968. viii, 330 pp. Biblio., notes.
  A unionist tract reviewing the collapse of the nineteenth-century Federation of Central America from the viewpoint of the theory of the state, and applying the lessons to a general discussion of Central American unionism. The author concludes that there is no such

thing as a Central American, and that consequently union, while necessary and desirable,
will be a slow process. He advocates a federal system and comments on the type of division of powers that would be necessary. DLC
LNHT

757 Reichardt, C.F. Centro-Amerika: nach den
gegenwärtigen Zuständen des Landes und Volkes,
in Beziehung auf die Verbindung der beiden
Oceane und im Interesse der deutschen
Auswanderung bearbeitet. Braunschweig: F.
Vieweg, 1851. 256 pp. Notes, maps.
    A basic geography, with brief historical
synopsis, designed for the potential German
immigrant. Includes accounts of the present
state of German immigration and data on the
location of the present German residents of
the nation, including distribution and location. DLC LNHT

758 Reina Valenzuela, José. Carrillo en Honduras.
San José: Imprenta Tormo, 1951. 28 pp.
Illus.
    A brief discussion, originally written as
an address, of the actions of Braulio Carrillo
during a residence in Honduras in the 1820s
and his role as a Costa Rican delegate to the
Congress of the Federation of Central America.
Defends his actions in separating Costa Rica
from the Federation during the 1840s. BNCR

759 _____. El prócer Dionisio de Herrera:
estudio biográfico. Tegucigalpa: Sociedad de
Geografía e Historia de Honduras, 1965. 277
pp. Notes, illus.
    A biography of one of the Hondurans in-
volved in the independence movement. Seeks to
restore him to his rightful position of glory
by tracing his career from independence advocate to opponent of the Mexican annexation to
Federation statesman. The focus is on his
service as governor of Nicaragua under the
Federation. Contains numerous documentary
excerpts. DLC LNHT

760 La República (Guatemala). Documentos
relacionados con la historia de Centro-
América. 2 vols. Guatemala: Tipografía
El Commercio, 1896. 208, 255 pp.
    A collection of documents relating to the
independence movement throughout Central America, offered without comment or explanation,
with no apparent order and no index or table
of contents. They range from 1813 through
1824 and include manifestos, speeches in the
assemblies, digests of the assemblies, declarations of the cities, selections from the
Memorias of Pedro Molina, and various letters.
LNHT

761 Reunión de presidentes de Centroamérica,
Panamá, y Estados Unidos de América: San
José, Costa Rica, marzo de 1963. San José:
Imprenta Vargas, 1963. 122 pp. Illus.
    The official programs and collected
speeches of the Central American summit
meeting of March 1963 with all the accompanying acts. LNHT

762 Reunión de presidentes de Centroamérica, y de
los Estados Unidos de América, julio 5-8,
1968. San Salvador: Imprenta Nacional, 1968.
143 pp. Illus.
    The collected public statements and
speeches attendent to the trip by President
Lyndon Johnson to meet with the Central American Executives. DLC

763 Revelo, Marco René, and José del Carmen
Pineda. Testimonios imparciales sobre el
conflicto bélico salvadoreño-hondureño y
actuación de la iglesia salvadoreña. San
Salvador: Imprenta Nacional, n.d. [1970].
29 pp.
    An official report by the Salvadoran
church, compiled by a priest and approved by
the archbishopric, defending the Salvadoran
stance and repeating the government charges of
genocide and the argument that Salvador is
defending human rights. DLC

764 Rey, Francis. La unión de Centro-América:
estudio relativo á las instituciones creadas
en Washington, por la Conferencia de Paz
Centro-Americana de 1907. Guatemala: Sánchez
& de Guise, 1911. 27 pp. Notes.
    A French professor and international lawyer
analyzes the 1907 Washington accords, in a
pamphlet that originally appeared as an article in the Revue Générale de Droit International Publique of Paris in 1911. The focus
is on the international legal precedents involved in the institutions created. The
author views the result as a contribution to
eventual federation, though he presumes that
this will require a period of years. DLC
BNCR

765 Rey, Julio Adolfo. Ensayos centroamericanos.
Santa Ana: Tipografía San José, 1955. 54 pp.
Biblio.
    An essay comparing the Central American
constitutions, seeking to show their similarities and differences and examine their implications for the unionist movement, followed by
a brief historical summary of the unionist
movement and discussion of the Organization of
Central American States. LNHT

766 Reyes, Rafael. Vida de Morazán. San
Salvador: n.p., 1883. 6th ed. San Salvador:
Ministerio de Cultura, 1957. 139 pp.
    An essay by a Salvadoran journalist that
has passed through many editions, extolling
Morazán and tracing his activities on behalf
of Central American independence, the Federation of Central America, and his efforts to
preserve it. Quotes liberally from various
volumes dealing with Morazán. DLC LNHT BNCR

767 Riba, Jorge Ricardo. Resumen de la monografía
"La vivienda en Centroamérica," cuyo autor
es . . . . San Salvador: ODECA, 1970. 28 pp.
    A summary of the author's larger study.
See item 768. LNHT BNG

768 _____. La vivienda en Centroamérica. San
Salvador: ODECA, 1969. iv, 107 pp. Illus.,
tables.

An analysis of the housing shortage in
Central America, with consideration of each
nation (including Panama), general analysis
for the entire region, and projections of
population-growth factors and their implications for future needs. Focuses on 1965
through 1980. LNHT BNG

769 Richmond, Doug. Central America: How to Get
There and Back in One Piece with a Minimum of
Hassle. Tucson, Ariz.: H.P. Books, 1974.
176 pp. Illus., maps, appendixes.
A profusely illustrated modern travel guide
for the novice, emphasizing procedures and
travel difficulties. Includes in its discussion of places to see not merely archeological
zones and tourist locales, but also local
industries and agriculture. Complete with
photos and explanations of procedures. DLC
LNHT

770 Rincón Coutiño, Valentín. Chiapas entre
Guatemala y México: injusto motivo de
discordias. Mexico: Sociedad Mexicana de
Geografía y Estadística, 1964. 32 pp.
A review of the boundary question in the
form of a paper presented in 1964 to the
Mexican Society of Geography and Statistics,
including discussion of a recent dispute involving a change of channel by the Suchiate
River that raised a new issue. The author
repeats the Mexican claims of facilitating the
independence of Central America, and argues
that the questions of Chiapas and Soconusco
are long since closed, but notes that Mexico
owes it to consistency to transfer the territory left on the Guatemalan side of the river
by the channel change, in view of its stand in
the Chamizal case involving a similar issue on
the Rio Grande with the United States. DLC

771 Rivas, Pedro. Límites entre Honduras y
Nicaragua en el Atlántico, historia
cartográfica documentada (1508 a 1821).
Tegucigalpa: Talleres Tipográficos
Nacionales, 1938. 131 pp. Illus., maps.
A detailed study of the question of Colonial jurisdiction as it relates to the boundary question, accompanied by numerous maps
from the time of discovery and the Colonial
era showing the jurisdictions, and a collection of documents. DLC LNHT

772 Rivera, Rubén. Apuntamientos históricos sobre
unión centroamericana. San Salvador:
Tipografía "La Unión," 1911. 54 pp. Notes.
A brief commentary on the 1903 unionist
attempt, by an associate of Tomás Regalado,
Salvadoran general and president who was its
chief promoter, consisting principally of a
series of letters he exchanged with various
prominent Central Americans, mainly congratulatory commentaries from a wide range of individuals to the author. Includes the text of
the accord, and a narration of the collapse of
the effort from the Salvadoran and unionist
viewpoint. LNHT

773 Rivera G., José Antonio. En defensa de la
integridad de Chiapas. Mexico: Imprenta de

Manuel León Sánchez, 1917. 32 pp. Biblio.,
notes.
While designed to argue against the transfer of a department from Chiapas to Tabasco,
this pamphlet, written from a Mexican prison,
provides a review of Chiapan history, arguing
for its uniqueness as against both Guatemala
and Mexico and commenting extensively on its
separateness during its Colonial linkage to
Guatemala. LNHT

774 Roberts, Morley. On the Earthquake Line:
Minor Adventures in Central America. London:
Arrowsmith, 1924. 310 pp. Index, illus.
An Englishman's adventure-travelogue, de-
scribing a trip in the four northern isthmian
republics during 1923, with emphasis on El
Salvador. Concentrates on physical descrip-
tion, narration, and adventure. Mirrors Euro-
pean prejudices and contrasts conditions with
European expectations. DLC LNHT

775 Roberts, Orlando W. Narrative of Voyages and
Excursions on the East Coast and in the Inte-
rior of Central America: Describing a Journey
up the River San Juan and Passage Across the
Lake of Nicaragua to the City of León: Point-
ing Out the Advantages of a Direct Commercial
Intercourse with the Natives. Edinburgh:
Constable, 1827. xxiii, 302 pp. Maps.
Latest ed. Gainesville: University of
Florida Press, 1965. xxiii, 302 pp. Illus.,
maps.
A descriptive travel account by a British
sea captain and merchant, covering the east
coast from Panama to Nicaragua, the San Juan
River, and the interior plain of Nicaragua.
The emphasis is on landforms, flora, and
fauna, with discussion of commercial prospects, economy, and potential harbors, but
there are also observations regarding social
customs. Although designed to orient potential traders to the region, the book also
provides an outsider's view of the independence movement.

776 Robleto, Hernán. Brújulas fijas. Madrid:
Cultura Clásica y Moderna, 1961. 254 pp.
A novel recounting the experiences of a
diverse group of people from different countries of Europe and the Caribbean who journey
to the new world to form a new community of La
Fortuna, where they undergo the rigors of the
frontier and in effect reexperience the problems, frustrations, and transformations of the
founding of the hemisphere. The format,
though hardly original, allows the author to
comment on the origins of many of the characteristics and problems of modern Central
America. DLC

777 Rodas M., Joaquín. Mis prisiones y
peregrinación por Centro América en aras del
ideal unionista. Quezaltenango: Tipografía
Suasnávar, 1936. 328 pp. 2d ed. Guatemala:
Tipografía Nacional, 1964. 415 pp. Illus.
The political memoirs of a Guatemalan unionist active in the movement during the early
years of the twentieth century. Recounts his
efforts, frequent imprisonment, and exile.

(Rodas M., Joaquín)
Provides insights, through the eyes of a participant and true believer, into the unionist movement and its political activities throughout the isthmus. DLC LNHT

778 _____. *Morazánida, de la epopeya, la tragedia, y la apoteosis.* Quezaltenango: Editora Suasnávar, 192?. Illus.
An admiring biography of General Morazán and his role in the independence and unification of the isthmus, by a Guatemalan intellectual who is an avowed unionist. DLC BNG

779 Rodman, Selden. *The Road to Panama.* New York: Hawthorn Books, 1966. 224 pp. Index, illus.
A well-known and experienced travel-book author brings his practiced eye to the Pan American Highway, describing a trip through Mexico and Central America during 1964-65, combining physical description, social observation, and conversation, interwoven with observations and historical background of the localities and events. DLC

780 Rodríguez, José Nery. *Estudios militares de Centro-América.* Guatemala: Tipografía Nacional, 1930. 383 pp. Biblio., illus., maps, appendixes.
A detailed history of Central American military conflicts from pre-Columbian times to the 1920s, discussing the causes of the conflicts and the conduct of the campaigns, with details of the various battles, complete with maps and analysis of the tactics involved, by a Guatemalan general. A standard source for details regarding the various battles, although the coverage is uneven. The discussions of the antecedents of the conflicts are somewhat partisan, though the main focus is on tactics and battlefield technicalities. DLC BNG

781 Rodríguez, Manuel Federico. *El centenario negro.* Buenos Aires: Editorial Claridad, 1936. 126 pp. Illus., tables.
A unionist appeal by a Honduran diplomat, emphasizing the harm done by the collapse of the Federation on the centennial of this event, and arguing for the indivisibility of the isthmus and the need to reunite. Despite the title there is little discussion of the collapse of the Federation. Instead, the book is principally devoted to arguments for a new unionist impulse, and an endorsement of the Unionist party and its platform, by one of its signers. DLC

782 Rodríguez, Mario. *The Cádiz Experiment in Central America, 1808-1826.* Berkeley: University of California Press, 1978. 316 pp. Index, biblio., notes, maps.
While focusing on the Spanish Cortes and the nation's Liberal constitution, this work details the impact of these important events in Central America. Based on extensive documentary research in the Spanish Archives, it traces the Central American role in the Spanish body and the isthmian reaction to its

work, linking the Spanish and Central American Liberals, showing the influence of the efforts to reform Spain in the isthmian colonies and the impact of the experience in politics on isthmian leaders. Includes a careful account of the Central American independence movement. DLC LNHT

783 _____. *Central America.* Englewood Cliffs, N.J.: Prentice-Hall, 1965. xi, 178 pp. Index, biblio., notes, maps.
América Central. Mexico: Editorial Diana, 1967. 203 pp. Biblio., notes, maps.
A succinct interpretation of the broad thrust of Central American history. Part of a series that seeks to attract the general reader by first considering the period since 1955 and then tracing the region's development from independence to 1955, in broad sweeps. The emphasis is on isthmian-wide trends, unionist efforts, states of development, and the dictatorships that exerted influence throughout the region. DLC LNHT BNG

784 _____. *La conspiración de Belén en nueva perspectiva.* Guatemala: Ministerio de Educación Pública, 1965. 56 pp. Notes.
An analysis of the Belén conspiracy and the impact of the Cádiz revolt and the Spanish constitution of 1813 on the Central American independence movement, particularly in Guatemala. Based on relevant archival materials. DLC LNHT

785 _____. *A Palmerstonian Diplomat in Central America: Frederick Chatfield, Esq.* Tucson: University of Arizona Press, 1964. 385 pp. Index, biblio., notes, illus., maps.
Chatfield, consul británica en Centro América. Tegucigalpa: Banco Central de Honduras, 1970. 526 pp. Biblio., notes, illus., maps.
A history, based on archival materials in England and several other countries, of British diplomacy in Central America from 1833 to 1852, by means of a biography of the principal British representative in the isthmus. Provides a clear account of British objectives and policy-making, of the changes in the British position, and the impact of the emergence of the United States. It also indicates that, contrary to previous assumptions, Britain was not responsible for the collapse of the Federation, but in fact actively supported it and the Liberal party, abandoning this position only in 1839 when the Federation was clearly in decline. DLC LNHT BNG

786 Rodríguez, Mario, and Vincent C. Peloso, eds. *A Guide for the Study of Culture in Central America: Humanities and Social Sciences.* Washington, D.C.: PAU, 1968. vii, 88 pp.
A basic list designed for the novice or generalist with little prior contact with the region, compiling over 900 of the general and best-known studies, with brief annotations. DLC LNHT

787 Rodríguez Beteta, Virgilio. *Aspectos geográficos del problema de la unión de Centro América.* Madrid: Imprenta del Patronato de

(Rodríguez Beteta, Virgilio)
Huérfanos de Intendencia e Intervención Militares, 1935. 19 pp.

A brief recapitulation of the unionist efforts in Central America, which apart from some references to the importance of the isthmus in world commerce has little pertaining to geography; by a prominent Guatemalan scholar who wrote this piece while serving as his nation's ambassador in Madrid. DLC LNHT

788 _____. Ideologías de la independencia: doctrinas políticas económico-sociales. Guatemala: Oficina Internacional Centro-Americana, 1912. 255 pp. 4th ed. Guatemala: Editorial Landívar, 1965. 248 pp.

An analysis of the ideas that dominated the independence era, considering such questions as political independence, economic development, Indian policy, and the role of the press in that era. LNHT BNG BNCR

789 _____. No es guerra de hermanos sino de bananos. Guatemala: Universidad de San Carlos, 1969. 209 pp.

A Guatemalan political figure, diplomat, and scholar provides an account of the Guatemala-Honduras border dispute in semi-memoir fashion, contending that the question reflected the rival claims of the banana companies operating in the region, Cuyamel in Honduras and United Fruit in Guatemala, both of which coveted the territory for their operations. This is hardly a new argument, but the volume provides a detailed study based in part on the author's service as Guatemalan minister to Honduras during the years 1927 to 1929. He contends that the countries were near war in 1928, reproducing the official correspondence that prevented the outbreak of a full-scale conflict, with the emphasis on the author's role and his mission. DLC LNHT BNG

790 _____. La política inglesa en Centroamérica durante el siglo XIX. Guatemala: Ministerio de Educación Pública, 1963. 242 pp. Notes, illus., maps.

A series of articles dealing with the Belize question, which were originally published in El Imparcial of Guatemala City during one of the periodic flareups of this long-standing dispute in 1961 and 1962. Based on research in secondary works and published documents, with some citations, they focus on British efforts to gain control of the coasts of Central America and the prospective canal routes, criticize the United States for being too timid in dealing with the British threat and "abandoning" Belize to the British, and excoriate British opportunism in taking advantage of Central American weakness. DLC LNHT BNG

791 Rodríguez Cerna, José. Centro América en el congreso de Bolívar. Guatemala: Tipografía Nacional, 1938. 323 pp. Illus. 2d ed. Guatemala: Ministerio de Relaciones Exteriores, 1956. 338 pp.

A collection of documents relating to the activities of the Federation of Central America during the Bolívar-inspired Congress of Panama in 1826, seeking to make the role of the Central American delegation and the proposals it made more widely known. The collection includes correspondence and the resolutions and treaties approved by the conference. DLC LNHT BNG

792 Rodríguez Guerrero, José. Los tres césares. Guatemala: n.p., 1903. 35 pp.

Yet another piece representative of the Guatemalan propaganda campaign during the isthmian crisis reflecting the ambitions of the various rulers, this one condemning José Santos Zelaya, Tomás Regalado, and Terencio Sierra as ruthless dictators plotting to take over the entire isthmus, and particularly Guatemala. BNG

793 Roemer, Hans Gustav. Die einmischungen der USA in die Revolutionen und Bürgerkriege der westindischen und zentralamerikanischen Republiken. Essen, Germany: Essener Verlagsanstalt, 1943. 137 pp. Notes.

A review of United States Caribbean policy in the 1920s, with chapters summarizing developments in several of the individual nations, including the Central American republics, based on the Foreign Relations volumes, newspapers, and secondary sources. DLC

794 Romero, Matías. Bosquejo histórico de la agregación á México de Chiapas y Soconusco, y de las negociaciones sobre límites entabladas por México con Centro América y Guatemala. Mexico: Imprenta del Gobierno, 1877. xxiv, 798 pp.

A massive collection of documents, with connecting narration, stating the Mexican case regarding the boundary dispute and the adherence of Soconusco to Mexico. Originally compiled in response to the volume by Andres Dardón and printed first in the Mexican Diario Oficial. Includes extensive material regarding the Colonial jurisdictions, the turmoil of the independence era, the annexation and separation of Central America from Mexico, and the jurisdictions of Chiapas and Soconusco and their decisions at the time of the split. DLC

795 Romero Vargas, German, et al. Ensayos de historia centroamericana. San José: CEDAL, 1974. 165 pp. Biblio., notes.

A collection of historical essays, originally prepared for a CEDAL conference. Most focus on the Colonial era but there are also essays by José Luís Vega Carbello dealing with the birth of the Costa Rican bourgeoisie and by Vilma Laines and Victor Meza on banana enclaves in Honduran history. BNCR

796 Rosa, Ramón. Biografía del licenciado don José Cecilio del Valle. Tegucigalpa: Tipografía Nacional, 1882. 162 pp. 5th ed. Tegucigalpa: Oficina de Relaciones Públicas de la Presidencia, 1971. 118 pp.

A brief biography, defending Valle and hailing his contributions to the independence movement. DLC

(Rosa, Ramón)
797 _____. *Historia del benemérito Gral. don Francisco Morazán, ex-presidente de la República de Centro-América.* Tegucigalpa: Instituto Morazánico, 1971. 193 pp. Notes.
  This incomplete manuscript was written during the 1880s at the same time as Rosa's work on Valle, but remained unpublished until this edition. Written by an avowed unionist, it is a sympathetic biography extolling Morazán's efforts, ideals, and work on behalf of the Federation. DLC LNHT

798 Rosa Chávez, Adolfo. *Grandeza y tragedia de la América Central.* Guatemala: Ministerio de Educación Pública, 1962. 190 pp. Illus.
  A series of essays regarding the various efforts to unify Central America, accompanied by essays hailing the potential of a unified isthmus and lamenting its failure, published under the patronage of the unionist movement of the Ydígoras Fuentes government. BNG.

799 Rowles, James. *El conflicto Honduras-El Salvador (1969) y el orden jurídico internacional.* San José: EDUCA, 1980. 320 pp. Notes.
  A study of the mediation efforts launched during the conflict, focusing on the role of international law and international bodies, providing an extremely detailed account, almost hour by hour, of the negotiations. The author concludes that Honduras negotiated more forthrightly while El Salvador dragged its feet, and emphasizes that the international mechanisms did successfully bring about a settlement, though in a painfully slow manner. BNCR

800 Rubio Melhado, Adolfo. *Próceres salvadoreños.* San Salvador: Ministerio de Cultura, 1959. 94 pp. Illus.
  A series of brief patriotic essays extolling the independence of Central America, written on the occasion of the centennial of that movement. Includes a general essay on independence and brief biographies of José Matías Delgado, José Simeón Cañas, Santiago José Celis, and Pedro Pablo Castillo, all designed to demonstrate their roles as national heroes of the movement. The accounts are intended for the general public. DLC

801 Ruhl, Arthur Brown. *The Central Americans: Adventures and Impressions between Mexico and Panama.* New York and London: Scribner's, 1928. x, 284 pp. Index, illus., maps.
  An account of a tour through the region by an experienced travelogue author, mixing his observations with explanations, comparisons, and background notes. DLC LNHT

802 Rull Sabater, Alberto. *La planificación económica y social en Centroamérica.* Madrid: Confederación Española de Cajas de Ahorros, 1971. 342 pp. Biblio., notes, tables.
  A detailed review of recent development and planning in Central America, emphasizing the linkage between economic and social planning. The author sees the division of the region into separate entities as a considerable problem, advocating more regional planning but noting that the separate states are part of the reality, and that cooperation rather than complete union must be sought. DLC LNHT

803 Sáenz, Alfredo. *La situación bananera en los países del Caribe.* San José: Imprenta Borrasé, 1928. 78 pp. Maps.
  A denunciation of the United Fruit Company and its operations in many countries, including Guatemala, Costa Rica, and Honduras, condemning all of its various actions and its control of railroads. Consists principally of folios, maps, and tabulations of profits, as well as statements by company officials some given in both English and Spanish. DLC DLC-LDS-519 LNHT BNCR

804 Sáenz, Vincente. *La actitud del gobierno de Washington hacia las repúblicas centroamericanas.* Mérida: n.p., 1919. 23 pp.
  One of the author's many clarion calls to battle against Yankee imperialism, denouncing the efforts at economic control and particularly the intervention in Nicaragua. DLC DLC-LDS-718

805 _____. *Cartas a Morazán.* Tegucigalpa: Imprenta El Sol, 1922. 220 pp.
  A Costa Rican journalist's series of pro-unionist essays about the 1920 unionist effort and the San José Conference, defending the role of Costa Rica and attacking the stand of Nicaragua as the reason for the failure of the conference. The essays deal with the preliminaries, the milieu, and the currents of the conference, and include exchanges with some of the presidents. BNCR

806 _____. *Centro América en pie: contra la tiranía; contra el crimen y la barbarie; contra el imperialismo en cualquiera de sus formas.* Mexico: Ediciones Liberación, 1944. 237 pp.
  A pro-unionist, antidictatorial call to revolution, attempting to express what the author considers the thinking of Central Americans in 1944. He speaks for the revolutionaries, condemning dictatorship as an American brand of fascism, criticizing the hegemony of the United States, and advocating the unification of the isthmus and a new posture in international affairs. Several of the chapters are reproductions of addresses delivered by the author during his residence in Mexico, including a eulogy of Morazán. DLC LNHT

807 _____. *¿Comunismo en los Estados Unidos? Respuesta de Sáenz a Turner.* Guatemala: Tipografía Nacional, 1950. 19 pp.
  An article that Sáenz wrote to contest a *New York Herald Tribune* series on "Communism in the Caribbean," by Fitzhugh Turner. Sáenz contends that there is no communism in Central America, denouncing the oppressive actions and unfavorable impact of Yankee companies in the region. Sáenz's reply originally appeared in *El Universal* of Mexico City. The folio also

(Sáenz, Vincente)
includes several other press articles related to the controversy. DLC LNHT

808 _____. Elogio de Francisco Morazán. Mexico: Gráfica Panamérica, 1942. 57 pp.
A speech hailing Morazán and his efforts on behalf of Central American union. DLC BNCR

809 _____. El Grito de Dolores, y otros ensayos. Mexico: Editorial América Nueva, 1959. 291 pp. Biblio., notes.
A commentary on hemispheric solidarity among the Latin American nations and criticism of the policy of the United States, which includes consideration of Latin American cultural themes. Among the diverse subjects is a section of the origin of Central American liberalism, focusing particularly on Francisco Morazán and the efforts to promote federalism, and a series of essays on the parallelism of peace and democracy in the hemisphere, emphasizing interaction among dictatorships and democracies, with references to Central America. DLC BNCR

810 _____. Norteamericanización de Centro América. San José: Talleres de La Opinión, 1925. 312 pp. Illus.
Perhaps fittingly in view of the author's style and views, the last chapter of this work is entitled "Termina la polémica." Traces the history of Yankee intervention in Nicaragua, and the various maneuvers and implications from the nineteenth century to the 1920s, flailing the Yankees and their tactics, and contending that they seek nothing less than the annexation of the entire region. American actions during that period provide plenty of ammunition for his call to arms to defend the region against the avaricious Gringos. The chapters originally appeared as newspaper articles, principally in La Opinión of San José. The author regards the articles as the basis for the history of Central America "as it ought to be written." DLC DLC-LDS-329 LNHT BNCR

811 _____. Nuestra América en la cruz: siete prólogos, varias apologías y otros apuntes. Mexico: Editorial América Nueva, 1960. 370 pp. Notes.
A collection of commentaries, written earlier, consisting principally of the prologues prepared by the author for the books of friends or for his own works. It also includes some addresses and commentaries on historical figures. Most reflect the author's strong stance within the Guatemalan revolutionary movement of the 1940s and 1950s, and stress the need for reform, opposition to dictatorship throughout the region, and denunciation of the role of the Yankees. DLC LNHT

812 _____. Opiniones y comentarios de 1943. Mexico: Ediciones Liberación, 1944. 270 pp.
A collection of commentaries on a wide range of themes covering contemporary world affairs, ranging from discussion of Central American problems to comments on fascism,

European countries, and Latin American themes, whose common denominator is denunciation of Yankee imperialism, which the author manages to somehow invoke in discussion of virtually every subject. There is no indication whether the items were written as speeches or newspaper commentaries, or if they were previously published. DLC

813 _____. Paralelismo de la paz y de la democracia. Mexico: Unión Democrática Centroamericana, 1946. 63 pp.
A political tract of the Unión Democrática Centroamericana that denounces dictatorship and calls for hemispheric action against incumbent dictatorships to promote democracy, continuing the author's other denunciations of tyrants and imperialism, but emphasizing the hemispheric aspects rather than the local issues in the Central American nations. The essay was originally published in the Mexican newspaper Excelsior in 1946, and reflected the propaganda duel between the Guatemalan regime of Juan José Arévalo and the surviving Central American dictatorships, while seeking to justify Arévalo's support of international rebel forces to aid local revolutionaries in those nations. DLC

814 _____. Rompiendo cadenas, las del imperialismo en Centroamérica y en otras repúblicas del continente. Mexico: Editorial CIADE, 1933. 315 pp. 4th ed. Mexico: Editorial América Nueva, 1962. 448 pp.
Another denunciation of the chicanery of the Yankee capitalist imperialists, detailing their efforts to dominate Central America and calling for rebellion throughout the isthmus to break the Yankee chains of enslavement. The work focuses on the years since 1920, considering the Nicaragua intervention and canal question, as well as other actions in the isthmus. Later editions carry the tirade forward to the 1950s. DLC LNHT

815 Sáenz Jimenez, Lenin. Integración y coordinación de los servicios de salud de Centroamérica. San Salvador: ODECA, 1971. 102 pp. Illus., maps, tables.
An ODECA-sponsored survey of the principal health organizations of the Central American nations, present programs, efforts at coordination, and discussion of possible means of coordination in the future, with extensive health statistics and graphs showing the situation in each nation. LNHT

816 Salas Marrera, Oscar A. Derecho notarial de Centroamérica y Panamá. San José: Editorial Costa Rica, 1973. 586 pp. Biblio., notes.
A detailed analysis of notary law in each of the countries of the isthmus, treated comparatively, with a history of notorial law and its antecedents, as well as copious excerpts from existing statutes. LNHT BNCR

817 Salazar, Carlos, ed. Anexos del alegato presentado por Guatemala ante el tribunal de

arbitraje integrado. Washington, D.C.:
Gibson Brothers, 1932. 664 pp.
    The documentation accompanying the Guate-
malan case in the arbitration of the boundary
with Honduras. DLC LNHT BNG

818 Salazar, Carlos. Arbitraje de límites entre
Guatemala y Honduras: alegato presentado por
Guatemala. 2 vols. Guatemala: Tipografía
Nacional, 1932. 240, 203 pp. Maps.
Guatemala-Honduras Boundary Arbitration: The
Case of Guatemala Submitted to the Arbitral
Tribunal. 2 vols. Washington, D.C.: Gibson
Brothers, 1932. 288 pp. Maps, tables.
    The Guatemalan case as presented by its
attorney. DLC LNHT BNG

819 ____. Arbitraje de límites entre Guatemala y
Honduras . . . 1931. Washington, D.C.: n.p.,
1931. 133 pp. 2d ed. Guatemala: Tipografía
Nacional, 1932. 333 pp.
    DLC LNHT BNG

820 ____. Arbitraje de límites entre Guatemala y
Honduras: replica de Guatemala. 2 vols.
Washington, D.C.: Judd & Detweiler, 1932.
Maps.
Guatemala-Honduras Boundary Arbitration: The
Counter Case of Guatemala Submitted to the
Arbitral Tribunal. 2 vols. Washington, D.C.:
Judd & Detweiler, 1932. Maps.
    DLC LNHT BNG

821 Salazar, Ramón Antonio. Los hombres de la
independencia. Guatemala: Tipografía
Nacional, 1899. 321 pp. Illus.
    Biographical sketches of the key figures of
the Central American independence movement,
including Manuel José Arce and Mariano de
Aycinena, by a well known conservative Guatemalan historian of the nineteenth century.
Reflects the early views of independence. DLC
LNHT BNG

822 ____. Manuel José Arce. 2d ed. Guatemala:
Ministerio de Educación Pública, 1952. xxx,
118 pp. Illus.
    Originally published as part of his Los
hombres de la independencia. DLC LNHT

823 ____. Mariano de Aycinena. 2d ed.
Guatemala: Ministerio de Educación Pública,
1952. 126 pp. Illus.
    A republication of part of the author's Los
hombres de la independencia. DLC LNHT BNG

824 Salazar Valiente, Mario, et al. El proceso
político centroamericano. San Salvador:
Editorial Universitaria, 1964. 124 pp.
Index.
    The proceedings of a September 1963 con-
ference at the University of El Salvador, with
two papers. Mario Salazar Valiente deals
sympathetically with the Guatemalan revolution
while denouncing the victory of the imperialists in 1954, and David A. Luna sympathetically recounts the 1931 leftist peasant
uprising in El Salvador, denouncing its

suppression and calling for an effort to solve
the social problems as well as for the political education of the army. Includes summaries of the discussion that followed. DLC
LNHT

825 Salvatierra, Sofonías. Contribución a la
historia de Centroamérica: monografías
documentales. 2 vols. Managua: Tipografía
Progreso, 1939. 568, 524 pp. Notes, illus.
    Principally Colonial, with only the final
fifty pages of the second volume dealing with
the independence movement. Sketches the leading figures of the era, with quotations from
proclamations and published statements. DPU

826 Samayoa, Julio, and R. Samayoa. Por la unión
de Centro-América. Guatemala: Sánchez & de
Guise, 1920. 48 pp.
    A unionist tract providing arguments for
the unification of the isthmus and suggestions
for the current effort, as well as analysis of
ways in which unification could benefit each
of the nations and the region as a whole.
LNHT

827 Sanborn, Helen Josephine. A Winter in Central
America and Mexico. New York: C.T.
Dillingham; Boston: Lee & Shepard, 1886. iv,
321 pp.
    The author traveled to Central America with
her father, James S. Sanborn, who went in
connection with the coffee trade of his firm,
Chase and Sanborn, just after she finished
college. A descriptive account originally
published as a series of articles in the New
England Grocer, reflecting the impressions of
a keen observer and including comments on
social customs, living conditions, culture,
and physical setting and transportation difficulties, though some Yankee prejudices remain.
DLC LNHT

828 Sánchez, Pedro C. Centro América: donde
principia, donde termina, regiones geológicas,
unidades geográficas. . . . Mexico: PAIGH,
1937. 30 pp. Maps.
    Basic geographic data, with emphasis on the
subregional zones, the volcanoes, and their
role in the region's development. DLC

829 Sánchez Sarto, Manuel. Comercio
internacional y economía centroamericana. San
José: ESAPA, 1956. 73 pp.
    A very general discussion of the develop-
ment of the world economy, its trade patterns,
and how Central America relates to them, focusing on such aspects as payments and accords
rather than on products or statistics. BNCR

830 Sancho, José. Unión económica y aduanera: su
coincidencia necesaria. San José: EDUCA,
1970. 142 pp. Biblio., notes.
    A study arguing that for the Common Market
to achieve maximum success a full and complete
customs union among the participants is necessary. This in turn, it is noted, will facilitate a unified economic policy, which will
also promote the region's development and

expand its market. The volume examines progress to date, and notes the future potential,
contending that the only obstacles to a full
customs union are political objections based
on a lack of understanding of the possible
economic gains. DLC LNHT

831 Sandner, Gerhard. La cartografía
centroamericana: su desarrollo e importancia
para la economía y planificación; cot de
Oreamuno; herencia colonial uso de la tierra,
problemas socioeconómicos; la Costa Atlántica
de Nicaragua, Costa Rica y Panamá; su
conquista y colonización desde principios de
la época colonial. San José: Instituto
Geográfico de Costa Rica, 1964. 178 pp.
Biblio., illus., maps.
      TxU

832 ____. Die Hauptstädte Zentralamerikas:
Wachatumsprobleme, Gestaltwandel und
Sozialgefüge. Heidelberg: Meyer, 1969.
198 pp. Index, biblio., illus., maps, tables.
      A detailed study of the growth of the capi-
tal cities of the six Central American nations, including Panama but excluding Belize,
from Colonial times to the present, but focusing on the period since 1920. Includes detailed maps and tables tracing the expansion
of the cities, population movement, their
physical setting, and facilities, as well as
details of transportation links between them.
A small section of photos drawn from the modern era is also appended. DLC

833 Sansón-Terán, José. El arbitraje
internacional y la controversia de límites
entre Nicaragua y Honduras. Barcelona:
Editorial Hispano Europea, 1959. 579 pp.
Biblio., notes.
      A restatement of the Nicaraguan case by the
diplomat who represented the Nicaraguan government before the International Court of
Justice, consisting of the Nicaraguan arguments regarding the validity of the arbitral
ruling of the king of Spain in 1906, with
extensive accompanying documents regarding
Colonial jurisdiction over the disputed
region. DLC

834 Sapper, Karl Theodor. Mittel-Amerika.
Hamburg: L. Friederischen, 1921. 132 pp.
Maps.
      A brief description of the contemporary
situation in the isthmus, focusing on economic, geographical, and social factors.
Includes extensive economic statistics for the
1910-18 period, encompassing trade and production by product and country. DLC

835 ____. Mittel-Amerika: ein praktischer
Wegweiser für Auswanderer, Pflanzer,
Kaufleute, Lehrer. Halle: Max Niemeyer
Verlag, 1927. viii, 128 pp. Index, tables.
      An extensive survey of the economy of the
region, with statistics covering the 1914-25
period. Includes discussion of the principal
products and comparative data regarding trade,
prices, and production for the various republics. Also contains brief discussion of the

press and recent literature, as well as of the
geographical setting. DLC LNHT

836 ____. Mittelamerikanische: Reisen und
Studien aus dem Jahren 1888 bis 1900.
Braunschweig: Friedrich Vieweg & Sohn, 1902.
xiii, 426 pp. Illus., maps, tables.
      A descriptive and analytical account of the
author's travels in Central America from 1888
through 1900 in the course of scientific expeditions to explore the region's geography and
geology. The reports are those of a trained
observer providing copious detail, though they
are presented basically in the form of a traveler's observations, with numerous illustrations, maps, and tables. Includes
descriptions of the culture of the inhabitants
of the interior regions as well as physical
data. DLC LNHT BNCR

837 ____. Die mittelamerikanischen Vulkane.
Gotha: Justus Perthes, 1913. 173 pp. Index,
notes, maps, tables.
Los volcanes de la América Central. Halle:
Verlag von Max Niemeyer, 1925. vi, 116 pp.
Index, illus., maps, tables.
      A detailed description of the geographical
region of each of the area's volcanoes, providing complete data on location, physical
dimensions, statistics, and classification,
with a chronological listing of volcanic eruptions from 1524 through 1913, and a table
listing all the volcanoes with their specifics. The tables in the Spanish edition are
updated. DLC DLC-LDS-382 LNHT

838 ____. A Modern Boundary Question.
Guatemala: Boundary Commission, 1928. 15 pp.
Maps. 3d ed. Guatemala: Boundary Commis-
sion, 1931.
      Originally an article in Geopolitik of
Berlin, this commentary by a well-known German
Central American geographer was translated
into English and published separately by the
Boundary Commission. It analyzes the
Guatemala-Honduras dispute and its persist-
ence, indicating previous accords that par-
tially resolved it and defining the problem.
Includes references to the Guatemala-Mexico
frontier. DLC

839 ____. Das Nördliche MittelAmerika nebst
einen Ausflug nach dem Hochland von Anahuac:
Reisen und Studien. Braunschweig: Friedrich
Vieweg & Sohn, 1897. xii, 436 pp. Maps,
tables.
      A detailed descriptive work based on his
researches and extensive travels in the isthmus. Most of these essays were previously
published in journals in Germany. The emphasis is on geography and economic and financial
aspects. The book focuses on Guatemala, particularly Verapaz (where the author's brother
resides), and the Petén, but also includes
material relating to Honduras, the Yucatan,
and El Salvador. DLC LNHT

840 ____. Über Gebirgsbau und Boden des
nördlichen Mittelamerika. Gotha: Justus

(Sapper, Karl Theodor)
Perthes, 1899. vi, 119 pp. Notes, illus.,
maps, tables.
A series of geographical-geological descriptions of the terrain and characteristics
of the region, offered for each specific segment, with narrative and figures providing
altitude and distances for the area from the
Yucatan through Honduras and Belize. A later
second volume covers Honduras through Costa
Rica (see next item). The second part of each
volume deals with regional features. Includes
extensive maps and tables, and provides some
of the earliest precise data about the remote
portions of the area. DLC LNHT

841 _____. Über Gebirgsbau und Boden des
südlichen Mittelamerika. Gotha: Justus
Perthes, 1905. 82 pp. Notes, maps, tables.
A continuation of the preceding item, covering the area south of Honduras. DLC LNHT

842 Savaria, Miguel G. Compendio de la historia
de Centro-América. Guatemala: Emilio
Goubard, 1881. 141 pp. Illus. Latest ed.
San Salvador: Imprenta Nacional, 1900.
A survey, from pre-Columbian times but
emphasizing the post-independence period, that
lists the principal accomplishments and events
of the various administrations. Commentary in
brief numbered paragraphs. DLC

843 Schatzschneider, Hellmut. Die neue Phase der
Monroe-Doktrin angesichts de kommunistischen
Bedrohung Lateinamerikas: unter besonderer
Berücksichtigung des Falles Guatemala vor der
Organisation Amerikanischer Staaten und den
Vereinter Nationen. Göttingen: Vandenhoeck &
Ruprecht, 1957. 80 pp. Notes.
A discussion of the Monroe Doctrine's evo-
lution into a collective security doctrine and
the Yankee use of it against communism.
Covers in particular the invocation of the
principle of hemispheric collective security
in the case of the 1954 Guatemalan interven-
tion and its use to circumvent the United
Nations. Based on the public declarations and
U.N. debates. DLC

844 Scherzer, Karl. Aus dem Natur und Völkerleben
im Tropischen Amerika. Leipzig: Georg
Wigand's Verlag, 1864. 380 pp.
A general introduction and collection of
data, based on the author's travels and research. Two thirds of the book deals with
Central America, treating the area topically
and generally. DLC LNHT

845 Scherzer, Karl, and Moritz Wagner.
Wanderungen durch die Mittelamerikanischen
Freistaaten Nicaragua, Honduras und San
Salvador. Vienna: n.p., 1854.
Travels in the Free State of Central America:
Nicaragua, Honduras, and El Salvador. 2 vols.
London: Longman, Brown, Green, 1857. 283,
320 pp. Maps. Reprint. New York: A.M.S.
Press, 1970.
A detailed account of wandering in the
remote backcountry of the area, by a German

geographer and a physician. They offer details and observations on all facets of the
lives of those they meet, consider social
customs and physical conditions, and make
comparisons with Europe. Particular emphasis
is placed on physical description of the terrain and the sanitary practices of the Indians
of the interior. DLC LNHT

846 Schiavo-Campo, Salvatore. Import Structure
and Import Substitution in the Central American Common Market. Río Piedras: University
of Puerto Rico, 1972. v, 122 pp. Biblio.
A survey and summary of the changes in the
import patterns of each country from 1953 to
1968, with a brief analysis. DLC LNHT

847. Schlesinger, Alfredo. El arma secreta: la
quinta columna. Guatemala: Centro Editorial,
1940. 74 pp. Tables.
A denunciation of Nazi fifth columns, with
a brief description of their role in the European war and a compilation of Central American
legislation designed to control them, along
with a discussion of potential activities in
Central America and a listing of supposed
Nazis among the Central American German community, clearly designed to expose suspects
and explain the need for legislation to the
general public. DLC BNG

848 _____. Centro América en peligro.
Guatemala: Unión Tipografía, 1942. 22 pp.
A wartime propaganda tract, written as a
call to arms for Central America, arguing that
just as in the case of Singapore, the logical
way to attack the Panama Canal would be by
land, not from the sea, and hence that all
Central America was in danger of Japanese or
German efforts to land there and use the isthmus as a base for an attack on Panama. Cites
the strategic location of the isthmus and the
danger of fifth columns among the German colonies in each of the nations. LNHT

849 Schmidt, George. Souvenir de América Central.
Matagalpa, Nicaragua, and San Francisco: G.
Schmidt, 1903. 49 pp. Illus.
A photo album, with identifying captions,
containing photos from all five republics,
showing city and rural scenes. DLC

850 Schmitter, Philippe C. Autonomy or Dependence
as Regional Integration Outcomes: Central
America. Berkeley: University of California
Press, 1972. viii, 87 pp. Biblio., notes,
tables.
This study contends that the Common Market
has shown considerable accomplishment as well
as severe limits, noting that it has facili-
tated both local development and the penetration of foreign companies and agencies. This,
the author concludes, reflects the limited
role of the technicians and integrationists,
the strength of local nationalism, and the
fact that all the member countries are closely
tied to a single external source, namely, the
United States, which limits their options and
prospects. It is noted that although the
Yankees have exhibited considerable policy

flexibility, allowing the Central American nations to decide in each case whether to act as a unit or separately, the fact that these small nations must deal with such a giant on all issues prevents experience in smaller markets. DLC LNHT

851 Schottelius, Herbert. Mittelamerika als Schauplatz deutscher Kolonisationsversuche, 1840-1865. Hamburg: Hans Christians Druckerei & Verlag, 1939. 111 pp. Biblio., notes.

A well-researched discussion of German colonization in the region, with particular emphasis on Guatemala, the Mosquito Coast, and Costa Rica, based on archival research in Germany and published works about German emigration. DLC LNHT

852 Schötz, Waltrand. Die Bananenkulturen in Mittelamerika und Westindien: eine wirtschaftsgeographische Studie. Ochsenfurt am Main: Buchdruckerei Fritz & Rappert, 1935. 95 pp. Tables.

A comprehensive study of the development of the banana industry, considering the physical and climatic conditions necessary, it's importance to the countries of Central America and the West Indies in which it is grown, and the role of the United Fruit Company in promoting the industry, with consideration of trade competition between American and British companies. Includes brief separate sections on the significance of the industry in each of the nations of the Caribbean and Central America, with trade statistics. NN

853 Schultze-Jena, Leonhard Sigmund. Indiana. 3 vols. Jena: Gustav Fischer, 1933-38. 394, 364, 384 pp.

A massive series tracing the culture and social and religious customs of the Indian groups of Middle America, based on extensive fieldwork during the 1930s, reproducing the legends collected, with analysis of the principal characteristics. The initial volume deals with the Quiché of Guatemala, the second with the Pipil of El Salvador, and the third with the groups of southern Mexico. The series encompasses the major linguistic groupings of the region, and while there is considerable focus on the present state of the Indians and their current beliefs and lifestyles, the effort to trace the influences upon them sheds considerable insight on the influence of the pre-Columbian societies and the persistence of their beliefs. DLC LNHT

854 Schumacher, Karl von. Mexiko und die Staaten Zentralamerikas: Geschichte, Politik, Wirtschaft. Zürich and Leipzig: Orell Füssli Verlag, 1928. 174 pp. Illus., maps.

A general introduction that surveys economic and political development and class structure. About half the volume is devoted to Central America. DLC

855 Secretaría Permanente del Tratado General de la Integración Económica Centroamericana. 5 años de labores en la integración económica centroamericana. Guatemala: n.p., 1967. 72 pp. Illus., maps, tables.

An official summary of the accomplishments and status of the market through 1967, as seen by its own secretariat. DLC

856 _____. La comercialización de los principales productos agropecuarios en el proceso de integración económica centroamericana. Guatemala: SIECA, 1967. 86 pp.

A study of the agricultural sector, with proposals for its improvement. Calls for efforts to commercialize the small holdings and promote a shift from subsistence agriculture to other crops. Emphasizes the need to increase credit, improve transportation facilities, and develop new markets and marketing systems to provide small landholders with the means to enter commercial agriculture. BNG

857 _____. Convenios centroamericanos de integración económica. 4 vols. Guatemala: n.p., 1963-68.

The official texts of the various agreements and codes involved in the Common Market. FU

858 _____. El desarrollo integrado de Centroamérica en la presente década: bases propuestas para el perfeccionamiento y la reestructuración del Mercado Común Centroamericano. 11 vols. Buenos Aires: Banco Interamericano de Desarrollo, 1973. Tables.

An exhaustive economic analysis of the Common Market, detailing its accomplishments during the 1960s, its problems at the end of the decade and its future prospects, with projections and recommendations for improvement. The initial volume summarizes the conclusions, with the detailed studies and recommendations in the others. The proposals call for increasing integration, uniform financial structures and requirements, free labor movement, uniform codes, and a full customs union. DLC

859 _____. Inventario de estudios básicos sobre recursos naturales de Centroamérica. Guatemala: n.p., 1964. ii, 127 pp. Biblio., illus., maps, tables.

An annotated bibliography of maps and geographical and geological studies of the region, covering topography, minerals, soils, vegetation, and water resources. Items are listed alphabetically by author under each of these headings. Includes brief introductions describing the regional characteristics under each of the above themes, but there is no indication of selection criteria. The majority of the entries are maps and journal articles, but also included are theses, mimeographed papers of official institutes and ministries, and some previously unpublished works. LNHT

860 _____. Resoluciones del Comité de Cooperación Económica del Istmo Centroamericano, 1952-1966. Guatemala: n.p., 1967. 254 pp. FU

(Secretaría Permanente del Tratado General de la
Integración Económica Centroamericana)

861 _____. Tratado General de Integración
Económica Centroamericana. Guatemala: Published by the Secretariat, 1964. 70 pp.
  The text of the 1960 accord establishing
the Common Market, with detailed tariff schedules and quotas as established by the agreement. LNHT

862 Seebach, Albert Ludwig Karl von. Über
Vulkane Zentralamerikas: aus
den nachgelassenen Aufzeichnungen. Göttingen:
Dieterische Verlag, 1892. 251 pp. Illus.,
maps, notes.
  Detailed descriptions of each of the
region's principal volcanoes, arranged by
country. Compiled by a German scholar and
mountain climber who was among the first to
scale and report scientifically on the
region's volcanoes during fieldtrips in the
1860s. Includes data on the region, vegetation, and specifics of the dimensions and
nature of each volcano, with some drawings and
maps. TxU

863 Sekai Bunkasha. Sekai Bunka Shirîzu No. 16,
Chuô Amerika [World Culture Series, no. 16:
Central America]. Tokyo, 1964. 146 pp.

864 Seminario de Integración Social de Guatemala.
Aspectos sociales y políticos de la
integración centroamericana. Guatemala:
Ministerio de Educación Pública, 1970. 549
pp. Biblio.
  A series of papers prepared for a conference conducted in 1969. Themes treated include integration, development, population,
agriculture, education, society, and regional
institutions. Under each subject there are
several papers, discussions, and conclusions
containing policy recommendations for the
future development of the Common Market and
the region, focusing on the social impacts.
DLC

865 Seminario sobre Aspectos Económicos, Sociales,
y Políticos de la Inversión Extranjera en
Centro América. Financiamiento extranjero en
América Central. San José: Centro de
Estudios Democráticos de América Latina, 1974.
192 pp. Biblio., tables.
  Papers presented at a seminar in 1973,
including studies of the entire isthmus and
specific papers regarding Guatemala, Honduras,
and Costa Rica. DLC

866 Seminario sobre la situación demográfica
de América Central: perspectivas y
consecuencias. San José: Published by the
Seminar, 1967. vii, 457 pp. Biblio., tables.
2d ed. San José: Published by the Seminar,
1972.
  A collection of papers and studies from a
conference held in San José during 1967. Sections on each of the countries provide projections for the future by age and sex, covering
the years 1960-80, with extensive discussions
of the implications and the methods of projection. They are followed by a regional

analysis of the economically active population, with projections and discussions of the
implications for the services, production, and
facilities needed. Extensive tables and
graphs provide the data and depict the trends.
LNHT

867 Serrano, Abelino. La unión centroamericana.
León: Editorial Metropolitana, 1952. 163 pp.
  A miscellany of speeches, letters, and
newspaper accounts from rallies of unionists
and other events, singing the praises of unionism in emotional rhetoric. DLC

868 Shaw, Royce Q. Central America: Regional
Integration and National Political Development. Boulder, Colo.: Westview Press, 1978.
x, 242 pp. Biblio., notes.
  A survey of the Common Market and its
actions, stressing the role of local politics
in its growth and problems. Rejects the dependency analysis, contending instead that
domestic factors in the various nations were
the principal source of the movement's problems. Concludes that the domestic elites were
heavily involved in the movement from the
outset and were its principal beneficiaries,
and hence that they needed no outside stimu-
lus. Based on secondary sources, the publications of the Market secretariat, and extensive
interviews. LNHT

869 Sibaja Chacón, Luís Fernando. Nuestro límite
con Nicaragua: estudio histórico. San José:
Comisión Nacional de Conmemoraciones
Históricas, 1974. 279 pp. Index, biblio.,
notes, illus., maps.
  A detailed and well-researched history of
the boundary questions between Nicaragua and
Costa Rica, from Colonial times through the
controversy regarding the Bryan-Chamorro
Treaty. Includes consideration of the various
treaties and arbitrations, the negotiations,
and the annexation of Guanacaste. Prints the
texts of the treaties and of the Cleveland
arbitral award, as well as maps of the contentions and changes. Based on appropriate secondary works and published documents. DLC
LNHT BNCR

870 Sicard, Félix. Simples notes sur l'Amérique
Centrale. Paris: Imprimerie de Paul DuPont,
1863. 18 pp.
  The head of a French maritime company
formed to conduct trade and expeditions to
Nicaragua and Costa Rica provides some general
comments, addressed to Napoleon III, about the
prospects of the region and its production,
urging greater French action in this region
and noting American and British efforts. DLC

871 Sierra Franco, Raúl, Napoleon Cueva, and Marco
Virgilio Carías. La industrialización en
Centroamérica y integración económica
centroamericana. San Salvador: Editorial
Universitaria, 1964. 124 pp. Biblio.
  Three separate essays, two dealing with
industrialization and one with the Common
Market, presented to the Seminar on Contempo-
rary History. Sierra Franco argues that

current industrial development does not make sufficient use of local raw materials. Cueva reviews the Salvadoran economy of the 1946-65 period, with statistics, advocating a continued thrust toward industry. Carías reviews the integration movement, seeing dependency and the paucity of agricultural technical assistance as the key problems. DLC

872 Silvela y de Vielleuze, Francisco. Limites entre la Colombie et la Costa-Rica: exposé présenté à Son Excellence M. le président de la Republique Français en qualité d'arbitre par don Francisco Silvela, avocat de la légation de Colombie en Espagne, Madrid, 8 décembre 1898. 2 vols. Paris: Imprimerie Réunies, Motteroz, 1898-99. 73, 106 pp.
    The Colombian case in the arbitral proceedings regarding the frontier between Costa Rica and Colombia, in two separate memoranda by the nation's attorney. DLC BNCR

873 Simposio y Seminario Técnico. La productividad, el desarrollo y la integración económica centroamericana. Guatemala: Centro de Desarrollo y Productividad Industrial, 1967. 133 pp. Illus., tables.
    A seminar for Central American businessmen, sponsored in part by the USAID-ROCAP office. Reproduces the various papers by businessmen describing the prospects of the Common Market and its implications for the region's industries in glowing terms and hailing its impetus for local production. LNHT

874 Sivers, Jegór von. Über Madeira und die Antillen nach Mittelamerika: Reisedenkwurdigkeiten und Forschungen. Leipzig: Carl F. Fleischer, 1861. xii, 388 pp. Index, biblio., notes.
    A descriptive travelogue-geography volume, including information about the economic development of the region during the mid-nineteenth century, recounting travels but also providing narrative backgrounds and basic data, clearly designed for the general audience in his homeland. About half the volume is devoted to Central America, with all countries covered. DLC LNHT

875 Slade, William Franklin. The Federation of Central America. Worcester, Mass.: n.p., 1917. 275 pp. Biblio., notes.
    Originally a doctoral dissertation in political science at Clarke University, published in full in the Journal of Race Relations and available in book form as an offprint. Based on published sources, it offers a survey of attempts at federation from independence to 1907, emphasizing the problems involved. The outlook is profederation, with explanations of the failure of the movements reflecting the prevailing Yankee and European stereotypes of the era of imperialism. Offers a highly critical perspective of the inadequacies and avariciousness of the local populace and politicians, frequently referring to the need for democracy and Yankee values. DLC LNHT

876 Solórzano, Carlos. Los falsos demonios. Mexico: Editorial Joaquín Mortiz, 1966. 217 pp.
    A novel commenting on dictatorship and tyranny, written in the form of a letter from a dying colonel who served in such a regime to his daughter, containing reminiscences, rambling thoughts, and preoccupations. DLC BNG

877 Somarriba Salazar, Jaime. Les limites entre le Nicaragua et le Honduras. Leiden, The Netherlands: A.W. Nijhoff, 1957. 338 pp. Biblio., illus., maps.
Limites entre Nicaragua y Honduras. Leiden, The Netherlands: A.W. Nijhoff, 1962. 349 pp. Biblio., maps, appendixes.
    Originally a legal thesis at the University of Paris, this work by a Nicaraguan reviews the history of the controversy and provides a detailed analysis designed to sustain the Nicaraguan contention that the decision of the king of Spain in 1906 was invalid due to legal technicalities and questions regarding his powers under the agreement. Reproduces all the pertinent accords in full. Contains a 125-page detailed chronology of the dispute, listing and summarizing all significant developments from 1502 through 1957. DLC LNHT

878 Sotela Bonilla, Rogelio. La Doctrina de Monroe desde un punto de vista subjetivo. San José: Imprenta Alsina, 1925. 34 pp.
    A Costa Rican writer's commentary on the Monroe Doctrine, noting its benefits for Latin America at independence and citing Secretary of State Charles Evans Hughes's comments on the doctrine's centennial. Hails the diminishing intervention of the Yankees and defends some of their actions as responding to internal conditions or solicitations in the various Latin American nations, while noting that the latest Nicaraguan elections were won by parties critical of the U.S. despite the Yankee presence. DLC BNCR

879 Soto Blanco, Ovidio. La educación en Centroamérica. San Salvador: ODECA, 1968. iv, 144 pp. Biblio., notes, illus., tables.
    A discussion of all aspects of contemporary education in Central America, including future projections, indicating deficiencies and needs, identifying similarities and common trends, and indicating the areas in which cooperation would be most beneficial. Includes statistics regarding the present situation and trends in students, classrooms, costs, facilities, salaries, employment prospects, and many more. DLC LNHT BNCR

880 _____. Situación actual y perspectivas hacia el futuro en el desarrollo de la educación pública centroamericana. San Salvador: ODECA, 1969. 51 pp.
    A summary of the author's La educación en Centroamérica, emphasizing the future projections. BNCR

881 Soto de Avila, J. Victor, ed. Hombres (Quién es Quién): diccionario biográfico

(Soto de Avila, J. Victor, ed.)
centroamericano. Guatemala: Editorial Istmo, 1944. 390 pp. Index.

A Who's Who type volume containing alphabetically arranged brief biographical listings for Central American university professors actively teaching at the time of publication, compiled by a professor and newspaper editor. Contains an index by country. Guatemala is most heavily represented, but all five countries are included. DLC LNHT

882 _____. Quién es quién en Centro-América y Panamá. Guatemala: Imprenta Hispánica, 1954. 218 pp. Illus.

A revised edition of the 1944 who's who volume, with photos and brief biographical listings for Central American university professors, arranged alphabetically by country. CU-B

883 Spain, Mildred W. "And in Samaria": A Story of Fifty Years' Missionary Witness in Central America, 1890-1940. Dallas: Central American Mission, 1940. 269 pp. Illus., maps. 2d ed. Dallas: Central American Mission, 1954. 328 pp. Illus., maps.

An account of the missionary activities of a fundamentalist but nondenominational Protestant group, stretching from its initial efforts in Costa Rica in 1890 and extending throughout the entire isthmus and into the mid-twentieth century. The second edition contains additional material bringing the narrative up to 1950, though the post-1940 section is rather brief. The emphasis is on the individuals who staffed the missions and the organizational basis, viewing the area as hostile and the effort as that of a crusade. DLC

884 Spitzler, James R., and Enrique Soto. Estudio centroamericano de transportes: informe resumido. Guatemala: SIECA, 1966. 129 pp. Maps, tables.
Central American Transportation Study: Summary Report. Guatemala: ROCAP, 1966. 129 pp. Maps, tables.

A comprehensive transportation survey of the entire region, considering use of the various types of transport, linkages between them, connections between countries, linkage of the interior and the ports, the importance of the various ports and zones, and imports and exports. Statistics refer to the 1964-74 period, with some projections to 1984. DLC BNCR

885 Squier, Ephraim George. Monograph of Authors Who Have Written on the Languages of Central America. London: Trübner & Co.; New York: J. Munsell, 1861. 70 pp.

A comment on the scholarship of the era dealing with the local languages and dialects. In the form of an annotated bibliography arranged alphabetically by author, it focuses on dictionaries of local speech and particularly on dictionaries and linguistic studies of the Indian dialects and languages. DLC

886 _____. The States of Central America. New York: Hurst, 1858. 3d ed. New York: Harper & Bros., 1878. xvi, 782 pp. Index, biblio., illus., maps.
Los estados de Centro América. San José: Imprenta Gutenberg, 1929.

A well-known U.S. diplomat in the isthmus and a prolific writer, Squier here offers an expanded version of his Notes on Central America (see HO422), covering all five countries and Belize in this volume. It combines personal observation with scholarly research in an effort to offer a comprehensive account, in encyclopedic detail, of the region as it was then, and to introduce it to a North American reading audience. DLC LNHT

887 Staudenmayer, L.R. The Loss of the [sic.] Central America: Or the Voice of God Upon the Waters. New York: Daniel Dana, Jr., 1857. 26 pp.
DLC

888 Stavenhagen, Rodolfo. Clases, colonialismo y aculturación: ensayo sobre un sistema de relaciones interétnicas en Mesoamérica. Guatemala: Ministerio de Educación Pública, 1968. 73 pp. Biblio., notes.

Examining the changes in the class structure since Colonial times, the author emphasizes that although some Colonial patterns persist, acculturation is changing the social structure, with the ladino class being different from that of Colonial days, and ethnic stratification being replaced by cultural and economic stratification. DLC BNG

889 Stephens, John Lloyd. Incidents of Travel in Central America, Chiapas, and Yucatan. 2 vols. Many editions, various pagings. New York: Harper & Bros., 1841.
Incidentes de viaje en Centro América, Chiapas y Yucatán. San José: Imprenta Gutenberg, 1929. 2d ed. Quezaltenango: Tipografía "El Noticiero Evangélico," 1939-40.
Reiseerlebnisse en Zentralamerika, Chiapas und Yucatan. Leipzig: n.p., 1854. 554 pp. Illus., maps.

A classic, consisting of the description and memoirs of a Yankee traveler and diplomat sent to Central America during 1839 as United States representative to the Federation. He used his stay to explore widely, discovering hitherto unknown Maya archeological zones. His volume combines accounts of travel, descriptions of the terrain, his initial impressions of and wonderment at the lost cities with discussions of his diplomatic efforts, contemporary politics, and graphic descriptions of the habitual internecine conflicts of the region. The account is also rich in detail regarding conditions of life and customs. It is the work of a professional observer who is an accomplished author and an artist who accompanied him. DLC DLC-LDS-532 LNHT BNCR

890 _____. Memoir of an Eventful Expedition in Central America, Resulting in the Discovery of the City of Iximaya. New York: Applegate, 1860. 35 pp.

General Central America

An account of the adventures and problems
of an expedition by Stephens and his discovery
of an archeological zone. Includes physical
description of the area, the transportation
difficulties, and his encounters with contemporary Indians of the region. DLC

891 Strandnaes, Børge. Fire lande uden vejskilt:
sorgløse rejseoplevelser fra Mellemamerika.
Copenhagen: Borgens Forlag., 1954. 196 pp.
Illus.
      A travelogue, emphasizing the Indians, but
including background notes and historical
outlines. DLC

892 Sue, Joseph. Henri le Chancelier: souvenirs
d'un voyage dans l'Amérique Centrale. Paris:
Pagnerre, Libraire-Éditeur, 1857. 234 pp.
      A travelogue, in semifictional form, re-
counting the travels of Henri, who served as
chancellor to the French consul in Guatemala
during the 1840s. Last names and dates are
used only in connection with Central American
historical figures, but not with the Frenchmen
or the individuals they met. Emphasis is on
description and travel, though some discussion
of political events in the isthmus is included. DLC

893 Suñol Leal, Julio C. El gran carnival:
reunión de presidentes de Centro América y los
Estados Unidos. San José: Imprenta Elena,
1963. 95 pp.
      Taking as its departure President Kennedy's
visit to Central America, this work mocks the
proceedings as a carnival with little accomplishment save for public relations, and argues that the development needs of the nation
require domestic decisions based on nationalism rather than cooperative ones with other
powers or through the Alliance for Progress.
Includes denunciation of the role of foreign
companies and investment in the nation. DLC

894 Szászdi, Adam. Nicolás Raoul y la República
Federal de Centro-América. Madrid: Gráficas
Bachende, 1958. 220 pp. Index, biblio.,
notes, illus.
      A revised version of the author's doctoral
dissertation, this work traces the participation of a former officer under Napoleon, whose
role in the combats of the 1820s illustrates
the importance of foreign adventurers and
officers in these civil wars. DLC LNHT BNG

895 Tamames Gómez, Ramón. Aspectos económicos de
la vinculación de Panamá al Mercado Común
Centroamericano. Panamá: Ministerio de
Relaciones Exteriores, 1966. 210 pp.
      An official report to the Panamanian gov-
ernment, providing a detailed analysis of the
potential implications for Panama of affiliation with the Common Market. Considers economic and social aspects, and potential
problems regarding the Colon Free Zone and the
Canal Zone. The focus is on the implications
within Panama, but it includes considerable
data regarding the trade potential between
Panama and the other isthmian republics, market possibilities, transportation links, and
similar themes that provide data about the

entire region and the degree to which Panama
is associated with the other states. DPU

896 Taplin, Glen W., ed. Middle American
Governors. Metuchen, N.J.: Scarecrow, 1972.
196 pp. Biblio.
      A chronological listing of the heads of
government (whatever their titles) of Mexico,
Panama, and each of the Central American nations. Includes Colonial and modern periods,
as well as heads of Indian groups in Mexico
and Guatemala. DLC LNHT

897 Tax, Sol, et al. Heritage of the Conquest:
The Ethnology of Middle America. Glencoe,
Ill.: Free Press, 1952. 312 pp. 2d ed. New
York: Cooper Square, 1968. 312 pp. Index,
biblio., maps.
      Papers presented at a conference of anthro-
pologists, focusing on the present-day Indians
of Meso-America and including transcripts of
the subsequent discussion. The distinguished
authors deal with such aspects as acculturation, the local economy, ethnic and communal
relations, and religious and political organization. DLC LNHT

898 Taylor, Bayard. Eldorado; or, Adventures in
the Path of Empire: Comprising a Voyage to
California . . . and Incidents of Mexican
Travel. London: H.G. Bohn, 1850, 360 pp.
Latest ed. Glorieta, N.M.: Río Grande Press,
1967. Illus.
      A travel account based on an 1884 trip.
DLC

899 Taylor, James Milburn. On Muleback through
Central America. Knoxville, Tenn.: James M.
Taylor, n.d. [1913]. 146 pp. Illus.
      The memoirs of an evangelical missionary
during a 1912 "crusade" traveling and preaching the gospel across Central America. The
emphasis is on travel, hardship, and local
conditions. The author clearly is an itiner-
ant preacher who spends at least as much time
traveling as preaching, but does reach some
remote locations. Includes descriptions of
his adventures and the places he visited while
traveling throughout the entire isthmus, as
well as choice words about the evils of the
Roman Catholic Church in the region, and its
promotion of "idols" such as the Black Christ
of Esquipulas. LNHT

900 Termer, Franz. Paisajes geográficos del
norte de la América Central. Madrid:
Imprenta del Intendencia e Intervención
Militares, 1933. 28 pp.
      A description of the general geographic and
climatic conditions of the region between the
Guatemala-Honduras border and the Isthmus of
Tehuantepec, viewing the area in terms of
geographic regions characterized by landforms
and flora and fauna, indicating the broad
patterns. LNHT

901 Thompson, Wallace. Rainbow Republics of Central America. New York: E.P. Dutton, 1926.
xi, 284 pp. Index, illus. 2d ed.
Chautauqua, N.Y.: Chautauqua Press, 1927.

An experienced travel-book author provides his impressions of the isthmus during a trip in the 1920s, covering geographical and physical features, cities, economies, and lifestyles, with expansive explanatory and background notes that place his observations in their context. DLC LNHT

902 Tikhomirov, V.P., ed. Strany Ameriki: Geograficheskie spravki: Meksiko, Gvatemala, Gonduras, Britanskii Gonduras, Salvador, Nikaragua, Kosta-Rika, Panama [The countries of Central America, geographical references: Mexico, Guatemala, Honduras, British Honduras, Salvador, Nicaragua, Costa Rica, Panama]. Moscow: Geograficheskaj Literatury, 1958. 54 pp.

903 Tilev, H. Ostrovna i Sredna Amerika [Central America and the Caribbean islands]. Sofia: Nauka i Izkustvo, 1960. 258 pp.

904 Tobar Cruz, Pedro. Valle: el hombre, el político, el sabio. Guatemala: Ministerio de Educación Pública, 1961. 355 pp. Biblio., notes, illus.
A biography of José Cecilio del Valle, emphasizing his role in the independence era and the politics of the Federation, originally inspired by a 1959 rumor that the Ministry of Education planned to omit Valle from its curriculum. The author seeks to show that although Valle was not involved in the initial movements for independence and opposed annexation to Mexico, he did support the ultimate efforts and worked diligently within the Federation government, and defends his stands. The volume quotes liberally from the documents and proclamations of the era. DLC LNHT BNG

905 Toledo Palomo, Ricardo. Las artes y las ideas de arte durante la independencia. Guatemala: Tipografía Nacional, 1977. 237 pp. Biblio., notes, illus.
After several chapters summarizing the Colonial era, this volume focuses on the 1791-1821 period, examining the intellectual currents and significant intellectual figures. Discusses the significance of the Academia de Pintura de Guatemala and the reformation of the Economic Society, indicating the relationship between the new currents of local influences in art on the tendencies toward independence. BNG

906 Tonblitz, C. Con la historia entre las manos. Tegucigalpa: Imprenta Atenea, 1965. 60 pp.
Part of the continuing polemic regarding the collapse of the Federation in the early years of independence and the role of Francisco Morazán and Rafael Carrera. Includes a statement by this Honduran scholar that was originally written in 1949 and some of his comments about various other scholars and responses, most directed at the newspaper commentaries of Clemente Marroquín Rojas. LNHT

907 Torres Rivas, Edelberto. Procesos y estructuras de una sociedad dependiente: Centroamérica. Santiago: Ediciones Prensa Latinoamericana, 1969. 210 pp. Biblio., notes, tables. 3d ed. San José: EDUCA, 1973. 319 pp.
A history of the unionist movement from the viewpoint of the dependency theory. Argues that the region's main problem is its external dependence and the internal dominance of its oligarchies, which increased with each stage of economic development. Repeats the charges that the Common Market favors external capital and hence increases dependency, thereby exacerbating the region's social problems. Later editions use the title Interpretación del desarrollo social centroamericano. DLC LNHT BNG BNCR

908 Torres Rivas, Edelberto, et al. Centro América hoy. Mexico: Siglo XXI, 1975.
A collection of dependency analyses, identifying what these Central American scholars describe as the critical problems of the present. Includes political and economic studies dealing with such themes as foreign investment, the Common Market, and rural conditions. DLC

909 _____. Financiamiento extranjero en América Central. San José: CEDAL, 1974. 192 pp. Index, notes, tables.
A series of essays dealing with various aspects of foreign financing in Central America, viewed within the dependency theory and focusing on the political rather than the economic implications. Includes specific essays on Guatemala, Honduras, and Costa Rica, as well as more general considerations, some historical and some contemporary, with statistics regarding loans by foreign banks to these nations. DLC LNHT BNCR

910 Townsend Ezcurra, Andrés. Fundación de la República. Guatemala: Ministerio de Educación Pública, 1958. 284 pp. Index, notes. 2d ed. San José: Editorial Costa Rica, 1973. 488 pp. Index, biblio., notes.
A careful study of the Constituent Assembly of the Federation of Central America and the constitution it prepared, covering the years 1823 and 1824. Based on research in the Archivo General de Centroamérica and appropriate secondary works, this work by a Peruvian historian considers the preliminaries, details each session of the Assembly and its debates, with appropriate excerpts, and then analyses the constitution by topic. The expanded second edition is entitled Las Provincias Unidas de Centroamérica: fundación de la República. DLC LNHT BNG BNCR

911 Toyama, Taeko. Chûnambei Hitori Tabi [My journey to Central America]. Tokyo: Asahi Shimbun Sha, 1964. 207 pp.

912 TSC Consortium. Central American Transportation Study, 1964-1965. 2 vols. Washington, D.C.: TSC Consortium, 1965. 656, 536 pp. Maps, tables.
A detailed survey of Central American transportation facilities and future needs, covering all forms of transport throughout the

region, conducted by consulting and engineering firms from the U.S. and Costa Rica. Tables and statistics generally cover the previous decade with projections to 1984. DLC LNHT

913 Tulane University, Middle American Research Institute. Department of Middle American Research of the Tulane University of America: Its Activities and Its Aims. New Orleans: MARI, 1928. 30 pp. Illus. 2d ed. New Orleans: MARI, 1932. 39 pp. Illus.

A history of the research institute and its work, expeditions, and museum. DLC LNHT

914 _____. An Inventory of the Manuscript Collection of the Department of Middle American Research. 4 vols. New Orleans: MARI, 1937-44.

A listing of the holdings of the various collections, with information and a useful index. Includes two volumes of maps, with a separate one for the F.D. Hoffman collection, and a volume of the Walker papers, as well as a volume of miscellaneous papers. DLC LNHT

915 Tunnermann Bernheim, Carlos. Pensamiento universitario Centro-Americano. San José: EDUCA, 1980.

916 Turcios Ramírez, Salvador. Al margen del imperialismo yanquí. San Salvador: Talleres Tipografía de Putriz, 1915. 291 pp.

A series of essays denouncing Yankee imperialism and the threat of economic domination of Central America, and reviewing the history of the nineteenth century, focusing on efforts to unify the isthmus and the campaigns against William Walker. Also included are commentaries on various general themes, and on historical ones such as independence and the unification campaigns of Gerrardo Barrios. DLC LNHT

917 _____. El prócer Dr. José Matías Delgado. San Salvador: Imprenta Nacional, 1917. 45 pp.

A sympathetic biographical sketch of one of the leaders of the independence movement, extolling his contributions. DLC

918 Unión Democrática Centroamericana. Carta dirigida a la Conferencia Interamericana de Chapultepec. Mexico: n.p., 1945. 15 pp.

An exile protest against the participation of the dictatorial isthmian governments in the hemispheric conference, equating them with the governments of Spain and Argentina, already under sanctions, and requesting similar action against the regimes in Honduras, Nicaragua, and El Salvador. DLC

919 _____. Por qué lucha Centro América. Mexico: Gráfica Panamericana, 1943. 77 pp.

An exile group operating from Mexico formed the Unión Democrática and herein states their principles, attacking what they call the "de facto" regimes and their tyranny in Guatemala, El Salvador, Honduras, and Nicaragua, with protests and letters linking their struggle to

democracy, the world war, the Atlantic Charter, the Four Freedoms, and all the other then-current catch phrases of wartime allied propaganda. DLC LNHT

920 United Fruit Company. The Story of the Banana. Boston: United Fruit Co., Educational Dept., 1931. 40 pp. Illus., maps. Latest ed. Boston: United Fruit Co., Educational Dept., 1941. 56 pp. Illus.

An account of the process of establishing and running a banana plantation, with comments on the state of the banana trade in 1938, designed for the general reader to provide information about the company's work and investments. DLC

921 United Nations. The Population of Central America (Including Mexico), 1950-1980: Future Population Estimates by Sex and Age. New York: U.N., 1954. 84 pp. Maps, tables. Reprint. Millwood, N.Y.: Kraus Reprint, 1974.

A series of population projections for the entire Middle American region, including Mexico and Panama as well as Central America, using 1950 census data to project population trends and characteristics through 1980. The methods employed are explained and the data are presented in tabular form, with the focus on age and sex distribution, in an effort to produce data useful for policy-making. LNHT

922 U.S., Congress. House. Committee on International Relations. Human Rights in Nicaragua, Guatemala, and El Salvador: Implications for U.S. Policy. Washington, D.C.: GPO, 1976. xi, 256 pp. Biblio., tables.
DLC

923 _____. Senate. Committee on Foreign Relations. Foreign Loans Hearings before Subcomittee, of the Committee on Foreign Relations, United States Senate, 69th Congress, 2nd Session pursuant to S. Con. Res. 15, Relative to engaging the Responsibility of the Government in Financial Relations between Its Citizens and Sovereign Foreign Governments. Washington, D.C.: GPO, 1927. iii, 94 pp. Tables.
DLC

924 U.S., Gov't of. Dept. of Navy, Hydrographic Office. Naval Air Pilot, Central America. Washington, D.C.: GPO, 1937. vi, 262 pp. Illus., maps, tables.

Descriptions of existing airfields and emergency landing sites, including those for seaplanes, in each country of the region, with full data. Includes photos and maps of many. DLC

925 _____. _____. Weather summary, Central America, for Use with Naval Air Pilot. Washington, D.C.: GPO, 1948. 166 pp. Illus.
DLC

926 _____. Dept. of State. Conference on Central American Affairs: Special Handbook for the

(U.S., Gov't of)
Use of the Delegates. Washington, D.C.:
GPO, 1922. 56 pp.
Contains the treaties of the 1907 Washington Conference, in Spanish and English, and the U.S. invitation to the 1923 conference. DLC

927 ____. ____. The Woven Strands: Cooperation in Central America. Washington, D.C.: GPO, 1968. iv, 20 pp. Illus.
Excerpts from President Johnson's statements during his Central American trip in July 1968, with profuse illustrations. DLC

928 Uriarte, Ramón [Renato Murray, pseud.]. La convención de 7 de diciembre de 1877: apuntes para la historia de la cuestión de límites entre Guatemala y México. Oaxaca: Imprenta de Gabino Marquez, 1882. 112 pp. 2d ed. Guatemala: Imprenta de Arenales, 1885.
The Guatemalan negotiator's account of the talks that led to the 1877 boundary treaty between Mexico and Guatemala, consisting primarily of the communications, letters, instructions, and documents attendant to the talks; the full accord; various newspaper accounts; and letters exchanged between the author and Guatemalan president Justo Rufino Barrios. The author states that he compiled these materials to defend the accord and himself against attacks in the Guatemalan press. DLC

929 Urquidi, Víctor L. Trayectoria del Mercado Común Latinoamericano. Mexico: Centro de Estudios Monetarios Latinoamericanos, 1960. 178 pp. Biblio., appendixes.
Free Trade and Economic Integration in Latin America: The Evolution of a Common Market Policy. Berkeley: University of California Press, 1962. 190 pp. Biblio.
A prominent Mexican economist traces the organization of the Central American Common Market, detailing the preliminary meetings and the accords and prospects shortly after its formation, with the texts of the treaties and optimistic projections. DLC LNHT

930 Urra Veloso, Pedro. La guerra del banano de la Mamita Yunai a la UPEB. Buenos Aires: Tierra Nueva, 1975. 90 pp. Biblio., tables.
A Costa Rican sociologist's account of the formation of the Union of Banana Exporting Countries in 1974, written with a sympathetic view of the workers' complaints and the standard denunciation of the imperialism of the banana companies, particularly United Fruit. Includes brief historical surveys of banana production and its consequences in Costa Rica, Honduras, and Panama, with Marxist overtones. Focuses on the 1970s. The final third of the volume reproduces the agreement and the initial policy statements of the group, while the earlier narrations are clearly viewed as justifications for these actions. DLC

931 Urrutia, Claudio. Memoria sobre la cuestión de límites entre Guatemala y México presentada al señor ministro de relaciones exteriores por

el jefe de la comisión guatemalteca. Guatemala: Tipografía Nacional, 1900. 325 pp. 2d ed. Guatemala: Tipografía Nacional, 1957. 247 pp.
An official report consisting of a compilation of historical documents regarding the agreements setting the line and detailed discussion of the proper location and the specific geographic landmarks and calculations involved in marking the precise location, and providing the justification for the Guatemalan interpretation of the correct location in accord with the previous agreements. DLC

932 Urtecho, José Andrés. Litigio entre Nicaragua y Honduras: párrafos de una conferencia dictada en Managua; nuestro derecho territorial en la Costa Atlántica y el laudo del rey de España. Guatemala: Tipografía "San Antonio," 1937. 55 pp.
A former Nicaraguan foreign minister defends his country's position in the dispute, reprinting the Bonilla-Gámez accord and reiterating the Nicaraguan contention that the ruling by the king of Spain violated its terms and hence was invalid. DLC LNHT

933 ____. Nuestro derecho territorial en la Costa Atlántica y el laudo del rey de España. Managua: Talleres Nacionales, 1937. 44 pp.
A summary of the dispute between Honduras and Nicaragua, from the viewpoint of a former foreign minister, with a detailed refutation of the ruling by the king of Spain that favored Honduras, disputing word by word the specifics of the ruling and stating the Nicaraguan contention that it violated the terms of the arbitration agreement and hence is not valid. DLC LNHT

934 Valdés Oliva, Arturo. Breves apuntes sobre la independencia. Guatemala: Ministerio de Educación Pública, 1969. 261 pp. Biblio., notes, illus.
A series of essays originally published in El Imparcial of Guatemala City, dealing with the events of 1811 through 1823. Stresses the role of various individuals in the independence movement, including all the well-known figures of the era as well as some lesser lights, and as such serves to clarify the role of these lesser-known figures. DLC LNHT BNG

935 ____. Caminos y luchas por la independencia. Guatemala: Ministerio de Educación Pública, 1956. 482 pp.
The author's major account of the independence movement, based on documentary research in the archives of Costa Rica and Guatemala, containing extensive quotations from the documents. Considers the situations that led to independence during the final days of the Colonial era, the events and leaders of the initial efforts, and the combats involved in attaining independence and in the Mexican incursion, criticizing the Mexican effort and its leader, General Vicente Filísola. DLC LNHT BNG

(Valdés Oliva, Arturo)

936 _____. Centro América alcanzó la libertad al precio de su sangre. Guatemala: Tipografía Nacional, 1965. 106 pp. Biblio., illus.

A series of accounts of early efforts at independence or rebellions against Spanish control, from 1808 to 1821, and the individuals who gave their lives in these efforts, whom the author considers the precursors of the Central American independence movement. Includes lengthy quotations from the documents of the era. DLC LNHT BNG

937 _____. La independencia en la realidad histórica. Guatemala: Tipografía Nacional, 1971. 228 pp. Biblio., notes, illus.

A detailed study of the independence movement in Central America, focusing on the years 1821 through 1823, though including appropriate Colonial background. Based on documents in the Archivo General de Centroamérica and on pertinent secondary works. In tracing the various juntas and congresses and their actions in each of the countries, as well as the Mexican intervention, the author concludes that it was the act of 15 September 1821 that definitively established the independence of Central America. LNHT BNG

938 _____. Los pasos por la independencia y después de la proclamación. . . . Guatemala: Tipografía Nacional, 1957. 130 pp. Biblio., illus., appendixes.

An analysis of the years 1811 through 1823 by a well-known historian of the independence era, consisting of brief factual accounts of the events of key days in the development of the independence movement and the activities of its heroes. Contains numerous photos of the principal figures. Pertinent documents are appended. DLC LNHT BNG

939 Valenciano Rivera, Rosendo de Jesús. ¿Enseñanza religiosa o enseñanza laica? Es la gran cuestión de actualidad. San José: Imprenta Lehmann, 1910. 83 pp.

A defense of Catholic education and the place of religious education in the schools, attacking the Liberal claims for secular education and what he calls a state monopoly of education, written by a priest and published with the support of the diocese. The author calls moral values coming from religion the basis of the nation, and defends the right of all to receive religious instruction. DLC DLC-LDS-160

940 Valladares, Paulino. Movimiento unionista (initiativa del señor presidente doctor Francisco Bertrand). Tegucigalpa: Tipografía Nacional, 1917. iii, 227 pp.

A collection of pro-unionist articles that originally appeared in El Cronista of Tegucigalpa, detailing the movement for isthmian federation in the years immediately preceding the centennial of independence. Focuses especially on and lauds the efforts of the Honduran government. The articles include the texts of the pertinent communications between the various governments. DLC LNHT

941 Valladares Rubio, Manuel [Frences Redish, pseud.]. Biografías: del Doctor Don José Matías Delgado y General Don Manuel José Arce. San Salvador: Tipografía "La Unión," 1911. 98 pp. 3d ed. Guatemala: Editorial Aguirre Velásquez, 1911. 140 pp. Biblio., illus.

Eulogistic biographies extolling their contributions to the independence movement, published on the occasion of the centennial of Central American independence. The third edition also contains a biography of Domingo Antonio de Lara and employs the title Próceres de la independencia: estudios biográficos. BNG

942 _____. Sucesos precursores de la independencia. Guatemala: Editorial del Ejército, 1971. 303 pp. Illus.

A study of the Guatemalan role in the Cortes of Cádiz, which the author contends was a precursor of independence in Central America. Based on the minutes of the Cortes. The major portion of the volume is devoted to a biography of Antonio Larrazábal, who headed the Guatemalan delegation; briefer biographies of all other delegates are also included. DLC LNHT BNG

943 Valle, José Cecilio del. Cartas de José Cecilio del Valle. Mexico: Secretaría de Educación Pública, 1943. 235 pp. 3d ed. Tegucigalpa: Universidad Nacional Autónoma de Honduras, 1963. 255 pp.

A compilation of the letters and correspondence that provides valuable documentation for the entire period and the complicated politics it entailed, as well as information regarding the role of Valle. DLC LNHT

944 _____. Discursos de José Cecilio del Valle en varios sesiones del Congreso Federal de 1826. Tegucigalpa: Tipografía Nacional, 1897. 80 pp.

Selections from the debates, providing the comments of this Central American independence leader on various legal and constitutional questions, particularly penal codes and security laws. The items under discussion are varied and the comments are offered without context, with the question under debate identified only by the speaker's allusions. LNHT

945 _____. Discursos de José del Valle en el Congreso Federal de Centro América de 1826. Guatemala: Imprenta La Unión, n.d. 16 pp. DLC

946 _____. Escritos del licenciado José Cecilio del Valle. Vol. 1, "El Amigo de la Patria." Guatemala: Ministerio de Educación Pública, 1969. 315 pp. Biblio., illus., maps. 2d ed. Tegucigalpa: Presidencia, Oficina de Relaciones Públicas, 1972. 340 pp. Illus., maps.

A reproduction of Valle's newspaper, El Amigo de la Patria, for 1820 and 1821, designed to show Valle's views and role in independence. The issues are reproduced in their

(Valle, José Cecilio del)
entirely, without comment. The second edition
uses only the newspaper name as its title.
LNHT BNG

947 ____. Pensamiento vivo de José Cecilio del
Valle . . . . Selección y prólogo de Rafael
Heliodoro Valle. San José: Ministerio de
Educación Pública, 1943. 2d ed. San José:
EDUCA, 1971. 285 pp.
A compilation of essays and articles written by Valle that show his universality and
the breadth of his ideas. Although most of
the articles are identified by date, there is
no indication as to the sources or whether,
and if so where, they were previously published. DLC LNHT BNG

948 Valle, José Cecilio del, and Jorge del Valle
Matheu, eds. Obras de José Cecilio del Valle.
2 vols. Tegucigalpa: Ministerio de
Instrucción Pública, 1906-14. 296, 380 pp.
Latest ed. Guatemala: Sánchez & de Guise,
1929-30. 316, 380 pp. Notes, illus.
A collection of manifestos, documents,
declarations, and random writings and comments
by Valle, including official documents. The
second volume, a reprinting of Valle's newspaper El Amigo de la Patria for the years
1820-22, details his stands in the independence struggle. Includes a brief biography of
Valle by Ramón Rosa and a collection of commentaries about Valle by various writers. DLC
LNHT

949 Valle, Rafael Heliodoro, ed. La anexión de
Centro América a México (documentos y escritos
de 1821). 6 vols. Mexico: Secretaría de
Relaciones Exteriores, 1924-49. Biblio.
A collection of documents relating to the
independence movement and the Mexican actions
in Central America. Consists primarily of
correspondence and proclamations selected from
the Archives of the Mexican Ministry of Foreign Relations and published sources. The
documents focus on requests for and protests
against Mexican annexation; they also include
the reports of Mexican government officials in
the isthmus. The first volume includes a
narrative by the editor dealing with "precedents," surveying contacts between Mexico and
Central America during pre-Columbian and Colonial times. DLC LNHT

950 ____. Bibliografía de don José Cecilio del
Valle. Mexico: Ediciones de "Numero," 1934.
38 pp. Biblio., illus.
A brief listing of Valle's writings, gathering books, periodical and newspaper articles, political proclamations, speeches, and
laws. Commentary is lengthy, but consists
principally of reproductions of the tables of
contents. Includes separate sections of
Valle's works and of works about him. DLC
LNHT

951 ____. Bibliografía de Rafael de Landívar.
Bogotá: Instituto Caro y Cuervo, 1953.
48 pp.

A brief biographical sketch of this intellectual and priest who served in Central America during the Colonial era; a list of his
publications and their various editions; and
an annotated bibliography of writings about
him, providing basic citations and some commentary, though the length and type of comment
varies greatly. DLC LNHT

952 ____. Cartas de Bentham a José del Valle.
Mexico: Editorial Cultura, 1942. 47 pp.
Biblio., notes, appendixes.
A brief introduction summarizing a series
of exchanges between philosopher Jeremy
Bentham and José Cecilio del Valle from 1821
to 1829, followed by the texts of the fifteen
letters involved. The two discussed the
political future of Central America, with
Bentham recommending works on the philosophy
of government and praising Valle as the best
hope for democracy in the isthmus. DLC LNHT

953 Valle, Rafael Heliodoro. Historia de las
ideas contemporáneas en Centro-América.
Mexico: Fondo de Cultura Económica, 1960.
306 pp. Notes.
A survey of the broad sweep of intellectual
trends in the isthmus, considering historical,
legal, scientific, economic, and philosophical
thought as well as literary trends and such
themes as union, democracy, social reform,
America, Spain, education, the Indians, and
religion. Concludes that despite the prominence of a few figures, intellectual development in the region leaves something to be
desired because of the restrictions imposed by
the political environment and the late development of the region's universities. The
footnotes indicate extensive use of published
works and the press of the various nations.
Includes a final chapter on Panama. DLC LNHT

954 ____. Tierras de pan llevar. Santiago:
Editorial Ercilla, 1939. 189 pp. 2d ed. San
José: EDUCA, 1970. 168 pp.
A series of sixty short stories by a prominent Honduran writer that depict various individuals from throughout Central America and
portray the life-style of the isthmus, using
the setting of its various countries. DLC
LNHT BNCR

955 Vallejo, Antonio Ramón. Historia documentada
de los límites entre la República de Honduras
y los de Nicaragua, El Salvador y Guatemala.
Tegucigalpa: Tipografía Nacional, 1905. 183
pp. 3d ed. New York: n.p., 1938. xvi, 184
pp. Biblio., notes.
A summary of the Honduran viewpoint of the
boundary question, written in 1898 for the
government. Traces the question, with the
usual legal citations and quotations through
the Colonial era and the nineteenth century,
somewhat more briefly than do the official
stands. Indicates through documents the
Colonial jurisdiction of Honduras using them
to support its claims against all of its
neighbors. DLC LNHT

(Vallejo, Antonio Ramón)

956   _____. Límites de Honduras con las repúblicas de Nicaragua, El Salvador, Guatemala, 1899-1926. Tegucigalpa: Tipografía Nacional, 1926. 314 pp. Maps.

Though under a slightly different title, this is in fact a continuation of his Historia documentada. This volume deals entirely with the ownership of the islands in the Gulf of Fonseca and hence with the dispute with El Salvador, tracing the issue from Pre-Columbian times through the conquest and Colonial era, combining some narration with lengthy documentary excerpts designed to buttress the Honduran claims. DLC

957   _____. Réplica al Dr. Santiago I. Barberena: la República de El Salvador no tiene ni nunca ha tenido documentos justificativos de poseer territorio hondureño. Comayagüela: Imprenta Cultura, 1971. 20 pp.

Originally written in 1899 as a newspaper series refuting a Salvadoran publication, this pamphlet constitutes a defense of the Honduran claims to the islands in the Gulf of Fonseca. It was published in the aftermath of the 1969 war with El Salvador to demonstrate that Salvador had always had designs on Honduran territory and that Honduras considered all such claims invalid. DLC

958   Van Sinderen, Adrian. Isthmus maximus. New York: Privately printed, 1948. 68 pp. Illus., maps.

A series of brief chapters, with the initial ones providing historical background for the later travelogue, lavishly illustrated. DLC LNHT

959   Varela, Arturo. Francisco Morazán, el alma centroamericana. Tegucigalpa: Imprenta Atenea, 1959. 108 pp. Illus. 2d ed. Tegucigalpa: Imprenta Esa, 1970.

An historical novel by a Honduran writer who seeks to bring Morazán to life and instill patriotism in the youth of the day by dramatizing his efforts on behalf of independence and union, portraying him as a heroic figure bravely fighting for his ideals. LNHT

960   Vásquez, Mariano. Alegato que el abogado de Honduras en el arbitramento de límites con Guatemala, presenta al Honorable Tribunal Especial, sobre la cuestión previa contenida en el Tratado de Arbitraje celebrado entre ambas repúblicas en 16 de julio de 1930. Tegucigalpa: Ministerio de Relaciones Exteriores, 1931. 40 pp. DLC

961   _____. Arbitraje de límites entre Honduras y Guatemala: alegato de la República de Honduras, sometido al Honorable Tribunal Especial de Límites. Tegucigalpa: Ministerio de Relaciones Exteriores, 1932. vii, 224 pp. Maps.

The Honduran case in the final arbitration of this vexing question. The arguments are based on Colonial jurisdiction and the situation at the time of independence: since

Honduras and Guatemala became independent at the same moment, each is said to have gained its rights only from Colonial jurisdictions. DLC

962   _____. Arbitraje de límites entre Honduras y Guatemala: impugnación de Honduras a la República de Guatemala; Honduras-Guatemala Boundary Arbitration: Rejoinder of Honduras to Counter Case of Guatemala. Tegucigalpa: Ministerio de Relaciones Exteriores, 1932. 560 pp.

The Honduran response to the Guatemalan case. DLC LNHT

963   _____. La cuestión de límites entre Honduras y Guatemala. San Salvador: Imprenta La Salvadoreña, 1928. 32 pp.

A summary of the Honduran case, by its attorney. DLC

964   _____. Informe del doctor don Mariano Vásquez sobre la conferencia de límites celebrada en Washington, del 20 de enero al 16 de julio de 1930. Tegucigalpa: Tipografía Nacional, 1930. 71 pp.

The Honduran attorney's report to his government regarding the mediation sessions. DLC

965   Vázquez, Andrés Clemente, ed. Bosquejo histórico de la agregación a México de Chiapas y Soconusco, y de las negociaciones sobre límites, entabladas por México con Centro América y Guatemala. Mexico: Secretaría de Relaciones Exteriores, 1932. xv, 655 pp. Latest ed. Mexico: Editorial Porrúa, 1971. xv, 661 pp.

A collection of documents from the Mexican Foreign Ministry archives relating to the annexation of Chiapas and Soconusco to Mexico and the resulting boundary dispute with Guatemala. Focuses on the years 1831-32 and covers the mission of Manuel Díaz de Bonilla, the Mexican envoy to Central America, and his efforts to negotiate with the Federation of Central America. Includes his full dispatches and instructions in addition to his reports on the state of Central America at the time and the problems of the Federation. Provides considerable data regarding conditions in Central America during the independence era, as well as about the Mexican intervention in the isthmus. DLC

966   Vega, Juan Ramón, and Greer Taylor. El concubinato en América Central. Cuernavaca: Centro Intercultural de Documentación, 1966. xv, 289 pp. Biblio., notes, tables.

The volume offers the thesis of Vega, a Roman Catholic priest from El Salvador, written in French, followed by a brief article in English by Taylor, an Episcopal priest, both commenting on the practice of consensual rather than legal marriage in the region. Vega views the problem as involving the place of the family in the integration of society, tracing the role of the family through the region's history and noting the failure of church and state to establish strong familial values sufficient to overcome the role of concubine. Taylor criticizes the Episcopal church for tolerating this. Vega concludes that the phenomenon is one of alienation in society as a whole and as such requires a new social integration at a broad level. Vega offers some statistics about the prevalence of concubinage before beginning his own analysis. LNHT

967 Velasquez, César Vicente. El dilema centroamericano. Quito: Casa de la Cultura Ecuatoriana, 1974. 90 pp.
    A study of the Central American Common Market and the 1969 war between El Salvador and Honduras, contending that the dispute involves fundamental differences that will impede the market unless solved. Concludes that frontiers are becoming problems for the Central American people and proposes union as the only solution. DLC

968 Velásquez, Rolando. Entre de selva de neón. San Salvador: Ministerio de Cultura, 1956. 265 pp.
    A novel about the trials and tribulations of life in a big city, focusing on its corrupting influence on the rural peasants who move to it, rather in the tradition of the viewpoint of the city as a monster that swallows up innocent people and changes their values and behavior. DLC LNHT

969 Velásquez Díaz, Max. La aplicación del tratado de Río y la agresión a Honduras. Tegucigalpa: Universidad Nacional Autónoma de Honduras, 1969. 126 pp. Illus., maps, appendix.
    The Honduran version of the 1969 war with Salvador, charging Salvador with aggression and contending that the other nations of the hemisphere were obligated to come to the assistance of Honduras under the Río hemispheric defense pact. DLC

970 _____. Las cuestiones pendientes entre Honduras y El Salvador. Tegucigalpa: 1976, n.p., 40 pp. Maps.
    A brief summary of the boundary question after the 1969 war, with a summary of earlier disputes. Seeks to demonstrate the narrowness of the areas still at issue and provides a dispassionate, if pro-Honduran, account of the negotiations to date. Designed for the general reader in Honduras. DLC LNHT

971 Vergara Escudero, Eduardo. Bases institucionales y jurídicas del Mercado Común Centroamericano. Santiago: Editorial Jurídica de Chile, 1969. 80 pp. Biblio., notes.
    A summary of the origins and early development of the Common Market, with a legal analysis of the key acts. Based on published reports of ODECA and secondary works. DLC LNHT

972 Viera Altamirano, Napoleón. La ciudad universitaria de Centro América. San Salvador: Imprenta Funes, 1940. 172 pp.
    A series of unionist articles, written as part of a campaign launched in 1936 by idealistic students, proposing the combination of the various universities of the Central American nations into a single institution. The articles detail the plans and reprint the proposal as a new impetus toward this long-standing goal. The author was the editor of the newspaper El Diario de Hoy of San Salvador, one of the most outspoken proponents of the plan. DLC

973 _____. Las fronteras malditas. San Salvador: El Diario de Hoy, 1947. 160 pp.
    A series of articles originally published in the author's paper, El Diario de Hoy of San Salvador. Advocates union, traces past efforts to achieve it, and hails the Pact of Santa Ana of 1946 between Guatemala and Salvador, which was the inspiration for the articles. Includes comments about hemispheric cooperation and the balkanization of Europe. DLC

974 _____. Integración económica de Centro América. San Salvador: n.p., 1957. 101 pp.
    A series of pro-unionist essays tracing the history of various unification efforts, hailing the ideal, and emphasizing the common elements in the region's culture and economy. Despite the title the emphasis is on the larger issue rather than the economic integration movement, and little is said about the latter. NN

975 Villagrán Kramer, Francisco. Aspectos jurídicos e institucionales de la integración económica centroamericana. Guatemala: Imprenta EROS, 1967. 198 pp. Biblio.
    Studies regarding the juridical aspects of Central American integration, originally presented at a 1966 congress of the Lawyers Association. Views union favorably, stressing the means of attaining it and the role of legal change, but also noting potential problems such as limitations on the sovereignty of the separate states and the lack of free movement by labor and capital throughout the region. DLC

976 _____. Integración económica centroamericana: aspectos sociales y políticos. Guatemala: Universidad de San Carlos, 1967. 374 pp. Biblio., notes, tables.
    A detailed examination of the various aspects of economic integration, by a proponent of the movement. Considers its effect on the social, political, and economic spheres; the legal, political, and economic bases for such a movement; and the various types possible. Draws upon general theoretical works and legal studies of the region, and applies the general theories to the specifics of Central America. DLC LNHT BNG

977 _____, ed. Mercado Común Centroamericano: regímenes especiales. Guatemala: Ministerio de Educación Pública, 1973. 399 pp. Biblio.
    A series of essays selected from previously published works by Central American scholars, describing the various special programs of the Common Market and containing excerpts from the

appropriate accords. The chapters cover the
various programs designed to offer incentives
to regional trade and businesses, and the
technicalities involved in utilizing them.
DLC

978 Villagrán Kramer, Francisco. Teoría general
del derecho de la integración económica
regional. San Salvador: Ministerio de
Educación, 1969. 383 pp. Notes.
    A legal study of economic unification,
awarded a prize by the Government of El
Salvador. Seeks to identify the various legal
forms such unification could take, and discusses the implications of each. BNG BNCR

979 Viteri Bertrand, Ernesto. El Pacto de Unión
de 1921: sus antecedentes, vicisitudes, y la
cesación de sus efectos. Guatemala:
Imprenta-offset, 1976. 87 pp. Notes.
    A brief, pro-unionist history of the Union-
ist party, the overthrow of the Estrada
Cabrera regime in Guatemala, the resulting
Unionist Pact of 1921, and its failure. Based
on published sources, collections of laws, and
the reports of the Unionist conference. DLC

980 Vivó Escoto, Jorge A. Estudio geográfico
económico de la América Central. Mexico:
PAIGH, 1956. 71 pp. Notes.
    A brief discussion of the principal agri-
cultural products of Central America and the
role of the area in world production, with
basic statistical data. DLC LNHT BNCR

981 Waggoner, George R., and Barbara Ashton
Waggoner. Education in Central America.
Lawrence: University of Kansas Press, 1971.
xi, 180 pp. Biblio., tables.
    A detailed description of education at all
levels throughout the isthmus, considering
primary through University schools and public
and private institutions. Each nation is
examined separately after a brief general
introduction to the isthmus and a history of
education in each nation. Includes consideration of curriculum, pedagogy, institutions,
professors, enrollment, and other factors of
educational concern, and a section dealing
with regional cooperation in the educational
field. DLC LNHT

982 Wagner, Moritz. Naturwissenschaftliche Reisen
im Tropischen Amerika aus geführt auf
Veranlassung und mit Unterstützung weiland Sr.
M. des Königs Maximilian II von Bayern.
Stuttgart: J.G. Cotta'schen. 632 pp. Notes,
tables.
    The main focus is the Central American
isthmus, which occupies over 400 pages, covering the region from Tehuantepec to Panama.
Written in the mid-nineteenth century by a
well-known German naturalist, the volume consists mainly of physical description of the
flora, fauna, and climate of each subregion.
Includes comments on the potential of various
canal routes. DLC

983 Wallström, Tord Kjell Engemund. Andarín:
resa i Centralamerika. Stockholm: Norstedt &
Söners, 1953. 219 pp. Illus., maps.

A Wayfarer in Central America. London:
Arthur Barker, 1955. 192 pp. Illus., maps.
Durch Zentralamerika: von Guatemala nach
Panama. Stuttgart: Pan Verlag, 1956. 248
pp. Illus., maps.
    An account of the adventures of a Swedish
traveler in the isthmus emphasizing physical
description, flora and fauna, the countryside,
adventure, and transportation difficulties,
but with comments also reflecting on customs
and life-styles. DLC LNHT

984 Wappäus, Johann Eduard. Geographie und
Statistik von Mexiko und Zentralamerika. . . .
Leipzig: J.C. Hinrich, 1863. 368 pp.
Tables.
    A standard physical geography, surveying
and providing data on climate, resources,
physical setting, and economy for each nation
and each department, as well as for Central
America in general. DLC LNHT

985 Wardlaw, Andrew B. Achievements and Problems
of the Central American Common Market.
Washington, D.C.: U.S. Dept. of State, 1969.
vi, 46 pp. Tables.
    A brief report for the External Research
Office of the State Department, summarizing in
a few pages each the Common Market programs in
topical areas such as agriculture, integration, external trade, and intraregional trade,
with statistical tables covering the years
1960-65. The author is optimistic about
accomplishments and future prospects. DLC
LNHT

986 Watkin, Virginia G. Taxes and Tax Harmoniza-
tion in Central America. Cambridge, Mass.:
Harvard University Press, 1967. xiii, 519 pp.
Biblio., notes, maps, tables.
    A discussion of the efforts to establish
uniform or at least similar tax structures
within the Central American Common Market to
facilitate trade. Provides a detailed summary
of the tax structures of each of the five
nations, including tax tables, indications of
rates and assessment patterns, and their legal
base. The emphasis is on the current system
and the cooperative efforts begun as part of
the economic integration program. ICU

987 Wauchope, Robert. Modern Maya Houses: A
Study of Their Archaeological Significance.
Washington, D.C.: Carnegie Institute, 1938.
vii, 181 pp. Index, biblio., notes, illus.,
maps, tables, appendixes.
    A detailed descriptive study of Mayan house
types of the 1930s, including both the Yucatan
and northern Central America, classifying them
by construction type and shape. While undertaken with an eye to understanding the works
found in archeological zones, the study provides a wealth of detail on architecture,
structure, construction materials, and the
function of the region's peasant housing. DLC

988 _____. They Found the Buried Cities.
Chicago: University of Chicago Press, 1965.
viii, 382 pp. Index, notes, illus.
    An enthusiastic account of the adventures
of the archeologists who engaged in the

exploration and discovery of various Maya ruins in Mexico and Central America, focusing on the specifics of their expeditions, conditions encountered, dangers braved, and the thrill of discovery. DLC LNHT

989 Wendt, Herbert. <u>Der schwarz, weiss, röte Kontinent: Latinamerika--Reformer und Rebellen</u>. Oldenburg, Germany: Gerhard Stalling Verlag, 1964. 518 pp. Index, maps. <u>The Red, White, and Black Continent: Latin America--Land of Reformers and Rebels</u>. Garden City, N.Y.: Doubleday, 1966. xxiii, 526 pp. Index, maps.

A survey of recent and contemporary conditions, written in picturesque language, that is critical of dictatorship, the upper class, business, and the United States, emphasizing the desire for reform and revolution. The Central American countries receive only forty-three pages, with provocative chapter titles. DLC

990 West, Robert Cooper, and John P. Augelli. <u>Middle America: Its Lands and Peoples</u>. Englewood Cliffs, N.J.: Prentice-Hall, 1966. 482 pp. Index, biblio., illus., maps. 2d ed. Englewood Cliffs, N.J.: Prentice-Hall, 1976. xvii, 494 pp. Index, illus., maps, tables.

Written as a text for a basic geography course dealing with the region, this work includes the island nations, Mexico, and the isthmian republics, employing a cultural approach. Mexico and Central America are covered jointly until independence (in three chapters), which means there is little emphasis on the isthmus. There are two chapters on contemporary Central America, organized topically and emphasizing the current economic and cultural situation. The individual countries are considered only briefly. DLC

991 Weyl, Richard. <u>Erdgeschichte und Landschaftsbild in Mittelamerika</u>. Frankfurt: Verlag Waldemar Kramer, 1965. 175 pp. Biblio., notes, illus., maps, tables.

A detailed geological study focusing on Costa Rica and Guatemala, with emphasis on fault lines but treating the entire range of geological formations and relating them to the entire Caribbean rim at large. Numerous illustrations and maps. DLC

992 _____. <u>Die Geologie Mittelamerikas</u>. Berlin: Gebrüder Bornträger, 1961. xv, 226 pp. Index, biblio., notes, illus., maps, tables.

A detailed geological analysis of the region, with extensive maps and charts, focusing particularly on earth movements, earthquakes, volcanoes, and seismography. Includes charts of the fault lines and the underlying structure of the region. A fifty-page supplement was published separately in 1971 to update the material. DLC LNHT

993 White, Edward Douglas. <u>Opinion and Decision of Edward Douglas White, Chief Justice of the United States in the Matter of the Arbitration of the Boundary Dispute between the Republics</u> of Costa Rica and Panama. Washington, D.C.: n.p., 1914. 37 pp. <u>Fallo arbitral del Chief Justice de los Estados Unidos de América en la controversia de límites de las repúblicas de Costa Rica y Panamá</u>. San José: Tipografía Nacional, 1914.

The White award, reaffirming the Loubet award and providing the ruling that finally settled the disputed frontier, though pressure by the United States was later necessary to secure Panamanian acceptance. The title varies in the editions of each nation. DLC DLC-LDS-143 LNHT BNCR

994 Wilgus, Alva Curtis, ed. <u>The Caribbean: The Central American Area</u>. Gainesville: University of Florida Press, 1961. xix, 383 pp. Index, biblio., notes, maps, tables. 2d ed. Coral Gables, Fla.: University of Miami Press, 1963.

A series of papers by various authors, all specialists in the region, prepared for delivery at one of the Caribbean conferences. The brief presentations encompass a broad range of topics, among them physical setting, culture and society, history, economic development, and international relations. Most of the papers contain footnotes or bibliographies. DLC LNHT

995 _____. <u>Latin America in the Nineteenth Century: A Selected Bibliography of Books of Travel and Description Published in English</u>. Metuchen, N.J.: Scarecrow Press, 1973. x, 174 pp. Biblio.

A listing of travel accounts, with brief commentaries but full citations. A considerable number of the entries relate to Central America. DLC

996 Williams, Mary Wilhelmine. <u>Anglo-American Isthmian Diplomacy, 1815-1915</u>. Washington, D.C.: American Historical Association, 1916. xii, 356 pp. Index, biblio., notes, maps. Reprint. Gloucester, Mass.: Peter Smith, 1965. xii, 356 pp. Index, biblio., notes, maps.

The standard account of the British-American competition for dominance in the Caribbean and control of the Central American canal routes. Though dated (coverage is from 1818 to 1915), it is still useful because it employs manuscript and documentary sources as well as secondary works. The focus is on the two world powers, with Central America viewed primarily as the object of their rivalry. The various efforts to secure and exert influence are meticulously chronicled, and the account is particularly valuable for the details of the British efforts with the Mosquito Indians and the various Anglo-American treaties regarding canal development. The rise of the United States to power status is clearly demonstrated. DLC LNHT

997 _____. <u>Cartographical and Geographical Report Bearing upon the Honduran-Guatemalan Boundary Question</u>. Baltimore: n.p., 1919. 57 pp. Maps. <u>Datos cartográficos y geográficos relacionados con la cuestión de límites entre Honduras y</u>

Guatemala. Tegucigalpa: Tipografía Nacional, 1929. iv, 73 pp. Maps.

A survey of ninety historical maps prepared by a technical expert engaged by the attorneys for Honduras in the boundary arbitration, describing the indications of the boundary location and concluding that throughout history the Honduran frontier has retreated eastward, but that most maps prepared during the Colonial period and through 1850 support Honduran claims to Cape Three Points and the Motagua River valley. The text is printed in English and Spanish, and a large number of maps is annexed. LNHT

998 Wilson, Charles Morrow. Books about Middle America: A Selected Bibliography. New York: Middle American Information Bureau, 1943. 23 pp.

An annotated guide prepared by a publicist associated with the United Fruit Company who was highly familiar with the area, focusing on travelogues and similar works in English, designed for the general reader. The entries are arranged alphabetically by country. DLC

999 ____. Challenge and Opportunity: Central America. New York: Henry Holt, 1941. x, 293 pp. Index, illus., maps. 2d ed. London: Allen & Unwin, 1942. 293 pp. Index, illus.

Written for the general reader, this work provides a brief overview of each country, strangely including Cuba, Jamaica, and Colombia, as well as the isthmian nations, though excluding Belize. The second portion of the volume considers the agricultural characteristics of the region in general by discussing each of the principal crops separately, providing a description of its cultivation and data regarding its importance to the region's economy, with optimistic comments about future prospects. DLC

1000 ____. Empire in Green and Gold: The Story of the American Banana Trade. New York: Henry Holt, 1947. 303 pp. Illus. Latest ed. New York: Greenwood Press, 1968. 303 pp.

An account of the banana industry, its foundation, growth, and organization, by a journalist familiar with the region. Includes discussion of production throughout the Caribbean and the organization necessary for marketing, as well as descriptions of the plantations themselves. The focus is on the early entrepreneurs. Particular attention is paid to the emergence of the Boston Fruit Company, an early predecessor of the United Fruit Company, with which the author was at times associated. Describes the company's facilities, emphasizing the costs and organization involved and the services it provides its laborers and the local populace. DLC LNHT

1001 ____. Middle America. New York: Norton, 1944. x, 317 pp. Index, illus., maps, tables. Reprint. Freeport, N.Y.: Books for Libraries Press, 1971. x, 317 pp. Index, illus., maps, tables.

A general account that includes geography and a brief historical synopsis but whose main focus is on agriculture, with over 100 pages dealing with individual crops, their uses, potential, and production. Includes discussion of air travel, health, a resource inventory, and a chapter dealing with the future. The emphasis is on economic potential, production useful to the United States, and international trade, reflecting the interests of the sponsoring United Fruit Company. DLC LNHT

1002 Winiarski, Andrzej. Strzały w Sierra Madre [Shots in the Sierra Madre]. Warsaw: Wydawn Ministerstwa Obrony Narodowej, 1971. 167 pp.

Though focusing on the Salvadoran-Honduran conflict of 1969, this volume treats all of Central America and is really a vehicle for repeating the standard communist charges of Yankee imperialism, employing all the catchwords while charging Yankee dominance and manipulation in collusion with the local oligarchies. DLC

1003 Woodward, Ralph Lee, Jr. Central America: A Nation Divided. London and New York: Oxford University Press, 1976. 344 pp. Index, biblio., notes, maps, tables.

An effective general survey from discovery to 1975, tracing the common elements and isthmian trends by topic, including the principal political eras and leaders, social trends, and the stages of economic development. The focus is primarily on Guatemala, though this results from that nation's key position in the isthmus. Reflecting Central American experience and viewpoints, Panama is excluded, but Belize is covered. DLC LNHT

1004 The World and Its Peoples: The Caribbean Region and Central America. New York: Greystone Press, 1968. 216 pp. Illus., maps.

A descriptive account for the general reader, with illustrations, focusing on the current situation. DLC

1005 Wylie, Kathryn H. Central America as a Market and Competitor for U.S. Agriculture. Washington, D.C.: GPO, 1959. iv, 35 pp. Illus., maps, tables.

A brief overview identifying the main crops that compete with U.S. exports, such as cotton, and the items that the region is likely to import from the U.S., such as wheat. Includes extensive statistical tables providing historical background regarding production and trade, extending from the 1930s to 1958. DLC

1006 Wynia, Gary W. Politics and Planners: Economic Development Policy in Central America. Madison: University of Wisconsin Press, 1972. xii, 227 pp. Index, biblio., notes, tables.

A detailed and careful account of planning efforts, their results, and their problems. Highlights the disputes between economic technical planners and politicians, which arise from their different focuses and approaches and explain the consistent gap between plans and reality. Includes extensive data regarding the current economy, as well as the history of the various planning agencies and their efforts. DLC LNHT

1007 Young, John Parke. <u>Central American Currency and Finance</u>. Princeton, N.J.: Princeton University Press, 1925. xviii, 258 pp. Biblio., maps.

A detailed account of the fiscal and monetary policies of Central American governments of the early years of the twentieth century, by a Yankee expert and consultant who worked in the area. Contains considerable data about Nicaragua and the Zelaya regime, as well as the impact throughout the isthmus of the economic problems of the post-World War I era, relations with external bankers, monetary instability, and the entire range of economic problems. DLC LNHT

1008 _____. <u>Central American Monetary Union</u>. Washington, D.C.: Agency for International Development, 1965. xv, 165 pp. Tables.

An economist who has served as a financial adviser in the isthmus presents a detailed plan for achieving isthmian monetary union to facilitate the operations of the Common Market, with supporting economic data. Includes capsule summaries of and comparisons to the experiences of the European Common Market. DLC

1009 Zamora Castellanos, Pedro. <u>Vida militar de Centro América</u>. Guatemala: Tipografía Nacional, 1924. 562 pp. Illus., maps. 2d ed. 2 vols. Guatemala: Editorial del Ejército, 1966-67. 277, 397 pp. Illus., maps.

A military history of Central America by a Guatemalan general, providing accounts of the causes, key figures, and campaigns of the region's conflicts. The first volume covers the period from pre-Columbian times through 1840, with emphasis on the independence era and the Federation; the second covers the years 1840 to 1907. They include detailed treatment of all combats and campaigns in the nineteenth century, as well as some concluding essays regarding changes in tactics through the years. There are numerous illustrations but few maps, although each battle is described in detail. DLC LNHT BNG

1010 Zelaya C., Antonio, ed. <u>Ante la conciencia de América: las conferencias de mediación en la controversia de fronteras entre las repúblicas de Honduras y Nicaragua</u>. San José: Imprenta Trejos, 1938. 249 pp. Illus.

The exchanges and documentation from the arbitration of the Honduran-Nicaraguan boundary dispute, held in San José before an arbitral panel representing the United States, Costa Rica, and Venezuela, which led to the definitive resolution of this long-standing dispute. DLC LNHT BNCR

1011 Zelaya Goodman, Chester José. <u>Las tres etapas de la independencia de centroamérica</u>. San José: Universidad de Costa Rica, 1967. 20 pp. Biblio., notes.

A well-known Costa Rican historian of the independence era provides a brief overview of the stages of independence, based on appropriate secondary sources. DLC BNCR

1012 Zeledón Matamoros, Marco Tulio. <u>El acta de independencia de Centro América a la luz de derecho y la razón</u>. San José: Instituto Cultural Costarricense Argentino, 1967. 58 pp. Biblio., notes.

A brief examination of the independence of Central America and its origins, concluding that the isthmus and the other Spanish colonies had a right to independence and were provoked to declaring it by a "cruel and despotic" Spanish administration. Provides various arguments based on Spanish law and on the contemporary situation to support this thesis. DLC LNHT BNCR

1013 _____. <u>Desde la tribuna de la ODECA</u>. San Salvador: ODECA, 1961. 94 pp.

A collection of addresses given by the secretary general of the Organization of Central American States during his first eighteen months in office. DLC LNHT BNCR

1014 _____, ed. <u>Digesto constitucional centroamericano</u>. San Salvador: Imprenta Nacional, 1962. 400 pp.

The secretary general of the Organization of Central American States compiled this volume, which consists of a reproduction of the current constitutions of all five of the isthmian republics as well as Panama, plus the 1824 constitution of the Federation of Central America. LNHT BNG BNCR

1015 Zeledón Matamoros, Marco Tulio. <u>Fronteras de Costa Rica</u>. San José: Imprenta Nacional, 1949. 16 pp.

A concise summary of the various boundary disputes and arbitrations involving Costa Rica with Nicaragua, Panama, and Colombia. DLC BNCR

1016 _____. <u>La ODECA, sus antecedentes históricos y su aporte al Derecho Internacional Americano</u>. San José: Imprenta Lehmann, 1966. xi, 192 pp. Index, biblio., notes, tables.

A detailed history of ODECA and the Common Market, citing precedents from international law and emphasizing the legal aspects. Includes a brief outline history of the previous attempts at union. DLC LNHT

1017 <u>Zentralamerika (Länder und Völker)</u>. Luzern, Switzerland: W. Schweizer; Herausgeber: Kunstreis-Buchverlag, 1965. 447 pp. Illus., maps.

A general, lavishly illustrated encyclopedia, part of a series dealing with various countries and regions. Encompasses geography, people, and culture, providing a brief description of each. The volume includes the Caribbean as well as the isthmus. DLC

1018 Zúñiga Huete, Ángel. <u>Morazán: un representativo de la democracia americana</u>. Mexico: Ediciones Botas, 1947. 434 pp. Illus.

A detailed biography of Morazán, portraying him as one of the heroes of the isthmus and an example for all to follow. The author, a Honduran Liberal political leader, emphasizes

Morazán's "ideology" in a chapter that identifies him with union and liberalism and surveys
subsequent unionist attempts. Includes a
summary of criticisms of the independence
leader. DLC LNHT BNCR

1019 Zúñiga V., Medardo. <u>Al margen de un folleto:
la cuestión de límites entre Honduras y
Guatemala</u>. Comayagüela: Imprenta El Sol,
1927. 27 pp. Maps.
    A brief statement of the Honduran case.
Some citations reverse the order of the title.
DLC

Belize

1 Alonso Chica, L. <u>Deberes</u> <u>de</u> <u>Centroamérica</u>
<u>con</u> <u>Guatemala</u> <u>ante</u> <u>el</u> <u>caso</u> <u>de</u> <u>Belice:</u> <u>la</u>
<u>liberación</u> <u>de</u> <u>Belice,</u> <u>es</u> <u>la</u> <u>causa</u> <u>del</u>
<u>derecho,</u> <u>la</u> <u>causa</u> <u>de</u> <u>la</u> <u>moral,</u> <u>la</u> <u>causa</u> <u>del</u>
<u>honor</u> <u>americano</u>. San Salvador: n.p., 1964.
247 pp.
   A discussion of the Belize question supporting the Guatemalan claim and denouncing
the actions of the British imperialists in
vivid prose; it calls for other Central American states to help their Guatemalan brothers
oust the imperialists.

2 Alvarado, Rafael. <u>La</u> <u>cuestión</u> <u>de</u> <u>Belice</u>.
Quito: Talleres Gráficos Nacional, 1948. 60
pp. Maps. Latest ed. Guatemala: Imprenta
Real, 1958. 60 pp. Maps.
   Excerpts from previous works, designed for
classroom use at the university and to introduce the general reader to the question and
the opinions regarding it. The author supports the Guatemalan claim and advocates
action by the United Nations. DLC LNHT BNG
BNCR

3 Alvarado, Ricardo E. <u>Lo</u> <u>que</u> <u>ha</u> <u>pasado</u> <u>con</u>
<u>Belice:</u> <u>breve</u> <u>bosquejo</u> <u>histórico</u> <u>jurídico</u> <u>de</u>
<u>política</u> <u>internacional</u>. Guatemala:
Ministerio de Educación Pública, 1959. 40
pp. Illus., maps.
   A brief folio outlining the history of the
dispute, with excerpts from key documents,
restating the Guatemalan legal arguments. DLC
LNHT BNG

4 Anderson, A.H. <u>A</u> <u>Brief</u> <u>Sketch</u> <u>of</u> <u>British</u>
<u>Honduras</u>. Belize: Government Printer, 1939.
55 pp. Biblio., maps. 8th ed. Belize:
Government Printer, 1963. 97 pp. Biblio.,
maps.
   Provides an effective summary of the geography and history of the nation, outlining its
social, political, and economic growth and
detailing its institutions and providing current economic statistics, written by a colonial official. A continuation of the series
<u>The</u> <u>Handbook</u> <u>of</u> <u>British</u> <u>Honduras</u> under a new
title. See item BE142. DLC

5 Anderson Morúa, Luís. <u>Estudio</u> <u>jurídico</u> <u>acerca</u>
<u>de</u> <u>la</u> <u>controversia</u> <u>entre</u> <u>Guatemala</u> <u>y</u> <u>la</u> <u>Gran</u>
<u>Bretaña,</u> <u>relativa</u> <u>a</u> <u>la</u> <u>convención</u> <u>de</u> <u>30</u> <u>de</u>
<u>abril</u> <u>de</u> <u>1859,</u> <u>sobre</u> <u>asuntos</u> <u>territoriales</u>.
Havana: Carasa y Cía., 1939. 71 pp.
   One of Latin America's most emminent international lawyers, a Costa Rican, offers his
opinion in support of the Guatemalan contention that the Treaty of 1863 was nullified by
the failure of Great Britain to comply with
article 7 and hence that things revert to the
<u>status</u> <u>quo</u> <u>ante</u>, citing legal precedents.
This, he concludes, means that Guatemala has
not relinquished its claim to Belize and that
new negotiations are necessary as the accord
does not give England legal title to it.
Anderson advocates arbitration <u>ex</u> <u>aequo</u> <u>et</u>
<u>bono</u>. DLC

6 Argueta Ruiz, José Dolores. <u>Estados</u> <u>Unidos,</u>
<u>fiel</u> <u>a</u> <u>la</u> <u>balanza</u> <u>en</u> <u>el</u> <u>caso</u> <u>de</u> <u>Belice</u>.
Guatemala: Editorial del Ejército, 1966. 75
pp. Biblio., illus., maps.
   A Guatemalan army colonel restates the
Guatemalan position, contending that the
United States has an obligation to support the
Guatemalan claim and that any other stance
will lead to loss of moral leadership since
Guatemala's case is just. DLC LNHT BNG

7 Ashcraft, Norman. <u>Colonialism</u> <u>and</u> <u>Under-</u>
<u>development:</u> <u>Processes</u> <u>of</u> <u>Political</u> <u>Economic</u>
<u>Change</u> <u>in</u> <u>British</u> <u>Honduras</u>. New York:
Teachers College Press, Columbia University,
1973. ix, 180 pp. Biblio., maps, tables.
   A dependency analysis focusing on Belize,
viewing it as a case study for underdevelopment. Generalizes about other third-world
states from the data on Belize and the theoretical framework of dependency, emphasizing
the impact of foreign interests and those of
the mother country, which, cooperating with
the local elite, pursued policies that restricted local rural development. DLC LNHT

8 Asturias, Francisco. <u>Belice:</u> <u>ampliación</u> <u>de</u>
<u>la</u> <u>conferencia</u> <u>del</u> <u>5</u> <u>de</u> <u>abril</u> <u>de</u> <u>1925</u>.
Guatemala: n.p., 1925. 92 pp. Illus., maps.
2d ed. Guatemala: Tipografía Nacional, 1941.
177 pp. Biblio., maps.
   Recounts the history of Belize and of the
controversy, with excerpts from correspondence
and the treaties, and analyzes the accords,

supporting the Guatemalan claim. The second edition contains an additional bibliography and a chapter lauding the efforts of the administration of Jorge Ubico to reassert Guatemalan claims. DLC LNHT BNG BNCR

9   Aycinena Salazar, Luís. La equidad en derecho internacional y la controversia sobre Belice. Madrid: Universidad de Madrid, 1952. 275 pp. Biblio., notes, maps.
An official description of Belize this extols its future prospects and provides basic information for the general reader in the rest of the world. Includes a brief historical sketch and a description of the U.N. action supporting independence. LNHT

Originally a doctoral thesis at the University of Madrid, this study begins with a general analysis of equity in international law, then applies the results to the Belize case, restating the history of the controversy and supporting the Guatemalan claim. BNG

10 Baranda Quijano, Joaquín. La cuestión de Belice. Campeche: Imprenta de la Sociedad Tipográfica, 1873. 92 pp.
DLC

11 Bardini, Roberto. Belice: historia de una nación en movimiento. Tegucigalpa: Editorial Honduras, 1978. 207 pp. Biblio., illus.
A brief sketch for the general reader by an Argentine journalist, tracing the history of the settlement and advocating independence while supporting British claims in the dispute with Guatemala.

12 Barrientos, Alfonso Enrique. Cuentos de Belice. Guatemala: Ministerio de Educación Pública, 1961. 113 pp. Index.
A series of short stories about Belize, with text in English and Spanish, by a Guatemalan writer depicting what he considers the frustrated hopes of the Belizan people under the subjugation of the British crown. They emphasize personal frustration and individual difficulties with the law, carrying the implication that the British government is oppressive and acting against the wishes of the Belizan people. DLC LNHT BNG

13 Bateson, J.H., and I.H.S. Hall. Reconnaissance: Geochemical and Geological Investigations of the Maya Mountains of Southern British Honduras. London: Institute of Geological Sciences, 1970. 43 pp. Biblio., maps, tables.
A geological report focusing on potential mineral resources, with technical data, discussion of soils, and recommendations on the most promising areas for further mineral exploration.

14 Belize, Gov't of. Belize: New Nation in Central America. Belmopan: Government Printer, 1976. 40 pp. Illus., maps.
A brief official description of Belize that extols its future prospects and provides basic information for the general reader in the rest of the world. Includes a brief historical sketch and a description of the U.N. action supporting independence. LNHT

15 ____. Information Service. Belmopan, Belize, C.A. Belize: Government Printer, n.d. 32 pp. Maps.

A detailed description of the plans for the new capital.

16 ____. ____. The New Capital for Belize. Belize: Government Printer, 1969. 12 pp. Maps.
An official presentation of the plans for the construction of the new capital, Belmopan.

17 ____. Ministry of Education. A Digest of Educational Statistics. Belmopan: Ministry of Education, 1979. 79 pp. Maps.
A compilation of educational statistics covering 1972–74, detailing all aspects and all levels. Includes some earlier data for comparison.

18 Bianchi, William J. Belize: The Controversy between Guatemala and Great Britain over the Territory of British Honduras in Central America. New York: Las Americas, 1959. 142 pp. Biblio.
A brief review of the legal dispute by a member of the New York bar who, while sympathetic to the Guatemalan claim, concludes that legally the Guatemalan case is far from strong. Emphasizes the symbolic and political importance of the case, calling for a political rather than a legal solution and viewing the Guatemalan stance as an effort to reduce great-power influence in Latin America that deserves hemispheric support. Several solutions are suggested, all emphasizing a larger role for the OAS and consultation with the population of Belize. DLC LNHT BNG

19 A Bibliography of Books on Belize in the National Collection. Belize: National Library Service, 1977. 102 pp.
A listing of holdings in the National Library of books by Belizan authors, arranged by subject, without annotation.

20 Bloomfield, Louis M. The British Honduras-Guatemala Dispute. Toronto: Carswell, 1953. 231 pp. Index, biblio., notes, tables.
A Canadian lawyer's summary of the dispute, focusing on the legal questions and quoting extensively from the governmental communications. Dispassionate but pro-British, it concludes that since international law recognized colonization the International Court of Justice could never rule in favor of returning the colony to Guatemala. Argues that the best possible outcome would be a court decision requiring Great Britain to compensate Guatemala for damages resulting from its refusal to renegotiate the disputed clause of the 1859 convention. DLC LNHT

21 Bolland, O. Nigel. The Formation of a Colonial Society; Belize, from Conquest to Crown Colony. Baltimore: Johns Hopkins University Press, 1977. 240 pp. Index, biblio., notes, maps, tables.
A dependency-theory analysis of Belize's economy in the early years, based on British government documents, stressing the impact of a plantation economy and monoculture. Emphasizes the unique aspects of a logging economy

and a severe labor shortage that differentiated this region from other plantation societies. Ironically, it was the appearance of British venture capital and governmental control from the mother country that reduced the local elite's power, though substituting greater dependence on England. DLC LNHT

22 Bolland, O. Nigel, and Assad Shoman. Land in Belize, 1765-1871: Law and Society in the Caribbean. Mona, Jamaica: University of the West Indies Press, 1977. 142 pp. Index, biblio., maps, appendix.

A detailed analysis of land use and land ownership, focusing on its concentration in the hands of an elite and on the racial barriers between owners and workers. Closely related to Bolland's earlier work. DLC

23 Bowman, W.A.J. Citrus Culture in British Honduras. 2d ed. Stann Creek, Belize: Franklin Printing Co., 1975. 58 pp. Illus.

A collection of commentaries on the development of the citrus industry in Stann Creek from 1913 to 1975. Many of the illustrations were previously published in the press.

24 Bradley, Leo H., ed. A Bibliography of the Published Material on the Country as Found in the National Collection. The Central Library, Bliss Institute, Belize City. 2d ed. Belize: Government Printer, 1964. 58 pp.

An unannotated list of the holdings of the Belize National Library, arranged alphabetically. A ten-page supplement was published in 1966. Covers all holdings, including journals and mimeographed local government reports. LNHT BNG

25 Bradley, Leo H. Glimpses of our Country. Belize: Government Information Service, 1964. 58 pp.

A series of radio broadcasts prepared by the director of the National Library, designed to capture the spirit of the nation, its people, and life-style in popular form. Covers all aspects of the nation, including its physical setting, history, and society.

26 Brindley, J.B. Sketches of the Wesleyan Mission in British Honduras to Commemorate the Jubilee of Wesley Church, Belize. Belize: Clarion Press, 1916.

Commentaries about the early efforts and the growth of the church in the colony.

27 Bristowe, Lindsay, and Phillip B. Wright. The Handbook of British Honduras: Comprising Historical, Statistical, and General Information Concerning the Colony, Compiled from Official and Other Reliable Records. Edinburgh and London: Blackwood, 1880. Latest ed. Edinburgh and London: Blackwood, 1892.

A continuation, under a new title, of the series The Handbook of British Honduras. See item BE142. CuB

28 British Honduras, Citizens of. The Defence of the Settlers of Honduras against the Unjust and Unfounded Representations of Colonel George Arthur, Late Superintendent of that Settlement, Principally Contained in His Correspondence Relative to the Condition and Treatment of the Slaves at Honduras, 1820-1823, and Printed by Order of the House of Commons, 16th June, 1823. Published by Order of the Inhabitants of Honduras, and By Whose Resolution Every Member of the Imperial Parliament is to be Presented with a Copy. Kingston: Alex Aikman, 1824. 101 pp.

Involves charges about the treatment of slaves, conditions in the colony, and its government. DLC

29 British Honduras Company, Ltd. The Colony of British Honduras: Its History, Trade, and Natural Resources. London: Pearson & Son, 1867. 40 pp. Maps.

A brief account of the situation of the colony at the date of publication, providing an indication of its known resources, economy, and settlement. DLC

30 British Honduras, Gov't of. Consolidated Laws of British Honduras. N.p., n.d.

The original compilation of the colony's laws was issued in 1887, with updated versions provided in 1914 and 1924, prior to the 1954 version by Alfred V. Crane and the 1958 edition by Cyril George Xavier Henriques.

31 _____. Education Department. Report on Elementary Education. Belize: Government Printer, 1923. 12 pp. Illus., tables.

A school inspector's report on the state of education in the colony, with statistics regarding 1922 enrollments, class sizes, and exam results, detailed by district. DLC

32 _____. Information Service. The P.U.P. Government and the Guatemalan Claim. Belize: n.p., 1959. 37 pp.

A collection of broadsides and statements by the Belizan People's United Party, rejecting the Guatemalan claims to Belize.

33 _____. Lands and Survey Department. Atlas of British Honduras. Belize: n.p., 1939. x, 17 pp.
DLC

34 _____. Medical Department. Field Study and Projected Proposal for the Extension of Health Services to the Rural Areas of British Honduras With Emphasis on Maternal and Child Health including the Training of Health Personnel. Belize: British Honduras Medical Department, 1956. 119 pp.

An official report projecting future health-care needs on the basis of contemporary population statistics, detailing the implications for the territory.

35 Bryce, William Gordon, ed. The Subsidiary Laws of British Honduras in Force on the 31st Day of December, 1963. 4 vols. London: R. Madley, 1964-68.

A compilation of legislation and ordinances.

36 Buhler, Richard O. <u>A History of the Catholic Church in Belize</u>. Belize: Belize Institute for Social Research and Action, 1976. 96 pp. Illus.

A brief résumé of the activities of the Catholic church in Belize since 1832, tracing the construction of the various churches and indicating the principal individuals involved in the church's leadership, written by a Jesuit. The focus is on the early twentieth century through 1939, with only brief comments about other eras. DLC LNHT

37 Burdon, John Alder, ed. <u>Archives of British Honduras</u>. 3 vols. London: Sifton, Praed & Co., 1931-35. 304, 436, 401 pp. Index, biblio., maps.

A selection of papers from the Archives, supervised by the colonial governor. Arranged chronologically with identifications, brief summaries of the documents, excerpts from them, and numerous maps. The first volume covers the years to 1800, the second from 1801 to 1840, and the third from 1841 to 1884. A group project; there is some unevenness in the entries and summaries. Contains chronologies of each era. DLC LNHT

38 Burdon, John Alder. <u>Brief Sketch of British Honduras: Past and Present and Future</u>. London: West India Committee, 1927. 42 pp. Biblio., maps. 2d ed. London: West India Committee, 1928. 52 pp. Biblio., maps.

A continuation, under a new title, of the series The <u>Handbook of British Honduras</u>. See item BE142. DLC LNHT

39 Bury, Herbert. <u>A Bishop amongst the Bananas</u>. London: Wells Gardner, Darton & Co., 1911. xvi, 236 pp. Illus. 2d ed. Milwaukee: Young Churchman Co., 1912. xvi, 236 pp.

The memoirs of a British cleric who served as Anglican bishop of British Honduras for three years, with responsibility for the rest of Central America. Intended for an English church audience, the descriptions of his experiences are designed to stimulate interest in the missions in Central America. Also included are reminiscences of the church, its activities and needs, as well as what the author regards as the terrible conditions throughout the region. There are accounts of visits to the other isthmian republics, but the bulk of the volume deals with Belize. LNHT

40 Caiger, Stephen Langrish. <u>British Honduras: Past and Present</u>. London: Allen & Unwin, 1951. 240 pp. Illus., maps.

A broad survey of Belizan history by an Anglican missionary resident in that nation, covering the sweep from Colonial times to the present and including a pro-British account of the boundary dispute with Guatemala. The final chapters emphasizing the commercial and agricultural potential of the colony, which the author feels has been neglected by the British government, are clearly designed to urge greater investment and attract businessmen. Based principally on published works. DLC LNHT

41 _____. <u>Honduras Ahoy! The Church at Work in Central America</u>. London: Society for the Propagation of the Gospel, 1949. 46 pp.

An Anglican priest's account of his missionary work in Belize, including a description of the church's various efforts in that nation. Also makes brief references to Guatemala, Honduras, and El Salvador.

42 Cain, Ernest E. <u>Cyclone: Being an Illustrated Official Record of the Hurricane and Tidal Wave which Destroyed the City of Belize (British Honduras) on the Colony's Birthday, 10 September 1931</u>. London: Arthur H. Stockwell, 1933. xv, 135 pp. Illus.

An account of the storm, with extensive description of the damage, relief efforts, reconstruction, assistance from abroad, lists of the deceased and damages, etc.; includes photos. LNHT

43 _____. <u>Cyclone Hattie</u>. Ilfracombe, England: Arthur H. Stockwell, 1963. 75 pp. Illus., maps.

An account of the damage caused by the hurricane that hit Belize City in October 1961 and of Hurricane Janet, which hit Corozal in 1955.

44 _____. <u>Cyclone "Hattie" Revised: Being a Record of the Hurricane and Tidal Wave which Destroyed the City of Belize in British Honduras</u>. Devon: Arthur H. Stockwell, 1964. 87 pp. Illus.

Further comment on the disastrous 1961 hurricane.

45 Calderón Quijano, José Antonio. <u>Belice, 1663(?)-1821: historia de los establecimientos británicos del Río Valis hasta la independencia de Hispano América</u>. Sevilla: Universidad de Sevilla, 1944. xix, 503 pp. Index, notes, illus., maps, appendixes.

A history of the development of British settlement in Belize from its origin to the independence of Central America, based on extensive research, primarily in Spanish archives and existing secondary works. The emphasis is on the contested title to the region with reference to Spanish claims and the treaty provisions resulting from European wars. DLC LNHT

46 Camejo Farfán, Hugo. <u>Belice: una cuestión continental</u>. Guatemala: Imprenta Universitaria, 1949. 23 pp. Illus., maps.

Part of the author's thesis at the University of Havana, published while he was serving in the Guatemalan government. Contends that the question of Belize has hemispheric implications, citing support for the Guatemalan position throughout the hemisphere and contending that all the nations of Latin America have an obligation to support the Guatemalan resistance to colonialism through this question. DLC BNG

47 Canales Salazar, Félix. <u>Derechos territoriales de la República de Honduras sobre Honduras Británica o Belice, Islas del Cisne y Costas de los Indios Mosquitos</u>. Mexico: n.p., 1946. 91 pp. Biblio., illus., maps.
A frequent spokesman on boundary questions asserts a potential Honduran claim to Belize, though focusing principally on strengthening its claim to the Bay Islands and the Atlantic coast of Nicaragua, where there was a pending dispute. FU

48 Carey Jones, N.S. <u>The Pattern of a Dependent Economy: The National Income of British Honduras</u>. Cambridge: Cambridge University Press, 1953. 162 pp. Index, biblio., notes, illus., tables, appendixes.
A colonial official's compilation and analysis of the income statistics for British Honduras during the 1940s, based on official reports and detailing the income and profitability of the various economic sectors as well as of the colony as a whole. Includes discussion of the role of the government, the high cost of labor as compared to that in the West Indies, and the implications of these factors and the predominantly agricultural economy for the future of British Honduras. DLC

49 Carpio Nicholle, Roberto. <u>Hacia donde Belice</u>. Guatemala: Ediciones Popular, 1977. 297 pp. Illus., maps, tables.
A Guatemalan newspaperman and Christian Democratic member of the National Congress reviews the Guatemalan claims, endorsing their validity but noting some errors in earlier efforts to assert them. Reproduces documents relating to the U.N. debates of 1968-75. The study is relatively objective, conceding that much of the population of Belize is not Guatemalan in culture and that this must be taken into account in an era of decolonization and self-determination, though asserting that union with Guatemala would serve Belizan interests. Interestingly, the author contends that the population of southern Belize is, in fact, of Guatemalan culture because it derives from Carib or Guatemalan origins. BNG

50 Carr, David, and John Thorpe. <u>From the Cam to the Cays: The Story of The Cambridge Expedition to British Honduras, 1959-1960</u>. London: Putnam, 1961. 190 pp. Biblio., illus., maps, appendixes.
Separate chapters written by the various members of the ten-man team, which included geologists, archeologists, botanists, photographers, and zoologists, that sought to travel throughout the territory and gather information to improve knowledge of it in England. These essays focus on their experiences, travels, and meetings with people rather than on reporting their studies. They are written in travel-book style, focusing on experience and observation, albeit some of it by trained observers. There is considerable comment about the people, their society, background, culture, and customs, though none of the members of the expedition were trained social scientists or historians, and British prejudices are evident. DLC LNHT

51 Carrillo, Alfonso. <u>Algunos aspectos jurídicos de la controversia angloguatemalteca sobre Belice</u>. Guatemala: Imprenta Universitaria, 1948. 48 pp.
A Guatemalan diplomat and professor defends the Guatemalan position in legalistic terms. This study, published under the sponsorship of the University of San Carlos as part of its effort to provide support for the government's position, was originally prepared for the Foreign Ministry for use at the Fifth Inter-American Legal Conference in Lima, Peru, in 1947. DLC LNHT

52 Carrillo y Ancona, Crescencio. <u>Correspondencia diplomática cambiada entre el gobierno de la república y el de Su Majestad Británica con relación al territorio llamado Belice</u>. Mexico: Imprenta Ignacio Cumplido, 1878. 94 pp.
A compilation of official notes from the nineteenth-century period when the regime of Porfirio Díaz was still asserting a claim on the territory and negotiating an accord with Guatemala regarding its disposition.

53 Castañeda, Gabriel Ángel. <u>Belikin: descripción monográfica de ventidós mil novecientos kilómetros cuadrados de centroamericanidad irredenta; centenario de la usurpación, 1859-1959</u>. Guatemala: Tipografía Nacional, 1969. 248 pp. Biblio., illus., maps.
A description of Belize, its physical setting and people, by a Guatemalan who is familiar with the territory and seeks to promote in each people a knowledge of the other, to demonstrate their similarities and common problems, and hence deal with the boundary dispute at the level of popular understanding rather than that of legal rights, while supporting the Guatemalan claim. Includes discussion of geography, flora, and fauna, with rich description; a résumé of the area's history; and a dictionary of place names giving their location, with explanations of their significance and their origin. Contends that the name Belize is derived from the Maya word <u>belikin</u>, meaning to the east. DLC LNHT

54 Castellanos, Francisco Xavier. <u>La intendencia de Yucatán y Belice</u>. Mexico: n.p., 1962. 62 pp. Notes, illus., maps.
A review of the question of Colonial jurisdictions, supporting the Mexican contentions and claims to Belize. DLC

55 Castellanos Sánchez, Miguel. <u>La cuestión de Belice</u>. Mérida: Imprenta Mercantil, 1897. 49 pp.
A senator from Yucatán states his opposition to the 1893 Anglo-Mexican treaty, arguing that Mexico does have a claim to Belize and must defend it. DLC LNHT

56 Charter, Cecil Frederick. <u>A Reconnaissance
Survey of the Soils of British Honduras North
of the Central Metamorphic and Igneous Massif,
with Special Reference to Their Utilization in
Agriculture</u>. Belize: Government Printer,
1941. 31 pp. Biblio., maps.
    A classification of the soil types, with
discussion of the crops for which they are
suited and the potential implications for the
Belizan economy. DLC

57 Chica, Luís Alfonso. <u>Deberes de Centroamérica
con Guatemala ante el caso de Belice</u>. San
Salvador: Editorial Helios, 1964. 245 pp.
Illus.
    A statement of support for the Guatemalan
claim, characterizing British control of the
territory as "permanent aggression" and calling for all Central American states to join in
the "liberation" of Belize. Includes excerpts
from statements of support over a period of
time from Latin American statesmen and international figures. DLC LNHT BNG

58 Cid Fernández, Enrique del. <u>Infundada
pretensión mexicana sobre el territorio de
Belice</u>. Guatemala: Editorial del Ejército,
1962. 66 pp. Biblio., notes, illus., maps.
    A refutation of the Mexican claims, con-
tending that the boundary between the Colonial
dependencies clearly placed Belize in the
Captaincy General of Central America rather
than of Mérida and citing previous Mexican
statements supporting the Guatemalan claim.
DLC LNHT BNG

59 Clayton, G., W.D. Garner, and E.T. York.
<u>Report of the Tripartite Economic Survey of
British Honduras</u>. Belize: Government
Printer, 1966. 158 pp.
    A survey of the local economy compiled by
representatives of Belize, Great Britain, and
the United States detailing the situation of
the nation in the early and mid-1960s, with
projections of future potential.

60 Clegern, Wayne M. <u>British Honduras: Colonial
Dead End, 1859-1900</u>. Baton Rouge: Louisiana
State University Press, 1967. vii, 214 pp.
Index, biblio., notes, maps, appendixes.
    A history of Belize in the nineteenth cen-
tury based principally on British documents,
emphasizing the lack of development and the
British neglect of what seemed in the context
of their empire a remote colony. The study
notes the limited attention paid Belize by the
home government, the concentration of land-
ownership, and the fact that Belize became a
backwater once it ceased to be a commercial
bridge between Europe (particularly England)
and the Central American nations. Includes
detailed examination of the diplomatic and
boundary disputes of the nineteenth century,
as well as consideration of the British-
American détente in the Caribbean, which
influenced British policy. DLC LNHT

61 _____. <u>Nueva luz sobre la disputa de Belice</u>.
Guatemala: Ministerio de Relaciones
Exteriores, 1959. 68 pp.

A translation of an article that appeared
in the <u>American Journal of International Law</u>
in April 1958, tracing the history of the
dispute and its legal aspects. It is published here in Spanish and English, under the
auspices of the Guatemalan Foreign Ministry.
BNG

62 Cleghorn, Robert. <u>A Short History of Baptist
Missionary Work in British Honduras, 1822-
1939</u>. London: Kingsgate Press, 1939. 71 pp.
    The observations of a Scottish missionary
who served extensively in Belize. Outlines
the development of missionary efforts in that
nation and comments on the local scene.

63 Collar, Jerry D., and Grant H. Collar, Jr.
<u>Belize: British Honduras, the Country and
People, Tourism and Investment</u>. Durango,
Mexico: Salas Offset, 1972. 52 pp. Maps.
    A brief overview designed to introduce the
layman to the area and encourage tourism and
investment. DLC LNHT

64 Collet, Wilfred. <u>British Honduras and Its
Resources</u>. London: West India Committee,
1909. 24 pp. Illus., maps.
    A description of the physical setting and
known resources of Belize, designed to encourage knowledge about and interest in the colony
on the part of the general British reader.
Includes advice about agriculture, timber, and
trade statistics. DLC

65 Crane, Alfred Victor, ed. <u>The Laws of British
Honduras</u>. Rev. ed. 6 vols. London:
Waterlow, 1954.
    A compilation of current statutes.

66 Cravioto, Adrián. <u>La paz de América:
Guatemala y Belice</u>. Mexico: Editorial
Cultura, 1943. 56 pp. Biblio., illus., maps.
    Originally a lengthy speech by a Mexican
army colonel. Reiterates the Guatemalan claim
to Belize, reviews the history of the controversy, and contends that the American nations
should receive some compensation for their
contributions during World War II; suggesting
that the appropriate form would be liberation
of all remaining colonies in the region, which
would entail the return of Belize to Guatemala.
DLC LNHT

67 Crowe, Frederick. <u>The Gospel in Central
America, Containing a Sketch of the Country,
Physical and Geographical, Historical, and
Political, Moral and Religious</u>. London:
Charles Gilpin, A.C. Black, 1850. xii, 588
pp. Maps.
    An early British Baptist missionary's view
of the region. Includes a brief history of
the area to 1850, with emphasis on what the
author regards as Indian idolatry, Spanish
popery, and the harm they did; a history of
the Baptist missions in British Honduras,
including the author's personal experiences;
and a brief essay on his own efforts in
Guatemala during Carrera's rule. Provides the
missionary view of the region and its needs,

as well as detailed observations and commentary about contemporary Belize, its
development, settlers, and society during
the mid-nineteenth century. DLC

68 Dillon, A. Barrow. <u>Geography of British
Honduras, Compiled from Various Sources</u>.
London: Waterlow & Sons, 1923. 39 pp. Maps.
    A detailed geographical survey, intended as
a text but including far more detail than is
usual in such efforts. Includes an account of
the state of the colony in 1922. LNHT

69 Dixon, C.G. <u>Geology of Southern British
Honduras, with Notes on Adjacent Areas</u>.
Belize: Government Printer, 1956. 85 pp.
Biblio., illus., maps, tables.
    A detailed survey and description of the
Maya mountains and the area south of Stann
Creek, undertaken to map the mountains and
search for mineral deposits. Fieldwork was
conducted between 1950 and 1956. Includes
consideration of sedimentary formations,
igneous rocks, minerals, and water supply, as
well as general geological and physical data
and detailed maps. DLC

70 ____. <u>Notes on the Geology of British
Honduras</u>. Belize: Government Printer, 1955.
12 pp.
    A detailed geological description of the
various subregions, based on extensive surveys
by the government geologist. Includes consideration of physical features, sedimentary
formations, igneous rocks, and regional tec-
tonics, providing a description of the terrain
that helped promote an understanding of the
transportation and water problems. LNHT

71 Dobson, Narda A. <u>A History of Belize</u>. Port-
of-Spain: Longman Caribbean, 1973. 362 pp.
Index, biblio., notes, illus., maps.
    A general history from 1798 to 1970 in
considerable detail, based on research in
British documents and secondary works, with
partial footnoting. DLC LNHT

72 Donohoe, William Arlington. <u>A History of
British Honduras</u>. Montreal: Provincial Publishing, 1946. 118 pp. Index, biblio.,
illus., maps. Latest ed. New York: Colorite
Offset Printing Co., 1947. 118 pp. Index,
biblio., illus., maps.
    A survey of the development of the colony,
particularly of the years 1900-1910, aimed at
the general reader. The section dealing with
the dispute with Guatemala presents a well-
balanced and succinct account of the various
issues. Concludes that England failed to
comply with the treaty of 1863 and has done
little to promote the development of the colony, though noting that any settlement would
have to consider the rights of the residents
of Belize, suggesting solution through the
United Nations. DLC

73 Downie, Jack. <u>An Economic Policy for British
Honduras</u>. Belize: Government Printer, 1959.
53 pp. Illus.

An official report, based on a one-month
visit by a colonial official, regarding the
situation in 1959. Details the economy of the
colony and concludes that its principal problems are an accumulation of minor difficulties
stemming principally from the small population, limited trade, and the absence of capital for investment. DLC

74 Dunlop, Walter Ronald. <u>Report on the Economic
and Natural Features of British Honduras in
Relation to Agriculture, with Proposals for
Development</u>. London: Crown Agents, 1921. 32
pp. Illus., maps, tables.
    A survey of agricultural potential, with
geographical detail and recommendations for
future development. DLC

75 Echánove Trujillo, Carlos Alberto. <u>Una tierra
en disputa: Belice ante la historia</u>. Mérida:
Editorial Yucatanese Club del Libro. 171 pp.
Biblio., maps.
    A defense of the Mexican claims, arguing
that Colonial jurisdictions placed Belize in
the Captaincy General of Yucatán and hence
that Mexico rather than Guatemala has rights
to the territory. LNHT

76 Edmond, Charles John. <u>A History of Orange
Walk Town, Belize</u>. Belize: n.p., 1977. 37
pp. Illus., maps.

77 Espino, Miguel Ángel. <u>Hombres contra la
muerta</u>. Guatemala: Tipografía Nacional,
1942. 330 pp. Latest ed. San Salvador:
Ministerio de Educación, 1976. 312 pp.
    A novel of human trials and tribulations in
the face of death, written during 1940 and set
in Belize and the jungle frontiers with
Guatemala and Mexico. There is some implicit
propaganda, since the plot involves the flight
of a group of whites and Indians from anarchy
and a massacre of whites by blacks in Belize,
their experiences while traveling through a
remote and hazardous region, and their cooperation during their journey. BNG

78 Espinosa, Antonio, ed. <u>Yucatán y Belice:
colección de documentos importantes que se
refieren al tratado de 8 de julio de 1893</u>.
Mérida: Tipografía de G. Canto, 1894. 173
pp. Maps.
    A collection of documents and testaments
relating to the 1893 Anglo-Mexican accord in
which Mexico ceded its claims to Belize and
recognized the British claim. The book is a
defense of this action, which was highly criticized, seeking to demonstrate that it was
correct, that Mexico had no legal claim, and
that Yucatán and its residents supported the
treaty. It contains the treaty, various legal
opinions, the report of Foreign Minister
Ignacio Mariscal to the Congress, and endorsements from the Yucatán state legislature as
well as from various other local officials and
bodies in that state. DLC

79 Estrada de la Hoz, Julio. <u>Belice</u>. Guatemala:
Tipografía Nacional, 1949. 90 pp. Biblio.

A legal thesis at UNAM, by a Guatemalan student, restating the Guatemalan case and reviewing the various episodes. It was later published by the Guatemalan Foreign Ministry. DLC LNHT

80 Evans, Geoffrey, et al. Report of the British Guiana and British Honduras Settlement Commission. London: HMSO, 1948. viii, 359 pp. Notes, illus., maps, tables, appendixes.
An official British government commission's examination of the development prospects of Belize and British Guiana as possible solutions to the overpopulation of the British West Indies, offering plans for expansion of the economy to enable the resettlement of West Indians in these territories. Includes analysis of the types of industries and agricultural efforts that would be possible, with specific programs detailing their operation and the necessary support facilities. DLC

81 Fabela, Isidro. Belice: defensa de los derechos de México. Mexico: Editorial Mundo Libre, 1944. 423 pp. Index, biblio., maps.
A well-known Mexican scholar and diplomat provides the most detailed statement of the Mexican claim, meticulously reviewing the questions of Colonial jurisdiction and quoting at length from the documents involved. Contends that Guatemala has a claim only to the southern half of Belize and that the northern half belongs to Mexico. DLC

82 Fairweather, D.N.A. A Short History of the Volunteer Forces of British Honduras, Now Belize. N.p.: n.p., 1977. 43 pp. Maps.
A brief history of the local armed forces from the seventeenth century to the present, written by one of its commanders. Provides a complete list of the officers who have headed the force.

83 Fairweather, Henry Clifton. The British Honduras-Guatemala Boundary. Bristol, England: Ernest E. Cain, 1969. 36 pp. Maps.
A member of a prominent Belizan family who served on the surveying team that marked the frontier in 1933 and whose work was later rejected by Guatemala provides the viewpoint of the local settlers, passionately rejecting Guatemalan claims, citing the rights of the populace to self-determination, and hailing the protection of the British. The presentation was originally prepared as a speech delivered in 1967.

84 Fonseca, Roberto Peragibe, da. The Question of British Honduras. 2d ser., A Defense of the Viewpoint of the Guatemalan Government. Rio de Janeiro: n.p., 1939. 84 pp.

85 Fowler, Henry. A Narrative of a Journey Across the Unexplored Portion of British Honduras, with a Short Sketch of the History and Resources of the Colony. Belize: Government Press, 1879. 64 pp. Maps. 2d ed. Belize: Government Printer, 1928. 38 pp.
A British official describes his adventures in the remote backlands, focusing on description, flora, and fauna, but recording the travels of an official expedition searching the interior for new resources with which to revive the colony's economy. DLC

86 Freisen, John D. Hurricane Hattie. London: Derksen Printers, 1965. 106 pp.
A detailed account of the hurricane that destroyed Belize City in 1961, with a supplemental account of the damage done by Hurricane Janet in 1955.

87 Furley, Peter A., ed. Expedition to British Honduras-Yucatán, 1966. Edinburgh: University of Edinburgh, 1968. 68 pp. Biblio., tables.
A detailed geographical description compiled by a group of British specialists from the university, based on fieldwork in 1966. Covers physical features, flora and fauna, agriculture, soils, forests, etc.

88 Furley, Peter A., and A.J. Crosbie. Geography of Belize. London: Collins Printing, 1974. 2d ed. London: Collins Printing, 1976. 48 pp. Index, illus., maps, tables.
Though intended as a text for the Belizan schools, this volume offers a detailed, if compact, survey of the nation's geography and climatic factors. LNHT

89 Gadsby, Walter J. On the Shores of the Caribbean Sea (Stories of Far-off British Honduras). London: J.W. Butcher, 1918. 128 pp. Illus.
A narrative about the experiences of a Methodist missionary in Belize, including some general comments on the history of the area and of the missions, but consisting principally of anecdotes, tales about the missionary effort, and descriptions of the physical setting and the people. NcD

90 Gall, Francis. Belice: tierra nuestra. Guatemala: Ministerio de Educación Pública, 1962. 197 pp. Biblio., notes, maps.
A prominent Guatemalan scholar's summary of the Guatemalan claim to Belize, with documentary excerpts from the pertinent accords. One of the most effective statements of the claim and its basis, reflecting the author's ties to the Guatemalan Academy of Geography and History. DLC LNHT BNG

91 _____. Opinion of the Geographical and Historical Society of Guatemala on Guatemala's Right to British Honduras. Guatemala: Geographical and Historical Society of Guatemala, 1939. 17 pp.
A brief official statement of the society, supporting the Guatemalan claim to Belize and stating that the members have reviewed the documentation in their capacity as historians and certify that it supports the Guatemalan position. DLC LNHT BNG

92 Gallegos, Anibal. El Belice mexicano. Mexico: UNAM, 1951. 110 pp. Biblio., notes.
A thesis restating the Mexican claims and the detailed legal arguments involved. The author contends that the 1893 accord is in-

valid, as Mexico signed under threat and then only ceded its de facto, not de jure, rights. While arguing the supremacy of Colonial jurisdiction from Yucatán, it adds a nuance by contending that Mexican claims encompass only part of Belize, namely, the area between the Río Hondo and the Río Sibun, and that it should negotiate with Guatemala, ceding the rest to the nation. DLC

93 García Bauer, Carlos. La controversia sobre el territorio de Belice y el procedimiento ex-aequo et bono. Guatemala: Imprenta Universitaria, 1958. 227 pp. Biblio., notes, maps.
   After reviewing the positions of Guatemala and Britain, the author argues the appropriateness of a juridical arbitration ex-aequo et bono, which would allow the court to make a direct territorial award if it judged that appropriate, rather than rule on a narrower issue that would require subsequent negotiation between the parties. His stand supports the Guatemalan position in favor of such a proceeding and criticizes England for refusing. Includes reproductions of the principal treaties in the case. DLC LNHT

94 Gibbs, Archibald Robertson. British Honduras (An Historical and Descriptive Account of the Colony from its Settlement, 1670). London: Sampson, Low, Marston, Searle, & Rivington, 1883. viii, 198 pp. Appendixes.
   A general account, written from the perspective of Great Britain, in which the colony is seen as a stirring instance of the success of British enterprise for the greater glory of the empire and the nation. The focus is on geography, living conditions, and settlement, particularly in the nineteenth century. Calls for greater self-rule. DLC LNHT

95 González-Blanco, Pedro. El problema de Belice y sus alivios. Mexico: Editorial Galatea, 1950. 129 pp. Biblio., notes.
   A restatement of the Guatemalan case, charging British conquest, refuting all other claims, and calling for the British to accept the Guatemalan arbitration proposal. DLC LNHT

96 González Davidson, Fernando. Belice: realidad y posibilidades. N.p., n.d. 33 pp. Biblio., notes, tables.
   A brief description of Belize and its current status, economy, and trade. Contends that if the nation becomes independent most of its foreign imports could come from the Central American Common Market, thus strengthening the new nation and the economies of its neighbors. LNHT

97 González Ramírez, Baltasar. Tratado Spenser-Mariscal: la cuestión de Belice. Mexico: Imprenta Moderna, 1962. 150 pp. Biblio.
   Originally a thesis at UNAM, restating the Mexican claim and seeking to refute the Guatemalan claims. DLC

98 Gottschalk, Kurt P. British Honduras (Belize) and Regional Economic Integration: An Analysis of Alternative Choices. Winston-Salem, N.C.: Wake Forest University Press, 1970. vii, 55 pp. Biblio., tables.
   A survey of the contemporary Belizan economy, matching it with both the Central American Common Market and the Caribbean Free Trade Association, contending that membership in CARIFTA would be more beneficial to Belize.

99 Grant, Cedric Hilburn. The Making of Modern Belize: Politics, Society and British Colonialism in Central America. Cambridge: Cambridge University Press, 1976. 400 pp. Index, biblio., notes, illus., tables.
   A study of Belizan development from 1931 through 1969 by a Guayanese political scientist. Based on secondary works, local newspapers, and local documents, it focuses on the new nation's cultural diversity and its implications for national unity and national identity. Includes comparisons to the West Indies, reflecting the author's Commonwealth perspective, and is pro-Belizan in discussing the boundary question. The role of the local elite and the changing nature of the ties to the mother country are also considered. LNHT

100 Great Britain, Gov't of. Central Office of Information. British Honduras. London: Swindom Press, 1960. 29 pp. Maps.
   Basic data about the colony, prepared by a government service. DLC

101 Gregg, Algar Robert. British Honduras. London: HMSO, 1968. 158 pp. Index, illus.
   A basic descriptive account written under the sponsorship of the British government as part of a series on the dependent territories and colonies. Designed to provide basic data, it replaces the old series of Bluebooks. The focus is on description and resources; the historical account deals only with the British colony and settlement, justifying the British claim to the region. DLC LNHT

102 Guatemala, Gov't of. Ministerio de Relaciones Exteriores. Breve resumen de la disputa guatamalteca con la Gran Bretaña sobre el territorio de Belice. Guatemala: Editorial del Ejército, 1976. 26 pp. Maps.
   A Brief Resume of Guatemala's Dispute with Great Britain over the Belize Territory (1783-1977). Guatemala: Ministry of Foreign Affairs, 1977. 34 pp.
   A brief summary of the Guatemalan claims and position, the history of the dispute, and the efforts to solve it. DLC BNG

103 _____. _____. El caso de Belice ante la conciencia de América; The Belize Question before the Conscience of America. Guatemala: Tipografía Nacional, 1948. 32 pp.
   A statement, in English and Spanish, made by the Guatemalan delegation to the Ninth Interamerican Conference in 1948, defending the Guatemalan claim. DLC LNHT

(Guatemala, Gov't of)

104 _____. _____. La controversia sobre Belice
durante el año de 1945. Guatemala:
Tipografía Nacional, 1946. 88 pp.
A folio containing the portions of the
Foreign Ministry's annual Memoria relating to
Belize, published separately to be grouped
with the White Book and containing the corre-
spondence between the two governments during
the year 1945. Text in Spanish and English.
DLC LNHT BNG

105 _____. _____. La controversia sobre Belice
durante el año de 1946; Status of the controversy over Belize during the year 1946.
Guatemala: Ministerio de Relaciones
Exteriores, 45 pp.
A continuation of the previous year's
volume. DLC LNHT

106 _____. _____. Libro Blanco: controversia
entre Guatemala y la Gran Bretaña relativa a
la Convención de 1859, sobre asuntos
territoriales: cuestión de Belice. 6 vols.
Guatemala: Tipografía Nacional, 1938-44.
Biblio., maps.
White Book: Controversy between Guatemala and
Great Britain Relative to the Convention of
1859 on Territorial Matters. 6 vols.
Guatemala: Tipografía Nacional, 1938-44.
The Guatemalan government's statement of
its case, detailing the history of the dispute, the basis of the Guatemalan claim, and
the controversy surrounding the 1859 treaty;
includes the Ubico Regime's correspondence
with the British government to 1938, when the
initial 491-page volume was issued. Several
supplemental volumes were issued periodically
under the title Continuation of the White
Book, each reproducing the latest exchanges,
demonstrating British intransigence and refusal to negotiate regarding the 1859 accord,
and compiling correspondence from other nations indicating support for the Guatemalan
claim. DLC LNHT BNG

107 _____. _____. Opinión centroamericana a
propósito del libro "Belice: tierra
irredenta." Guatemala: Tipografía Nacional,
1944. 125 pp. Maps.
A series of excerpts and reproductions from
various newspapers, journals, and letters
repudiating the thesis of Ramón López
Jiménez's Belize: tierra irredenta. An opening commentary by the Guatemalan Foreign Ministry states that the book is anti-Central
American and rejects López Jiménez's contention that all Central American republics have
a joint claim to Belize since all were part of
the Federation, which inherited Spanish
claims. A careful selection of reprints of
statements from the other countries and
governments rejects this thesis and reiterates
their support for the Guatemalan claim. DLC
LNHT BNG

108 _____. _____. Puntos capitales que sostiene
el gobierno de Guatemala en la controversia
anglo-guatemalteca, para reivindicar el
territorio de Belice. Guatemala: Tipografía
Nacional, 1945. 12 pp. 2d ed. Guatemala:
Tipografía Nacional, 1950. 12 pp.
A succinct restatement of the Guatemalan
position and the basis of its claims on
Belize. DLC LNHT BNG

109 _____. Presidencia, Secretaría de Información.
Cruceros británicos amenazan a Guatemala:
mensajes enviados al gobierno de la república
expresando solidaridad y simpatía con
oportunidad de la presencia de grandes barcos
de guerra ingleses en aguas de Belice.
Guatemala: Tipografía Nacional, 1948.
173 pp.
The speech of Guatemalan president Juan
José Arévalo on 4 March 1948 protesting the
visit of British naval vessels to Belize and
reiterating Guatemalan claims. The correspondence exchanged with various nations and
citizens regarding the resulting crisis is
collected to show the overwhelming international support for the Guatemalan claim; it
includes hundreds of letters and telegrams of
support. DLC LNHT

110 Gullick, C.J.M.R. Exiled from St. Vincent:
The Development of Black Carib Culture in
Central America up to 1945. Malta: Progress
Press, 1976. 152 pp. Biblio., maps.
An account of the transfer of the Caribs
from St. Vincent in 1797 to the coast of
Belize and Nicaragua, tracing their subsequent
development and the preservation of their
traditions and life-style.

111 Hadel, Richard E. Three Early Censuses, 1816,
1820, 1823, of Belize. Belize: Belize Institute for Social Research and Action, 1974.
22 pp. Tables.
An analysis of data from the three censuses, with tables and statistics.

112 Henderson, George. An Account of the British
Settlement of British Honduras to which Are
Added Sketches of the Manners and Customs of
the Mosquito Indians. London: C. & R.
Baldwin, 1809. xi, 203 pp. Maps. 2d ed.
London: C. & R. Baldwin, 1811. xi, 237 pp.
Maps.
A general descriptive account by a British
army officer. Focuses on geography and early
settlement by Europeans, indicating the condi-
tions of life. The emphasis is on physical
description, though the history of the early
settlements in Belize is also covered.
British efforts at expansion into the Mosquito
Territory are included, reflecting the
author's service as superintendent of Belize
and his visit to the Mosquito region in 1804.
DLC LNHT

113 Henriques, Cyril George Xavier, ed. The Laws
of British Honduras in Force on the 15th day

of September 1958. 6 vols. London:
Waterlow, 1960.
    An updated compilation of the current
legislation.

114 Hershey, Samuel. Samuel Hershey's Travels in
Central America and Elsewhere. Springfield:
Illinois State Register, 1897. 36 pp. Index.
    A travelogue recounting an 1895 trip to
Belize, which he calls "this strange land."
Emphasis is on physical description. DLC

115 Hill, David O., Charles H. Hartwell, and
Jitendra Kohli. Report of the Commission of
Enquiry on a Review of the Public Service in
Belize, 1973. Belize: Government Printer,
1974. 289 pp. Tables.
    A review of the government service, its
current condition and future needs, with statistical projections and recommendations.

116 Howard, Michael C. Ethnicity in Southern
Belize: The Kekchi and the Mopan. Columbia:
University of Missouri Museum, 1975. 111 pp.
Biblio., maps.
    A study of two Indian cultures of Belize,
their interaction, and their isolation from
the rest of society within the country. DLC

117 Hubbe, Joaquín. Belice. Mérida: Tipografía
Yucateca, 1940. 164 pp.
    A series of essays, originally published in
1880 and 1881 in the newspaper El Eco de
Comercio of Yucatán, arguing that Mexico has a
legitimate claim to Belize and meticulously
tracing the Mexican case. They initially
constituted part of the debate regarding the
Díaz regime's treaty with England relinquish-
ing Mexican claims, and were republished as
part of the effort to reassert these claims in
the 1940s. DLC LNHT

118 Humphreys, Robert Arthur. The Diplomatic
History of British Honduras, 1638-1901.
London: Oxford University Press, 1961. 196
pp. Biblio., notes, maps.
    A summary of the Belize dispute from the
British point of view, carefully written from
British Foreign Office documents by a well-
known historian. Provides an effective outline of the dispute, the British position, and
the British attitude toward it. DLC LNHT

119 Hurtado Aguilar, Luís Alberto. Belice es de
Guatemala: tratados, situación jurídica,
actuaciones, opiniones. Guatemala: Imprenta
Hispania, 1958. 128 pp.
    A restatement of the Guatemalan position,
with extensive excerpts from previous treaties
and diplomatic exchanges, relevant constitutional clauses, and Inter-American agreements
and declarations. Emphasizes actions since
the 1930s. DLC LNHT BNG

120 Hyde, Evan X. The Crowd Called UBAD: The
Story of a Peoples Movement. Belize: Modern
Printers, 1970. 90 pp. Illus.
    The program of the United Black Association
for Development, and an account of its formation and activities.

121 King, Emory. "Hey Dad, This Is Belize."
Belize: Tropical Books, 1977. 167 pp.
    A collection of essays originally published
in the local press, humorously recounting the
local life and customs.

122 Latin American Bureau. The Belize Issue.
London: Latin American Bureau, 1978. 77 pp.
Biblio., maps.
    A survey of the boundary issue from the
British perspective, criticizing the Guatemalan claim and calling it an impediment to
the development of Belize. Focuses on the '
recent claims and negotiations, providing only
a brief historical sketch of the dispute.
Includes a summary of the current situation in
Belize, with up-to-date figures regarding its
economy and population.

123 Lewis, D. Gareth. The History of St. John's
Cathedral, Belize. Belize: St. John's
Cathedral, 1976. 20 pp. Illus.
    A lavishly illustrated pamphlet tracing the
history of the Anglican Cathedral of Belize,
with very brief text and a list of its rectors, compiled by the present rector. LNHT

124 Leyton Rodríguez, Rubén. Belice es tierra de
Guatemala. Mexico and Guatemala: Ediciones
Rubén Leyton Prado, 1953. 228 pp. Biblio.,
illus.
    A restatement of the Guatemalan position
and of Latin American support for it, by a
prolific writer who traces the history of the
dispute and supports the Guatemalan claim.
BNG

125 _____. Carta de Belice. Guatemala:
Ediciones Rubén Leyton Prado, n.d. 84 pp.
Biblio.
    Another statement of support for the Guate-
malan claims to Belize, with historical refer-
ences to various stages of the dispute. LNHT
BNG

126 _____. La puerta de Guatemala en el Caribé, y
la inseguridad de América. Guatemala:
Ediciones Rubén Leyton Prado, 1971. 212 pp.
Biblio., illus., maps.
    A restatement of the Guatemalan case re-
garding its rights to Belize, with excerpts
from the treaties and various other statements
that the author feels are relevant. Contends
that possession of Belize is essential to the
development of the Petén, which would be impossible without a Caribbean port, and hence
is vital to the fulfillment of Guatemala's
potential. Concludes that because colonialism
is the source of much of the region's unrest,
the Caribbean can be calmed by British cession
of Belize to Guatemala, thereby eliminating
the last vestige of colonialism. DLC LNHT
BNG

127 Llanas Sánchez, Enrique. México y sus
derechos sobre Belice. Mexico: Talleres
Gráficos de Impresiones Modernos, 1958.
Biblio., maps, appendixes.
    A thesis at UNAM; retraces the legal argu-
ments in detail, along with the history of the

dispute, and staunchly defends the Mexican claim. DLC

128 López, Francisco Marcos. Dos momentos dramáticos y una sola cuestión. Belice (año de 1783-1859); I. Los efectos de los "pactos de familia," en el status de Belice (1783); II. El momento curcial de Guatemala; III. El desenlace del drama de Belice. Guatemala: Secretaría de Información de la Presidencia de la República, 1959. 35 pp.
     Another restatement of the Guatemalan claims to Belize, based on the broken agreements of the mid-nineteenth century. TxU

129 _____. Quiebra y reintegración del derecho de gentes: Gibraltar, Belice, Las Malvinas. Guatemala: Imprenta Hispania, n.d. 78 pp. Illus.
     A discussion of British "opportunism," condemning the British seizures of the various territories in question as contrary to the rights of man and existing law and as indicative of British actions throughout the world. Supports the Guatemalan claim to Belize and the British evacuation of all the colonies in question. DLC LNHT BNG

130 López Jiménez, Ramón. Belice: tierra irredenta. Mexico: Editorial Mundo Actual, 1943. 232 pp.
     Contends that the 1863 treaty surrendered Guatemala's claim to Belize, but that since all of the Central American republics inherited a share of the Spanish title as successor states, the other four nations retain their claims. After much legal argument regarding this position the author, a Salvadoran historian, concludes that the other four nations should press their claims against Great Britain to obtain the territory, and should then give it to Guatemala, its rightful owner. DLC

131 López Mayorical, Mariano. Aspectos reales sobre Belice. Guatemala: Ministerio de Educación Pública, 1977. 39 pp. Maps.
     A series of articles, restating the Guatemalan case, published in various Guatemalan newspapers between 1967 and 1976. BNG

132 Maher, John, ed. Readings in Belizean History. Belize: Belize Institute for Social Research and Action, 1973. 75 pp. Maps.
     A collection of articles from the journal Belizan Studies dealing with the early settlement of the colony, its ethnic groups, and the independence movement. Intended as the initial volume in a series for classroom use.

133 Marín, Rufino. Las 3 bombas de tiempo en América Latina: devolución de Belice a Guatemala; acceso propio y soberano al Marañón para Ecuador; salida al mar Pacífico para Bolivia. Quito: Editorial Universitaria, 1959. 265 pp. Index, biblio., maps. 2d ed. Guatemala: Tipografía Nacional, 1959. 195 pp. Index, biblio., maps.
     An analysis of what the author calls three time bombs in the hemisphere, namely, Belize,

Bolivian access to the sea, and Ecuadorian access to Marañón. He contends that these are the three key issues most likely to cause crises, that they will have to be faced sometime in the future if the peace of America is to be maintained, that all are consequently hemispheric problems rather than local ones, and that they merit the attention of the Organization of American States. LNHT BNG

134 Mariscal, Ignacio. Informe del C. Ignacio Mariscal, secretario del despacho de relaciones exteriores, rendido ante el Senado acerca del Tratado de Límites entre Yucatán y Belice, con un apéndice de notas y piezas justificativas. Mexico: Imprenta de F. Díaz de León, 1893. 55 pp. Maps.
     The foreign minister's official statement of the rationale for the controversial Anglo-Mexican Treaty of 1893 (sometimes known as the Mariscal-St. John Treaty) in which Mexico recognized the British claim to Belize. Contains the full text of the treaty. DLC

135 Marroquín Rojas, Clemente. México jamás ha poseído territorio propio al sur del Río Hondo. Guatemala: Editorial del Ejército, 1962. 102 pp.
     A well-known Guatemalan newspaperman and political figure refutes Mexican claims, contending that Belize was part of the Captaincy General of Central America based in Guatemala throughout most of the Colonial period. The strong feelings engendered by the dispute are reflected in the author's comparison of Mexico's claim with the nineteenth-century expansionist attitude of the United States toward Mexico, his references to Mexican efforts to annex Guatemala at independence and their success in detaching a Guatemalan province, and in his paraphrase of the common Mexican statement of that century, contending that Guatemala is "so far from God and so close to Mexico." The volume meticulously reviews the various disputes regarding the Colonial jurisdictions, and cites the Guatemalan-Mexican treaty with the Díaz regime in which Mexico relinquished its claims to Belize. DLC LNHT BNG

136 Martínez Alomía, Santiago. Belice: estudio histórico político, y legal sobre el proyecto de tratado de límites concertado entre el Lic. Ignacio Mariscal, secretario de rel. ex. y Sir Spencer St. John, ministro plenipotenciario de Inglaterra. Campeche, Mexico: Departamento Cultural del Gobierno del Estado de Campeche, 1945. 374 pp. Maps.
     A series of articles written by a leading intellectual of Campeche during 1894 when the Anglo-Mexican Treaty was under discussion, originally published in the newspaper El Reproductor Campechano, denouncing the treaty and defending the Mexican claim to Belize. The articles argue that the treaty constitutes a unilateral surrender of Mexican claims without compensation or any assurances from England, thereby suggesting that the question is not merely one of national honor and

Mexican rights, but of using these rights to secure compensation and concessions. DLC

137 Martínez Palafox, Luís. La cuestión de Belice: relación documental. Mexico: UNAM, 1944. 117 pp. Notes. 2d ed. Mexico: Editorial Polis, 1945. 135 pp. Illus.

A graduate thesis at UNAM recounting the history of the dispute to the 1890s from the Mexican point of view, although focusing on the problems of the dispute rather than on a legalistic analysis of the positions of the claimants. Based on documents from the Mexican Ministry of Foreign Relations. DLC LNHT

138 Mendieta, Salvador. La cuestión anglo-centroamericana de Belice. Guatemala: Imprenta Hispania, 1958. 63 pp.

A leading unionist argues that the Belize question concerns all of Central America and hence that all the republics should support the case of Guatemala, implying that it can be a basis for isthmian unity. BNG

139 Mendoza, José Luís. Belice pertenece a Guatemala: la propaganda británica tergiversa la historia; Belize Belongs to Guatemala: The Britannic Propaganda Tergiversates History. Guatemala: Tipografía Nacional, 1947. 39 pp.

A series of articles from the Guatemalan press, praising the Guatemalan Libro Blanco and attacking the British case as baseless, criticizing British propaganda over the years. With text in English and Spanish. DLC LNHT BNG

140 _____. Inglaterra y sus pactos sobre Belice: Guatemala tiene derecho a reivindicar el territorio íntegro de Belice. Guatemala: Tipografía Nacional, 1942. 287 pp. Biblio., maps.
Britain and her Treaties on Belize (British Honduras). Guatemala: Tipografía Nacional, 1947. 301 pp. Biblio. 2d ed. Guatemala: Tipografía Nacional, 1954.

A detailed legal analysis of the various accords, stating the Guatemalan case that Britain acquired usufruct, not territory; that Guatemala is the heir to the Spanish sovereignty; and that the 1863 treaty is null and void because of the failure of England to comply with the article providing compensation to Guatemala, leaving Guatemalan claims intact. DLC LNHT BNG

141 Metzgan, Monrad Sigrid, and Henry Conrad Cain, eds. The Handbook of British Honduras: Comprising Historical, Statistical, and General Information Concerning the Colony. London: West India Committee, 1925. 460 pp. Index, illus., maps, tables.

Part of a continuing official series of volumes, intended to be annual but issued intermittantly, to provide basic information about the colony, its geography, history, people, and economy, with many statistics. It was later discontinued in favor of a briefer more general account, becoming A Brief Sketch, which also appeared irregularly. Includes a description of the colony's current state, and basic facts about it, its people and economy, a history, lists of governers and office-holders, and numerous tables, as well as a digest of current laws and other pertinent data. DLC

142 Mexico, Gov't of. Correspondencia diplomática cambiada entre el gobierno de la república y el de Su Majestad Británica con relación al territorio llamado Belice; 1872-1878. Mexico: Imprenta de Ignacio Cumplido, 1878. 94 pp.

A collection of missives from a period when formal diplomatic relations were suspended and hence involving direct communication of the ministries, which was initiated when the vice-governor of Belize complained about incursions by Mexican Indians into Belize. The Mexican government noted the problems of policing the remote area, and then took the occasion to raise the question of the status of the territory, contending that British occupation was temporary and unsanctioned, and reasserting the Mexican claim. The rest of the exchanges argue the positions of the respective governments. DLC LNHT

143 _____. Ministerio de Relaciones Exteriores. Tratado de límites Estados-Unidos Mexicanos y Honduras Británica, seguido de los principales documentos que á él se refieren. Mexico: Tipografía de J. Aguilar Vera, 1897. 130 pp. Maps.

The official version of the Anglo-Mexican Treaty of 1893, with full text, the foreign minister's report to the Congress, the congressional approval and ratification, and a justification. DLC

144 _____. Defensa del tratado de límites entre Yucatán y Belice, con respuesta á las objecciones que se han hecho en su contra, apoyada en algunos documentos inéditos y seguida de otros ya conocidos así como de los principales artículos de prensa metropolitana y yucateca. Mexico: Imprenta de El Siglo Diez y Nueve, 1894. xxxii, 368 pp. 3d ed. Guatemala: Ministerio de Educación Pública, 1958. xxxiv, 381 pp.

The Foreign Ministry's official response to the opposition to the Treaty of 1893, containing a new statement of its rationale and reproducing the full treaty, statements by the British government, Mariscal's original Informe to the Senate, and a long list of acts and adhesions by various state legislatures and groups, as well as newspaper articles of endorsement. DLC BNG

145 Minkel, Clarence W., and Ralph H. Alderman. A Bibliography of British Honduras, 1900-1970. East Lansing: Michigan State University, 1970. vii, 93 pp.

An unannotated alphabetical listing encompassing over 1,000 entries, including books and periodical articles, arranged by subject. Only specific studies relating to Belize are included. DLC LNHT

146 Morris, Daniel. The Colony of British Honduras: Its Resources and Prospects, with Particular Reference to Its Indigenous Plants

and Economic Productions. London: Edward
Stanford, 1883. xiii, 152 pp. Index, illus.,
maps.

A survey resulting from an official inspection visit by a British official. Emphasizes
the climate, flora and fauna, and economy,
urges settlement, and extols the prospects for
economic development of the colony. Notes the
current lack of development and sparcity of
settlement, observing that the largest export,
mahogany, produces only as much revenue as the
citrus trade of Jamaica. DLC LNHT

147 Narváez López, Carlos. Justicia internacional
sometida a prueba: estudio jurídico de la
controversia entre Guatemala y la Gran Bretaña
por el dominio de Belice. Guatemala:
Tipografía Nacional, 1946. 16 pp.

A Nicaraguan jurist's legal treatise supporting the Guatemalan claim and contending
that the result of the dispute will determine
the impartiality of the international justice
system, for in his view the legal claims all
belong to Guatemala. DLC

148 Nicolle, Roberto Carpio. Hacia donde va
Belice. Guatemala: Editorial Girblán, 1977.
297 pp. Biblio., notes, maps, tables.

An expanded version of a political science
thesis at the Universidad Landívar by a member
of the Guatemalan Congress who has represented
Guatemala in debates regarding Belize at the
United Nations. The work surveys the question
of jurisdiction, supporting the Guatemalan
claims but noting international sympathy for
Belizan independence. The author concludes
that Belizan union with Guatemala would offer
the best prospects; he stresses the economic
benefits while recognizing the political problems and noting that union would have to be
accomplished voluntarily by both peoples. DLC

149 Ower, Leslie Hamilton. The Geology of British
Honduras. Belize: Clarion, 1928. 24 pp.
Maps.

A brief description and summary of the
principal features and characteristics, designed for the general reader. DLC LNHT

150 Pallottine Missionary Sisters. Fifty Golden
Years: 1913-1963 in British Honduras.
Limburg, Belgium: Pallottine Fathers, 1963.
157 pp.

A history of the order's activities in
staffing the schools at each of its principal
towns.

151 Pardo Ruiz, German. Un nuevo enfoque sobre el
problema de Belice. Guatemala: Ministerio de
Educación Pública, 1977. 39 pp.

A statement by a Colombian scholar rejecting the new British moves to invoke self-
determination in the Belize case before the
United Nations, contending that it is solely a
bilateral question, that the presence of the
populace of Belize reflects the British occupation, and that since they have been ruled as
a colony they have little experience in such
matters. Therefore, he contends, self-
determination does not apply in this case,

since legal rights supercede and predate it.
BNG

152 Pasos, Gabriel. Belice: patrimonio de
Guatemala. Granada: Escuela Tipografía
Salesiana, 1944. 106 pp. Biblio.

A brief summary of the principal events in
the controversy and a legal analysis of the
various agreements and stands. Supports the
Guatemalan claims to Belize and hails Ubico's
campaign to regain the territory for
Guatemala. The United States position in the
question is hailed, with citations of the
protections provided by the Monroe Doctrine
and the Anglo-American accords of the nineteenth century. DLC

153 Paz Salinas, María Emilia. Belice: el
despertar de una nación. Mexico: Siglo XXI,
1979. 188 pp. Latest ed. Mexico: Siglo XXI
Editores, 1980. 192 pp.

A summary of the development of Belize from
its foundation to the verge of independence,
by a Mexican writer seeking to show its unique
traditions and cultural orientation. Includes
discussion of the boundary dispute with
Guatemala. The focus is on internal development and the readiness for independence, and
the volume is written with the intention of
increasing knowledge of Belize in the Spanish-
speaking world, which largely ignores it.

154 Paz y Paz, L. Alberto. La cuestión de Belice:
compromidos históricos. Guatemala: Imprenta
Universitaria, 1949. 108 pp.

A series of articles supporting the Guatemalan claim to Belize and harshly criticizing
the British "piracy" in retaining control by
force of arms. Originally appeared in La
Estrella de Panamá during 1945. DLC LNHT

155 People's United Party. Twenty-Five Years of
Struggle and Achievement, 1950-75: Short
History. Belize: National Printers, 1975.
36 pp.

An official summary of the activities of
the nation's major party.

156 Pérez Trejo, Gustavo A., ed. Documentos sobre
Belice o Balice. Mexico: Secretaría de
Hacienda y Crédito Público, 1958. 209 pp.
Biblio., notes, illus., maps.

A collection of excerpts from the pertinent
documents in the dispute, including the Royal
Cédulas regarding Colonial jurisdictions,
treaties, the statements of the positions of
the various governments, and resolutions of
Inter-American and International bodies and
conferences. DLC LNHT

157 Polanco R., Raúl. Los derechos de un pueblo a
través del tiempo: Belice, territorio
guatemalteco. Guatemala: Ministerio de
Educación Pública, 1959. 95 pp. Biblio.,
illus., maps.

An official account designed to explain the
Guatemalan claims to young people and schoolchildren, and to raise the national consciousness regarding this question. Portrays

England as a colonial power; summarizes the standard Guatemalan arguments. DLC BNG

158 Posnett, N.W., and P.M. Reilly, eds. Belize (British Honduras). Surbiton, England: Land Resources Division, Overseas Development Administration, 1973. vi, 92 pp.
    A topically arranged unannotated bibliographical list, covering all aspects of agriculture. Includes periodical articles as well as books.

159 Prats y Beltrán, Alardo. Visión actual de Belice. Mexico: Libro Mex, 1958. 194 pp. Illus., appendixes.
    A contemporary discussion of Belize, its desire for independence, and its leaders; critical of Guatemalan and Central American claims, but includes a discussion of the Mexican position. DLC

160 Rebolledo, Miguel. Quintana Roo y Belice. Mexico: Published by the Author, 1946. 106 pp. Maps.
    An account of the development of these regions, seeking to tie the evolution of Belize to Yucatán and contending that while Mexico surrendered its claims in favor of Britain, if the territory were turned over to Guatemala this would be a new situation that would enable the revival of a Mexican claim to part of it, since it is economically and historically part of Yucatán. DLC

161 Recinos, Marco Augusto. Les droits de Guatemala sur Belice; conférence. Paris: Publications de la Légation du Guatemala, 1948. 32 pp.
    An official publication restating the Guatemalan case, seeking to familiarize Europeans with the details and legal basis of the claim. TxU

162 Rodríguez, Manuel Eduardo. Impresiones de mi visita a Belice. Guatemala: Talleres Gráficos Díaz-Paiz, 1958. 31 pp.
    A series of articles by a Guatemalan journalist, originally published in El Imparcial during 1958. Details the current situation of Belize, its politics and economy; argues that the "highest sectors" favor union with Guatemala and that Guatemala needs to launch a major campaign to attract Belizans to the idea of joining with Guatemala, since the British must pull out eventually and the nation is too small and impoverished to stand alone. DLC BNG

163 Rodríguez Beteta, Virgilio. El libro de Guatemala Grande, Petén-Belice: estudio geográfico e histórico. 2 vols. Guatemala: Tipografía Nacional, 1951. xxii, 251, 231 pp. Index, illus., maps.
    Combines a history of the region, with the emphasis on Colonial and pre-Columbian times, with the history of the English usurpation of Belize; restates the Guatemalan case regarding its claims. DLC LNHT BNG

164 _____. Solidarity and Responsibilities of the United States in the Belize Case. Guatemala: Tipografía Nacional, 1965. 137 pp. Biblio., illus., maps.
    A discussion of the Belize question, supporting the claims of Guatemala and citing Yankee precedents, contending the Anglo-American agreements and the Monroe Doctrine represented attempts by the Northern Colossus to remove British influence from Central America and hence defend the region's liberty, and that since British actions in Belize violated this objective, the United States has an obligation to secure British withdrawal and the return of the territory to Guatemala. DLC LNHT BNG

165 Rogers, Ebenezer. Honduras Británica: sus recursos y desarrollo. Mérida: Tipografía Yucateca, 1938. 34 pp. Maps.
    A summary of the current economic situation and future potential. ICN

166 Romney, D.H., et al., eds. Land in British Honduras: Report of the British Honduras Land Use Survey Team. 2 vols. London: HMSO, 1959. 327 pp. Maps, tables.
    A detailed official survey of land use, with extensive statistics detailing its ownership and the nation's agriculture. Includes consideration of soils, native vegetation, common plants and animals, an economic history of the colony, and a discussion of its future potential, with extensive maps and statistics. DLC

167 Rubio Alpuche, Néstor. Belice: apuntes históricos y colección de tratados internacionales relativos a esta colonia británica. Mérida: Imprenta de La Revista de Mérida, 1894. 194 pp. Maps.
    Part of the controversy revolving around the Anglo-Mexican Treaty of 1893, this is a survey of the colony and the dispute, concluding with a recommendation that the treaty be rejected to preserve Mexico's claim, which the author considers legitimate. DLC LNHT

168 Santiso Gálvez, Gustavo. El caso de Belice a la luz de la historia y el derecho internacional. Guatemala: Ministerio de Relaciones Exteriores, 1941. 236 pp. Biblio. Latest ed. Guatemala: Ministerio de Relaciones Exteriores, 1975. 290 pp. Biblio.
    A thesis, by a Guatemalan national at UNAM, reviewing the legal aspects of the question, analyzing the treaties regarding it, and staunchly defending Guatemala's claim to the territory. Argues that none of the accords ceded any rights to England and contends that in any event the 1859 accord was nullified by the British nonfulfillment of the highway clause. The thesis was reprinted in Guatemala, with the endorsement of the Foreign Ministry, and conforms closely to the Guatemalan position. DLC LNHT BNG

169 _____. La condición resolutoria tácita por incumplimiento en las tratados internacionales y su aplicación al caso de la convención

angloguatemalteca de 30 de abril de 1859.
Guatemala: Tipografía Nacional, 1946. 27 pp.
    The Guatemalan minister in Lima restates
the Guatemalan position in an address at the
University of San Marcos, emphasizing the
Guatemalan willingness to agree to arbitration
only if all aspects of the dispute are considered. Emphasizes that the nonfulfillment
of the 1859 treaty clause by England nullifies
the treaty and returns the dispute to its
previous status under international law. DLC
LNHT

170 Schlesinger, Alfredo. Tópicos del momentos:
de Suez, Chipre, Gibraltar, Islas (Malvinas), a
Nuestro Belice. Guatemala: Tipografía
Nacional, 1956. 29 pp.
    The author links the controversies of Suez,
Gibraltar, the Falkland Islands, and Belize,
citing all as cases of British intransigence
and outdated imperialism based on force. BNG

171 Setzekorn, William David. Formerly British
Honduras: A Profile of the New Nation of
Belize. Newark, Calif.: Dumbarton Press,
1975. ix, 291 pp. Index, biblio., maps.
    A survey attempting to present basic data
about Belize, compiled from published sources,
in usable form. The focus is on the present,
though a historical sketch comprises a major
portion of the volume. Includes sections on
geography, economy, and people. DLC LNHT

172 Sharpe, Reginald. British Honduras: Report
of an Inquiry into Allegations of Contacts
between the People's United Party and
Guatemala. London: HMSO, 1954. 36 pp.
    An inquiry into allegations that the party
had sought financial assistance from the
Guatemalan government to enable an uprising.
Concludes that the Guatemalan consul in Belize
had provided some funds. DLC

173 Silva Badillo, José. Los derechos de México
en su frontera sur. Mexico: UNAM, 1965. 128
pp. Biblio., notes, maps, appendixes.
    A legal thesis contending that Mexico has
sovereignty over Belize because Belize was
under the jurisdiction of the Captaincy General of Yucatán during the Colonial period,
and was governed from Mexico City as part of
the Viceroyalty at the time of independence.
Argues that the 1893 Anglo-Mexican accord
conceded only usufruct to England, as did
previous Anglo-Spanish accords, and that consequently sovereignty still lies with Mexico.
The various treaties are reproduced in the
appendixes. DLC

174 Straughan, Robert P.L. Adventure in Belize.
London: Thomas Yoseloff; New York: A.S.
Barnes, 1975. 215 pp. Index, biblio.,
illus., maps.
    A travelogue, focusing on description of
flora and fauna, with extensive illustrations.
DLC

175 A Summer in Central America: The Record of a
Trip to the Land of Manana [sic] Written by

Members of the Party. Pulaski, Tenn.: L.D.
McCord, 1915. 45 pp.
    The adventures of a group of Yankees,
focusing on Belize with some references to
Guatemala. DLC

176 Swan, Michael. British Honduras. London:
Phoenix House, 1957. 39 pp. Maps.
    A brief background sketch summarizing the
colony's history, origins, economy, and present situation, written to promote knowledge
about it in England and among the nations of
the British West Indies. TxU

177 Swett, Charles. A Trip to British Honduras,
and to San Pedro, Republic of Honduras. New
Orleans: George Ellis, 1868. 125 pp.
    A diary giving a day-by-day account of the
author's trip to British Honduras and
Honduras, focusing on physical description and
living conditions. The trip was undertaken by
a Mississippian, in the company of friends who
were seeking to emigrate to British Honduras
in search of a better life in the wake of the
fall of the Confederacy and the destruction
caused by the Civil War. The author disa-
greed, and his doubting attitudes and contempt
for other customs and cultures are evident in
his account. He left and returned fully con-
vinced of the merits of the United States and
contemptuous of those who wished to flee. His
account consequently emphasizes all the nega-
tive aspects and the problems of life in the
tropics, and particularly in British Honduras.
His descriptions are nonetheless detailed and
illustrative of life there in the 1860s. DLC
LNHT

178 Taylor, Douglas MacRae. The Black Carib of
British Honduras. New York: Wenner-Gren
Foundation, 1951. 176 pp. Biblio., notes,
illus., maps, appendixes.
    An anthropological study emphasizing the
effects of the assimilation of escaped slaves
into the existing black Carib society on the
island of Saint Vincent, off British Honduras.
Combines observation with historical accounts,
considering life-style, social organization,
life cycles, and religious beliefs. Seeks to
identify the origins and traits of the society
that resulted from the black former slaves
adopting the Arawak language and the culture
of the local Carib Indians, whom the Europeans
considered useless as slaves. DLC LNHT

179 Thompson, John Eric Sidney. Ethnology of the
Mayas of Southern and Central British
Honduras. Chicago: Field Museum of Natural
History, 1930. 213 pp. Biblio., maps,
appendixes.
    Based on four expeditions to the region by
an experienced observer, this study examines
its agriculture, religion, social life, industry, and folklore, detailing practices observed and the surviving elements of the traditional culture. DLC

180 Vela, David. Nuestro Belice. Guatemala:
Tipografía Nacional, 1939. 195 pp. Biblio.

A lengthy exposition, by the editor of El Imparcial of Guatemala City, of the Guatemalan case throughout the controversy, emphasizing the legal questions. Originally appeared in that paper during 1938. DLC LNHT BNG

181 Vickers, Thomas Douglas. The Legislature of British Honduras. Belize: Government Printer, 1955. 26 pp.
A sketch of the history of the legislature and its role, by the acting governor, tracing its emergence and role since the Colonial era but focusing on the years since 1931.

182 Viejo del Carmen, Benque. Atlas of Belize. Belize: Cubola Productions, 1976. 36 pp.
An oversized volume with thirteen maps and a brief gazeteer giving current information. The maps include political, physical, and economic features, communications, climate, and similar items. Economic statistics and communications distances are also indicated.

183 Villaseñor y Villaseñor, Alejandro. La cuestión de Belice y el informe del señor secretario de relaciones. Mexico: Imprenta El Tiempo, 1894. 141 pp.
Part of the debate regarding ratification of the Anglo-Mexican treaty of 1893, this was originally a series of articles analyzing and replying to Mariscal's report that appeared in the newspaper El Tiempo opposing ratification of the accord. DLC

184 Waddell, David Alan Gilmour. British Honduras: A Historical and Contemporary Survey. London: Oxford University Press, 1961. 151 pp. Biblio., illus., maps.
An overview of the history of the colony from its origin to the present, based on secondary works and emphasizing the perspective of the British Empire. Includes consideration of the economy, social conditions, ethnic factors, political development, the planter class, relations with the mother country, and the British view of the boundary dispute with Guatemala. DLC LNHT

185 Walker, S.H. Summary of Climate Records for Belize. Surrey, England: Foreign and Commonwealth Office, Land Resources Division, 1973. 145 pp. Maps.
Consists of rainfall and temperature data recorded at twenty-six observation stations from 1882 to 1970.

186 Wallace, James Allen, and Angelo F. Spano. An Annotated Bibliography on the Climate of British Honduras. Washington, D.C.: GPO, 1962. 17 pp. Illus.
An annotated listing of studies of the climate of British Honduras, consisting principally of periodical articles, items from meeting proceedings, or studies by official agencies, many available only in mimeographed form. WU

187 Woodward, Ralph Lee, Jr. Belize. Santa Barbara, Calif.: Clio Press, 1980. xxii, 229 pp. Index, maps.

An annotated bibliography of selected works dealing with the nation, encompassing a broad range of topics of interest to tourists as well as to students and general readers. Includes books and articles from journals and periodicals, providing the most complete listing available. Provides full bibliographic data and annotations, though the arrangement of the entries within the topical chapters is not clear, with titles listed before author, and the entries not arranged alphabetically by title or author. The index and extensive cross-references facilitate searching out particular entries. DLC LNHT

188 Woolrich B., M.A. Bibliografía sobre Belice. Mexico: Editor Vargas Rea, 1957. 45 pp.
A small, limited edition printed on odd-sized and curiously aged paper, listing volumes and articles regarding Belize and the boundary question and covering the Colonial and modern eras. Some are annotated, others have only partial data. The emphasis is on Mexican volumes that refer to Belize, but it includes items relating to the boundary dispute in general, especially those in Spanish. DLC BNG

189 Ydígoras Fuentes, Miguel. Belice, Guatemala, La Gran Bretaña, y Centro América. Guatemala: Sánchez & de Guise, 1976. 23 pp.
A brief summary by a former president of Guatemala of his efforts while in office to secure control of Belize and assert the Guatemalan claims, with an account of the problems encountered and the British stand. DLC

190 Zammit, J. Ann. The Belize Issue. London: Latin American Bureau, 1978. 77 pp. Biblio., maps.
A summary of the boundary dispute from the Belizan viewpoint, with an overview of the present state of the territory and its economy.

Costa Rica

1 Abadie Santos, Aníbal Raúl. Cartas a mi sobrino. San José: Imprenta Greñas, 1916. 33 pp.
Ten letters commenting on the contemporary political scene, reflecting the disputes and polemics of the era. BNCR

2 Acosta, José, María. Prontuario de las leyes de Costa Rica. San José: Tipografía Nacional, 1893. 40 pp.
An alphabetically arranged series of definitions of legal terms and terminology as used in Costa Rica. Unfortunately this pamphlet covers only items beginning with the letter A. DLC-LDS-694

3 _____. Vocabulario del derecho patrio. San José: Tipografía Nacional, 1902. 207 pp.
An expansion of the author's earlier work, providing definitions of legal terms as used in Costa Rica, with explanations and commentary. DLC

4 Acosta Valverde, Adán. Anecdotario. San José: n.p., 1966. 103 pp. Illus.
A collection of anecdotes and jokes characteristic of Costa Rica, selected to provide insights into the national outlook and character and to illustrate the local sense of humor. LNHT BNCR

5 Acuña de Chacón, Angela. La mujer costarricense a traves de cuatro siglos. 2 vols. San José: Imprenta Nacional, 1969-70. 443, 665 pp. Biblio.
A compilation of information regarding the role of women in Costa Rican society from pre-Columbian times to the present, divided by sectors such as education, art, and charitable services and consisting principally of brief descriptions of the work of particular individuals important in each field. Both the length and the content of the descriptions vary, sometimes including laws or excerpts from writings or works. Based on secondary sources. The selection criteria for those included is not readily apparent, though the sheer bulk of the data and number of essays makes the work useful. DLC BNCR

6 Acuña Valerio, Miguel Ángel. El 48 (Cuarenta y ocho). San José: Imprenta Lehmann, 1974. 386 pp. Maps.
A detailed and sympathetic account of the 1948 revolution in Costa Rica, its background and development. Focuses on the military campaigns rather than the political realm, providing detailed histories of the combats and maneuvers and extolling the exploits of the revolutionaries. Based on interviews with numerous veterans of the campaign, their diaries, and commentaries written at the time, with extensive quotations from their accounts and from the proclamations of the era. LNHT BNCR

7 _____. Jorge Volio: el tribuno de la plebe. San José: Imprenta Lehmann, 1972. 198 pp. Notes, illus.
A biography of General Jorge Volio, whose leftist reformist party was among the first to pursue the "reformist" line of "leftist but-non-communist." His call for improved conditions for the poor and semisocialist outlook was considered radical and demagogic at the time. Traces his entire career, based on newspapers of the day and on proclamations. Includes his political efforts, his service as director of the National Archives, his links with and support of the Calderón Guardia administration, and his opposition to the Revolution of 1948. LNHT BNCR

8 Adis Castro, Gonzalo, et al. Algunos aspectos sociográficos del area metropolitana de San José; Costa Rica. San José: Universidad de Costa Rica, 1974. 105 pp. Biblio., illus. BNCR

9 Agüero, Arturo. El español de América y Costa Rica. San José: Universidad de Costa Rica, 1960. 2d ed. San José: Imprenta Lehmann, 1962. 285 pp. Index, biblio.
Designed originally for use in classes at the University of Costa Rica, the initial third of this volume treats the entire hemisphere generally, describing the characteristics of the Spanish brought by the conquistadores and the various changes common to the hemisphere. The latter two-thirds focuses on the evolution of the language as spoken in

Costa Rica, providing specific analysis of the various pronunciations, a linguistic history of the nation, a survey of the studies of its linguistic characteristics, and details regarding the various regional dialects. NN

10 Aguilar Bulgarelli, Oscar R. Breve reseña de algunas ideologías políticas de Costa Rica. San José: Universidad de Costa Rica, 1968. 38 pp. Biblio., notes.
A brief essay focusing on socialism, communism, and reformism in Costa Rica during the 1920s, 1930s, and 1940s, emphasizing the "Liberal era" of the coffee planters and the limits of its policies as contributing factors to the Revolution of 1948. BNCR

11 _____. La constitución de 1949: antecedentes y proyecciones. San José: Editorial Costa Rica, 1973. 188 pp. Biblio., notes. 2d ed. San José: Editorial Costa Rica, 1974. 188 pp. Biblio., notes.
A brief analysis, clause by clause, of the present constitution and a discussion of its origins, objectives, and its reflection of the political situation in which it was written. The author, a history professor at the University of Costa Rica, contends that the 1949 constitution closely parallels its 1871 predecessor, which he feels was unjustly converted into a national monument. He characterizes the 1949 document as conservative when compared to the social reforms of the early 1940s, but notes that these had bankrupted the nation and brought it to crisis. He clearly feels that some of the provisions are not suited to the modern world and to economic development, though he refrains from offering recommendations, limiting himself to an analysis of the existing document. BNCR

12 _____. Costa Rica y sus hechos políticos de 1948. San José: Editorial Costa Rica, 1969. 443 pp. Biblio. 2d ed. San José: EDUCA, 1974. 568 pp. Biblio.
A detailed account of the 1948 revolution, originally a thesis at the University of Costa Rica, beginning with the antecedents in the Calderón Guardia administration and ending with a discussion of the 1948 provisional government. Based on extensive research in published works and the polemics and periodicals of the time, it includes extensive documentary excerpts. Concludes that the revolution was not very revolutionary, with a change in government but little social or economic reform save for the new constitution and the bank nationalization, which were primarily a reaction to the electoral fraud of the preceding regimes. What social and economic changes occurred, the author contends, began during the Calderón Guardia regime and constituted a reaction to the changing world and national conditions. DLC LNHT BNCR

13 _____. Democracia y partidos políticos en Costa Rica, 1950-1962. San José: n.p., 1977. 175 pp. Biblio.
LNHT

14 _____, ed. El desarrollo nacional en 150 años de vida independiente. San José: Universidad de Costa Rica, 1971. 401 pp. Biblio., notes, illus.
Essays by leading Costa Rican historians from the University of Costa Rica, concisely summarizing the various aspects of national development on the occasion of the 150th anniversary of independence. Chapters deal with constitutions and economic, literary, educational, financial, and journalistic development, all in brief summary form to provide an overview, with some quotations from pertinent documents. DLC LNHT BNCR

15 Aguilar Bulgarelli, Oscar R. Evolución político-constitucional de Costa Rica. San José: Imprenta Lehmann, 1976. 126 pp. Biblio.
An overview of Costa Rican constitutional development considering each of the nation's constitutions, its democracy, its institutions, and the changing times. An effort is made to cast each constitution in the perspective of the politics of its era, differentiating between what it borrowed from tradition and its innovations. Focuses on political generations and the need to change the institutions periodically while remaining within the national tradition. BNCR

16 _____. José Santos Lombardo. San José: Ministerio de Cultura, Juventud y Deportes, 1973. 162 pp. Biblio., notes, illus.
A biography of a Costa Rican who served as a colonial official and then participated in the independence movement, tracing his activities and service in the Constituent Assembly and his political stances. Based on secondary sources and documentary research it sheds light on a little-known figure of this era. DLC BNCR

17 Aguilar J., Emanuel. Don Miguel Obregón Lizano: fundador y organizador de bibliotecas públicas. San José: Imprenta La Tribuna, 1935. 52 pp. Illus.
A sketch of the early career of this well-known Costa Rican educator, recounting his role in the construction, foundation, and development of its most significant libraries during the 1880s and 1890s. Deals only with that portion of his life and hence does not discuss his later and more important positions or his influence on the nation's educational system. DLC DLC-LDS-835 LNHT BNG

18 _____. Don Miguel Obregón y el instituto de Alajuela. San José: Imprenta Elena, 1950. 19 pp. Illus.
A brief account of the dedication to and promotion of the secondary school in Alajuela, Costa Rica, by one of the nation's leading educators. BNCR

19 Aguilar Machado, Alejandro. Miscelánea. San José: Editorial Aurora Social, 1948. 134 pp. Index, illus.
A series of essays and speeches by a Costa Rican intellectual and diplomat of the 1920s,

(Aguilar Machado, Alejandro)
1930s, and 1940s. They include commentaries on Costa Rican historical themes and figures, which predominate, as well as essays regarding hemispheric themes and historical figures, and a collection of speeches that includes his address as head of the Costa Rican delegation to the Ninth Inter-American Conference. BNCR

20 _____. *Opiniones y discursos*. San José: Imprenta Alsina, 1929. 159 pp. Index.
A series of commentaries and collected speeches by the author, consisting primarily of brief résumés of the careers of significant figures in Costa Rican nineteenth- and early twentieth-century development, but also including comments on contemporary politics and on the unionist movement, whose cause the author expounds. DLC DLC-LDS-436 BNCR

21 Aguilar Meza, Ricardo. *Cum Laude, historia de un cirujano o 50 años de mi vida*. Guatemala: Unión Tipográfia, 1941. 355 pp. Illus.
The memoirs of a Costa Rican surgeon who worked for United Fruit Company hospitals in Honduras and Costa Rica, focusing on medical problems and surgical techniques then in use. Provides detailed descriptions and photos of the facilities in the United Fruit hospitals, noting their advantages over those of others in the nation. The discussion of medical problems serves to illustrate the types of accidents that occurred on the company's plantations, though the analysis of techniques is quite technical. DLC BNCR

22 Alajuela, Instituto de. *Libro del centenario de Juan Santamaría y algunas otras paginas cívicas de Alajuela*. San José: Imprenta Nacional, 1934. 312 pp. Illus.
A series of essays regarding important personages from and events in the history of the city of Alajuela, with the title essay devoted to the national military hero of the campaigns against William Walker. DLC DLC-LDS-608 BNCR

23 Albertazzi Avendaño, José. *Unos apuntes simples sobre democracia costarricense*. San José: Imprenta Nacional, 1941. 26 pp.
A brief essay extolling the benefits of Costa Rican democracy and the origins of this nation's unique democratic tradition, written in patriotic terms. BNCR

24 _____. *Palabras al viento*. San José: n.p., 1936. 162 pp. Index, illus.
Speeches and commentaries by a Costa Rican political orator, including commentaries on such themes as rural schools and their role in the nation. DLC DLC-LDS-848 BNCR

25 _____. *El perfil moral costarricense*. San José: Imprenta Lehmann, 1967. 144 pp.
A series of essays dealing with Costa Rican freedom and its traditions, comparing the nation with others in Latin America, hailing its moralistic tradition, and offering suggestions for expanding the absence of restrictions even more. DLC LNHT

26 Alfaro Arguedas, Gregorio. *Problemas que afectan el desarrollo agropecuario en cuatro cantones de la Península de Nicoya*. San José: Ministerio de Agricultura y Ganadería, 1966. 64 pp. Illus., maps, tables.
A tabulation of data from a survey of the Nicoya Peninsula, providing detailed breakdowns of land ownership and use, occupations, income, labor resources, and other economic factors. DLC

27 Alleger, Daniel E., ed. *Fertile Lands of Friendship: The Florida-Costa Rican Experiment in International Agricultural Cooperation*. Gainesville: University of Florida Press, 1962. xi, 312 pp. Biblio., illus., maps.
A detailed account of the cooperative program between the University of Florida School of Agriculture and the Servicio Técnico Interamericano de Cooperación Agrícola for the improvement of agriculture in Costa Rica between 1954 and 1960. Each phase of the broad effort that involved technical services to existing farms and experimental stations throughout the republic is meticulously described, offering detailed information about the nation's agriculture as well as the results of the various programs. DLC

28 Alvarado Quirós, Alejandro. *La democracia; una conferencia y varios artículos*. San José: Imprenta Trejos, 1939. 86 pp.
Essays on wide-ranging themes, including the title piece on democracy, a discussion of contemporary Costa Rican political parties, and commentaries on several events in countries outside the isthmus. DLC

29 _____. *Ecos de la vida parlamentaria*. San José: Imprenta Gutenberg, 1930. 137 pp.
Speeches by an important congressional deputy covering the years 1926 through 1929 and dealing with both domestic and international politics. Includes comments on presidential elections, the contract with the United Fruit Company, canal projects, and many other subjects. DLC DLC-LDS-486

30 _____. *El licenciado don Alejandro Alvarado García*. San José: Imprenta Trejos, 1939. 116 pp. Illus.
A brief biography of a Costa Rican jurist whose career included service as president of the Supreme Court during the 1920s, tracing his judicial and legal positions and his educational efforts; followed by tributes at the time of his death. The essays hail democracy in general, refer to the development of the various Costa Rican parties, and acclaim them as becoming more representative and less doctrinaire. DLC-LDS-841 BNCR

31 _____. *Nuestra tierra prometida*. San José: Imprenta Trejos, 1925. 227 pp. Notes.
The initial half of the volume is devoted to essays regarding Costa Rican and isthmian themes and historical figures, encompassing a description of the different cities of Costa Rica and biographical sketches of Central

American figures. The second portion deals with South American and hemispheric themes. DLC-LDS-340 BNCR

32 Alvarez Cañas, Alberto. La République de Costa Rica. Paris: A. Michalon, 1905. 44 pp.

A glowing description of the nation and its future prospects, by the Costa Rican consul in France. Clearly designed to familiarize the general French audience with the nation and to encourage trade and investment. DLC DLC-LDS-490

33 Alvarez Melgar, Mariano. Breve reseña de la República de Costa Rica y algunas consideraciones sobre su provenir. Barcelona: Tipografía La Académica de Serra y Russell, 1919. 45 pp. Illus., map.

A brief description of the current state of Costa Rica, giving basic physical, political, and economic data. Emphasizes the economy, the Spanish culture, and the potential for linkage with Spain. DLC DLC-LDS-173

34 Amador, Francisco de Paula. Pro-Puntarenas. San José: Imprenta Moderna, 1914. 176 pp.

A brief historical sketch of the city, followed by a collection of annual reports and legislative decrees relative to its development, particularly port development. The topics are broad and the selection criteria are not clear, while the chronology is widely spaced. BNCR

35 Amador Guevara, José, et al. Nuestro problema demográfico. San José: Ministerio de Salubridad Pública, 1966. 26 pp. Biblio., tables.

A brief analysis of population growth, including statistical projections and discussion of birth control programs, their present extent and their potential effects. BNCR

36 Ameringer, Charles D. The Democratic Left in Exile: The Antidictatorial Struggle in the Caribbean, 1945-1959. Coral Gables, Fla.: University of Miami Press, 1974. 352 pp. Index, biblio., notes, maps.

A study of the political Left that analyzes both regimes in power and exile movements in a manner that unifies the entire Caribbean-Central American region. Contains extensive data regarding Guatemala and Costa Rica during these years, demonstrating that, along with Cuba, they were the key supporters of revolutionary efforts directed against incumbent dictatorships such as the Somoza regime in Nicaragua. Though arguing that the so-called "Caribbean Legion" never really existed, the author demonstrates considerable cooperation among a group of political parties, whether in or out of power, and indicates joint efforts to acquire arms and sponsor revolts, with cooperative efforts leading to interlocking leadership and the use of nations with "reformist" governments as bases for expeditions against the dictatorships, which of course were engaged in similar efforts against the reform governments. DLC LNHT

37 _____. Don Pepe: A Political Biography of José Figueres of Costa Rica. Albuquerque: University of New Mexico Press, 1978. x, 324 pp. Index, biblio., notes.

An examination of the career of Costa Rica's dominant political figure during a pivotal era, based on research in Figueres's private archives, extensive interviews, and appropriate secondary works. Includes consideration of Figueres's struggle for power, his formation of the National Liberation party, his service on the junta, and his first presidential term. The focus is on the years 1958-70, when Figueres's archive is the fullest, though the 1948-58 era is also treated extensively. The years after 1970 are examined more lightly, from secondary works and periodical literature. DLC LNHT

38 Amighetti, Francisco. Francisco en Costa Rica. San José: Editorial Costa Rica, 1966. 223 pp. Illus. 2d ed. San José: Editorial Costa Rica, 1972. 161 pp. Illus.

A Costa Rican writer and artist's remembrances of his life in his native land, offering views of his childhood and other experiences, in both prose and drawing, seeking to show the nature of Costa Rican society, its culture, and customs. DLC LNHT BNCR

39 Angulo Novoa, Alejandro. Familia, educación y anticoncepción: análisis comparativo de tres encuestas de fecundidad en Bogotá, Panamá y San José. Bogotá: Fundación para la Educación Superior y el Desarrollo, 1974. viii, 101 pp. Biblio., illus., tables.

A comparative analysis of family planning in three cities, based on data gathered in field research during the 1960s, indicating the impact of education and industrialization on attitudes and family size. DLC

40 Unos apuntes simples sobre democracia costarricense. San José: Imprenta Nacional, 1941. 26 pp.

A brief essay on Costa Rican democracy that was awarded a prize in a competition in Argentina. It stresses the fact that the nation has real and effective democracy, tracing this to the national unity, its long tradition, the absence of barriers in the society, and the honesty of the governments. Ironically, the work was awarded the Calderón Guardia prize, in honor of the then-incumbent executive whose actions contributed to a later revolution. DLC-LDS-907

41 Arango, Jacinto P. Las instituciones del estado creadas por don Tomás Soley Güell y sus defectos. San José: Imprenta La Tribuna, 1931. 73 pp.

A series of articles that appeared in La Tribuna of San José, detailing and analyzing the current economic crisis, and particularly El Crédito Hipotecario Nacional, which the author contends is insolvent. He provides details about the bank's operation, alleging irregularities and poor practices, and advocates government action to correct the situation and reinforce the bank. Includes

discussion of other financial institutions of
the government and refutation of the arguments
and responses by Soley Güell.   DLC

42   Araya Incera, Manuel E.   Materiales para la
historia de las relaciones internacionales de
Costa Rica: bibliografía, fuentes impresas.
San José: Universidad de Costa Rica, 1980.
91 pp.
An alphabetical listing, with bibliographical information but without annotation,
within topical headings, focusing on works
published in Central America. Despite the
title, it includes many general items that
have only limited information on the subject.
BNCR

43   Araya Pochet, Carlos.   Historia de los
partidos políticos: Liberación Nacional.
San José: Imprenta Lehmann, 1968. 203 pp.
Biblio., notes.
Originally written as a thesis, this
slender volume presents a eulogistic account
of the role of Liberación Nacional in Costa
Rica since the Revolution of 1948, covering
the following twenty-five years. DLC LNHT
BNCR

44   _____. Historia económica de Costa Rica,
1950-1970. San José: Editorial Fernández-
Arce, 1975. viii, 158 pp. Biblio., illus.,
tables.
A dependency-based analysis that reviews
the various sectors of the economy and contends that although Costa Rica entered a new
era in 1950 little has changed because what
has occurred is growth rather than development, with economic expansion but little
social reform, and with the nation retaining
the same capitalist economy. The author contends that agriculture, based on latifundia
and minifundia, is neglected, just as in other
Latin American countries, and that the nation's focus is toward industry, which has
little social benefit and promotes dependence.
DLC LNHT BNCR

45   Araya Pochet, Carlos, et al.   El desarrollo
nacional en 150 años de vida independiente.
San José: Universidad de Costa Rica, 1971.
401 pp. Biblio., illus.
BNCR

46   Araya Rojas, José Rafael.   Vida musical de
Costa Rica. San José: n.p., 1943. 39 pp.
2d ed. San José: Imprenta Nacional, 1957.
142 pp.
The first part, originally published separately in 1942, contains a series of single-
paragraph commentaries on various aspects of
musical development in Costa Rica. The second
portion offers similar commentaries on significant Costa Rican composers and artists and
their works, arranged alphabetically. Portions of this second part were also published
during the 1940s, like the first, as articles
in Revista Educación.   DLC BNCR

47   Arce, José M.   Manuel González Zeledón: vida
y obra. San José: Editorial Universitaria,

1947. 2d ed. New York: Hispanic Institute,
1948. 37 pp. Illus.
A brief biographical sketch of a leading
Costa Rican writer who used the pseudonym
Magón on many of his works, tracing his life
and the influences that affected his short
stories of the costumbrista school. Includes
a collection of his short stories from the
Costa Rican press that have not previously
appeared in book form. DLC LNHT

48   Arce C., Jorge.   Evolución de la enseñanza
normal en Costa Rica. San José: Ministerio
de Educación Pública, 1957.
A synopsis of the evolution and growth of
Costa Rica's normal schools, providing information on the development and state of teacher
training in that nation.

49   Arce Vargas, Mariano.   Reseña histórica del
Cantón de Orotína. Orotína: Imprenta
Borrasé, 1923. 50 pp.
A brief history of the canton, focusing on
local development and local institutions,
especially schools, from the founding of the
town in Colonial days to the present. BNCR

50   Architects Collaborative.   Housing in Costa
Rica: A Report on Housing and Community Development Made Possible by Cooperation Between
the Government of Costa Rica and the Government of the United States; La vivienda en
Costa Rica: un informe sobre la vivienda y
desarrollo de la comunidad que ha sido posible
gracias a la cooperación de los gobiernos de
Costa Rica y de los Estados Unidos de América.
Cambridge, Mass.: n.p., 1951. xiv, 104 pp.
Biblio., illus., maps, tables.
A study of the nation's housing situation
and needs, conducted by the Architects Collaborative of Cambridge, Massachusetts, under the
auspices of the U.S. Technical Cooperation
Administration. The technicians were Rafael
Espino and Leonard Currie, and the text is
printed in English and Spanish, with ample
maps, charts, and illustrations. It surveys
existing housing conditions in various sectors
of the republic and recommends detailed and
elaborate programs for future construction,
including projects, financing, type of construction, and priorities in various areas.
DLC BNCR

51   Arenys de Mar, Zenon de.   Los RR. PP.
Capuchinos en Costa Rica: breve historia.
Cartago: El Heraldo de la Archdiocese de San
José, 1936. 50 pp. Illus.
The history of the Capuchin fathers in
Costa Rica, written by one of its priests,
previously published in the order's magazine,
El Heraldo Seráfico, including essays on its
principal activities and heroes in Costa Rica,
followed by a province-by-province résumé of
its responsibilities. The focus is on the
nineteenth century, though data on the Colonial era and the 1930s are included. Includes
illustrations of figures mentioned and of the
current churches. DLC DLC-LDS-843

52 Argüello, Rosendo. <u>Quienes</u> <u>y</u> <u>cómo</u> <u>nos</u>
<u>traicionaron</u>. N.p.: n.p., 1952. 172 pp.
Illus.
    A tract by a Nicaraguan exile who partici-
pated in the 1948 Costa Rican revolution and
later held offices in the resulting governments. Includes an account of the combat in
Costa Rica and a denunciation of Figueres's
later actions, charging that he failed to
honor his pledges to help the Nicaraguan
exiles overthrow the Somoza regime. The
author assails Figueres for qualifying his
pledges of aid and for reassessing his crusade
for democracy in the Caribbean, charging that
Figueres was too pragmatic and not loyal to
his ideology. Includes a collection of documents and letters exchanged between the author
and Figueres. FMU

53 _____. <u>La</u> <u>verdad</u> <u>en</u> <u>marcha</u>: <u>timos</u>,
<u>delaciones</u> <u>e</u> <u>imposturas</u> <u>en</u> <u>el</u> <u>Caribe</u>. Mexico:
Imprental Nonpareil, 1950. 172 pp. Illus.
Latest ed. Mexico: Imprenta Nonpareil, 1951.
172 pp.
    A Nicaraguan attorney and historian's
account of the Costa Rican crisis of 1948,
consisting primarily of an attack on the
alleged corruption and irregularities of the
Calderón Guardia and Picado regimes, and
written from a viewpoint sympathetic to the
National Liberation Movement. BNCR

54 Argüello Mora, Manuel. <u>La</u> <u>bella</u> <u>Herediana</u>:
<u>el</u> <u>amor</u> <u>a</u> <u>un</u> <u>leproso</u>. San José: Imprenta de
Alfredo Greñas, 1900. 50 pp.
    Costumbrista short stories dealing with
peasant life in the rural countryside.

55 _____. <u>Costa</u> <u>Rica</u> <u>pintoresca</u>: <u>sus</u> <u>leyendas</u> <u>y</u>
<u>tradiciones</u>. San José: Imprenta María
Viuda de Lines, 1899. 320 pp.
    A prominent Costa Rican writer of the late
nineteenth century composed this series of
short (and not-so-short) stories based on his
nation's traditions and folklore. They seek
to preserve the local lore and are rich in
description of the country and its beauties.
BNCR

56 _____. <u>Un</u> <u>drama</u> <u>en</u> <u>el</u> <u>Presidio</u> <u>de</u> <u>San</u> <u>Lucas</u>,
<u>un</u> <u>hombre</u> <u>honrado</u>, <u>las</u> <u>dos</u> <u>gemelas</u> <u>del</u> <u>mojón</u>.
San José: Tipografía La Paz, 1900.
    A collection of costumbrista short stories
emphasizing the nation's tradition and folklore. BNCR

57 _____. <u>Novelitas</u> <u>de</u> <u>costumbres</u>
<u>costarricenses</u>. San José: Imprenta María
Viuda de Lines, 1900.
    Another collection of costumbrista short
stories emphasizing the rural and folkloric
traditions of the nation. BNCR

58 _____. <u>Obras</u> <u>literarias</u> <u>e</u> <u>históricas</u>. San
José: Editorial Costa Rica, 1963. 495 pp.
Index, biblio., notes, illus.
    An anthology of the works of a Costa Rican
writer of the late nineteenth century who
spent much of his career abroad in the United
States and Europe. Includes historical

essays, memoirs of his trips, and literary
commentaries. The largest segment consists of
short stories based on Costa Rican folklore
and regional traditions. LNHT BNCR

59 _____. <u>Páginas</u> <u>de</u> <u>história</u>: <u>recuerdos</u> <u>e</u>
<u>impresiones</u>. San José: Tipografía El Fígaro,
1898. iv, 212 pp.
    A volume of commentaries combining a series
of essays on the career of Juan Rafael Mora
and various newspaper articles commenting on
life in Costa Rica, including the author's
observations during his various travels
abroad. The essays on Mora hail the projects
he promoted during his tenure as president,
his role in the campaign against Walker, and
his negotiations with the United States and
Nicaragua regarding the canal question. They
include commentaries on his political role and
his exile, in which the author defends the
actions of Mora, who was his uncle. DLC DLC-
LDS-34 LNHT BNCR

60 _____. <u>La</u> <u>trinchera</u> <u>y</u> <u>otras</u> <u>páginas</u>
<u>históricas</u>. San José: Editorial Costa Rica,
1975. 153 pp. Biblio., notes.
    A series of historical novelettes set in
the nineteenth century. Drawn from the larger
<u>Obras</u> <u>literarias</u> <u>e</u> <u>históricas</u> by Argüello
Mora. DLC LNHT

61 Arias, Tomás. <u>Tres</u> <u>mesas</u> <u>en</u> <u>Costa</u> <u>Rica</u>.
Panamá: Panama Star and Herald, 1928. 27 pp.
    A Panamanian visitor's brief summary of the
cities and locations he visited in Costa Rica
during 1928, along with commentaries on the
nation and its people. Originally prepared
for publication in the Panamanian press. BNCR

62 Arias Sánchez, Oscar. <u>Grupos</u> <u>de</u> <u>presión</u> <u>en</u>
<u>Costa</u> <u>Rica</u>. San José: Editorial Costa Rica,
1971. 130 pp. Biblio., notes.
    Originally a thesis, this brief volume
analyzes the role of political pressure groups
in Costa Rica, drawing upon published works in
political theory and the writings of Costa
Rican political figures. Contends that pressure groups are inevitable in a democracy, but
that they exercise more influence in Costa
Rica than might be the case because of the
lack of party solidarity. Includes a brief
mention of the various current groups that
participate in the political system. DLC
LNHT BNCR

63 _____. <u>Nuevos</u> <u>rumbos</u> <u>para</u> <u>el</u> <u>desarrollo</u>
<u>costarricense</u>. San José: EDUCA, 1980.
150 pp.

64 _____. <u>¿Quién</u> <u>goberna</u> <u>en</u> <u>Costa</u> <u>Rica</u>? <u>Un</u>
<u>estudio</u> <u>del</u> <u>liderazgo</u> <u>formal</u> <u>en</u> <u>Costa</u> <u>Rica</u>.
San José: EDUCA, 1976. 378 pp. Biblio.
    A detailed analysis of the social origins
of the Costa Rican leadership since 1920,
concluding that despite the changes brought
about by the 1948 revolution, the vast majority of those in government still come from the
upper classes, though they now are more careful to represent a middle-class viewpoint.
Argues that the middle class has played a

larger role in the legislature, but offers no comment on the distribution of power between the legislature and the executive. Notes that the vast majority of the political leaders come from urban areas, but adds that the National Liberation party shows a higher percentage of those from rural sectors. Concludes that while there has been an opening of the political system to ideas and a broadening of participation by parties and by the electorate, the background of the leadership has changed very little, and that while the middle class now at least partly shares power with the upper class, the latter remains dominant. LNHT BNCR

65 Armijo, Roberto, and José Napoleón Rodríguez Ruíz. <u>Francisco Gavidia: la odisea de su genio</u>. 2 vols. San Salvador: Ministerio de Educación Pública, 1965-67. 301, 213 pp. Index, biblio., notes, illus.
    A detailed study of the works and outlook of Gavidia, with extensive quotations and excerpts from his publications. The first volume discusses modernism in general and Gavidia's relationship to Darío, focusing on his poetry. The second volume deals with his philosophy, focusing on his short stories and plays. The analysis considers both content and literary style, seeking to identify influences upon him, indicate his principal characteristics, and extol his literary contributions. DLC LNHT BNCR

66 Arrieta Quesada, Santiago, ed. <u>El pensamiento político de monseñor Sanabria</u>. San José: EDUCA, 1977. 332 pp. Biblio.
    A collection of writings and speeches by the bishop of Costa Rica who headed the church from 1940 to 1952, was active in promoting social reform during the turbulent 1940s, and hence participated in the political events of this pivotal era. The excerpts and analyses demonstrate his support of church involvement in politics and reform, as well as his role as a mediator between political factions during the civil war, which led to his later being declared Benemérito de la Patria. BNCR

67 Arroyo Soto, Victor Manuel. <u>El habla popular en la literatura costarricense</u>. San José: Universidad de Costa Rica, 1971. 320 pp. Biblio., notes.
    An analysis of the use of Costa Rican idioms and modisms in the work of Costa Rican authors Arturo Agüero Chaves, Fabián Dobles, Luís Dobles Segreda, Aquileo Echeverría, Carlos Luís Fallas, Ricardo Fernández Guardia, Joaquín García Monge, Manuel González Zeledón, Adolfo Herrera García, Carmen Lyra, José Marín Cañas, Jorge Montero Madrigal, and Carlos Salazar Herrera. Originally a thesis, it includes definitions and detailed analyses of the various forms and types that appear in the nation's literature. DLC BNCR

68 ____. <u>Pedro Pérez, candidato</u>. San José: Ediciones Aula, 1975. 32 pp.
    A brief farce, written for the theater, lampooning politics by recounting the experiences of a small-town barber who becomes a candidate for political office and narrating the effect on his life. DLC BNCR

69 Asociación de Maestros de la República de Panamá. <u>El viaje a Costa Rica de los maestros panameños</u>. Panamá: Imprenta Nacional, 1927. 110 pp. Illus.
    A collection of material relating to the April 1927 visit of a group of Panamanian teachers to Costa Rica; includes photos, press commentary, public declarations and official acts, and comments by the visitors and about the visit. DLC

70 Azofeifa, Isaac Felipe. <u>Cómo pronunciamos nuestra lengua y conversaciones sobre literatura costarricense</u>. San José: J. Bejarano, n.d. 116 pp.
    A commentary on the local Costa Rican idioms and a collection of commentaries on the nation's literature and writers. TxU

71 ____. <u>Don Mauro Fernández: teoría y práctica de su reforma educativa</u>. San José: Editorial Fernández Arce, 1975. 69 pp. Biblio., illus.
    A study of the educational reforms of the nineteenth century in Costa Rica, their basis and their impact, focusing on the role of the key promoter of the changes and quoting extensively from his commentaries and the laws. KU

72 ____. <u>El viejo liceo</u>. San José: Ministerio de Cultura, Juventud y Deportes, 1973. 103 pp. Illus.
    An analysis of the Liceo in Costa Rica from its founding in 1887, noting its important role in spreading culture and education in the nation, arguing that the strength of education is the primary contributor to the tradition of Costa Rican democracy. BNCR

73 Backer, James. <u>La iglesia y el sindicalismo en Costa Rica</u>. San José: Editorial Costa Rica, 1974. 268 pp. Biblio., notes. 3d ed. San José: Editorial Costa Rica, 1978. 335 pp. Biblio., appendix.
    A study of the relation between the church and labor unions, consisting of brief narrations of each administrative and church era from the mid 1800s to the present, followed by an appendix with pertinent statements and correspondence. Concludes that the church in Costa Rica has been conservative, and that only Bishop Sanabria in the mid-twentieth century promoted unionization. DLC BNCR

74 Baeza Flores, Alberto. <u>Daniel Oduber: una vida y cien imagenes</u>. San José: Editorial Eloy Morúa Carrillo, 1976. 303 pp. Illus.
    A biography of the recent Costa Rican president. Traces his life and career, with emphasis on the post-1948 era. Covers his service in Congress, as foreign minister, as candidate, and as president. The volume consists principally of excerpts from various speeches by and commentaries about Oduber, along with numerous photos showing him with world leaders and on the political trail. The connecting narration is sparse. LNHT BNCR

(Baeza Flores, Alberto)

75   _____. La lucha sin fin. Mexico: B. Costa-
Amic, 1969. 432 pp. Biblio., map.
A Chilean scholar's history of the Costa
Rican Revolution of 1948, viewed sympatheti-
cally as a victory for democracy over tyranny.
The focus is on the key figure, José Figueres
Ferrar, whom the author ranks among the out-
standing democratic leaders of the hemisphere.
Includes liberal quotations from the speeches
and broadsides of the time and from secondary
works. DLC LNHT BNG BNCR

76   Barahona Jiménez, Luís. Anatomía patriótica.
San José: Universidad de Costa Rica, 1970.
98 pp.
A call for political change to deal with
pressing social problems caused by maldistribution of income and by population growth,
criticizing personalismo and the stability of
the current system while indicating a need for
new leadership to enable the nation to solve
its problems and preserve its integrity. LNHT

77   _____. El gran incógnito: visión interna del
campesino costarricense. San José: Editorial
Universitaria, 1953. 164 pp. Biblio., notes.
Latest ed. San José: Universidad de Costa
Rica, 1975. 223 pp. Biblio., notes,
appendix.
A psychological discussion of the Costa
Rican peasants, providing a view of their
personalities, lives, and desires, ennunciat-
ing the typical characteristics of this group
and the societal factors that are important in
their lives. Includes discussion of their
patriotism, nationalism, and relation to
national life. DLC LNHT BNCR

78   _____. El pensamiento político en Costa Rica.
San José: Editorial Fernández-Arce, 1971.
180 pp.
A brief history of Costa Rican political
thought from Colonial times to the 1960s,
consisting of a series of commentaries with
quotations regarding each of the nation's most
influential political leaders and theorists.
The essays are short, ranging from a single
paragraph to several pages, and hence provide
an outline of the nation's political history.
DLC BNCR

79   _____. La Universidad de Costa Rica, 1940-
1973. San José: Editorial Universidad de
Costa Rica, 1976. 408 pp. Biblio., notes.
An official history of the University of
Costa Rica during recent years, viewing the
institution functionally and topically rather
than chronologically, based on research in the
university's documents and minutes. Includes
consideration, in separate chapters, of such
themes as the professors, research, students,
extension services, and the university's influence on the national culture. DLC LNHT
BNCR

80   Barahona Streber, Oscar, ed. Pensamiento y
acción. Cartago: Colegio Vocacional de Artes
y Oficios de Cartago, 1971. 413 pp. Illus.
A collection of statements regarding and
press commentaries about the actions of Oscar

Barahona Streber during his service as minister of hacienda of Costa Rica from 1969 to
1970, with a collection of his speeches and
declarations from the period. Indicates the
financial policies of the government as well
as his own views. BNCR

81   Barahona Streber, Oscar. Principios y
objectivos de la integración. San José:
Imprenta Trejos, 1970. 39 pp.
A brief summary of the official Costa Rican
positions toward the Central American economic
integration movement, by the nation's minister
of hacienda, indicating the problems and the
benefits as seen by that nation. BNCR

82   Barrantes Ferrero, Mario. Evolución de la
división territorial en la provincia de San
José. San José: Instituto Geográfico
Nacional, 1968. v, 120 pp. Illus., maps,
tables.
A listing for each canton of the department, indicating the legal changes in its
boundaries and dependencies since independence. Arranged chronologically, with explanations of the details and maps of the present
lines. DLC LNHT

83   _____. Orígenes de los costarricenses: los
Barrantes de Costa Rica. San José: n.p.,
1967. ii, 114 pp. Biblio., illus., map.
A family genealogy focusing on Colonial
days but extending to the mid-nineteenth century, following a "typical founding family" of
Costa Rica. BNCR

84   Baruch, Bernardo. Los orígenes del Partido
Liberación Nacional en Costa Rica. San José:
Editorial Eloy Morúa Carrillo, 1969. 24 pp.
Biblio.
A brief essay, originally a speech, summarizing the birth of the PLN in the crisis of
the 1940s and the formation of its organization and constitution during the 1950s, providing only brief and basic data. DLC BNCR

85   Beeche Argüero, Octavio. Índice general de la
legislación vigente en Costa Rica. . . . 5
vols. San José: Imprenta Nacional, 1935-49.
Alphabetical listings, under topical headings, of all current Costa Rican legislation,
each with a brief description and a citation
of the appropriate law. The series keeps
moving with the times. Hence the first three
volumes cite laws in force for 1934, the
fourth updates the citations to 1940, and the
fifth updates again for laws in force in 1948.
DLC-LDS BNCR

86   Bell, John Patrick. Crisis in Costa Rica:
The Revolution of 1948. Austin: University
of Texas Press, 1971. 192 pp. Index,
biblio., notes.
Guerra civil en Costa Rica. San José: EDUCA,
1976. 222 pp. Index, biblio., notes
A revisionist analysis of the 1940-48
period, seeking to identify the origins of the
conflict that eventually split the nation and
led to the Revolution of 1948. The author
contends that the dispute was really a clash

126

between middle- and upper-class reformers over methods, involving personal ambitions. The Calderón Guardia administration is presented as reformist, though patronizing, while Figueres appears as ambitious and using anticommunism to his own advantage. Contains detailed information about the state of Costa Rican society, its problems, and the political scene. DLC LNHT BNCR

87 Bello, Leoncio N. El problema agrícola. San José: Imprenta Alsina, 1907. 24 pp.

A discussion of the role of the banana industry in the Costa Rican economy and its regulation, part of a political polemic regarding legislation to control and tax the industry. This tract seeks to reject the idea of Ricardo Jiménez Oreamuno that all revenues from the banana tax be earmarked for payment of the foreign debt; it includes particulars about the amount of the intended tax, and discusses the related question of the concentration of landownership. The author proposes the creation of a Ministry of Agriculture to regulate the industry, including railroads, which he views as associated with banana production. DLC DLC-LDS-39

88 Benavides, Enrique. Nuestro pensamiento político en sus fuentes. San José: Editorial Costa Rica, 1976. 226 pp.

A series of interviews by a journalist with the leading political figures of the current generation of his nation, seeking to provide insights into their thinking. Concludes that Costa Ricans are pragmatic rather than doctrinaire, and that liberalism is the dominant philosophy of the nation, though without dogmatic inflexibility. Included are interviews with Manuel Mora Valverde, Rodrigo Carazo Odio, José Joaquín Trejos Fernandez, Fernando Trejos Escalante, Alfonso Carro Zúñiga, Luís Alberto Monge, Mario Echandi J., Daniel Oduber Quirós, and José Figueres Ferrar. DLC LNHT BNCR

89 Benavides, Héctor. León Cortés: apasionantes páginas de la vida del último caudillo del pueblo costarricense. San José: Editorial Victoria, 1949. 40 pp.

A narration of a series of episodes from the life of León Cortés, president of Costa Rica from 1940 to 1944, to illustrate his passions, causes, and personality. The events are disparate. LNHT BNCR

90 Benavides Robles, Rafael. Límites entre Heredia y Alajuela. Heredia: Campaña de Cubujuquí, 1950. 44 pp.

A discussion of a jurisdictional dispute between these two neighboring provinces of Costa Rica, inevitably tracing the antecedents back to Colonial days but continuing to the present, and defending the position of Heredia. BNCR

91 Benavides Sánchez, Manuel. Análisis de los precios de los productos agrícolos básicos de Costa Rica. San José: Banco de Costa Rica, 1974. 220 pp. Biblio., tables.

A discussion and analysis of price changes in Costa Rican basic food products during the 1950s and 1960s, including rice, corn, black beans, and meat, with numerous statistics. Each product receives detailed analysis of the reasons for past changes, future prospects, and the market and production situation. BNCR

92 Benharis, Ruma, ed. Garzaleida. San José: Imprenta Soley y Valverde, 1937. 51 pp.

A collection of short stories (most only one or two pages long) recounting folktales, principally from Guanacaste. DLC-LDS-848 BNCR

93 Berggren, Karl. Svenska Kolonien "Nueva Suecia," San Carlos, Costa Rica. Upsala: Harold Wretman, 1893. 32 pp.

A pamphlet by a Swedish settler, describing the town and concession in which the small Swedish colony is located. Provides details about terrain, crops, and climate on a month-by-month basis, as well as other aspects; designed to encourage further emigration to Costa Rica. DLC DLC-LDS-367

94 Besso, Henry V. A Guide to the Official Publications of the American Republics. Vol. 6, Costa Rica. Washington, D.C.: Library of Congress, 1947. 92 pp.

A listing of the publications of each of the various governments, arranged by ministry or agency, with some explanations of the date of the creation of the agency or the period covered by periodical publications, but without annotation. DLC

95 Biesanz, John Berry, and Mavis Biesanz. Costa Rican Life. New York: Columbia University Press, 1944. 272 pp. Index, biblio., notes, illus., map. Reprint. Westport, Conn.: Greenwood, 1979. 272 pp. Index, biblio., notes, illus., map.
La vida en Costa Rica. San José: Ministerio de Cultura, 1975. 415 pp.

A well-known and detailed description of Costa Rican life and social customs, based on observations during service as visiting professors in that nation, by a team of Yankee sociologists who spent much of their lives in Latin America and particularly the isthmus. Focuses exclusively on describing the then-current situation. Reflecting the training of the authors, it provides an effective glimpse of the society, standard of living, lifestyles, and customs; it is quite popular in Costa Rica. DLC LNHT BNCR

96 Biesanz, Mavis, Richard Biesanz, and Karen Biesanz. Los costarricenses. San José: Editorial Universidad Estatal a Distancia, 1980. 730 pp. Illus.
The Costa Ricans. Englewood Cliffs, N.J.: Prentice-Hall, 1980.

A comprehensive sociological examination of contemporary Costa Rican society, with voluminous data and extensive statistics, seeking to identify its predominant characteristics and test the veracity of the national myths about

the country and its people. The work emphasizes the characteristics that are unique to
Costa Ricans, while demonstrating that some of
its most cherished myths, such as that of a
classless society, have no foundation. BNCR

97 Biolley, Paul. Costa Rica et son avenir.
Paris: A. Giard, 1889. 127 pp. Biblio.,
notes, map, tables.
Costa Rica and Her Future. Washington, D.C.:
Judd & Detweiler, 1889. v, 96 pp. Biblio.,
map.
Costa Rica und seine Zukunft. Berlin:
Thormann & Goetsch, 1890. 88 pp. Index, map,
tables.
      A compilation of basic data about Costa
Rica in an effort to make it better known to
Europeans and Yankees, by a Swiss professor
residing in Costa Rica. Includes geographic,
economic, social, and political information,
stated briefly in general terms. DLC DLC-
LDS-44 LNHT BNCR

98 ____ . Cuestión Banco de la Unión en el
Congreso Constitucional de 1890. San José:
Tipografía de V. Lines, 1891. 127 pp.
      Resulting from the political polemic re-
garding a series of monetary reform efforts
establishing the bank as the sole emitter of
currency, this volume includes the text of the
law, congressional speeches, newspaper editorials and commentary, as well as various
essays and speeches on the subject, indicating
the course of the debate. DLC DLC-LDS

99 Blanco Segura, Ricardo. Historia eclesiástica
de Costa Rica: del descubrimiento a la
erección de la diócesis, 1502-1805. San José:
Imprenta Nacional, 1960. 299 pp. Index,
biblio., notes. 2d ed. San José: Editorial
Costa Rica, 1967. 401 pp. Biblio., illus.,
map.
      A history of the Costa Rican church. The
first edition focuses on the Colonial era, but
includes fifty pages on the period from independence to the formation of the diocese. The
second edition is greatly expanded. Still
focusing on the Colonial era, it offers
greater coverage of the post-independence
years. LNHT BNCR

100 ____ . Monseñor Sanabria. San José:
Editorial Costa Rica, 1962. 315 pp. Biblio.,
notes, illus., appendixes. 2d ed. San José:
Editorial Costa Rica, 1971. 371 pp. Biblio.,
illus.
      A biography of the second archbishop of the
relatively recent archdiocese of Costa Rica,
who served in that post from 1940 through 1952
and whose career thus spanned the turbulent
years of political unrest that led to and
followed the Revolution of 1948. The archbishop's activist role and intervention in the
conflict is analyzed, in addition to the
account of his prolific efforts at building
the structure and facilities of the diocese.
Includes numerous quotations from his commentaries, declarations, pastorals, and writings.
DLC LNHT BNCR

101 ____ . Obispos y arzobispos de Costa Rica.
San José: Imprenta Nacional, 1966.
      A series of biographical sketches tracing
the careers of the principal ecclesiastical
leaders of Costa Rica, written by a well-known
church historian of that nation. BNCR

102 Blutstein, Howard. Area Handbook for Costa
Rica. Washington, D.C.: GPO, 1970. xiv, 323
pp. Index, biblio., illus., map.
      Part of a series of volumes prepared under
the auspices of the American University for
the U.S. government. Provides concise, up-to-
date basic information about each nation for
the general reader. Includes capsule descriptions, some statistics, an historical overview, and geographic description, with
recommended reading in English. DLC LNHT

103 Bonilla, Harold H. Figueres and Costa Rica:
An Unauthorized Political Biography. San
José: Editorial Texto Limitada, 1975. ccii,
214 pp. Biblio.
Figueres y Costa Rica: una biografía política
independiente. San José: Editorial Sol,
1977. cxxxviii, 274 pp. Index, biblio.,
illus.
      A series of essays on various portions of
Figueres's career, covering the years through
the early 1970s, written by a major in the
Costa Rican armed forces. Discusses disparate
aspects of Figueres's life, with liberal expressions of the author's opinions, which are
favorable to the National Liberation leader.
DLC LNHT BNCR

104 ____ . Nuestros presidentes. San José:
Imprenta Soley y Valverde, 1942. 227 pp.
Biblio., illus.
      Biographical essays of the presidents of
Costa Rica, arranged by era but not chronologically within eras, providing brief overviews of their careers and particularly their
policies and actions in office; with numerous
photos. DLC DLC-LDS-900

105 Bonilla Baldares, Abelardo, ed. Estilística
de lenguaje costarricense. San José:
Universidad de Costa Rica, 1967. 82 pp.
Index, notes.
      A study of Costa Rican Spanish, focusing on
its internal development and uniqueness and
stressing the factors that contributed to the
emergence of a distinct Costa Rican dialect
during the Colonial era. The author emphasizes isolation, natural beauty, individual-
ism, resentment of the mother country, and
similar factors, quoting from various documents and works by Costa Rican authors to
illustrate his points. DLC

106 ____ . Historia de la literatura
costarricense. San José: Editorial
Costa Rica, 1967. 408 pp. Index, notes.
      A revision and updating of the initial
volume of the author's Historia y antología de
la literatura costarricense, reissued separately to offer the literary history without
the anthology contained in the second volume
of the original work. See next item. DLC
BNCR

(Bonilla Baldares, Abelardo, ed.)

107 _____. Historia y antología de la literatura costarricense. 2 vols. San José: Imprenta Trejos & Universidad de Costa Rica, 1957-61. 447, 590 pp. Index, biblio., notes.

Volume 1 is a history of Costa Rican literature, including discussions of the best-known authors in the fields of novels, short stories, theater, history, law, poetry, and essays. They are grouped by subject, time period, and school, each emphasizing the twentieth century. The essays include data regarding each author and his principal works, with emphasis on the latter, including excerpts. The second volume consists of an anthology of the best-known writers, providing what the editor considers representative samples. Works are identified only by title, usually with date, but with no more bibliographical information. DLC LNHT BNCR

108 Borge C., Carlos, ed. La Virgen de Los Angeles coronada: Cartago, 1635-1926. San José: Imprenta Lehmann, 1927. 244 pp. Illus., tables.

The initial hundred pages of this commemorative volume reproduce the history of the shrine at Cartago and the emergence of the cult, previously published by Eladio Prado. The remaining pages commemorate the coronation ceremony of 1926, in which the statue was named the patroness of Costa Rica. Includes the correspondence and minutes of the organizing committee that prepared the event, and the speeches, prayers, and hymns that constituted the ceremony; with illustrations. See item CR902. DLC-LDS-391.

109 Borges Pérez, Fernando. Historia del teatro en Costa Rica. San José: Imprenta Española, 1942. 106 pp. Illus.

A newspaper reporter's account of the various theater companies, individuals, and buildings that constitute the Costa Rican dramatic scene, with highlights of the various seasons covering the nineteenth and twentieth centuries. DLC DLC-LDS-874 LNHT BNCR

110 Bosch, Juan. Apuntes para una interpretación de la historia costarricense. San José: Editorial Eloy Morúa Carrillo, 1963. 38 pp. Latest ed. San José: Editorial Liberación Nacional, 1966. 38 pp.

The president of the Dominican Republic, whose party is closely allied with the governing Partido de Liberación Nacional of Costa Rica, provides a brief overview of the main themes of Costa Rican history, focusing on the 1948 revolution and viewing the movement sympathetically. Contends that despite rhetoric about fighting for democracy the real crisis involved oligarchic control of the economy and its resulting absorption of all investment funds into the coffee sector, which prevented industrial development and stifled the middle class. The Revolution of 1948 responded to this situation by assuring that the middle class rather than the oligarchy would control the nation, hence that the nation would follow the path of economic development, enabling it

to offset its trade deficit; this would in turn enhance the situation and status of the middle class, as well as improve economic opportunities for all. LNHT

111 Boza McKellar, Amadeo. Dos años de gobierno local bajo la presidencia de don Leonidas Poveda Echeverría: ligera reseña de la actuación de la Municipalidad de Puntarenas durante los años de 1920 y 1921. San José: Imprenta Nacional, 1921. 75 pp. Illus., tables.

A detailed account of the public-works projects of the city, with illustrations and statistics about the city, its residents, and its economy during the period covered, compiled by the secretary of the municipality. DLC-LDS-295

112 Bozzolli de Wille, María Eugenia. Localidades indígenes costarricenses, 1960-1968. San José: Universidad de Costa Rica, 1969. 82 pp. Index, biblio., illus., maps, tables, appendixes. 2d ed. San José: EDUCA, 1975. 231 pp. Biblio., illus., maps, tables.

Originally published as a short description of the life-styles and living circumstances of the Indian villages of Costa Rica from 1960 to 1968, a much more extensive section was added to the second edition providing similar analysis for 1973 and a comparison of the situation in 1968 to that in 1973, thus greatly enhancing the value of the work. It presents descriptive and social-science analysis under topics such as housing, health and educational services, educational facilities, traditions, land tenure, internal governance, etc. rather than by site, but focuses on common elements and trends. DLC

113 Braulio Carrillo: tributo patrio consagrado a su memoria en celebración del primer centenario de su natalicio. San José: Tipografía Nacional, 1900. 64 pp. Illus. 2d ed. San José: Editorial Costa Rica, 1971. 115 pp.

Essays about the career of this first Costa Rican chief of state, as well as excerpts from various publications and studies from his era, accompanied by several of his letters and proclamations. DLC LNHT BNCR

114 Brenes, Rafael. Primera parte del bosquejo sobre algunos pasajes de la historia de Costa Rica. San José: Imprenta de la Libertad, 1885. 44 pp.

A priest imprisoned during the 1870s recounts his version of the political maneuverings of that era and the clash between the church and the liberals. DLC DLC-LDS-90

115 Brenes Cordoba, Alberto. Derecho civil de Costa Rica. 3 vols. San José: Tipografía Nacional & Imprenta Trejos, 1906-25. 394, 576, 334 pp. Latest ed. San José: Editorial Costa Rica, 1974.

A legal treatise that emphasizes general theoretical discussions of the basis and purposes of the law, but includes references to Costa Rican legal practice and comparisons of the provisions of Costa Rican laws to those of other countries; by a professor at the nation's law school. LNHT

116   Briceño Baltodano, Leonidas. Incorporación del Guanacaste a Costa Rica. San José: Imprenta del Comercio, 1910. 33 pp.
       A brief and general essay regarding the shift of this province to Costa Rica at the time of independence, with justification for the actions and support for the Costa Rican position in the boundary dispute with Nicaragua. DLC DLC-LDS-52

117   Bruño, Pedro, pseud. Cuestion bananera: los dictamenes sobre el impuesto bananero. San José: Imprenta Alsina, 1929. 56 pp.
       Part of the polemic regarding banana taxes, this series of articles, which originally appeared in La Tribuna of San José, rejects the arguments of the congressional commission that proposed placing an export tax on bananas and argued, with the support of a number of the nation's banana producers, that such a move would be counterproductive and would drive the producers, including the United Fruit Company, to seek greener pastures outside Costa Rica and hence retard the industry. The author notes that Costa Rica is a small producer of bananas and that export is their only possible use, arguing that the Congress should be seeking to promote the expansion of production, which can best be accomplished by abolishing taxes. Indeed, he proposes a constitutional amendment guaranteeing that the export of bananas would be forever free of taxation. DLC-LDS-458

118   Buckingham, James Silk. Colonisation of Costa Rica, for the Development of Its Rich Mines of Gold, Silver, Lead, Copper, Iron, and Coal, and for Opening a New Route Between the Atlantic and Pacific, thus Avoiding the Tedious and Circuitous Navigation Round Cape Horn and the Cape of Good Hope, and Shortening the Voyages to Either Ocean; Creating, at the Same Time, New Homes for British Emigrants, New Sources of Supply for Tropical Productions, and New Markets for British Manufacturers. London: E. Wilson, 1852. vi, 34 pp. Maps.
       A pamphlet written to encourage British interest in the isthmus, reflecting the British focus on control of key locations in the world's sea lanes and the tendency toward independent action by individuals of that nation. It seeks to portray the potential of Costa Rica in glowing terms to encourage British immigration to that nation, while arguing for the desirability of British control of its potential canal route. DLC

119   Bula, Clotilde A. Estadística demográfica. San José: Universidad de Costa Rica, 1960. 306 pp. Biblio., illus., tables.
       A discussion of the use of census and population data to provide a profile of the nation, focusing on Costa Rica but using some figures from Central America for comparison. Covers the entire span from independence to

the present, although the tables for each subject do not always correspond to the period covered. The figures are considered in various topical headings to show how they can be used to gather information on such factors as unemployment, migration, births, deaths, etc., with calculation formulas shown and analyzed. BNCR

120   Burch, Conde de. Estudios económicas derivadas de las consecuencias de la Guerra Europea sobre los paises prósperos de la América Latina. Vol. 1, La República de Costa Rica. Barcelona: Tipografía La Académica de Serra Hnos. y Russell Rondas, 1915. 107 pp.
       A general description of Costa Rica that provides basic data about the nation, with emphasis on economic factors, purporting to focus on the effects of World War I on the nation as part of a series dealing with this theme. In fact, the focus is on the nation in general during the 1910 to 1915 period, although the trade data drawn from the Memorias of the various ministries for these years does indicate some impact of the European conflict. DLC-LDS-141 BNCR

121   Busey, James L. Notes on Costa Rican Democracy. Boulder: University of Colorado Press, 1962. iv, 84 pp. Biblio., notes, illus., maps, tables, appendixes. Latest ed. Boulder: University of Colorado Press, 1967. 84 pp. Biblio., illus., maps.
       Notas sobre la democracia costarricense. San José: Editorial Costa Rica, 1968. 159 pp. Biblio.
       A political scientist's descriptive survey of the nation's political system, emphasizing the 1949 constitution and the political parties of the succeeding era. He surveys the principal characteristics of the society and economy, arguing that the pattern of small landholding rather than the concentration of land ownership characteristic of other Latin American nations is the principal factor in the development of the Costa Rican democratic tradition. DLC LNHT BNCR

122   Cabrera, Victor Manuel. Guanacaste: libro conmemoratico del centenario de la incorporación del Partido de Nicoya a Costa Rica, 1824-1924. San José: Imprenta María Viuda de Lines, 1924. 486 pp. Illus., maps.
       A compilation of data and a general description of Guanacaste, focusing on its geography and resources but including a discussion of the contemporary scene, its economy, government, and facilities, with illustrations. Also includes the laws incorporating the region into Costa Rica in 1824 when it seceded from Nicaragua, the acts and proclamations celebrating the centennial, and newspaper commentaries on the occasion. DLC LNHT BNCR

123   Calderón, José Tomás. Anhelos de un ciudadano. San Salvador: Tipografía La Unión, 1961. 366 pp.
       Selected speeches and articles by this Costa Rican leader, covering the years from 1912 through the 1940s. He comments on a wide

range of political issues and events, as well as on broader themes such as communism and militarism, and the issue of Central American unification. FU

124 Calderón, Próspero. <u>Vistas de Costa Rica</u>. San José: Imprenta de La República, 1901. Pages unnumbered. Illus.
A collection of photos showing Costa Rica at the turn of the century. Includes major public buildings in the capital and rural scenes from various parts of the nation. BNCR

125 Calderón Guardia, Rafael Ángel. <u>El gobernante y el hombre frente al problema social costarricense</u>. San José: n.p., 1942. 45 pp.
A brief commentary in which the Costa Rican president speaks as an individual as well as in his official capacity, citing the nation's social problems of poor living conditions and inequality while advocating a new labor code to assure social guarantees and decent living standards and wages, which he feels will alleviate the problems. DLC BNCR

126 Calvo, Francisco. <u>Los muertos en la campaña nacional de 1856-1857</u>. San José: Imprenta Lehmann, 1932. 65 pp.
A list, by the chaplain of the Costa Rican unit, of those Costa Ricans who died in the campaign against Walker. Includes an introduction by Victor Sanabria Martínez, to whom authorship of the book is sometimes mistakenly attributed. DLC

127 Calvo Mora, Joaquín Bernardo. <u>La campaña nacional contra los filibusteros en 1856 y 1857: breve reseña histórica</u>. San José: Tipografía Nacional, 1909. viii, 94 pp. Illus. 3d ed. San José: n.p., 1954. 74 pp.
A basic and concise account of the various battles of the campaign. Prepared for the Historical Commission of Costa Rica from published secondary sources and documents. The Costa Rican role and the joint efforts of the several Central American nations in the face of this threat are emphasized. DLC DLC-LDS-43 LNHT BNCR

128 _____. <u>Estudio e informe sobre el café de Costa Rica</u>. San José: Tipografía Nacional, 1900. 48 pp. Tables.
A detailed report, with statistics, about the status and potential of Costa Rican coffee exports, particularly to the United States, as well as comments about its quality. Prepared by the Costa Rican minister in Washington, drawing upon the consular reports of the U.S. and various other studies of the coffee market, world production, and the quality of Costa Rican samples. DLC-LDS-308

129 _____, ed. <u>Las fiestas del 15 de septiembre de 1895</u>. San José: Tipografía Nacional, 1897. 321 pp. Illus.
An account of the celebrations and official acts attendant to the dedication of the monument to the heroes of the 1856-57 military campaign against William Walker, with the official addresses, and a history of the campaign by the editor. DLC

130 Calvo Mora, Joaquín Bernardo. <u>República de Costa Rica: apuntamientos geográficos, estadísticos e históricos</u>. San José: Imprenta Nacional, 1887. 325 pp. Tables, appendixes.
<u>The Republic of Costa Rica</u>. Chicago: Rand, McNally, 1890. 292 pp. Illus., tables.
An officially sponsored compilation of the state of the Costa Rican economy and its potential, including basic geographic and climatic data, a summary of the political situation, and biographical sketches of the nation's presidents. DLC DLC-LDS-527 LNHT BNCR

131 _____. <u>The Republic of Costa Rica</u>. Washington, D.C.: PAU, 1894. 56 pp. Notes, illus., maps.
One of the Pan American Union "facts and figures" series providing basic data on Costa Rica in 1893, followed by a brief article dealing with the Costa Rican exhibit at the World Columbian Exposition in Chicago. Provides information about the state of the nation and its development at that time. DLC DLC-LDS-366 LNHT BNCR

132 Calzada Bolandi, Jorge. <u>Orientación</u>. San José: Imprenta Atenea, 1950. 223 pp.
Commentaries extolling liberty, personal freedom, and democracy in general terms, while condemning the actions of the Calderón Guardia regime as excessive oppression and heavy-handed use of state power. DPU

133 Camacho, Viriato. <u>Apuntes sobre la personalidad de Doris Stone y su obra en Costa Rica</u>. San José: Imprenta Ernesto Ortiz, 1951. Pages unnumbered.
A sketch of the work of Doris Stone, a Yankee and daughter of the president of the United Fruit Company, who lived in Costa Rica for many years during the 1940s. Describes her anthropological studies and their contributions to knowledge of the nation's Indian cultures, as well as her efforts on behalf of the National Museum. DLC BNCR

134 Camisa, Zulma C. <u>Costa Rica: comparación entre tres proyecciones de población</u>. San José: CELADE, 1969. 33 pp. Tables.
A comparison of three population projections, noting their differences and analyzing the calculations that explain them. DLC LNHT BNCR

135 Campos Jiménez, Carlos María. <u>Apuntes para el estudio de uno de los aspectos de la estratificación social en Costa Rica</u>. San José: Caja Costarricense de Seguro Social, 1969. Pages unnumbered. Biblio., illus.
A collection of statistics and data indicating the social structure of the nation and emphasizing the changes of the 1950s. BNCR

136 _____. <u>Las ciencias sociales en Costa Rica</u>. Rio de Janeiro: Centro Latinaméricano de

Investigaciones en Ciencias Sociales, 1959.
62 pp. Tables.

A brief overview of the expansion and development of the social sciences in Costa Rica, considering investigations, teaching in the schools, publications, and graduates in the various fields as compared to other faculties. DLC LNHT BNCR

137 Cañas, Victor Manuel. El caso Vincenzi. San José: Imprenta Trejos, 1935. 20 pp.

A brief essay about the life, works, and philosophy of Moises Vincenzi, extolling his significance for and influence in the Costa Rican literary and educational scene. DLC

138 Cañas Escalante, Alberto F. Aquí y ahora. San José: Editorial Costa Rica, 1965. 249 pp.

A fictionalized perspective on life in San José, focusing on the urban middle and upper classes and detailing the foibles and limits of modern society and the adjustments made by the people caught in it. Could be called a collection of short novelettes, or a series of long short stories, depending on the reader's viewpoint. DLC LNHT BNCR

139 _____. Una casa en el barrio del Carmen. San José: Editorial Costa Rica, 1976. 129 pp.

A short novel again focusing on the problems of modern city life and its effects on the people caught in it. BNCR

140 _____. La exterminación de los pobres y otros piensas. San José: Editorial Costa Rica, 1974. 107 pp. Illus.

A series of short stories by this well-known Costa Rican writer, focusing as usual on the foibles of modern society. Includes a wide range of characters from various classes. BNCR

141 _____. Los 8 años. San José: Editorial Liberación Nacional, 1955. 120 pp. Index, notes.

An interpretation of the 1948 crisis, written by a journalist sympathetic to the National Liberation Movement. He offers a particularly harsh criticism of the Calderón Guardia and Picado administrations and the situation that led to the crisis, and justifies the National Liberation position. DLC LNHT BNCR

142 Cardona, Jorge. Hombres y máquinas. San José: Imprenta Lehmann, n.d. 178 pp.

A novel about life on the Pacific Railroad shortly after the turn of the century, describing the experiences of several workers and the interaction of man and machine in the difficult terrain. BNCR

143 Cardona-Hine, Alvaro. Agapito. New York: Scribner's, 1969. 117 pp.

An emotional account of peasant life and death in the countryside, as seen through the innocent eyes of a child who observes all in detail and wide-eyed wonderment. WU

144 Cardona Peña, Alfredo. Fábula contada: narrativa fantástica. San José: EDUCA, 1972. 257 pp.

Over forty short stories focusing on diverse aspects of Costa Rican life and narrating everyday events. DLC

145 Cardona y Valverde, Jenaro. Del calor hogareño. San José: Imprenta Alsina, 1929. 172 pp.

A short-story collection of the Costa Rican costumbrista school, focusing on the lives of the humble peasants of the interior and their daily struggles and problems, using their language and idioms. DLC-LDS-427 BNCR

146 _____. El primo. San José: Tipografía Nacional, 1905. 289 pp.

A Costa Rican novel of the costumbrista school, focusing on the lives of the rural peasants and their trials and tribulations. The author's best-known work. DLC DLC-LDS-7 BNCR

147 Carlomagno. Reflexiones políticas. San José: Imprenta San José, 1924. 43 pp.

A discussion of the various political forces in the Costa Rican scene of the 1920s, focusing on the latest elections and including commentaries on all the leading groups and personalista parties and their leaders and ambitions, particularly Ricardo Jiménez Oreamuno, Alberto Echandi Montero, and Jorge Volio Jiménez. Notes the ties or opposition of each to the Tinoco regime and laments the disarray of the political scene in the wake of the Tinoco break in the previous electoral continuum. DLC-LDS-312

148 Carmona, José Daniel. De San José al Guanacaste é indios Guatusos: descripción religiosa, política, tipográfica e histórica de esos pueblos y lugares. San José: Tipografía de San José, 1897. 236 pp.

A priest's account of his travels and experiences among the Indians of Guanacaste, with emphasis on their life-style, customs, religious practices, social organization, and government, providing an account of their culture as well as of his travels and difficulties, though seen through his eyes and reflecting his attitudes and prejudices. DLC DLC-LDS-18 LNHT

149 Carter, William E., ed. Cannabis in Costa Rica. Philadelphia: Institute for the Study of Human Issues, 1980. 352 pp. Biblio., notes.

A study of the effects of long-term regular use of marihuana, based on interviews with "traditional" users in San José and focusing on those who had smoked the drug regularly for ten years or more. DLC LNHT

150 Carvajal, Manuel J., ed. Políticas de crecimiento urbano: la experiencia de Costa Rica. San José: Dirección General de Estadísticas y Censos, 1977. 288 pp. Maps, notes, tables.

A study of urbanization in Costa Rica, detailing the policies necessary to deal with it by providing services, infrastructure, and jobs at a suitable pace. Includes contributions by both Costa Rican and Yankee scholars. Contains considerable statistical information in tabular and graphic form, as well as maps. DLC BNCR

151 Carvajal, Manuel J., and James E. Ross. Foreign, Regional, and International Organizations Affecting Agricultural Development in Costa Rica. San José: Ministerio de Agricultura y Ganadería, 1968. 24 pp.
A listing, with single-paragraph descriptions, of the agencies and agreements that affect Costa Rican agriculture, prepared under a cooperative program between the Costa Rican Ministry of Agriculture, the Agency for International Development, and the University of Florida. Also available in a combined edition with item CR152, with same date and publisher. BNCR

152 _____. Public Institutions Affecting Agricultural Development in Costa Rica. San José: Ministerio de Agricultura y Ganadería, 1968. 64 pp.
An expanded version of the preceeding item, listing and describing each of the domestic agencies involved in agriculture in Costa Rica, including nonprofit organizations; provides expanded data regarding functions and organization. Also available in a combined edition with item CR151, with same date and publisher. BNCR

153 Carvajal, Manuel J., David T. Geithman, and Patrick R. Armstrong. Pobreza en Costa Rica. San José: Dirección General de Estadísticas, 1977. 330 pp. Biblio., notes, tables.
A statistical look at poverty and its characteristics, with brief descriptive text seeking to define the subject and a compilation of statistical material to demonstrate it. The tables of figures and graphs are by far the most valuable aspect. They include breakdowns of income and population characteristics by province and age group, and figures on income distribution and sources. Families are examined by age, services available, income, land ownership, and many other factors. Figures are drawn from the 1973 housing census. LNHT

154 Carvajal Herrera, Mario. La planificación en Costa Rica. San José: Universidad de Costa Rica, 1972. 134 pp. Biblio., notes.
A discussion of the origins of planning in Costa Rica at the governmental level, of the national needs, the specific legal basis necessary, and role of planning in the national economy and the government. Emphasizes the need for a single centralized planning entity within the government to coordinate official activities and set priorities. DLC BNCR

155 Casal Viuda de Quirós, Sara. El voto femenino. San José: Imprenta Nacional, 1925. 16 pp.
An early feminist leader's petition seeking voting rights for Costa Rican women, with

letters of support from several leading political figures including Pedro Pérez Zeledón and Alberto Brenes. DLC-LDS-322

156 Casorla, J.R. Apuntes de un diario por una de las víctimas de general Guardia. Panamá: Imprenta de La Estrella de Panamá, 1876. 68 pp.
A prison diary recounting the author's trials and tribulations during his imprisonment by the Guardia regime, narrating his activities, protests of innocence, and transfer to various locations, including a period of house arrest, and denouncing the government and its unfairness. DLC DLC-LDS-89

157 Castro, Salomón. Educación nacional. San José: Imprenta Alsina, 1910. 30 pp.
A collection of commentaries about the type of education most suited to Costa Rica and its national educational needs, calling for government financing of the entire educational system and appending proposed educational laws and an organizational system for the schools. DLC DLC-LDS-51

158 Castro, Zenón. Rafael Iglesias ante la historia. San José: Imprenta Alsina, 1903. 27 pp.
An "open letter" denouncing the regime of Rafael Yglesias and particularly recounting events of 1902. Includes commentary allegedly made to the author by Guatemalan president José María Reina Barrios. Though a political polemic, the letter sheds some light on the complexities of Costa Rican politics during the 1890-1902 era, and also on the interrelationships between the politics of the various Central American nations. DLC-LDS-145 BNCR

159 Castro Carazo, Miguel Ángel. Breve reseña del ferrocarril al Pacífico: desde sus comienzos hasta nuestros días. San José: Imprenta Nacional, 1933. 36 pp. Illus.
A brief sketch of the Costa Rican Pacific Railroad from its foundation, though with emphasis on the contemporary. Includes a complete list of the company's equipment, useful statistics for the years 1904 through 1933, and an extensive album of photos of the various stations and track construction. DLC DLC-LDS-763 BNCR

160 Castro Cartin, José Enrique, and Hiram Sotela Montagne. Reseña de la industria turistica en Costa Rica. San José: Instituto Costarricense de Turismo, 1971. 43 pp.
A brief history of the nation's tourist industry, with emphasis on the coordinative efforts of the Institute since its foundation in 1931, consisting chiefly of a series of brief résumés of its departments and services. BNCR

161 Castro Esquivel, Arturo. José Figueres Ferrer: el hombre y su obra. San José: Imprenta Tormo, 1955. 274 pp. Illus.
A detailed account of the Costa Rican crisis of the mid-1940s. Follows the efforts of the National Liberation party and its

(Castro Esquivel, Arturo)
leader from his 1942 radio speech through the 1949 constitution, as well as the work of the revolutionary junta; lavishes praise on Figueres and quotes liberally from his speeches and proclamations. DLC LNHT BNCR

162   ____. Junto al surco. San José: Imprenta Borrasé, 1931. 205 pp.
A novel of the trials and tribulations of life on a coffee finca near Cartago, following the adventures and activities of a young man who frequently consults with the village priest, who serves as a fount of knowledge. LNHT

163   ____. El médico del pueblo. San José: Imprenta Trejos, 1934. 233 pp.
A novel about life in Costa Rica, focusing on the differing life-styles of the various classes and observing the social situation and political maneuvering through the eyes of a doctor. NcU

164   Castro Fernández, Héctor Alfredo. Vincenzi: su personalidad y su obra literaria. San José: Editorial Atenea, n.d. 62 pp.
A brief and somewhat anecdotal and disorganized commentary on the Costa Rican philosopher, based on the author's friendship with him and focusing on his personality, with some discussion of his writings. BNCR

165   Castro Rawson, Margarita. El costumbrismo en Costa Rica. New York: n.p., 1964. vii, 449 pp. 3d ed. San José: Editorial Costa Rica, 1971. 478 pp. Biblio.
Originally a doctoral dissertation, the initial one-third by this Yankee university professor consist of a comprehensive history of Costa Rican literature, placing costumbrismo in the context of the nation's literary development, contending that it was the nation's dominant literary trend, and also comparatively placing Costa Rican costumbrismo in its broader Latin American context. Includes discussion of the work of significant authors and of the role of the press in disseminating short stories and legends involved in the costumbrista movement. The remaining pages consist of an anthology of brief selections, usually only two to three pages, from the works of various Costa Rican costumbristas. DLC LNHT BNCR

166   Castro Rivera, Victor M. Un héroe nacional. San José: Imprenta Falcó y Borrasé, 1920. 32 pp.
A brief essay and collection of testimonies regarding the assassination of Joaquín Tinoco, brother of the president who had seized power by coup. Hails the assassin as the true restorer of Costa Rican liberty and democracy, since this act led to the fall of the government. DLC-LDS-183 BNCR

167   Castro Saborío, Luís. Biblioteca de derecho vigente en Costa Rica. 8 vols. San José: Imprenta Lehmann, 1913-16.

A detailed compilation of then-current law codes in Costa Rica, with commentary. DLC

168   ____. Estudios penales. San José: Tipografía Nacional, 1914. 486 pp.
A critical analysis of the existing Costa Rican penal code, placing it in the context of legislation in various nations and examining the origins of the theories on which the legislation was based. DLC

169   ____. Formulario de actuaciones penales. San José: Librería María Viuda de Lines, 1910. 142 pp.
A collection of legal formulae for the preparation of documents necessary to file required reports and conduct legal proceedings under then-current Costa Rican law, with explanations. DLC

170   ____. Guía práctica de legislación y jurisprudencia penales. San José: Imprenta Alsina, 1911. 221 pp.
Alphabetically arranged headings, with citations to the appropriate prevailing codes and related legal cases, most focusing on the laws of the 1890s and early 1900s. References indicate only date or law and are offered without comment. DLC

171   Castro Saborío, Octavio. Bernardo Augusto Thiel en la historia. San José: Imprenta Nacional, 1915. Latest ed. San José: Imprenta Nacional, 1959. 163 pp. Biblio., illus.
An address delivered in 1957 to the Costa Rican Academy of History, tracing the career of the second archbishop of San José, whose career spanned the turbulent church-state conflict. The study focuses principally on his religious activities, such as his work as a professor at the seminary and his influence on the development of the Costa Rican church, but also includes a brief outline of his expulsion from the country and subsequent glorification as a national hero. The absence of chapter titles renders the work difficult to use, and the various episodes are not examined in the same depth; but the work does provide an overview of the prelate's role in the nation's history. BNCR

172   ____, ed. El centenario del benemérito de la patria; ex-presidente de la república general don Juan Rafael Mora, 1814-1914. San José: Tipografía Nacional, 1915. 132 pp. Illus.
A collection of speeches by and articles about Mora, extolling his heroics during the campaign against William Walker and barely mentioning his presidency. Includes the addresses and acts of the ceremonies commemorating the centennial. LNHT BNCR

173   Castro Saborío, Octavio. Laude: evocación de Mora; el hombre, el estadista, el héroe, el mártir. 2d ed. San José: Editorial Aurora Social, 1955. 78 pp.
A summary of the career of General Juan Rafael Mora, discussing his role in the Costa Rican Liberal party and his actions as president, in addition to extolling his heroics in

defending the nation and detailing his participation in the campaign against William Walker as commander of the Costa Rican forces. DLC LNHT BNCR

174 CEDAL. <u>Costa Rica</u>: <u>centros regionales universitarios</u>. San José: CEDAL, 1973. 126 pp. Notes.
A collection of articles by various scholars regarding the efforts and experiments toward establishing regional educational centers and satellite campuses of the University of Costa Rica, focusing principally on plans and projected activities. BNCR

175 _____. <u>El movimiento sindical costarricense</u>. San José: CEDAL, 1971. 114 pp.
A collection of articles by several economists analyzing the labor movement in Costa Rica during the recent era. Stresses its problems and accomplishments, and legislation regarding the organization of labor unions, with recommendations for future legislation to further promote their development. BNCR

176 _____. <u>Panorama del sindicalismo costarricense</u>. San José: CEDAL, 1977. Pages not consecutively numbered.
A collection of articles regarding labor organizations in Costa Rica, including a commentary on their early development, some suggestions for the future, and the positions and platforms of various unions. BNCR

177 _____. <u>Socialismo Democrático en Costa Rica y Venezuela</u>: <u>los partidos Liberación Nacional y Acción Democrática</u>. San José: CEDAL, 1976. 71 pp.
Basic descriptive data regarding the organization and political positions of these two parties, preceded by an essay by Luís Alberto Monge regarding the social democratic idea and its development in Latin America and Costa Rica, tracing the influence in broad terms. BNCR

178 <u>Centenario Jesús Jiménez</u>: <u>compilación de los documentos relativos a su celebración y de las leyes y disposiciones a que se refiere la obra educacional del ex-presidente de la República de Costa Rica, benemérito licenciado don Jesús Jiménez</u>. San José: Imprenta Nacional, 1923. 168 pp.
While containing laudatory declarations, the majority of this volume consists of a compilation of the laws and decrees relating to the subject's work in developing the Costa Rican educational system. DLC-LDS-290 BNCR

179 Cerdas Cruz, Rodolfo. <u>La crisis de la democracia liberal en Costa Rica</u>: <u>interpretación y perspectiva</u>. San José: EDUCA, 1972. 2d ed. San José: EDUCA, 1976. 191 pp. Biblio., notes, tables.
A dependency analysis briefly tracing Costa Rican development from Colonial times to the present and contending that the introduction of export crops made the nation dependent while creating a new oligarchy during the late nineteenth century, and that the Central American Integration Movement is making the nation

even more dependent by facilitating the entry of foreign capital and creating a new managerial class, thereby expanding the oligarchy while rendering it even more externally oriented. The author contends that the solution must be political, in the form of a turn to social democracy and social democratic approaches. Includes tables regarding long-term trade and crop trends. DLC LNHT

180 _____. <u>Formación del estado de Costa Rica</u>. San José: Universidad de Costa Rica, 1967. 208 pp. Index, biblio.
A Marxist interpretation of the origins of the Costa Rican state, based on documentary research in the National Archives as well as on appropriate secondary works and containing considerable historical data. The author argues that the formation of the independent state of Costa Rica began immediately upon independence and continued throughout the existence of the Federation, and reflected the needs of the nascent bourgeoisie to consolidate its control and dominate the masses, which he contends it did through what he characterizes as the "dictatorship" of Braulio Carrillo during the Federation era. DLC LNHT BNCR

181 Cersosimo, Gaetano. <u>Los estereotipos del costarricense</u>: <u>un análisis de estereotipos sociales como instrumento de control y dominación</u>. San José: Universidad de Costa Rica, 1977. 131 pp. Biblio.
An examination of the Costa Rican self-image as seen through the media, viewing the stereotypes skeptically and arguing that they represent efforts at social control through the media, which seeks to promote conformity to the perceived national norm. The conclusions are limited by a small sample. DLC BNCR

182 Céspedes Marin, Armando. <u>Crónicas de la visita oficial y diocesana al Guatuso</u>. San José: Imprenta Lehmann, 1923. 176 pp. Illus.
A copiously illustrated description of the diocese of Alajuela, Costa Rica and the surrounding areas, with statistics regarding the diocese and an account of travels throughout the region. DLC-LDS-314 BNCR

183 Céspedes Solano, Victor Hugo. <u>Costa Rica</u>: <u>la distribución del ingreso y el consumo de algunos alimentos</u>. San José: Universidad de Costa Rica, 1973. xi, 132 pp. Biblio., illus., tables.
A detailed study of contemporary income, production, and consumption patterns, focusing particularly on the distribution of income and its effects on consumption. Includes tables, statistical calculations, and comparisons to other countries. Based on a nationwide poll of a sample of 3,100 families, including both urban and rural residents. DLC BNCR

184 Chacón, Lucas Raúl. <u>Aclaremos</u>: <u>estudio jurídico de la nacionalidad del Lic. don</u>

(Chacón, Lucas Raúl)

Octavio Beeche. San José: Imprenta La Tribuna, 1935. 15 pp.

The usual pre-election debate regarding the citizenship status of prospective candidates for the presidency, this time involving the question of whether Octavio Beeche, though clearly a Costa Rican, had forfeited his citizenship by virtue of the fact that he served as the minister of El Salvador in Washington during the early twentieth century when the Julio Acosta administration had not yet been recognized by the Washington government. Concludes that since this violated the constitution and since he never reapplied for citizenship, he had lost his citizenship despite his birth in the nation and hence was ineligible to serve as president despite the fact that he later held several posts in the Costa Rican diplomatic service and Cabinet. DLC

185 _____. Biografía del expresidente de la república: general y benemérito de la patria D. Juan Rafael Mora. San José: Imprenta San José, 1929. 32 pp.

A brief laudatory essay tracing the career of Juan Rafael Mora and singing his praises, focusing particularly on his heroism in defending the nation and the isthmus during the Walker episode. Includes brief excerpts from speeches and proclamations. DLC-LDS-430

186 _____. Saber ponderar. San José: Imprenta Borrasé, 1930. 15 pp.

A series of political commentaries originally published in La Nueva Prensa of San José during September and October 1930, comparing the Costa Rican domestic crisis to those that led to military coups in several South American countries, concluding that social stability was dependent on economic stability and that the government needed to give its primary attention to the economic crisis. DLC-LDS-863

187 Chacón Chaverri, Tranquilino. Información ad perpetuam heroismo de Juan Santamaría Batalla del 11 de abril de 1856, Alajuela, Costa Rica, 15 de septiembre de 1891. San José: Imprenta de José Canalías, 1891. 27 pp.

A collection of documents regarding the exploits of the Costa Rican military hero of the campaign against William Walker, designed to glorify his name. DLC DLC-LDS-89

188 _____. Proceso historico . . . 27 de enero de 1917, o el bochorno nacional. San José: Imprenta Falcó y Borrasé, 1920. 193 pp. Notes, illus.

An indictment of the Tinoco regime in Costa Rica that focuses on its alleged crimes and errors, by a member of the opposition. Prepared in newspaper fashion, with liberal excerpts from proclamations and reports and the commentaries of others involved. Provides the view of the "outs" who eventually ousted the regime and restored Costa Rica to its tradition of democratic elections. DLC DLC-LDS-176 BNCR

189 Chacón Pacheco, Nelson. Reseña de nuestras leyes electorales. San José: Imprenta Lehmann, 1975. 384 pp.

A summary of all the electoral laws of Costa Rica and the pertinent provisions of its various constitutions, from independence to the Constitution of 1949, with a summary and quotations from each, as well as narration of the intervening elections. BNCR

190 Chacón Trejos, Gonzalo. Costa Rica es distinta en Hispano América. San José: Imprenta Trejos, 1969. 47 pp.

A brief essay on what makes Costa Ricans unique, commenting on the national characteristics and citing cultural heritage, traditions, and racial unity as the key factors. LNHT BNCR

191 _____. El crimen de Alberto Lobo. San José: Editorial Trejos, 1928. 118 pp. 2d ed. San José: Editorial Costa Rica, 1971. 124 pp.

A novel of political intrigue and frustration set in a mythical Republic of Ticonia or Ticolandia, whose place names and figures closely resemble Costa Rica. Traces the political and military maneuverings attendant to a disputed election and coup, with the title figure vainly struggling to prevent the uprising. Touches on many of the political characteristics and problems of Central America, noting the predictability of some of the reactions, the ease of manipulation of the political figures and the military, and the fragile nature of electoral politics. The novel was initially published in 1928 and the events relate to the Tinoco coup and regime. DLC LNHT

192 _____. Maquiavelo: Maquiavelismo del presidente Ricardo Jiménez, a-Maquiavelismo del presidente Alfredo González. San José: Imprenta Trejos, 1935. 64 pp.

Originally a speech delivered in 1934, this essay reflects the political passions of the time when Jiménez was serving his third term as president. His realistic political maneuvering is compared to that of an ex-president whose ineffective government was overthrown by the Tinoco revolt in 1917. Acclaims the political ability of Jiménez as good for the nation. DLC BNCR

193 _____. Tradiciones costarricenses. San José: Imprenta Trejos, 1936. Latest ed. San José: Imprenta Trejos, 1964. 176 pp.

A series of short stories dealing with Costa Rican legends, folktales, heroes, and historical heroes. DLC DLC-LDS-916 LNHT

194 Chanto Méndez, Marcos. Tarrazú en su centenario. San José: Imprenta Lehmann, 1968. 20 pp.

A very brief history of the Canton of Tarrazú, Costa Rica, followed by an equally brief description of its contemporary situation and facilities. BNCR

195 Chase, Alfonso. Max Jiménez. San José: Ministerio de Cultura, Juventud y Deportes, 1973. 114 pp. Biblio., illus.

(Chase, Alfonso)
A brief biographical sketch of this prominent Costa Rican writer, noting his contributions in the arts as well as literature, with an anthology of selections from his poetry and short stories. TxU

196 ____. Mirar con inocencia: narraciones. San José: Editorial Costa Rica, 1975. 178 pp. Biblio., illus.
A series of humorous short stories drawing on the author's memories of his youth, using vivid descriptions as well as magic realism to show the experiences of adolescents and children growing up, and their efforts to come to grips with the world. DLC BNCR

197 ____, ed. Narrativa contemporánea de Costa Rica. 2 vols. San José: Ministerio de Cultura, Juventud y Deportes, 1975. 467, 521 pp.
Compiled by a Costa Rican literary scholar who also provides an introduction and notes on the authors, this valuable anthology includes the nation's best-known authors of this century. Included are Max Jiménez, José Marín Cañas, Carlos Salazar Herrera, Carlos Luis Fallas, Aldolfo Herrera Garcia, Yolanda Oreamuno, Alfredo Cardona Peña, and Joaquín Gutierrez. In his introduction Chase notes that most of these authors focus on the social and agrarian problems of the nation and on the lives of the peasants, and that some are Marxists. This, he says, represents an indigenous movement and not an imitation of the European style as in earlier times. While considering this a major departure point in the nation's literary history, he also notes that most of the authors, rather than conjure up fictional situations, draw upon their own experience, which he says limits their use of imagination, the parameters of the story, and the development of its characters. DLC BNCR

198 ____, ed. Poesía contemporánea de Costa Rica. Mexico: Ministerio de Educación Pública, 1967. 78 pp.
A brief anthology of Costa Rican poetry, with a concise and valuable introduction that surveys its development. The editor concludes that although the country has many poets, its poetry was not particularly distinguished until the twentieth century, and that a Costa Rican form and theme that won recognition outside the nation did not appear until the generation of 1940 and the Revolution of 1948, when poetic themes paralleled the new novel of social consciousness and when the nation's poetry became more sophisticated in form. BNCR

199 Chavarría, Lisímaco. Manojo de guarias. San José: Imprenta Moderna, 1913. 63 pp.
Another collection of poems of the Costa Rican countryside, reflecting the author's preferred theme. DLC-LDS-151 BNCR

200 ____. Nomadas. San José: Imprenta Nacional, 1906. 205 pp.
A collection of poetry that centers on the Costa Rican countryside and employs the idioms and simple vocabulary of the peasantry, reflecting the author's origins, yet also exhibits some experimentation in form as his style evolved. DLC-LDS-2 BNCR

201 Chavarria F., Rafael A. Primer centenario del monopolio de fabricación de licores en Costa Rica, 1851-1951. San José: Fábrica Nacional de Licores, 1951. 232 pp. Illus., tables.
An official centennial volume tracing the history of the government-operated liquor factory and its national monopoly. Although the focus is principally on the laws, directorates, and types of products manufactured, the volume includes both tables and graphs showing production from the 1860s to 1950, as well as graphs regarding production quality, though these are of more recent origin. BNCR

202 Chaves Vargas, Luís Fernando. Tipos de hábitat en el norte de la región cafetalera central de Costa Rica. Mérida, Venezuela: Universidad de Los Andes, 1966. 50 pp. Biblio., notes, illus., maps, tables. 2d ed. San José: Ministerio de Transportes, Instituto Geográfico de Costa Rica, 1967. 50 pp. Biblio., notes, illus., maps, tables.
Combines information drawn from existing reports and statistics with personal observation to describe the various types of living facilities and neighborhoods in the region. DLC

203 Church, George Earl. Report upon the Costa Rica Railway. London: Waterlow & Sons, 1895. 91 pp. Maps.
A detailed description of the company, its operations, and its holdings, as well as of traffic on it and the commerce of Costa Rica. Written as a report to the stockholders by a member of its board of directors who visited and inspected the line. Contains specifics about existing and proposed facilities, as well as comments about the importance of the railroad in Costa Rica and the implications for relations with the government and necessary policies. DLC DLC-LDS-259

204 La ciudad de San José, 1871-1921. San José: Banco Nacional de Costa Rica, 1972. Pages unnumbered. Illus.
A collection of photos showing the changes in the city of San José from 1871 to 1921. DLC

205 Clark, David S. Renting, Sharecropping, and Other Indirect Land Tenure Forms in Costa Rica: A Legal and Economic Analysis. San José: Universidad de Costa Rica, 1971. 191 pp. Notes.
An analysis of the nation's different land-tenure forms, including both formal and informal rental agreements, focusing on the decade of the 1960s. Analyzes the forms, size of holdings, regional distribution, settlement

of disputes, etc., and concludes with recommendations for new legislation designed to
formalize the system and provide protection to
all. The study shows that tenancy is limited
to less than 10% of the nation's land. BNCR

206 Coen, Elliot. Introducción al estudio de las
erupciones del Volcán Irazú. San José:
Universidad de Costa Rica, 1964. 78 pp.
Maps, tables.
     A geologic analysis of the 1963 eruptions
of the Irazú volcano in Costa Rica, including
discussion of possibly related meteorological
conditions and detailed readings of the various aspects of the eruption and the resulting
dust cloud that enveloped the capital. BNCR

207 Colegio Superior de Señoritas de Costa Rica.
Ideas sobre el periodismo nacional moderno.
San José: Imprenta Alsina, 1934. 54 pp.
     The Colegio surveyed all of Costa Rica's
leading editors of newspapers and journals,
asking each what changes they would consider
most beneficial in the nation's press. The
results are printed in this volume. The responses, ranging from single sentences to
several pages, provide a unique inside view of
the nation's press, with the answers ranging
from a belief that the press is sufficiently
vigorous that no changes are necessary, to
comments regarding technical improvements or
focus, to discussions of what is covered and
what is omitted, to suggestions for particular
types of new publications that would be useful
DLC-LDS-812 LNHT

208 Comisión de Festivos, Centenario de la Villa
de Barba. Centenario de la Villa de Barba.
San José: Imprenta Lehmann, 1924. 56 pp.
Illus.
     A brief history of the town and description
of its current state, with emphasis on its
churches. DLC

209 Conard, Louis. La République de Costa Rica.
Paris: Imprimerie Générale Lahure, 1913. 50
pp. Maps, tables.
     A brief description and compilation of
basic data, with emphasis on existing fate
his birth in the nation and hence was ineligible to serve as president despite the fact
that he 1tline. BNCR

210 Conejo Guevara, Adina. Henri Pittier. San
José: Ministerio de Cultura, Juventud y
Deportes, 1975. 162 pp. Biblio.
     A series of essays on the life and work of
this well-known tropical botanist, emphasizing
his efforts in and influence upon Costa Rica.
Also includes excerpts from some of his obser-
vations, reports, and correspondence. DLC
BNCR

211 Congreso Centroamericano de Historia
Demográfica, Económica y Social. Ensayos de
historia centroamericana. San José: CEDAL,
1974. 165 pp. Biblio.
     Six essays on demographic history presented
at the conference, with only two dealing with
the postindependence era. They focus on the
role of coffee and bananas in the local economies and societies. DLC

212 Consultecnica, Ltda., San José, Costa Rica.
Proyecto preliminar de canalización Lagunas
del Atlántico. San José: Consultecnica
Ltd., 1961. 198 pp. Notes, illus., maps,
tables.
     A detailed analysis and plan for canalizing
the marshy rivers along the Caribbean coast of
Costa Rica near Limón to provide protected
inland waterways to encourage development,
prepared by an engineering firm under contract
with the government. Includes detailed plans
and financial analysis. KU

213 Conte, Josefa. Impresiones de un viaje a
Costa-Rica. Panamá: Times Publishing Co.,
1928. 19 pp.
     A glowing description of the author's
travels in Costa Rica, emphasizing the
economic prospects and progress while
describing his experiences. DLC-LDS-718

214 Conway, Hobart McKinley, Jr. Costa Rica:
Where You'll Find Friends and Opportunity.
Atlanta: Conway Productions, 1963. 48 pp.
Biblio., illus., maps, tables.
     A lavishly illustrated discussion of prog-
ress and economic possibilities in Costa Rica,
designed to encourage investment. BNCR

215 Cooper, Enrique. Informe sobre el camino a
Matina y la Costa del Norte presentado al
gobierno. . . . 2d ed. San José: Tipografía
Nacional, 1896. 26 pp.
     An account of a trip in 1838 to the then-
remote North Coast of Costa Rica, describing
the rigors of the journey. Provides a vivid
description of the region and a graphic account of the monumental obstacles that confronted even the stout-hearted traveler during
the independence era. BNCR

216 Cordero R., Oscar. Diario. San José:
Imprenta de Soley Hermanos, 1948. 63 pp.
Illus.
     A diary and commentaries by a Costa Rican
who fought with the forces of José Figueres in
the Revolution of 1948, presenting the revolutionaries' view of the nation and its problems, and chronicling the campaigns in which
he participated. BNCR

217 Cordero Solano, José Abdulio. El ser de
la nacionalidad costarricense. Madrid:
Editorial Tridente, 1964. 179 pp. Biblio.,
notes.
     An intellectual history of Costa Rica re-
viewing the Colonial era, independence period,
and early nineteenth century and seeking to
identify the intellectual factors that made it
a nation and unified its culture. The author
focuses on the University of Santo Tomás as
the key element in evolving independent intellectuals who eventually became the core of the
new nation and shaped its culture. DLC LNHT
BNCR

218 Cordoba, Julio. La capacidad inversionista del sector público en Costa Rica. San José: Instituto Centroamericano de Administración Pública, 1978. v, 97 pp. Notes, tables.

A detailed analysis of the 1974 national plan, focusing on the role of the public sector and its investment; with tables and analysis of the role of the various sectors, objectives, and sources of funds. KU

219 Córdoba Zeledón, Alberto. Biografía y vida de un hombre: el Dr. Rafael Ángel Calderón Guardia, candidato a la presidencia de la República de Costa Rica, postulado por el Partido Republicano Nacional para el período de 1940-1944. San José: Imprenta Borrasé, 1939. 31 pp.

A campaign biography providing a laudatory sketch of the candidate's life and accomplishments, with excerpts from his speeches. BNCR

220 Corrales Briceño, Juan Bautista. La anexión de Guanacaste a Costa Rica. San José: Imprenta Nacional, 1962. 32 pp. Notes.

A collection of documents, with some connecting narration, regarding the annexation of the province of Guanacaste to Costa Rica during the independence era and the resulting disputes with Nicaragua, including the arbitral rulings in the case and some Colonial documents supporting the Costa Rican claims. DLC LNHT BNCR

221 Cortés Castro, Claudio. Álbum del ferrocarril eléctrico al Pacífico. San José: Imprenta La Tribuna, 1940. 91 pp. Illus., tables.

A profusely illustrated commemorative album reporting on the Pacific Railroad of Costa Rica and its facilities, operations, and routes, including statistics regarding operation during the 1930s, tables and graphs and commemorative rhetoric. BNCR

222 Cortés Chacón, Rafael. Necesidad de una reorganización del sistema educativo costarricense. San José: Esquela Superior de Administración Pública, 1957. xxiv, 199 pp. Biblio., notes, illus., tables.

A study of the Costa Rican educational system and its growth, and a call for administrative reform to allow better control and faster development. Includes statistics from throughout the twentieth century, although primarily from the 1941-55 period. DLC BNCR

223 _____. El pensamiento de Omar Dengo en la educación costarricense. San José: Imprenta Vargas, 1956. 56 pp. Illus.

An analysis of the educational thinking of one of Costa Rica's most influential professors during the initial two decades of the twentieth century, emphasizing what the author calls his "practical idealism," that is, his insistence that education was a separate field with its own theories, his practicality in emphasizing teacher preparation and methodological training, and his support of the nation's first normal school. Dengo also fought for the introduction of modern educational methods developed abroad. He was offered the post of minister or vice-minister of education by two different regimes, but preferred to remain in the classroom and continue his writings, though always fighting for educational reform within the g`>ernment and even in appearances before Congress. The essay is followed by a series of brief single-paragraph quotations from Dengo's commentaries on education, which the author feels indicate his thinking. DLC BNCR

224 Costa Rica, Academia de Geografía e Historia. Centro América en las vísperas de la independencia. San José: Imprenta Trejos, 1971. 457 pp. Biblio., notes.

A series of papers presented at conferences commemorating the sesquicentennial of Central American independence, held in San José during November 1970. There are contributions by leading Costa Rican historians that deal with many aspects of Central American life during the late Colonial and independence period, including political, economic, and social questions. Most reflect research in pertinent secondary works and published documents from the era. BNG BNCR

225 Costa Rica, Centro Para El Estudio de los Problemas Nacionales. La administración Calderón Guardia. San José: Editorial Surco, 1949. 97 pp.

A critique of the Calderón Guardia administration by a group that supported the 1948 revolution, this work traces the consequences of the regime's policies. BNCR

226 _____. Ideario costarricense: resultado de una encuesta nacional. San José: Editorial Surco, 1943. 437 pp.

The political plans of this young Social Democratic group, with a critique of the present state of the nation and a discussion of its heritage, representing their outlook on a broad range of problems confronting the nation. DLC

227 _____. El Partido Comunista de Costa Rica enjuiciado por sus hechos. San José: Imprenta Borrasé, 1943. 31 pp.

A critique of the Communist party, one of the group's favorite targets, citing the party's statements and actions as indications that it is inappropriate for the Costa Rican tradition. KU

228 Costa Rica, Cooperativa Bananera Costarricense. Certamen del patriotismo: trabajos y opiniones sobre la cuestiones agraria y ferrocarrilera, en relación con los concesionarios extranjeros en Costa Rica. San José: Imprenta La Tribuna, 1928. 191 pp.

A series of essays on the boundary dispute with Panama and the imperialism of foreign corporations in the banana and railroad fields, prepared by various authors for a patriotic contest sponsored by the Costa Rican Banana Owners Cooperative, a domestic agency of native banana producers. The essays are patriotic and anti-imperialistic in tone, advocating limitation of foreign capital and fostering of domestic enterprise as well as supporting the Costa Rican position in the boundary dispute. A series of addresses by Costa Rican political figures and a collection of documents about the various foreign contracts in Costa Rica is included. DLC DLC-LDS-415 BNCR

229   Costa Rica, Ferrocarril de. Documentos sobre la cuestión de cruces ventilada entre el señor subsecretario de estado en el despacho de Fomento y el agente general de la Compañía del Ferrocarrill de Costa Rica, mayo-junio, 1902. San José: Imprenta Lehmann, 1902. 33 pp.

A dispute involving railway rights and contracts in which the Ferrocarril de Costa Rica objects to a government grant allowing the Tropical Trading and Transport Company to cross its lines, despite contractual stipulations protecting them from any interference with their traffic by such crossings. DLC-LDS-74

230   Costa Rica Oil Corporation. Estudio sobre la ley del subsuelo y observaciones a la misma. San José: Imprenta Alsina, 1921. 103 pp. Appendixes.

A collection of legal opinions by well known jurists, prepared as part of a controversy regarding ownership of subsoil petroleum rights that is often characteristic of Latin American nations, reflecting the conflict between the Roman and Anglo-Saxon property concepts. The Costa Rica Oil Corporation had the opinions prepared to support legislation in Costa Rica declaring subsoil rights national property, which would enable honoring a concession to the company while effectively revoking property rights held by the United Fruit Company, which claimed that its land-ownership included title to subsoil resources. The incident was a major political issue in that nation. DLC-LDS-261

231   Costa Rica, Pacific Railroad. Estudios del ferrocarril a Quepos. San José: Published by the Railroad, 1958. 68 pp. Illus., maps.

A preliminary study by the railroad of the possibility of extending the track along the Pacific Coast from Puntarenas to the southern part of the province, to the town of Quepos, to link two separate existing sections of track completing a circle from San José, and an exposition of the problems, costs, and potential of such an effort. BNCR

232   Costa Rica, University of. El desarrollo económico de Costa Rica. 5 vols. San José: Universidad de Costa Rica, 1958-62. Pages unnumbered. Tables.

A massive description and analysis of the then-current state of the economy, with historical background, consisting of several team-written volumes focusing on the various economic sectors. Includes statistics and econometric analysis, as well as projections. DLC

233   _____. Estudio del sector externo de la economía costarricense con una descripción del desarrollo económica durante el período 1946-1954. San José: Universidad de Costa Rica, 1958. 72 pp. Illus., tables.

A survey of the Costa Rican economy during the years 1946-54, including a general description and a product-by-product survey of the principal exports, with appropriate statistics and graphs to indicate the trends. Includes projections for the export products to 1966. LNHT

234   _____. Estudio integral de las necesidades de la Universidad de Costa Rica para un período de diez años. San José: Universidad de Costa Rica, 1962. 98 pp. Tables.

The university's projection of its needs for the next ten years. Includes detailed lists of necessary equipment, studies of job demand in various fields, and projected numbers of students and graduates in each. BNCR

235   _____. Financiación de la Ciudad Universitaria: antecedentes y problemas. San José: Universidad de Costa Rica, 1960. 34 pp.

The University's official proposal to the Congress, reporting on its internal finances and proposing a law allowing the university to establish its own stamp tax for revenue purposes. BNCR

236   _____. Terremoto de Cartago: 1910. San José: Universidad de Costa Rica, 1974. Pages unnumbered. Illus.

Photos of the damage caused by the Cartago earthquake of 1910. BNCR

237   _____. Tesis de grado presentados a la Universidad de Costa Rica. 2 vols. San José: Universidad de Costa Rica, 1957-68.

An alphabetical list of the theses at the university, by faculty and then by authors. The first volume covers the years to 1947, and the second 1957-68. Since that date there has been an annual edition to keep the listing current. There are both subject and author indexes. Each listing contains title, year, and length, and an indication whether it has been subsequently published and if so by which press, but without date of publication. LNHT BNCR

238   Costa Rica, Gov't of. Compañía Bananera de Costa Rica, Chiriqui Land Company, United Fruit Company: leyes, contratos y resoluciones relativos a las industrias de banano, abaca, cacao, y palma africana oleaginosa, 1930-1953. San José: Imprenta Tormo, 1953. 97 pp.

A compilation of Costa Rican laws regarding the cultivation of these crops, and the contracts with the companies involved, covering the years 1930 through 1953. BNCR

239   _____. Contestación que el supremo gobierno del estado de Costa Rica dío a la protesta que la legación de Nicaragua le hizo por la retención de los pueblos del partido de Nicoya. San José: Imprenta de Estado, 1843. 21 pp.

(Costa Rica, Gov't of)

One of the many exchanges between Costa Rica and Nicaragua regarding the dispute that resulted from the shift at independence of the province of Guanacaste to Costa Rica, this note is the Costa Rican statement of its case in response to the latest Nicaraguan note, and became the basis of many later statements and exchanges. It bears the signature of Foreign Minister José María Castro. DLC DLC-LDS-195

240 _____. Contratos bananeros 1940-1957. San José: n.p., 1958.
The full text of all the accords for the years in question. BNCR

241 _____. Contratos presentados por la United Fruit Co. y M.M. Marsh al Congreso Nacional. San José: Imprenta La Tribuna, 1926. 168 pp. 2d ed. San José: Imprenta La Tribuna, 1927. 116 pp. Maps, tables.
A collection of materials pertinent to the 1926 contract between Costa Rica and the United Fruit Company, including documents and press articles, drawn mainly from the pages of La Tribuna. Includes the contract, speech of President Ricardo Jiménez Oreamuno, official reports of the company and statements of various outside experts, and memorials from local banana growers and associations interested in the railroad, which was part of the contract. DLC DLC-LDS-380

242 _____. Costa Rica as the Much Desired Home for the Homeless. San José: Tipografía Nacional, n.d. [190-?]. 24 pp. Illus.
A government pamphlet designed to encourage immigration and tourism, extolling the virtues of the nation in sometimes uncertain English, with extensive illustrations. DLC DLC-LDS-307

243 _____. Costa Rica Railway Company Ltd., and Northern Railway Company. San José: Printed by the Company, 1953. 200 pp. Illus., maps.
A brief résumé of the company and its evolution, followed by a photo essay emphasizing its facilities, problems, and importance to the economy. DLC BNCR

244 _____. Documentos relativos a la controversia (en juicio arbitral) entre el gobierno de la República de Costa Rica y la Simmons Construction Corporation. San José: Imprenta Nacional, 1933. 168 pp.
A collection of court decisions and submissions regarding a controversy in which the government broke its road-construction contract with the Simmons Company, alleging noncompliance, and the company sought to collect its payments according to the contract through the courts, which straddled the issue by ruling that the contract was valid and could not be broken by the government, but assessed penalties against the company for the alleged noncompliance. The issue became a political question inspiring considerable debate. DLC-LDS-727

245 _____. Documentos relativos a la disolución del Congreso Constitucional y convocación de las Asambleas Electorales. San José: Tipografía Nacional, 1892. 17 pp.
The presidential decree of General José J. Rodríguez dissolving Congress and charging that it had violated the constitution and then adjourned illegally. DLC-LDS-98

246 _____. Documentos relativos a la Guerra Nacional de 1856 y 57 con sus antecedentes. San José: Tipografía Nacional, 1914. 330 pp.
A compilation covering the years 1855 to 1857, consisting principally of official government communications with representatives abroad and with the other Central American nations, relative to the William Walker expedition and the resulting military campaign, reproduced without comment or annotation. DLC

247 _____. Documentos relativos a las tentativas de asesinato contra la persona del señor presidente de la república don Rafael Yglesias. San José: Tipografía Nacional, 1894. 261 pp.
A collection of documents, consisting principally of the interrogations and declarations of those arrested and the officials involved in frustrating the assassination attempt against the Costa Rican president during September 1894. DLC-LDS BNCR

248 _____. Documentos relativos a la transacción verificada entre los partidos políticos de la república, con el fin de elegir presidente para el período constitucional de 1902-1906. San José: Tipografía Nacional, 1901. 30 pp.
A series of exchanges involving the chiefs of all the Costa Rican political parties and principally Rafael Yglesias and Cleto González Víquez, regarding a pact to prevent a bitter electoral combat by naming a single candidate for the 1902 elections. BNCR

249 _____. Documentos relativos al proyecto de contrato petrolero Pinto-Greulich. San José: Imprenta Nacional, 1920. 106 pp.
A collection of documents regarding a controversial petroleum exploration contract that dates from 1915, reflecting the various congressional debates and actions regarding it. DLC-LDS-180 BNCR

250 _____. Exposición de los motivos del cambio político acaecido en Costa-Rica el 14 de agosto de 1859. San José: Imprenta Nacional, 1860. 37 pp.
A catalog of the charges against Juan Rafael Mora justifying the revolution that overthrew him, compiled by the revolutionaries, accusing him of arbitrary and high-handed methods and illegal activities to promote his own financial gain, and condemning what is characterized as a dictatorial regime that violated the constitution and Costa Rican traditions. DLC-LDS

251 _____. Exposición histórica de la revolución del 15 de septiembre de 1859, acompañada de algunas reflecciones sobre la situación del

(Costa Rica, Gov't of)

país, antes y después del 14 de agosto de 1859. San José: Imprenta del Gobierno, 1861. xii, 100 pp. Maps.

An account of the maneuvers and campaigns attendant to the overthrow of the government of Juan Rafael Mora, detailing the successful revolution and Mora's later invasion seeking to regain power, and providing elaborate justification for the movement by reprinting various commentaries on the state of the nation and the faults of the Mora regime. Includes the proclamations and polemics of the movement, lists of wounded in the battles, and a map of Puntarenas detailing the defeat of Mora's invasion. DLC DLC-LDS-68

252 _____. Las fiestas del 15 de septiembre de 1895: celebradas con motivo de la inauguración del monumento nacional erigido en San José a los héroes de 56 y 57. San José: Tipografía Nacional, 1897. iv, 321 pp. Notes, illus.

A compilation of historical data regarding the heroism of Juan Santamaría in the campaign against Walker, and an account of the festivities for the inauguration of the monument to him in San José in 1895. Includes a substantial collection of contemporary accounts of the military campaign and of documents from the era. DLC BNCR

253 _____. Nacionalización de la Fuerza Eléctrica y creación del Servicio Nacional de Electricidad en Costa Rica. San José: Editorial Gutenberg, 1929. 39 pp.

A collection of the laws and decrees involved in the nationalization of the electric service and the creation of the entities that would administer them for the government; drawn from the government Gaceta. DLC-LDS-432

254 _____. Nacionalización de las Fuerzas Hidráulicas y Eléctricas: creación del Servicio Nacional de Electricidad. San José: Imprenta Trejos, 1931. 80 pp.

A compilation of the laws and decrees creating and governing the new entity after the nationalization that completed the lengthy political debate. DLC-LDS-526

255 _____. Archivo Nacional. Acta de Independencia de Costa Rica. San José: Imprenta Nacional, 1971. 37 pp. Biblio., notes.

A reprinting of the Costa Rican Declaration of Independence of 29 October 1821 and several essays describing the event. BNCR

256 _____. _____. Índice de los protocolos de Alajuela, 1793-1850. San José: Tipografía Nacional, 1908. 511 pp.

A listing, by date and year, of the contents of each file and hence of each transaction legally recorded in the district, including land and house purchases, property deeds, wills, debts, court cases, and much more. The arrangement by date renders finding anything specific about given individuals laborious, but does parallel the files. The

indexes invariably start in Colonial days, with some extending into the mid-to-late nineteenth century. A potentially valuable and little-used source regarding the economic and social history of the nation, especially family linkages. DLC LNHT

257 _____. _____. Índice de los protocolos de Cartago. 6 vols. San José: Tipografía Nacional, 1909-30.
DLC LNHT See item CR256.

258 _____. _____. Índice de los protocolos de Guanacaste, 1756-1850. San José: Tipografía Nacional, 1909. 368 pp.
DLC LNHT See item CR256.

259 _____. _____. Índice de los protocolos de Heredia, 1721-1851. San José: Tipografía Nacional, 1904. 724 pp.
DLC LNHT See item CR256.

260 _____. _____. Índice de los protocolos de San José. 2 vols. San José: Tipografía Nacional, 1905-6. 576, 559 pp.
DLC LNHT See item CR256.

261 _____. _____. Índice de los protocolos del Archivo Nacional. 21 vols. San José: n.p., 1891.
DLC See item CR256.

262 _____. Asamblea Constituyente de 1949. Asamblea Nacional Constituyente de 1949. 3 vols. San José: Imprenta Nacional, 1952-56. 675, 648, 702 pp.

The minutes of the Constituent Assembly, including related correspondence and proposals brought before it, reflecting the deliberations that produced the 1949 constitution. DLC BNCR

263 _____. Banco Central. Documentos relacionados con la situación fiscal de Costa Rica y con las medidas financieras propuestas para nivelar el presupuesto nacional. San José: Imprenta Lehmann, 1957. 48 pp.

A collection of documents and exchanges regarding the internal bonding operations of the Banco Central, including the bank's announcements of the various loans and written exchanges regarding them between the bank, the National Assembly, and ex-president Figueres. DLC

264 _____. _____. Estadísticas economías, 1966-1971. San José: Banco Central, 1972. 31 pp. Tables.

A compilation of monthly statistical data relating to economic and financial matters for the years 1966-71. BNCR

265 _____. _____. Reseña de los principales acontecimientos monetarios y cambiarios en Costa Rica, 1969-1970. San José: Banco Central, 1971. 91 pp. Tables.

A brief compilation of information on the Costa Rican economy in 1971, focusing on legislation regarding monetary policy, trade, and the balance of payments, as well as full

(Costa Rica, Gov't of)
information regarding internal and external
debt. BNCR

266 _____. Banco Nacional. La Ciudad de San
José, 1871-1921. San José: Imprenta Lehmann,
1972. Pages unnumbered. Illus.
A collection of historical photos of the
city of San José, showing its development and
the principal buildings throughout the fifty-
year period in question. DLC BNCR

267 _____. _____. Prontuario de legislación
bancaria, 1914-1964. San José: Banco
Nacional de Costa Rica, 1965. 452 pp.
A fifty-year compilation of the banking
legislation of Costa Rica, arranged chronologically from the initial efforts to create a
national banking system in 1912 through 1964.
Provides a title, date, and brief description
of each piece of legislation or decree regarding banking during this era. DLC BNCR

268 _____. Banco Nacional de Seguros. El alcohol
y la gasolina. San José: Banco Nacional de
Seguros, 1936. 34 pp. Tables.
A study conducted by the state gas monopoly
in 1933, proposing that the nation seek to cut
its dependence on foreign petroleum imports by
refining alcohol from cane sugar plants and
requiring that all gasoline sold in the nation
be 10% alcohol. DLC-LDS-813

269 _____. Caja Costarricense de Seguro Social.
Apuntes para el estudio de uno de los aspectos
de la estratificación social en Costa Rica.
San José: n.p., 1969. Illus.
BNCR

270 _____. Centro de Promoción de Exportaciones e
Inversiones. El macrocosmos de un punto. San
José: Imprenta Lehmann, 1971. Pages
unnumbered. Illus., tables.
A collection of economic statistics from
the 1960s accompanied by lavish photos of
ports and industrial facilities, designed to
encourage trade and investment. BNCR

271 _____. Comisión de Investigación Histórica de
la Compaña de 1856-1857. Batalla de Rivas.
San José: Editorial Aurora Social, 1955. 77
pp. Index, illus., maps.
A collection of documents regarding the
battle in which Costa Rican troops confronted
Walker, including a complete medical report
listing all those killed or wounded, and an
account of the cholera epidemic that followed
the campaign. Includes the official orders
and reports of the Costa Rican army regarding
the events. DLC LNHT BNCR

272 _____. _____. Batalla de Santa Rosa. San
José: Tipografía Nacional, 1954. 67 pp.
A history of the Costa Rican participation
in the fight against the Walker intervention,
consisting primarily of reproductions of contemporary documents, including the call to
arms and orders, the contemporary accounts by
participants, and excerpts from existing
secondary accounts and historical studies,

accompanied by an itinerary of the army and a
list of its members. Includes a selection of
popular folk songs of the day supposedly sung
by the troops on the march. DLC LNHT BNCR

273 _____. _____. Crónicas y comentarios: año
centenario, 1856-1956. San José: Imprenta
Universal, 428 pp. Index, illus.
A collection of documents and excerpts from
contemporary newspaper accounts and existing
secondary works regarding the Walker intervention in Central America. The illustrations
from the period are also useful. DLC LNHT
BNCR

274 _____. _____. Documentos relativos a la
guerra contra los filibusteros. San José:
Tipografía Nacional, 1956. 416 pp. Biblio.,
illus.
A collection of documents from 1855 and
1856 relating to the Walker intervention,
principally consisting of interchanges between
the various Central American republics regarding cooperation in the face of the Yankee
threat. DLC LNHT BNCR

275 _____. _____. Juan Santamaría. San José:
Tipografía Nacional, 1954. 65 pp.
Despite its title, this is not another
account of Juan Santamaría's actions during
the campaign against Walker, but rather a
collection of documents in which the various
cantons and towns praised his action and honored him, accompanied by excerpts from various
existing descriptions of the campaign and the
documentation regarding the granting of
Santamaría's mother a pension after he was
declared a national hero. DLC LNHT BNCR

276 _____. _____. Proclamas y mensajes. San
José: Tipografía Nacional, 1954. 59 pp.
A collection of proclamations by various
Costa Rican officials relating to the campaign
against Walker, including calls to arms, etc.,
all drawn from the era. DLC LNHT BNCR

277 _____. _____. La segunda campaña. San José:
Tipografía Nacional, 1956. 63 pp. Illus.
A brief narration of Walker's final efforts
and his surrender, with a discussion of the
situations of Nicaragua and Costa Rica at the
end of the conflict, accompanied by various
documentary excerpts and proclamations regarding the termination of the conflict. DLC
LNHT BNCR

278 _____. Comisión Nacional del Sesquicentenario
de la Independencia de Centro América. Actas
y correspondencia del ayuntamiento de Cartago,
1820-1823. San José: Imprenta Nacional,
1971. 394 pp.
The minutes of the city council of Cartago
and its correspondence during the independence
era, including the initial organization of the
government in the aftermath of independence.
BNCR

279 _____. _____. Antología filatélica
costarricense. San José: Imprenta Lehmann,
1971. 183 pp. Illus., tables.

(Costa Rica, Gov't of)
    A collection of articles about various
aspects of the history of postage stamps in
Costa Rica, with discussions of particular
issues and changes in the locations, etc.
LNHT BNCR

280   _____. Consejo Superior de Educación.
    Oficina de Planeamiento Integral de la
    Educación. Informaciones preliminares para el
    diagnóstico de la situación del sistema
    educativo costarricense. San José: n.p.,
    1964. 196 pp.
        A legal and statistical report about the
    state of the Costa Rican educational system,
    emphasizing its organization, legal basis,
    facilities, programs, and the national needs,
    providing a summary of the organization and
    law, and indicating the problems, national
    needs, and the gap between official rhetoric
    and the actuality of the existing system and
    facilities. DLC

281   _____. Dirección General de Artes y Letras.
    Arte costarricense: estudios, biografías y
    laminas. San José: Imprenta Lehmann, 1968.
    48 pp. Illus.
        An overview of Costa Rican art, with bio-
    graphical sketches of sixteen artists and
    black and white illustrations of their work.
    IEdS

282   _____. Dirección General de Estadística.
    Resúmenes estadísticos años 1883 a 1910. 2
    vols. San José: Imprenta Nacional, 1912.
    155, 135 pp. Tables.
        A massive compilation of census data com-
    paring information from the surveys of 1883,
    1888, and 1892, in tabular form, in numerous
    classifications including population, distri-
    bution by sex and age, and data by province.
    The material varies, with some tables offering
    partial information, others employing odd
    dates in between, and several covering a
    broader span for comparative purposes, ranging
    back to 1844. DLC DLC-LDS-92 LNHT

283   _____. _____. Resúmenes estadísticos
    publicados por orden del señor secretario de
    estado en el despacho de Fomento, doctor don
    Juan J. Ulloa G. 3 vols. San José:
    Tipografía Nacional, 1895-96. 180, 134, 272
    pp. Tables.
        Another massive compilation of statistics,
    in tabular form, with most tables offering
    annual figures in each category and some pro-
    viding broader figures that extend back to
    independence for comparative purposes. The
    initial volume focuses on demography, the
    second on agriculture, and the third on trade.
    A useful source of data that also stands as a
    monument to the positivistic era and its ef-
    forts to focus on scientific approaches and
    statistics as the basis of development. DLC
    DLC-LDS

284   _____. Instituto Costarricense de Turismo.
    Costa Rica Offers Great Advantages for Retired
    People. San José: Instituto Costarricense de
    Turismo, 1965. 55 pp. Illus., tables.

    A pamphlet in English published by a gov-
ernment institute and designed to encourage
Yankees to take advantage of the possibilities
of retirement in Costa Rica, with emphasis on
the provisions of law 3393 of 1964 designed
for this purpose. Explains the provisions of
the law and provides basic data on the country
and life in it, with lists of social clubs,
discussions of the existing retirement community, and examples of then-current prices for
standard items such as food and clothing to
illustrate the cost of living. DLC BNCR

285   _____. Instituto de Tierras y Colonización.
    Estudio de comunidades indígenas: zonas
    Boruca-Térraba y China Kichá. San José:
    Published by the Institute, 1964. vi, 203 pp.
    Illus., maps, tables.
        An ethnographic survey and economic study
    of two areas of the Costa Rican interior,
    providing descriptive and statistical data on
    the populations and on economic and social
    change. DLC

286   _____. _____. Estudio de la región de Upala.
    San José: Published by the Institute, 1964.
    v, 153 pp. Biblio., illus., maps, tables.
        A survey of the Costa Rican side of its
    frontier with Nicaragua, emphasizing popula-
    tion, land tenure, land use, natural re-
    sources, and economic prospects. The study
    stresses the potential for increased produc-
    tion as well as the limits of the natural
    resources, concluding that further development
    of infrastructure to improve transportation
    and access would enable increased agricultural
    production, but that colonizing new settlers
    in the region would be counterproductive. DLC

287   _____. Instituto Geográfico. Guía para
    investigaciones de Costa Rica. San José:
    PAIGH, 1977. 138 pp.
    Research Guide to Costa Rica. San José:
    PAIGH, 1977. 138 pp.
        Prepared as part of the Institute of Pan
    American Geography and History series, this
    volume offers a bibliography of books and maps
    dealing with Costa Rica, with an emphasis on
    geography. DLC BNCR

288   _____. _____. El Instituto Geográfico de
    Costa Rica; un organismo público al servicio
    de la comunidad y la ciencia geográfica. San
    José: Published by the Institute, 1961. 21
    pp. Illus., maps.
        A brief summary of the history and activi-
    ties of the National Institute of Geography.
    DLC LNHT

289   _____. _____. Nuevos apuntes y bibliografía
    de la Isla de Coco. San José: Published by
    the Institute, 1964. viii, 79 pp. Illus.,
    maps.
        A series of studies of Cocos Island by
    members of the Institute, and an extensive
    bibliography regarding it consisting almost
    entirely of articles from journals and period-
    icals, though also citing general books that
    briefly mention the island. DLC BNCR

(Costa Rica, Gov't of)

290 _____. _____. Reproducciones científicas, una expedición y legislación de la Isla de Coco. San José: Published by the Institute, 1963. 125 pp. Biblio., illus., maps.

The preliminary map of Cocos Island, based on aerial photography by the U.S. Air Force, with reproductions of several of the original exploration reports from the 1890s, and a bibliography of Costa Rican legislation about it. DLC LNHT BNCR

291 _____. Ministerio de Cultura, Juventud y Deportes. La Costa Rica del año 2000. San José: Imprenta Nacional, 1977. 711 pp. Tables.

The addresses and documents of a planning symposium sponsored by the government during 1976 in which the development of the nation in all fields, including political, economic, social, and cultural, was projected to the year 2000 by various specialists, though with few statistics. BNCR

292 _____. Ministerio de Economía y Hacienda. Manual de organización de la administración pública de Costa Rica. San José: ESAPAC, 1962. 382 pp. Illus., tables. 2d ed. San José: Imprenta Nacional, 1968. 468 pp.

A general description and organization charts of the various agencies of the Costa Rican government and their interrelationships. BNCR

293 _____. Ministerio de Educación Pública. Cartilla antialcohólica para uso de las escuelas y colegios de la República: escrita por varios maestros y miembros de la liga antialcohólica de Costa Rica. San José: Imprenta Nacional, 1929. 41 pp.

A pamphlet designed for classroom use, detailing the evils of alcoholism and its consequences. DLC

294 _____. _____. Centenario del nacimiento de don Miguel Obregón Lizano. San José: Imprenta Revista Educación, 1961. 65 pp. Illus.

A brief summary of the career of one of the nation's leading educators, followed by excerpts from commentaries on his works, and commentaries and addresses commemorating his centennial; accompanied by appropriate photos. BNCR

295 _____. _____. Costa Rica. San José: Ministerio de Educación Pública, 1963. 111 pp. Illus., maps, tables.

A compilation of brief summaries of basic data about the nation in the 1960s, including geographic, economic, and cultural factors, with brief summaries of its history and a discussion of the national symbols. Intended for basic education or popular consumption. BNCR

296 _____. _____. Expansión y rendimiento del sistema educativo costarricense: 1960-1970. San José: Ministerio de Educación Pública, 1971. 137 pp. Tables.

A detailed report regarding growth and expansion of the Costa Rican educational system at all levels, replete with extensive statistics for the ten-year period indicated. BNCR

297 _____. Ministerio de Fomento. Documentos relativos al contrato celebrado entre la Secretaría de Fomento y la United Fruit Company incremento de la industria bananera. San José: Imprenta Nacional, 1934. 38 pp.

The contract of the early 1930s, with related documents. BNCR

298 _____. _____. Informes de las comisiones nombrados por el gobierno para estudiar los diferentes sistemas de construcciones contra temblores. San José: Tipografía Nacional, 1910. 74 pp. Illus.

Reports of various official commissions studying the most effective earthquake-proof construction methods available with existing technology. No conclusion was reached because Congress rejected the idea of legislation in this area. DLC DLC-LDS-96

299 _____. _____. Nomina de las concesiones hidráulicas y eléctricas existentes hasta el 15 de abril de 1934. San José: Imprenta Nacional, 1934. 16 pp.

A listing, alphabetically by holder within each province, of legally confirmed water-rights concessions, covering the years 1917 to 1934. Includes holder, place, and specifics regarding extent and type of use, as well as decree number. The vast majority of the listings are in the province of San José, with Cartago the next most significant and the other provinces only sparsely represented. DLC-LDS-782

300 _____. Ministerio de Gobernación. Guanacaste: libro conmemorativo del centenario de la incorporación del partido de Nicoya a Costa Rica, 1824-1924. San José: Imprenta María Viuda de Lines, 1924. 486 pp. Illus., maps, tables.

A commemorative volume issued on the centennial of the incorporation of the province into Costa Rica after its separation from Nicaragua at independence. Details its history, present development, and services with extensive illustrations, excerpts from official documents attendant to its joining Costa Rica, description of its terrain, and various pieces commemorating the occasion from speeches and the press. The area's history is considered topically, with chapters devoted to railroads, mining, agriculture, roads, and the various services. DLC DLC-LDS-319 LNHT

301 _____. Ministerio de Hacienda. Compilación de leyes y documentos oficiales relativos a la evolución monetaria de Costa Rica. San José: Tipografía Nacional, 1900. 125 pp.

This compilation covers the changes in the Costa Rican banking system during the regime of Rafael Yglesias from 1896 through 1900. DLC BNCR

(Costa Rica, Gov't of)

302 _____. Ministerio de Hacienda y Comerico. Documentos concernientes al contrato de empréstito para la construcción de la Carretera Interamericana. San José: Imprenta Nacional, 1941. 75 pp.

The Ministry's report to Congress, calling for approval of the loan contracts, with the full text of the documents and loan agreements providing 50% funding by the U.S. Export-Import Bank and construction supervision by Yankee engineers. Also contains a summary of congressional debate and the report of the relevant commission, along with estimates of costs, repayment schedules, and the impact of the road program on government revenues. DLC LNHT

303 _____. Ministerio de Obras Públicas. Anteproyecto portuario: obras terrestres y marítimas para la Península de Nicoya. San José: Ministerio de Obras Públicas, 1960. 98 pp. Biblio., illus., maps, tables.

A government study regarding the construction and facilities necessary to establish a second Pacific port in Costa Rica on the Nicoya Peninsula, with extensive maps and charts of the area and recommendations for the necessary facilities. DLC BNCR

304 _____. _____. Características del tránsito en el área metropolitana de San José, 1957-1962. San José: Published by the Ministry, 1963. 132 pp. Biblio., illus., tables.

A comprehensive study of the capital's transportation system, with monthly statistics, comparative tables, and graphs. Considers seasonal and hourly fluctuations, types preferred, directions, sources, etc., encompassing private vehicles and the various types of public transportation. DLC BNCR

305 _____. Ministerio de Relaciones Exteriores. The Case of Costa Rica in the Matter of Claims Presented by His Britannic Majesty's Government against the Republic of Costa Rica before the Chief Justice of the United States of America, Arbitrator. 2 vols. Washington, D.C.: Press of Byron S. Adams, 1923. 165, 608 pp. Appendixes.

306 _____. _____. Colección de tratados celebrados entre Costa Rica y varias naciones extranjeras. San José: Imprenta de la Paz, 1861. 258 pp.
See item CR307. DLC BNCR

307 _____. _____. Colección de tratados: contiene solamente los tratados vigentes en la fecha del 31 de diciembre de 1926: edición ordenada por la Secretaría de Relaciones Exteriores. San José: Imprenta Alsina, 1927. 435 pp.

The official compilation of Costa Rican treaties in force, arranged by country. Contains full text without comment. There have been several editions, though their timing is unpredictable. DLC-LDS-699 LNHT BNCR

308 _____. _____. Colección de tratados: edición ordenada por la Secretaría de Relaciones Exteriores. San José: Tipografía Nacional, 1896. iii, 245 pp.
See item CR307. DLC-LDS-112 BNCR

309 _____. _____. Colección de tratados internacionales celebrados por la República de Costa Rica. 2 vols. San José: Tipografía Nacional, 1892-93. 391, 434 pp.
See item CR307. DLC BNCR

310 _____. _____. Counter-Case of Costa Rica in the Matter of Claims Presented by His Britannic Majesty's Government against the Republic of Costa Rica before the Chief Justice of the United States of America, Arbitrator. Washington, D.C.: Press of Byron S. Adams, 1923. 290 pp.

311 _____. _____. Índice completo por orden alfabético de las opciones, inscripciones y naturalizaciones practicadas desde el año de 1829 hasta septiembre de 1927. San José: Imprenta Nacional, 1927. 290 pp.

A complete list of all individuals registered or nationalized in Costa Rica during the nineteenth century and initial portion of the twentieth century, providing name, city of residence, date of inscription or naturalization, and previous nationality. DLC-LDS-429 BNCR

312 _____. _____. Notas crusadas entre las cancillerías de Costa Rica y Nicaragua, relativas a la abrogación del pacto de Corinto de 20 de enero de 1902. San José: Tipografía Nacional, 1907. 41 pp.
DLC DLC-LDS-45

313 _____. _____. Reunión de presidentes de Centroamérica, Panamá y Estados Unidos de América. San José: Imprenta Vargas, 1963. 122 pp.

The program and addresses of the chief executives during their March 1963 meeting in San José. BNCR

314 _____. Ministerio de Seguridad Pública. Información seguida para averiguar los autores de un proyecto de sedición. San José: Imprenta Nacional, 1882. 34 pp.

The testimonies and confessions of individuals regarding an attempted coup, implicating Demetrio Tinoco as their leader and providing details regarding the effort; published without narration or comment. BNCR

315 _____. _____. Revolución de Federico Tinoco y Demetrio Iglesias. San José: Imprenta Nacional, 1902. 201 pp.

A collection of testimonies and confessions regarding an uprising in the principal military barracks of San José, allegedly headed by Tinoco and Iglesias. Provides details of the plot and implicates these two individuals; published without narration or further comment. BNCR

316 _____. _____. Sumaria de los sucesos acaecidos en Liberia el 13 de septiembre de

(Costa Rica, Gov't of)
1926. San José: Imprenta Nacional, 1926.
123 pp. Illus., maps.
     The court proceedings and signed testimony
of the various participants in a plot in
Liberia, involving General Jorge Volio Jiménez
in an attempt to seize control of the city.
Provides the details of the plot and maps of
the combat, though without any overall narration of the complete episode. DLC LNHT BNCR

317 _____. _____. Sumaria levantada con motivo
de asalto al cuartel de artillería. San José:
Tipografía Nacional, 1899. 213 pp. Index.
     A collection of testimonies resulting from
the investigations and court proceedings regarding an attempted coup that included an
attack on the artillery barracks in San José.
There is no overall narration, just the collection of declarations and confessions. DLC
DLC-LDS-62 BNCR

318 _____. _____. Sumaria levantada con motivo
de la rebelión del cuartel principal y
comandancia de plaza ocurrida el 3 de mayo de
1902. San José: Tipografía Nacional, 1902.
201 pp. Index.
     The official report and record of the
proceedings of the investigation and the
testimony of the suspects involved in the
unsuccessful uprising. DLC DLC-LDS-33 BNCR

319 _____. _____. Sumaria por sedición:
noviembre y diciembre, 1906. San José:
Tipografía Nacional, 1906. 147 pp. Index.
     The testimony and transcripts of the judi-
cial proceedings resulting from the investigation of the uprising in Puntarenas on 13
November 1906, published without further
comment or narration. DLC-LDS-33 BNCR

320 _____. _____. Sumaria sobre la conspiración
contra el gobierno de la república. San José:
Imprenta Nacional, 1880. 20 pp.
     The official account and confessions of a
group of plotters who planned to infiltrate
the galleries of the Constituent Assembly and
disrupt it in September 1880, providing the
government's version of the frustrated plot.
DLC-LDS-116

321 _____. Ministerio de Transportes. Reseña
histórica de los transportes en Costa Rica.
San José: Ministerio de Transportes, 1967.
84 pp. Biblio., tables.
     A brief history of transportation in Costa
Rica from the Colonial period to the present,
with chapters on the development of the railroads, the ports, the highway network, and air
services. Graphs showing the significance of
the various forms from 1910 through the present provide useful data on exports and their
routes. A helpful overview, though in brief
outline and focused on the present. DLC BNCR

322 _____. Oficina de Planeamiento y
Coordinación. Características de la actividad
agropecuaria en Costa Rica 1950-1964. San
José: Published by the Office, 1965. 278 pp.
Maps, tables.

A summary of Costa Rican agriculture and
its development during these years, replete
with extensive statistics. Includes consideration of land ownership; physical setting;
demography; demand for various crops, both
foreign and domestic; prices; markets; production methods; credit, etc. The statistics and
tables are particularly helpful for an overview of the nation's agricultural development
and trends. BNCR

323 _____. Oficina de Planificación. Previsiones
del desarrollo económico y social 1969-1972, y
planes del sector público. 2 vols. San José:
Oficina de Planificación, 1970. 265, 420 pp.
Biblio., tables.
     The official government plan for 1969-72
governing its investment and public works
priorities, replete with extensive statistics
and explanations. DLC BNCR

324 _____. Oficina Nacional de Censo.
Alfabetismo y analfabetismo en Costa Rica.
San José: Imprenta Alsina, 1928. 65 pp.
Tables.
     A province-by-province description of the
extent of illiteracy based on the 1927 census
data, with comparative sections by sex and
age, and data regarding schools and students
enrolled. The tables provide these figures
for each municipality in the republic,
arranged by province. DLC-LDS-404

325 _____. _____. Estadística Vital (1906-1925):
natalidad, nupcialidad, mortalidad general,
mortalidad infantil. San José: Imprenta
Lehmann, 1927. 87 pp. Illus., tables.
     DLC LNHT

326 _____. Patronato Nacional de la Infancia. 10
años de labor, 1930-1940. San José: Imprenta
Nacional, 1941. 154 pp. Illus., tables.
     A summary of the office's programs and
accomplishments during its initial ten years
of existence. The volume is much more valuable, however, for its statistical tables and
graphs, which provide a great deal of information about Costa Rican children, their health,
social problems, delinquency, and other aspects not readily available from other
sources. DLC LNHT BNCR

327 _____. Presidencia, Secretaría de
Información. Cuatro años de la administración
Cortés: obras de provecho público, 1936-1940.
San José: Imprenta Nacional, 1940. Pages
unnumbered. Illus.
     An item-by-item description of the public-
works projects of the regime of President León
Cortés, extolling the regime's extensive con-
struction efforts and emphasizing highways.
Includes extensive photos of the projects.
LNHT

328 _____. _____. Dos años de labor de la
administración Calderón Guardia. San José:
n.p., 1942. Pages unnumbered. Illus.
     A lavishly illustrated description of the
public works of the Calderón Guardia administration during 1940-42, compiled by the regime

(Costa Rica, Gov't of)
and stressing the many buildings and services
and their distribution around the country, at
a time most were still in progress. Contains
brief descriptions of each, along with photos;
projects are listed by province. BNCR

329 _____. _____. 15 días en Costa Rica. San
José: Tipografía Nacional, 1972. Pages
unnumbered. Illus.
A collection of speeches, photos, and reports regarding the activities of the Figueres
regime. In commemoration of a visit to Limón
and the nationalization of the Northern Railroad of Costa Rica, but encompasses visits to
many other local plants, projects such as port
works in Limón, and even a speech by the
foreign minister at the U.N. BNCR

330 _____. Servicio Nacional de Electricidad.
Proyecto de contrato con las Compañías
Eléctricas: texto, comentarios, anexos. San
José: Imprenta La Tribuna, 1931. 71 pp.
The proposed contract forcing the three
electric companies operating in Costa Rica to
consolidate into a single national company
incorporated in Costa Rica and establishing a
regulatory board that would control rates and
service, though allowing the companies a
profit. Includes legal studies by attorneys
retained by the National Electric Commission
arguing that this arrangement does not violate
the concessions previously granted to the
companies. DLC-LDS-508

331 _____. Sociedad Económica de Amigos del País.
Estudio de la Sociedad . . . relativo a los
contratos bananeros celebrados entre el
gobierno de Costa Rica y Mr. M.M. Marsh y la
United Fruit Co. respectivamente, presentados
al Congreso en la Legislatura de 1927. San
José: Imprenta Nacional, 1929. 33 pp.
A series of studies and commentaries by the
society, urging the Congress to reject the new
accord with the United Fruit Company contending that while the nation should welcome foreign investment, the contract gives the
company unfair monopoly privileges that will
harm the interests of domestic growers. DLC
DLC-LDS-458

332 Costa Rica y Morazán. San José: Imprenta de
Jose Canalías, 1887. 79 pp.
A collection of Costa Rican newspaper articles by various authors, some anonymous, all
dated 1887, dealing with Morazán and generally
criticizing his actions in Costa Rica. The
longest series is by Jorge Volio and is drawn
from La República. DLC-LDS-89 BNCR

333 Coto Conde, José Luís. Don Ricardo Fernández
Guardia: ensayo biográfico. San José:
Imprenta Nacional, 1957. 20 pp. Notes.
A brief biographical sketch tracing the
career of a Costa Rican educator, historian,
and diplomat of the late nineteenth century
and early twentieth centuries. Originally
prepared as an address to the Costa Rican
Academy of History, the focus is on his

historical studies but all aspects of his
career are briefly outlined. DLC BNCR

334 Creedman, Theodore S. Historical Dictionary
of Costa Rica. Metuchen, N.J.: Scarecrow,
1977. xi, 251 pp. Biblio.
Part of a series of volumes providing
alphabetically arranged brief definitions and
identifications of terms, places, individuals,
parties, and events of the nation's history.
Contains a fuller bibliography and is more
careful in providing full double names than
some other volumes in the series. Like the
others, it is useful yet limited. DLC LNHT

335 CSUCA. El sistema educativo en Costa Rica:
situación actual y perspectivas. San José:
CSUCA, 1964. x, 242 pp. Illus., tables.
A detailed overview of the educational
system during the post-1950 era, including
copious statistics regarding the population,
age groups, school children, and the growth in
all, as well as occupational and income statistics for the nation. Provides a description of its administrative apparatus at all
levels and a survey of resources, as well as a
discussion of future needs with statistical
projections. DLC LNHT BNCR

336 Cuestión político-religiosa: discusión sobre
los artículos 2 y 6 del decreto de elecciones,
dictado por el gobierno provisorio, en lo que
concierre el clero. San José: Imprenta
Nacional, 1870. 52 pp.
A series of exchanges, essays, press commentaries, and pamphlets concerning the rights
of priests in the body politic, reflecting the
Liberal reforms of the era. Focuses on the
government regulations for the forthcoming
Constituent Assembly, which barred priests
from voting and thereby in effect also from
serving in the Assembly, since all those
elected had to be selected from the voting
lists. Includes a protest by several clerics
who cite the role of priests in leading the
independence movement, and responses. Indicates the tenor of the exchange but is clearly
compiled in a form that favors the government
position, and argues for the separation of
church and state. DLC DLC-LDS-103

337 Curtis, William Elroy. La más pequeña de las
repúblicas americanas. San José: Imprenta
Nacional, 1887. 60 pp.
A brief general description of Costa Rica
and its physical setting and people, originally published in Harpers New Monthly
Magazine. DLC DLC-LDS-23 BNCR

338 Darío, Rubén. Rubén Darío en Costa Rica. San
José: Ministerio de Educación Pública, 1967.
59 pp.
Selections from item CR339. DLC BNCR

339 _____. Rubén Darío en Costa Rica: 1891-1892,
cuentos y versos, artículos y crónicas. 2
vols. San José: Editorial García Monge,
1919-20. 148, 108 pp.
A collection of articles and poems written
by Darío during a visit to Costa Rica in 1891

and 1892 and published in the local press at that time. Includes commentaries on and reactions to various Costa Rican themes, customs, events, and places, as well as some more general pieces. There are also some articles about Darío, from the Costa Rican press of that time. DLC BNCR

340 DeBravo, Jorge. Canciones cotidianas. San José: Editorial Costa Rica, 1967. 67 pp.
A collection of poems focusing on the daily lives of the workers, constituting part of the social-protest poetry associated with the author. DLC LNHT BNCR

341 _____. Los despiertos. San José: Editorial Costa Rica, 1972. 86 pp.
The author's last book of poetry, published posthumously, reflecting his focus on the lives of the poor and the lower classes, particularly the peasants. He considers himself a militant, using his poetry to fight for justice and brotherhood by crying out against abuse. DLC BNCR

342 _____. Nosotros los hombres. San José: Editorial Costa Rica, 1966. 112 pp. 2d ed. San José: Editorial Costa Rica, 1974. 109 pp.
A collection of poetry focusing on human emotions and the lives of the poor workers, which won the national prize for 1966 for this Costa Rican poet. The themes reflect his association with the modern school of social protest. This is considered his major work. DLC LNHT BNCR

343 Delgado Aguilera, Ulises. Maceo en Costa Rica. San José: Imprenta Nacional, 1969. 83 pp. Illus.
A brief account of the presence in Costa Rica of Cuban guerrilla and liberator Antonio Maceo and his efforts to promote a Cuban colony in Costa Rica and launch a sugar mill, detailing the resulting difficulties until his return to his homeland in 1892 to renew his efforts for independence. Contains accompanying documentation from the period. BNCR

344 Dengo, Gabriel. Bibliografía de la geología de Costa Rica. San José: Universidad de Costa Rica, 1959. iii, 27 pp. 2d ed. San José: Universidad de Costa Rica, 1962. 67 pp.
DLC LNHT

345 _____. Estudio geológico de la región de Guanacaste, Costa Rica. San José: Instituto Geográfico, 1962. ix, 112 pp. Biblio., illus., maps.
A geological study of the oldest region of the Central American mountain range, providing clues to its development in ancient times. Focuses on the Pacific highlands of northwestern Costa Rica, giving specific descriptions of its regions, formations, and sediments, and hence of its evolution, upheaval, and volcanic activity; with appropriate maps and illustrations. DLC LNHT BNCR

346 Dengo, Omar. Meditaciones. 2 vols. San José: Imprenta Alsina, 1929-30. 174, 179 pp.
A collection of essays and commentaries on diverse themes by one of Costa Rica's most influential educators and well-known intellectuals. The subjects are varied, though they include observations regarding education and Costa Rican politics of the 1900-1920 era. Most, however, deal with general subjects and reflect the breadth of the author's interests rather than his specific influences. The work is announced as the beginning of an intended collected writings of Dengo. DLC DLC-LDS-463 BNCR

347 Dengo de Vargas, María Eugenia, ed. Omar Dengo: escritos y discursos. San José: Ministerio de Educación Pública, 1961. 479 pp. Biblio., appendixes.
A lengthy selection from the writings of this well-known and influential Costa Rican educator and intellectual, compiled by his daughter. The volume includes selections from his early works, his literary and philosophical writings, his political and educational commentaries, and his critical reviews, and hence covers a broad range of themes that serves to demonstrate both his thinking and the breadth of his activities. DLC LNHT BNCR

348 _____. Roberto Brenes Mesén. San José: Ministerio de Cultura, Juventud y Deportes, 1974. 437 pp. Biblio., notes, illus.
A brief biographical sketch of a Costa Rican educator and modernist poet whose works include poetry and prose as well as educational studies, and whose career includes service as director of various schools as well as in ministerial posts. His educational works helped set the programs and curricula of the nation's schools during his fifty-year career, which began during the 1890s. Includes an anthology of his works. LNHT BNCR

349 Denton, Charles F. La política del desarrollo de Costa Rica. San José: Novedades de Costa Rica, 1969. 164 pp.
Patterns of Costa Rican Politics. Boston: Allyn & Bacon, 1971. 113 pp. Index, biblio., tables.
Part of a political science series aimed at the general reader with no knowledge of the country, this work provides a concise summary of the current social, economic, and political state of the nation, though within a viewpoint that is highly critical of the system, differing with most existing interpretations by contending that the nation's famous democracy is limited to a small part of the population and ignores the lower classes. DLC LNHT

350 Desamparados, Comisión del Centenario. Memoria del centenario de Desamparados, 1862-- 4 de noviembre--1962. San José: Comisión del Centenario de la Creación de Desamparados, 1964.
A collection of material, documents, literary excerpts, etc. about the canton, with

accounts of and writings by its leading citizens. Includes a description of the founding of the town and of its principal institutions. DLC BNCR

351 DeWitt, R. Peter, Jr. The Inter-American Development Bank and Political Influence: With Special Reference to Costa Rica. New York: Praeger, 1977. 197 pp. Index, biblio., notes, tables.

A dependency-based analysis written from secondary sources, condemning the Yankee role in the bank and characterizing the institution as an instrument of Yankee imperialism. Includes an effective overview of Costa Rican development policy and statistics regarding the bank's lending that indicate a shift from social projects to infrastructure during the course of the bank's existence. DLC LNHT

352 Díaz, Hugo. El mundo de Hugo Díaz. San José: Editorial Costa Rica, 1977. 271 pp. Illus.

A collection of cartoons and comic strips from the late 1960s and early 1970s by a prominent Costa Rican artist, offering humorous portrayals of world events, Costa Rican domestic problems and political events, as well as of contemporary society. BNCR

353 Un Diputado. Una conversación con el pueblo. San José: Tipografía Nacional, 1916. 48 pp.

A discussion of the Costa Rican tax system, with a call for its reform, contending that as presently constituted it falls more heavily on the poor. Written as part of a political polemic, the account is highly critical of foreign debts and calls for taxing foreigners living or investing in the nation, whom it says are now exempt. DLC DLC-LDS-154

354 _____. Una conversación con un trabajador de los campos. San José: Imprenta Nacional, 1916. 34 pp.

Part of a political dispute, this pamphlet deals with agricultural credit. It condemns the profits of the past and hails the government's new efforts, which it says constitute the first governmental attempt to provide ample credit for the agricultural sector at reasonable rates. Written in the form of a dialogue with a peasant, it explains the issues in simple terms. DLC-LDS-154

355 Dobles, Fabián. Aguas turbias. San José: Imprenta Trejos, 1943. 392 pp.

A novel set in a small town in the Costa Rican countryside, focusing on the lives of the peasants and emphasizing their desire for land and their struggle for a decent living standard. DLC LNHT BNCR

356 _____. Cuentos de Fabián Dobles. San José: EDUCA, 1971. 141 pp.

A collection of short stories featuring elaborate descriptions of both settings and characters, focusing, as usual, on the struggles of the oppressed peasants in the Costa Rican countryside, though including some stories based in San José. About half had been previously published. DLC LNHT BNCR

357 _____. En el San Juan hay tiburón. San José: Editorial L'Atelier, 1967. 112 pp.

A novel of Costa Rican peasant life, broadening the theme to include all of Central America. Emphasizes the common links among the peoples who live on the frontiers in times of crisis and their cooperation to resolve their problems, leaving the reader to draw his own conclusions about applying such techniques to social as well as physical situations. DLC LNHT BNCR

358 _____. Ése que llaman pueblo. San José: Editorial Letras Nacionales, 1942. 320 pp. 3d ed. San José: Editorial Costa Rica, 1977. 306 pp.

Another of this influential author's works focusing on the lives of the rural peasants in his native Costa Rica, emphasizing their hardships and problems, narrating their efforts to survive in the harsh world of the interior. In this case the focus is on the trials and tribulations of a youthful peasant seeking to build a decent life for his family. He is treated as a representative unsung hero of the lumpen proletariat of the countryside, for whom all life is a struggle against exploiters and mere survival a victory. DLC DLC-LDS-938 LNHT BNCR

359 _____. Historias de Tata Mundo. 2 vols. San José: Imprenta Trejos, 1955-56. 6th ed. San José: Editorial Costa Rica, 1977. 293 pp.

One of the best known of the author's works focusing on the harsh life of the rural peasants. The setting is the Costa Rican countryside, with specific locations, but the focus is on describing the people rather than the setting, and the resulting picture is applicable to all of Costa Rica. The work uses a narrator and mythical figure whose tale enables analysis of the peasants' experiences and narration in popular idioms to capture the feelings and expressions of the campesinos. DLC LNHT BNCR

360 _____. Los leños vivientes. San José: Imprenta Elena, 1962. 136 pp.

A novel focusing on life in the Costa Rican countryside. As do most of the author's efforts, it contains themes of social protest and decries the harsh life and poverty. This one seems to be seeking to justify a new revolution against oppression. The 1947-48 period, indicated as the setting, suggests a relationship to an attempted uprising in 1948. DLC LNHT BNCR

361 _____. El maijú, y otras historias de Tata Mundo. San José: Ediciones Repertorio Americano 1957. 99 pp. Illus.

In effect a sequel to his earlier Historias de Tata Mundo. Uses this Costa Rican mythical figure to narrate the short stories based on local folklore and imagery. DLC LNHT

362 _____. El rescoldera. San José: Editorial L'Atelier, 1947. 88 pp.

Among the earliest works by an author who later would become prominent, these short

(Dobles, Fabián)
   stories, written in 1941 and 1946 but not
   published until 1947, focus on a clash between
   rural peasants and a powerful banana company.
   LNHT BNCR

363 _____. El sitio de las abras. Guatemala:
Ministerio de Educación Pública, 1950. 216
pp. Illus. Latest ed. San José: Editorial
Costa Rica, 1975. 207 pp.
   A novel emphasizing the struggle for control of land, a struggle that pits all the
members of a community against each other.
Demonstrates the importance of land ownership
to status and a decent life-style, as well as
its implications for the social class system.
DLC LNHT BNCR

364 _____. El violín y la chatarra. San José:
Editorial Pablo Presbere, n.d. [1965?].
75 pp.
   Another in the series of short stories
describing the life of the peasants in the
countryside and emphasizing their traditions
and problems, though in this case using a
shorter form and a more rigid, doctrinaire
approach that focuses on the class struggle.
DLC LNHT BNCR

365 Dobles Segreda, Gonzalo. La voz de la
campaña. Cartago: Imprenta El Heraldo, 1928.
16 pp.
   A brief novellette about life in the rural
countryside; it was awarded a prize in a 1927
national competition. DLC-LDS-405

366 Dobles Segreda, Luís. Caña brava: leyendas,
paisajes y tipos de la ciudad de Heredia. San
José: Imprenta Trejos, 1926. Latest ed. San
José: Editorial Costa Rica, 1975. 100 pp.
   A prominent Costa Rican writer's description of life in his native city of Heredia at
the turn of the century. Based on local lore,
it demonstrates the conflict between the
city's rich tradition and cultural heritage
and the changes brought by the modern world.
DLC LNHT BNCR

367 _____. Fadrique Gutierrez: hombre
extravagante de muchas andanzas. San José:
Imprenta Trejos, 1954. xviii, 182 pp. Illus.
San José: Editorial Costa Rica, 1975.
167 pp.
   An historical novel of life in the Costa
Rican countryside during the mid-nineteenth
century, set in the author's native Heredia
and based on one of its legendary figures,
whose life combines art with politics and a
military career through participation in local
revolutions. The volume focuses particularly
on description of Heredia and its life during
the nineteenth century. DLC LNHT BNCR

368 _____, ed. Heredia: geografía, historia,
literaria. Heredia: Editorial, ALA, 1935.
642 pp. Biblio., illus.
   A commemorative volume on the province's
200th anniversary. Incorporates reproductions
of the editor's previously published work on
its geography and the Colonial history of the
province by Cleto González Víquez. The editor

added a massive annotated bibliography of
Heredian writers (pp. 276-642), arranged alphabetically and with most entries coded to
his own Letras patrias collection. Despite
this restriction to Heredian authors, the fact
that this bibliography is arranged alphabetically rather than by year and appeared late
in his life makes it far easier to use than
his longer Indice bibliografico. DLC-LDS-810

369 Dobles Segreda, Luís. Índice bibliográfico de
Costa Rica. 9 vols. San José: Imprenta
Lehmann, 1927-36.
   Intended as a comprehensive bibliographical
study of the nation but falls short of this
objective despite being one of the best available guides. The volumes are arranged by
subject matter, with citations to the various
collections. The annotations are mainly excerpts from tables of contents or introductions. Within the subject areas the order is
unpredictable; though partially alphabetical
within years, it varies considerably, making
it necessary to go through the entire section
to find a particular item. In addition, there
is only a single volume for each subject, and
since they appeared at intervals, each contains only the citations of which the author
was aware at the time. No supplements were
ever issued. This affects comprehensiveness
as well as codings, for each volume covers
only a portion of the author's own vast collection, which he continued to enlarge without
adding to the index. Selection criteria are
not indicated, and books and journal articles
are mixed. Citations do not always use standard form, and punctuation can create confusion
for those not familiar with the authors or
titles. DLC DLC-LDS

370 _____. El libro del héroe: documentos y
elogios acerca de Juan Santamaría. San José:
Imprenta Lehmann, 1926. vii, 335 pp.
   A collection of documents and essays about
Juan Santamaría, one of the Costa Rican military heroes of the William Walker intervention
in Central America. DLC DLC-LDS-351 BNCR

371 _____. Lista de mapas parciales o totales de
Costa Rica. San José: Imprenta Lehmann,
1928. 64 pp.
   A listing of maps, arranged chronologically, with a brief paragraph describing
each, published separately for the use of
geographers although it was originally prepared as part of the second volume of the
Índice bibliográfico. The descriptions indicate content and preparer but not location.
DLC DLC-LDS-421

372 _____. La obra de Joaquín García Monge. San
José: Imprenta Borrasé, 1944. 16 pp.
   One prominent Costa Rican writer comments
on another during an address that was part of
an awards ceremony. Hails the works of
Joaquín García Monge and his efforts to
portray Costa Rican life, and also extols his
service as a professor. BNCR

(Dobles Segreda, Luís)

373 _____. Obras del profesor Luís Dobles Segreda. San José: Imprenta Lehmann, 1935. 56 pp.

An annotated bibliographical listing of the author's works extracted from the bibliography in his volume on Heredia. DLC DLC-LDS-819

374 _____. Por el amor de Dios. . . . Heredia: Imprenta Alsina, 1918. 114 pp. Latest ed. San José: Ministerio de Educación Pública, 1968. 92 pp. Biblio., illus.

Among the earliest works by this now-prominent author, this volume was one of a series focusing on life in Heredia, his native city. It emphasizes its traditions and the conflicts with modern society at the turn of the century, during his youth. Though some critics categorize him as a costumbrista because his focus is on the interior, the author himself contends that he is not of this school but rather that he seeks to preserve tradition and its values, and to assure the retention of the memory of this era. He also notes that the writings focus on experiences from his life and reflect the particularly rich heritage of his native city. DLC DLC-LDS-164 LNHT BNCR

375 _____. La provincia de Heredia: apuntamientos geográficos. San José: Imprenta Lehmann, 1934. 160 pp. Illus., maps.

A geography of the province of Heredia in Costa Rica, a history of the area from Colonial times to the 1930s, and a compendium of information about it and its prominent citizens, including lists of school graduating classes. Although the emphasis is on the Colonial period, modern statistics are included. DLC-LDS-796 LNHT BNCR

376 _____. Rosa mística. Heredia: Imprenta Alsina, 1920. 306 pp. Illus.

The second in the series of works based on life in Heredia at the turn of the century, reflecting the rich cultural traditions of that region of Costa Rica as seen through the eyes of one of its natives. The stories are told in the form of observations of scenes in the principal church and are drawn from real life and the author's youth. DLC BNCR

377 Documentos para escribir la historia de la revolución de Costa-Rica, que estalló en fin de septiembre del año de 1835. San José: Imprenta de la Paz, 1836. 47 pp.

A collection of proclamations, letters, petitions, and municipal resolutions from the Costa Rican National Archives relating to the revolt against the Central American Federation. The items are miscellaneous and merely compiled rather than selected, but they are arranged chronologically. DLC

378 Dondoli B., César, and J. Alberto Torres M. Estudio geoagronómico de la región oriental de la meseta central. San José: Ministerio de Agricultura e Industrias, 1954. 180 pp. Biblio., illus., maps, tables.

A detailed geology of Costa Rica, focusing particularly on soil classification but including other aspects. Profusely illustrated, with appropriate tables and maps. DLC BNCR

379 Dos Jóvenes Colombianos. Costa Rica al día: impresiones del país recogidas sin infulas de sociólogos, ni mucho menos. San José: Imprenta Borrasé, 1923. 64 pp.

General data by two Colombian journalists describing their visits to numerous governmental institutions and embassies, as well as to the principal cities of the nation, all in short paragraphs emphasizing hospitality and friendliness. Includes advertising, apparently directed at encouraging tourism from Colombia, though the ads seem more suited to the domestic market. DLC-LDS-346

380 Duncan Moodie, Quince. Una canción en la madrugada. San José: Editorial Costa Rica, 1970. 81 pp.

A series of short stories that were among the earliest efforts of this black Costa Rican writer from Limón, who first provided the viewpoint of this ethnic group in Spanish literary form and hence contributed to a better understanding of his people in the nation at large. The stories deal with everyday life experiences, the traditions and culture of black Costa Ricans, and their life in the Atlantic coastal region. DLC LNHT BNCR

381 _____. Los cuatro espejos. San José: Editorial Costa Rica, 1973. 162 pp.

A novel focusing on the lives of the workers on the banana and cacao plantations of the Atlantic coastal region. Describes their distinct cultural heritage and traditions as well as their daily lives, providing insights into their situation in the nation, their isolation from its cultural mainstream, and the problems of integration into the nation. DLC BNCR

382 _____. Hombres curtidos. San José: Cuadernos de Arte Popular, 1971. 141 pp.

A collection of essays on the traditions and folklore of the black population of Limón, tracing its origins and beliefs and its role in the nation, prepared by a native of that region. MU

383 _____, ed. El negro en la literatura costarricense. San José: Editorial Costa Rica, 1972. 190 pp. 3d ed. San José: Editorial Costa Rica, 1975. 190 pp.

Excerpts from various Costa Rican authors, demonstrating the appearance of the black residents of Limón in Costa Rican literature. Notes the evolution of the appreciation of the negro in Costa Rican literature, comparing it with the history of this ethnic group in the nation, emphasizing that the group remained cut off from the national culture in their own enclave in Puerto Limón to the point that even their schoolteachers were imported from Jamaica until the 1940s. The selections were designed, he explains, not to show the typical view of the blacks in Costa Rican literature but to focus on authors who attempt to rise above the stereotypes to present a more realistic picture. DLC LNHT BNCR

384 Durán Ayanegui, Fernando. Dosreales y otros cuentos. San José: Asociación Nacional de Fomento Económico, 1961. 60 pp. Illus.

A collection of short stories dealing with life in modern Costa Rica, particularly as it affects the poor. DLC LNHT BNCR

385 Durán Escalante, Santiago [Un Costarricense, pseud.]. La hora presente: diciembre de 1932, febrero de 1933. San José: Imprenta Tormo, 1933. 43 pp.

A series of letters to the local press written under the pseudonym "un costarricense," commenting on the nation's political situation, emphasizing the economic crisis and the failure of the government to deal with it, and criticizing various government loans and concessions to foreign companies, contending that in the present crisis the government should focus on domestic matters and not contract new debts or seek to pay off old ones. DLC-LDS-725

386 Echavarría Campos, Trino. Historia y geografía del cantón de San Ramón. San José: Imprenta Nacional, 1966. 107 pp. Biblio.

A résumé of the development of the canton of San Ramón in the Costa Rican province of Alajuela from its founding in 1842 to the present, with brief accounts of the foundation of its principal services as well as essays regarding its illustrious citizens. A geographical and economic description follows, arranged by district. LNHT BNCR

387 Echeverría, Aquileo J. Concherías. Barcelona: Imprenta de Borrás y Mestres, 1909. Latest ed. San José: Editorial Costa Rica, 1973. 127 pp.

A series of poems dealing with the various regions of Costa Rica and reflecting the local lore. Its representations of the humor, modisms, speech, and customs of the countryside and its peasants make it widely known as one of the most typical of such collections. DLC DLC-LDS-388 LNHT BNCR

388 _____. Concherías, romances, epigramas. San José: Editorial Universitaria, 1950. 307 pp. 2d ed. San José: Imprenta Trejos, 1953. 318 pp.

A collection of poetry by an early twentieth-century Costa Rican poet. It reflects his focus on the regionalism and the customs and lore of the rural countryside, but also includes his romantic poetry and other disparate verse. DLC LNHT BNCR

389 _____. Crónicas y cuentos míos. San José: Imprenta La Tribuna, 1934. 261 pp.

A collection of short stories and commentaries based on the author's experiences in his native Costa Rica. The short stories include some elements of modernism. Many of the items in this volume are essays that comment on various public and literary figures in contemporary Costa Rica. DLC-LDS-788 BNCR

390 Echeverría, Carlos Francisco. 8 artistas costarricenses y una tradición. San José: Ministerio de Cultura, Juventud y Deportes, 1977. 179 pp. Illus.

A series of essays on the life and works of eight Costa Rican artists. The accompanying photos of their works are unfortunately in black and white. The author contends that all are part of a single national Costa Rican tradition that developed during the nineteenth century and that readily separates Costa Rican art from that of the rest of Latin America, and even Central America. This tradition, he says, does not indicate a resistance to impulses and influences from abroad, but is rather a result of the striking scenery of the nation, which focuses its artists on portraying rural homes and landscapes, which he characterizes as artistic realism. BNCR

391 Echeverría Jiménez, Luís. Historia del Banco Nacional de Costa Rica. San José: Banco Nacional de Costa Rica, 1964. 257 pp. Illus., tables.

A history of the Costa Rican National Bank on the occasion of its fiftieth anniversary, covering the years 1914 through 1964. Includes a year-by-year account, stressing its management, expansion, and development, with photos of its facilities and statistics regarding its transactions. Ample excerpts from annual reports and legislation are included. BNCR

392 La electrificación del Ferrocarril al Pacífico contrada por la AEG de Berlin. San José: Imprenta Trejos, 1926. 38 pp. Illus.

A collection of documents and judgments relating to the electrification contract, with photos of the types of equipment to be employed, discussions of the company's experience in Europe, and cost figures and specifications of the project. DLC-LDS-350

393 Elizondo Arce, Hernán. La calle, jinete y yo. San José: Editorial Costa Rica, 1975. 122 pp.

An account of an average town and the lives of its various citizens and institutions, set in the author's native Costa Rica. The author employs description, lyrical phrases, and satire to emphasize the problems of daily life anywhere, focusing on the mythical average citizen. Though not published until 1975, this work was actually written in 1965 and 1966 and consequently represents one of the author's earliest efforts. DLC BNCR

394 _____. La ciudad y la sombra. San José: Imprenta Lehmann, 1971. 131 pp.

A novel of Costa Rican life, its evolution and problems, focusing on the limits of modern society but including accounts of various periods of Costa Rican history from pre-Columbian times to the present to demonstrate the changes in life-style and emphasize the impact of modern society. BNCR

395 _____. Memorias de un pobre diablo. San José: Editorial Costa Rica, 1964. 268 pp.

2d ed. San José: Editorial Costa Rica, 1969. 190 pp.

The author's best-known work, a prize-winning study by a contemporary Costa Rican who is part of the generation of novelists who focus on the limits of modern society and the problems of humans who must exist in it. The story focuses on the life of a faceless, nameless rural peasant in an equally nameless location in rural Guanacaste, who recounts his sad and troubled life, his struggle against hunger, his hard labor, and his spartan existence. DLC LNHT BNCR

396 Elizondo Mora, Víctor Manuel. Bajo el manto de temis y otros cuentos. San José: Imprenta Lehmann, 1972. 103 pp.

A series of short stories, in effect memoirs, by a Costa Rican judge. He views humanity and its problems and sins from the perspective of his experience on the bench, seeing himself as the patron of justice. One of his earliest works, it is set in Costa Rica and employs local modisms. LNHT BNCR

397 _____. De mi Heredia de antaño. San José: Imprenta Lehmann, 1969. 115 pp. Illus.

A nostalgic autobiographical novel of the author's youth, extolling the idyllic existence in his native city of Heredia. The essays were originally published in the Costa Rican press and focus on primary school days and the traditions and customs of the city. BNCR

398 _____. Recuerdos de la vida de un juez. San José: Imprenta Lehmann, 1970. 221 pp.

The memoirs of a Costa Rican judge whose comments on his forty-year career and on his experiences on the bench provide an insider's view of the Costa Rican judicial and legal system in operation. BNCR

399 Elliot, Elisabeth. Who Shall Ascend: The Life of R. Kenneth Strachan of Costa Rica. London: Hodder & Stoughton, 1968. xii, 171 pp. Illus., maps.

A biography of a Costa Rican evangelical minister, tracing his trials and tribulations while preaching the gospel throughout the isthmus. Emphasizes his role in the foundation and nurturing of the community and institute in San José that became an important base for the evangelical effort throughout Latin America. Based on his private papers and interviews with associates and family members, it focuses on the man, detailing his dedication, work, and problems. DLC

400 Empresa Alsina. Monografía: opiniones de distinguidas personalidades. San José: Imprenta Alsina, 1912. 61 pp. Illus.

A collection of statements from prominent Costa Ricans praising the role of the publishing house and its founder, Avelino Alsina, for its contributions to the nation and providing historical accounts of its development, with illustrations of the plant. DLC DLC-LDS-95

401 English, Burt H. Liberación Nacional in Costa Rica: The Development of a Political Party in a Transitional Society. Gainesville: University of Florida Press, 1971. 185 pp. Biblio., tables.

Originally a dissertation, this work analyzes the Costa Rican National Liberation party. Based on secondary works, Costa Rican publications, and a survey of 103 political leaders, it outlines the growth of the various movements that united to form the party, its institutionalization, platforms, and success in four elections through 1966. Concludes that its success reflected the popularity of its leader, the fact that it appeared at a critical time in response to a national need, and the ability of those who constituted its leadership. DLC LNHT

402 Erba, Adolfo. La Repubblica di Costa Rica. Genoa: Tipo-Litográfico Pietro Pellas, 1897. 53 pp. Tables.

A collection of basic geographic data, followed by a discussion of the economy that includes the monetary situation, agriculture, and exports, with statistics from the era. Clearly designed to promote trade and encourage interest by Italian businessmen in Costa Rica. BNCR

403 ESAPAC. Algunas características demográficas del área metropolitana de San José. San José: ESAPAC, 1957. 68 pp. Maps, tables.

A collection of statistical tables and maps showing the expansion of the capital city of Costa Rica from 1927 through 1955, replete with statistics on population density, death rates, etc. BNCR

404 Escóbar, Francisco. Juventud y cambio social: apuntes desde una perspectiva sociológica. San José: Ministerio de Cultura, Juventud y Deportes, 1972. 142 pp. Biblio. 2d ed. San José: Ministerio de Cultura, 1975. 176 pp.

Focusing on the role of youth in transforming society, this volume includes general comments as well as discussion of the role of youth in Costa Rica. Emphasizing the generational gap and the changes in values experienced by youth, it seeks to portray the young adults as a pivotal driving force in the modernization process. Includes extensive population statistics about Costa Rica, encompassing the years 1927 through 1963. DLC

405 La Escuela Normal en sus bodas de plata, 1915-1940. Heredia: La Escuela Normal, 1940. 92 pp. Illus.

A brief history of the Normal School of Costa Rica on the occasion of its twenty-fifth anniversary, with speeches, the alma mater, lists of faculty and graduating classes, and documents related to its foundation and significant events in its history. LNHT

406 Estrada, Rafael. Aspectos del problema eléctrica en Costa Rica: las "holding companies." San José: Ediciones del Repertorio Americano, 1931. 15 pp.

(Estrada, Rafael)
   A brief address that constituted part of
the dispute and debate regarding electric
regulation in Costa Rica. Draws from the
investigations of trusts in the U.S. to contend that the Costa Rican actions were designed to prevent these types of evils, not
just to respond to the existing situation, and
that this perspective was essential to understanding the government action. DLC-LDS-521

407 _____. Como la mentira comercial extranjera
absorbe nuestras riquezas y destruye nuestra
soberanía. San José: n.p., 1930. 30 pp.
   A nationalistic call for the defense of the
nation's resources against foreign domination,
and a condemnation of the imperialists and
their avaricious ways. DLC-LDS-503 BNCR

408 Estrada Molina, Ligia, ed. Teodoro Picado
Michalski: su aporte a la historiografía.
San José: Imprenta Nacional, 1967. 253 pp.
Biblio., notes, illus.
   A collection of the historical articles
published by Picado Michalski, who later
served as president of the republic, with a
brief introduction. The articles come from
various San José newspapers, but unfortunately
are not dated. Includes a bibliography of
writings by Picado. DLC LNHT BNCR

409 Un estudiante de derecho. El doctor Durán no
puede ser presidente de Costa Rica porque no
es ciudadano costarricense. San José: n.p.,
1913. 16 pp.
   A pamphlet arguing that Dr. Carlos Durán is
ineligible to be elected president because his
father was a citizen of El Salvador for several years during his residence in Costa Rica
before becoming a naturalized Costa Rican; the
candidate was thus born to a foreigner, was
registered legally as the son of a foreigner,
and hence fails to meet the constitutional
qualifications for the presidency. See
Leonidas Pacheco for the response in this
political polemic, item CR843. DLC DLC-LDS-
119

410 Exposición de los motivos del cambio político,
acaecido en Costa Rica, el 14 de agosto de
1859. San José: Imprenta Nacional, 1860.
37 pp.
   A polemic recounting the charges against
the regime of Juan Rafael Mora Fernández,
which was ousted in 1859. Justifies the
actions of the provisional regime, details
charges of corruption and wrongdoing, and
criticizes his efforts to return to power
through revolution, which eventually led to
his execution. DLC

411 Facio, Justo. Temas de educación. San José:
Editorial Gutenberg, 1929. 152 pp.
   A collection of essays written at different
times, dealing with proposals for the nation's
educational system and containing general
comments on the philosophy of education. Includes the author's proposals for specific
courses of study in primary and secondary
schools, focusing on social activity with an

emphasis on the development of individual
personalities. DLC-LDS-453

412 Facio Brenes, Rodrigo. Estudio sobre la
economía costarricense. San José: Editorial
Soley y Valverde, 1942. 174 pp. Biblio.,
tables. 3d ed. San José: Editorial Costa
Rica, 1975. 424 pp. Biblio., illus., tables.
   A study of contemporary Costa Rican economic problems, by one of the nation's leading
economists. An historical introduction provides perspective on the evolution and growth
of the economy; there is a commentary on each
of the present problems, such as monoculture,
foreign capital, the absence of production for
the internal market, balance of payments,
etc.; the conclusion calls for national economic planning to enable the rational use of
scarce resources to serve the nation's internal needs. DLC DLC-LDS-935 LNHT BNCR

413 _____. La moneda y la banca central en Costa
Rica. Mexico: Fondo de Cultura Económica,
1947. 325 pp. 2d ed. San José: Editorial
Costa Rica, 1973. 325 pp.
   A history of money and banking in Costa
Rica by one of the nation's best-known economists, focusing particularly on the crisis of
the 1930s; the post-World War II arrangements,
including Bretton Woods; and the future prospects of the nation. Includes careful analysis of the crises, a clear account of the
various pieces of legislation and regulatory
statutes involved, and full consideration of
the past and future role of the central bank
in regulating the nation's banking system.
Also discusses the Costa Rican position in the
world economy. DLC LNHT BNCR

414 _____. Obras de Rodrigo Facio. 3 vols. San
José: Editorial Costa Rica, 1972-77.
   A collection of the works of a Costa Rican
economist and scholar who served as university
rector for many years and whose name was given
to the University of Costa Rica campus. The
first volume reproduces his Estudio sobre la
económica costarricense, and the second his La
moneda y la banca central en Costa Rica, while
the third volume consists of his university
addresses and commentaries about the development and administration of the institution.
DLC BNCR

415 _____. Proceso de la separación de Costa Rica
de la República Federal y de su constitución
como república soberana libre e independiente.
San José: ESAPAC, 1970. 48 pp. Notes.
   A Costa Rican scholar's concise account,
based on appropriate secondary works, of the
creation of Costa Rica as an independent nation through its separation from the Central
American Federation. A useful summary of the
legal steps and the Costa Rican viewpoint
regarding the problems of the Federation.
BNCR

416 Facio Segreda, Gonzalo J. Costa Rica y el
levantamiento de las sanciones contra el
gobierno de Cuba. San José: Imprenta
Lehmann, 1975. 79 pp. Illus.

(Facio Segreda, Gonzalo J.)
The Costa Rican foreign minister states his government's position in favor of lifting the economic sanctions against Cuba and stresses its leading role in the efforts. The folio also contains his speeches to the two meetings that considered this question, as well as various related documents. BNCR

417 _____. México y Costa Rica: una política exterior paralela. San José: Imprenta Nacional, 1973. 28 pp.
A brief statement regarding the advantages of and points of potential cooperation between Costa Rica and Mexico in the isthmus and the Caribbean. BNCR

418 _____. Nuestra voz en el mundo. San José: Imprenta Trejos, 1977. 263 pp.
A statement and outline of the general foreign policy of the National Liberation party and of Costa Rica by the foreign minister and longtime PLN party militant, written in the form of a personal statement which, though expressing policy positions in general terms, also stresses his own role in enunciating them. He refers to the 1970s as the era of "maturity" in Costa Rican foreign policy and emphasizes the universalist nature of its stances in favor of pluralism, democracy, human rights, disarmament, peaceful settlement of disputes, and international organization. BNCR

419 Faerron, Francisco. Tierra guanacasteca. San José: Imprenta Universal, 1933. 36 pp.
A journalist from this region of Costa Rica comments on what he considers its vitality, stressing its natural resources and location. He responds to the book by Ramón Zelaya criticizing the region, although he is himself critical of the local divisions and rivalry as well as of the current congressional delegation, which he feels is performing less effectively than that in which he served. DLC-LDS-770

420 Faerron, Francisco, and Luís Anderson Morúa. Sobre la ley de puniciones y otros extremos en relación con la industria eléctrica: carta del licenciado don Luís Anderson y contestación de éste. San José: Imprenta Borrasé, 1930. 95 pp. Notes.
This exchange regarding the proposed law nationalizing the electricity industry was part of the political and constitutional debate regarding this issue. Anderson was the company's attorney, and Faerron wrote to disagree with his arguments, prompting a lengthy missive from Anderson citing legal and constitutional authorities and precedents from throughout the world. Both "open letters" were published in the local press as part of the debate. DLC-LDS-500

421 Fallas Monge, Carlos Luís. Alfredo González Flores. San José: Ministerio de Cultura, Juventud y Deportes, 1976. 377 pp. Biblio., tables.

An account of his regime, emphasizing the impact of World War I on the nation and detailing its economic and political problems with extensive documentary excerpts. Provides useful background on the crisis that led to the Tinoco coup, as well as on the regime. DLC BNCR

422 Fallas S., Carlos Luís. Gentes y gentecillas. San José: n.p., 1947. 319 pp. 2d ed. San José: Imprenta Trejos, 1967. 384 pp.
A dramatic novel about the lives of poor peasants working on a coffee estate that was formerly a banana plantation. This work is among the author's best-known efforts and is considered by his countrymen as his finest work. It reflects his focus on external exploitation and his association with the poor and oppressed, portraying their lives and especially their hardships vividly, passionately, and with explosive force. It is clearly a novel of social consciousness, focusing on all the evils of contemporary society, its injustices and brutality, and evoking strong emotions in behalf of the lower classes. DLC LNHT BNCR

423 _____. La gran huelga bananera del Atlántico de 1934. San José: Publicaciones de la CGTC, 1955. 2d ed. San José: Editorial Principios, 1966.
A Marxist analysis of the strike, by a party member and strike leader who became a well-known novelist of the social protest school. BNCR

424 _____. Mamita-Yunai. Many editions. San José: Editorial Soley y Valverde, 1941. 248 pp.
The best-known of Fallas's works outside his native country, though hardly considered his best within Costa Rica, this is an anti-imperialist novel focusing on the cruel life of the workers on the Yankee banana plantations and their oppression by the imperialists. Written so as to emphasize their exploitation and the brutality of their existence, it reflects the feelings engendered by the banana strikes that occurred in his nation, as well as Fallas's experience as an adolescent banana worker and his Marxist ideology. DLC DLC-LDS-898 LNHT BNCR

425 _____. Marcos Ramirez: aventuras de un muchacho. Many editions. San José: Editorial Falcó, 1952. 207 pp.
Another in the author's series of stories of the life of the poor, employing a child and his adventures as his vehicle. DLC LNHT BNCR

426 _____. Mi madrina. Many editions. San José: n.p., 1954. 184 pp.
Another of the author's novels focusing on peasant life in Costa Rica, with a sympathetic eye and emphasis on the hardships involved. The author uses the life of a child to portray the situation of these people, using his eyes, perspective, and innocence to full advantage

(Fallas S., Carlos Luís)
   to emphasize the worst aspects of poverty.
   DLC LNHT BNCR

427 _____. El peligro de la dictadura: las
     elecciones y la organización sindical. San
     José: Imprenta Falcó, 1935. 40 pp.
        An early work that predates the author's
     prominence as a writer of "social novels"
     depicting the oppression of the banana workers
     and lower classes, this pamphlet was written
     in his capacity as secretary general of the
     Federación de Trabajadores del Atlántico,
     strike leader, and affiliate of the Inter-
     national Red Syndicate and the Communist
     International. It employs the standard
     communist terminology to exhort the workers to
     unite under the communist banner and decries
     what he calls the "dictatorship" of the Cortés
     regime and the threat posed by the Pan Amer-
     ican Highway, which he sees as merely a means
     of enabling the imperialist Yankees to move
     their troops throughout the region, facilitat-
     ing intervention. The volume contains the
     official endorsement of the Communist party
     and the symbol of the International Red
     League. DLC-LDS-846

428 _____. Reseña de la intervención y
     penetración yanqui en Centro América. Mexico:
     Fondo de Cultura Popular, 1954. 16 pp.
        A well-known Costa Rican novelist's summary
     of all the signs of Yankee imperialism, in a
     mere sixteen pages. Includes brief commentar-
     ies on subjects ranging from the Walker inter-
     vention and the Panama Canal to the Costa
     Rican civil war of 1948 and the Yankee inter-
     vention in Guatemala in 1954, all viewed as
     examples of the Yankee menace, with appro-
     priate derision of the use of the "Moscow
     phantom." BNCR

429 _____. Tres cuentos. San José: Editorial
     Costa Rica, 1967. 152 pp. 2d ed. San José:
     Editorial Costa Rica, 1973. 132 pp.
        Three short stories by a well-known Costa
     Rican novelist that deal with the lives of the
     poor and include some of his early efforts.
     DLC LNHT BNG BNCR

430 Fallas S., Carlos Luís, Eduardo Mora, and
     Arnoldo Ferreto. Calderón Guardia, José
     Figueres y Otilio Ulate. San José: n.p.,
     51 pp.
        A discussion of the events of 1948 in Costa
     Rica and the succeeding crisis, by the leaders
     of the leftist political parties, particularly
     of the Vanguardia Popular. They attack the
     activities of the supporters of Calderón
     Guardia and Picado, contending that they cur-
     ried favor with the Yankee imperialists in an
     effort to seek support, and condemn the efforts
     of the Somoza regime in Nicaragua to oppose
     the National Liberation Movement, labeling the
     Nicaraguan efforts as intervention on behalf
     of the Yankees. BNCR

431 Fernández, Guido. Los caminos del teatro en
     Costa Rica. San José: EDUCA, 1977. 186 pp.
     Illus., notes.

A collection of reviews of plays, originally published in the Diario de Costa Rica
between 1970 and 1976, commenting on the writers of this era, evaluating the plays, and
focusing on their social-reform content and
the use of the theater as a means of communi-
cating these concerns to the populace. DLC
BNCR

432 Fernández Arias, Mario E., ed. La población
     en Costa Rica. San José: Universidad de
     Costa Rica, 1976. 199 pp. Maps, tables.
        A detailed statistical study of Costa Rican
     population and migration trends, focused on
     the 1950-76 period. Historical data are in-
     cluded, although unevenly, as are tables pro-
     jecting the trends to the year 2000 and a
     consideration of their implications for devel-
     opment. The chapters deal with such themes as
     growth trends, age distribution, location and
     migration, birth and death rates, labor, sex
     distribution, etc. DLC LNHT BNCR

433 Fernández Bonilla, León. Índice general de
     los documentos del archivo de Cartago,
     anteriores al año 1850 inclusivo. 4 vols.
     San José: Imprenta Nacional, 1883-98.
        A listing by date of the holdings of the
     archive. The initial three volumes deal with
     the Colonial era, and the fourth with the
     independence era. DLC-LDS-666

434 Fernández Bonilla, León, and Ricardo Fernández
     Guardia, eds. Colección de documentos para la
     historia de Costa Rica. 10 vols. San José:
     Imprenta Nacional, 1881-1907.
        A massive collection of documents, that
     unfortunately ends with independence, though
     the final volumes contain some interesting
     items from this era. The series was begun by
     Fernández Guardia and completed by León
     Fernández. DLC DLC-LDS-81-84 LNHT BNCR

435 Fernández Durán, Gerardo. La venta de la
     bandera. San José: Imprenta Trejos, 1974.
     239 pp. Notes.
        An analysis of Costa Rican legislation
     regarding extraditions, criticizing its limits
     and loopholes, and citing cases in which it
     would prove inoperative. BNCR

436 Fernández Durán, Roberto. La huelga de brazos
     caídos. San José: Editorial Liberación
     Nacional, 1953. 39 pp.
        An account of the general sit-down strike
     of July 1947 in Costa Rica, in protest against
     the electoral fraud of the outgoing adminis-
     tration. The strike succeded in compelling
     appointment of an investigating commission,
     which virtually amounted to a bloodless coup.
     This maneuvering was part of the crisis that
     led to the Revolution of 1948, itself in part
     a response to the same electoral fraud. LNHT
     BNCR

437 Fernández Ferraz, Juan [J.E. Fernández,
     pseud.]. Conversaciones políticas con el
     pueblo. San José: Imprenta La Prensa Libre,
     1889. 29 pp.

(Fernández Ferraz, Juan)

A series of general essays calling for more democracy, stressing popular rights, seeking to encourage more participation in political events, and warning against tyranny. The articles frequently refer to the contemporary era in Costa Rica as a critical period, but fail to provide any details. DLC-LDS

438 _____. Librito de los deberes. San José: Imprenta La Prensa Libre, 1880. 32 pp.

A sequel to the author's Conversaciones políticas con el pueblo, continuing his call for a responsible citizenry and citizen control of the government through more democracy. Argues for obeying the laws and accepting democratically made decisions and court rulings, while calling for more active popular participation in government. Combines citations of Catholic doctrine with those of Yankee democrats, while condemning tyranny and socialism. DLC-LDS

439 _____. Nahuatlismos de Costa Rica: ensayo lexicográfico acerca de las voces mejicanas que se hallan en el habla corriente de los costarricenses. San José: Tipografía Nacional, 1892. xxv, 148 pp.

An alphabetical dictionary of terms and idioms of Nahua origin in use in Costa Rica, giving an explanation of the derivation and a definition of each. DLC BNCR

440 Fernández Guardia, León, and Armando Céspedes Marín. El temblor de Cartago de 4 de mayo de 1910. San José: n.p., 1910. 52 pp. The Cartago Earthquake, 1910. San José: Imprenta Lehmann, 1910. 51 pp. Illus.

An account of the earthquake that destroyed Cartago on 4 May 1910, with photos of the damage and discussion of the origins of the quake and its effects. DLC-LDS-49 BNCR

441 Fernández Guardia, Ricardo. Cartilla histórica de Costa Rica. Many editions. San José: Imprenta Alsina, 1909. 132 pp. Illus., maps.

A general history of the nation, from Colonial times to 1948, consisting of very brief single-paragraph narrations of each era and regime. It has passed through many editions, extending its coverage and adding illustrations. DLC DLC-LDS-45 LNHT BNCR

442 _____. Cosas y gentes de antaño. San José: Imprenta Trejos, 1935. 388 pp. Notes. 2d ed. San José: Imprenta Trejos, 1939. 425 pp.

A prominent Costa Rican historian prepared this series of essays on disparate historical themes ranging from Colonial times to the mid-nineteenth century. The major portion of the volume refers to the events of the Federation period and particularly of 1840-42 when the Federation was weakening. DLC BNCR

443 _____, ed. Costa Rica en el siglo XIX: antología de viajeros. San José: Imprenta Gutenberg, 1929. 508 pp. 2d ed. San José: EDUCA, 1970. 585 pp.

An anthology of travelers' accounts describing Costa Rica, covering the years 1825 through 1863. Collected and excerpted from the writings of the best-known foreign travelers, it offers only those portions of their accounts that deal with Costa Rica. Introductory commentaries and annotations by the editor. DLC DLC-LDS-988 LNHT BNCR

444 Fernández Guardia, Ricardo. Costa Rican Tales. Girard, Kansas: Haldeman-Julius Co., 1925. 64 pp.

Selections from the author's Cuentos ticos, translated into English. DLC

445 _____. Los cuentos. San José: Imprenta Lehmann, 1971. 310 pp.

A compilation of the author's short stories, including in one volume his separate volumes Cuentos ticos, Hojarasca, and La miniatura. BNCR

446 _____. Cuentos ticos. Many editions. San José: Imprenta María Viuda de Lines, 1901. 317 pp.
Cuentos ticos. Cleveland: Burrow Bros., 1905. 293 pp. Illus., maps.

A series of short stories reflecting Costa Rican traditions and customs and focusing on the countryside, by a prolific writer who was one of the earliest proponents of the short story as a preserver of local traditions. The stories span the range from pirate treasure to an account of heroism in the war against Walker. DLC DLC-LDS-353 LNHT BNCR

447 _____. Espigando en el pasado. San José: Imprenta Atenea, 1946. 95 pp. Index.

A series of essays by a well-known and prolific Costa Rican historian, dealing with the contributions and activities of various figures significant in Costa Rican history, literature, and education. Many were previously published, but some are new. The individuals and themes selected are diverse, and no criterion is indicated. BNCR

448 _____. La guerra de la liga y la invasión de Quinjano. San José: Imprenta Nacional, 1934. 69 pp. Illus. Latest ed. San José: Librería Atenea, 1950. 60 pp. Notes, illus.

A detailed account of Costa Rica's second civil war in 1834-35, based on documents from the National Archives. Provides the specifics of the complex maneuverings by the numerous caudillos and potential caudillos of the Liberal and Conservative factions and of the rivalry between Cartago and San José. The defeat of the revolt of the so-called league, in which Alajeula, Heredia, and Cartago joined to oppose San José, resulted in the confirmation of Braulio Carrillo as the dominant political figure in Costa Rica. DLC DLC-LDS-785

449 _____. La independencia: historia de Costa Rica. San José: Imprenta Lehmann, 1941. 162 pp. Index, notes. Latest ed. San José: Comisión Nacional del Sesquicentenario de la

(Fernández Guardia, Ricardo)
Independencia de Centro América, 1971. 162 pp. Biblio.
A brief account of the years 1821 through 1824 in Costa Rica, based on published works and focusing on the debates in the various councils and temporary authorities regarding the future course of the area and particularly the question of the future form of government in the wake of the independence declaration in Guatemala. DLC LNHT BNG BNCR

450 _____. La independencia y otros episodios. San José: Editorial Trejos, 1928. 410 pp. Index, appendixes. Latest ed. San José: Comisión Nacional de Sesquicentenario de la Independencia de Centro América, 1971.
A detailed account of the independence era covering the years 1821 through 1835 and focusing on the organization of the Costa Rican state, its relations with the Federation of Central America, and the conflicts resulting from the Federation's instability. Reprints of significant documents from this era are appended. DLC DLC-LDS-900 LNHT BNCR

451 _____. La miniatura. San José: García Monge y Cía, 1920. 115 pp. Latest ed. San José: Librería Universal, 1944. 155 pp.
Another group of Costa Rican short stories reflecting the nation, its setting, people, and customs. DLC-LDS-184 LNHT BNCR

452 _____. Morazán en Costa Rica. San José: Imprenta Nacional, 1942. 28 pp. 2d ed. San José: Imprenta Lehmann, 1943. 188 pp.
Originally a series of newspaper articles in honor of the centennial of Morazán's death, focusing particularly on the latter portion of his career and his unsuccessful attempt to use Costa Rica as a base from which to restore the crumbling Federation in the face of the rise of localist and Conservative caudillos in the northern states. DLC LNHT BNCR

453 _____. Reseña histórica de Talamanca. San José: Imprenta Alsina, 1918. 198 pp. Index. 3d ed. San José: Imprenta Nacional, 1968. 135 pp. Notes, map.
A history of the city of Talamanca from Colonial times through 1914, emphasizing the Colonial years. Includes consideration of the role of the city in Costa Rican history, discussion of development of the Atlantic coastal region, and both the effects upon and the role of Talamanca in this process. DLC DLC-LDS-155 LNHT BNCR

454 Fernández Güell, Rogelio. Lola: romance de costumbres nacionales. San José: Imprenta Alsina, 1918. 31 pp.
A posthumously published costumbrista poem. DLC-LDS-149

455 Fernández Güell, Victor. Consideraciones sobre política de actualidad. San José: Imprenta del Comercio, 1909. 15 pp.
A brief essay, part of the political maneuvering of the time, contending that Costa Rican politics had become too personalized around the three dominant figures, Rafael Yglesias, Ricardo Jiménez Oreamuno, and Panfilo J. Valverde. Argues that none of them had enunciated a clear political program, and calls for a national insistence that they announce their stands and plans prior to any voting. DLC DLC-LDS-69

456 Fernández Mira, Ricardo M. Juan Santamaría: el soldado-héroe de Costa Rica. Buenos Aires: Talleres Gráficos Contreras, 1937. 70 pp. Illus.
A summary of the moment of glory that made a Costa Rican national hero of Juan Santamaría, who volunteered for a mission that meant certain death during the campaign against William Walker. DLC DLC-LDS-854 BNCR

457 Fernández Montúfar, Joaquín. Bocteco histórico del Ferrocarril Nacional. San José: Imprenta Nacional, 1934. 48 pp. Illus.
A brief summary of the principal developments in the history of the Costa Rican railroads, including lists of the dates of the openings of the various lines and a chronological list of all legislation relating to the railroads and their financing. Includes extensive illustrations of the types of equipment and installations, and commentary on the impact of the railroads on the coffee industry. DLC-LDS-782

458 _____. Historia ferrovial de Costa Rica: galería de progreso nacional. San José: n.p., 1935. 221 pp. Illus., map.
The initial 200 pages contain a résumé of the history of the railroads, with particular emphasis on their foundation and expansion. Includes considerations of the construction of the ports, electrification, cooperation with the government, and the influence of the railroad on development. The remaining portion of the volume is a photo album of railroad facilities, with brief descriptions. DLC DLC-LDS-814 BNCR

459 Fernández Mora, Carlos. Anecdotario nacional. 3 vols. San José: n.p., 1953-70. 228, 280, 387 pp. Illus.
A collection of miscellaneous anecdotes from and about Costa Rica, providing a glimpse of Costa Rican life and attitudes through humor. They deal with disparate themes; the selection criteria is uncertain and no order is apparent. Volume 3 includes caricatures by Costa Rican cartoonists to illustrate some of the tales. DLC LNHT BNCR

460 _____. Calderón Guardia, líder y caudillo. San José: Editorial José Martí, 1939. 38 pp. Illus.
A brief campaign biography summarizing the career of the presidential candidate and hailing his actions and leadership potential as just what the nation needs. DLC DLC-LDS-845 LNHT

(Fernández Mora, Carlos)

461 _____. Semblanzas: algunas valores de Costa Rica. San José: Imprenta Vargas, 1956. 81 pp.
  A series of brief biographical sketches of Costa Ricans whose careers caused them to be known outside the republic. The figures come from several fields, though most are political or literary, and span the nineteenth and early twentieth centuries. A two- to three-page commentary on each is included, emphasizing his contributions and the reasons for his fame, frequently including basic biographical data. DLC LNHT BNCR

462 Ferrero Acosta, Luís. Amighetti: grabador, engraver, Holzschneider. San José: Editorial Don Quijote, 1967. xii, 20 pp. Illus.
  A brief commentary on the art of Francisco Amighetti, a Costa Rican muralist and engraver, followed by a selection of photos of his works. His career spanned the mid-twentieth century, with his best-known works beginning in the 1930s; his themes were invariably rural scenes from the Costa Rican countryside and peasant life. DLC BNCR

463 _____. Andrés Bello en Costa Rica. San José: Ministerio de Educación Pública, 1962. 24 pp. Biblio., notes, illus.
  A brief essay that traces the influence of the Venezuelan scholar on Costa Rican letters, learning, and politics, by citing references to his works in Costa Rican writings. FU

464 _____. Arte costarricense: grabados en madera de F. Zúñiga. San José: Imprenta Lehmann, 1973. 31 pp. Illus.
  An illustrated essay on the works and techniques of a well-known Costa Rican woodcarver, providing insights not only into his work but into the craft of woodcarving, which is prominent in Costa Rica and Central America. BNCR

465 _____. Brenes Mesén: prosista. San José: Imprenta Trejos, 1964. 29 pp. Biblio., illus.
  A critical commentary on the prose of this well-known Costa Rican writer and poet, emphasizing his use of description and moralism and arguing for the study of his works and the publication of his collected works. DLC BNCR

466 _____. La clara voz de Joaquín García Monge. San José: Editorial Don Quijote, 1963. xvi, 126 pp. Notes, illus.
  A discussion of the theories and attitudes of Joaquín García Monge, emphasizing his focus on the entire American hemisphere and his dedication to democracy and education in his own life and in his career as a professor. DLC LNHT BNCR

467 _____. Enrique Echandi: vida y obra, 1866-1959 San José: Editorial Don Quijote, 1963. 29 pp. Notes, illus.
  A brief sketch of a Costa Rican artist of the late nineteenth and early twentieth centuries who helped define a distinctive Costa Rican art tradition separate from the Colonial heritage. His work as a professor and his studies of primary education helped shape art education in the nation. DLC LNHT BNCR

468 _____. Manuel de Jesús Jiménez. San José: Editorial Don Quijote, 1963. 25 pp. Biblio., notes.
  A brief account of the life of a Costa Rican scholar and educator of the turn of the century whose historical works are well known, and who was also instrumental in the reconstruction of his native city of Cartago after the 1910 earthquake, based on his writings. LNHT BNCR

469 _____, ed. La poesía folklórica costarricense. San José: Imprenta Trejos, 1964. 27 pp. Notes.
  A collection of poems based on Costa Rican folklore recounting the local traditions and legends, with introductory comments. In some cases, more than one version of the legend is offered, to allow comparison. LNHT BNCR

470 Figueres Ferrer, José. Cartas a un ciudadano. San José: Imprenta Nacional, 1956. 280 pp.
  A series of commentaries about the government, its functioning, and national problems, by the president of Costa Rica, written in the form of letters to each individual citizen seeking to communicate with the average citizen privately. In the prologue, he states that the book is like a private visit with him, which he has little opportunity to grant to individuals, but that through it he hopes to reach all with a simple and direct explanation of the government and its efforts. DLC LNHT BNCR

471 _____. Cubaces tiernos en abril. San José: Excelsior de Costa Rica, 1975. 29 pp. Illus.
  A brief story by the ex-president, originally published in the local press, regarding the difficulties of travel in the mountains of the nation and focusing on a railroad accident in 1926 that took many lives. The volume is fancifully illustrated with photos inspired by phrases in the story. LNHT BNCR

472 _____. Los deberes de mi destino. San José: Imprenta Vargas, 1957. 38 pp. BNCR

473 _____. Doctrina social y jornadas crecientes. San José: Imprenta Nacional, 1949. 20 pp. BNCR

474 _____. Las elecciones de 1958 y el futuro de un gran movimiento popular. San José: Imprenta Nacional, 1958. 23 pp. BNCR

475 _____. Estos diez años: discurso pronunciado por el señor presidente de la república don José Figueres, el día 29 de enero de 1958. San José: Imprenta Nacional, 1958. 29 pp.
  A speech by the Costa Rican president detailing the accomplishments of the revolutionary regimes in their initial ten years in

(Figueres Ferrer, José)
power, and indicating those of which the
leader was most proud. BNCR CU-B

476 _____. Nacionalización bancaria en Costa
Rica. Many editions. San José: Imprenta
Nacional, 1951. 48 pp.
A brief summary of Costa Rican banking
history and its problems, followed by the
details of the nationalization of banking in
1948, with various supplemental documents and
approving statements, compiled officially and
issued by the head of the junta to demonstrate
the regime's rationale and seek public support
for its decision. BNCR

477 _____. Orientación política de la Junta
Fundadora de la Segunda República. San José:
Imprenta Nacional, 1949. 16 pp.
A summary of the positions and actions of
the junta, by its leader, emphasizing its
goals and political ideals. TxFTC

478 _____. Palabras gastadas. Many editions.
San José: Editorial Soley y Valverde, 1943.
36 pp.
A collection of early speeches, delivered
during 1942 by the influential Costa Rican
leader who in later years served as president,
dealing with the importance of democracy and
liberty, and supporting democratic socialism.
DLC BNCR

479 _____. Una tesis nacionalista: discurso
sobre la Banca Nacionalizada pronunciado en
televisión el 17 de julio de 1967. San José:
Talleres Altas, 1967. 20 pp.
A 1967 speech by the Costa Rican leader,
extolling the benefits of the Revolution of
1948, focusing particularly on the nationalization of the banking industry, citing the
case for the value of government control of
the financial sector, and arguing that the
banks benefit the ordinary citizen and support
the national development program better if
government controlled. Includes comments on
the Central American Common Market and references to the Costa Rican social security system. Several editions were published the same
year, some bearing the title Temas du nuestro
tiempo: una tesis, países en desarrollo.

480 Fonseca, Jaime M. Communication Policies in
Costa Rica. Paris: UNESCO, 1977. 89 pp.
Notes, tables.
A survey of mass communications policy in
Costa Rica, compiled as part of a UNESCO series. Designed to identify the state of enun-
ciation of government policy and suggest
future directions, it traces recent training,
growth, and regulation. Concludes that more
regulation, better training facilities for
professionals, more sophisticated assessment
of the type of information needed by the public, and study of the degree of dependency on
external sources are needed. DLC LNHT

481 Fonseca, Virginia S. de. Manuel González
Zeledón: Magón. San José: Ministerio de

Cultura, Juventud y Deportes, 1974. 198 pp.
Illus.
A biographical sketch of a well-known Costa
Rican poet who also served in the diplomatic
corps, with an anthology of his writings.
Intended for the general public. DLC BNCR

482 Fonseca Corrales, Elizabeth. Juan Manuel de
Cañas. San José: Ministerio de Cultura,
Juventud y Deportes, 1975. 194 pp. Notes,
illus.
A biography of the last Spanish governor of
Costa Rica that provides considerable information regarding the independence era, the origins of the independence movement in Costa
Rica, and local reactions to it. Written with
ample attention to background and setting,
which helps place the movement and the actions
of the governor in their proper context.
Based on documentary research. BNCR

483 Fonseca Tortos, Eugenio, et al. Algunos
aspectos sociográficos del área metropolitana
de San José Costa Rica. San José:
Universidad de Costa Rica, 1969. Pages not
consecutively numbered. Illus., tables.
A general sociological and statistical
profile of the present San José metropolitan
area, with emphasis on social statistics.
BNCR

484 Fradín, Elisio P. Documentos relacionados con
la navegación de los Ríos San Juan, Colorado,
Sarapiquí y San Carlos. San José: Tipografía
Nacional, 1898. 53 pp.
A description of the rivers, based on
government-sponsored expeditions into the
region in 1893, 1894, and 1895; compiled for
the Costa Rican government. DLC-LDS-43 BNCR

485 _____. Estudios del Golfo de Nicoya de la
Bahía del Cocos y del Golfo de Culebra, 1891-
1892. San José: Tipografía Nacional, 1892.
109 pp.
A descriptive geographical study, considering the physical and climatic characteristics of this coastal sector. DLC-LDS-46 LNHT
BNCR

486 _____. Ferrocarril al Pacífico: defensa por
Puntarenas. San José: n.p., 1907. 17 pp.
Part of a domestic political debate about
the most suitable location for a Pacific port
in Costa Rica, and hence where the Pacific
Railroad should terminate. The Congress selected Puntarenas after extended debate, but
the discussion continued as rival cities
forced reconsideration. This piece defends
Puntarenas as the logical spot and decries the
politics of the issue, while reproducing
statements from seafarers indicating the un-
suitability of its rival Tivives. DLC DLC-
LDS-16

487 _____. Puntarenas y Tivives: exposición
presentada al señor gobernador y municipalidad
de Puntarenas. San José: Tipografía
Nacional, 1903. 19 pp.
A brief speech, part of the contest between
Puntarenas and Tivives over which would be

designated the terminus of the Pacific Railroad and hence the nation's principal Pacific
port, praising the facilities and prospects of
Puntarenas and denigrating Tivives as a hick
town in comparison. This essay was part of
the propaganda attendant to the initial campaign, in which Puntarenas emerged victorious.
DLC DLC-LDS-69

488 Frantzuis, Alexander von. La ribera derecha
del Río San Juan. San José: Tipografía
Nacional, 1895. 57 pp. Notes.
     An account of an 1862 expedition into the
Río San Juan region by a German explorer,
written during his travels. Includes a careful description of the geological and geographical features of the area, as well as
observations about the local population in the
towns passed during the early portions of the
trip. DLC DLC-LDS-45 BNCR

489 Freemasons of Costa Rica, Grand Lodge.
Efforts of the Costa Rican Freemasonry for the
Independence of Central America; Labor de la
masonería costarricense de favor de la
independencia de Centro América. San José:
Grand Lodge of Freemasons, 1913. 77 pp.
     The Costa Rican Lodge of the Masons, sensi-
tive about Yankee intervention in Nicaragua,
reacted to a press report that the United
States government had hinted at establishing a
protectorate over all of Central America with
this scathing attack on the Woodrow Wilson
administration, sent as a letter asking support to all the masonic lodges in Central
America, Spain, and the United States. The
manifesto and the responses are printed in
Spanish and English. The contrast between the
alarmed cries of the Central American lodges,
who see this move as the first step in a new
colonialist-imperialist expansion by the
United States, and the incredulous responses
of the Yankee lodges, who cannot understand
the source of this mistrust of their country
given its good intentions and disclaimers, is
indicative of the differing perspectives that
lie at the heart of many of the problems in
inter-American relations. DLC DLC-LDS-694

490 Fumero Paez, Alejo. Juan Rafael Chacón. San
José: Ministerio de Cultura, Juventud y
Deportes, 1977. 220 pp. Biblio., illus.
     A brief biography and discussion of the
works of this Costa Rican modernist sculptor
of the human figure. Accompanied by a portfolio of photographs of his works, which depict the life of the rural peasant and the
mileau in which he originated. BNCR

491 Furbay, John Harvey. Education in Costa Rica.
Washington, D.C.: GPO, 1946. vi, 62 pp.
Biblio., notes, illus., tables.
     Another in the U.S. education series of
surveys of present data and educational programs. DLC LNHT

492 Gabb, William M. Informa sobre la exploración
de Talamanca, verificada durante los años
1873-1874. San José: Tipografía Nacional,
1894. 89 pp.

One of the first efforts to provide a geological description of this region, based on
the author's travels in it during 1873-74.
Primarily a physical description by a trained
observer. DLC DLC-LDS-655 LNHT

493 Gagini Chavarria, Carlos. Al través de mi
vida. San José: Editorial Costa Rica, 1961.
207 pp. Biblio., illus. 2d ed. San José:
Editorial Costa Rica, 1965. 207 pp.
     The autobiography of a prominent and influ-
ential Costa Rican educator and linguistic
scholar, published long after his death in the
1920s. It focuses on his early years as a
student, professor, and school director, and
includes his travels, concluding in 1908.
Consequently it offers no comments on his
subsequent service as director of the National
Library and the National Printing Company.
Includes a list of his publications and key
dates in his life, as well as tributes by
well-known contemporaries. DLC LNHT BNCR

494 _____. El árbol enfermo: novela. Many editions. San José: Imprenta Trejos, 1918. 115
pp. Latest ed. San José: Editorial Costa
Rica, 1973. 130 pp.
     A Costa Rican writer's analysis of his
nation, accomplished through comparison with
the Yankees. The story concerns the rivalry
of two individuals, one Costa Rican and one
Yankee, whose personal duel extends to many
fields and leads to a self-examination by the
Costa Ricans of why they are losing to the
Yankees in all fields. Gagini faults such
things as alcoholism, the abandonment of traditional methods and views, and the lack of
entrepreneurial spirit, as well as the decline
of the peasantry. DLC-LDS-146 LNHT BNCR

495 _____. La caída del águila: novela. San
José: Imprenta Trejos, 1920. 181 pp. Latest
ed. San José: Editorial Costa Rica, 1973.
136 pp.
     A Costa Rican writer's anti-imperialist
novel warning of the Yankee danger. The novel
recounts an era of prosperity when all of
Central America has become a Yankee colony and
the Isle of Cocos has become a major Yankee
military base, describing the resulting conditions, the yearning of Central Americans for
justice, and the collapse of the Yankee empire. DLC DLC-LDS-182 LNHT BNCR

496 _____. Cuentos grisas. Many editions. San
José: Imprenta Falcó & Borrasé, 1918. 81 pp.
     A series of short stories dealing with
Costa Ricans and national themes and settings.
Written by an early exponent of this form, it
has been reissued several times for use in the
nation's schools. DLC DLC-LDS-149 LNHT
BNCR

497 _____. Cuentos y otras prosas. San José:
Editorial Centroamericana, 1969. 86 pp.
Biblio. 2d ed. San José: Imprenta Lehmann,
1971. 87 pp.
     A collection of Gagini's short stories and
other writings, excerpted from his previously
published works. BNCR

(Gagini Chavarria, Carlos)

498 _____. *Diccionario de barbarismos y provincialismos de Costa Rica*. San José: Tipografía Nacional, 1892. 604 pp. Latest ed. San José: Editorial Costa Rica, 1975. 243 pp.

Although now dated, this compilation is the definitive collection of Costa Rican idioms and regional modisms; with definitions and identifications, arranged alphabetically. It has passed through several editions, some of which employ the title *Diccionario de costarriqueñismos*. DLC DLC-LDS-19 LNHT BNCR

499 Galdames, Luís. *La universidad autónoma*. San José: Editorial Borrasé, 1935. 519 pp.

A detailed discussion of the role of the University of Costa Rica, its organization and future, by the dean of the faculty of Philosophy of the University of Chile, who served as a consultant in drawing the new legislation and regulations involved in the reestablishment of the University of Costa Rica in 1935. Provides general background regarding the role of universities in Latin America, details regarding his proposals, the various programs of study, and the organization and operation of the new university, as well as explanations of its potential contributions to the nation. DLC

500 Gallegos Salazar, Demetrio. *Vida privada y hecho heroico de Juan Santamaría*. San José: Imprenta Nacional, 1966. 63 pp. Biblio., notes, illus.

An address to the Costa Rican Academy of History tracing what is known about the life of the Costa Rican military hero who gave his life in the combat against William Walker. It seeks to refute attacks on the hero, hails his action, wrapping him in nationalism, and provides concrete data to convince the skeptics who question whether he is a real or mythical figure. Based on secondary sources. Includes commentary on the need for such a hero from the masses in promoting patriotism and nationalism. DLC BNCR

501 Gamboa, Elisa María, ed. *Los vetos del presidente Echandi, sus razones y justificación, 1958-1962*. San José: Imprenta Nacional, 1962. 848 pp. Index.

An official compilation, by a functionary of the presidency, of the full texts of the various veto messages sent by the Conservative president Echandi to the Congress, which was controlled by Liberación Nacional. The differences in their views resulted in a large number of vetoes with accompanying political polemics. BNCR

502 Gamboa Alvarado, Emma. *Educación en una sociedad libre: fundamentos y ejemplario*. San José: Editorial Costa Rica, 1976. 168 pp.

A theoretical analysis of the linkage between democracy and a strong educational system, citing the case of Costa Rica as an example. DLC BNCR

503 _____. *Educación primaria en Costa Rica: síntesis de una investigación y recomendaciones: informe al gobierno de la república*. San José: Imprenta Nacional, 1952. 31 pp. Notes.

A brief outline of the needs of Costa Rican primary education, with recommendations for improvement and standardization of the program, prepared by the subsecretary of education in the Ulate regime. TxU

504 Gamboa Alvarado, Gerardo. *Del folklore costarricense: relatos de la bajura y de la serranía*. San José: Editorial Fernández-Arce, 1975. xvi, 205 pp.

A series of folktales often told in the form of dialogue with local residents, drawn primarily from the Alajuela and Guanacaste provinces of Costa Rica. The oral traditions recorded include jokes, superstitions, and legends regarding real life and supernatural creatures. DLC BNCR

505 Gamboa Alvarado, José. *Memorias*. San José: Imprenta Trejos, 1960. 130 pp. Illus.

A novel about life in the Costa Rican countryside at the turn of the century, describing the haciendas and the campesinos in the "good old days" of horseback and oxcart transportation, emphasizing the remoteness and beauty of the rural areas. The work employs regional idioms and seeks to emphasize the local traditions. Includes a glossary of regionalisms. BNCR

506 Gamboa Guzmán, Francisco. *Costa-Rica: de la flibuste au Pentagone*. Paris: Editions Sociales, 1973. 280 pp. Maps.

A Marxist interpretation of Costa Rican history by a member of the Vanguardia Popular party, professor, and journalist, who served as a correspondent for the Soviet news agency Tass. It stresses the threat of Yankee intervention, which it describes as constantly hanging over the entire isthmus, while condemning the efforts of the dictatorships from the other Central American nations to dominate Costa Rica, implying that they act at Washington's behest. Attacks the role of foreign enterprises, contending that the Common Market is a plot by the multinational corporations and the pro-Yankee dictatorships of the northern states to enhance the profits of the imperialists, which Costa Rica has heroically resisted. While the history emphasizes the Yankee role in Costa Rica and criticizes interventionism, it carefully avoids mention of Woodrow Wilson's intervention in that nation in opposition to one of its dictatorships. DLC LNHT

507 _____. *Costa Rica: ensayo histórico*. Havana: Librería Internacional, 1962. 5th ed. San José: Imprenta Elena, 1974. 193 pp.

Reflecting the author's Marxist viewpoint, stresses the bourgeoisie's dominant position and its manipulation of the nation's democratic institutions, charging that it has ignored the needs of the lower classes. The

(Gamboa Guzmán, Francisco)
various strikes, especially on the banana plantations, are emphasized, while the National Liberation Movement is viewed as an anticommunist tool of the imperialists, which made some changes but is not sufficiently revolutionary to deal with the nation's problems. BNCR

508 ____. Costa Rica: monografía económica y social. Havana: Editorial Nacional, 1963. 271 pp. Maps.
A Marxist interpretation of the social and economic problems and needs of the nation, continuing the author's previous works. CSt-H

509 García Carrillo, Eugenio, ed. Cosas de don Joaquín: como las vio su hijo. San José: Imprenta Trejos, 1962. 78 pp. Biblio.
A collection of brief writings by the prominent Costa Rican novelist Joaquín García Monge, compiled by his son. Includes a very brief autobiography and some of his early works. DLC LNHT BNCR

510 García Monge, Joaquín. Abnegación. San José: Imprenta de Padrón y Pujol, 1900. 87 pp. 3d ed. San José: Ministerio de Cultura, Juventud y Deportes, 1977.
One of the earlier efforts by this now well-known author. Reflects, as do his other works, the class struggle, focusing on the poor living conditions of the rural peasants and on domestic themes involved in a search for national identity. LNHT BNCR

511 ____. Hijas del campo. San José: Imprenta de Alfredo Greñas, 1900. 168 pp.
One of the earliest efforts of the later well-known novelist, this work is still virtually unknown. It reflects his initial focus on the lives of the rural peasants, a trend developed in his later works, but emphasizes love as its main theme. DLC BNCR

512 ____. La mala sombra y otros sucesos. San José: Ediciones de Autores Costarricenses, 1917. 53 pp. 3d ed. San Salvador: n.p., 1960. 43 pp.
An influential and well-known collection of short stories. With it the author changed the nature of costumbrismo from description of settings and regional lore to a portrayal of the lives of the lower classes and peasants, thereby contributing to the shift to the so-called novel of social consciousness. DLC-LDS-150 LNHT

513 ____. El moto. San José: Imprenta de Alfredo Greñas, 1900. 50 pp. 6th ed. San José: Imprenta Lehmann, 1968. 62 pp. Biblio., illus.
In this his initial novel, employing impassioned narration, simple verbiage, and the idioms and regionalisms of the nation, García Monge began his shift from the costumbrismo theme of an idyllic life in the countryside toward the concentration on the hardships and problems of the rural peasants that became

characteristic of the novel of social protest. DLC DLC-LDS-7 LNHT

514 ____. Tres novelas: el moto, hijas del campo, abnegación. San Salvador: Ministerio de Cultura, 1959. 345 pp. Illus.
A combined edition of three of the author's works. See items CR510-11, 513. DLC LNHT BNG BNCR

515 García Solano, Arturo. Gobierno municipal: disposiciones que lo regulan. San José: Imprenta María Viuda de Lines, 1924. 207 pp. 2d ed. San José: Imprenta Nacional, 1927. iv, 259 pp.
A general treatise on municipal government, but geared specifically to Costa Rica, spelling out the author's proposals for the regulation and operation of municipal government in the nation and its relationship to the national government. DLC-LDS-486

516 Garnier, José Fabio. La esclava. San José: A. Greñas, 1905. 31 pp.
A brief novelette about life in Costa Rica, emphasizing the traditions and the pace of life. DLC

517 Garro, Joaquín. La derrota del Partido Liberación Nacional. 2d ed. San José: Imprenta Vargas, 1958. 53 pp.
Essays of "self-criticism" designed to examine all possible factors in the defeat of the PLN in the 1958 elections. They consider the campaign, the party's platform, its candidates, its governmental record, and its recent actions, concluding that new organization and leadership is necessary to enable future victories. DLC BNCR

518 ____. Veinte años de historia chica: notas para una historia política costarricense. San José: Imprenta Vargas, 1967. 116 pp. Index, biblio., notes.
A narration of the period from 1948 through 1966 in Costa Rica, drawn from press commentaries and the laws passed, criticizing and praising all political groups and leaders. Though inclining toward the opposition to the National Liberation party, the author dispassionately analyzes the various political campaigns and explains the results. LNHT BNCR

519 Gil Pacheco, Rufino. Ciento cinco años de vida bancaria en Costa Rica y algunos hechos sobresalientes de nuestra economía. San José: n.p., 1958. xvi, 524 pp. Biblio., tables. 2d ed. San José: Editorial Costa Rica, 1974. 415 pp. Biblio., illus., tables.
A history of banking in Costa Rica from the 1900s through the nationalization of 1948, by a Costa Rican economist, diplomat, and journalist. Includes description and analysis of the various actions and their effects, extensive statistics about the economy, the monetary and banking system, and the individual banks, and discussion of the impact of the global and national currents on the banking system, focusing particularly on the crisis of the 1930s and 1940s. LNHT BNCR

520 Gólcher, Federico. <u>Acerca</u> <u>de</u> <u>la</u> <u>inicitiva</u>
<u>presentada</u> <u>por</u> <u>la</u> <u>junta</u> <u>Pro-Limón</u> <u>para</u> <u>la</u>
<u>nacionalización</u> <u>de</u> <u>las</u> <u>tierras</u> <u>y</u> <u>de</u> <u>la</u>
<u>industria</u> <u>bananera</u>. Limón: Published by the
Junta, 1929. 30 pp.
    A proposal for the nationalization of the
nation's banana production, advocated by a
group in Limon connected to the banana workers' union. Contains the proposed law and the
group's resolutions supporting the proposal.
DLC-LDS-466

521 Goldrich, Daniel. <u>Sons</u> <u>of</u> <u>the</u> <u>Establishment:</u>
<u>Elite</u> <u>Youth</u> <u>in</u> <u>Panama</u> <u>and</u> <u>Costa</u> <u>Rica</u>.
Chicago: Rand-McNally, 1966. viii, 139 pp.
Notes, maps.
    A comparative study of the high-school age
scions of the elites of these two nations,
based on surveys conducted in the high schools
from 1961 through 1963, with comparative statistical analysis of their views regarding
politics, legitimacy, national planning, the
current situation, social issues, Latin American political issues, and similar themes.
Provides a glimpse of the views of those who
are presumed to be the most likely heirs to
the positions of power in their respective
countries, and comparison of the variances and
similarities of viewpoint between youth from
two very different political and social situations. DLC LNHT

522 Gómez Barrantes, Miguel. <u>Estimaciones</u> <u>de</u>
<u>población</u> <u>para</u> <u>Costa</u> <u>Rica</u> <u>en</u> <u>el</u> <u>período</u> <u>1950-</u>
<u>78</u> <u>por</u> <u>sexo,</u> <u>grupos</u> <u>de</u> <u>edades</u> <u>y</u> <u>zonas</u> <u>urbana</u> <u>y</u>
<u>rural</u>. San José: Universidad de Costa Rica,
1967. 91 pp. Illus., tables.
    A statistical study, with narration, re-
garding the population trends of the nation.
Uses data for 1950-67 as a basis for projections through 1978. Tables and graphs offer
various divisions by age, sex, population
centers, etc., with explanations of the calculations. DLC BNCR

523 Gómez Miralles, Manuel. <u>Costa</u> <u>Rica,</u> <u>América</u>
<u>Central,</u> <u>1922</u>. San José: n.p., 1922. Pages
unnumbered. Illus., tables.
    A collection of about 200 photos of urban
and rural Costa Rica in 1922, including buildings, people, and transportation facilities,
that provides a glimpse of the nation at that
time. DLC-LDS-342

524 Gomez Urbina, Carmen Lila. <u>Actitud</u> <u>del</u> <u>pueblo</u>
<u>costarricense</u> <u>ante</u> <u>la</u> <u>presencia</u> <u>del</u> <u>general</u>
<u>Morazán</u>. San José: Universidad de Costa
Rica, 1969. 23 pp.
    A brief summary of the Costa Rican role in
the struggles of the Federation in the immediate post-independence era. CU-BANC

525 _____. <u>Corte</u> <u>Superior</u> <u>de</u> <u>Justicia</u> <u>del</u> <u>estado</u>
<u>de</u> <u>Costa</u> <u>Rica,</u> <u>1825-1833</u>. San José:
Universidad de Costa Rica, 1945. 31 pp.
    An examination of the judiciary in the
early years after independence, noting that
because of the confusion, lack of experience,
and frequent resignations, the courts only
functioned intermittently, and hence that for

practical purposes there was no judiciary in
the new nation. CU-BANC

526 _____. <u>Costa</u> <u>Rica</u> <u>y</u> <u>la</u> <u>federación</u> <u>durante</u> <u>los</u>
<u>gobiernos</u> <u>constitucionales</u> <u>de</u> <u>Juan</u> <u>Mora</u>
<u>Fernández</u>. San José: Universidad de Costa
Rica, 1969. 36 pp.
    An overview of the Costa Rican role in the
civil wars of 1826-29 during the struggles
regarding the Central American Federation in
the immediate post-independence era. CU-BANC

527 _____. <u>Los</u> <u>gobiernos</u> <u>constitucionales</u> <u>de</u> <u>don</u>
<u>Juan</u> <u>Mora</u> <u>Fernández,</u> <u>1825-1833</u>. San José:
Universidad de Costa Rica, 1974. 294 pp.
Index, biblio., notes, tables.
    A detailed history of the administration of
the Costa Rican head of state during the early
years of the Central American Federation, and
of the problems of organizing the newly independent region. Sheds considerable light on
the origins of Costa Rican institutions as
well as on the problems of the Federation.
Based on documentary research in the Costa
Rican National Archives and on appropriate
secondary sources. DLC LNHT BNCR

528 _____. <u>Juan</u> <u>Mora</u> <u>Fernández</u>. San José:
Ministerio de Cultura, Juventud y Deportes,
1973. 145 pp. Biblio., notes.
    A brief biographical sketch of one of the
Costa Rican independence leaders, who represented Costa Rica in the Federation Congress,
served as one of the nation's first chiefs of
state after the collapse of the Federation, and
held several governmental positions in
that nation during the late 1830s and early
1840s. Includes an outline of his outlook and
actions, lists of his laws, and excerpts from
his messages and proclamations. Based on
documentary research in the Costa Rican
National Archives. BNCR

529 Góngora Herrera, Federico. <u>Documentos</u>
<u>históricos</u> <u>de</u> <u>la</u> <u>masonería</u> <u>centroamericana,</u>
<u>1824-1933</u>. San José: Imprenta Española,
1937. 356 pp.
    A collection of documents regarding the
history and significant actions of the masonry, including data on its foundation, the
acts of its various grand meetings, and correspondence with political figures. Despite
the title, the volume deals almost exclusively
with the Costa Rican branch. LNHT

530 González Campo, Federico. <u>Frutos</u> <u>de</u> <u>sombra</u>.
Guatemala: Ministerio de Educación Pública,
1955. 92 pp.
    A brief novel of social criticism, empha-
sizing the rigors and problems of peasant life
in Costa Rica, that was awarded second prize
in the contest commemorating literary pieces
in honor of the anniversary of the 1948 Costa
Rican Revolution. DLC LNHT BNG

531 González Flores, Alfredo. <u>La</u> <u>crisis</u> <u>económica</u>
<u>de</u> <u>Costa</u> <u>Rica:</u> <u>su</u> <u>origen,</u> <u>proceso</u> <u>y</u> <u>factores</u>
<u>que</u> <u>la</u> <u>han</u> <u>agravado;</u> <u>medidas</u> <u>recomendables</u>
<u>para</u> <u>procurar</u> <u>al</u> <u>reajuste</u> <u>económico</u>. San

(González Flores, Alfredo)

José: Imprenta Trejos, 1936. 125 pp. Notes, tables.

An account of the financial crisis in Costa Rica resulting from the Depression. Traces its local origins in the 1920s and uses financial statistics to detail the impact of the international crisis on that nation. Suggestions for dealing with the crisis include a balanced budget, banking regulation, and currency control. DLC DLC-LDS-841 BNCR

532   _____. Manifesto a mis compatriotas: noviembre de 1919._ San José: Imprenta Minerva, 1919. 16 pp.

A former president's denunciation of the Tinoco regime, hailing the Woodrow Wilson administration's refusal to recognize it. DLC

533   _____. El petróleo y la política en Costa Rica._ San José: Imprenta Trejos, 1920. 92 pp.

A political tract charging that the coup by Federico Tinoco in 1914 was related to the petroleum contract known as the Pinto-Gruelich accord and arguing that the agreement is without validity. The tone reflects the political passion of the era. DLC

534   González Flores, Luís Felipe. _Benefactores de Heredia._ San José: Imprenta Gutenberg, 1930. 51 pp. Illus.

A series of short biographical sketches of the lives of significant figures from the Costa Rican city of Heredia, including individuals born there and those whose careers were centered there. Deals mainly with the eighteenth and nineteenth centuries, but includes individuals born during the later half of the nineteenth century whose public life was in the twentieth century. Encompasses individuals from a wide range of careers, including many from the political and literary scene. DLC DLC-LDS-503

535   _____. Biografía del Lic. Cleto González Víquez en conmemoración del centenario de su nacimiento, 1858-octubre-1958._ San José: Imprenta Lehmann, 1958. 47 pp. Illus.

A brief biography of an influential political figure of the late nineteenth and early twentieth centuries who served as president of Costa Rica from 1906 to 1910 and again from 1928 through 1932, and who with Ricardo Jiménez Oreamuno dominated the nation's political scene from the turn of the century to the mid-1930s. This work, published to commemorate the centennial of his birth, is brief and laudatory, furnishing only an outline of his career and excerpts from some of his writings. DLC LNHT BNCR

536   _____. La casa de enseñanza de Santo Tomás: apuntes acerca de su origen y desarrollo hasta la erección en universidad._ San José: Imprenta Nacional, 1941. 21 pp.

A brief history of the foundation in 1812 of what became the University of Costa Rica, reprinting its initial regulations of 1822. LNHT BNCR

537   _____. Educación vocacional, compilación de los artículos que bajo ese título fueron publicados por su autor en "El Republicano."_ San José: Imprenta Lehmann, 1913. 48 pp.

A series of essays discussing vocational education and its proper place in the Costa Rican school system, arguing that this aspect has been neglected and advocating greater development of such teaching in the rural schools as a means of making them more appropriate to local needs. DLC DLC-LDS-115

538   _____. La evolución de la instrucción pública en Costa Rica._ San José: Imprenta Nacional, 1934. 41 pp.

A short summary of the evolution of public education in Costa Rica since independence, continuing through 1921 but emphasizing the nineteenth century. All levels are covered. DLC DLC-LDS-787 BNCR

539   _____. Heredia en los albores de la independencia._ San José: Editorial La Tribuna, 1942. 30 pp. Illus.

A discussion of the situation and actions of this Costa Rican province at the time of independence, including ample background regarding life at that time. DLC-LDS-938 BNCR

540   _____. Historia de la influencia extranjera en el desenvolvimiento educacional y científico de Costa Rica._ San José: Imprenta Nacional, 1921. 317 pp. Notes, illus., appendixes. 2d ed. San José: Editorial Costa Rica, 1976. 296 pp.

A history of foreign influences in Costa Rican education, considering such broad themes as the French Revolution but focusing on the influence of individuals, grouped by nation. Includes chapters dealing with many European and most Latin American nations, citing their use as models, sources of reforms, sources of scholars, places of study, etc. through a series of brief chronicles of the contributions of individuals from those nations or who studied there. Based on publications of the subjects. DLC DLC-LDS-266 LNHT BNCR

541   _____. Historia del desarrollo de la instrucción pública en Costa Rica._ 2 vols. San José: Imprenta Nacional, 1945-61. 143, 434 pp. Notes, illus.

A detailed history of education at all levels, with the initial volume covering the Colonial era and the second the period from independence to 1884. Includes discussion of the development of the principal educational institutions, methods and curriculum, and the contributions of particularly important leaders, with separate discussion of the national trends during individual presidential regimes or eras. DLC LNHT

542   _____. La obra cultural de don Miguel Obregón._ San José: Imprenta Nacional, 1919. 46 pp. 3d ed. San José: Imprenta Nacional, 1956. 61 pp. Illus.

A brief résumé of the career of this influential educator who served as minister of education during the 1920s. Emphasizes his

(González Flores, Luís Felipe)
efforts to reform the nation's educational system and libraries, and his ideas regarding the appropriate curriculum. DLC DLC-LDS-169 LNHT BNCR

543 _____. Omar Dengo: estudio de su personalidad. San José: Imprenta Nacional, 1929. xxiii, 88 pp. Notes, illus.
A loving portrait of a prominent Costa Rican educator, extolling his efforts as a teacher and his devotion to his pupils and emphasizing his personality through the use of anecdotes. Includes a biographical sketch of Dengo. The essays were originally published as a series in the Diario de Costa Rica. DLC-LDS-417

544 González Ramos, José Luís, and John C. Hammock, eds. Seis comunidades costarricenses. San José: n.p., 1973. 294 pp. Notes, tables.
A sociological study based on direct observation and fieldwork during 1972 in six selected Costa Rican rural towns. Provides basic description of the towns and their social, political and economic infrastructure, focusing on the existing institutions, their functioning, the local social customs, and factors for potential change. BNCR

545 González Truque, Guillermo. Apuntes sobre economía costarricense. San José: Universidad de Costa Rica, 1978. 191 pp. BNCR

546 _____. Los topes selectivos de cartera como instrumento de política monetaria: la experiencia de Costa Rica. Mexico: Centro de Estudios Monetarios Latinoamericanos, 1964. 63 pp.
A brief overview of the installation and use of loan ceilings as an instrument of monetary control in Costa Rica, tracing their initial adoption in 1947, their institutionalization by the Revolutionary Junta in 1948, and their subsequent use. Notes that loan ceilings began as limits for individual banks but later were set by economic sector and loan purpose, thus serving an allocating function as well as a monetary one. DLC

547 González Víques, Cleto. De actualidad: colección de los artículos de don Cleto González Víquez publicados ultimamente el "La Tribuna." San José: Imprenta Trejos, 1920. 27 pp.
A discussion of the monetary crisis and foreign-exchange situation, which were then acute, calling for banking reform, new regulations, and changes in the banks of emission, by one of the nation's leading political figures whose basic contention is that the situation is serious enough to warrant drastic governmental action. He discusses a number of alternatives, stressing the need for prompt action whatever course the government decides to adopt. Originally prepared as a series of newspaper articles, the series was published collectively in book form by the national

chambers of commerce and agriculture, indicating the concern of the business community. DLC-LDS-346

548 _____. Apuntes estadísticas sobre la ciudad de San José. San José: Imprenta Alsina, 1905. 34 pp. Tables.
A compilation of current statistics. DLC-LDS-16

549 _____, ed. Compilación de leyes no insertas en las colecciones oficiales, 1821-1831. 2 vols. San José: Imprenta Nacional, 1937-47. 655, 363 pp.
A former president's compilation of laws that somehow were overlooked and hence do not appear in the official collections and series. LNHT BNCR

550 González Víques, Cleto. Heredia: su nacimiento y primeros pasos. San José: Universidad de Costa Rica, n.d. 110 pp.
A history of the Colonial origins of the province and city of Heredia, focusing on the Colonial era with but a few references to the nineteenth century. The volume was reproduced in Luís Dobles Segreda's edited bicentennial history during the 1930s. DLC-LDS-810

551 _____. Historia financiera de Costa Rica. San José: Universidad de Costa Rica, 1965. 207 pp. 2d ed. San José: Editorial Costa Rica, 1977.
A collection of articles originally published in the Revista de Costa Rica by the former chief executive, tracing the nation's financial history during the nineteenth century, focusing particularly on the British loans. Contains full statistics and the history of each loan, including the subsequent disputes, litigations, and payments. DLC BNCR

552 _____. Límites entre San Juan y San Vicente. San José: Tipografía Nacional, 1906. 20 pp. Maps.
A legal and historical study prepared in response to an 1894 protest by residents of the San Juan district of the central canton of San José, who requested that the government delineate the boundary between their district and the neighboring one. Recommends the appropriate lines and provides justification. DLC DLC-LDS-106 BNCR

553 _____. Obras históricas. San José: Imprenta Lehmann, 1958. 510 pp. Illus., appendix.
Despite the title this is not a collection of all the author's historical writings, but his effort to prepare a complete history of Costa Rica. It covers the years from independence to 1871 in 315 pages, followed by an appendix reproducing appropriate documents from the period. Although intended as the first volume of a series, it is the only one he completed. The commentaries originally appeared in the Costa Rican press. The narration is brief and includes copious excerpts from documents and proclamations of the period, as well as details of all election results. DLC LNHT BNCR

(González Víques, Cleto)

554 _____. Personal del poder ejecutivo de Costa Rica, 1821-1956. San José: Imprenta Moderna, 1958. 32 pp. Illus. 2d ed. San José: Instituto Geográfico Nacional, 1970. 45 pp.

A chronological listing of all individuals who held the position of president or chief of state of Costa Rica from independence to 1936, followed by a list of the vice-presidents or designates, also chronological. A single-paragraph outline curriculum vita of each of the presidents is also provided. DLC BNCR

555 _____. El puerto de Puntarenas: algo de su historia. San José: Imprenta Gutenburg, 1933. 124 pp. Maps.

A series of articles, originally published in the Diario de Costa Rica, about the city and port of Puntarenas, tracing its history and discussing its possibilities as a port. Articles and correspondence on the subject from throughout the nineteenth century are reprinted. DLC-LDS-752 LNHT BNCR

556 _____. Temblores, terremotos, inundaciones y erupciones volcanicas en Costa Rica, 1608-1910. San José: Tipografía Alsina, 1910. 200 pp. Illus., maps, tables.

A listing and description in Spanish and English of earthquakes and floods affecting Costa Rica from Colonial times to 1910. Presents brief descriptions; comparative tables; lists of damage and affected areas; and when available, photos. DLC-LDS-74 LNHT BNCR

557 González Víques, Cleto, and Pedro Pérez Zeledón. Dos próceres. San José: Imprenta Nacional, 1918. 35 pp.

Two brief and unconnected essays, one by González Víques extolling the contributions of the regimes of Ricardo Jiménez Oreamuno to the national educational system, and the other by Pérez Zeledón, tracing the role of José María Castro in the independence movement. DLC DLC-LDS-155

558 González y González, Ricardo. Costa Rica Railway: Section Cartago to Santiago. San José: Imprenta El Comercio, 1887. 34 pp.

A glowing series of articles describing the progress of construction and the economic prospects of the region. Emphasizes both the benefits to the nation of the link with the Atlantic and the prospects for banana production along the coast. Written in optimistic terms and offered in English, it is clearly designed to encourage Yankee investment. The editor's articles were originally published in his newspaper. They include construction details and physical descriptions of the region. DLC-LDS-691

559 González Zeledón, Manuel [Magón, pseud.]. Cuentos de Magón. San José: Editorial Universitaria, 1947. xlvi, 329 pp. Biblio., illus. 2d ed. San José: Imprenta Lehmann, 1968. xlv, 416 pp. Biblio., illus.

A collection of short stories by a humorist from Costa Rica whose writings spanned the 1910-45 era. The edition includes a biographical sketch and critical introduction by José M. Arce. The stories deal with Costa Rican customs, themes, and settings, reflecting the nation's humor, traditions, and the character of its people. DLC LNHT BNCR

560 _____. La propia. San José: n.p., 1910. Latest ed. San José: Imprenta Lehmann, 1920. 295 pp.

Another collection of short stories by this well-known Costa Rican writer. Most are drawn from the pages of his newspaper, El País, some from later works. All employ the Costa Rican settings, themes, customs, and idioms that are his trademark and capture the spirit of the times. DLC LNHT

561 Guardia Quirós, Víctor. El arbitraje anglo-costarricense y la ley de nulidades. San José: Imprenta Lehmann, n.d. 87 pp.

An impassioned commentary regarding an arbitration by Chief Justice Taft of the United States of a claim by Great Britain involving a loan by the Royal Bank to Federico Tinoco while the latter was president and a subsequent law that retroactively made the state responsible for what was originally a personal loan, which resulted in Taft's rejection of the claim on the grounds that the law's retroactivity violated the Costa Rican constitution and hence that the debt remained private rather than becoming an obligation of the state. The essay hails this decision and contains a good deal of rhetoric about the law and other allegedly related factors. DLC-LDS-314 BNCR

562 _____. Escarceos literarios. San José: Editorial Borrasé, 1938. 226 pp. Illus.

The initial portion of this volume consists of a series of essays by the author defending the Costa Rican position in its border dispute with Nicaragua and answering the Nicaraguan arguments. The second portion is a series of literary works dealing with diverse themes, all previously published. DLC DLC-LDS-841 LNHT BNCR

563 Gudmundson Kristjanson, Lowell. Estratificación socio-racial y económica de Costa Rica, 1700-1850. San José: Editorial Universidad Estatal a Distancia, 1978. 178 pp. Biblio., notes, maps, tables, appendixes.

Three separate essays dealing with the impact of economic change on social stratification. The first deals with the freedom of the African slaves during the Colonial era and their intermixture with the populace, the second with cattle-ranching on a large hacienda during the early independence years, and the last with the changes caused by the introduction of coffee cultivation in the latter part of the nineteenth century. The volume is based on secondary works and contains extensive statistics regarding the economy, population, and land ownership. DGU

564 Güell, Cipriano. De la ruta de la vida. San José: Editorial Trejos, 1940. 179 pp. 2d

ed. San José: Editorial Costa Rica, 1968.
147 pp.
   The memoirs and commentaries of a Costa
Rican journalist of the 1910-30 era, covering
a broad range of themes including his journalistic career and his impressions during his
travels. BNCR

565 La Guerra de la Liberación 1948. San José:
Imprenta Atenea, 1949. 27 pp. Illus., map.
   A brief pamphlet lauding the National Liberation Movement and hailing the heroes who
gave their lives in the 1948 civil war. Includes a summary of the military conflict and
its principal battles. BNCR

566 Guerrero, José. Estadística vital, 1906-1925.
San José: Imprenta Lehmann, 1927. 88 pp.
Tables.
   A valuable collection of figures, tables,
and graphs by the director of the Costa Rican
census office. Traces the various trends in
births and deaths, infant mortality, sex,
civil status, etc., both nationally and for
each province. DLC DLC-LDS-395

567 Guevara Solano de Pérez, Raquel. Estudio
sobre el Lic. Pedro Pérez Zeledón. San José:
Asamblea Legislativa, 1968. 148 pp. Biblio.,
maps. 2d ed. San José: Ministerio de
Cultura, Juventud y Deportes, 1971. 204 pp.
Notes, illus., maps.
   Originally written as a thesis, this volume
provides a brief overview and compilation of
data and documents about a well-known historian and government servant whose career
spanned the early twentieth century, as well
as his historical writings dealing with the
Colonial era in Costa Rica. His career included service in the boundary dispute with
Panama, the post of minister of fomento, and
that of foreign minister. The brief biography
includes excerpts from his writings and the
rulings, as well as a chronological list of
his publications. Based on research in documents and periodicals of the era. LNHT BNCR

568 Gutiérrez, Joaquín. Cocorí. Santiago:
Editorial Rapa Nui, 1947. 77 pp. Illus.
   A brief novel about childhood and growing
up. Although set in the author's native province of Limón in Costa Rica, it was first
published in Chile, where he lived for many
years. LNHT BNCR

569 _____. Manglar. Santiago: Editorial
Nacimiento, 1947. 246 pp. Illus. Latest ed.
San José: Editorial Costa Rica, 1972.
140 pp.
   A novel based on life in the Costa Rican
hinterland, focusing on the activities of a
schoolteacher in Guanacaste. DLC LNHT BNCR

570 _____. Murámonos, Federico. San José:
Editorial Costa Rica, 1973. 214 pp.
   A novel about middle-class life. Following
the experiences of a number of distinct characters, it depicts the foibles of the class,
its life-style, and how it differs from that
of other Costa Ricans. DLC BNCR

571 _____. Puerto Limón. Santiago: Editorial
Nacimiento, 1950. 380 pp. Illus. Latest ed.
San José: Editorial Costa Rica, 1973.
250 pp.
   A novel set in the author's native region.
It differs from some of his other works in
that in seeking to capture its beauty and
traditions, he emphasizes description of the
region and the group rather than the individual. One of his best-known works. DLC
LNHT BNCR

572 Gutiérrez Braun, Federico. Expedición del
doctor Richard Weyl al macizo del Chirripó:
bosquejo geológico de la Cordillera de
Talamanca. San José: Instituto Geográfico,
1955. 56 pp. Illus.
   An account of the mission of German geologist Richard Weyl and the reports of his
studies of the Talamanca mountain region,
conducted during 1954-55. DLC

573 Gutiérrez Braun, Federico. Reseña geográfica
de Costa Rica. Rio de Janeiro: PAIGH, 1955.
27 pp. Biblio., illus., maps, tables.
   A very brief description containing basic
data regarding physical features, based on
fieldwork conducted during the late 1950s as
part of the Institute's basic series. DLC
BNCR

574 Gutiérrez Carranza, Claudio. Análisis de
información sobre rendimiento académico de
estudiantes. San José: Universidad de Costa
Rica, 1972. 67 pp. Tables.
   A profile of the 13,000 students who entered the University of Costa Rica between
1965 and 1971, with statistical data and
tables providing information about the origins, preparation, and achievements of the
youth seeking to take advantage of the opportunity of a university education. DLC BNCR

575 Gutiérrez Gutiérrez, Carlos José, ed. Costa
Rica: Constitución Política, anotada y
síntesis del proceso constitucional. San
José: Equidad de Centroamérica, 1975. 256
pp. Index.
   The nation's current constitution and its
first, along with a brief historical essay
regarding the country's constitutional evolution and its various other fundamental documents, followed by an index aiding in locating
specific provisions. BNCR

576 Gutiérrez Jiménez, Mario. Vida y obra de don
Ricardo Jiménez. San Salvador: ODECA, 1960.
48 pp.
   A brief summary of the political career of
the three-time Costa Rican president, emphasizing his agricultural efforts and political
and development programs, which are outlined.
BNCR

577 Hall, Carolyn. El café y el desarrollo
histórico-geográfico de Costa Rica. San José:
Editorial Costa Rica, 1976. 208 pp. Index,
biblio., notes, maps, tables, appendixes.
   An analysis and history of coffee cultivation in Costa Rica since 1935, though with a

brief introduction regarding the nineteenth century. Focuses on the role of coffee in the nation's economy and development, particularly in the various regions, and on the expansion of coffee culture. Uses geographic data and methods, as the author is a geographer who began her study as a dissertation and later expanded it with fieldwork. DLC LNHT BNCR

578 Hancock, Ralph, and Julian A. Weston. The Lost Treasure of Cocos Island. New York: Thomas Nelson & Sons, 1960. 325 pp. Index, illus.

Two newsmen describe the legends regarding the alleged pirate treasures buried on Cocos Island, efforts to locate them, and shipwrecks in the area, providing data to verify their claims as far as possible. They include the story of the burying of the treasure taken from Lima, Peru, to avoid its falling into the hands of the victorious revolutionaries during the independence era. DLC BNCR

579 Hecht, Rudolf S. "More Teachers Than Soldiers": Recent Impressions of Costa Rica. New Orleans: Mississippi Shipping Co., 1953. 14 pp.

A general description of Costa Rica, its life, and its institutions, emphasizing the positive impact of recent changes. LNHT BNCR

580 Herbster de Gusmao, Oswaldo. Estudio sobre las instituciones autónomas de Costa Rica. San José: ESAPAC, 1968. 129 pp. Notes.

A concise survey of the evolution of the autonomous institutions created by the Costa Rican government since the 1948 revolution, viewing them as means of decentralizing administration. Makes some comparisons to Panamanian efforts to decentralize through other methods. Examines the details of the institutions, their legal structure, and the problem of coordination among autonomous agencies, as well as the means of control available to the executive, though it is noted that so drastic a remedy as intervention could be invoked only in dire circumstances. DLC LNHT BNCR

581 Hernández, Francisco. Caricaturas de Hernández. San José: Diario de Costa Rica, n.d. 223 pp. Illus.

A collection of political cartoons and caricatures by a Costa Rican artist whose drawings appeared in the Diario de Costa Rica, covering the years 1922 through 1924. They portray Central American and domestic events, noting the overwhelming presence of the Yankees in those days, and offer a Costa Rican view of isthmian events as well as a humorous look at domestic problems and politics. The frequent use of the theme of Don Quixote reflects Spanish influence. DLC-LDS-392 BNCR

582 Hernández, Rubén. Las libertades políticas en Costa Rica. San José: Editorial Juricentro, 1980. 250 pp.
BNCR

583 Hernández Carvajal, Efraín. Monografía del cantón de San Isidro de Heredia. San José: Imprenta Nacional, 1955. 58 pp. Illus.

A brief history and description of the town, with emphasis on the current situation and its leading citizens of the contemporary era, published on the occasion of its fiftieth anniversary. BNCR

584 Hernández de Jaen, Mireya. Monografía del cantón Carrillo, 1877-1977. San José: Universidad de Costa Rica, 1977. 132 pp. Biblio., illus., maps.

A centennial summary of the town, its history, and the current state of its institutions and principal buildings. BNCR

585 Hernández h., Hermogenes. Refranes y dichos populares usuales en Costa Rica. San José: Imprenta Elena, 1969. 62 pp.

A disparate collection of one-liners drawn from popular sayings and phrases in Costa Rican usage, arranged alphabetically by first word. LNHT BNCR

586 Hernández Poveda, Rubén. Desde la barra: cómo se discutió y emitió la Constitución Política de 1949. San José: Editorial Borrasé, 1953. 323 pp.

A Costa Rican journalist's daily accounts of the Constituent Assembly of 1949 and its deliberations, providing an outside view of the activities, which can be used in conjunction with the official minutes. Includes the author's reactions to the events. DLC

587 Herrera García, Adolfo. Vida y dolores de Juan Varela. 3d ed. San José: Editorial Costa Rica, 1966. 106 pp. Illus. 4th ed. San José: Editorial Costa Rica, 1968. 87 pp.

A brief novel about the trials and tribulations of the small farmer. Using vivid and dramatic dialogue and narration, traces the problems and efforts of a peasant who homesteads on unowned virgin territory. Later editions are entitled simply Juan Varela. KU

588 Herrera García, Adolfo, Enrique Mora V., and Francisco Gamboa G. Partido Vanguardia Popular: breve esbozo de su historia. San José: Imprenta Elena, 1971. 56 pp. Illus.

A brief summary of the party and its activities.

589 Herrick, Bruce, and Barclay Hudson. Urban Poverty and Economic Development. New York: St. Martin's Press, 1980. xiii, 188 pp. Index, biblio., notes, illus.
DLC

590 Herzfeld, Anita, and Teresa Cajiao Salas. El teatro de hoy en Costa Rica. San José: Editorial Costa Rica, 1973. 268 pp. Biblio., appendixes.

Two Latin American but non-Costa Rican scholars provide critical looks at contemporary theater in that country. Provides a brief historical outline of the development of theatrical writing in Costa Rica and a discussion of the works of several prominent playwrights, including a brief biographical sketch and list of works of each, along with analysis of one or two of their best-known pieces. Authors considered include Alberto Cañas, Samuel Rovinski, Daniel Gallegos, Antonio Yglesias, and William Reuben. Includes lists of all the works offered during the 1968-70 seasons in San José, with the works, authors, companies, directors, and theaters. DLC LNHT BNCR

591 Hess Estrada, Raul. Rodrigo Facio: el economista. San José: Universidad de Costa Rica, 1972. 223 pp.
A biography of a Costa Rican economist, political figure, and professor of economics whose contributions to the nation were of such significance that the campus of the University of Costa Rica now bears his name, by one of his former students. Includes discussion of his educational efforts, his articles in the press, and his economic studies of the nation, in addition to analysis of his political career, which included service in the Constituent Assembly of 1948. DLC BNCR

592 Hidalgo, Alfredo. Apuntes de la santa visita canónica a Tarrazú, Buenos Aires, General y Golfo Dulce. San José: Imprenta Lehmann, 1922. 87 pp.
A presbiter's account of the visit by the bishop of San José, Monsignor Castro, to the interior regions of Costa Rica in 1922, containing rich description of the area and the church facilities. BNCR

593 Hill, George W., Manuel Gollas Quintero, and Gregorio Alfaro. Un área rural en desarrollo: sus problemas económicos y sociales; Costa Rica. San José: Instituto Universitario Centroamericano de Investigaciones Sociales y Económicas, 1964. 56 pp. Illus., maps, tables.
A study of rural development in Costa Rica, in the Rio del Coto Brus under an AID contract, considering land tenure, workforce, investment, production, expenses, and other factors affecting both land use and production. The conclusions emphasize the many influences and the need for broad governmental programs that encompass health, education, land tenure, and transportation. DLC LNHT BNCR

594 _____. Frontier Rural Development in Costa Rica. San José: n.p., 1964. 127 pp.
An examination of colonization projects in the Costa Rican interior that notes the wide range of needs and stresses the importance of government programs to provide services in such areas as health, education, and transportation. WU

595 Homenaje a los combatientes costarricenses en la segunda guerra mundial. San José: Imprenta La Tribuna, 1946. 40 pp. Illus.
A collection of photos and brief biographical sketches of Costa Ricans who died fighting for the Allied forces, principally the U.S. Army, during World War II. The introduction invokes patriotism and friendship between the U.S. and Costa Rica, hailing continental solidarity. BNCR

596 Huffman, Maxine Fish. Tico Tales. New York: Exposition Press, 1963. 63 pp. Illus.
A collection of Costa Rican legends, compiled by a Yankee educator, seeking to provide the English-speaking audience access to Costa Rican folklore. DLC BNCR

597 Ibarra Bejarano, Georgina. Aquileo J. Echeverría: estudio crítico-biográfico. San José: Imprenta Trejos, 1946. 49 pp. Biblio.
A brief sketch of the life of this Costa Rican folklorist, followed by a discussion of what are called the principal themes of his works, consisting mainly of quotations with introductions and without critical comment. The themes are the usual societal values and issues of the peasants, including work, the home, and similar subjects. DLC LNHT

598 Ibarra Mayorga, Francisco. La tragedia del nicaragüense en Costa Rica. San José: Imprenta Borrasé, 1948. 16 pp.
A commentary on Nicaraguan influence in Costa Rica focusing on the 1940s, citing the Nicaraguan intellectual contribution while lamenting the involvement of Nicaraguans in the internal politics of Costa Rica and particularly their role in the crisis of the 1940s, which the author contends made the Nicaraguan community in Costa Rica a target of criticism and reprisals. Stresses that Nicaraguans were active in support of both sides in the Costa Rican civil war, despite the fact that the role of Nicaraguans in support of the National Liberation Movement is less well known. DLC

599 Ideario costarricense: resultado de una encuesta nacional. San José: Editorial Surco, 1943. 437 pp. Illus.
Part of the political maneuvering in Costa Rica during the 1930s, this volume presents the responses of a number of leading citizens to a survey seeking ideas about changes necessary in the governmental structure to enable the nation to deal with its present problems. Editorial Surco was an arm of the Centro para el Estudio de Problemas Nacionales, one of the groups that joined with the Partido de Liberación Nacional during the 1948 crisis and revolution, and many of the persons involved in the survey were subsequently associated with the 1948 revolution. Responses are printed as received, along with an introductory explanation. The tendency of the comments is toward the need for constitutional reform to make the government more responsive and effective, a later position of the PLN. DLC

600 Iglesias, Francisco María de, ed. Braulio Carrillo: tributo patrio y consegrado á su memoria en celebración del primer centenario de su natalicio. San José: Tipografía Nacional, 1900. 2d ed. San José: Editorial Costa Rica, 1971. 115 pp.

A collection of commentaries about and writings and proclamations by an individual who served as head of the state of Costa Rica during 1835-36, and again as its first president from 1838 through 1842, during which time it separated from the Federation of Central America. His tenures were turbulent and his methods harsh in the face of various uprisings, and he remains controversial despite his role in the founding of Costa Rica as an independent nation. The commentaries are drawn from contemporaries and scholars of that era. DLC-LDS-25 BNCR

601 Iglesias, Francisco María de. *Pro patria: una biografía y algunos recuerdos históricos.* San José: Tipografía Nacional, 1899. 70 pp.
An essay dealing with the late-Colonial and independence eras recounting the efforts of various Costa Rican figures, particularly Joaquín Iglesias, and their actions in gaining independence and in the matter of relations with the Federation. DLC-LDS-11 LNHT BNCR

602 Iglesias Hogan, Rubén. *La casona.* San José: Imprenta Trejos, 1975. 88 pp.
A novel set in Costa Rica at the turn of the century, designed to preserve the traditions of the nation by showing the life-style of these years. BNCR

603 _____. *Costa Rica y la Federación de Centro América: las actas municipales de Cartago.* San José: Tipografía La Tribuna, 1933. 52 pp. Notes.
A brief essay, based on published secondary sources and documents, recounting the Costa Rican activities during the independence era. Focuses on the city council's actions and on the various local proclamations regarding independence and adhesion to the Central American Federation, particularly those of Cartago, the government seat. There is also a brief essay on Costa Rican positions regarding the 1920 Federation attempt. DLC DLC-LDS-731 LNHT BNCR

604 _____. *Tierras de sol y otros relatos.* San José: Imprenta La Tribuna, 1935. 2d ed. San José: Imprenta Trejos, 1970. 87 pp.
A series of short stories set in Guanacaste province depicting its beauties and providing a somewhat idylic image of life there, emphasizing its tranquillity. DLC-LDS-825 BNCR

605 Ignotus, pseud. *Cuestión bananera: ¿es que deseamos suicidarnos?* San José: Imprenta Alsina, 1929. 24 pp.
A series of articles that originally appeared in *La Tribuna* of San José, republished under the auspices of the city of Limón. The viewpoint of the banana port is sympathetic to the company that provides its chief economic impulse, and the articles vigorously condemn opponents of the new banana contract, dubbing the banana tax a case of "killing the goose that laid the golden egg" and an act of "national suicide" at a time when banana production was already declining, citing the

importance of the banana trade and industry to the nation. They also note that the Atlantic Railroad would collapse without the banana trade and hence destroy the nation's access to the outside world. DLC

606 El Imparcial (San José). *Lo del 28 de abril.* San José: Imprenta de El Imparcial, 1915. 75 pp. Index.
A series of newspaper exchanges regarding negotiations among the contenders for the Costa Rican presidency in 1914 and 1915 and the resulting election, in which no one received a majority of the votes. The two leading candidates then resigned, thereby preventing the Congress from choosing between them. They had hoped to force a new election, but Congress named a designate as temporary president, resulting in a dispute over the constitutionality of such an action. Parties involved in the exchange were Ricardo Jiménez Oreamuno, Rafael Yglesias, and Carlos Durón. DLC BNCR

607 *Índice general de la legislación promulgada, 1948-1970.* Oxford, N.H.: Equity Publishing, 1972. xviii, 463 pp. Illus.
An alphabetical index to recent Costa Rican legislation, with citings to appropriate laws by topic and codings to enable consultation of the earlier Beeche index as well. DLC BNCR

608 Instituto de Nutrición de Centro América y Panamá. *Evaluación nutricional de la población de Centro América y Panamá: Costa Rica.* Guatemala: Ministerio de Salubridad Pública, 1969. Various pagings. Illus., tables.
A detailed report of the nutritional state of the rural Costa Rican populace, based on surveys and medical examinations conducted during 1965-69. Provides extensive data regarding the diet, food, distribution, shortages, and medical implications. DLC

609 International Bureau of the American Republics. *Costa Rica: A Handbook.* Washington, D.C.: GPO, 1892. iv, 146 pp. Biblio., illus., maps, tables.
Part of the Bureau's series providing general data regarding the republic, with emphasis on its economy and trade, followed by a series of tables listing import duties. Clearly designed to encourage trade. See item GU729. DLC BNCR

610 Istituto Italo-Latino Americano. *Costa Rica.* Rome: Istituto Italo-Latino Americano, 1971. 35 pp. Biblio., tables.
A description of the current situation, with emphasis on the economy, for the general reader. DLC

611 Jaksch, Hans Jüergen. *Optimale Investitionsvarianten in Costa Rica von 1961 bis 1966.* Frankfurt: Vittorio Klostermann, 1966. 156 pp. Biblio., notes, tables.
A study of recent Costa Rican developments. DLC LNHT

612 Jiménez, Carlos María, ed. El petróleo para los costarricenses: estudios jurídicos sobre la ley del subsuelo. 3 vols. San José: Imprenta Lehmann, 1920-21. 30, 51, 60 pp.
A collection of material relating to the petroleum contracts in Costa Rica, particularly the issues surrounding the Pinto-Greulich contract, which involved the question of the rights of landowners over subsoil deposits and the powers of the government. The law involved gave the government licensing rights and provided taxes, hence disallowing the contract, which was based on absolute ownership rights. The resulting debate involved all the leading political and legal figures of the day. The first two volumes contain political speeches and legal studies; the third indicates the support of fifty of the nation's fifty-six municipalities for the law providing government control, proposed by Deputy Jorge Suarez. Volume 3 is subtitled El ley del subsuelo, adhesiones de municipios. DLC DLC-LDS-185

613 Jiménez, Enrique, and Gerardo Jiménez. Higiene de la habitación y del agua en Costa Rica. San José: Tipografía Nacional, 1901. 252 pp. Biblio., illus., tables.
A discussion of types of housing construction and their implications for health and water supply, by a medical doctor and an agricultural engineer. Although they discuss the construction types in general terms, they focus on problems and conditions particular to Costa Rica. They consider the need for water purification and the conditions required for it, particularly in San José, proposing possible methods and water works. DLC DLC-LDS-20

614 Jiménez, Manuel de Jesús. Páginas escogidas. San José: Ministerio de Educación Pública, 1959. 156 pp. Biblio., notes.
A collection of writings by a prominent Costa Rican political and intellectual figure of the late nineteenth century. Includes brief novels and short stories based on Costa Rican national themes and regional customs, encompassing Colonial life and the patriotism inspired by the mid-nineteenth century campaign against the Walker expedition, as well as commentaries on life and customs in the nineteenth century. DLC LNHT BNCR

615 _____. Selecciones. San José: Editorial Costa Rica, 1964. 182 pp. Biblio.
A collection of novels and short stories, partially duplicating those in Páginas escogidas, but with additional essays on the independence era. DLC LNHT BNCR

616 Jiménez, Manuel de Jesús, and Faustino Víquez, eds. Documentos relativos a la Guerra Nacional de 1856 y 1857, con sus antecedentes. San José: Tipografía Nacional, 1914. 330 pp.
A collection of documents from the Costa Rican Archives covering the years 1855-56. Included are the Foreign Ministry's correspondence with England and the Central

American governments regarding the Walker intervention of the 1850s. BNCR

617 Jiménez, Salvador. Elementos de derecho civil y penal de Costa Rica. 2 vols. San José: Imprenta de Guillermo Molina & Tipografía Nacional, 1874-76. 454, 470 pp.
Intended as a law school text, this work combines general definition of legal terms, a survey of Costa Rican legal history, detailed discussion of the existing laws, and an historical survey indicating the evolution of the national legislation. DLC-LDS-60

618 Jiménez Castro, Wilburg. Análisis electoral de una democracia: estudio del comportamiento político costarricense durante el período 1953-1974. San José: Editorial Costa Rica, 1977. 43, 94 pp. Illus., maps, tables.
An analysis of voting patterns from 1953 to 1974, by a Costa Rican professor and government official. The narration is brief, with the bulk of the outsized volume devoted to elaborate and multicolored maps and charts showing the voting patterns and shifts in each of the nation's cantons for each of the elections, as well as the percentage of voters and other relevant details. The votes are also tabulated by province. Such factors as blank ballots and abstentions are also considered. DLC BNCR

619 _____. Importancia de la modernización de la administración pública para el programa de integración del Istmo Centroamericano. San José: ESAPAC, 1966. 43 pp.
A call for better training of personnel and more professional administration of the various state entities throughout Central America, emphasizing the importance of effective national and regional planning and control to the success of the various economies and to the integration movement. DLC LNHT BNCR

620 _____. Migraciones internas en Costa Rica. Washington, D.C.: PAU, 1956. 163 pp. Biblio., illus., maps, tables.
A detailed statistical and historical study of the Costa Rican population and its internal migrations from Colonial times to the present. Includes statistical tables, graphs, and maps showing movement, distribution, and origin of individuals in each province and distribution of population by age and sex in the various regions. The text is relatively brief but does furnish an account of the shifts and the possible reasons, and indicates the trends. The bulk of the volume consists of statistics and charts. DLC LNHT BNCR

621 _____. Planificación operativa o caos nacional. San José: n.p., 1960. xiv, 103 pp. 3d ed. San José: ESAPAC, 1965. xxiv, 103 pp. Biblio., tables.
An examination of planning, its various forms and functions, and its importance in the governmental systems of Central America. Contends that central planning is essential to development, especially in countries with limited resources, and emphasizes the need for

the establishment of central planning entities in each nation to coordinate all governmental activities and set priorities as a means of rationalizing planning. DLC LNHT

622 Jiménez Gutiérrez, Carlos María. La legión Caribe. San José: Editorial Borrasé, 1948. 113 pp. Illus.
The memoirs of a member of the Caribbean Legion, recounting its role in the Costa Rican civil war of 1948 and hailing its activities. Includes a list of all members of the legion and photos of most. BNCR

623 _____. Historia de la aviación en Costa Rica. San José: Imprenta Elena, 1962. 187 pp. Appendix.
After briefly discussing the origins of flight, the author focuses on the initial pioneers of aviation in Costa Rica, cataloging in short descriptive sketches all the first flights and records, the construction of the airport, and the formation of the national airline. The appendix provides a list of aviation accidents in Costa Rica, giving full details regarding the plane, the occupants and their fate, and statistics regarding flights and passenger traffic for the 1952–61 decade. DLC LNHT BNCR

624 Jiménez Oreamuno, Ricardo. Colegio de Cartago. San José: Imprenta Alsina, 1921. 73 pp.
Part of a polemic regarding educational policy in which an ex-president of Costa Rica responds in detail to a series of newspaper articles by the director of the Colegio de Cartago. The themes are diverse, and include educational policy. DLC BNCR

625 _____. Como vieron los sucesos del 7 de noviembre del 89 algunos ciudadanos que participaron en ese journada. San José: n.p., n.d. [1889]. 121 pp. Illus.
A criticism of the installation of José Joaquín Rodríguez in the presidency, contending that the election was fraudulent and that what amounted to a coup had been staged to prevent the incumbent president, General Bernardo Soto, from turning power over to the first designate, Carlos Durán. DLC-LDS-930

626 _____. La noche del 28 de abril. San José: Imprenta Alsina, 1919. 35 pp.
A Costa Rican president's version of the events of 1914 that led to the coup by Federico Tinoco, emphasizing Jiménez's actions and those of his party in opposing the coup. Provides considerable detail regarding the maneuvering that preceded the coup and the electoral controversies involved. BNCR

627 _____. Selección de artículos originales del prócer. San José: Imprenta Nacional, 1946. 82 pp. Index.
A collection of articles and commentaries by an influential Costa Rican political figure who served as president three times and dominated his nation's politics for two decades from 1917 through 1936, intended to preserve

some of his many observations during his active political campaigns and polemics. The themes are diverse, but principally national and political. DLC BNCR

628 Jiménez Ortiz, Manuel Francisco. Breve reseña de la economía costarricense. San José: Comisión Costarricense de Fomento Interamericano, 1944. 51 pp. Tables.
A brief résumé of the Costa Rican economy and its historical development, principally through compilations of available statistics, along with brief résumés of the trends. Includes consideration of all important products and production and of significant imports and exports, viewed in long-range perspective. Some of the figures provide continuous data from the mid-nineteenth century to the 1940s, though the range covered in any particular sequence varies. A valuable compilation of historical statistics regarding the economy that helps place any particular era in its context, despite the limits of the available statistics that cause variations in the years available. BNCR

629 _____. El convenio commercial entre los Estados Unidos de América y Costa Rica: la política de tratados bilaterales de comercio en el Continente Americano. San José: Imprenta La Tribuna, 1937. 89 pp.
A commentary on the reciprocal trade agreements policy of the Franklin D. Roosevelt administration, reflecting local needs and other tensions in the isthmus. DLC LNHT

630 _____. Intervenciones públicas. San José: Imprenta La Nación, 1951. 156 pp.
A series of essays by a representative of the Constitutional party to the Constituent Assembly of 1949. Part of the political exchanges of those years about the future of the nation, they advocate moderate changes and favor basing the new constitution on the previous one of 1871. The essays cover the years 1946–49, and focus on economic and constitutional issues, but include the author's explanation of his role in the political turmoil of this era. DLC

631 Jiménez Quesada, Mario Alberto. Obras completas. 2 vols. San José: Editorial Costa Rica, 1962. 282, 307 pp. Index, biblio., notes, illus.
A collection of the writings of a Costa Rican professor. Volume 1 contains a series of essays on diverse themes, the majority dealing with Costa Rican historical subjects, but some with general themes. The second volume contains his thesis on the relation of the executive and legislature in Costa Rica and their influence in foreign relations (see item CR632), followed by three other essays. DLC LNHT BNCR

632 _____. Sobernía externa y relaciones entre el legislativo y ejecutivo en nuestra evolución constitucional. San José: n.p., 1951. 170 pp. Biblio., notes. 2d ed. San José:

Editorial Costa Rica, 1973. 170 pp. Biblio.,
notes.

An essay on the powers of the two governmental branches, particularly in matters regarding foreign relations, tracing the various
disputes in Costa Rican history though focused
chiefly on theoretical and philosophical aspects of the question; based on secondary
works. The second edition bears the title
Desarrollo constitucional de Costa Rica. DLC
LNHT BNCR

633 Jiménez Quirós, Otto [Ocho-Ji-Kiros, pseud.].
Árbol criollo. Cartago: Editorial Irazú,
1964. 296 pp. Notes, illus.

A series of humorous essays by a Costa
Rican writer. Using national themes and
attempting to capture the local humor tradition, he traces the Quirós family tree and
provides information about some of the leading
members of this illustrious Costa Rican family. DLC LNHT BNCR

634 Jinesta, Carlos. Braulio Carrillo y su
tiempo. San José: Imprenta Lehmann, 1940.
68 pp. Illus.

A brief chronicle of the first Costa Rican
chief of state. Comments on his harsh methods
and on his role in securing the nation's independence upon the collapse of the Central
American Federation. Includes both praise and
criticism of his actions, seeking to emphasize
the limits of his methods and the necessities
of the times. DLC LNHT BNCR

635 _____. Carlos Gagini: vida y obras. San
José: Imprenta Lehmann, 1936. 32 pp. Illus.

A brief summary of the life of a prominent
and influential Costa Rican professor and
school director who left his mark on the nation's educational system during the the late
nineteenth and early twentieth centuries. A
résumé of his writings in the fields of language and linguistics is also included, with
commentaries on his focus on this theme. DLC-
LDS-833 BNCR

636 _____. Cromos. San José: Imprenta Alsina,
1932. viii, 101 pp.

A prominent and prolific Costa Rican writer's collection of short stories based on the
regional folklore and local traditions of his
native country. DLC-LDS-547 BNCR

637 _____. Elogio: Claudio González Rucavado.
San José: Imprenta Alsina, 1930. 30 pp.
Illus.

A brief essay hailing the contributions and
tracing the life of a Costa Rican law professor and author who served in the national
Congress during the years 1910 through 1924.
DLC LNHT BNCR

638 _____. Epinicio: Juan Santamaría. San José:
Imprenta Alsina, 1931. 37 pp. Illus.

An essay on the life and exploits of Juan
Santamaría, the Costa Rican military hero of
the war against William Walker, detailing his
heroism and tracing his life, with background

comments about Walker and Central America at
that time. DLC DLC-LDS-504 LNHT BNCR

639 _____. José Martí en Costa Rica. San José:
Imprenta Alsina, 1933. 46 pp. Illus.

An account of two visits to Costa Rica by
Cuban liberator José Martí, in 1893 and 1894,
during periods of exile in which he was organizing new revolts in his homeland. This brief
study details his arrivals and departures, and
his activities while in Costa Rica. DLC DLC-
LDS-764 BNCR

640 _____. Juan Mora Fernández, 1784-1854. San
José: Imprenta Lehmann, 1938. 43 pp. Illus.

A brief essay summarizing the contributions
of the leader of the Costa Rican state during
the days of the Federation, hailing his
actions and his role in the independence
movement and in seeking to continue the
Federation. DLC

641 _____. Juan Rafael Mora. San José: Imprenta
Alsina, 1929. 32 pp. Illus.

A brief eulogy of the career of Juan Rafael
Mora, this work was awarded a prize by the
Ministry of Education. It hails his contribution to the nation and his dynamism, offering
him as a model of patriotism to the nation's
youth. Includes excerpts from several of his
speeches and decrees. DLC DLC-LDS-425 LNHT

642 _____. Manuel María Gutiérrez. San José:
Imprenta Feniz y Rojas, 1929. 29 pp. Illus.

A brief biographical sketch of a long-time
director of the national band of Costa Rica
during the mid-nineteenth century, who was the
author of the music for the national anthem.
DLC-LDS-461 LNHT BNCR

643 _____. Omar Dengo. San José: Imprenta
Alsina, 1929. 32 pp. Illus.

A brief summary of the career and writings
of this well-known Costa Rican educator. DLC-
LDS-418 LNHT

644 _____. Rubén Darío en Costa Rica. Mexico:
n.p., 1944. 75 pp.

An account of the Nicaraguan poet's nine
months in Costa Rica in 1891 and 1892, and a
discussion of references to the country in his
subsequent writings and letters. DLC LNHT
BNCR

645 Jinesta, Ricardo. La evolución penitenciario
en Costa Rica. San José: Imprenta Falcó,
1940. 286 pp.

A survey of penal institutions and conditions in Costa Rica from Colonial times, noting recent trends toward rehabilitation and
less cruelty. Traces the laws that govern the
institutions and offenses, including judicial
rulings and sentences. Concludes with a proposal for a new penal code, which the author
feels would be a culmination of the present
trends. DLC LNHT

646 _____. La garganta del Guanacaste. San José:
Imprenta Falcó, 1938. 29 pp. Map.

(Jinesta, Ricardo)
A geographical study of this coastal region of Costa Rica, focusing on its characteristics and precise dimensions. DLC BNCR

647 _____. La Isla del Coco. San José: Imprenta Falcó, 1937. 24 pp. Maps.
A brief description of the geography, flora, and fauna of Cocos Island. DLC-LDS-872 BNCR

648 _____. El oro en Costa Rica. San José: Imprenta Falcó, 1938. 32 pp.
A brief history of gold mining in Costa Rica, including descriptions of the mines and their rise and fall, spanning the Colonial and post-independence eras. DLC DLC-LDS-863

649 Jinesta, Ricardo, and Carlos Jinesta. La instrucción pública en Costa Rica. San José: Imprenta Falcó y Borrasé, 1921. 291 pp.
A brief essay regarding the educational reforms of Mauro Fernández, followed by a more detailed history of education in Costa Rica from Colonial times to 1910, with narrations of the principal educational events of each year. DLC DLC-LDS-265 BNCR

650 Jones, Chester Lloyd. Costa Rica and Civilization in the Caribbean. Madison: University of Wisconsin Press, 1935. ix, 171 pp. Biblio., illus., maps. Latest ed. New York: Russell & Russell, 1967. 172 pp. Biblio., tables.
La República de Costa Rica y los civilizaciones en el Caribé. San José: Editorial Borrasé, 1940. 171 pp. Illus., maps. 2d ed. San José: Editorial Borrasé, 1941. 160 pp.
A topical survey of then-contemporary problems by a well-known scholar, originally written in 1935, focusing on the economic, social, and political problems of the nation and considering each topically. Includes brief historical background on each topic. The principal focus is the economy and particularly monoculture and the role of the great foreign enterprises in agriculture. Also included are chapters dealing with public health, education, population, foreign trade, communications, and similar themes. DLC DLC-LDS-903 LNHT

651 Jore, Émile. République de Costa Rica: movement maritime et commerciale, années 1901-1902-1903. San José: Imprimerie Nationale, 1905. 65 pp. Tables.
A detailed report by the French consul and chargé in Costa Rica, providing extensive statistics regarding trade, imports, and exports, by class and product, including source, destination, data regarding the ports, facilities, laws regarding foreigners, the French colony, and shipping. DLC-LDS-257

652 Julio Sánchez Lépiz. Heredia: Imprenta Lehmann, 1934. 188 pp. Illus.
A series of articles by various authors eulogizing the contributions of the Costa Rican "coffee king," sponsored and compiled by

his native city. Includes descriptions of his activities and photos of his ranches and collaborators. BNCR

653 Junoy, Ramón, ed. Homenaje póstumo a la memoria del excelentísimo e ilustrísimo monseñor doctor don Claudio María Volio Jiménez. San José: Imprenta Trejos, 1946. 122 pp. Illus.
A series of brief essays by various authors commenting on the life and works of a Costa Rican priest and bishop, focusing principally on his activities during the early portion of the twentieth century. The topics are disparate and the result is not a full biography. DLC BNCR

654 Kalnins, Arvids. Tributos municipales costarricenses: análisis crítico y perspectivas. San José: Instituto de Fomento y Asesoría Municipal, 1972. x, 193 pp. Illus., tables.
A compilation of data and laws regarding local taxes in Costa Rica focusing on the sources of revenue for the municipal governments, prepared by a U.N. technician. A pioneering compilation on a much-neglected subject, it provides basic data for future efforts. DLC

655 Kantor, Harry. Bibliography of José Figueres. Tempe: Arizona State University Press, 1972. 50 pp.
An unannotated listing of the numerous pieces written by Costa Rica's leading twentieth-century political figure, arranged alphabetically by title, and a briefer list of studies about and commentaries on Figueres. Focuses on Figueres's numerous newspaper essays. DLC LNHT

656 _____. The Costa Rican Election of 1953: A Case Study. Gainesville: University of Florida Press, 1958. vii, 68 pp. Tables.
A brief review of the election and its background, emphasizing its free and democratic nature. Includes a brief overview of the Revolution of 1948 and the developments that led to the election, as well as summaries of the contesting parties and their platforms. A handy and concise summary of the forces and issues. DLC

657 Karsen, Sonja. Desenvolvimiento educacional de Costa Rica con la asistencia técnica de la UNESCO, 1951-1954. San José: Ministerio de Educación Pública, 1954. 175 pp. Biblio., illus., maps, tables, appendix.
Educational Development in Costa Rica, with UNESCO's Technical Assistance, 1951-1954. San José: Ministerio de Educación Pública, 1954. 167 pp. Biblio., notes, maps, tables, appendix.
Développement de l'éducation de Costa Rica avec l'assistance technique de l'UNESCO, 1951-1954. San José: Ministerio de Educación Pública, 1954. 193 pp. Biblio., illus., maps, tables, appendix.
An assessment of the three-year UNESCO mission and its impact on the Costa Rican

educational system, with recommendations for
the activities of similar missions in other
Latin American countries on the basis of the
results and experience of this one. It seeks
to emphasize the role of the mission and includes a compilation of all the newspaper
commentaries about it in the bibliography.
The mission focused on developing plans for
modernizing the rural, secondary, vocational,
and teacher-training sectors. Includes extensive statistics about enrollment patterns and
needs. The recommendations for the future
relate principally to administration and coordination of the personnel of the assistance
team, though they do stress the need for careful surveys of the country at the outset. DLC

658 Keith, Minor C. Contestación de Minor C.
Keith a lo dicho en "La República" de 3 de
mayo último sobre el negocio de bananos. San
José: Imprenta Alsina, 1907. 15 pp.
     A reply to an article in La República of
San José by Manuel de Jesús and Ricardo
Jiménez, which contained statistics regarding
United Fruit Company investment and profits
that Keith says are incorrect. He provides
the correct figures to the public and denies
the allegations about profits. The item contains extensive figures regarding the contemporary operations of the company in Costa Rica
and other nations. DLC-LDS-144

659 Keith Alvarado, Henry M. Historia de la
familia Alvarado-Barroeta. San José: Gráfica
Pipa, 1972. xi, 104 pp. Illus., tables.
     A combination genealogy-family history
tracing the origins and contributions of the
Alvarado and Barroeta families, the former in
the conquest and the latter in the independence era. The historical essays focus on
these eras, though the genealogy extends to
the mid-nineteenth century. DLC BNCR

660 Koberg Bolando, Max. Mi derecho a relevo.
San José: Published by the Author, 1935.
47 pp.
     An engineer who served as head of the Costa
Rican National Junta Eléctrica after the
nationalization writes his observations and
reflections after seven years of service, as
his farewell legacy. Provides a succinct
account of the history of the electric service
of the nation and the financial and political
crisis that led to the nationalization, citing
the profits and the cutting of voltage as well
as the benefits of a policy that placed San
José among the world's leaders in electric
stoves in the 1920s. Recounts the formation,
organization, and functioning of the National
Electric Service and its dealings with the
private firms. Concludes with a consideration
of future policy, calling for constant revision of the law, continued expansion, continued regulation, and private participation
subject to government regulation. DLC DLC-
LDS-817

661 _____ . La tracción eléctrica en el
Ferrocarril al Pacífico. San José: Imprenta
Lehmann, 1928. 27 pp. Illus.

An elaborate description, in laymen's
terms, of plans for the possible conversion of
the Pacific Railroad to electric power. Emphasizes the practicality of such an action
and seeks to win popular support for this
long-discussed project. DLC-LDS-429

662 Koninklijk Institut voor de Tropen. Costa
Rica: Landendocumentatie. Amsterdam:
Published by the Institute, 1974. 55 pp.
Biblio., illus., maps, tables.
     General geographic data, with details on
economic development and land use for the
1950s and 1960s. DLC

663 Kümpel, Juan. ¡Abajo las caretas! San José:
Imprenta Greñas, 1920. 22 pp.
     Writing in the form of a letter to Costa
Rican president Francisco Aguilar Barquero
regarding the politics of the 1917-20 era, the
author recounts his services to a previous
government and the charges of corruption
against him, appealing for presidential intervention in his behalf. The letter refers to
many of the figures of the times and discusses
the charges and countercharges in detail. DLC
BNCR

664 Kurtze, Francisco. The Interoceanic Railroad
Route through the Republic of Costa Rica. New
York: J.A. Gray & Green, 1866. 29 pp. Maps.
La ruta ferroviaria interoceánica a través de
la República de Costa Rica, 1866. San José:
Imprenta Alsina, 1918. 45 pp. Maps.
     A study conducted in 1866 by the Costa
Rican director of public works to elaborate an
interoceanic rail route in Costa Rica and
convince the United States of the advantages
of a route within that country. Published in
the annual report of the ministry in 1876, it
is here reprinted. Includes a geographic
study of the proposed route. DLC BNCR

665 Lafond de Lurcy, Gabriel. Notice sur le Golfo
Dulce dans l'état de Costa-Rica (Amérique
Centrale) et sur un nouveau passage entre les
deux océans. Paris: A. Fontaine, 1856.
58 pp.
     A description of a potential canal route
through Costa Rica, part of the continuing
efforts during the late nineteenth century to
select and dominate a route. Prepared by a
Frenchman who sought to form a company to
construct and control the route, it emphasizes
the benefits of the route to prospective investors and its potential advantages to European governments. DLC

666 Laporte, Gilbert. Reseña del desarrollo del
Banco Anglo-Costarricense a partir de su
nacionalización, 1948-1960. San José: Banco
Anglo-costarricense, 1961. 56 pp.
     A history of the operations and development
of the most important British bank in Costa
Rica, beginning with its nationalization in
the takeover of the banking system that followed the 1948 revolution. Provides narration
and statistics regarding its transactions and
facilities. BNCR

667   Lara, Gerardo, and Diego Chamorro, eds.
      *Índice alfabético y cronológico de los
      protocolos del Archivo Nacional*. 23 vols.
      San José: Imprenta Nacional, 1888-91.
          Indexes of the municipal registries and
      court archives of the various provinces of
      Costa Rica, covering the years 1851 through
      1888. Particularly useful for tracing land
      ownership, citizenship, or similar records.
      DLC

668   Láscaris Comneno, Constantino. *El
      costarricense*. San José: EDUCA, 1975. 477
      pp. Notes.
          A discussion of Costa Rican culture and its
      various aspects, considering everything from
      history and folklore to idioms and humor, with
      emphasis on idioms, speech usages, and customs
      peculiar to the nation and its interior re-
      gions. LNHT BNCR

669   _____. *Desarrollo de las ideas filosóficas
      en Costa Rica*. San José: Editorial Costa
      Rica, 1965. 631 pp. 2d ed. San José:
      Editorial Costa Rica, 1975. 512 pp. Index,
      biblio., notes.
          A history of philosophy in Costa Rica, from
      independence to the present. Consists of
      brief essays on the writings and thinking of
      each scholar who contributed to this realm,
      arranged by schools, with a bibliography of
      the works of each. Virtually all the nation's
      important thinkers are included, as are some
      from other isthmian nations. The individual
      essays are short, ranging from two to ten
      pages, including bibliography. DLC BNCR

670   Láscaris Comneno, Constantino, and Guillermo
      Malavassi Vargas. *La carreta costarricense*.
      San José: Ministerio de Cultura, Juventud y
      Deportes, 1975. 210 pp. Biblio., illus.
          A study of the Costa Rican oxcart, the
      national symbol. Discusses its evolution and
      the origins of the traditions behind its dis-
      tinctive decorations, providing details re-
      garding utility, durability, forms of
      construction, and decoration. Unfortunately,
      the photos are in black and white. Includes
      selections from poetry and other commentaries
      regarding the carts. DLC BNCR

671   Leíva Quirós, Elias. *Comentario político*.
      San José: Imprenta Gutenberg, n.d. 34 pp.
          A series of articles originally published
      in the *Diario de Costa Rica*, dealing with the
      complicated political maneuvers in 1926 when a
      section of the army attempted to prevent
      Ricardo Jiménez Oreamuno from taking office to
      succeed Cleto González Víquez. The articles
      are impassioned commentaries rather than re-
      portage, with numerous historical references.
      DLC-LDS-526 BNCR

672   _____. *Estudio sobre el desarrollo económico,
      social y político de la República de Costa
      Rica presentado al congreso científico de
      Chile*. Santiago: Imprenta "El Globo," 1909.
      57 pp.
          A glowing official account by the Costa
      Rican delegate to the Pan American Scientific
      Congress in Santiago, Chile, in 1908-9, hail-
      ing the economic progress of Costa Rica during
      the nineteenth century and offering it as an
      example of rapid growth, change, and democ-
      racy. Discusses the changes, focusing on the
      railroad and agricultural production. DLC
      DLC-LDS-46

673   León, Jorge. *Nicoya: el ambiente y la vida
      de un pueblo antiguo*. San José: Imprenta
      Nacional, 1942. 28 pp. Biblio., illus.,
      maps.
          A brief description of geography and life-
      style in the coastal region of Costa Rica,
      including discussion and diagrams of house-
      holds indicating the type of lodgings and
      their facilities. DLC DLC-LDS-928 BNCR

674   _____. *Nueva geografía de Costa Rica*. San
      José: Soley y Valverde, 1943. 174 pp. 10th
      ed. San José: Librería La Española, 1952.
      170 pp. Index, biblio., maps.
          A basic physical geography, which has
      passed through many editions, that provides
      data for the various sectors of Costa Rica as
      well as numerous maps. DLC BNCR

675   León Sánchez, José. *A la izquierda del sol*.
      Barcelona: Editorial Novaro, 1972. 214 pp.
      6th ed. San José: Editorial Costa Rica,
      1975. 239 pp.
          A collection of short stories drawn from
      the author's earlier works *La cattleya negra*
      and *Cuando canta el caracol*. DLC BNCR

676   _____. *La cattleya negra*. San José:
      Editorial Costa Rica, 1967. 123 pp.
          A collection of semi-autobiographical short
      stories in vivid prose, all dealing with the
      lives and problems of Costa Rican peasants.
      The title story is the first item the author
      ever published. DLC LNHT

677   _____. *La colina del buey*. Mexico:
      Editorial Novaro, 1972. 210 pp. Latest ed.
      San José: Editorial Costa Rica, 1977. 264
      pp. Notes.
          A novel describing the harsh life of the
      miners in the Pacific gold mines of Costa
      Rica, written in the form of the memoirs of a
      seventy-year-old ex-miner. The volume has
      gone through numerous editions, principally in
      Mexico, and reflects the author's focus on and
      sympathy for the struggles and sufferings of
      the poor. DLC BNCR

678   _____. *Cuando canta el caracol*. Guatemala:
      J.A. Núñez, 1967. 209 pp. 2d ed. San José:
      Imprenta Lehmann, 1970. 204 pp. Illus.
          A collection of short stories awarded a
      prize in a Guatemalan literary festival, deal-
      ing with Costa Rican themes and customs. BNG

679   _____. *Una guitarra para José de Jesús*. San
      José: Biblioteca Manuel I. Guerra T., 1964.
      23 pp.
          One of the author's earlier works, this
      short story, written from prison, provides a
      vivid picture of the struggles of the poor and

(León Sánchez, José)
the minor triumphs that become pivotal points in their lives. LNHT BNCR

680 ____. *La isla de los hombres solos*. San José: Privately published, 1963. Latest ed. Barcelona: Editorial Novaro, 1976.
A vivid novel of prison life in the Costa Rican penal colony of San Lucas, written while the author was incarcerated there. Includes commentary on the desperate conditions, mistreatment, despair, and other factors that affect the prisoners, narrated in emotional terms. DLC BNCR

681 ____. *José León Sánchez visto por José León Sánchez*. Mexico: Editorial Novaro, 1977. 302 pp.
Autobiographical comments and essays by a well-known Costa Rican novelist, who examines influences on his life and important phases of it in his usual vivid style. BNCR

682 ____. *La niña que vino de la luna*. San José: Editorial Zaidem, 1964. 21 pp.
One of the earlier works of this now well-known author, this short story written in prison focuses on the life of the Costa Rican peasants, its harshness and hardships, as seen by someone who comes from another world, which the author contends is the perspective of those who live in the city or in middle- or upper-class society. BNCR

683 ____. *Picahueso*. San José: Imprenta Lehmann, 1971. 206 pp.
A novel about a lone miner in the western Costa Rican mountains, his search for gold, and his efforts to mine it. Written with an understanding of the struggles involved in the contest between man and nature, as well as of the loneliness and harshness of the life of a miner. BNCR

684 ____. *El poeta, el niño y el río*. Heredia: n.p., 1964. 59 pp.
First-person accounts of childhood memories, in short-story form, written in the Heredia jail with feeling and containing vivid portrayals. One of the author's earlier works, for which he was awarded a prize. DLC LNHT

685 León Villalobos, Edwin. *Monografía del cantón de San Pablo de Heredia*. San José: Imprenta Nacional, 1971. 202 pp. Biblio., notes.
Originally a thesis presenting an effective and detailed history based on research in documentary and secondary sources, this work pays ample attention to the physical setting and the contemporary situation. BNCR

686 Liga Espiritual de Profesionales Católicos. *Costa Rica: un estado católico*. San José: Imprenta Nacional, 1955. 202 pp.
A collection of essays discussing the church-state relationship in Costa Rica, focusing particularly on article 76 of the 1949 Constitution but also referring to historical antecedents and extolling Catholic values as those fundamental to the nation.

Includes discussion of church practices regarding some political questions, advocating the position of Christian Democracy. DLC BNCR

687 Lines, Jorge A. *Libros y folletos publicados en Costa Rica durante los años 1830-1849*. San José: Universidad de Costa Rica, 1944. 151 pp. Biblio., illus.
A listing of early Costa Rican publications, with physical descriptions and some reproductions of title pages, arranged chronologically without annotation, with each entry occupying an entire page. Most of the items are governmental proclamations or religious works. No selection criteria are indicated. DLC

688 Lino Paniagua Alvarado, Rafael. *Apuntes históricos y crónicas de la ciudad de San Ramón en su centenario*. San José: Imprenta La Tribuna, 1943. 111 pp. Illus.
A history of the city of San Ramón in the province of Alajuela in Costa Rica, narrating its development and role in the nation from its founding in Colonial times to the present, with particular attention to local organizations and native sons who became prominent in the nation. BNCR

689 [Lira, Carmen, pseud.]. María Isabel Carvajal. *Los cuentos de mi Tía Panchita: cuentos populares recogidos en Costa Rica*. San José: García Mongey Cía, 1920. 160 pp. Latest ed. San José: Empresa Editora Las Américas, 1956. 210 pp. Illus.
A series of short stories constituting the last book of this well-known Costa Rican author and communist militant. It is based on regional tales and folklore, and has been compared by one literary scholar of her country to the Uncle Remus tales, in that it recounts regional lore and records oral tradition, using regional idioms to present vivid pictures of the local figure and to preserve their traditions and customs. DLC DLC-LDS-172 LNHT

690 ____. *El grano de oro y el peón*. San José: Publicaciones del Partido Comunista, n.d. 24 pp.
A brief but scathing attack on the owners of the coffee estates, portraying them as exploiters of their peons who seek to cheat all whom they come in contact with, ending with a call for the union of the workers under the banner of the Communist party; by one of the nation's leading writers of social novels portraying the hard life of the peasants. DLC-LDS-722

691 ____. *Obras completas de María Isabel Carvajal: Carmen Lyra*. San José: Editorial Patria Libre, 1972. 354 pp.
The first volume of a series designed to include all the published and unpublished works of this well-known Costa Rican novelist, political activist, and sometime communist. This volume includes two general stories, *En una silla de ruedas* and *Fantasia de Juan*

Silvestre, as well as her Historia de Costa
Rica. The latter views her nation from a
Marxist ideological perspective, and the editors of the series note that it contains numerous errors and ignores the beneficial
aspects of some of the imperialists she
condemns, but feel that it is worth reproducing for its "literary value" and to assure
that the collection of her works is complete.
BNCR

692 Lizano Fait, Eduardo. Cambio social en Costa
Rica. San José: Editorial Costa Rica, 1975.
352 pp. Notes.
A collection of essays by a Costa Rican
economist that focus on the social ramifica-
tions of national politics, agricultural development, and the Central American economic
integration movement. They place principal
emphasis on political change as a stimulant
for social change. DLC LNHT BNCR

693 _____. Comentarios sobre economía nacional.
San José: Universidad de Costa Rica, 1971.
355 pp. Biblio., notes.
A collection of articles regarding current
Costa Rican economic questions, written by a
leading economist between 1954 and 1968. Most
were previously published, either in the press
or in professional journals. All are identified as to time and place of original publication or preparation. Includes a wide range of
economic themes characteristic of this era,
ranging from Central American integration to
inflation, from agriculture to banking reform,
and from pressure groups to balance of payments. DLC BNCR

694 _____. La organización institucional de la
agricultura nacional. San José: Universidad
Nacional de Costa Rica, 1969. 80 pp. Biblio.
An analysis of the agricultural sector and
its role in the national economy, stressing
the need to augment production and promote
social stability, with proposals for implementing these objectives. DLC

695 Lizano Hernández, Victor. Leyendas de Costa
Rica. San José: Editorial Soley y Valverde,
1941. 167 pp.
A collection of Costa Rican legends and
folktales from the various regions of the
country, with identification as to source,
dates, and location, intended to preserve the
local lore and make it available for school
use. DLC DLC-LDS-879 LNHT BNCR

696 Lombardo, Heraclio A. Análisis de una
economía agrícola dentro de la meseta central
de Costa Rica. San José: Inter-American
Institute of Agricultural Sciences, 1965. 116
pp. Biblio., illus., maps, tables.
A study of the Costa Rican agricultural
economy, based on the Central Valley, followed
by general theory regarding the role of agriculture in underdeveloped nations and a discussion of alternative development plans for
the nation. Provides detailed data regarding
land tenure, crops, income, methods, and
trends during the 1950s and 1960s. LNHT BNCR

697 Loomis, Charles P., et al., eds. Turrialba:
Social Systems and the Introduction of Change.
Glencoe, Ill.: Free Press, 1953. viii, 288
pp. Notes, illus., maps, tables.
A series of essays on various aspects of
change in this Costa Rican city. Compiled by
an interdisciplinary team from the Inter-
American Institute of Agricultural Sciences in
Turrialba and from Michigan State University,
it is based on field research and surveys of a
population sample during 1948. Separate chapters deal with such themes as social status,
small and large landholdings, communications,
ecology, demography, religion, education, and
agricultural extension systems. DLC LNHT
BNCR

698 López, Jacinto. La caída del gobierno
constitucional en Costa Rica: el golpe de
estado del 27 de enero de 1917. New York:
Laisne & Carranza, 1919.
A critical account of the 1917 coup that
brought Federico Tinoco to power, ousting
Alfredo González Flores.

699 López Guzmán, Leyla. Estudio monográfico del
cantón de Atenas. San José: Imprenta
Lehmann, 1968. 67 pp. Biblio., illus.
A history of a town in the Central Valley
of Costa Rica in the province of Alajuela,
founded in 1868. Includes an historical
résumé, a current description, and essays
regarding its leading citizens. BNCR

700 Lundberg, Donald E. Adventure in Costa Rica.
Tallahassee, Fla.: Dixie Publishers, 1960.
238 pp. Index, biblio., illus., maps.
Costa Rica. San José: Juan Mora, 1968. 224
pp. Biblio., illus., maps.
A basic travelogue designed to encourage
tourism, but including discussion of such
factors as culture shock, differences in customs, living, and food in addition to the
standard information about facilities, economy, and trade. Written with an understanding
of the country and of Yankee attitudes, and
designed to alleviate the difficulties Yankees
sometimes encounter abroad by indicating the
customs and identifying the attitudes that
cause them. Data in the more recent Spanish
edition has been updated. DLC LNHT BNCR

701 Lynch, David. Tariff Policy in Costa Rica.
San José: Ministerio de Hacienda, 1951. 68
pp. Tables.
A brief examination of present Costa Rican
tariff policy by a consultant appointed by the
U.S. State Department, with specific recommen-
dations for changes designed to strengthen the
Costa Rican trade and economy and facilitate
linkages with new Yankee tariff structures.
DLC

702 Maccio, Guillermo A. Costa Rica:
proyecciones de población por sexos y grupos y
edad, 1950-1978. Santiago: CELADE, 1968.
ii, 48 pp.
Population projections, based on the 1950
census, seeking to show the consequences by
1978 of continued growth, and hence facilitate

planning to meet the social, economic, and educational needs of the larger population. BNCR

703 MacDonald, Mary B., and Dwight H. McLaughlin. <u>Vida y obras de autores de Costa Rica</u>. Havana: Editorial Alfa, 1941. 99 pp.

A list Though part of a Cuban series on authors of the various Latin American countries, this particular volume dealing with Costa Rica was prepared by a pair of schoolteachers from Minneapolis. It offers brief biographies of various Costa Rican authors, with a list of their books and articles. There is no explanation of the selection criteria or the arrangement, though most of the writers were born during the late nineteenth century and published during the years 1900 through 1935. DLC LNHT BNCR

704 Madrigal G., Rodolfo. <u>Geología del mapa casico "Barranca," Costa Rica</u>. San José: Universidad de Costa Rica, 1970. 55 pp. Biblio.

A geographical survey of Costa Rica, employing photo analysis to provide a basic description of its regions and geological formations. BNCR

705 Madrigal J., Abraham. <u>El general Próspero Fernández</u>. San José: Imprenta Alsina, 1904. 21 pp.

A brief essay defending the actions of General Próspero Fernández and noting the controversy surrounding his regime, during which the archbishop of Costa Rica, Bernardo Thiel, and the Jesuits were expelled from the nation by the Liberal government. The account is dispassionate, though clearly supporting Fernández. DLC DLC-LDS-23

706 Madriz, Federico. <u>El desastre de Costa Rica</u>. San José: Imprenta Falcó y Borrasé, 1917. 16 pp.

The author's view of the social ills of the nation, which he blames on corrupt politics and a lack of effort to promote intellectual development. DLC-LDS-149

707 Malavassi Vargas, Guillermo, ed. <u>Los principios cristianos de justicia social y la realidad histórica de Costa Rica</u>. San José: Imprenta Trejos, 1977. 345 pp. Illus.

A collection of church documents, ranging from papal encyclicals to pastoral messages of Costa Rican bishops, regarding the question of social justice, accompanied by some of the speeches and legislation of Rafael Calderón Guardia, whose administration professed to be responding to the Costa Rican situation by applying this doctrine. BNCR

708 Mallagaray. <u>Marxista pero . . . ¡Cristiano!</u> San José: Imprenta Lehmann, 1973. 167 pp.

A series of radio talks by a well-known Costa Rican radio commentator denouncing communism, with other similar pronouncements. Reflects the internal political and ideological confrontation in that nation, though the terms are general rather than specific to the nation. BNCR

709 Maluquer y Salvador, José. <u>República de Costa Rica: notas bibliográficas</u>. Madrid: Imprenta de la Revista de Legislación, 1888. 30 pp.

A brief paper prepared for a bibliographic conference by the consul of the Costa Rican legation in Spain, providing brief commentaries, in paragraph form, on the state of the library and on contemporary writers. Lists government and general publications, providing title, author, city, and date, and a single-sentence indication of focus or contents. DLC-LDS-695

710 Marín Cañas, José. <u>Los bígardos del ron: cuentos</u>. San José: Imprenta Borrasé, 1929. 177 pp.

A collection of short stories by this well-known writer, all stressing the problems of life among the lower classes of his native land. NcU

711 _____. <u>Coto: la guerra del 21 con Panamá</u>. San José: La Hora, 1934. 3d ed. San José: Editorial Costa Rica, 1976. 105 pp.

A novel based on and critical of the Costa Rican-Panamanian frontier conflict over the Coto district in 1921. The author notes that no one questioned such activities then as it was a heroic and infantile era. Returns to the theme employed in some of his earlier and better-known works, emphasizing the horrors of war and its effect on the individuals caught in it. DLC DLC-LDS-780 BNCR

712 _____. <u>Julio Sánchez</u>. San José: Ministerio de Cultura, Juventud y Deportes, 1972. 103 pp. Illus.

A brief biography of a Costa Rican "coffee king" and hacienda owner, discussing his contributions to the national economy and his efforts to promote the growth of coffee cultivation in the nation during the first half of the twentieth century. Includes descriptions and photos of his estate in Heredia. BNCR

713 _____. <u>Pedro Arnáez</u>. San José: Imprenta Trejos, 1942. 4th ed. San José: Editorial Costa Rica, 1977. 215 pp.

A novel set in 1914 and focusing on the world war, the decline of civilization it represented, and its impact on the Costa Rican peasants. DLC LNHT BNCR

714 Marsden, Howard J. <u>Preliminary Survey: The Port of Limón, the Port of Puntarenas</u>. Washington, D.C.: U.S. Department of Commerce, 1952. 28 pp. Illus., maps.

A brief technical survey of the port facilities of Costa Rica's principal ports, by the U.S. technician under the Point-Four Program. Includes recommendations for construction of additional facilities and improvements, especially to eliminate customs delays. BNCR

715 Martén, Alberto. <u>El comunismo vencido</u>. San José: Imprenta Borrasé, 1952. 30 pp.

Part of the Costa Rican political confrontation of the late 1940s and early 1950s, this
volume denounces communism and particularly
its propaganda efforts in that nation, providing figures on alleged subsidies to propaganda
publications within Costa Rica. BNCR

716 Martín Carranza, Ernesto. Refutación del
comunismo. San José: Imprenta Soley y
Valverde, 1947. 24 pp.
A Costa Rican intellectual's denunciation
of communism, reflecting that nation's political crisis of the late 1940s in which the
role of the communists in the future of the
nation played a part. The terms are general
and do not refer directly to Costa Rica. BNCR

717 Martín Carranza, Ernesto, and Stuart H.
Benton. Latin American Commercial Law: Cuba,
Mexico, Costa Rica. New York: Latin American
Adviser, 1926. 256 pp.
The full text and English translation of
selected articles of Costa Rica's commercial
code and legislation regulating trade and
investment in that nation, clearly designed to
encourage trade and investment from the United
States. DLC

718 Martínez, Fernando. El presidente Cortés a
través de su correspondencia: apuntes
biográficos y discursos. San José: Imprenta
Lehmann, 1939. 213 pp.
A collection of speeches by the president
of Costa Rica from 1940 to 1944, preceded by a
brief biographical sketch and several contemporary commentaries. Includes some anecdotes
designed to illustrate his humor, and a summary of the actions of his administration.
DLC DLC-LDS-845 LNHT BNCR

719 Martínez, Juan P. Costa Rica en sus hombres
notables. San José: Librería Española, 1908.
Pages unnumbered.
A series of single-page essays extolling
the work of various figures of Costa Rican
politics in the nineteenth and twentieth centuries. The commentaries are emotional and
seek to portray the individual and his dynamism and character rather than describe his
career. No selection criteria are indicated
and the arrangement is random. DLC-LDS-548

720 Martínez, Modesto. Héroes de campo: escena y
paisajes de la vida rural de Costa Rica. San
José: Talleres Gráficos de La Tribuna, 1929.
236 pp.
A series of short stories focusing on the
rural peasants of Costa Rica and discussing
everyday occurrences in their lives. Written
during the 1920s and originally published in
various newspapers, they were designed to
preserve local and regional traditions and to
focus interest on the importance of the peasants in the nation and its economy. DLC-LDS-
461 LNHT BNCR

721 Masferrer, Alberto. En Costa Rica. N.p.,
n.d. 55 pp.
A Salvadoran social commentator's views of
Costa Rica, focusing on its people, economy,
and social conditions as he observed them,

inevitably with some emphasis on the differences with other parts of Costa Rica. He
comments on the trend toward concentration of
land ownership, the lightness of the Indian's
skin, the European nature of the society, the
agricultural organization, and many other
subjects. The selections are not dated. DLC
DLC-LDS-151

722 Mata Gamboa, Jesús. Historias de Cartago.
San José: Imprenta Moderna, 1970. 301 pp.
Illus.
A series of articles dealing with events in
the history of the city of Cartago in the
nineteenth and twentieth centuries. The focus
is on the religious institutions of the community and the role of the local priests,
though other themes are also included. Lavishly illustrated. BNCR

723 ____. Monografía de Cartago. Cartago:
Imprenta El Heraldo, 1930. 631 pp. Illus.
A series of articles and essays, originally
published in the Costa Rican press, describing
various incidents and significant individuals
in the history of the city of Cartago, from
Colonial times to the present. Includes considerations of significant institutions, such
as schools and hospitals, as well as historical events and all the leading citizens. DLC
LNHT BNCR

724 Mata Oreamuno, Alberto, ed. Ramillete de
recuerdos a la grata memoria del doctor don
Rafael Ángel Calderón Guardia en la
aniversaria de su sentida muerte. San José:
n.p., 1971. 174 pp. Illus.
Brief commentaries about the career of the
Costa Rican president, reproduced from the San
José press on the anniversary of his death.
BNCR

725 May, Stacey, et al. Costa Rica: A Study in
Economic Development. New York: Twentieth
Century Fund, 1952. 374 pp. Biblio., maps,
tables.
A detailed survey of the current state of
Costa Rica, focusing on its economy and detailing its situation, facilities, needs,
prospects, and resources, with extensive statistics and tables. Includes specific recommendations for future economic policy,
stressing the promotion and diversification of
agricultural production, and recommendations
for United States aid patterns. The volume
was written as part of a series designed to
provide aid recommendations and examine the
impact of previous efforts. DLC LNHT

726 Meagher, Thomas Francis. Vacaciones en Costa
Rica. San José: Imprenta Trejos, 1923. xii,
138 pp. Notes, illus.
A travel account, originally published in
Harper's New Monthly Magazine in 1859 and
1860, recounting the travels of an Irishman
during the 1850s in Costa Rica. The account
is rich in description of travel conditions,
people, cities and villages, scenery, and
customs, with some background information.
DLC DLC-LDS BNCR

727 Meléndez Chaverri, Carlos, ed. Carl Hoffmann: viajes por Costa Rica. San José: Ministerio de Cultura, Juventud y Deportes, 1976. 217 pp. Notes, illus.
    A brief biography of a German physician and surgeon who emigrated to Costa Rica in 1854 and lived there for five years, followed by excerpts from the chronicles of his trips throughout the country to collect scientific data regarding botanical species, which he published in Europe, helping to encourage knowledge of Costa Rica there. He also served as a physician during the military campaigns against the forces of William Walker. DLC LNHT BNCR

728 _____. Cincuentenario de la letra del himno nacional de Costa Rica, 15 de septiembre, 1903-1953. San José: Ministerio de Educación Pública, 1953. 90 pp. Illus. 2d ed. San José: Imprenta Nacional, 1954. 90 pp. Illus.
    A series of essays and commentaries on the origins of the Costa Rican national anthem; biographies and commentaries on the life of its author, José María Zeledón B.; and commentaries on the contest held in 1903 to pick the words for the anthem, which resulted in the selection of his entry. Published in commemoration of the fiftieth anniversary of the event. DLC LNHT BNCR

729 Meléndez Chaverri, Carlos. Costa Rica: evolución histórica de sus problemas más destacados: ¿A donde vamos? San José: Imprenta Atenea, 1953. 85 pp. Biblio., illus.
    A brief pamphlet intended as a guide to the National Museum's exhibits. Discusses the history of agriculture and social evolution in Costa Rica, focusing principally on the Indian and Colonial eras but tracing the trends to the present. Points to the increased significance of agriculture and diversity, and the ethnic unification of the nation. Contains photos of the exhibits. LNHT

730 _____. D. Rafael Moya M.: esbozo de su biografía. San José: Imprenta Nacional, 1964. 29 pp.
    A brief biographical sketch of the prominent landowner and political figure of the first half of the nineteenth century who is characterized as representative of his generation; based on appropriate documentation. DLC BNCR

731 _____, ed. Documentos fundamentales del siglo XIX. San José: Editorial Costa Rica, 1978.
    A collection of important documents in the nation's development, focusing on the independence era. BNCR

732 Meléndez Chaverri, Carlos. Dr. José María Montealegre: contribución al estudio de un hombre y una época poco conocida de nuestra historia. San José: Academia de Geografía e Historia de Costa Rica, 1968. 207 pp. Biblio., notes, illus., maps, tables.
    A detailed biography of a physician who played a key role in the Costa Rican political maneuvers of 1858-60 when Juan Rafael Mora was overthrown, and who served as president from 1861 to 1863, carefully tracing the era and his participation and following his career through various governmental posts. In the process, it clarifies the political maneuvers and coups of this period. DLC LNHT BNCR

733 _____, ed. Heredia: ayer, hoy y siempre. Heredia: n.p., 1963. Pages not consecutively numbered. Biblio., illus., maps.
    A compilation of material about the history of the province of Heredia, prepared by a professional historian in honor of the bicentennial of Cubujuquí. Includes information about geography and agricultural regions in addition to the history, which focuses on the Colonial period but continues beyond. Also contains data regarding the region in the nation's literature, with excerpts. BNCR

734 Meléndez Chaverri, Carlos. Un héroe olvidado: don Luís Pacheco Bertoa; apuntes sobre su vida y notas sobre su acto heroico del 11 de abril de 1856. San José: Imprenta Tormo, 1958. 16 pp. Biblio., illus.
    A brief account of the exploits of another of the heroes of the war against Walker about whom little is known. TxU

735 _____. Historia de Costa Rica. San José: Editorial Universidad Estatal a Distancia, 1979. 174 pp. Index, biblio., maps, tables.
    A succinct overview of Costa Rican development to the present, designed as a text, with about half the volume covering the era from independence to 1978. In true educationist fashion it includes suggested readings, objectives and review questions. The focus is on social and economic aspects, though the political and cultural trends are treated in brief. BNCR

736 _____, ed. Homenaje al Lic. don Julio Acosta García. San José: Academia de Geografía e Historia de Costa Rica, 1972. 69 pp. Illus.
    A collection of writings about and speeches and writings by a Costa Rican figure whose political career spans four decades of the twentieth century and included service as president during the 1920s, published on the occasion of the centennial of his birth. Includes an essay hailing his contributions to the nation and a chronology of his posts and awards. BNCR

737 Meléndez Chaverri, Carlos. Juan Santamaría. San José: Imprenta Nacional, 1956.
    A brief sketch of the Costa Rican hero of the campaigns against William Walker. Written by a professional historian, it provides a more balanced and detailed account than some, though it still reflects the patriotism that Santamaría inspired. BNCR

738 _____, ed. Legislación indigenista de Costa Rica. Mexico: Instituto Indigenista Interamericano, 1957. 50 pp.

(Meléndez Chaverri, Carlos)
A collection of laws and decrees relating to the treatment of the Indians in Costa Rica, covering the nineteenth century. LNHT

739 _____. Viajeros por Guanacaste. San José: Ministerio de Cultura, Juventud y Deportes, 1974. 557 pp. Notes, maps.
A collection of descriptions of the Guanacaste region on the Pacific coast of Costa Rica, taken from various travel accounts written between 1523 and 1935. Includes excerpts from many of the well-known travel accounts of the region, as well as from more obscure studies. The selections serve to indicate the change in and development of the region. DLC BNCR

740 Meléndez Chaverri, Carlos, and Quince Duncan, eds. El negro en Costa Rica: antología. San José: Editorial Costa Rica, 1972. 281 pp. Index, biblio., illus. 3d ed. San José: Editorial Costa Rica, 1976. 258 pp. Index, biblio., illus.
A collection of commentaries on the role of the black population in Costa Rica and its image in the nation. The most valuable portions are the editors' introductory essays tracing the history of the nation's black population and its contributions. The anthology itself, which occupies about half the volume, consists of a number of commentaries and essays dealing with various aspects of these themes, including biographical sketches of significant figures and some bibliographical commentaries, as well as journalistic articles from various eras. DLC BNCR

741 Meléndez Chaverri, Carlos, and José Hilario Villalobos. Gregorio José Ramírez. San José: Ministerio de Cultura, Juventud y Deportes, 1973. 242 pp. Biblio., notes, illus., maps, tables, appendixes.
An account of the life of one of the figures of the Costa Rican independence movement who, after serving as an envoy and in the Spanish coast guard, distinguished himself in commanding the independence forces against resistance from the province of Cartago, and later served briefly as governor of Cartago. The volume is based on primary and secondary sources, has a documentary appendix, and includes passages setting the stage by describing the state of Costa Rica at the time of independence and the various phases of that movement. DLC BNCR

742 Meléndez Ibarra, José. La columna liniera. San José: Ediciones Revolución, 1969. 85 pp.
A brief discussion of events leading to the 1948 Costa Rican revolution. Stresses the earlier struggles for social legislation, and particularly the role of the workers on the banana plantations, as preliminaries to the later National Liberation Movement. LNHT BNCR

743 Menton, Seymour, ed. El cuento costarricense: estudio, antología y bibliografía. Mexico: Antologías Stadium, 1964. 184 pp. Biblio.

An anthology of Costa Rican short-story writers. The critical introduction classifying the various writers, schools, and generations is more valuable than the anthology because it presents an overview of the development of this important art form, which was predominant in the nation until very recently. The study covers the late nineteenth and twentieth centuries, with particular focus on the latter. Includes a comprehensive bibliography of the Costa Rican short story. DLC BNCR

744 Merlos, Salvador, R. La poesía en Costa Rica. San Salvador: Imprenta Nacional, n.d. [1916]. 66 pp.
A brief overview of Costa Rican poetry and its principal poets. Classifies the poets, praises their writing, notes their public careers, and prints excerpts from their works. Includes discussion of many poets, but the major focus is on Pío Víquez, Aquileo J. Echeverría, Lisímaco Chavarría, and Rafael Cardona. DLC DLC-LDS-146

745 Merz, Karl Franz. Algunos aspectos de la crisis fiscal y económica de Costa Rica: estudio estadístico--analítico respecto a su origen y sus efectos. Panamá: Tipografía "La Moderna," 1938. 59 pp. Tables.
A brief summary of the financial problems of Costa Rica during the 1930s, reflecting the worldwide depression and the unsound programs of the 1920s; by a well-known economist of that era, replete with statistics. DLC

746 _____. El comercio internacional de la República de Costa Rica: estudio analítico de la estadística comercial. San José: Imprenta Nacional, 1929. 125 pp. Illus., tables.
A comprehensive study of Costa Rican exports and imports, covering the years 1924-28, with extensive statistics and some comparison to other Central American nations. A valuable collection of data regarding commerce in the 1920s that serves to indicate the trends of the period. DLC BNCR

747 _____, ed. Compendio estadístico, demografía, comercio internacional y finanzas de la República de Costa Rica. San José: Imprenta Nacional, 1932. 50 pp. Tables.
A statistical collection focusing on the years 1927-31, that is, those of the regime of Ricardo Jiménez Oreamuno, but including some figures that go back to 1907 for comparative purposes. Includes figures on population, births and deaths, production, trade, etc. DLC-LDS-699

748 Merz, Karl Franz. Finanzhaushalt, Produktion und Handel der Republik Costa Rica. San José: C. Federspiel, 1928. 102 pp. Tables.
A detailed economic summary of trends in Costa Rica during the mid-1920s, focusing on the years 1924-27, though with some statistics that extend further back. Provides product-by-product figures for production and export. Includes data regarding the quality and value of each crop, export details by country, percentage figures covering the years 1913

(Merz, Karl Franz)
    through 1927, and specifics of railroad con-
    struction. Clearly seeks to provide German
    readers with details that will heighten their
    interest in trade and investment. DLC DLC-
    LDS-419 LNHT

749   _____. Las relaciones mutuas entre los
    ingresos generales y las entradas de aduana de
    la República de Costa Rica. San José:
    Imprenta Alsina, 1930. 26 pp. Tables.
        A study of tariff and tax revenues in Costa
    Rica, pointing out the close relationship
    between them due to a tax structure in which
    import and export taxes constitute 65% of
    government revenue. Examines various poten-
    tial changes in tariffs and export taxes and
    notes the impact of the new systems dealing
    with value or weight that were then being
    advocated in other parts of the world. Orig-
    inally prepared for the Ministry of Hacienda
    by the director of statistics for the customs
    service. DLC

750   _____. Ricardo Jiménez el economista. San
    José: Imprenta La Tribuna, 1946. 90 pp.
    Illus.
        A discussion of the Costa Rican economy
    during the era of Ricardo Jiménez and the
    effect of his policies on his nation's devel-
    opment. Emphasizes that he focused his ef-
    forts on agriculture in the countryside;
    praises his efforts to stress education and
    maintain political calm, which aided the
    economy. BNCR

751   México/Costa Rica: pueblos hermanos. N.p.,
    n.d. 171 pp. Illus.
        A lavishly illustrated commemorative volume
    regarding the meeting in Mérida, Mexico, of
    presidents Figuerres and Echeverría in 1971.
    Prints the texts of their various speeches and
    press conferences, and photos of the various
    activities. BNCR

752   Michaud, Madame. Cuentos de Madame Michaud.
    San José: Imprenta Gutenberg, n.d. 128 pp.
    Illus.
        A foreigner's view of Costa Rica, presented
    as short stories rather than memoirs, but
    recounting with lavish description the various
    events she witnessed and places she visited.
    DLC

753   Miranao, Juan. Un pensamiento y una idea.
    Heredia: Tipografía Herediana, 1900. 36 pp.
        A pamphlet suggesting that Costa Rica would
    be better off if it were annexed to the United
    States: it would have all the material bene-
    fits of the Northern Colossus, and furthermore
    would not have to worry about dictatorships,
    since neither Texas nor California will ever
    again be ruled by Latin despots. BNCR

754   Molina, Felipe. A Brief Sketch of the Repub-
    lic of Costa Rica. London: P.P. Thomas,
    1849. 15 pp. Maps.
    Bosquejo de la República de Costa Rica seguido
    de apuntamientos por su historia. Madrid:
    Imprenta de la Viuda de Calero, 1850. 44 pp.

Maps, tables. 2d ed. New York: S.W.
Benedict, 1851. 128 pp. Index, maps, tables.
Coup d'oeil rapide sur la République de Costa
Rica. Paris: Imprimerie D'aubusson, 1850.
33 pp. Maps, tables.
Die Republik Costa Rica in Central Amerika.
Hamburg: R. Kittler, 1849. 30 pp. Maps,
tables.
    A brief historical sketch of the nation,
followed by a descriptive account arranged by
topics such as rivers, lakes, climate, imports, exports, etc., usually treated in a
single page. DLC DLC-LDS-65 LNHT BNCR

755   _____. Der Freistaat Costa Rica in Mittel
Amerika, und seine Wichtigkeit für den
Welthandel, den Ackerbau und die Kolonisation.
Berlin: G. Hempel, 1850. xiv, 87 pp. Map.
    A brief discussion of geography and cli-
mate, followed by a discussion of colonization
in Costa Rica and its suitability as a site
for immigrants; clearly designed to encourage
German immigration to that nation. DLC LNHT
BNCR

756   Moncado G., Arturo. Historia de San Ramón.
San José: Tipografía de San José, 1917.
25 pp.
    A brief account of the founding of San
Ramón in 1844 by settlers from nearby
Alajuela, with an account of its growth and
development. Includes reproductions of documents and decrees from the National Archives.
Concludes with a brief description of contemporary San Ramón. DLC-LDS-146

757   Monge, Luís Alberto. Somos un partido joven.
San José: Ediciones Victoria Liberacionista,
1969. 20 pp.
    TxU

758   Monge Alfaro, Carlos. La educación superior
en Costa Rica. San José: Oficina de
Planificación de la Educación Superior, 1975.
152 pp. Tables.
    An educational scholar's history of higher
education in Costa Rica, focused on the University of Costa Rica but including other
institutions. Considers changes in curriculum, growth of programs offered, and the expansion of the student population and its
relationship to general population growth.
Originally prepared as a background study for
the council that designed the five-year plan
for the national higher education policy.
BNCR

759   _____. Historia de Costa Rica. San José:
Talleres Tipográficos, 1947. 211 pp. 14th
ed. San José: Trejos Hermanos, 1976. 313
pp. Notes, illus.
    Though intended as a text, this volume by a
well-known Costa Rican scholar provides a
useful overview of the nation, including its
geography, economic and social development,
and politics. Covering the span from discovery to 1970, its brief essays include basic
data on each of the nation's regimes with some
documentary excerpts, as well as sufficient

(Monge Alfaro, Carlos)
　　narration to link the eras and indicate the
　　general trends. DLC LNHT BNCR

760 　　____. Manual del guía de turistas:
República de Costa Rica. San José:
Secretaría de Integración Turística
Centroamericana, 1972. 226 pp. Biblio.,
illus.
　　Designed for tour guides, this work provides an indication of the official view of
what they should know and the viewpoints the
government hopes they will promote, as well as
basic data regarding places to go, stay, and
see, and transport facilities. The background
provided on each event and location provides
insights into the nation's history. DLC

761 　　____. Nuestra historia y los seguros. San
José: Editorial Costa Rica, 1974. 542 pp.
Biblio., notes.
　　A history of the Costa Rican national insurance institute on the occasion of its fiftieth anniversary, based on detailed research
in its records and the Costa Rican press, as
well as appropriate legislation. Includes
consideration of the various types of insurance offered by the institute and their evolution, and of the political effects of the
various eras on its efforts. Emphasis is
placed on its internal development and on the
impulse provided by various political leaders.
Contains extensive quotations from the pertinent legislation, and considers the institution's role in the nation's development. BNCR

762 Monseñor Stork ante la historia. San José:
Imprenta Lehmann, 1930. 67 pp. Illus.
　　A collection of speeches and the public
acts of the dedication of the monument to the
third archbishop of Costa Rica, Juan G. Stork,
who served from 1904 through 1920. Includes
several accounts of his career and his pastoral work. DLC-LDS-503

763 Montero Barrantes, Francisco. Apuntamientos
sobre la provincia de Guanacaste en la
República de Costa Rica. San José:
Tipografía Nacional, 1891. 38 pp.
　　A physical description of the then-current
situation of this Costa Rican coastal province, including geography, population, and
data regarding facilities. DLC DLC-LDS-44
LNHT BNCR

764 　　____. Campaña nacional. San José:
Academia Costarricense de la Historia, 1955.
60 pp. Illus.
　　A brief narration of the overall era of the
Walker intervention and the campaign against
him, with emphasis on the Costa Rican role,
covering the years 1856-57. The résumé is
reprinted from the author's Elementos de
historia de Costa Rica. DLC LNHT

765 　　____. Elementos de historia de Costa Rica.
2 vols. Tipografía Nacional, 1892-94. 349,
320 pp. 2d ed. San José: Imprenta Nacional,
1922.

　　This work, which constitutes one of the
earliest attempts to provide a domestic syn-
thesis of Costa Rican history, was written in
response to legislation requiring the teaching
of the nation's history in the elementary
schools and designed for use by the nation's
teachers. Volume 1 covers the period from
discovery through 1856, and volume 2 from 1856
through 1890. The work consists of a detailed
narration, with liberal quotations from documents, laws, and official reports. The Colonial era is treated briefly, with the focus on
the nineteenth century, particularly its political events. DLC DLC-LDS-28 BNCR

766 　　____. Geografía de Costa Rica. San José:
Imprenta Nacional, 1886. 50 pp. 4th ed.
Barcelona: Tipografía de José Cunill Sala,
1892. 350 pp. Maps.
　　A detailed description of the different
portions and regions of Costa Rica, prepared
under official auspices by a well-known geographer for use at the Universal Exposition in
Chicago and the American Historical Exposition
in Madrid, and hence designed to provide Europeans and Americans with basic information
about the republic, its physical setting,
economy, people, and political system. Emphasizes physical features and description, with
enough detail to provide a valuable indication
of the state of the nation at the turn of the
century and also to indicate what the government wished to stress. DLC DLC-LDS-91 LNHT
BNCR

767 Montero Umaña, Lilia. Resumen de la
legislación tributaria costarricense, 1900-
1970. San José: Universidad de Costa Rica,
1972. 572 pp. Tables.
　　A compilation of brief descriptions of tax
laws of Costa Rica from 1900 through 1970,
with most of the statistics pertaining to the
post-1950 era. The volume consists of brief
résumés, usually one or two pages, of each
statute, with its date and basic provisions,
some with tables indicating the revenue realized from it since 1950. Taxes are arranged
by type, with all the income taxes or all the
coffee taxes considered together, chronologically. BNCR

768 Montero Vega, Arturo. Poemas de la
revolución. San José: Ediciones Revolución,
1969. 60 pp.
　　A collection of brief poems evoking the
emotion of the Costa Rican revolutionaries of
1948, acclaiming their ideals and struggles
and indicating the conditions against which
they fought. MU

769 Montes de Oca Ramírez, Faustino. Para la
historia. San José: Tipografía El Diario,
1898. 15 pp.
　　A brief account of the author's experiences
during and condemnation of the 1898 coup by
Rafael Iglesias. DLC DLC-LDS-123

770 Mora, Federico. Colección de artículos
publicados en "La República" en el debate

sobre la industria cafetera. San José: Tipografía Nacional, 1910. 57 pp.

A collection of articles that originally appeared in La República, dealing with the future of coffee culture in Costa Rica and responding to questions raised in an earlier series by Pedro Pérez Zeledón. The debate produced a detailed consideration of the future of coffee in that nation and its implications for the national economy. DLC-LDS-50 BNCR

771 Mora, Nini de. En pos de un gobierno eclesiástico y la estructuración fiscal, 1824-1825. San José: Universidad de Costa Rica, 1970. 95 pp. Biblio., notes, appendixes.

A study of the problems of independence, including discussions of the church and its governance, the mines and their operation, and other institutions; based on documentary research and accompanied by reproductions of documents from the era. BNCR

772 _____. Manifestaciones de progreso, 1824-1825. San José: Universidad de Costa Rica, 1970. 117 pp. Biblio., notes, appendixes.

A description and analysis of Costa Rica at independence, including considerations of commerce and economy, land tenure, agriculture, the press, and the annexation of Nicoya; based on documentary research and appropriate secondary sources, with a collection of appended documents from the era. DLC LNHT BNCR

773 _____. Obra de Juan Mora Fernández y alcances de la tertulia patriótica, 1824-1825. San José: Universidad de Costa Rica, 1970. 155 pp. Biblio., appendix.

An essay on the independence period, hailing the actions of the chief of the Costa Rican state within the Federation and his efforts to establish freedom and liberty in the province. Based on documentary research and appropriate secondary sources, with an appendix of documents from the period. LNHT BNCR

774 Mora Barrantes, Carlos. Cantón de Tarrazú en su centenario. San José: Imprenta Metropolitana, 1968. 124 pp. Biblio., illus.

A description of the town and its present facilities, combined with a brief account of its history and essays regarding its leading citizens. BNCR

775 Mora Valenzuela, Arturo. La marcha del hombre hacia su meta social: problemas sociales de la democracia, Estados Unidos de América defensores de los derechos humanos. Many editions. Guatemala: Ministerio de Educación Pública, 1955. 181 pp.

A Costa Rican writer discusses the issue of human rights, contending that it is the most important in the world and placing it in the context of the Cold War, condemning communism and endorsing the West and the Yankees as the defenders of human rights. DLC LNHT BNG

776 Mora Valverde, Manuel. Crisis y revolución. San José: Imprenta Elena, 1963. 52 pp.

A call for socialism in Costa Rica by a socialist leader of that country, condemning the sins of imperialism and arguing that only socialism can save the nation and promote its development. BNCR

777 _____. Dos discursos en defensa de Vanguardia Popular. San José: n.p., 1959. 62 pp.

The leader of the Costa Rican Vanguardia Popular (Socialist) party defends his party's stance in two radio addresses during early 1958. Replying to speeches by José Figueres and Otilio Ulate, he provides his view of Costa Rican politics and the solutions offered by socialism. BNCR

778 _____. Nuestra soberanía frente al Departamento de Estado. San José: n.p., 1940. 136 pp.

A series of articles originally published in the Costa Rican press by the leader of that nation's Socialist party, constituting a ringing denunciation of the sins of the imperialists, focusing particularly on the confrontation with the Mexican government of Lázaro Cárdenas and condemning pressure on the Calderón Guardia government of Costa Rica, and referring to previous military interventions in Central America. BNCR

779 _____. Por la afirmación de nuestra democracia: por el progreso y de nuestra nación. San José: Comité Central del Partido Comunista, 1939. 24 pp.

A speech by Manuel Mora Valverde, the secretary-general of the Costa Rican Communist party, defining the party position and platform, calling for drastic reforms to benefit the proletariat, and stressing that the party was nationalist in outlook. DLC

780 Muñoz Fonseca, Enrique. El seguro social: su desarrollo en Costa Rica. San José: Imprenta Trejos, 1944. 129 pp.

An account of the origins of the Costa Rican social security law, with detailed discussions of its provisions and the available benefits. DLC

781 Muñoz Q., Hugo Alfonso. La Asamblea Legislativa en Costa Rica. San José: Editorial Costa Rica, 1977. 305 pp. Biblio., notes.

A theoretical political science analysis of the Costa Rican Legislative Assembly, examining its organization, functioning, place in the political system, etc., and suggesting improvements in its organization and operation. Written by a Costa Rican professor, it considers all aspects of the Congress, the functions of majority and minority, elections, powers, and relation to other governmental entities, focusing on the contemporary era. DLC BNCR

782 Murchie, Anita Gregorio. Imported Spices: A Study of Anglo-American Settlers in Costa Rica, 1821-1900. San José: Ministerio de Cultura, 1980. 344 pp. Biblio., illus., tables.

An account of the Yankee, Canadian, and
British settlers in Costa Rica, based on interviews with descendants and archival research. Written in the form of a series of
letters by a ficticious settler, it describes
meetings and interviews with the subjects.
While the theme is historical, the methods are
anthropological and the vivid prose is almost
akin to that of a novel. This combination is
used to focus on a small number of residents
and through them illuminate the contributions
of the entire colony to the development of the
nation, its traditions, and culture. The
author, an anthropologist, is the wife of a
U.S. Foreign Service officer and has resided
in Costa Rica for several years. BNCR

783 Naranjo Cote, Carmen. _Camino al mediodía_.
San José: Imprenta Lehmann, 1968. 69 pp.
    A member of the new generation of Costa
Rican writers provides another view of the
difficulties of modern society, the stifling
nature of its structure, and its effects on
human lives. He seeks to show that the norms
imposed by modern society frustrate the individual and change his behavior. DLC LNHT
BNCR

784 _____. _Diario de una multitud_. San José:
EDUCA, 1974. 297 pp.
    By one of Costa Rica's best-known contempo-
rary novelists, this work reflects the trend
in fiction toward themes of social consciousness. It focuses on the lives of the poor,
depicting a society composed of classes of
exploiters and exploited that is caught up in
and in effect held prisoner by technology and
mechanization, to the point that all are un-
happy and unable to change their lives. The
emphasis is on the cruel realities of life,
the dominance of machines and systems over
human needs and emotions, and on the growing
feeling of helplessness. DLC LNHT BNCR

785 _____. _Hoy es un largo día_. San José:
Editorial Costa Rica, 1974. 123 pp.
    A collection of short stories focusing on
the problems of lower- and middle-class life,
particularly in the city, and the prevalence
of the norms imposed by modern society, with
its machines, complications, dislocations, and
emphasis on punctuality, which clash with
basic human predilections and needs. DLC
BNCR

786 _____. _Memorias de un hombre palabra_. San
José: Editorial Costa Rica, 1968. 172 pp.
    Reflecting the author's focus on the sti-
fling nature of modern society and bureaucracy, this novel, written in the form of an
autobiography, describes the life of a faceless middle-class bureaucrat who, though troubled by the directions of modern society and
constantly trying to change them, fails just
as consistently in his efforts. He continues
to be a small cog in the bureaucracy, trapped
in its vast structure and his own mediocrity
and unable to promote change in its impact on
people's lives despite his ability to identify
the problems. DLC BNCR

787 _____. _Los perros no ladraron_. San José:
Editorial Costa Rica, 1966. 457 pp. 2d ed.
San José: Editorial Costa Rica, 1974.
208 pp.
    A prize-winning novel focusing on the mid-
dle class and its frustrations with the structure of modern society, emphasizing the
bureaucracy and its foibles. LNHT BNCR

788 _____. _Responso por el niño Juan Manuel_.
San José: Ediciones Conciencia Nueva, 1971.
192 pp.
    Another novel focusing on the dehumanizing
aspects of modern society, emphasizing the
isolation of the individual within the multi-
tude and the necessity of struggling for survival and material goods while feeling a
spiritual and moral void due to the conflict
between basic human nature and the methods of
filling these needs imposed by modern society.
This is portrayed through the eyes and experiences of a recently deceased young child
named Juan Manuel. DLC BNCR

789 Navarro, Carlos F. _Pasado y futuro de Costa
Rica_. San José: Talleres Gráficos Ortiz,
1963. 64 pp.
    Though focusing on Costa Rica and its prob-
lems, this volume includes extensive discussions of and comparisons to the United States
and Europe, and their experiences. It focuses
on the needs of the peasants in Costa Rica,
but only after an extensive discussion of
other countries, particularly the United
States, which comprises nearly half the volume, reflecting the author's residence in that
country. DLC LNHT BNCR

790 Navarro Bolandi, Hugo. _La generación del 48:
juicio histórico-político sobre la democracia
costarricense_. Mexico: Editorial Olimpio,
1948. 150 pp. 2d ed. Mexico: Editorial
Olimpio, 1957. 238 pp.
    An account of the 1948 crisis in Costa
Rica, lauding the efforts of José Figueres and
the National Liberation Movement and condemning the previous regimes, but also criticizing
the result. The author devotes considerable
attention to the old regime, and contends that
the problem in Costa Rica is that there were
no true political parties but rather strictly
personalistic groupings. He argues that the
National Liberation Movement failed to overcome this and became simply another personalistic grouping aspiring to continuation in
power, but that it still has an opportunity to
change the nation due to the intellectual
prowess and social vision of its leaders,
particularly Figueres. BNCR

791 _____. _José Figueres en la evolución de Costa
Rica_. Mexico: Imprenta Quirós, 1953.
111 pp.
    A series of newspaper articles published in
La República of San José during the course of
the 1952 election campaign, supporting the
candidacy of Figueres, defending the work of
the National Liberation party, and hailing the
1949 Constitution and legislation of the Revolutionary Junta headed by Figueres. Though

part of the campaign, they serve to illustrate the views and political platform of the National Liberation party. BNCR

792 Nicholson, Thomas Herbert. Exposición que las compañías de electricidad hacen al Congreso con motivo del proyecto de ley sobre puniciones y otros extremos en relación con la Industria Eléctrica. San José: Imprenta Borrasé, 1930. 16 pp.
    The manager of the British-owned Costa Rican Light and Traction Company responds to proposed legislation before the Congress to regulate the industry, explaining the company's position, stressing its good intentions, and seeking to show that portions of the proposed laws violate existing laws and contracts and would seriously impede the company's operation. DLC-LDS-495

793 Niederlein, Gustavo. The Republic of Costa Rica. Philadelphia: Philadelphia Commercial Museum, 1898. 127 pp. Index, maps, tables.
    A general description, focusing on geology, geography, flora, fauna, climate, and economic situation at that time, designed for the layman. Though brief, the descriptions are comprehensive and offer statistics for the years 1897-98, when the research and visits took place. DLC LNHT

794 Noguera, María Leal de. Cuentos viejos. San José: Repertorie Americane, 1938. xvi, 198 pp. 4th ed. San José: Imprenta Lehmann, 1963. 178 pp.
    A collection of short stories from Costa Rica's Guanacaste province, many of them children's fables, compiled by a schoolteacher, representing the region's folklore. They were originally published as part of a larger work edited by Joaquín García Monge in 1923. DLC DLC-LDS-908 LNHT

795 Noriega, Félix F. Diccionario geográfico de Costa Rica. San José: Tipografía Nacional, 1904. 247 pp. 3d ed. San José: Imprenta Nacional, 1923. 247 pp.
    An alphabetically arranged dictionary of names and places in Costa Rica, with brief definitions and locations. DLC DLC-LDS-99 LNHT BNCR

796 Nuhn, H., and S. Pérez Q., et al. Estudio geográfico regional: zona atlántica norte de Costa Rica. San José: Instituto de Tierras y Colonización, 1967. xv, 360 pp. Illus., maps, tables.
    A technical study of the northern region and Atlantic coast of Costa Rica, conducted under the auspices of a government institute with the technical assistance of the German government, seeking to promote settlement in and outline the economic development possibilities of the area. Includes consideration of physical features, soils, climate, flora and fauna, population, communications and transportation facilities, social services, and economic regions, as well as recommendations for a development program and an assessment of its agricultural potential. BNCR

797 Núñez Monge, Francisco María. Anecdotario costarricense. San José: Editorial Aurora, 1953. 112 pp.
    A collection of Costa Rican anecdotes that provide insights into the national character and values. The items are miscellaneous, without any particular arrangement or classification. DLC

798 _____. Atisbos y comentos: cuarenta años de diarismo, 1911-11-junio 1951. San José: Imprenta La Española, 1951. 36 pp. Biblio.
    A well-known Costa Rican writer's commentaries on journalism, its traditions, and its responsibilities, followed by some general essays, principally dealing with Costa Rican themes. The initial commentaries regarding journalism provide some insights into the issues in this field in Costa Rica. DLC BNCR

799 _____. Braulio Carrillo: representativo de su época, organizador de nuestra nacionalidad. San José: Imprenta Soley y Valverde, 1945. 31 pp. Illus.
    A brief commentary on the actions of the first Costa Rican chief of state and the controversies surrounding him, including brief excerpts from various historical studies and commentaries. Prepared under the auspices of the National Society of Geography and History of Costa Rica. DLC BNCR

800 _____. Décadas: diez esbozos biográficos. San José: Editorial Aurora Social, 1951. 47 pp.
    A series of brief essays on ten significant Costa Rican figures from diverse fields, principally the intellectual and professorial realm but including some political figures, describing their contributions. All were originally published in that nation's press, over a period of fifteen years, and are dated, though without publication data. DLC BNCR

801 _____. Desamparados: tierra nutricia. San José: Imprenta Lehmann, 1967. 123 pp. Illus.
    A series of essays on the author's native city, reflecting his love for his homeland and for his nation. Includes commentaries on various historical events and on personages of the region, plus a collection of documents about the town. BNCR

802 _____. Dos Cercas. San José: Editorial Adecas, 1971. 117 pp.
    A series of acute and impassioned descriptions of the author's native canton, Desamparados, using its original name, Dos Cercas. The second portion contains essays dealing with famous people of the town, followed by a series of local legends. BNCR

803 _____. La evolución del periodismo en Costa Rica, 1883-1946. San José: Imprenta Minerva, 1921. 86 pp. Latest ed. San José: Imprenta Soley y Valverde, 1946. 15 pp.
    The major portion of this volume consists of a listing of all newspapers published in Costa Rica during this period, with brief

(Núñez Monge, Francisco María)
descriptions of each providing data regarding
their foundation, location, type, directors,
and contributors. The entries are arranged
chronologically, in accordance with the
appearance of the periodicals. Includes the
text of the laws relating to publication and
the press, as well as an introduction and
brief linking narrations that outline the
general trends. DLC DLC-LDS-270 LNHT

804   _____. Grecia en su centenario: recopilación
de datos y documentos relativos a la fundación
y desarrollo de Grecia, ordenada al celebrarse
al primer centenario de su fundación, el 27 de
abril de 1938. San José: Imprenta Nacional,
1939. 108 pp.
    A brief, topical history of the town of
Grecia in the province of Alajuela, from its
founding in the 1830s through the 1930s. Includes chapters on the history of the church,
the local government, the schools, social
life, prominent personages, agriculture, and
physical facilities, as well as some historical documents regarding the region. LNHT
BNCR

805   _____. Iniciación y desarrollo de las vías de
comunicación y empresas de transportes en
Costa Rica. San José: Imprenta Nacional,
1924. 336 pp. Latest ed. San José:
Imprenta Nacional, 1925. 8, 336 pp.
    A study and outline of the development of
transportation facilities in Costa Rica from
Colonial times to the 1920s, providing descriptions of and legislation regarding the
advance of roads, railroads, street-car systems, and the telephone and telegraph. DLC
DLC-LDS-320 LNHT BNCR

806   _____. Itinerario de la novela costarricense.
San José: Imprenta Soley y Valverde, 1947.
46 pp. Biblio.
    A brief overview of the development of the
novel in Costa Rica, contending that there
were no significant national novelists until
the end of the nineteenth century and noting
that the short story developed first. Focuses
on the generation of the 1940s as the first
identifiable grouping that produced a national
form that was not a copy of the European
styles, concluding with a paragraph-length
listing of each author and his works. LNHT
BNCR

807   _____. Julio Acosta. San José: Ministerio
de Cultura, 1973. 120 pp. Biblio., notes,
illus.
    Part of a series of brief biographies de-
signed for the general reader, this volume
focuses on a well-known Costa Rican hero who
led the opposition to the Tinoco dictatorship
and later served as president during the
1920s. Emphasizes his thought and personality. Thematic chapters stressing his dedication to democracy and unionism are followed by
an anthology of brief excerpts from his writings and speeches, a chronology of his life,
and a bibliography of his writings. DLC

808   _____. Mi tierra nativa: estudio histórico,
geográfico y estadístico del cantón de
Desamparados. San José: Imprenta Nacional,
1917. 169 pp. Illus. 2d ed. Cartago:
Editorial ADECAS, 1974. 181 pp.
    A history of the canton of Desamparados by
a native of the town, reflecting his tender
feeling for his home. Includes an economic,
demographic, and political history of the town
and all of its districts, as well as an anthology of references to it in Costa Rican
literature. DLC-LDS-173 BNCR

809   _____. Recopilación de artículos publicados
con motivo del debate del contrato petróleo
Pinto-Greulich en el Congreso. San José:
n.p., 1916. 76 pp.
    A series of articles originally published
in La Época of San José, part of the polemic
in the controversy that arose when a congressional committee recommended rejection of the
petroleum-concession contract on the grounds
that the nation needed to control the rights;
others, including the administration and its
minister of fomento, who signed the accord,
contended that development could be achieved
only with foreign technology and investment.
The accord became a major political issue
involving all of the nation's leading politicians. Carefully outlines the controversy,
drawing comparisons with other Latin American
nations and narrating the extensive congressional debate. DLC BNCR

810   _____. Tres ensayos de Francisco María Nuñez.
San José: Banco Nacional de Costa Rica, 1971.
78 pp. Illus.
    Three essays dealing with various figures
of Costa Rican history, delivered as speeches
during the 1940s and collected here as part of
the celebration of independence. They deal
with José María Castro Madriz, Braulio
Carrillo, and Francisco Morazán. BNCR

811 Nunley, Robert E. The Distribution of Population in Costa Rica. Washington, D.C.:
National Academy of Sciences, 1960. 71 pp.
Biblio., maps, tables.
    An historical economic geography employing
census and government records to trace the
movement and distribution of the Costa Rican
population from the conquest to the present.
Notes its shifts and concentrations, which the
study relates to the pattern of economic
growth and the development of the nation's
transportation system. DLC

812 La obra cultural de don Miguel Obregón. San
José: n.p., 1917. 46 pp. Illus.
    A brief sketch of the educational efforts
of this well-known Costa Rican scholar, tracing his work as a professor and his administrative efforts to promote standardized
requirements and new methods of instruction.
DLC-LDS

813 La obra social del presidente Calderón
Guardia. San José: n.p., 1942. 61 pp.
Illus.

A laudatory official description of the government's program and actions, stressing its social-reform efforts and their controversial nature while extolling its goals and progress. Includes comments regarding the labor code, the foundation of the University of Costa Rica, and other reform measures and laws, all written as brief summaries. DLC LNHT BNCR

814 Obregón Loría, Edgar A. Miguel Obregón. San José: Ministerio de Cultura, Juventud y Deportes, 1974. 219 pp. Biblio., illus.

A biography of a well-known Costa Rican professor and intellectual figure of the late nineteenth and early twentieth centuries, written by his son. Miguel Obregón Lizano, who held numerous important positions in his nation's educational system including that of minister of education and was the author of several texts, exerted considerable influence on his nation's intellectual development. The volume is filled with the author's boyhood memories of his father's advice and quotations of him; the latter portion consists of reproductions of commentaries on the nation's education written by the title figure. BNCR

815 Obregón Loría, Rafael. La campaña del tránsito, 1856-1857. San José: Imprenta Lehmann, 1956. 383 pp. Biblio., illus., maps. 2d ed. San José: Editorial Costa Rica, 1976. 246 pp. Biblio., illus., maps.

A leading Costa Rican historian's well-researched and detailed account of Costa Rica's participation in the campaign against the filibustering expedition of William Walker and of its efforts in the campaign along the Nicaraguan frontier to maintain control of the San Juan River and prevent Walker from expanding into Costa Rica. Based on extensive research in the Costa Rican National Archives and in appropriate secondary sources, this study serves to illustrate the confluence of local national interest with the needs of the entire isthmus. The title has changed in the various editions, with the original title as listed using the latest but the latest using the title Costa Rica y la guerra del 56, with the original title as a subtitle. DLC LNHT BNCR

816 ____. Conflictos militares y políticos de Costa Rica. San José: Imprenta La Nación, 1951. 127 pp. Biblio., illus.

A series of brief single-paragraph résumés providing basic data on Costa Rican military actions, including domestic uprisings and foreign conflicts, covering the years 1823 through 1932, many with illustrations of the participants. The focus is on the military details. Based on secondary sources and newspapers. A handy guide for anyone desiring the basic outline of the nation's coups and internal turmoil. LNHT BNCR

817 ____. Costa Rica en la independencia y en la Federación. San José: Editorial Costa Rica, 1977. 254 pp. Biblio., notes, appendixes.

A reissue of two works, originally published separately in mimeograph form in 1971

and 1974, respectively, dealing with the early days of Costa Rica, prepared by a prominent Costa Rican historian and based on research in documents and appropriate secondary works. The first narrates and examines the Costa Rican independence movement from the Mexican declaration through the local actions, including those of the various cities and regions, and contains documentary appendixes. The second analyzes the Federation of Central America and Costa Rica's role in it, emphasizing the interaction of Costa Rica and the Federation and the differences of this state with the aggressive policies of Morazán and his military campaigns to preserve unity. It is also accompanied by appropriate documents from the era. DLC-LDS-153 BNCR

818 ____. Dr. José María Castro Madriz: paladín de la libertad y de la cultura. San José: Editorial La Nación, 1949. 44 pp. Illus.

A brief biography of a nineteenth-century political and intellectual figure who held numerous governmental and educational positions, served as head of state during the 1840s, and was one of the founders of the independent nation. Follows his career through his many positions until his death in 1892. LNHT

819 ____. Gangellini: organizador de la masonería en Costa Rica. San José: Imprenta Trejos, 1941. 110 pp. Illus., appendixes.

A brief history of the founding of the Masonic Order in Costa Rica in 1865, focusing on its founder, a priest, followed by appended photos and documents involving significant members. LNHT BNCR

820 ____. De nuestra historia patria. 8 vols. San José: Universidad de Costa Rica, 1966-74. Biblio.

A massive series on various aspects of the independence era, by a prominent Costa Rican historian. Some volumes were published in mimeograph form by the university's Institute of History and Geography; others appeared in regular printed form, usually some years later. Includes considerations of stages of the independence era and existing historical scholarship regarding it, and of Costa Rican relations with the Federation of Central America. All are based on documentary research and secondary sources. DLC LNHT BNCR

821 ____. Nuestros gobernantes. San José: Editorial Aurora Social, 1948. 58 pp. Illus.

Single-page vitas, with photos, of each of the presidents and acting heads of government of Costa Rica from independence through 1948, arranged chronologically. BNCR

822 ____. El poder legislativo en Costa Rica. San José: Imprenta Nacional, 1966. 538 pp. Notes, illus.

A brief history of each session of the Costa Rican legislature, with a list of members and summary of its actions, from independence to 1949. Preceded by an alphabetical listing of all individuals who served in it

(Obregón Loría, Rafael)
during these years, with photos and single-page biographical sketches of each. Concludes with a discussion of the powers of the legislature under the 1949 Constitution. BNCR

823 _____. Presbítero doctor Francisco Calvo (Gangellini), organizador de la masonería en Costa Rica. San José: Imprenta Borrasé, 1963. 114 pp. Biblio., notes.
A biography of a nineteenth-century priest who founded the Masonic Order in Costa Rica in 1865. Includes a history of the order and its political activities during its early days in the republic. Contains considerable data regarding the church, church-state relations, and the foundation of the diocese of Costa Rica. Based on documentary research and appropriate secondary sources, and prepared by a professor of history. DLC LNHT BNCR

824 _____. Los rectores de la universidad de Santo Tomás de Costa Rica. San José: Editorial Universitaria, 1955. 181 pp. Illus.
A series of biographical sketches, with illustrations of the rectors and acting heads, of the Costa Rican university from its foundation in 1844 through its suppression in 1888. DLC LNHT BNCR

825 Obregón Loría, Rafael, and George F. Bowden. La masonería en Costa Rica. 4 vols. San José: Editorial Trejos, 1938-50.
A detailed history of masonry in Costa Rica, prepared by a professional historian who was active in the movement. Includes minutes, resolutions, lists of members, etc. Also offers insights into the group's political involvements and stands at various times. Based on research in the organization's records. Volume 1 covers the years through 1870, volume 2 through 1889, volume 3 through 1899, and volume 4 the entire twentieth century. DLC-LDS-482 BNCR

826 Oduber Quirós, Daniel. Apuntes para un congreso ideológico del Partido Liberación Nacional. San José: Editorial Eloy Morúa Carrillo, 1969. 61 pp.
A collection of commentaries by this Costa Rican leader, inspired by the worldwide student unrest of 1968. Analyzes the present situation and differentiates between "impossible" aspirations and a "possible revolution." The author criticizes doctrinaire Marxism and defends democratic socialism as the most realistic solution, while restating the position of the National Liberation party in terms of the present crisis. IEdS

827 _____. Una campaña: artículos y discursos de la campaña electoral, 1966-67. San José: Editorial Eloy Morúa Carrillo, 1967. 445 pp.
A collection of the most important speeches of the unsuccessful Liberación Nacional presidential candidate during the 1967 elections, designed to preserve his principal platform and positions. He later served as president during the 1970s. The volume also includes

essays on his early years and the formation of the party, its growth, and his role in previous PLN governments. LNHT BNCR

828 Oficina Internacional Centro-Americana. El arreglo de la deuda externa de Costa Rica: documentos y opiniones relativos a tan importante asunto. Guatemala: Tipografía El Nacional, 1911. 87 pp.
A collection of documents, statements, and political exchanges attendant to the Costa Rican debt renegotiation that was concluded in 1910 to refund the debt, whose payment had been suspended by the government several times due to economic and political crises in the nation. The introduction presents a brief sketch of the Costa Rican foreign debt and its history. The figure of Minor C. Keith bobs in and out of the documents as one of the intermediaries involved in the negotiations among the bondholders, banks, and government. Includes the accords and opinions about them by the nation's leading political figures. DLC-LDS-169

829 Oficina Internacional del Trabajo. Los trabajadores de las plantaciones: sus condiciones de empleo y sus niveles de vida. Geneva: OIT, 1966. xii, 317 pp. Notes, tables, appendixes.
A global topical analysis of plantation labor and the working conditions and standards of living of the people involved, using as a base countries from Africa, Asia, and Latin America. Costa Rica was one of the countries included, but there is little specific data regarding it save in the discussion of plantations growing products typical of that nation, namely, coffee and bananas. DLC BNG

830 Operations and Policy Research, Inc. Costa Rica Election Factbook, February 6, 1966. Washington, D.C.: Institute for the Comparative Study of Political Systems, 1966. 44 pp. Illus., maps, tables.
A brief summary of the issues, candidates, parties, and background of the election, including an overview of the political developments since 1948, details regarding the electoral laws, registration statistics, and similar data. DLC LNHT

831 Oreamuno, José Rafael, ed. La caída del gobierno constitucional en Costa Rica: el golpe de estado del 27 de enero de 1917. New York: De Laisne & Carranza, 1919. 79 pp. Illus.
A compilation of information and reporting about the 1917 coup by General Federico Tinoco Granados in Costa Rica, compiled by the secretary of the Costa Rican legation in Washington. It includes a series of reports by Jacinto Lopez detailing the events, originally published in the journal La Reforma Social, and a series of articles regarding the events and the Yankee reaction from the New York Herald. DLC DLC-LDS BNCR

832 Oreamuno Quirós, Alfredo. El callejón de los perdidos. San José: Imprenta Lehmann, 1972. 134 pp.

A novel viewing alcoholism through the eyes of an alcoholic, depicting his tortured life, his experiences, and his efforts to overcome his problem. BNCR

833 _____. Un harapo en el camino: caída, vida y redención de un alcohólico. 3d ed. San José: Imprenta Lehmann, 1970. 130 pp.

The autobiography of a Costa Rican alcoholic, tracing his life and recuperation. Serves to supply some clues into alcoholism and its treatment in that nation, and provides insights into the "underworld" of society that are seldom available to readers or observers. BNCR

834 Organización Iberoamericana de Seguridad Social. Los seguros sociales en Costa Rica. Madrid: Organización Iberoamericana de Seguridad Social. 42 pp. Illus.

A brief summary of the Costa Rican social security law and its implementation and functioning. DPU

835 ORIT. Costa Rica: documentos para la historia. Mexico: ORIT, 1955. 47 pp.

A series of letters and resolutions from various countries of the hemisphere, expressing the labor organization's support of the Costa Rican National Liberation Movement. Accompanied by excerpts from press commentaries. BNCR

836 Orozco, Rafael. Elementos de derecho penal de Costa Rica. San José: Imprenta Nacional, 1882. 502 pp.

A treatise on Costa Rican penal law, with extensive reproduction of the existing statutes. DLC

837 Orozco Castro, Jorge. Bajo el sol tropical. San José: Editorial Maucci, 1932. 238 pp.

A novel about life and its problems in the Costa Rican banana region, involving the struggle against the Caribbean Fruit Company, an oppressive Yankee company that monopolizes banana growing through its control of the railroads, with no benefits to the nation. This is attributed to poor government at the national level. The work indicates the anti-Yankee feeling that results from dislike of the company and its exploitive tactics, and makes references to longings to emulate the "heroes" who liberated Cuba from foreign control. DLC-LDS-792 LNHT

838 Ortega, Ernesto. Cuentos del terruño. San José: Imprenta Alsina, 1933. 90 pp.

A collection of short stories drawn from and set in the Turrialba-Cartago region of Costa Rica, dealing with a broad range of themes. DLC-LDS-761

839 Ortiz Cartín, Bienvenido. Índice alfabético de leyes de Costa Rica . . . comprende las leyes emitidas desde 1824 hasta 1924. . . . 3

vols. San José: Imprenta Nacional, 1925-30. 601, 284, 302 pp.

An alphabetical index to the laws of Costa Rica during this period. The series never got beyond the third volume, hence the coverage is from A through J. DLC-LDS-484 BNCR

840 Ortuño Sobrado, Fernando. El monopolio estatal de la banca de Costa Rica. San José: Imprenta Trejos, 1963. 194 pp.

Originally a thesis, this work briefly surveys Costa Rican financial history. Gives a detailed account of the creation of the Banco Central by the 1949 Constitution and the consolidation of its control of the nation's financial institutions, with a detailed analysis of the provisions of the laws involved, the powers granted to the bank, and the impact of the nationalization. Concludes that the system was not working well and that either new legislation to restructure it or a return to private banking was necessary for the economic health of the nation. DLC LNHT BNCR

841 Pacheco, León. Mauro Fernández. San José: Ministerio de Cultura, Juventud y Deportes, 1972. 121 pp. Illus.

A brief account of the life and contributions of this Costa Rican statesman of the late nineteenth century, written in sympathetic though straightforward fashion. Provides an overview of his career that lists his principal accomplishments in each of his various political posts and seeks to place him in the context of the political and intellectual currents of his era. Includes an anthology of selections from his governmental reports and speeches to show his viewpoints, the breadth of his activities, and what the author calls his "combative" approach to politics. PPiU

842 Pacheco, Leonidas. Algunos apuntes sobre inmigración. San José: Tipografía Nacional, 1909. 36 pp.

A general discussion of immigration, its problems, and its benefits, citing the needs for immigrants in Costa Rica. DLC DLC-LDS-35 BNCR

843 _____. El doctor Durán es ciudadaño costarricense y si puede ser presidente de Costa Rica. San José: Imprenta Moderna, 1913. 20 pp.

Part of a political campaign and the attendant polemic, this volume seeks to rebuff the arguments against the presidential candidacy of Dr. Carlos Durán in the 1914 election. The dispute involved his citizenship, with some contending that he did not fulfill the constitutional stipulations. This pamphlet argues that whatever the status of his father, the latter became a Costa Rican citizen before the presidential candidate reached the age of majority, and that this fulfills the constitutional qualification. For the charges see item CR409. DLC DLC-LDS-119

844 _____. Los hechos y el derecho: el contrato petrolero ante el Congreso. San José: Imprenta Moderna, 1916. 30 pp.

A collection of statements supporting the legality of the Pinto-Greulich contract for oil-exploitation rights, compiled by Greulich's lawyer in support of the accord. Includes statements by various attorneys and prominent political figures, including several ex-presidents. The issue dealt with the powers of the executive in making the agreement, and the role of Congress. DLC DLC-LDS-698

845 Pacheco Cooper, Federico, ed. Costa Rica en 1842: Morazán, Saravia, Pinto: documentos históricos. San José: Imprenta Alsina, 1904. 88 pp.
A series of documents regarding the 1842 political maneuvering in Costa Rica during the waning days of the Central American Federation, when a revolt in protest against governmental changes and the prospect of Costa Rican troops being sent outside the state to fight for the Federation resulted in the arrest of Morazán and his cohorts. The correspondence includes letters, reports from military commanders, and proclamations. The editor provides brief introductions for the documents, which are drawn from the Costa Rican Archives and are grouped according to which of the three figures they pertain to. DLC DLC-LDS-18 BNCR

846 Padilla Castro, Guillermo. El caso de Costa Rica ante la Sociedad de Naciones. San José: Imprenta Soley y Valverde, 1936. 16 pp.
A brief discussion of the League of Nations and Costa Rica's role in it, through Costa Rica's withdrawal. Focuses on the withdrawal and the justifications for it, though faulting the Costa Rican diplomatic stance and concluding with a call for a greater effort to develop a more professional diplomatic corps. DLC-LDS-861 BNCR

847 ____. Derecho penal costarricense: parte general. San José: Universidad de Costa Rica, 1966.
Intended as the initial volume in a series examining the practices of Costa Rican penal law, this portion contains a general discussion of the theory and evolution of penal law on a global and historical basis, seeking to demonstrate the antecedents of local practice. TxU

848 Padilla Castro, Noé. Álbum social costarricense: cien mujeres bellas; prosa y verso. San José: Imprenta Alsina, 1926. Illus. 2d ed. San José: Imprenta Alsina, 1927. Illus.
A collection of photographs of prominent Costa Ricans including influential socialites and attractive women, with identification but no biographical data. The text consists of poetry and passionate commentary about the beauty of the nation and the ideals of its citizens. BNCR

849 Palmerlee, Albert Earl. Maps of Costa Rica: An Annotated Cartobibliography. Lawrence: University of Kansas Press, 1965. 358 pp.
A bibliography of maps of Costa Rica, arranged in five sections from general

national maps to specific city plans. Within sections, the listing is alphabetical by type, such as population, railroad, etc. The listing provides complete information regarding type of map, scale, what it shows, when made, and author, and also a location coding. Covers the complete collection of the Library of Congress and the University of Kansas, and shows other locations only for maps not in either of these. Users will need to remember that the collection of the American Geographic Society has moved from New York to the University of Wisconsin-Milwaukee. DLC LNHT

850 Partido Liberación Nacional. José Figueres: su gesta libertaria. San José: Editorial Eloy Morúa Carrillo, 1952.
An official party statement extolling its founder and leader, acclaiming his actions and his plans for his nation.

851 ____. Los pagos de la guerra de Liberación Nacional. San José: Editorial Liberación Nacional, 1953. 80 pp.
The financial records of the PLN, indicating its expenses during the nation's civil war, its sources of credit, and the names of the individuals and enterprises to whom it made payments. The publication was designed to encourage open and honest politics by countering rumors and making a public record of the financing of the effort. DLC BNCR

852 Partido Vanguardia Popular de Costa Rica. Partido Vanguardia Popular de Costa Rica: breve esbozo de su historia. San José: Ediciones Revolución, 1968. 56 pp. Illus. 2d ed. San José: Ediciones Revolución, 1971. Illus.
A brief account of the principal events in the history of the Costa Rican Marxist party, formed in 1929 in response to the Russian Revolution, and of its leader, Manuel Mora Valverde, outlining its stances and principal actions. BNCR

853 Peralta, José F. de. La propriété foncière à Costa-Rica. Brussels: Imprimerie-Mertens, 1888. 80 pp.
A brief historical overview of Costa Rica and a description of its current situation, particularly focusing on the economy and development, detailing laws regarding investment and property ownership. Clearly designed to interest Europeans in investment and provide them with general information about the nation. DLC DLC-LDS-147

854 Peralta, Manuel María de. Costa Rica: Its Climate, Constitution and Resources, with a Survey of Its Present Financial Position. London: Straker Brothers, 1873. 16 pp.
One of many publications by the indefatigable Costa Rican envoy to Europe, designed to encourage European investment in his homeland by extolling its development, resources, and prospects. In this case he includes an overly optimistic account of the prospects for constructing an interoceanic railway from its own

(Peralta, Manuel María de)
finances, with fanciful comments on the potential impact on the nation's economy. DLC

855 _____. La République de Costa Rica (Amérique Centrale): appel a l'émigration européenne. . . . Geneva: Imprimerie Georg, 1871. 18 pp.
The Costa Rican envoy strikes again, this time with a pamphlet seeking to encourage immigration and extolling the virtues of Costa Rica as a location for European colonists. CU-B

856 Peralta Quirós, Hernán G. Agustín de Iturbide y Costa Rica. San José: Imprenta Soley y Valverde, 1944. 329 pp. Latest ed. San José: Editorial Costa Rica, 1968. 526 pp. Notes, illus.
A review of Costa Rican, Central American, and Mexican independence, which despite its title is more a study of Iturbide's entire career than of his efforts to annex Central America. Only a few chapters actually deal with the specifics of the annexationist movement. The heart of the volume deals with the Costa Rican viewpoint of the independence movement and of the Central America efforts, as well as with the course of the independence movement in Costa Rica. Provides a useful summation of the debates among the Costa Rican leaders and of their uncertainty in the face of several options provided by the era. DLC LNHT BNCR

857 _____. El Colegio de San Luís Gonzaga: datos relativos a su fundación. San José: Imprenta Nacional, 1941. 30 pp. Illus.
A brief history of the Colegio founded in the 1840s in Cartago, emphasizing its early days and initial directors. DLC DLC-LDS-815 LNHT

858 _____, ed. Las constituciones de Costa Rica. Madrid: Instituto de Cultura Hispánica, 1962. xix, 660 pp.
The full text of each of Costa Rica's various constitutions, with an introductory essay regarding the nation's legal history by the editor, who is a well-known scholar. LNHT BNCR

859 Peralta Quirós, Hernán G. Costa Rica y la fundación de la república. San José: Imprenta Española, 1948. 36 pp.
NN

860 _____. El derecho constitucional en la independencia de Costa Rica. San José: Imprenta Trejos, 1965. 56 pp.
An essay examining the legalities of the Costa Rican independence movement, concluding that all governmental agencies acted within their proper powers and hence that the action was entirely legal. The second half consists of a collection of documents from the independence period. LNHT BNCR

861 _____. La diplomacia en Costa Rica. San José: Imprenta Trejos, 1969. 81 pp.

Originally a speech, this pamphlet provides a brief overview of Costa Rican diplomacy and its main actions since independence. DLC LNHT BNCR

862 _____. Don José María de Peralta. San José: Imprenta Trejos, 1956. 217 pp. Notes.
A biography of one of the leaders of the Costa Rican independence movement, tracing his governmental positions in the late Colonial period, his service in the Congress, and his career in the government of the newly independent Central American Federation during the 1820s and 1830s. Continues well beyond the death of its title character in 1836 by following the development of some of his projects through the 1890s and tracing the controversy over his activities in politics and as head of the National Tobacco Factory, though the relationship is not always clear. Based on secondary works and documents. DLC LNHT BNCR

863 _____. Don Rafael Yglesias: apuntes para su biografía. 2 vols. San José: Imprenta Trejos, 1928. Latest ed. San José: Editorial Costa Rica, 1968. 171 pp. Notes.
After narrating Yglesias's early career until his assumption of the presidency of Costa Rica in 1894, the author analyzes the church-state conflict in each of the Central American countries. Contends that the persecution of the church in Costa Rica was an unjustified effort to imitate the Liberal party of Guatemala, which led to the emergence of the Catholic Union party, which stimulated the formation of the Civil party headed by Yglesias. A projected second volume, which never appeared, was to cover his presidency. Based on secondary sources. DLC-LDS-412 LNHT BNCR

864 _____. El Pacto de Concordia: orígenes del derecho constitucional de Costa Rica. San José: Editorial Trejos, 1952. 126 pp. 3d ed. San José: Imprenta Lehmann, 1969. 126 pp. Biblio.
A reprinting of the text of Costa Rica's first constitution, an unofficial pact established during the early days of independence as a provisional measure that became the basis for the government of the region during its time as a state of the Federation of Central America. Preceded by a brief essay explaining its origins and significance. DLC LNHT BNCR

865 _____. El 3 de junio de 1850. San José: Imprenta Española, 1950. 48 pp. Illus., notes.
An account of the various maneuvers involved in an attempted coup in Costa Rica, providing all the details and focusing on the activities of General José Manuel Quirós, the commander of the Costa Rican Army who was the pivotal figure in the dispute. Accompanied by documents concerning the episode. DLC BNCR

866 Pérez Cabrera, Ricardo. Asuntos educacionales. San José: Imprenta Cartín, 1939. 111 pp. Illus., tables.

The author's suggestions for reforms of the Costa Rican primary schools. Centers principally on the idea of using student interests as the focus of organization for studies instead of the rigid government curriculum, but ranges from methods to specific activities and proposals about the course of study. DLC

867   Pérez Pancorbo, Humberto. Educación y desarrollo: reto a la sociedad costarricense. San José: Editorial Costa Rica, 1971. 112 pp. Biblio., illus., tables.
      A critical analysis of the Costa Rican educational system, noting that despite its extent, success, and reputation, it is not devoid of problems. DLC

868   Pérez Zeledón, Pedro. El Banco de Costa Rica en la Legislatura de 1891, o refutación de los errores económicos en que se funda la ley número 15 de 25 de junio del mismo año. San José: Imprenta de José Canales, 1891. 41 pp.
      The bank's defense against charges against it and its response to efforts to remove its powers to emit currency, prepared by its attorney as a response to the political debate. The bank, formed as the Banco de la Unión in 1888, was still a new entity in the nation, and hence a controversial one, and efforts to end its role as the sole emitter of bills in favor of the other banks continued to agitate the political scene. DLC-LDS

869   _____. Colección de artículos sobre política agrícola. San José: Tipografía Nacional, 1910. 56 pp.
      A collection of articles that originally appeared in La República and provoked considerable debate in Costa Rica about the nation's agricultural development and the role of coffee in its economy. The author challenged the existing assumptions by raising questions about the advantages and disadvantages of coffee cultivation and its expansion. His series drew answers from Federico Mora and J.E. Van Der Laat, which can be found under those authors. DLC DLC-LDS-50 BNCR

870   _____. El empréstito. San José: Imprenta Borrasé, 1922. 16 pp.
      The author's comments on the latest foreign loan and refunding of the national debt. Criticizes the accord, contending that its terms are unfavorable to the nation and that the citizens have forgotten the meaning of the word economy and continue to demand more external funds to fuel an imbalanced budget. Includes commentary on the economic problems of the nation. DLC

871   _____. Gregorio José Ramírez y otros ensayos. San José: Editorial Costa Rica, 1971. 227 pp. Biblio.
      An anthology of historical studies by a prominent Costa Rican political figure of the late nineteenth century who held numerous cabinet posts. Preceded by a brief biographical essay by Carlos Meléndez Chaverri. Most of the themes are Colonial, but the volume also includes essays dealing with political

figures of the early and mid-nineteenth century. DLC LNHT BNCR

872   Périgny, Maurice C. de. La République de Costa Rica: son avenir économique et la canal de Panama. Paris: Libraire Félix Alcan, 1918. 238 pp. Index, illus., maps.
      The initial portion of this volume consists of a brief historical outline, followed by a general discussion of the economy, transport facilities, and related factors from 1910 through 1917. The second portion consists of a description of the various regions of the country, emphasizing economics. Despite the title, only the final chapter refers to the potential economic impact of the Panama Canal. DLC DLC-LDS-309 LNHT BNCR

873   Peterson, Arthur W., and Quentin M. West. Agricultural Regions of Costa Rica. Turrialba, Costa Rica: Inter-American Institute of Agricultural Sciences, 1953. Pages not numbered consecutively. Biblio., tables.
      A summary of the various agricultural regions of Costa Rica, followed by a collection of detailed regional statistics for the year 1950. BNCR

874   Peyroutet, H. Apertura del mercado francés al café de Costa Rica: proyecto de convenio comercial entre Costa Rica y Francia. San José: Imprenta Borrasé, 1930. 32 pp.
      A defense of the recently signed trade treaty, in reply to Costa Rican opponents who charged that the tariff reductions given to France were excessive. Recounts the history of the negotiations and compares the treaty to others, contending that it would benefit Costa Rica while granting tariff concessions parallel to those France received from Guatemala. DLC

875   Picado Chacón, Manuel. Vida y obra del doctor Clodomiro Picado Twight. San José: Editorial Costa Rica, 1964. 286 pp.
      A biography of a scientist and doctor whose efforts in Costa Rica from 1910 to 1943 contributed to the nation's health and sanitation programs. Hails his efforts and chronicles his scientific researches and discoveries. DLC BNCR

876   Picado Michalski, Teodoro. El Pacto de la Embajada de México. Managua: n.p., 1949. 48 pp. 2d ed. Managua: n.p., 1950.
      A discussion of the negotiations, under the auspices of the diplomatic corps, to end the Costa Rican civil war in 1948. Traces the various proposals and the eventual agreement, signed by representatives of both sides in the Mexican embassy 19 April 1948, which provided for the resignation of the government and a transitional provisional regime. The author contends that the revolutionaries failed to respect the pact once the government resigned, and prints the various resulting exchanges and protests. Reflects the political passions of the times but indicates the various behind-the-scenes maneuvers. BNCR

877 Picado Michalski, Teodoro, and Carlos Cuadra
Pasos. Dos hombres, dos historias: don
Ricardo Jiménez y general José Santos Zelaya.
Managua: Academia Nicaragüense de la Lengua,
1960. 119 pp.
     The addresses delivered by a Costa Rican
and a Nicaraguan, both political figures and
scholars, on the occasion of Picado's induc-
tion into the academy in 1949. Picado analyzes the career of Ricardo Jiménez, while
Cuadra Pasos deals with José Santos Zelaya and
compares his political stances to those of
Jiménez. Both extol the contributions of
their figures. Picado's essay occupies two
thirds of the volume. BNCR

878 Picado Soto, Francisco [Alarmvogel, pseud.].
Apuntes para la historia de la Ciudad de
Alajuela. San José: Imprenta Nacional, 1966.
162 pp.
     A history of the city of Alajuela from
Colonial times to 1966, with emphasis on its
institutions and their development. Includes
lists of the governors, comments on customs
and traditions, a history of the city and its
various institutions, and a discussion of the
current situation. BNCR

879 _____. La ciudad de Alajuela y sus templos
católicos. San José: Imprenta Nacional,
1951. 56 pp. Illus.
     Descriptions and photos of the town's
churches, with accounts of their foundation
and history. DLC

880 _____. En el 50 aniversario de la erección
del monumento de Juan Santamaría. San José:
Imprenta Nacional, 1941. 56 pp. Illus.
     A collection of the speeches and official
acts on this occasion, with various congratulatory telegrams and photos. DLC-LDS-912

881 _____. General Tomás Herrera Sanchez. San
José: Imprenta Nacional, 1968. 29 pp.
Illus.
     A brief biographical sketch of a Costa
Rican military officer who distinguished him-
self in the campaigns against William Walker.
BNCR

882 _____. La instrucción pública en Alajuela.
San José: Imprenta Nacional, 1953. 143 pp.
Illus.
     A history of the various schools in the
city, focusing principally on the nineteenth
century. Includes mention of prominent professors and the development of facilities.
There are chapters on art and music, the public library, and other educational institutions. BNCR

883 Pinaud, José María. El 7 noviembre de 1889.
San José: Imprenta La Tribuna, 1942. 123 pp.
Illus.
     A series of essays discussing the Costa
Rican governmental crisis of 1889, when street
demonstrations protesting alleged electoral
fraud provoked clashes with police and troops.
The major portion of the volume contains a
series of commentaries by Pinaud, editor of La

Tribuna, hailing the actions of then-President
Bernardo Soto in alleviating the bloodshed and
preventing a major confrontation. It is followed by a discussion of the same situation by
Liberal party leader and later president
Ricardo Jiménez Oreamuno, who was a
participant in the Liberal protests, and by
essays on this incident by several Costa Rican
historians. DLC DLC-LDS-930 BNCR

884 _____. Las verdaderas causas de mi rebeldía
frente al presidente Cortés. San José:
Imprenta La Tribuna, 1940. 28 pp.
     The editor of La Tribuna reproduces some of
his editorials of February 1940, which were
part of the polemic he engaged in with then-
President León Cortés Castro. The editor
argues that the president is seeking to muzzle
the press by criticizing his commentaries and
denying their accuracy, while the president
accuses the paper of printing falsehoods in a
smear campaign against him and his son, Otto
Cortés, who was president of Congress. The
editor opposes the president's methods and
tendency toward a strong executive, seeing
himself as the defender of the free press.
DLC DLC-LDS-482

885 Pinto, Julieta. A la vuelta de la esquina.
San José: Editorial Conciencia Nueva, 1975.
121 pp.
     A collection of short stories by a well-
known writer whose works emphasize Costa Rican
settings, customs, idioms, speech patterns,
and the plight of the lower classes and rural
peasants. DLC

886 _____. Cuentos de la tierra. San José:
Ediciones L'atelier, 1963. 154 pp. Illus.
     A series of short stories set in various
locations in Costa Rica, emphasizing the beauties of the countryside. Includes drawings by
Francisco Amighetti, one of the nation's best-
known artists. DLC LNHT BNCR

887 _____. La estación que sigue al verano. San
José: Imprenta Lehmann, 1969. 148 pp.
     Another of the author's novels of social
consciousness that focus on the different
life-styles of the various classes in her
native Costa Rica and on the plight of the
poor. The account is written with vivid description and passion. BNCR

888 _____. Los marginados. San José: Editorial
Conciencia Nueva, 1970. 131 pp. Illus.
     A collection of eighteen short stories
about the life of Costa Rican peasants, focusing on their marginal existence and their
separation from the economy. DLC BNCR

889 Pittier de Fábrega, Henri François.
Apuntaciones etnológicas sobre los indios
Bribri. San José: Imprenta Nacional, 1938.
28 pp.
     An anthropological study describing the
then-current life-style of the Indians inhab-
iting the Talamanca region, written in the
late 1930s by an aging but prominent scholar

(Pittier de Fábrega, Henri François)
of the region. Includes a brief account of
such factors as religion, superstitions, bur-
ial practices, diet, and village organization.
DLC

890   _____. Apuntaciones sobre el clima y
geografía de la República de Costa Rica:
observaciones y exploraciones efectuadas en el
año de 1888. San José: Tipografía Nacional,
1889. 56 pp. 2d ed. San José: Tipografía
Nacional, 1890. 41 pp.
A naturalist's studies of the Costa Rican
climate that offer some of the earliest scientific observations and data. DLC-LDS-43 LNHT
BNCR

891   _____. Capítulos escogidos de la geografía
física y prehistórica de Costa Rica. San
José: Imprenta Nacional, 1938. 56 pp.
Tables. 2d ed. San José: Imprenta Nacional,
1942.
Some basic geographical description, combined with historical meterological data regarding temperatures and rains during the
years 1889-1903. The latter are particularly
valuable for the historical record. LNHT
BNCR

892   _____. Kostarika: Beiträge zur Orographie
und Hydrographie. Gotha: Justus Perthes,
1912. 48 pp. Maps.
A detailed study of the rivers and water
resources of Costa Rica, giving the location
and geographic, geologic, and climatic data
for each river. DLC-LDS-382

893   _____. La lluvia en Centro América:
exploraciones en Talamanca. San José:
Tipografía Nacional, 1895. 24 pp.
A naturalist's observations and analysis of
the rainfall patterns in Central America, and
his description of the region of Talamanca in
Costa Rica, emphasizing its flora and fauna.
DLC-LDS-43 LNHT BNCR

894   _____. Nombres geográficos de Costa Rica, I:
Talamanca. San José: Tipografía Nacional,
1895. 46 pp.
An alphabetical listing of place names in
the province, with an explanation of their
derivation. DLC-LDS-112 LNHT

895   _____. Notas sobre la geografía de Costa
Rica. San José: Tipografía Nacional, 1893.
18 pp.
A geographic account focused principally on
the San Juan River Valley. Also discusses the
mountain ranges and historical geography,
referring to the initial maps and geographic
commentaries on these regions. DLC-LDS-181
LNHT BNCR

896   _____. Viaje de exploración al valle del Río
Grande de Terraba. San José: Tipografía
Nacional, 1891. 138 pp. Map.
A diary kept by a leading naturalist and
botanist during an official expedition to this
remote region, rich in description of the
landforms and particularly the flora and fauna

of the region. Includes accounts of the ecology and detailed discussion of the plant species encountered and their habitat. DLC-LDS-
14 BNCR

897 Pittman, Marvin S. Algunos problemas
educativos de Costa Rica: informe sobre la
educación secundaria en Costa Rica. San José:
Ministerio de Educación Pública, 1954. 95 pp.
Tables.
A detailed analysis of the Costa Rican
educational system at the secondary level and
its characteristics and problems, prepared by
a UNESCO adviser. Includes extensive statics,
consideration of enrollment characteristics,
student views of the usefulness of subjects
studied, and recommendations for modernizing
the curriculum. DLC

898 Piza, Rodolfo E. Situación actual de los
productores de bananos y los proyectados
contratos con la United Fruit Company. San
José: n.p., 1926. 16 pp.
A protest against the new contract with the
United Fruit Company, which was designed to
open new areas of the nation to banana production, by the owner of a Costa Rican banana
plantation who views the contract from the
perspective of the native producers. He argues that the contract will give competitive
advantages to the company and that unless the
government provides assistance to the national
producers, the opening of new productive areas
will redound solely to the credit of the company. He argues that this is the reason for
their concern, and that charges that they are
involved in a personal vendetta with President
Ricardo Jiménez Oreamuro, who owns land in the
areas to be opened to production by the company, are baseless. DLC DLC-LDS-367

899 Pougin, Edouard. L'état de Costa Rica et ce
qu'on pourrait y faire dans l'intérêt de
l'industrie, du commerce et de l'émigration
Belge. Antwerp: Kornicker, 1863. 24 pp.
Biblio., notes, maps.
An optimistic view of the Costa Rican econ-
omy and its potential, seeking to encourage
Belgian investment and trade. CU-B

900 Prado, Eladio. Juan Santamaría y el libro de
defunciones de la campaña nacional. San José:
Imprenta Lehmann, 1926. 24 pp.
An essay raising doubts about the authen-
ticity of the exploits of the nation's sole
military hero, famed for his bravery in battle
against the filibusterers of William Walker.
Citing inconsistencies in the records that
suggest that Santamaría might have died of
cholera rather than in battle, the author
notes many omissions from the lists of names,
observing that Juan Santamaría might have been
only a partial name, since there were several
individuals named Juan, Santa, and María, with
different last names. The entire controversy
(which in Costa Rica might be called heresy)
is based exclusively on the problems of inac-
curate and inconsistent records. DLC DLC-
LDS-350

(Prado, Eladio)
901 _____. Monografía del Santuario de Nuestra
Señora de los Ángeles de Cartago. San José:
Imprenta Lehmann, 1926. 101 pp. Illus.
    A revision and expansion of the author's
earlier work detailing the history of the
shrine and its significance, with appropriate
prayers and details of its official sanction.
See item CR902. LNHT

902 _____. Nuestra Señora de Vjarrás: historia
del pueblo de Ujarrás y sus leyendas. San
José: Imprenta Lehmann, 1920. 81 pp.
Illus., Maps. 2d ed. San José: Imprenta
Lehmann, 1960. 139 pp.
    An account of the legend of Our Lady of
Ujarrás, patroness of Costa Rica, recounting
the apparition and the miracles attributed to
her, mainly from Colonial days. Followed by
an account of the shrine, its festivities,
devotions, and administration. DLC DLC-LDS-
174

903 _____. La orden franciscana en Costa Rica.
Cartago: Imprenta El Heraldo, 1925. 220 pp.
Biblio., illus., tables.
    Traces the development of the various in-
stitutions of the Franciscans church by church
and post by post. The focus is on the Colonial era, but some of the narrations extend
into and even through the nineteenth century,
to the 1920s. DLC-LDS-365 LNHT BNCR

904 _____. Lo que reclamamos los católicos. San
José: Imprenta Lehmann, 1920. 16 pp.
    A defense of Catholic education, supporting
a bill that would restore it to Costa Rican
schools. Written by a priest and well-known
religious propagandist, it argues that Catholic education is entirely consistent with the
values of the Costa Rican constitution and the
state, and would be good for the nation. DLC

905 Prado, Eladio, and Victor Ortiz. Breve
compendio de la historia de la milagrosa
imagen de Nuestra Señora de Los Ángeles que se
venera en la Ciudad de Cartago, Costa Rica y
piadosa relación en romance de la aparición de
la imagen. San José: Imprenta Lehmann, 1942.
79 pp. Illus., appendix.
    A brief history of the veneration of the
image and the construction and care of the
church, by Prado, followed by a lengthy narration, in poetry, of the legend of the apparition, written by the aging priest who heads
the shrine. The appendix contains church and
governmental documents recognizing the shrine,
and prayers to the virgin. DLC DLC-LDS-349
LNHT

906 Prado Quexada, Alcides, ed. Costa Rica su
música típica y sus autores. San José:
Imprenta Lehmann, 1962. 67 pp. Illus.
    A collection of folksongs, with words and
music. Some selections include biographical
sketches of their authors, with photos, which
provide some background regarding the music as
well. No selection criteria are indicated.
DLC

907 Prieto Tugores, Emilia. Escritos y grabados.
San José: Ministerio de Cultura, Juventud y
Deportes, 1977. 319 pp. Index, biblio.,
illus.
    A collection of essays by a Costa Rican art
professor, with some illustrations by her,
presenting her observations about the development and state of art in Costa Rica and her
commentaries upon and exchanges with various
Costa Rican artists. Most have been previously published during the 1930s and 1940s,
and all are identified as to date and place of
original appearance. BNCR

908 Protti Martinelli, Eduardo. Publicaciones del
Instituto Geográfico Nacional: XV aniversario
(1954-1969), indice bibliográfica. San José:
Instituto Geográfico Nacional, 1970. 16 pp.
    A listing of the Institute's publications
throughout its existence, including books,
pamphlets, maps, journal articles, and mimeographed items. DLC

909 Pucci, Enrique. Plan de una empresa
industrial agrícola en Costa Rica, litoral del
Pacífico; Plan of an Industrial-Agricultural
Enterprise Possible on the Pacific Coast of
Costa Rica. San José: Imprenta Alsina, 1912.
141 pp. Illus.
    A prospectus, with supporting documents and
endorsements, by a prominent Costa Rican attempting to organize a firm in the United
States and secure financing for the purpose of
creating an agricultural project to grow bananas on his land in the Nicoya Peninsula on
the Costa Rican Pacific coast. He details his
plan, describes the area and its prospects,
and includes official endorsements from prominent Costa Ricans and the government. The
text is in both Spanish and English. DLC
DLC-LDS-119

910 Pupo Pérez, Carlos. El doctor don Carlos
Durán. San José: Imprenta Nacional, 1924.
21 pp. Illus.
    A synopsis of the career of a Costa Rican
medical doctor and political figure of the
late nineteenth century who founded the tuber-
culosis sanitarium and served as rector of the
university, president of the National Congress, and president of the Republic. TxU

911 Quesada, Octavio. Breve noticia sobre el
diccionario de legislación de Costa Rica. San
José: Imprenta Alsina, 1904. 80 pp.
    A brief description of the author's two-
volume work of the same title, with the index
and tables of contents, and commentaries by
other lawyers. Yet no citation of the volume
described has been found, hence its fate seems
questionable; this pamphlet appears to be an
advertisement for the forthcoming work. Volume 1, the author says, covers the decrees
and contracts of the government from 1824
through 1900, and volume 2 the circulars,
acuerdos, etc., attendant to the contracts
from 1824 through 1888. DLC DLC-LDS-68

(Quesada, Octavio)

912 _____. Informe: límites entre Alajuela y Heredia. San José: Imprenta Alsina, 1907. 91 pp. Maps, appendixes.

The official report regarding the boundary dispute between these Costa Rican provinces. Contains the historical investigations, geographical data, and a recommendation, with supporting data and documents. DLC-LDS-46 BNCR

913 _____. Límites: San José y Heredia y de Santo Domingo y San Isidro de Heredia. San José: Tipografía Nacional, 1910. 112 pp. Maps, tables.

An official report regarding these boundary disputes in Costa Rica, providing a history, a recommendation for a boundary, and a rationale for the lines proposed. DLC DLC-LDS-96 BNCR

914 _____. Santa Anna, límites del nuevo cantón. San José: Tipografía Nacional, 1908. 134 pp. Illus., maps.

An official report regarding the boundaries of the newly created canton, establishing its jurisdiction. KU

915 Quesada H., Fenelon. Monografía de San Carlos. Alajuela, Costa Rica: Imprenta Falcó, 1958. 32 pp. Illus.

A brief history and description of the canton of San Carlos with illustrations. DLC BNCR

916 Quesada Picado, Máximo, ed. Disposiciones legales relacionadas con el gobierno municipal. San José: Imprenta Nacional, 1939. 332 pp.

A compilation of Costa Rican legislation regulating municipalities. Because there is no formal unified municipal code, this constitutes the best approximation of a comprehensive guide. DLC

917 Quesada Vargas, Octavio. Proceso de la resturación; o la intervención Americana en Costa Rica. San José: Imprenta Alsina, 1922. 328 pp.

A compilation of press articles and legislation, with some linking narration, covering the era of the Tinoco regime. Contends that the Wilson administration went too far in insisting on the return of particular individuals to the presidency; condemns the Yankee intervention while simultaneously criticizing the Tinoco regime as illegal, yet notes that the succeeding regime was just as despotic. In effect it endorses Wilson's purpose but decries his method as a poor precedent constituting a second coup d'état conducted by the Yankees. The selections all appeared in the San José press between 1919 and 1922 and recount the various events, charges, and countercharges of the era, providing an indication of the various political currents and viewpoints of this turbulent period. BNCR

918 Quinjano, Aníbal, and Francisco C. Weffort. Populismo, marginalización y dependencia. San

José: EDUCA, 1976. 284 pp. 2d ed. San José: EDUCA, 1977. 330 pp. BNCR

919 Quinjano Quesada, Alberto. La campaña electoral de 1939 y el gobierno del presidente Cortés. San José: Imprenta Borrasé, 1939. 32 pp.

A tract favoring the candidacy of Calderón Guardia in the Costa Rican election campaign of 1940. Traces his participation in earlier electoral struggles and the Liberal opposition to him while warning against interference by the government of León Cortés in the electoral campaign. The account is somewhat episodic and the focus, despite the title, is on Calderón Guardia rather than León Cortes. DLC-LDS-841 BNCR

920 _____. Costa Rica ayer y hoy, 1800-1939. San José: Imprenta Borrasé, 1939. 771 pp. Biblio., illus.

A history of foreigners in Costa Rica and their contributions to national development. Consists chiefly of brief paragraphs describing the principal foreigners and their business activities, with photos of the individuals and their enterprises. Includes discussions of their cultural influence and the formation of institutions, their contributions in the fields of medicine and public health, their effect on international relations, and various other aspects of national development. All are covered in very brief commentaries, but the collection serves to gather references to foreigners in a single volume, suggesting the importance of their contributions to the nation. DLC LNHT BNCR

921 Quintana, Emilio. Bananos: la vida de los peones en la Yunai. Managua: Ediciones Culturales, 1976. 64 pp.

A brief novelette focusing on the lives of the peasants working in the foreign-owned banana plantations and the indignities to which they are subjected. Describes the dehumanizing experiences in vivid and emotional prose, emphasizing the cultural conflicts involved in such work and in the operation of the plantations. LNHT

922 Quirós, Manuel A. Prontuario de legislación financiera y de leyes de banco. San José: Imprenta Alsina, 1916. 46 pp.

A chronological listing of laws regulating finance and banking in Costa Rica, listed topically, covering the period from the 1840s to 1916. Most of the legislation was enacted after 1890. DLC-LDS-699

923 Quirós Aguilar, Ernesto. Historia de la cruz roja costarricense. San José: Imprenta La Tribuna, 1928. 36 pp.

A brief collection of documents and official acts tracing the activities of the Costa Rican Red Cross from its foundation in 1885 through 1928. The emphasis on changes in structure and on associated agencies, focused particularly on the 1920s. Only brief

(Quirós Aguilar, Ernesto)
  connecting narrations supplement the documents. DLC-LDS-404

924 _____. Los Quirós en Costa Rica. San José: Imprenta Trejos, 1948. 48 pp. Biblio., illus.
  A genealogy and history of a particularly well-known family, tracing it from Colonial times to World War I; compiled by one of its members. The focus is on the nineteenth century. DLC LNHT BNCR

925 Quirós Amador, Tulia. Geografía de Costa Rica. San José: Ministerio de Obras Públicas, 1954. iii, 192 pp. Biblio., notes, maps, tables.
  Though general in approach, this volume is not a school text but a scholarly work. It covers the usual topics of climate, physical setting, landforms, flora and fauna, population, economy, resources, commerce, etc., in general terms but nevertheless contains considerable data for the specialist. DLC BNCR

926 Ramírez Arias, Mariano. Algunas características demográficas del área metropolitana de San José. San José: Ministerio de Economía y Hacienda, 1957. 68 pp. Maps, tables.
  A detailed study of the growth of the San José metropolitan area from 1927 through 1955. Extensive tables, graphs, and maps show the changes, the rates of change, the directions of movement, and the problems involved in providing services and transportation. Prepared under the auspices of the Department of Statistics and Census. DLC

927 _____. Crecimiento de la población estudiantil universitaria. San José: Universidad de Costa Rica, 1959. 249 pp. Biblio., tables.
  A detailed study of the university's past growth containing graphs and tables showing the trends and projections based on these trends, extending into the 1970s. Includes many educational statistics for the primary and secondary schools as well as for the university. DLC BNCR

928 Ramírez Fajardo, Aníbal. Las formas de tenecia de la tierra en Costa Rica y algunos otros aspectos de la actividad agropecuaria. San José: Universidad de Costa Rica, 1961. 270 pp.
  A compilation of data about landholdings and agriculture in Costa Rica. Drawing principally on the 1965 agricultural census, it presents extensive statistics and includes classification of landholdings by size. BNCR

929 Ramos, Lilia, ed. Júblio y pena del recuerdo. San José: Ministerio de Educación Pública, 1965. 439 pp. Index, biblio., illus.
  An anthology of writings on the history of San José, Costa Rica. Drawn from the previously published works of various historians and writers, it consists mainly of essays

regarding its significant figures and institutions. DLC LNHT BNCR

930 Reni, Aníbal. Estampas guanacastecas: recados criollos. San José: n.p., 1944. 68 pp. Illus.
  A rich description of the author's native Guanacaste region of Costa Rica, in the form of a series of short stories set in this area and based on local people, life, and folklore. BNCR

931 _____. Sacan juches: cuentos guanacastecos. San José: Editorial Costa Rica, 1976. 109 pp.
  A collection of short stories set in and based on the folklore of the Guanacaste region of Costa Rica, rich in description of the area. DLC BNCR

932 La República. Una polémica memorable. San José: Imprenta Moderna, 1914. 61 pp.
  A political debate that took place in the Costa Rican Congress in December 1913 between Alejandro Rivas Vázquez and Manuel Diéguez, regarding the political confrontation between Máximo Fernández and Rafael Yglesias. DLC-LDS BNCR

933 La República de Costa Rica. Barcelona: La Industria de Manuel Tasís, 1914. 39 pp. Tables.
  A compilation of general data, focusing principally on facilities and the contemporary situation. DLC-LDS-145 BNCR

934 La République de Costa Rica: notice géographique et statistique. Paris: Louis Conard, 1913. 50 pp. Maps, tables.
  General descriptive data designed to interest Europeans in trade and investment, providing current information. The topical arrangement provides cultural, climatic, and physical data but is focused on economics and finance. DLC DLC-LDS-257

935 Retana, Marco. La noche de los amadores: cuentos. San José: Editorial Costa Rica, 1975. 86 pp. Illus.
  A collection of twelve short stories depicting in vivid prose the life of the rural peasants of Costa Rica, their everyday problems, trials, tribulations, and emotions. Reflects the author's residence in the rural areas and his familiarity with their lifestyle and problems. DLC

936 Reuss, Lawrence A., and J.F. Montoya R. Tipo y tamaño de finca en el cantón de Atenas, 1959. San José: Ministerio de Agricultura e Industrias, 1960. 90 pp. Illus., tables.
  A study of farm operation and management in Costa Rica, based on a survey of seventy-nine farms in this canton in the province of Alajuela. Not surprisingly, the authors find that return on capital increases with the size of the farm and are critical of the lack of intensive cultivation and the scant use of fertilizer and scientific methods, which they conclude limit yields and will cause long-term

problems in view of increasing population.
DLC

937 Revista de Costa Rica en el siglo XIX. San
José: Tipografía Nacional, 1902. 404 pp.
Illus., tables.
   A useful compilation of information by and
about Costa Rica's leading literary figures of
that century, with essays on the nation's
history, economy, and culture, and several
bibliographical studies. In fact, it was
edited by Juan Fernández Ferraz and Francisco
M. Iglesias, but that is indicated in the
volume rather than on the title page or cover,
and hence it is usually cited by title only.
DLC

938 La revolución del 22 de febrero de 1918. 2
vols. San José: Imprenta Falcó y Borrasé,
1919. 32, 64 pp.
   Part of a series of folios for popular
use, this item contains a brief summary and
reproductions of documents and press articles
regarding the 1918 maneuvering involving the
Tinoco regime and what it calls the "semana
trágica," supposedly taken from the memoirs of
an unidentified "revolutionary compatriot" of
Rogelio Fernández Güell. It recounts an
attempted uprising and the arrest and prosecu-
tion of a large number of individuals. DLC

939 Reyes H., Alfonso. Así es Costa Rica: visión
de un mexicano. San José: n.p., 1945.
83 pp.
   A descriptive account by the head of the
Mexican Tourist Office in Central America,
clearly designed to encourage visits to the
isthmian republic. Includes basic descriptive
data not only of facilities, but also of social life and customs. DLC LNHT BNCR

940 Roberts, W. Dayton. Strachan of Costa Rica:
Missionary Insights and Strategies. Grand
Rapids, Mich.: William B. Eerdmans Co., 1971.
187 pp. Index.
   An evangelical missionary's account of the
activities of a fellow missionary, his
brother-in-law R. Kenneth Strachan, who served
for thirty years in the Protestant missions in
Central America, much of it in Puerto Limón,
Costa Rica, and later headed the Latin American Mission. A combination memoir by the
author, loving history of his friend, and
account of the growth of the evangelical missions and their activities. DLC

941 Roberts Smith, Edward. Maestros de
juventudes: Brenes Mesén y García Monge. San
José: Editorial Don Quijote, 1971. 75 pp.
Biblio., notes, illus.
   Brief essays on two significant Costa Rican
educators of the early twentieth century.
Discusses their careers and outlooks, emphasizing their positivism and their impact.
Based on their writings and on appropriate
secondary sources regarding Costa Rican education and intellectual currents. BNCR

942 Rodríguez, Juvenal Valerio. Turrialba: su
desarrollo histórico. Turrialba: Talleres
Gráficos Tormo, 1953. 197 pp. Illus., maps.

A history of the city of Turrialba, consisting of extensive quotations from appropriate documents, with connecting narration.
Includes physical description. The history of
the region is traced from Colonial times to
the present, including its use as a penal zone
in the 1840s, the commentaries of various
travelers who passed through it, and the development of the city. Considerations of the
significance of the Atlantic railroad and the
impact of the world depression of the 1930s on
the local economy are included. BNCR

943 Rodríguez Camacho, Francisco. Glorias de
Costa Rica. San José: n.p., 1895. 44 pp.
   A brief account of the battles of Santa
Rosa and Rivas, hailing the actions and brav-
ery of the Costa Rican troops who confronted
the forces of William Walker. DLC-LDS-120
BNCR

944 Rodríguez López, Alcides. En el sendero de mi
vida. San José: Imprenta Lehmann, 1974. 78
pp. Illus.
   A series of semi-autobiographical short
stories set in the author's native San Ramón
in the province of Alajuela, based on his
youth in the days before electricity reached
the town. He describes the town, its people,
institutions, illustrious citizens, and traditions. BNCR

945 Rodríguez Porras, Armando. Juan Rafael Mora
Porras y la guerra contra los filibusteros.
San José: Imprenta Las Américas, 1955. 212
pp. Biblio., appendixes.
   A history of Costa Rica during the 1850s,
focusing on the man who served as president
throughout much of the period and including
considerable detail regarding the campaign
against William Walker. DLC LNHT BNCR

946 Rodríguez Vega, Eugenio. Apuntes para una
sociología costarricense. San José:
Editorial Universitaria, 1953. 130 pp.
Biblio.
   An effort to describe the social reality of
Costa Rica. Includes an historical survey of
the development of the nation focusing on its
effects on the society's outlook and composition. Describes and analyzes the various
facets of the collective Costa Rican character
and its mannerisms. Discusses the various
social classes in the nation, their position,
and their life-styles. An influential piece
whose author later became rector of the University of Costa Rica. DLC LNHT

947 _____. Los días de don Ricardo Jiménez. San
José: Editorial Costa Rica, 1971. 188 pp.
2d ed. San José: Editorial Costa Rica, 1974.
188 pp.
   A sympathetic biography of Ricardo Jiménez
Oreamuro, based principally on the newspapers
of the era. Frequently cites his public
statements, hails his career as the essence of
Costa Rican Liberal beliefs and hence acclaims
his leadership of that party. The author
emphasizes Jiménez's quarrels with the United
Fruit Company as particular manifestations of

his stance as spokesman for the nation. DLC
LNHT BNCR

948 Rojas Corrales, Ramón. La infancia
delincuente en Costa Rica. San José:
Tipografía Nacional, 1914. 159 pp. Illus.,
tables.
    An early study of juvenile delinquency in
Costa Rica, complete with statistical tables.
Includes discussion of the causes and some
proposals regarding programs to alleviate
them, though the viewpoint reflects the more
rigid views of its day. DLC DLC-LDS-140
BNCR

949 Rojas Solano, Hector. Monografía de
Alajuelita. San José: Imprenta Lehmann,
1973. 248 pp. Illus.
    A topical history of the canton of
Alajuelita in Costa Rica. Includes a
description of its current facilities and a
genealogy of its leading families, with appropriate illustrations. BNCR

950 _____. Santa Rosa: cuña de nuestra soberanía
y hermandad centroamericana. San José:
Ministerio de Agricultura y Ganadería, 1972.
76 pp. Biblio., illus.
    A history of the Battle of Santa Rosa and a
description of the national park that now
occupies the site of this confrontation between Costa Rican forces and those of William
Walker during the campaigns of the mid-1850s.
BNCR

951 Rojas Suárez, Juan Francisco, ed. Costa Rica
en la segunda guerra mundial: 7 de diciembre
de 1941, 7 de diciembre de 1943. San José:
Imprenta Nacional, 1943. 342 pp. Illus.,
tables.
    A collection of documents, consisting prin-
cipally of laws passed between 1941 and 1943
during the Calderón Guardia administration.
Includes public declarations and proclamations
covering internal as well as external affairs,
with brief introductions to the documents but
no general narration. Focuses on the Calderón
Guardia regime rather than World War II. DLC
LNHT BNCR

952 Rojas Vincenzi, Ricardo. Crítica literaria.
San José: Imprenta Borrasé, 1929. 63 pp.
    An essay on the life of Joaquín García
Monge, seeking to identify the influences upon
his education and writing by describing his
experiences and listing the writers whose
works influenced him, followed by brief commentaries on Auristela C. De Jiménez and
Francisco Rodríguez Ruiz. DLC DLC-LDS-422
LNHT

953 _____. Mosáicos: vida y obra de Luís Dobles
Segreda. San José: Imprenta Trejos, 1927.
38 pp. Illus.
    A brief biographical sketch and review of
the career of Luís Dobles Segreda, providing
single-paragraph summaries of the main themes
of his literary works and his literary criticism, as well as an outline of his career as a
professor. DLC DLC-LDS-370 LNHT

954 Romero, Mario. La deserción estudiantil en
la Universidad de Costa Rica. Guatemala:
Universidad de San Carlos, 1964. 96 pp.
Tables, appendix.
    A professor at the University of Costa Rica
studies student attrition at his school
through the use of interviews and questionnaires. He details the patterns for 1962,
indicating the numerous factors involved in
interruptions of studies. These include family background, economic status and age, job
opportunities, personal and family problems,
and problems adjusting to the university milieu. The questionnaire is printed as an
appendix. BNCR

955 Romero Pérez, Jorge Enrique. Contribución a
la comprensión del estado moderno de Costa
Rica: el reformismo político y el pensamiento
de Rodrigo Facio Brenes. San José:
Universidad de Costa Rica, 1976. 260 pp.
Biblio., notes.
    A study of the political activity and ideas
of an important figure of the National Liberation party. Covers his early years at the
University of Costa Rica and at the Center for
the Study of National Problems, as well as his
later governmental career. Particular emphasis is placed on his role in the formation and
development of the Center. The author concludes that Facio is a reformer who favors
modernization of Costa Rican society and its
economy through a free system and a mixed
economy. Provides details regarding Facio's
expressions on these subjects and his analytical efforts by quoting from his studies,
some of which are not well known. BNCR

956 _____. La licitación pública en Costa Rica.
San José: Universidad de Costa Rica, 1975.
434 pp.
    Originally a thesis, this volume consists
of a handbook for lawyers, outlining the current laws and practices affecting basic legal
activities in the nation. BNCR

957 Rosenberg, Mark B. Las luchas por el seguro
social en Costa Rica. San José: Editorial
Costa Rica, 1980.

958 Ross, Delmer G. Rails Across Central America:
The Development of the Costa Rican Interoceanic and Other Railways. Mobile, Ala.:
Institute for Research in Latin America, 1976.
153 pp. Index, notes, maps.
    A survey tracing the broad outline of the
development of Costa Rica's rail lines, covering construction programs, financing, and
maintenance. Based on secondary sources and
some United Fruit Company documents. Provides
an effective overview of the various aspects
of railroad development and their linkage.
DLC

959 Rovinski, Samuel. Las fisgonas de paso ancho.
San José: Editorial Costa Rica, 1975. 45 pp.
Illus.
    A play offering a satirical treatment of
Costa Rican institutions and life, casting the
nation and its problems in a different light

by indicating the foibles of its institutions while capturing its spirit. DLC BNCR

960 Ruíz Solórzano, Vilma. 25 dibujos de Francisco Alvarado Abella. San José: Editorial Costa Rica, 1971. 34 pp. Biblio., illus.
    A collection of pen-and-ink drawings by this Costa Rican artist, with descriptive text. Originally prepared as a university thesis. DLC

961 Saborio Montenegro, Alfredo. Teatro costarricense: la Virgen de Los Ángeles y Juan Santamaría. San José: Imprenta Nacional, 1942. 141 pp.
    Two plays with Costa Rican national themes, one dealing with the national patroness and the other with the national military hero of the campaign against William Walker. DLC BNCR

962 Sáenz, Alfredo, ed. Contratos y actuaciones de las compañías del Ferrocarril de Costa Rica, la Northern Railway Company, la United Fruit Company en Costa Rica. San José: Imprenta La Tribuna, 1929. vii, 478 pp. Tables.
    A compilation of documents by the former Costa Rican inspector general of railroads, focusing particularly on the provisions of the railroad concessions and the various contracts, but also including data regarding exports. Designed as a critical review of corporate actions, with the intention of providing the government information with which to secure better terms when the contracts are renegotiated. Includes allegations regarding the companies' role in the boundary dispute with Panama and the actions of the United Fruit Company. Presents documents, contracts, laws, letters, newspaper reports, and charges and countercharges. Though the value of the material varies, this is a useful collection of data for the operation of the railroads and the United Fruit Company from 1907 through 1928. DLC-LDS-419 LNHT

963 Sáenz, Alfredo. Se denuncian ante el juzgado primero del crimen irregularidades cometidas por la Compañía del Ferrocarril de Costa Rica, la Northern Railway Co., y la United Fruit Co. San José: Imprenta Española, n.d. 45 pp.
    A series of charges and annexed documents filed in legal proceedings against the railroads, charging that they abused their privileges and ignored contractual terms, particularly in importing duty-free items not included in the concessions. BNCR

964 Sáenz, Vicente. Traidores y déspotas de Centro-América. San José: Imprenta Falcó y Borrasé, 1920. 140 pp. 2d ed. San José: Imprenta Falcó y Borrasé, 1920. 140 pp.
    A series of press articles and speeches written or published during 1917 and 1918, condemning the Tinoco regime as an effort to impose despotism on Costa Rica and break its tradition of democracy. The commentaries focus on the coup, the assassination of

Fernández Güell, and the ambitions of Tinoco. DLC-LDS-182 BNCR

965 Sáenz Cordero, Manuel. Los ferrocarriles en Costa Rica. San José: Imprenta del Comercio, 1911. 39 pp. Illus., tables.
    Discusses each of the separate railroad lines in the nation, providing basic outline data on formation, origin, extent, and construction, with current statistics about traffic, equipment, and financial position. DLC DLC-LDS-104

966 Sáenz Elizondo, Carlos Luís. Costarriqueñas del 56: 15 de Septiembre de 1956. San José: Imprenta Las Américas, 1956. 46 pp.
    A collection of stories about Costa Rican women who played a part in the campaigns against the Walker intervention, ranging from a soldier to the wife of the president to the flag maker. BNCR

967 Sáenz Maroto, Alberto. Historia agrícola de Costa Rica. San José: Universidad de Costa Rica, 1970. 1,087 pp. Biblio., illus.
    A formidable tome, consisting primarily of a compilation of laws relating to agriculture and brief histories of the various crops, with a chronological outline of single-paragraph descriptions of each. Contains a great deal of useful information, but hardly constitutes a real history of the nation's agriculture. BNCR

968 ____. Suelos volcánicos cafeteros de Costa Rica. San José: Universidad de Costa Rica, 1966. 355 pp. Biblio., illus., maps, tables.
    A geographical and geological history of Costa Rica focusing on soils and climate, particularly on the soil types resulting from volcanic erruptions and their implications for coffee cultivation. The final chapters constitute a classification of the soils of the central valley. BNCR

969 Sáenz Maroto, Alberto, Luís Ángel Vives Fernández, and Jesús M. Bárcenas Barreto. Estudio estadístico matemático del clima del Valle Central de Costa Rica. San José: Universidad de Costa Rica, 1963. 169 pp. Biblio., maps, tables.
    A statistical analysis of climatic conditions in the Costa Rican plateau, based on the years 1949-57, concluding that there are in fact several regional variations within the valley and defining each of these "mini climates," with monthly characteristics; includes extensive maps and statistical tables. LNHT BNCR

970 Sáenz P., Carlos, and C. Foster Knight. Tenure Security, Land Titling, and Agricultural Development in Costa Rica. San José: Universidad de Costa Rica, 1971. 107 pp. Notes, illus., maps, tables.
    An AID-financed study designed to emphasize the role of the Costa Rican legal system and national law in the development of the agricultural sector. Contains data regarding land tenure, distribution and size of holdings in

various selected regions, and extensive tables
and graphs regarding the identifiable trends
and the comparative distribution in the outlying areas. BNCR

971 Salas Marrera, Oscar A., and Rodrigo Barahona
     Israel. Derecho agrario. San José:
     Universidad de Costa Rica, 1973. xxvi, 897
     pp. Biblio., notes, tables.
     A general treatise on all aspects of agrar-
     ian law, but focusing sharply on Costa Rica
     and drawing most of its cases and examples
     from the modern era in that nation. Discusses
     all aspects, including land ownership, coloni-
     zation, labor contracts, and commerce as well
     as the specifics of many of the region's pre-
     dominant crops. BNCR

972 Salazar, Eduardo. A los que se preocupan por
     los problemas eléctricos in Costa Rica. San
     José: Imprenta La Tribuna, 1971. 60 pp.
     A response to and critique of the proposal
     of the Servicio Nacional de Electricidad and
     its head, Alfredo González Flores, rejecting
     its arguments. Contends that what is involved
     is nationalization and confiscation rather
     than regulation, and that the proposal vio-
     lates the legal rights granted to the com-
     panies by Costa Rica in their concessions.
     Denies the practicality of the arrangement,
     concluding that it is all illegal under Costa
     Rican law. DLC-LDS-508

973 Salazar Arrué, Salvador [Salarué, pseud.].
     Cuentos de Barro. San Salvador: Editorial la
     Montaña, 1933. 180 pp. Latest ed. San
     Salvador: Ministerio de Educación, 1975.
     208 pp.
     A series of short stories focusing pri-
     marily on the life of the poor, whether
     Indians, peasants, or laborers. Represents
     the new emphasis on social consciousness in
     the region's literature. DLC LNHT BNCR

974 Salazar García, Salomón. Diccionario de
     provincialismos y barbarismos centro-
     americanos y ejercicios de ortología clásica.
     2d ed. San Salvador: Tipografía La Unión,
     1910. 312 pp.
     A dictionary of Costa Rican idioms,
     phrases, and local works, with definitions and
     explanations of their origin. DLC

975 Salazar Mora, Jorge Mario. Calderón Guardia.
     San José: Publicaciones del Ministerio de
     Cultura, Juventud y Deportes, 1980. 240 pp.

976 _____. La iglesia rebelde de América Latina:
     el caso de Costa Rica. San José: Universidad
     de Costa Rica, 1978. 46 pp. Biblio.
     A brief survey of the role of the church in
     Costa Rica, followed by a discussion of the
     so-called rebel or reformist elements of the
     mid-twentieth century and their efforts to
     ally the church with the underprivileged.
     Provides a handy guide to the stances of va-
     rious Costa Rican priests in recent times.
     BNCR

977 Salazar Mora, Orlando. Máximo Fernández. San
     José: Ministerio de Cultura, Juventud y
     Deportes, 1975. 345 pp. Biblio., notes.
     A biography of the founder of the Costa
     Rican Republican party, whose career extended
     from the 1880s through 1917 and included ser-
     vice as head of his party, several terms in
     Congress, two unsuccessful presidential candi-
     dacies, and the role of chief negotiator of
     the Costa Rican national debt. Based on re-
     search in the National Archives, a newspaper
     of the day, and appropriate secondary sources,
     this volume traces his entire career in de-
     tail; it includes discussion of and extracts
     from his political polemics, and also provides
     an ample sketch of the political scene of this
     era. Noting Fernández's peasant origins, the
     author considers his party a challenge to the
     oligarchy that dominated the nation's poli-
     tics. BNCR

978 Salazar Obando, Omar. Monografía de
     Turrialba. San José: Imprenta Lehmann, 1953.
     338 pp. Biblio., illus.
     A geographical description of the city of
     Turrialba and a history of its development
     from pre-Columbian times to the present, with
     copious documentary excerpts. Discusses its
     various entities and organizations and covers
     such topics as education, sports, social
     classes, newspapers, etc. BNCR

979 Un Saleriano. Vocabulario de palabras-
     modismos y refranes ticos. Cartago: Escuela
     Tipografía Salesiana, 1938. 132 pp. Biblio.
     A collection of Costa Rican modisms and
     idioms, arranged alphabetically, with defini-
     tions. DLC-LDS-897

980 Sanabria Martínez, Víctor Manuel. Anselmo
     Llorente y Lafuente, primer obispo de Costa
     Rica: apuntamientos históricos. San José:
     Imprenta Universal, 1933. 403 pp. Index,
     biblio., notes, tables, appendixes. 2d ed.
     San José: Editorial Costa Rica, 1972.
     397 pp. Biblio., notes, tables, appendixes.
     The initial study by a now well-known Costa
     Rican historian, clergyman and later bishop,
     this volume traces the life and works of the
     first bishop of Costa Rica from his ap-
     pointment in 1851 through his death in 1871.
     It also encompasses the formation of the dio-
     cese which makes it also a history of the
     church in Costa Rica during these years. Con-
     tains valuable information about the number of
     priests; enumerates the various parishes,
     offering statistics on their baptisms and
     funerals; and encompasses the entire realm of
     church activity, including the role of the
     church in politics. A collection of church
     documents and statistics is appended. DLC
     LNHT BNCR

981 _____. Bernardo Augusto Thiel, segundo obispo
     de Costa Rica: apuntamientos históricos y
     primeros. San José: Imprenta Lehmann, 1941.
     650 pp. Index, biblio., notes, illus.,
     appendixes.
     A biography of the second bishop of the
     diocese of San José, providing a highly

(Sanabria Martínez, Víctor Manuel)
detailed account of his turbulent life. Thiel
served as bishop from 1880 through 1910, during the Liberal-Conservative confrontation
over the relationship between the church and
state, and his activities in defense of the
church resulted in his expulsion by General
Prospero Fernández in 1884. He was declared a
"Benemérito" of the nation during the twentieth century. Traces his political and religious activities, as well as his travels
throughout Central America during his exile.
Provides as much data about the church in
Central America during the nineteenth century
as it does about Thiel, and hence is partially
a history of the church-state confrontation
and political problems that resulted from it
throughout the late nineteenth century. Discusses other isthmian republics in addition to
Costa Rica. Appended documents include pastorals and letters by the subject. DLC-LDS-
911 BNCR

982   _____. Episcopologio de la diócesis de
Nicaragua y Costa Rica. San José: Imprenta
Lehmann, 1943. 88 pp.
     A listing, with brief biographical data, of
all the bishops of Nicaragua and Costa Rica
from Colonial times, when the diocese was
combined, to the mid-nineteenth century, when
they were separated to reflect the national
boundaries. BNCR

983   _____. Genealogías de Cartago hasta 1850. 6
vols. San José: Privately published, 1957.
Index.
     A genealogy of Cartago province in Costa
Rica, from Colonial times to 1850, based on
documentary research in the region. Includes
all the area's families, many of which played
important roles in the development of the
nation. Published in mimeograph. The volumes
contain an alphabetical listing of individuals, with lists of children, births, and
deaths. An extensive index occupies more than
200 unnumbered pages of the final volume. DLC
LNHT

984   _____. La primera vacante de la diócesis de
San José, 1871-1880. San José: Imprenta
Lehmann, 1935. 399 pp. Notes, illus. 2d ed.
San José: Editorial Costa Rica, 1973. 282
pp. Index, notes, illus.
     A history of the Costa Rican church during
a particularly crucial period between the
death of its first prelate and the appointment
of his successor, which coincided with a period of considerable church-state conflict in
the rest of Central America, including the
reexpulsion of the Jesuits from Guatemala.
DLC-LDS-812 LNHT BNCR

985   _____. Últimos años de la orden franciscana
en Costa Rica. San José: Imprenta Lehmann,
1931. 59 pp.
     Commenting that the work on the Franciscans
in Costa Rica by Eladio Prado, published by
the Capuchin order, focuses on the Colonial
era more than on the nineteenth century and is
inadequate in dealing with the latter, this
priest offers his own version, focusing on the
role of the Franciscans from independence
through their expulsion in 1878. He provides
a detailed history of the order, particularly
of its headquarters monastery in Cartago,
including complete lists of all the abbots and
priests at the monastary during that era,
their years and place of service in Costa
Rica, and a full inventory of the possessions
of the monastery. DLC DLC-LDS-504

986 Sánchez Bonilla, Gonzalo. El pobre manco.
San José: Imprenta del Comercio, 1910.
44 pp.
     A brief costumbrista novel set in Costa
Rica and based on local customs. Frequently
uses local modisms and idioms, which are defined in a glossary. Awarded a prize in a
literary competition in 1909. DLC DLC-LDS-
160

987 Sánchez García, Álvaro. Resumen biográfico de
don Ricardo Jiménez O. San José: Editorial
Covao, 1959. 18 pp.
     Brief essays concerning episodes in the
career of the three-time president of Costa
Rica. BNCR

988 Sánchez Ruphuy, Rodrigo. El impacto de la
comunicación en el desarrollo rural: una
investigación en Costa Rica; un estudio
adicional. San José: Programa Interamericano
de Información Popular, 1968. 64 pp.
Biblio., illus., tables.
     A brief overview of rural change resulting
from this program. The program's pamphlets
and the lengthy survey used occupy most of the
volume. DLC

989 Sancho, Mario. Costa Rica: suiza
centroamericana. San José: Imprenta La
Tribuna, 1935. 57 pp.
     A general critical analysis of Costa Rican
society and problems. Criticizes the classes,
noting the differences between them, their
attitudes, and their desires and placing them
in a broader global context. The work offers
commentary on a wide variety of social customs
and life-styles within the nation, as well as
on the political sphere. It is generally
critical of the nation, and of the divergent
focuses of the classes and the communications
gaps between them, and hence is skeptical of
Costa Rica's ability to solve its contemporary
problems. DLC DLC-LDS-831 BNCR

990   _____. El doctor Ferraz: su influencia en la
educación y en la cultura del país. San José:
Imprenta La Tribuna, 1934. 59 pp. Illus.
     A tribute to Dr. Valeriano Fernández
Ferraz, a native of Spain who taught at the
Colegio de San Luís in Cartago, Costa Rica,
from 1869 through 1913, and had as his pupils
many of the nation's intellectual and political leaders. Extols and summarizes his
career and his dedication to education, noting
some of his eminent pupils and reproducing a
number of his speeches and orations about him.
DLC DLC-LDS-789

991 Sandner, Gerhard. Agrakolonisation in Costa Rica. Keil: Schmidt & Klaunig, 1961. 199 pp. Biblio., illus., maps, tables. La colonización agrícola de Costa Rica. San José: Instituto Geográfico de Costa Rica, 1962. 168 pp. Illus., maps.

A detailed study of the history of internal migrations to rural areas in Costa Rica, emphasizing rural colonization efforts from the Colonial era to the present. Aerial photography is used to follow the migration routes, and extensive statistics provide an indication of the scope of the population movements and their significance. The focus is on Colonial times and the nineteenth century. Numerous photos, tables, and maps. DLC LNHT BNCR

992 _____. Turrubares, estudio de geografía regional: problemas sociales y económicos de la expansión agrícola de Costa Rica. San José: Instituto Geográfico de Costa Rica, 1960. 95 pp. Biblio., illus., maps.

A geographical study of the mountains of the northern Pacific coast region of Costa Rica. Includes illustrations and maps as well as detailed descriptions and climatic data. Based on fieldwork conducted during 1958 and 1959 by a German geographer. DLC LNHT BNCR

993 Sandner, Gerhard, and H. Nuhn. Das nördliche Tiefland von Costa Rica: Geographische Regionalanalyse als Grundlage für die Entwicklungsplanung. Berlin: Walter de Gruyter, 1971. 202 pp. Biblio., illus., maps, tables.

A detailed geographical study considering climate, physical setting, development, human resources, etc.; with excellent maps. DLC LNHT

994 Sandoval de Fonseca, Virginia, ed. Manuel González Zeledón (Magón). San José: Ministerio de Cultura, 1974. 198 pp. Illus.

A short biography and analysis of the writings of a well-known Costa Rican short-story author of the late nineteenth century, who closed his career in the United States. This is followed by an anthology of selections from his works. Hails him as the discoverer of the theme of national customs and praises his use of national themes and settings in his short stories. DLC LNHT BNCR

995 Sanfuentes, Julio. La mujer costarricense: su fisomonía moral, su influencia en la evolución de nuestra sociedad. San José: Imprenta Alsina, 1906. 15 pp.

A brief speech, without specifics, extolling the role of women of all classes and their influence on Costa Rican development. DLC-LDS-42

996 Santoro, Gustavo, et al. Algunos aspectos de la vida urbana en San José: tres problemas apremiantes. San José: Universidad de Costa Rica, 1962. 62 pp. Illus., tables.

A detailed study of four neighborhoods of San José, conducted under the auspices of the University of Costa Rica. Provides detailed information regarding the population, density, age groups, housing facilities, communications, transport, and public services and identifies problems for future consideration. The statistics and charts are particularly useful. DLC LNHT BNCR

997 Sapper, Karl. Viajes a varias partes de la República de Costa Rica: 1899 y 1924. San José: Imprenta Universal, 1942. 140 pp.

A series of selections from this well-known German geographer's journals and published accounts of his travels and observations on two trips to Costa Rica. Most of it is based on a visit in 1899 and includes commentaries on the capital, the volcanoes, and many parts of the republic. His 1924 visit was more limited and for the purpose of presenting an address, which is included. LNHT BNCR

998 Sariola, Sakari. Social Class and Social Mobility in a Costa Rican Town. Turrialba: Inter-American Institute of Agricultural Sciences, 1954. vi, 136 pp. Biblio., notes, maps, tables, appendixes.

A study of the city of Turrialba and its change during recent years, based on a questionnaire and field work by a Finnish scholar during 1950-54. The focus is on the concept of class and its influence, status, and social mobility as measured by various attitudes and levels of living. The various classes in the town and their characteristics are all defined. DLC BNCR

999 Schaufelberger, Paul. Costa Rica. San José: Imprenta Universal, 1931. 83 pp. Illus., maps, tables.

A geological study of Costa Rica, with detailed description of the evolution of the landforms of the nation and with particular emphasis on volcanoes. Includes discussion of fossils characteristic of the area and of each specific volcano. DLC DLC-LDS-509

1000 Schaufelberger, Paul, and Emel Jiménez S. Apuntes de geología: algunas nociones sobre terremotos y temblores en Costa Rica. San José: Imprenta La Tribuna, 1933. 31 pp. Illus., maps, tables.

A brief analysis of the locations and causes of Costa Rican earthquakes, combining observation with discussion of the geological development of the republic. DLC-LDS-764

1001 Schiffer, Jacobo. La fase oculta de la guerra civil en Costa Rica. San José: EDUCA, 1979. 160 pp.

1002 Schroeder, John. Costa Rica: Immigration Pamphlet with Two Maps: A Guide for the Agricultural Class Coming from Other Countries to Make Costa Rica Its Home. San José: Tipografía Nacional, 1893. 173 pp. Illus., maps, tables.

A volume designed to explain procedures and encourage immigration to Costa Rica. Presents the usual basic descriptive data, with explanations of the pertinent laws and a prospective budget for the first two years. Contains

considerable data about the efforts to encourage immigration and also about the nation.
DLC DLC-LDS-112 LNHT BNCR

1003 Schurr, Anton. Costa Rica und seine Wirtschaftlichen Verhältnisse. Würzburg: n.p., 1919. 54 pp. Biblio., tables.
A general survey, written from secondary sources, originally as a doctoral dissertation, providing basic descriptive data on geography, politics, and economy, with particular emphasis on the latter. DLC-LDS-389

1004 Segarra, José, and Joaquín Julio Segarra. Excursión por América: Costa Rica. San José: Imprenta Alsina, 1907. 655 pp. Index, illus., maps.
A detailed travelogue providing considerable descriptive data regarding Costa Rica in 1905. Emphasizes people, customs, lifestyles, and places visited during an extensive tour of much of the republic. Includes illustrations. DLC DLC-LDS-36 LNHT BNCR

1005 Segura, Rosalía de. Biografía de Florentino Castro Soto. San José: Editorial Borrasé, 1954. 178 pp. Illus.
A collection of data about the life of a Costa Rican finquero, describing his life and estates, and his political activities during the early 1940s, as indicated through the reproduction of a series of newspaper articles from that era. The material is disparate and deals with only a few aspects of his life and career. BNCR

1006 Segura Paguaga, Alfonso. El petróleo en Costa Rica. San José: Imprenta Borrasé, 1941. 34 pp. Illus.
A brief summary of petroleum explorations in Costa Rica. Makes a theoretical argument that there should be deposits in the nation, given its geology. DLC

1007 Seligson, Mitchell. El campesino y el capitalismo agrario de Costa Rica. San José: Editorial Costa Rica, 1980. 232 pp.
BNCR

1008 Shaw, R. Paul. Land Tenure and the Rural Exodus in Chile, Colombia, Costa Rica, and Peru. Gainesville: University Presses of Florida, 1976. 180 pp. Index, biblio., tables.
A member of the Population Division of the United Nations seeks to develop a statistical model for predicting out-migration from the rural areas of underdeveloped countries with high rates of population growth, using as his test cases Chile from 1952 to 1960, Peru from 1940 to 1961, Costa Rica from 1950 to 1963, and Colombia from 1951 to 1964. His main concern is the statistical model and the calculations involved; he provides extensive discussion of the methods and variances, with tables of statistics and computations. The Central Americanist will find the comparative

figures demonstrating that Costa Rica, with a more equitable land distribution, experienced a significantly lower rate of migration from rural areas than did the other nations with more rigid landholding patterns of greater interest than the question of the validity of the formula. DLC LNHT

1009 Sibaja Chacón, Luís Fernando, and Chester José Zelaya Goodman. La anexión de Nicoya. San José: Imprenta Nacional, 1974. 185 pp. Index, biblio., notes, illus., maps.
A detailed study of the annexation of Nicoya and Guanacaste to Costa Rica at the time of independence, tracing the political and economic aspects and noting that the region was already closely linked economically to the central valley and San José during the late Colonial era. Based on research in the National Archives and appropriate secondary sources. An effective study of an episode that is little known outside the region, but important to the nations involved. BNCR

1010 Sladek, Jaromir. Sun over Costa Rica. New York: Pageant Press, 1957. 317 pp.
A novel by an American businessman seeking to portray the poverty of the peasants and their lives, though also presenting them as somewhat childlike and naive and given to simple tastes. It does capture some of the emotions of frustrated lives and provides vivid descriptions of poverty. DLC BNCR

1011 Solano, Juan Andres. Alma nativa. Cartago: Imprenta Covao, 1960. 135 pp.
The memoirs of a Costa Rican, constituting an episodic history of his native Cartago during the 1940s. Encompasses the political stances of the city and its role in the 1948 revolution; the focus is on the protests and maneuverings that took place in the days preceding the full-scale armed revolution. Includes references to the regimes of León Cortés, Calderón Guardia, and Picado. BNCR

1012 Solera Rodríguez, Guillermo, ed. Beneméritos de la patria y ciudadaños de honor costarricense. San José: Imprenta Lehmann, 1958. 238 pp. Biblio., illus. 2d ed. San José: Imprenta Lehmann, 1963. 303 pp. Biblio., illus.
A collection of biographical sketches, with illustrations, of significant figures from Costa Rican history. Covers individuals from many fields, emphasizing their careers rather than biographical data. Includes documentary excerpts and covers some "honorary citizens" such as Franklin D. Roosevelt. DLC BNCR

1013 Solera Rodríguez, Guillermo. El cantón de Barba: apuntes históricos de su fundación y progreso, 1562-1964. San José: Imprenta Nacional, 1964. 191 pp. Biblio., notes, illus.
A brief history of a Costa Rican town, with emphasis on the present and on its facilities but also including such items as lists of the local priests and accounts of the town's

(Solera Rodríguez, Guillermo)
    various social institutions and public ser-
    vices, tracing the origins of each.   LNHT
    BNCR

1014   ____. Costarricenses: ilustres servidores
de la enseñanza. San José: Imprenta Lehmann,
1963. 96 pp. Biblio., notes, illus. 2d ed.
San José: Imprenta Nacional, 1971. 208 pp.
Biblio., illus.
    A series of brief biographical sketches and
descriptions of the careers of significant
figures in Costa Rican education, designed for
use as a school text. Covers the nineteenth
and twentieth centuries. The expanded second
edition is entitled Ilustres servidores de la
enseñanza and includes lists of the subjects'
publications where appropriate. DLC LNHT
BNCR

1015   ____. Expresidentes de la Corte Suprema de
Justicia, 1825-1955. San José: n.p., 1966.
89 pp. Illus.
    A series of brief biographical essays on
the individuals who have headed the Costa
Rican Supreme Court. Arranged chronologically, with illustrations.   LNHT BNCR

1016   ____, ed. Principales leyes y decretos en la
educación costarricense de 1824 a 1958. San
José: Ministerio de Educación Pública, 1958.
    A collection of legislation dealing with
education. BNCR

1017 Soley Güell, Tomás. Compendio de historia
económica y hacendaria de Costa Rica. San
José: Imprenta Soley y Valverde, 1940. 200
pp. Biblio. 2d ed. San José: Editorial
Costa Rica, 1975. 135 pp. Index, biblio.
    A condensed version of the author's
Historia económica y hacendaria de Costa Rica,
covering the years 1850 through 1940. As in
the larger work, the focus is on public finance rather than production. DLC LNHT BNCR

1018   ____. Evolución monetaria: artículos de
divulgación sobre la caja de conversión. San
José: Imprenta Nacional, 1924. 93 pp.
    An account of the creation in 1922 of the
Caja de Conversión to regulate the nation's
money supply, and its early operation and
effects. Includes the text of the law creating it, statistics regarding the money supply, and a sympathetic discussion of the necessity of the institution. DLC-LDS-322

1019   ____. Historia económica y hacendaria de
Costa Rica. 2 vols. San José: Editorial
Universitaria, 1947-49. 367, 361 pp.
    These volumes provide a major economic
history of Costa Rica from Colonial times
through 1940, with emphasis on the independence period. They offer a summary and narrative of the economic and financial actions of
each regime, concentrating on finance and
loans rather than on production and trade,
though there is also some data regarding the
latter. Private enterprise receives scant
mention. There is also considerable information regarding transport and communications,

as well as foreign immigration. DLC DLC-LDS-
879 LNHT BNCR

1020   ____. Historia monetaria de Costa Rica. San
José: Imprenta Nacional, 1926. 287 pp.
Tables.
    A detailed and careful study of the mone-
tary history of Costa Rica, covering pre-
Columbian, Colonial, and national times, with
80% of the volume on the latter period. The
author narrates the numerous changes that took
the small nation through a dizzying series of
monetary and banking experiments ranging from
gold, silver, and bimetalism to unsecured
paper money and gold certificates until the
1920s, when a system of gold certificates with
limited convertibility finally ended the chaos
in foreign-exchange conversions. Includes
statistics and legal excerpts, careful explanations of all the various systems, their
monetary denominations, and their economic
consequences. Discusses taxes and government
revenues, as well as monetary expansion. DLC
DLC-LDS-366

1021 Solórzano Calvo, Fabio, ed. Índice alfabético
de leyes y acuerdos del Poder Legislativa de
1920 hasta . . . 1947. San José: Imprenta
Nacional, 1947. 215 pp.
    A topical index of legislative texts. BNCR

1022 Solow, Anatole A. Proyecto para el desarrollo
urbano de la capital de Costa Rica.
Washington, D.C.: PAU, 1949. vii, 55 pp.
Illus., maps. 2d ed. San José: n.p., 1956.
vii, 67 pp. Illus.
    A study of the urban situation of the Costa
Rican capital and the central valley, conducted by the Pan American Union at the request of the national and city governments.
Includes analysis of the then-current situation, identification of problem areas, and
detailed plans for the development of parks
and highways and the improvement of housing
and deteriorated zones. Useful as a standard
of comparison for later developments and development plans. DLC LNHT BNCR

1023 Soto Blanco, Ovidio, Alfonso Carro, and
Claudio Gutiérrez. Consideraciones
preliminarias sobre la creación de los centros
universitarios regionales. San José:
Universidad de Costa Rica, 1967. 33 pp.
Tables.
    The University of Costa Rica's proposal for
the creation of regional centers. Including
the analysis on which the proposal is based,
projections of needs, specifics of location
and budget, and proposed programs. BNCR

1024 Soto-Hall, Máximo. Un vistazo sobre Costa
Rica en el siglo XIX, 1800-1900. San José:
Tipografía Nacional, 1901. 302 pp. Index,
notes.
    A series of brief biographical sketches of
the leading figures of nineteenth-century
Costa Rica. Offers basic data about birth,
death, positions, education, and, in some
cases, principal actions in office. Also
includes essays dealing with specific events

or setting the scene for a decade, though most of the volume is devoted to the biographical information. DLC DLC-LDS-10 BNG BNCR

1025 Stephens, John Lloyd. <u>Viajes por la América Central: Costa Rica, 1841</u>. San José: Imprenta Nacional, 1921. 64 pp.

A translation of the portions of the author's <u>Incidents of Travel in Central America</u> that deal with Costa Rica. See item CA889. DLC-LDS-215 BNCR

1026 Stewart, Watt. <u>Keith and Costa Rica: A Biographical Study of Minor Cooper Keith</u>. Albuquerque: University of New Mexico Press, 1964. xiii, 210 pp. Index, biblio., notes, illus., maps.
<u>Keith y Costa Rica</u>. San José: Editorial Costa Rica, 1967. 243 pp. Biblio.

A scholarly biography of that portion of Keith's career spent in Costa Rica, detailing his efforts to build railroads and develop the banana industry. Based on pertinent secondary literature, newspapers from the era, and some manuscript sources. The focus is on the enterprises rather than the man, but it effectively tells the story of an individual who was pivotal in the development of Costa Rica. The broader implications for the banana industry and the developmental pattern of the region receive only limited attention. DLC LNHT BNCR

1027 Stone, Doris Zemurray. <u>The Boruca of Costa Rica</u>. Cambridge, Mass.: Peabody Museum, 1949. 50 pp. Biblio., illus., maps, tables. Latest ed. New York: Kraus Reprint, 1968. viii, 50 pp.

A report of systematic observations of the Boruca Indians made during four visits in the early 1940s, with data regarding life-styles, social customs, religious beliefs, medicinal practices, economy, and virtually all facets of their culture. DLC

1028 Stone, Samuel. <u>La dinastía de los conquistadores: la crisis del poder en la Costa Rica contemporánea</u>. San José: EDUCA, 1975. 623 pp. Biblio., illus., tables.

This volume purports to be a history of the Costa Rican elite. Focuses on its dominance of the nation's society, economy, and politics, tracing its actions and changes in outlook from the conquest through the present. Includes genealogical tables indicating the prevalence of certain families, as well as tables, and commentaries serving to identify the growth and the different sectors and emphases in various eras. The volume indicts the elite's dominance, employing a dependency analysis charging cooperation with foreign elites, emphasizing class divisions, and making broad comparisons with various other Latin American nations and their elites. Based on pertinent secondary works, contemporary periodicals and appropriate documentary depositories, as well as general books of less obvious relevance that provide ideological or analytical frameworks. LNHT BNCR

1029 Strachan, R. Kenneth. <u>The Inescapable Calling</u>. Grand Rapids, Mich.: William B. Eerdman Co., 1968. 120 pp.

A collection of inspirational lectures and accounts of the experiences of an evangelical missionary in Costa Rica, prepared as notes for lectures delivered to prospective missionaries during a teaching assignment at Fuller Theological Seminary in 1964. Draws on thirty years of his own experience in the field, as well as that of his parents. He emphasizes a "total evangelization" approach involving community development, schooling and social service, and religious mission. DLC

1030 Stucky, Milo. <u>A Report on the Teacher Preparation Program of the School of Education of the University of Costa Rica, with Emphasis on the Secondary and Administration Areas</u>. Lawrence: University of Kansas Press, 1969. 25 pp.

A proposal for changes in the education of teachers in Costa Rica, without explanation of rationale or even of the current practice. DLC

1031 Suñol, Julio. <u>La noche de los tiburones</u>. San José: Imprenta Lehmann, 1977. 174 pp.

A novel based on the Robert Vesco incident in Costa Rica. Concerns the efforts of a foreign-expatriate to purchase control of a nation by corrupting its political figures and leaders. Includes all the key symbols and code words, such as discussion of whether he is a CIA agent and argument about whether it was easier to corrupt a democracy than a military dictatorship, since the latter might seize him and his property whereas a democracy without an army did not present this risk. Much of the story is told by observers watching the efforts of John Goldsmith, and the title invokes the symbolism of Juan José Arévalo's volume about the Yankees in Latin America. The story ends before the election, and the volume comes complete with several blank pages and an explanation that they are included to allow the reader to write his own conclusion about the success of the effort, with several possibilities suggested. The use of the form of a novel allows this journalist to speculate on occurrences and motives and hence carry his inuendo well beyond that of his earlier volume, which dealt with the issue in a less thinly veiled manner. LNHT

1032 _____. <u>Robert Vesco compra una república</u>. San José: Imprenta Trejos, 1974. 315 pp. Index, illus.

A collection of press commentaries and speeches regarding the Vesco affair and Vesco's relationship with the regimes of José Figueres and Daniel Oduber. Contains the charges and the political polemics resulting from his presence and investment in Costa Rica. The commentaries reflect the political passion with which this issue became associated. DLC BNCR

1033 Taft, William Howard. <u>Fallo arbitral del chief justice de los Estados Unidos de América</u>

sobre las reclamaciones del Royal Bank of
Canada y de John M. Amory and Son. San José:
Imprenta Nacional, 1924. 64 pp.
    DLC

1034 Thiel, Bernardo Augusto. Monografía de la
población de la República de Costa Rica en el
siglo XIX. San José: Ministerio de Economía
y Hacienda, 1900. 43 pp. Tables. 2d ed.
San José: n.p., 1951. 43 pp.
    A Costa Rican bishop's careful examination
of the nation's population during the nineteenth century, focusing on the years 1864-93,
with discussion of the Colonial background and
the situation at independence. Drawn from
census data, it constitutes one of the best
available population studies of that era.
Includes breakdowns by age and sex, religion,
region, and literacy. DLC

1035 ____. Tratado escrito con ocasión de la
encíclica de N.S. Pedro León XIII del 29 de
junio de 1881 por el ilustrísimo y
reverendísimo señor obispo de Costa Rica, don
Bernardo A. Thiel, el verdadero y genuino
carácter de la autoridad, dedicado a la
juventud estudiose de Costa Rica. San José:
Imprenta Nacional, 1882. 67 pp.
    Although a general treatise, this discus-
sion of the principle of authority, its importance, its derivation, and the relationship of
the church and state expresses succinctly the
church position in Costa Rica and throughout
the isthmus, in addition to discussing the
encyclical. DLC

1036 ____. Viajes a varias partes de la República
de Costa Rica, AC, 1881-1896. San José:
Tipografía Nacional, 1896. 93 pp. Latest ed.
San José: Trejos Hermanos, 1927. 151 pp.
Illus.
    A series of accounts of trips throughout
Costa Rica by the bishop of the nation during
the 1880s, when travel was difficult and in-
frequent. The accounts are rich in description and in data regarding the church and its
facilities in various parts of the republic.
The essays in the 1927 edition are annotated
by Henry Pittier, one of the best-known botan-
ical scholars of this area, whose commentaries
add to the descriptions. DLC DLC-LDS-387
BNCR

1037 Thomas Gallardo, Frank J., and Claudio
Gallardo Volio. Nuestros presidentes. San
José: Editorial Texto, 1968. 48 pp.
    Extremely brief biographical sketches of
the various individuals who headed Costa Rica
since independence. BNCR

1038 Thompson Quirós, Emmanuel. Defensa de
Carrillo: un dictador al servicio de América.
San José: Imprenta Borrasé, 1945. 216 pp.
Illus.
    A detailed history of the first Costa Rican
head of state. Defends his actions and responds to a newspaper criticism of him, seeking not to defend his harsh and dictatorial
methods but to place them in the context of
their times and indicate the choices that

faced Carrillo. Contends that given the turbulent times and resort to force and revolution, he had little choice if he was to hold
the nation together and successfully separate
it from the Federation of Central America.
DLC LNHT

1039 Tinoco, Luís Demetrio. Apuntes de finanzas y
derecho fiscal costarricense. San José:
Escuela de Derecho. 1940. 154 pp. Notes.
    A general text on financial law, but fo-
cused on Costa Rica and its financial history.
Uses local laws as examples and cites domestic
precedents. DLC DLC-LDS-904

1040 ____, ed. Población de Costa Rica y orígenes
de los costarricenses. San José: Editorial
Costa Rica, 1977. 404 pp. Notes, maps,
tables.
    A collection of excerpts from various stud-
ies bearing upon the Costa Rican population,
its origins, growth, and migrations, including
commentaries on the census statistics, followed by an extensive series of tables indicating the population trends and the presence
of foreigners from Colonial days to the 1970s.
The statistical tables and compilations are
particularly valuable. Includes complete reproduction of the volume edited by Mario E.
Fernández Arias (see item CR432), and works by
Bernardo A.C. Thiel, Cleto González Víquez,
Norberto Castro Tosi, Víctor Sanabria M., and
others. DLC BNCR

1041 Tinoco Granados, Federico. Páginas de ayer.
Paris: Imprimerie Solsona, 1928. 154 pp.
    The political memoir of the Costa Rican
military officer who seized power in 1914 and
was denied recognition by the Woodrow Wilson
administration, written from exile, explaining
his view of the situation and his rationale
for acting, depicting fraud and corruption by
the preceding regimes and defending his actions as president. Contains a number of
excerpts from various commentaries and contemporaries relating to the events of this
era. BNCR

1042 Torres Padilla, Oscar. Diagonóstico sobre la
utilización de los recursos humanos y su
relación con las necesidades educativas. San
José: Instituto Nacional de Aprendizaje,
1971. 73 pp. Tables.
    A description and projection of supply and
demand for trained educators in the nation.
DLC

1043 Torres Vicenzi, Fernando. Dr. Rafael Ángel
Calderón Guardia. San José: Imprenta
Lehmann, 1940. 48 pp.
    A laudatory campaign biography that in-
cludes a brief summary of his training and
medical career, and an outline of his political activity stressing his programs, dedication, and patriotism. DLC DLC-LDS-860

1044 Tovar, Rómulo. Un discurso y una campaña.
San José: Imprenta Lines, 1928. 110 pp.
Illus.

(Tovar, Rómulo)
     This volume opens with and is based on a
speech by the president of the United Fruit
Company, Victor M. Cutter, delivered 28 March
1928 to the New York Bond Club, discussing the
company's actions and seeking to interest
Yankee investors in Latin America, which he
says is about to enter a period of development and constitutes the best prospective
market for the United States and its industries. It is followed by a lengthy series of
articles by Tovar, originally published in the
Diario de Costa Rica, noting the importance of
the company in the Costa Rican economy, citing
its contribution to investment and development, and hailing the UFCO president for his
efforts to interest the Yankees in investing
in and assisting the development of Latin
America. Tovar notes that the withdrawal of
such a company from the nation would be an
economic disaster that could be remedied only
by seeking investment from other foreign companies, and comments extensively on the trade
potential and role of Yankee investment. DLC
DLC-LDS-412

1045   _____. Don Mauro Fernández y el problema
escolar costarricense. San José: Imprenta
Alsina, 1913. 80 pp.
     A brief biography of a turn-of-the-century
Costa Rican educator, emphasizing his efforts
to organize and reform the national educational system, though also discussing his
career as a lawyer and his various ministerial
and diplomatic posts, his years in Congress,
and his contributions to the codification of
the nation's laws during a career that spanned
the years 1866 through 1905. DLC DLC-LDS-115
BNCR

1046   Trejos, José Francisco. Origen y desarrollo
de la democracia en Costa Rica: apuntes para
estudio. San José: Imprenta Trejos, 1939.
66 pp.
     A brief essay regarding democracy in Costa
Rica. Traces its origins to Colonial times,
when there was some local control of city
government, and contends that this was its
origin. DLC LNHT BNCR

1047   Trejos, Juan. Geografía ilustrada de Costa
Rica. San José: Imprenta Trejos, 1916. 96
pp. Latest ed. San José: Imprenta Trejos,
1948. 142 pp. Illus.
     A general descriptive geography with exten-
sive illustrations. Includes sections dealing
with the nation's political organization,
economy, and physical features province by
province. DLC-LDS-141 BNCR

1048   Trejos Escalante, Fernando. Artículos y
discursos. San José: Imprenta Lehmann, 1972.
230 pp. Index, illus.
     An anthology of commentaries by a prominent
Costa Rican political figure, most of which
were previously published in La Nación of San
José. The author has served as a deputy in
Congress as well as pursuing his medical career, and not surprisingly has placed considerable emphasis on the development of medical

services for his nation in his political activities. The articles include many dealing
with this theme, general political commentaries indicating his differences with the
National Liberation party, discussion of
themes such as liberty and the role of the
state, and several historical essays. LNHT
BNCR

1049   _____. Libertad y seguridad: libertad
económica y seguridad social. San José:
Asociación Nacional de Fomento Económico,
1963. 197 pp.
     A medical doctor and political figure's
comments on the concept of health care and
social security in Costa Rican history. He
argues that provisions for public assistance
or private help existed throughout history,
long before the national social security program was created, and criticizes the present
program for its restriction to union members
and the gainfully employed, arguing the necessity for broader provisions and specifically
proposing old-age and disability pensions.
DLC LNHT BNCR

1050   Trejos Fernández, José Joaquín. Ocho años en
la política costarricense: ideales políticos
y realidad nacional. 4 vols. San José:
Editorial Hombre y Sociedad, 1973-74.
     A collection of writings and speeches by
the Costa Rican president from 1966 to 1970,
detailing what he considers the nation's political agenda for the period 1965-70 and his
programs for the solution of the nation's
problems. The volumes are arranged themat-
ically and cover significant areas such as
education, economic problems, and social problems. Most of the entries are selected from
his presidential speeches, with the original
date and place of delivery indicated. DLC
LNHT BNCR

1051   _____. Un programa de gobierno: ideales y
realizaciones. San José: Imprenta Nacional,
1969. 127 pp.
     An explanation of the government program of
the Trejos regime and an analysis of its
achievements to date, emphasizing its contributions to the nation. TxU

1052   _____. Reflexiones sobre la educación. San
José: Editorial Costa Rica, 1963. 168 pp.
2d ed. San José: Imprenta Trejos, 1968.
184 pp.
     A noted Costa Rican educator and political
figure discusses the trends in his field in
general terms, analyzing their implications
for his nation. A lengthy essay on the academic reforms of the University of Costa Rica
comprises the most valuable part, indicating
his role in the changes there and the problems
involved. Several other essays deal with the
university and its role in society. DLC LNHT

1053   Tristán Fernández, José Fidel. Baratijas de
Antaño. San José: Editorial Costa Rica,
1966. 185 pp. Biblio., illus.
     A series of essays by a well-known Costa
Rican naturalist and biologist. Here he deals

(Tristán Fernández, José Fidel)
not with his areas of speciality but provides commentaries on contemporaries and predecessors in the Costa Rican educational field, discussing the various significant professors and schools, their characteristics, and their contributions. Provides an "inside" view of Costa Rican education that contributes to the educational history of the nation. DLC BNCR

1054 _____, ed. Dos documentos históricos. San José: Imprenta Lehmann, 1924. 47 pp.
Two documents, one about the 1723 eruption of the Irazú volcano, and the other an account by a soldier, Jacinto García, who fought in the 1856-57 campaign against William Walker, describing his experiences while serving with the Costa Rican contingent. DLC-LDS-322

1055 Trullás y Anlet, Ignacio. Escenas josefinas. San José: Imprenta María Viuda de Lines, 1913. 207 pp.
A series of short stories set in contemporary San José and based on the author's experiences there, drawing on real life to portray the customs, mores, and culture of the city and its residents, as well as their idiosyncrasies. DLC DLC-LDS-148

1056 Tulio Salazar, Marco. Palabras del director. Heredia: Liceo de Heredia, 1955. 38 pp.
The director of the secondary school in the city of Heredia offers a series of speeches commenting on the city's famous sons and significant figures in its history, followed by some disparate commentaries. Figures included are Cleto González Víquez, Tranquilino Sáenz, Luís R. Flores, Santiago Zamota, and Joaquín García Monge. BNCR

1057 Ulate Blanco, Otilio. A la luz de la moral política. San José: Imprenta Trejos, 1976. 475 pp. Illus.
A collection of letters, speeches, and diary like notations covering important events in his career, assembled by the ex-president of Costa Rica and published posthumously by his wife, Olga Marta Ulate. Includes a description of his funeral and a number of tributes to him on that occasion. The papers and commentaries cover the years 1961 through 1973 after he left the presidency but continued in the leadership of his party, including his second candidacy for the presidency. LNHT

1058 _____. ¿Hacia dónde lleva a Costa Rica el señor presidente Figueres? San José: Imprenta Universal, 1955. 35 pp. Illus.
A series of articles published by the Costa Rican ex-president as part of a polemic between him and ex-President José Figueres during 1955. Figueres had charged that Ulate was conspiring against the Costa Rican government and seeking external support for a coup against the revolutionary regimes, and Ulate denied the charges, countering with accusations that Figueres had cooperated with Guatemalan President Juan José Arévalo to sponsor military expeditions to aid revolutions throughout the Caribbean. The details

and accompanying letters provide information about the so-called Caribbean Legion and the links between Figueres and Arévalo. The entire dispute reflects the turbulence of the 1954 coup in Guatemala and its effect on the isthmus. KU

1059 Ulloa Zamora, Alfonso. El teatro nacional. San José: Editorial Costa Rica, 1972. 147 pp. Biblio., notes, illus.
A history of the Costa Rican National Theater and its antecedents, construction, and architecture, written in the form of a biography of the building. DLC BNCR

1060 Últimas comunicaciones cruzadas entre la junta del servicio nacional y las compañías eléctricas. San José: Imprenta Borrasé, 1931. 32 pp.
Exchanges between the Costa Rican Electric Light and Traction Company, the Compañía Nacional de Electricidad, the Compañía Nacional Hidroeléctrica, and the government electricity service, regarding proposals to nationalize the companies or consolidate their separate lines into a single national system, that constituted part of the continuing political debate about the future of electric service in the nation. Includes the government's new proposal, favoring consolidation, with the company responses and objections. DLC-LDS-504

1061 The United Fruit Co., La compañía del Ferrocarril de Costa Rica y La Northern Railway Co. ante el Congreso Nacional. San José: Imprenta Alsina, 1907. 107 pp. Maps.
The company's view of the proposal by Ricardo Jiménez Oreamuno to establish a national railway commission to regulate the companies operating in Costa Rica, contending that some of the proposed functions of the regulatory commission would violate the existing contracts and law. DLC-LDS-717

1062 U.S., Gov't of. International Cooperation Administration. El punto cuatro en acción en Costa Rica. San José: Imprenta Trejos, 1956. 40 pp. Illus., tables.
A brief summary of the Point Four Program and its activities in Costa Rica, with statistics and illustrations. DLC BNCR

1063 Urbano, Victoria. Una escritora costarricense: Yolanda Oreamuno, ensayo crítico. Madrid: Ediciones Castilla de Oro, 1968. 246 pp. Index, biblio., notes.
A detailed critical analysis of the writings of Costa Rican essayist and novelist Yolanda Oreamuno, viewing her works sympathetically. Classifies Oreamuno as a naturalist and suprarealist of the new generation of socially conscious writers who rebelled against pure folklore but used rural settings for their stories and associated with the peasants. Notes her emphasis on description and her love of nature, which reflect her early life. DLC LNHT BNCR

1064 Urbina Castro, Cornelio. La carrera administrativa en Costa Rica. San José:

Dirección General de Servicio Civil, 1966. 48 pp.

An official pamphlet explaining the civil-service law and regulations of the nation, and their implications for government employment and employees. BNCR

1065 Ureña Morales, Gabriel, ed. Memoria del centenario de Desamparados: 1862–4 de noviembre, 1962. San José: Comisión Central del Centenario, 1964. 371 pp. Illus.

In addition to the usual collection of decrees and minutes of the commission and the speeches made on the occasion, this volume includes a history of the canton and anthologies of writings about it and by its literary figures and intellectuals, providing data on its history, geography, and folklore. LNHT BNCR

1066 Ureña Morales, Gabriel. Presencia del padre Matías Zavaleta en Desamparados, 1847–1898. San José: Comisión Central del Centenario, 1962. 75 pp. Biblio., illus.

Published as part of the centennial of Desamparados, this work sketches the life and contributions of the local parish priest, stressing his efforts during his long tenure to improve the community, promote education, and encourage agricultural development. DLC LNHT BNCR

1067 Ureña Morales, Gabriel, and René Moser. Costa Rica: La Suiza de centroamérica. San José: Imprenta Lehmann, n.d. Pages unnumbered. Illus., maps. Latest ed. Paris: Delroisse, 1977. 134 pp. Illus., maps.

A brief description of the marvels of Costa Rica, in English, Spanish, French, and German. Designed to encourage tourism by emphasizing the flora, fauna, colorful local customs, and tourist facilities. Lavish photographs. DLC BNCR

1068 Valenciano Rivera, Rosendo de Jesús. Derecho de la Santa Iglesia Católica en la enseñanza religiosa. San José: Imprenta Lehmann, 1912. 36 pp.

A defense of religious education, reflecting the nineteenth-century polemics and attacking the legal limitations imposed by the reform era. DLC-LDS-89

1069 _____. Reminiscencias históricas: 7 de noviembre de 1889. San José: n.p., 1951. 14 pp.

A priest's reminiscences of an attempted coup during his youth, and his comments on other themes of the times. BNCR

1070 Valentine, Lincoln G. The Case of Costa Rica. Washington, D.C.: Gibson Brothers, 1919. 107 pp. Illus.
El caso de Costa Rica. Washington, D.C.: Gibson Brothers, 1919. 107 pp. Illus.

A series of articles that originally appeared in the New York Herald, charging manipulations by oil companies and by Germany in the Costa Rican political crisis that led to the Tinoco coup, with supporting documents and commentaries on U.S. policy in this situation. The dispute involved the Woodrow Wilson administration's commitment against dictatorship; its perception of the German "threat" in relation to World War I; and the struggle for petroleum that was then raging in the region, including the much-disputed Greulich contract in Costa Rica. DLC DLC-LDS-664 BNCR

1071 Vallbona, Rima de. Yolanda Oreamuno. San José: Ministerio de Cultura, Juventud y Deportes, 1973. 159 pp. Biblio., illus.

A brief biographical sketch and analysis of the novels of a Costa Rican writer who lived a substantial portion of her life in Mexico and Guatemala and whose writings spanned the 1940s and 1950s. Included is consideration of her style, themes, principal works, and the feminist tendencies and social commentaries contained in her works, with excerpts from her principal volumes and essays. DLC BNCR

1072 Van der Laat, J.E. La sombra en los cafetables: artículos publicados en el periódico "La Prensa Libre." San José: Tipografía Nacional, 1910. 22 pp.

Part of a debate regarding the desirability of the then rapidly expanding coffee culture in Costa Rica and its implications for the future, the economy, and the nation's international position. See also citations under Pedro Pérez Zeledón and Federico Mora. DLC-LDS-50 BNCR

1073 Vargas, Guillermo. El benemérito licenciado don Jesús Jiménez. San José: Tipografía Nacional, 1903. 22 pp. Illus.

A brief biographical sketch of a Costa Rican president during the 1860s, tracing his ministerial positions during the 1850s and the turbulent years and politics after his inauguration in 1863. He is remembered principally for launching the highway to the Atlantic Coast and for establishing free public education in Costa Rica. DLC-LDS-308 BNCR

1074 Vargas Coto, Joaquín. Biografía del Lic. Ricardo Jiménez Oreamuro. San José: Imprenta Vargas, 1959. 24 pp.

A brief and sympathetic biographical sketch of the life of the man who dominated his country's politics from 1910 through 1936 and served as president three times. Compiled on the centennial of his birth. DLC BNCR

1075 _____. Cartas de don Camilo. San José: Editorial Costa Rica, 1969. 316 pp. Index.

A collection of essays written during the 1950s and originally published as letters in the newspaper La Nación, describing life, customs, and folklore in Guanacaste in short-story form. While not a native of the Guanacaste region, the author is noted as its best interpreter and conserver of its lore, customs, culture, and idioms. DLC LNHT BNCR

1076 Varona, Esteban Antonio de. Costa Rica. Mexico: Unión Gráfica, 1957. 43 pp. Illus.

A brief description of contemporary Costa Rica in words and pictures, with the photo essay constituting the principal portion of the volume. DLC BNCR

1077 Vega Rodríguez, Jorge. A la sombra del caduceo. San José: Imprenta Lehmann, 1972. 176 pp. Biblio., illus.
     The memoirs of a surgeon who served as vice-president of Costa Rica during the regime of President José Joaquín Trejos from 1966 through 1970. Focuses mainly on his medical career, emphasizing that this was his chosen field, but also provides commentaries about politics and particularly the negotiations that led to the coalition that launched the Trejos candicacy. Includes commentaries on disparate subjects, such as individuals he met during the course of his career and travels. LNHT BNCR

1078 Venero, Juan. Aniversario de la revolución de 27 de abril de 1870: bosquejo histórica. San José: Imprenta Nacional, 1880. 55 pp. Tables.
     A defense of the 1870 revolution in Costa Rica that eventually led to the installation of General Tomás Guardia in the presidency, hailing it as dedicated to progress, recounting its projects, and providing tables of economic statistics that demonstrate the development of the nation during his years in power. BNCR

1079 Villafranca, Richard. Costa Rica, the Gem of American Republics: The Land, its Resources and its People. New York: Sackett & Wilhelms, 1895. 139 pp. Notes, illus., tables.
     A compendium of information about Costa Rica written for the Cotton States Exposition, designed to introduce Costa Rica to North Americans and encourage interest in trade and investment. Includes geographical, geological, and climatic information, but the emphasis is on the economy and resources, with detailed tables and statistics regarding economy, financial situation, and agriculture covering the 1883-93 decade. There is even a complete list of coffee plantations and their owners, and production figures broken down by region. The author is a former government official and former consul general in San Francisco. DLC LNHT BNCR

1080 Villalobos, Asdrúbal. Apuntes sobre el voto femenino. San José: La Tribuna, 1926. 26 pp.
     A statement opposing granting women voting rights, contending that since the constitution does not mention women in its citizenship clause, taking into the account the spirit of the time in which it was written it must be assumed that, without specific mention, it did not confer citizenship on women, and hence that they cannot possibly vote. The author argues that the feminist movement in the nation is new and opposed by most women and hence that the Congress reflected the national will in rejecting the idea. Contends that Costa Rican women have enough responsibility as the transmitters of the nation's culture to its youth and hence that men should bear the burden of politics and shield women from it. DLC DLC-LDS-349

1081 Villanueva, Luís Manuel. Una infame dictadura y la gesta cívica de un pueblo campesino. N.p., 194? 56 pp. Illus.
     An account of a peasant uprising in Llano Grande, Costa Rica on 13 February 1944 against the Calderón Guardia regime, hailing the rebels as heroes and condemning the "tyranny" of the administration. The uprising was against the electoral fraud of 1944, and the author notes its relationship to José Figueres and the degree to which it anticipated later Costa Rican protests. BNCR

1082 Villar, Salvador. Guanacaste: monografía histórica y geográfica. San José: Imprenta Borrasé, 1934. 31 pp.
     A very brief geographical description with a general historical outline, printed in both Spanish and English. Includes some contemporary description. DLC-LDS-784 LNHT BNCR

1083 Villasuso Estomba, Juan Manuel, and Alvaro Vargas Marín. Índices estacionales de los precios al por mayor al por menor de 18 frutas y hortalizas en Costa Rica. San José: Instituto de Fomento y Asesoría Municipal, 1973. 146 pp. Illus., tables.
     A study of the prices of basic food products and their monthly fluctuations, including elaborate graphs and tables, focusing on the early 1970s but with some data extending to the 1960s. Includes virtually all fruits and vegetables, but omits the basics such as corn, rice, beans, and wheat. BNCR

1084 Villegas, Rafael, ed. El ejército y la política. San José: Tipografía Nacional, 1906. 26 pp.
     Although Villegas appears as the editor, the bulk of this pamphlet consists of an address by Gerardo Zúñiga Montúfar dealing in a theoretical sense with the role of the military in politics, criticizing the politization of the military in Latin American, and calling for new legislation and military reorganization in Costa Rica to guarantee that the army would be removed from politics. DLC DLC-LDS-44

1085 Villegas, Rafael. Por el porvenir de Costa Rica: consideraciones acerca de la necesidad de fundar in el país un Banco Agrícola Hipotecario. San José: Tipografía Nacional, 1914. 60 pp.
     Analyzing the current economic crisis of Costa Rica, the author concludes that the cause of the malaise is a shortage of credit, since in his view money serves the same function in an economy that blood does in the human body. He argues that the most effective measure the government could take would be to create an agricultural mortgage bank to pump money into the agricultural sector. DLC DLC-LDS-119

1086 Vincenzi Pacheco, Moises. <u>Geografía de Costa Rica</u>. San José: Imprenta Nacional, 1936. 71 pp. Tables.

Although this volume begins with a brief general geographical description, the main portion is devoted to hydrography, with extensive discussion of the nation's river basins. The final portion provides a general description and listing of flora and fauna. BNCR

1087 _____. <u>Guía del maestro costarricense</u>. San José: Soley y Valverde, 1941. 102 pp.

A general educational text by one of the nation's leading educators and intellectuals, dealing with theory but relating these considerations to the Costa Rican scene, stressing those methods and subjects most useful in that setting. DLC-LDS-892

1088 _____. <u>Mensaje a las juventudes de nuestra América</u>. San José: n.p., 1921. 40 pp.

A prominent Costa Rican writer calls for a critical self-examination by Latin Americans of their own area and countries, criticizing both foreign influences and the idea that such external influences will solve the region's problems. He contends that only the people themselves can do this, and criticizes Latin American intellectuals for looking elsewhere or blaming external factors rather than focusing on internal problems. DLC-LDS-330 BNCR

1089 _____. <u>Mensaje a los jóvenes Yanquis</u>. San José: Imprenta Trejos, 1926. 31 pp.

A critique of inter-American relations by a well-known Costa Rican writer who warns of the lack of understanding between North and South America and criticizes the Yankee methods as well as the Latin tendency toward anti-imperialistic polemics. His message is that a change of tactics by the Yankees is necessary to prevent a clash, and that the hemisphere needs to work cooperatively toward common objectives, with understanding of each other's viewpoints and culture. He calls on the Yankee intellectuals to bring about this understanding. DLC-LDS-350 BNCR

1090 Víquez, Pío J. <u>Relación del viaje del señor presidente de Costa Rica, general don Bernardo Soto a la República de Nicaragua 10 de julio-10 de agosto de 1887</u>. San José: Tipografía Nacional, 1887. 227 pp.

An account of an official visit by the president of Costa Rica to Nicaragua in 1887, which took over a month in those days of limited transportation facilities and constituted a significant event in this era before summitry became fashionable. The account is descriptive of the rigors of the trip and of the terrain encountered, as well as of the official ceremonies and conferences. DLC-LDS-100 BNCR

1091 Vives, Juan Luís. <u>Tabulación para uso agrícola de los datos climáticos de Costa Rica</u>. San José: n.p., n.d. xxi, 222 pp. Tables.

A tabulation of statistics regarding climate for each of the zones of Costa Rica; based on the years 1951-69, though samples for all regions are not identical. The study consists principally of tables showing the average monthly temperature, rainfall, wind, etc. for each of the provinces and many of the specific cities. Provides a comprehensive overview of the climatic conditions in Costa Rica and their seasonal and regional variances. BNCR

1092 <u>Vocabulario de palabras-modismos y refranes ticos: por un salesiano</u>. Cartago: Escuela Tipografía Salesiana, 1938. 132 pp. Biblio.

A dictionary, with definitions, of Costa Rican phrases and idioms. DLC

1093 Vogel, Robert Cross, and Claudeo González Vega. <u>Agricultural Credit in Costa Rica</u>. San José: n.p., 1969.
<u>Crédito agrícola en Costa Rica</u>. San José: Associated Colleges of the Midwest, 1969. ii, 163 pp.

Prepared by a visiting scholar under an AID contract, this volume surveys agricultural credit in Costa Rica during the 1955-67 period. Each of the credit sources and each of the nation's principal agricultural products is reviewed separately, to demonstrate the distribution of credit and its impact on the production and exports of the nation. The study concludes that Costa Rican landowners tend to resist borrowing to finance their crops, that the banking system, which is the principal source of credit, favors the coffee sector excessively, and that a broader use and distribution of credit is necessary in the agricultural sector. BNCR

1094 Volio, Jorge. <u>El año funesto y la traición del 27 de enero de 1917</u>. Panamá: Imprenta Católica, 1918. 55 pp.

An attack on the Tinoco regime, part of the political polemics of the era, leveling all sorts of charges and hailing the opposition of Woodrow Wilson to the regime. DLC

1095 Volio, Marina. <u>Jorge Volio y el Partido Reformista</u>. San José: Editorial Costa Rica, 1972. 318 pp. Biblio., illus., notes.

Originally a thesis, this analysis of the early political life of General Jorge Volio and his founding of the Reformist party during the early 1920s was written by his daughter, a history professor. The work reflects his passionate appeal for social change and reform to assist the masses, and includes the party's platforms and Volio's principal declarations. Based on extensive research in documentary sources, her father's private papers, interviews with contemporaries, and appropriate secondary works. Though clearly sympathetic to the general's viewpoint, the volume provides useful information about his early career and the origins of his party. DLC LNHT BNCR

1096 Wagner, Moritz, and Carl Scherzer. <u>Die Republik Costa Rica in Central Amerika mit besonderer Berücksichtung der Naturverhaltnisse und der Frage der deutschen</u>

Auswanderung und Colonization, Reisestudiern
und Skizzen aus den Jahren 1853-1854.
Leipzig: Arnoldische, 1856. xvi, 578 pp.
Maps. 2d ed. Leipzig: Arnoldische, 1857.
578 pp. Maps.
La República de Costa Rica en Centro América.
San José: Imprenta Lehmann, 1944. x, 353 pp.
Maps. Latest ed. San José: Ministerio de
Cultura, 1974.
   A collection of articles written by two
German geographers during the 1850s, describ-
ing their explorations of various portions of
the republic. The emphasis is on landforms
and flora and fauna, but all aspects including
population, social customs, life-styles, and
economy are included. DLC LNHT BNCR

1097 Waisanen, F.B., and Jerome A. Durlak. Estudio
sobre actitudes hacia la dinámica de población
en Costa Rica. San José: American International Association for Economic and Social
Development, 1966. 195 pp. Biblio., tables,
appendixes.
A Survey of Attitudes Related to Costa Rican
Population Dynamics. San José: American
International Association for Economic and
Social Development, 1966. 189 pp. Biblio.,
tables, appendixes.
   A report on a national survey of 1,500
people conducted during 1961-64 to determine
attitudes toward family planning and abortion
in the central plateau. Includes details of
the survey, the sample, and the questions and
analyzes the results, with appropriate tables
and statistics. A 64% majority reacted favorably to family planning. BNCR

1098 Wilson, H.G. El contrato Pinto-Greulich ante
el Congreso: exposición del representante de
The Costa Rica Oil Corporation. San José:
Imprenta Alsina, 1920. 35 pp.
   The company's summary and view of the controversy surrounding the oil exploitation
treaty and the resulting political confrontation, with appended supporting opinions by
several ex-presidents of the nation. Provides
a brief summary of the role of the various
individuals and their linkages to Yankee companies, and stresses the company's independence and its willingness to accept the
disposition of the Costa Rican government.
The pamphlet is written in response to the
charges made in the Costa Rican Congress and
seeks to clarify the issue, as well as present
the company's version of the evolution of the
accord. DLC-LDS-174

1099 Wolters, J. Costa Rica: régime monétaire,
finances publiques, commerce international,
voies de communication, agriculture.
Brussels: Imprimer Duroi, 1902. 146 pp.
Tables.
   An official governmental report prepared in
1901 by the Belgian mission to Central
America, focusing primarily on economy and
commerce and the resultant trade and investment possibilities. Includes discussion of
the laws regulating the economy and finances,
and a brief description of the contemporary
legal and political systems. BNCR

1100 Woodbridge, Paul. Los contratos Webster-Mora
y las implicaciones sobre Costa Rica y
Nicaragua. San José: Editorial Costa Rica,
1968. 94 pp. Biblio.
   A brief study of a contract signed by the
government of Juan Rafael Mora during the mid-
1850s with William Webster, which contained
provisions affecting the navigation of the San
Juan River that caused considerable concern
regarding whether they potentially forfeited
the government's rights to river navigation
and hence any influence it might have on canal
development in this region, as well as upon
the existing boundary disputes. Based on
secondary sources. DLC LNHT BNCR

1101 Yglesias Castro, Rafael. Apuntes de don
Rafael Yglesias Castro sobre su vida privada y
actuaciones públicas. San José: Imprenta
Lehmann, 1917. 48 pp. 2d ed. San José:
Imprenta Lehmann, 1961. 48 pp.
   A brief autobiography, combined with several speeches by a Costa Rican political figure of the 1880-1920 era who served in
Congress and as president for two terms from
1894 through 1902. It contains a brief résumé
of his principal actions and a defense of his
stances, though its value is limited by its
brevity. DLC BNCR

1102 _____. Compilación de leyes y documentos
oficales relativos a la evolución monetaria
de Costa Rica, iniciada y llevada á término
por la administración de don Rafael Iglesias,
1896-1900. San José: Tipografía Nacional,
1900. 125 pp.
   A reproduction of the various monetary laws
during the author's tenure as subsecretary of
hacienda, a brief overview of the nation's
situation, and the history of its monetary
legislation, taken from the 1900 Memoria of
the Ministry. DLC-LDS

1103 Zamora, Blas. Reseña histórica de la Iglesia
del Carmen de Heredia. Heredia: Imprenta L.
Cartín G., 1909. 24 pp.
   A brief account of the foundation of the
parish in the 1830s, its destruction by earthquake in 1851, and its reconstruction during
the 1870s as a symbol of the devotion of the
populace. DLC-LDS

1104 Zamora, Ciriaco. La tierra para todos. San
José: Imprenta Nacional, 1942. 160 pp.
Biblio., illus.
   A light historical account of Costa Rica
that won a prize in a contest for the "best
historical work written in literary style
suitable for propaganda in favor of tourism to
the republic." It represents a history in
"popular form" written for the general audience, illustrated by drawings, stressing the
pleasantness of life in Costa Rica and its
picturesque traditions. DLC DLC-LDS-930
LNHT BNCR

1105 Zamora Corletto, José H., et al. Costa Rica:
tierra de trabajo y esperanza, impresiones de
un viaje. San José: Imprenta Nacional, 1956.
50 pp.

A collection of articles by several Guatemalan journalists reporting a visit to Costa Rica in 1956. The commentaries are laudatory and sympathetic to the nation and its government, hailing the work of José Figueres. BNCR

1106 Zanetti, Antonio. Il territorio de Costa Rica: apunti sulle sue condizioni climatiche, agricole ed economiche. San José: n.p., 1893. 28 pp.
    A compilation of basic and current economic and trade data, designed for the European reader and seeking to emphasize the possibilities for trade and investment. DPU

1107 Zelaya C., Antonio, ed. La inflación y sus consecuencias en la economía costarricense: contribución al estudio de los problemas económicosociales. San José: Imprenta Nacional, 1944. 147 pp. Index, tables.
    A study of the wartime inflation in Costa Rica, its cause, impact, and the failure of government control programs. Contains a proposed law to regulate money, foreign exchange, and international transfer of funds, prepared by Robert Triffin. DLC

1108 _____. Por la dignidad y el honor de Costa Rica. San José: Imprenta Alsina, 1921. 40 pp.
    An essay regarding the Tinoco regime, originally written for the Costa Rican press by an attorney and former judge. Denounces the Woodrow Wilson administration for its opposition to the Tinoco coup and contends that Wilson's stand had nothing to do with democracy but was interventionist, reflecting the fact that Tinoco was not a supporter of Yankee interests. DLC BNCR

1109 Zelaya Goodman, Chester José. El bachiller Osejo. 2 vols. San José: Editorial Costa Rica, 1971. 249, 419 pp. Index, biblio., notes, illus.
    A detailed and well-researched study of the life of an influential Costa Rican of the early nineteenth century who served as a Supreme Court Justice, philosophy professor, and congressman whose contributions span the economic, political, and intellectual realms. Based on the Costa Rican archives, periodicals from the era, the subject's writings, and appropriate secondary works. The second volume contains a collection of the subject's writings, both published and unpublished, as well as a portion of his letters and correspondence. DLC BNCR

1110 _____. El bachiller Osejo y la introducción de las ideas ilustradas en Costa Rica. San José: Universidad de Costa Rica, 1967. 18 pp. Biblio., notes.
    A brief preliminary sketch of the life and work of Rafael Francisco Osejo and his influence during the independence era and the early nineteenth century. The subject was a member of the Costa Rican Assembly from 1823 through 1829. DLC LNHT BNCR

1111 _____, et al. ¿Democracia en Costa Rica? Cinco opiniones polémicas. San José: Editorial Universitaria, 1977. 249 pp. Biblio., notes.
    A series of essays about democracy and its evolution in Costa Rica. They include several historical essays regarding various phases of its development by Zelaya, Oscar Aguilar Bulgarelli, and Daniel Camacho, and some discussions of the contemporary scene by Rodolfo Cerdas and Jacabo Schifter S. Together they provide different perspectives and different answers regarding the origins and state of Costa Rican democracy. LNHT BNCR

1112 Zelaya Villegas, Ramón. El contrato Aguilar-Wicker sobre el Litoral Atlántico. San José: Imprenta Alsina, 1918. 35 pp.
    A reproduction of and commentary on a contract granting Cyrus French Wicker, a Yankee, rights in a vast zone along the Atlantic Coast for agricultural development, specifically in coconuts. Zelaya contends that while the nation should do all in its power to attract investment, the eight-year accord gives Wicker rights that are excessively broad, would allow interference with maritime traffic, and are extended for too little in return, as he contends that the grant would cost Wicker only $566.66. DLC-LDS-504

1113 _____. El derecho mercantil, de cambios, de quiebras y marítimo de Costa Rica: tratado y comento; Das Handelsrecht, Wechselrecht, Konkursrecht und Seerecht von Costa Rica: Bearbeitet und Erlautert. Berlin: R. von Decker, 1907. 252 pp.
    A bilingual compilation, with Spanish and German in parallel columns, of the laws pertaining to commerce and trade, clearly designed to encourage additional trade from Germany. Reproduces all the appropriate laws currently in force, with specifics on when passed, etc. DLC-LDS-487

1114 _____. Estudio sobre comprobaciones históricas y sobre el liberalismo. San José: Imprenta de Alfredo Greñas, 1900. 80 pp.
    Though officially an essay on liberalism, this article is in fact a reply to the Memoirs of Rafael Montúfar. It defends the activities of Francisco María Iglesias, a Costa Rican statesman whom Montúfar called an "agent of Jesuits." Zelaya replies by disputing the principles of liberalism and attacking Montúfar as inaccurate. DLC-LDS-548 LNHT BNCR

1115 _____. Mea culpa centroamericana. San José: Imprenta Alsina, 1920. 58 pp.
    A discussion of the unionist movement and its problems, contending that there is a lack of leadership in Central America because the politicians of each nation prefer to maintain themselves in power and hence oppose union while resorting to dictatorial methods to retain their posts. The author specifically criticizes Ricardo Jiménez for his inaction on this theme, characterizing him as an idealogue rather than a man of action, and contends that

(Zelaya Villegas, Ramón)
even in Costa Rica there is a ruling clique that maintains itself at the expense of the people. DLC-LDS-178 BNCR

1116 ____, ed. Minor C. Keith: contestación a los señores Villafranca. San José: Imprenta Alsina, 1913. 14 pp.
A response to an "open letter" printed in the local press, this essay constitutes a defense of Keith and his actions. DLC-LDS-144 BNCR

1117 ____. De la oposición en política y de la alternabilidad. San José: A. Font, 1897. vii, 179 pp.
A series of newspaper articles and exchanges of letters among leading political figures, part of a political polemic in Costa Rica between 1889 and 1897 regarding presidential reelection and its desirability, at a time when a constitutional provision imposing what was called the "alternative" system barring immediate reelection but enabling a return after one intervening term was being debated. The later adoption of this system led to alternation in power by two powerful political figures in the early twentieth century. The exchanges include Zelaya's statements and the letters by all the ex-presidents and leading politicians expressing their views on the subject. DLC DLC-LDS-11

1118 Zelaya Villegas, Ramón. Una prisión honrosa. San José: Imprenta Alsina, 1919. 270 pp. Illus., appendixes.
An account of the author's imprisonment by the Tinoco regime, detailing his experiences and those of others he encountered in jail and attacking the regime. Includes a list of political prisoners he identified as victims of the regime, as well as general comments indicting it and denouncing its political tyranny. DLC DLC-LDS-310

1119 ____. Las sociedades mercantiles extranjeras en Costa Rica. San José: Imprenta Trejos, 1923. 31 pp.
A discussion of the problems of Costa Rican commercial law relating to the operation of foreign firms in the nation, using a particular case involving Grace and Company to demonstrate the faults of current legislation. Contends that Costa Rican law is out of step with that of Europe and that this will cause problems for the nation as it becomes more active in the world economy. Argues for more effective legislation and more enforcement of the provisions for local incorporation or the registration of foreign companies and their authorized agents. DLC DLC-LDS-313

1120 Zeledón, José María. El Banco Nacional de Seguros y sus impugnadores. San José: Imprenta Alsina, 1928. 63 pp.
Originally a series of articles in La Nueva Prensa of San José, these commentaries are the bank's official reply to criticisms regarding a contract with Pan American Underwriters of New York providing an effective insurance monopoly in the nation. Details the process by which the contract was signed and contends that other funds were not available, since the company was the only Yankee insurance and banking firm willing to put money into such ventures in Latin America. DLC DLC-LDS-886

1121 Zeledón Matamoros, Marco Tulio. Bosquejo biográfico del benemérito don Joaquín García Monge. San Salvador: Imprenta Nacional, 1960. 27 pp. Illus.
A brief outline of the life of a prominent Costa Rican novelist, writer, and journalist, providing the basic data regarding his education, career, posts, and publications. BNCR

1122 ____. Columnas de la prensa. San José: Imprenta La Tribuna, 1946. 136 pp.
A collection of articles originally published in the San José newspaper La Prensa between 1940 and 1946, dealing with various themes and questions that were national issues during this era. Appended is a series of commentaries by other writers and journalists about the author and his work. Covers the entire range of social, political and economic questions of this era. DLC BNCR

1123 ____. La constitución política del 49: ensayo de derecho político. San José: Imprenta La Nación, 1950. 15 pp.
A commentary on the then-new constitution of 1949, contending that it is in fact less effective than and inferior to the 1871 document that served as its model. Discusses its provisions clause by clause. BNCR

1124 ____. XVIII años de vida estudiantil: crónicas. San José: Imprenta Nacional, 1959. 80 pp. Illus.
A series of essays, really memoirs, of a well-known Costa Rican writer's student days. Discusses his life, studies, friends, professors, and similar concerns. Provides a look at Costa Rican student life and the intellectual currents therein. DLC LNHT BNCR

1125 ____, ed. El digesto constitucional de Costa Rica. San José: Colegio de Abogados, 1946. 318 pp.
A collection of all of Costa Rica's various constitutions, plus provisional executive decrees and enabling legislation. LNHT BNCR

1126 Zeledón Matamoros, Marco Tulio. Don Miguel Obregón: benemérito de la enseñanza. San José: Imprenta Nacional, 1956. 30 pp.
A speech tracing the career of a Costa Rican intellectual on the occasion of the author's admission to the Costa Rican Academy of History in 1956. Drawing upon existing biographies, it briefly summarizes the subject's career in the late nineteenth century. DLC BNCR

1127 ____. Historia constitucional de Costa Rica en el bienio 1948-49. San José: Franklin Aguilar, 1950. 73 pp. 2d ed. San José: Imprenta La Nación, 1950. 77 pp.

(Zeledón Matamoros, Marco Tulio)
A brief essay regarding the political events of the 1948-49 period and the constitutional gap that resulted under the Provisional Junta while the Constituent Assembly elaborated the nation's new 1949 constitution. Most of the space is devoted to reprinted documents, exchanges, and decrees from the era. DLC BNCR

1128 _____. Reseña histórica del régimen constitucional de Costa Rica. San José: Imprenta Nacional, 1941. 19 pp.
A brief essay regarding the legal basis of the early governments of Costa Rica from de facto independence through the Mexican intervention, the establishment of the Federation, and the dictatorship that governed the state during part of the Federation era. DLC DLC-LDS-917 BNCR

1129 Zumbado, Fernando. Asignaciones familiares en Costa Rica: impacto en la economía y el desarrollo demográfico. San José: Universidad de Costa Rica, 1973. 103 pp. Tables, appendixes.
A study of family income in Costa Rica, based on interviews with various workers and providing extensive statistical data regarding income distribution, expenditures, future plans, and potential effects of increased income or changes in distribution. The study covers the period 1969 through 1972, and the questionnaire is appended. BNCR

1130 Zúñiga, Francisco. Zúñiga: grabados en madera. San José: Ministerio de Educación Pública, 1971. Pages unnumbered. Illus.
A collection of photos of woodcarvings showing scenes from Costa Rican society. Illustrates the work of one of the nation's most prominent artists in this form and the use of carving to produce what appear almost as paintings. BNCR

1131 Zúñiga Díaz, Miguel [Miguel Salguero, pseud.]. A través del terruño. San José: Editorial Costa Rica, 1967. 148 pp. Illus.
A description of Costa Rica and its various towns, in the form of tales about them and dialogues regarding events in their history; arranged canton by canton. DLC BNCR

1132 _____. Así vivimos los ticos. San José: EDUCA, 1976. 398 pp. Illus.
Excerpts from interviews with forty-two Costa Ricans in various walks of life, recounting their opinions of the nation and its society and their views of their own lives, satisfactions, and complaints. Many of the questions used follow a pattern providing a profile of attitudes toward national institutions, customs, dress, and such aspects as news sources and use of public facilities. An interesting view of Costa Rican life seen from its various levels, albeit in a somewhat disparate manner. The criteria used in excerpting the interviews are not indicated, and the overall plan of the questions used is also not reproduced. DLC BNCR

1133 _____. Crónicas de tierra adentro. San José: Editorial Costa Rica, 1975. 179 pp. Illus.
A description of various parts of Costa Rica, including places and festivals, with extensive photos. Provides views of the nation, its people, its recreational facilities, and its physical landforms, including underground caves and jungle forests. The selection criteria for the items included are not apparent, but they are arranged by sector of the nation. DLC LNHT BNCR

1134 Zúñiga Montúfar, Tobías. El contrato Pinto-Greulich y el estado: el problema de la caducidad. San José: Imprenta Alsina, 1922. 143 pp.
An analysis of a controversial petroleum contract of the 1920s, including a full discussion of its terms and provisions, prepared for the local Costa Rican press by the company's attorney. DLC-LDS BNCR

1135 _____. Dos sedes vacantes y monseñor Victor Sanabria. San José: Imprenta Trejos, 1952. 87 pp. Illus.
Correspondence between the author, in his capacity as minister of foreign relations, and the archbishop, regarding the appointment of bishops to two of the nation's dioceses. Covers the years 1937-40 and demonstrates the linkages and issues between church and state. DLC

1136 _____. El problema del Pacífico: exposición y proyecto de ley relativos al ferrocarril y puerto terminal del Pacífico. San José: Imprenta Alsina, 1904. 27 pp.
A discussion of various aspects of the Pacific Railroad contract, written by a Costa Rican congressman during the course of the railroad's construction. Suggests changes in the accord and discusses possible locations for the Pacific port to be constructed at the railway terminus, arguing in favor of Puntarenas. DLC-LDS-89 BNCR

1137 _____. Selecciones de La Tribuna y de la Prensa. San José: Editorial Apolo, 1953. 222 pp. Index.
An anthology of the writings of a Costa Rican figure, selected by himself; most concern individuals in Costa Rican history, particularly political figures. Also includes some general political commentary and several excerpts from other authors commenting on Zúñiga Montúfar. DLC DLC-LDS-840 BNCR

1138 _____. Tierras y ferrocarriles: informe jurídico. San José: Imprenta Alsina, 1928. 67 pp.
An official report by the Costa Rican attorney for the United Fruit Company regarding various political polemics and criticisms directed at the company in an effort to restrict its operations. Summarizes the complaints and proposed remedies, examining their legality. The proposals, by various groups in the Costa Rican Banana Cooperative, an association of private producers, include efforts

to limit the land owned by foreign companies
to prevent the company's expansion of banana
lands and tightening of the railroad restrictions to control the firm's Northern Railroad
Company. The summary of the various political
proposals is very handy in enabling the reader
to understand concisely the various issues in
the complex polemic. The report indicates the
legal channels that each of the proposed reforms would have to follow. DLC DLC-LDS-418

1139 Zúñiga Tristan, Virginia. El anglicismo en el
      habla costarricense. San José: Editorial
      Costa Rica, 1976. 166 pp. Biblio., illus.
         A dictionary of English usage in Costa
      Rican Spanish and the resulting derivatives,
      with definitions and explanations of their
      origins. Preceded by a brief introductory
      essay describing the degree of English forms
      modified for Spanish use and their prevalence.
      BNCR

El Salvador

1 Aguilar, Juan J., and Judith Lovato, eds.
Bibliografías agrícolas de América Central:
El Salvador. Turrialba, Costa Rica:
Instituto Interamericano de Ciencias
Agrícolas, 1974. 147 pp.
 One of a series by the institute, this
provides a listing of books and journal arti-
cles, focusing on locally published items,
relating to agriculture and to the crops grown
in El Salvador. BNCR

2 Aguilar Chávez, Manuel. Puros cuentos.
San Salvador: Ministerio de Cultura, 1959.
145 pp.
 Emotional short stories focusing on the
lives of the peasants and employing local
Salvadoran settings, customs, and idioms,
effectively capturing the outlook, attitudes,
and life-styles of the poor. DLC LNHT BNCR

3 Aguirre Cardona, Francisco Osmín. La historia
constitucional de El Salvador y el movimiento
unionista centro americano. Talca: Talleres
Gráficos Poblette, 1954. 195 pp. Biblio.
 A survey of the Federalist movement during
the nineteenth century and a discussion of the
1944 Salvadoran constitution, describing its
various headings and sections. Originally
written as a law thesis at the University of
Chile. DLC

4 Albayeros-Sosa, Fernando. Pedagogia social:
curso doctrinario de sociología salvadoreña.
San Salvador: n.p., 1959. 131 pp. Illus.
 Though identified as a course in national
sociology delivered over Radio Vanguardia by
the author, this work is in fact a summary of
a series of propaganda broadcasts extolling
and explaining the work of the regime of
Colonel José María Lemus and identifying his
activities with the nation, patriotism, and an
effort to solve the national problems. LNHT

5 Alemán Bolaños, Gustavo. El oso ruso:
historia novelada del primer levantamiento
comunista en América. Managua; Editorial
Atlántida, 1944. 112 pp.
 A novel by a Nicaraguan journalist-
polemicist citing the then-current Yankee
concern about the spread of communism in Latin
America and recounting a fictionalized version

of the uprising in El Salvador in 1931 and the
communist involvement in that movement. This
work is out of character with the author's
usual condemnation of the Yankees and dictatorship. DLC

6 Alens Z., Alex A. República de El Salvador:
proyección de la población por sexo y grupos
de edad, 1961-1981. Santiago: CELADE, 1964.
iii, 49 pp. Biblio., illus., tables.
 A statistical projection employing census
data to indicate the impact of current trends
over the next twenty years, showing the change
in the age, sex, and income groups in the
populace, as well as the totals, thus hinting
at the economic and social consequences and
needs. DLC

7 Alvarado, Gustavo. El alma de la patria. San
Salvador: Imprenta Nacional, 1951. 140 pp.
 A brief volume designed for the troops and
the general populace by the Defense Ministry,
evoking patriotism and moral virtues while
extolling the nation and its symbols. DLC

8 Alvarado h., Hermogenes. Organización
administrativa de la República de El Salvador.
San Salvador: Imprenta Nacional, 1918. 151
pp. Tables.
 Includes theoretical essays regarding administration, description of the jurisdictional divisions in the nation, and specific
discussion of organizational and administrative procedures in use. DLC

9 Alvarenga, Ivo P. Temas de derecho agrario y
reforma agraria. San José: EDUCA, 1977.
294 pp.
 An examination of the general issues involved in agrarian and land reform. Emphasizes the legal aspects and includes the
theoretical basis of such actions, with
analysis of the economic, political, and
social goals and implications. Although the
discussion is general, the work includes a
proposed agrarian reform law for El Salvador,
dating from 1971, with an analysis and recommendations. DLC

10 Alvarenga, Jorge Arturo. Anaconda. San
Salvador: Imprenta Nacional, 1975. 117 pp.

A novel of emotion, bravery, and valor, set in the interior of El Salvador. Follows the career of a military officer who is confronted with peasant and Indian mobs in civilian life and saves the lives of several friends through his actions. DLC

11 Ambrogi, Arturo. Crónicas marchitas. San Salvador: Imprenta El Centroamericano, 1916. 125 pp. 2d ed. San Salvador: Ministerio de Educación, 1962.

A series of essays by a well-known Salvadoran writer. Includes vivid descriptions of his country, social commentary, and several essays relating to his meetings with such literary figures as Rubén Darío and Enrique Gómez Carrillo. LNHT BNG BNCR

12 ____. Cuentos y fantasias. San Salvador: Imprenta Nacional, 1895. 225 pp. 2d ed. San José: n.p., 1898.

A collection of short stories, among the earliest works of this prominent writer, which like his other efforts consist of realistic and vivid portrayals of life in his native El Salvador. This group includes both urban and rural life, with discussion of the problems of the citizens and extensive description. BNCR

13 ____. El Jetón. San Salvador: Editorial La Prensa, 1936. 236 pp. 2d ed. San Salvador: Ministerio de Educación, 1961. 266 pp.

A collection of short stories, most dealing with the hardships of life of the rural peasants and their struggle against nature and those who exploit them. The lengthy stories combine description and emotion, though emphasizing social themes, thus encompassing costumbrismo and social protest. DLC LNHT BNCR

14 ____. El libro del trópico. San Salvador: Samuel C. Dawson, 1907. 102 pp. Latest ed. San Salvador: Ministerio de Educación, 1973. 371 pp.

A novel depicting life in the small towns and plantations of the tropical regions of Central America, focusing on the peasants, customs, and life-styles. The description of the scenery and the setting are particularly vivid. DLC BNG BNCR

15 ____. Muestrario. San Salvador: Ministerio de Cultura, 1955. 197 pp.

A collection of essays compiled from commentaries published in the Salvadoran press during the 1910-20 period and reflecting life in and the concerns of that city during those years. Unfortunately, the articles are not dated or identified as to the newspapers in which they appeared. They include commentaries on contemporary political figures in other Latin American nations, such as the fall of Estrada Cabrera in Guatemala. DLC LNHT BNG BNCR

16 ____. El segundo libro del trópico. San Salvador: Imprenta Nacional, 1916. 186 pp.

A continuation of the author's earlier volume, again including short stories focusing on rural life, combining costumbrista-style description with social-protest themes. DPU

17 Anderson, Thomas P. Matanza: El Salvador's Communist Revolt of 1932. Lincoln: University of Nebraska Press, 1971. 175 pp. Index, biblio., notes, maps.
El Salvador, 1932: los sucesos políticos. San José: EDUCA, 1976. 250 pp. Biblio., notes.

A detailed account of the 1932 peasant rebellion with comment on the accompanying political crisis, based on some of the pertinent State Department documents and extensive interviews in El Salvador, as well as appropriate secondary works. Emphasizes the social, economic, and racial tensions that led to the uprising, including the impact of the depression. Provides ample evidence of communist organizers while emphasizing that this element provided organization rather than constituting the cause of the uprising. Includes details of the military repression and the blood-bath that followed. The events described constitute an important departure point for all subsequent Salvadoran politics. DLC LNHT

18 Anderson Morúa, Luís. Estatus del gobierno que preside en la República de El Salvador el general Maximiliano Hernández Martínez, conforme a la constitución y tratados de Washington. San José: Imprenta Lines, 1931.

A legal brief by Costa Rica's outstanding international lawyer, supporting the government of General Maximiliano Hernández Martínez in El Salvador and stating the case for its constitutionality while contending that the general's rise did not violate the 1923 Washington pacts. The work was published as part of the Martínez regime's effort to win recognition from its neighbors as a counter to Washington's efforts to oust him from office, presaging the later Costa Rican support of his regime that led to the 1934 Central American Conference and the demise of the treaties. DLC-LDS-756

19 Andino, Manuel [Mateo Abril, pseud.]. Mirando vivir. San Salvador: Ministerio de Instrucción Pública, 1926. 141 pp. 2d ed. San Salvador: Ministerio de Cultura, 1960. 144 pp.

A collection of short stories set in and based on life in El Salvador in the 1920s, including many of its public figures, though focusing on the humorous, ironic, and romantic. DLC LNHT BNCR

20 ____. Tomás Regalado: notas y documentos para un ensayo sobre el caudillo. Santa Ana: Editorial Santa Ana, 1940. 288 pp. Illus.

A compilation of contemporary press articles, essays, and commentaries about the career of Regalado, who served as president of El Salvador from 1899 to 1902 and was an important figure in the nation's politics and military affairs throughout the 1890s and early 1900s. The author states that he is not an historian and hence seeks to provide not a history but rather a collection of material relating to his title character for use by later historians. He contends that Regalado was a caudillo in the true sense of the term, and hails his policies and efforts as beneficial to El Salvador. DLC

21 Andino, Manuel, and Raúl Andino. <u>La obra del gobierno del doctor Quiñónez Molina: primer años de su administración pública, 1923-1927</u>. San Salvador: Imprenta Nacional, 1925. 363 pp. Illus., maps, tables.
An official publication lauding the regime's programs and tracing them in detail. Includes extensive photos of its personnel, projects, and of festivities on official days, as well as trade and production figures for its years in power. The emphasis is on road construction, government buildings, and educational activities. DLC BNCR

22 _____. <u>El padre de la democracia: revelaciones de un periodísta sobre la compaña electoral, 1921-1931</u>. San Salvador: Tipografía "La Unión," 1931. 119 pp.
A collection of material and commentaries about the career of Pío Romero Bosque, tracing his career through his service in the national judiciary and the regime of Alfonso Quiñónez Molina and his tenure as president of El Salvador from 1927 to 1931. Hails his efforts and particularly acclaims his conduct of the 1931 election, whose free and open balloting gave him the title "the father of Salvadoran democracy."

23 Arévalo, Adrian Meléndez. <u>El 63 episodios nacionales, histórico-novelescos</u>. San Salvador: Imprenta "Arévalo," 1916. 179 pp.
An historical novel dealing with the events leading to the fall of Gerado Barrios from power in El Salvador. Barrios is hailed as having done much for his country, yet the volume contends that he was overthrown as much by domestic opposition as by the invading Guatemalan forces. DLC

24 Argueta, Manlio. <u>El Valle de las Hamacas</u>. Buenos Aires: Editorial Sudamericana, 1970. 157 pp.
A novel of social protest recounting the brutal suppression of a student demonstration by Salvadoran police and the resultant conversion of a student group into guerrillas after they escaped their native country. The story traces their guerrilla training in Nicaragua and their subsequent defeat by the military, focusing on their alienation and desperation. Employs first-, second-, and third-person narration. DLC

25 Arias Gómez, Jorge. <u>Esbozo biográfico: Farabundo Martí</u>. San José: EDUCA, 1972. 157 pp. Biblio., illus. 2d ed. San José: EDUCA, 1980. 162 pp.
A biography of a leading Salvadoran communist, tracing his career in the Party, his service with the forces of Augusto César Sandino in Nicaragua, his role in organizing the 1932 peasant uprising in El Salvador, and

his execution by firing squad after the failure of the revolt. The volume is sympathetic to its title figure, but dispassionate in its account. Its focus on Martí requires presentation of the rebel viewpoint. Though based mainly on the press and secondary works, it provides an account of the activities of a revolutionary who is difficult to trace. DLC LNHT

26 Arrieta Gallegos, Benjamín. <u>The Republic of El Salvador: A Land of Opportunity</u>. Baltimore: Sun Book, 1925. 67 pp. Illus., tables.
A concise review of the condition of El Salvador and particularly its economy and commercial possibilities, written to encourage Yankee investment and trade. Stresses the advantages of the nation as the most highly populated of the region with the most fertile soil, and hence with the land, conditions, and labor possibilities most favorable to development and investment. The work was prepared by the consulate general in New York and presents an official view, reflecting the official goals of seeking investment and trade for development. DLC

27 <u>Atlas económico de El Salvador, 1974</u>. San Salvador: Itzalco, 1974. 181 pp. Biblio., illus., maps, tables.
A collection of maps and economic statistics that portray the current state of the nation's economy.

28 Avila, Julio Enrique. <u>Mitología de Cuscatlán</u>. San Salvador: Ministerio de Educación, 1967. 77 pp.
A series of short stories by a well-known Salvadoran writer recounting the various legends that comprise Salvadoran mythology. The stories reflect both Indian and Colonial origins, and are still current in the rural areas. BNG

29 Barba Salinas, Manuel. <u>Memorias de un espectador: seguidas de cuentos, ensayos conferencias y artículos diversos</u>. San Salvador: Ministerio de Cultura, 1957. 381 pp. Illus.
A collection of articles and essays by a popular newsman, many from the column he wrote under the title of the volume, dealing with a wide range of events during his lifetime, which spanned the first half of the twentieth century, and also with historical and philosophical themes. DLC LNHT BNCR

30 Barberena, Santiago Ignacio. <u>Convención celbrado en Washington el 20 de diciembre de 1907, sobre futuras conferencias centroamericanas . . . estudio que, por encargo del Ministerio de Relaciones Exteriores, ha elaborado el Dr. Santiago Ignacio Barberena, sobre el sistema monetario de la república, en relación con lo dispuesto en dicho convenio, para ser presentado á la 1. conferencia que se reunirá en Tegucigalpa el 1 de enero próximo entrante</u>. San Salvador: Imprenta Nacional, 1908. 16 pp.

(Barberena, Santiago Ignacio)
A brief summary of the current state of the
Salvadoran monetary and financial system,
prepared for a regional conference under the
sponsorship of the government. DLC

31 _____. Descripción geográfica y estadística
de la República de El Salvador. San Salvador:
Imprenta Nacional, 1892. 114 pp. Maps,
tables.
Contains numerous tables and statistics and
a description of the nation's physical resources and climate. DLC LNHT

32 _____. Estudios estadísticos respecto a las
riquezas naturales, industrias, y comercio de
la República de El Salvador. San Salvador:
Imprenta Nacional, 1907-8. 50 pp.
A compendium of statistical information
about the state of the Salvadoran economy, its
development and potential, providing a look at
the state of the nation at that time. DLC
LNHT

33 _____. Nuevas y fehacientes pruebas de que el
Archipiélago de la Bahía de Fonseca pertenece
a la República del Salvador. San Salvador:
n.p., 1899.
A statement and collection of documents
pertaining to the boundary dispute with
Honduras involving the islands in the Gulf of
Fonseca. DLC

34 Barberena, Santiago Ignacio, and Pedro S.
Fonseca. Monografías departamentales. 14
vols. San Salvador: Imprenta Nacional, 1909-
14. Illus., maps, tables.
A series of brief volumes, one on each of
the nation's departments, ranging from twenty
to ninety pages each, published over a five-
year span under the auspices of the Dirección
General de Estadística. Each provides a brief
historical narration of each department, district, and municipality, with some current
data. The emphasis is on the historical outlines, each of a few pages. The majority were
prepared by Barberena, with Fonseca completing
the last three volumes in the series. Offers
basic historical data such as foundation
dates, important transitional points, and key
individuals. DLC LNHT

35 Barón Castro, Rodolfo. José Matías Delgado y
el movimiento insurgente de 1811. San
Salvador: Ministerio de Educación, 1962. 239
pp. Biblio.
A carefully researched study of Delgado's
role in the 1811 independence movement in El
Salvador, emphasizing his earlier career. The
work is based on extensive research in the
Archive of the Indies in Spain, as well as on
a lengthy list of appropriate secondary
sources. DLC LNHT BNCR

36 _____. La población de El Salvador: estudio
acerca de su desenvolvimiento desde la época
prehispánica hasta nuestros días. 3 vols.
Madrid: Instituto Gonzalo Fernández de
Oviedo, 1942. 644, 625, 650 pp. Index,
biblio., illus., maps, appendixes. 2d ed.

Madrid: Instituto Gonzalo Fernández de
Oviedo, 1978.
A monumental study which, despite its
title, focuses mainly on the Colonial era and
the foundation of the various cities of the
nation. Only about 150 pages deal with the
nineteenth century and postindependence era.
They include essays summarizing the various
censuses of the nation and the formation of
additional towns and provinces, with extensive
statistical data. DLC LNHT

37 Barón Ferrufino, José René. Comunismo y
traición. San Salvador: n.p., 1971. 459 pp.
Illus., tables.
Written as a sequel to the author's earlier
work, this one continues the rambling denunciation of communism as the evil force in the
world and the greatest threat to El Salvador,
though most of the discussion is general.
Includes comments opposing all revolution or
any agitation that might disturb public order,
as well as just about every other ideology,
cause, or organization that occurred to the
author. DLC LNHT

38 _____. Penetración comunista en El Salvador y
viente años de traición. San Salvador:
Editorial Ahora, n.d. [1970]. 332 pp.
Illus., maps.
A rambling denunciation of Salvadoran politics, blaming the communists for all evils,
but also discussing the Salvadoran border
conflict of 1969. The commentary jumps about
from independence to the 1970s without any
evident pattern, but focuses on the post-1950
era, particularly criticizing the revolutionary Osorio regime of that time. DLC LNHT

39 Basauri, Daniel. Contribución a la
mineralogía y geología de El Salvador. San
Salvador: Tipografía "La Unión," 1945. 207
pp. Biblio., illus., maps.
A collection of articles dealing with various aspects of the minerology and geology of
El Salvador, originally published in various
scientific journals of that country during the
years 1943-45. Includes discussion of the
mineral resources of the nation and regional
treatments of geological phenomena, with extensive illustrations and maps. DLC

40 Belot, Gustave de. La République du Salvador
(commerce, agriculture, population, moeurs,
etc.). Paris: Dentu, 1865. 90 pp.
A brief volume in large print providing
current information about the nation, seeking
to encourage greater European efforts to utilize the economic resources and opportunities
of Central America in general and El Salvador
in particular. The data is keyed to trade and
French industry, and the author even advocates
emigration by stressing the need for Europe in
general and France in particular to become
active to forestall the advance of the Yankees, already begun in Mexico, so as to avoid
a Yankee monopoly and hegemony over the region
and its resources. DLC

41 Beltrand, Manuel, ed. <u>Orientaciones económicas del Sr. presidente Meléndez</u>. San Salvador: Imprenta Meléndez, 1917. vi, 97 pp. Biblio., illus.

A reproduction of an open letter written by Salvadoran President Carlos Meléndez in September 1917, dealing with economic affairs in the nation and calling for an economic policy that is based on nationalism and self-sufficiency to reduce the impact of world commodity-price fluctuations. DLC

42 Bermúdez, Alejandro. <u>El Salvador al vuelo: notas, impresiones y perfiles</u>. San Salvador: Imprenta Moisant Bank Note Co., 1917. 279 pp. Illus.

A detailed discussion of the current state of the republic, focusing on economy, finance, resources, trade, and potential, but also including brief résumés of the culture and of the nation's stand in regard to the Bryan-Chamorro Treaty. The work hails the peace of the nation, its trend away from government by force, and its material prosperity, foreseeing a rosy future for an industrious people in a richly endowed land, and seeks to acquaint the nation and the rest of the world with these prospects. DLC LNHT BNCR

43 Blutstein, Howard. <u>Area handbook for El Salvador</u>. Washington, D.C.: GPO, 1971. xii, 259 pp. Index, biblio., illus., maps. 2d ed. Washington, D.C.: GPO, 1979. 259 pp. Index, biblio., illus., maps.

Like other volumes in this series, this work provides concise and up-to-date basic information about the nation for the general reader, with capsule descriptions, some statistics, geographic description, and historical overview. DLC LNHT

44 Bonilla, Tiburcio P. <u>Comentarios al código civil salvadoreño</u>. San Salvador: Imprenta Nacional, 1884.

An overview of Salvadoran civil law, including a brief introductory summary and excerpts from the various laws. DLC

45 Brannon, Max P. <u>Las deudas privadas en la crisis contemporánea; teoría económica aplicada en El Salvador para la solución del problema y sus resultados. Editado por la Secretaría de Hacienda de El Salvador</u>. San Salvador: Imprenta Nacional, 1937. 131 pp.

An essay about the problems of debt during the depression, with suggestions for bankruptcy laws and payment moratoriums as a means of dealing with the situation, drawing comparatively upon the legislation of other nations and suggesting similar action in El Salvador. The focus is more on theory and proposed legislation than on the details of the Salvadoran situation at the time. DLC LNHT

46 Brannon de Samayoa, Carmen [Claudia Lars, pseud.]. <u>Tierra de infancia</u>. San Salvador: Ministerio de Cultura, 1958. 205 pp. 3d ed. San Salvador: Ministerio de Educación, 1974. 215 pp.

The childhood memoirs of a well-known Salvadoran poet, recounting with feeling and enthusiasm the experiences of her youth in Sonsonate and in the process providing a look at the culture of the region and the influences upon her writing. DLC LNHT

47 Browning, David. <u>El Salvador: Landscape and Society</u>. Oxford: Clarendon Press, 1971. xx, 329 pp. Index, biblio., notes, illus., maps. <u>El Salvador: la tierra y el hombre</u>. San Salvador: Ministerio de Educación, 1975. 482 pp. Index, biblio., notes, illus., maps.

A careful and detailed study, by a British geographer and diplomat, of the relationship between man and land in El Salvador, covering the use of land and agriculture from Colonial times to the present. Stressing the population pressure on the land, the author traces the introduction of the various crops that compete for land usage, emphasizing the significance of the shift to coffee in the nineteenth century and of the addition of cotton production in the twentieth century. Contends that throughout Salvadoran history there has been a fundamental conflict between those who see land as a basis of sustenance and those who view it as a source of wealth, and that this conflict grows worse with population expansion. Ample consideration is given to the types of agrarian production, their implications for the national economy and local life, and the problems and prospects of both subsistence and commercial farming. DLC LNHT BNG

48 Bustamante Maceo, Gregorio. <u>Historia militar de El Salvador</u>. San Salvador: Talleres Gráficos Cisneros, 1935. 150 pp. Illus. 2d ed. San Salvador: Imprenta Nacional, 1951. 211 pp. Illus.

A brief sympathetic outline history of the Salvadoran military and its principal combats and heroes, followed by a series of brief biographical sketches of the leading officers in Salvadoran history and a collection of military anecdotes, written by a Salvadoran army colonel. The first edition extended through the 1906 war with Guatemala (though its title indicated a broader coverage), while the second edition terminated with the 1931 coup that ousted Arturo Araujo from the presidency, expanding and extending the existing biographies as well. Though providing a convenient list of Salvadoran military heroes and the battles that nation's army considers its key exploits, the descriptions are rarely more than a single page in length, providing little detail. DLC LNHT BNCR

49 Calderón, José Tomás. <u>Prontuario geográfico y comercial, estadística y servicios administrativos de El Salvador</u>. San Salvador: Imprenta La Salvadoreña, 1927. xii, 329 pp. Illus., maps, tables. 3d ed. San Salvador: Tipografía "La Unión," 1939. xv, 440 pp. Index, biblio., illus., maps, tables.

An alphabetical listing of places in the republic and a general compilation of current data regarding all aspects of the nation and

its people, with extensive tables, illustrations, and maps.   DLC LNHT BNCR

50 Calderón, Julio César. Episodios nacionales:
Anastasio Aquino y él por qué de su rebelión
en 1833 en Santiago Nonualco. San Salvador:
Imprenta Moreno, 1957. 56 pp. Illus.
    An account of an Indian rebellion in El
Salvador in 1833 led by the title figure,
seeking to restore his rightful place in history by viewing his actions sympathetically
and comparing his efforts to those of the
national heroes of Guatemala and El Salvador.
This is followed by commentaries about other
rebellions and the later war between El
Salvador and Guatemala reflecting the
nineteenth-century efforts to impose
unification of the isthmus by force.   LNHT

51 Campos, Camilo. Normas supremas. San
Salvador: C.E. Lobo & H. Aguilar, 1938. 106
pp. 5th ed. San Salvador: Ministerio de
Educación, 1976. 155 pp.
    A discussion of national values and accom-
plishments and educational goals, originally
written in the 1920s by the founder of the
National Normal School for the preparation of
teachers in El Salvador. A biography of the
author prepared by Ceferino E. Lobo is appended to the later editions. Campos emphasizes the problems and accomplishments of the
nation and the values its teachers should seek
to encourage, as well as the educational process and role of the Normal School.   DLC

52 Canales, José María. Organización y
contabilidad bancarias: evolución bancaria en
El Salvador, 1880-1935. San Salvador:
Imprenta Funes, 1942. 380 pp.
    A detailed history of the financial system
of El Salvador, focusing on the commercial
banks and the Central Reserve Bank, with appropriate statistics. Includes a practical
manual of contemporary banking and financial
practices in that country.   DLC

53 Cardenal, Rodolfo. El poder eclesiástico en
El Salvador. San Salvador: UCA, 1980.
342 pp.

54 Cárdenas, Joaquín E. San Miguel y sus
hombres: apuntes biográficos e históricos.
San Salvador: Editorial Ahora, 1962. 271 pp.
Illus.
    A series of brief biographical sketches,
ranging from a single paragraph to three pages
in length, of the figures from the district
the author judges to be the most important in
the nation's history, many with illustrations.
Most are from the nineteenth century, and
there is no apparent pattern to the order of
the listings.   DLC LNHT

55 Cardona, Jorge. Convención unionista de Santa
Ana y impresiones de El Salvador. San José:
Imprenta Minerva, 1921. 39 pp.
    A report of a unionist meeting and a jour-
nalist's account of the travels en route,
originally written for El Diario de Costa
Rica. DLC-LDS-215

56 Cardona Lazo, Antonio. Diccionario geográfico
de la República de El Salvador. San Salvador:
Talleres Nacional de Grabados, 1945. 246 pp.
    A compendium of towns, rivers, provinces,
haciendas, etc., providing brief explanations,
locations, descriptions, and statistical data,
including the population and in many cases its
composition.   DLC

57 ____. Monografías departmentales. 3 vols.
San Salvador: Imprenta Nacional, 1938. 102
pp. 2d ed. San Salvador: Imprenta Nacional,
1939. 203, 316 pp. Tables.
    A series of brief descriptions providing
data on each of the nation's departments,
prepared under the sponsorship of the
Dirección General De Estadística. Each is
arranged by district and municipality, providing current description of its resources,
production, population, and physical features,
as well as thumbnail historical summaries of
each city and town, with the entries for each
comprising a few pages.   DLC LNHT

58 El caso salvadoreño, la verdadera situación
del país: constitucionalidad del gobierno
provisorio del coronel Osmín Aguirre y
Salinas. San Salvador: Imprenta Nacional,
1944. 22 pp.
    A defense of the constitutionality of the
regime of Colonel A. Osmín Aguirre y Salinas
and his seizure of power in 1944, arguing that
he merely took power from the satraps of the
regime of General Maximiliano Hernández
Martínez, and hence that his ousture of
General Andres I. Menéndez did not violate the
spirit of the constitution due to the latter's
service under Martínez, which made it necessary to end the regime's tenure by ousting the
Martínez partisans from control.   DLC

59 Castañeda, Francisco. El general Menéndez y
sus victimarios: páginas de la historia
contemporánea de la República de El Salvador.
Guatemala: Tipografía La Unión, 1892. xx,
292 pp. Notes, illus. 3d ed. San Salvador:
Ministerio de Educación, 1966. 193 pp.
Illus.
    A somewhat episodic account of the career
of General Francisco Menéndez, written by a
contemporary during the 1890s. Portions of
his political and military careers receive
attention, the latter consisting principally
of exploits in opposing the unionist ambitions
of Justo Rufino Barrios of Guatemala.   DLC
LNHT BNCR

60 ____. Nuevos estudios (historia, política,
literatura, crítica, arte, sociología, derecho
international, enseñanza, etc.). 2 vols. San
Salvador: Imprenta Nacional, 1919. 294, 377
pp. Illus.
    A series of miscellaneous essays by a
Salvadoran official, written between 1909 and
1919, many of which had previously appeared in
the journal Centro-América. They cover a wide
range of subjects, with the emphasis on political and historical aspects of union, of which
the author is an avowed partisan.   DLC LNHT
BNCR

61 Castillo, Daniel de J., ed. Índice de leyes militares y de marina del año de 1872 a 1902, formado en orden de tratados y fechas. San Salvador: Imprenta Nacional, 1902. 15 pp.
    An index to the author's larger compilation, providing access to the nation's military code by topic.

62 _____. Recopilación de leyes militares y de marina del año de 1872 a 1902 (por el general Daniel J. Castillo de orden del Ministerio de Guerra). San Salvador: Imprenta Nacional, 1902. 416 pp.
    The full text of the nation's laws pertaining to its military for the years in question, arranged chronologically.

63 Castro Ramírez, Manuel. Derecho penal salvadoreño: exégesis y crítica del título VIII del libro segundo del código penal salvadoreño. San Salvador: Universidad Autónoma de El Salvador, 1947. xx, 251 pp. Notes.
    A brief summary of the current statute, with critical comments, compiled by a Salvadoran law professor. DLC

64 _____. Frente a la historia. San José: Imprenta Moderna, 1913. 47 pp.
    A brief account of the accomplishments of the Manuel Enrique Araujo regime in El Salvador from 1911 until the assassination of the president in 1913, defending its actions against later accusations and praising its accomplishments. DLC-LDS-695

65 Cea, José Roberto. El solitario de la habitación 5 Guión 3. San Salvador: Ministerio de Educación, 1970. 33 pp.
    A short story focusing on life in San Salvador, seen through the eyes of a resident who observes the monotony of street life, which changes only with the seasons. TxU

66 Cevallos, José Antonio [Justo Franco, pseud.]. Recuerdos salvadoreños. 3 vols. San Salvador: Imprenta Nacional, 1891-1920. 365, 436, 487 pp. 3d ed. San Salvador: Ministerio de Educación, 1964. 315 pp.
    Though titled as a single work, these three volumes by a prominent Salvadoran jurist of the late nineteenth and early twentieth centuries contain two distinct items. The first volume, published under the pseudonym Justo Franco in 1891, consists of a narration of the author's alleged travels through El Salvador in 1875, with rich description and frequent digression to comment on historical themes relating to the places he passed. The other two volumes, published posthumously, consist of a history of the independence movement in El Salvador from 1810 through 1832, with extensive documentary excerpts. DLC LNHT BNCR

67 Chacón, Enrique. El presidente Dr. Francisco Dueñas y su época. San Salvador: Tipografía "La Unión," 1911. 187 pp.
    A history of mid-nineteenth-century El Salvador written by a nineteenth-century intellectual and published posthumously by the Salvadoran Academy of History. It focuses principally on the prominent political figures of the 1840-60 era, Francisco Dueñas, Gerardo Barrios, Miguel Santín Del Castillo, and Rafael Campos, with Dueñas as the central focus. Includes considerable excerpts and reproductions of correspondence, public declarations, and press commentary. The efforts of Dueñas to counter the influence of Gerardo Barrios are viewed sympathetically. DLC

68 Choussy, Félix. Economía agrícola salvadoreña: producción agrícola e industrias conexas. San Salvador: n.p., 1950. 485 pp. Illus.
    DLC

69 _____. Nuestra crisis actual y las soluciones propuestas: ensayo sobre una posible adaptabilidad de nuestra política monetaria de cambio fijo a una política monetaria condicional. Santa Ana: Junta Departamental de la Asociación Cafetalera, 1935. 37 pp. Tables.
    NN

70 Colindres, Eduardo. Fundamentos económicos de la burguesía salvadoreña. San Salvador: UCA, 1977. 590 pp. Biblio., notes, tables.
    Originally a thesis at the university, this volume focuses on the economic history of the nation since 1950, though with a brief review of the earlier years. Noting fundamental changes as cotton and sugar joined coffee as export products, and as industrialization via import substitution with foreign capital occurred in the 1960s, it contends that the landowners have firmly controlled the government since 1930, but that the burgeoisie constitutes a new force, which though created by the new industrialization is too closely linked to the landowning class to become "progressive" in regard to landownership, and hence that this modernization did not alter the balance of power within the nation. Includes extensive tables of statistics regarding the economy during the 1950-70 period. Based on a small number of secondary sources and government reports. LNHT

71 Colindres, Rafael B., ed. Jurisprudencia salvadoreña. 2 vols. Santiago de María: Imprenta Colindres, 1914. 2d ed. San Salvador: Tipografía La Vanguardia, 1924.
    A selection of court decisions, focusing on the most important rulings during the period.

72 Comité de Investigaciones del Folklore Nacional y Arte Típico Salvadoreño. Recopilación de materiales folklóricos salvadoreños: primera parte. San Salvador: Imprenta Nacional, 1944. 412 pp.
    A massive compilation of Salvadoran folklore, including popular verses, song lyrics, wise sayings, proverbs, legends, riddles, children's games, slang, idioms, etc., covering a wide range of fields, though offered without comment and arranged only by being grouped together with similar items (i.e., folk songs). Compiled through the efforts of

a national committee, with the cooperation of the nation's schoolteachers. DLC

73 Comité Salvadoreño de Liberación Nacional. El caso salvadoreño ante la conferencia de cancilleres. Guatemala: Talleres Gutenberg, 1945. 24 pp.

An appeal by the defeated Salvadoran exiles to the hemispheric meeting of foreign ministers requesting nonrecognition of the regime of General Osmín Aguirre y Salinas, which is characterized as a military dictatorship. The United States did withhold recognition for several months.

74 _____. Crónica salvadoreña. Guatemala: Talleres Gutenberg, 1945. 19 pp.

A propaganda pamphlet by the unsuccessful revolutionaries in El Salvador, reflecting the movements that swept the isthmus during 1944 against the various dictatorships, stating their reform objectives and condemning the regime of General Osmín Aguirre y Salinas, which seized control from the revolutionaries to preserve military dominance.

75 Contreras Castro, Julio. De cómo fue traicionado el presidente ingeniero Arturo Araujo por Maximiliano Hernández Martínez. San Salvador: n.p., 1944.

An account of the overthrow of Araujo in late 1930, charging that General Maximiliano Hernández Martínez was involved in the plot.

76 Cortés, Emiliano. Biografía del capitán general Gerardo Barrios. San Salvador: Editorial Lea, 1965. 279 pp. Illus., maps.

A laudatory, anecdotal account of Barrios's life and efforts to unite Central America, viewing him as the maximum hero of the nation and one of the extraordinary figures of his era. Includes copious excerpts from documents. Though treating Barrios's entire career, the emphasis is on his unionism and his heroics on the battlefield. DLC LNHT

77 CSUCA. El sistema educativo en El Salvador: situación actual y perspectivas. San José: CSUCA, 1965. xviii, 140 pp. Tables, illus.

See item CR335. LNHT BNCR

78 Cuenca, Abel. El Salvador: una democracia cafetalera. Mexico: ARR-Centro Editorial, 1962. 175 pp.

An analysis of the contemporary situation of El Salvador by a longtime exile who participated in all the region's revolutions and was exiled by all its dictatorships since the 1930s, contending that the real problem is the dominance of the nation's oligarchy of landowners through a closed democracy, and that the key is the clash between the interests of industrial development and the landowners rather than a class struggle, with the coffee growers preventing industrialization by holding down wages and hence the internal market. Contends that the populace should ally with the burgeoisie to promote rapid industrialization, and that the Common Market is an attempt by the elite to find external-regional markets

for industrial products and thus satisfy the industrialists by allowing continued industrial growth without dealing with the problem of internal income distribution. LNHT

79 Dada Hirezi, Héctor. La economía de El Salvador y la integración centroamericana, 1945-1960. San Salvador: UCA, 1978. 110 pp. Index, biblio., tables.

80 Dalton, Roque. El Salvador. Havana: Casa de las Américas, 1963. Biblio., illus., maps.

A brief description of the nation, designed as part of a series for use in Cuban schools. Provides basic historical data, always comparing the figures and events with Cuba and viewing the nation from a Marxist perspective. DLC LNHT

81 _____. Las historias prohibidas del pulgarcito. Mexico: Siglo XXI, 1974. vii, 232 pp. Biblio.

A revolutionary version of Salvadoran history in poetry, designed to show the exploitation of the poor by the rich and the foreigners from pre-Columbian times to the present. Emphasizes the conditions of the peasants, the concentration of landownership, and the inequities that exist, and hails the efforts at reform and revolt. DLC

82 _____. Miguel Mármol: los sucesos de 1932 en El Salvador. San José: EDUCA, 1972. 564 pp. Biblio., illus.

An account by a member of the Salvadoran Communist party based on interviews during 1966 with longtime Salvadoran Communist leader Miguel Mármol, focusing on the latter's role in and organizing efforts on behalf of the party, emphasizing its formation and role in the 1931 uprising. Mármol was shot during the resulting massacre but survived to reorganize the party. The volume includes his account of its later reorganization, its role in the 1944 revolution, and its view of subsequent Salvadoran politics. DLC LNHT BNCR

83 Dárdano, Marietta, ed. El Dr. Carlos F. Dárdano y sus victimarios: documentos para la historia. San Salvador: Imprenta Cisneros, 1912. 80 pp.

A collection of commentaries about the author's brother, a physician imprisoned for political activities and rebellion, combining praise for his medical career with comments on his political stances and denunciations of his arrest and trial as violations of the constitution. LNHT

84 Deger, Erwin Conradin. Las cenizas y arenas volcánicas de Guatemala y El Salvador en relación con su rol en la formación del suelo agrícola. Guatemala: Tipografía Amos & Anderson, 1932. 23 pp. Illus.

A study of the volcanic soil of the area, with details of its properties, composition, variances, moisture, and potential uses. DLC

85 Domínguez Sosa, Julio Alberto. Génesis y significado de la Constitución de 1886. San

Salvador: Ministerio de Cultura, 1958. 82 pp. Biblio.

An account of the Assembly with a discussion of the constitution and its text. DLC LNHT

86 Durán, Miguel Ángel. *Ausencia y presencia de José Matías Delgado en el proceso emancipador historia salvadoreña.* San Salvador: Tipografía Guadalupe, 1961. 385 pp. Illus.

A detailed account of the role of Delgado in the independence era, tracing his service and positions within the various twists and turns of the turbulent era, with extensive quotations from published works and documents. Provides an overview of the role of this liberal cleric in the various independence efforts, the Mexican annexation, and the final achievement of the region's independence. DLC LNHT

87 _____. *Historia de la Universidad de El Salvador, 1841-1930.* San Salvador: Talleres Gráficos Ariel, 1941. 236 pp. Illus.

A history of the university that traces its long-term evolution and linkage to the political scene, narrated regime by regime. Includes discussion of student political activities and protests, lengthy quotations from legislation and decrees, and analysis of how the university changed, whether its existence was continuous, the autonomy movement, etc. The account is general but catches the main trends. DLC LNHT

88 _____. *En torno al mensaje presidencial, 14 de diciembre de 1951.* San Salvador: Imprenta Nacional, 1952. 57 pp.

An official commentary on and glowing abridgment of the presidential message of 1951, prepared for popular circulation among those who could not be expected to read the entire message by the Presidential Information Secretariat. It hails the acts of President Oscar Osorio, the recent revolution of 1950, and its objective of creating a "new" Salvadoran man, combining brief quotations from the president's speech with comments acclaiming his objectives, relating them to the revolutionary goals, and noting the regime's accomplishments. DLC

89 Ebaugh, Cameron Duncan. *Education in El Salvador.* Washington, D.C.: GPO, 1947. vi, 81 pp. Biblio.

A general description of existing educational facilities and their organization, with plans for future development. DLC

90 ECLA. *Agricultural Credit in El Salvador.* New York: U.N., 1950. 59 pp.

A survey of the availability and sources of credit for the nation's agricultural sector, calculating the needs and noting the inadequacy of the existing sources while suggesting improvements in its administration as well as expansion in view of the needs identified. DPU

91 _____. *Analysis and Projections of Economic Development, VIII; El desarrollo económico de El Salvador.* New York: U.N., n.d. v, 175 pp. Tables. 3d ed. Mexico: U.N., 1955.

A survey of the economy, covering 1945 through 1955, examining all sectors, consumption, exports, imports, needs, labor, and similar factors, with statistical tables. DLC

92 Ehrhardt, Lucien André. *La hacienda pública en El Salvador.* New York: U.N., 1954. 125 pp. Tables.

A United Nations technical report prepared in 1951. Reviews Salvadoran financial policy, providing appropriate statistics and making some recommendations for its improvement, including suggested modifications of the codes and areas from which revenue could be increased. DLC

93 El Salvador, Academia Salvadoreña de la Historia. *Biografía de vicentinos ilustres: homenaje al tercer centenario de la fundación de la ciudad San Vicente.* San Salvador: Imprenta Nacional, 1935. 214 pp. Illus., tables. 2d ed. San Salvador: Imprenta Nacional, 1962. 178 pp. Illus.

Brief biographical sketches of twenty-seven figures from the city of San Vicente. Encompasses clerics, generals, intellectuals, and public figures. The length and quality of the essays vary, and the emphasis is on the early nineteenth century. DLC LNHT

94 _____. *San Salvador y sus hombres.* San Salvador: Imprenta Nacional, 1938. 423 pp. Illus. 2d ed. San Salvador: Ministerio de Educación, 1967. 424 pp. Illus., maps.

A series of brief biographical sketches, ranging from two to ten pages, of leading figures of the city of San Salvador, originally compiled by the Salvadoran Academy of History in 1938. The focus is on the nineteenth and early twentieth centuries. Includes a wide range of individuals from many fields but provides only basic data about each. There are also some single-paragraph biographical capsules of less prominent figures, and an account of the founding of the city. DLC LNHT

95 El Salvador, Asociación Salvadoreña del Café. *Legislación salvadoreña del café, 1846-1955.* San Salvador: Editorial Ahora, 1956. 706 pp.

A compilation of laws relating to coffee production, marketing, financing, and landholding. DA

96 El Salvador, Centro Nacional de Información. *Reportajes y comentarios de las elecciones: los comicios del 8 de marzo de 1970 constituyeron un voto de confianza para el gobierno.* San Salvador: Imprenta Nacional, 1970. 43 pp. Illus., tables.

A collection of newspaper articles commenting on the elections for city and local governments, with introductory narration. Hails the result as a vote of confidence in the government of General Fidel Sánchez Hernández and the ruling Partido de

Conciliación Nacional, and as a demonstration of the vigor of Salvadoran democracy and the unity of its people. DLC

97 El Salvador, Constitutions. Constitución del estado del Salvador. San Salvador: n.p., 1824. 21 pp.
    LNHT

98 El Salvador, Cooperativa de Abogados de. Cooperativismo en El Salvador: legislación y doctrina. San Salvador: Cooperativa de Abogados de El Salvador, 1971. 200 pp. Tables.
    A history of the cooperative movement, with excerpts from pertinent legislation and data on the history of the lawyer's association. DLC

99 El Salvador, Universidad de. Catálogo de Tesis de todas las facultades. San Salvador: Universidad de El Salvador, 1937. 101 pp.
    A listing of the theses for degrees granted at the university through 1936, arranged alphabetically by author within faculty, with author, title, and date provided. LNHT

100 _____. Ensayos sobre la incidencia de la caficultura en algunos aspectos de la economía nacional. San Salvador: Editorial Universitaria de El Salvador, 1958. 72 pp. Notes, illus., tables.
    A collection of unsigned essays under the sponsorship of the university's economics faculty, surveying the broad trends of coffee cultivation and its internal economic impacts, covering the years 1925 through 1956. Includes essays, tables, graphs, and statistics covering such aspects as prices, taxes, exports, population growth, cost of living, and the interrelationship between each of these factors. DLC

101 _____. Estudios históricos. San Salvador: Imprenta Nacional, 1941. 344 pp.
    A collection of essays on various themes, including the study of history, histories of the University of El Salvador, essays on leading historical figures of the nation, and patriotic round-table discussions. The main focus of the various contributors is the independence of El Salvador, with separate essays on each of the leading figures of that era. DLC

102 _____. Guión histórico de la Universidad Autónoma de El Salvador. San Salvador: Editorial Ahora, 1949. 84 pp. Illus.
    A collection of material about the university's history, with brief biographical sketches of all its rectors, arranged chronologically. Includes brief histories of each of its faculties, usually consisting of information about their foundation, followed by a discussion of the current status, and in some cases comparing the courses required at the foundation and at the date of publication. Includes photos, among them shots of the new campus under construction. DLC LNHT

103 _____. Impuesto sobre la renta. San Salvador: Editorial Universitaria de El Salvador, 1968. 209 pp.
    A collection of studies dealing with the general aspects of income-tax law and the history of the income tax in El Salvador, followed by the opinions of two experts regarding the tax reform of 1966 that provoked considerable controversy by granting special tax credits to domestic corporations. It had been hoped the volume would contribute to the national debate by printing the opinions of a large number of experts from the nation, but only two replied to the survey. LNHT

104 El Salvador, Gov't of. Álbum patriótico. San Salvador: Imprenta Nacional, 1915. 266 pp. Illus.
    A collection of biographies of the president, Carlos Meléndez, and of his vice-president and designated successor, Alfonso Quinoñéz M. Includes selected reprints of articles hailing them and their work, excerpts from their statements and letters, and descriptions of ceremonies of support throughout the republic, accompanied by photos of the regime's leading figures and some of its public works. DLC

105 _____. Labor del gobierno del general Fernando Figueroa, presidente constitucional de la república, 1907-1909. San Salvador: Imprenta Meléndez, 1909. 209 pp. Illus.
    A summary listing of the regime's projects and budget listed by ministry, with brief biographies of all its ministers and principal figures. DLC

106 _____. Recopilación de leyes y reglamentos sobre trabajo y securidad social. San Salvador: Imprenta Nacional, 1951. 298 pp. 2d ed. San Salvador: Imprenta Nacional, 1960. 493 pp.
    A collection of current laws regarding labor and those establishing and regulating the nation's social security system. DLC

107 _____. Archivo General de la Nación. Documentos relativos al Dr. y presbitero José Simeón Cañas y Villacorta, libertador de los esclavos de Centro América. San Salvador: Ministerio de Educación, 1966. 91 pp. Illus.
    A collection of testaments, documents, and excerpts from previous biographies of Cañas, issued on the occasion of the bicentennial of his birth and designed to extol his contributions. DLC

108 _____. Asamblea Legislativa. Guión histórico del poder legislativo de El Salvador: constituyentes-legislaturas: síntesis biográficas de sus presidentes. 2 vols. San Salvador: Asamblea Legislativa, 1966-69. 336 pp. Illus.
    A series of biographies of the individuals who served as president of the Salvadoran Assembly from 1822 through 1900. DLC LNHT

109 _____. Asamblea Nacional Constituyente, 1950. Documentos históricos de la constitución

(El Salvador, Gov't of)
política salvadoreña de 1950. San Salvador:
Imprenta Nacional, 1951. 331 pp.
   The records of the constitutional convention and the new constitution. DLC LNHT

110 _____. Banco Hipotecario. 26 años del Banco
Hipotecario de El Salvador. San Salvador:
Imprenta Criterio, 1951. 53 pp.
   A résumé of the bank's creation and its
growth and policies during its twenty-six
years of existence.

111 _____. Banco Salvadoreño. Memoria 75
aniversario 1885-1960. San Salvador: Banco
Salvadoreño, 1960.
   An official volume commemorating the bank's
anniversary, with data regarding its creation,
an outline of its history and growth, and
information about its current facilities and
officials.

112 _____. Biblioteca Nacional. Apéndice al
Catálogo Alfabético y por materias de la
Biblioteca Nacional de El Salvador. San
Salvador: Tipografía El Cometa, 1890.
   A supplement listing items acquired since
publication of the earlier published catalog.

113 _____. _____. Bibliografía salvadoreña:
lista preliminar por autores. San Salvador:
n.p., 1952. 430 pp.
   An alphabetical listing, by author, of the
library holdings at the time of publication,
without annotations but with full publication
data. The overwhelming majority of the works
are published in El Salvador, with theses and
government reports comprising the largest
segments. DLC

114 _____. _____. Catálogo alfabético y por
materias de todos los libros que contiene la
Biblioteca Nacional de El Salvador formado por
Rafael U. Palacios. San Salvador: Imprenta
Nacional, 1887. 128 pp. 2d ed. San
Salvador: Tipografía El Cometa, 1887.
152 pp.
   A listing of the books then in the National
Library, arranged by author within subjects,
with city and date but no further informa-
tion. The volumes are mainly European, particularly
Italian and French, and the section on Central
American history contains only nine entries.

115 _____. _____. Catálogo general alfabético de
la Biblioteca Nacional de El Salvador, por
orden de autores, 1896: D. Meany, director.
San Salvador: Imprenta Nacional, 1896.
244 pp.
   Another catalog of the National Library,
updating previous publications. DLC

116 _____. _____. Documentos y datos históricos
y estadísticos de la República de El Salvador.
San Salvador: Imprenta Nacional, 1926. 155
pp. Notes, tables.
   Excerpts from the official reports of the
various Salvadoran ministries during 1827 and
1828 detailing the foundation of the state and
the difficulties with its neighbors during the
turbulent post-independence era when conflict

regarding the Federation was constant. The
introduction notes that the work was published
to refute the statements of Manuel Montúfar in
his Memorias de Jalapa. DLC LNHT

117 _____. Comisión Organizadora de las
Celebraciones de Septiembre. Septiembre
histórico. San Salvador: Imprenta Nacional,
1966. 171 pp. Illus.
   A collection of short works, scholarly and
journalistic, dealing with the independence
movement and offered, along with orations and
papers, in a commemoration of independence
during Salvadoran celebrations in 1966. Brief
biographical sketches of leaders, photos, and
documentary excerpts are appended to the articles, which were prepared, published, and
awarded prizes as part of the occasion. DLC

118 _____. Comité pro-centenario José Matías
Delgado. Delgado: el padre de la patria.
San Salvador: Imprenta Nacional, 1932. 119
pp. 2d ed. San Salvador: Ministerio de
Educación, 1961. 204 pp. Notes, illus.
   A series of essays about the founder of the
Salvadoran nation, compiled by the centennial
committee under the auspices of the Salvadoran
Academy of History. Includes several brief
biographies of Delgado as well as studies of
specific aspects of his career written by
leading Salvadoran historians, in addition to
poetry and speeches. Some of the studies are
footnoted to secondary works. DLC LNHT

119 _____. Consejo de Gobierno Revolucionario.
Justicia social en El Salvador. San Salvador:
Imprenta Nacional, 1949. 75 pp.
   DLC LNHT

120 _____. Consejo Nacional de Planificación y
Coordinación Económica. El Salvador: su
desarrollo económico y su progreso social.
San Salvador: Imprenta Nacional, 1966. 250
pp. Illus., tables.
   A lavishly illustrated folio with statistics describing the current state of the national economy and the nation, with emphasis
on development from 1962 to 1965 and details
of the projects planned for 1965-69. DLC
LNHT

120A _____. Consulate of El Salvador. The Republic of El Salvador; a land of Opportunity.
Baltimore: Sun Book, 1925. 67 pp. Illus.,
tables.
   A concise review of the condition of El
Salvador, and particularly its economy and
commercial possibilities, written to encourage
Yankee investment and trade, and stressing the
advantages of the nation as the most highly
populated of the region with the most fertile
soil, and hence with the land, conditions, and
labor possibilities most favorable to development and investment. The work was prepared by
the Consulate General in New York, and presents an official view, reflecting the official goals of seeking investment and trade for
development. DLC

121 _____. Dirección General de Caminos. Diez
años en la historia de El Salvador. San

(El Salvador, Gov't of)
Salvador: Tipografía "La Unión," 1943. 60
pp. Illus.
    A collection of photos of various road and
construction projects, including customs
houses, hospitals, and drainage ditches and
sewers, with cost figures. Designed to show-
case the works of the regime of General
Maximiliano Hernández Martínez from 1932 to
1942. LNHT

122   _____. Dirección General de Estadística y
Censos. Diccionario geográfico. San
Salvador: Imprenta Nacional, 1940. 360 pp.
3d ed. San Salvador: Dirección General de
Estadística y Censos, 1959. 258 pp. Illus.
    An exhaustive description of the geograph-
ical features and characteristics of El
Salvador. DLC

123   _____. _____. Índice de precios al
consumidor obrero en San Salvador, Mejicanos y
Delgado 1960-1969. San Salvador: n.p., 1970.
103 pp. Illus., maps, tables.
    A nine-year tabulation of monthly prices in
three Salvadoran cities for various products
and staples, including data on the cost of
living for a family of five, using 1954 as the
base year. DLC

124   _____. _____. La República de El Salvador:
Synopsis; The Republic of El Salvador: Synopsis. San Salvador: Dirección General de
Estadística, 1924. 200 pp. Biblio., illus.,
tables.
    A bilingual general description of the
current state of the nation, intended for
foreigners. Includes geographical data and
historical summaries but focuses on the current situation and the economy; presents some
statistics regarding production and export of
various products. Clearly designed to promote
interest in trade and investment. DLC LNHT

125   _____. Instituto Geográfico Nacional.
Diccionario geográfico de El Salvador. 4
vols. San Salvador: Instituto Geográfico
Nacional, 1970-76. Biblio., illus., maps,
tables.
    An encyclopedic compilation of geograph-
ical, climatic, physical, and demographic data
about El Salvador, including general sections
and discussion of each province and municipality. DLC LNHT

126   _____. Ministerio de Defensa. Principios y
objetivos del gobierno de la Revolución. San
Salvador: Departamento de Publicaciones e
Información, 1955. 75 pp.
    A government-sponsored review of the accom-
plishments of the 1948 junta, sympathetically
tracing its political, economic and social
programs and indicating the results. DLC

127   _____. Ministerio de Economía. Primera
reunión de inversionistas centroamericanos.
San Salvador: Tipografía "La Union," 1959.
74 pp.
    The report of a meeting of Central American
businessmen held in San Salvador in October

1959 to identify and discuss the implications
of the new Common Market on regional trade and
investment. Includes a list of those attending and summaries of the discussions that
provide lists of problems the businessmen
consider important, in some cases with proposals. The focus is on increasing regional
trade by facilitating investment and economic
expansion and eliminating bottlenecks, whether
in transport, law, or financing, to enable
larger exchanges of goods and services. Provides a businessman's eye view of the problems
of conducting trade and business in the region
and the impact of existing regulations. LNHT

128   _____. _____. Proyecto de aprovechamiento
hidroeléctrico del Río Lempa: antecedentes y
documentos, 1949-1951. 2 vols. San Salvador:
Imprenta Nacional, 1953. 763 pp. Illus.,
maps.
    A compilation of data and reports about the
Rio Lempara electrification project, including
the legislation and engineering and financial
feasibility studies, all reporting favorably
on the government's plans for this controversial endeavor. DLC

129   _____. Ministerio de Educación. Diagnóstico
estadístico y proyecciones de la educación
primaria en El Salvador. San Salvador:
Ministerio de Educación, 1970. 106 pp.
Tables.
    A study of the educational system, with
extensive current statistics and projections
to 1976. Examines the current problems and
concludes that more rural schools are needed
and that the attrition rate in the early
grades, particularly the first, is a serious
problem; recommends that the promotion requirements in the first grade be reduced and
promotion from it made automatic so as not to
discourage pupils at the start of school,
since the result is often early dropouts. DLC

130   _____. _____. Documentos para la historia:
las elecciones de 1964. San Salvador: n.p.,
1964. 246 pp. Illus.
    A compilation of material relevant to the
1964 elections that led to the installation of
the regime of Colonel Julio Rivera. Includes
election laws, press accounts of the campaign
and the balloting, and various public statements from participants and observers, as well
as the inaugural ceremonies and address, all
designed to emphasize the openness and fair-
ness of the election. DLC

131   _____. _____. Recopilación de documentos
históricos relativos a la administración del
general Francisco Menéndez. San Salvador:
Imprenta Nacional, 1974. 495 pp.
    After a sympathetic preface, presents a
collection of official documents from the
regime that governed the nation from 1885 to
1890, extolling its programs and accomplishments. Includes speeches, proclamations,
treaties, laws and statements regarding economic reforms and public-works projects, and
miscellaneous routine appointments, all from
the National Archives. DLC LNHT

(El Salvador, Gov't of)

132 _____. _____. El sistema educativo:
fundamentos doctrinarios, estructuras, planes
y programas. San Salvador: n.p., 1970. 75
pp. Biblio.
   A brief historical overview of the
Salvadoran educational system since 1939, with
the basic plans of the existing programs and
summaries of appropriate legislation. DLC

133 _____. _____. Situación demográfica, social,
económica y educativa de El Salvador. San
Salvador: Ministerio de Educación, 1963. 131
pp. Illus., tables.
   A statistic-packed report summarizing the
status and problems of the educational system
in 1962, prepared for a conference on education and economic and social development in
Latin America held in 1962. Includes information on the effects of population growth,
cultural diversity and its impact on the educational system, and preparation of students,
as well as on budgetary trends, administrative
patterns, and future plans. DLC

134 _____. Ministerio de Hacienda. El Salvador:
la política económica internacional y la
cláusula de la nación mas favorecida. San
Salvador: Imprenta Nacional, 1939. 95 pp.
Tables.
   Prepared for an inter-American meeting of
treasury ministers. Most of this volume summarizes the origins and usefulness of the
most-favored-nation clause, but the latter
portion does include an overview of Salvadoran
trade policy, stressing the 1930s. DLC

135 _____. Ministerio de Hacienda y Crédito
Público. Estudio sobre la situación económica
de El Salvador. San Salvador: Imprenta
Nacional, 1912. 33 pp.
   DLC

136 _____. Ministerio de Instrucción Pública. La
cuestión económica. San Salvador: Imprenta
Nacional, 1919. 351 pp.
   A series of papers by members of the government and the university examining the monetary question that was plaguing the nation and
contributing to a financial crisis. The
papers discuss monetary theory, the national
situation, and actions of the United States,
most concluding that the only appropriate
response was a return to the gold standard,
which is what ultimately resulted from the
discussion. Contains the text of the congressional decrees providing for gold coinage,
paper bills redeemable in gold, and government
regulation of emitting banks to restore confidence in the nation's currency. DLC LNHT

137 _____. Ministerio de Obras Públicas. Guía
para investigadores, República de El Salvador.
San Salvador: PAIGH, 1977. 81 pp. Biblio.,
maps.
   Another in a series of bibliographical
guides focusing on geography. See CR287. DLC

138 _____. Ministerio de Relaciones Exteriores.
Condición jurídica del gobierno del presidente
Gral. Maximiliano Hernández Martínez ante la
constitución política de la República de El
Salvador y el Tratado General de Paz y Amistad
Centroamericano suscrito en Washington en
1923. San Salvador: Imprenta Nacional, 1932.
16 pp.
   A brief preliminary statement of the
Salvadoran position, expanded in a subsequent
publication, arguing that the regime assumed
power in accordance with the constitution,
that Martínez took no part in the coup,
and that the treaty did not apply because of
Salvadoran reservations at the time of ratification. DLC

139 _____. _____. El gobierno del presidente
Gral. Maximiliano Hernández Martínez ante la
constitución política de El Salvador y el
Tratado de Paz y Amistad, suscrito por las
repúblicas de Centroamérica en la ciudad de
Washington el 7 de febrero de 1923: diversas
opiniones. San Salvador: Imprenta Nacional,
1932. 153 pp.
   The Martínez regime's statement of its case
against the policy of nonrecognition, designed
to establish its constitutionality and legal
position. Includes official declarations,
legislative acts, signed petitions, and manifestos designed to demonstrate popular support, as well as newspaper commentaries from
the local press and excerpts from the appropriate documents such as the constitution and
the treaty. The heart of the effort is a
series of commentaries by internationally
known lawyers and jurists regarding the significance of nonrecognition and offering interpretations of the treaty. DLC DLC-LDS-821

140 _____. _____. Libro Rosado: contiene la
actuación de la cancillería salvadoreña
relativa a la aceptación y adhesión de El
Salvador al pacto international Liga de las
Naciones. San Salvador: Ministerio de
Relaciones Exteriores, 1920. 40 pp.
   The official decrees and exchanges by which
El Salvador joined the League of Nations. DLC
LNHT

141 _____. _____. Pactos internacionales de El
Salvador. San Salvador: Tipografía "La
Unión," 1911.
   A collection of the texts of treaties in
force.

142 _____. _____. Tratados, convenciones y
acuerdos internacionales vigentes en El
Salvador. 6 vols. San Salvador: Imprenta
Nacional, 1938-60.
   The full texts of all the nation's international agreements, constituting a continuing
series issued irregularly. The 1938 volume
began with accords for the years 1865 through
1929, with subsequent volumes continuing the
chronology through 1960. DLC

143 _____. Ministerio de Trabajo y Previsión
Social. Esbozo de la situación económico-
social en las materias más estrechamente
relacionadas con la seguridad social en la
República de El Salvador. San Salvador:
Ministerio de Trabajo y Previsión Social,
1951. 42 pp. Illus., tables.

(El Salvador, Gov't of)
Statistics about contemporary El Salvador, covering population, economy, and medical facilities, with information about social groups and living standards. DLC

144 _____. Ministerio del Interior. Catorce de diciembre de 1951: tercer aniversario de la revolución salvadoreña. San Salvador: Imprenta Nacional, 1952. 102 pp. Illus.
An official volume containing excerpts of speeches at and reportage about the celebration of the anniversary of the 1948 revolution. Emphasizes the official actions of the regime of Colonel Oscar Osorio and prints photos of the demonstration. Includes a succinct summary of the regime's official view of the objectives of the revolution, stressing its democratic, law-and-order, and reformist goals. DLC

145 _____. Poder Ejecutivo. Homenaje al prócer José Simeón Cañas en el primer centenario de su muerte, 1838-1938. San Salvador: Tipografía "La Unión," 1939. 54 pp. DLC

146 _____. Presidencia, Secretaría de Información. Aquí Chaltenango. San Salvador: Imprenta Nacional, 1969. 51 pp. Illus.
A series of public speeches and statements extolling the regional development program for this Salvadoran district, delivered during the visit of President Fidel Sánchez Hernández to dedicate the works and inspect progress. DLC

147 _____. _____. El Salvador: país en marcha ascendente. San Salvador: Imprenta Nacional, 1953. 119 pp. Illus.
A collection of newspaper articles published in the press of El Salvador and Honduras, consisting of the comments and observations of a group of Honduran journalists during a visit to El Salvador in March 1953. Includes general description, historical and cultural comment, and interviews with important government figures. DLC

148 _____. _____. Gerardo Barrios: héroe nacional de El Salvador. San Salvador: Imprenta Nacional, n.d. 61 pp. Illus.
A collection of photos and documents relating to the national hero of El Salvador, including press commentaries eulogizing him. DLC LNHT

149 _____. _____. Homenajes al presidente Lemus. San Salvador: Imprenta Nacional, 1959. 209 pp. Illus.
A collection of articles, speeches, commentary, and photos recounting the popular outburst of sympathy and support for President Lemus inspired by his visit to the United States at the invitation of President Eisenhower and represented in the huge demonstration that greeted him on his return. Contains his addresses and the official declarations for the occasion, with numerous photos and favorable press commentaries. Compiled by the regime. DLC

150 _____. _____. Labor del gobierno del general Fernando Figueroa, presidente constitucional de la república, 1907-1909. San Salvador: Imprenta Meléndez, 1909. 209 pp. Illus.
The regime's catalog of its works and their benefits, focusing on a detailed list of all its projects. Includes thumbnail biographies of all important officials, with photos; details regarding trade and commerce; and summaries of the projects of each of the ministries, based on their annual reports. Although the reports are current, some of the statistics on trade and finance extend back to the previous decade for comparison. DLC

151 _____. _____. Legalidad constitucional de la Asamblea Legislativa. San Salvador: Imprenta Nacional, 1951. 138 pp.
A collection of articles, proclamations, acts, letters, and Supreme Court decisions regarding the 1951 Constituent Assembly, its powers, and its legality reflecting the continuing disputes from the 1948 revolution in that nation. They trace the legal maneuvers and political polemics in the press regarding the revision of the constitution. DLC

152 _____. _____. Me enorgullezco de ser salvadoreño. San Salvador: Editorial Ahora, 1951. 193 pp.
A collection of miscellaneous historical documents and essays, designed to encourage patriotism. Includes the nation's declaration of independence, portions of the latest presidential message to congress, and comments on the military. DLC LNHT

153 _____. _____. El poder constituyente en El Salvador. San Salvador: Imprenta Nacional, 1962. 23 pp.
An official account of the process by which the military government called the constitutional convention of 1961, with justifying statements referring to the political situation and to previous constituent assemblies in the nation. DLC

154 _____. _____. Viaje a una revolución. San Salvador: Imprenta Nacional, 1953. 79 pp. Illus., tables.
A collection of articles prepared by a group of Guatemalan journalists who visited El Salvador during August 1953 at the invitation of Colonel Oscar Osorio, hailing the progressive and revolutionary works of the Osorio regime. LNHT

155 _____. _____. El Salvador: The Development of the People's Struggle. Birmingham, England: Tricontinental Society, 1980. 37 pp.
A sympathetic view of the guerrilla movement, detailing the governmental abuses and societal problems that constitute its basis.

156 El Salvador: un pueblo perseguido: testimonios de cristianos. 2 vols. Lima: Centro de Estudios y Publicaciones, 1980. 148, 250 pp. Biblio., illus.
A collection of reports and statements about the Salvadoran crisis. Denounces the brutality, violence, and oppression of the

peasants and focuses on the church's role, though the emphasis on class structure has Marxist overtones. The first volume covers 1977 through 1980; the second focuses on statements by and the murder of Archbishop Oscar Romero. AzU

157 Erdozain, Placido. <u>Archbishop Romero: Martyr of Salvador</u>. Maryknoll, N.Y.: Orbis, 1980. 128 pp. Illus.
A loving biography of the archbishop of San Salvador by a priest who, though not among his earliest adherents, had worked with him. Hails Romero's courage and love for the poor, drawing upon his own recollections and those of other priests who knew the archbishop. Clearly seeking to claim him for the revolutionaries, it emphasizes his association with the plight of the poor and his martyrdom. DLC

158 Escuela Normal de Maestras "España." <u>Algunas maestras, pintores, músicos, y escritores salvadoreños</u>. San Salvador: Escuela Normal de Maestras "España," 1953. 309 pp. Illus.
A collection of single-page biographical sketches of leading Salvadoran artists, musicians, teachers, and scholars, with photos. Designed for students and teachers, it provides basic data about their lives and works. Includes some photos of paintings and samples of music. No editor is indicated and the selection criteria are not explained. DLC LNHT

159 Espino, Francisco. <u>Folk-lore salvadoreño</u>. San Salvador: Talleres Gráficos Cisneros, 1946. 123 pp.
A collection of folk-song lyrics, riddles, nicknames, and placenames from El Salvador, offered without comment. LNHT

160 _____. <u>Panorama de la escuela salvadoreña</u>. San Salvador: Talleres Gráficos Cisneros, 1941. 20 pp.
A compilation of data, statistics, and laws regarding the Salvadoran educational system, with the current basic programs for the schools. NN

161 Espino, Miguel Ángel. <u>La vida de José Simeón Cañas, padre de los esclavos</u>. Guatemala: n.p., 1938. 29 pp. 2d ed. San Salvador: Ministerio de Cultura, 1955. 42 pp.
Part of the "Biblioteca Mínima" series designed to present brief biographical sketches of national heroes and significant figures in Salvadoran history in a form that will encourage greater knowledge of and identification with them by students and the public. DLC LNHT

162 Falconio, Leda de [Aldef, pseud.]. <u>Cuentos de tierra y mar</u>. San Salvador: Ministerio de Educación, 1974. 128 pp.
A collection of short stories dealing with Salvadoran life and folklore, written by an Italian now resident in El Salvador. DLC

163 Federación de Cajas de Crédito de El Salvador. <u>Monografía de El Salvador: los problemas del crédito agropecuario y el desarrollo económica</u>. San Salvador: Federación de Cajas de Crédito, 1968. 137 pp. Biblio., tables.
An economic overview of the nation, focusing on the problems of agriculture and the role of credit in fostering agricultural development. Identifies the problems and prospects in Salvador in question-and-answer form. DLC

164 Fernández, Julio Fausto. <u>Patria y juventud en el mundo de hoy</u>. San Salvador: Ministerio de Cultura, 1956. 262 pp.
A series of essays analyzing the political and social conditions in El Salvador and the current crisis, written by a young lawyer who seeks to demonstrate the need for action but rejects foreign doctrines and calls for an indigenous model that reflects local needs and nationalism. His inclusion of Christianity as one of the bases for such a plan suggests ties to the reformist Christian Democratic party, and the rationale fits its stance of seeking to reject extremes on both sides of the political spectrum. DLC

165 Fernández, Manuel. <u>Bosquejo físico, político e histórico de la República de El Salvador</u>. San Salvador: Imprenta Nacional, 1869. 166 pp. Latest ed. San Salvador: Biblioteca Nacional, 1926. 158 pp. Illus.
A narrative description of the principal geographic and physical features of the republic. DLC LNHT

166 Figeac, José Flores. <u>La libertad de imprenta en El Salvador</u>. San Salvador: Universidad Autónoma de El Salvador, 1931. Latest ed. San Salvador: Universidad Autónoma de El Salvador, 1947. 592 pp. Illus., tables.
A series of brief essays tracing the history of the press and its regulation from independence to 1947, with brief essays summarizing the policies of each of the nation's governments, quotations from the laws regarding the press, and single-paragraph references to each new newspaper founded or suppressed and to significant press events. Includes a list of all the papers published during each administration, and of all the editors of the various newspapers throughout Salvadoran history. DLC LNHT

167 _____. <u>Recordatorio histórico de la República de El Salvador</u>. San Salvador: Talleres Gráficos Cisneros, 1934. Latest ed. San Salvador: Talleres Gráficos Cisneros, 1938. 500 pp. Illus.
A history of nineteenth-century El Salvador, though the first 391 pages contain a broad overview of the Colonial era. It is based on documentary research in the Archivo General de Centro América and the Salvadoran government archives, though citations are limited to extensive quotations incorporated into the text. The final portion consists of a series of brief essays on the history of each of the provincial capitals of the nation. The narration is sufficient to provide an overview, though not detail, and the documentary excerpts are extensive. DLC LNHT

168 Flakoll, Darwin J., and Claribel Alegría.
     Cenizas de Izalco. Barcelona: Seix Barras,
     1966. 175 pp. 2d ed. San Salvador:
     Ministerio de Educación, 1976. 230 pp.
          A novel by a husband-and-wife team includ-
     ing a Yankee and a Nicaraguan raised in
     Salvador. Focuses on the problems, emotions,
     and tribulations of life in the Salvadoran
     countryside, emphasizing emotions rather than
     the locale. DLC

169 Flemion, Philip F. *Historical Dictionary of
     El Salvador*. Metuchen, N.J.: Scarecrow
     Press, 1972. 157 pp. Biblio.
          The thinnest of the Central American
     volumes in this series, this work, like the
     others, provides an alphabetical listing and
     brief definitions of names, places, groups,
     and institutions in the nation's history. The
     bibliography is brief, and the definitions are
     extremely cryptic. The emphasis is on places
     and people. As is often the case in the
     series, maternal names are not consistently
     included. DLC LNHT

170 Flores, Saúl. *Nuestros maestros: notas para
     una historia de la pedagogía nacional*. San
     Salvador: Editorial Ahora, 1963. 635 pp.
     Index, illus.
          A collection of brief biographical sketches
     of various Salvadoran teachers, with emphasis
     on the contemporary generation but including
     nineteenth-century figures as well. Arrange-
     ment is disparate and selection criteria not
     evident. The commentaries do provide an out-
     line of the careers of most of those covered,
     though some include funeral orations or ex-
     cerpts from their publications instead. DLC
     LNHT

171 Fonseca, Pedro S. *Demografía salvadoreña*.
     San Salvador: Imprenta Rafael Reyes, 1921.
     84 pp. Illus., maps, tables.
          A writer and professor of statistics exam-
     ines the available indicators regarding the
     population of the nation by comparing the
     birth and death rates with those of other
     nations, using registrations of births,
     deaths, and marriages to compensate for the
     absence of census data. Examining the repub-
     lic's first hundred years, he notes the high
     birth rate, but focuses on the illigitimacy
     rate, which he attributes to inadequate sala-
     ries, poor living conditions, and laws that
     fail to enforce the responsibilities of par-
     ents, which he says encourage abandonment of
     children in view of poor economic conditions.
     He calls on the upper classes to remedy the
     economic and social problems that contribute
     to this situation. DLC

172 _____. *La moneda salvadoreña*. San Salvador:
     Imprenta Nacional, 1924. 36 pp. Notes,
     illus., tables. Latest ed. San Salvador:
     Talleres Nacional de Grabados, 1929. 29 pp.
     Notes.
          A brief overview of the Salvadoran monetary
     and banking system from Colonial times to the
     1920s, with details of the coinage, currency,
     exchange, loans, and volume, as well as ex-
     cerpts from the pertinent legislation. DLC

173 Fortín Magaña, Romeo. *Conferencias y
     discursos universitarios*. San Salvador:
     Editorial Universitaria, 1963. 416 pp.
          A collection of speeches and commentaries
     by the rector of the National University of El
     Salvador, written between 1955 and 1959 when
     the institution was fighting for its autonomy
     and its identity, reflecting these struggles
     and the problems of the university in that
     era. Includes commentaries on a wide range of
     educational problems, speeches on various
     historical and intellectual figures of the
     nation, and discussion of a range of political
     and economic themes. DLC LNHT

174 _____. *Democracia y socialismo: seguida de
     otros breves estudios*. San Salvador:
     Talleres Gráficos Cisneros, 1953. xx, 355 pp.
          A collection of wide-ranging theoretical
     essays on disparate themes, including democ-
     racy, socialism, corporations, laws, etc.
     Most focus on general themes, though some
     provide specifics regarding El Salvador and
     others are very narrowly focused, for example
     a discussion of a particular paving project in
     Santa Ana. DLC

175 _____. *Inquietudes de un año memorable, 1944*.
     San Salvador: Talleres Gráficos Cisneros,
     1945. viii, 298 pp.
          A series of essays about and inspired by
     the 1944 revolution in El Salvador. Includes
     a lengthy study of the 1886 constitution the
     revolutionaries sought to restore, as well as
     commentaries on Salvadoran democracy and
     national problems, with discussion of the
     revolutionary aims. Includes an extensive
     collection of documents relating to the 1886
     constitution and the 1944 upheaval. NN

176 Galdames Armas, Juan, ed. *Hombres y cosas de
     Santa Ana: crónicas históricas documentadas
     de hechos u obras notables de la ciudad y
     rasgos de la vida de sus hijos más ilustres*.
     Santa Ana: Imprenta Gutenberg, 1943. 245 pp.
     Illus.
          A collection of documents and commentaries
     about the Salvadoran city of Santa Ana and its
     leading citizens throughout its history, with
     some introductory and connecting narration.
     The editor notes that data for the earlier
     years are limited by the fact that the city
     archives were destroyed in the 1870 volcanic
     eruptions. Includes a list of all mayors and
     city councilmen during the existence of the
     republic. DLC

177 Gallardo, Miguel Ángel, ed. *Cuatro
     constituciones federales de Centro América y
     las constituciones políticas de El Salvador*.
     San Salvador: Tipografía "La Unión," 1945.
     xxxix, 380 pp.
          The complete text of the ten constitutions
     that have governed El Salvador through 1944,
     as well as those of the various attempts at
     Central American Federation, with a brief
     introduction tracing constitutional trends in
     Latin America. DLC LNHT

(Gallardo, Miguel Ángel, ed.)

178 _____. Papeles históricos. 3 vols. San
Salvador: Imprenta Nacional, 1954. 228, 279,
307 pp.
A diverse collection of documents, primarily dealing with the nineteenth century but
including some Colonial items. Originally
launched on the occasion of the centennial of
the city of Santa Tecla and focusing on that
region, it encompasses political subjects as
well as biological and geographical ones. DLC
LNHT

179 Gallardo, Ricardo, ed. Las constituciones de
El Salvador. Madrid: Ediciones Cultura
Hispánica, 1961. 2 vols. 803, 1269 pp.
Biblio., notes.
Part of a collection designed to provide a
convenient compilation of texts of all twelve
constitutions in the history of El Salvador
from 1824 to 1950, this volume offers much
more than the title implies. In addition to
the constitutions it contains a narrative
history of El Salvador, prepared by one of its
leading scholars and carefully researched in
pertinent government reports, published as a
series of essays commenting upon and analyzing
the current constitution by subject, function,
and governmental division. DLC

180 Gallegos Valdés, Luís. Panorama de la
literatura salvadoreña. San Salvador:
Ministerio de Educación, 1962. 238 pp.
Index, illus., notes.
A broad survey of literary trends in El
Salvador, focusing on the various generational
changes and characteristics, though including
some essays on significant writers. Each of
the generational chapters offers single-page
biographical sketches of its principal writers, and a list of their publications. DLC
LNHT

181 _____. Plaza mayor. San Salvador:
Ministerio de Cultura, 1960. 62 pp. 2d ed.
San Salvador: Ministerio de Educación, 1970.
74 pp.
Twenty short stories about life in the
Salvadoran countryside, in the costumbrista
tradition. FU

182 Gámez, José Dolores. Gerardo Barrios ante la
posteridad: apuntes y documentos para su
biografía en el XXXVI aniversario de su
muerte. Managua: Tipografía Nacional, 1901.
603 pp. 2d ed. San Salvador: Ministerio de
Educación, 1965. 486 pp. Illus.
A Nicaraguan writer's compilation of documents regarding Barrios's years as president
of El Salvador, covering the period from 1858
to his death. The author contributes brief
introductions and commentaries to link some of
the documents and hail his subject. Most of
the items consist of Barrios's correspondence,
though they also include treaties and proclamations, official exchanges, and some excerpts
from the press. Republished as part of the
official Salvadoran celebration of the centennial of the hero's death. DLC LNHT

183 Garcés Pachano, Wilson. Estudio sobre la
vivienda en El Salvador. New York: U.N.,
1954. 86 pp.
An analysis of housing conditions and
needs, with detailed data about the present
situation. DLC

184 García, Joaquín. Lucha de San Salvador contra
el imperio, 1821-1823. San Salvador:
Imprenta Nacional, 1940. 95 pp. Biblio.
An account of the Salvadoran resistance to
the Mexican efforts to annex Central America,
its rejection of Emperor Iturbide, and its
separation from Guatemala. Consists primarily
of extensive documentary excerpts. Details
the domestic political situation and the campaign against General Filísola, but also provides summations of the arguments for and
against annexation, though defending the
Salvadoran position and hailing the resistance
that gave birth to the nation. Based on secondary works and published documents dealing
with El Salvador and Mexico. DLC

185 García, Miguel Ángel, ed. Diccionario
histórico enciclopédico de la República de El
Salvador: anecdotas centroamericanos. 13
vols. San Salvador: Tipografía del Diario
Latino, Imprenta Salvadoreña, & Imprenta
Nacional, 1927-50.
A continuing series, arranged alphabetically, consisting of a collection of excerpts
from documents about the leading figures and
events of Salvadoran history. Provides basic
data regarding birth and death of the subjects, but the data is disparate. Entries are
primarily documentary rather than biographical, resembling a scrapbook or set of notes,
and the length varies widely. Several volumes
were devoted to Gerardo Barrios, while some
figures receive only a few paragraphs. Only
thirteen volumes, covering the letters A
through Col were completed before the author's
death, but several separate volumes dealing
with individual themes also bear the series
title, causing considerable confusion about
the number of volumes, much less the sequence
and proper citation. DLC LNHT

186 _____. El doctor José Matías Delgado:
homenaje en el primer centenario de su muerte,
1832-1932: documentos para el estudio de su
vida y de su obra. 2 vols. San Salvador:
Imprenta Nacional, 1933-39. 656, 628 pp.
Notes, illus.
A massive collection of studies of and
documents regarding one of the leading figures
of Salvadoran independence, published in honor
of the centennial of his death. Includes
correspondence, government documents, his publications, items from the contemporary press,
contemporary political polemics and pamphlets,
and several biographical studies by various
contributors. Nubmered as the initial volumes
of the Diccionario histórico though clearly a
separate series within it. DLC LNHT

187 _____. Universidad Nacional: homenaje en el
primer centenario de su fundación. 2 vols.
San Salvador: Imprenta Nacional, 1941.

Volume 1 contains a collection of significant speeches about the university, arranged chronologically but with selection criteria not clear, and a series of brief biographical sketches of its professors through the years, arranged alphabetically. The second volume consists of the text of laws relating to the university, arranged chronologically, covering the full sweep of the 1841-1941 era. The title page identifies these as part of the larger Diccionario histórico enciclopédico though they are numbered separately and clearly outside the regular sequence. DLC LNHT

188 Garzona S., Fernando, José María Sifontes, and J. Antonio Gutiérrez, eds. Álbum histórico de Sonsonate. N.p., 1926. Pages unnumbered. Illus.
A volume commemorating the fourth centennial of the foundation of the city in May 1924, with photos of the celebrations, brief historial résumés of the city's institutions, and descriptions of its current facilities and services. LNHT

189 Gavidia, Francisco Antonio. 1814. San Salvador: Tipografía "La Unión," 1905. 64 pp.
An account of the events of 1814 in Salvador that provides details of early phases of the independence movement, based on documents from the Biblioteca Nacional of El Salvador. DLC

190 _____. Historia moderna de El Salvador. 2 vols. San Salvador: Imprenta Meléndez, 1918. 2d ed. San Salvador: Ministerio de Cultura, 1958. 494 pp.
A documentary compilation, with brief narrations connecting the excerpts, focusing on the independence era, its origins and leaders. The 1958 edition is part of the Obras completas. DLC LNHT

191 _____. Obras de Francisco Gavidia. San Salvador: Imprenta Nacional, 1913. 500 pp. Latest ed. San Salvador: Ministerio de Educación, 1976. 464 pp.
The collected works of this influential Salvadoran writer, including poetry, essays, short stories, and theater, mirroring his shift from romanticism to modernism. All editions after the first employ the title Obras completas de Francisco Gavidia. DLC

192 Geoffroy Rivas, Pedro. El español que hablamos en El Salvador. San Salvador: Instituto Salvadoreño del Seguro Social, 1969. 4th ed. San Salvador: Ministerio de Educación, 1978. 131 pp.
An alphabetically arranged dictionary of Salvadoran idioms and local terms, with definitions, accompanied by a brief essay explaining the various currents that affected the adoption of idioms in this nation and their sources in the Indian languages and Spanish. The later editions use the title La lengua Salvadoreña. DLC

193 Gierloff-Emden, Hans Günter. Die Küste von El Salvador: eine morphologisch-ozeanographische Monographie. Wiesbaden: Franz Steiner, 1959. Biblio., illus., maps.
La Costa de El Salvador: monografía morfológica-oceanográfica. San Salvador: Ministerio de Educación, 1976. 273 pp. Illus., maps.
A detailed geological study of the nation's coastline. DLC LNHT

194 Gómez Campos, José. Semblanzas salvadoreñas. San Salvador: Talleres Gráficos Cisneros, 1930. 131 pp. Illus.
A series of satirical and humorous caricatures of the leading Salvadoran literary figures of the day, seeking to portray their personality. IaU

195 González, Darío. Estudio histórico y geográfico de la República del Salvador seguido de algunos datos estadísticos. New York: Appleton, 1894. 569 pp. Illus., maps, tables.
A brief historical narration covering the conquest, Colonial era, and independence period through the dissolution of the Federation, followed by an extensive geographical and geological description of the nation, with an account of each of the departments as they stood in 1891 and a collection of statistics relating to the budget and state of the nation in that year. The historical narration is straightforward and the descriptive data are massive. LNHT

196 González Montalvo, Ramón. Barbasco. San Salvador: Ministerio de Cultura, 1960. 203 pp.
A novel of social protest featuring the inevitable theme of a greedy landowner, who in this case is a former peasant become wealthy, brutally exploiting the peasants and confiscating their land to enhance his holdings until he eventually goes too far by killing their leader. The enraged peasants then rise up and kill him, destroying his hacienda and dispersing, thus ending their world along with the oppression, though not necessarily living happily ever after. DLC

197 _____. Las tinajas. San Salvador: n.p., 1935. 2d ed. San Salvador: Ministerio de Cultura, 1956. 283 pp.
A novel set in the Salvadoran countryside, focusing on the problems of the peasants and the exploitation of the landowners. Emphasizes love for the land and the importance of new technical and scientific methods of farming over social protest. DLC LNHT

198 González Ruíz, Ricardo. El Salvador de hoy. San Salvador: Talleres Martínez, 1952. 367 pp. Illus., maps, tables.
A series of brief descriptions, with lavish photos, of the various places of interest in the nation, including cities and geographic regions. Also presents a review of the current state of the nation, concentrating on the economy and productive facilities but containing sections regarding the social,

governmental, and educational facilities. Emphasizes the works of the current regime and the 1950 constitution and acclaims the recent progress of the nation and its government. DLC LNHT

199 González Sol, Rafael. Fiestas cívicas, religiosas y exhibiciones populares de El Salvador. San Salvador: Talleres Editorial Cisneros, 1945. 84 pp. Biblio., illus., tables. 2d ed. San Salvador: Talleres Gráficos Cisneros, 1947. 82 pp.
A brief discussion of Salvadoran regional fiestas, with a calendar of dates and places, followed by description of the various dances of the nation; includes verses and photos of the dances and celebrations. DLC LNHT

200 _____. Índice geográfico de la República de El Salvador. San Salvador: Editorial Ahora, 1948. 208 pp. Biblio., maps.
An index of cities, towns, and geographical features. Arranged by province, with information, location, etc. DLC

201 González y Contreras, Gilberto. Historia de una persecución: epístolas de burlas y picardías. Mexico: Ediciones Mexicanas, 1946. 99 pp. Illus.
A Salvadoran exile's commentaries, in the form of letters, newspaper columns, and essays, written in Cuba during the regime of General Maximiliano Hernández Martínez. The author comments on a wide range of themes and defends himself against what he characterizes as attacks upon him from Salvador and by the Cuban press. In the process, he states his position on numerous political and social themes and denounces the regime that governed his country. ICarbS

202 Guandique, José Salvador. Gavidia, el amigo de Darío. San Salvador: Ministerio de Educación, 1965. 378 pp. Biblio., notes.
A biography of Gavidia and a study of his literary significance that employs comparison with Darío for emphasis, though it also deals with their friendship, similar techniques, and influence on each other. Based on extensive use of secondary works and literary criticism, as well as on the works of the subject. DLC LNHT

203 _____. Presbítero y doctor José Matías Delgado: ensayo histórico. San Salvador: Ministerio de Educación, 1962. 349 pp. Index, biblio., notes.
An interpretation of the Salvadoran struggle for independence, based on secondary works, which despite its title focuses more on the situation of the nation and the conditions that led to the the independence movement than on Delgado. Draws wide-ranging comparisons with other nations. DLC LNHT

204 _____. Roberto Edmundo Canessa: directivo, fundador, ministro, candidata, víctima. San Salvador: Tipografía Ungo, 1962. xviii, 222 pp. Notes, illus.
A sympathetic biography of a leading Salvadoran political figure and statesman who served as his nation's foreign minister during 1950–54, was one of the founders of the Organization of Central American States, as well as a founder of the Partido Acción Nacional of El Salvador and its presidential candidate in the election of 1955. He died in 1961 after his arrest, beating, and flight into exile. The author emphasizes his contributions to the nation and his persecution after his unsuccessful candidacy. Based on published government reports, press accounts, and the subject's statements and writings. DLC LNHT

205 Guerra, Tomás. El Salvador: octubre sangriento. San José: n.p., 1979. 158 pp.
A hasty analysis of the October 1979 coup that overthrew the Romero regime in El Salvador. Reflects the leftist viewpoint that it was a move contrived to present an appearance of change so as to short-circuit a leftist uprising and hence prevent El Salvador from following the path of Nicaragua.

206 Guerrero, Francisco José. El Salvador ante los organismos internacionales: discursos del Sr. ministro de relaciones exteriores de El Salvador, Dr. Francisco José Guerrero, en la ONU y en la OEA, octubre de 1969. San Salvador: Imprenta Nacional, 1969. 43 pp.
Two speeches stating the official Salvadoran position, one before the U.N., dealing with general topics, and the other before the OAS, dealing more specifically with the conflict with Honduras. DLC

207 Guidos Véjar, Rafael. El ascenso del militarismo en El Salvador. San Salvador: UCA, 1980. 156 pp. Biblio., notes.
A study of the years 1929–32, based on secondary sources, stressing the problems of the nation during the world depression. Argues that the civil governments failed to deal with the situation, demonstrating the failure of the local bourgeoisie and leaving the path open for the rise of the military. Includes extended discussion of the regime of Arturo Araujo, and a survey of the Liberal regimes from 1871 to 1929 focusing on how their economic policies contributed to the problems of the nation. FU

208 Guzmán, David Joaquín. Apuntamientos sobre la topografía física de la República del Salvador. San Salvador: Tipografía El Cometa, 1883. 525 pp. Illus., tables.
A general geographical description providing details regarding the republic's location, landforms, flora, fauna, and Indians. Includes descriptions of the contemporary agriculture and economy, some tables regarding haciendas, and climatic data. DLC LNHT

209 Guzmán, Mauricio. La acción de divorcio en la ley salvadoreña. San Salvador: Ministerio de Cultura, 1956. 163 pp.
A brief survey of the divorce laws of El Salvador, originally prepared as a legal thesis. Includes description and summary of current law, and discussion of the causes and types of proof necessary, based on existing cases. LNHT

210 Haverstock, Nathan A., and John P. Hoover. El
     Salvador in Pictures. New York: Sterling,
     1974. 64 pp. Index, illus.
          Part of the visual geography series, this
     volume is designed to introduce children to
     the country. Provides brief general accounts
     of landforms, climate, economy, government,
     culture, etc., to link the black-and-white
     photographs that constitute the heart of the
     work. DLC

211 Hernández Aguirre, Mario. Gavidia: poesía,
     literatura, humanismo. San Salvador:
     Ministerio de Educación, 1968. 498 pp.
     Biblio., notes, illus., appendix.
          A comprehensive literary study, with a
     bibliography of Gavidia's works and a chro-
     nology of his life. Includes consideration of
     his relationship to the romanticist, modern-
     ist, and humanist schools of writing and con-
     sideration of his plays, essays, narratives,
     and poetry. The bibliography provides a list
     of studies of his works and commentaries about
     them. DLC LNHT

212 Hernández Segura, Roberto Emilio. La
     planeación y el desarrollo económico de El
     Salvador. Mexico: n.p., 1956. 143 pp.
     Biblio., notes, illus., tables. 2d ed. San
     Salvador: Imprenta Nacional, 1957. 85 pp.
     Biblio., notes, illus., tables.
          A discussion of the need for centralized
     economic planning, including consideration of
     the theoretical basis and objectives of plan-
     ning in general and a survey of specific needs
     in El Salvador. Emphasizes the importance of
     planning for all classes of the population and
     of broad input. The author criticizes the
     Liberal economic system for overlooking the
     lower classes and yet is careful to separate
     general planning for key sectors from total
     state control of the economy, which he also
     rejects. Includes economic and population
     statistics covering a broad span of years,
     some running from 1930. DLC

213 Herradora Alcántara, María Luisa. Puntitos
     sobre geografía económica de El Salvador. San
     Salvador: Ministerio de Instrucción Pública,
     1927. 47 pp. Biblio., notes, illus., maps,
     tables.
          A brief geographical summary designed for
     use by secondary teachers. Principally a
     listing of current economic production and
     transportation facilities, with descriptive
     and climatic information. DPU

214 Herrera Vega, Adolfo. El indio occidental de
     El Salvador y su incorporación social por la
     escuela. Izalco, El Salvador: Tipografía
     Comercial de Nicolas Cabezas Duarte, 1935.
     110 pp. Illus.
          A tract calling for the schools of the
     nation to assume the responsibility for edu-
     cating the Indian in practical skills to im-
     prove his life-style, patronizingly stressing
     his poor habits, morals, and living condi-
     tions. Argues that the school is the only
     appropriate vehicle to teach him new values
     and is shirking its responsibility if it does
     not do so. Calls for the incorporation of the
     Indian into the mainstream of the nation,
     through education that will convert him to
     ladino values. DLC

215 Herrera Velado, Francisco. Agua de coco. San
     Salvador: n.p., 1926. 4th ed. San Salvador:
     Ministerio de Educación, 1961. 224 pp.
     Kokosovoe moloko: rasskazy [Coconut milk:
     stories]. Moscow: Izdatel'stvo Inostrannoi
     Literatury, 1962. 136 pp.
          A collection of short stories based on the
     regional folklore and traditions of western El
     Salvador, employing local customs and idioms,
     and seeking to capture the local color and
     feeling. DLC LNHT

216 Hoselitz, Berthold Frank. Industrial Develop-
     ment of El Salvador. New York: U.N., 1954.
     104 pp. Tables.
     Desarrollo industrial de El Salvador. New
     York: U.N., 1954. 107 pp. Notes, tables.
          A U.N. Technical mission survey detailing
     the current state of Salvadoran industry and
     future prospects, with discussions of each
     sector. DLC

217 Huezo Selva, Rafael. Agenda demográfica de El
     Salvador. San Salvador: Asociación
     Demografía Salvadoreña, 1974. 74 pp. Illus.,
     maps, tables.
          A pamphlet designed to alert the general
     public to the problems posed by the rapid
     population increase in the nation, with
     cartoon-style illustrations. DLC

218 _____. El espacio económico más singular del
     Continente Americano. San Salvador: Pub-
     lished by the Author. 1972. 201 pp. Maps,
     tables.
          A Salvadoran economist's view of his nation
     and its prospects, with extensive comparison
     with other Latin American nations and numerous
     comparative tables and graphs. He emphasizes
     the role of coffee, the population problem,
     and the usefulness of the Common Market. DLC
     LNHT

219 Ibarra, Cristóbal Humberto. Tembladerales.
     San Salvador: Ministerio de Cultura, 1957.
     210 pp.
          A novel set in the Salvadoran countryside
     detailing the trials and tribulations of the
     peasants during the regime of General
     Maximiliano Hernádez Martínez, combining
     costumbrista descriptive passages and local
     dialect with social protest, focusing on the
     harshness of the regime. DLC

220 Iglesias, Luís. Los misioneros redentoristas
     y la República de El Salvador, C.A.: apuntes
     para la historia religiosa de El Salvador.
     Mexico: Gerardo Mayela, 1956. 147 pp.
     Illus.
          A history of the activities of the Redemp-
     torist order in El Salvador from 1928 through
     1955, written by a member of the order. In-
     cludes a brief history of missionary activi-
     ties in the nation in earlier years and of the
     foundation of the order, but consists princi-
     pally of descriptions of the activities in
     each of the cities and towns in which the

order works. Includes statistics regarding numbers of sermons, classes, communions, etc., for each location. LNHT

221 Instituto de Nutrición de Centro América y Panamá. Evaluación nutricional de la población de Centro América y Panamá: El Salvador. Guatemala: Ministerio de Salubridad Pública, 1969. 142 pp. Illus., tables.
       Like others in this series, provides details regarding the nutritional state of the rural populace. See item CR608.

222 Instituto Nacional de Informare si Documentare Stiintifica si Tehnica. El Salvador: dezvoltarea stiintifica, tehnica si economica. Bucharest: Published by the Institute, 1974. 43 pp. Biblio., tables.
       A general economic survey of the early 1970s designed to make data about the nation available in Romania. DLC

223 Istituto Italo-Latino Americano. El Salvador. Rome: Istituto Italo-Latino Americano, 1971. 41 pp.
       See item CR610. DLC

224 Jiménez, Lilian. Condiciones de la mujer en El Salvador. Mexico: Editorial Muñoz, 1962. 76 pp.
       A descriptive survey of the place of women in Salvadoran society, focusing on the various roles they fill and the careers open to them, as well as on the conditions in each and in the home. DLC LNHT

225 Jiménez, Tomás Fidias. Toponimia arcaica de El Salvador: significado de los nombres geográficos indígenas. San Salvador: Tipografía "La Unión," 1936. xii, 123 pp. Biblio.
       An explanation of the significance and origin of place names, arranged alphabetically by department within sections devoted to towns and physical features. DLC LNHT

226 Jiménez Gómez, Carlos. Estudio económico y social de la familia del área metropolitana de San Salvador, agosto 1964. San Salvador: n.p., 1965. xiv, 171 pp. Tables.
       A report and statistical information based upon a survey conducted in 1964 examining the status of the nation's families. Includes information about economic standing, education, social views, and birth control information and attitudes as reflected in the responses of housewives. DLC

227 José María Peralta: biografía, producciones, homenajes. San Salvador: Tipografía "La Unión," 1949. 287 pp. Illus.
       A brief biography of General José María Peralta Lagos, whose career, which spanned the late nineteenth and early twentieth centuries, included service in the military, the cabinet, and the nation's military academy, as well as a candidacy for the vice-presidency. A large portion of the volume consists of tributes by friends after his death in 1944 and excerpts from some of his speeches; the biography,

focused on his political career, which ended in 1931, is the most useful. DLC

228 Lardé, Jorge. Geología general de Centroamérica y especial de El Salvador. San Salvador: Imprenta Nacional, 1924. 82 pp.
       A general descriptive survey of existing knowledge, prepared for a 1924 Pan American Scientific Congress. DLC LNHT

229 _____. Obras completas. San Salvador: Ministerio de Cultura, 1960. 597 pp.
       A compilation of the most important works of this Salvadoran geologist, educator, and scientist of the early twentieth century, with a brief biographical sketch. DLC LNHT

230 _____. El volcán de Izalco; viaje geológico a ese volcán; descripción del mismo y de sus contornos; sus últimos erupciones; origen e historia documentada de ese volcán desde el año 1524 hasta nuestros días, año 1923. San Salvador: Imprenta Nacional, 1923. 120 pp. Illus.
       A detailed description of the volcano and a history of its eruptions since the conquest, arranged chronologically. DLC

231 Lardé y Larín, Jorge. El Salvador: historia de sus pueblos, villas y ciudades. San Salvador: Ministerio de Cultura, 1957. 571 pp. Tables.
       An alphabetical listing of all the cities, towns, and villages of the nation, with a brief historical outline of each ranging from a single paragraph to several pages. Includes population statistics as of 1953. DLC LNHT

232 _____. Guía histórica de El Salvador. San Salvador: Ministerio de Cultura, 1952. 126 pp. Index, illus. 2d ed. San Salvador: Ministerio de Cultura, 1958. 170 pp. Illus.
       A brief volume combining three essays by a well-known Salvadoran scholar. Originally published separately, they are gathered here to make them available to the nation's secondary schoolteachers. They consist of a brief chronological outline of Salvadoran history from pre-Columbian times to 1950, emphasizing the heroes of the nation and providing appropriate photos; a short patriotic description of the nation's flag and symbols; and a series of single-paragraph essays providing the outline of the key historical events in each of the nation's municipalities. DLC LNHT

233 _____. Himnología nacional de El Salvador. San Salvador: Imprenta Nacional, 1954. 80 pp.
       A history of the national anthem of El Salvador, the various versions that were used, and the disputes regarding them, detailing the several laws and the date on which the current anthem became effective in the late nineteenth century. DLC LNHT

234 _____. Monografías históricas del departamento de Santa Ana. San Salvador: Imprenta Nacional, 1955. 126 pp. Illus. DLC

(Lardé y Larín, Jorge)

235 _____. <u>Ramón Belloso</u>. San Salvador: Imprenta Nacional, 1957. 182 pp. Illus.
A brief biography of a Salvadoran military officer of the mid-nineteenth century who led the Salvadoran troops who entered Nicaragua to assist in the campaign against William Walker. DLC

236 _____, ed. <u>Recopilación de leyes relativas a la historia de los municpos de El Salvador</u>. San Salvador: Ministerio de Interior, 1950. 459 pp. Index, illus.
Reprints all Salvadoran legislation relating to the organization and governance of municipalities from independence to 1850, arranged chronologically. Includes brief descriptions of each municipality and an index. DLC LNHT

237 Latin American Bureau. <u>El Salvador under General Romero</u>. London: Latin American Bureau, 1979. 254 pp. Notes.
A highly critical summary of events in El Salvador during the initial portion of the Romero government. Decries oppression and human rights violations and sympathizes with the calls for revolution. Provides up-to-date information about the nation and insights into the leftist viewpoint and the conditions contributing to the civil war and guerrilla activities. DLC LNHT

238 _____. <u>Violence and Fraud in El Salvador: A Report on the Current Political Events in El Salvador</u>. London: Latin American Bureau, 1977. 48 pp. Notes.
A brief review of the violence in El Salvador during the Romero government, of which it is highly critical. Focuses on official repression as the basic problem. DLC LNHT

239 <u>Lecciones de historia del departamento de San Salvador</u>. San Salvador: Imprenta "La República," 1912. 47 pp. Illus.
A brief sketch of the department, with reproductions of documents regarding its foundation and single paragraph résumés of each of its towns. DLC

240 Leistenschneider, Maria, ed. <u>Dr. Rafael Zaldívar: recopilación de documentos históricos relativos a su administración</u>. 2 vols. San Salvador: Ministerio de Educación, 1977. Illus.
A collection of documents regarding the Liberal who ruled Salvador from 1876 to 1885, emphasizing his promotion of railroad construction and limitations of the power of the church, as well as his role in the war against Justo Rufino Barrios of Guatemala. LNHT

241 Lemus, José María. <u>Entrevistas y opiniones</u>. San Salvador: Imprenta Nacional, 1955.
A collection of commentaries by the minister of defense published as part of the campaign for the presidency, designed to provide his viewpoints and outlook through excerpts from statements and press interviews that constituted the principal vehicle for the

campaign of 1956, in which he was unopposed. The comments are designed to emphasize his association with the reformist regime of Oscar Osorio.

242 _____. <u>Mensajes al pueblo salvadoreño</u>. San Salvador: Imprenta Nacional, 1956. 57 pp. Illus.
A collection of speeches during 1956 by the president of El Salvador. DLC

243 _____. <u>Mensajes y discursos</u>. 4 vols. San Salvador: Ministerio de Cultura, 1957-59. Illus.
Selected speeches of the Salvadoran president, covering the years 1956-59. Does not include the official annual message or other official statements to Congress, but rather focuses on his political orations to various groups and audiences and on ceremonial occasions. The emphasis is on reform, public works programs, and his association with the revolution of his predecessor, Oscar Osorio. DLC LNHT

244 _____. <u>Pensamiento político-revolucionario del teniente coronel José María Lemus</u>. San Salvador: n.p., 1956. 91 pp. Illus.
A collection of speeches by the president-elect, drawn from his campaign, with illustrations of various demonstrations of support. Many of the speeches are excerpted rather than quoted in full. They all are identified as to place and date, with a brief introduction explaining the theme and circumstances. His reformist views and anticommunism are evident throughout. DLC LNHT

245 _____. <u>Por la patria y por la libertad: el ejército, temas militares</u>. San Salvador: Imprenta Nacional, 1949. 123 pp. Illus., tables.
Essays, speeches, and commentaries by the then minister of the interior and later president, dealing with a broad range of themes, principally military but including comments on democracy, government, and Salvadoran historical figures. TxU

246 _____. <u>El Presidente Lemus en defensa de las fuerzas armadas</u>. San Salvador: Imprenta Nacional, 1959.
A defense of the role of the Salvadoran army in the nation's politics by the incumbent president, himself a military officer, replying to charges of repression and condemning opposition to the regime as communist-inspired, while hailing the importance and benefits of the military's participation in and dominance of the nation's political system.

247 Leyton Rodríguez, Rubén. <u>El Salvador, tierra de porvenir</u>. San Salvador: Imprenta El Porvenir, 1952. 233 pp. Illus.
A collection of material describing in an enthusiastic and emotional manner the present state of El Salvador and its future prospects. Includes poetry, short commentaries, and photos referring to its institutions, symbols,

cities, leading citizens, and other themes. LNHT

248 Lindo, Hugo. <u>Cada día tiene su afán</u>. San Salvador: Ministerio de Educación, 1965. 196 pp.

A novel focusing on the lives of several upper-class individuals, particularly a doctor, dealing with their response to a political crisis in which the characters are forced to confront such issues as dictatorship by being drawn into service in a revolutionary government. Follows their debates about this situation, their efforts to contribute to their nation, and the resulting problems. In the process it deals with the attitudes of the upper class and the effect of politics on their lives. ICU

249 _____. <u>El divorcio en El Salvador: historia legislativa, jurisprudencia, anotaciones críticas</u>. San Salvador: Universidad Autónoma de El Salvador, 1948. 223 pp.

A legal analysis detailing the legislation and case law regarding divorce, its accepted causes, necessary proof, and such factors as child custody. DLC LNHT

250 _____. <u>Recuento: anotaciones literarias e históricas de Centro-América</u>. San Salvador: Ministerio de Educación, 1969. 422 pp. Biblio.

A series of essays, originally written separately and published over a period of years by a well-known Salvadoran writer and literary scholar, dealing with various aspects of Salvadoran literary history and its principal writers, including considerations of trends in poetry, the short story, and the novel, with separate commentary on several of the nation's most significant writers and the impact of the Salvadoran milieu on their works. DLC LNHT

251 López, Matilde Elena. <u>Masferrer: alto pensador de Centroamérica</u>. Guatemala: Ministerio de Educación Pública, 1954. 299 pp. Illus.

A brief biography and extensive analysis of the writings of the journalist and intellectual Alberto Masferrer, who was associated with the 1931 communist-inspired uprising in El Salvador. The author contends that although Masferrer was a rebel in thought and a reformer, he was not a communist. The volume concludes with a listing of what the author considers the principal bases of Masferrer's ideology. DLC LNHT BNG

252 López Jiménez, Ramón. <u>Mitras salvadoreñas</u>. San Salvador: Imprenta Nacional, 1960. 185 pp. Index, illus.

Brief biographical sketches of the seven individuals who served as bishop or archbishop of San Salvador from independence to the present, providing an outline of their careers, their principal pastorals, and the significant accomplishments of their tenures. Includes some quotation from their public proclamations, and accounts of their political stances and clashes with the governments. DLC LNHT

253 López Trejo, Roberto. <u>El drama de la república (1961-1962)</u>. San Salvador: Editorial Ahora, 1962. 64 pp.

The political statements of a Salvadoran army major, defining what he considers the current needs of the nation. The messages were broadcast on the radio or published in the local press during the years in question. DLC

254 _____. <u>Realidad dramática de la república: 25 años de traición a la fuerza armada y a la patria</u>. San Salvador: Editorial Ahora, 1974. 420 pp.

A Salvadoran army major defends the armed forces against what he sees as a communist plot to defame them throughout the world through propaganda, yet criticizes all the military regimes since 1944 as inadequate. He hails the regime of General Maximiliano Hernández Martínez as the only honest government and as the regime that accomplished the most in terms of public works, contending that current income is being wasted. He calls for greater responsibility by the elite and armed forces, and a greater willingness to act for the good of the nation to improve the lot of the populace rather than for their personal interests, yet clearly sees the army as the only basis for sound stable government. The focus is on the years 1961-72. Includes his earlier works <u>Rescate</u> and <u>El drama de la república</u>. DLC LNHT

255 _____. <u>Rescate</u>. San Salvador: Editorial Ahora, 1963. 72 pp.

The theme of this series of essays is better indicated by the prologue title "Rescatando la república." Originally published in various Salvadoran newspapers during the fall of 1973, these commentaries by an army major provide his view of what is needed for the improved welfare of the nation. His views include a condemnation of communism, an argument for the institutional responsibility of the armed forces to protect the constitution, and advocacy of a broader social welfare state, whose support he urges on the upper and middle classes. He also calls for higher prices in the international basic commodities trade. These broad stands are offered as warnings, without specific policy recommendations for implementation. DLC

256 _____. <u>La verdad nacional, 1962-1963</u>. San Salvador: Editorial Ahora, 1963. 72 pp.

A compilation of newspaper articles by a Salvadoran army major and political figure, giving his views on the current state of the nation and its future. The emphasis is on criticizing national policy, while hailing the army and condemning communism. DLC

257 López Vallecillos, Ítalo. <u>Gerardo Barrios y su tiempo</u>. 2 vols. San Salvador: Ministerio de Educación, 1967. 325, 516 pp. Biblio., notes, illus., maps.

A massive review of the Salvadoran caudillo's career, with ample excerpts from the documents. Based on research in documents, press, and secondary works, with

(López Vallecillos, Ítalo)
footnotes, though they are sparse in places.
Volume 1 covers his early years and rise
(1815-58) and volume 2 his years in power
(1858-65). The work is controversial, having
been awarded second prize in the competition
on the occasion of the centennial of Barrios;
the award was made by a divided vote of the
commission, which considered none of the
entrants worthy of the first prize and hence
awarded only a second prize, with one member
objecting to that. This may reflect the fact
that it is less laudatory of Barrios than some
other studies (though it is by no means unfavorable to him) and contains references to
Barrios as a product of the "feudal" economy
of his time. DLC LNHT

258 ____. El periodismo en El Salvador:
bosquejo histórico-documental. San Salvador:
Editorial Universitaria, 1964. 478 pp.
Index, illus.
A valuable collection of material, offering
brief summaries of the birth, death, and focus
of each of the various newspapers of the
nation's history, with an illustration of a
sample number. The data are quite complete,
down to editor and political stance. The
principal drawback is that the publications
are arranged by theme, such as political
papers, social papers, literary papers, etc.,
and chronologically within them. Includes, at
the end of the volume, the vitae of then-
active Salvadoran editors and journalists.
DLC LNHT

259 Lucientes, Francisco. Regalado. San José:
Editorial Borrasé, 1933. 98 pp.
A brief essay on General Tomás Regalado,
who governed El Salvador during the era of
Manuel Estrada Cabrera in Guatemala. The
author details several episodes of the politics of the initial years of the twentieth
century, but confines himself to episodes. He
characterizes Regalado as the Salvadoran who
most closely fits the caudillo type typical of
the era. The absence of chapters renders use
of the volume difficult. DLC DLC-LDS-761
LNHT BNCR

260 Luna, David. Análisis de una dictadura
fascista latinoamericana. San Salvador:
n.p., n.d.
A condemnation of the dictatorship of
General Maximiliano Hernández Martínez,
attacking its repressive measures and militarism and comparing it with European fascism.

261 ____. Manual de historia económica de El
Salvador. San Salvador: Editorial
Universitaria, 1971. 230 pp. Biblio.,
illus., tables.
Despite its title, this volume is really a
general historical overview of El Salvador.
About 60% of it deals with the pre-
independence era, with the years after 1919
covered in a single chapter. Although it
gives more emphasis to economics than is usual
in such brief narrations, its focus is not
sharp enough to merit classification as an
economic history, and its treatment of

individual topics and eras is extremely brief.
There are also discussions of developments in
the United States and comparisons with El
Salvador. The economic portions are Marxist
in tone. DLC LNHT

262 Machón Vilanova, Francisco. Ola roja.
Mexico: n.p., 1948. 416 pp.
A novel about peasant life and agrarian
problems set in the author's native El
Salvador, based on that nation's experience
with the communist-influenced uprising of
1931. Emphasizes the need for programs to
deal with rural development; condemns the
communist solutions as worse than the existing
problems. TxU

263 Magaña Menéndez, Enrique. Gobernantes
salvadoreños, libertad de imprenta,
comentarios, cuartillas y crónicas.
Ahuachapán, El Salvador: Imprenta Kelly,
1956. 192 pp. Maps.
A series of disparate essays, originally
published in the Salvadoran press between 1920
and 1955, reflecting the author's writings on
various Salvadoran themes. They include commentaries on various governments and political
events, such as constitutional reforms,
Salvadoran historical events and anniversaries, and observations regarding typical
Salvadoran customs. BNG

264 Magaña Menéndez, Gustavo. Estudios sociales,
políticos y económicos. San Salvador:
Talleres Gráficos Cisneros, 1950. xvi, 149
pp. Illus.
A posthumous collection of the author's
writings. The majority are commentaries on
agriculture in Salvador, but they include some
historical and political references, as well
as a collection of speeches from his university days. The agricultural essays refer to
the cultivation of coffee and its role in the
Salvadoran economy. BNG

265 Magaña Menéndez, Gustavo, and Enrique Magaña
Menéndez, eds. Francisco Menéndez a través de
sus anécdotas: junio 22 de 1932. San
Salvador: Talleres Gráficos Cisneros, 1932.
109 pp.
A collection of commentaries about
Francisco Menéndez, who served as president in
the 1880s. Taken from newspapers, letters,
speeches, and stories, they are grouped according to the aspect of his public life to
which they refer and provide an anecdotal
account of his various activities. Compiled
by two family members to assure him his proper
place in history. DPU

266 Malaina, Santiago. La compañía de Jesús en El
Salvador, C.A., desde 1864 a 1872. San
Salvador: Imprenta Nacional, 1939. 125 pp.
Maps.
A history of the brief interlude of the
Jesuit functioning in nineteenth-century
Salvador, covering the years from the bishop's
request in 1864 for the assignment of Jesuits
through their expulsion in 1872 by the Lib-
erals. The author, a Jesuit, views their
actions sympathetically, employing church

(Malaina, Santiago)
documents and published documents and secondary works. Provides background regarding the church-state dispute in El Salvador, details of the polemic, and biographical sketches of the five Jesuits involved. LNHT

267 _____. *Historia de la erección de la diócesis de San Salvador*. San Salvador: Talleres Gráficos Cisneros, 1944. 152 pp. Biblio., illus.

A brief and pro-church account of the church-state conflict during the initial decades of independence, written by a cleric. Covers the years from independence through 1844. Includes an account of the efforts to establish a separate diocese in San Salvador, which did not succeed until after the collapse of the Federation rendered a national bishopric essential. Most of the volume consists of a collection of over 100 pertinent documents, which are printed in full. TxU

268 Márquez, Adolfo de Jesús. *Leyendas salvadoreñas*. San Salvador: Imprenta "La República," 1942. 130 pp. Notes, illus.

A compilation of very short stories and poems (most a page or two in length) by various authors, recounting the legends and folklore of the nation, covering a wide range of themes from pre-Colonial to modern times. Authors and dates of writing are usually provided, though there is no background or indication of the origin or region of the individual stories. DPU

269 Marroquín, Alejandro Dagoberto. *Apreciación sociológica de la independencia salvadoreña*. San Salvador: Universidad de El Salvador, 1964. 108 pp. Biblio.

An analysis of the independence era in Salvador. Emphasizes the class and ethnic conflicts and their role in the movement; consequently places more emphasis on the role of the lower classes and their resentment of the Spaniards than do must such studies. Also considers the local resentment of the domination of Guatemala City during the Colonial era, and the effect of this on the later federalist maneuverings. Based on secondary works. DLC LNHT

270 _____. *Panchimalco, investigación sociológica*. San Salvador: Editorial Universitaria, 1959. 454 pp. Biblio., illus., maps, tables.

A detailed sociological survey of a small town near the Salvadoran capital, conducted by a Salvadoran professor and six of his students during the Holy Week vacations of 1958. Includes a brief historical essay and considerable data regarding the life-style, educational facilities, attitudes, economy, social organization, community life, and aspirations of the town and its residents. Based on observations and interviews, with elaborate tables and graphs as well as numerous illustrations. DLC LNHT

271 _____. *San Pedro Nonualco: investigación sociológica*. San Salvador: Editorial

Universitaria, 1964. 336 pp. Biblio., notes, illus., tables.

A study of a town in Salvador, by a sociology professor at the national university. Provides a detailed description of its culture, lore, economy, population, social organization, and services. Concludes that the town is typical of the villages of El Salvador and is characterized by economic underdevelopment, social stratification on a near-feudal model, resistance to change, a gradual population increase, and mestizo values. Includes statistical tables regarding population, literacy, and the economy. DLC LNHT

272 Martin, Percy Falcke. *Salvador of the Twentieth Century*. London: Edward Arnold, 1911. 2d ed. New York: Longman's Green, 1911. xvi, 328 pp. Index, illus., maps.

The observations of the British travel-book author during his sojourn in El Salvador, emphasizing contemporary economic data and his impressions of the people and nation but also offering a brief, if biased, historical outline. The author was an experienced observer, but his historical comments are limited by his contemporary impressions. A call for more British interest in the area and an eye for potential commercial advantages to England are evident. DLC LNHT

273 Martínez Vargas, Isidro. *Cien años de actuaciones presidenciales, 1862-1962*. San Salvador: Isidro Martínez Vargas e Hijos, 1962. 78 pp. Illus.

Brief summaries of the principal events in the terms of the various Salvadoran presidents during this period. FU

274 Masferrer, Alberto. *Cartas a un obrero*. San Salvador: n.p., n.d.

The author's clearest statement regarding the need for land reform, and a ringing denunciation of the power of the landowners in El Salvador, condemning their monopoly of the life-giving land and calling for drastic change. DLC

275 _____. *El dinero maldito*. San Salvador: Imprenta "La República," 1927. 82 pp. Latest ed. San Salvador: Ministerio de Educación, 1968. 60 pp.

One of the area's earliest social commentators and critics prepared this series of essays dealing with the problem of alcoholism among the campesinos. It was initially published in 1927. In it he chronicles the tragedy of the peasants, whose only diversion from a miserable existence is a weekend drinking trip to the cantinas of the city. The author discusses at length the resulting fights, injuries, and tragedies; he advocates prohibition, a national campaign against alcoholism, and a social program to aid the peons. DLC DLC-LDS-844 LNHT BNG

276 _____. *Ensayo sobre el destino*. San José: El Convivio, 1925. 136 pp. Latest ed. San Salvador: Ministerio de Educación, 1963. 137 pp.

(Masferrer, Alberto)

A general and fatalistic discussion of destiny and its effect on human life, written in the disillusioning aftermath of World War I, which contradicted the author's view of Europe as an example to the rest of the world and the center of knowledge. The volume also reflects the author's despair during a three-year period when he was paralyzed. DLC LNHT

277 _____. Estudios y figuraciones sobre la vida de Jesús. San Salvador: Tipografía "La Unión," 1927. 195 pp. 3d ed. San Salvador: Ministerio de Cultura, 1956. 163 pp.

A symbolic autobiography in which the author combines religion and his life. He views both himself and Jesus as confronting the great problems of humanity, suffering persecution, struggling against heavy odds, reaching out to the masses, spreading hope and ideals of conduct; he reveals much about his view of his life and his own mission, though always through the study of the life of Christ. DLC LNHT

278 _____. Helios: visión de Alberto Masferrer. San Salvador: Imprenta "La Salvadoreña," 1928. 75 pp. 2d ed. San Salvador: Ministerio de Educación, 1963. 80 pp.

A collection of poems and short essays and stories involving religious faith and grand ideals as the basis of human conduct. Stresses the importance of striving for justice, equality, improvement, and ideals. DLC LNHT

279 _____. Leer y escribir, y la cultura por medio del libro. Tegucigalpa: Tipografía Nacional, 1922. 45 pp. Latest ed. San Salvador: Ministerio de Educación, 1968. 70 pp.

Written in 1913 in Europe, one of the early works of this Salvadoran scholar, educator, sociologist, and reformer. In it he indicates his concern for the lower classes by emphasizing the importance of a national effort to provide literacy training for all as the basis for improving the standard of living of the poor. DLC LNHT

280 _____. El libro de la vida. Guatemala: Casa Editora "Orientación," 1932. 56 pp.

One of the most political of the author's works and written in the heat of his reformist political career, this work spells out clearly his opposition to capitalism and his call for a minimum standard for all in a communalistic society based on land reform. Should be read with his other political works, El mínimo vital and La patria. DLC

281 _____. El mínimo vital. San Salvador: Editorial Helios, 1929. 51 pp. Latest ed. San Salvador: Ministerio de Educación, 1968. 46 pp.

A series of sociological essays by a well-known Salvadoran scholar and commentator, focusing on the living conditions of the poor and emphasizing the necessity of reforms to improve their lives. He contends that every member of society is entitled to a minimum standard of existence that enables the satisfaction of basic needs. The various essays emphasize the plight of the poor and offer suggestions for improving their life. This attitude made Masferrer a controversial figure in his nation, and ultimately led to accusations of involvement with the 1931 peasant uprising in that nation. Some of the numerous editions combine this seminal piece with his other writings, employing the title El mínimo vital y otras obras de carácter sociológica. DLC LNHT BNG

282 _____. Obras completas. 2 vols. San Salvador: Tipografía "La Unión," 1935-45.

Volume 1, entitled La rosa deshojado, contains essays, newspaper articles, and poetry; it includes social commentary and general themes, but none of the principal works for which the author is primarily known. There is no explanation of the selection or organization. Some items are identified by date of writing but not original location of publication. Volume 2, bearing the title La misión de América, continues with newspaper articles, mainly from the 1920s, focusing on his effort to promote Central American unification and on statements in support of democracy and social justice throughout the hemisphere. DLC

283 _____. Obras escogidas. San Salvador: Editorial Universitaria, 1971. 527 pp.

A collection of the most important works of this Salvadoran social reformer, with a valuable introduction that summarizes his career, outlook, and influence in Salvadoran thinking and politics. DLC LNHT

284 _____. Páginas escogidas. Buenos Aires and New York: W.M. Jackson, 1945. xxxiv, 386 pp. Latest ed. San Salvador: Ministerio de Educación, 1976. 283 pp.

Selections from Masferrer's various writings, including newspaper editorials and books, and even some unpublished items, designed to provide an overview of his social criticism. His essays point out the problems of the poor and their mistreatment, as well as other national problems such as alcoholism and underdeveloped educational systems; he calls for reforms to benefit the campesinos, who had long been neglected. DLC LNHT BNG

285 _____. Patria. San Salvador: Editorial Universitaria, 1960. 241 pp.

A collection of editorials published by this noted Salvadoran social reformer in his newspaper Patria during its existence from 1928 through 1931. Provides his thoughts in brief, employing much of the terminology of his larger works; indicates his fervor and crusading spirit; clearly demonstrates his political agitation, which contributed to the unrest that surfaced in 1930. Includes his call for a minimum standard of living for all, his denunciation of capitalism, and his explosive call for land reform, all stated more

(Masferrer, Alberto)
    succinctly than in his other writings. DLC
    LNHT

286   ____. Pensamientos y formas: notas de
viaje. San José: J. García Monge, 1921.
125 pp.
    This volume offers some of the author's
literary works; a collection of short stories;
and some notes made during his travels, extolling the beauties of the places he visited.
They deal with disparate locations in Central
America and elsewhere. DLC DLC-LDS-624 LNHT

287   ____. Las siete cuerdas de la lira;
materia, animia, lumén. San Salvador:
Tipografía "La Unión," 1926. 200 pp. Latest
ed. San Salvador: Ministerio de Educación,
1963. 205 pp.
    A poetic and almost musical invocation of
the mysteries of nature as a symbolism and the
basis of his idealism, emphasizing the links
to religion and creation and the mystical
nature of his quest for social justice, which
he views as being within the tradition of
Saint Augustine and Christ. DLC LNHT

288   ____. Una vida en el cine: el buitre que se
tornó calandria. San José: J. García Monge,
1922. 128 pp. Latest ed. San Salvador:
Ministerio de Cultura, 1955. 108 pp.
    A novel written in the form of a dialogue
between a man and a woman in a movie theater.
Examines the societal values and attitudes of
El Salvador, demonstrating how the traditions
of the nation limit the lives and potential of
some of its citizens, and in effect calling
for new attitudes in the nation, particularly
in its educational system. DLC

289 Masferrer C., Manuel. Biografía del escritor
Alberto Masferrer. San Salvador: Tipografía
Canpress, 1957. 164 pp.
    A collection of material relating to this
well-known Salvadoran writer and social reformer. Assembled by his brother, it includes
a brief biographical sketch emphasizing his
earlier years and personal activities but
consists principally of a collection of his
letters and writings, followed by commentaries
about him and his work by a number of individuals. LNHT

290   ____. Vida anecdótica de Alberto Masferrer.
San Salvador: n.p., 1957.
    A compilation of stories about incidents in
the private life of the reformer, compiled by
his brother; sheds light on the influences
upon him.

291 Mata Gavidia, José. Francisco Gavidia;
artifice de nuestra nacionalidad. San
Salvador: Ministerio de Educación, 1965. 69
pp. Biblio., illus.
    A profusely illustrated series of brief
essays extolling the career of this late
nineteenth- and early twentieth-century
Salvadoran teacher and intellectual who
founded the National Theater, pioneered the
use of local idioms on the stage, and produced

considerable poetry. Contains a bibliography
of his works and a record of his honors. DLC
LNHT

292   ____. Magnificencia espiritual de Francisco
Gavidia. San Salvador: Ministerio de
Educación, 1968. 268 pp. Index, biblio.,
notes, appendixes.
    A well-researched and detailed biography of
a Salvadoran literary figure and scholar whose
life spans the late nineteenth and early twentieth centuries. Traces his experiences,
analyzes his works, and prints excerpts. DLC
BNG

293 Mayo, John K., Robert Hornik, and Emile G.
McAnany. Educational Reform with Television:
The El Salvador Experience. Stanford, Calif.:
Stanford University Press, 1976. xi, 216 pp.
Index, biblio., illus., maps, tables.
    A study of the origins and organization of
educational television in El Salvador that
details its uses and impact. DLC LNHT

294 Mayora C., Manuel. Dr. Manuel E. Araujo: su
vida, su obra, su sacrificio. San Salvador:
Published by the Author, 1913. 102 pp.
    A brief work extolling Araujo, hailing his
patriotism, his medical skills, and his political career, with a summary of his years in
power from 1911 through 1913. DLC

295 Meléndez, Carlos. Cartas políticas cruzadas
entre los presidentes de El Salvador y de los
Estados Unidos. San Salvador: Imprenta
Nacional, 1918. 85 pp.
    An exchange of letters between President
Meléndez and Woodrow Wilson in which the
Salvadoran executive, responding to a Wilson
statement to reporters on 9 June 1918 advocating an American League of Nations as part of
the larger world body, endorsed the concept,
hailed Wilson's emphasis on the juridicial
equality of states, and added that the Monroe
Doctrine was a problem in the Western Hemisphere because of its unilateral nature.
Meléndez suggested that the Monroe Doctrine be
multilateralized and converted into a mutual
security guarantee by all the hemispheric
states. Wilson's reply avoids reference to
the latter suggestion, focusing on the ideal
of cooperation. Includes the notes exchanged
and press commentary. DLC

296   ____. Las relaciones entre los Estados
Unidos de América y El Salvador. Washington,
D.C.: PAU, 1918. 22 pp. Illus.
Relations between the United States of America
and El Salvador. Washington, D.C.: PAU,
1918. 20 pp. Illus.
    A brief summary of Salvadoran relations
with the United States, written during World
War I by a Salvadoran president. NN

297 Meléndez Palacios, Roberto D. Catecismo de la
constitución política de la República de El
Salvador. San Salvador: Tipografía "La
Unión," 1940. xv, 195 pp. Index.
    A clause-by-clause examination of the new
constitution, in question-and-answer form,

designed to provide simplified information for the average citizen and schoolchild. Includes discussion of constitutional theory. DLC

298 Melgar Callejas, José María, and J. Armando Dueñas C. Historia del Ministerio del Interior. San Salvador: Imprenta Nacional, 1976. 135 pp. Index, biblio., illus., tables, appendixes.

A collection of documentation regarding the organization of the ministry, with organization charts, followed by single-paragraph sketches of the careers of all the ministers and subministers throughout the nation's history. DLC

299 Membreño, Alberto. Nombres geográficos de la República de El Salvador. Mexico: Imprenta de I. Escalante, 1908. 53 pp.

A collection of brief definitions of the meaning and origins of Salvadoran place names, arranged alphabetically. DLC

300 Mena, Alberto. Índice de las leyes emitidas desde el año 1875 hasta el de 1900. San Salvador: Tipografía La Salvadoreña, 1900. 174 pp.

A listing of the various laws dealing with specific topics, intended to facilitate consultation of the nation's legislation.

301 Méndez, Joaquín. Los sucesos comunistas en El Salvador. San Salvador: Imprenta Funes y Ungo, 1932. 209 pp. Illus.

A reporter's version of the 1931 uprising, providing summaries of what he observed and was told when he visited each of the provinces involved shortly after the event. He says that he offers his narration without comment to portray what occurred accurately. He talked with government officials, troops, army officers, and ordinary citizens in each of the region's principal towns. The illustrations show the damage done in the rioting. The work clearly indicts the rebels and the destruction, though it offers various views on their communism and portrays the situation as one of mobs of anarchists on a rampage, with only the army defending order and society. DLC LNHT

302 Méndez, José María. Tres mujeres al cuadrado. San Salvador: Ministerio de Educación, 1963. 225 pp.

A collection of satirical short stories by a well-known humorist dealing with El Salvador, its people, problems, and political scene, criticizing all in a humorous vein and emphasizing human frailty and the limits of government. DLC

303 Méndez, José María, et al. El constitucionalismo y la vida institucional centroamericana. San Salvador: Editorial Universitaria, 1964. 90 pp.

A collection of papers from a conference on contemporary history which, despite its title, deal principally with the current political situation in El Salvador and the need for constitutional reform, citing the problems of

the situation and the provisions of previous constitutions. TxU

304 Menéndez, Isidro. Recopilación de las leyes del Salvador en Centro América, 1821-1855. 2 vols. Guatemala: Imprenta La Luna, 1855-56. 456, 528 pp. Index. 2d ed. San Salvador: Imprenta Nacional, 1956.

The first catalog and index to the laws of El Salvador, covering the years from independence through 1855. The laws are conveniently listed chronologically within chapters arranged by subject. The full text or at least the core of all pertinent legislation is listed for each legal category. DLC LNHT BNG

305 Menéndez Rodríguez, Mario. El Salvador. San José: EDUCA, 1980. 228 pp.

306 Menjívar, Rafael. Crisis del desarrollismo: caso El Salvador. San José: EDUCA, 1977. 139 pp. Notes, tables.

A survey of Salvadoran economic development, with emphasis on its present situation. Contends that the dominance of the land-owning, coffee-growing oligarchy has meant a development program focused exclusively on economic modernization with total disregard for the social aspects, resulting in a crisis because development has benefited only a small segment of the population. The author contends that if the government changed its development policy and gave the same degree of aid to the lower classes that it now gives to the oligarchy, the national situation would improve. LNHT

307 _____. El Salvador. San José: EDUCA, 1980. 240 pp.

308 _____. Formas de tenencia de la tierra y algunos otros aspectos de la actividad agropecuaria. San Salvador: Editorial Universitaria, 1962. 86 pp. Biblio., tables.

A technical description of the land-tenure situation in El Salvador, based on the 1950 census, detailing the landholding pattern and emphasizing the use of human labor and primitive methods on the large number of small holdings. DLC LNHT

309 Mestas, Alberto de. El Salvador: país de lagos y volcanes. Madrid: Ediciones de Cultura Hispánica, 1950. xii, 672 pp. Biblio., illus., maps, tables.

The first 200 pages of this volume by a Spanish diplomat offer an economic history of El Salvador, with emphasis on the period since 1930, treating such items as commerce, transport, and the various crops topically, with considerable statistical information spanning the 1930-50 period. The middle portion is a historical narrative from pre-Colonial times to the present; the period through independence occupies 270 pages, while the years since independence are covered in 20 pages. The final portion offers essays on the present political structure, the nation's literary production, culture, education, social scene,

and current communications and transport
facilities. DLC LNHT

310 Miranda Ruano, Francisco. Los voces del
terruño. San Salvador: Imprenta "La
República," 1929. xv, 223 pp. Illus. Latest
ed. San Salvador: Ministerio de Cultura,
1955. 155 pp.
A series of commentaries and essays reflecting life in the Salvadoran countryside
during the 1920s, focusing on the people,
their customs, and everyday activities. DLC
LNHT BNG

311 Molina, Arturo Armando. Ideario político
democrático del señor presidente de la
república coronel Arturo Armando Molina. San
Salvador: Imprenta Nacional, n.d. [1974].
90 pp.
A series of "quotations from President
Molina," compiled by the presidential public
relations secretariat. Consists of brief
paragraphs from his various speeches, divided
by subject and provided with a thumb index for
easy consultation of particular themes. Concepts indexed are political, economic, cultural, social, and civic. Each entry cites
the speech from which it is excerpted. The
emphasis is on democracy, cooperation, nationalism, and responsibility. Includes a curriculum vita of the chief executive. DLC

312 ____. Mensajes y discursos del señor
presidente de la república coronel Arturo
Armando Molina. 8 vols. San Salvador:
Imprenta Nacional, n.d. [1973]. Various
pagings.
The collected speeches of the Salvadoran
president, issued by his Department of Public
Relations every six months throughout his
term, providing the full text of his major
addresses. LNHT

313 Molina, José Lino. El educador nacional:
tratados de moral y enseñanza cívica. 2 vols.
San Salvador: Imprenta Nacional, 1948-49.
198, 264 pp.
A discussion of Salvadoran teaching methodology that is related to the official school
program and includes the official syllibi in
the areas of social and civic education, which
serves to demonstrate the interpretation
emphasized as well as the organization and
methods employed in the Salvadoran schools.
DLC

314 ____. Ennoblezcamos la escuela primaria.
San Salvador: Imprenta Nacional, 1922. 231
pp. Illus.
A collection of essays and letters dealing
with methods for improving the Salvadoran
primary schools. Includes proposals for improving facilities, increasing the status of
teachers, encouraging parent cooperation and
similar programs. DLC

315 Molina y Morales, Roberto. Guión histórico
del poder legislativo de El Salvador:
constituyentes-legislaturas, síntesis
biográficas de sus presidentes. 2 vols. San

Salvador: Imprenta Nacional, 1966-69. 291,
336 pp. Illus.
A collection of brief vitae outlining the
careers of each of the members of the various
Salvadoran legislatures, including constituent
assemblies. Arranged alphabetically within
congresses and chronologically by legislature,
with photos where available. The initial volume covers the years 1822-70, and the second
from 1870 to 1900. DLC LNHT

316 ____. Los ministros de hacienda, 1838-1871.
San Salvador: Ministerio de Hacienda, 1970.
290 pp. Illus.
A collection of brief biographies, arranged
chronologically, of all the individuals who
held the post of minister of hacienda during
the years indicated. The sketches trace their
overall careers, before and after holding the
position, rather than their tenure in the
office, saying little about their policies in
that post but offering data regarding their
backgrounds and relations with the presidents
under whom they served. LNHT

317 Monedero, Oscar Manuel. Historia de la
arquitectura contemporánea en El Salvador.
San Salvador: Editorial Universitaria, 1970.
157 pp. Biblio., illus.
A discussion of the characteristic architecture of El Salvador, covering the years
since 1900 and inevitably focusing on churches
and public buildings. With illustrations.
DLC

318 Monterrey, Francisco J. Historia de El
Salvador: anotaciones cronológicas 1810-1871.
2 vols. San Salvador: Talleres Gráficos
Cisneros, 1943. 536 pp. Index. 2d ed. San
Salvador: Editorial Universitaria, 1977. 379
pp. Index.
As the title implies, the volume consists
entirely of chronologically arranged single-
paragraph descriptions of significant events
in Salvador. The so-called index lists names,
with the years in which they are referred to
rather than pages, and a similar list of names
precedes each year, providing the dates, meaning that two indexes are necessary to locate
each entry. DLC LNHT

319 Montes, Segundo. Estudio sobre
estratificación social en El Salvador. San
Salvador: UCA, 1979. 504 pp. Biblio., maps,
tables.
A massive compilation of statistics and
computer analyses focusing on the years 1960-
77, demonstrating the impact of diverse vari-
ables when applied to population statistics,
to identify the key aspects of social stratification. Although available only in photo-
offset from typescript, it is included because
of the utility of the statistics and the
uniqueness of some of the analytical frameworks applied. DLC

320 ____. Tercer mundo: educación. San
Salvador: UCA, n.d. [197?]. 136 pp. Biblio.
Originally published as a series of sep-
arate articles, these essays examine the

sociological situation of present-day El
Salvador and the role of education and Christian aspiration in the future development of
the nation. The essays, written by a Spanish-
born Jesuit who has spent his career at the
Universidad Centroamericana José Simeón Cañas,
range widely in theme and constantly evoke
Vatican pronouncements or Catholic doctrine as
the basis for reform. LNHT

321 Morán, Francisco. Alberto Masferrer o la
consciencia social de un pueblo. San
Salvador: Ministerio de Cultura, 1951. 42
pp. Biblio.
    A brief essay on the life of this
Salvadoran social reformer, calling him the
nation's social conscience; this is followed
by a bibliography of his works and brief commentaries on some of the most significant
ones, relating them to events in his life and
his overall outlook. DLC

322 Muguerza y Sáenz, Simeón. El Salvador:
bosquejo histórico, geográfico, estadístico y
comercial de dicha república. Barcelona:
Imprenta Hijos de Domingo Casanovas, 1912.
119 pp. Illus., maps.
    A description of the economic situation of
El Salvador in the early 1900s, focusing on
its products and the potential for Spanish-
Salvadoran trade and economic cooperation.
Provides then-current information on production, trade, and finance. DLC LNHT

323 Narvaez García, Emilio. Rutas terrestres de
El Salvador: kilometraje, 1939-1940. Santa
Ana: Tipografía Comercial, 1940. 80 pp.
Illus.
    A catalog of the nation's road system,
hailing the construction efforts of the regime
of General Maximiliano Hernández Martínez;
reflects the emphasis placed on highways by
many of the regimes of that era. TxU

324 Nathan, Robert R., Associates, Inc. Investment and Industrial Development in El
Salvador: A Report for the International
Cooperation Administration. Washington, D.C.:
Nathan Associates, 1961. vi, 215 pp. Tables,
appendixes.
    A report prepared for the International
Cooperation Administration by a consulting
firm suggesting financial policies to promote
further investment in Salvadoran industry,
describing the current economy and resources
and providing detailed recommendations for
statutes and financial facilities. Also recommends a conservation corps. DLC LNHT

325 Nitoburg, Eduard L'vovich. Sal'vador [El
Salvador]. Moscow: Gosudarstvennoe
izdatel'stvo geograficheskoi literartury,
1953. 43 pp.
Salvador. Leipzig: Veb. Bibliographisches
Institut, 1955. 47 pp. Illus.
    A brief overview of twentieth-century
Salvadoran history from a Marxist perspective,
emphasizing the role of the Communist party
and the proletariat as well as the frustration
of their aspirations by the oligarchy and the

capitalist-imperialist Yankees. Includes descriptive data regarding the economy and geography. DLC

326 Operations and Policy Research, Inc. El
Salvador: Election Factbook, March 5, 1967.
Washington, D.C.: Operations and Policy
Research, 1967. 40 pp. Maps, tables.
    A brief summary of the issues, candidates,
parties, and background for the election, with
comparative data from previous votes. DLC
LNHT

327 Organización Iberoamericana de Seguridad
Social. Los seguros sociales en El Salvador.
Madrid: n.p., 1961. 27 pp.
    Another in a series summarizing the na-
tion's social security law and describing the
resulting program and its operation.

328 Osborne, Lilly de Jongh. Four Keys to El
Salvador. New York: Funk & Wagnalls, 1956.
221 pp. Index, biblio., illus., maps.
    A compilation of information about and
observations of El Salvador by an experienced
travel-book writer and Central American resident. The focus is on physical description
and information regarding the Indians, particularly their arts, crafts, and culture,
written on the pattern of her works about
Guatemala. Includes brief historical synopses
of the pre-Conquest and Colonial eras. DLC
LNHT BNG

329 Osorio, Miguel Ángel [Ricardo Arenales,
pseud.]. El terremoto de San Salvador.
Corpus Cristi, junio 7 de 1917. San Salvador:
Imprenta del Diario del Salvador, 1917. 64
pp. 2d ed. San Salvador: Ministerio de
Educación, 1961. 139 pp.
    A journalist's graphic description of this
destructive quake. Describes the damage in
San Salvador and the reaction of its people,
focusing on the Hospital Rosales. DLC BNCR

330 Pan American Union. Division of Labor and
Social Information. La vivienda en El
Salvador: análisis del problema con
recomendaciones para una programa nacional de
la vivienda. Washington, D.C.: PAU, 1950. 36
pp. Biblio., illus.
    A survey of existing housing and estimates
of future needs based on population projections, with policy proposals for meeting those
needs; designed for planners. DLC

331 Parada, Alfredo. Etapas políticas. 2 vols.
San Salvador: Tipografía "La Unión," 1950-75.
281, 88 pp.
    A nationalistic account of Salvadoran his-
tory defending the nation against its neighbors, based on and liberally quoting the
contemporary press and the Diario Oficial.
The initial volume, covering the years 1885-
1912, offers a somewhat more detailed coverage
than the second volume, which spans the years
1918 through 1950 with very brief chapters
that are more opinionated. The author is
highly critical of Guatemala and of General
Maximiliano Hernández Martínez. DLC

332 Paredes, Jacinto. <u>Vida</u> <u>y</u> <u>obras</u> <u>del</u> <u>Dr.</u> <u>Pío</u> <u>Romero</u> <u>Bosque:</u> <u>apuntes</u> <u>para</u> <u>la</u> <u>historia</u> <u>de</u> El <u>Salvador.</u> San Salvador: Imprenta Nacional, 1930. 455 pp. Illus.

An adulatory discussion and summary of the career and presidency of Pío Romero Bosque, whom the author hails as a man of rare perception and an intellectual whose goals brought the nation back to its true heritage and prospects. Seeking to show his influence, it includes a detailed account of all the works of his regime, with summaries of laws and descriptions of each project, building, reorganization, and initiative, as well as of his relations with the various national organizations and institutions. DLC LNHT

333 Paredes, Jacinto Rodríguez. <u>Salvadoreños</u> <u>de</u> <u>estripe:</u> <u>libro</u> <u>de</u> <u>entrevistas.</u> Guatemala: Unión Tipografía, n.d. [1943]. 272 pp. Illus.

A series of articles about prominent Salvadorans whom this Guatemalan physician and journalist has met and interviewed, though most of the articles are descriptions and commentaries rather than interviews. DLC

334 Parra Pradenas, Ortelio. <u>Sindicalización</u> <u>racional</u> <u>de</u> <u>los</u> <u>trabajadores.</u> San Salvador: Partido Revolucionario de Unificación Democrática, 1951. 37 pp.

Comments on the labor-union movement in El Salvador by a local professor, inspired by the recent enactment of legislation legalizing and regulating the unions. Seeks to emphasize the constructive nature of labor unions and reject radicalism. TxU

335 Partido Araujista. <u>El</u> <u>Partido</u> <u>Araujista.</u> San Salvador: n.p., 1910. 428 pp. Illus.

An alphabetical listing, by municipality, of the members of the party backing the candidacy of Manuel Enrique Araujo for the Salvadoran presidency. DLC

336 Peccorini Letona, Francisco. <u>La</u> <u>voluntad</u> <u>del</u> <u>pueblo</u> <u>en</u> <u>la</u> <u>emancipación</u> <u>de</u> <u>El</u> <u>Salvador.</u> San Salvador: Ministerio de Educación, 1972. 131 pp. Biblio., notes.

A study of the independence movement in El Salvador, contending that the leaders of the movement differed from the desires of the populace, which was overwhelmingly opposed to domination by Spain but preferred rule by a monarch and union with Mexico, while the leaders maneuvered for a separate independence and a republic. Contains extensive quotations from documents previously published in secondary sources. DLC LNHT

337 Peña Kampy, Alberto. <u>El</u> <u>general</u> <u>Martínez:</u> <u>un</u> <u>patriarcal</u> <u>presidente</u> <u>dictador:</u> <u>vívidos</u> <u>relatos</u> <u>históricos,</u> <u>con</u> <u>comentarios</u> <u>de</u> <u>actualidad,</u> <u>de</u> <u>algunos</u> <u>destacados</u> <u>y</u> <u>auténticos</u> <u>sucesos</u> <u>políticos,</u> <u>sociales</u> <u>y</u> <u>económicos;</u> <u>ocurridos</u> <u>en</u> <u>una</u> <u>época</u> <u>en</u> <u>la</u> <u>República</u> <u>de</u> <u>El</u> <u>Salvador</u> <u>en</u> <u>Centro</u> <u>América.</u> Santa Anita, Mexico: Editorial Tipografía Ramírez, n.d. [197?]. 207 pp. Illus.

A sympathetic view of the Martínez regime based on accounts given to the author, often without dates, discussing various aspects of the regime, though without any pretext of completeness, organization, or chronology. The author emphasizes Martínez's imposition of order and organization of the nation in a time of chaos and stresses the value of his saving the country from communism and its misleading promises. DLC LNHT

338 Peralta Lagos, José María [T.P. Mechin, pseud.]. <u>Brochazos.</u> San Salvador: Imprenta "La República," 1925. Latest ed. San Salvador: Ministerio de Educación, 1975.

A collection of short stories by this well-known writer, designed to emphasize Salvadoran customs, traditions, and humor; focused particularly on life in the countryside. DLC

339 _____. <u>Burla</u> <u>burlando.</u> San Salvador: Imprenta Rafael Reyes, 1923. 238 pp. Latest ed. San Salvador: Ministerio de Cultura, 1955. 262 pp. Biblio., illus., appendixes.

A collection of humorous short stories, among the earliest works of this well-known Salvadoran writer, focusing on local customs and life-styles and using the local idioms. Includes a glossary of idioms. DLC LNHT

340 _____. <u>Candidato.</u> San Salvador: Imprenta "La República," 1931. xii, 191 pp. Latest ed. San Salvador: Ministerio de Educación, 1976. 247 pp.

A play, in comedy form, using the Salvadoran election of 1931 and the milieu of that time to portray the problems and the social crisis that faced the nation, the new political formulas and ideals attempted by the Araujo regime, and the political scene in general, emphasizing the difficulties of elections and the posturing of the candidates. DLC LNHT

341 _____. <u>La</u> <u>muerte</u> <u>de</u> <u>la</u> <u>tórtola,</u> <u>o</u> <u>malandanzas</u> <u>de</u> <u>un</u> <u>corresponsal.</u> San Salvador: Imprenta Funes y Ungo, 1933. 235 pp. 2d ed. San Salvador: Ministerio de Cultura, 1958. 249 pp. Index.

A novel, written in the form of a series of newspaper reports from the Salvadoran festival of San Miguel, recounting the events and using this as a base to comment on and portray Salvadoran customs, culture, humor, and modisms, all within the picturesque setting of the fair. DLC LNHT

342 Pérez, Marchant, Braulio, ed. <u>Diccionario</u> <u>biográfico</u> <u>de</u> <u>El</u> <u>Salvador.</u> San Salvador: Escuela Tipográfica Salesiana, 1937. 220 pp. Illus. 2d ed. San Salvador: Dutriz Hermanos, 1942. 230 pp. Illus.

A series of single-paragraph entries, arranged alphabetically, providing outline data on the careers of significant Salvadorans throughout the nation's history. Includes some figures from neighboring nations who affected Salvador during their careers, as well as separate sections dealing with current officials and the diplomatic corps in the capital. DLC LNHT

343 Pohl, Carlos. Gentes de mi tierra. Santa Ana: Tipografía Comercial, 1975. 211 pp. Illus.

A collection of short stories based on the traditions and folklore of eastern El Salvador, mirroring the Indian and Colonial heritage and the characteristics of the region. DLC LNHT

344 Pons, Gabriel. Ecología humana en Centroamérica: un ensayo sobre la regionalización como instrumento de desarrollo. San Salvador: ODECA, 1970. 247 pp. Illus., maps, tables.

A discussion of population distribution and its relation to resources, emphasizing the need for and possibilities of a regional population and development policy for all of Central America. Prepared under the sponsorship of the Organization of Central American States. Contains numerous tables and maps showing the population, transport facilities, and resources. Valuable for showing the current situation. DLC LNHT BNG

345 Porras Mendieta, Nemesio. Estructura económica de El Salvador. Tegucigalpa: Instituto Nacional Agraria, 1976. 53 pp. Biblio.

A general overview of the current Salvadoran economy. Considers agriculture, industry, land use, human resources, forms of production, and income distribution. DLC

346 PRELAC. Situación y prespectivas del empleo en El Salvador. Santiago: PRELAC, 1977. 453 pp. Notes, tables.

A detailed analysis of employment and unemployment in El Salvador, based on a technical mission from the labor organization that studied the situation during 1974 at the request of the Salvadoran government. The study covers the trends of the 1961-71 decade and also employs the agricultural census of 1973. It identifies the problems, including the fact that population growth is outstripping the creation of new jobs and that 41% of the population receives income below the legal minimum wage, and analyzes the specific characteristics of the growth of the industrial and agricultural sectors and their implications for employment. BNG

347 Quijano Hernández, Manuel. Dejados de la mano de Dios: una tiranía audaz y un pueblo inerte. San Salvador: Talleres Gráficos Cisneros, 1931. 103 pp.

A novel that satirizes the political methods of dictators and condemns the methods of control by force, by describing the misadventures in a mythical Central American country. The volume also contains a number of short reviews of the author's previous works. DLC

348 _____. En la montana; o el alma del indio. San Salvador: Talleres Gráficos Cisneros, 1930. iii, 187 pp.

A collection of essays describing the life and customs of the peasants in the countryside, based on the author's experiences in his country home in the eastern part of the nation and his observations of and conversations with the peasants there. He seeks to portray their values, concerns, and manner by narrating their folklore and their responses to various situations, emphasizing the local Indian traditions. CSt

349 Quiñónez, Lucio. La cuestión económica: contribución al estudio de la reforma monetaria en El Salvador. San Salvador: Imprenta Nacional, 1919. 154 pp. Illus., tables.

A detailed study of the Salvadoran economy during the 1910-19 period, contending that the main problem is monetary instability and calling for a broad governmental financial program to stabilize the value of the money and regulate it. The author also notes the problems of expenditure imbalances and calls for tighter government budgets, while arguing that the high prices of coffee offer an opportunity for monetary stabilization and that such an action would aid economic development and promote investment. Includes tables regarding the money supply and government finances. DLC

350 Rafael Zaldívar: recopilación de documentos históricos relativos a su administración. 2 vols. San Salvador: Ministerio de Educación, 1977. 293, 175 pp.

A collection of documents relating to the president who governed El Salvador from 1876 to 1885. Details his promotion of railroad construction in an effort to develop his nation; reflects his stormy relationship with Guatemalan president Justo Rufino Barrios, whose unification efforts eventually led to a war in 1885.

351 Ramírez Peña, Abraham, ed. Pactos internacionales de El Salvador. 3 vols. San Salvador: Tipografía "La Unión," 1910-11.

A collection of the full texts of Salvadoran treaties, arranged by region and nation, then chronologically.

352 Rasgos biográficos del Dr. Sixto Alberto Padilla. Ahuachapán, El Salvador: n.p., n.d. 37 pp.

A brief résumé of the career of a nineteenth-century Salvadoran medical doctor, military surgeon, and military commander. His political career was based principally around the regime of General Menéndez, during which he served in Congress and was a close confidant of the president, though it also included service to Gerrardo Barrios. LNHT

353 Raynolds, David R. Rapid Development in Small Economies: The Example of El Salvador. New York: Praeger, 1967. xvii, 124 pp. Maps, tables, appendixes.

A former foreign service officer's optimistic survey of the Salvadoran economy for the general reader, focusing on the late 1950s and early 1960s. He hails the development of the nation and the U.S. aid, which he cites as facilitating this growth while leaving the decisions to the Salvadorans; he offers this as an example to other nations and advocates that the emphasis in U.S. aid be placed on small nations, where greater short-term impact can be achieved. Briefly discusses each industry and product, with emphasis on recent growth and change. DLC LNHT

354 Regalado Dueñas, Miguel, and José Salvador Guandique. El repliegue político de la oligarquía cafetalera. San Salvador: Tipografía Santa Anita, 1975. 91 pp.

An examination of contemporary El Salvador, arguing that interpretations based on Marxist theories of class conflict are not appropriate because in the present state of the economy the fundamental conflict has become that between the government and private enterprise. DLC

355 República El Salvador, América Central, 1924: 200 fotografías de la República de El Salvador. N.p., n.d. [192?]. Pages unnumbered. Illus.

· A collection of photos taken in El Salvador showing its life, people, and facilities in the 1920s, offered without comment. LNHT

356 Reyes, Rafael. Apuntamientos estadísticos sobre la República del Salvador. San Salvador: Imprenta Nacional, 1888. 104 pp. Tables.

A brief description of the then-current situation of El Salvador, written for the Paris Universal Exposition of 1889. Includes, in addition to the usual physical and economic data, brief essays on a wide range of subjects such as political and cultural institutions and organizations. DLC LNHT

357 _____, ed. Colección de tratados del Salvador. San Salvador: Imprenta del Dr. Francisco Sagrini, 1884. 334 pp. 2d ed. San Salvador: Imprenta Nacional, 1896. 471 pp.

A collection containing the full text of the nation's international accords.

358 Reyes, Rafael. El Salvador: la reorganización bancaria. San Salvador: Imprenta Nacional, 1939. 47 pp.

A brief overview of Salvadoran monetary and banking policy from 1929 through 1939, focusing particularly on the Central Bank. Prepared by a government official for an international conference, it provides a general view of the problems of the depression in that nation and the adjustments that were necessary to combat them. DLC

359 Rivera, Abrahám. Apuntes biográficos del honorable ex-presidente de El Salvador, don Rafael Campo. San Salvador: Tipografía "La Unión," 1913. 152 pp.

A sketch of the life of a Conservative who served as president from 1856 to 1858 and later held the posts of foreign minister and president of the Constituent Assembly. NN

360 _____. Problema bancaria en relación con el sistema monetario. Sonsonate: Tipografía Heraldo de Sonsonate, 1941. 44 pp.

Reflecting the depression-induced financial crisis, this collection of articles advocates abandoning the gold standard in favor of a system of foreign currency convertibility. DLC

361 _____. Pro-reestablecimiento económico de El Salvador, 1921-1933. Sonsonate: Tipografía Heraldo de Sonsonate, 1933. 36 pp.

Another series of articles discussing the financial and economic plight of El Salvador during the depression era, this one surveying the 1920s and early 1930s and drawing lessons for future policy from previous experience.

362 _____. Segundo folleto sobre el problema bancaria en relación con el sistema monetario. Sonsonate: Tipografía Heraldo de Sonsonate, 1941. 44 pp.

A continuation of the author's articles on the nation's economic problems.

363 Rochac, Alfonso, and Rafael Reyes. La reforma bancaria en la República de El Salvador. Panamá: Universidad de Panamá, 1937. 55 pp.

A survey of Salvadoran monetary and financial history, emphasizing the problems of the depression era. DLC

364 Rodríguez González, Salvador. Derecho público salvadoreño: historia de las constituciones de El Salvador, en la América Central, pleno concepto de la soberanía del pueblo salvadoreño: diferencia sustancial entre los vocablos reelección y continuismo. San Salvador: Imprenta Diario del Salvador, 1926. 46 pp.
NN

365 Rodríguez Ruíz, José Napoleón. Discursos universitarios. San Salvador: Editorial Universitaria, 1962. 150 pp.

A collection of addresses by the rector of the University of El Salvador, though not necessarily from his years in office. Most deal with professional themes relating to teaching, the university, and scholarship, but a few discuss historical figures. Includes a report on the functioning of CSUCA. DLC LNHT

366 _____. Historia de las instituciones jurídicas salvadoreñas. San Salvador: Editorial Ahora, 1951. 304 pp. Notes.

Intended as a text for general legal history courses at the university level, this volume discusses general concepts of law and the state, surveys the Colonial institutions, and devotes the last half of its pages to a legal history of El Salvador since independence, summarizing constitutions, legal codifications, and the role of the individual institutions such as the various branches of

(Rodríguez Ruíz, José Napoleón)
the government, and reprinting excerpts from
the pertinent laws and documents. LNHT

367   ____. El janiche y otros cuentos. San
Salvador: Ministerio de Cultura, 1960.
282 pp.
    A collection of twenty-six short stories
about the life of rural peasants in El
Salvador. Emphasizes the hardships but avoids
social protest, simply portraying the problems
and actuality of peasant life as realistically
and vividly as possible; thereby effectively
captures the essence of the peasants' concerns. DLC LNHT

368   ____. Jaraguá: novela de las costas de El
Salvador. San Salvador: Editorial
Universitaria, 1950. 366 pp. 2d ed. San
Salvador: Ministerio de Cultura, 1958.
436 pp.
    A novel set in the Salvadoran countryside
and based on the folklore of the region, dramatically presenting the life of the peasants,
their beliefs and culture. Makes extensive
use of local idioms and modisms. Includes
rich description and considerable emotion in
presenting the primitive conditions of life in
the countryside and illuminating both the
regional aspects and the sociopolitical crisis
that eventually led to the difficulties of
1931. DLC LNHT

369 Romeu, José Tomás. La Guardia Nacional
Salvadoreña, desde su fundación, año 1912, al
año 1927. San Salvador: Imprenta Nacional,
1927. 208 pp. Illus., maps, tables.
    An account of the formation and history of
the Guardia Nacional, by its head, explaining
its duties and functions as a rural police
force. Details its growth, organization, and
equipment, and presents an extensive documentary collection of orders regarding its organization and functions. Includes a complete
list, by rank, of its officers on duty at the
time of publication, and extensive illustrations of its men, ceremonies, facilities, and
equipment. IU

370 Rubio Melhado, Adolfo. Manuel José Arce,
fundador del ejército salvadoreño. San
Salvador: Ministerio de Cultura, 1958. 60
pp. Illus.
    An official publication issued shortly
after the Salvadoran National Congress declared a day of the soldier. Focuses on Arce
as the founder of the Salvadoran army and
provides a brief laudatory biographical sketch
of this exemplary hero of the republic. DLC

371   ____. Los padres Aguilar: héroes ejemplares
de nuestra independencia. San Salvador:
Ministerio de Cultura, 1960. 69 pp. Illus.
    A series of brief essays on Nicolas,
Vicente, and Manuel Aguilar, three of the
lesser-known figures of Salvadoran independence. Written for the celebrations on the
centennial of independence, it is designed to
assure them their place among the heroes of
the movement. Each of the three brothers is
treated separately; references to their ecclesiastical careers are brief, since the emphasis is on their role in the independence
movement. DLC

372 Salazar Arrué, Salvador [Salarrué, pseud.].
El Cristo Negro: leyenda de San Uraco. San
Salvador: Tipografía "La Unión," 1936. 3d
ed. San Salvador: Ministerio de Cultura,
1955. 74 pp.
    The legend connected with the "Black
Christ," with accounts of the veneration,
rituals, and the shrine itself. DLC

373   ____. Obras escogidas. 2 vols. San
Salvador: Editorial Universitaria, 1969-70.
561, 680 pp.
    A collection of the works of a well-known
and influential Salvadoran writer of novels
and short stories who focuses on rural folklore, and particularly on the Indian traditions of the nation, frequently employing the
figures of Indian myths or setting his works
in the Colonial era to portray the clash of
cultures. DLC

374 Sánchez Hernández, Fidel. Discursos del señor
presidente de la república general Fidel
Sánchez Hernández. 4 vols. San Salvador:
Departamento de Relaciones Públicas de la
Presidencia, 1968-71. 116, 120, 71, 130 pp.
    The principal speeches of the Salvadoran
president, issued in annual volumes. The
complete texts are arranged chronologically,
with indication of place, date, and occasion.
DLC LNHT

375 San Salvador, Municipality of. El Salvador
monumental: homenaje de la municipalidad de
San Salvador al general Francisco Morazán.
San Salvador: Published by the Municipality,
1942. Pages unnumbered. Illus.
    A collection of speeches commemorating the
centennial of Morazán's death, with accompanying documentation of his speeches and decrees, followed by illustrations and brief
descriptions of the city's various monuments
to its historical heroes, starting with those
to Morazán. DLC LNHT

376 Saravia, Mario [Marconte, pseud.]. Fuerzas en
marcha. Guatemala: Tipografía Nacional,
1949. 138 pp. Tables.
    A series of essays on the state of
Salvadoran agriculture and its problems, by a
well-known commentator and observer. Originally published in the local press, the essays
provide an indication of the local viewpoint
and include comparisons of Salvadoran agricultural practices with those of other nations.
DLC LNHT

377 Schlesinger, Jorge. Revolución comunista.
Guatemala: Unión Tipográfica, 1946. 284 pp.
Illus.
    A detailed examination of the 1931 uprising
in El Salvador, tracing its communist inspiration. Emphasizes the chaos, destruction, and
loss of life, with numerous photographs depicting destruction and death. Stressing that

this was the result of communism, the author views his book as a means of ensuring that the populace does not forget the 1931 tragedy, so as to prevent them from being misled by contemporary agitators. DLC LNHT BNG

378 Seminario Latinoamericano sobre Crédito Rural. <u>Monografía de El Salvador: los problemas del crédito agropecuario y el desarrollo económico.</u> San Salvador: Federación de Cajas de Crédito, 1968. 137 pp. Biblio., tables.

A brief overview of the national economy and the role of agricultural credit in its development, with a description of current credit facilities and needs. The statistical data covers the years 1960-67. The volume is entirely descriptive, with no recommendations. DLC LNHT

379 Silva, José Enrique. <u>Estudios de moneda y banca de El Salvador.</u> Santa Ana: Tipografía Comercial, 1979. 143 pp.

380 Sol, Ricardo. <u>Para entender El Salvador.</u> San José: Departamento Ecuménico de Investigaciones, 1968. 161 pp.

381 Sonnenstern, Maximilian von. <u>Descripción de cada uno de los departamentos del Estado del Salvador, relativamente á su topografía, suelo, minerales, agua y temperatura.</u> New York: Published by the Author, 1858. 35 pp. Tables.

A series of brief essays, usually about one or two pages in length, describing the geographical and physical features of the departments of El Salvador, with some references to climate and transportation. DLC LNHT

382 Suárez, Belarmino. <u>Pláticas populares.</u> San Salvador: Tipografía "La Unión," 1921. 162 pp. Latest ed. San Salvador: Banco Agrícola Comercial, 1974. 179 pp.

An examination of the state of the Salvadoran economy and its problems, focusing on the monetary question. Originally written as a series of articles in <u>La Prensa</u> of San Salvador, it examines banking, the gold standard, credit needs and facilities, and other aspects in brief pieces written for the layman, arguing for improved banking and credit facilities and criticizing the concept of paper money. The series reflected the continuing financial crisis and the unfavorable balance of trade that adversely affected the economy in the immediate postwar era. DLC LNHT

383 Suay, José E. <u>Doce años de labor en el Ramo de Hacienda y de Crédito Público en la República de El Salvador, abril 1909-marzo 1921.</u> Guatemala: Sánchez & de Guise, 1921. 206 pp. Tables.

The political memoirs of an individual who held numerous financial posts in El Salvador between 1909 and 1921, including that of minister of hacienda. The memoirs span the political campaigns as well as his official posts, with appropriate reproduction of documents. DLC BNG

384 ____. <u>La obra económica del Dr. don Manuel E. Araujo, presidente de la República.</u> San Salvador: Imprenta Nacional, 1913. 35 pp.

A summary of the financial aspects of El Salvador during 1911-13, emphasizing the foreign loans, payments, refinancing, and government revenues, with full statistics. Includes information about export and import taxes at the various ports. DLC

385 Sutter, Victor Arnoldo. <u>Informe de un estudio sobre algunas condiciones de vida de los trabajadores agrícolas e industriales de la casa H. de Sola e Hijos en El Salvador Centro América.</u> San Salvador: n.p., 1945. 122 pp. Tables.

A company-sponsored study of the living conditions of its workers at its agricultural enterprises, focusing principally on housing and medical services that are provided by the company. Includes statistics regarding the workforce, its origin and makeup, with age and sex breakdowns, as well as housing and medical data, followed by recommendations for improving company services. The data clearly show how the company aids its employees, and provide a good deal of information about a particular enterprise and its impact on the nation. DPU

386 Tercero, Rafael Antonio. <u>Masferrer, un ala contra el huracán.</u> San Salvador: Ministerio de Cultura, 1958. 85 pp.

A brief sketch of the life of the Salvadoran social reformer, with emphasis on his early years, tracing the experiences that contributed to his later stands. DLC LNHT

387 ____. <u>La verdad sobre las elecciones del marzo de 1950.</u> San Salvador: Imprenta "La República," 1950. 72 pp.

A brief pamphlet that was part of the electoral propaganda. Rejects the charges of fraud by the Partido Acción Renovadora, which alleged the use of disturbances and intimidation to affect the voting, responding that PAR did not come close to victory and that there was no evidence of wrongdoing on the part of the official slate. DLC

388 <u>En torno a Masferrer.</u> San Salvador: Ministerio de Cultura, 1956. 282 pp. Biblio.

A collection of excerpts from commentaries about Masferrer and his writings, discussing his significance and critically examining his ideas. Includes excerpts from works by more than twenty-five scholars and writers. While many are highly laudatory, the volume does provide some indication of the Salvadoran view of Masferrer and his significance for the nation. LNHT

389 Toruño, Juan Felipe. <u>Desarrollo literario de El Salvador: ensayo cronológico de generaciones y etapas de las letras salvadoreñas.</u> San Salvador: Ministerio de Cultura, 1958. 440 pp. Biblio.

A prize-winning survey of Salvadoran literary development and trends from pre-Colonial

(Toruño, Juan Felipe)
to modern times, reviewing the field chronologically by generation and focusing on the
principal writers. The chapters consist of
single-page biographical sketches of the
authors that emphasize the influences on their
lives, followed by brief selections from their
works. DLC LNHT

390 _____. Gavidia entre raras fuerzas étnicas:
de su obra y de su vida. San Salvador:
Ministerio de Educación, 1969. 260 pp.
Biblio., notes, illus.
A sympathetic biography of this influential
Salvadoran writer, emphasizing and hailing his
aesthetic and moral values. Includes discussion of his use of Salvadoran settings and
local culture and idiom in his works, which
are extensively excerpted. DLC LNHT

391 Turner, George P. An Analysis of the Economy
of El Salvador, April, 1961. Los Angeles:
Published by the Author, 1961. xviii, 107 pp.
Biblio., notes, illus., tables.
A survey of the current state of the
Salvadoran economy, with some recommendations
for industrial development. DLC

392 Ulloa, Cruz, ed. Codificación de leyes
patrias de la República del Salvador, desde la
independencia hasta el año de 1875. San
Salvador: n.p., 1879. 369 pp.
An official compilation of and index to
Salvadoran legislation since independence.

393 Uriarte, Juan Ramón. La esfinge de Cuzcatlan
(El presidente Quiñónez). Mexico: Imprenta
Manuel León Sánchez, 1929. 67 pp.
A sympathetic account of the administration
of Alfonso Quiñónez Molina and his service as
vice-president and president of El Salvador
from 1919 through 1927, written by a supporter
who admits that the regime was dictatorial and
oppressive but notes its accomplishments in
such fields as monetary stabilization.
Quiñónez was known as the sphinx because of
his habit of remaining silent at meetings but
acting later, and the source of this nickname
is evident from the events narrated here.
LNHT

394 Urrutia Flamenco, Carlos. La ciudad de San
Salvador, capital de la República de "El
Salvador" o la ciudad Fénix: América Central,
1924. San Salvador: Imprenta Nacional, 1925.
268 pp. Illus.
A description of the city and its current
facilities. LNHT BNG

395 _____. Recopilación de documentos importantes
para la historia del Ramo de Comunicaciones
Eléctricas de El Salvador. San Salvador:
Imprenta Diario del Salvador, 1928. 62 pp.
A collection of material relating to electric communications in the nation and their
foundation and expansion, emphasizing the
pertinent laws and concessions as well as the
formation of the regulatory agencies. BNG

396 Valiente, Gilberto, and Carlos Monterrosa.
Metapán: monografía del distrito. San
Salvador: Imprenta Nacional, 1931. 104 pp.
Illus. 2d ed. San Salvador: Imprenta
Nacional, 1932. 106 pp. Illus.
A series of essays on the province of
Metapán dealing with its history, principal
figures, economy, agriculture, and literature,
with numerous illustrations of the region and
its people. DLC LNHT

397 Vanni, Manfredo. Salvador: condizioni
naturali ed economiche. Rome: Fratelli
Treves, 1926. 159 pp. Biblio., illus., maps.
NN

398 Vaquero, Francisco, ed. Codificación de las
leyes de El Salvador desde 1875 hasta 1889
compilación de Francisco Vaquero. San
Salvador: n.p., 1890.
An official index to Salvadoran laws for
the period in question.

399 Vásquez, Juan Ernesto. El Salvador:
actividades hacendarias en lo que se refiere a
los aspectos monetarios, cambiarios y
bancarios, década 1929-1939. San Salvador:
Imprenta Nacional, 1939. 26 pp.
A summary of Salvador's problems and policies in the financial and monetary sphere
during the turbulent period of the depression,
reflecting the problems involved and the cor-
rective measures attempted. Compiled as
an official report for an international
conference. DLC

400 Velasco, Miguel Ángel. Monografía histórica
de la ciudad de Sensuntepeque, departamento de
Cabañas, República de El Salvador, Centro
América. Sensuntepeque: Imprenta Mercurio,
1949. 95 pp. Illus.
An alphabetically arranged collection of
material about the town and its present state
and facilities, consisting principally of a
series of brief biographical sketches of its
leading figures throughout its history. LNHT

401 Velásquez, Rolando, et al. Libro blanco: El
Salvador y su diferendo con Honduras: nuestra
lucha por los derechos humanos. San Salvador:
Imprenta Nacional, 1970. 239 pp. Illus.,
maps.
An officially sponsored statement of the
Salvadoran position regarding the 1969 border
war with Honduras, containing press accounts
alleging Honduran atrocities and charging
"genocide" against Salvadorans in Honduras.
Includes Salvadoran protests, and seeks to
portray Honduras as having initiated the conflict, contending that Salvadorans were defending human rights. DLC

402 Veloz Goiticoa, Nicolás. El Salvador at the
Pan American Exposition. Buffalo, N.Y.:
n.p., 1901. 34 pp. Illus.
An account of Salvadoran activities at the
exhibition, its exhibits, prizes won, and a
brief description of the nation for visitors.
Contains some statistics regarding agricultural production at that time. DLC

403 Ventocilla, Fleodoro. Lemus y la revolución
     salvadoreña. Mexico: Ediciones
     Latinoamérica, 1956. 190 pp. Illus.
        A sympathetic biography of Colonel José
     María Lemus, who became president of El
     Salvador in 1956. Seeks to show his vast
     popular support and his dedication to reform
     and democracy in fulfillment of the popular
     desires that supported the revolution that put
     him in power. DLC LNHT

404 Vidal, Manuel. Nociones de historia de Centro
     América. San Salvador: Talleres Gráficos
     Cisneros, 1935. 257 pp. Index, biblio. 6th
     ed. San Salvador: Editorial Universitaria,
     1961. 392 pp. Biblio.
        A Salvadoran professor's textbook, based on
     his researches and notes prepared for class-
     room use, dealing with the entire isthmus but
     focusing on El Salvador. A relatively well-
     balanced survey noting the pros and cons of
     each regime and taking into account the con-
     troversies and historiography involved, ending
     in the 1920s. DLC LNHT

405 Vilanova, Santiago Ricardo. Apuntamientos de
     historia patria eclesiástica. San Salvador:
     Imprenta Diario de El Salvador, 1911. 319 pp.
        A detailed history of the Salvadoran church
     from its foundation in Colonial times to the
     end of the nineteenth century, with narrations
     of the significant events and biographies of
     the principal individuals who headed the
     church and its various administrative sub-
     divisions, written as the official history of
     the diocese by its vicar general. Includes
     the church's version of its disputes with the
     state and of its role in politics, with expla-
     nations of the basis of the official stances
     it adopted. TxU

406 Villalobos, Lisandro. El último señor de
     Moropala: cuentos y artículos. San Salvador:
     Editorial Ungo, 1939. 127 pp.
        A collection of short stories and articles,
     some previously published, seeking to capture
     the cultural traits of El Salvador and its
     milieu. Focuses specifically on the tendency
     of caudillismo as a type of political and
     social leadership that the author considers
     lamentable but a fact of life in all of Latin
     America. DLC

407 Vincenzi Pacheco, Moisés. Vida ejemplar del
     general don Francisco Menéndez: mensaje a los
     políticos de América. San Salvador:
     Imprenta Ahora, 1955. 261 pp.
        A biography extolling the works of General
     Francisco Menéndez, who served as president of
     El Salvador from 1885 to 1890, and hailing him
     as a deserving hero of the nation. Includes
     an account of his childhood and early partici-
     pation in the various political and military
     confrontations and revolutions, and details of
     his regime and programs, all emphasizing his
     glories. LNHT BNCR

408 Wallich, Henry Christopher, et al.
     Proyecciones económicas de las finanzas
     públicas, un estudio experimental en El

Salvador. Mexico: Fondo de Cultura
Económica, 1949. 363 pp. Tables.
Public Finance in a Developing Country: El
Salvador--A Case Study. Cambridge, Mass.:
Harvard University Press, 1951. 346 pp.
Index, tables. Reprint. New York: Greenwood
Press, 1968. 346 pp. Index, tables.
   A study of the financial problems of El
Salvador during the 1940s, though with some
data covering the 1920s and 1930s. Focuses on
government finance and programs as well as on
the strains of economic development and expansion of social services in a developing nation. Considers taxation, services, and government budget balances. Salvador is viewed
as having progressed further than many other
nations and as having a more favorable revenue
pattern, yet still lacking in data. The study
was assisted by the Salvadoran government.
DLC LNHT

409 Webre, Stephen. José Napoleón Duarte and the
     Christian Democratic Party in Salvadoran Poli-
     tics, 1960-1972. Baton Rouge: Louisiana
     State University Press, 1979. xiii, 233 pp.
     Index, biblio., notes.
        A scholarly overview of the Salvadoran
     Christian Democratic leader and the rise of
     the party. Based on secondary sources and
     newspapers, and originally written as a mas-
     ter's thesis. Covers the years from the
     party's formation in 1960, through its rise,
     and the disputed 1972 election that resulted
     in Duarte's exile; an introduction provides
     historical context. Although reflecting the
     limits of contemporary history, it provides an
     overview of the party, its stances, and the
     role of its leader. DLC LNHT

410 White, Alastair. El Salvador. New York:
     Praeger, 1973. 288 pp. Biblio., illus.
        A general survey of Salvadoran history from
     discovery to the present, with emphasis on the
     twentieth century, economic growth, and social
     problems. Based on secondary literature and
     written by a British scholar specializing in
     social problems of the lower classes. DLC
     LNHT

411 Wirtschaftsbericht El-Salvador. Hamburg:
     Deutsch-Südamerikanische Bank, 1958. 57 pp.
     Maps, tables.
        A survey of Salvadoran economic develop-
     ment. DLC

412 Wright, Hamilton Mercer. El Salvador of the
     Magic Table Lands. Washington, D.C.: PAU,
     1918. 24 pp. Illus.
        A brief description originally written for
     the Bulletin of the PAU. DLC

413 Wright, Marie Robinson. Salvador. New York:
     l'Artiste, 1893. 46 pp. Illus.
        A brief travelogue-style description extol-
     ling the virtues of visiting El Salvador, with
     extensive illustrations of the nation, its
     facilities, and buildings. DLC LNHT

414 Yanes Díaz, Gonzalo. <u>El Salvador y su
     desarrollo urbano en el contexto centro-
     americano</u>. San Salvador: Ministerio de
     Educación, 1976. 102 pp. Biblio., maps,
     tables.
         An architect's survey of the trends in
     urban development in El Salvador, with excel-
     lent maps showing the growth of the cities.
     Concludes that unplanned urban spread is
     creating a situation in which the capital
     dominates and all other cities are dependent,
     a situation that duplicates the international
     economy. Argues for a greater planning effort
     and utilization of the Common Market as an
     opportunity to reorient urban development
     toward autonomous urban centers apart from the
     capital. LNHT

Guatemala

1 Abascal, Valentín. *Santiago de los Caballeros de Goathemala*. Guatemala: Ministerio de Educación Pública, 1961. 237 pp. Biblio., illus.

   A series of essays about the various aspects and areas of Guatemala City and portions of its history, emphasizing its churches and the Colonial era. DLC LNHT BNG

2 _____. *Tierra nuesta: reportajes*. Quezaltenango: Tipografía del Escuela de Artes y Oficios de Varones de Occidente, 1935. 118 pp.

   A series of descriptive essays chronicling the author's travels in Guatemala, including visits to Atitlán, San Pedro La Laguna, San Juan Bautista, Chicacao, and San Miguel Panán. His commentaries include both descriptions and the thoughts inspired by his visits. DLC

3 Aceña Durán, Ramón. *Tiruliro y otras historias sin motivo*. Guatemala: Tipografía El Progreso, 1926. 159 pp.

   The life of a typical Guatemalan hero, a composite figure covering accomplishments in many fields. Traces his youth, success, failure, corruption by the United States during a visit there, etc., ironically combining the many limitations of Guatemalan leaders and heroes and creating a figure to contrast with Juan Chapin, the common Guatemalan, thereby commenting on many of the problems of the nation and its values. Includes the stories of several other individuals from various walks of life, demonstrating the same factors in shorter form. DLC

4 Aceña I., Ramón. *Estos mis paisanos*. Guatemala: Tipografía El Progreso, 1922. 192 pp.

   Essays and short stories, written during the previous decade, detailing the author's travels in his homeland and describing individuals he came into contact with. DLC

5 Acuña, G., Augusto. *La Escuela Politécnica y su próximo centenario*. Guatemala: Tipografía Nacional, 1973. 160 pp. Biblio., illus.

   A brief and profusely illustrated account of principal events of the Guatemalan military academy, focusing on the years from 1871 through 1920. The volume is somewhat anecdotal and consists of brief descriptions of a series of incidents rather than a full history. DLC BNG

6 Adamic, Louis. *The House in Antigua: A Restoration*. New York and London: Harper, 1937. x, 300 pp. Illus.

   A travel-book author's account of the romance and history of a house in Antigua and its present resident, Dorothy Hughes Popenoe. In describing the house and recounting its history, examines life in Colonial Guatemala and the restoration efforts in Antigua. DLC LNHT BNG

7 Adams, Richard Newbold. *Un análisis de las creencias y prácticas médicas en un pueblo indígena de Guatemala*. Guatemala: Ministerio de Educación Pública, 1952. 105 pp. Biblio.

   An anthropological study of the Guatemalan town of Magdalena Milpas Altas, focusing on the beliefs of the populace regarding the causes and cures of diseases. These explanations are classified, analyzed, and compared to those of other towns in northern Guatemala. Based on fieldwork conducted in 1951. DLC LNHT BNG BNCR

8 _____. *Crucifixion by Power: Essays on Guatemalan National Social Structure, 1944-1966*. Austin: University of Texas Press, 1970. xiv, 553 pp. Biblio., illus., map, tables.

   A major work in political anthropology, examining the power basis of the political and social relationships in contemporary Guatemala. Based on an investigation during the years 1963-67 by a research team directed by Adams, who prepared the final text. The volume is considered a pioneering effort toward bringing the perspectives of other disciplines to bear on the rural social problems studied by anthropologists. Includes study of such important institutions as the military, the church, the landowning elite, the peasant organizations, and regional power blocs. Despite the title, the initial years and the pre-1944 period are treated briefly and within revolutionary stereotypes; the most valuable portion of the work is consequently that dealing with the 1954-66 era. Most of

(Adams, Richard Newbold)
the statistical tables focus on the 1950s and
1960s. Includes chapters by Adams, Brian
Murphy, and Bryan Roberts. The extensive
theoretical framework in the nearly 100-page
opening chapter has potential application to
other nations. DLC LNHT

9 _____. Encuesta sobre la cultura de los
Ladinos en Guatemala. Guatemala: Ministerio
de Educación Pública, 1956. 288 pp. Biblio.,
illus. 2d ed. Guatemala: Ministerio de
Educación Pública, 1964. 300 pp. Biblio.
Based on observations made during extensive
travels throughout Guatemala by a well-known
anthropologist. Seeks to define the ladino
culture in that country and emphasizes the
variations between city and rural ladinos.
The volume includes consideration of the
Indian and black Carib cultures of the nation,
but it focuses on the life of the ladino,
considering agriculture, economic activities,
household, family, social structure, politics,
religion, and health. DLC LNHT BNG BNCR

10 _____. Migraciones internas en Guatemala:
expansión agraria de los indígenas kekchíes
hacia El Petén. Guatemala: Ministerio de
Educación Pública, 1965. 34 pp. Maps,
tables. Latest ed. Guatemala: Seminario de
Integración Social, 1978.
A brief examination of the migration of the
Kekchi Indians into the Petén region since
1950, though with longer-range comparisons in
the table that extends from 1936. Considers
the various factors involved in the migration,
the routes, types of people, and problems
encountered. Based on data collected in 1963
and 1964, the study concludes that the 1950s
witnessed an important shift, with the Kekchi
immigrants seeking permanent settlement in the
Petén rather than viewing themselves as seeking only temporary work. The implications for
the area's development and the potential integration problems are discussed. LNHT

11 Adams, Richard Newbold, et al. Social Change
in Latin America Today: Its Implications for
United States Policy. New York: Vintage,
1960. xiv, 353 pp. Index, notes.
Cambios sociales en América Latina: sus
derivaciones para la política de los Estados
Unidos. Mexico: Libreros Mexicanos Unidos,
1965. 448 pp.
A collection of separate country studies by
social anthropologists, prepared for the Council on Foreign Relations, focusing on the
problems of social change and the implications
for U.S. policy. Richard Adams prepared the
chapter on Guatemala, the only Central American nation represented; it offers a concise
outline of findings available in more detail
in his other works. DLC LNHT BNCR

12 Adler, John Hans, Eugene R. Schlesinger, and
Ernest C. Olson. Public Finance and Economic
Development in Guatemala. Palo Alto, Calif.:
Stanford University Press, 1952. xix, 282 pp.
Tables. Reprint. Westport, Conn.: Greenwood
Press, 1970. xix, 282 pp. Tables.

Las finanzas públicas y el desarrollo
económica de Guatemala. Mexico: Fondo de
Cultura Económica, 1952. 338 pp. Tables.
A study of the role of public finance in
economic development, dealing with the role of
government fiscal policy in a stage of rapid
development. The statistics were prepared by
the Banco de Guatemala. The focus is the
post-1944 era, though some of the figures
extend back to the 1920s and 1930s. The study
devotes principal attention to financial legislation, including taxation, expenditures,
foreign loans, etc. Includes budget analysis
by category. DLC LNHT

13 Agüero, Raúl. Guatemala: la revolución
Liberal de 1871 y las administraciones del
benemérito licenciado don Manuel Estrada
Cabrera. San José: Imprenta Alsina, 1914.
67 pp. Illus.
A highly laudatory view of the 1871 revolution, detailing its accomplishments, with
accompanying photos. DLC DLC-LDS-294

14 _____. Guatemala y el licenciado Estrada
Cabrera: perfil biográfico; 21 de noviembre
de 1857--21 de noviembre de 1911. San José:
Imprenta Alsina, 1911. 19 pp. Illus.
A brief biographical sketch of the career
of Estrada Cabrera and the public works program of his presidency. Seeks to counter the
critical propaganda by hailing his accomplishments, stating that these must be taken into
account along with the criticism of his political methods. DLC-LDS-663

15 Aguilar, Octavio. El Juez Olaverri y Juan
Canastuj; historias policíacas. Guatemala:
Editorial Landívar, 1956. 91 pp.
Published under the sponsorship of the
Secretaría de Divulgación de la Presidencia as
part of the commemoration of the second anniversary of the National Liberation Movement,
this political novel deals with a young judge
who had not quite terminated his legal studies
before being assigned to a remote and crime-
ridden village, and a drunkard whom he re-
leases to become his servant. It traces the
problems and political life of the town
through their interaction and the cases that
come before the judge. DLC LNHT

16 Aguilar P., J. Humberto. El drama político de
Guatemala: vida y muerte de una dictadura.
Mexico: Tipográfica Nieto, 1944. 65 pp.
Illus.
An anti-Ubico tract, criticizing the regime
and recounting the author's experiences in its
prisons and his mistreatment by it. DLC LNHT

17 Aguilar Peláez, Víctor. Diccionario
geográfico de la República de Guatemala, año
1930. Guatemala: Tipografía San Antonio,
1930. 120 pp. plus advertising.
A list of cities and places, providing
basic data, location by province, and population. DLC

18 Aguilera, Julio Fausto, ed. Antología de poetas revolucionarios. Guatemala: Asociación de Estudiantes "El Derecho," 1973. 56 pp.
A collection of poems by the so-called poets of the Guatemalan revolution of 1944, containing works by Enrique Juárez Toledo, Otto Raúl González, Miguel Ángel Vásquez, Oscar Arturo Palencia, Otto René Castillo, Luís Alfredo Arango, Julio Fausto Aguillera, José Luís Villatoro, Francisco Morales Santos, Roberto Obregón, and Marco Antonio Flores. BNG

19 Aguilera, León. Treinta años de "El Imparcial": o la lucha de un diario por su independencia. Guatemala: Unión Tipográfia, 1952. 419 pp. Illus.
A history of the important Guatemalan newspaper El Imparcial, recounting its struggles, trials, and triumphs from 1922 through 1952. Highlights its efforts to remain independent, its political struggles with the various regimes, its principal reporters and contributors, and above all the efforts of its founder and editor, Alejandro Cordova. Includes reproductions of many of its front pages reporting major domestic and international events. The comments about difficulties regarding press control with the various regimes are particularly interesting and reveal a great deal about the governments. LNHT BNG

20 _____. Urnas del tiempo. Guatemala: Imprenta Hispania, 1956. 238 pp.
A selection of the author's daily commentaries that have appeared in El Imparcial since 1942, focusing on contemporary themes. Unfortunately, there is no indication of the dates or the selection criteria, and the themes are disparate. DLC LNHT BNG BNCR

21 Aguilera de León, Carlos. Libro-centenario de Guatemala, 1835-1935: conmemorativo del aniversario natal del general Justo Rufino Barrios, reformador de Guatemala. Guatemala: Tipografía Nacional, 1935. 242 pp. Illus.
An official project to commemorate the centennial of the birth of the Guatemalan Liberal hero and reformer Justo Rufino Barrios. Although focusing on the accomplishments of Barrios and the Liberal tradition, this work carefully links the incumbent regime of Jorge Ubico to that tradition, in some instances by direct comparison of the legislation of Ubico and Barrios, and in others by placing photos of Ubico's public works projects within a text describing the projects of Barrios. DLC LNHT BNCR

22 Aguilera Peralta, Gabriel Edgardo. La violencia en Guatemala como fenómeno político. Cuernavaca, Mexico: Centro Intercultural de Documentación, 1971. 169 pp. Biblio., tables.
A brief résumé of the various guerilla groups in Guatemala, their origins, leadership, and ideology, with an outline of the stance of the societal groups and organizations opposed to them and a discussion of the effects of the violence. The author concludes that political violence has been a part of Guatemala for a long time and that the prevalence of this method forces all to adopt it. He notes that the prevalence of violence has served to help polarize the political scene and harden positions on all sides, which could lead to broader conflict. DLC LNHT

23 Aguirre Beltrán, Gonzalo, and Emil J. Sady. The Indian Economic Development Service of Guatemala. New York: U.N., 1960. iii, 46 pp. Illus., maps.
An official summary, by a well-known Mexican anthropologist, of the Indian life in Guatemala and the work of the Servicio de Fomento de la Economía Indígena. DLC LNHT

24 Aguirre Cinta, Rafael. Lecciones de historia general de Guatemala. Guatemala: Tipografía Nacional, 1899. 248 pp. Illus.
A series of commentaries and documentary selections compiled by a Mexican historian, dealing with important episodes from Guatemalan development. Approximately half the volume pertains to pre-Colonial and Colonial times, with the remaining portion covering the years from independence through the Barrios regime. Includes a mixture of entire documents, excerpts from documents, and extremely brief narrations in numbered paragraphs. DLC LNHT BNCR

25 Aguirre Godoy, Mario, ed. Reportorio de jurisprudencia: fallos de la Corte Suprema de Justicia en los ramos procesal civil, mercantil y contencioso administrativo, en un períodó de 10 años comprendido de 1950-1959. 2 vols. Guatemala: Editorial Universitaria, 1962. 666, 442 pp.
A collection of rulings by the Supreme Court dealing with civil, commercial, and administrative law during the period 1950-59. MH-L

26 Aguirre Matheu, Lily. The Land of Eternal Spring: Guatemala My Beautiful Country. New York: Patio Press, 1949. 253 pp. Index, biblio., illus. Latest ed. Guatemala: Editorial Landivar, 1959. 160 pp. El país de la eterna primavera. Guatemala: Ministerio de Educación Pública, 1950. 239 pp. Biblio., illus.
A series of essays describing Guatemala, its life, history, and Indian traditions, designed to familiarize Yankees with the nation and encourage tourism. Written by a Guatemalan novelist who long resided in the United States and hence seeks to bridge the two countries. The 1959 edition is titled Guatemala My Beautiful Country. DLC BNG

27 Albizurez Palma, Francisco. La novela de Asturias. Guatemala: Editorial Universitaria, 1975. 210 pp. Biblio. LNHT

28 Álbum gráfico centenario de la Escuela Politécnica. Guatemala: Editorial del Ejército, 1973. Pages unnumbered. Illus.

A photographic album including many photos and commentaries regarding the various classes of the Guatemalan military academy, lists of all classes in graduation rank, and photos of the ceremonies and the school. Most interesting and useful is the collection of photos and minibiographies of each of the directors and subdirectors throughout the history of the academy, many of whom later rose to prominent governmental positions. BNG

29   Álbum gráfico Quetzaltenango [sic]: homenaje al señor presidente constitucional de la república. Quezaltenango: E. Cifuentes, 1936. 212 pp. Illus.
A collection of photos of the city and region and its facilities, with emphasis on the works of the Ubico administration. Includes single-page descriptions and commentaries. LNHT

30   Alemán Bolaños, Gustavo. Vida agrícola de Guatemala. Guatemala: Editorial Hispania, 1946. 98 pp.
A brief description of each of the nation's largest estates, giving location, use, facilities, production, and ownership. Particular emphasis is placed on the prominence of foreign ownership. DLC LNHT

31   Alianza de la Juventud Democrática Guatemalteca. Alianza de los sectores de la juventud guatemalteca en la lucha nacional por la democracia, la libertad y la paz mundial. Guatemala: Tipografía Nacional, 1949. 71 pp.
A collection of political broadsides issued by the party during the previous sixteen months, detailing its political position and goals. DLC

32   Alonso, Antonio. Monografía de Mixco. Guatemala: Tipografía San Antonio, 1932. iii, 64 pp. Illus., maps.
A brief résumé of the leading citizens of the town and of its development, with emphasis on the present. DLC LNHT

33   Alonzo de Rodríguez, Josefina, ed. Arte contemporáneo: occidente – Guatemala. Guatemala: Imprenta Universitaria, 1966. 507 pp. Biblio., illus., maps.
The first 100 pages contain a series of analytical essays on the development of art in Guatemala, written by a group of artists from that nation who are members of the Faculty of Humanities of the University of San Carlos. The remaining portion consists of supporting illustrations, black-and-white photos of architecture and sculpture and both black-and-white and color prints of paintings. DLC LNHT

34   Los Altos, Gov't of. Origen histórico del Estado de los Altos. Quezaltenango: n.p., 1836. 22 pp. Illus.
A reproduction of the documents from the 1824 creation of the state of Los Altos.

35   Altuve, Arturo. Ligeros apuntamientos bibliográficos del teniente coronel don Nicolás Mazariegos. Guatemala: Tipografía Luís de Guise, 1925.
A brief essay extolling the contributions of the title figure to the 1871 Liberal revolution. DPU

36   Alvarado, Gregorio. Leyendas de Guastatoya y escenas de la vida real. Guatemala: Ministerio de Educación Pública, 1964. 233 pp. Illus., appendix.
A collection of legends from the eastern coastal region of Guatemala and the author's recollections of his life there. Many of the legends are religious in nature, though they also include ghosts and witches, as well as Indian tales. The remaining third of the book consists of the author's recollections, appearing as a series of short stories. Includes a glossary of regionalisms employed DLC LNHT BNG

37   Alvarado, Miguel T. Pro patria: pequeñas biografías: general Justo Rufino Barrios. Quezaltenango: n.p., 1925. 52 pp. Biblio., illus.
A brief account of the life of Justo Rufino Barrios, based on published sources and emphasizing his unionist efforts. Praises his works and his regime, and includes a list of accomplishments. DLC

38   Alvarado Arellano, Huberto. Exploración de Guatemala. Guatemala: Ediciones Revista de Guatemala, 1961. 95 pp. Index.
Analysis of the use of prominent Guatemalan themes in the works of its writers and novelists, discussing and tracing through the works of many authors such themes as magic realism, naturalism, internal passion, incipient nationalism, regionalism, and social criticism. The author contends that these themes reflect the Guatemalan people's struggle for identity while interpreting and defining their own culture, and that the reoccurrence of these themes indicates that they do represent the Guatemalan reality and constitute literature's contribution to the evolution of the national culture. DLC BNG BNCR

39   _____. Por un arte nacional, democrático y realista. Guatemala: Ediciones Saker-Ti, 1953. 40 pp. Illus.
A brief overview and self-criticism of the Saker-Ti group, restating its focus in the field of art and its efforts to promote the growth of a national culture and break the bonds of old forms in literature and the arts. Also indicates its birth in the revolutionary era and its support of the anti-imperialist, antidictatorial efforts of the revolution that sought to improve the living standards of the poor. Indeed, the essay notes that absorption in politics has sometimes interfered with the literary efforts of the group's members. DLC LNHT

40   _____. Preocupaciones. Guatemala: Ediciones Vanguardia, 1967. 200 pp. Biblio.
An outline of the factors the author feels hinder the proper development of art and

literature in Central America. Denounces
bourgeois attitudes and the problem of cultural dependency. DLC

41 Alvarado Fajardo, Federico. Calcomanías: el
clamor de la tierra, prensa y política.
Guatemala: Editorial El Sol, 1928. 146 pp.
    A collection of political commentaries and
editorials from newspapers, decrying the economic crisis and ineffectiveness of the government in responding. DLC

42 _____. El liberalismo y su evolución
progresista. Guatemala: Tipografía Libertad,
1931. 175 pp. Illus.
    A discussion of Guatemalan politics of the
1920s, partially in response to the work of
Gustavo Schwartz, seeking to clarify the origins of the Progressive party and its doctrines. The emphasis is upon General Jorge
Ubico as the "decisive factor" in the evolution of the Progressive movement, hence his
activities and his role in the political scene
are defended. The Progressive party platform
is reproduced and closely linked to the previous Liberal tradition. LNHT BNG

43 _____. Lo que pensamos los locos. Guatemala:
Editorial El Sol, 1921. 197 pp.
    A volume reflecting the experience of the
regime of Manuel Estrada Cabrera and the eu-
phoria that greeted its overthrow. Denounces
caciquismo and rigidity, adopts the view of
the lower classes and calls for attention to
their needs, and idealistically emphasizes the
need for universal democracy; catalogs the
excesses of the long dictatorship and supports
the then-current unionist movement. LNHT

44 Alvarado Pinetta, Rony S. La Transformación
agraria en Guatemala. Guatemala: Instituto
Nacional de tranformación Agraria, 1964. 125
pp. Illus., maps, tables.
    A lavishly illustrated description of the
agricultural programs of the Peralta regime.
DLC LNHT BNG

45 Alvarado Pinto, Carlos Román. Ahora que me
acuerdo. Guatemala: Editorial del Ejército,
1977. 114 pp. Illus.
    A series of essays recounting the principal
events and important individuals of
Quezaltenango, seeking to preserve the
memories of its leading citizens and its
traditions. The themes and individuals are
disparate, with no indication of time or means
of selection. BNG

46 Alvarado Rubio, Mario, and Rodolfo Galeotti
Torres. Índice de pintura y escultura.
Guatemala: Unión Tipográfica, 1946. 95 pp.
Illus.
    An alphabetical listing of Guatemalan
artists and sculptors, with brief biographical
sketches in Spanish and English accompanied by
photos of samples of their work. In some
cases self-portraits of the artists are substituted. Includes artists from the Colonial
era to the present. DLC BNG

47 Álvarez, Juan. Dos palabras al folleto
titulado "Centro América: su presente, su
pasado y porvenir." San José: Imprenta
Nacional, 1879. Latest ed. Guatemala:
Tipografía El Progreso, 1880. 16 pp.
    A reply to a folio by Luís Batres, bitterly
denouncing the latter's activities and attacking the Liberal regimes in Guatemala. An
example of the vitriolic polemics that characterized the region's politics. BNCR

48 Álvarez Elizondo, Pedro. El presidente
Arévalo y el retorno a Bolívar: un
panamericanismo revolucionario. Mexico:
Ediciones Rex, 1947. 232 pp.
    An enthusiastic account of Arévalo's life
and the initial years of his tenure in the
Guatemalan presidency, acclaiming his efforts
and initiatives and extolling his efforts to
promote Central American unification and Latin
American cooperation. Declares him a new
Bolívar who seeks to reunify the region and
promote cooperation in meeting its needs.
Most of the book consists of excerpts from
Arévalo's writings and speeches strung together with brief phrases and short narratives
of praise. DLC LNHT BNG

49 Amaro, Nelson, ed. El reto del desarrollo en
Guatemala: un enfoque multi-disciplinario.
Guatemala: Editorial Financiera Guatemalteca,
1970. 482 pp. Illus., maps, tables.
    Compiled under the auspices of the bank and
the Instituto para el Desarrollo Económico y
Social de América Central, this volume con-
tains a number of studies by leading Central
American scholars that deal with various as-
pects of development in the region. The con-
tributors come from several disciplines, and
the topics include ideology, ecology, social
structure, cultural change, and political
alternatives. Some of the studies deal with
Guatemala, and others with the entire isthmus.
Contributors include René de León Schlotter,
Nelson Amaro, Enrique Torres Lezama, Leonel
González, Josef Thesing, Miguel Ángel Reyes,
Gabriel Aguilera, Carlos Gehlert Mata, Vinicio
José Aguilar, Elmar René Rojas, Rolando
Marroquín, and Mauro Cuevas. DLC LNHT

50 Amaya Amador, Ramón. Amanecer. Tegucigalpa:
Tipografía Nacional, 1953. 265 pp. 2d ed.
Tegucigalpa: Tipografía Nacional, 1956.
265 pp.
    An account of the Guatemalan revolution as
seen through the sympathetic eyes of a member
of the Honduran Communist party who fled to
Guatemala after being expelled from his own
nation. To him the movement was a social-
democratic effort toward justice for the peasants, one that opposed the exploitive foreign
corporations in the banana zone, where he had
personal experience. He later spent years in
exile in Argentina and Eastern Europe. DLC

51 _____. Operación Gorila. Moscow: n.p.,
1970.
    A Honduran Communist party member and so-
cial novelist's work denouncing the CIA intervention in Guatemala in 1954, which forced him

to flee that nation. Written in Eastern
Europe and not yet published in Spanish. One
of many such works flowing from his prolific
pen. DLC

52 Amurrio González, Jesús Julián. El
positivismo en Guatemala. Guatemala:
Editorial Universitaria, 1970. 228 pp.
Biblio.
    A survey of positivism and its influence in
Guatemala, based on secondary sources and
written by a Guatemalan philosophy professor.
Focuses on the Liberal governments of the late
nineteenth century that based their develop-
mentalist approach on its tenets, but also
considers influences during the early twentieth century. Includes discussion of the
doctrine, its introduction and spread in
Guatemala, its role in the nation's educational system, and the role of its principal
proponents on the local scene. DLC LNHT BNG

53 Anderson, Marylyn. Guatemalan Textiles Today.
New York: Watson-Guptill, 1978. 200 pp.
Index, biblio., illus., maps.
    A survey of the entire Guatemalan highlands
region, considering both design and technique;
with extensive and excellent photos. DLC
LNHT

54 Anderson, Young. Memoir contenant un aperçu
statistique de l'état de Guatemala: rapports
et correspondance relative à la colonisation
du Vera Paz S. Tomas de M. Young Anderson.
Brussels: n.p., 1840. 158 pp. Maps.
    A prospectus designed to encourage emi-
gration to the Belgian settlement in Alta
Verapaz. Includes the text of the Guatemalan
government's concession to the Belgian company, statistical information about Guatemala
emphasizing its commercial and agricultural
prospects, and plans for the colony and facilities available in it.

55 Anino C., Juan. La República de Guatemala
América Central: apuntes sobre su situación
geográfica y política, y datos acerca de sus
riquezas agrícolas, comercio é industriales y
guía de la ciudad de Guatemala. Guatemala:
Tipografía Nacional, 1894. 177 pp.
    A compilation of current data about the
nation, listing each city and province and
explaining everything from taxes to schools,
with lists of insurance firms, printers, companies, and similar data. Designed to promote
greater knowledge of Guatemala abroad and
encourage investment and trade. BNCR

56 Aparicio y Aparicio, Edgar Juan. Los
Gutiérrez Marroquín y sus descendientes.
Guatemala: Talleres Gutenberg, 1956. 160 pp.
    A genealogy that traces an illustrious
family from Colonial days by listing all the
children and birthdates of the various lines.
BNG

57 Applebaum, Richard P. San Ildefonso
Ixtahuacán, Guatemala: un estudio sobre la
migración temporal, sus causas y
consecuencias. Guatemala: Ministerio de

Educación Pública, 1967. 82 pp. Biblio.,
notes, tables.
    A study of seasonal migration of laborers
in Huehuetenango, based on fieldwork conducted
in 1965. Originally published as an article
in the Princeton University journal Public and
International Affairs in 1966, under the title
"Seasonal Migration in San Ildefonso
Ixtahuacán." It describes the town and the
agriculture of the region, including its
cycles and labor needs, and analyzes the
migration, its causes, and its effects,
placing it in the overall social-economic
context of the town and the region. DLC LNHT
BNG

58 Arana Osorio, Carlos. Discursos del
Presidente Arana Osorio. Guatemala:
Tipografía Nacional, 1970. 76 pp. Illus.
Latest ed. Guatemala: Tipografía Nacional,
1972. 80 pp. Illus.
    A collection of the speeches of the
Guatemalan president during 1972, consisting
principally of orations connected with the
visits to Guatemala of the presidents of El
Salvador, Honduras, and Nicaragua. Only the
speeches of the host are included. LNHT

59 _____. En ruta hacia la muerte. Many
editions. Guatemala: n.p., 1956. 48 pp.
Illus.
    A nephew of Colonel Francisco J. Arana,
himself a future president, recounts his imprisonment and torture by the Arbenz government and includes photos of numerous other
individuals identified as the victims of its
terrorism. The pamphlet went through several
editions in the same year. DLC

60 Aranda, José, and J. Samuel Gálvez. Manuel
Estrada Cabrera y Guatemala de triunfo.
Guatemala: Tipografía A.M. Anderson, 1904.
27 pp.
    A campaign folio endorsing the Liberal
party's candidate, General Manuel Estrada
Cabrera, as just the type of leader the nation
needs.

61 Arce, Francisco de. Impresiones sobre
Guatemala: apuntes de viaje. Guatemala:
Tipografía Nacional, 1907. 40 pp. Illus.
    A description of the nation under the
Estrada Cabrera regime, originally published
in the Spanish press and later reprinted in
book form by the Guatemalan government. The
author hails Guatemala, its potential, and the
works of the incumbent regime, describing the
institutions and programs of the nation. Includes comments on schools, the military,
government buildings, programs, society, and
the government, providing an indication of the
state of the nation in the early twentieth
century. LNHT

62 Arce y Valladares, Manuel José. Diario de un
escribiente. Guatemala: Editorial Piedra
Santa, 1979. 204 pp.

63 _____. Síntesis de Guatemala. Guatemala:
Editorial del Ejército, 1966. 45 pp. Illus.

A brief summary of Guatemalan history and description of the present situation, designed to provide basic information for outsiders. LNHT BNG

64   Archila Lemus, José. <u>Monografía del departamento de Zacapa</u>. Guatemala: Tipografía Nacional, 1928. 211 pp. Illus., maps.
      A description of the department and each of its municipalities including physical setting, resources, flora and fauna, customs, economy, history, and holidays. DLC LNHT BNG

65   Archivo General de Centro América. <u>Guatemala: el acta de patzicía</u>. Guatemala: Comité Central pro-Conmemoración del Centenario, 1971. 239 pp.
      A reproduction of the pact that launched the Liberal revolution of 1871, issued on the centennial of the event, with accompanying contemporary documentation consisting of the exchanges and pledges of support that followed, which enabled the triumph of the movement that terminated the rule of the Conservative party and began the Guatemalan era of reform. LNHT BNG

66   Ardón F., José Enrique. <u>La revolución Liberal término el 80</u>. Guatemala: Tipografía Nacional, 1972. 288 pp. Illus., maps.
      A history of the Guatemalan Liberal revolution of 1871, extolling its virtues and leaders and its impact on Guatemala, but arguing that there is a distinction between the revolution and the reforms it brought about. The revolution proper constituted the era of the struggle for control of the nation and, in the author's view, ended with the new constitution entering into force in 1880. This left the Liberals in complete control and able to carry out the reform program they had already initiated. The years after 1880, the author argues, constitute a separate period made possible only by the first, and represent an era of more arbitrary rule and less creative actions. The work includes biographical sketches of many of the key figures of this important era as well as anecdotes drawn from published works. DLC LNHT BNG

67   _____. <u>El señor general Ubico</u>. Guatemala: Comercial Tipografía, 1968. 119 pp. Illus.
      A brief biographical sketch of the dictator who ruled Guatemala from 1931 through 1944, with commentary hailing the accomplishments of his regime and cataloging many of his projects and the honors bestowed upon him. Includes photos of many of the edifices constructed during his tenure. DLC LNHT BNG

68   _____. <u>Tito</u>. Guatemala: Tipografía Nacional, 1964. 105 pp. Illus.
      A collection of autobiographical essays recounting various episodes in the author's life. Though providing glimpses into the episodes that he remembers, they offer little insight into the era; the author carefully avoids dates, his military career, and political events, and focuses on personal and formative incidents. DLC LNHT BNCR

69   Arévalo, Teresa. <u>Rafael Arévalo Martínez: biografía de 1884 hasta 1926</u>. Guatemala: Tipografía Nacional, 1971. 422 pp. Biblio., notes.
      A loving biography by the daughter of one of Guatemala's best-known writers. Recounts in detail the first forty-two years of his life, employing anecdotes and insights from his private life to illustrate his character while drawing upon her conversations with him to demonstrate his views and reactions to events and people. Despite its obvious bias, it helps round out knowledge of the man and demonstrates the effect of the political events of his lifetime upon his outlook. Particular stress is placed on his years under the dictatorship of Manuel Estrada Cabrera. A second volume covering the remainder of his life is intended. DLC LNHT BNG

70   Arévalo Bermejo, Juan José. <u>La adolescencia como evasión y retorno</u>. Buenos Aires: Imprenta Lopez, 1941. 118 pp. Biblio. 4th ed. Caracas: Instituto Pedagogico, 1961. 107 pp.
      A series of essays on adolescence and the education of adolescent children, with discussion of their attitudes and needs and the requisite courses. Among the author's earlier works, it focuses entirely on educational policy, though it foreshadows some of his later concern for education as president. DLC

71   _____. <u>Antikomunismo en América Latina: radiografía del proceso hacia una nueva colonización</u>. Many editions: Mexico: Editorial América Nueva, 1959. 206 pp. 3d ed. Havana: Ediciones La Tertulia, 1960. 206 pp. <u>Anti-Kommunism in Latin America: An X-Ray of the Process Leading to a New Colonialism</u>. New York: Lyle Stuart, 1963. 224 pp. Biblio.
      A vitriolic denunciation of Yankee policy by a bitter crusader, written in the aftermath of the 1954 CIA intervention in Guatemala that overthrew his successor. Attacks the rigid anticommunism that characterized the Yankee stance during the Cold War years, citing the efforts of dictatorships to use anticommunism to seek support from the Northern Colossus while shielding their excesses, and noting the gullibility of the Yankees to such contentions. In his view blind anticommunism is the basis of the Yankee errors in the hemisphere and of their failure to understand the problems of the region, causing them to reject its reform movements. DLC LNHT BNCR

72   _____. <u>Carta política al pueblo de Guatemala con motivo de haber aceptado la candidatura presidencial</u>. Mexico: B. Costa-Amic, 1963. 46 pp. Illus. 2d ed. Guatemala: Tipografía San Antonio, 1963. 50 pp. Biblio.
      The political platform on which the ex-president declared his candidacy for the 1963 elections. Restates his ideals of "spiritual socialism" and defends the goals of the revolution and the actions of his administration, calling for a return to the principles of the

(Arévalo Bermejo, Juan José)
1944 movement and denouncing the foreign corporations and special interest groups allied to the counterrevolution. LNHT

73   _____. La carta política del ciudadano._
Guatemala: n.p., 1965. 116 pp.
    A continuation and elaboration of the Carta política al pueblo of 1963, written after a military coup prevented the election in which Arévalo was to seek a return to the presidency. Stresses nationalism and "spiritual socialism" while defending the actions of his earlier revolutionary government and criticizing his constant enemies, the imperialists and the United Fruit Company.

74   _____. Discursos en la presidencia._
Guatemala: Tipografía Nacional, 1947. 237 pp. 2d ed. Guatemala: Tipografía Nacional, 1948. 314 pp.
    A collection of speeches from the years 1945-47, the initial period of Arévalo's presidency. Includes his first annual report on his stewardship, his inaugural address, salutes to significant constituencies such as labor, and disparate routine statements such as New Year's greetings, inaugurations of various institutions, and exchanges of greetings with foreign dignitaries and visiting statesmen. Contains some of his efforts to flesh out his theory of "spiritual socialism." DLC LNHT BNG

75   _____. Escritos pedagógicos y filosóficos._
Guatemala: Tipografía Nacional, 1945. 291 pp.
    Essays on educational subjects, written from exile in Argentina during the years the Ubico administration dominated Guatemala, focusing principally on pedagogical and educational issues and reflecting the years of Arévalo's academic career. DLC LNHT BNCR

76   _____. Escritos políticos._ Guatemala: Tipografía Nacional, 1945. 205 pp. Illus.
    A collection of speeches and essays covering the years 1935-44, including pleas for Central American unification but consisting principally of political statements and attacks on the government of Jorge Ubico. The author uses broad themes rather than specific events, condemning militarism, fascism, dictatorship, and servitude. He thus attacks the regime by implication, maintaining an intellectual facade while engaged in politics. The essays also hail revolution and popular government and speak of a "new Guatemala," providing insights into his doctrine of "spiritual socialism." The speeches from 1944 that comprise the final section are more politically overt. DLC LNHT BNG BNCR

77   _____. Escritos políticos y discursos._
Havana: Ediciones Cultural, 1953. 515 pp.
    A two-volume reprint combining the Escritos políticos and the Discursos en la presidencia. DLC

78   _____. Fábula del tiburón y las sardinas, América Latina estrangulada._ Many editions. Santiago: Ediciones América Libre, 1956. 274 pp. Notes. 6th ed. Buenos Aires: Editorial Palestra, 1965. 221 pp.
The Shark and the Sardines. New York: Lyle Stuart, 1961. 256 pp.
    An impassioned cry against Yankee imperialism, big business, and capitalism, by a leading Guatemalan political figure who was one of its victims. The original fable, which opens the volume, is one of the classic intellectual statements of the leftist view, offering in allegory form the leftist stereotype of the pervasive Yankee, presaging the later dependency theory. The subsequent chapters are far more doctrinaire and rabidly Yankeefobic, yielding to Marxist terminology and vitriolic condemnation based on sweeping generalities. Despite its one-sidedness, it illustrates a widely held viewpoint, and has been read extensively throughout Latin America. DLC LNHT BNG

79   _____. La filosofía de los valores en la pedagogía 1939._ Buenos Aires: Imprenta López, 1939. 78 pp. 2d ed. Guatemala: Tipografía Nacional, 1946. 75 pp.
    A piece dealing with significant new trends in education, reflecting the educational scene in Argentina, where the author taught during his exile, but also mirroring his own educational and political views. DLC

80   _____. Guatemala, la democracia y el imperio._ Many editions in several countries during 1954. 7th ed. Buenos Aires: Editorial Palestra, 1964. 241 pp.
    An ex-president of Guatemala and leader of the revolutionary governments provides his thoughts on and reactions to the Yankee intervention that overthrew his successor. Written immediately after the fact, it is a scathing condemnation of Yankee imperialism reflecting the passion of the moment. DLC LNHT BNG BNCR

81   _____. La inquietud normalista: estampas de adolescencia y juventud, 1921-1927._ San Salvador: Editorial Universitaria, 1970. 316 pp.
    A former president of Guatemala provides his memoirs of his years at the nation's Normal School in the 1920s. He describes his studies, thoughts, friends, teachers, and travels, and makes comments on the contemporary political situation. The volume was written immediately prior to publication, largely from memory, and hence provides as much information about Arévalo's memories of the situation and what parts influenced him as about the distant events themselves. The reminiscences also help to show the evolution of his political thought, as he remembers it, and the factors he considers most influential in shaping his credo. DLC LNHT

82   _____. Istmania o la unidad revolucionaria de Centroamérica._ Guatemala: Editorial

(Arévalo Bermejo, Juan José)
Indoamérica, 1945. 3d ed. Buenos Aires: Editorial Indoamérica, 1954. 62 pp.

The title essay was written in 1935, though not previously published. It argues for the need for revolution in all of Central America and offers the solutions of a "new generation." Points to an evolution of societies from monostructures, in which there is only one power center, the executive, to polistructures, in which there are several loci of power; contends that it is time that Central America passed from the former to the latter. In the process, it distinguishes between personality and individuals and hints at a distinction between economics and spiritual things; it is thus an early precursor of the author's later doctrine of "spiritual socialism." The remaining essays deal with the role of education, and were previously published in the 1930s in Argentine educational journals. They reflect the author's career as an educator and also foretell his later stance in support of education as a key factor in the revolution. The preface and cover notes by the publisher denounce imperialistic intervention by the Yankees in Guatemala and also reject the Stalinist solution, but bear little relation to the contents of the book. DLC LNHT

83 _____. La personalidad, la adolescencia, y los valores y otros escritos de pedagogía y filosofía. Guatemala: Ministerio de Educación Pública, 1974. 598 pp. Biblio.

A series of essays, speeches, and commentaries by the Guatemalan president, spanning a broad range of themes and the years 1928 through 1949, and offering his views on instructional methodology and general philosophy. They comprise his professional writings as an educational scholar, collected in a single edition, with the dates and places noted. His early commentaries on the Mexican Revolution and its instructional methods are particularly interesting in view of his later efforts. Most of the writings, however, refer to educational method, indicating his view of the school as an institution for social change. LNHT BNG

84 _____. Venezuela y Guatemala: discursos con motivo de la visita del presidente Betancourt a Guatemala, 26 de julio de 1946. Guatemala: Tipografía Nacional, 1946. 19 pp. Illus.

A collection of speeches during the official acts of the Venezuelan president's visit, emphasizing the reformist rhetoric of both regimes. TxU

85 _____. Viajar es vivir. Buenos Aires: Imprenta Mercatal, 1933. 157 pp. 2d ed. Guatemala: Tipografía Nacional, 1950. 157 pp.

A series of essays dealing with diverse themes that the author describes as an effort to liberate himself from the confines of his own experience through the broadening impact of travel. They include commentaries about travelers and about various items he saw, and the thoughts inspired thereby. The themes range from the tropics and natural forces to the modern city as contrasted with the backwardness of the interior. DLC

86 Arévalo Bermejo, Juan José, and Alfredo Aldana H. Que significan las escuelas "federación": solución guatemalteca en un conflicto universal entre la arquitectura y la pedagogía; cómo funciona la escuela "federación" de Palencia. Guatemala: Tipografía Nacional, 1949. 78 pp. Illus.

Two separate papers extolling the new type of school designed by the revolutionary government, which is explained and acclaimed as a purely domestic design and a solution to a domestic need, a primary school that allows flexibility and permits many diverse types of education as well as community use. The idea features a large central assembly hall and garden, surrounded by dispersed classrooms. The president describes the plans, while a member of the Ministry of Education provides details regarding costs, facilities, and the functioning of one such school. Extensive illustrations of schools and plans for the new form are included. DLC LNHT

87 Arévalo Martínez, Rafael, ed. Catálogo de la Biblioteca Nacional. Guatemala: n.p., 1932. 257 pp. Index.

A catalog of the Guatemalan National Library's holdings in the 1930s, when Arévalo Martínez was serving as its director. The initial section is arranged by subject according to the Dewey Decimal classification, with the second portion consisting of works dealing with Central America. Not all listings contain full information, and unfortunately it cannot be assumed that volumes in the library in the 1930s remain in its collection years later. LNHT BNG BNCR

88 Arévalo Martínez, Rafael. Concepción del cosmos. Guatemala: Editorial Landívar, 1954. 157 pp.

At the age of seventy the author returns, this time in a clear philosophical discussion, to the theme he treated allegorically in El hombre que parecía un caballo. The first and last chapters of this new work are both entitled "El hombre es un animal," and the volume deals with the uncertainties of life, the factors that influence human behavior, and the peculiarities of these animals. Includes discussion of such themes as religion, imagination, and philosophy. DLC LNHT

89 _____. ¡Ecce Pericles! Guatemala: Tipografía Nacional, 1945. xxv, 649 pp. 2d ed. 2 vols. San José: EDUCA, 1971. 396, 404 pp.

A novelized description of the regime of Manuel Estrada Cabrera and the terror by which it ruled, based on the author's recollections. The emphasis is on the brutality of the regime, and the portions dealing with the dictatorship parallel Asturias's El señor presidente, which deals with the same regime. Includes an account of the unionist movement

(Arévalo Martínez, Rafael)
and the demonstrations that eventually brought down the regime; hails the Unionist party, its goal, and its efforts in the confrontation. DLC LNHT BNG

90 _____. El embajador de Torlania. Guatemala: Editorial Landívar, 1960. 88 pp.
A short story, which actually occupies only about half the volume after a lengthy prologue, set in a diplomatic reception in the post-World War II world. The story is in a sense a sequel to Viaje a Ipanda. It deals with various schemes for a world league of states and the advantages they gave the respective nations. Employing a modern setting, with references to the Cold War, the investment patterns of the superpowers, etc., it portrays the world of diplomacy and the aspirations of the states and their representatives. DLC LNHT

91 _____. El hombre que parecía un caballo. Many editions. Quezaltenango: Tipografía Arte Nuevo, 1915. 70 pp.
A discussion of human foibles and behavior through comparison of human and animal behavior, one of the author's favorite themes. His best-known work, more a short story than a novel, it has passed through numerous editions and has often been published with various of his other works. The author excelled at this type of psychozoological story in which he considers many of the characteristics of the Latin culture. Some of the later editions combine this volume with others by the author, a situation that is reflected in the titles used. DLC DLC-LDS-623 LNHT BNG BNCR

92 _____. Hondura. Guatemala: Folletín de La Hora, 1947. 170 pp. Latest ed. Guatemala: Ministerio de Educación Pública, 1959. 254 pp. Illus.
Although the cover refers to this work as a novel, it is more like a series of semiautobiographical short stories dealing with Guatemalan life, particularly that of university students during the 1910-20 era. There are numerous references to figures from Guatemala, Honduras, El Salvador, and Nicaragua then studying in Guatemala, describing the author's contacts with them and the events of their student days. The essays are episodic and the subjects disparate; although they include commentaries on general questions and world politics as well as domestic political themes reflecting the dictatorship of Manuel Estrada Cabrera, the emphasis remains on the idylic days of student life and intellectual companionship among a group that included many subsequent literary figures from the region. DLC BNG

93 _____. Manuel Aldano: la lucha por la vida. Guatemala: Talleres Gutenberg, 1922. 149 pp.
An autobiographical novel published several years after its completion, dealing with the author's adolescence. It represents one of his earliest efforts, revealing much about his character and outlook as well as his talent for capturing emotion. The emphasis on the struggle for existence and the hardships of life that came to characterize his later works are evident here, indicating their origins in his own experience. The work indicates the author's view of the indolence that characterized tropical lands, his critical view of the Indians, and also his rejection of the imperialism of the Anglo-Saxons. DLC LNHT BNG

94 _____. El mundo de los maharachías. Guatemala: Unión Tipográfica, 1938. 126 pp.
A fanciful visit to a fictional land inhabited by monkeys who live in an idyllic socialistic world without cares, one of the author's numerous works using animals to satirically portray human foibles. The tale is one of imperialism, conquest, intrigue, international rivalry, and treachery, with the various races of semihuman animals struggling in the same way as human nations. Clearly reflecting the author's view of Yankee imperialism trying to dominate the innocents of the hemisphere, a theme that appears in his other works. DLC LNHT BNG

95 _____. Obras escogidas. Guatemala: Editorial Universitaria, 1959. 525 pp.
A collection of Arévalo Martínez's works, covering fifty years of his career and including poetry, short stories, and even some of his novels. The works are reprinted without commentary or analysis. DLC LNHT BNG BNCR

96 _____. La oficina de paz en Orolandia: novela del imperialismo yanqui. Guatemala: Sánchez & de Guise, 1925. 2d ed. Guatemala: Editorial Landívar, 1966. 118 pp.
One of the best-known works of this prominent Guatemalan novelist. Uses the allegory of a ficticious governmental unit of an imaginary country, detailing its efforts, its foibles, and its effect on others to assail Yankee imperialism. The office is clearly a satirical portrayal of the Pan American Union, seen as a vehicle for Yankee dominance of the hemisphere. DLC LNHT BNG BNCR

97 _____. El señor Monitot. Guatemala: Sánchez & de Guise, 1922. 215 pp.
A series of short stories written between 1914 and 1920, set in his native land and dealing with varied Guatemalan themes. They include tales of Colonial days and more modern themes, including the Yankees. Most of the stories deal with the similarity of people to animals, thus satirizing the types of individuals discussed. One of the studies, "Las fieras del trópico," was originally written as part of a trilogy that included the well-known El hombre que parecia un caballo, but its publication was delayed because it was feared that the government of Manuel Estrada Cabrera would consider it too political. DLC LNHT BNG BNCR

98 _____. La signatura de la esfinge. Guatemala: Imprenta Electra, 1933. 53 pp.
Another of the author's psychological short stories employing animals to satirize human behavior. DLC LNHT

(Arévalo Martínez, Rafael)

99 _____. *Viaje a Ipanda, 1939.* Guatemala: Centro Editorial, 1939. 228 pp.

Using the familiar vehicle of a description of a trip to a mythical land inhabited by animals, this work provides a picture of an ideal democracy leaning toward socialism but functioning entirely within the Liberal-Democratic tradition, and operating within the limits of constitutionalism under a law of peace and contentment, where the people rule and the role of the state is limited to supporting the individual and the family. Written at the end of the depression and on the eve of World War II, it reflects a time when the forces of communism, fascism, and democracy were contending strongly for support; it clearly was written as an endorsement of democracy and hence a rejection of communism and fascism. DLC LNHT BNG

100 _____. *Una vida.* Guatemala: Imprenta Electra, 1914. 46 pp. Illus.

The world through the eyes of a child, which is in fact an autobiographical account of the author's youth. DLC LNHT

101 Arévalo Morales, Rafael. *Verapacenses de valía.* Guatemala: Impresos Arte y Creación, 1977. 226 pp. Illus.

A series of short biographies of illustrious personages from the Verapaz region of Guatemala, drawing upon individuals from throughout history and briefly describing their deeds. BNG

102 Arévalo Zelaya, Rubén. *Empresa Guatemalteca de Electricidad Inc.* Guatemala: Imprenta Hispania, 1945. 38 pp.

Part of the revolutionary regime's case against foreign companies, this booklet contains the government's claim for payment of back taxes from an American company. It details the history of a firm that had been founded by German investors, then expropriated by the government and sold to an American owner in 1918.

103 Argüello, Santiago. *Barrios y Ubico: la obra creadora de dos constructores de la nación.* Havana: Tipografía Aguilar, 1937. 36 pp.

A brief tract in which the unionist leader hails the works of Ubico and his contribution to Guatemala, comparing Ubico to his hero, Barrios. Though more of the essay deals with Barrios than with Ubico, the acclaim for Ubico's creative impetus, energy, and various projects is clear. While the author stops short of calling Ubico a new leader of unionism, this is implicit in the parallel drawn with Barrios, especially since the section dealing with Barrios notes that a man of such creative impulses could not be expected to limit himself to a single country. LNHT

104 Arias, Arturo. *Ideologías, literatura y sociedad durante la revolución guatemalteca, 1944-1954.* Havana: Casa de las Américas, 1979. 304 pp. Biblio., notes, tables.

A sociological study, written from a Marxist and dependency perspective, that seeks to study commentary about the 1944-54 era. Though it employs some literary works and contends that its purpose is to apply sociological analysis to literature, it actually focuses on political and economic studies of this period of Guatemalan history, particularly on the writings of the participants and on studies by later scholars. References to literary works are few. The author argues that the scholarship of the 1960s regarding this era reflected cultural dependency and the dominance of Yankee investigators, all of whom cast the era in terms of a problem of social integration and ladinization. This, the author contends, is a misinterpretation that serves imperialistic interests by ignoring the real class conflicts in the nation and failing to apply the true Marxist theoretical perspective, which he feels alone provides an explanation of the events of these years. He contends that Guatemalans themselves are coming to this conclusion during the 1970s. DLC

105 Armas, Daniel. *Diccionario de la expresión popular guatemalteca.* Guatemala: Tipografía Nacional, 1971. 423 pp. Biblio.

An alphabetical listing, by initial word, of words and idioms peculiar and common to Guatemala, with definitions and examples of their use. DLC

106 Armas Lara, Marcial. *El folklore guatemalteco en la tradición y leyenda a través de los siglos.* Guatemala: Tipografía Nacional, 1970. 200 pp. Illus.

Principally a catalog of Guatemalan public celebrations and holidays, describing the dances and functions that characterize them and commenting on their significance, origin, and religious links. Includes some disparate folktales. DPU

107 _____. *Origen de la marimba, su desenvolvimiento y otros instrumentos músicos.* Guatemala: Tipografía Nacional, 1970. 116 pp. Illus.

A discussion of Guatemalan musical instruments, emphasizing the Guatemalan argument that the marimba is native to that nation and citing evidence of precursors in the Indian codices, though without demonstrating a linkage with later instruments. Includes discussion of other instruments and musical tradition, focusing primarily on the Indian, as well as comments on prominent Guatemalan marimba players and groups. DLC

108 _____. *El renacimiento de la danza guatemalteca y el origen de la marimba.* Guatemala: Ministerio de Educación Pública, 1964. 452 pp. Illus.

The president of the Guatemalan Folklore Society presents a collection of random descriptions of various regional dances and their origins, as well as a history of dance and musical instruments in Guatemala. Most are traced to the pre-Columbian era, with emphasis on their local roots and patriotic implications. Regional customs and their origin and persistence in modern times are also noted. Many specific and typical dances are described, with illustrations of the costumes. DLC LNHT BNG

109 Arriola, Jorge Luís, ed. Cultura indígena de Guatemala: ensayos de antropología social. Guatemala: Seminario de Integración Social Guatemalteca, 1956. 302 pp. 2d ed. Guatemala: El Seminario, 1959. 326 pp.
    The papers presented at the first conference sponsored by the Seminario de Integración Social during June 1956, containing contributions by leading scholars from throughout the world. The papers are broad, encompassing history, economy, social relations, psychological aspects, and cultural change among the Indians. BNG

110 ____. Economía de Guatemala. Guatemala: Ministerio de Educación Pública, 1958. 313 pp.
    A collection of nine previously published essays by well-known economic scholars dealing with various aspects of the Guatemalan economy and its development, problems, characteristics, and dominant sectors, including the financial sector. Some consider broader isthmian aspects, though most focus on Guatemala. DLC LNHT BNCR

111 Arriola, Jorge Luís. Ensayos sobre psicología indígena. Guatemala: Sánchez & de Guise, 1933. 49 pp. Biblio.
    A discussion of native Indian religious beliefs and mythology, with emphasis on their origins and impact on Guatemalan culture, contending that religious beliefs constitute the key to understanding Indians and that the impact of these beliefs on Guatemalan society constitutes an important aspect of the national culture. BNG

112 ____. Gálvez en la encrucijada: ensayo crítico en torno al humanismo político de un gobernante. Mexico: B. Costa-Amic, 1961. 467 pp. Biblio., notes, appendixes.
    A detailed, sympathetic biography of Gálvez, attempting to link him to the present by comparing him to Arévalo and contending that only these two presidents were humanistically inclined, in the sense that they focused on human problems and services to the people. Includes a large section of reprinted documents and is based on research in secondary literature and documents. DLC LNHT

113 ____, ed. Integración económica de Centroamérica. Guatemala: Ministerio de Educación Pública, 1959. 383 pp.
    The addresses, papers, and commentaries presented at the First Seminar of Central American Integration, held in San Salvador in November 1957. Includes addresses by the Salvadoran president and the secretary general of ODECA, and papers on various pertinent themes by Central American scholars and political figures, with extensive commentaries.

Also includes transcripts of the round-table discussions. The papers focus on the major themes defined by ODECA as central to the success of the integration movement. DLC LNHT BNG

114 ____. Integración social en Guatemala. 2 vols. Guatemala: Ministerio de Educación Pública, 1956-59. 429, 454 pp. Biblio.
    A collection of papers and commentaries from a conference of this title sponsored by the Seminario de Integración Social and held in Guatemala during December 1956. The leading Guatemalan, American, and foreign scholars participated, studying social integration at the national and regional levels and examining the prevailing anthropological theories and their applicability to Guatemala. The papers stress the impact of the changes on both the Indians and the entire nation, considering cultural, social, and economic aspects. The second volume, published later, contains transcriptions of the round-table discussions that followed the papers. The papers are briefly summarized, their texts having been already published in the first volume. DLC BNG

115 Arriola, Jorge Luís. El libro de las geonomías de Guatemala: diccionario etimológico. 3d ed. Guatemala: Ministerio de Educación Pública, 1973. 710 pp. Biblio.
    A dictionary of the place names of Guatemala, providing data on the origin and significance of the terms. DLC

116 ____. Pequeño diccionario de voces guatemaltecas: ordenadas etimologicamente. Guatemala: Tipografía Nacional, 1941. 194 pp. 2d ed. Guatemala: Ministerio de Educación Pública, 1954. 199 pp.
    A dictionary of Guatemalan place names and words of Indian origin, arranged alphabetically, with definitions, explanations of the origins of the terms, and location of the villages. The emphasis on place names leaves little space for discussion of idioms in rural conversation. DLC BNG BNCR

117 Arriola, Osmundo, ed. Quezaltenango: álbum conmemorativo de la inauguración del ferrocarril nacional de Los Altos, patrocinado por el comité de festejos y la municipalidad de mil novecientos treinta. Quezaltenango: Tipografía Arte Nuevo, 1930. 48 pp. Illus.
    A collection of photos accompanied by brief emotional statements and poetry acclaiming the ill-fated effort to construct an electric railroad in western Guatemala that was to provide passenger service to the region through tramlike single and double cars. Includes photos of the bridges, stations, cars, track, etc. LNHT

118 Arrocha, Angela Delli Sante. Juan José Arévalo: pensador contemporáneo. Mexico: B. Costa-Amic, 1962. 112 pp. Biblio., notes.
    A sympathetic analysis of Arévalo's ideas, based on his published works. Emphasizes the

consistency of his viewpoint, seeing the policies of his regime as the logical outcome of
his views. DLC LNHT

119 Arzú, José. El diálogo de los bostezos y
otros motivos nacionales. Guatemala:
Tipografía Nacional, 1945. 348 pp.
    A series of radio skits portraying various
aspects of Guatemalan life from the viewpoint
of the man in the street, showing the everyday
trials and tribulations of the poor. DLC BNG

120 _____. Pepe Batres íntimo: su familia, su
correspondencia, sus papeles. Guatemala:
Sánchez & de Guise, 1940. 268 pp. Illus.
    A biography, with annexed letters, of a
Guatemalan poet and political figure of the
late nineteenth and early twentieth century,
focusing on his family and private life. The
initial chapters consist of fifty pages devoted to the genealogy of his ancestors. The
final half of the volume consists of a series
of letters, excerpts from his writings, and
commentaries on his works. DLC LNHT BNG

121 Asturias, Francisco. Historia de la medicina
en Guatemala. Guatemala: Tipografía
Nacional, 1902. 557 pp. Illus. Latest ed.
Guatemala: Editorial Universitaria, 1958.
477 pp. Illus.
    Contains chapters describing each of the
significant hospitals in the nation, giving
its date of construction and discussing its
history and facilities. Other chapters describe the lives of well-known Guatemalan
medical specialists and of the evolution of
medical education in Guatemala. Written in
1902, the volume focuses on the nineteenth
century, though many institutions are traced
back to the Colonial era. DLC LNHT BNG

122 _____. Recordatorio: breve panorama
histórico de la medicina. Guatemala: Sánchez
& de Guise, 1943. 63 pp.
    A physician's overview of the development
of medical practice in Guatemala from the
conquest to 1943. LNHT

123 _____. La reforma: San Marcos. Guatemala:
Unión Tipográfica, 1958. 96 pp.
    A compilation of data regarding the impact
in San Marcos of the Liberal reforms of the
latter portion of the nineteenth century.
Includes reproductions of documents and excerpts from existing historical studies. DLC

124 Asturias, Miguel Ángel. Hombres de maíz.
Buenos Aires: Editorial Losada, 1949. 285
pp. Latest ed. San José: EDUCA, 1974.
Men of Maize. New York: Delacorte Press,
1975. 337 pp.
    A novel of Indian traditions in a modern
setting. By mixing realism and mysticism,
this work focuses on the problems of the
Mayans in a modern age and the conflict between their heritage and the demands of modern
civilization. The focus is the sacred nature
of corn as the staff of life and its corruption by modern consumerism and commerce. The
characters move between the real and mystical

worlds, the latter populated by the ancient
Maya deities who seek to protect the Indians
and punish those committing injustices against
them. DLC LNHT BNG BNCR

125 _____. Leyendas de Guatemala. Madrid:
Imprenta Argis, 1930. 207 pp. Illus. 5th
ed. Buenos Aires: Editorial Losada, 1973.
169 pp.
    A series of essays and short stories based
on the Indian traditions and folklore of
Guatemala, recounting the nation's folkloric
heritage in vivid prose. Depicts the folklore
as literary works of art as well as the basis
of the nation's character. DLC LNHT BNG

126 _____. Mi mejor obra: autoantología.
Mexico: Editorial Novaro, 1973. 236 pp. 2d
ed. Mexico and Barcelona: Editorial Novaro,
1974. 236 pp.
    A selection by the author of parts of all
of his major works. Provides an indication of
the portions he considers most interesting and
important. The 1974 edition uses the title Lo
mejor de mi obra. DLC LNHT

127 _____. Mulata del Tal. Buenos Aires:
Editorial Losada, 1963. 280 pp. 3d ed.
Buenos Aires: Editorial Losada, 1968.
300 pp.
The Mulatta and Mr. Fly. New York:
Delacorte, 1967. 307 pp. Latest ed.
Harmondsworth: Penguin, 1970. 332 pp.
    One of the author's best-known and most
complex novels. Draws heavily upon the Indian
mythology that he loves, mixing the mystical
and magical with the reality of the present
lives of the Indians of his native land. DLC
LNHT BNG

128 _____. Novelas y cuentos de juventud. Paris:
Centre de Recherches de l'Institut d'Etudes
Hispaniques, 1971. 359 pp.
    A collection of the author's earliest
essays, which are not easily obtainable
elsewhere. DLC LNHT

129 _____. Obras completas. 3 vols. Madrid:
Ediciones Aguilar, 1967. 1087, 932, 1108 pp.
3d ed. Madrid: Ediciones Aguilar, 1969.
1087, 932, 1108 pp.
    A collection of Asturias's works, in fine
print on thin paper to enable the inclusion of
all in a minimum of volumes, gathered following his Noble Prize in literature to provide a
handy means for consulting all his works. DLC
LNHT BNG

130 _____. Obras escogidas. 2 vols. Madrid:
Ediciones Aguilar, 1955. 2d ed. Madrid:
Ediciones Aguilar, 1964. 1275 pp. Index.
    Principally poetry, arranged by year of its
writing, but also including reproductions of
several of his novels and essays. DLC LNHT

131 _____. Los ojos de los enterrados. Buenos
Aires: Editorial Losada, 1960. 482 pp. 5th
ed. Buenos Aires: Editorial Losada, 1972.
492 pp.

(Asturias, Miguel Ángel)
The Eyes of the Interred. New York:
Delacorte, 1973. 695 pp. Latest ed. London:
Cape, 1974. 695 pp.

This series of novels constitutes the so-called banana trilogy focusing on the clash between development and traditional Guatemalan (and Latin) values and between the new ways and the traditional societies of the indigenous cultures. These novels were instrumental in Asturias's being awarded the Nobel Prize for literature. The series details the impact of an unscrupulous Yankee entrepreneur, focusing on the role of the banana companies in Central America, a regional preoccupation widely reflected in literary and intellectual circles. The novels also encompass broader themes regarding the impact of modernization and the role of the multinational corporations. As such, they reflect significant trends in both the Central American and the Latin American novel, which in the name of "realism" are increasingly adopting political and social reformist themes. The portrayal of political events reveals considerable stereotyping, condemning the Yankee emphasis on power and the Green Pope who worships the dollar, but effectively conveys the feelings of helplessness and exploitation of the poor and the stifling psychological impact of external forces. DLC LNHT BNG BNCR

132   . El papa verde. Buenos Aires:
Editorial Losada, 1954. 319 pp. Latest ed.
Buenos Aires: Editorial Losada, 1973.
315 pp.
The Green Pope. New York: Delacorte, 1971.
386 pp.
Zelenyi papa; roman. Moscow: Isdatel'stvo
khudozhestvennoi literatury, 1964. 340 pp.
See item GU131. DLC LNHT BNG BNCR

133   . El señor presidente. Mexico: n.p.,
1946. Many editions in several languages.
An early and by far the most famous of Asturias's novels, this work details the corrupt and brutal actions of a military dictatorship in his homeland, portraying the awesome power of total control of the citizenry and the arbitrary actions of the regime. While written as a denunciation of all dictatorships, the book actually refers to the regime of General Manuel Estrada Cabrera, which dominated Guatemala during the initial decades of the twentieth century and fell from power in 1920. Although the subsequent revolutionaries employed it as propaganda against the Ubico regime, it clearly reflected the methods of the nineteenth-century dictator characteristic of Asturias's youth, which were outdated by the time the work was published. The work is an effective portrayal of the methods of the nineteenth-century regimes and the despair they inspired. DLC LNHT BNG BNCR

134   . Sociología guatemalteca: el problema
social del indio. Guatemala: Sánchez & de
Guise, 1923. 59 pp. Latest ed. Paris:

Centre de Recherches d'Institut d'Études Hispanques, 1971. 146 pp.
Originally Asturias's thesis at the University of Guatemala, it deals with sociological subjects at a time when the discipline was new to the nation. One of the first writers to call attention to the plight of the Indians and propose measures to improve their lives. His attention to this subject is reflected in his later novels, and a reading of this thesis is essential to an understanding of the sources of his concern for and identification with the Indians. DLC LNHT

135   . Viento fuerte. Buenos Aires:
Editorial Losada, 1950. 205 pp. 6th ed.
Buenos Aires: Editorial Losada, 1972.
The Cyclone. London: Peter Owen, 1967.
238 pp.
Strong Wind. New York: Delacorte, 1968.
242 pp.
See item GU131. DLC LNHT BNG BNCR

136   . Viernes de dolores. Buenos Aires:
Editorial Losada, 1972. 314 pp. 2d ed.
Buenos Aires: Editorial Losada, 1972.
314 pp.
A novel set in the days of the Estrada Cabrera dictatorship that served as the basis for El señor presidente, this time focusing on the Holy Week festivities and the tradition of lampooning the powers and elites by the university students. This feature allows for criticism of the regime and its supporters, though the emphasis is on general revelry and local color, with extensive use of Guatemalan idioms, modisms, and local humor. DLC LNHT

137   . Weekend en Guatemala. Buenos Aires:
Editorial Goyanarte, 1956. 228 pp. Latest
ed. Buenos Aires: Editorial Losada, 1971.
233 pp.
Uik-end v Gvatemale; rasskazy. Moscow:
Izdatel'stvo inostrannoi literatury, 1961.
236 pp.
The most overtly political of Asturias's works, this ringing denunciation of Yankee imperialism was written as a protest against the CIA-sponsored revolt in 1954 that overthrew the leftist government of Jacabo Arbenz; it was written shortly after the event. It condemns all Yankees and intervention, portraying the Yankees as heinous beasts responsible for the destruction caused by the conflict as well as for the nation's problems, while continuing his attack on the United Fruit Company and its economic domination of the nation. Seeking to portray the outrage of Guatemalan peasants, the work offers stereotypes in which all Yankees are villains and are responsible for all evil, and all Guatemalans are innocent victims. This novel is less complex than his other writings and clearly constitutes the bitter cry of a partisan of Arbenz, written from exile after the new regime of Carlos Castillo Armas had revoked his Guatemalan citizenship because of his association with Arbenz. DLC LNHT BNG BNCR

138 Asturias Montenegro, R., and G. García Trejo.
     Terremoto 76. Guatemala: Ediciones Pop,
     1976. 128 pp. Illus., maps.
        A detailed discussion of the 1976 earth-
     quake, with photos of the damage, statistics,
     and maps showing the affected areas. DLC
     LNHT BNG

139 Aybar, Jose M. de Soto. Dependency and Inter-
     vention: The Case of Guatemala in 1954.
     Boulder, Colo.: Westview Press, 1978. xxi,
     374 pp. Index, biblio., notes, tables,
     appendixes.
        An ideological, dependency-based analysis
     originally prepared as a political science
     dissertation, employing secondary works and
     focusing on theory. The author argues that
     Guatemala is a typical "case study" and gen-
     eralizes from the Guatemalan data. DLC LNHT

140 Badescu, S. Guatemala. Bucharest: Editura
     Ştiinţifică, 1957. 119 pp.

141 Baglay, Marat Viktorovich. Gosudarstvennyĭ
     stroĭ Gvatemaly. Moscow: Gosudarstvennoe
     Izdatel'stvo iuridicheskoi literatury, 1959.
     59 pp. Illus.
     DLC

142 Bahiana, Henrique Paulo. A Guatemala em
     marcha. Rio de Janeiro: Gráfica Tupy
     Editôra, 1962. 110 pp. Illus., maps.
        A general description of present-day
     Guatemala, its geography, culture, and cus-
     toms. Designed to acquaint the Brazilian
     public and Portuguese readers with that na-
     tion, and serve as an introduction to en-
     courage interest in, travel to, and business
     with Guatemala. DLC BNG

143 Balsells Rivera, Alfredo. El venadeado y
     otros cuentos. Guatemala: Imprenta
     Universitaria, 1958. 194 pp.
        A series of short stories describing
     Guatemalan life during the author's career
     from 1904 to 1940, originally published in
     contemporary newspapers. The stories mirror
     the problems of life during the dictatorships
     that characterized these years. DLC BNG

144 Barahona Streber, Óscar, and J. Walter Dittel,
     eds. Bases de la seguridad social en
     Guatemala. 2 vols. Guatemala: Instituto
     Guatemalteco de Seguridad Social, 1948-49.
     366, 260 pp. Tables.
        An official summary of the plan and origins
     of the Institute of Social Security's program
     of accident insurance. The first volume re-
     produces, analyzes, and acclaims the prelim-
     inary studies that enabled a systematic
     launching of the Institute. The second volume
     quotes extensively from the appropriate legis-
     lation establishing the program, adding ex-
     planatory text. DLC LNHT BNG BNCR

145 Barcarel, Ángel Horacio. La vialidad en
     Guatemala. Guatemala: Sánchez & de Guise,
     1928. 53 pp. Notes, maps.
        A brief history and analysis of the highway
     labor tax, tracing its origins to Colonial

times and discussing its use by the governments of the late nineteenth and early twentieth centuries in seeking to maintain and
expand the nation's highway network. Contains
useful tables regarding the state of the highways and the budget of the Highway Department
and the use of labor under the vialidad from
the 1880s to 1928. DLC LNHT

146 Barillas, Manuel L. La administración del
     general don Manuel L. Barillas 1885-1892.
     Guatemala: Tipografía Nacional, 1892.
     420 pp.
        An officially sponsored volume extolling
     the regime's programs and projects, with de-
     tails of all the various activities. It pro-
     vides considerable data about the state of the
     nation. BNG

147 Barnoya Gálvez, Francisco. Fray Ignacio
     Barnoya: prócer ignorado: su actuación en
     pro de la independencia de Guatemala y en
     contra de la anexión de Chiapas a México.
     Guatemala: Editorial del Ejército, 1967. 238
     pp. Biblio., illus. 2d ed. Guatemala:
     Ministerio de Educación Pública, 1970. 462
     pp. Biblio., illus., maps.
        A brief essay, followed by excerpts from
     appropriate documents from the Archivo General
     de Centroamérica and the church archives in
     Guatemala City. They comprise all but forty
     pages of the volume and detail the activities
     of the title character, a cleric who played a
     considerable role in the independence movement
     and was a staunch opponent of the Mexican
     efforts to annex Central America. The focus
     is on the Mexican annexation of Chiapas, which
     the friar opposed vigorously. The documents
     provide insights into the politics of the era,
     in addition to illuminating the role of Fray
     Barnoya. DLC LNHT BNG

148 ____. Genealogía de la familia Verdugo.
     Guatemala: Editorial del Ejército, 1969. 63
     pp. Illus.
        A family genealogy from Colonial days,
     listing by birthdate all children of the
     various lines, with single-paragraph descrip-
     tions of some of their careers. DLC BNG

149 ____. Genealogía de las familias Barnoya de
     España y de Guatemala, 1614-1966. Guatemala:
     Editorial del Ejército, 1967. 48 pp. Notes,
     illus.
        A family genealogy listing birthdates for
     all the various lines, with brief résumés of
     the lives of some of the individuals. DLC
     LNHT BNG

150 ____. Han de estar y estarán: cuentos y
     leyendas de Guatemala. Santiago: Zig-Zag,
     1938. 169 pp. Latest ed. Guatemala:
     Editorial Piedra Santa, 1974. 173 pp. Illus.
        A series of short stories based on
     Guatemalan legends, designed to popularize and
     preserve them. The stories include pre-
     Columbian Indian legends, Colonial tales, and
     folktales from the modern era. Some of the
     titles indicate the regions from which the

stories come. Includes a glossary of Indian
terms and modisms. DLC LNHT BNG

151 Barquero, Antonio. En Guatemala: crónicas.
Guatemala: Tipografía Nacional, 1913. 80 pp.
Illus.
A description of Guatemala hailing the
impact of the government and projects of the
Estrada Cabrera regime. Includes photos.
Provides a look at the republic during this
period through physical descriptions of the
cities. DLC

152 Barreda, Pedro Froilán. Geografía e historia
de correos y telecomunicaciones de Guatemala:
sus estudios. Guatemala: Tipografía
Nacional, 1960. 439 pp. Illus., maps,
tables.
A detailed examination of the expansion of
postal and telegraph service in Guatemala from
independence through the 1930s, replete with
appropriate maps to show the extension of
departmental service. Although there are
references to the 1950s and photos are from
this era, most of the discussion refers to
earlier times, with only brief mention of
contemporary service. Treatment is topical in
the different realms, though with departmental
consideration in a separate section that emphasizes the extension of service throughout
the nation. DLC LNHT BNG

153 _____. Guía de comunicaciones: informativa
sobre los servicios de correos, fardos
postales, telégrafos, teléfonos, cables
submarinos, ferrocarriles y vapores.
Guatemala: Tipografía Nacional, 1927. 686
pp. Illus., tables.
A brief history of the Guatemalan postal,
telegraph, and transportation services, from
the Liberal revolution of 1871 until the
1920s, recounting the expansion of service and
the professionalization of the personnel,
followed by an extensive listing of the contemporary services. Includes reproduction of
appropriate laws and decrees, as well as the
existing customs regulations and duty lists
from the contemporary era, and an exhaustive
listing of the various stations and services.
DLC LNHT BNG BNCR

154 _____. Ligeros apuntes relacionados con el
servicio de Correos Nacionales de la República
de Guatemala, a base de las leyes locales e
internacionales del ramo. Guatemala:
Tipografía Nacional, 1923. 152 pp.
An official statement by the Postal Service, describing its activities and functions,
listing its districts and classification, and
explaining rates. BNG

155 Barreda Avila, Rubén. Castillo Armas el
quinto jinete del apocalipsis (drama
nacional). Guatemala: Imprenta Iberia, 1954.
28 pp. Illus. 2d ed. Guatemala: Impreso
EGSA, 1958. 27 pp.
A condemnation of the Castillo Armas regime
and the National Liberation Movement, written
by a supporter of the Arbenz regime. Employs
picturesque language to charge that Castillo

Armas and his supporters are destroying the
nation, its people, and its culture. TxU

156 _____. Guaridas infernales: mi drama vivida
durante, 1096 días en las mazmorras
penitenciarias, en el período en el que Carlos
Castillo Armas detentó poder y ultrajó la
dignidad nacional. Guatemala: n.p., 1960.
176 pp.
The memoirs from prison of a supporter of
the Arbenz regime, recounting his mistreatment
and experience in prison during the regime of
Castillo Armas. DLC LNHT

157 Barrera Túnchez, J. Antonio. Tablas de vida:
República de Guatemala, 1964. Guatemala:
Dirección General de Estadística, 1967. 67
pp. Illus., tables.
Life expectancy tables for Guatemalans,
based on the 1964 census data, with comparative figures for Costa Rica, Panama, and the
U.S., presented by age group in tabular and
graphic form. DLC LNHT

158 Barreto, Mariano. Carta histórica,
filosófica, religiosa. León: Tipografía La
Patria, 1924. 127 pp.
A letter to the bishop of Guatemala criticizing his stands, written as part of the
Liberal confrontation with the church. It
specifically challenges censorship, although
it deals with the entire question of the basis
of religion and the nature of man, quoting
extensively from various classical and biblical scholars and church edicts. While the
author claims that he writes as a Catholic, he
includes an edict by the bishop declaring the
volume heretical and banning its reading by
practicing members of the church. DLC BNCR

159 Barrientos, Alfonso Enrique. Enrique Gómez
Carrillo. Barcelona: n.p., 1959. 2d ed.
Guatemala: Ministerio de Educación Pública,
1973. 306 pp. Index, biblio., notes, illus.
A study of the life and works of this
prominent Guatemalan writer, with chapters
analyzing the principal influences on his life
through discussion of the places he lived,
their characteristics, and the events that
influenced him, followed by critical analysis
of the themes and techniques he employed. The
work hails Gómez Carrillo's contributions, and
was published on the occasion of the centennial of his birth. LNHT

160 _____. Gómez Carrillo: 30 años después.
Barcelona: Ediciones Rumbos, 1959. 253 pp.
Notes, illus.
A detailed biography of one of Guatemala's
best-known writers, based on extensive study
of his works, his correspondence, and interviews with those who knew him. This volume
seeks to reveal his personality, emphasizing
personal details and employing a rich lore of
anecdotes. The author even retraced many of
Gómez Carrillo's travels, and takes care to
provide the context of his trips by sketching
events in Guatemala and other spots at the
time of his visits. Offers new insights into

its subject through its imaginative use of
sources. DLC LNHT BNG

161 Barrington and Company, Inc., New York.
Industrial Development of Guatemala. New
York: Agency for International Development,
1962. 190 pp. Illus., tables.
    A survey of the current state of industry,
its problems, and future prospects. Based on
interviews with over 100 executives in that
nation, it provides insights into the perceptions of industrialists and managers, as well
as into the economy. DLC

162 Barrios, Justo Rufino. Carta que el general
J. Rufino Barrios, presidente constitucional
de la República de Guatemala, dirige a sus
amigos del Partido Liberal de Centro América,
con motivo de los trabajos sobre la unión de
estas repúblicas. Guatemala: n.p., 1883.
15 pp.
    An official statement of Barrios's unionist
program, which eventually led to his efforts
to impose his program by force of arms. Cst-H

163 Barton, Edwin. Physician to the Mayas: The
Story of Dr. Carroll Behrhorst. Philadelphia:
Fortress Press, 1970. 208 pp. Illus., maps.
    A well-written account of some of the expe-
riences of a Yankee missionary doctor who went
to work among the Cakchiquel Indians of
Guatemala. Details his struggle for acceptance, his efforts on behalf of the health of
the Indians in Chimaltenango, and his eventual
construction of a modern clinic there. DLC
LNHT

164 Bascom Jones, J., ed. El "Libro Azul" de
Guatemala (the "Blue Book" of Guatemala),
1915: relato e historia sobre la vida de las
personas más prominentes; Narrative and History of the Lives of the Most Prominent People; Historia condensada de la república;
Condensed History of the Republic; Artículos
especiales sobre el comercio, agricultura y
riqueza mineral basado sobre las estadísticas
oficiales; Special Articles Relative to the
Commerce, Agriculture and Mineral Wealth,
Based on Official Statistics. New Orleans:
Searcy & Pfaff, 1915. 406 pp. Illus., maps.
    An elaborate volume with text in both
Spanish and English, designed to commemorate
the Estrada Cabrera regime but containing a
compendium of material including a brief historical overview of the republic, essays on
its most prominent historical figures, and
articles on its economic and agricultural
development and prospects, all, of course,
hailing the efforts of the regime and its
accomplishments. There are extensive illustrations of the nation, particularly of the
regime's public works. Includes articles about
the leading figures of the regime, as well as
of principal businessmen, the diplomatic
corps, military officers, and other significant groups. DLC LNHT

165 Batres, Luís. Centro América: su presente,
su pasado y porvenir. San José: Imprenta
Nacional, 1879. 48 pp.

A Conservative denunciation of the Barrios
regime, written from exile by a former minister of the ousted Carrera government, arguing that the prosperity of the nation
reflected the coffee growing stimulated by the
Carrera era rather than the programs of
Barrios. DLC

166 Batres Jáuregui, Antonio. Bosquejo de
Guatemala, en la América Central. New York:
Imprenta Las Novedades, 1883. 70 pp.
Sketch of Guatemala in Central America. New
York: Imprenta Las Novedades, 1883. 78 pp.
Notes, tables.
    A province-by-province description empha-
sizing the economic development prospects,
climate, and agricultural products as well as
physical description, written in English and
clearly designed to promote investment and
interest in trade with Guatemala. Includes
glowing accounts of the nation's central location to world trade and port and coastal facilities. LNHT

167 _____. El Dr. Mariano Gálvez y su época.
Guatemala: Sánchez & de Guise, 1925. 117 pp.
Illus. 2d ed. Guatemala: Ministerio de
Educación Pública, 1957. 146 pp. Illus.
    A brief sympathetic and enthusiastic ac-
count of the life of a leading Guatemalan
political figure of the independence era,
focusing particularly on his efforts to reform
education. DLC LNHT BNG BNCR

168 _____. Literatos guatemaltecos: Landívar e
Irisarri, con un discurso preliminar sobre el
desenvolvimiento de las ciencias y las letras
en Guatemala. Guatemala: Tipografía
Nacional, 1896. 312 pp. 2d ed. Guatemala:
Ministerio de Educación Pública, 1957.
192 pp.
    Sympathetic biographies of two well-known
Guatemalan figures of the late Colonial and
independence era, by another prominent
Guatemalan writer and scholar. The portion of
the volume dealing with Landívar is rather
short and consists of literary criticism and
excerpts from his poems, with some biographical data. The major portion of the work is
devoted to Irisarri, emphasizing his travels
throughout the hemisphere and Europe and his
service to many countries during the independence era, but also including chapters of
literary criticism and a discussion of his
philosophy. The second edition is entitled
Landívar e Irisarri: literatos guatemaltecos.
DLC LNHT BNG BNCR

169 _____. 1821-1921: Memorias de un siglo.
Guatemala: Tipografía Nacional, 1949. 706
pp. Vol. 3 of La América Central ante la
historia.
    A detailed and documented general history
of the region by a well-known Guatemalan lawyer and scholar who was one of the republic's
leading Conservative historians. The third
volume deals with the nineteenth century and
was published posthumously in 1949. It mixes
recollection of his youth during the days of
Carrera and a scholarly account of his regime,

(Batres Jáuregui, Antonio)
replete with extensive anecdotes about the
era. The account of subsequent regimes,
though still Conservative in tone, continues
the same mix but includes the political memoirs of the author, who served as a diplomat
and a cabinet member under serveral presidents. The first two volumes, titled La
América Central ante la historia, provide an
effective survey of the scholarship about the
pre-Hispanic and Colonial eras during the
nineteenth century, were published in 1915 and
1920 respectively. DLC LNHT BNG BNCR

170 _____. Vicios del lenguaje y provincialismos
de Guatemala: estudio filológico. Guatemala:
Encuadernación y Tipografía Nacional, 1892.
560 pp.
A dictionary of Guatemalan idioms, regionalisms, and modisms, alphabetically arranged.
Each is defined giving both its meaning in
traditional Spanish and its colloquial implication, with an explanation of its origin and
regional base, and a phonetic spelling. There
is no discussion of the extent of the use of
the terms. The introduction provides a brief
philological analysis of the Spanish language.
DLC LNHT BNCR

171 Batres Montúfar, José. Tradiciones de
Guatemala: poesías. Guatemala: n.p., 1940.
Latest ed. Guatemala: Imprenta Casa
Gutiérrez, 1966. 200 pp.
A series of lengthy poems relating prin-
cipally to Colonial days and recounting the
regional legends of Guatemala. DLC LNHT BNG

172 Bauer Paíz, Alfonso. Catalogación de leyes y
disposiciones de trabajo de Guatemala del
período 1872 a 1930. Guatemala: Universidad
de San Carlos, 1965. 222 pp.
A chronological listing, by topic, of the
laws pertaining to each aspect of labor regulation, with a single-paragraph summary of
their stipulations and a page reference to the
collected laws of Guatemala series, where the
full text can be consulted. LNHT

173 _____. Cómo opera el capital yanqui en
Centroamérica: el caso de Guatemala. Mexico:
Editorial Ibero-Mexicana, 1936. 415 pp.
Tables, appendixes. Latest ed. Mexico:
Editorial Ibero-Mexicana, 1956. 415 pp.
Tables, appendixes.
A pro-revolutionary and anti-Yankee study
contending that the 1944 revolution drasti-
cally changed the nation and sought to end its
control by foreign companies. The detailed
chapters focus on the United Fruit Company,
International Railways of Central America, and
the Electric Bond and Share Company, three of
the largest foreign enterprises in Guatemala,
examining their actions critically and denouncing their monopolistic practices and what
the volume calls their exploitive and colo-
nialist tendencies. Despite the bias against
the companies, the volume contains considerable data about their operation, and also
illustrates the view of the Guatemalan revolution. DLC LNHT

174 _____. Destellos y sombras en la historia
patria. Guatemala: Editorial Escolar Piedra
Santa, 1966. 193 pp. Illus.
A prominent Guatemalan writer, who is primarily a sociologist, provides a pro-liberal
panorama of the major periods in Guatemalan
development in the nineteenth century, written
not as history but to bring modern sociology
to the study of these eras. Accordingly, his
focus is on the general sweep of each era
rather than the specifics, considering the
principal institutions and major trends in the
economy, society, and culture. DLC LNHT

175 _____. La frutera y la discriminación:
réplica al senador Lodge y Cía. Guatemala:
Tipografía Nacional, 1949. 25 pp.
Part of the political outcry involved in
the expropriation by the Guatemalan revolutionaries of United Fruit Company land, replying to company allegations that the
Guatemalan legislation discriminated against
it, a position supported by numerous U.S.
senators. This folio offers the speech of a
Guatemalan legislator contending that the law
was equitably applied, citing the domestic
court recourses available to the company and
charging that it was the latter that had ignored Guatemalan law during its operation in
that nation. DLC LNHT

176 Bauer Paíz, Alfonso, and Julio Valladares
Castillo. La frutera ante la ley: los
conflictos laborales de Izabal y Tiquisate.
Guatemala: Tipografía Nacional, 1949. Latest
ed. Guatemala: Ministerio de Economía y
Trabajo, 1952. 103 pp.
An official publication written by
Arévalo's minister of economy, this volume
states the government case in a dispute with
the United Fruit Company and its subsidiaries
regarding a labor conflict and strike in the
UFCO plantations in eastern Guatemala. It is
designed to indicate the positions of both
sides and demonstrate that the company has
violated Guatemalan law by refusing to accept
compulsory arbitration by the government,
which the company charges is allied with the
unions. The dispute, one of the key episodes
of this era, led to the company-government
confrontation and eventual expropriation. The
documents and official statements of all parties are reproduced. DLC LNHT BNG

177 Beals, Carlton. Land of the Mayas: Yesterday
and Today. New York: Abelard-Schuman, 1966.
158 pp. Biblio., illus.
A description of contemporary Mayan society
in Mexico and Guatemala, with comparisons to
their previous civilization. Written by a
well-known travel-book author. Includes consideration of cultural and social aspects of
everyday life, with comments about continuing
cultural customs and their ties to the past,
as well as about adaptation to the modern
world. DLC LNHT

178 Die belgischen Kolonien in Guatemala und
Brasilien: Versuch einer Darstellung des
thatsächlichen, mit einen Hinblick auf die

Hoffnungen, welche sich daran knüpfen.
Cologne: L. Kohnen, 1844. 152 pp. Tables.
A chronicle of the Belgian colonies in Santo Tomás, Guatemala, and in Brazil, with about half the volume devoted to each. Includes physical descriptions of climate and setting, historical accounts of the settlements, and discussion of their produce and trade. Particular attention is paid to trade with Germany, it being demonstrated that nearly all of the agricultural production is sent to Europe, particularly Germany. DLC

179 Bellini, Giuseppe. La narrativa di Miguel Ángel Asturias. Milan: La Goliardica, 1965. 217 pp. Notes.
An analysis of Asturias's novels by theme and technique, focusing on his political narratives and mythical novels, with liberal quotations from the author. The volume is intended for the European literary audience. LNHT

180 Beltranena Sinibaldi, Luís. Como se produjó la caída de Estrada Cabrera. Guatemala: Imprenta Eros, 1970. 45 pp. Illus.
A series of brief essays, originally published in Guatemala City newspapers, regarding the fall of the longtime dictatorship in 1920, detailing the maneuvering. The author contends that what was involved was not a rebellion but rather a unionist effort that was not directed at internal politics. DLC

181 _____. Fundación de la República de Guatemala. Guatemala: Tipografía Nacional, 1971. 303 pp. Biblio., illus., maps.
Offers a new perspective of the early years of the nation and its foundation, focusing on the role of the Conservative dictator Rafael Carrera. Views him as the individual who consolidated independence through the foundation of the state of Guatemala and hence launched the new nation on a secure course. Includes discussion of the principal societal factors during the late Colonial period and a brief discussion of the early independence movement and the Federation, but the focus is on Carrera as consolidator of the nation. Based on research in documentary and unpublished sources, though without footnotes; includes extensive excerpts. DLC BNG

182 Benítes, Tulio. Meditaciones de un católico ante la reforma agraria. Guatemala: Ministerio de Educación Pública, 1952. 111 pp. Biblio., illus.
A statement regarding the controversy about the agrarian reform laws of the Arbenz administration in Guatemala, contending that it is false to say that all land reform is communistic and anti-Catholic. Cites various papal encyclicals from the nineteenth century to argue that land reform is indeed within the Christian tradition, and that the church recognizes limits on private property. DLC LNHT BNG

183 Benítez Porta, Oscar Rodolfo. Secesión pacífica de Guatemala de España. Guatemala:

Ministerio de Educación Pública, 1973. 674 pp. Biblio., notes, illus.
Originally a thesis at the University of San Carlos, this volume provides a detailed survey of the independence era from its origins to its consumation, emphasizing the legal processes and justifications employed. The study is based on documentary research and appropriate secondary sources. DLC

184 Besso, Henry V. A Guide to the Official Publications of the Other American Republics. Vol. 11, Guatemala. Washington, D.C.: Library of Congress, 1947. 88 pp. Latest ed. New York: Johnson Reprint Corp., 1964.
See item CR94. DLC

185 Beteta, José Antonio. Edmundo. Guatemala: Tipografía Nacional, 1896. 154 pp.
A novel set in Guatemala in the turbulent 1860s, dealing with the everyday concerns of the lives of ordinary citizens as they cope with illness, hardship, and encounters with the authorities. LNHT BNCR

186 _____. Refutación a un folleto. Guatemala: Unión Tipográfica, 1925. 56 pp.
Part of the political polemics that characterized the early 1920s, after the fall of Estrada Cabrera, involving the various accusations of brutality and arbitrary actions between the supporters of the fallen regime and those of the unionist government of Carlos Herrera. This pamphlet presents counterarguments involving alleged lynchings. DLC

187 Bianconi, F., and Crisanto Medina. Texte et carte commerciale de la République du Guatemala avec notice descriptive. Paris: Imprimerie Chaix, 1890. 31 pp. Maps.
A brief summary of the current state of Guatemala, with emphasis on economy, transport, finances, and economic potential. Includes trade statistics. DLC LNHT

188 Bílak, León. Centenario de los primeros sellos postales de Centro América, 10 de diciembre de 1862-1962. Guatemala: Tipografía Nacional, 1963. 47 pp. Illus.
A history of Guatemalan postage stamps and collectors' exhibitions, with photos of rare items and explanations of the various issues, as well as those exhibiting printing mistakes. DLC LNHT

189 Billig, Otto, John Gillin, and William Davidson. Aspectos de la personalidad y la cultura en una comunidad guatemalteca: métodos etnológicos y de Rorschach. Guatemala: Universidad de San Carlos, 1966. 78 pp. Biblio.
Analysis by Billig of data collected in San Luís Jilotepeque by Gillin and Davidson during their studies of the town, in 1942 and 1946 respectively, when they administered Rorschach tests to the population, using these tests to study personality traits and examine their relationship to the culture. The ladino and Indian groups are studied separately to note the general traits of each and the differences

between them. Both groups are shown to be bound by cultural traditions and authoritarianism, but differences resulting from the social status are noted. DLC LNHT

190 Binckum, J. Vandenberghede. Rapport de M. le chevalier Vandenberghe de Binckum, membre de la députation permanente du Brabant, et membre de la commission d'exploration dans l'Amerique Central, à MM, les fondateurs de la Compagnie Belge de Colonisation. Brussels: n.p., 1824. 16 pp.
     An early summary of the progress of, and conditions in, the Belgian colony at Santo Tomás, Guatemala, written by one of the initiators of the project. DLC

191 Bjerregaard, Lena. Idianvervaevning fra Guatemala: mayarnes laendvaev, fremstilling, opsaetning, vaevning, mønstre. Copenhagen: Høst, 1976.
Techniques of Guatemalan weaving. New York: Van Nostrand, 1977. 96 pp. Index, biblio., illus.
     A careful description of techniques in language understandable to the layman, written at the beginning design level and focusing on the San Andres region, with black-and-white pattern photos and drawings as well as color photos. DLC

192 Blaffer, Sarah C. The Black-Man of Zinacantan: A Central American Legend. Austin: University of Texas Press, 1972. 194 pp. Index, biblio., illus., maps, tables.
     Though focusing primarily on research in Chiapas, this study of demonology in Maya folklore includes data from throughout the Tzotzil-Maya speaking area, including Guatemala. It narrates legends about demons, noting the particular emphasis on were-animals and the relationship of humans to beasts. The title refers to a black batlike demon particularly prominent in the tales. DLC

193 Blondeel van Cuelebrouck, Édouard. Colonie de Santo-Tomás: enquête de M. Blondeel van Cuelebrouck, . . . déposée sur le bureau de la Chambre des Représentants, le 10 juin, 1846, par M. le ministre des affaires étrangères. Brussels: Ministre des Affaires Étrangères, 1846. 240 pp. Illus., maps, tables.
     An official report by a Belgian diplomat, submitted to the Legislature in 1846, tracing the history of the settlement, describing conditions in it and facilities available, and explaining all aspects of life there in question-and-answer form, with appended reports and maps. The format indicates debate as to whether Belgium should seek to assert official control over the region. Includes data on colonists, health, government, services, economy, work conditions, and many other aspects of the colony. DLC

194 _____. Colonie de Santo-Tómas: suite de l'enquête. Brussels: Published by the Company, 1846. 50 pp. Maps, tables.
     A series of answers to questions before the Parliament by Blondeel van Cuelebrouck,

providing details about the colony and its commerce, and the region of Guatemala, its government, commerce, and contacts with the rest of the world. DLC

195 _____. Colonie de Santo-Tómas: suite de l'enquête. Brussels: Ministre des Affaires Étrangères, 1846. 136 pp. Illus., maps, tables.
     A continuation of the author's earlier report on the colony, stressing its potential value to Belgian commerce, with detailed economic and trade statistics. The author clearly feels the enterprise is useful to Belgium but is also concerned about relations with Guatemala, emphasizing economic rather than political value and linkages. DLC

196 Bocanegra Gutiérrez, Mario. Fundamentos para la auditoria interna de Bancos Centrales aplicables al sistema guatemalteco. Guatemala: Imprenta Universitaria, 1956. 65 pp. Biblio.
     A guide for bank auditors, with citations and excerpts from appropriate Guatemalan statutes, demonstrating the specific system in use in that nation. DLC BNG

197 Boddam-Whetham, John. Across Central America. London: Hurst & Blackett, 1877. xii, 353 pp. Illus.
     One of the classic travelogues by an experienced travel-book author, recounting his observations during a visit to Guatemala and the Yucatan during 1873. Provides detailed descriptions of physical setting, people, places, life-styles, and customs, with particular attention to rural Indians, furnishing an account of Guatemalan life during the Barrios regime. DLC LNHT

198 Bodenheimer, Susanne Jonas, and David Tobis, eds. Guatemala. Berkeley, Calif.: NACLA, 1974. 264 pp. Biblio., illus., maps, tables, appendixes.
Guatemala: una historia inmediata. Mexico: Siglo XXI Editores, 1976. 346 pp. Tables.
     A joint effort by the North American Congress on Latin America, this volume reflects the ideological militancy of that group, offering a survey of Guatemala from 1954 to 1974 drawn from secondary sources, which indicts Yankee imperialism, dependency, and the local bourgeoisie as the causes of all Guatemalan problems. Includes statistics on the economy and social structure, and offers an effective summary of the dependency viewpoint as applied to Guatemala and Central America. DLC LNHT

199 Bonilla Aquino, Daniel. La enseñanza de la lectura y la escritura iniciales en Guatemala. Guatemala: Ministerio de Educación Pública, 1971. 350 pp. Biblio., illus., tables.
     Originally a thesis in education at the University of San Carlos, this volume consists of a criticism of the instructional methods used in Guatemalan primary schools to teach reading and writing at the present time, and a comparison of those methods to educational theories. Includes test results of Guatemalan

students during the early 1960s. Notes that most Guatemalan elementary teachers are not knowledgeable about the various educational theories and methods, and that a major effort to disseminate such knowledge is necessary. BNG

200 Bonilla Ruano, José María. <u>Anotaciones criticodidácticas sobre el poema del himno nacional de Guatemala</u>. Guatemala: Unión Tipográfica, 1935. 351 pp. Notes, illus., appendixes.

An exhaustive and detailed discussion of the national anthem and its symbolism, including comparison to other anthems, consideration of the values represented in it, and discussion of the various references to other national symbols such as the Quetzal, as well as literary and critical analysis and a detailed account of the origin of the anthem and its official adoption. DLC

201 _____. <u>Mosaico de voces y locuciones viciosas</u>. Guatemala: Unión Tipográfica, 1939. 400 pp. Index, illus.

Over 300 poems illustrating local usage, idioms, and errors, with footnotes explaining the origins and meaning of over 1,200 idioms and so-called barbarisms. The arrangement employing poetry renders the volume difficult to use, though there is an alphabetical index of words that partially alleviates the problem. Identified as volume 3 of the author's <u>Gramática castellana</u>, but stands alone as the other volumes of that series deal with conventional Spanish, with no references to specifically Guatemalan terms. DLC LNHT BNG

202 Bonis, Samuel B. <u>Geología del área de Quezaltenango, República de Guatemala</u>. Guatemala: Instituto Geográfica Nacional, 1965. 84 pp. Notes, illus., maps.

A description and compilation of basic data designed to accompany the appropriate section map prepared by the Institute. Emphasizes physical description of landforms, and includes tables of volcanic eruptions in the region. DLC

203 Bordas, P.H., J.P. Gagnere, and Oliver Martel. <u>Guatemala</u>. Paris and Boulogne: Editions Delroisse, n.d. [1976?]. 151 pp. Illus.

A bilingual (French and Spanish) general description of places and events of contemporary Guatemala, with extensive color photos. DLC

204 Bosch, José María. <u>Financiamiento de la educación en Guatemala</u>. Guatemala: Ministerio de Educación Pública, 1973. 19 pp. Tables.

A discussion of the sources of and disposition of the educational budget of the nation from 1963 through 1973, recommending an expansion of the educational effort. BNG

205 Bower, Reuben Edward. <u>Our Friends in Guatemala</u>. Kansas City: Church of the Nazarene, 1924. 61 pp. Illus.

An account of the observations of a dedicated student of Indian life in the United States during a missionary tour of Guatemala, focusing mainly on the conditions of the Indians in Alta Verapaz. Highly critical of the local governments, contending that the Indians are living in worse conditions than prior to the conquest, it calls for expanded missionary efforts to improve their lives and save their souls. DLC

206 Bran Azmitia, Rigoberto. <u>Historia de los cuadros de la independencia</u>. Guatemala: Ministerio de Educación Pública, 1962. 49 pp. Illus.

A brief account of the life and work of the Guatemalan painter Agustín Iriarte Castro, on the occasion of his death. Includes a description of his most important works, which are historical paintings, many focusing on the independence movement. BNG

207 _____. <u>El libro de los reportajes: 12 galardones de prensa</u>. Guatemala: Tipografía Nacional, 1960. 170 pp. Illus.

A series of prize-winning articles and interviews written by the author between 1951 and 1959 and awarded prizes by the Guatemalan Association of Reporters. Includes interviews with many political leaders of these years; a history of the association is appended. BNG

208 _____, ed. <u>La Politécnica en sus primeros tiempos</u>. Guatemala: Editorial del Ejército, 1975. 249 pp. Illus.

A compilation of contemporary press commentaries regarding the founding of the Guatemalan military academy, with selections from the memoirs of various early officials and cadets, as well as the appropriate excerpts of the <u>Memorias</u> of the Ministry of War during the Academy's early years, detailing the curriculum. The focus is on the late nineteenth-century formative years, but the volume extends its coverage to 1922. BNG

209 Bran Azmitia, Rigoberto. <u>Vida y misión de una hemeroteca: panorama del periodismo guatemalteco</u>. Guatemala: Ministerio de Educación Pública, 1967. 91 pp. Illus.

Originally a series of articles in the newspaper <u>El Imparcial</u>, this volume offers an account of the development of the national newspaper library of which the author is director; emphasizing its role as the storehouse of the nation's journalistic output and hence of much of its history. DLC LNHT BNG

210 Brañas, César. <u>Antonio Larrazábal: un guatemalteco en la historia</u>. 2 vols. Guatemala: Editorial Universitaria, 1969. 233, 459 pp. Illus.

A sympathetic and detailed history of the life of a leading Guatemalan political and literary figure whose varied career spans the late Colonial and independence eras to the mid-nineteenth century, recounting his many efforts on behalf of independence, his negotiations with Mexico, his service as Guatemalan representative at the Panama

(Brañas, César)

Conference, and his long political career.
The author is a well-known Guatemalan novelist, most of whose works focus on human emotions rather than on political or social
themes. LNHT BNG

211 _____. La finca: monografía sentimental.
Guatemala: Unión Tipográfica, 1946. 132 pp.
A series of essays about life on a
Guatemalan finca in the interior, written
independently over a period of years and hence
constituting a series of commentaries rather
than a novel. The setting is wholly ficticious and is not based on any particular region of the nation, though there are ample
indications of the various aspects of finca
life. DLC LNHT BNG

212 _____. José Rodríguez Cerna o el esplendor de
la crónica literaria. Guatemala: Unión
Tipográfica, 1956. 213 pp. Illus.
A brief sketch of the life and writings of
a prominent Guatemalan journalist, by a longtime friend, with extensive excerpts from his
writings. DLC

213 Brief Statement, Supported by Original Documents of the Important Grants Conceded to the
Eastern Coast of Central America Commercial
and Agricultural Company, by the State of
Guatemala. London: Whitaker & Co., 1839.
137 pp. Maps. 2d ed. London: Manning &
Mason, 1840. 174 pp. Maps.
A description of the potential of eastern
Guatemala, designed to convince Europeans to
immigrate to the region. Prepared by the
faltering Eastern Coast Company, which held a
concession in the region and was unsuccessfully seeking to secure enough colonists to
avoid revocation of its grant and its transfer
to a Belgian company. Includes the text of
the original agreements involved in the grant.

214 Brigham, William Tufts. Guatemala: The Land
of the Quetzal, a Sketch. New York:
Scribner's Sons, 1887. 453 pp. Latest ed.
Gainesville: University of Florida Press,
1965. 453 pp. Illus., maps.
One of the earliest English-language travel
accounts of the region, detailing the wanderings and observations of a Bostonian in
Guatemala during trips in 1869 and the 1880s.
Brigham provides detailed descriptions of
flora and fauna, and seeks to awaken Yankee
interest in the economic potential of the
region, particularly in the mineral and agricultural realms. The account also includes
his various adventures and hardships along the
way, exhibiting the usual Yankee stereotypes
and attitudes characteristic of that era, and
hence highly critical of the natives he met.
He was, however, impressed by the reforms of
Justo Rufino Barrios, in power during his
latter trips, and extolled their potential for
the nation and the leadership of Barrios. DLC
LNHT

215 Brine, Lindesay. Travels amongst American
Indians: Their Ancient Earthworks and

Temples; Including a Journey in Guatemala,
Mexico, and Yucatan, and a Visit to the Ruins
of Patinamit, Utatlan, Palenque, and Uxmal.
London: S. Low, Marston & Co., 1894. xvi,
429 pp. Illus., maps.
An account of the travels of a British
admiral in the Maya regions of Guatemala and
the Yucatan, providing detailed observations
on the Indians and their life and art. Includes description of archeological zones and
of the lives of the Maya in the nineteenth
century, when these regions were still quite
remote and unknown. DLC LNHT

216 Buenaventura de Cogollos-Vega, Padre. Los
capuchinos en Guatemala (conmemorado un
centenario: 1872-1972). Sevilla: Talleres
de El Adalid Seráfico de los Padres
Capuchinos, 1972. 85 pp. Illus.
A centennial history of the work of
the capuchin fathers in Guatemala from 1872
through 1972, describing their efforts, expul-
sions, and successes, with photos of Colonial
and contemporary churches in their charge.
The order was expelled from Guatemala in 1872
and allowed to return only in 1956. The portion on the recent era emphasizes the social
and health-care aspects of the missions. DLC
BNG

217 Bunzel, Ruth. Chichicastenango: A Guatemalan
Village. Locust Valley, N.Y.: American
Ethnological Society, 1952. xxvi, 438 pp.
Biblio., appendixes. Latest ed. Seattle:
University of Washington Press, 1959. xxvi,
438 pp. Biblio.
A detailed anthropological study by a young
researcher, based on fieldwork conducted during 1931-32 just before the isolated village
was reached by the road-construction program
of the Ubico regime, constituting a last look
at an Indian town before it became connected
to the rest of the nation. The major focus is
on religion and festivals, with textual translations, although the volume covers government, family life, and social life as well.
The research was conducted in Spanish, which
limited the author's contacts because many
inhabitants of the village spoke only Quiché.
Her comments about the villagers' reactions to
her and the disturbing role of an outsider in
the community are also illuminating. DLC
LNHT

218 Burbank, Addison. Guatemala Profile. New
York: Coward-McCann, Inc., 1939. x, 296 pp.
Illus., maps.
A vivid description of Guatemala and the
author's experiences in that nation, illustrated by her own drawings and focusing particularly on the Indians of the highlands.
The portrait is sympathetic and good-humored,
seeking to understand the local customs and
providing anecdotes from personal experience
as examples. Includes descriptions of markets, social customs, agriculture, and especially the local lore and crafts, emphasizing
the color and uniqueness. DLC LNHT

219 Burgess, Paul. <u>Justo Rufino Barrios</u>: <u>A Biography</u>. Philadelphia: Dorrance, 1926. xxi, 286 pp. Illus.
<u>Justo Rufino Barrios</u>: <u>una biografía</u>.
Guatemala: Editorial del Ejército, 1971. xxxi, 285 pp. Illus. 2d ed. San José: EDUCA, 1972. 437 pp. Notes.
    The only scholarly English biography of this major Guatemalan figure, this volume is the result of research on the scene, particularly in published materials. Although making the usual comparison between Barrios and Abraham Lincoln, it presents a relatively balanced account, noting both his accomplishments and his failures. DLC LNHT BNG

220 Bush, Archer C. <u>Organized Labor in Guatemala, 1944-1949</u>: <u>A Case Study of an Adolescent Labor Movement in an Underdeveloped Country</u>. Hamilton, N.Y.: Colgate University Press, 1950. Biblio., notes, illus., maps. Latest ed. Ann Arbor, Mich.: University Microfilms, 1964.
    Originally a master's thesis, this volume, based on contemporary published materials and newspapers, summarized the organizational expansion and efforts of the Guatemalan labor movement under the Arévalo administration. It notes the political nature of the Guatemalan labor movement, its concentration in the urban areas, its efforts to extend its organization to the rural area where the bulk of the population resides, and the government's involvement in the movement. DLC LNHT

221 Cabrera, Roberto. <u>El grabado guatemalteco</u>. Guatemala: Dirección General de Cultura, 1973. Pages unnumbered.
    A short illustrated history of Guatemalan engravings and the development of the art in that country, with appropriate samples. BNG

222 Cáceres, Eduardo. <u>Historia de la odontología en Guatemala</u>. Guatemala: Tipografía Nacional, 1938. 315 pp. Biblio., illus.
    A detailed history of dentistry in Guatemala, from the practices and deformations of pre-Columbian days to the 1930s. Particular emphasis is placed on various institutes, facilities, and organizations in the dental field, efforts to improve methodology, and governmental regulations. Includes texts of appropriate decrees and reports of pertinent conferences. DLC BNG BNCR

223 Cáceres, Ziola Aurora [Evangelina, pseud.]. <u>Mi vida con Enrique Gómez Carrillo</u>. Madrid and Buenos Aires: Editorial Renacimiento, 1929. 302 pp.
    The memoirs of one of the wives of the Guatemalan scholar and writer, detailing her recollections of their marriage, offering anecdotes about him, and reproducing letters between them. The author, a daughter of a former president of Peru, married Gómez Carillo during the early days of his residence in Paris but wrote her story only after his death. DLC

224 Caille, Alexis. <u>Au pays de printemps éternel</u>: <u>la Guatemala et son avenir économique</u>. Paris: Chez Louis Cunard, 1914. 72 pp. Illus.
    A survey of Guatemala for the general European reader, providing basic geographic information and historical overview while hailing the works of the Estrada Cabrera regime. Focuses principally on economic development, agricultural products, and the prospects for the future. LNHT

225 Caivano, Tommaso. <u>Il Guatemala</u>. Florence: Tipografía di Salvador Landi, 1895. viii, 310 pp. Biblio.
<u>Guatemala</u>. Florence: Tipografía de Salvador Landi, 1895. viii, 331 pp. Biblio.
    Combines a general narration of Guatemalan history with a critical look at the present state of the nation, situation, culture, population, and economy. The author has written several books on various South American nations. DLC BNCR

226 Calder, Bruce Johnson. <u>Crecimiento y cambio de la iglesia católica guatemalteca, 1944-1966</u>. Guatemala: Ministerio de Educación Pública, 1970. 193 pp. Biblio., notes, maps.
    A study of the church, emphasizing its tremendous growth since the 1940s and the pivotal role of foreign impulses in the modern church. Expansion is evident in church institutions and services, particularly in the rural areas, but the volume demonstrates that the urban and rural churches are quite distinct, with the urban church focusing on the spiritual realm and the rural church emphasizing the social and political aspects. Notes that the growth in priests primarily reflects the presence of foreign clergy from the United States and Spain. DLC LNHT BNG

227 Calderón de Muitoz, Alba Rose, and Lourdes Benefeldt Rojas, eds. <u>Registro bibliográfico de publicaciones de catedráticos de la Facultad de Humanidades</u>. Guatemala: Imprenta Universitaria, 1962. 77 pp. Index.
    An alphabetical listing of all the professors (full- and part-time) at the University of San Carlos in 1962. Full bibliographic information on their scholarly publications, including books, journal articles, and newspaper articles appears after each name, alphabetized by title. An index enables location of similar disciplines or titles. A useful recent bibliography that encompasses a large portion of current Guatemalan scholarship. DLC LNHT BNG

228 Calderón Salazar, José. <u>Letras de liberación</u>: <u>homenaje al Movimiento de Liberación Nacional, en el I aniversario de aquella cruzada que devolvio a la patria la dirección de su destino histórico</u>. 2 vols. Guatemala: Tipografía Nacional, 1955. 119, 254 pp.
    Excerpts and selections from the broadcasts of Radio Liberación in the early days after Castillo Armas assumed the presidency. Although enunciating and extolling the movement and its program, the essays are primarily emotional appeals to patriotism and attacks

on the Arbenz regime and the opponents of
Castillo Armas. They were written for oral
delivery rather than to be read. DLC LNHT
BNG

229 Cambranes, J.C. El imperialismo Alemán en
Guatemala: el tratado de comercio de 1887.
Guatemala: Universidad de San Carlos, 1977.
xii, 348 pp. Biblio., notes, tables,
appendixes.
    A detailed examination of the negotiations
that led to the Commercial Treaty of 1887,
tracing the role of the German minister and
the officials of the Barrios regime. Contends
that the treaty opened the way for the entry
of German capital into Guatemala and hence
formed the basis of the subsequent substantial
investment in that nation, promoting German
control of the coffee production that constituted the nation's most significant and rapidly growing export and facilitating the
establishment of Germany as the primary market
for Guatemalan coffee. This, it is contended,
illustrates the operation of German imperialism in Guatemala. Based on existing secondary
works and research in the Archivo General de
Centro América, with an extensive documentary
appendix. IU

230 Cambronero Salazar, Miguel Ángel. La escuela
secundaria guatemalteca: problemas y
soluciones. Guatemala: Ministerio de
Educación Pública, 1961. 157 pp. Biblio.,
tables, appendixes.
    An analysis of the status of secondary
education in Guatemala, with proposals for the
future. Originally prepared as a thesis at
the University of San Carlos. DLC LNHT BNG

231 Camisa, Zulma C. Las estadísticas
demográficos y la mortalidad en Guatemala
hacia 1950 y 1964. San José: CELADE, 1969.
ix, 109 pp. Biblio., notes, tables.
    A detailed study of mortality, using com-
parative figures from the 1950 and 1964 censuses, with breakdowns by age and sex. DLC

232 _____. Guatemala; proyecciones de la
población total, 1965-2000. San José:
CELADE, 1970. iii, 36 pp. Tables.
    Population projections by age and sex, with
an explanation of the methods involved and a
brief discussion of the impact of changes in
birth rates that might be possible. Most of
the volume consists of tables of figures. DLC
LNHT

233 Campos Jiménez, Carlos María. Organización y
desarrollo de la comunidad para el bienestar
social. Guatemala: Tipografía Nacional,
1956. 282 pp. Biblio., tables.
    A general manual on community organization
that was published officially by the Dirección
General de Desarrollo Socio-Educativo Rural
and consequently indicates the type of program
it was promoting. Discusses the purposes and
methods of organizing voluntary community
action groups, emphasizing education and presenting potential classroom discussion materials. The organization's program constitutes

the answer of the postrevolutionary regimes to
the revolutionary communitarian efforts. DLC
LNHT

234 Canella, Francisco. Independencia de
Guatemala. Rio de Janeiro: Journal do
Comercio, 1935. 20 pp.
    A brief summary (in Portuguese) by the
Guatemalan consul in Rio de Janeiro, of the
independence movement in Central America;
originally delivered as an address to the
Brazilian Society of Geography. DLC

235 Canton, Wilberto L. Genio y figura de
Guatemala. Guatemala: Tipografía Nacional,
1946. 79 pp.
    An account of various scenes and inspira-
tions during a tour of Guatemala. Includes
historical references combined with praise of
the Arévalo regime. Takes a pessimistic view
of the past and hails the future under the new
revolution that will free the nation from
tyrants. DLC LNHT BNG

236 Capella, Jacinto. La ciudad tranquila
(Guatemala): impresiones de un viaje a través
del país de la eterna primavera. Madrid:
Imprenta La Moderna Poesía, 1916. 221 pp.
    The author's impressions of and reactions
to Guatemala during a tour of the country,
written to acquaint Spaniards with the republic and encourage them to visit it. Includes
comments on places, customs, and people, and
notes the Guatemalan love for Spain. DLC BNG

237 Caplow, Theodore. La ecología social de la
Ciudad de Guatemala. Guatemala: Ministerio
de Educación Pública, 1966. 60 pp. Notes,
tables.
    Originally published as an article in
Social Forces in 1949. Draws upon observation, anthropological studies, and maps of
the city to trace its expansion since Colonial
days. The work emphasizes the problems of
size and the concentration of population and
business as the city grew. LNHT BNG

238 Cardona, Rafael. El hombre, la tierra, y el
alfabeto en Guatemala. Guatemala: Tipografía
Nacional, 1957. 50 pp.
    A brief essay extolling the new agrarian
and rural school plans of the Castillo Armas
government, contrasting it with that of the
revolutionary regimes and hailing its potential for improving the life of the peasants.
DLC LNHT BNG BNCR

239 _____. Rasgos biográficos del general Jorge
Ubico, presidente de la república para el
período constitucional de 1931-1937.
Guatemala: El Liberal Progresista, 1931. 32
pp. Illus.
    An official publication of Ubico's party,
issued shortly before his inauguration, this
brief pamphlet contains a sketch of his life
and his previous official posts, an outline of
the history of the party, and a collection of
anecdotes about Ubico purporting to show his
character and humor, all written in the manner
of a campaign biography. It provides a

glimpse of how he wished to be seen and of the official party viewpoint. LNHT BNG

240 Cardoza y Aragón, Luís. Guatemala: las líneas de su mano. Mexico: Fondo de Cultura Económica, 1955. 304 pp. Notes. 3d ed. Mexico: Fondo de Cultura Económica, 1976. 452 pp.

A ringing denunciation of Yankee imperialism, by a collaborator of Arbenz who condemns dictatorship and the authoritarian heritage of the Colonial era and denounces economic dependence. Includes a broad description of Guatemala and some discussion of its history, as well as a chapter surveying Guatemalan literature and extolling the nation's culture. DLC LNHT BNG BNCR

241 _____. La revolución guatemalteca. Mexico: Ediciones Cuadernos Americanos, 1955. 215 pp. 2d ed. Montevideo: Ediciones Pueblos Unidos, 1956. 233 pp.

Part of the propaganda barrage that characterized the mid-1950s in Guatemala, this volume offers sympathetic essays recounting the programs of the Arévalo and Arbenz regimes, followed by a bitter denunciation of Yankee capitalist monopolies, their attack on the revolution, and the Yankee intervention that resulted in what the author, who served as president of the National Assembly during the Arbenz regime, calls a temporary interruption in the march of the Guatemalan people. The account, written in the immediate aftermath of the fall of the regime, is bitter about the Yankee role and totally supportive of the revolutionary goals, which, in the author's view, were in the best interests of the people and were opposed only by the capitalists. DLC LNHT

242 Carranza, Jesús Enríquez. Algunos datos e referencias para la biografía del benemérito general Justo Rufino Barrios, reformador de Guatemala y caudillo de la Unión de Centro América. Guatemala: Tipografía Popular-Totonicapán, 1901. vii, 134 pp. Illus. 3d ed. Guatemala: Ministerio de Educación Pública, 1956. 139 pp. Illus.

A succinct biography of the Guatemalan Liberal hero, extolling his virtues, refuting all criticism, and hailing him as a Liberal statesman, reformer of the nation, and fighter for Central American unity. Includes reproductions of portions of his correspondence and other supporting documents. The third edition bears the title El general Justo Rufino Barrios. DLC LNHT BNG BNCR

243 _____. Un pueblo de los Altos: apuntamientos para su historia; Totonicapán. Totonicapán: Tipográfico Popular, 1897. x, 326 pp.

A collection of essays dealing with portions of the history of the department of Totonicapán in Guatemala, including essays regarding the pre-Columbian period, a discussion of its role in the so-called sixth state of Los Altos during the Federation era, and a collection of various documents and commentaries from that era and the nineteenth century.

Includes geographic description and discussion of culture and customs. DLC LNHT BNG

244 _____. Sobre la tumba del héroe de Chalchuapa. Guatemala: Tipografía Nacional, 1900.

An essay dedicated to Justo Rufino Barrios, effusively hailing his leadership of the nation and his fight for isthmian union.

245 Carranza Cervantes, Francisco Javier. La escuela activa como función social. Guatemala: Tipografía Nacional, 1927. 354 pp. Illus., tables.

A discussion of the social functions of the school and the role it should play in the nation, followed by suggested lessons and themes appropriate to these objectives and the national curriculum. The focus is on using the primary school to teach national values and practical skills such as agriculture, and hence as an instrument of governmentally sponsored social change and self-improvement. Most of the volume is devoted to proposed lesson plans to aid the nation's teachers. IU

246 Carrera, Sotero. Bando de policía y buen gobierno, expedido para el departamento de Sacatepéquez, por su corregidor y comandante general brigadier Sr. Sotero Carrera. Guatemala: Imprenta de la Aurora, 1846. 51 pp.

A governmental plan for the Guatemalan province of Sacatepéquez prepared by the brother of Rafael Carrera, constituting a clear statement of the paternalistic, law-and-order emphasis of the Conservative regime.

247 Carrillo, Alfonso. La mujer guatemalteca y su situación jurídica. San José: Imprenta Lehmann, 1940. 14 pp.

The Guatemalan minister in Costa Rica presents an official view, based principally on constitutional clauses and recent legislation, noting the improvement in the legal status and stressing the rights and responsibilities of women under then-current Guatemalan law. He argues that women in Guatemala have all rights except the vote. DLC LNHT BNCR

248 Carrillo Ramírez, Alfredo. Evolución histórica de la educación secundaria en Guatemala, desde el año 1831 hasta el año 1969. 2 vols. Guatemala: Ministerio de Educación Pública, 1971-72. 443, 396 pp. Biblio., illus.

Volume 1 is organized chronologically, discussing the educational policy of each regime that governed Guatemala from 1831 to 1969. Volume 2 proceeds topically, discussing each type of school and educational extension effort throughout its existence, compiling course plans and pertinent decrees regarding education for each regime. DLC BNG

249 Carrillo Ramírez, Salomón. Tierras de oriente: ensayo monográfico. Guatemala: Tipografía Nacional, 1927. 142 pp. Illus.

An emotional description and history of the eastern regions of Guatemala and their role in

Guatemalan development. The work encompasses the Verapaz sector, Jutiapa, Chiquimula, Jalapa, Zacapa, and Izabal, treating the area in general. Discussions focus on the Indian civilizations; the Colonial era; and the nineteenth century, particularly the Carrera and Barrios regimes. Geographical description and the legends of the region are also included. DLC LNHT BNG

250 Carter, William E., and Samuel C. Snedaker. New Lands and Old Traditions: Kekchi Cultivators in the Guatemalan Lowlands. Gainesville: University of Florida Press, 1969. 153 pp. Biblio., notes, illus., maps, tables.
    A detailed anthropological survey of a milpa community of highland Kekchi migrants to the lowlands of Izabal, describing their settlement, life cycle, and agriculture in detail. The survey provides considerable information about the agriculture of the ancient Maya civilizations as well as about the present, and the author notes that it appears to indicate that despite the difficulties highland Indians can successfully adjust to the lowlands. The detailed description provides information about social and cultural life, family ties, and other related items, as well as about agriculture. A discussion of the implications for Guatemalan agricultural development plans for the lowlands is also included. DLC LNHT

251 Casa de la Cultura de Occidente. Biografías ilustres. Quezaltenango: Editorial Casa de Cultura, n.d. [1967?]. 156 pp. Biblio., illus.
    A collection of brief biographies of individuals awarded the Botón de Oro of Quezaltenango from 1961 to 1966. DLC

252 Casariego, Mario. Cartas pastorales y discursos. San Salvador: Escuela Tipografía Emiliani, 1967. 248 pp.
    A collection of pastorals and speeches by the archbishop of Guatemala, all dating from the 1960s, dealing with religious and church questions and patriotic themes, as well as with general issues such as the changing role of the family in modern society. LNHT

253 Casasola Saavedra, Carlos Egberto. Monografía del municipio de El Jicaro. Guatemala: Ministerio de Educación Pública, 1961. 107 pp. Illus.
    A brief description of a municipio in the department of El Progreso, with emphasis on the present state of the community and its society, economy, and culture. DLC LNHT BNG

254 Casasola y Casasola, Oliverio. Grandezas y miserias del Petén. Guatemala: Ediciones Indiana, 1968. 65 pp.
    A description of the Petén and a brief summary of its history, discussing its problems and prospects and hailing it as the key to the future of Guatemala. DLC LNHT BNG

255 Castañeda, Francisco. Una ciudad histórica: Antigua, Guatemala; su pasado y su presente. Guatemala: Imprenta La República, 1907. 176 pp. Biblio., illus., maps.
    An illustrated history of the various buildings of Antigua, focusing on the Colonial period but including accounts of the nineteenth century and reconstruction efforts. The commentary is short, with photos the most valuable part of the work. LNHT

256 _____. Guía del viajero en la República de Guatemala; The Traveler's Guide in the Republic of Guatemala. Guatemala: Artes Gráficos Electra, 1909. 272 pp. Biblio., illus., maps.
    A detailed bilingual description of the nation, its tourist attractions and principal cities, compiled under government auspices and providing an indication of development at the time of publication. DLC LNHT BNG BNCR

257 Castañeda, Gabriel Ángel. Esquipulas: descripción geográfica, histórica, legendaria, y etimológica del municipio y de la villa de Esquipulas. Mexico: B. Costa-Amic, 1955. 140 pp. Biblio., illus.
    A history and description of the city of Esquipulas. Combines detail about the town, its origins, traditions, and legends with the history and legends of the shrine located therein. The author argues that as the most significant religious edifice in the region, it can serve the cause of Central American unification. BNG

258 _____. Ismael Cerna boceto para su estatua literaria previa a su fundición en bronce, 1856 centenario, 1956. Guatemala: Tipografía Nacional, 1962. 207 pp. Biblio., illus.
    A brief biography of a Guatemalan writer of the nineteenth century who was a nephew of General Vicente Cerna, published on the centennial of his death. Traces his life and writings and his role in the politics of the nineteenth-century Liberal revolutions. Reproduces several of his works, among them an historical drama entitled La penitenciaria de Guatemala. See item GU284. DLC LNHT BNG

259 _____. Quetzal-Tenán: monografía sesquicentenaria de la Ciudad de Quezaltenango. Guatemala: Impresos Miranda, 1975. 253 pp. Illus.
    A compendium of information regarding Guatemala's second-largest city, published in honor of its 150th anniversary. Contains basic geographical and descriptive information, a historical synopsis, a glossary of regionalisms, and a discussion of the modern city, with illustrations of significant figures in the city's history. LNHT BNG

260 Castañeda, Ricardo C. Análisis de don Mariano Salas, licenciado, presentado ante la Asamblea Nacional. Guatemala: Tipografía A. Siguere, 1908. 32 pp.
    A Guatemalan congressman's critical analysis of the legislative procedures during the Estrada Cabrera regime. CU-B

(Castañeda, Ricardo C.)

261 _____. Principios de derecho público: la
política en Guatemala. Madrid: Editorial
"Guatemala," 1931. 273 pp.
   A series of essays regarding the legal
system and politics, written by the president
of the Western Court of Guatemala, who also
served as a national deputy. The author
offers wide-ranging comments on the political
system, explaining its procedures and the
powers of the various arms of the government,
analyzing the nation's problems, offering
solutions, and concluding with praise for the
Liberal Progressive party and its program.
DLC LNHT BNG

262 _____. Prontuario de los procedimientos
judiciales. Guatemala: Imprenta Marroquín,
1922. iv, 118 pp.
   A Guatemalan judge provides an outline of
Guatemalan judicial practice and procedure.
DLC

263 Castaño, Camilo. Dieci Giorni in Guatemala.
Milan: Librería Deltrinelli, 1967. 69 pp.
   An Italian reporter's account of his visit
to Guatemala, including interviews with several officials and guerrilla leaders. DLC

264 Castello, Julio. Así cayó la democracia en
Guatemala: la guerra de United Fruit.
Havana: Ediciones Faro, 1961. 174 pp.
   A scathing attack on the Yankee intervention of 1954, consisting of the memoirs of an
official of the Arbenz government, written
from exile as a series of newspaper articles
describing his experiences and contending that
the entire Castillo Armas movement was a crea-
ture of the United Fruit Company, which controlled American policy. The volume collecting the articles was published by the Castro
government, with an appropriate introduction
focusing on the episode as a case study of
Yankee imperialism. DLC

265 Castelpoggi, Atilio Jorge. Miguel Ángel
Asturias. Buenos Aires: Editorial La
Mandrágora, 1961. 222 pp.
   An analysis of the themes of Asturias's
various works, seeking common elements in them
and emphasizing the use of the past and tradition, the focus on the problems of the poor,
and the use of clearly defined right and wrong
in his works. DLC LNHT

266 Castillo, Efren. Monografía del departamento
de Chimaltenango. Quezaltenango: Imprenta E.
Cifuentes, 1943.
   A description of the department and a
compendium of information about its current
state, development, economy, population, and
facilities. BNG

267 _____. Monografía del departamento de
Quezaltenango. Quezaltenango: Imprenta E.
Cifuentes, 1942.
   See item GU266. BNG

268 _____. Monografía del departamento de San
Marcos. Quezaltenango: Imprenta E.
Cifuentes, 1940.
   See item GU266. BNG

269 _____. Monografía del departamento de
Totonicapán. Quezaltenango: Imprenta E.
Cifuentes, 1924. 77 pp.
   See item GU266. BNG

270 Castillo, Otto René. Informe de una
injusticia: antología poética. San José:
EDUCA, 1975. 419 pp. Biblio.
   A series of new-left poems denouncing the
injustices of Guatemalan life, extolling the
campesinos, and hailing the forthcoming revolution and liberation, by a poet who served
with the guerrillas of the FAR and died in
combat. Provides a statement of the movement's ideology in poetic form. DLC LNHT
BNG

271 Castillo Armas, Carlos. Discursos del
presidente de Guatemala. Guatemala: Imprenta
Hispania, 1957. 223 pp. Illus.
   A collection of speeches by Castillo Armas
during his presidency, arranged by topic, with
excerpts from the various statements said to
embody the core of his thought and plans for
the nation. BNG

272 _____. Una era de labor constructiva en
Guatemala. Guatemala: Tipografía Nacional,
1956. 441 pp.
   A volume detailing the programs and hailing
the accomplishments of the Castillo Armas
regime, emphasizing the differences between
its programs and those of the revolutionary
regimes and its anticommunism. DLC LNHT BNG

273 _____. Pensamiento del presidente Carlos
Castillo Armas. Guatemala: Secretaría de
Divulgación, Propaganda y Turismo, 1955. 95
pp. Illus.
   A collection of excerpts from speeches by
Castillo Armas during the period from July
1954 to July 1955. The comments reflect his
return to the country and the political turbulence and rhetoric of the period. LNHT BNG

274 Castillo Cordero, Clemente, and Juan Alfredo
García O. Atlas político-administrativo de
la República de Guatemala. Guatemala:
Ministerio de Educación Pública, 1953. 62 pp.
Illus., maps.
   Brief data for each province, listing the
political subdivisions and their population,
along with a description of the state and a
map. DLC BNG

275 Castillo Prado, Emilia. Una experiencia con
el test Ballard en Guatemala: la actividad
mental de los niños de 10 a 12 años.
Guatemala: Universidad de San Carlos, 1954.
86 pp. Biblio., illus.
   Data collected by administering the test to
a sample of Guatemalan schoolchildren, with
analysis of the results and their implications
for the nation and its educational system.
TxU

276 Castro, José Rafael. <u>Política internacional</u>
<u>de Guatemala</u>. Havana: Imprenta H.C., 1951.
190 pp.
   An account of the principal foreign-policy
stands of the Arévalo regime, written shortly
after he left office by a Honduran who was a
personal friend of the Guatemalan revolutionary president, hailing his efforts to unify
the region and oppose dictatorship and acclaiming his moral leadership. Includes a
summary of the Guatemalan regime's initiatives
in regard to the Franco government in Spain,
Central American federation, the Palestinian
question, efforts to promote a democratic
front against dictatorship in the region,
colonialism, and diplomatic asylum. TxU

277 _____. <u>La revolución desde el poder</u>: <u>viaje</u>
<u>de ida y vuelta a Guatemala</u>. Havana: Arrow
Press, 1948. 30 pp.
   A collection of articles lauding the revo-
lution, by a personal friend of President
Arévalo. Based on a visit to Guatemala and
interviews with Arévalo.

278 Castro, Julio. <u>Bombas y dólares sobre</u>
<u>Guatemala</u>. Montevideo: Editorial Marcha,
1954. 23 pp.
   A denunciation of the 1954 Yankee intervention in Guatemala, attacking the United Fruit
Company as the perpetrator and contending that
the real objection was to the agrarian reform
law that sought to confiscate the company's
lands.

279 Cayetano, El Padre. <u>Explicación de la</u>
<u>doctrina cristiana</u>, <u>según el método con que la</u>
<u>enseñan los padres de las escuelas pías a los</u>
<u>niños que cuentan sus escuelas dispuesta en</u>
<u>forma de diálogo entre maestro y discipulo</u>.
Guatemala: n.p., 1860. 120 pp. Latest ed.
Mexico: C. Bouret, 1882.
   An official teacher's manual for religious
instruction in the primary schools of
Guatemala, showing the doctrine and teaching
methods that prevailed during the Carrera
regime. NNH

280 CEDAL. <u>La situación política en Guatemala</u>.
San José: CEDAL, 1974. 66 pp.
   A study group focusing on sociopolitical
conditions in the hemisphere presents its view
of Guatemala, considering the constitution,
the present government and its policies, and
the economy. Concludes that Guatemala was not
a democracy in 1974 when the book was published because its constitution was written by
a body appointed by a junta, and because the
government is one that maintains power by
force. DLC LNHT

281 Centeno Cordon, Carlos Enrique. <u>Cooperativos</u>
<u>de El Petén</u>: <u>situación socioeconómica</u>.
Guatemala: Universidad de San Carlos, 1973.
194 pp. Biblio., notes, illus., tables.
   A study of cooperatives functioning in the
Petén, based on fieldwork conducted there
during 1972 by university students participating in the first program of "supervised professional study." The work emphasizes "social

economy" and notes that, although members of
the cooperatives own their own land, they are
still "exploited" by the distribution system
for their products. BNG

282 Cerezo Dardón, Hugo, et al. <u>Coloquio con</u>
<u>Miguel Ángel Asturias</u>. Guatemala: Editorial
Universitaria, 1968. 37 pp. Illus.
   A transcription of a University of San
Carlos round-table discussion about Asturias's
works, with scholars commenting on their sig-
nificance, themes, and style. Much of the
discussion focused on <u>El señor presidente</u>.
DLC LNHT

283 _____. <u>Ensayos</u>. Guatemala: Ministerio de
Educación Pública, 1975. 383 pp. Notes.
   A series of essays commenting on the work
of Guatemalan literary figures and on recent
trends in literature. They include biographical sketches and literary analyses of the
work of eleven Guatemalan writers, focusing on
Ramón Salazar, Domingo Estrada, and Alberto
Velázquez. There are also a number of general
essays dealing with such themes as modernism
in Guatemala and with the city of Antigua.
BNG

284 Cerna, Ismael. <u>La penitenciaría de Guatemala</u>:
<u>drama histórico nacional en tres actos y en</u>
<u>verso</u>. Guatemala: Imprenta El Comercio,
1891. 96 pp.
   A play set in the Guatemalan jail during
the regime of Justo Rufino Barrios, criticizing the dictator by stressing political arrests and the hardships of prison life. LNHT

285 Chamorro Zelaya, Pedro Joaquín. <u>El patrón</u>.
Managua: Editorial La Prensa, 1966. 498 pp.
Biblio., appendixes.
   A critical biography of the well-known
Guatemalan reformer Justo Rufino Barrios, seen
from a Conservative viewpoint, attempting to
portray the man as an individual rather than
describe his official acts. It contends that
although he professed to be a democrat, he
governed by methods as arbitrary and despotic
as any caudillo; emphasizes his intervention
in other Central American states and his ambitions, all without denying his considerable
accomplishments. DLC LNHT

286 Chavarría Flores, Manuel. <u>Analfabetismo en</u>
<u>Guatemala</u>: <u>informe de seis años</u>. Guatemala:
Imprenta Universitaria, 1952. 115 pp. Illus.
   A report, with statistics, about literacy
in Guatemala and the efforts and plans of the
national program to combat illiteracy. DLC

287 _____. <u>Hacia una sistema nacional de</u>
<u>educación</u>. San Salvador: Ediciones
Masferrer, 1956. 140 pp. Biblio., tables.
   A proposed national law regulating the
educational system of Guatemala, by a leading
educational scholar. Contains discussion, the
full text, and organization charts. Includes
a brief history of education in Guatemala and
discussion of other educational systems. LNHT
BNG

(Chavarría Flores, Manuel)

288 ____. *Política educacional de Guatemala.*
Guatemala: Imprenta Universitaria, 1951. 220
pp. Biblio., illus.
   An analysis of the Guatemalan educational
system, its evolution, traditions, and present
state, with recommendations for a systematic
education policy for the future. Discusses
the previous impact of politics on education
and notes the many changes in policy, which
the author attributes to politics. Contends
that the absence of continuity could be remedied by a professionally conceived long-range
plan. DLC LNHT BNG

289 ____. *Tezulutlán.* Guatemala: Sánchez & de
Guise, 1936. 184 pp. Illus.
   A series of essays dealing with the Verapaz
region of Guatemala, discussing its geography,
history, and customs. DLC LNHT BNG

290 Chávez Zelaya, Enrique. *Índice de libros
escolares autores guatemaltecos.* Guatemala:
Instituto de Investigaciones y Mejoramiento
Educativo, 1963. 34 pp.
   A listing of textbooks available in
Guatemala, arranged by subject and designed to
aid teachers in selecting texts for the
schools. DPU

291 Chinchilla Aguilar, Ernesto. *Formación y
desarrollo del ejército de Guatemala.*
Guatemala: Editorial del Ejército, 1964.
31 pp.
   A very brief résumé of the development of
the Guatemalan army, including Colonial antecedents, and appropriate legislation from the
nineteenth and twentieth centuries. DLC

292 ____. *Historia del arte en Guatemala, 1524-
1962: arquitectura, pintura, y escultura.*
Guatemala: Ministerio de Educación Pública,
1963. 229 pp. Biblio., illus. 2d ed.
Guatemala: Ministerio de Educación Pública,
1965. 261 pp. Biblio., illus.
   A history of Guatemalan architecture,
sculpture, and painting in the Colonial and
modern eras, focusing particularly on architecture. Emphasis is on the Colonial years.
DLC LNHT

293 ____. *Historia y tradiciones de la Ciudad de
Amatitlán.* Guatemala: Ministerio de
Educación Pública, 1961. 261 pp. Biblio.,
illus.
   The history of the city of Amatitlán and
its lake, treated topically and with a compilation of folktales from the region; based on
secondary sources. The emphasis is on the
Colonial era, but coverage extends to the mid-
twentieth century. Includes a number of poems
about the city and lake, as well as discussion
of local festivals, life-styles, facilities,
and agriculture. DLC LNHT BNG

294 Chinchilla Aguilar, Ernesto, and Francis Gall.
*Historiadores de América: Alejandro Marure y
José Milla y Vidaurre.* Mexico: PAIGH, 1966.
50 pp. Biblio., illus.
   Brief sketches and critical summaries of
the works of two Guatemalan historians (Marure

by Chinchilla Aguilar, Milla by Gall), providing analysis by well-known contemporary
Guatemalan historians of the works of an earlier scholarly generation. DLC

295 Choza, Arcadio, ed. *La personalidad del
consejero de estado José León Castillo.*
Guatemala: Sánchez & de Guise, 1920. 45 pp.
   A collection of contemporary material about
this Guatemalan Liberal leader who was a candidate for the presidency of his nation and
opposed the regime of Manuel Estrada Cabrera.
The collection includes proclamations,
speeches, newspaper reports, and political
polemics from the press and propaganda sheets,
as well as reprints of some of his letters.
LNHT

296 Cid Fernández, Enrique del. *Antecedentes e
historia de la fundación de la asociación de
la Cruz Roja guatemalteca; octubre 12 de 1922-
abril 9 de 1927.* Guatemala: Ministerio de
Educación Pública, 1963. 151 pp.
   A brief description of the origins of the
Red Cross, chiefly consisting of a reproduction of its articles of incorporation, lists
of its directors, and a calendar of its activities for the years indicated. LNHT

297 ____. *Cruz y Barrios: incendia y saqueo á
la villa de Huehuetenango.* Guatemala:
Editorial del Ejército, 1967. 61 pp.
Biblio., illus.
   An account of the siege and burning of
Huehuetenango in 1869 by the forces of Marshal
Serapio Cruz and Justo Rufino Barrios, during
the Liberal-Conservative civil wars that
wracked Guatemala. Provides a narration of
the siege of the town and its destruction when
Cruz and Barrios were compelled to abandon it,
setting it afire as they retreated. Includes
photos of the participants and reproductions
of various letters and decrees relevant to the
campaign, including a report of the incident
by a village priest. LNHT

298 ____. *Don Gabino de Gaínza y otros estudios.*
Guatemala: Imprenta Universitaria, 1959. 337
pp. Biblio., notes, illus.
   The title study examines the role of the
acting captain general of Central America in
the independence movement, arguing that
whereas some authors attribute his lack of
resistance to cowardice, he was in fact a
secret partisan of independence and hence was
unwilling to use repression to preserve
Spanish rule. The study quotes liberally from
the work of previous scholars and from documents. The remaining essays in the volume
deal with the Colonial era. DLC LNHT BNG

299 ____, ed. *Epistolario inédito de Antonio
José de Irisarri, 1857-1868.* Guatemala:
Editorial del Ejército, 1966. 295 pp.
   A book of previously unpublished letters,
containing the communications of Antonio José
de Irisarri, longtime representative of
Guatemala and several other Central American
republics in Washington, to Guatemalan foreign
minister Pedro de Aycinena, and his correspondence with the Nicaraguan representative

in Washington, covering the years 1857-68. The letters provide a Central American viewpoint of the Yankee actions of the time and indicate the diplomat's efforts to disuade the Yankees from intervention and to explain the Yankee actions to his government. Includes communications relative to the William Walker filibustering efforts, the French intervention in Mexico, and contemporary political trends in both Central America and the United States. The letters are printed in full, without analysis, and there is no index. DLC LNHT BNG

300 Cid Fernández, Enrique del. Grandezas y miserias de la vida diplomática. Guatemala: Editorial del Ejército, 1966. 745 pp. Illus., maps.

A detailed study of Guatemalan border disputes during the nineteenth century, based on extensive research in documentary and secondary sources and excerpting liberally from each, by a prominent Guatemalan scholar who served as historian of the Foreign Ministry for many years. The volume deals with all the various disputes, focusing on those with Mexico and on the Belize question, and emphasizes that Guatemala has lost territory from its original independence claims to both Mexico and England. Appropriate documentary excerpts from the correspondence and the resulting agreements are appended to the narration at the end of each chapter. BNG

301 _____. Orígin, trama y desarrollo del movimiento que proclamó vitalicia la presidencia del general Rafael Carrera. Guatemala: Editorial del Ejército, 1966. 123 pp. Biblio., notes, illus.

A brief account of the Carrera regime, focusing on the individuals who supported and served it, offering a more realistic view than most historical accounts. Notes that both Liberals and Conservatives of the era gained power by military force, established dictatorships, and retained office as long as possible. Describes the key supporters of the regime and reprints the declarations of support and the appointment as perpetual president, narrating the acts and meetings and describing each of the supporters and their stands. LNHT

302 100 industrias guatemaltecas. Guatemala: n.p., 1968. 209 pp.

Catalog of the nation's largest industries in 1967, with a one- or two-page description, providing basic data on location, plant, production, etc., though the entries are not arranged in any particular order. Though up to date only for a given period, a useful source of information about the size and scope of industry in the nation. DLC

303 Cifuentes, Edwin. Carnaval de sangre en mi ciudad. Guatemala: Editorial Contemporánea, 1968. 60 pp.

A novelistic account of the impact of the violence and terrorism in Guatemala City during the late 1960s on the lives of its inhabitants, stressing the disruption of lives,

human tragedy, the arbitrary nature of the combat, deaths, and arrests. DLC

304 _____. Cuentos de tiempos universitarios. Guatemala: Editorial Contemporánea, 1969. 52 pp.

A collection of short stories of social protest, most set in Guatemala, decrying racial discrimination, the treatment of the Indians, the conditions of the peasants, and the plight of the modern urban resident. DLC

305 _____. Jesús Corleto. San José: Ministerio de Cultura, 1972. 114 pp.

A social-reform novel by a Guatemalan writer, demonstrating the frustrations of the lower classes and the petite bourgeoisie, which are depicted as the groups whose condition render drastic change necessary. The title character is a charismatic and idealistic leader, who often appears through reports of his actions rather than in person, who with another reformer seeks to promote the revolution needed to improve the life of the masses by removing the restrictions that hold them down. LNHT

306 Cobos Batres, Manuel. Carrera. Guatemala: Sánchez & de Guise, 1935. 84 pp.

An attempted biography of the Guatemalan Conservative leader, written by a nonhistorian who, though he states that he seeks an unbiased view, is a well-known partisan and distant relative of the former caudillo. The work is primarily a collection of excerpts about Carrera drawn from previously published works, with the author disputing the prevailing interpretation about Carrera by replying, in brief connecting narrations between the excerpts, to the various allegations against him and about his ancestry. Includes a genealogy of the Carrera family designed to show that the general was of pure Spanish extraction rather than of mixed blood. LNHT

307 Colby, Benjamin, and Pierre L. van den Berghe. Ixil Country: A Plural Society in Highland Guatemala. Berkeley: University of California Press, 1969. xviii, 218 pp. Index, biblio., notes, illus., maps, tables, appendixes.
Ixiles y ladinos: el pluralismo en el altiplano de Guatemala. Guatemala: Ministerio de Educación Pública, 1977. Biblio., illus., tables.

A study of the Ixil Indians of northwestern Guatemala, based on fieldwork conducted in 1966-67, using informants, questionnaires, and existing texts. The authors emphasize the pluralistic nature of Ixil society, the interaction between Indians and ladinos, and the impact of modernization on the ancient beliefs and practices. The volume includes consideration of their history and religion, though the emphasis is on modern times and recent changes in society, government, religion, and ethnic relations. DLC LNHT BNG

308 Colón y Gómez Carrillo, Julio. Origen y desarrollo de la empresa hidroeléctrica del

estado. Guatemala: Centro Editorial, 1943.
64 pp. Illus.
   An outline of the electric utilities of
Guatemala. Provides a brief historical background of early unproductive efforts; stresses
the revitalization brought about in the 1930s
by the Ubico regime and describes the facilities and transmission lines. The majority of
the volume consists of the full text of the
laws regulating the industry and specifying
its operational procedures. DLC

309 Comité Coordinador Anticomunista. El caso de
Guatemala ante el Primer Congreso contra la
penetración soviética en América Latina
celebrado en México en mayo de 1954.
Tegucigalpa: ITS Publicaciones, 1954. 79 pp.
Illus.
   Apparently a propaganda pamphlet of the
Castillo Armas forces, this small folio pro-
vides evidence of communist control of
Guatemala, attacks the Arbenz government,
notes hemispheric alarm, and hails Castillo
Armas as a leader of the movement to liberate
the nation. DLC

310 Comité Interamericano de Desarrollo Agrícola.
Tenencia de la tierra y desarrollo
socioeconómico del sector agrícola:
Guatemala. Washington, D.C.: PAU, 1965. xx,
244 pp. 2d ed. Guatemala: Editorial
Universitaria, 1971. 395 pp. Biblio.,
tables.
   An analysis of Guatemalan land tenure and
the structure of the agricultural sector of
the economy, with detailed statistics regarding land use, ownership, and crop production,
including descriptions of the agricultural
policies of the Arbenz regime and the succeeding governments of the late 1950s and early
1960s. DLC

311 Comité Organizador de la Conmemoración del
Sesquicentenario de la independencia de
Centroamérica. Actas de la Junta Provisional
Consultiva de 1821. Guatemala: Editorial del
Ejército, 1971. 512 pp.
   Photographic reproductions of the entire
handwritten set of minutes of sessions of the
Provisional Junta of Central America, which
sat from 17 September 1821 through 21 February
1822 in Guatemala. BNG

312 Compagnie Belge de Colonisation. Amérique
Centrale: colonisation du district de Santo-
Thomás de Guatemala par la Communauté de
L'Union fondée par la Compagnie Belge de
Colonisation: collection de renseignements.
Paris: Rignoux, 1844. 520 pp. Illus., maps.
   A report by de Puydt on the territory and
its prospects, followed by a collection of
comments by various travelers and by the
Belgian press about the area and the project,
all published by the company. DLC LNHT

313 _____. Belgische Compagnie zur Colonisation
des Districts Santo Thomás, staat Guatemala.
Dresden: Walther'schen Hofbuchhandlung, 1842.
58 pp. Maps.

A description of the company, its grant and
colonization project, designed for recruitment
of potential settlers. DLC

314 _____. Collection de tous les documents
relatifs au Guatemala. Brussels: Compagnie
Belge de Colonisation, 1842. 203 pp. Maps.
   A collection detailing the company's rights
and grants in Guatemala and its plans for and
organization of its colony there. DLC

315 _____. Colonisation dans l' Amérique Centrale
du district de Santo Thomás de Guatemala par
la Communauté de l'Union fondée par la
Compagnie Belge de Colonisation. Paris:
Rignoux, 1844. 147 pp. Maps.
   Another of the official reports detailing
the company's plans and efforts, while propa-
gandizing the potential of the colony. CU

316 _____. Communauté de l'Union. Brussels:
Compagnie Belge de Colonisation, 1842. 23 pp.
   The company regulations to govern the operation of the colony of Santo Tomás, providing the specifications of the jurisdiction,
the parceling out of the land, sizes of holdings, costs, rights and duties of the inhabitants, and similar specifics. DLC

317 _____. De l'organisation du travail à propos
de la Compagnie Belge de Colonisation.
Brussels: Compagnie Belge de Colonisation,
1843. 23 pp.
   An article combining theory about the value
of work and its social role with a statement
of the company's goals, presented as offering
a new opportunity for the downtrodden and poor
to make a fresh start in a land of opportunity
that needs their labor and offers them equality of status and an absence of slavery or any
form of peonage. Clearly part of the company's efforts to encourage settlement, it
also mirrors the need for labor. DLC

318 _____. Essai sur la colonisation de la Vera-
Paz. Brussels: Librairie Polytechnique,
1841. 95 pp. Maps, tables.
   A brief summary of the various colonization
attempts along the Guatemalan Caribbean coast,
followed by a collection of documents about
the Belgian Company's Santo Tomás colony, with
government statements, grants detailing its
rights, and a glowing account of the efforts
to date. Published under the auspices of the
company to promote colonization. DLC

319 _____. Status, contrats et chartes.
Brussels: Lesigne, Frères, Imprimeurs, 1841.
57 pp.
   An official report, consisting principally
of a reproduction of the various grants and
documents. DLC

320 Consuegra, Sfelino. Monografía del municipio
de San Pedro Sacatepéquez. Guatemala: n.p.,
1967. 64 pp. Maps.
   A series of brief descriptions of the city,
its history, geography, facilities, illustrious citizens, customs, etc., with lists of

the mayors, holidays, professionals in the
city, etc. LNHT

321 Contreras, Gregorio, and Joaquín Díaz Durán.
Crónicas de la campaña revolucionaria de 1871.
Guatemala: Editorial del Ejército, 1971. 52
pp. Illus.

   An account of the military campaigns of the
Liberal revolution of 1871 that installed that
party in power, written at the time by two
Liberal military officers and initially published in El Progreso Nacional in 1895. The
account is reprinted here as part of the efforts of the centennial committee of the revolution. BNG

322 Contreras Reinoso, José Daniel. Breve
historia de Guatemala. Guatemala: Ministerio
de Educación Pública, 1951. 135 pp. Illus.,
maps. 2d ed. Guatemala: Ministerio de
Educación Pública, 1961. 143 pp. Biblio.,
illus., maps.

   An outline of Guatemalan history (in the
form of brief paragraphs) from the Liberal
viewpoint, focusing mainly on the Indian,
Colonial and independence eras, with only
thirty pages devoted to the era since the
collapse of the Federation. Based primarily
on the author's notes from the history of
Central America course taught by Joaquín Pardo
in the faculty of Humanities of the University
of San Carlos. DLC LNHT BNG BNCR

323 _____. Una rebelión indígena en el partido de
Totonicapán en 1820. Guatemala: Imprenta
Universitaria, 1951. 90 pp. Biblio. 2d ed.
Guatemala: Universidad de San Carlos, 1968.
92 pp. Biblio., notes.

   A study of a little-known Quiché Indian
rebellion in the town of Totonicapán in 1820,
led by Atanasio Tzul, which the author contends was a precursor of the independence
movement that demonstrates that the Indians
did participate in the independence efforts.
Based on published sources, principally the
Colonial accounts and documents. The effort
to associate the Indian with independence
reflects historiographical trends throughout
Latin America in recent years. DLC LNHT BNG

324 Contreras Vélez, Álvaro. ¡A la orden de
usted, general Otte! Guatemala: Editorial La
Prensa Libre, 1966. 247 pp.

   A humorous novel dealing with military
dictatorship in Central America, using farce
to ridicule all its characteristics and drawing upon the Guatemalan sense of humor and
Guatemalan terminology. Set in the mythical
land of Parsimonia, the story details the
foibles of a dictatorship, to snipe at over-
reactions to and misinterpretations of student
demonstrations, terrorism, and similar events,
while assailing the concept of dictatorship
and its pomp and ritual, portraying the regime
as clumsy and error-prone. Yankee intervention is also criticized. DLC LNHT

325 _____. En el XXX aniversario de la revolución
de octubre: apuntes para la historia en

remembranzas de CACTO. Guatemala: Editorial
La Prensa Libre, 1974. 124 pp. Illus.

   A well-known Guatemalan journalist whose
column has been a fixture in the capital press
for thirty years provides a fragmentary account of the 20 October 1944 uprising that
overthrew the regime of Federico Ponce Vaides,
reporting the mileau of the time and the
events he participated in. The comments are
those of an observer rather than a participant, though clearly those of a supporter of
the revolution who was active in the subsequent events in behalf of the junta and ac-
quainted with its members, providing insights
into the way the events affected contemporaries. DLC LNHT

326 Córdoba, Horacio de. Mis nueve horas con el
diablo: prisión, torturas, destierro.
Mexico: Talleres de Técnica Litográfica,
1957. 240 pp. Illus.

   An account of the author's imprisonment by
the Arbenz regime and of his political activities against communist domination of it,
attacking Arbenz and his cohorts while hailing
Castillo Armas. DLC BNG

327 _____. Sonetos "reaccionarios" xx: a mi
patria. Guatemala: Editorial Trópico, 1954.
Pages unnumbered.

   A series of sonnets by a member of the
National Liberation Movement, written in exile
and upon his return to Guatemala, condemning
communism, extolling the movement, and expressing his longing for a return to his
homeland and for the coming of the revolution
to free it from communism. Part of the propaganda of the era. LNHT BNG

328 Córdoba González, Jacinto. Papeles íntimos.
2 vols. Guatemala: Sánchez & de Guise, 1907-
47. 87, 403 pp.

   The memoirs and commentaries of the
Guatemalan unionist and Liberal, whose career
in journalism included publication and editing
of several regional newspapers in the western
highlands in and around Quezaltenango. These
are essentially political essays, memoirs, and
speeches, most of which previously appeared in
the author's papers; they deal with a wide
range of themes including political events,
historical figures, localities of his region,
and his own political activities and credos.
BNG

329 Cordón de Franco, Aída. Medio siglo y un poco
más: vida y costumbres de un pueblo.
Guatemala: Imprenta Propsa, 1975. 335 pp.
Illus.

   A description and informal history of
Teculután, Zacapa, written by a native of the
town. Combines present descriptions, discussions of various traditions and narration of
the town's development with references to its
leading families and personages. BNG

330 Córdova, Alejandro. Espigas al viento.
Guatemala: Ediciones El Imparcial, 1926.
110 pp.

A series of commentaries by a well-known
Guatemalan newspaper editor, including de-
scriptions of the rural areas of the coast of
Guatemala and a series of wide-ranging commen-
taries about themes such as adolescence. DLC
LNHT BNG

331 Córdova de Rojas, Sara. Córdovita: biografía
del prócer guatemalteco Lic. Dn. José
Francisco de Córdova. San Diego, Calif.:
Neyenesch Printers, 1947. 72 pp. Illus.
     A biography of a Guatemalan political and
literary figure of the independence era and
early nineteenth century by his granddaughter,
providing a brief summary of his life and
extolling his contributions to the nation.
Based on the notes and papers in her possession and her recollection of family traditions. The title character helped draft the
declaration of independence and opposed the
Mexican intervention, and the volume seeks to
establish his place in history. DLC LNHT

332 Coronado Aguilar, Manuel. Apuntamientos para
la historia de Guatemala. Guatemala:
Editorial del Ejército, 1975. 2d ed.
Guatemala: Ministerio de Educación Pública,
197? 561 pp. Biblio.
     A history of Guatemala from independence to
1869, focusing on the Federation period and
the Carrera administration, based on secondary
works. The volume is highly critical of
Francisco Morazán, contending that he favored
the other states of the Federation and justifying the Guatemalan independence effort in
view of this, criticizing Gerardo Barrios in
El Salvador, and viewing the Carrera regime
dispassionately, emphasizing its accomplishments rather than the standard Liberal criticisms. Much of the volume is devoted to
extensive quotations from laws and proclamations, with but brief connecting narration.
LNHT BNG

333 _____. El general Rafael Carrera ante la
historia. Guatemala: Editorial del Ejército,
1965. 61 pp.
     A speech discussing the historiography of
the Carrera regime and anticipating some of
the viewpoints evident in the author's subsequent detailed study of this era in his volume
Apuntamientos para la historia de Guatemala.
BNG

334 _____. Retazos de la vida: coram veritate.
Guatemala: Tipografía San Antonio, 1942.
323 pp.
     The memoirs of a Guatemalan judge and law
professor, recounting his life, his posts, and
the individuals who made the greatest impression on him. The majority of the volume is
devoted to his formative years, spent studying, working, and traveling. The author
served in minor judicial posts during the
regime of Carlos Herrera in the early 1920s.
DLC BNG

335 Coronado Lira, Luís. Totalitarismo
espiritualista: tres panoramas y un caso de

nacionalidad. Alajuela: Imprenta Venus,
1946. 26 pp.
     A well-known Guatemalan scholar writing
from exile assails the Arévalo regime, charging that it is maintained in power by brute
force and detailing the tortures of various
prominent Guatemalan intellectuals in its
prisons. BNCR

336 Coronado P., J. Adrián. Monografía del
departamento de Sacatepéquez. Guatemala:
Ministerio de Educación Pública, 1953. 226
pp. Illus.
     A detailed description of the present state
of the department, including all aspects of
life, resources, climate, ethnography, and
agriculture, as well as a discussion of notable citizens of the region. DLC LNHT BNG

337 Coronado y Pacheco, Ángel B. La ruina de
Guatemala, capital de la República de
Guatemala, América Central acaecida durante
la noche de 25 de diciembre de 1917.
Guatemala: Sánchez & de Guise, 1918. 32 pp.
Illus.
     A description of the Christmas earthquake
that destroyed the city, the subsequent relief
efforts, and a detailed account of the extent
of the damage, hailing the efforts of the
government and the various agencies that sent
aid. LNHT

338 Correa, Gustavo. El espíritu del mal en
Guatemala, ensayo de semántica cultural. New
Orleans: Tulane University, MARI, 1955. 103
pp. Index, biblio., notes.
     A survey of the concept of evil in
Guatemala, focusing on separating the Indian
and European origins and the mixture of concepts resulting from the Conquest, seeking to
show the continued existence of influence from
both cultures in modern Guatemala. Based on
published works and commentaries. LNHT

339 Corro, Alejandro del, ed. Guatemala: La
violencia. 3 vols. Cuernavaca, Mexico:
Centro Intercultural de Documentación, 1968.
Various pagings. Index, biblio., illus.
     A bibliography and compilation of publica-
tions from 1960 to 1967 regarding the
Guatemalan violence, drawn principally from
the local press, but also including clandestine pamphlets and publications from both
right and left, with appropriate citations.
Includes photos of victims. Volume 1 covers
the press for 1960-65, volume 2 for 1966-67,
and volume 3 has the clandestine material and
illustrations. DLC

340 Cosenza S., Roberto. Los hombres del banano.
Mexico: Siglo XXI, 1951. 75 pp.
     A novel about life in the banana planta-
tions, focusing on the changing life-style and
increasing conscientiousness of the workers
and their ability to adapt. Rejects the neglect of the dictatorial regimes, the excessive idealism of the reformers, and the
doctrinaire stances of the communists, contending that the nation must deal with its
reality and that the peasants are capable of

improving their lives and supporting democracy. The work is clearly based on experience in the banana zone and in the regimes of Ubico and Arévalo. LNHT

341 Cospín, Miguel Ángel. Ydígoras Fuentes ante la faz de sus contemporáneos. Mexico: Ediciones Ley, 1970. 396 pp. Illus.
A sympathetic journalistic account of the administration of Ydígoras Fuentes, emphasizing the rebellions with which it had to contend, its programs and accomplishments, the plans that were frustrated by its overthrow, and his efforts to promote union. Hails the president as an able leader and criticizes his successors for deviating from his plans. Includes extensive quotations from official statements and laws as well as from the commentary on the regime in the contemporary press, both internal and external. LNHT BNG BNCR

342 Cotero Aragón, Manolo. Guatemala en al corazón de Antigua: exaltación a Escuintla. Antigua: n.p., 1968. 43 pp.
A speech recounting the history of Escuintla. DLC

343 Crosby, Elisha Oscar. Memoirs of Elisha Oscar Crosby: Reminiscences of California and Guatemala from 1849 to 1864. San Marino, Calif.: Huntington Library, 1945. xxvi, 119 pp. Index, biblio., notes, illus., appendixes.
These memoirs include the author's impressions of Guatemala during the Carrera regime, where he stopped on a diplomatic mission related to the U.S. Civil War. His comments provide a view of Guatemala during Carrera's administration and a favorable view of the president, his works, and his relationship to the Indian peasants. The account includes discussion of a scheme to promote the settlement of freed black slaves from the southern United States in Central America, much akin to the Liberia effort, which the author contends was part of his secret instructions during his mission to Guatemala. DLC

344 Cruz, Fernando, and Antonio Machado. José Batres y Montúfar y Alejandro Marure. 2d ed. Guatemala: Ministerio de Educación Pública, 1957. 138 pp.
A reprinting of two scholarly essays. The first, by Fernando Cruz, which occupies more than two-thirds of the volume, consists of a critical evaluation of the poetry of José Batres y Montúfar, hailing his work. It was originally written in 1889. The second and shorter essay, written in 1888 by Antonio Machado, is a brief biographical sketch of Alejandro Marure. It discusses his role in the early nineteenth century, particularly his service in the Gálvez administration, and examines the historical and literary publications of this Conservative historian who wrote extensively of his own epoch, employing quotations from his volumes in detailing his life. DLC LNHT BNG

345 Cruz Torres, Mario Enrique de la. Monografía del municipio de Senahú del departamento de Alta Verapaz. Guatemala: Ministerio de Educación Pública, 1978. 234 pp. Biblio., illus.
A compilation of information about the town, its history, facilities, legends, and famous citizens. BNG

346 _____. Rubelpec: cuentos y leyendas de Senahú, Alta Verapaz. Guatemala: Ministerio de Educación Pública, 1965. 382 pp. Illus.
A collection of legends from the Quiché region of Alta Verapaz, designed to preserve the Indian folklore, most of which comes from pre-Hispanic times. DLC LNHT

347 _____. Valores de la Alta Verapaz: exaltación de una noble tierra. Guatemala: Tipografía Nacional, 1968. 27 pp. Illus.
An essay extolling the significance of Alta Verapaz and listing, chronologically, important events in the province's history. DLC

348 CSUCA. El sistema educativo in Guatemala: situación actual y perspectivas. San José: CSUCA, 1964. xxii, 283 pp. Tables.
See item CR335. DLC LNHT BNCR

349 Dardón Córdova, Gonzalo. Identificación de autores guatemaltecos. Guatemala: Universidad de San Carlos, 1962. 10 pp. 2d ed. Guatemala: Instituto Guatemalteco-Americano, 1963. 17 pp.
An alphabetical list providing the birth and death dates of prominent Guatemalan authors, but without other biographical material. DLC

350 _____, ed. Series guatemaltecas en el campo de las humanidades, 1886-1962. Guatemala: Instituto Guatemalteco-Americano, 1962. 137 pp. Index.
A bibliography that lists works alphabetically within series, providing full bibliographical information but without annotation. The organization by series is problematical. There is an author index, but no subject index. DLC LNHT

351 Dardón R., Félix. Maya Quiché: Método para la desanalfabetización del indígena y el soldado guatemalteco. Guatemala: Tipografía Nacional, 1939. 72 pp. Illus. 2d ed. Guatemala: Tipografía Nacional, 1944. 72 pp. Illus.
A reader designed for the literacy program of the army during the regime of General Jorge Ubico, which initiated an effort to teach army draftees from the Indian regions to read. The stories employed clearly reflect nationalism, glorification of the noble calling of the military, and the values of the caudillo (e.g., the importance of highways). DLC

352 Dávila, Fernando Antonio. Bosquejo del curato de Quezaltenango por el cura encargado de la misma parroquia. Guatemala: Imprenta La Paz, 1846. 115 pp.

A history of the parish of Quezaltenango by the priest in charge, summarizing its origins, activities, and facilities, and including official reports regarding it. Provides considerable statistical information about the city and its people, as well as about the church. LNHT

353 Davion, L., and C. Loretz. L'avenir du Guatémala: ses ressources, sa prospérité, sa population et ses moeurs. Paris: Librairie Orientale et Américaine, 1909. 86 pp. Illus.

A description of Guatemala during the regime of Estrada Cabrera, written to emphasize the possibilities for investment by French companies. Stresses the economic development programs of the regime and its desire for foreign investment. Includes a descriptive survey of the nation and its resources, and photos of the regime's public works projects, as well as a brief historical sketch. DLC LNHT

354 Deambrosis Martins, Carlos. La Conferencia de Bogotá y la posición de Guatemala. Guatemala: Departamento de Publicidad de la Presidencia de la República, 1948. 23 pp.

An account of the Bogotá Conference presented as an address to the law and social science faculty of the University of San Carlos, summarizing the actions of the conference, hailing the cooperation among the Latin American nations, and stressing that the Guatemalan claims to Belize require joint action by all the nations of the hemisphere, while emphasizing the Guatemalan role in promoting the condemnation of colonialism. TxU

355 Deger, Erwin Conradin. Álbum petrográfico de la América Central: I--La zona de Amatitlán. Guatemala: Tipografía Nacional, 1939. 78 pp. Illus., maps, tables.

A descriptive survey of the rock formations of the Amatitlán region of Guatemala, with discussion of its geological origins and structure and discussion of the properties of each of the various rocks and minerals identified. TxU

356 Déleon, Manfredo L. Monografía del departamento de Quezaltenango. Quezaltenango: Talleres de Diario de la Tarde, 1925. 86 pp. plus advertising. Illus., maps.

A locally sponsored description of this Guatemalan department, with sections on each municipality and jurisdiction indicating its present condition and facilities, and including essays on its history and culture. Lavishly illustrated. DLC LNHT

357 Delgado, Rafael. Falange en Guatemala: una amenaza para la democracia. Mexico: Gráfica Panamericana, 1948. 127 pp.

Part of the propaganda characteristic of the immediate postwar era. Reflecting both the efforts of Spanish exiles in Mexico against the Franco regime in Spain and the turmoil in Guatemala resulting from the revolution, this tract charges that Guatemala is a key propaganda base of the Spanish Falange in its efforts to win support in Latin America.

358 Delli Sante-Arrocha, Angela. Arévalo: pensador contemporáneo. Mexico: B. Costa-Amic, 1962. 112 pp. Biblio.

An overview of Arévalo's beliefs, based on his writings, placing him within the mainstream of Western thought, calling him a neo-idealist, and stressing his rejection of positivism; cites the intellectual origins of his principal beliefs in a long list of Western thinkers. TxU

359 Descamps, Emilio. Nomenclator de Guatemala, diccionario geográfico y guía de communicaciones. Guatemala: Tipografía San Antonio, 1937. 598 pp. Latest ed. Guatemala: Talleres Tipográficos San Antonio, 1942. 580 pp.

An alphabetical guide to all the cities and facilities of Guatemala, in separate sections by category, emphasizing transport but including information on sundries such as local market days and laws affecting travel and tourists. The latest edition is entitled Diccionario geográfico y guía de communicaciones de la República de Guatemala, recopilado y ordenado. DLC LNHT

360 Deutschmann, Paul John, Alfredo Méndez, and William Herzog. Adoption of Drugs and Foods in Five Guatemalan Villages. San José: American International Press, 1967. 69 pp. Notes, tables.

A study of the diffusion process in Guatemalan villages, focusing on the means of transmission of new products. DLC LNHT

361 Díaz, Eliseo J. Bosquejo biográfico del señor licenciado don Manuel Estrada Cabrera. Guatemala: Tipografía Nacional, 1915. 68 pp.

A brief biographical sketch extolling the impulse the Guatemalan president gave to the nation, associating him with the national heroes and the Liberal party with references and quotations from his speeches and those of historical figures, and providing accounts of various incidents said to illustrate his character and style of action. LNHT

362 Díaz, Víctor Miguel. Las bellas artes en Guatemala. Guatemala: Tipografía Nacional, 1934. 600 pp. Illus.

Rather than a complete history, this volume consists of a series of sketches of a wide range of individuals and organizations that have played an important role in the Guatemalan fine arts, emphasizing the contribution of each. The focus is on the Colonial era and the nineteenth century. Includes a section discussing architecture, especially of churches, and monuments as elements of the arts. DLC LNHT BNG

363 _____. Boceto biográfico del doctor Mariano Gálvez: homenaje de la municipalidad de 1925, la capital a la memoria del jefe del estado de

(Díaz, Víctor Miguel)
Guatemala. Guatemala: Sánchez & de Guise,
1925. 132 pp. Biblio., illus.
A study of the life of Doctor Mariano
Gálvez published on the occasion of the return
of his remains to Guatemala, describing his
role in the separation of Guatemala from the
Federation of Central America and his reformist efforts in the field of education. Includes excerpts from various studies of Gálvez
and reproductions of descriptions and illustrations of Guatemala City in the 1830s. LNHT
BNG

364   . Breve historia del periodismo en
Guatemala: desde la época colonial hasta los
primeros años del presente siglo. Guatemala:
Folletín del Diario de Centro América, 1929.
538 pp. Illus.
A detailed account of the principal developments in the nation's journalism. Covers
the Colonial era and the nineteenth century,
focusing on significant editors and their
newspapers. DLC

365   . Bronces patrios: Barrios ante la
posteridad. Guatemala: Tipografía Nacional,
1935. 736 pp. Illus.
A compilation of documents about Barrios,
linked by short narrations of events and biographical sketches of his associates, detailing the accomplishments of his regime. The
bulk of the volume consists of documentation
from the era, including letters, speeches, and
transcripts of the Constituent Assembly. DLC
LNHT BNG

366   , ed. Guatemala independiente:
recopilación de documentos históricos después
de la independencia de Centro América.
Guatemala: Tipografía Nacional, 1932.
308 pp.
Contains the "Actas inéditas" of the
"diputación provincial," from March 1822
to January 1823, all drawn from the official
Diario, detailing the debates of the
Guatemalan legislative body regarding the
union with Mexico. DLC LNHT BNG

367 Díaz, Víctor Miguel. História de la imprenta
en Guatemala desde los tiempos de la colonia
hasta la época actual, 1660-1930. Guatemala:
Tipografía Nacional, 1930. xii, 181 pp.
Illus.
A history of printing in Guatemala, providing brief descriptions of all the printing
presses and establishments in the country from
Colonial times, as well as brief discussions
of leading Guatemalan writers. The volume was
published in honor of the opening of the new
plant of the Tipografía Nacional, and provides photos and descriptions of the new
facilities and the staff. Includes a listing
of all printing presses and publishers in
Guatemala, giving locations and foundation
dates. DLC LNHT BNG

368   . Narraciones. Guatemala: Tipografía
Nacional, 1918. 259 pp.
An emotional account of the Christmas 1917
earthquake that destroyed Guatemala City.

Provides a vivid account of the damage, the
dead, the injured, the ruined buildings, and
the action of the government of General Manuel
Estrada Cabrera to help the victims. The
first half of the volume is an account of
earlier earthquakes in the region, included
for comparative purposes. LNHT

369 Díaz Castillo, Roberto, ed. Legislación
económica de Guatemala durante la Reforma
Liberal: catálogo. Guatemala: Universidad
de San Carlos, 1973. 428 pp. Tables. Latest
ed. San José: EDUCA, 1980. 428 pp.
A compilation of the laws, decrees, and
projects of the Barrios regime, detailing its
programs, plans, and rationale. This is projected as the first of two volumes, with the
second to focus on presidential messages and
annual Memorias of the various ministries
during the regime. DLC BNG BNCR

370   . Museo de la farmacia de Guatemala.
Guatemala: Editorial Universitaria, 1976.
160 pp. Biblio., illus.
A photographic history of pharmacies, with
some comment tracing the development of that
science in Guatemala. BNG

371 Díaz Durán, Enrique. Fincas de café,
República de Guatemala. Guatemala:
Tipografía Nacional, 1910. 70 pp.
An official compilation of statistics relating to the then-current state of coffee
production in Guatemala, with a history of its
expansion, compiled by the director general of
agriculture. Includes commentary extolling
the virtues of the nation for coffee production, contending that a large portion of its
arable land is suited to this crop and calling
for expansion of its cultivation. BNG

372 Díaz Laparra, Marco. Eugenio María de Hostos
y Fray Matías de Córdova. Guatemala:
Ministerio de Educación Pública, 1950. 86 pp.
Biblio., illus.
Brief biographical sketches of the lives of
two writers, with Matías de Córdova representing the late Colonial and independence
era, and de Hostos the early nineteenth
century. DLC

373 Díaz Lozano, Argentina. Aquí viene un hombre:
biografía de Clemente Marroquín Rojas;
político, periodista y escritor de Guatemala.
Mexico: B. Costa-Amic, 1968. 251 pp.
A journalist's biography of a leading colleague, who is also a political figure of
importance and whose life spans the nation's
most significant epochs in the twentieth century. The focus is on his earlier years,
particularly the 1920s and his years in exile
during the Ubico regime, though it covers his
career until 1966 when he became a candidate
for vice-president, a fact not mentioned in
the volume. The focus is on his combative
style, his political struggles, and his tendency to place himself at the center of the
national political debates; characterizes him
as "the most typical Guatemalan" of his day.
Although unfootnoted, the book is based on his
writings in his newspaper, La Hora, on his

(Díaz Lozano, Argentina)
many publications, and on interviews with friends; includes liberal quotations. DLC LNHT BNG

374 _____. *Il faut vivre*. Brussels: Messaco, 1959.
Y tenemos que vivir. Mexico: Editorial Latinoamericana, 1961. 186 pp. Latest ed. Guatemala: Tipografía San Antonio, 1963. 174 pp.
Another of the author's novels of Indian-peasant life in Guatemala, this purporting to be set in the years of the dictatorship of Jorge Ubico and showing the authoritarianism of that era and its effects on the Indians, who remained second-class citizens. The Indian is vividly portrayed as isolated, neglected, oppressed, and struggling with everyday problems and hostile authorities. The image conveyed reflects the revolutionary stereotype of the Ubico regime, extolling the subsequent revolution by focusing on the life of an idealistic youth who seeks to improve his nation and people. LNHT

375 _____. *Mansión de la bruma*. Guatemala: Autores Nacionales, 1965. 124 pp. 2d ed. Guatemala: Editorial del Ejército, 1968.
A story of life in the countryside and the status of the peasants, detailing their frustration and the failure of the 1944 revolution to solve their problems, and indicating the need for further revolutionary change if the attitudes of the elite are to be erased. DLC

376 _____. *Topacios, cuentos*. Tegucigalpa: Editorial Calderón, 1940. 137 pp. Illus.
A collection of short stories dealing realistically with the everyday concerns of life among the peasants and with their problems. Includes a variety of themes and fictional individuals. DLC

377 Díaz Rozzotto, Jaime. *El carácter de la revolución guatemalteca: ocaso de la revolución democrático-burguésa corriente*. Mexico: Ediciones Revista Horizonte, 1958. 312 pp. Index, biblio.
Charakter gvatemal'skoĭ revoliûtsii: zakat traditŝionnoĭ burzhauzno-demokraticheskoi revoliûtsii. Moscow: Izsatel'stvo inostrannoi literatury, 1962. 350 pp.
La révolution au Guatemala, 1944-1955. Paris: Editions Sociales, 1971. 270 pp. Notes.
A marxist interpretation of recent Guatemalan events and what it calls the "bourgeoisie revolution" of 1944, emphasizing the raising of a class consciousness and the organization of the Labor party as the decisive elements that can change the future. Calls the revolution antifeudal, but not anti-imperialist until its later phases. Originally a thesis at UNAM. DLC LNHT

378 Díaz Vasconcelos, Luís Antonio. *Autores nacionales*. Guatemala: Tipografía Nacional, 1971. 236 pp.
A collection of critical essays reviewing and commenting on various Guatemalan authors and their works, written by this well-known literary figure over a period of years and first collectively published here, though some have served as prologues for the volumes involved. They include commentaries on most of the current generation of authors. In the fashion of Latin literary figures, some are reviews but most are commentaries about the author and enthusiastic pieces extolling the latest work. DLC BNG

379 _____. *Conociéndonos*. Guatemala: Ministerio de Educación Pública, 1966. 477 pp. Illus.
The impressions of a Guatemalan congressman, recorded in diary form for publication in the contemporary press during a visit to the United States by a group of members of the Guatemalan Congress. Serves to indicate the reaction of Guatemalans to American society, production, products, and life-styles, and hence to illustrate the differences between the nations. LNHT BNG

380 _____. *El impuesto sobre la renta con dimensiones centroamericanas*. Guatemala: Tipografía Nacional, 1966. 602 pp. Biblio.
A complete text of the Guatemalan income tax law and an explanation and analysis of its provisions, with some background notes regarding earlier taxation in Central America. DLC

381 Diez de Arriba, Luís. *Un pueblo en la montaña: el cura y su perrita*. Guatemala: n.p., 1967. 159 pp.
The commentaries of a Spanish priest who spent several years teaching in San Pablo, Guatemala. They deal with a wide range of subjects, some recounting events, many in the form of homilies or commentaries on contemporary problems and society as he sees them. As such, they provide some indication of a sympathetic outsider's view of Guatemalan society, though in a rather haphazard and paternalistic manner. BNG

382 Dimes, Lemus. *Reforma y antireforma en Guatemala: es la Guatemala de 1971, digna sucesora de la reforma del siglo pasado*. Guatemala: Editorial Eros, 1971. 229 pp.
An impassioned plea for a new direction for Guatemala, emphasizing basic economic development and liberty, tracing these from the Liberal reforms of the late nineteenth century, and contending that some of the heirs of the movement betrayed it by changing its programs. Advocates a new impulse for basic development and a return to the original principles of the nineteenth-century movement as the key to the nation's future. IEdS

383 Dimitrov, T. *Gvatemala (Političesko-Geografski očerk)* [Guatemala: a politico-geographic sketch]. Sofia: Nacionalen Săvet na Otečestvenija Front, 1967. 79 pp.

384 Dion, Marie Berthe. *Las ideas sociales y políticas de Arévalo*. Santiago: Prensa Latinoamericana, 1958. 197 pp. 2d ed. Mexico: Editorial América Nueva, 1958. 172 pp. Biblio.

Originally a master's thesis translated into Spanish and published only in that language, this work analyzes the ideas expressed by Arévalo in his publications, focusing on his social and political thinking in generally sympathetic terms. DLC

385 Dittel, J. Walter. La doctrina de presupuesto social como base de los regímenes de previsión social obligatoria. Guatemala: Instituto Guatemalteco de Seguridad Social, 1950. ii, 35 pp. Biblio.

A theoretical explanation of the concept of social budgeting, which the author, an official of the Guatemalan Social Security Institute, contends should be substituted for social security. DLC

386 Dodge, David. How Lost Was My Weekend: A Greenhorn in Guatemala. New York: Random House, 1948. 247 pp. Illus. 2d ed. London: Home & Van Thal, 1949.
Vater Fliegt ins Blaue: Fröhlich Irrfahr durch Guatemala und Honduras. Ruschlikon-Zurich: Alb. Müller, 1955. 246 pp.

A colorful account of the author's year-and-a-half residence in Guatemala, with emphasis on the physical setting, the life-style, the people he met, and how different the life was from the Yankee style. DLC LNHT

387 Dombrowski, John, et al. Area Handbook for Guatemala. Washington, D.C.: American University Press, 1970. xiv, 361 pp. Biblio., illus., maps.

Another in the series of area handbooks prepared under the auspices of the American University. Provides basic current information in concise form for the general reader needing an introduction to the country. DLC LNHT

388 Donis Kestler, Agustín. Azul y grana. Managua: Editorial Novedades y Pinsa, 1973. 118 pp. Illus.

The memoirs of a military officer and graduate of the Guatemalan Escuela Politécnica, detailing his life as a cadet and the course of studies, published in honor of the centennial of the Academy. Includes comments regarding his later service and a list of brief résumés of fellow students who have died in the line of duty. BNG

389 Donoso, Ricardo. Antonio José de Irisarri: escritor y diplomático. Santiago: Universidad de Chile, 1934. xii, 319 pp. Biblio., illus.

A biography of a Guatemalan journalist who fought in the wars of independence of both Central America and Chile, and served in the Chilean diplomatic corps. His contribution was primarily to Chile, where he spent most of his adult life. Includes a bibliography and extensive quotations from other studies. DLC LNHT

390 Dotti, Victor. "Toda la verdad" sobre Guatemala: dos conferencias leídas en el ateneo, en julio de 1954. Montevideo:

Movimiento Juvenil Antitotalitario, 1954. 37 pp.

A denunciation of the revolutionary propaganda about Guatemala, criticizing the Arbenz regime as communist, rejecting the "Yankee-fobia" of the revolution's defenders, and seeking to detail the communist involvement and the excesses of the Arbenz government. Cst-H

391 Dunlop, Robert Glasgow, and Robert Wallace. Travels in Central America, Being a Journal of Nearly Three Years Residence in the Country. Together with a Sketch of the History of the Republic and an Account of Its Climate, Production, Commerce, etc. London: Longman, Brown, Green & Longmans, 1849. viii, 358 pp. Maps.
Viajes en Centro América. San José: Talleres Gutenberg, 1929.

A Scottish merchant's account of a residence in Guatemala from 1843 to 1846. More than just a travelogue or journal, it includes historical accounts drawn from the existing literature. Despite his European-Protestant biases, his accounts of contemporary political maneuvers and revolts are valuable to the historian of this era. DLC LNHT

392 Dunn, Henry. Guatimala [sic], or The Republic of Central America in 1827-1828: Being Sketches and Memorandums made during a 12 Month Residence. New York: G.C. Carvill, 1828. 318 pp. Latest ed. Detroit: Blaine Ethridge, 1981.
Guatemala, o las Provincias Unidas de Centro América, durante 1827-1828. Guatemala: Tipografía Nacional, 1960. 234 pp.

One of the classic travelogues, written by an Anglican clergyman traveling in company with the Dutch consul general during the conflicts relating to the independence movement. His account emphasizes travel difficulties, poor conditions, and the remoteness of the region but also provides a description of life in Guatemala City at the time and its relative isolation due to the lack of transportation facilities. The account is highly descriptive of terrain, and includes accounts of the Indians and other people he met, though with the British-Protestant prejudices characteristic of that era. DLC LNHT BNG

393 Durston, John W. La estructura de poder en una región ladina de Guatemala: El departamento de Jutiapa. Guatemala: Ministerio de Educación Pública, 1972. 178 pp. Biblio.

An anthropological survey of a Guatemalan rural department examining the social structure, the organization of the governmental system and economic activity, and the role of various types of organizations that reveal the local structure of control. The author concludes that the principal landowners, while deriving their power base from the region, are primarily absentee owners who ignore the area and focus on the national political scene. This leaves local power in the hands of the government and party officials, administrators of the estates, and the businessman, subject to some variances for personal ties with the landowners and others in the community. The groups in control cooperate to preserve the status quo. DLC LNHT

394 Eastern Coast of Central America Commercial and Agricultural Company. Brief Statement, Supported by Original Documents, of the Important Grants Conceded to the Eastern Coast of Central America Commercial and Agricultural Company by the State of Guatemala. London: Whittaker, 1839. 137 pp. Maps, appendixes.

A description of the territory, accompanied by the charter and other documents, designed to promote immigration from England to Verapaz. DLC

395 Esbaugh, Cameron Duncan. Education in Guatemala. Washington, D.C.: GPO, 1947. vi, 82 pp. Biblio. 2d ed. Washington, D.C.: Federal Security Agency, 1949.

A general description of the current system and plans for future development, with brief background. Includes plans of study for the school system and university faculties. DLC LNHT

396 Echeverría S., Buenaventura. Derecho constitucional guatemalteco. Guatemala: Tipografía Nacional, 1944. xxi, 657 pp.

A reproduction, explanation, and critical analysis of the Guatemalan constitution and its independence acts, tracing their origins through a brief legal history and through considerations of general constitutional law. The various clauses, laws, and powers of the government are all discussed separately. DLC LNHT BNG

397 Echevers, Malín d'. Metal noble. Guatemala: Ministerio de Educación Pública, 1966. 300 pp.

A novel set in Guatemala in 1914, focusing on the oppressiveness of the regime of Manuel Estrada Cabrera and on its effect on the lives of the citizens of the capital, especially of the poor. DLC

398 ECLA. Agricultural Credit in Guatemala. New York: U.N., 1950. 77 pp.

An overview of the current state of agricultural credit in the nation and a projection of future needs, prepared by a visiting U.N. mission. DPU

399 Economía de Guatemala en los siglos XVIII y XIX. 3d ed. Guatemala: Universidad de San Carlos, 1970. 134 pp. Notes.

Four separate essays regarding the Guatemalan economy, three concerning the Colonial era, with only the final work, by Sanford Mosk, focusing on the nineteenth century. It deals with the coffee economy of the latter half of the century. DLC BNG

400 El Salvador, Gov't of. Presidencia, Secretaría de Información. De la neutralidad vigilante a la mediación con Guatemala: gráficos, documentos, informaciones, comentarios: contribución en el primer aniversario de la pacificación guatemalteca. San Salvador: Imprenta Nacional, 1954. 255 pp. 2d ed. San Salvador: Imprenta Nacional, 1955. 279 pp. Illus.

Reproduces documents and newspaper accounts demonstrating Salvador's interest in and neutrality regarding the Guatemalan withdrawal from ODECA, and its role in enabling the Guatemalan military chiefs to reach agreement during the 1954 fighting attendant to the fall of Arbenz. Includes photos. DLC

401 Emery, Gennet Maxon. Protestantism in Guatemala: Its Influence on the Bicultural Situation with Reference to the Roman Catholic Background. Cuernavaca, Mexico: Centro Intercultural de Documentación, 1970. Pages not consecutively numbered. Index, biblio., illus., maps.

An analysis of Protestantism in Guatemala, including a brief historical résumé and a discussion of its present state, institutions, organization, and effects. The author concludes that Protestantism has introduced a new set of moral values that are essentially North American, and therefore is associated with Yankee cultural values; adds that thus far Protestantism has been less flexible in terms of adjustment of beliefs and institutions to local conditions than has Catholicism. DLC LNHT

402 Empresa Eléctrica de Guatemala, S.A. Memorial en que la Empresa Eléctrica de Guatemala, S.A., hace aclaraciones al informe rendido por el Consejo Técnico del Ministerio de Economía y Trabajo, con fecha 11 de febrero de 1950, respecto a la situación de la mencionada empresa. Guatemala: Centro Editorial, 1950. 80 pp.

The company's reply to the accusations of the revolutionary government, providing extensive data regarding production costs and activities to justify its pricing policy, and offering the corporations' interpretation of the agreement with the government under which it operated. BNG

403 Episodios nacionales: lectura para el pueblo. Guatemala: Tipografía Nacional, 1926. 88 pp.

An anonymous tract consisting primarily of excerpts from published works and documents, recounting supposedly typical or important events in Guatemalan history. The pamphlet is clearly the product of a Liberal pen (excerpting heavily from Montúfar) and attacks the regime of Rafael Carrera. DLC

404 Escobar Pérez, Francisco. Palencia en la historia. Guatemala: Editorial Landívar, 1966. 123 pp. Biblio., illus., maps.

A brief description of the town, including excerpts from Villacorta's monograph regarding it in 1926, and brief minibiographies of important figures from the town. DLC LNHT BNG

405 Espinosa Altamirano, Horacio. El libro del ciudadano, doctrinas jurídicas contemporáneas.

Guatemala: Tipografía Nacional, 1930.
191 pp.

Designed for general civic instruction, this volume contains chapters discussing such themes as the origins of society, sovereignty, liberty, and law, as well as the Guatemalan governmental system and its history; employs examples and excerpts from Guatemalan legislation. DLC BNG

406   Estrada, Hugo. Veneno tropical. Guatemala: Editorial Landívar, 1966. 146 pp.

A series of short stories about life among the peasants in the tropics, written by a priest who mixes fantasy and reality. Focuses on human needs and the improvement of living conditions by portraying the situation of the poor. DLC LNHT

407   Estrada Cabrera, Manuel. Escrito de defensa. Guatemala: Unión Tipográfica, 1923. 191 pp. Tables.

A commentary by the ex-president, submitted to a court in response to charges of arbitrary arrests and executions during his long tenure, defending his actions and denying the charges. Accompanied by various letters and telegrams endorsing or refuting the accusations. A useful collection on the Estrada Cabrera regime, providing data not normally available regarding internal judicial proceedings. DLC LNHT

408   Estrada H., Ricardo. Flavio Herrera: su novela. Guatemala: Imprenta Universitaria, 1960. 151 pp. Biblio., illus.

An analytical study of the novels of Flavio Herrera, by a close friend. Concludes that his works emphasize vivid action and intense images, portray real-life situations, reflect Guatemalan society, people, and emotions, and focus on the problems of the peons in a sympathetic manner that constituted social criticism. His works also reflect the problems of the small farmer as against the large landowner, and as such favor land distribution, the author concludes. Includes topical consideration of the themes of the Indian, popular spirit, human ties to the soil, music, and others. DLC BNG

409   Estrada Monroy, Agustín. Datos para la historia de la iglesia en Guatemala. 2 vols. Guatemala: Sociedad de Geografía e Historia, 1972. 438, 804 pp. Illus., maps, tables.

Brief narrations of each bishop's tenure and its principal events, to introduce collections of documents from the ecclesiastical archive, consisting principally of pastorals and correspondence. Focuses on church affairs but includes items relating to the participation of clerics in such events as the independence movement, which occupies much of the second volume. The first volume extends to the early 1700s, the second from 1736 through 1860. LNHT

410   _____. Hombres, fechas, y documentos de la patria. Guatemala: Ministerio de Educación Pública, 1977. 188 pp. Illus.

A listing of the governors and presidents of Guatemala, with photos and dates of office, and of the mayors of Guatemala City (without photos), plus reproduction of important historical documents from Guatemalan history. BNG

411   Estrada Paniagua, Felipe [Barbaroux, pseud.]. Administración Estrada Cabrera: reseña de los progresos alcanzados en los ramos de adjudicación de terrenos, ferrocarriles, carreteras, puentes, comunicaciones por correo, telégrafo y teléfono, y producción agrícola. Guatemala: Tipografía Nacional, 1904. 247 pp. Illus., maps, tables.

An official volume, cataloging the public works of the Estrada Cabrera regime from 1898 through 1903 and hailing his accomplishments, with statistics regarding trade and finance for this era and those immediately preceding it. Emphasis is placed on the internal development aspects in the fields of communications and transport, at which the regime was most effective. DLC LNHT BNG

412   _____. El 9 de febrero de 1898 en Guatemala. 2 vols. Guatemala: Arturo Síguere y Cía, 1899. 94, 128 pp.

A brief account of the assassination of José María Reyna Barrios, denouncing the role of the Conservatives in the episode, contending that they tried to seize power in the aftermath and describing the chaos that followed the act. A postscript that is longer than the initial essay describes the roles of various individuals, further criticizes the Conservative party, and details the laws, regulations, and corruption that provided various individuals and officers with motives for acting during the crisis. Implies that Manuel Estrada Cabrera, the first designate and constitutional successor, was somehow involved, or at least was not the logical successor and clearly profited from the event. The second part, published later the same year under the author's real name, pursues this line further and seeks to refute the response of Salvador Toledo, a functionary of both regimes. LNHT

413   Estrella de Centroamérica. Transformación económica de Guatemala: hacia una reforma agraria. Guatemala: Tipografía Nacional, 1951. 251 pp. plus advertising. Illus., tables.

A collection of materials and statements regarding the agrarian-reform program of the regime of Jacabo Arbenz Guzmán, with texts of the law, public statements, and official studies extolling its prospects and hailing its significance in creating the "new" Guatemala. DLC

414   Ewald, Robert Harold. Bibliografía comentada sobre antropología social guatemalteca, 1900-1955. Guatemala: Tipografía Nacional, 1956. 132 pp.

A bibliographical essay providing basic descriptive information regarding existing sociological literature relating to Guatemala, with the commentary in essay form and the citings of the works listed by year. Includes books and articles, as well as microfilm collections of field notes available in Guatemala. DLC LNHT

415 No entry

416 Fabrega, José Isaac. <u>Guatemala visto por un panameño</u>. Guatemala: Tipografía Nacional, 1944. 46 pp. Illus.

A series of descriptive articles recounting the impressions of a Panamanian journalist during a visit to Guatemala in 1944, originally published in <u>La Estrella de Panamá</u>. DLC

417 Fabri, Joseph. <u>Los belges au Guatemala, 1840-1845</u>. Brussels: Academie Royale des Sciences Coloniales, 1955. 266 pp. Index, biblio., notes, maps.

A history of the Belgian efforts to colonize Santo Tomás in Guatemala, tracing this little-known episode through the publications of the company and the government archives, and providing details of the plans, difficulties, and personages. Beginning during a period immediately after independence when the Central American region was in disarray, the effort lost viability as the Guatemalan government stabilized, despite the presence of military colonists. DLC LNHT

418 Fajardo Cadena, Hector, ed. "Gaceta de los Tribunales": <u>número extraordinario con motivo de la glorificación del general don Justo Rufino Barrios en el primier centenario de su nacimiento</u>. Guatemala: Published by the Gaceta, 1935. 70 pp. Illus.

A lavishly illustrated folio published as a separate volume annexed to a periodical, containing accounts of Barrios, his government, and his collaborators, all hailing his works. DLC

419 Falla, Ricardo. <u>Quiché rebelde: estudio de un movimiento de conversión religiosa, rebelde a las creencias tradicionales, en San Antonio Ilotenango, Quiché (1948-1970)</u>. Guatemala: Editorial Universitaria, 1978. 574 pp. Biblio., notes, illus., maps, tables.

An anthropological study of changing cultural and religious values in the Quiché community of San Antonio Ilotenango, written by a priest. Focuses on the social and political structure and the shifting location of power, and describes the resulting conflicts in values and beliefs, as well as the impact on the community. Although it concentrates on the years 1948-70, the volume encompasses the entire era from the Colonial period on in defining the societal characteristics and values and the impact of religion and the centralization of government. Originally prepared as a dissertation in anthropology at the University of Texas. LNHT

420 Fanjil, Vivian, and Héctor Gaitán. <u>Imágines de la ciudad de Guatemala</u>. Guatemala: Editorial Plus Ultra, 1977. 90 pp. Illus.

A collection of photographs of Guatemala City and various buildings within it, from diverse historical eras, arranged by street and barrio. LNHT BNG

421 Fergusson, Erna. <u>Guatemala</u>. New York: Knopf, 1937. x, 320 pp. Index, biblio., illus., maps. Reprint. New York: Knopf, 1946. x, 320 pp. Index, biblio., illus., maps.

An experienced travel-book author's perceptions of Guatemala based on travel during the 1930s, providing a vivid view of the country, its facilities and conditions, and a perceptive account of its people, focusing on the Indian traditions, exotica, and customs. Employs witty and understanding anecdotes reflecting personal experience to recount the life of the people and the Indians. The author's experience makes her a keen observer with an eye for the significance of events. DLC LNHT

422 Fernández, Orlando. <u>Turcios Lima; biografía y documentos</u>. Havana: Ediciones Tricontinental, 1968. 2d ed. Montevideo: Ediciones de la Banda Oriental, 1969. 155 pp.

A sympathetic treatment of one of the leftist guerrilla leaders of the 1960s, eulogizing his role. The actual biography is extremely short, with most of the volume given over to documents comprising his writings and manifestos. Also contains a prologue by César Montes. DLC

423 Fernández Marroquín, Vitalino. <u>Remembranzas de Esquipulas</u>. Guatemala: Tipografía Nacional, 1972. 127 pp. Biblio., illus.

A history of the city and its shrine, with extensive illustrations, including a contemporary description of facilities and culture as well as brief biographical sketches of its most illustrious citizens throughout history. DLC LNHT

424 Ferrús Roig, Francisco. <u>General mayor de la Universidad de San Carlos en Guatemala de la Asunción: reseña histórica</u>. Guatemala: Universidad de San Carlos, 1962. 92 pp. Illus.

A history of the University of San Carlos, Guatemala's national university, from its foundation in Colonial times to the present, emphasizing its heads, traditions, and particularly its movement as new facilities were needed. Includes discussion of its expansion, changes in its operation, and relations with the various regimes that governed the nation. DLC

425 Figueroa Ibarra, Carlos. <u>El proletariado rural en el agro guatemalteco</u>. Guatemala: Universidad de San Carlos, 1976. xxii, 428 pp. Biblio., notes.

A semi-Marxist theoretical analysis by a member of the faculty of the University of San Carlos disputing the nature of the rural labor and whether it is a real proletariat or in fact a semiproletariat. Argues that the distinction between Indian and ladino is artificial and condemns capitalism, exploitation,

and the landowners for the nation's ills.
Contends that the landowners deliberately
depress the rural laborers and the subsistence
economic sector, and that the capitalism is
too underdeveloped to create a real rural
proletariat, which is the reason for the use
of minifundia whose owners constitute a semiproletariat. TxU

426 Flamenco, José. La beneficencia en Guatemala:
reseña histórica. Guatemala: Tipografía
Nacional, 1915. 365 pp. Illus.
    The history of the various hospitals of
Guatemala, with appended biographies of lead-
ing medical figures in Guatemalan history.
The author hails the efforts of the Estrada
Cabrera regime to expand the health services
of the nation. DLC LNHT BNG

427 Fletcher, Lehman B. Guatemala's Economic
Development: The Role of Agriculture. Ames:
Iowa State University Press, 1970. ix, 212
pp. Illus., maps, tables.
    An econometric study of Guatemalan agricul-
ture by four economists working under the
auspices of AID. Focuses on the current
situation with extensive data and statistics,
most covering the period from 1950 through
1968. Includes projections for the future,
assuming continuation of current trends. A
valuable collection of economic and agricultural statistics and information. DLC LNHT

428 Florencia Calderón, Juan. Historia de la
farmacia en Guatemala. Guatemala: Tipografía
Nacional, 1924. 132 pp. Biblio., illus.,
tables.
    A discussion of the development of phar-
macies and the pharmaceutical sciences in
Guatemala, emphasizing Colonial days but covering the years through the regime of Estrada
Cabrera, with an additional chapter regarding
the history and founding of the faculty of
pharmacy at the University of San Carlos,
where the author teaches. BNG

429 Flores, Marco Antonio. Los compañeros.
Mexico: Joaquín Mortiz, 1976. 237 pp.
    A novel focusing on the guerrilla groups of
the new left in Latin America in the 1960s,
written by a Guatemalan poet and playwright
and set in that nation. Seeks to convey the
emotions and conviction of the warriors, the
brutality of their existence, and the tragedy
that pervades their lives. The constant
strain, the problem of living with death, and
the desire to avenge compatriots provide
strong emotion for this sympathetic view of
the guerrillas. DLC

430 _____. Muros de luz. Mexico: Siglo XXI,
1968. 109 pp. 2d ed. San Salvador:
Ministerio de Educación Pública, 1968.
134 pp.
    A collection of social protest poems ex-
tolling revolution and emphasizing the need
for social justice and drastic action to promote reform. The short poems, set in his
native land, treat various topical themes
related to the injustices of modern society,

the plight of the poor, and the role of revolution in promoting change. DLC

431 Flores Avendaño, Guillermo. Memorias (1900-
1970). 2 vols. Guatemala: Editorial del
Ejército, 1974. 365, 507 pp.
    The memoirs of a Guatemalan army officer
who served as president of the republic during
1957 and 1958. His long career spans the
history of the republic from the regime of
Estrada Cabrera to 1960, and hence his memoirs
include commentaries on his experiences and
activities during the Ubico regime, the revolution, and the counterrevolution. LNHT BNG

432 Flores Avendaño, Humberto. El adamscismo y
la sociedad guatemalteca. Guatemala:
Editorial Piedra Santa, 1973. 339 pp.
Biblio., tables.
    A critique of the interpretation of Richard
Newbold Adams in his studies of Guatemalan
society, arguing that his conclusions were
influenced by his Yankee-capitalist origin,
which caused him to overlook the role of
Marxist theory in his studies. The author
stresses that Adams viewed Guatemala as lacking social and economic integration, and as
racially divided; he saw the integration of
the Indians into mainstream society through
ladinization as the solution to the nation's
problems. The author of this work contends
that the real divisions in Guatemalan society
are those of class conflict in classic Marxist
terms and hence have little to do with culture
or race. He contends that Adams's interpretation served the purposes of the imperialists
who wish to deny the existence of class conflict. DLC

433 _____. Proletarización del campesino de
Guatemala. Guatemala: Editorial Piedra
Santa, 1970. 289 pp. Biblio., tables.
    A Marxist interpretation of Guatemalan
society. Contends that the rural laborers are
becoming increasingly conscious of their role
as landless laborers exploited, like all
others in their class, by the imperialists,
and that this increasing awareness of the
rural proletariat is the basis for the continuing crisis, which is in fact a class
conflict.

434 Flores M., Rosa. Chiquimula en la historia.
Chiquimula: n.p., 1952. 475 pp. Illus. 2d
ed. Guatemala: Ministerio de Educación
Pública, 1973.
    A detailed study of the history and devel-
opment of the city and province and their role
in the nation, based on archival research and
extensive interviews. Includes discussion of
the leading citizens and their role in the
national scene. DLC LNHT BNG

435 Florida, University of. An Interdisciplinary
Approach to Earthquake Redevelopment: A Case
Study of El Progreso, Guatemala. Gainesville:
University of Florida Press, 1977.
    A detailed study of El Progreso, using the
earthquake reconstruction to assess the com-
munity, its resources, and needs. Considers

agriculture, housing, demography, and other social and economic indicators. FU

436 Flynn, Gerard, Kenneth J. Grieb, and Richard J. Callan. Essays on Miguel Ángel Asturias. Milwaukee: University of Wisconsin--Milwaukee, 1973. 32 pp. Biblio.

Essays dealing with the political content, mythical structure, and recent criticism of Asturias's novels. Includes a discussion of the portrayal of the revolution of 1944 and of dictatorship, which is contrasted with the reality in Guatemala during these years. DLC BNG

437 Fortuny, José Manuel. Informe sobre la actividad del Comité Central del Partido Comunista de Guatemala. Guatemala: Partido Guatemalteco del Trabajo, 1953.

An official report of the activities of the Guatemalan Communist party during the Arévalo regime, prepared by its secretary general, who also served in the regime.

438 Fotografía Industrial, S.A. Todo Guatemala. Guatemala: Editorial Centroamericana Sello de Oro, 1974. 126 pp. Illus., maps.

A photo essay emphasizing the progress of modern Guatemala, contrasted with the archeological zones. DLC

439 Fox, John W. Quiché Conquest: Centralism and Regionalism in State Development in the Guatemalan Highlands. Albuquerque: University of New Mexico Press, 1978. xii, 322 pp. Index, biblio., maps.

440 Frente Popular Liberador de Guatemala. Por la patria, por la juventud y por el pueblo: reseña biográfica del licenciado Manuel Galich. Guatemala: Imprenta Hispania, 1950. 20 pp.

A campaign biography of Manuel Galich published by his party, emphasizing his role in the Arévalo regime and his activities as a leader of the revolution of October 1944. BNG

441 Frey, Martin, ed. Deutschtum in der Alta Verapaz. Stuttgart: Deutschen Verlag-Unstalt Stuttgart, 1938. 74 pp. Illus., tables.

A history of the German colony in Cobán from 1888 to 1938. Includes physical description, discussion of the role of important individuals in the community, complete statistics regarding German immigration, and a list of all families and individuals involved in the colony, with vital statistics. DLC LNHT

442 Frison, Bruno. Pahula: estudio histórico pastoral sobre la parroquia de San Cristobal Tontonicapán desde su origin hasta nuestros días. Guatemala: Instituto Teológico Salesiano, 1975. 184 pp. Biblio., illus.

A history of the village church from its foundation/by Franciscan missionaries during the Colonial era. Most of the volume deals with the years preceding independence, except for the list of pastors that provides brief biographical data to the present and the final chapter on the present organization and operation of the church. DLC LNHT

443 Fryd, Norbert. Ulybaiushchaiasia Gvatemala: putevye ocherki i zarisovki [Smiling Guatemala: travel notes and sketches]. Moscow: Gosudarstvennoe izdatel'stvo geograficheskoi literatury, 1958. 368 pp. Uśmiechnięta Gwatemala. Warsaw: Wiedza Powszecna, 1958. 379 pp. Mosolygo Guatemala: Utirajzok utikepek. Forditotta Zador Margit. Budapest: Godolat Konykiado, 1960. 294 pp. Illus., maps.

444 Fuentes, Mariano [Emirio Fuensanta, pseud.]. Bronces preclaros. Quezaltenango: Imprenta Elsmar, 1959. 107 pp.

A biography of General Francisco Fuentes, a native of Quezaltenango who began his career in that city and rose to the posts of first designate to the presidency (in 1893) and minister of war (in 1923), describing his career and service in the various Liberal regimes of the day and his role in both the politics and the civil wars of the time. BNG

445 Fuentes Castillo, Alberto. Así no da pena gastar su plata. Guatemala: Ministerio de Educación Pública, 1967. ix, 269 pp. Illus.

A collection of short stories combining naturalistic description with folklore and myth while focusing on the little trials and tribulations of everyday life among the Indian peasants, in both humorous and mystical tales that reflect the folklore and traditions of rural Guatemala as well as social protest themes. The characters include oppressive landowners and Gringos, along with long-suffering peasants who somehow manage to exist despite their trials and hence emerge as the heroes. DLC LNHT

446 Fuentes Mohr, Alberto. Secuestro y prisión: dos caras de la violencia en Guatemala. San José: EDUCA, 1971. 211 pp. Illus.

Two lengthy letters by a leading Guatemalan political figure and foreign minister, recounting day by day his kidnapping by the guerrillas. Also deals with his aspirations and plans for his country and for the Revolutionary party with which he was associated, and his activities during 1970-71. DLC LNHT BNG

447 Funes, José Alberto. Carlos Castillo Armas, presidente de la república. Guatemala: Tipografía Nacional, 1955.

Speeches exchanged between the Salvadoran army colonel serving as ambassador to Guatemala and dean of the diplomatic corps in Guatemala City and Guatemalan president Carlos Castillo Armas, on the occasion of a banquet by the diplomatic corps in honor of the Guatemalan president, with the usual official declarations of good will and cooperation. BNG

448 Gaitán, Héctor. Historias de la ciudad de Guatemala. Guatemala: Editorial Plus Ultra, 1977. 56 pp.

A discussion of the history of various buildings in Guatemala City, tracing their origins and significance in local history. BNG

449   Gaitán, Luís. *Biografía del Dr. Juan J. Ortega*. Guatemala: Universidad de San Carlos, 1958. 42 pp.
A brief biography of a Guatemalan diplomat and medical educator who headed the medical school and the general hospital during a career spanning the years 1882 through 1930. The essay was originally written in 1940 by a former student, and was published in 1958 in commemoration of the centennial of his birth. DLC

450   Galeano, Eduardo H. *Guatemala, clave de Latinoamérica*. Montevideo: Ediciones de la Banda Oriental, 1967. 166 pp. Maps.
A series of essays written from a Marxist perspective and originally published as newspaper articles, tracing the oppression of the rural peasants in Guatemala by the landowners, aided and abetted by Yankee imperialists. Includes discussion of the situation of the peasants during the 1950s and 1960s, a sympathetic account of the guerrilla movement of the 1960s, and discussion of the agrarian-reform efforts of the revolutionary governments of 1944-54, with emphasis on their frustration by Yankee intervention. DLC

451   ____. *Guatemala: país ocupado*. Mexico: Editorial Nuestro Tiempo, 1967. 129 pp. Notes, maps, appendixes. 2d ed. Paris: n.p., 1968.
Guatemala: Occupied Country. New York: Monthly Review, 1969. 159 pp. Biblio., maps.
A Marxist Uruguayan journalist's indictment of Yankee imperialism in Guatemala, with details of the oppression of the peasants. DLC LNHT

452   Galich, Luís Fernando. *Vida del guatemalteco de América: don Antonio José de Irisarri*. Guatemala: Tipografía Nacional, 1968. 48 pp. Biblio.
A brief sketch of the life and work of Antonio José de Irisarri, published on the occasion of his centennial and hailing his contributions to Latin America during the early nineteenth century in the fields of literature, diplomacy, and politics as well as to the political life and independence movements of both Central America and Chile. DLC BNG

453   Galich, Manuel. *El canciller Cadejo, historia de espantos*. Guatemala: Ministerio de Educación Pública, 1945. 94 pp.
A play from the grotesque theater, using allegory to depict the rise of totalitarianism and the impending loss of liberty, and fantasy and symbolism to depict the problems of a dictator and his actions. The play was originally written in 1940, during the Ubico regime and World War II. DLC BNG

454   ____. *Del pánico al ataque*. Guatemala: Tipografía Nacional, 1949. 362 pp.
An account of the origins of the 1944 Guatemalan revolution, by one of its leaders. Focuses on the initial resistance and organization among the student and lawyers' groups of which he was a part, tracing the initial efforts against the Ubico regime and detailing the maneuvers of 1944 from an insider's vantage point. The account is more accurate about the revolutionaries than in its interpretation of the Ubico regime, reflecting the author's viewpoint and his greater familiarity with the movement he led, as well as revolutionary stereotypes. DLC LNHT BNG

455   ____. *Guatemala*. Havana: Casa de las Américas, 1968. 88 pp. Illus., maps.
A general description and brief historical chronology, from the viewpoint of the left, condemning the effects of imperialism and calling for revolution, with comments about the contemporary guerrilla campaigns. Hails Arbenz and Arévalo, condemns Arana as a reactionary, and, of course, criticizes Castillo Armas. DLC LNHT

456   ____. *Ida y vuelta*. Guatemala: Tipografía Nacional, 1949. 87 pp.
A play about the nineteenth-century Liberal movement in Guatemala, depicting family and private lives of historical figures from 1837 and 1838. DLC BNG

457   ____. *M'hijo el bachiller*. Guatemala: Ministerio de Educación Pública, 1953. 142 pp.
A play that portrays the experiences of a Guatemalan family in which the father is a shoemaker who wins the national lottery, expands his business, and seeks to provide the best of education for his son. The play focuses on the changes in Guatemala, on the rise of the middle class and its implications for the national life-style. DLC BNG

458   ____. *La mugre: comedia en tres actos*. Guatemala: Ministerio de Educación Pública, 1953. 143 pp.
A sequel to *Papá-Natas*, this play begins in 1944 and criticizes corrupt union leaders who are linked to the previous tyrannical dictatorship, while hailing the ideals of the 1944 revolution. DLC

459   ____. *Obras de teatro*. Guatemala: Tipografía Nacional, 1946. 177 pp.
A collection of the plays of a well-known Guatemalan playwright and social commentator. Those in this volume, however, are his comedies, including *Papá-Natas*, *De lo vivo a lo pintado*, and *M'hijo el bachiller*. DLC LNHT BNG

460   ____. *Papá-Natas*. Guatemala: Ministerio de Educación Pública, 1953. 128 pp.
A satirical play portraying the oppression of the poor and their hard life, criticizing the pursuit of material well-being by individuals at the expense of others. DLC

(Galich, Manuel)

461 _____. Por qué lucha Guatemala. Arévalo y Arbenz: dos hombres contra un imperio. Buenos Aires: Elmer, 1956. 374 pp.

A defense of the Arévalo and Arbenz regimes and an indictment of Yankee intervention in Guatemala, written from exile by the former foreign minister who served the revolutionary regimes. It shows the usual bitterness against the Yankee-capitalists and the U.S. participation in the overthrow of the revolution, charging corporate opposition to meaningful reform and denying all links to communism. DLC LNHT

462 _____. El tren amarillo: drama del Caribé, en tres actos. Buenos Aires: Ediciones Transición, 1955. 93 pp. Latest ed. Havana: Editorial Tierra Nueva, 1961. 118 pp.

A revolutionary play depicting the exploitation of the peasants on the banana plantations of Central America, written by a leader of the Guatemalan revolution. Stresses the evil effects of the foreign imperialists on the region and portrays in vivid terms the impact on the peasants. DLC

463 Gall, Francis. Cerro quemado: volcán de Quezaltenango. Guatemala: Ministerio de Educación Pública, 1966. 115 pp. Biblio., illus., maps.

A history of the Cerro Quemado volcano in Quezaltenango, by a longtime officer of the Guatemalan Society of Geography and History. Studies its eruptions throughout the eighteenth and nineteenth centuries and suggests the possibility that this, rather than the volcano of Santa María, as is generally believed, is the volcano on the coat of arms of the state. The volume also includes reprints of earlier descriptions of the volcano, including that by Karl Sapper and Howel Williams. DLC LNHT BNG

464 _____. Contribución a los nombres geográficos de Guatemala. Guatemala: Instituto Geográfico Nacional, 1962. 59 pp. Maps.

A discussion of the progress and the problems involved in the study of geographic names in Guatemala, considering such questions as the definition of terminology. Prepared for the Pan American Institute of Geography and History by one of Guatemala's best-known scholars and longtime secretary of the nation's Society of Geography and History. DLC LNHT

465 _____. Estudio sobre nombres geográficos de Guatemala. Rio de Janeiro: PAIGH, 1961. 66 pp. Maps.

A compendium of basic geographical information, including a list of provincial and municipal names and a study of their derivation, along with map coordinates of each. DLC LNHT

466 Gálvez Estrada, Héctor. Rendención. Guatemala: Secretaría de Divulgación de la Presidencia, 1956. 257 pp.

A novel recounting the efforts of the National Liberation Movement and its struggles against the Guatemalan revolutionary governments, emphasizing the evils of communism, the difficulties of the liberation effort, and the oppression and atrocities allegedly committed by its communist opponents. DLC LNHT BNG

467 Gálvez García, María Albertina. Símbolos nacionales. Guatemala: Ministerio de Educación Pública, 1966. 47 pp. Illus.

One of many editions, under various similar titles, of a brief official pamphlet describing the history and origins of the Guatemalan national emblems, tracing the origins of the use of the quetzal and the changes in the national flag and coat of arms, and including discussion of the national anthem and flower. Designed for the general public, it provides basic information and a history of the emergence and significance of these items, with photos of the various flags and coats of arms. DLC LNHT BNG

468 _____. Síntesis bio-bibliográfica de don José Toribio Medina y su "Historia de la imprenta en Guatemala." Guatemala: Ministerio de Educación Pública, 1960. 46 pp. Illus.

A brief sketch of the life of the author and of the origins of the volume Historia de la imprenta en Guatemala by José Toribio Medina, explaining that the work began as a series of articles in his magazine in his native Chile. DLC LNHT BNG

469 Gámez, José Dolores, and Enrique Guzmán. Rafael Carrera y Justo Rufino Barrios ante al historia: discusión entre J.D. Gámez y Enrique Guzmán en el año 1889. Managua: Tipografía Internacional, 1907. 133 pp.

A series of letters originally published in 1889 in El Diario Nicaragüense and republished in book form by the Nicaraguan Liberal party, consisting of a debate about the historical standing and alleged abuses of the Guatemalan Conservative and Liberal leaders that constituted part of the continuing polemic among their respective supporters and led to numerous exchanges of charges and countercharges. LNHT

470 Gandarias, León de. Jornadas periodísticas: etapas notables de la prensa guatemalteca. Guatemala: n.p., 1959. 80 pp. Illus.

A series of brief essays discussing significant figures from the history of Guatemalan newspapers and the role of the various publications in their eras, with photos of the principal editors and journalists. DLC LNHT BNG

471 _____. La reforma social. Mexico: Editorial Studium, 1954. 156 pp.

An attack on socialism that condemns violence, emphasizes the need to resolve social problems on a global scale and the need for progressive legislation, and defends the capitalist system and individual rights. Part of the political polemics that characterized the clash between the Guatemalan socialists and revolutionaries and the right-wing counterrevolutionaries. BNG

472 Garavito, Humberto, ed. <u>Francisco Cabrera:</u>
<u>miniaturista guatemalteco 1781-1845.</u>
Guatemala: Tipografía Nacional, 1945. xx,
167 pp. Illus.
        A brief biographical sketch of a Guatemalan
miniaturist, followed by an extensive album of
his paintings of significant individuals of
his era. The collection provides a view of
the life and life-style of his years, particularly of the upper class. BNG

473 García, A.V. <u>Guatemala y sus progresos en</u>
<u>presencia de la reacción.</u> Guatemala:
Tipografía "El Progreso," 1878. 20 pp.
Latest ed. Guatemala: Tipografía Nacional,
1906. 26 pp.
        A defense of the Estrada Cabrera regime and
a reply to the Conservative party criticisms,
contending that all such attacks reflect politics and the party's ambitions. LNHT

474 García Acietuna, José Luís. <u>Don Rufino.</u>
Guatemala: Tipografía Nacional, 1959.
525 pp.
        An historical novel, which the author con-
tends represents historical reality, provides
a "true" account of the era despite being a
novel, and is based on documentary research,
though it contains neither bibliography nor
footnotes. Extolls the virtues of Barrios,
the Liberal tradition in Guatemala, and the
glories of the Guatemalan army, in that order.
Includes some criticism of the Liberal party
before Barrios's term, but the emphasis in
dealing with Barrios is entirely positive.
BNG

475 _____. <u>Esquipulas: reseña histórica del</u>
<u>culto del Señor Crucificado que se venera en</u>
<u>este santuario; origen de la imagen y las</u>
<u>romerías; crónicas, leyendas y tradiciones;</u>
<u>documentación histórica desde los tiempos de</u>
<u>la colonia hasta nuestros días.</u> Jalapa:
Editorial Oriental, 1940. 348 pp. Illus.,
maps. 2d ed. Jalapa: Editorial Oriental,
1954. 327 pp. Illus., maps.
        A history of the shrine of Esquipulas, its
legends, origins, and role in the religious
life of Guatemala and Central America, with
appropriate illustrations. The shrine dates
from 1594. The volume includes descriptions
of the shrine's important festivals, directions as to how to get there, accounts of the
legends associated with its "Black Christ,"
and a catalog of "miracles" ascribed to it. A
brief history of the city of Esquipulas is
appended. DLC LNHT BNG

476 _____. <u>Leyendas indígenas de Guatemala.</u>
Guatemala: Editorial Oriental, 1942. 272 pp.
Illus. 2d ed. Guatemala: Editorial
Oriental 1959. 251 pp.
        A collection of Indian legends, narrated in
poetic verse but without specific identifica-
tion as to origin or culture. DLC

477 _____. <u>El movimiento armado del 13 de</u>
<u>noviembre de 1960.</u> Guatemala: Tipografía
Nacional, 1962. 330 pp. Illus.

        A government account of the 1960 uprising
in the province of Zacapa against the regime
of General Miguel Ydígoras Fuentes, detailing
the rebellion and the campaigns that defeated
it. Hails the leadership of Ydígoras Fuentes,
his government, and the popularity that
brought it support from the masses, while
charging that the rebellion was encouraged and
supplied from Cuba. Provides detailed evidence of communist influence and Cuban provision of supplies and training, and includes a
selection of contemporary press accounts. DLC
LNHT BNG

478 García Bauer, Carlos. <u>Antonio José de</u>
<u>Irisarri: diplomático de América; su</u>
<u>actuación en los Estados Unidos, la</u>
<u>colonización negra y la invasión filibustera.</u>
Guatemala: Editorial Universitaria, 1970.
125 pp. Biblio., notes, illus.
        A well-known Guatemalan scholar provides a
useful study of some aspects of Irisarri's
diplomatic missions in the United States,
based on documentary research in the Archivo
General de Centroamérica and the papers of the
U.S. Department of State. Irisarri, at the
end of a varied and distinguished career,
represented Guatemala, Nicaragua, and El
Salvador in Washington from 1855 to 1868 and
served as dean of the diplomatic corps there
during the 1860s. The volume focuses on the
questions of American attempts to promote
black settlement in Central America, the era
of the Yankee filibustering during the 1850s,
and Irisarri's efforts to defend Central
American interests against the aggressive
Northern Colossus. DLC LNHT BNG

479 _____. <u>En el amanecer de una nueva era:</u>
<u>espisodios de la participación de Guatemala en</u>
<u>la vida internacional.</u> Guatemala: Tipografía
Nacional, 1951. 203 pp. Illus.
        A series of speeches by the Guatemalan
representative to the U.N. that deal with
various international themes, such as human
rights, Spain, and Jerusalem. DLC LNHT BNG

480 _____. <u>Jorge García Granados: humanista y</u>
<u>político.</u> Guatemala: Editorial Prensa Libre,
1967. 94 pp. Illus.
        A eulogy of the Guatemalan diplomat and
political figure by an equally eminent figure
in these fields, extolling his work and emphasizing his role in Israel with the U.N. commission. DLC BNG

481 García Bauer, José. <u>Digesto constitucional</u>
<u>centroamericano.</u> Guatemala: Tipografía
Nacional, 1971. 206 pp.
        A collection of documents pertaining to the
origins of constitutionalism in Central
America. Includes Spanish constitutions of
the Colonial era, the initial decrees regarding Central American independence, and the
Constitution of 1823 of the Federation of
Central America, with brief introductory descriptions by the author. The volume is intended as the first of a series covering all
of Guatemalan constitutional history, but is
the only one to date. DLC

(García Bauer, José)

482 _____. *Filosofía social cristiana a propósito de sus principios, doctrinas y valores, con algunas referencias en Guatemala.* Guatemala: Tipografía Nacional, 1967. 798 pp. Notes, appendix.

A major treatise discussing the general basis of all aspects of Christian social philosophy, emphasizing the family as the foundation of society, the role of Christian outlook, and the idea of property, as well as the role of education. Includes a chapter on the Guatemalan church and its role in dealing with social problems, which is based entirely on the post-1962 era and the encyclical *Mater et Magistra.* The appendix includes reproductions of numerous papal encyclicals and pronouncements of the Vatican II Council. The statement emphasizes the importance of the church's role in solving social problems, advocates an active church role in national society, and stresses the duty of all Christians to seek social justice. Enunciates the new activist role of the Guatemalan church, which is consistent with the attitude of the Latin American churches during the 1960s and 1970s. Though the work of the author, support by the church is evident in the introduction by the papal nuncio. DLC LNHT BNG

483 _____. *Nuestra revolución legislativa.* Guatemala: Tipografía Nacional, 1948. 207 pp. 2d ed. Guatemala: C.A. Press, 1949. 267 pp.

A series of essays by a Guatemalan congressman, written while still a law student, discussing the philosophical origins of the law and such questions as political and economic equality, communism, materialism, aristocracy, and the family. The latter section focuses on the Guatemalan legal system and recent congressional actions, emphasizing the positive impact of the laws. DLC LNHT BNG

484 _____. *Religión y comunismo.* Guatemala: Ministerio de Educación Pública, 1954. 54 pp. Illus.

In addition to the title essay, the pamphlet contains a pastoral letter by the archbishop of Guatemala, Mariano Rossell Arellano. Both are part of the propaganda of the 1950s and the clash of ideologies in Guatemala, emphasizing the religious persecution by communism while contending that Catholicism and communism are incompatible. BNG

485 García Goyena, Rafael. *Fábulas del doctor don Rafael García Goyena.* Guatemala: n.p., 1825. Latest ed. Guatemala: Ministerio de Educación Pública, 1965. 204 pp.

A series of poetic fables dealing with disparate Guatemalan themes, reflecting the concerns of the independence era. Originally written in 1825 by a Guatemalan poet and scion of a prominent family, these verses are considered to reflect the transition in literature from Colonial to national themes. They include some political commentaries on the new situation of the nation and its form of government. The volume has gone through many editions in Europe and Guatemala and is considered one of the classics of that nation's literature. DLC

486 García Granados, Jorge. *Ensayo sobre sociología guatemalteca.* Guatemala: Sánchez & de Guise, 1927. 68 pp. Notes, tables.

Though a thesis, this work is interesting in terms of the subsequent prominence of its author. It consists of a general survey of the characteristics of Guatemalan society from the Conquest to 1920, characterizing the process as the substitution of armed conquest, rejection of authority of the motherland, solidification of the predominance of the oligarchy, and finally the substitution of economic interests for personal ones as the dominant elements. LNHT

487 _____. *Evolución sociológica de Guatemala ensayo sobre el gobierno.* Guatemala: Sánchez & de Guise, 1927. 164 pp. Latest ed. Guatemala: Sánchez & de Guise, 1930. 164 pp.

An essay examining the state of the nation during the government of Mariano Gálvez in the 1830s, outlining the structure of society, examining the problems of the day, and placing the political situation in that overall context. The author concludes that the oppressive and dictatorial governments were in fact a product of their time, reflecting the conditions of society. He advocates a typically upper-class viewpoint, positing that the country consists of "the governed," mainly the Indians who have degenerated and are incapable of anything, and "the leaders," mainly the upper class of Spanish descent, and that the nation must be consequently characterized by a hierarchial society and government. DLC LNHT BNG

488 García Granados, Miguel. *Memorias del general Miguel García Granados.* 2 vols. Guatemala: Imprenta de El Progreso and Tipografía Nacional, 1877-94. 282, 272 pp. 2d ed. Guatemala: Ministerio de Educación Pública, 1952. 551 pp. Index, illus.

The memoirs of an important Liberal political figure, published in two parts. The initial volume covered the years to 1829, while the second volume spanning the period 1829 to 1838 was published many years later, reflecting its political sensitivity. Provides a detailed account of the author's actions and career as well as of the events of these years, including observations about the origins of the two major political parties and their disputes that illuminate the century's political scene. DLC LNHT BNG

489 García Laguardia, Jorge Mario. *Antecedentes del seguro social en Guatemala: la responsabilidad civil y los infortunios de trabajo.* Guatemala: Imprenta Universitaria, 1964. 195 pp. Biblio., notes.

A legal study of the antecedents and structure of Social Security in Guatemala, tracing the idea of employer responsibility for his workers back to Roman law and discussing the

(García Laguardia, Jorge Mario)
effects of the various legislation regarding
the relationship of workers and employers.
LNHT   BNG

490   _____. La génesis del constitucionalismo
guatemalteco: estudio preliminar selección de
documentos y notas. Guatemala: Editorial
Universitaria, 1971. lxii, 456 pp. Illus.
A detailed study of the Central American
and Guatemalan participation in the Cádiz
government and constitution. Stresses French
influence and reprints the pertinent documents
at length, including the minutes of the
meetings. LNHT BNG

491   _____, ed. El pensamiento Liberal en
Guatemala: antología. San José: EDUCA,
1976. 362 pp. Notes.
A well-known scholar of the Guatemalan
Liberal movement provides a brief summary of
the impact of the reforms of the late nineteenth century and a collection of documents
from the era. Focused on the Liberal leaders,
the book is designed to provide convenient
excerpts for classroom use. LNHT

492   García Laguardia, Jorge Mario. La reforma
Liberal en Guatemala: vida política y orden
constitucional. Guatemala: Editorial
Universitaria, 1972. 457 pp. Biblio., notes,
illus., appendixes. Latest ed. Mexico:
UNAM, 1980. 266 pp. Biblio., notes, illus.
A history of the Liberal movement during
the 1870s concentrating on its early phase and
the constitutions of 1872 and 1876. The latter half of the volume is devoted to reproductions of appropriate documents from the era.
Based on documentary sources, it uses memoirs,
official acts, proclamations, newspapers, and
political pamphlets from the era, supplemented
by secondary sources. The focus is on the
political and ideological aspects of the Liberal movement, the constitution and its origins, and the conflict between Miguel García
Granados and Justo Rufino Barrios. The 1876
constitution is characterized as representing
"democratic dictatorship." DLC LNHT BNG

493   García Mejía, René. Golpe a las 2 A.M. Ensayo
teatral en dos actos. Guatemala: Imprenta
Romero, 1958. 32 pp.
A brief play detailing an attempted coup in
a small country, supposedly one that could be
any of the Latin American nations in the mid-
1950s but based on the September 1955 uprising
in Guatemala, to whose dead it is dedicated.
The entire episode is seen from a distance,
with the play set in an embassy residence
where reports of the episode are followed with
some of the participants passing through.
LNHT

494   García Salas, José María. Panorama
guatemalteco: bellezas naturales de la
República de Guatemala. Guatemala: Imprenta
"El Comercio," 1891. 318 pp.
Descriptions of physical settings and locations in Guatemala, collected from various
writings by nationals and foreign visitors,
emphasizing the beauty of the country. LNHT
BNG

495   Gardner, Mary A. The Press of Guatemala.
Lexington, Ky.: Association for Education in
Journalism, 1971. 48 pp. Biblio.
A brief overview of the present situation
of the Guatemalan press, emphasizing the legal
climate and the political orientations of the
various newspapers, with details about each
publication and its editors. Contains some
historical background in summary fashion. DLC

496   Gehlert Mata, Carlos. Análisis y
consideraciones sobre problemas sanitarios de
Guatemala: sus posibles soluciones.
Guatemala: Ministerio de Educación Pública,
1966. 199 pp. Biblio., maps, tables.
A discussion of the current health situation of Guatemala, with profiles and discussion of such aspects as birth and death rates,
abortions, availability of water and sanitary
services, and population growth. Seeks to
emphasize the differences between rural and
urban areas as well as between the various
social classes, arguing in favor of a massive
effort to provide services to the lower levels, which suffer much higher rates of disease
and death than the upper and middle sectors.
DLC LNHT

497   Geiger, Theodore. Communism Versus Progress
in Guatemala. Washington, D.C.: National
Planning Association, 1953. 90 pp. Illus.,
maps, tables.
A brief statement of the case charging that
the government of Guatemala was increasingly
coming under communist influence. Includes,
in addition to a listing of evidence and recent actions, a discussion of the role of the
various political and social segments and a
brief summary of previous Guatemalan history.
DLC

498   Gereda Asturias, Ramiro. Un militar en el
servicio diplomático. Guatemala: Tipografía
Nacional, 1958. 121 pp. Illus.
The memoirs and commentaries of a
Guatemalan army colonel who served in that
nation's diplomatic service. Includes general
commentaries on the nature of the diplomatic
service, descriptions of the author's travels
and experiences, principally in Mexico, New
York, and especially Panama, where he served.
The essays were previously published in
Guatemalan newspapers, though they are not
identified and dates are not provided. BNG

499   _____. Táctica general aplicada al medio
centroamericano. Guatemala: Tipografía
Nacional, 1938. 372 pp. Illus.
A manual of military tactics for the
Guatemalan army that focuses more sharply than
most on the Central American terrain and the
adaptations it requires. BNG

500   Giacomán, Helmy F., ed. Homenaje a Miguel
Ángel Asturias: variaciones interpretativas
en torno a su obra. New York: Las Américas,
1972. 334 pp. Biblio., notes.

A collection of analytical pieces dealing principally with the themes of Asturias's novels, all previously published by various authors. The banana triology and El señor presidente receive the most coverage. DLC

501 Gillin, John Phillip. The Culture of Security in San Carlos: A Study of a Guatemalan Community of Indians and Ladinos. New Orleans: MARI, 1951. vii, 128 pp. Biblio., tables. San Luís Jilotepeque: la seguridad del individuo y de la sociedad en la cultura de una comunidad guatemalteca de indígenas y ladinos. Guatemala: Ministerio de Educación Pública, 1958. 366 pp. Biblio., tables.
A careful study, based on fieldwork conducted during several stays between 1942 and 1948, of a Pokomám Indian community in Guatemala. Focuses on local beliefs and the social situation, emphasizing the ties to the old system and the community's outlook, which provide the security of a stable social and economic situation that, despite the fact that it provides only a meager existence, assures all a niche and provides a certain outlook toward the future. Includes consideration of the resistance to and impact of change, the role of the church, the mixing of Catholicism with native beliefs, the local political structure and economy, agriculture, nutrition, family structure, and the common value system of the residents, as well as of the impact of ladinos with ties to the rest of the nation and differing values. The name used in the title is ficticious to preserve the identity of the actual community. DLC LNHT BNG

502 Gómez, Ignacio. Biografía del ilustre centro americano licenciado don Miguel Larrenaga. Guatemala: Imprenta La Aurora, 1847. Pages unnumbered.
A brief biographical sketch of the career of the president of the Supreme Court during the original Federation of Central America in the immediate post-independence era. BNG

503 Gómez Carrillo, Agustín. Biografías de presidentes del Poder Judicial. Guatemala: Tipografía Nacional, 1902. 191 pp. 2d ed. Guatemala: Ministerio de Educación Pública, 1967. 168 pp.
Chronologically arranged biographies of the six individuals who served as president of the Judicial Power or Supreme Court of Guatemala from 1821 through 1893. The career of each prior to his appointment is traced, including publications, schooling, political service, and legal experience, though there is no discussion of their service on the Supreme Court itself or of their decisions. LNHT BNG

504 Gómez Carrillo, Enrique. El despertar del alma: treinta años de mi vida. Guatemala: Ministerio de Educación Pública, 1966. 239 pp.
A reprinting, under a different title of GU509. LNHT

505 _____. Historia del gobierno de don Manuel Estrada Cabrera. Barcelona: Casa Editorial Sopena, n.d. 237 pp. Illus.

A detailed account of the events of the regime of Estrada Cabrera, defending the actions of the dictator and emphasizing the positive aspects of his rule. The biography includes a discussion of his outlook as well as topical considerations of the most important aspects of his regime, such as the development program, educational expansion, the financial crisis, and the various revolts with which he had to contend. BNG

506 _____. Manuel Estrada Cabrera: MDCCCXCVIII. Guatemala: Tipografía de Arturo Siguere, 1898. 31 pp.
A brief campaign pamphlet describing Estrada Cabrera in glowing terms, reflecting Gómez Carrillo's journalistic career. BNG

507 _____. Obras completas. 26 vols. Madrid: Editorial Mundo Latino, 1919-23.
The collected works of a well-known Guatemalan writer, whose efforts include novels, short stories, chronicles, and memoirs, but predominantly short stories. He lived much of his life in Spain and traveled widely throughout the world during the first two decades of the twentieth century, hence most of his literary production deals with European or foreign themes rather than Guatemalan subjects. DLC

508 _____. Páginas escogidas. 3 vols. Guatemala: Ministerio de Educación Pública, 1954. xxx, 372 pp. Illus.
A series of essays, short stories, and memoirs, including his impressions of the places he visited on his various travels, plus essays on disparate subjects. DLC LNHT BNG

509 _____. Treinta años de mi vida. Madrid: Tipografía Yagües, 1919. 24 pp.
The initial volume in a series of memoirs by this Guatemalan literary figure. Covers his youth, adolescence, and school years, focusing on his companions and the experiences that affected his attitudes, ends with his departure from Guatemala for Europe in the 1890s. DLC

510 González, Nicolás Augusto. Desde el llano. Guatemala: Sánchez & de Guise, 1908. 68 pp. Illus.
The memoirs of an Ecuadorian exile who lived in Guatemala, recounting his acquaintances and dealings with the leading figures of the Liberal era. The focus is particularly on Manuel Estrada Cabrera, seeking to show the dictator as an individual with a warm personality, while briefly narrating the author's own participation in various events spanning the era and his contacts with Justo Rufino Barrios, Miguel García Granados, and others. His comments were written in Peru after his return to South America. LNHT

511 _____. Mis presidentes. Guatemala: Tipografía Nacional, 1915. 29 pp.
A series of brief essays recounting the author's contacts with various Guatemalan and

Salvadoran presidents, covering the late nineteenth and early twentieth centuries, condemning some and hailing others, and emphasizing physical description and his own acquaintance with them. DPU

512 González, Otto-Raúl. Poesía fundamental, 1943-1967. Guatemala: Editorial Universitaria, 1973. 523 pp.
A collection of poetry covering the author's works from 1943 to 1967 by one of the "Generation of 1940," that is, the writers associated with the Guatemalan revolution of 1944 and subsequently embittered by the 1954 counterrevolution. His poetry reflects the leftist ideals of the revolutionaries and the changes in outlook they underwent from the optimistic years of the revolutionary governments to the disillusion of defeat and exile, focusing on the peasant discontent and the injustices of life as seen by the lower classes. DLC LNHT BNG

513 González Campo, Enrique. Casos y cosas. Guatemala: n.p., 1966. 107 pp. Illus.
A collection of anecdotes set in the Empresa Eléctrica de Guatemala, which the author recalls from his twenty-five years of employment there. DLC

514 González Campo, Federico. Fiesta de remembranzas: periodismo y periodistas. Guatemala: Tipografía Nacional, 1967. 98 pp.
A well-known Guatemalan newspaperman writes a series of essays about journalism, including a history of journalism in Central America, focusing particularly on his own country. He covers radio reporting in addition to newspapers, and comments on the impact of the news media. DLC BNG

515 González Orellana, Carlos. Historia de la educación en Guatemala. Mexico: B. Costa-Amic, 1960. 462 pp. Biblio. 2d ed. Guatemala: Ministerio de Educación Pública, 1970. 564 pp. Biblio.
A Guatemalan professor who served as subsecretary of education during the revolutionary regimes provides this history of Guatemalan education, written in exile in Mexico. The volume covers the entire span of Guatemalan history from Maya times to the end of the revolutionary era in 1954, offering a narrative and analysis which, though well researched, reflects his biases when dealing with the Ubico and revolutionary regimes, with a disproportionate share of the volume devoted to praise of the Revolutionary programs. Provides an effective overview of educational development in Guatemala during the pre-1930 era. DLC LNHT BNG

516 González Quezada, Carlos Alfonso. Monografía del municipio de Santa Lucía Cotzumalguapa. Guatemala: Ministerio de Educación Pública, 1974. 320 pp. Illus., maps.
A monograph of a city in Escuintla, providing a history of the area and its Indian cultures; extensive descriptive data on

current facilities, accompanied by illustrations; and a detailed discussion of the work at its archeological zone, which is also illustrated. DLC LNHT

517 González R., Mario Gilberto. Distinciones otorgadas a la muy noble y muy leal ciudad de Santiago de los Caballeros de Guatemala. Guatemala: Ministerio de Educación Pública, 1964. 92 pp. Illus.
A collection of various significant laws and grants regarding the city, and distinctions regarding its buildings and institutions. Covers the entire history of the city, though the emphasis is on the Colonial era. DLC BNG

518 _____. El divino jesuita: Rafael Landívar. Guatemala: Ministerio de Educación Pública, 1962. 31 pp. Illus.
A brief sketch acclaiming the contribution of Landívar to the independence movement and outlining his life, with illustrations and selections from his poetry. Part of a popular series for the general reader and the schools. LNHT

519 _____. Pequeña reseña bio-bibliográfica de Carlos Wyld Ospina. Guatemala: Ministerio de Educación Pública, 1957. 53 pp. Illus.
A very brief sketch of the life of a major Guatemalan literary figure, with excerpts from contemporary newspaper reviews of his works and selections from his poetry. The actual biography comprises less than ten pages. DLC BNG

520 González Ruiz, Ricardo, ed. Guatemala de hoy. Guatemala: Imprenta Sansur, 1949. 231 pp. Illus., maps.
A general appreciation of contemporary Guatemala, providing basic data and focusing on the changes of the Guatemalan revolution, with chapters dealing with the new governmental institutions designed to provide additional services to the populace. Lavishly illustrated and also containing advertisements. The subject matter is quite disparate. DLC BNG

521 González Saravia, Antonio. Derecho patrio. 2 vols. Guatemala: Tipografía Nacional, 1910-14. 181, 323 pp.
A collection of basic Guatemalan legislation and court cases, compiled by the president of the Guatemalan Supreme Court under the regime of Manuel Estrada Cabrera. Intended as a handbook for lawyers, it offers limited commentary. DLC BNG

522 Goodman, Roland A. Guatemala: A Handbook on the Postal History and Philately of Guatemala by the International Society of Guatemalan Collectors. 2 vols. London: Robson Lowe, 1969-74. 277 pp. Illus.
A detailed history of Guatemalan postage stamps, with color photos and full specifications for each issue regarding design, denominations, size, quantity printed, etc., for use by collectors. The first volume covers issues

through 1902 and the second from 1902 to 1971. Includes discussions of preprinted envelopes, postal meter designs, postmarks, and the various exhibitions of Guatemalan stamps. DLC LNHT

523 Goubaud Carrera, Antonio. Distribución de las lenguas indígenas actuales de Guatemala. Guatemala: Instituto Indigenista Nacional, 1946. 16 pp. Biblio., map, tables.
 A province-by-province listing of the prevailing Indian languages of Guatemala, with a map tracing their distribution, a bibliography, and definitions of the terms employed in the study. DLC

524 _____. Indigenismo en Guatemala. Guatemala: Ministerio de Educación Pública, 1964. 259 pp. Biblio., illus., maps, tables.
 A series of studies by the founder of the Guatemalan Indigenous Institute, who led the way in promoting domestic anthropological studies of the Indians, both modern and past. The essays were previously published in newspapers or served as speeches on various occasions, and are here gathered in one place posthumously under the auspices of the Seminario de Integración Social. They cover a broad range of topics, from analysis of the Maya numerical system to a study of the diet of Guatemalan Indians during the 1940s. DLC LNHT BNG

525 Gracias, Domingo. Contribución a la defensa de Estrada Cabrera. Guatemala: Unión Tipografía, 1924. 26 pp.
 A statement supporting the former president, describing his numerous programs and public works and the state of the country at the time. DLC

526 Gramajo, José Ramón. Monografía histórica: las traiciones militares del 97. Quezaltenango: Torres Hermanos, 1934. 116 pp. Illus.
 A participant's account of the unsuccessful revolution against the regime of Reyna Barrios in eastern Guatemala in 1897. Details the events, plans, combats, and failures. Most of it was previously published in various newspapers. Includes interviews with veterans of the rebel forces. The account supplements and overlaps the author's previous writings from exile in 1898. DLC BNG

527 _____, ed. Reproducción de los datos históricos de la revolución de Guatemala en 1897. Managua: Talleres Gráficos Cisneros, 1898. 3d ed. San Salvador: Talleres Gráficos Cisneros, 1931. 94 pp.
 An account of the unsuccessful 1879 revolt in western Guatemala against the regime of José María Reyna Barrios, originally published in exile in the Managua newspaper El Liberal in 1898. Details the events, emphasizing the brutality of the repression by the regime, and charges that the revolutionary effort was betrayed. Includes some documents regarding those later charged, some of whom the author contends had nothing to do with the uprising.

The Guatemalan edition, published in Jalapa in 1930, employed the title Fiat Lux. LNHT BNG

528 Gramajo, José Ramón. Las revoluciones exteriores contra el ex-presidente Estrada Cabrera. 2 vols. Mazatenango and Coatepeque: Torres Hermanos, 1937-43. 183, 100 pp.
 A series of articles, some previously published in Nuestro Diario of Guatemala City, detailing the various uprisings against the Estrada Cabrera regime, with particular attention to the leaders. The author states that he wishes to be sure that the role of these "heroes" is preserved, claiming that he is the first to write about this period. Includes some of the correspondence involved. DLC LNHT BNG

529 Granados, Jenny. Doña María Teresa Laparra de Ydígoras Fuentes: su vida y su obra. Guatemala: Ministerio de Educación Pública, 1962. 41 pp. Illus.
 A brief biographical sketch of the wife of the then-president of Guatemala, hailing her efforts to promote the national culture and expand social and health services. BNG

530 Great Britain, Gov't of. Foreign Office. Report on Events Leading up to and Arising out of the Change of Regime in Guatemala, 1954. London: HMSO, 1954. iv, 125 pp.
 A compilation of the OAS and U.N. documents and proceedings regarding the 1954 overthrow of the Arbenz revolutionary government. DLC

531 Grieb, Kenneth J. Guatemalan Caudillo: The Regime of Jorge Ubico, Guatemala, 1931-1944. Athens: Ohio University Press, 1979. xv, 384 pp. Index, biblio., notes, maps, tables.
 A detailed study of the Ubico regime, based on U.S. and Guatemalan documents, interviews, and the local press and focusing on a pivotal period of Guatemalan development that constitutes a watershed in the nation's politics. Includes consideration of the regime's extensive development efforts and the effects on the economy and nation, as well as examination of all aspects of foreign policy, including the twists and turns of isthmian rivalries, relations with Europe, the Yankees, Mexico, and the revival of the Belize question. Provides a scholarly and dispassionate analysis that penetrates the political polemics and the resulting mythology that surround this era. Includes consideration of the origins of the revolutionary movement, its sources, and leaders, as well as of its stereotyped view of the Ubico regime. DLC LNHT

532 Griffith, William Joyce. Empires in the Wilderness: Foreign Colonization and Development in Guatemala, 1834-1844. Chapel Hill: University of North Carolina Press, 1965. x, 332 pp. Index, biblio., notes, maps.
 A careful monograph based on documents, examining the efforts of the regime of Mariano Gálvez to promote European and specifically British colonization along Guatemala's remote northern frontier and east coast during the

(Griffith, William Joyce)

years 1834-44, indicating the hopes and problems involved in the venture, which ultimately failed. A detailed study of one of the much-neglected colonization schemes that reflected the outlook of the day and the problems of settling the remote coastal and interior portion of the nation, which played an important role in its development and later politics and economy. DLC LNHT BNG

533 _____. Santo Tomás: anhelado emporio del comercio en el Atlántico. Guatemala: Tipografía Nacional, 1959. 50 pp. Notes.

A valuable overview of Guatemalan efforts to develop Santo Tomás and Alta Verapaz, including the foreign colonization efforts during the first half of the nineteenth century. Based on research in documents and published works. DLC BNG

534 Guardia, Manuel César de la. Libertador y mártir. Guatemala: Editorial Indoamérica, 1957. 383 pp. Illus.

A collection of emotional prose extolling the virtues of Colonel Carlos Castillo Armas and his wife Odilia Palomo de Castillo, recounting the liberation of the nation and tracing the widow's subsequent political activities. Included are sections providing accounts of the key era, a biography, discussions of political views and philosophy, and excerpts from the press and foreign commentary, all ringing with praise. LNHT

535 Guatemala, Academia Guatemalteca. Biografías de literatos nacionales: publicación de la Academia Guatemalteca correspondiente de la Real Academia Española. Guatemala: Tipografía La Unión, 1889.

A series of brief biographical sketches, by various contributors, of several leading Guatemalan authors. The volume includes excerpts from their works and literary criticisms by the contributors. DLC LNHT BNG

536 Guatemala, Arzobispado de. Segundo centenario de arzobispado de Guatemala. Guatemala: Arzobispado Metropolitano de Guatemala, 1947. 126 pp. Illus.

A volume commemorating the 200th anniversary of the founding of the archbishopric of Guatemala, published by the archbishopric and reviewing its history from 1743 to 1943. The acts of celebration and the attendant speeches are reproduced, along with documents from the founding of the diocese and photos of Guatemalan churchmen and churches. LNHT BNG

537 Guatemala, Asociación Nacional de Constructores de Viviendas de. El problema habitacional en Guatemala. Guatemala: Published by the Association, 1977. 27 pp. Illus.

A discussion of the housing shortage and a projection into the future, noting the mounting deficit and calling for an expanded government program of construction. BNG

538 Guatemala, Ayuntamiento de. Instrucciones para la constitución fundamental de la monarquía española y su gobierno de que ha de tratarse en las próximas Cortes Generales de la nación, dadas por el M. I. ayuntamiento de la M. N. y L. ciudad de Guatemala a su diputado el Sr. D. Antonio de Larrazabal. Guatemala: Ministerio de Educación Pública, 1953. xx, 86 pp.

The instructions of the Guatemalan ayuntamiento to its delegate to the Cortes of Cádiz of 1810, which many Guatemalans consider a precursor to independence. They mirror the views of the leading citizens as to the form and method of government appropriate to their nation as well as to Spain and its empire, and as such reflect one of the earliest formal statements of thoughts regarding government in Guatemala. DLC BNG

539 Guatemala, Comité Central Pro Centenario de la Revolución de 1871. El acta de patricia. Guatemala: Tipografía Nacional, 1971. 239 pp.

The original declaration of the Liberal Revolution of 1871 against the government of Vicente Cerna, reproduced photographically in its original handwritten form, followed by reprintings of the various declarations of support from the diverse municipalities of the republic. BNG

540 _____. Índice general de las leyes emitidas por los gobiernos de la revolución de 1871 (la reforma): época de los presidentes Miguel García Granados y Justo Rufino Barrios. Guatemala: Tipografía Nacional, 1971. 194 pp.

An index to the reform legislation of the Liberal reform era, published on the centennial of the revolution that brought the Liberals to power. LNHT BNG

541 _____. Índice de las leyes de reforma emitidas por el gobierno de la República de Guatemala establecido después de la revolución de 1871, desde junio del mismo año, hasta noviembre de 1879 año en que se instala la Asamblea Nacional Constituyente. Guatemala: Tipografía Nacional, 1971.

See item GU540. LNHT BNG

542 Guatemala, Comité Central Pro Festejos de la Revolución de 1871. Antecedentes históricos de la Revolución de 1871. Guatemala: Ministerio de Educación Pública, 1971. 139 pp.

One of many pamphlets published in honor of the centennial of the Liberal revolution, this volume consists of a collection of documents and laws, reproduced from the pages of La Gaceta and La Semana, offering some of the ultimate actions of the Vicente Cerna administration and the initial actions of the Liberal revolutionary movement. LNHT BNG

543 Guatemala, Comité de Estudiantes Universitarios Anticomunistas de. El calvario de Guatemala. Guatemala: Tipografía Nacional, 1955. 397 pp. Illus.

(Guatemala, Comité de Estudiantes
Universitarios Anticomunistas de)
  A compilation of the allegations and
charges against the Guatemalan revolutionary
governments detailing the crimes, massacres,
and tortures of which their opponents accused
them. Focusing particularly on the last year
of the Arbenz regime, the volume offers accounts of the various executions, arrests, and
other oppressive actions from diverse parts of
the republic and identifies the "martyrs."
Includes a discussion of the policies of the
Castillo Armas regime for the future. DLC
BNG

544   ____. Del comunismo en Guatemala.
Tegucigalpa: Imprenta Calderón, 1954. 29 pp.
  A statement addressed to the Tenth Inter-
american Conference in Caracas, stating the
rightist case against communist infiltration
in Guatemala and listing the various positions
held by communists and the actions of the
government in various ministries that followed
its doctrine. DLC

545   ____. Plan de Tegucigalpa: el coronel
Carlos Castillo Armas ha dicho. N.p.:
Talleres Gráficos Liberación, 1953. 65 pp.
  The governmental plan and platform of the
Liberación Nacional movement, announced and
prepared in exile in Tegucigalpa, indicating
its intentions after seizing power, condemning
communism, and citing the movement's links
with Guatemalan history. DLC LNHT BNG

546 Guatemala, Comité Guatemalteco de Defensa de
los Derechos Humanos. La violencia en
Guatemala: dramática y documentada denuncia
sobre el tercer gobierno de la revolución, la
democracia de Méndez Montenegro. Mexico:
Fondo de Cultura Popular, 1969. 215 pp.
  A detailed report of the violence and victims in Guatemala from 1967 to 1969, focusing
on the actions of the rightist terrorist
groups. DLC

547 Guatemala, Congreso Nacional de Economistas,
Contradores Públicos y Auditores. Una
política para el desarrollo económico de
Guatemala. Guatemala: Universidad de San
Carlos, 1969. 386 pp. Tables.
  An economic and financial survey of the
present state of the nation, with extensive
statistics, considering natural and human
resources, infrastructure, production, fiscal
situation, trade, and balance of payments,
followed by specific policy recommendations in
each of these areas. The proposals focus on
the need for more planning and coordination at
the national level, as well as increased
attention to social factors. DLC LNHT

548 Guatemala, Sociedad de Geografía e Historia
de. La Sociedad de Geografía e Historia de
Guatemala: breve recuento de sus labores al
cumplir sus bodas de plata. Guatemala: Published by the Society, 1948. 74 pp. Index.
  A brief volume published to commemorate the
twenty-fifth anniversary of the Society, which
was founded in 1923. Summarizes its goals,
lists its present and past members, and, most
useful, provides a list of all its publications, including the tables of contents of
each volume of its journal, Anales de la
Sociedad de Geografía e Historia de Guatemala.
A comprehensive author index covers its entire
span from 1924 through 1947. LNHT

549 Guatemala, Universidad de San Carlos. Costa de
la vida: sistema de números índices.
Guatemala: Universidad de San Carlos, 1974.
169 pp. Tables, appendixes.
  An effort to establish uniform indexes for
the cost of living in Guatemala, defining the
categories, regions, etc.; conducted by the
Institute of Economic and Social Investigations with the collaboration of the Banco de
Guatemala. Previous indexes were limited to
the capital. The volume explains the system
and the categories, the mathematical formulas,
and methods employed, while the appendixes
provide current calculations based on the new
indexes. BNG

550   ____. Guatemala: estructura agraria del
Altiplano Occidental. Quezaltenango: Centro
Universitario de Occidente, Universidad de San
Carlos, 1976. 575 pp. Biblio., maps, tables.
  A study of the agricultural characteristics
of the Western Highlands coffee-growing region, designed to enunciate its characteristics and development to provide data for
effective planning. The study states that
while it is common to assume that agrarian
development means land distribution, such a
move must be planned carefully and limited by
such factors as productivity, use, application
of technology, investment, education of the
peasants, and capability of the zone. Seeks
to identify these factors in this region and
notes that there is considerable intensive
cultivation, application of technology, and
technical education of the peasants already in
progress there. The area covered is an officially designated government planning zone
that includes portions of the departments of
Quezaltenango, San Marcos, Sololá, and
Totonicapán. The volume provides a comprehensive statistical picture of the region,
encompassing soil types, climates, land ownership and use, crops, application of technology, education, equipment, migration, labor,
and much more, all for the 1974-75 period in
which the survey was conducted. LNHT

551   ____. Periódicos de la independencia:
selección. Guatemala: Universidad de San
Carlos, 1967. 283 pp.
  Selected articles from three of the leading
Guatemalan newspapers of the independence era,
El Editor Constitucional, El Amigo de la
Patria and El Genio de la Libertad, princi-
pally covering the years 1820 and 1821 and
selected to show the political thought of the
era. LNHT

552   ____. Selección de documentos de la vida
independiente. Guatemala: Editorial
Universitaria, 1974. 210 pp.

(Guatemala, Universidad de San Carlos)
A collection of significant documents in
Guatemalan history, focusing on the independence movement but including various proclamations from the Liberal revolution of the late
nineteenth century and even single items from
the Unionist party and the 1944 revolutionary
junta. The arrangement is chronological and
no explanation of the selection criteria is
offered. LNHT BNG

553 _____. Universidad de San Carlos de
Guatemala: publicación conmemorativa
tricentenario, 1676-1976. Guatemala:
Editorial Universitaria, 1976. 341 pp.
Illus.
A lavishly illustrated commemorative volume
celebrating the tricentennial of the national
university. Includes a brief history of the
institution and descriptions of its most illustrious professors and officials, as well as
discussion and photos of the present university, its physical facilities and organization. BNG

554 Guatemala, Gov't of. La administración del
general don Manuel L. Barillas: 1885-1892,
documentos oficiales. Guatemala: Tipografía
El Modelo, 1892. 632 pp.
A collection of documents from the various
ministries, compiled by the regime in its
final months in office. Provides an overview
of its coming to power, its activities, programs, politics, and accomplishments, as the
regime wished itself to be remembered. Includes excerpts from official reports for 1891
detailing actions in each department of the
republic, as well as the annual presidential
messages to Congress. DLC LNHT

555 _____. La administración del general José
María Orellana y el arreglo económico de
Guatemala: documentos para la historia.
Guatemala: Tipografía Nacional, 1926. 48 pp.
Illus., maps.
An official publication issued in the regime's final year, emphasizing its efforts to
stabilize the economy and financial system
through the establishment of a central bank
and sweeping montetary reform laws. Argues
that this had fully stabilized the nation,
enabling the amnesty and pardon decrees (also
included) by which Orellana attempted to end
internal divisions and promote national unity
by pardoning most prisoners on 15 September,
independence day. As things worked out, this
was accomplished only a few days before he
died of a heart attack. MH

556 _____. Álbum gráfico: administración del
general Ubico. Guatemala: Tipografía
Nacional, 1935. 104 pp. Illus.
Photos of the various public works projects
and government offices of the Ubico administration, commemorating his accomplishments.
Includes descriptive text of works in progress. DLC BNG

557 _____. Apuntamientos sobre la República de
Guatemala, sus progresos desde 1871 a 1884

bajo el gobierno del general J. Rufino
Barrios: condiciones favorables para una
inmigración de extranjeros laborioses en la
república: rasgos biográficos del general J.
Rufino Barrios, presidente constitucional de
la república. Guatemala: Tipografía El
Progreso, 1885. 66 pp.
A brief official volume hailing Barrios and
the accomplishments of his regime and emphasizing the prospects for European immigrants
in Guatemala by stressing the progress of the
nation and the attitude of its government.
Clearly intended as part of the effort to
attract European immigrants to foster development, a strategy in vogue among positivist
regimes in Latin America at that time. DLC

558 _____. Documentos fundamentales de la
independencia de Guatemala. Guatemala:
Ministerio de Educación Pública, 1967. 45 pp.
Reprints the independence acts and the
reports of the Constituent Assembly. DLC
LNHT

559 _____. Documentos relativos a la elección
popular para la presidencia constitucional de
la república en la persona del general J.
Rufino Barrios. Renuncia del general Barrios
y reptida denegación de la Asamblea
Legislativa: toma de posesión y manifiesto
del presidente constitucional a los
guatemaltecos. Guatemala: Tipografía de El
Progreso, 1880.
An official volume detailing Barrios's
reelection by the legislature after he engi-
neered the preparation of a new constitution.
Designed to emphasize his popularity and
stress his offers to resign, which of course
were rejected by his legislature, which "insisted" that he continue to serve the nation
for another term. DLC LNHT

560 _____. Génesis de la reforma constitucional
de la República de Guatemala en el año de
1927. Guatemala: Tipografía Nacional, 1931.
xxxi, 195 pp.
The proceedings of the Constituent Assembly
and a collection of documents attendant to its
origin, with the text of the new constitution.
DLC

561 _____. Guatemala: General Description.
Guatemala: Tipografía Latina, 1922. 29 pp.
Illus., maps.
General basic data for the layman. Pro-
vides some statistics and impressions of the
nation in 1922. DLC LNHT

562 _____. Guatemala: un año. Guatemala:
Tipografía Nacional, 1964. Pages unnumbered.
Illus.
An account of the projects and accomplish-
ments of the Peralta regime, with extensive
photos of projects and officials. DLC

563 _____. Guatemala y la Revolución del 1871:
crónica. Guatemala: Tipografía Nacional,
1917. 51 pp. Illus.
An account of the celebration in 1917 of
the anniversary of the revolution of 1871,

(Guatemala, Gov't of)
with copies of the speeches and the declarations of loyalty to the Liberal party and the regime of Manuel Estrada Cabrera, and various poems to the heroes of the revolution. LNHT

564   ____. Índice de los expedientes tramatados desde 1786 a julio de 1943 en la Escribanía del Gobierno y Sección de Tierras. Guatemala: Tipografía Nacional, 1944. 288 pp.
A listing of documents for the indicated years, arranged by province, covering terrenos baldios that the state awarded to municipalities, communities, and private holders. A separate section of biennes del estado covers the years 1842 to 1922. BNG

565   ____. Índice General del Archivo de Tierras que se custodia en la Escribanía del Supremo Gobierno. Guatemala: Tipografía Nacional, 1889. 332 pp.
A list of records in the Archivo relating to land ownership from discovery to the date of publication, arranged by province. BNG

566   ____. Informe al III Congreso contra la intervención soviética en la América Latina. Guatemala: n.p., 1957. 24 pp.
A summary of the accomplishments of the Castillo Armas regime and its efforts to counter the propaganda against it, which it views as of communist inspiration. DLC

567   ____. Política nacional de desarrollo regional. Guatemala: M.C.O.P., 1967. 87 pp. Maps, tables. 2d ed. Guatemala: Editorial Martí, 1969. 87 pp. Maps, tables.
A study conducted by several governmental entities delimiting and examining the various national regions. Replete with numerous graphs, tables, and maps that indicate the distribution of people, land, and resources in the various parts of the republic. The information is current, with no attempt to provide historical context. DLC BNG

568   ____. El primer libro del soldado guatemalteco. Guatemala: Tipografía Nacional, 1936. 190 pp. Illus. 2d ed. Guatemala: Tipografía Nacional, 1938. 196 pp. Illus.
An official publication designed for soldiers and the populace in general. Includes a brief history of the republic through the regime of Barrios, a geographic description, and a declaration of civic duties, citizens' rights, and the values of the regime. Serves to illustrate official doctrine and views of the Ubico regime. DLC BNG

569   ____. Proyecto de constitución para la República de Guatemala, presentado al supremo gobierno en julio de 1847 por la Comisión encargada de formarlo de orden del mismo supremo gobierno. Guatemala: Imprenta de la Paz, 1848. 57 pp.
The outline of the 1851 constitution, with the discussions of the commission that drafted it and a commentary by Alejandro Marure, placing the issues in the context of the politics

of the time, explaining the role of the author on the commission and providing a justification for his shift from his earlier liberalism to the conservatism reflected in this document. DLC LNHT

570   ____. Recopilación de leyes emitidas por el gobierno democrático de la República de Guatemala, desde el 3 de junio de 1871, en que el ejército libertador, al mando de los generales don Miguel García Granados y don Justo Rufino Barrios, desconoció la administración de Don Vicente Cerna. Numerous volumes and many editions. Guatemala: Various publishers, 1874-.
The initial series was edited by Manuel Pineda de Mont, and appears under his name. It covered the years from independence to 1871, with several later annual supplements. There have been many editions of this standard and official compilation of Guatemalan legislation, periodically updating the list and reproducing the original volumes. The collection had reached twenty-five volumes by 1924 and fifty-one volumes by 1935. BNG

571   ____. La verdad sobre los sucesos de junio de 1956. Guatemala: Tipografía Nacional, 1956. 129 pp. Illus.
An official account of the demonstrations of 25 June 1956 against the government of Carlos Castillo Armas, when a student meeting spawned a riot and a clash with security forces. Includes an account of the event, lists of those arrested and police wounded in the melee, photos of weapons confiscated, telegrams of support and loyalty from the parties, towns, and citizens, and reproductions of items that the government charges prove that the effort was orchestrated by the Communist party. Part of the continuing propaganda and political maneuvering of this controversial era. LNHT

572   ____. Asamblea Constituyente. Diario de las sesiones de la Asamblea Constituyente de la República de Guatemala, celebrada el 15 de julio de 1927. Guatemala: Tipografía Nacional, 1927. 599 pp.
DLC LNHT

573   ____. ____. Diario de las sesiones de la Asamblea Constituyente de 1879 reimpreso por acuerdo de la Comisión de Régimen Interior de la Asamblea Constituyente de 1927 en observancia de las disposiciones de la Asamblea Legislativa de 1925. Guatemala: Tipografía Nacional, 1927. 189 pp. Illus.
DLC

574   ____. ____. Diario de sesiones de la Asamblea Constituyente de 1945. Guatemala: Tipografía Nacional, 1951. 928 pp.
DLC LNHT

575   ____. Banco de Guatemala. Ingreso nacional de Guatemala, 1950-59. Guatemala: Banco de Guatemala, 1960. 17 pp. Illus.
A compilation and description of the national income statistics, offering several

(Guatemala, Gov't of)
years of data to allow comparison. The figures indicate the drastic shifts resulting
from the 1954 policy changes, yet also show
the constant elements that continued with
little impact. DLC LNHT

576 _____. Congreso Regional de Economía. El
triángulo de Esquintla: el estado, el
capital; los trabajadores. Guatemala:
Tipografía Nacional, 1946. 390 pp. Illus.,
maps, tables.
    The report of a government-sponsored re-
gional conference promoting a linkage between
the government, labor, and capital, which was
a project of the Arévalo regime. DLC LNHT
BNG

577 _____. Consejo de Bienestar Social.
Introducción al estudio de la asistencia
gerontológica en Guatemala. Guatemala:
Ministerio de Educación Pública, 1959. 98 pp.
    A discussion of the existing services for
the aged in Guatemala and the need for such
services, with a plan for their expansion in
the future. DLC BNG

578 _____. Consejo de Economía. La Empresa
Eléctrica de Guatemala, S.A.: un problema
nacional. Guatemala: Ministerio de Educación
Pública, 1950. 155 pp. Illus., tables.
    A discussion of the role of the electric
company in the Guatemalan economy, issued by
the revolutionary government. Views foreign
control and ownership of such facilities as a
problem that threatens the nation. Includes a
discussion of the history of the company, its
finances, profits, and services, with reproduction of appropriate documentation. DLC
LNHT BNG

579 _____. Consulado General en Barcelona.
Guatemala. Barcelona: López, Robert y Cía,
1915. 20 pp. Illus.
    General data regarding the country and its
government during the regime of Estrada
Cabrera. DLC

580 _____. Consulat Général à Paris. Le
Guatemala: section de publicité du consulat
général de Guatemala à Paris. Paris:
Kauffmann Editores, 1927. 40 pp. Illus.,
maps.
    General data regarding the country for the
European reader; designed to encourage investment, trade, and tourism. NN

581 _____. Crédito Hipotecario Nacional. 25 años
del Crédito Hipotecario Nacional. Guatemala:
Byron Zadik, 1955. 73 pp. Illus.
    A history of the bank, with lavish photos
of its officials and statistics regarding its
activities and loans. BNG

582 _____. Department of Public Works. A
Descriptive Account of the Republic of
Guatemala, Central America. Chicago:
Courrier de Chicago, 1893. 39 pp.
    General data about the republic, designed
to encourage Yankee interest, investment, and
tourism. DLC

583 _____. Dirección General de Asuntos Agrarios.
La evidencia de los hechos: la prensa ante la
reforma agraria de Guatemala, juicios y
comentarios de periodistas guatemaltecos y
extranjeros, con relación al programa agrario
del gobierno de la república. Guatemala:
Imprenta Hispania, 1957. 119 pp.
    A collection of reproductions of newspaper
commentaries on the agrarian reform of the
Castillo Armas regime, drawn principally from
Guatemalan papers but including some from
papers outside the nation. DLC BNG

584 _____. Dirección General de Caminos. Guía
kilométrica de las 23 rutas nacionales de la
República de Guatemala. Guatemala:
Tipografía Nacional, 1942. 185 pp. Map. 2d
ed. Guatemala: Tipografía Nacional, 1949.
211 pp. Maps.
    The first edition, an official publication
of the Ubico regime, features a photo of the
caudillo astride his motorcycle, provides a
detailed map of the roads of the republic and
descriptions of each of the twenty-three newly
designated national highways, indicates the
state of transportation development, and provides detailed locations. The second edition
omits the photo and the large map but reproduces the data for each route, with updated
information. Many subsequent editions have
followed. The second edition in 1949 initiated the pattern of two separate volumes,
the first containing detailed maps and descriptions of the national routes, the second
listing secondary roads by department and
including distances between towns, without
maps. Subsequent editions, which appear periodically, are not listed, but bear the shorter
title Guía kilométrica de la República de
Guatemala. DLC BNG

585 _____. Dirección General de Cartografía.
Anteproyecto de un plan para el desarrollo
socio-económico de Guatemala en 21 años.
Guatemala: Dirección General de Cartografía,
1964. 58 pp. Tables.
    A proposal for an elaborate development
plan drawn by the Dirección, using as a base
the statistics and information in its Atlas
preliminar de Guatemala, published the same
year. Emphasizes the general objectives and
financing needed, while avoiding discussion of
the specific management of the projects, the
choices necessary, and the tax and revenue
implications. DLC BNG

586 _____. _____. Atlas preliminar de Guatemala.
Guatemala: Dirección General de Cartografía,
1964. 74 pp. Illus., maps. 3d ed.
Guatemala: Dirección General de Cartografía,
1966. 78 pp. Illus., maps.
    A collection of detailed maps and accompa-
nying charts and tables that provide physical
information about the present state of the
nation, its roads, population distribution,
economy, etc. DLC BNG

587 _____. _____. Diccionario geográfico de
Guatemala. 4 vols. Guatemala: Tipografía
Nacional, 1961-68. Tables.

(Guatemala, Gov't of)
A guide in the form of an alphabetical listing of all place names and political designations, providing general information about the current situation of each and including geographic location, population, etc. DLC LNHT

588 _____. Dirección General de Cultura y Bellas Artes. Danzas folklóricas de Guatemala. Guatemala: Dirección General de Cultura y Bellas Artes, 1971. 38 pp. Illus., maps, tables.
A brief discussion of typical regional dances, with tables indicating the regions in which each is used. DLC

589 _____. Dirección General de Desarrollo Socioeducativo Rural. Desarrollo integral de las comunidades rurales en Guatemala. Guatemala: Ministerio de Educación Pública, 1956. 89 pp. Illus.
A series of articles from the Diario de Centro América, printed in September 1956, describing the efforts of the Castillo Armas regime in the field of rural education and development, and hailing the program. BNG

590 _____. Dirección General de Estadística. Demarcación política de la República de Guatemala. 2 vols. Guatemala: Tipografía Nacional, 1893. 315 pp. Latest ed. Guatemala: Tipografía Nacional, 1902. 94, 83 pp.
A listing of each municipio, by department, with a detailed description of each. DLC

591 _____. _____. Estudio sobre las condiciones de vida de 179 familias en la ciudad de Guatemala. Guatemala: Tipografía Nacional, 1948. 126 pp. Biblio., illus.
A study conducted in 1946 using random selection and interviews to describe the living standards of families in the capital. The volume contains elaborate tabulations and statistics regarding all aspects of life, including food, dress, budget, age, size of family, and many other factors, which provide a useful overview of the standard of living and the conditions in the capital. DLC BNG

592 _____. _____. Índices de precios en la ciudad de Guatemala, 1954-1969. Guatemala: Dirección General de Estadística, 1970. 70 pp. Illus., tables.
A study of the cost of living, based on government indexes and prices of specific goods, providing detailed figures for many products as well as graphs and tables illustrating the rise in prices in the capital, with monthly increments. Some of the statistics encompass the entire period, while others cover only the 1960s. DLC

593 _____. Dirección General de Obras Públicas. Análisis urbano de Colombia. Guatemala: Dirección General de Obras Públicas, 1964. 39 pp. Illus., maps, tables. 3d ed. Guatemala: Dirección General de Obras Públicas, 1966. 39 pp. Illus., maps, tables.

A detailed study of this small town in the coffee-growing district of Quezaltenango, describing its current facilities and population distribution, with extensive maps and charts. Covers the years 1950-64 when the study was originally prepared. LNHT

594 _____. _____. Estudio geográfico Champerico. Guatemala: Dirección General de Obras Públicas, 1965. 90 pp. Maps, tables. 3d ed. Guatemala: Dirección General de Obras Públicas, 1968. 90 pp. Illus., maps, tables.
A detailed description and compilation of geographical data regarding Champerico. Considers resources, services, and agriculture and makes recommendations for development. DLC BNG

595 _____. FYDEP. El Petén: la lucha por su desarrollo. Guatemala: Ediciones FYDEP, 1969. 140 pp. Illus., maps.
A publication of the Empresa Nacional de Fomento y Desarrollo Económico de El Petén (FYDEP), a government agency in charge of promoting the development of this vast region. The volume provides a brief overview of the Petén, a survey of its known resources, and a discussion of the plans and objectives of the agency, which was created in 1964. BNG

596 _____. Instituto Guatemalteco de Seguridad Social. Informe sobre el problema de la clases pasivas en Guatemala. Guatemala: Imprenta Hispania, 1948. 139 pp. Tables.
A study of the problem of unfunded and underfunded pensions in Guatemala, with proposals for the Institute to assume control of all pensions and suggestions for using the Institute to remedy the problem. BNG

597 _____. _____. Seguridad Social en Guatemala. Guatemala: Instituto Guatemalteco de Seguridad Social, 1955. 129 pp. Illus., tables.
A description of the social security program, its coverage and facilities, with lavish illustrations. BNG

598 _____. Instituto Indígenista Nacional de Guatemala. Chinautla: síntesis socioeconómica de una comunidad indígena de Guatemala. Guatemala: Ministerio de Educación Pública, 1948. x, 57 pp. Illus., maps, tables.
Part of a series by the Institute designed to survey the current situation of Indian communities. Includes a description of the town, its physical setting, life-style, customs, economy, facilities, and services, with accompanying statistics and tables regarding the economy and population, all based on observations and data gathered by Institute personnel. DLC BNG

599 _____. _____. Chuarrancho: síntesis socioeconómica de una comunidad indígena guatemalteca. Guatemala: Ministerio de Educación Pública, 1948. x, 52 pp. Maps, tables.
See item GU598. DLC BNG

(Guatemala, Gov't of)

600 _____. _____. Parramos: síntesis socio-económica de una comunidad indígena guatemalteca. Guatemala: Ministerio de Educación Pública, 1948. 56 pp. Illus., maps, tables.
   See item GU598. DLC BNG

601 _____. _____. ¿Porque es indispensable el indígenismo? Guatemala: Talleres del Instituto Lingüístico de Verano, 1969. 95 pp.
   Written in response to attacks on indígenismo as paternalism, this volume argues that special treatment of the Indians is essential because they are not reached by ordinary institutions of the nation--because of social and linguistic barriers--contending that the ultimate objective of indígenismo is to promote the integration of the Indian into the national culture. DLC BNG

602 _____. _____. San Antonio Aguas Calientes: síntesis socio-económica de una comunidad indígena guatemalteca. Guatemala: Ministerio de Educación Pública, 1948. xi, 56 pp. Illus., maps, tables.
   See item GU598. DLC BNG

603 _____. _____. San Bartolomé Milpas Altas: síntesis socio-económica de una comunidad indígena guatemalteca. Guatemala: Ministerio de Educación Pública, 1949. 58 pp. Illus.
   See item GU598. DLC BNG

604 _____. _____. San Juan Sacatepéquez: síntesis socio-económica de una comunidad indígena guatemalteca. Guatemala: Ministerio de Educación Pública, 1948. x, 63 pp. Illus., maps, tables.
   See item GU598. DLC BNG

605 _____. _____. Santa Catarina Barahona: síntesis socio-económica de una comunidad indígena guatemalteca. Guatemala: Ministerio de Educación Pública, 1948. x, 49 pp. Illus., maps, tables.
   See item GU598. DLC BNG

606 _____. _____. Santa Eulalia: tierra de nuestros antepasados y esperanzas para nuestros hijos. Guatemala: Published by the Instituto, 1968. 86 pp. Illus., appendixes.
   See item GU598. DLC BNG

607 _____. _____. Santo Domingo Xenacoj: síntesis socio-económica de una comunidad indígena guatemalteca. Guatemala: Ministerio de Educación Pública, 1949. 58 pp. Illus.
   See item GU598. DLC BNG

608 _____. Instituto Nacional de Electrificación. Plan maestro de electrificación nacional. 5 vols. Guatemala: Published by the Instituto, 1976. Various pagings.
   A detailed plan for the development of the electricity generation and transmission facilities of the nation, prepared with the technical assistance of a German firm and governmental agency. The plan extends to the year 2000 and seeks to estimate demand and needs in terms of volume and location, as well as potential, to enable development of appropriate facilities. BNG

609 _____. Instituto Nacional de Geografía. Atlas nacional de Guatemala. Guatemala: Published by the Instituto, 1972. 83 pp. Illus., maps, tables.
   A collection of large and well-executed multicolor maps of Guatemala showing the distribution of population, resources, crops, etc., as well as physical and political divisions. Prepared by the Institute. DLC

610 _____. _____. Guía para investigadores de Guatemala. Guatemala: PAIGH, 1978. 157 pp.
   Another in a series of bibliographic guides focusing on geography. See item CR287. DLC BNG

611 _____. Ministerio de Defensa Nacional. El capitán general Rafael Carrera, 1814-1865. Guatemala: Editorial del Ejército, n.d. 15 pp. Illus.
   A very brief sketch of the military career of Carrera, designed for use by military officers. BNG

612 _____. _____. Distrito portuario Matías de Gálvez. Guatemala: Editorial del Ejército, 1959. 45 pp. Illus.
   An explanation of the naming of this district, with a brief history of the military installations at Puerto Livingston and a brief biography of Matías de Gálvez. BNG

613 _____. Estado Mayor del Ejército. Visión de Guatemala: cifras e informes de interés sobre un pueblo. Guatemala: Editorial del Ejército, 1957. 128 pp. Biblio., illus., maps, tables.
   A collection of general information about the nation, its people and facilities, emphasizing such items as roads, education, transportation and communication facilities, including descriptions of each of the government ministries; designed for the general foreign reader. DLC LNHT BNG

614 _____. Ministerio de Economía y Trabajo. Política económica del Gobierno de Liberación. Guatemala: Tipografía Nacional, 1957. 58 pp.
   A summary of an official conference regarding the future economic policy of the nation, chaired by the president, including the various official reports by the appropriate governmental officials and the remarks by the president. BNG

615 _____. Ministerio de Educación Pública. Diagnóstico de la educación en Guatemala: programa de la educación para la República de Guatemala. Guatemala: Ministerio de Educación Pública, 1965. 57 pp. Illus., tables.
   A brief survey of Guatemalan education and an outline plan for the years 1965-69. BNG

616 _____. _____. La educación guatemalteca: bases para un planeamiento integral.

(Guatemala, Gov't of)
   Guatemala: Ministerio de Educación Pública,
   1962. 118 pp. Biblio., tables.
      A study of the Guatemalan educational sys-
   tem, its prospects and problems. Devoted
   principally to statistics, it is designed to
   comprise the base for future planning. The
   volume covers such aspects as facilities,
   schools, preparation of teachers, libraries,
   teaching materials, and student population and
   distribution, from the primary through the
   university level. The statistics are for
   1959-62. An extensive series of tables and
   graphs is included. BNG

617 _____. _____. Extensión de la escuela
   primaria en Guatemala. Guatemala: Ministerio
   de Educación Pública, 1958. 117 pp. Tables.
      An analysis of the present school system in
   the rural areas, with details of location and
   type, and full statistical data, followed by a
   plan for its extension into more remote villages and neglected areas. BNG

618 _____. _____. La juventud y el comunismo.
   Guatemala: Talleres Gutenberg, 1956. 48 pp.
   Illus.
      A propaganda folio reflecting the political
   and ideological conflict of the 1950s. Prepared by the Castillo Armas government, it is
   designed to expose the "infiltration" of the
   Ministry of Education by communist elements
   during the Arbenz regime and the "indoctrination" effort directed at Guatemalan youth
   through the school system. DLC BNG

619 _____. _____. Plan nacional de educación
   para la República de Guatemala. Guatemala:
   Ministerio de Educación Pública, 1969. 391
   pp. Tables.
      A detailed study by the Ministry of Educa-
   tion describing the educational resources of
   the nation and projecting future needs, with
   emphasis on the 1969-72 period. Includes
   consideration of employment possibilities,
   trends, and national needs, as well as discussion of facilities and programs needed at all
   levels. Contains a useful compilation of
   educational statistics for the period 1956 to
   1967. BNG

620 _____. _____. Profesionalización de maestros
   empíricos de primaria en servicio. Guatemala:
   Ministerio de Educación Pública, 1965. 29 pp.
   Tables.
      A study of Guatemalan teachers and their
   levels of study, with a plan for in-service
   and extension programs to improve their compe-
   tence. BNG

621 _____. _____. Situación demográfica,
   económica, social y educativa de Guatemala.
   Guatemala: Ministerio de Educación Pública,
   1963. 251 pp. Tables.
      Statistical data regarding population and
   educational needs, based on census data; analysis and discussion of the educational levels
   of the populace and their implications for the
   future. DLC

622 _____. Ministerio de Fomento. Álbum del
   Ferrocarril Interoceánico de Guatemala.
   Guatemala: Tipografía Nacional, 1908. xvi,
   160 pp.
      A folio-size, lavishly illustrated volume
   published by the Estrada Cabrera regime in
   commemoration of the inauguration of the railroad from Puerto Barrios to the capital in
   1908. Contains the official speeches given on
   the occasion, including due reference to the
   foresight and contributions of the incumbent
   regime of Manuel Estrada Cabrera in promoting
   this project. Includes poems and essays in
   honor of the event. DLC LNHT

623 _____. _____. Ferrocarril a El Salvador:
   documentos relativos a la caducidad del
   contrato Mendez-Williamson. Guatemala:
   Imprenta Nacional, 1921. 82 pp.
      A series of documents and opinions regard-
   ing the fulfillment of the contract of 1908
   and the governmental subvention involved. The
   volume contains official government statements, congressional investigations and statements, press commentaries regarding the
   obligations of the railroad and government,
   and reproductions of the original contract and
   appropriate documents. BNG

624 _____. _____. Los ferrocarriles en
   Guatemala. Guatemala: Tipografía Nacional,
   1952. 533 pp.
      A collection of documents, laws, and con-
   cessions concerning the principal railroads in
   Guatemala compiling all appropriate items from
   the initial laws and concessions in the nineteenth century to 1944. The documents are
   arranged chronologically with chapters pertaining to each of the separate lines and to
   general questions, such as mail service and
   land grants. DLC BNG

625 _____. Ministerio de Hacienda y Crédito
   Público. Las experiencias de Guatemala en los
   aspectos monetario, bancario y cambiario,
   durante el decenio comprendido de 1929 a 1939:
   exposición de la Secretaría de Hacienda y
   Crédito Público a la Primera reunión de
   ministros de hacienda de los países
   americanos, celebrada en Guatemala en
   noviembre de 1939. Guatemala: Tipografía
   Nacional, 1939. 72 pp. Tables.
      A summary of the financial history of
   Guatemala during this period, serving to
   indicate the impact of the Great Depression on
   that nation. The emphasis is on the policies
   of the Ubico regime and its success in reviv-
   ing the nation's financial system and economy.
   DLC LNHT BNG

626 _____. Ministerio de Relaciones Exteriores.
   Aporte de Guatemala a la solidaridad y
   cooperación interamericana. Guatemala:
   Tipografía Nacional, 1942. 50 pp.
      A collection of official statements and
   documents from the 1930s tracing the steps by
   which the American nations acted jointly to
   neutralize the hemisphere and ally against
   aggression, with emphasis on the Guatemalan
   role. Includes statements by Franklin D.

(Guatemala, Gov't of)
Roosevelt and Guatemalan president Jorge Ubico
regarding the various measures. DLC LNHT

627 _____. _____. Centenario del fallecimiento
de don Antonio José de Irisarri. Guatemala:
Editorial del Ejército, 1971. 387 pp.
A series of commentaries by various scholars analyzing the contributions and diplomatic
career of the longtime representative of
Guatemala and other Central American countries
in Washington during the early and mid-
nineteenth century. BNG

628 _____. _____. Denuncia de Guatemala de la
Carta de San Salvador y retira de la
Organización de Estados Centroamericanos.
Guatemala: Imprenta Nacional, 1953. 31 pp.
The Guatemalan note of 4 April 1953 with-
drawing from ODECA in protest against the
efforts of the other Central American states
to include discussion of anticommunist methods
and their stand against the spread of communism, which was directed at the Guatemalan
regime. The folio also contains the replies
of the other governments and the Guatemalan
complaint to the U.N. Security Council, charging that its neighbors were aiding counterrevolutionary factions operating within their
territory in preparation for armed action
against the Guatemalan revolutionary government. DLC BNCR

629 _____. _____. Documentos justificativos de
la guerra declarada por el gobierno de
Guatemala al del Salvador. New York:
Imprenta de Esteban Hallet, 1863. 31 pp.
A collection of documents regarding the war
between Guatemala and El Salvador, consisting
of exchanges about the conflict between the
Guatemalan foreign minister and the U.S. minister; states the Guatemalan case and includes
Guatemalan-Salvadoran communications. The
Guatemalan statements condemn the unionist
efforts of Gerardo Barrios of El Salvador,
accusing him of intervention in Honduras and
conspiracy through secret treaties to arrange
a coalition against Guatemala. Printed in
Spanish and English. BNG

630 _____. _____. Guatemala ante América: la
verdad sobre la Cuatra Reunión de Consulta de
Cancilleres Americanos. Guatemala:
Ministerio de Relaciones Exteriores, 1951.
174 pp. Illus.
The Guatemalan position at the March 1951
foreign ministers' meeting. Complete with
press excerpts, the conference declarations,
speeches by the Guatemalan delegates, and
other pertinent items, all defending the
Arbenz regime and its stand in rejecting
continental defense at the conference. The
Guatemalan stance rejected accusations of
communism and stressed self-determination and
democracy. DLC LNHT BNG

631 _____. _____. Libro Blanco de Guatemala:
sobre el incidente del 31 de diciembre de
1958. Guatemala: Tipografía Nacional, 1959.
142 pp. Illus., maps.

The diplomatic correspondence between
Guatemala and Mexico in a case involving
fishing rights and the seizure by Guatemala of
several Mexican fishing vessels accused of
poaching in Guatemalan waters. DLC BNG

632 _____. Poder Judicial. Álbum, Palacio de
Justicia, 1938: homenaje del poder judicial
al señor general don Jorge Ubico, presidente
constitucional de la república. Guatemala:
Tipografía Nacional, 1938. 83 pp. Illus.
An album of photos of the Palace of Justice
constructed by the Ubico regime to house the
nation's judiciary and Supreme Court, showing
its various facilities; there is no text.
LNHT

633 _____. Presidencia, Secretaría de
Información. A los dos años de la revolución.
Guatemala: Tipografía Nacional, 1946. 76 pp.
Illus.
A collection of speeches given during
September and October of 1945 and 1946, com-
memorating the Guatemalan Revolution and ex-
tolling its accomplishments and goals, by
various officials of the government. DLC
LNHT

634 _____. _____. Comentarios al discurso en
Panamá, del presidente de Guatemala, coronel
Carlos Castillo Armas. Guatemala: Imprenta
Real, 1956. 23 pp.
An address stating his foreign-policy aims,
emphasizing anticommunism, Central American
and Inter-American solidarity, and the need
for cooperation and strength. BNG

635 _____. _____. Crítica al proyecto de Ley
Agraria de la Asociación General de
Agricultores (AGA). Guatemala: Secretaría de
Propaganda y Divulgación de la Presidencia,
1952. 37 pp.
TxU

636 _____. _____. El cuatro poder en funciones
con el grandioso marco de la verdad.
Guatemala: n.p., 1955. Illus.
An official publication consisting of photos of a celebration in honor of the press,
with identifying paragraphs hailing its role
in the nation. Designed to emphasize the
value that the National Liberation Movement
placed on the press and its freedom of action
in that nation. LNHT

637 _____. _____. Democracia amenazada: el caso
de Guatemala. Guatemala: Tipografía
Nacional, 1954. 98 pp. Illus.
An official statement of the Arbenz government revealing details it has obtained regarding Castillo Armas's efforts through the
National Liberation Movement to launch a revolt against the Arbenz regime. TxU

638 _____. _____. Dentro del círculo vicioso:
el ataque a comunismo es un ataque al
gobierno, el ataque al gobierno es un ataque a
la patria: bajo este sofismo tenebroso la
prensa independiente de Guatemala vivió años
de terror durante el régimen de los

(Guatemala, Gov't of)
comunistas. Guatemala: Imprenta Iberia, n.d.
[1954]. Pages unnumbered. Illus.
Focuses on press control during the Arbenz
regime, providing evidence of pressure. DLC
LNHT

639 _____. _____. Después supimos la verdad.
Guatemala: n.p., 1954. 64 pp. Illus.
A collection of photos of captured materials revealing the extent of the communistic
propaganda of the Arbenz regime and emphasizing the Marxist content of its official
publications. TxU

640 _____. _____. Discursos del doctor Juan José
Arévalo y del teniente coronel Jacabo Arbenz
Guzmán en el acto de transmisión de la
presidencia de la república, 15 de marzo de
1951. Guatemala: Tipografía Nacional, 1951.
31 pp. Illus.
The official speeches at the ceremony in
which Arbenz succeeded Arévalo as president.
DLC

641 _____. _____. Documentos que la historia de
Guatemala conservará para asignarle a cada
quien, el lugar que justamente le corresponde.
Guatemala: n.p., 1954. Pages unnumbered.
Illus.
A summary of the propaganda efforts and
"secret expenditures" of the Arbenz regime,
condemning its use of communist propaganda and
its efforts to spread it abroad as well as
within the country. Reflects the continuing
propaganda effort of the Castillo Armas regime
to condemn the Marxist tendencies of its predecessor. BNG

642 _____. _____. 2 años de gobierno del general
e ingeniero don Miguel Ydígoras Fuentes, 1958-
1960. Guatemala: Tipografía Nacional, 1961.
103 pp. Illus.
A lavishly illustrated volume describing
and praising the projects of the initial two
years of the Ydígoras Fuentes government. DLC
LNHT BNG

643 _____. _____. Dos pueblos amigos.
Guatemala: Tipografía Nacional, 1956. Pages
unnumbered. Illus.
A volume commemorating Castillo Armas's
visit to the United States, with profuse illustrations and reproductions of the speeches
and ceremonies, clearly implying that the
visit constituted Yankee endorsement of the
regime. DLC LNHT

644 _____. _____. Genocidio sobre Guatemala:
exposición del monstruoso crimen cometido
contra el pueblo de Guatemala, durante los
últimos días del gobierno comunista, presidido
por Jacobo Arbenz, derrotado por la conciencia
nacional y gracias el ejército de liberación
comandado por el coronel Carlos Castillo
Armas. Guatemala: Tipografía Nacional, 1954.
139 pp. Illus.
A denunciation of the excesses of the
Arbenz regime, published by the Castillo Armas
regime as part of the propaganda battle. Denounces tortures and executions, detailing

them with captured photos of prisoners under-
going torture, gruesome photos showing the
wounds of survivors and exhumed bodies, as
well as with lists of victims. The pamphlet
charges systematic elimination of opponents,
genocide, crimes against humanity, etc. DLC
LNHT

645 _____. _____. El gran argumento de los
comunistas. Guatemala: Unión Tipografía,
1954. 15 pp.
Reproductions of newspaper front pages and
various journalistic accounts relating to the
National Liberation Movement and the alleged
communism of the Arbenz regime. LNHT

646 _____. _____. Guatemala, 1963: Historia de
su resurgimiento económico. Guatemala:
Secretaría de Información del Gobierno
Militar, 1964. 206 pp. Tables.
A description of the economic policies of
the government of Colonel Enrique Peralta
Azurdia, with accompanying criticism of the
policies of his predecessor, hailing the new
efforts and contending that the government has
placed Guatemala on the road to economic re-
covery. Includes excerpts from many decrees.
LNHT BNG

647 _____. _____. Guatemala: un pueblo amigo.
Guatemala: Talleres Gutenberg, 1955. 82 pp.
Biblio., illus., maps.
A general description of the country pub-
lished on the occasion of the visit by Presi-
dent Carlos Castillo Armas to the United
States. Emphasizes the defeat of communism in
Guatemala, depicting the government of Jacabo
Arbenz as communistic and hailing the men who
fought for liberation with Castillo Armas.
The text is printed in English and Spanish,
with some poor translation. Included are
photos of the nation, the freedom fighters,
the leftists, and the visit to Guatemala by
Nixon. DLC LNHT

648 _____. _____. Hacia un futuro mejor:
importantes documentos para la historia
patria. Guatemala: Tipografía Nacional,
1932. 63 pp.
Documentation regarding the early acts of
the Ubico regime, including the president's
inaugural address, the inventory of his personal property that he filed on taking office,
and the Law of Probity, the latter printed in
Spanish, English, French, and German. DLC
LNHT

649 _____. _____. El hombre liberado en
Guatemala. Guatemala: Tipografía Nacional,
1956. 127 pp. Illus., maps.
An official description and a collection of
photos of the projects of the Castillo Armas
regime, hailing its activities, the freedom of
the populace to engage in development under
its rule, and the potential benefits of its
programs for the populace. DLC LNHT

650 _____. _____. Índice de las principales
obras materiales realizadas en cuatro años de
gobierno del doctor Arévalo. Guatemala:
Tipografía Nacional, 1949. 35 pp.

(Guatemala, Gov't of)
An official tabulation of the regime's accomplishments, acclaiming the benefits to the country. LNHT

651 _____. _____. La intriga roja en Guatemala. Guatemala: Imprenta Iberia, 1954. Pages unnumbered. Illus.
A denunciation of the communist role in the revolution and its government, charging tortures, large-scale executions, and all manner of excesses. Photos designed to emphasize the role of the communists, showing figures before photos of Stalin, an East European ship delivering arms, etc., are followed by photos of the celebration of the victory of the forces of Carlos Castillo Armas. LNHT

652 _____. _____. Liberación. Guatemala: n.p., 1954.
Another propaganda piece; hails the victory of the National Liberation Movement as the second independence of the nation and details the military campaign involved.

653 _____. _____. Nuestro pueblo . . . derramó lágrimas . . . al conocer el látigo y el crimen de la justicia comunista en Guatemala. Guatemala: Talleres Gutenberg, 1955. Pages unnumbered. Illus.
A compilation of the charges against the Arbenz regime by the victorious National Liberation forces, this work consists of gruesome photos and descriptions of assassinations, tortures, imprisonments, etc., contending that it was the darkest moment in Guatemalan history and that the brutality of the leftist regime surpassed that of the Middle Ages. Accounts by the victims are printed in lurid detail. ViU

654 _____. _____. La opinión pública condena la violencia. Guatemala: Ministerio de Relaciones Públicas de la Presidencia, 1967. 183 pp.
A compilation of Guatemalan press commentaries from 1967 referring to the violence in the country and condemning terrorism, compiled by the government as part of its propaganda effort. Authors, papers, and dates of original publication are all identified. DLC

655 _____. _____. Pasado y presente. Guatemala: n.p., 1956. Illus.
A collection of photos and commentaries contrasting the turmoil and problems of the Arbenz years with the peace, prosperity, progress, and tranquillity of the Castillo Armas regime. Compares the situation in various social sectors and organizations, economic activity, etc. BNG

656 _____. _____. Los pueblos de la república contra la conspiración No. 27. Guatemala: Tipografía Nacional, 1950. 323 pp.
Details the reaction of the Arévalo government to the attempted demonstrations and rebellion of July 1950, on the anniversary of the assassination of Colonel Francisco Arana. The bulk of the volume consists of telegrams and lettes sent to Arévalo pledging adhesion

to his government; these are arranged by department. The preface describes the riot in the capital, reflecting the strength of feeling regarding the political confrontations of the revolutionary era; it assails the rebels, charging that they were supported by the United Fruit Company, all the previously defeated regimes, the wealthy classes, and virtually every other group possible, seeking to discredit the movement by linking it with all the so-called privileged classes. LNHT BNG

657 _____. _____. Realizaciones del régimen democrático del coronel Carlos Castillo Armas. Guatemala: Imprenta Hispania, 1956. Pages unnumbered. Illus.
A collection of photos, with brief descriptions, of the major public-works projects of the Castillo Armas regime, compiled principally by journalist Carlos de León Paz working under the auspices of the presidential office that is listed as author. BNG

658 _____. _____. Representante de un pueblo amigo: visita de su excelencia, el coronel Carlos Castillo Armas. New York: IBM World Trade Corporation, 1956. 36 pp. Illus.
A volume commemorating the visit to the U.S. of Colonel Carlos Castillo Armas during the fall of 1956, clearly seeking to portray the state visit as official U.S. support for the National Liberation Movement. The volume includes the official speeches and acts in which Castillo Armas emphasized cooperation against communism, along with Guatemalan press commentary hailing the visit as a highpoint in U.S.–Guatemalan relations and symbolizing the alliance between the two nations. Lavishly illustrated. DLC

659 _____. _____. Tres mentiras comunistas sobre Guatemala. Guatemala: Imprenta Arimany, 1954.
Another denunciation of the alleged communism of the Arbenz regime. BNG

660 _____. _____. La verdad sobre la última conspiración del comunismo. Guatemala: Tipografía Nacional, 1957. 71 pp. Illus.
A government account of a student conspiracy in July to seize Puerto San José, denouncing it as another effort of international communism to regain control of the nation. NcD

661 _____. _____. La voz del pueblo aclama al jefe del Movimiento de Liberación Nacional, coronel Carlos Castillo Armas. Guatemala: Talleres Gutenberg, 1954. Pages unnumbered. Illus.
Another photographic collection showing the enthusiasm with which the public greeted Castillo Armas and acclaiming his programs. TxU

662 _____. Sociedad Protectora del Niño. Sociedad Protectora del Niño, 1920/1945. Guatemala: Tipografía Nacional, 1945. 122 pp. Illus.
A brief history of the organization and its work. DLC

(Guatemala, Gov't of)
663 _____. Tipografía Nacional de Guatemala. <u>Catálogo general de libros, folletos y revistas editados en la Tipografía Nacional de Guatemala desde 1892 hasta 1942</u>. Guatemala: Tipografía Nacional, 1944. xiv, 374 pp.
A year-by-year listing, arranged alphabetically by title, of all the works published by the government printing establishment. Most are official documents and memorias. Includes official reports, periodicals, and books, indiscriminately mixed. BNG

664 _____. _____. <u>Cincuenta años de la Tipografía Nacional de Guatemala, 1894-1944: 7 de enero</u>. Guatemala: Tipografía Nacional, 1944. 38 pp. Illus.
A brief summary of the origins and growth of the official national press of Guatemala, with extensive illustrations of its facilities and equipment as of 1944. DLC

665 <u>Guatemala</u>. Guatemala: Tipografía Latina, 1922. 29 pp. Illus., maps, tables.
An official pamphlet of the Estrada Cabrera regime describing the current state of the nation and its facilities, with illustrations and references to each of the provinces. The focus is clearly on economic development, trade, tourist potential, and stability. Includes geographical and climatic information, trade and economic statistics for the years from 1910 to 1919, and provides an indication of the type of construction undertaken by the regime and the projects it sought to support. DLC LNHT

666 <u>Guatemala: la república progresista de Centro América</u>. Mexico: Editorial El Globo, 1925. 38 pp. Illus.
A profusely illustrated official summary of the policies of the regime of General José María Orellana, with descriptions and photos indicating the state of the nation's facilities and its capital at that time. LNHT

667 <u>Guatemala y su dolor: corona fúnebre sobre la tumba del coronel Carlos Castillo Armas</u>. Guatemala: Tipografía Nacional, 1957. 143 pp. Illus.
A volume commemorating the death of Coronel Carlos Castillo Armas and eulogizing his work. Contains the various condolences sent by other governments, and lavish photos of the funeral. DLC LNHT BNG

668 Guerra Borges, Alfredo. <u>Evaluación de la política fomento industrial en Guatemala</u>. Guatemala: Delgado Impresores, 1971. ii, 150 pp. Notes, illus., tables.
A study of government programs to attract industry between 1961 and 1967, analyzing the industries and their impact upon imports, with emphasis on the latter. The author concludes that the policy has often attracted industry that depends on imported raw materials rather than industry that processes domestic resources, and that import-substitution has been illusory, with only the nature of the imports changing. He notes that the exemptions

granted to attract industry result in a large portion of the new imports being duty-free. DLC LNHT BNG

669 _____. <u>Geografía económica de Guatemala</u>. Guatemala: Editorial Universitaria, 1969. 416 pp. Illus., maps, tables.
A detailed economic and geographical survey of the nation by a well-known scholar. Replete with extensive statistics, it focuses on the present state of the economy, drawing upon census data, published works by other scholars, and the author's own investigations. DLC LNHT

670 Guevara Paniagua, Arturo. <u>Forjadores de nuestra libertad (1821-15 de septiembre 1966)</u>. Guatemala: Tipografía Nacional, 1966. 68 pp. Biblio., illus.
A series of brief essays, with photos, providing biographical sketches of the principal figures of Guatemalan independence. LNHT BNG

671 Guillén, Fedro. <u>Guatemala: genio y figura</u>. Guatemala: Ministerio de Educación Pública, 1954. 190 pp.
A collection of commentaries, some previously read as speeches or published in the press, dealing with significant figures in Guatemalan development and with various places and events. DLC LNHT BNG

672 _____. <u>Guatemala: prólogo y epílogo de una revolución</u>. Mexico: Cuadernos Americanos, 1964. 91 pp.
Reflections on the fall of the Arbenz regime, summarizing its good works, contending that it epitomized the ideals of Latin America, and comparing it favorably with the Mexican Revolution. Includes lavish praise for Juan José Arévalo and the 1944 movement, and denunciation of Yankee intervention in opposition to the regime. DLC LNHT

673 Guillén, Flavio. <u>Polvo de oro</u>. Tapachula, Mexico: El Sur de Mexico, 1913. 213 pp. 2d ed. Mexico: Federico Guillén, 1971. 213 pp.
A collection of speeches, short stories, and excerpts from the correspondence of a Guatemalan journalist, covering a wide range of subjects and personages, commenting on factors in everyday life, and describing localities in Mexico. BNG

674 Guillén, Juan Ramón. <u>Miscelánea de historia Centro-Americana</u>. Quezaltenango: Editorial "C.D.S.," 1926. 202 pp.
A series of essays relating to episodes of Guatemalan history ranging from discovery through the 1890s, with about half the volume devoted to Colonial times. Designed for consultation by teachers and students, and hence devoted principally to brief biographies and basic data. LNHT BNG

675 Guillén Castanon, Flavio, and Armando Gálvez Castro. <u>50 años de escultismo</u>. Guatemala: Ministerio de Educación Pública, 1972. 411 pp. Illus.

A history of Boy Scouting in Guatemala, from its origins in 1918 to the present, consisting principally of a listing of inscriptions of individuals and the honors they earned, though also including descriptions of significant programs and methods. The absence of chapters makes the volume difficult to use. BNG

676 Guinea, Gerardo. Armas para ganar una nueva batalla. Guatemala: Tipografía Nacional, 1957. 129 pp. Illus.

A survey of Guatemalan developments, published on the occasion of the third anniversary of the National Liberation Movement. Hails the educational and developmental programs of the new regime; argues that the school is the heart of the community and that education is the key to the future development of the nation. Particular attention and praise are lavished on the rural-education effort, which is seen as the opportunity for the peasants to enter the modern world, and, by implication, as a far more positive measure to help them improve their lives than the agrarian-reform efforts of the Arévalo and Arbenz regimes. DLC BNG

677 Guinther, Mercedes. Desarrollo y rendimiento de la educación primaria en Guatemala: estudio comparativo en cuatro departamentos. Guatemala: Ministerio de Educación Pública, 1973. 82 pp.

A study of the existing primary-education system in four rural Guatemalan departments-- Totonicapán, El Quiché, Izabal, and Zacapa-- including numerous statistics regarding enrollments, teachers, and graduates from 1966 through 1971. Concludes that education is primarily a service for the upper classes, with little provision for the Indians, since the vast majority of the students drop out before completing primary school; calls for a larger-scale program in the rural areas, but notes the difficulties of financing and staffing such an effort. BNG

678 Guiteras Holmes, Calixta. Perils of the Soul: The World View of a Tzotzil Indian. New York: Free Press, 1961. 371 pp.

An anthropological study outlining the attitudes of the Tzotzil Indians, based on fieldwork conducted in San Pedro Chenalho during 1953. Includes a biographical sketch of the principal informant; the author's notes on his interviews with him; and an analysis of the attitudes and beliefs of this individual about human nature, the world in general, and his place in it. There is also information about the town, its people, and its setting. DLC

679 Gutiérrez G., Víctor Manuel, and Gabriel Alvarado. Breves resúmenes de economía política. Guatemala: Ministerio de Educación Pública, 1950. 107 pp.

A brief outline of the current Guatemalan financial and social security legislation, preceded by a general treatise on economic principles; intended for the general audience or the introductory classroom. DLC

680 Gutiérrez G., Víctor Manuel. Guatemala contra Ydígoras. Guatemala: n.p., 1962. 40 pp. Illus.

A brief account of the various uprisings against the Ydígoras Fuentes regime, denouncing him as a puppet of the imperialists and the exploitive classes who serves the United Fruit Company. Calls for continued efforts to overthrow his government, charging repression and excesses. LNHT

681 Guzmán Anléu, Mario Alfonso. Supervivencias del pensamiento mágico en las costumbres de una comunidad indígena de Guatemala. Quezaltenango: n.p., 1965. 52 pp. Biblio.

Originally a thesis, this brief work focuses on the myths, legends, and traditions of the Indians regarding birth, death, marriage, etc., focusing on San Cristóbal Totonicapán. Concludes that these events are so closely bound with tradition that rural social workers must have a detailed knowledge of these traditions to be successful. DLC LNHT

682 Guzmán-Böckler, Carlos, and Jean-Loup Herbert. Guatemala: Una interpretación histórica-social. Mexico: Siglo XXI Editores, 1970. vii, 205 pp. Biblio., notes, tables. 5th ed. Mexico: Siglo XXI Editores, 1975. 205 pp. Biblio., notes, tables.
Indianité et lutte des classes. Paris: Union Générale d'Editions, 1972. 317 pp. Biblio., notes, maps, tables.

A major sociological study of Guatemalan society from pre-Conquest days to the present, but with emphasis on the present. Presents a number of separate essays by the two authors, focusing on the cultural diversity of the nation, the Indian heritage, the class structure, and the survival of what is called internal colonialism. Emphasizes class struggle and exploitation of the Indians and the lower classes, contending that the ladino is a figment of the imagination, since in fact the society consists of the masses and the exploiters. DLC LNHT BNG

683 Guzmán Selva, Enrique. Diario íntimo: relaciones políticas y personales entre el 25 de agosto de 1884 y el 2 de octubre de 1885. Managua: Tipografía Nacional, 1912. xviii, 199 pp.

An excerpt from the diary of a prominent Nicaraguan journalist of the late nineteenth century, revealing his personal reactions to the events of these years and to the Guatemalan regime of Justo Rufino Barrios. Describes his travels in Barrios's Guatemala, discusses the caudillo's projects and ambitions, and describes various officials of his government, hailing some and criticizing others. The complete diary, covering the years 1878-1911, was serialized in the Revista Conservador from 1960 to 1964 but has not appeared in book form. LNHT

684 Haefkens, Jacob. <u>Centraal Amerika, uit een geschiedkundig, aardrijkskundig en statistiek oogpunt beschouwd</u>. Dordrecht, The Netherlands: Blussé & van Braam, 1832. 488 pp. Illus., maps.

The author was a Dutch diplomat who served as the consul general in Guatemala from 1828 through 1829 and dedicated his efforts to visiting remote parts of the republic and assembling as much information about it as possible, later publishing several volumes that combine his observations with the data he gathered about the history of the area and about the contemporary scene. Provides historians with valuable insights into the situation during the 1820s. DLC LNHT

685 _____. <u>Reize naar Guatemala: Behlzende eene reize door de provincie San Salvador, alsmede keen verslad der gerschiedenis en des handles Centraal Amerika</u>. The Hague: W.K. Mandemaker, 1827. iv, 119 pp. Illus.

See item GU684. DLC LNHT BNG

686 _____. <u>Viaje a Guatemala y Centroamérica</u>. Guatemala: Editorial Universitaria, 1969. xxii, 342 pp. Index, notes, illus.

A Spanish translation combining items GU684-85. DLC LNHT BNG

687 Hegel, Carlos Augustin Enrique. <u>Die historische Entwicklung der Plantagenwirtschaft in Guatemala bis zum Ende des 19. Jahrhunderts</u>. Munich: Druck von V. Hofling, 1930. 63 pp.

An overview of the expansion of plantation agriculture during the nineteenth century. DLC

688 Heredia, Manuel de. <u>Atención Guatemala: el general Ydígoras Fuentes y la realidad histórica de Guatemala</u>. Madrid: Editorial Española, n.d. [196?]. 283 pp. Index, illus.

A Spanish journalist and prize-winning novelist provides a sympathetic account of Guatemala and its situation during the regime of Ydígoras Fuentes, with discussion of the president, his rise, his programs, and future prospects of the nation. DLC LNHT

689 Hereford, Karl Thomas. <u>Formación del personal para la enseñanza media: estimación de costos</u>. Guatemala: Instituto de Investigaciones y Mejoramiento Educativo, 1964. 22 pp.

A brief summary of the projection of the costs of mounting a massive training program for high-school teachers sufficient to fulfill the vast needs of the nation if it is to make education available to all. DLC

690 Hernández Cardona, Romeo Manuel. <u>El salario mínimo en Guatemala</u>. Guatemala: Tipografía Nacional, 1963. 325 pp. Index, biblio., notes, tables.

An overview of Guatemalan minimum-wage regulations and their application, considering historical antecedents and the theory of such regulations in general as well as the current system in Guatemala, written as a thesis by an official of the Ministry of Labor. Includes summaries of and excerpts from legislation and regulations, tables regarding the limits, and data on such issues as the minimum standards of living and the cost of basic items used to compute it, with explanation of the specific rules for the different economic sectors and categories of labor. FU

691 Hernández Cobos, Humberto. <u>Las casas sin paredes: rapsodia novelada</u>. Guatemala: Ministerio de Educación Pública, 1965. 259 pp.

A novel describing life in urban Guatemala. LNHT BNG

692 Hernández de León, Federico. <u>A lo largo del camino andanzas, venturas y malaventuras: alegrías y quebrantos en torno a una vida</u>. Guatemala: Editorial Landívar, 1957. 192 pp.

A semimemoir relating various events in the life of a prominent Guatemalan journalist, including references to Central American figures he has known. It focuses on his remembrances of his youth during the early years of the twentieth century, ranging from personal life and schooling to commentaries on contemporary political figures and issues. TxU

693 _____. <u>La deuda Inglesa, su orígen, desarrollo y cancelación</u>. Guatemala: Tipografía Nacional, 1958. 153 pp.

A series of essays originally published in the <u>Revista de la Economía Nacional</u> during the 1940s. They detail the history of one of the most famous, and infamous, debts in Guatemalan history, the so-called English debt, contracted in 1824 and a subject of continued dispute between Guatemala and England until it was paid in full by the regime of Jorge Ubico during the final days of his tenure. The view reflects the official attitude of the caudillo: the debt is portrayed as an onerous load for the nation to carry, one that prevented further progress and proved profitable for the British moneygrabbers; its full payment is hailed as a national victory liberating the nation from this unjust burden left over from the past. DLC BNG

694 _____. <u>De las gentes que conocí, desfile arbitrario de personajes que se mueven al recuerdo simple</u>. 2 vols. Guatemala: Tipografía Nacional, 1958. 317, 329 pp.

A series of brief descriptions of the individuals in the circle of this prominent Guatemalan journalist, including nearly all the leading journalists and intellectuals of the nation. The passages combine description with characterization, discussing the personality and outlook of the individuals, their friendships in the society, and their intellectual orientation. The haphazard arrangement is offset by a table of contents. It is interesting that few of the political figures of the contemporary era are included, and that those present are from the 1920s; the listing is confined to longtime associates, and does not include those with whom he had contact as a journalist while reporting the national

(Hernández de León, Federico)
scene. The sketches provide useful, though personal, views of many significant figures. LNHT

695   ____. El libro de las efemerides: capítulos de la historia de la América Central. 8 vols. Guatemala: Sánchez & de Guise, 1925-30, 1959-68.
An historical calendar consisting of a series of essays briefly summarizing the historically significant events of each day in Guatemalan history, drawing from all historical eras. They are arranged day by day and include several complete cycles employing distinct events. Quotations from documents and published works are included, with journalistic-style reporting showing the pros and cons of the various individuals and regimes. The last four volumes were published posthumously. DLC LNHT BNG

696   ____. El libro de las entrevistas en nuestro recuerdo, la verdad de ayer revienta de pronto como una fruta madura. Guatemala: Sánchez & de Guise, 1922. 238 pp. Latest ed. Guatemala: Sánchez & de Guise, 1932. 238 pp.
Interviews by a prominent Guatemalan journalist, originally conducted for his newspaper, Nuestro Diario, presenting the views of the leading figures of the Guatemalan political scene during the turbulent years following the overthrow of the regime of Manuel Estrada Cabrera and the political turmoil that characterized the short-lived regime of Carlos Herrera. Includes all the leading political figures of the various parties and factions, but unfortunately the interviews are not dated. IU

697   ____. Viajes presidenciales: breves relatos de algunas expediciones administrativas del general D. Jorge Ubico, presidente de la república. 2 vols. Guatemala: Publicaciones del Partido Liberal Progresista, 1940-43. 574, 546 pp. Illus., maps.
The coeditor of Nuestro Diario, who was also a close friend of Ubico and accompanied him on his journeys to the interior, provides detailed accounts of Ubico's numerous annual inspection trips throughout the entire country. Originally prepared for the newspaper, these sympathetic accounts provide illustrations of Ubico's activities and personality, including a rich collection of tales and the caudillo's favorite sayings, and as such constitute one of the most valuable sources regarding this controversial dictator. LNHT BNG

698   Hernández Linares, Tadeo, ed. Álbum gráfico: asistencia social y sanidad pública en los departamentos. Guatemala: Tipografía Nacional, 1960. 46 pp. Illus.
A collection of brief descriptions of the nation's health-care facilities, with photos and text hailing the expansion of the facilities under the revolutionary governments. LNHT

699   Hernández Sifontes, Julio. Realidad jurídica del indígena guatemalteco. Guatemala: Ministerio de Educación Pública, 1965. 413 pp. Biblio., illus., maps, tables.
A study of the role of Indians in Guatemala and their present condition, written by a member of the faculty of the University of San Carlos. The first half consists of an historical analysis focusing on the pre-Colonial and Colonial days and the life-style of the Indians; the second half is devoted to an analysis of Guatemalan legislation relative to the Indians, from independence to the present. The author concludes that the legal system is unfavorable to the Indian and that the government serves the interests of the dominant classes. He recommends a larger role by the university in defense of the Indian, larger budgetary appropriations, and more programs by the government to improve the lot of the Indians. LNHT BNG

700   Herrera, Flavio. Caos. Guatemala: Editorial Universitaria, 1949. 187 pp. Latest ed. Guatemala: Editorial Universitaria, 1974. 187 pp.
A novel sympathetically depicting the life of the Indian peasants in the Guatemalan countryside, focusing on their traditions, folklore, and trials and tribulations. Demonstrates both the problems of their lives and the fatalism and hopelessness that characterize their traditions and attitudes. DLC LNHT

701   ____. La tempestad. Guatemala: Unión Tipográfica, 1935. 331 pp. Illus. Latest ed. Guatemala: Ministerio de Educación Pública, 1963. xxii, 300 pp.
A novel set in the coffee-growing hinterlands of Guatemala, dealing with the lives of the people and stressing the plight of the campesino and his low state. It also provides an account of the life-style on the coffee estates and the methods employed in growing the crop, but its importance derives from its portrayal of the contrast between the lives of the peasants and the landowners. DLC LNHT BNG

702   Herrera, Francisco. Agrarismo guatemalteco: sinopsis histórica. Guatemala: Editorial Landívar, 1966. 48 pp. Biblio., tables.
A history of agriculture, focusing particularly on land tenure during the post-1950 era, which occupies half the volume. DLC LNHT

703   Herrera, Marta Josefina. Semblanzas. Guatemala: Tipografía Nacional, 1966. 372 pp. Illus.
A series of brief biographical sketches of illustrious Guatemalans of the mid-twentieth century, as well as of citizens from all walks of life, accompanied by photos. DLC LNHT

704   Herrera Muñoz, Francisco. Manual para comités de educación. Guatemala: Escuela de Cooperativismo Chimaltenango, n.d. 112 pp. Biblio., illus.

A handbook designed for use by organizers of cooperatives in the rural areas, providing instruction, objectives, and definitions of the various processes and institutions and their functions. BNG

705 Herrick, Thomas R. Desarrollo económico y político de Guatemala durante el periódo de Justo Rufino Barrios, 1871-1885. Guatemala: Editorial Universitaria de Guatemala and San José: EDUCA, 1974. 369 pp. Biblio., notes, tables.
A history of the regime of Justo Rufino Barrios, emphasizing his impact on the nation and his place in the Liberal movement. Based on published documents and pertinent secondary works. The author stresses Barrios's successful efforts at economic development while criticizing his dictatorial methods, but notes that he still managed to capture the political ideals of an era, since the constitutions he wrote lasted well beyond his regime. DLC LNHT BNG

706 Hersey, Jean. Half-Way to Heaven: A Guatemalan Holiday. New York: Prentice-Hall, 1947. xii, 259 pp. Illus., maps.
A well-known travel author's impressions of Guatemala, mixing observations during a visit, experiences with the people he met, and folktales and Indian legends drawn from other writers and from personal accounts. Vivid prose and the practiced eye of a seasoned observer are evident, producing an account focusing on the people and their traditions and life-styles while including descriptions of the various regions of the nation, though of course stressing the unusual and exotic. The emphasis is on the Indians, the pace of life, and the natural beauty. Written for the general reader. DLC LNHT

707 Hidalgo, J., ed. Encuesta provocada por "El Imparcial" y sus colegas afiliados a propósito de una petición de justicia de algunos amigos de Cabrera. Guatemala: n.p., 1924. 106 pp. Illus.
A collection of articles, commentaries, and letters from the Guatemalan press, covering 1923-24, all identified as to original publication data, reflecting the controversy over the fate of Manuel Estrada Cabrera after his overthrow. They were occasioned by a petition for his release from prison by some of his former supporters. The communications trace the resulting polemic, with its charges and countercharges by supporters and enemies, reflecting the turbulence of the era and the controversial nature of his regime. LNHT

708 Hidalgo N., J. El general Cayetano Sánchez: rasgos biográficos. Guatemala: Tipografía Popular, 1904. 23 pp. Illus.
A brief biographical sketch of the hero of the Battle of Coco. DLC

709 Hinshaw, Robert E. Panajachel: A Guatemalan Town in Thirty-Year Perspective. Pittsburgh: University of Pittsburgh Press, 1975. xxvii, 203 pp. Index, biblio., maps, tables.
An anthropological study of an Indian community, testing and refuting some of the hypotheses made in a similar study of a neighboring community twenty years earlier by Sol Tax. The author was part of the team of the Seminario de Integración Social of Guatemala headed by Tax, which restudied the entire region to test change in the years since Tax's original work. He notes a greater adaptation to external contact, particularly in the economic sphere, and emphasizes the role of the Catholic church in assisting change and adapting to the local culture, citing the abolition of mandamientos during the 1920s and of debt peonage during the 1930s as the most significant changes in the Indian's lives in this century. DLC LNHT

710 Hints on Colonization, Particularly with Reference to the Valuable Grant Made by the Supreme Government of Central America to the Eastern Coast of Central America Commercial and Agricultural Company. London: Robert Sears, n.d. 16 pp.
A folio describing a grant for the colonization and development of Verapaz, made in 1834 by the Federation government to a British company; seeks settlers for the area by extolling the virtues and potential of the region. DLC

711 Holleran, Mary P. Church and State in Guatemala. New York: Columbia University Press, 1949. 359 pp. Biblio., notes, illus., maps.
A detailed study of the role of the church in nineteenth-century Guatemala and in its politics, focusing principally on the independence-Federation period and the Liberal revolution. Based on extensive research in secondary works, newspapers, and Guatemalan documents. Includes consideration of the major church-state issues and their role in the nation's politics, with attention to the positions of the leading parties and political figures as well as of churchmen. While the volume covers the years to the date of publication, the twentieth century is considered only in very general terms in a few pages, with the major focus of the volume remaining the nineteenth century. DLC LNHT BNG

712 Honduras, Universidad Nacional Autónoma de. Clementina Suárez. Tegucigalpa: Universidad Nacional Autónoma de Honduras, 1969. Pages unnumbered. Illus.
A collection of brief commentaries about and appreciations of this well-known Guatemalan writer extolling her work and emphasizing her contributions to the literature of social protest; includes a series of paintings and drawings of her. DLC

713 Hoppenot, Hélène. Guatemala. Lausanne, Switzerland: Editions Clairefontaine, 1955. xix, 80 pp. Notes, illus., maps.
A collection of photos showing contemporary life in Guatemala, with views of cities, countryside, and particularly of the Indians. The only text is an excerpt from the work Four Keys to Guatemala. DLC

714 Hurtado Aguilar, Luís Alberto. <u>Así</u> <u>se</u> <u>gestó</u>
<u>la</u> <u>Liberación</u>. Guatemala: Tipografía
Nacional, 1956. 434 pp. Illus.
    The official history of the National Lib-
eration Movement, offering its version of the
events in Guatemala. Traces the leftward
trend of the nation; what it calls the communist infiltration; and the "heroic" struggle
for liberation, featuring coronel Carlos
Castillo Armas. Includes the acts of the
various political meetings and the orders and
decrees of the movement and its government,
detailing its fight and eventual takeover of
the nation. Includes a vitriolic attack on
the Arbenz regime, with photos of its victims
and of other aspects of the effort. Reprints
voluminous documentation regarding the communist role, and quotes extensively from
Castillo Armas. DLC LNHT BNG

715 _____. <u>Castillo</u> <u>Armas</u>. Guatemala: Imprenta
Hispania, 1956. 36 pp.
    A laudatory official biography hailing the
president and tracing the important stages of
his life in brief single-page journalistic
essays. BNG

716 _____. <u>Efemérides</u> <u>de</u> <u>la</u> <u>Liberación</u>: <u>junio</u>
<u>y</u> <u>julio</u> <u>de</u> <u>1954</u>. Guatemala: Tipografía
Nacional, 1955. 72 pp.
    An account of the National Liberation Move-
ment, beginning on 1 June 1954. Contrasts the
actions of the Arbenz regime with those of the
movement; includes the usual accusations
against the Arbenz government and a laudatory
account of the heroism of the liberators and
their triumph, which "saved" the nation from
communism and terror. BNG

717 _____. <u>Historia</u> <u>de</u> <u>un</u> <u>golpe</u> <u>rojo</u>. Guatemala:
Imprenta Hispania, 1956. 84 pp. Illus.
    An account of the attempted countercoup of
June 1956 and the resulting confrontation and
deaths. Contains photos and reprints of documents and newspaper accounts. Justifies the
government stand, picturing the incident as a
communist attempt to regain control of the
country. Includes lists of the individuals
arrested in connection with the coup or
wounded in the clashes. The publication is
particularly critical of the alleged involvement of university students in the plot. DLC
BNG

718 <u>Hombres</u> <u>de</u> <u>la</u> <u>Liberación</u>. Guatemala: n.p.,
1955. 95 pp. Illus.
    A history of the National Liberation Move-
ment, with an account of its formation, principal actions, and triumph. Makes the usual
charges against the Arbenz regime but focuses
on a description of the movement's various
leaders, with laudatory comments about the
actions of each and some background information about them. Published on the first anniversary of the movement's victory. DLC

719 Idell, Albert Edward. <u>Doorway</u> <u>in</u> <u>Antigua</u>: <u>A</u>
<u>Sojourn</u> <u>in</u> <u>Guatemala</u>. New York: William
Sloane, 1949. 210 pp. Illus.

A novelist's account of his stay in Antigua
and the house he bought, focusing on the
changes he made in it and his contacts with
people to study their customs. DLC LNHT BNG

720 El Imparcial (Guatemala). <u>Artículos</u> <u>relativos</u>
<u>a</u> <u>la</u> <u>reforma</u> <u>monetaria</u> <u>de</u> <u>Guatemala</u>.
Guatemala: Tipografía Nacional, 1924.
108 pp.
    A series of articles that originally
appeared in <u>El</u> <u>Imparcial</u> during the fall of
1924 and in the <u>Diario</u> <u>de</u> <u>Guatemala</u> during the
spring of 1925, discussing the need for mone-
tary reform and stabilization in Guatemala,
including possible reserve systems. The un-
signed articles emphasize banking problems and
serve to indicate the debate in the nation
regarding the need for regulation and for a
central bank, as well as the controversy regarding the new legislation, its necessity,
and efficacy. BNG

721 Inman, Samuel Guy. <u>A</u> <u>New</u> <u>Day</u> <u>in</u> <u>Guatemala</u>:
<u>A</u> <u>Study</u> <u>of</u> <u>the</u> <u>Present</u> <u>Social</u> <u>Revolution</u>.
Wilton, Conn.: Worldover Press, 1951. iv,
58 pp.
    A sympathetic summary of the Guatemalan
revolution by a prominent scholar of Latin
America, designed to counter the criticism of
the regime in the United States, which the
author views as inspired by the United Fruit
Company. Hails the reforms and objectives of
the governments of the revolution and acclaims
the leadership and idealism of Juan José
Arévalo. The author draws heavily on press
commentary, his own experiences, and interviews with individuals who have met Arévalo.
Quotes liberally from statements extolling
Arévalo's abilities, goals, and leadership,
while condemning economic exploitation. DLC
LNHT

722 Instituto Centroamericano de Población y
Familia. <u>Actitudes</u> <u>de</u> <u>obstetras</u> <u>y</u> <u>ginecólogos</u>
<u>de</u> <u>Guatemala</u> <u>sobre</u> <u>la</u> <u>regulación</u> <u>de</u> <u>la</u>
<u>natalidad</u>. Guatemala: Instituto
Centroamericano de Población y Familia, 1968.
46 pp. Tables.
    A study, sponsored by the institution and
the Regional Organization for Central America
and Panama, regarding the role of doctors in
birth-control programs. The study concludes
that the doctors are not passing sufficient
information on to their patients, and that
Catholicism is not an impediment to birth
control. It advocates a larger effort on the
part of the medical community, contending that
the main problem is a lack of information
available to families. DLC BNG

723 _____. <u>Fecundidad</u> <u>en</u> <u>Guatemala</u>. Guatemala:
Instituto Centroamericano de Población y
Familia, 1972. 709 pp. Tables.
    A collection of studies dealing with
various aspects of birth rates, birth control,
and attitudes toward them, including a 1967-68
survey. DLC

724 Instituto de Nutrición de Centro América y
Panamá. <u>Evaluación</u> <u>nutricional</u> <u>de</u> <u>la</u>

población de Centro América y Panamá:
Guatemala. San José: Instituto de Nutrición
de Centro América y Panamá, 1969. Various
pagings. Illus., tables.

 A detailed survey of the nutritional state
of the rural Guatemalan populace, based on
surveys and medical examinations conducted
during 1965-67. Provides extensive data regarding the diet, food distribution, shortages, and medical implications. DLC

725 Instituto Guatemalteco Americano. Books about
Guatemala. Guatemala: Instituto Guatemalteco
Americano, 1960. 34 pp.
 A brief, unannotated list of books about
Guatemala, compiled by Gonzalo Dardón Córdova.
There are separate sections for titles in
Spanish and English, arranged by subject.
Despite its brevity, it includes many signifi-
cant titles. DLC LNHT

726 Instituto para el Desarrollo Económico y
Social de América Central. El reto del
desarrollo en Guatemala. Guatemala:
Editorial Financiera Guatemalteca, 1970. 428
pp. Maps, tables.
 A detailed overview of the present state of
Guatemala's society and economy, focusing on
the recent socioeconomic development and its
impact; replete with statistics and appropriate maps. DLC

727 Inter-American Peace Committee. Report of the
Inter-American Peace Committee on the Contro-
versy Between Guatemala, Honduras, and
Nicaragua. Washington, D.C.: PAU, 1954. v,
71 pp.
Informe sobre la controversia entre Guatemala,
Honduras y Nicaragua. Washington, D.C.: PAU,
1954. 70 pp.
Rapport sur le différend entre le Guatemala le
Honduras et le Nicaragua. Washington, D.C.:
PAU, 1954, 76 pp.
 A chronological account of the committee's
efforts in response to the Guatemalan claim of
invasion from Honduras and Nicaragua attendant
to the overthrow of the government of Jacabo
Arbenz by the movement of Carlos Castillo
Armas, followed by the official exchanges
between the governments and the committee.
The mediation and investigation ended shortly
after the governmental change in Guatemala
rendered it pointless. DLC LNHT

728 International Bank for Reconstruction and
Development. The Economic Development of
Guatemala: Report of a Mission Sponsored by
the International Bank for Reconstruction and
Development in Collaboration with the Government of Guatemala. Washington, D.C.: International Bank for Reconstruction and Development, 1951. xviii, 305 pp. Maps.
El desarrollo económico de Guatemala: resumen
del informe de la misión que bajo los
auspicios del Banco Internacional de
Reconstrucción y Fomento y con la colaboración
del gobierno de la república realizo un
estudio de la economía del país. Guatemala:
Tipografía Nacional, 1951. 122 pp. Maps.

 A report resulting from a 1951 mission by
the bank to study the Guatemalan economy. The
mission was headed by George E. Brintell, a
Canadian scholar. Includes a survey of the
existing conditions in several key economic
sectors, such as agriculture, industry, mining
and petroleum, communications, transport,
electricity, and finance, with plans for
further development emphasizing short-term
policies designed to rapidly stimulate
agriculture. DLC LNHT BNG

729 International Bureau of American Republics.
Guatemala. Washington, D.C.: GPO, 1892. 192
pp. Illus., maps.
 A collection of general data and descriptive material. Originated in 1892 as a for-
midable volume compiling considerable
information, but issued intermittently. After
the turn of the century, it became more frequent (with one for each country), and was cut
to a brief pamphlet. DLC BNCR

730 International Court of Justice. Nottebohm
Case: Liechtenstein vs. Guatemala. 2 vols.
The Hague: International Court of Justice,
1955. 561, 708 pp. Index, appendixes.
Recueil des arrets avis consultatifs et
ordonnances, Affaire Nottebohm (Liechtenstein
c. Guatemala). 2 vols. London: A.W.
Sijthoff's, 1955. 65, 65 pp.
 The proceedings of a case before the International Court of Justice resulting from the
Guatemalan seizure during World War II of the
German-owned Nottebohm Bank, among the largest
in the republic. After the war Nottebohm
sued, contending that because it was incorporated in Liechtenstein it was not subject to
seizure as a German asset. The Guatemalan
government countered with information supplied
by the United States. The documentation and
arguments provide a complete record of the
Nottebohm Corporation's operations in
Guatemala, the appropriate contracts and concessions, the Guatemalan laws regulating
German-owned firms during the war, and the
financial records of the firm since its seizure by the government during 1944, furnishing
useful data regarding the firm, its holdings
and operations, and the role of foreign corporations, and particularly of the German community, in Guatemala. The Court's decision
was published in French and English under the
French title. DLC

731 International Railways of Central America.
International Railways of Central America:
Documents referring to the Nullification of
the Concession of February 19, 1908. New
York: Phillips & Van Brunt, 1921. 273 pp.
Maps, tables.
 The company's protest regarding the revocation of its 1908 concession in 1921 by the
Herrera regime, the documents submitted in
support of its stand, and the subsequent exchanges regarding the question. Includes
legal opinions regarding the company's rights,
the original concession, various company contracts and subcontracts for railroad work in

the nation, and statements contending that the company acted properly and fulfilled its contractual obligations under the concession terms.   DLC LNHT

732 International Union of Students. Ten Years of Student Struggle for Freedom and Democracy: Guatemala--1954-1964. Prague: International Union of Students, n.d. [1964]. 36 pp.
  A pamphlet commemorating the twentieth anniversary of the Revolution of 1944. Discusses the Guatemalan situation in Marxist terms, condemning feudalism and Yankee imperialism and extolling the role of students in the revolution. Contains resolutions of the group's congress declaring solidarity with the Guatemalan leftist student movement. DLC

733 Irisarri, Antonio José de [Hilarion de Altagumea, pseud.]. El cristiano errante: novela que tiene mucho de historia. Bogotá: Imprenta de Espinosa, 1847. Latest ed. Guatemala: Ministerio de Educación Pública, 1960. xxx, 449 pp. Illus.
  A semiautobiographical novel by a well-known and well-traveled Guatemalan author, recounting his observations during his travels. DLC LNHT BNG

734 _____. History of the Heroic Epaminondas of Cauca. 2 vols. New York: Hallet, 1863. 347 pp. Illus.
Historia del perínclito Epaminondas del Cauca. 2 vols. Guatemala: Ministerio de Educación Pública, 1951. xxxix, 347 pp. Illus.
  A novel by a prominent Guatemalan writer of the mid-nineteenth century, portraying the life of an autocrat and using irony and sarcasm to detail his many escapades, his misdeeds, and the form of his government. The novel, which uses a broad Latin American setting, is written in a timeless form to deal with all dictators. It clearly refers to the early nineteenth-century type of strong-man characteristic of the post-independence era. DLC LNHT

735 Irungaray, Ezequiel C., ed. Índice del Archivo de la Enseñanza Superior de Guatemala. Guatemala: Editorial Universitaria, 1962. 300 pp.
  A complete shelf listing, volume by volume and letter by letter, of the holdings of the Archive of Higher Education of Guatemala, housed at the University of San Carlos. Arranged chronologically by issuing agency. The largest portions date from Colonial times (70 vols.) but a "modern" section covers the Academia de Estudios from 1832 to 1839 (13 vols.), the Consejo Superior de Instrucción Pública from 1875 through 1881 (2 vols.), the university, from 1821 to 1879 (96 vols.), and the Faculty of Law from 1880 to 1899 (150 vols.). These files consist of the records of the educational entities, principally student records and degrees granted, but also encompass some business records and account books and the correspondence of the directorates. A useful guide to a little-known archive that contains significant information regarding

educational policy and the history of education in Guatemala. DLC LNHT

736 Istituto Italo-Latino Americano. Guatemala. Rome: Istituto Italo-Latino Americano, 1971. 55 pp.
  See item CR610. DLC

737 Jackson, Joseph Henry. Notes on a Drum: Travel Sketches in Guatemala. New York: Macmillan, 1937. x, 276 pp. Illus.
  An experienced travel-book author's descriptive account of a two-week swing through Guatemala, emphasizing the unique and the unusual with vivid description and a practiced eye. The focus is on the landforms, flora and fauna, the people, and the Indians, though description of the principal cities and their tourist attractions, particularly colonial buildings, is also extensive. DLC LNHT

738 Jacob, Jeffrey C. Rural-to-Urban Migration: The Rural Normal School Students of Guatemala. Syracuse, N.Y.: Syracuse University Press, 1971. v, 48 pp. Tables.
  A brief study of the career plans of students at the Normal School who come from rural areas, focusing on the reasons they gave for settling in the city or returning to a rural environment. DLC

739 James, Daniel. Red Design for the Americas: Guatemalan Prelude. New York: John Day, 1954. 347 pp.
Tácticas rojas en las Américas. Mexico: Editorial Intercontinental, 1955. 245 pp.
  A journalist's summary of the Guatemalan crisis, indicting the Arbenz regime for communism and detailing the revolution's reforms and leftward shift, drawing some generalizations regarding the potential effects on the rest of Latin America. The account is primarily factual, based on available information with extensive quotations from official statements, and clearly written from the perspective of the Cold War. The author advocates strong Yankee support for democracy in Latin America, though warning against the temptation to substitute one type of dictatorship for another. DLC BNG

740 Jenness, Aylette, and Lisa W. Kroeber. A Life of Their Own: An Indian Family in Latin America. New York: Crowell, 1975. xiii, 133 pp. Index, illus.
  Aimed at a junior-high audience, this volume discusses typical facets of the life of a Guatemalan Indian family by means of presentation of typical chores, meals, and activities, based on the observations of the authors. Intended to acquaint young people with the basic aspects of Indian life rather than to analyze. DLC

741 Jensen, Amy Elizabeth. Guatemala: A Historical Survey. New York: Exposition Press, 1955. 263 pp. Index.
  A broad narration of Guatemalan history, with strong emphasis on the crusade against communism, written for the general reader by a

schoolteacher drawing on uncited secondary sources. Provides an overview of the nation's development from Colonial times, though with definite heroes and villains among the nation's presidents and dictators. Clearly reflects the Cold War mentality in its latter portions by denouncing the dangers of the communist "virus" and calling for Yankee vigilance in the hemisphere. DLC LNHT

742 Jesús, Felipe de. María, historia de una mártir. Guatemala: Tipografía Musical, 1897. Latest ed. Guatemala: Ministerio de Educación Pública, 1967. 279 pp.

A novel set in Guatemala in 1847 that recounts the life of the peasants and their trials and tribulations under the arbitrary dictatorships. Emphasizes the use of force against the populace by following the life of a woman and her clashes with the authorities. DLC LNHT

743 Jiménez España, Julio Ernesto. El derecho de trabajo y la indemnización por despido injustificado: problema jurídico y económico de Guatemala. Guatemala: Ministerio de Educación Pública, 1965. 252 pp. Biblio.

An analysis of current labor law and future needs. DLC

744 Jiménez G., Ernesto Bienvenido. La educación rural en Guatemala. Guatemala: Ministerio de Educación Pública, 1967. 340 pp. Biblio., illus., maps, tables.

A study of rural education in Guatemala, briefly tracing its history from Colonial times to 1944. Details its problems and deficiencies, describes the changes of the revolutionary era, and discusses the various aspects of the modern system while emphasizing the changes in the various governmental agencies in charge of the program. The author concludes that rural education remains a problem in Guatemala, as it has been throughout history, and recommends more vigorous efforts to improve it, including better teacher training and more incentives for teachers to work in rural areas, as well as more assistance to help them meet the special problems encountered. BNG

745 Johnson, George B. Guatemala en el año 2000: o el despertar de una raza. Mexico: Ediciones Iximche, 1950. 434 pp.

A novel by a Yankee nuclear engineer who has long resided in Guatemala, presenting his view of what Guatemala might be like in the year 2000 and commenting on the social and political changes that might occur. BNG

746 Johnson, Kenneth F. The Guatemalan Presidential Election of March 6, 1966: An Analysis. Washington, D.C.: Institute for the Comparative Study of Political Systems, 1967. 25 pp. Biblio., tables.

A brief summation of the issues, conduct, and candidates in the 1966 Guatemalan election, with analysis of the voting statistics. Seeks to emphasize the choice between a civilian and a military candidate. The author concludes that the populace was disillusioned with the nation's recent political history, but that the election was fair. DLC LNHT

747 Jones, Chester Lloyd. Guatemala: Past and Present. Minneapolis: University of Minnesota Press, 1940. xii, 420 pp. Index, biblio., illus., maps.

A broad survey of Guatemalan developments of the late nineteenth and early twentieth centuries that focuses on economic and social conditions and includes brief historical background from Colonial times. Includes economic statistics and topical chapters examining such themes as agriculture, labor, population, and social life, all considered within a realistic view of the starting point and the nation's potential, as well as political chapters discussing the role of the nation's parties and leaders. The concluding chapter, "If I were Dictator," provides a useful perspective on the problems facing any government in an underdeveloped nation. DLC LNHT

748 Jones, J. Bascom, Maximo Soto Hall, and William T. Scoullar, eds. El "Libro Azul" de Guatemala, 1915. New Orleans: Searcy & Pfaff, 1915. 406 pp. Index, illus., maps.

Designed to provide basic information for the prospective investor and tourist, this bilingual volume (Spanish and English) includes a brief historical synopsis, descriptions of places, hotels, clubs, etc., and alphabetized lists of significant officials and diplomats, all with extensive photos. DLC

749 Juárez Muñoz, J. Fernando. El indio guatemalteco: ensayo de sociología nacionalista. 2 vols. Guatemala: Tipografía Latina and Tipografía San Antonio, 1931-46. 179, 127 pp.

A discussion of the role of Guatemala's Indians, their style and cultures, but particularly their interaction with the rest of society. Advocates new labor laws to protect the Indian. Volume 2 focuses more on the Indian life-style and its problems, discussing their effects and the means of dealing with them. DLC LNHT BNG

750 ____. Nuestros problemas: apuntes del ambiente. Guatemala: Tipografía Nacional, 1926. 140 pp.

A series of essays discussing what the author considers Guatemala's principal problems, including agriculture, industry, economy, education, labor, and alcoholism. DLC BNG

751 Juárez y Aragón, José Fernando. Cuentos del mar. Guatemala: Unión Tipográfica, 1941. 62 pp.

A series of short stories dealing with the life-style and customs of the tropical coastal regions of Guatemala. DLC LNHT BNG

752 ____. Ésta es Guatemala. Guatemala: Imprenta Iberia, 1950. 245 pp.

A series of essays describing significant cities, buildings, and events in Guatemala,

(Juárez y Aragón, José Fernando)
giving the history of each and the inspirations they provided the author. The result is a somewhat disorganized discussion of various aspects of Guatemalan history and the characteristics of the nation and its culture. DLC LNHT BNG

753 _____. *Hacia el futuro Petén*. Guatemala: Unión Tipografía, 1955. 53 pp. Illus.
An optimistic description of the prospects of the Petén and of the various development projects under way as part of the effort of the regional development agency promoted by the Ydígoras Fuentes regime. Reports a visit to the region by three congressional deputies inspecting the works. Extensive photos of the projects are included. DLC LNHT

754 _____. *El milagro: novela criolla en el corazón del trópico*. Guatemala: Imprenta M. Ortiz H., 1952. 84 pp.
A novel about peasant life that deals with its problems and tribulations and seeks to offer hope for improvement and salvation. The peasants in the story place their faith in religion and pray to the Christ of Esquipulias for assistance, and this plus their hard work pays off. LNHT

755 Kapuściński, Ryszard. *Dlaczego zginał Karl von Spreti* [Why Karl von Spreti died]. Warsaw: Ksiazka i Wiedza, 1970. 92 pp.
A Marxist interpretation, in brief outline fashion, of Guatemalan events from Ubico through the guerrilla movement. DLC

756 Karen, Ruth. *Hello Guatemala*. New York: Grosset & Dunlap, 1970. 123 pp. Index, biblio., illus.
Narrations of various events, designed to typify current local life and emphasize social factors and physical description. Contains a brief historical introduction. DLC

757 Kelsey, Vera, and Lilly de Jongh Osborne. *Four Keys to Guatemala*. New York and London: Funk & Wagnalls, 1939. xiv, 332 pp. Index, biblio., illus., maps. Latest ed. New York: Funk & Wagnalls, 1961. 332 pp. Index, biblio., illus.
A general descriptive survey and a travel guide that examines the current state of the nation as of 1936 when it was written; focuses topically on the visible aspects of the Colonial, Indian, and modern cultures, as well as on the economy. Includes information on things to see, hotels, entertainment, etc.; only these aspects were revised in the later editions, with the cultural portion remaining as written in the 1930s. DLC LNHT BNG

758 Kendrick, John William. *A Report upon International Railways of Central America: Located in the Republics of Guatemala and Salvador*. Chicago: n.p., 1921. xv, 233 pp. Illus., maps, tables.
DLC

759 Kestler Farnés, Maximiliano. *Introducción a la teoría constitucional guatemalteca*. Guatemala: Sánchez & de Guise, 1950. 2d ed. Guatemala: Ministerio de Educación Pública, 1964. 510 pp. Biblio., notes.
Originally a thesis at the University of San Carlos, this text examines the Guatemalan constitution in the light of general constitutional theory, commenting on the strengths and weaknesses as well as the legal basis for the present Guatemalan governmental system. LNHT BNG

760 King, Arden R. *Cobán and the Verapaz: History and Cultural Process in Northern Guatemala*. New Orleans: MARI, 1974. xi, 379 pp. Biblio., maps, tables.
Based on fieldwork conducted during 1950–56, this volume studies the cultural assimilation and situation in the capital of Alta Verapaz in Guatemala, where the Indians are located within an area of intensive agriculture and coffee fincas populated principally by individuals of German origin, providing a glimpse of the cultural evolution of this isolated and very distinct region. The emphasis is on the 1950s and the impact of the German settlers, with historical background to provide an overview of the changing patterns. The area is examined topically, considering such questions as business, religion, education, family, courtship, marriage patterns, recreation, and others. DLC LNHT

761 Kint de Roodenbeek, Auguste T'. *Rapport présenté à M. le ministre de L'intérieur . . . sur les résultats de sa mission comme membre de la Commission du Government pour l'exploration de la Vera-Paz et du district de Santo-Thomas*. Brussels: Lesigne Frères, 1842. 74 pp.
The author's impressions of a visit to the region, focusing on general description but also including comments regarding the inhabitants and the state of Guatemala at that time. DLC

762 Kusch, Eugen. *Guatemala im Bild: Land der Maya*. Nurenburg: Hans Carl, 1962. 161 pp. Biblio., Illus.
Imágenes de Guatemala, el país de los Mayas. Nurenburg: Hans Carl, 1962. 161 pp. Biblio., illus.
Guatemala in Pictures. Nurenburg: Hans Carl, 1962. 160 pp. Biblio., illus. Latest ed. New York: n.p., 1965. 160 pp.
A photo essay, with a brief explanatory text, showing various aspects and regions of Guatemala. DLC LNHT

763 L., F. *Lecciones de geografía de Centroamérica: precedidas de nociones de geografía universal*. Guatemala: n.p., 1889. 297 pp. Illus., maps. 4th ed. Guatemala: Librería de Antonio Partegás, 1896.
A basic geography that, despite the title, focuses on Guatemala, which is the only country described province by province; the rest

(L., F.)
are treated in brief chapters on each nation
or in the general introductory section. BNG

763a _____. Notes of the Republic of Guatemala:
Her Progress from 1871 to 1884 Under the Government of Gen. J. Rufino Barrios. New York:
Nesbitt, 1885. 47 pp.
   A tract extolling the accomplishments of
the Barrios regime, designed to stimulate
interest in trade, investment, and immigration. Contains descriptions of his various
projects, commentaries on his stabilization of
the nation and on its potential, and a brief
biographical sketch. LNHT

764 LaCharité, Norman A., et al. Case Study
in Insurgency and Revolutionary Warfare:
Guatemala, 1944-1954. Washington, D.C.:
American University Press, 1964. vii, 116 pp.
Index, biblio., notes, illus., maps.
   A summary of the organization, position,
and role of the military and of the Communist
party, the two principal power groups struggling for control of Guatemala during the
turbulent years of 1944-54. Prepared under
government contract; draws primarily upon
existing literature, particularly Ronald M.
Schneider's Communism in Guatemala. The
account emphasizes the internal splits and
rivalries in both groups as key factors in
reducing their respective influence, and notes
that the Communist party appealed to the dis-
affected groups that were not part of the
political power structure, particularly labor
and the middle class, while the military reflected the predominance of middle-class officers among the graduates of the academy. DLC

765 La Farge, Oliver. Santa Eulalia: The Religion of a Cuchumatan Indian Town. Chicago:
University of Chicago Press, 1947. xix, 211
pp. Index, biblio., illus., maps.
   An anthropological study based on fieldwork
during 1932, when the area was still isolated
and without access roads. Among the subjects
discussed are myths, ceremony, ritual, and the
mixture of native beliefs with Christianity.
DLC LNHT

766 La Farge, Oliver, and Douglas Byers. The Year
Bearer's People. New Orleans, MARI, 1931.
xii, 379 pp. Biblio., illus., maps, tables.
   A detailed and descriptive anthropological
study of the Jacalteca Indians, based on
fieldwork conducted in 1927. Focuses on
customs, folklore, religion, dance, and life-
style, with particular emphasis on the survival of the Maya calendar and religious ritual
and their blend with the local brand of
Catholicism. DLC

767 Laferrière, Joseph. De París à Guatémala:
notes de voyages au Centro-Amérique, 1866-
1875. Paris: Garnier Frères Editeurs, 1877.
vi, 450 pp. Illus., tables.
   A description of the author's observations
during a trip through the West Indies to Central America, with chapters on each of the
five isthmian republics and Panama. The

emphasis is on physical description but data
regarding economics and trade, as well as
social observations, are included. Other
chapters list Central American agricultural
products and contain reproductions of the
constitution of El Salvador and the trade
treaty between Salvador and France, as well as
a discussion of contemporary European efforts
to settle colonies in the region. The author
clearly seeks to encourage European trade with
and interest in the area, reflecting his service as French vice-consul in San Salvador.
DLC

768 Lainfiesta, Eduardo, et al. Homage to a
Patriot: His Excellency Manuel Estrada
Cabrera. New Orleans: n.p., 1915. Pages
unnumbered. Illus.
   A brief pamphlet extolling the virtues of
Estrada Cabrera and the benefits his regime
brought to Guatemala, with photos of public-
works projects. DLC

769 Lainfiesta, Francisco. Apuntamientos para la
historia de Guatemala. Guatemala: Ministerio
de Educación Pública, 1975. xxxi, 487 pp.
   A history of Guatemala from 1865 through
1885. Written in the form of a memoir from
exile by a defender of Justo Rufino Barrios it
hails his progressive administration and its
benefits for Guatemala. The author was a
political supporter of Barrios who served in
Congress and as minister of fomento and wrote
shortly after the regime's collapse in the
1880s. He claims to be speaking impartially
and does manage to present the facts clearly,
despite his bias. A brief biography of the
author by David Vela provides an introduction.
LNHT BNG

770 Landini, Piero. Guatemala: condizioni
naturali ed economíche. Rome: Instituto
Cristoforo Colombo, n.d. [1925]. 164 pp.
Biblio., illus., tables.
   A basic description encompassing geography,
geology, and culture but focusing on economic
development, written during the 1920s and
designed to encourage Italian trade with and
knowledge about Guatemala. The final chapters
focus on agriculture, communications and
transport, and finance. DLC

771 Lanning, John Tate. The Eighteenth Century
Enlightenment in the University of San Carlos
de Guatemala. Ithaca, N.Y.: Cornell University Press, 1956. xxv, 372 pp. Index, notes,
illus.
   While focusing on the Colonial era and the
1700s in tracing the early development of the
university, this volume examines the impact of
the university experience on its graduates by
considering the role of the university in
educating the leaders of the independence
movement and in exposing them to the prevailing European doctrines of the Enlightenment.
DLC

772 Lara F., Celso A. Leyendas y casos de la
tradición oral de la ciudad de Guatemala.

(Lara F., Celso A.)
Guatemala: Editorial Centroamérica, 1973. xxi, 217 pp. Biblio., illus., maps.

A detailed study of Guatemalan folktales, including over 2,000 stories collected by the author during fieldwork in 1967-68 in Guatemala City. Offers a theoretical framework for studying the stories, and applies it in classifying the various legends recounted. DLC

773 _____. Por los viejos barrios de la Ciudad de Guatemala. Guatemala: Universidad de San Carlos, 1977. 265 pp. Biblio., illus.

A folklore specialist's continuing study. Includes a theoretical framework for the study of folkloric themes in literature but consisting principally of a series of short stories summarizing the tales of Guatemala City that the author collected, transcriptions of the oral legends used as the bases of his stories, and details regarding the parts of the capital in which he encountered them. DLC

774 Larraínzar, Federico. Carta sobre los últimos sucesos de Centro-América. Mexico: Imprenta Literia, 1864. 66 pp.

A Guatemalan general's version of the causes of the war between Guatemala and El Salvador, narrating the combats, explaining the reasons for the Guatemalan victory, and commenting extensively on the current situation and the actions of the other isthmian republics. As a detailed account of the military campaigns of the conflict between Carrera and Gerardo Barrios, written by a participant on the Guatemalan side, it illuminates important aspects of the conflict. DLC BNG

775 _____. La revolución de Guatemala. Mexico: Valle Hermanos, 1872. 149 pp. Latest ed. Mexico: Valle Hermanos, 1873. 96 pp.

A survey of the turbulent era from independence through 1872. Although written from a Conservative perspective, it is critical of both Liberals and Conservatives. The emphasis is on the many changes of government and the revolutions and civil wars involved. DLC LNHT

776 Leal, Héctor Alfonso. Tierra de liberación para el campesino: colonias agrícolas autenticamente nacionales. Guatemala: Tipografía Nacional, 1955. 190 pp. Illus., tables.

A description of the internal colonization program of the Castillo Armas government, focusing on the Pacific Coast pilot projects and hailing the new effort as a means of liberating the peasants and promoting the national economy. DLC BNG

777 Leíva, Raúl. Palabra en el tiempo. Guatemala: Editorial Universitaria, 1975. 772 pp.

A massive collection of poems written between 1944 and 1974 by one of the best-known of the generation of poets and intellectuals associated with the Guatemalan revolution of 1944-54, in which he expresses his love for his country, his revolutionary ideals, social conscience, and frustration. DLC BNG

778 Lemale, Carlos. Guía geográfica descriptiva de los centros de población de la República de Guatemala. Guatemala: Diario de Centro América, 1881. 421 pp.

An alphabetically arranged collection of brief, single-paragraph descriptions and identifications of places and place names in Guatemala. It includes cities, towns, and barrios, each briefly described and identified as to location. DLC LNHT

779 _____. El maestro Pedro Antonio Zea: su obra y su consagración biográfica. Guatemala: Ministerio de Educación Pública, 1957. 58 pp. Illus.

A biography of a schoolteacher from Chiquimula, Guatemala, written on the occasion of the naming of a school in his honor. Recounts his life through his teaching career, service in the municipal government, exile during the early portion of the twentieth century, and his retirement in 1947. DLC LNHT BNG

780 Lemus Mendoza, Bernardo. Vías para el desarrollo de Guatemala. Guatemala: Ediciones Piedra Santa, n.d. [1966]. 81 pp. Biblio., notes.

Originally a thesis, this work summarizes recent Guatemalan economic trends for each sector and then applies developmental theory to the situation, arguing against the route of dependent capitalism. Notes the limits imposed by the superdeveloped states, and calls instead for state control of the economy and an effort to promote internal development in both social and economic spheres. LNHT

781 Lentz, Joseph. Die Abtragungsvorgänge in den vulkanischen Lockermassen de Republik Guatemala. Wurzburg: Kabitzsch & Monnich, 1925. xi, 96 pp. Illus., maps.

A geological study of landforms and their relationship to the volcanoes of Guatemala and their eruptions. Includes considerable data regarding river valleys, mountain and cliff formations, and the geological origins and formation of the area. DLC LNHT

782 León, J. Romeo de. Contribución al conocimiento de la transmisión de la oncocera volvulvus por los simulados de Guatemala. Guatemala: Imprenta Universitaria, 1961. 52 pp. Biblio., illus.

A study of the parasite onchocerca volvulvus and its spread, concluding that simulium flies are the principal agent for its dissemination in Guatemala. The author is the chief of the parasite investigation institute of the Faculty of Medicine of the University of San Carlos. BNG

783 León, Juan María de. Contribución y bases estadísticas para el estudio de nuestro desequilibrio económico. Guatemala: Imprenta Electra, 1921. 105 pp. Tables.

A compilation of statistics and material regarding the Guatemalan economy, covering the years 1860 through 1921. Includes tables of exchange value, import and export data, and extensive tables regarding the principal nations exporting Guatemala's chief products throughout the world, supplemented by a chronological listing of Guatemalan legislation regarding economic matters, which includes global events affecting its trade and reproduction of a general economic study by Argentine scholar Juan Alberdi. DPU

784 León Aragón, Oscar de. Los contratos de la United Fruit Co. y las compañías muelleras en Guatemala. Guatemala: Ministerio de Educación Pública, 1950. 301 pp.

A denunciation of the role of the United Fruit Company in Guatemala, tracing its history through its contracts, particularly the 1924, 1930, and 1936 accords. Details the talks and the terms, contending that the company outmaneuvered the governments and secured vast concessions at little cost. The author is particularly bitter about the release of the company from the obligation of constructing a port on the Pacific Coast. DLC BNG

785 _____. La planificación en Guatemala: su historia, problemas y perspectivas. Guatemala: Tipografía Nacional, 1969. 162 pp. Maps, tables.

A report by the secretary general of the Consejo Nacional de Planificación Económica to the president of the republic. Reviews the history of previous planning efforts and their results, concluding that the 1968 plan was 41% complete by the time the report was written. Also analyzes the limitations of the planning process and present organization, recommending a streamlining of the organization and expansion of its power by placing its secretariat general under the presidential office. DLC LNHT BNG

786 León Hill, Eladia. Miguel Ángel Asturias: lo ancestral en su obra literaria. Eastchester, N.Y.: Editorial Torres, 1972. 250 pp. Biblio.

A study of the use of Indian legends and folklore in Asturias's works, concluding that he draws on these themes to provide a focus of identity with which the peasants can associate and that he employs these themes as a common unifying base in all his works. Includes discussion of the legends in specific volumes and of the use of the idylic version of the Maya cultural past in the Banana Trilogy. DLC

787 León Porras, Fernando de. Intereses vocacionales de la adolescencia en Guatemala. Guatemala: Universidad Autónoma de San Carlos, 1952. 73 pp. Biblio., appendixes.

A study analyzing the results of a sample of 4,200 student responses to a standard vocational interest test used in Guatemala for the first time. The sample, selected from a much larger group of participants, was balanced between sexes and ages throughout the adolescent years. Includes discussion of psychological theories regarding adolescence and

analysis of the results, concluding that they demonstrate the failures of the Guatemalan educational system by indicating that it is oriented toward the humanities and the professions, rather than the areas in which there are more job opportunities and greater national needs. TxU

788 León Schlotter, René de. El reto del desarrollo en Guatemala. Guatemala: Editorial Financiera Guatemalteca, 1970. xiii, 428 pp. Illus., maps, tables.

The head of the Christian Democratic party presents his views of the current state of the Guatemalan economy and the policies needed for its future development. DLC

789 Lewis, A.B. Santa Ana Mixtan: A Bench Mark Study on Guatemalan Agriculture. East Lansing: Michigan State University Press, 1973. x, 87 pp. Illus.

A detailed study of the agricultural economy in a small Guatemalan town in Escuintla that provides a wealth of statistics and information about crops, land tenure, methods of farming, production, and similar items. Demonstrates the local adaptations and practices as well as the impact of broader policies on the peasant and the village. DLC

790 Leysbeth, Nicolas. Historique de la colonisation Belge à Santo-Tomás, Guatemala. Brussels: Nouvelle Société D'Éditions, 1938. 350 pp. Illus., maps.

A detailed history of the Belgian Colonization Company and its colony in Alta Verapaz, including the various authorizations and annual reports of the company, lists of settlers, and all basic data. A valuable source for the nineteenth century and the efforts to attract foreign settlers to the country. Includes the experiences of the colony as well as the intergovernmental relations, reproducing considerable documentation. DLC LNHT

791 Leyton Rodríguez, Rubén. Barrundia: su lección y mensaje. Guatemala: Ediciones "Rubén Leyton Prado," 1967. 191 pp. Biblio., illus.

A wordy discussion of facets of the career of José Francisco Barrundia, one of the lesser-known leaders of the independence movement, who served in the first Congress of the Central American Federation and was also a journalist. The emphasis is on his views regarding various subjects, such as personal rights, rather than on his political career. Since the author adds his personal views regarding the questions under discussion and the importance of the isthmus, the reader does not receive a very clear view of Barrundia and his role. DLC LNHT

792 _____. Doctor Pedro Molina o Centro América y su prócer. Guatemala: Editorial Iberia, 1958. 221 pp. Biblio., illus. Latest ed. Guatemala: Ediciones "Rubén Leyton Prado," 1965. 129 pp. Biblio.

A biography of one of the leading Liberal intellectuals of the independence era, with emphasis on his doctrines and writings. Since the author is an avowed unionist, the book emphasizes Molina's efforts to support and defend the Federation. Includes the author's call to unionism and excerpts from correspondence and documents of the day. DLC LNHT BNG

793   Lizardo Díaz O., José. <u>De la democracia a la dictadura</u>. Guatemala: Imprenta Hispania, 1946. 133 pp. Illus.

A sympathetic history of the revolution of 1897 in Quezaltenango in western Guatemala. Despite some early success in its home territory, the uprising against the regime of José María Reyna Barrios was ultimately defeated. Includes a discussion of the rise of Estrada Cabrera and the initial rebellions against his regime. Profusely illustrated with photos from the revolutionary campaigns. The volume is based on research in memoirs and records in Quezaltenango and on interviews with surviving members of the rebel forces. DLC LNHT BNG

794   _____. <u>Estrada Cabrera, Barillas y Regalado: la revolución entre Guatemala, San [sic] Salvador y Honduras en 1906</u>. Guatemala: Editorial San Antonio, 1962. 224 pp. Illus., maps.

A history of the revolution of General Manuel Lisandro Barillas, organized from exile in El Salvador, against the regime of General Manuel Estrada Cabrera, and of his ill-fated attempt to launch an invasion of Guatemala from Salvadoran territory. In providing a detailed account of the battles and maneuvering, the author copiously quotes Estrada Cabrera's contemporary letters and communications. LNHT BNG

795   _____. <u>Estrada Cabrera, Barillas y Regalado: refutaciones a la campaña que entabló el director del diario "La Hora."</u> Guatemala: Editorial San Antonio, 1962. 72 pp. Illus., maps.

Seeks to refute the charges made by Clemente Marroquín Rojas about the campaign of 1906 in his newspaper articles attacking the author's earlier study of the same incident (see previous item). Díaz provides another account of the campaign, referring to the specific accusations and reprinting documents and some of the articles from La Hora. The pamphlet is part of a personal polemic between the men, former political allies who had become opponents. DLC LNHT BNG

796   Lonteen, Joseph Anthony. <u>Interpretación de una amistad intelectual y su producto literario: el hombre que parecía un caballo</u>. Guatemala: Editorial Landívar, 1968. 107 pp.

Originally a master's thesis, this volume describes the Guatemalan literary scene in 1914 and relates Arévalo Martínez's volume to that setting, tracing the influences on its composition, relating its themes to that context, and explaining the subsequent controversy regarding the volume. The effort is descriptive rather than interpretative. BNG

797   López, Francisco Marcos. <u>¿Qué es liberarse?</u> Guatemala: Imprenta Hispania, 1955. 85 pp.

Part of the propaganda of the National Liberation Movement, this pamphlet extols liberty and defines liberation as a love of liberty and a willingness to seek individual liberty. Associates the concept with the goals of the movement and with anticommunism, and supports the Plan of Tegucigalpa.

798   López Alvarez, Luís. <u>Conversaciones con Miguel Ángel Asturias</u>. Madrid: Editorial Magisterio Español, 1974. 215 pp. Biblio., illus. Latest ed. San José: EDUCA, 1976. 215 pp. Index, biblio., illus.

A series of extensive taped interviews with Asturias by a Spanish poet, recorded in Paris in 1973. Covering all aspects of his career, as well as literary themes, they include discussion of his major novels, his diplomatic posts, and his career as a journalist. Asturias comments on the political aspects of the revolution, his service to it as a diplomat, and the Estrada Cabrera regime. DLC LNHT

799   López L., Roger. <u>¿Cómo es quién en Guatemala: figuras conocidas?</u> Guatemala: Artes Gráficas, 1945. Pages unnumbered. Illus.

A series of caricatures of leading and well-known contemporary Guatemalans, with a few words of description. BNG

800   López Larrave, Mario. <u>Breve historia del movimiento sindical guatemalteco</u>. Guatemala: Editorial Universitaria, 1976. 82 pp. Biblio., notes, illus. 2d ed. Guatemala: Editorial Universitaria, 1979. 82 pp. Biblio., notes, illus.

A summary overview of the Guatemalan labor movement in the twentieth century by a member of the faculty of the University of San Carlos. Emphasizing the efforts to unify the labor movement, its growth and its problems, stressing the need for governmental support. The revolutionary years of 1944-54 are described as the heyday of the labor movement in the nation, with the post-1954 period denounced as one of suppression of unions. Invokes comparisons with Panama to show the importance of governmental support to the success of large-scale unionization in a nation with a relatively small industrial labor segment. DLC LNHT

801   López Rivera, Lionel Fernando. <u>Discursos y conferencias</u>. 3 vols. Guatemala: Tipografía Nacional, 1971-74. 62, 114, 136 pp.

A collection of speeches by the Guatemalan minister of trabajo y previsión social regarding disparate themes and the activities of his ministry. BNG

802   López Valdizón, José María. <u>La carta</u>. Guatemala: Ediciones de la Unión de Escritores y Artistas de Guatemala, 1958. 118 pp. Illus.

A series of short stories by a Guatemalan writer associated with the social criticism of the revolutionary era, viewing the reforms of

(López Valdizón, José María)
the Arévalo and Arbenz regimes favorably and
condemning the programs of the National
Liberation Movement. Written in exile in
Ecuador, the stories focus on the incidents of
peasant life, emphasizing the poor conditions
and the oppression in rural Guatemala, but
also showing the everyday lives of the people
and their ability to survive such conditions.
DLC LNHT BNG

803 _____. La sangre del maíz. Guatemala:
Ediciones Nuevo Día, 1966. 197 pp.
A novel set in the Guatemalan countryside,
sympathetically depicting the lives and hardships of the peasants while presenting the
reforms of the Arévalo and Arbenz regimes as
offering the promise of improvement in the
future. Includes regional backgrounds and
customs, showing some folkloric influence.
DLC LNHT

804 _____. Sudor y protesta. Guatemala:
Ministerio de Educación Pública, 1953.
224 pp.
A series of short stories written during
1949-51. The author uses incidents in the
lives of various peasants to demonstrate the
brutal aspects of rural life and condemn what
he sees as feudalism. BNG

805 López Villatoro, Mario. Por los fuerzos de la
verdad histórica: una voz de la patria
escarnecida, Guatemala ante la diatriba de uno
de sus hijos renegados. Guatemala:
Secretaría de Divulgación Cultura y Turismo,
1956. 222 pp.
A pro-Liberación Nacional polemical reply
to Arévalo's Guatemala, la democracia y el
imperio, detailing what it calls the communist
conspiracy to seize control of Guatemala,
justifying the concern of the Yankees, and
hailing the liberators and particularly
Castillo Armas, while discussing the cost to
the nation of Arévalo's rule. It also cites
the danger to other hemispheric nations and
alleges an international conspiracy in favor
of communism that includes figures from several countries (e.g., Rómulo Betancourt),
along with Arévalo. DLC LNHT

806 _____. ¿Por qué fue derrotado el comunismo en
Guatemala? Guatemala: Talleres Gráficos
Díaz-Paiz, 195? 63 pp.
Discusses the meaning of communism for
Guatemalan citizens, cataloging the abuses of
the revolutionary governments and contending
that they were repudiated by the citizens who
abandoned the regime of Arbenz and rallied
around the heroic figure of Castillo Armas.
DLC BNG

807 Lorand de Olazagasti, Adelaida. En Indio en
la narrativa guatemalteca. San Juan:
Editorial Universitaria de Puerto Rico, 1968.
277 pp. Biblio., notes.
Originally a doctoral thesis at the University of Puerto Rico, this well-researched
volume offers a detailed analysis of Indian
themes and the indigenista movement as

reflected in Guatemalan literature from Colonial times to the present. Authors receiving
major consideration include Carlos Wyld
Ospina, Flavio Herrera, Carlos Samayoa
Chinchilla, Miguel Ángel Asturias, and Mario
Monteforte Toledo. Includes briefer considerations of many other authors, categorizing
Guatemalan writers in terms of other
indigenista movements, contending that in
recent times the emphasis has shifted from
description to social protest, and that there
is a dearth of writing from the Indian's point
of view since Asturias. DLC LNHT BNG

808 Lorang, Mary Corde. Footloose Scientist in
Mayan America. New York: Scribner, 1966.
xi, 320 pp. Index, biblio., illus.
A Maryknoll nun describes her experiences
and observations during a year's teaching
assignment in Guatemala and her travels in the
countryside. Emphasizes people, life-styles,
living conditions, customs, and religion of
the Indian community. DLC LNHT

809 Luján, Herman D., ed. Estudios sobre
administración pública en Guatemala.
Guatemala: Editorial del Ejército, 1969.
xii, 188 pp. Maps, tables.
A study of public administration in
Guatemala, conducted during 1967 and 1968 by a
group of investigators from Guatemala and the
University of Kansas. Focuses on human resources and bureaucratic organization, concluding that the greatest need for improvement
lies in the areas of agrarian reform, marketing, and improved training and security for
civil servants. Includes extensive statistics, tables, and graphs. LNHT BNG

810 Luján Muñoz, Jorge. Permanencia de Antigua.
Guatemala: Universidad de San Carlos, 1966.
92 pp. Biblio., illus.
A discussion not only of the history of
Antigua, but of the preservation of the city
as a historical monument as well as of the
laws and efforts involved, and a passionate
call for more enforcement of the rules to
protect the character of the city. DLC LNHT

811 Luján Muñoz, Luís. Apuntes para la historia
de la fotografía en Guatemala en el siglo XIX:
Edward Muybridge. Guatemala: N.p., n.d. 24
pp. Illus.
A collection of rare early photos of the
capital and other parts of Guatemala, dating
from 1875, by a pioneer American photographer.
DLC

812 _____. Legislación protectora de los bienes
culturales de Guatemala. Guatemala:
Instituto de Antropología e Historia, 1974.
175 pp. Illus.
Texts of the legislation designed to protect the national patrimony, prevent the theft
of artifacts, and regulate archeological exploration, including sections of many laws
that are partially applicable. LNHT

813 _____. Síntesis de la arquitectura en
Guatemala. Guatemala: Universidad de San

Carlos, 1968. 31 pp. Biblio., illus. 2d ed.
Guatemala: Universidad de San Carlos, 1972.
36 pp. Biblio., illus.

A broad survey of Guatemalan architecture
from Colonial times to the present, considering the various styles, construction types,
and the types of buildings, with photos and
plans. The focus is naturally on massive
constructions, such as churches and government
buildings, but includes chapters on houses and
popular architecture. LNHT BNG

814 Lumen, Enrique. Entre lagos y volcanes:
realidad Centro-Americana y Venezolana.
Mexico: B. Costa-Amic, 1949. 250 pp.

A Mexican reporter's observations, written
for the newspaper El Universal during a trip
through the region in the late 1940s, commenting on the nations he visited and the leaders
he met. The focus is on Central America, with
the largest portions devoted to Guatemala,
Honduras, and Nicaragua, but the other states
are also included. He views the Guatemalan
revolution sympathetically, given his own
experience in the Mexican Revolution, and
clearly regards some of the other nations as
despotisms ripe for explosions. Description,
emotional observations, and comments on such
items as religion and intellectual trends are
mixed with the basic political commentary
about current conditions. LNHT

815 McArthur, Harry S., and Roland H. Ebel.
Cambio político en tres comunidades indígenas
de Guatemala. Guatemala: Ministerio de
Educación Pública, 1969. 89 pp. Notes,
tables.

A political scientist and an anthropologist
return to three communities, Ostuncalco,
Concepción Chiquirichaoa, and Aguacatán in
1965-66, three years after their initial
study, to assess the changes in the interim.
They conclude that there has been little real
change in the political rule of the villages,
despite the separation of church and municipal
authority and an increasing ladinization. DLC
LNHT BNG

816 Machado, J. Tible. Le Guatemala en 1898.
Guatemala: Tipografía Nacional, 1898. 65 pp.
A description of Guatemala emphasizing
business, commerce, and immigration. Prepared
by the Guatemalan consul in Bordeaux and published in French to encourage contacts between
Guatemala and France. BNG

817 Macías del Real, A. Perfiles biográficos del
licenciado don Manuel Estrada Cabrera,
presidente de la República de Guatemala.
Guatemala: Tipografía el Demócrata, 1898.
34 pp.

Despite the title, this pamphlet consists
of a narration of the governmental changes
that brought Estrada Cabrera to power, and
includes the addresses and decrees regarding
his assumption of office. DLC

818 Maestre Alfonso, Juan. Guatemala:
subdesarrollo y violencia. Madrid: IEPAL,
1969. 254 pp. Biblio., illus., maps.

Guatemala: Unterentwicklung und Gewalt.
Frankfurt: Suhrkamp, 1971. 162 pp. Biblio.
A leftist interpretation of recent
Guatemalan history and politics, combining
short chronological chapters with thematic
ones focusing on the principal institutions
and problems of the republic. Emphasizes the
role of imperialism and Yankee dominance,
contending that the nation did not win its
independence until 1944, and then lost it
again in 1954. The chapters dealing with the
revolutionary governments are highly laudatory, and Castillo Armas is viewed as a Yankee
tool. The discussion of agriculture, the
economy, social factors, and the institutions
provide insight into the leftist interpretation. DLC LNHT

819 Maldonado Robles, Manuel. Síntesis histórica
de la academia militar. Guatemala: Editorial
del Ejército, 1961. 105 pp. Illus.
A brief historical sketch of the academy,
covering the years 1912 to 1920, with photos
of the classes and commanders, and lists of
the students. BNG

820 Mancilla, A. Autobiografía. Guatemala:
Tipografía El Esfuerzo, 1899. 39 pp.
A rambling description of the author's
perceptions of the leading figures of his
youth, Justo Rufino Barrios, Miguel García
Granados, and Lorenzo Montúfar y Rivera
Maestre, followed by a denunciation of the
Mexican detachment of the provinces of Chiapas
and Soconusco from Guatemala at independence.
LNHT

821 Manson, Anne. Guatemala. Lausanne: Éditions
Rencontre, 1965. 191 pp. Illus., maps.
A travelogue in French, with extensive
illustrations, focusing heavily on contempo-
rary Indian cultures and archeological zones.
Includes a general historical account, though
this is fragmented by the narration of trips.
DLC

822 Mantovani, Juan. Juan Enrique Pestalozzi.
Guatemala: Tipografía Nacional, 1946. 36 pp.
A brief biographical sketch of a Guatemalan
educator whose work spanned the last years of
the Colonial era and the initial years of
independence, emphasizing his impact upon
education and intellectual currents in
Guatemala. DLC

823 _____. Misión de la universidad en nuestra
época. Guatemala: Tipografía Nacional, 1946.
32 pp.

A speech delivered by a faculty member at
an official celebration of the first anniversary of the granting of university autonomy.
After reviewing the traditional functions of
the university, he argues that it must also
provide the intellectual orientation for all
of society and be the "conscience" of American
unity. DLC

824 Mariñas Otero, Luís, ed. Las constituciones
de Guatemala. Madrid: Instituto de Estudios
Políticos, 1958. xvi, 818 pp. Notes.

A collection of the full texts of the eighteen constitutions of Guatemala and all revisions of each, that of the initial Federation, and supplemental documents related to the nation's political process. Covers the years 1823 through 1956 and includes a summary of Guatemalan political developments, arranged by historical period, that provides an effective overview of the nation's development and of the maneuvering that led to the frequent changes in constitution. LNHT

825 Marinello Vidaurreta, Juan. <u>Guatemala nuestra</u>. Havana: Imprenta Nacional de Cuba, 1961. 176 pp.

A Cuban perspective written during the heady days after Fidel Castro achieved power. Condemns imperialism and the Yankees, calling for an uprising of the masses to liberate Guatemala and bring it to its second independence as part of the continental movement begun by the Cuban Revolution. Cites the events of 1944 and 1954 in Guatemala as examples for the present, and includes a discussion of the country in general leftist terms. The articles that comprise this volume originally appeared in a book entitled <u>Meditación americana</u> (Buenos Aires, 1959). DLC

826 Marroquín A., J. Emilio. <u>Monografía elemental del departamento de Quezaltenango</u>. Guatemala: B. Zadik, 1937. 16 pp. Illus., maps.

A capsule description of the department, emphasizing social services and communications facilities. DLC

827 _____. <u>Monografía elemental del departamento de San Marcos</u>. Guatemala: B. Zadik, 1937. 16 pp. Illus., maps.

A capsule description of the province. DLC

828 Marroquín Rojas, Clemente. <u>La bomba, los cadetes; historia de dos atentados contra Estrada Cabrera</u>. Guatemala: n.p., 1974. xi, 171 pp. Illus.

A combined edition of <u>La bomba</u> (GU829) and <u>Los cadetes</u> GU830). TxU

829 _____. <u>La bomba: historia del primer atentado contra Estrada Cabrera</u>. Many editions. Guatemala: Imprenta Muñoz Plaza, 1930. xvi, 213 pp. Illus. Latest ed. Guatemala: n.p., 1967. 234 pp.

A detailed account of the unsuccessful effort to assassinate General Manuel Estrada Cabrera in 1906, leading to a new wave of repression in which the author's uncle perished. Includes a history of the regime, emphasizing its brutality and unpopularity. LNHT BNG

830 _____. <u>Los cadetes: historia del segundo atentado contra Estrada Cabrera</u>. Many editions. Guatemala: Sánchez & de Guise, 1930. Latest ed. Guatemala: Tipografía Nacional, 1974. 208 pp.

A history of a second unsuccessful rebellion against the regime of Manuel Estrada Cabrera, in 1907, led by cadets of the Military Academy. Includes a highly critical

account of the regime, particularly of its actions against the army and its use of the institution for political purposes, which led to the rebellion. Details the subsequent repression and reprisals. DLC LNHT BNG

831 _____ [Canuto Ocaña, pseud.]. <u>La "carta política" del ciudadano Juan José Arévalo</u>. Guatemala: Editorial San Antonio, 1965. 116 pp.

Originally a series of articles appearing in La Hora during 1963, written under a pen name by its editor, Clemente Marroquín Rojas, who acknowledges that it is a "political polemic." It quotes extensively from Arévalo's many statements during his 1963 presidential campaign, and then provides counterarguments, paragraph for paragraph, comparing his actions during his previous term in 1945-49 with his oratory and disputing his impact on the nation. Includes examination of many of his statements from exile about the political situation after the fall of the revolution in 1954, again disputing his attacks point by point. DLC

832 Marroquín Rojas, Clemente. <u>Crónicas de la Constituyente del 45</u>. Guatemala: Imprenta La Hora Dominical, 1955. 112 pp. 2d ed. Guatemala: Tipografía Nacional, 1970.

A leading Guatemalan newspaper editor who served as a member of the Constituent Assembly of 1945 provides an insider's view of its functioning. The volume contains a compilation of the author's daily summaries of the debate and functioning of the Assembly as prepared for his newspaper, La Hora, and published therein at the time, as well as a later speech evaluating the Assembly. The summaries are brief, with quotations from debate rather than the full proceedings, and as such provide a useful overview. DLC LNHT

833 _____. <u>La derrota de una batalla: réplica al libro, "La battalla de Guatemala" del ex-canciller Guillermo Toriello</u>. Guatemala: n.p., n.d. [1957]. 187 pp.

Originally published as a series of articles in the author's newspaper, La Hora, these essays reply to and challenge the volume La batalla de Guatemala by Guillermo Toriello, who served as foreign minister during the revolutionary era, and constitute part of the political polemic of those years. Marroquín Rojas refutes Toriello's version of the revolution, depicting the revolutionary regimes as dictatorships that imposed their will in the same manner as the governments they denounced. He details their abuses and tyranny, and denounces their support of leftist revolutionaries of other nations. The two volumes should be read together for an understanding of both sides in the Revolutionary era and an appreciation of the passion of the confrontation. LNHT BNG

834 _____. <u>Desnudando al ídolo: relato de algunos de los crímenes cometidos por Jorge Ubico</u>. Guatemala: Imprenta La Hora, 1926.

(Marroquín Rojas, Clemente)

A series of scathing attacks on General Jorge Ubico y Castañeda, written by a bitter opponent during Ubico's unsuccessful 1926 presidential campaign. Seeks to challenge Ubico's reputation and contest the validity of the acclaim he received for the various projects in which he had engaged. BNG

835 _____. Ecce Homo; mi campaña política de 1926. Paris: Editorial Paris-América, 1927. 178 pp.

An account of the author's role in and thoughts regarding the 1926 electoral campaign in Guatemala, focusing principally on his opposition to Jorge Ubico, whom he denounces, and his support of the efforts of the incumbent, General Lázaro Chacón. Written from exile in Paris after the campaign, it is in effect a memoir, justifying and explaining the actions of its author, then a young newspaperman and later one of the principal journalists of his country. Offers insights into the campaign maneuvers, while serving to explain the sources of the antagonism between its author and Ubico, who became political opponents throughout their respective careers. BNG

836 _____. En el corazón de la montaña: pequeños cuadros de la vida real. Guatemala: Sánchez & de Guise, 1930. 96 pp.

A series of short stories dealing with life in the mountains of Guatemala, emphasizing the calm and peacefulness of the society save for the intrusion of outside authority. The prologue states that the stories were originally written in the form of fiction as a means of circumventing official pressure from the regime of General Lázaro Chacón, which objected to his criticism of the disruption of local life by the programs of the Ministry of Agriculture. DLC LNHT BNG

837 _____, ed. En el mundo de la polémica. Guatemala: Tipografía Nacional, 1971. 514 pp.

A representative collection of the author's most notable polemics with various other prominent political figures from his country. The volume focuses on Marroquín Rojas's commentaries, though it includes some responses by the other parties if they were submitted in the form of letters to the author's newspaper, La Hora. Encompasss the major national issues of the post-1944 era and a wide variety of historical and political subjects, though not all are dated. Includes exchanges with Adrián Recinos, Luís Cardoza y Aragón, Eurique Muñoz Meany, Guillermo Toriello, Mario Monteforte Toledo, and Ramón Blanco Casteñada. DLC LNHT

838 Marroquín Rojas, Clemente. Francisco Morazán y Rafael Carrera. Guatemala: Imprenta Marroquín, 1965. 410 pp. Illus. Latest ed. Guatemala: Ministerio de Educación Pública, 1971. 398 pp.

Focusing on the careers of the leading protagonists of the independence era and their conflict, the author rejects as a fiction of the Liberal movement the standard interpretation that Morazán was the hero of the Federation movement and Carrera the destroyer of this great ideal, contending instead that Morazán sought to dismember Guatemala into at least two separate states within the Federation, and that it was this that caused Carrera to oppose him. In this light the roles are reversed, and Carrera emerges as the creator and savior of Guatemala who prevented its dismemberment. Marroquín Rojas notes that although several other Central American states at the time had more than one center of culture, Morazán contemplated dividing only Guatemala, and views this as a plot against that state. DLC LNHT BNG

839 _____. Historia de Guatemala. Guatemala: Tipografía Nacional, 1971. 362 pp. Index, biblio., notes, illus.

A history of the Guatemalan independence movement and the struggle over Mexican annexation, covering the years 1808 through 1840, based on secondary sources. The author contends that the independence era constituted a period of ideological confrontation between the "new" foreign ideal of Liberal democracy and the traditional Guatemalan mode of monarchy and dictatorship, which he says was the style of Spain, its colonies, and Indian cultures. This confrontation, the author feels, explains the loss of the province of Chiapas to Mexico, for in this area the residents feared the new ideology and opted for the Mexican system, which seemed more attuned to the traditional modes. The rest of Guatemala continued in the ideological struggle through the collapse of the Federation to the latter portion of the century. This volume was to be the first of a new series covering all of Guatemalan history that was cut short by the author's death. DLC LNHT

840 _____. Historia del movimiento unionista. Barcelona: Talleres Gráficos R. Llauger, 1929. 95 pp. Illus.

A brief account, by one of its adherents, of the Unionist party in Guatemala, its efforts during 1919-20, and its role in the overthrow of the regime of Manuel Estrada Cabrera. Much of this brief volume consists of reproductions of the various manifestos and descriptions of the demonstrations held by the party. LNHT BNG

841 _____. Memorias de Jalapa: o recuerdos de un remichero. Guatemala: Editorial del Ejército, 1977. 561 pp.

The author's reminiscences of his early days in Jalapa combining the attributes of an autobiography and a set of memoirs. Includes comments on the various events and an account of his early experiences; as such it indicates the influences upon him as well as his view of the region and its traditions. The account covers the years through 1938 but is not entirely chronological, and there are no chapters, just a flowing essay broken by asterisks. BNG

(Marroquín Rojas, Clemente)

842 _____. El retorno a Bolívar. Guatemala: Tipografía Nacional, 1972. 366 pp.

Originally a series of essays written during 1948 for his newspaper, La Hora, rejecting efforts to associate Juan José Arévalo with the memory of Bolívar, refuting the volume El presidente Arévalo y el retorno a Bolívar point for point, and denouncing the Arévalo regime. Includes excerpts from Arévalo's newspaper column, "Carta política," with counterarguments, as well as a series of commentaries denouncing the Ubico regime. LNHT BNG

843 Martí y Pérez, José Julián. Guatemala. Mexico: Imprenta de I. Cumplido, 1878. 119 pp. Latest ed. Guatemala: Ministerio de Educación Pública, 1953. 88 pp. Illus.

Commentaries about Guatemala by the Cuban liberator, published in Mexico and reflecting his residence in Guatemala during the early 1870s when General Justo Rufino Barrios governed the nation. Martí offers his favorable and optimistic impression of the nation and the Barrios reforms. DLC LNHT BNG

844 Martí y Pérez, José Julián, and Rafael Esténger. Guatemala: seguido de Martí en la tierra del Quetzal. Guatemala: Ministerio de Educación Pública, 1952. xxx, 105 pp. Illus.

A reprint of Martí's volume recounting his days in Guatemala and his impressions of that nation, combined with a short essay by Esténger regarding Martí's stay in Guatemala and commenting on his volume. DLC LNHT BNG

845 Martínez Durán, Carlos. Las ciencias médicas en Guatemala: origen y evolución. Guatemala: Sánchez & de Guise, 1941. 439 pp. Biblio., illus. 3d ed. Guatemala: Editorial Universitaria, 1964. 710 pp. Biblio., illus.

A survey of Guatemalan medicine from pre-Conquest times to 1900, with only 100 pages devoted to the national era in the third and largest edition. Surveys and describes significant events such as hospital construction, and provides brief sketches of the lives of the nation's prominent medical figures. DLC LNHT BNG

846 _____. Discursos universitarios, 1945-1950. Guatemala: Universidad de San Carlos, 1950. xiii, 136 pp.

A collection of speeches given on various occasions by the rector of the University of San Carlos, dealing with a broad range of themes including educational problems, the contemporary scene, and the intellectual community of the hemisphere and Guatemala. DLC BNG

847 _____. Discursos universitarios, 1958-1962. Guatemala: Universidad de San Carlos, 1962. xxvi, 229 pp.

A sequel to the previous item. DLC BNG

848 _____. Realidad y ensueño del peregrino. Guatemala: Editorial Universitaria, 1972. 516 pp. Illus.

A series of disparate essays by a well-known Guatemalan medical doctor, diplomat, scholar, and rector of the University of San Carlos. The themes include national subjects, reflections on a European trip, meditations, and commentaries on Guatemalan intellectual figures. DLC BNG

849 _____. Tiempo y substancia del estudiante eterno. Guatemala: Editorial Universitaria, 1956. 196 pp. Illus.

The reminiscences of a prominent Guatemalan intellectual's school days, covering the years 1919-31; includes portraits of friends and teachers, and notes the influential events of his formative years. TxU

850 Martínez Ferraté, Rodolfo. Una política rural para el desarrollo: esquemas de medidas aplicables a Guatemala. Santo Domingo: Consejo de Fundaciones Americanas de Desarrollo, 1976. xv, 217 pp. Biblio., tables.

Originally a thesis at the University of San Carlos, this study surveys rural problems in Guatemala, proposing more extensive government efforts to improve living standards and reach into the rural sectors to combat poverty and isolation. Particularly recommends land redistribution, the extension of credit to small landowners, and an expanded educational effort. DLC

851 Martínez-Holgado, Arturo C. La secteur agricole du Guatemala. Austin: University of Texas Press, 1969. 268 pp.

A detailed survey of Guatemalan agriculture, its current situation, and its development. TxU

852 Martínez Morales, Antonio. Versión histórica-geográfica de Chiquimula. Guatemala: Ministerio de Educación Pública, 1973. 50 pp.

A brief pamphlet, sponsored by the Instituto Normal para Varones de Oriente in Chiquimula on the occasion of its centennial, written by professors at the school. Provides an outline of the history and setting of Chiquimula, and recounts the history of the Institute. BNG

853 Martínez Nolasco, Gustavo. El movimiento armado de diciembre de 1930. Guatemala: Tipografía Nacional, 1931. 94 pp. Illus.

A history of Guatemalan politics from 1926 through 1930, dealing with the rise and fall of General Lázaro Chacón, and the military movement that displaced him. The volume is clearly pro-Ubico, holding that he was the popular candidate in 1926 and that only fraud denied him power, emphasizing the poor performance and unpopularity of the Chacón regime. LNHT BNG

854 Martínez Sobral, Enrique. Artículos relativos a la reforma monetaria de Guatemala. Guatemala: Tipografía Nacional, 1925. 108 pp.

A series of newspaper articles written by the special advisor to the minister of

(Martínez Sobral, Enrique)
hacienda that explain and defend the
Guatemalan monetary reforms, and seek to
present them in the context of the local and
global problems of the 1920s; intended to
inspire confidence in the nation's financial
system as changed by the new laws. Includes a
history of the nation's recent monetary experience, discussion of the rationale of the
program, and explanations of the specific
steps and laws involved. The articles originally appeared in the Guatemalan newspaper El
Imparcial during 1924. DPU

855   _____. Humo. Guatemala: Síguere, 1900.
152 pp.
A novel set in the Guatemalan countryside
in the nineteenth century, dealing with the
problems of the landowners and residents and
the difficulties caused by the political turmoil of the era. LNHT

856   _____. Inútil combate. Guatemala: Síguere,
1902. 133 pp. 2d ed. Guatemala: Ministerio
de Educación Pública, 1957. 133 pp.
The memoirs of a well-known Guatemalan
writer, which, though recounting his observations during his travels, give more attention
to his thoughts and hence assume the aspect of
a series of essays about general topics. DLC
LNHT BNG

857   _____. Prosas. Guatemala: Síguere, 1899.
xxiii, 274 pp.
A collected volume containing several of
the author's previous publications, including
the memoirs of his travels, and his works
Humo, Su matrimonio, and Los de Peralta. LNHT

858   Martini Orozco, Margarita. Hacia la escuela
activa en la educación guatemalteca.
Guatemala: Universidad de San Carlos, 1951.
126 pp. Index.
A brief overview of the educational history
of Guatemala, with a call for a new focus,
emphasizing practical learning-by-doing rather
than the traditional method, calling for the
creation of a laboratory school to bring this
method to the nation, and extolling its advantages. DLC

859   Martz, John D. Central America: The Crisis
and the Challenge. Chapel Hill: University
of North Carolina Press, 1959. ix, 356 pp.
Index, biblio., appendixes.
A discussion of the problems of the region
during the post-World War II era, considered
country by country, with emphasis on the political situation and the importance of the
area to the United States. Written for the
general Yankee reader and designed to combat
inattention to the isthmus by the United
States. Includes consideration of political
change, economic and societal gaps, and the
communist threat. DLC LNHT

860   _____. Communist Infiltration in Guatemala:
A Study of Subversion. New York: Vantage
Press, 1956. 125 pp. Biblio., notes.

An overview of the period from 1944 to
1954, based on published sources, with particular attention to the communist organizational efforts and methods of seizing power.
Originally written as a thesis. DLC

861   _____. Justo Rufino Barrios and Central American Union. Gainesville: University of
Florida Press, 1963. 51 pp. Biblio., notes.
A brief but well-researched and balanced
account of Barrios's unionist efforts.
Focuses exclusively on the unionist campaigns
rather than on his domestic policy, stressing
his final effort to impose his personal hegemony, which led to war and his death on the
battlefield. DLC

862   Marure, Alejandro. Catálogo de las leyes
promulgadas en el estado de Guatemala, desde
su erección en 15 de septiembre de 1824 hasta
5 de octubre de 1841. Guatemala: Imprenta de
la Paz, 1941. 143 pp. Index, illus.
A topically arranged listing of the laws
for the years in question.

863   _____. Observaciones sobre la intervención
que ha tenido el ex-presidente de Centro-
América, general Francisco Morazán, en los
negocios políticos de Guatemala, durante las
convulsiones que ha sufrido este estado de
mediados de 837 a principios de 839.
Guatemala: Imprenta de la Academia de
Estudios, 1839. 17 pp.
Brief essays detailing the role played by
Morazán in mediating political confrontations
within Guatemala, noting the problems involved
and lamenting the fact that this meant that
the ultimate authority was outside Guatemala
and hence beyond the reach of its popular
opinion. LNHT

864   Marure, Alejandro, and Andrés Fuentes Franco,
eds. Catálogo razonado de las leyes de
Guatemala: comprende todas las que han sido
promulgadas desde la independencia hasta el 30
de septiembre de 1856. Guatemala: Imprenta
de la Paz, 1856. 361 pp.
An expanded version of item GU862, covering
additional years.

865   Marx, Paul, ed. The Death Peddlers: War on
the Unborn. Collegeville, Minn.: St. Johns
University Press, 1971. xvi, 191 pp.
Los mercaderes de la muerte. Guatemala:
Simposio sobre el Aborto, 1971. 215 pp.
A collection of papers and panel discussions from a 1971 conference opposing abortion, reflecting the spread to Guatemala of
the global concern with population control and
the discussion of the appropriate methods.
The arguments presented are quite standard to
all such debates in any country. BNG

866   Matta Retana, Rafael. Nuestra época.
Guatemala: Ministerio de Educación Pública,
1973. 83 pp. Illus.
A volume designed to commemorate the centennial of the Instituto Normal para Varones
de Oriente in Chiquimula, written by a journalist for one of the capital's newspapers who

was a member of the class of 1941-45. Recounts the principal events of that era as
they affected the lives of the students,
though it does not focus exclusively on their
involvement. The result is a description of
national events of the 1940s and 1950s as seen
from Chiquimula, showing how they affected
that city and detailing the Ubico regime, the
revolution, and the counterrevolution. LNHT

867 Maudslay, Ann Cary, and Alfred Percival
Maudslay. A Glimpse at Guatemala and Some
Notes on the Ancient Monuments of Central
America. London: John Murray, 1899. xvii,
289 pp. Index, illus., maps, tables.
    A travelogue describing an expedition that
passed through a substantial part of the
nation. Although the emphasis is on archeological zones, there is also rich description
of the terrain, the people, and the conditions
in much of the country. DLC LNHT

868 Mazariegos, Alfonso A. Sangre y luto: hoy
como ayer el Partido Conservador se destaca
ante la historia como siniestro abanderado del
crimen. Guatemala: Tipografía Latina, 1922.
28 pp. Illus.
Blood and Sorrow: Now as Always the
Guatemalan Conservative Party Shows Up, True
to its History, as the Sinister Standard-
Bearer of Crime. Guatemala: Tipografía
Excelsior, 1932. 31 pp.
    A propaganda tract denouncing the Conserva-
tive role in the revolt that overthrew the
Estrada Cabrera regime. Attacks the unionists
and the resulting governments, lists those
executed by the revolutionaries, and calls for
a counterrevolution. LNHT

869 Meany, Jorge. Semblanza de Francisco Vela.
Guatemala: Ministerio de Educación Pública,
1959. 43 pp. Illus.
    A brief biography tracing the life and
extolling the contributions of a Guatemalan
general, engineer, and teacher whose service
spans the late nineteenth and early twentieth
centuries and whose legacy to the nation includes a huge relief map of Guatemala, completed in 1905. DLC

870 Medina Ruiz, Fernando. En pos de las
luciérnagas: cuentos de altiplano y litoral.
Guatemala: Ministerio de Educación Pública,
1961. 161 pp.
    A series of short stories based on the
legends of the Guatemalan highlands and
coastal regions. DLC BNG

871 _____. Tres cuentos guatemaltecos.
Barcelona: Savia, 1963. 56 pp. 2d ed.
Guatemala: Ministerio de Educación Pública,
1966. 90 pp.
    Short stories based on regional folktales.
The second edition is entitled Tres cuentos
guatemaltecos y uno más. DLC

872 Mejía, José Víctor. Geografía de la República
de Guatemala. Guatemala: Sánchez & de Guise,
1922. 408 pp. Maps. 2d ed. Guatemala:

Tipografía Nacional, 1927. iv, 400 pp.
Biblio., tables.
    A detailed text with sections dealing with
physical, economic, and ethnographic aspects
of the nation. Each topic is discussed re-
gionally. Though basically descriptive, the
discussions are extensive, and the volume
provides useful data regarding this era. DLC
LNHT BNG

873 _____. Geografía médico-militar de la
República de Guatemala. Guatemala:
Tipografía Nacional, 1928. 195 pp. Index,
biblio., illus.
    A geographical study of Guatemala, with
particular emphasis on military implications,
including considerations of medical factors,
geology, population, water, terrain, and mete-
orology. After a general discussion there is
a brief consideration by sections of the country. The author is a Guatemalan army general.
DLC LNHT BNG

874 _____. El Petén: datos geográficos e
históricos. Guatemala: Tipografía Nacional,
1904. 68 pp. Maps.
    A basic geographical description of the
Petén region, representing an early study and
mirroring Guatemalan hopes for this remote
frontier area. The volume includes a brief
historical summary and description of the
major geographic features and the political
divisions. DLC BNG

875 Mejía, Medardo. Juan José Arévalo o el
humanismo en la presidencia. Guatemala:
Tipografía Nacional, 1951. 358 pp. Biblio.
    A sympathetic view of Arévalo's philosophy,
outlook, programs, goals, and accomplishments,
originally published as a series of articles
in the official Diario de Centro América, the
"voice of the Revolution" at the time
Arévalo's term was nearing its culmination.
The emphasis is on Arévalo's doctrine of
humanism; the articles liberally quote his
speeches and official acts, and summarize each
of his annual Informes, hence his accomplishments. The short bibliography includes works
by Marx, Lenin, Hitler, and Bolívar, but few
volumes about Guatemala, save for some by the
revolutionaries. DLC LNHT BNG

876 _____. El movimiento obrero en la revolución
de octubre. Guatemala: Tipografía Nacional,
1949. 219 pp. Illus.
    An account of the Guatemalan revolution of
1944, written from the revolutionary viewpoint
by a participant, emphasizing the October
phase and the role of the urban labor organizations. The portion regarding the revolutionary planning and actions is more accurate
than the discussion of the reaction of the
incumbent regime, for the latter, unlike the
former, is an outsider's view based on stereotype and rumor. DLC LNHT BNG

877 Melville, Thomas, and Marjorie Melville.
Guatemala: Another Vietnam? Middelsex,
England: Penguin Books, 1971. 312 pp.
Illus., maps.

(Melville, Thomas, and Marjorie Melville)
The impressions of two Yankee Catholic
Maryknoll missionaries who worked among the
Guatemalan peasants and became associated with
the leftist guerrilla movement. Contains their
comments on the role of the United States, the
importance of land ownership, and Guatemalan
politics, as well as narrations of episodes
from their experiences, quoting liberally from
leftist Guatemalans and President Arbenz. DLC
LNHT

878   _____. Guatemala: The Politics of Land Ownership. Riverside, N.J.: Free Press, 1971.
xv, 320 pp. Index, biblio., maps, tables,
appendixes.
Tierra y poder en Guatemala. San José:
EDUCA, 1975. 306 pp. Notes, appendixes.
A scathing critique of the Guatemalan agricultural scene, focusing on land tenure and
its power implications, social structure, and
conservative government policy, by two former
Maryknoll missionaries who served in that
nation as a priest and a nun for ten years
during the 1950s and 1960s before being expelled from Guatemala on charges of promoting
peasant unrest, written after they left their
order and married. They are critical of all
regimes since Arévalo and of U.S. aid policies, focusing on the situation of the poor
and the concentration of wealth. Their interpretation, based on class conflict, might be
called a precursor of Liberation theology.
Although the account is written from a rigidly
ideological perspective, it offers considerable information on the land-ownership and
agricultural policies and their impact on the
rural peasants, as well as on lower-class
living conditions. DLC LNHT BNG

879   Mencos Franco, Agustín. La revolución de 71:
sus efectos fueron bochornosos para el honor
de la patria, y prepararon la semilla, que al
desarrollarse, la enfermó de la "pandemia" del
Cabrerismo, que mató el honor de la nación y
la vida del ciudadano. Guatemala: Imprenta
"La Patria," 1921. 52 pp.
A denunciation of the Estrada Cabrera
regime and the entire Liberal era. TxU

880   Mendelson, E. Michael. Los escándalos de
Maximón: un estudio sobre la religión y la
visión del mundo en Santiago Atitlán.
Guatemala: Tipografía Nacional, 1965. 209
pp. Biblio., notes, illus., appendixes.
A study of Santiago Atitlán, originally
prepared as a doctoral thesis, focusing on
religion and the world view of the community.
The emphasis is on the coexistence of and
conflict between the traditional Indian religious beliefs and ceremonies and those of
Christianity, with comparison of the two and
the impact of each on the community and its
political and social life. The clandestine
nature of the native practices hampered the
study but enhance its value as a description
of a native mentality and psychology and their
implications for the nation and its culture.
DLC LNHT BNG

881   Méndez, Francisco, and Raúl Carrillo Meza.
Cuentos de Francisco Méndez y Raúl Carrillo
Meza. Guatemala: Dirección Nacional de
Bellas Artes, 1957. 179 pp.
A prize-winning collection of short stories
combining folkloric tradition, Indian symbolism, and social protest. Some focus on each
of these, others link them through accounts of
contemporary problems in Indian peasant communities. References to the past are mixed
with mystical allusions. DLC

882   Méndez, Joaquín. Guatemala de fiesta:
unión de los ferrocarriles del centro y
occidente, 21 de noviembre de 1903.
Guatemala: Tipografía Nacional, 1904. 76 pp.
A brief history of the Guatemalan Central
Railroad, extolling its progress and significance for the nation. Published to commemorate the completion of one of its lines, that
to Mazatenango, in November of 1903. TxU

883   _____. Guatemala en 1897, obsequio de "El
Progreso Nacional" a sus lectores el 24
diciembre de 1897. Guatemala: Tipografía
Nacional, 1897. 237 pp. Illus.
A collection of descriptions and photos of
the buildings and constructions of the regime
of Justo Rufino Barrios and a set of descriptions and photos commemorating the Central
American Exposition in Guatemala City in 1897,
showing the state of the nation and hailing
the Liberal regime and the progress it brought
to the nation. Compiled by the newspaper El
Progreso Nacional. Many of the buildings
pictured no longer exist. BNG

884   _____. Guía del inmigrante en la República de
Guatemala. Guatemala: Tipografía Nacional,
1895. 272 pp. Tables.
A government-sponsored volume designed to
encourage immigration to Guatemala, providing
detailed information about the nation, its
facilities, economy, climate, society, standard of living, transportation system, contacts
with the outside world, development, services,
foreign trade, etc., along with appropriate
legislation and data regarding immigration in
the past. Contains a great deal of data about
the nation during the latter half of the nineteenth century, with extensive statistics
focusing mainly on the 1890s but extending as
far as the 1850s in some cases. DLC BNG

885   Méndez, Rosendo P. Índice general de la
recopilación de leyes en orden cronológico y
ligera síntesis para facilitar la consulta de
disposiciones legales vigentes de observancia
general en los diferentes ramos de la
administración pública: apéndice de
disposiciones que se incluyen por su
importancia histórica. Guatemala: Tipografía
Nacional, 1925. 102 pp.
An index to the initial ten volumes of the
standard compilation of Guatemalan laws. BNG

886   Méndez Cifuentes, Arturo. Nociones de tejidos
indígenas de Guatemala. Guatemala:
Ministerio de Educación Pública, 1967. 194
pp. Biblio., illus.

A study of the textile designs and techniques of San Juan Sacatepéquez, using this
area as a means of preserving the traditions,
methods, and designs of the Indian weaving
craft of that portion of Guatemala. Includes
discussion of looms and methods, with extensive illustrations, as well as a large collection of design illustrations. DLC LNHT BNG

887 Méndez Dominguez, Alfredo. Zaragoza: la
estratificación social de una comunidad ladina
guatemalteca. Guatemala: Tipografía
Nacional, 1967. 246 pp. Biblio., maps,
tables, appendixes.
   A study of a ladino community, with particular emphasis on the impact of urbanization on
the ladino culture, a factor that the author
considers of pivotal importance to Guatemala.
He stresses the various effects of economic
modernization on the culture, the movement
from rural to urban settings, the changing
hierarchy, and the implications for the nation. The developments observed in this town
are placed in their broader national and anthropological context. Extensive statistical
data is appended. DLC LNHT BNG

888 Méndez Hidalgo, Julián [Julius Pater, pseud.].
La venganza de Tonino. Guatemala: Talleres
Gráficos Díaz-Píaz, 1958. 31 pp.
   Autobiographical short stories recounting
the author's youth in Esquipulas. The stories
make use of the local setting, but the emphasis is on youthful hijinks and childhood games
and activities. DLC

889 Méndez Montenegro, Julio César, ed. 444 años
de legislación agraria, 1513-1957. Guatemala:
Imprenta Universitaria, 1960. 919 pp.
   A compilation of Guatemalan agrarian legislation dating from Colonial days, written by a
leader of the Revolutionary party who was
devoted to agrarian reform. Contains the
texts of the many laws and seeks to provide a
single unified source for their study and
improvement. BNG

890 Mendoza, José Luís, ed. Tratados y
convenciones internacionales vigentes para
Guatemala. 4 vols. Guatemala: n.p., 1958-
60. Illus.
   Reproduction of the texts of all treaties
presently in force in Guatemala, regardless of
when signed, grouped in volumes by subject,
and within each volume by year signed. The
series covers accords of all types dating from
1884 to its printing. DLC LNHT

891 Mendoza, Juan Manuel. Enrique Gómez Carrillo:
estudio crítico-biográfico: su vida, su obra
y su época. 2 vols. Guatemala: Unión
Tipográfica, 1940. xxii, 397, 419 pp. Illus.
2d ed. Guatemala: Tipografía Nacional, 1946.
1i, 394, 505 pp. Illus.
   A detailed biography of an influential
Guatemalan intellectual, scholar, journalist,
and Liberal ideologue of the nineteenth century who was one of the leaders of the Liberal
movement that eventually secured control of
the nation. As a scholar and literary figure

he wrote on varied themes, while also contributing political polemics and editing an influential Liberal journal. The account is mainly
biographical, eulogizing his contributions, as
the author indicates that he views the book as
a monument to Gómez Carillo. Some commentary
on his writings and analysis of his ideas is
also included. DLC LNHT BNG

892 _____. Una vez por todas: refutación al
foleto intitulado "Para la historia de
Guatemala: datos sobre el gobierno del
licenciado Manuel Estrada Cabrera" por Felipe
Pineda C. Guatemala: Tipografía de Arturo
Síguere, 1902. 409 pp. Illus.
   A pro-Estrada Cabrera polemic, answering
and attacking in strong language the pamphlet
by Felipe Pineda C., and defending the actions
of the regime. The author notes that Pineda
was imprisoned in 1898 for opposing Estrada
Cabrera and had been released into exile by
one of the caudillo's amnesties. He disputes
Pineda sentence for sentence, quoting his
accusations and countering with extensive
excerpts from documentation to show that
Estrada Cabrera assumed office legally and
governed in full accord with the law. DLC
LNHT

893 Menjívar, Rafael. Reforma agraria:
Guatemala, Bolivia, Cuba. San Salvador:
Editorial Universitaria, 1969. 475 pp.
Biblio., illus., maps, tables.
   A summary of three different land-reform
efforts, by the former dean of the School of
Economics of the University of El Salvador.
His research is designed to survey potential
models for what he considers the inevitable
effort at land reform in El Salvador. Each
movement is surveyed separately, with extensive statistics and graphs to demonstrate its
impact and extent, as well as a description of
its legal structure and terms, but without
comparisons among them. Concludes that partial efforts are futile, since they allow
opposition by the landowners and do not change
the social implications of concentration of
ownership. Views the Guatemalan reform,
treated in 200 pages, as too restricted because it applied only to unused land, allowing
underutilized land to be protected. States
that the intervention and the efforts of the
United Fruit Company demonstrate that no Latin
American nation can afford to allow United
States citizens or companies to own land
within its borders. Praises the Cuban system
for showing that rapid and drastic change is
feasible, while warning about the lessons of
its futile efforts to diversify production and
the unmanageability of its state farms, which
were too large. Hails the cooperative approach to land use to preserve productive
entities as the most effective, and stresses
the need for drastic and rapid rather than
limited change. DLC LNHT

894 Menton, Seymour. Historia crítica de la
novela guatemalteca. Guatemala: Editorial
Universitaria, 1960. 332 pp. Index,
biblio., illus.

The most important study to date of the
Guatemalan novel and its development, covering
the principal authors from independence
through the 1950s. Combines analysis of individual authors, making comparisons with the
literature of other Latin American nations and
with world literary trends, and an overall
commentary on the development of the
Guatemalan novel as an entity. Includes
biographical data and analysis of the works of
the nation's most prominent writers. DLC
LNHT BNG

895 Mexico, Gov't of. Correspondencia oficial con
motivo de invasiones de Guatemala en
territorio mexicano, con los antecedentes y el
arreglo final. Mexico: Imprenta de F. Díaz
de León, 1895. 246 pp. Maps.
A collection of official correspondence
concerning border disputes and various complaints by the Mexican government of Porfirio
Díaz alleging Guatemalan invasions of southern
Mexico or complicity in revolutionary movements in this area. Contains the agreement
signed by the two governments to eliminate the
problems. DLC LNHT BNG

896 Meza, César. San Bartolomé Milpas Altas:
síntesis socio-económica de una comunidad
indígena guatemalteca. Guatemala: Ministerio
de Educación Pública, 1949. 58 pp.
A description of the principal characteristics of a Guatemalan Indian community, designed to show the current situation. BNG

897 Meza, Rafael. Centro-América: campaña
nacional de 1885, aumenta con las memorias del
doctor Meza y el derrumbe de la dictadura
zaldivarista. Guatemala: N.p., n.d. [1910].
204 pp. Latest ed. Guatemala: Ministerio de
Defensa Nacional, 1971. 404 pp. Illus.,
appendixes.
A sympathetic account of Justo Rufino
Barrios's tragic campaign to unite the isthmus
and of his resulting death, written in 1906 by
the secretary of his Jefetura Militar, based
on his notes from that campaign. Meza, a
strong adherent of the Guatemalan leader and a
devoted unionist and Liberal, provides a detailed account of Barrios's activities and the
military campaign from Barrios's point of
view, though his comments about the background
and other leaders reflect his own outlook.
The 1934 edition is dedicated to Ubico and
hails him as the heir of Barrios and the new
leader of isthmian unification. This dedication is omitted from the 1958 edition, which
also adds several appendixes designed to provide some balance by briefly indicating the
Conservative interpretation through the use of
contemporary documents and commentaries by
opponents. DLC LNHT BNG

898 Mezzera, Baltasar Luís. Guatemala.
Montevideo: Artes Gráficas Covadonga, 1966.
39 pp. Biblio.
A series of random comments about the
nation, designed for the general Uruguayan
reader. DLC

899 Middeldyk, Rudolph Adams van. Guatemala:
Some Facts and Figures for the Information of
Visitors Compiled and Arranged for the
Guatemala Central Railroad Company. New York:
George F. Nesbitt, 1895. 70 pp. Illus.
An account of a trip along the Central
Railroad Company's line, which the author
calls the best in Central America, with drawings of track and bridges. Describes the
country and particularly the railroad service,
commenting on facilities and economic production. Optimistically urges a visit, hailing
the nation's stability. DLC LNHT

900 Milla y Vidaurre, José [Salome Gil, pseud.].
El canasto del sastre: cuadros de costumbres.
Guatemala: Imprenta de la Paz, 1865. Many
editions, various pagings.
A series of essays written in the 1860s by
a well-known Guatemalan author and literary
commentator who sought to record Guatemalan
folklore and provide social commentary through
novelettes and essays dealing with various
customs, traditions, and outlooks characteristic of his native land. The title varies in
the numerous reprintings, with some using only
one of its two parts. DLC LNHT BNG

901 ____. El esclavo de don Dinero en el canasto
del sastre. Guatemala: Tipografía Nacional,
1935. Latest ed. Guatemala: Ministerio de
Educación Pública, 1965. 207 pp. Illus.
A brief novelette, designed as a commentary
on the growing materialism of the late nineteenth century, detailing the adventures of an
individual so dedicated to money that he is
enslaved by his pursuit of wealth. The prologue states that although slavery has long
been abolished in Guatemala, many people remain slaves to their desire for wealth. BNG

902 ____. Historia de un pepe: don Bonifacio.
Guatemala: Tipografía "El Modelo," 1890.
362 pp. 7th ed. Guatemala: Ministerio de
Educación Pública, 1967. 398 pp.
A novel by one of Guatemala's best-known
literary figures, who was also a Conservative
politician and longtime diplomat representing
Guatemala in the United States and Europe. He
is known for his astute observations of society and human fraility, and his keen sense of
humor. This romantic-historical novel is the
product of his years in exile in Europe, emphasizing the tragic aspects of life. Its
locale is Guatemala City during the Colonial
era. DLC LNHT BNG

903 ____. Libro sin nombre: artículos varios.
Guatemala: Imprenta de la Paz, 1870. 120 pp.
5th ed. Guatemala: Ministerio de Educación
Pública, 1964. 326 pp. Illus.
A series of miscellaneous essays discussing
the national outlook, the heritage of the
Colonial era, and the nation's picturesque
traditions. The essays in this volume are not
among his best-known or most-acclaimed pieces,
but nonetheless serve to illustrate his style
and to preserve the Guatemalan traditions that
are reflected in nearly all his works. DLC
LNHT BNG

(Milla y Vidaurre, José [Salome Gil, pseud.])

904 _____. *Obras completas.* 6 vols. Guatemala:
E. Goubaud, 1897-99.
The collected works of this well-known
Guatemalan writer. LNHT

905 _____. *Un viaje al otro mundo, pasando por
otras partes 1871 a 1874.* 3 vols. Guatemala:
Imprenta del Comercio, 1875. 511, 511, 512
pp. Latest ed. Guatemala: Ministerio de
Educación Pública, 1962-63.
An autobiographical memoir of the author's
travels abroad, describing the travels of "Don
Chapin," a typical Guatemalan, and his reactions to the new worlds he finds outside his
native land. The first volume deals with his
adventures and observations in the United
States, the second with Europe. In all cases
observations are combined with literary references and commentaries on his homeland. DLC
BNG

906 Miller, Hubert J. *La Iglesia católica y el
estado en Guatemala en tiempo de Justo Rufino
Barrios.* Guatemala: Editorial Universitaria,
1977. 514 pp. Biblio.
A study of the church-state conflict during
the nineteenth-century Liberal era, based on
church archives showing the church's viewpoint. Details the dispute and demonstrates
that the Liberals effectively destroyed the
church's economic and political power. BNG

907 Miolan, Ángel, and David Aizcorbe. *Guatemala,
democracia revolucionaria: juzgada por dos
antillanos eminentes.* Guatemala: Tipografía
Nacional, 1949. 16 pp.
A sympathetic view of the Guatemalan revolutionary regime by a Dominican exile and a
Cuban journalist. They hail the reforms,
democracy, and the socialistic tendencies of
the regime, clearly reflecting the problems in
their own nations. The commentaries were
originally published in *El Crónica de la
Habana* during 1949, and include an official
account of the events of 18-19 July 1949, when
the regime faced its severest test to date
with the assassination of armed forces chief
Colonel Francisco Arana and a revolt by the
Presidential Guard; details of the counter-
maneuvers that enabled the government to retain control; and praise for the loyalty of
various groups and forces. LNHT

908 Molina Sierra, Beatriz. *Estudio de los
intereses vocacionales en un grupo de
adolescentes guatemaltecas.* Guatemala:
Imprenta Universitaria, 1963. 79 pp.
Biblio., illus.
Report of a survey of Guatemalan high-
school students regarding their career aspirations, with comment about the implications for
the nation, its development, and educational
needs. DLC

909 Molina y Mata, Marcelo. *Exposición a la
Convención de los Estados Centroamericanos
protestando contra la usurpación de Los Altos.*
Mexico: Imprenta Ignacio Cumplido, 1841.
54 pp.

The appeal of the state of Los Altos after
the Carrera forces invaded to prevent its
succession from Guatemala, directed to the
Congress of the Federation; with accompanying
documentation.

910 _____. *Ligeros apuntamientos acerca de los
principales sucesos de la carrera literaria y
vida pública de Marcelo Molina.*
Quezaltenango: Editorial Casa de Cultura,
1971. Pages unnumbered.
The only known memoirs of the Guatemalan
journalist who served as the president of the
incipient state of Los Altos during the early
years of independence, published posthumously.
Despite their brevity they do provide some
insights into the era and its maneuvering.
BNG

911 Moncada, José María. *Pepe Batres.* Guatemala:
Tipografía Nacional, 1910. 41 pp.
A brief study of the Guatemalan poet, with
liberal quotations from his works and a brief
introduction describing his principal characteristics and hailing his contributions to the
literary world and to the culture of his nation. LNHT

912 Monge, Luís Alberto, ed. *Posición de la
O.R.I.T. y sus filiales en el caso de
Guatemala.* Mexico: O.R.I.T., n.d. [1954].
20 pp.
A statement of the official position of the
labor organization, defending its stance in
opposition to the allegedly communist government of Guatemala, which had led to charges of
assisting the Yankee imperialists. Cites the
organization's various positions against Yankee imperialism, supports the land reforms of
the Guatemalan revolution, criticizes the
United Fruit Company, and contends that the
organization favors reform but draws the line
at communism, since it seeks above all to
promote democracy. Includes several statements and resolutions defining these stands.
FU

913 Monteforte Toledo, Mario. *Anaité.* Guatemala:
Editorial "El Libro de Guatemala," 1948.
320 pp.
A novel, originally written in 1939 and
awarded the national prize in literature, but
not published until 1948. It is set in the
tropical jungles of the nation's east coast
and Petén region, and focuses on the conditions of the peasants in that area and their
struggle with nature and oppressive landlords,
tracing their trials and tribulations with
sympathy and feeling. The Ubico regime judged
the subject matter too sensitive for publication, and it did not reach print until after
the revolution, in which the author played a
role. DLC LNHT

914 _____. *Casi todos los cuentos.* Barcelona:
Barral Editores, 1974. 362 pp.
A collection of short stories by this social reformer and novelist, focusing on a
variety of themes, principally the life of the
rural peasants and their problems, struggles,
and plight. LNHT

(Monteforte Toledo, Mario)

915   _____. Cuentos de derrota y esperanza.
Jalapa: Universidad Veracruzana, 1962.
261 pp.
    A collection of short stories dealing with
the problems of contemporary Latin America by
focusing on the last days of the Arbenz regime, its overthrow, and the Castillo Armas
regime. The stories reflect the author's
sympathy with Arbenz and seek to depict the
problems of the poor, the hopelessness of
their situation, and the prospects offered by
the revolutionary regimes. Hence the various
stories assail the military, landowners, Yankee imperialists, and foreign enterprises.
The author seeks to offer hope by showing how
these forces can be overcome through action by
the poor, and sees promise in the assassination of Castillo Armas. DLC LNHT

916   _____. La cueva sin quietud. Guatemala:
Ministerio de Educación Pública, 1949. 267
pp. Illus.
    A series of short stories with disparate
themes portraying Guatemalan life and culture
and accenting social conditions, particularly
the plight of the poor and the rural
campesinos. DLC LNHT BNG

917   _____. Una democracia a prueba de fuego.
Guatemala: Tipografía Nacional, 1949. 47 pp.
Illus.
    An account of the attempted coup of October
1949 attendant to the assassination of Colonel
Arana. Denounces the alleged barbarity of the
rebels, hailing the suppression of the revolt
as a victory for the people and acclaiming the
Arévalo regime. The author was president of
the National Assembly during Arévalo's tenure.
LNHT

918   _____. Los desencontrados. Mexico:
Editorial Joaquín Mortiz, 1976. 190 pp.
    A novel of contemporary life and its con-
tradictions, including themes of cultural
conflict and foreign dominance. Based on the
author's experiences, it traces the activities
of exiles living in Mexico, their life-style,
adjustments to the local culture, and relations with friends and co-workers, emphasizing
their adjustment problems, the difficulties
inherent in their state of exile, and their
attitudes. LNHT

919   _____. Donde acaban los caminos. Guatemala:
Tipografía Nacional, 1953. 313 pp. Latest
ed. Santiago: Zig-Zag, 1966. 199 pp.
    A novel by a well-known Guatemalan sociolo-
gist associated with the revolution, focused
on peasant life, its frustrations, and its
brutality. Using the life of a doctor working
in rural areas as his point of observation, he
seeks to portray the difficulties encountered
by those seeking to help the peasants. He
emphasizes the government's lack of interest
and denial of problems in its effort to present the best image to the outside world.
Concludes that this situation demonstrates the
irrelevance of existing institutions to peasant life. LNHT BNG

920   _____. Entre la piedra y la cruz. Guatemala:
Editorial "El Libro de Guatemala," 1948. 302
pp.
    A novel of peasant life that focuses on the
oppression of the Indian peons by the landowners, upper classes, and foreign businessmen, and on the conditions in which the
campesinos live. The incompatability of the
Indian culture, tradition, and life-style with
modern capitalist society is emphasized, with
the focus on the Indian's struggle to find
their own way and maintain their culture in a
changing world. DLC LNHT BNG

921   _____. Guatemala: monografía sociológica.
Mexico: UNAM, 1959. 2d ed. Mexico: UNAM,
1965. 682 pp. Biblio., notes, illus.,
tables.
    Part of a series of sociological monographs
on each Latin American country, sponsored by
the National University of Mexico. Provides
detailed discussion and semi-Marxist analysis
of all aspects of society, including demography, culture, social structure and institutions, labor, political structure, economic
factors, and the principal institutions. The
emphasis is on the contemporary class struggle
and the problems of the poor. Extensive survey and census data are employed, particularly
from 1950, and items discussed are placed in
the context of general sociological theory.
Demonstrates the viewpoint of the young intellectuals of the nation, as well as the usual
comments on Yankee imperialism and the United
Fruit Company. DLC LNHT BNG

922   _____. Llegaron del mar. Mexico: Editorial
Joaquín Moritz, 1966. 235 pp.
    Another of the author's vivid novels of
social justice; focuses on the lives and problems of the lower classes and on their oppression, seeking to offer the hope of a new day.
Portrays an indigenous culture, subdued by
foreign invaders, which preserves its traditions and engages in passive resistance, ultimately to rebel to seek its freedom. The
story mixes contemporary overtones with Indian
mythology, invoking the gods of the civilizations of pre-Columbian times. Despite the use
of terms such as imperialism, the focus is on
the Indian peasants, and the novel deals with
warfare among Indian nations. LNHT

923   _____. Una manera de morir. Mexico: Fondo
de Cultura Económica, 1957. 393 pp.
    A semi-autobiographical novel that deals
with the efforts at change in the countryside
and the effects of the Guatemalan revolution,
emphasizing the difficulties and frustrations.
In the process it portrays the hopes, life-
style, attitudes and skepticism of the peasants, and the oppressiveness of government.
Awarded first prize in the 1955 international
novel competition of the Union of Latin American Universities. LNHT BNG

924   Montgomery, George Washington. Narrative of a
Journey to Guatemala in Central America, in
1838. New York: Wiley & Putnam, 1839. viii,
195 pp.

The notes of a U.S. envoy to the Central American Republic in 1838, recounting his visit to Guatemala. His sympathies clearly lay with the Federation, and this as well as the prevailing stereotypes and attitudes of Yankees and Europeans of that day are evident in his comments on Carrera and his revolution. Despite these biases, however, his comments do provide considerable information about Carrera and his uprising. DLC

925 Montúfar, Rafael. Caída de una tiranía. Guatemala: Sánchez & de Guise, 1923. 298 pp. Index, illus.
An account of the fall of Estrada Cabrera, by a victim of his regime who details the many facets of the series of events and plots that led to the fall of the dictatorship. Includes a discussion of the state of the nation and the problems it faced. The work, covering the years 1919-22, is a sequel to the author's Memorias de una prisión and continues the account of the regime. DLC LNHT BNG

926 _____. Comprobaciones históricas: el doctor Lorenzo Montúfar y el partido jesuítico. Guatemala: Tipografía Nacional, 1899. 102 pp.
A defense of the actions of the author's father, Lorenzo Montúfar, in reply to the attacks on him by Francisco María Iglesias; quotes liberally from his father's Memorias, the critics, and appropriate documentation from the era. The author emphasizes that the criticism reflects the political passions of the era, which have lingered well beyond their time, and calls Iglesias an agent of the Jesuit party. DLC-LDS-367 LNHT BNG

927 _____. El deslinde de los partidos: artículos publicados en "El Imparcial." Guatemala: Unión Tipográfica, 1925. 141 pp.
A series of articles that originally appeared in El Imparcial of Guatemala City, discussing the role of political parties in nations in general and Guatemala in particular, stressing their importance and insisting on the impossibility of a one-party state. Although criticizing both parties for their splits, personalismo, and the taking of stands that sometimes render it difficult to tell them apart, the series defends the Liberals, with whom both the author and his father are associated. DLC LNHT BNG

928 _____, ed. Discursos del doctor Lorenzo Montúfar y Rivera Maestre. Guatemala: Tipografía La Unión, 1897. xx, 322 pp. 2d ed. Guatemala: Sánchez & de Guise, 1923. xx, 298 pp.
A collection of speeches by one of the leading nineteenth-century Liberal statesmen and scholars of Guatemala, compiled by his son. They emphasize the need for principles to supersede individuals, extolling all the typical Liberal programs. A considerable portion were delivered to the constituent assemblies of 1876 and 1879, while others are miscellaneous speeches or addresses to Congress; spans the years 1862 through 1885. DLC LNHT BNG

929 Montúfar, Rafael. Estudios económicos. Guatemala: Tipografía de Arturo Siguerra, 1899. 118 pp. Biblio.
An analysis of the economic crisis that affected Guatemala at the turn of the century, contending that it was due to deficit spending and unsound financial practices such as the use of paper money. Reflects the worldwide disputes of the time about the use of silver and paper money, and endorses the gold standard. LNHT

930 _____. Labor de un diputado a la Asamblea Legislativa de Guatemala en el período de 1922-1925. Guatemala: Unión Tipográfica, 1926. 435 pp. Appendix.
The memoirs of a Liberal member of the Guatemalan Congress from 1922 to 1925, providing insights into three years of congressional maneuvering and hence into the legislative and general politics of the nation during the early 1920s. While emphasizing the author's role and initiatives, the volume touches all the leading political issues of the day, especially those concerned with foreign investment, legal codification, and interisthmian relations. The appendix reproduces important documents and treaties of the era. LNHT BNG

931 _____. Memorias de una prisión: páginas de la historia de Centro-América. Guatemala: n.p., 1908. 270 pp. Illus. Latest ed. New York: Harper & Row, 1917.
The memoirs of a former official of the Estrada Cabrera regime who was later arrested and accused of plotting against it, recounting his imprisonment and discussing the regime, listing its limitations and its accomplishments, and criticizing the dictatorship. DLC LNHT BNG

932 Montúfar y Coronado, Manuel. Estado político de Guatemala--últimas ocurrencias de aquel país--derrota del general Morazán. Mexico: Ignacio Cumplido, 1840. 17 pp.
A Conservative account of the political maneuvering of the late 1830s regarding the Federation, explaining the failure of a Conservative revolt.

933 Montúfar y Rivera Maestre, Lorenzo. Contestación a don Antonio José de Irisarri. London: C. Whiting, 1863. 28 pp. 2d ed. Guatemala: Tipografía La Unión, 1891. 34 pp.
Part of the continuing polemic in the Liberal-Conservative wars, reflecting the intensity of the political scene and involving two of its leading figures. Pits the Guatemalan minister in Washington, Irisarri, representing the government of Rafael Carrera, against a Liberal leader then in exile and accused of assisting the Salvadoran government of Gerrardo Barrios in its war with Guatemala. DLC

934 _____. El evangelio y el syllabus: opúsculo escrito y dedicado al autor de los siete tratados de las Catilinarias y de la marcurial eclesiástica. San José: Imprenta Nacional,

(Montúfar y Rivera Maestre, Lorenzo)
1884. 53 pp. Latest ed. Guatemala:
Tipografía Nacional, 1961. 100 pp.
Part of a series of polemical attacks on
the church in Central America; this one
attacks its educational indoctrination and
supports the separation of church and state.
DLC   DLC-LDS-89

935   _____. Los jesuítas impugnados por el señor
dr. Lorenzo Montúfar y defendidos por el R.P.
León Tornero. Riobamba, Ecuador: Imprenta
del Colegio, 1876. 480 pp.
A collection of the anti-Jesuit writings of
a leading Liberal propagandist, gathering the
entire series of pamphlets he prepared during
the church-state clash in the isthmus. In
sarcastic tones he characterizes the Jesuits
as reactionary, counterrevolutionary businessmen defending what he calls "dictatorial the-
ocracy." Details their political activities
against various governments throughout Europe
and charges subversion of Latin American governments. The volume provides a good indication of the tone of the dispute and the
intense feeling involved. This version
includes counterarguments of similar length
and tone. TxU

936   _____. Los jesuítas: opúsculo escrito por el
doctor Lorenzo Montúfar del colegio de
abogados de Lima: individuo correspondiente
de la Academia Española dedicado al sr.
licenciado don José Antonio Pinto, presidente
actual de Costa-Rica, en testimonio de aprecio
por haber prohibido a los jesuítas la entrada
en esta república. San José: Imprenta
Nacional, 1872. 29 pp.
See item GU935. DLC DLC-LDS-104

937   _____. Los jesuítas, opúsculo segundo:
dedicado a los supremos gobiernos de Guatemala
y El Salvador en testimonio de respeto por la
expulsión de los individuos de la compañía
fundada por Loyola. San José: Imprenta
Nacional, 1872. 37 pp.
See item GU935. DLC-LDS-104

938   _____. Los jesuítas: tercer opúsculo
dedicado a la juventud de Centro-América. San
José: Imprenta Nacional, 1872. 107 pp.
See item GU935. DLC-LDS-89

939   Memorias autobiográficas. Guatemala:
Tipografía Nacional, 1898. 614 pp. Illus.
The memoirs of a militant and prolific
Guatemalan Liberal whose political career and
writings constituted an important part of the
politics of nineteenth-century Guatemala and
the ultimate triumph of the Liberals in that
nation. These memoirs detail his efforts,
views, and several periods of exile, as well
as his early life, reflecting his numerous
polemics. The account ends in the mid-1870s.
BNG   BNCR

940   Moore, G. Alexander. Life Cycles in Atchalán:
The Diverse Careers of Certain Guatemalans.
New York: Teachers College Press, 1973. x,

220 pp. Biblio., illus., maps, tables,
appendixes.
An anthropological-educational study, based
on fieldwork conducted between 1960 and 1970,
that focuses on the different cultures--
ladino, Indian, and cosmopolitan--in a
Guatemalan village (with a fictitious name)
near Antigua, emphasizing the persistence and
transmission of culture. Focussing on ten
individuals, the author traces the various
"rites of passage" that characterize key
phases of life, noting that these rites transmit culture and knowledge more effectively
than does the formal educational system and
observing that the schools have failed to
create a national mentality. He also describes various adult education programs,
noting that ad-hoc efforts that focus on practical skills are the most successful. In the
process, he reviews the various stages in the
careers of individuals in each of the three
cultures of the town as they climb the ladder
of success, noting the skills necessary and
the differing values and methods involved.
DLC LNHT

941   Moore, Richard E. Historical Dictionary of
Guatemala. Metuchen, N.J.: Scarecrow Press,
1967. 187 pp. Biblio. 2d ed. Metuchen,
N.J.: Scarecrow Press, 1973. 285 pp.
Biblio.
One of the thinner volumes in this series,
a surprising situation in view of the larger
amount of scholarship dealing with Guatemala
and its central role in isthmian affairs,
this volume offers extremely brief definitions
of names and terms, with identification of
people and places. The second edition is a
bit fuller than the first, but still limited,
and the extreme brevity of the entries continues to be a problem. The emphasis is still
on place names rather than people or events,
though the ratio in the second edition is
better. The other limitations characteristic
of the series remain. DLC LNHT

942   Morales, Baltasar. La caída de Jorge Ubico:
derrocamiento de una tiranía; reseña de la
gesta cívica de junio de 1944. Guatemala:
Sánchez & de Guise, n.d. [1944]. 110 pp. 3d
ed. Guatemala: Tipografía Nacional, 1966.
A revolutionary account by a participant in
the overthrow of the Ubico regime in July
1944. Covers the maneuvers, protests, and
memorials that led to the caudillo's resigna-
tion, but not the succeeding regime or the
second stage of the revolution. The author,
a member of the Social Democratic party,
stresses his own role, with the result that
his account focuses more on the events in the
capital, the involvement of the intellectuals
and the professionals, and the diplomatic
mediations than do the accounts by other participants; he emphasizes the role of these
groups and downplays that of the students and
labor. He also views the Ubico regime with
more balance than most revolutionaries, granting that it accomplished much in the 1930s,
though the account of the regime's response to

the crisis reflects many of the usual revolutionary stereotypes. Some editions bear only
the shorter title Derrocamiento de una
tiranía. DLC LNHT BNG

943 Morales Urrutia, Mateo. La división política
y administrativa de la República de Guatemala,
con sus datos históricos y de legislación. 2
vols. Guatemala: Editorial Iberia, 1961.
748, 830 pp. Biblio.
     A listing of the services and facilities of
each municipio of the republic, listed by
department, with appropriate excerpts from the
legislation and a chronology of the significant institutions. Useful in tracing the
internal boundary changes and the accompanying
disputes, as well as the shifting status of
the various towns in the republic. LNHT BNG

944 Morán Chinchilla, Sarbelio. Guía geográfica
de los departamentos de Guatemala. Guatemala:
Imprenta Mansilla, 1971. 239 pp. Maps,
tables.
     A compilation of basic contemporary data,
by department, with useful tables and maps,
indicating the distribution of production,
population, etc. BNG

945 Morelet, Arthur. Voyage dans L'Amérique
Centrale, L'île de Cuba et le Yucatan. 2
vols. Paris: Gide & J. Baudray, 1857. 337,
323 pp. Illus., maps.
Travels in Central America: Including
Accounts of Some Regions Unexplored since the
Conquest. New York: Holt & William, 1871.
xvi, 430 pp. Biblio., illus., maps.
Viaje a la América Central y el Yucatan.
Madrid: Gaspar y Roig, 1861.
Reisen In Zentral Amerika. Jena: n.p., 1872.
362 pp. Illus., maps.
     A detailed descriptive account of a French
naturalist's trip through the then virtually
unexplored regions of the Petén and Verapaz,
from Campeche to Guatemala City. His emphasis
is on flora, fauna, and physical features.
Includes descriptions of the towns visited,
the population, Indian cultures, customs, and
social practices, complete with musical scores
from songs he heard. The detail is encyclopedic. While the descriptions of Guatemalan
life pay little attention to politics, there
is a pro-Carrera trend. DLC LNHT

946 Moreno, Laudelino. Derecho consular
guatemalteco. Guatemala: Tipografía
Nacional, 1946. 696 pp. Biblio., maps,
tables.
     A treatise explaining the various aspects
of existing Guatemalan consular law, and the
various regulations and procedures pertaining
to travel or the conduct of business abroad
and the importation of products. Reproduces
the laws, providing explanations of how to use
the services and maps and tables regarding the
consular service. DLC BNG

947 Morren, F.W. Koffiecultuur in Guatemala, met
aanteekeningen betreffende de overige
cultures, de mijnen en den economischen
toestand van deze republiek. Amsterdam: J.H.

de Bussy, 1899. 142 pp. Illus., maps,
tables.
     A volume designed to introduce the Dutch
public to Guatemala and its economic prospects, particularly seeking to encourage Dutch
investment in coffee plantations there. Includes a brief historical overview, a general
geographic description, a discussion of coffee, and a survey of current economy. Prints
the text of the fiscal code and other laws
regulating investment and trade. DLC

948 Morton, Friedrich. Xelahuh: Abenteuer im
Urwald von Guatemala. Salzburg: Otto Müller
Verlag, 1950. 388 pp. Illus., maps.
In the Land of the Quetzal Feather. New York:
Devin-Adair, 1960. 208 pp. Illus.
     An adventure-memoir based on the author's
residence on a Guatemalan coffee finca, but
emphasizing his experiences and encounters
with animals, volcanoes, and people. These
are grouped by subject in the form of a story-
telling session, without specific details or
chronology. DLC LNHT

949 Mosquera Aguilar, Antonio. La organización
popular en Guatemala. Guatemala: Universidad
de San Carlos, 1976. 180 pp.
     BNG

950 Movimiento Revolucionario 13 de Noviembre.
Primera Declaración de la Sierra de las Minas:
documento de la dirección del movimiento
revolucionario 13 de noviembre. Montevideo:
Edición del Comité Bancario de Lucha
Antiimperialista, 1965. 46 pp.
     The revolutionary manifesto and platform of
the Guatemalan leftist group known as the 13th
of November group. Signed by Marco Antonio
Yon Sosa, Luís Augusto Turcios Lima, and others, and dated 20 December 1964, it provides
their interpretation of Guatemalan society and
their version of Guatemalan history viewed in
the light of the Russian and Chinese revolutions; they denounce the puppet regimes they
contend serve the interests of the upper
classes and the imperialists, and state a case
for all the oppressed workers of Latin America. Some introductory data about the movement are included. DLC LNHT

951 Moya Posas, Emma. La jornada épica de
Castillo Armas vista desde Honduras.
Tegucigalpa: Imprenta La República, 1955.
108 pp. Illus.
     A detailed and sympathetic account of the
National Liberation Movement from its foundation to its triumph. Focuses on the exile
period in Honduras and the preliminary phases,
but also includes an account of the military
campaign. TxU

952 Müeller, Adrian. Guatemala: Ein Bildbuch.
Zurich and Stuttgart: Fretz & Wasmuth Verlag,
1963. 50 pp. Biblio., illus., maps.
     A photo essay of Guatemala, with brief
accompanying descriptive text. DLC LNHT

953 Muñoz, Joaquín. Guatemala: From Where the
Rainbow Takes Its Colors--Ancient, Historical,

Colorful, Picturesque, Modern. Guatemala: Tipografía Nacional, 1940. 328 pp. Illus., maps. Latest ed. Guatemala: Serviprensa Centroamérica, 1975. 290 pp.

A combination guidebook and brief historical and cultural synopsis providing descriptions of locations, services, and transportation facilities, along with background sketches designed to inform and pique the curiosity of the potential visitor. DLC LNHT BNG

954 Muñoz, Joaquín, and Anna Bell Ward. Guatemala: Ancient and Modern. New York: Pyramid, 1940. xviii, 318 pp. Index, illus., appendixes.

A travelogue written as a kind of guidebook to the nation by one of its intellectuals and a North American tourist, providing an account of their travels and experiences. Includes historical background, though in sketchy form, and discussion of the archeological zones, Colonial artifacts, Antigua, the Indians, markets, textiles, places of natural beauty, and the capital. DLC LNHT

955 Muñoz Meany, Enrique. Crónicas y apuntes. Guatemala: Ediciones Revista de Guatemala, 1961. 228 pp.

A compilation of essays and literary commentaries, written during the years 1925 to 1930 under various pseudonyms by a well-known Guatemalan scholar and political figure who was active in the 1944 revolution. The commentaries reflect the idealism and emotion of youth and offer vignettes of Guatemalan life under the various dictatorships, emphasizing the oppression of these regimes. LNHT BNG

956 _____. El hombre y la encrucijada. Guatemala: Tipografía Nacional, 1950. 263 pp. Notes.

A compilation of speeches, by the foreign minister of the Revolutionary Junta and of the Arévalo administration, dealing with a wide variety of issues but focusing on what he calls the defense of democracy. Topics range from domestic affairs and the role of the university in the revolution to speeches concerning the Guatemalan position in regard to Israel and in support of the Spanish exile government; commentaries on international law, inter-American relations, and Latin American solidarity; and denunciations of dictatorship and Yankee imperialism. DLC

957 _____. La palabra de Guatemala en Bogotá: discurso del canciller. Guatemala: Tipografía Nacional, 1948. 17 pp. Illus.

An official statement of the Guatemalan defense against accusations of communism at the Bogotá conference. LNHT

958 Munson, Donn. Zacapa: The Inside Story of Guatemala's Communist Revolution. Canoga Park, Calif.: Challenge Books, 1967. 256 pp.

A journalist's memoirs of his days in Guatemala and his contacts with the guerrillas, whose story he tells, along with

personal observations. His account of the procedures necessary to gain access to the movement provides interesting insight on its security and operation. DLC

959 Nach, James. Guatemala in Pictures. London and Melbourne: Oak Tree, 1966. 64 pp. Illus., maps. Latest ed. New York: Sterling, 1970. 64 pp. Illus.

Basic information provided principally through photos and brief explanation. DLC

960 Nájera Cabrera, Antonio. Mensaje político a los guatemaltecos en general y en particular a las generaciones nuevas y nacientes, indígenas y ladinas o mestizas. Guatemala: Imprenta Valenzuela, 1957. 31 pp.

An emotional and patriotic discussion of the nation's problems. Criticizes foreign influence, materialism, the lack of education, and political corruption while calling for national renovation, new leadership, and reliance on domestic ideas, national unification, and patriotism. The volume is sometimes cited by its shorter cover title Mensaje político al pueblo de Guatemala, though the full title appears on the title page. TxU

961 Nájera Farfán, Mario Efraín. Del capitalismo al comunismo. Guatemala: Unión Tipográfica, 1962. vii, 473 pp. Notes.

A Guatemalan lawyer, writer, and political figure whose career spans the 1940s and 1950s provides an analysis of communism, rejecting it and contending that it has support in Guatemala only because of ignorance of its operation. Nájera Farfán served in the 1945 Constituent Assembly, helped install Arévalo in the presidency, and served in his government before becoming disillusioned with the leftist trend and dictatorial nature of the new regime. He later served the rightist counterrevolutionary movement in the government of Castillo Armas. He draws upon his experience in this exposé, analyzing Marxist doctrine at length and always stressing the difference between doctrine and practice. His cover inscription indicates his views that communism takes from all, not just the rich, and deprives all of their liberty. DLC LNHT

962 _____. Cuando el árbol cae . . . un presidente que murió para vivir. Mexico: Editorial Stylo, 1958. 291 pp. Illus.

A defense of the Castillo Armas regime published by the secretaría general de la presidencia of his regime in honor of the anniversary of his assassination. The volume mixes memoirs of the activities of the author with discussion of Castillo Armas and his actions, stressing Castillo Armas's anti-communism, praising his impact on Guatemala, and emphasizing the loss to the nation in his death. LNHT BNG

963 _____. ¡¡Delenda est Wall Street¡¡ Guatemala: Editorial San Antonio, 1961. 66 pp.

A series of articles, originally published in the newspaper La Prensa Libre of Guatemala

(Nájera Farfán, Mario Efraín)
City in April of 1960, commenting on the book The Shark and the Sardines by Juan José Arévalo. The articles summarize the book, agreeing with its charges of Wall Street financial domination of the hemisphere but also criticizing it, particularly for its imagery. The author concludes that Arévalo has raised a cry of complaint, but has failed to provide proposals for the best means for Latin America to deal with the Yankees. BNG

964 _____. Los estafádores de la democracia: hombres y hechos en Guatemala. Buenos Aires: Editorial GLEM, 1956. 301 pp.
The memoirs of a participant in the Guatemalan revolution, covering the years 1945-55 and reflecting a transition from the author's early idealism, during which he helped lead the overthrow of the old regime, the installation of the Arévalo regime, and to his growing disillusion with the reform efforts and a denunciation of Marxism. The author concludes that Arévalo was a stalking-horse for the Marxists to whom he ultimately delivered the Revolution, thereby betraying it, and is particularly bitter in his attacks on Arbenz. As such, this insider's account traces the path of the moderate supporters of the revolution, who became disenchanted as it swung leftward. DLC LNHT BNG

965 _____. Máximos y mínimas para un gobernante ideal: pasatiempo político-literario. Guatemala: Imprenta Eros, 1972. 154 pp.
A well-known Guatemalan writer and commentator provides his version of the ideal president, not necessarily for Guatemala, but for every democracy, describing what he considers desirable traits of a chief executive, his associates, and of governments. The subtitle suggests that he wrote the book to pass the time, and expects it to be read in a similar vein. BNG

966 _____, ed. La realidad de un mensaje: pláticas presidenciales. Guatemala: Tipografía Nacional, 1957. 394 pp. Illus.
A record of the 1957 inspection trips to all the provinces of the republic by then-President Colonel Carlos Castillo Armas, reproducing the speeches he made at each location along with the replies of the local figures, with illustrations from his trip; compiled by the secretary general of the presidency. The tour is summarized in tables and the route detailed, while the introduction hails the regime's programs. The volume parallels the Viajes presidenciales of Federico Hernández de León, and it is interesting that the introduction credits Ubico with instituting the tradition and hails Castillo Armas's revival of the custom after its abandonment during what it calls the "pro-Soviet" governments. DLC BNG

967 Narisco, Vicente A. Álbum de recuerdos: expedición musical al Petén y Belize [sic], 1910-1911. Guatemala: Imprenta de Síguere, 1911. 94 pp. Illus.

The observations, in diary form, of a music professor during a visit to this region. Encompasses culture, life-styles, the life of the chicleros, and other aspects of the region, as well as the lyrics and music for the folk songs he heard and description of the predominent forms of music. LNHT

968 Narod Gvatemaly i iunajted frut kómpani [The people of Guatemala and the United Fruit Company]. Moscow: Izdatelstvo Inostrannoj Literatury, 1954. 50 pp. Biblio.
A denunciation of the U.S. intervention in Guatemala and the role of the United Fruit Company, viewing the situation in Marxist terms. DLC

969 Nash, Manning. Machine Age Maya: The Industrialization of a Guatemalan Community. Glencoe, Ill.: Free Press, 1958. 118 pp. Biblio., illus. 2d ed. Chicago: University of Chicago Press, 1967. xv, 155 pp. Index, biblio., maps, tables.
Los Mayas en la era de la máquina. Guatemala: Ministerio de Educación Pública, 1970. 238 pp. Biblio., illus.
A detailed study of Cantel, a small Indian community in Western Guatemala, based on fieldwork during the 1950s. Details the social changes brought by industrialization, focusing on cultural adaptation. The author concludes that local control of social factors is important to such a transition, and specifies the compromises and alterations in life-style that resulted from changing productive systems and urbanization. Includes assessment of the impact of the revolution in the community, concluding that it brought considerable change, but that the local residents resisted surrendering authority to the central government. DLC LNHT

970 _____. Primitive and Peasant Economic Systems. San Francisco: Chandler, 1966. viii, 166 pp. Biblio.
A survey of the problems of acculturation and the various aspects of a peasant economy, based on the author's earlier research in Guatemala and Indonesia. Provides a comparative and theoretical anthropological overview of the problems involved in changing a traditional system. DLC

971 The Netherlands, Gov't of. Wenken voor exporterus: Guatemala. Gravenhagen: n.p., 1957. 124 pp. Illus., tables.
Part of a general series designed to encourage Dutch companies and investors, this volume provides details about Guatemala's current economy, trade, and production. DLC

972 Neutze de Rugg, Carmen. Diseños de los tejidos indígenas de Guatemala. Guatemala: Imprenta Universitaria, 1976. 107 pp. Biblio., illus.
Designs in Guatemalan Textiles. Guatemala: Editorial Piedra Santa, 1977. 107 pp. Index, biblio., notes, illus.
A detailed discussion of both designs and weaving techniques, with extensive color

photos of the designs and elaborate drawings
to show the techniques. Text in English and
Spanish. Includes discussion of pre-Colonial,
Colonial, and modern times. LNHT

973 Newbold, Stokes, pseud. A Study of Recep-
tivity to Communism in Rural Guatemala.
Washington, D.C.: Department of State, 1954.
viii, 49 pp. Maps, tables.
     This analysis is based in part on inter-
views with individuals incarcerated in the
Central Penitentiary in the capital on charges
of communism. DLC

974 Niederlein, Gustavo. The Republic of
Guatemala. Philadelphia: Philadelphia
Commercial Museum, 1898. 63 pp. Maps.
     A brief descriptive survey of the situation
in Guatemala during 1897-98. Follows the
pattern of the author's volumes on other isthmian countries written during the same tour,
emphasizing physical description, flora,
fauna, climate, resources, and the economy.
DLC LNHT

975 Noval, Joaquín. Materiales etnográficos de
San Miguel. Guatemala: Universidad de San
Carlos, 1964. 99 pp.
     A description of the economic and social
structure of San Miguel Milpas Alpas, based on
fieldwork in 1960 and 1961, emphasizing the
social organizations in the town. Concludes
that the town is part of the national economy
rather than being devoted wholly to subsistence agriculture, but that national law has
few effects. Includes a summary of the various social classes identifiable in the town
and the factors that distinguish them from
each other. DLC

976 _____. Resumen etnográfico de Guatemala.
Guatemala: Universidad de San Carlos, 1961.
162 pp. Biblio. 2d ed. Guatemala:
Universidad de San Carlos de Guatemala, 1972.
180 pp. Biblio.
     A description of the principal characteris-
tics of the Indian and ladino elements of the
population, treated as units with no distinction among Indian ethnographic groups and
concluding with a commentary on national integration. Covers distribution, economy, and
social organization of each group, with the
major focus on the Indians, calling for
greater attention and more programs for this
group. DLC LNHT BNG

977 _____. Tres problemas de la educación rural
en Guatemala. Guatemala: Ministerio de
Educación Pública, 1959. 43 pp. Biblio.
     A brief discussion of the practices and
problems of rural education as it relates to
the Indian community, by a leading Guatemalan
anthropologist. He suggests more flexibility
in method and awareness of the diversity of
the cultural backgrounds, while stressing
literacy and greater effort to expand the
educational system in the rural areas. DLC
LNHT

978 Nuestro Diario (Guatemala). Apertura de un
puerto moderno en el Pacífico: entrevistas
tomadas de las ediciones de "Nuestro Diario."
Guatemala: Unión Tipográfica, 1930. 108 pp.
Maps.
     A series of interviews with leading citi-
zens of the Pacific coast regarding the need
for a port in the region, and the possible
means of financing it. The opinions on methods and location are diverse, though most
emphasize the importance of such a port to
national development. The series is indicative of the debates over methods and the frustration regarding the long-hoped-for port, and
illustrates the many problems involved. BNG

979 _____. Consideraciones sobre la situación
económica de Guatemala: comentarios al margen
del libro "Central American Currency and
Finance" por John Parke Young. Guatemala:
Publicaciones Selca, 1925. 228 pp.
     A detailed chapter-by-chapter analysis of
Young's volume, originally published in the
newspaper. There is no indication of the
author of the commentaries, which are critical
of the volume, contending that Young, despite
his good intentions, did not spend sufficient
time in the area to fully appreciate conditions in Central America, and condemning Yankee interventionism, suggesting that the
Yankees can best help by letting the region
solve its own problems. Despite these criticisms, the essays hail the effort, and support
trade with the Yankees. LNHT BNG

980 _____. Reflexiones para comprender la
situación política de Guatemala en noviembre
de 1949. Guatemala: Nuestro Diario, 1949.
28 pp.
     A collection of editorials from the news-
paper, published during 1949, defending the
revolutionary regime and explaining its program. Reproduced in pamphlet form to provide
revolutionary leaders throughout the country
with a handbook for use to promote support for
the movement and its government. Reflects the
leftward shift of the movement, emphasizing
class struggle and calling for drastic reforms, particularly in the agricultural realm.
TxU

981 Núñez de Rodas, Edna Isabel. El grabado en
Guatemala. Guatemala: Instituto Geográfica
Nacional, 1970. 186 pp. Index, biblio.,
notes, illus.
     A history of engraving in Guatemala from
pre-Conquest times to 1970, with over 100
black-and-white illustrations, all properly
identified and cataloged. The principal prac-
ticioners and schools of the republic are also
discussed. Clearly based on extensive research, with appropriate documentation from
all the logical repositories, an extensive
bibliography, and a full categorization of the
engravings presented as examples. BNG

982 O., S.L. J. Rufino Barrios y los infortunios
de Guatemala. Alajuela, Costa Rica: Imprenta
de la República, 1878. 13 pp.
     A condemnation of Barrios as an ambitious
usurper who was not effectively in the

tradition of the Guatemalan Liberal movement, and of Miguel García Granados; characteristic of the polemics of the day. BNCR

983 Oakes, Maud van Cortlandt. Beyond the Windy Place: Life in the Guatemalan Highlands. New York: Farrar, Straus & Young, 1951. 338 pp. London: Victor Gollancz, 1951. 338 pp.

Draws on data used in the author's earlier work; presents the material in popular format, employing a diary form to describe the author's experiences and observations. DLC LNHT

984 ____. The Two Crosses of Todos Santos: Survivals of Mayan Religious Ritual. New York: Pantheon Books, 1951. xiii, 274 pp. Index, biblio., illus., maps. 2d ed. Princeton, N.J.: Princeton University Press, 1969. viii, 274 pp. Index, biblio., illus.

A detailed analysis of the religious life of a Guatemalan town (Todos Santos Cuchumatán), examining the influences of Mayan and Catholic traditions. Includes basic data as well as description and analysis of the various ceremonies, narrating the author's experiences and observations. DLC LNHT BNG

985 O.A.S. Tenencia de la tierra y desarrollo socioeconómico del sector agrícola en Guatemala. Guatemala: Editorial Universitaria, 1971. 395 pp. Biblio., tables.

A detailed study of land holdings and use, prepared in 1965 by an O.A.S mission. Extensive statistical data for late 1950s and early 1960s show the changes in ownership and usage, and their impact on the economy. DLC

986 Obando Sánchez, Antonio. Memorias: la historia del movimiento obrero en Guatemala en este siglo. Guatemala: Imprenta Universitaria, 1978. 161 pp. Illus. BNG

987 Obert, L.J.C. Mémoire contenant un aperçu statistique de l'état de Guatemala ainsi que des renseignements précis sur son commerce, son industrie, son sol, sa température, son climat, et tout ce qui est relatif à cet état. . . . Brussels: Imprimerie de Lesigne, 1840. xi, 158 pp. Maps, appendixes.

The report of an agent of the Belgian Compagnie Commerciale et Agricole des Côtes Orientales de L'Amérique Centrale, which had been offered a concession for colonization by the Guatemalan government, who visited the country to assess its situation and prospects. His account was sent to the Belgian government as well as to the company. Includes copies of relevant correspondence, the charters and concession agreements, and details of Guatemalan organizations such as the National Bank, along with basic geographical and climatic factors. The author concludes that such a colonization project would be of commercial value. DLC LNHT

988 Obregón Loría, Rafael. José Quirce Filguera: fundador de la masonería en la República de Guatemala. San José: Imprenta Tormo, 1951. 15 pp.

A brief essay on the founding of Masonic societies in Guatemala in 1861 and the individual who started the first lodge. BNCR

989 Oehler, Klaus, ed. Las minifundistas de Guatemala: situación y perspectivas; enfoque especial del indígena. Guatemala: Editorial Financiera Guatemalteca, 1971. 467 pp. Illus., maps, tables.

A compilation of available data regarding the current situation of the nation's small landholders in the rural interior, with particular emphasis on the Indian communities. BNG

990 Olivera, Otto. La literatura en publicaciones periódicas de Guatemala: siglo XIX. New Orleans: Tulane University, 1974. 273 pp. Index, biblio., notes.

An analysis and summary of literary works published in seventeen nineteenth-century Guatemalan periodicals, with discussion of the authors, analysis of the works, and excerpts from them. DLC

991 Oliveros, Augusto César. Cuentos, leyendas, e historietas mínimas. Guatemala: Ministerio de Educación Pública, 1964. 139 pp. Illus.

A series of short stories and legends from Antigua that describe local life and customs. DLC LNHT BNG

992 O'Neale, Lila Morris. Textiles of Highland Guatemala. Washington, D.C.: Carnegie Institution, 1945. x, 319 pp. Biblio., illus., maps. 2d ed. New York: Johnson Reprint, 1966.
Tejidos de los Altiplanos de Guatemala. 2 vols. Guatemala: Ministerio de Educación Pública, 1965. 787 pp. Illus.

This volume combines photographs and comprehensive descriptions of the characteristic textile materials and designs of the various regions of Guatemala, arranged by region. The fieldwork by an experienced anthropologist was conducted during 1936. Includes chapters describing the materials, weaving, dyes, loom types, and procedures, as well as a survey of design motifs and garments. The Spanish edition is substantially expanded. DLC LNHT BNG

993 Operations and Policy Research, Inc. Election Factbook, March 6, 1966. Washington, D.C.: Institute for the Comparative Study of Political Systems, 1966. 43 pp. Illus., maps.

Following the pattern of other volumes in this series, this item provides specifics regarding candidates, parties, electoral laws, background, and other data that help in understanding the current campaign. DLC LNHT

994 Ordóñez, López R., Rosales Cerna, and Girón Cerna. Guatemala: un pueblo amigo. Guatemala: Imprenta Iberia, n.d. Pages unnumbered. Illus.

A brief description, with lavish photos, of the nation and particularly the capital, designed for the tourist. BNG

995 Ordóñez Argüello, Alberto, ed. <u>Arévalo visto por América: la opinión continental en torno a la personalidad del primero presidente de la nueva Guatemala</u>. Guatemala: Ministerio de Educación Pública, 1951. 342 pp. Illus.
A government-sponsored compilation of editorials and press comment from throughout Latin America hailing Arévalo and his leftist regime and particularly praising its antidictatorial stances. Includes excerpts from speeches and official statements. DLC LNHT

996 _____. <u>Transformación económica de Guatemala: hacia una reforma agraria</u>. Guatemala: Tipografía Nacional, 1951. 251 pp. Tables.
A series of studies regarding the agrarian-reform efforts of the Arévalo and Arbenz regimes, viewing the programs sympathetically as Guatemala's hope for the future. The bulk of the study consists of official reports and statements. BNG

997 Ordóñez Jonama, Ramiro. <u>Las cárceles en Guatemala: visión histórico-legal</u>. Guatemala: Imprenta Iberia, 1970. vii, 203 pp. Biblio., notes.
Written as a thesis, this work surveys the history and evolution of prisons in Guatemala from the Colonial era, noting the principal trends and the foundation of the various institutions and stressing the improvement of conditions while recommending further improvements, more effective budgeting, and control by the government. LNHT

998 Orellana González, René Arturo. <u>Análisis estadístico del costa de la vida en Guatemala</u>. Guatemala: Dirección General de Estadística, 1967. ii, 80 pp. Tables.
A detailed study of the cost of essentials and of price levels in the capital in 1967, with analysis of the long-term cycles. Includes comparison with other countries and a discussion of the purchasing power of the quetzal. BNG

999 _____. <u>Encuesta sobre ingresos y gastos de la familia del campesino asalariado de Guatemala, 1966</u>. Guatemala: Universidad de San Carlos, 1972. 531 pp. Illus., maps, tables.
A detailed study, under the auspices of the Institute for Social and Economic Investigations, that examines the income and expenditures of Guatemalan rural families; based on interviews with 1,800 families in all districts of the nation. The data are tabulated and analyzed exhaustively by family size, educational level, employment, etc., though not by region, to provide an overview of the portions of income that come from given sources and the percentage of expenditures on the various necessities of life. Extensive graphs illustrate the findings. DLC

1000 Orellana González, René Arturo, and Adolfo Enrique de León L. <u>Ingresos y gastos de</u>

<u>familias urbanas de Guatemala</u>. Guatemala: Universidad de San Carlos, 1972. 234 pp. Tables.
A study of the income and expenditure pattern of Guatemalan families from urban areas. Based on interviews with 2,800 families, three-quarters of them from the capital and the remainder from the next four largest cities, with detailed statistical analysis broken down by sex, size of family, size of income, educational level, etc. The tabulations and analysis are presented as a single sample, without regional distinctions. DLC

1001 Orr, Paul G., and Karl T. Hereford. <u>Necesidades de personal en la educación media</u>. Guatemala: Imprenta Universitaria, 1963. 19 pp. Tables.
A brief report projecting the need for teachers for 1964 through 1970, based on the activities of the first Central American Conference Regarding the Preparation of Teachers for Educación Media. BNG

1002 Ortiz Passarelli, Miguel. <u>Hacia una democracia Guatemalteca: principio y acción del orticismo</u>. Guatemala: Imprenta El Nacionalista, 1957. 50 pp.
A statement of objectives by a candidate for the presidency in the 1957 elections who was running with the support of the Movimiento Democratico Nacional. TxU

1003 Osborne, Lilly de Jongh. <u>Así es Guatemala</u>. Guatemala: Ministerio de Educación Pública, 1960. 385 pp. Biblio., illus.
An anthropological descriptive account of the Indian cultures in present-day Guatemala, their life, customs, arts, and traditions. It is similar in form to the author's <u>Four Keys to Guatemala</u>, but focuses exclusively on the Indians and contains updated and more extensive data. DLC BNG BNCR

1004 _____. <u>Folklore, supersticiones, y leyendas de Guatemala</u>. Guatemala: Tipografía Nacional, 1965. 70 pp. Biblio.
A collection of folktales from various parts of the republic, gathered by a longtime investigator. The initial portion of the volume discusses the customs and religion of the area as background for the stories that comprise the second half. LNHT BNG

1005 _____. <u>Guatemala Textiles</u>. New Orleans: Tulane University, MARI, 1935. 110 pp. Index, illus.
A full discussion of the various types of textiles, considering their design, function, and the different weaving techniques. DLC LNHT

1006 _____. <u>Indian Crafts of Guatemala and El Salvador</u>. Norman: University of Oklahoma Press, 1965. 278 pp. Index, biblio., illus., maps, appendixes. 2d ed. Norman: University of Oklahoma Press, 1975. xxvi, 385 pp. Index, biblio., illus., maps, appendixes.
A descriptive account of the weaving techniques and varieties of costume in Guatemala and El Salvador, including discussion of

costume types, design, looms, dyes, coloration, etc., with illustrations in color. DLC LNHT

1007 Osegueda, Raúl. *Operación Centro-América: £$ OK £$*. Mexico: Editoria Ibero-Mexicana, 1957. 239 pp. Biblio. 2d ed. Santiago: Prensa Latinoamericana, 1958. 263 pp. Biblio.

A scathing denunciation of Anglo-Saxon influence and actions in Central America from the era of Monroe to that of McCarthy. Acknowledges an exchange of mutually beneficial ideas and technology, but is highly critical of the imperialists and their impact on the region. The author calls for more independent action on the part of Central America; more equality in international affairs; and reduction of Yankee and English dominance in all fields, noting that because of the size and wealth of the United States and Britain, Central America becomes a pawn in their struggles. He emphasizes the role of money and capitalism, commenting on foreign debts and spelling "United $tate$" and "Eng£and" with monetary symbols; he traces the history of their interventions in the region and of their struggle to dominate the interoceanic canal routes, employing picturesque and condescending terminology. The work is a product of the immediate post-intervention era of 1954, and constitutes an effective statement of the disillusionment of the isthmian left. DLC LNHT BNG

1008 _____. *Operación Guatemala: $$ OK $$*. Mexico: Editorial América Nueva, 1955. 306 pp. Biblio.

An impassioned denunciation of the Yankee attacks on the Guatemalan revolutionary governments of the 1944 to 1954 era and a ringing defense of the Guatemalan position, by a leftist sympathizer of the movement. He focuses on American diplomats and corporations, denouncing their influence and efforts to control the country, reprinting many of the diplomatic, verbal, and press exchanges of the era regarding the mutual accusations of communism, profiteering, and interference. The volume presents the Guatemalan viewpoint and captures the intensity of the confrontation and the verbiage. DLC LNHT BNG

1009 Osorio García, Miguel. *Semblanza de un patriota guatemalteco*. Mexico: n.p., 1958. 62 pp.

A laudatory biography of Colonel Moisés Evaristo Orozco Carranza in the form of a letter to the minister of agriculture, Lázaro Chacón Pazos, acclaiming the colonel's services and noting his association with the minister's father, General Lázaro Chacón. The account hails the colonel's ideals and service to the nation and details his career, which spanned the period from 1920 through the fall of the regime of General Federico Ponce Vaides in 1944, when the colonel was forced into exile. FMU

1010 Osorio S., J. Adalberto. *Santa Catarina Mita: ensayo monográfico*. Guatemala: Tipografía

Nacional, 1964. 205 pp. Biblio., illus., maps.

A description of the physical setting, life-style, and history of the town, including discussion of its current facilities, services, and customs. DLC LNHT BNG

1011 Ovalle, Néstor K. *Industrial Report on the Republic of Guatemala*. Washington, D.C.: Inter-American Development Commission, 1946. 163 pp. Tables.

A detailed statistical compilation about the Guatemalan economy, treating each of its significant sectors and industries separately. Provides tabulations of production by department, including statistics on the 1930s and 1940s and predictions about expansion and costs for the future. DLC LNHT

1012 Ovalle Samayoa, Oscar. *El hijo de la costurera y otros cuentos desde Senahú*. Guatemala: Ministerio de Educación Pública, 1977. 264 pp.

A series of short stories based on the regional folklore and life-style of Alta Verapaz. Includes stories of life in the various sections of the area and emphasizes the brutality of the life of the campesinos. BNG

1013 Ovidio Rodas, Héctor. *Lucía Estrada*. Guatemala: Ministerio de Educación Pública, 1956. 127 pp.

A verse novel that traces the life and extols the heroism of Estrada, who fought in the army of Justo Rufino Barrios; details her experiences in the unionist forces. BNG

1014 Oviedo, Matías. *Un año de labor administrativo bajo el gobierno del general Chacón, 1927-1928*. Guatemala: Tipografía Nacional, 1928. 281 pp. Illus.

A summary of the accomplishments of the regime and its programs. DLC LNHT

1015 *Páginas para la historia: juicios de la clase obrera*. Guatemala: Guatemala Artística, 1917. 117 pp. Illus.

A detailed résumé of the works of the Estrada Cabrera regime, with appropriate illustrations, signed by "the working class of Guatemala" and acclaiming his efforts. BNG

1016 Palacios, Julio E. *La "huelga" de 1944*. Guatemala: Ministerio de Educación Pública, 1950. 54 pp.

An account of the 1944 strike at the Normal School, by a professor at this institution, emphasizing the role of its students in the political movements and in the university student movement that led to the fall of the Ubico regime. Provides an interesting viewpoint, as most accounts of the era focus on the university and say little about the role of the other schools. BNG

1017 Palencia, Oscar Arturo. *Con los brazos abiertos: poemas, 1959-1961*. Guatemala: Editorial Universitaria, 1967. 89 pp. Illus.

(Palencia, Oscar Arturo)
A series of poems written between 1959 and 1961 that focus on Guatemalan themes and reflect the violence and disillusion of that era. DLC BNG

1018   _____. Recuento de poesía, 1969-1974.
Guatemala: Editorial Universitaria, 1977. 154 pp.
A revolutionary statement in the form of a series of impassioned poems depicting the nation, imprisonment, exile, and other aspects of the frustration of the supporters of the revolution of 1944-54. BNG

1019   Palma Sandoval, Alvaro Enrique. Cien años de Zacapa y sus antecedentes históricos.
Guatemala: Ministerio de Educación Pública, 1973. 409 pp. Biblio., illus., maps, tables.
A compilation of material about the department of Zacapa. The first part focuses on geography, history, and current statistics; the remainder of the volume traces the various services presently available in the department, noting their foundation and development, and reprints various municipal acts and documents relating to them. Such items as drinking water, rail service, the market, the slaughterhouse, etc., are considered. There are also chapters detailing current regulations and discussing significant events, such as visits to the area by presidents and foreign dignitaries. LNHT

1020   _____. Huité: pequeña monografía.
Guatemala: Ministerio de Educación Pública, 1960. 102 pp. Biblio., illus., maps.
A brief history of the origins and development of a town recently elevated to the status of municipio in the province of Zacapa. Includes physical setting, formation, services, economy, and customs. DLC

1021   _____. Monografía de Mixco. Guatemala: Imprenta Hispania, n.d. 52 pp. Biblio., illus., maps.
A very brief physical description, sketch of the history of the town, and discussion of some of its folklore. DLC LNHT BNG

1022   _____. Monografía mínima del departamento de Jutiapa. Guatemala: Imprenta Real, 1959. 104 pp. Biblio., illus.
Briefly lists the principal features, statistics, and facilities of each municipio of the state. DLC

1023   Palma y Palma, César Augusto. El bayo corredor de los Flandes: cuentos camperos del Suchitán y sus laderas. Guatemala: Imprenta Eros, 1970. 214 pp. Appendixes.
A collection of short stories about the eastern region of Guatemala, specifically Suchitán, seeking to capture the local spirit and culture. The author emphasizes the existence of a unique cooperative spirit in the community, which transcends class lines. The stories deal with all aspects of town and rural life, its trials, tribulations, joys, and heroes. DLC LNHT

1024   Palmieri, José Alfredo. Terror rojo en Guatemala. Guatemala: Imprenta Norte, 1954. 14 pp. Illus.
Red Terror in Guatemala. n.p., n.d.
The editor of El Espectador of Guatemala City gives his version of the misdeeds and tortures of the Arbenz regime, accompanied by photos of victims. DLC LNHT

1025   Palomo, J. Antonio. Breves apuntes acerca de las riquezas agrícolas, comerciales é industriales, etc., que posee la República de Guatemala, América Central. Guatemala: Tipografía Nacional, 1910. 54 pp. Illus.
A brief summary of the situation in the nation in 1910, designed to attract foreign investment. Emphasizes the nation's stability, transportation facilities, and mineral wealth. A list of transportation links with the rest of the world and a list of the consular corps in the nation are appended. LNHT

1026   Paniagua Santizo, Benjamin. Vida y obra de militares ilustres: año del centenario de la Escuela Politécnica. Guatemala: Editorial del Ejército, 1973. 279 pp. Illus.
Despite its title, this volume is in fact a history and a eulogy of the role of the Escuela Politécnica in Guatemalan history, published as one of several works issued in honor of its centennial. It does include several brief chapters regarding various military officers significant in Guatemalan development, but they are incidental to the volume, and exclude all the well-known figures and ex-presidents. Lavishly illustrated with photos of the academy, the cadets, military officers, and troops in review. BNG

1027   Pardo Gallardo, José Joaquín, ed. Bibliografía del doctor Pedro Molina.
Guatemala: Ministerio de Educación Pública, 1954. 55 pp.
An alphabetical but unannotated list of books and journal and newspaper articles containing references to Pedro Molina. LNHT BNG

1028   _____. Índice de los documentos existentes en el Archivo General del Gobierno. Guatemala: Tipografía Nacional, 1936. 524 pp.
A detailed listing of the documents in the archivo that had been cataloged by 1936, providing details regarding a large portion of its holdings. Most of the documents pertain to the Colonial era and the nineteenth century. BNG

1029   Paredes, Lucas. Símbolos nacionales de Guatemala: obra declarada texto oficial para la enseñanza cívica. Guatemala: Tipografía Nacional, 1927. 127 pp. Illus.
A history of the Guatemalan flag, coat of arms, and the quetzal, detailing how each became a national symbol. The histories of the flag and coat of arms are most significant, indicating the changes, the various decrees that brought them about, and the reasons for them. Includes essays regarding the Indian and the marimba. DLC LNHT BNG

1030 Paredes Moreira, José Luís. <u>Estudios sobre</u> <u>reforma agraria en Guatemala: aplicación del</u> <u>decreto 900: Cuadro No. 1.</u> Guatemala: Universidad de San Carlos, 1964. 87 pp. Biblio., illus., maps, tables.

A brief study of the application of the 1953 agrarian-reform decree through 1954, when it was frozen by the revolution. Makes little comment, simply providing the facts and figures regarding the land seized and its distribution. Prints the texts of the laws stipulating the conditions of expropriation and lists the specific tracts of land, all of them belonging to the United Fruit Company and its subsidiaries. Includes lists of the numbers and distribution in each province of affected owners of unexploited land, to which the decree specifically applied. LNHT

1031 _____. <u>Reforma agraria: una experiencia en</u> <u>Guatemala.</u> Guatemala: Imprenta Universitaria, 1963. ix, 195 pp. Biblio., maps, tables.

A survey of the program of the Arbenz regime, which the author views sympathetically as a practical and potentially effective approach to the problem. Notes that any such program needs to set flexible standards that allow variances by province in the size of land parcels, according to fertility and land usage, so as to avoid minifundia. He feels that the 1953 effort was well designed and gave sufficient attention to financing and technical assistance within the limits of the national resources, and notes that the termination of the program in 1954 left the nation still confronting the problem. He characterizes the agrarian-reform programs since 1954 as confused and changing too frequently to be effective. DLC LNHT

1032 Paret-Limardo de Vela, Lise. <u>Folklore musical</u> <u>de Guatemala.</u> Guatemala: Tipografía Nacional, 1962. 54 pp. Illus.

A brief essay regarding the regional music of Guatemala and the instrumentation and verses characteristic of each sector of the nation, with illustrations, followed by a collection of music and words for the folk songs collected by the author. DLC LNHT

1033 Partido Guatemalteco del Trabajo. <u>El camino</u> <u>de la revolución guatemalteca.</u> Mexico: Ediciones de Cultura Popular, 1972. 150 pp.

The official program of the Guatemalan communist party and its version of conditions in Guatemala, continuing the call for armed struggle and support of the guerrillas, though noting that the forms of the revolutionary struggle may vary with the situation of the moment. Includes the usual denunciations of the classes, the oligarchy, and the imperialists, as well as support of international communist stands. LNHT

1034 _____. <u>La intervención norteamericana en</u> <u>Guatemala y el derrocamiento del régimen</u> <u>democrático.</u> Guatemala: n.p., 1955. 62 pp.

The Guatemalan Communist party's version of the events of 1954, condemning Yankee imperialism and the United Fruit Company and accusing Honduras of committing aggression against Guatemala, while recounting the principles of the Arbenz regime and extolling its effort to throw off the yoke of foreign corporations through its agrarian-reform program. TxU

1035 _____. <u>Situación y perspectivas de la</u> <u>revolución guatemalteca.</u> Mexico: Published by the Party, 1968. 35 pp.

The Guatemalan Communist party's version of Guatemalan history and current problems, with its platform, advocating revolutionary struggle and support of the guerrillas, citing such examples as Russia, Vietnam, and Cuba. The problems of doctrinaire political positions in regard to current events are illustrated by the passages dealing with the capitalist-imperialist plot to impoverish the small nations by depressing world coffee prices. LNHT

1036 Partido Liberal. <u>Gratitud y lealtad:</u> <u>manifestaciones con motivo del aniversario de</u> <u>la gloriosa revolución del 71.</u> Guatemala: Tipografía Nacional, 1907. 244 pp.

A collection of pledges of loyalty and congratulations to General Manuel Estrada Cabrera from various towns, individuals, and entities, on the anniversary of the triumph of the 1871 Liberal revolution. LNHT

1037 Partido Liberal Progresista. <u>Dos lustros de</u> <u>obra sanitaria en la República de Guatemala.</u> Guatemala: Partido Liberal Progresista, 1942. 189 pp. Illus., maps, tables.

A detailed and lavishly illustrated account of the health program of the Ubico regime, emphasizing the expansion of services and construction of new facilities. Contains charts and graphs detailing the efforts to reach into the rural areas and the services available, and photos of the showpiece facilities. DLC LNHT BNG

1038 _____. <u>Guatemala en 1943: álbum gráfico.</u> Guatemala: Partido Liberal Progresista, 1943. 290 pp. Illus., maps.

A collection of photos of the public-works projects of the Ubico administration, with brief laudatory descriptions, compiled by his party. DLC

1039 _____. <u>La obra del general Ubico: asilo de</u> <u>ancianos.</u> Guatemala: Partido Liberal Progresista, 1940. 31 pp. Illus.

An account of the campaign Ubico led to raise money for the construction of a new old-folks home, with photos of the building and its facilities. DLC

1040 _____. <u>Ramo de Comunicaciones: labor</u> <u>realizada en la administración del señor</u> <u>general de división don Jorge Ubico,</u> <u>Presidente de la República de Guatemala,</u> <u>durante los años de 1931 a 1941.</u> Guatemala: Partido Liberal Progresista, 1941. 413 pp. Illus., maps.

An official summary of the Ubico regime's programs in the communications field,

(Partido Liberal Progresista)
emphasizing the completion of the "Communications Palace" to house its offices and telegraph facilities. Provides descriptions and
maps of the new lines, the distribution of
service, and the growth of the agency, covering telegraph, telephone, postal services,
etc. Contains lavish illustrations of the
personnel and facilities. DLC LNHT BNG

1041 _____. Seis años de gobierno presidido por
el general Jorge Ubico: la directiva del
Partido Liberal Progresista presenta a la
consideración nacional una relación sucinta y
gráfica de la obra gubernativa realizada de
1931 a 1936. Guatemala: Tipografía Nacional,
1937. 392 pp. Illus., maps.
Yet another official compilation of Ubico's
public works projects, with laudatory text and
suitable photos. DLC LNHT

1042 _____. Ubico: el actual gobernante de
Guatemala; su obra y sus calumniadores.
Guatemala: Imprenta El Liberal Progresista,
1933. 180 pp.
An official party portrayal of Ubico during
the early years of his regime, attempting to
capture his personality and dynamism and show
him as "sympatico," though of course doing so
in flattering terms and refuting his critics
by presenting him in a different light than
that sometimes seen by the public. The emphasis is on his patriotism, his concern for his
people, and his ambitions for his nation. DLC

1043 _____. Vías de comunicación, síntesis de la
obra de vialidad desarrollada por el gral.
Jorge Ubico, presidente de la república de
Guatemala; carreteras, puentes, canales:
siete mil kilómetros de carreteras en ocho
años. Guatemala: Tipografía Nacional, 1941.
415 pp. Illus., maps, tables.
An official publication, with illustrations
and maps, tracing the road-construction and
transportation programs of the Ubico regime.
Since highways were a passion with Ubico and
the construction program was one of his principal legacies to the nation, there was much
to be acclaimed, and the party publication
contains lavish praise for and numerous references to the caudillo's personal involvement
and effort and the contribution the roads,
bridges, and canals made to the national
economy. DLC LNHT BNG

1044 Partido Nacional de Trabajadores. Partido
Nacional de Trabajadores al pueblo de
Guatemala. Guatemala: Sánchez & de Guise,
1946. 191 pp.
The platform and ideological statement of
the Guatemalan labor party, published shortly
after its emergence during the Revolution of
1944. Provides a lengthy exposition of the
nation's ills, as seen by the party, and its
program for change. LNHT BNG

1045 Partido Revolucionario. Así se hace
revolución. Guatemala: Partido
Revolucionario, n.d. [1968]. Pages
unnumbered. Illus.

A propaganda piece by the official party,
detailing the accomplishments of the government of Julio Méndez Montenegro. Aimed at the
general populace, it presents the program and
its accomplishments in the form of cartoons
and drawings. Very brief accompanying narration, in large print, highlights the campaign
to eradicate illiteracy, which is described as
a national problem. LNHT

1046 Paul, Benjamin David. La vida de un pueblo
indígena de Guatemala. Guatemala: Ministerio
de Educación Pública, 1959. 67 pp.
Though listed as a special issue of the
Seminario de Integración Sociales Cuadernos,
this is a separate volume in which a study
originally published in 1950 in English in
Patterns for Modern Living is translated into
Spanish for the first time. It provides a
comprehensive description of folk culture,
customs, and life-styles in the village of San
Pedro La Laguna on Lake Atitlán in Guatemala.
Subjects treated include childhood, courtship
and marriage, the family, death, and social
organization, all based on the author's fieldwork in the village and drawing on his personal observations in this isolated village.
Dates of the research are not provided. DLC
LNHT

1047 Paul, Lois, and Benjamin D. Paul. Cambios en
los modelos de casamiento en una comunidad
guatemalteca del altiplano. Guatemala:
Ministerio de Educación Pública, 1966. 36 pp.
Notes.
This article examining San Pedro La Laguna
in Solalá was originally published in the
Southwestern Journal of Anthropology in 1963.
It compares the new and old styles of courtship and marriage, noting the social implications of the changes. BNG

1048 Payne, Walter. A Central American Historian:
José Milla (1822-1882). Gainesville:
University of Florida, Press, 1957. vi, 77
pp. Biblio., notes. Reprint. New York:
Kraus Reprint, 1972. vi, 77 pp. Biblio.,
notes.
An analysis of the career and writings of
Guatemalan Conservative historian and literary
figure José Milla, focusing on his transformation from a romantic novelist to a national
historian and discussing the events that influenced his work. DLC

1049 Paz Solórzano, Juan. Historia del Señor
Crucificado de Esquipulas, de su santuario:
romerías; antigua provincia eclesiástica de
Chiquimula de la Sierra y actual vicaría
foránea; como también de otras muchas cosas
dignas de saberse: todos estos datos han sido
recogidos por el actual capellán del
santuario. 2 vols. Guatemala: Imprenta
Arenales Hijos, 1914-16. 129, 33 pp. Index,
illus. 2d ed. Guatemala: Unión Tipográfica,
1949. 218 pp. Illus.
A history of the devotion to the "Black
Christ" of Esquipulas, written by the chaplain
of the shrine, detailing the belief, the construction of the church, the devotees of the

cult, and the various miracles credited to it, with extensive photos of the church. The title varies slightly in the second volume, and the second edition combining the two volumes uses a somewhat different wording: Historia del Santo Cristo de Esquipulas. TxU

1050 Paz y Paz, Alberto. "Lampocoy" y "Taguayní": historia de mi fuga. San José: Unión Tipográfía, 1936. 159 pp.

The memoirs and commentaries of a former Guatemalan Supreme Court justice and minister of gobernación, written in the form of letters to his wife from exile after he fled from the Ubico regime in 1934. The comments describe his travels and problems and provide his view of the situation in Guatemala. This he manages with some balance, for although he is critical of the Ubico regime and condemns what he considers its oppressive methods, unlike most exiles he notes that Ubico is not the first Guatemalan president to employ such methods, and that Guatemala is scarcely the only country characterized by such governments. The memoirs detail the author's flight and stay in El Salvador, Honduras, Nicaragua, and finally Costa Rica. DLC LNHT BNG

1051 Paz y Paz, Roberto. Sin coco roneles. Guatemala: Editorial Landívar, 1970. 48 pp.

A series of short essays using irony and ridicule to describe the life of a military officer serving a dictatorship. Comments sarcastically upon the life of the upper class and military officers who comprise the beneficiaries of the regime. BNG

1052 Paz y Paz G., Leonor. La mujer de pelo largo. Guatemala: Editorial Landívar, 1967. 202 pp.

A novel focusing on the problems of the poor and criticizing the church by contrasting the lives of the clerics with the stark poverty of the bulk of the populace. DLC

1053 Pellecer, Carlos Manuel. ¡Camino equivocado, Che! Guatemala: Editorial del Ejército, 1971. 297 pp.

A collection of essays written during 1970 and 1971 in various places, indicating the author's thoughts about the state of Latin American revolutions and terrorism. Though sympathetic to the objectives of the revolutionaries, the author betrays frustration with terrorist tactics, which tend to backfire by alienating public opinion and forcing the supporters of the system to coalesce to defend it. He is particularly critical of the terrorism in Guatemala against the regime of his friend Julio César Méndez Montenegro. BNG

1054 _____. Llamarada en la montaña. Guatemala: Tipografía Nacional, 1947. 104 pp.

A series of brief impassioned essays denouncing the Ubico regime, focusing on brutality and the oppression of the peasants; written from exile in Mexico by a young leftist student who later embraced and then rejected communism, and who was an adherent of the revolution of 1944-54. LNHT BNG

1055 _____. Memoria en dos geografías. Mexico: B. Costa-Amic, 1964. 521 pp. Index.

The memoirs of a well-known Guatemalan leftist politician and sociologist. He recounts his childhood in Antigua, Guatemala, and his youth during the Ubico dictatorship, which shaped his views and led to his political sympathy with the peons, his exile in Mexico, where he served as a rural schoolteacher, his support for the Guatemalan opposition to the dictatorship, and his reaction to the 1944 revolution, which he later served as a member of the 1945 Constituent Assembly. The account of the 1944 uprising is clearly secondhand. DLC BNG

1056 _____. Renuncia al comunismo. Mexico: B. Costa-Amic, 1963. 127 pp. 6th ed. Mexico: Costa-Amic, 1967. 127 pp.

An impassioned statement by a former member of the Guatemalan Communist party's directorate, breaking with communism, denouncing the failures of the Castro revolution in Cuba and the Soviet repression of the East European revolts as betrayals of slogans and of the hopes of the populace and as impositions of tyranny. LNHT BNG

1057 _____. Tierra ancha y rebelde. Guatemala: Tipografía Nacional, 1948. 115 pp.

A well-known Guatemalan political figure associated with the 1944 revolution provides an account of the rural Indians and their status, with historical allusions to Colonial days designed to explain their subjugation and neglect, stressing the role of education in providing the means of uplifting their status. DLC BNG

1058 Pepper, Charles Melville. Guatemala: The Country of the Future. Washington, D.C.: Legation of Guatemala, 1906. 80 pp. Illus.

A physical description emphasizing resources and future possibilities, along with a brief account of the then-current situation and the policies of the government of Manuel Estrada Cabrera, praising his actions. Includes lists of current officials. DLC LNHT

1059 Pepper B., José Vicente. Soviet's Claws on Central America: Las garras del Soviet sobre Centro América. Ciudad Trujillo, Dominican Republic: Papelera Industrial Dominicana, 1948. 74 pp.

A series of exposé-type articles, originally published in La Nación of Ciudad Trujillo, charging that the Arévalo government is part of a Soviet plot to subvert all of Central America as a means of gaining control of the Panama Canal. The text is published in both Spanish and English, and includes charges and innuendoes regarding the involvement of Arévalo and communist agents in various problems throughout the isthmus. DLC LNHT

1060 Peralta Méndez, Carlos Enrique. Política económica del gobierno militar. Guatemala: Editorial del Ejército, 1966. 170 pp. Illus.

A summary report of the economic policies of the Peralta government, prepared by the

minister of economy, detailing the regime's
various programs, with excerpts from appropriate decrees and official reports. BNG

1061 Pérez, J.P. El Lic. Estrada Cabrera y el
arreglo de la hacienda pública en Guatemala.
Tapachula, Mexico: n.p., 1899.
    A reply to charges in the Mexican newspaper
El Universal, which the author contends ma-
ligned Guatemalan president Manuel Estrada
Cabrera, defending the latter's financial
policies.

1062 Pérez Maldonado, Raúl [Stelio Spino, psued.].
Por opeustos rumbos. Guatemala: Tipografía
Nacional, 1964. 147 pp.
    Part of a series of "novelas de costumbres
guatemaltecas," but in fact a work of social
protest rather than costumbrismo. Set in
Guatemala and using the local idiom, it focuses on the problems of the poor, their
exploitation by the upper class and by officials, and on the corruption and abuses of
power. Officialdom is portrayed as oppressors
using arbitrary tactics to take advantage of
those under their control, indifferent to the
problems and lives of those around them. DLC
LNHT

1063 _____. La sangre no es azul.
Chichicastenango: Editorial San Antonio,
1964. 277 pp.
    See previous item. DLC LNHT

1064 _____. Un virtuoso del arte. Guatemala:
Tipografía Nacional, 1964. 136 pp.
    See item GU1062. DLC LNHT

1065 Pérez Valenzuela, Pedro. Santo Tomás de
Castilla: apuntes para la historia de las
colonizaciones en la Costa Atlántica.
Guatemala: Tipografía Nacional, 1956. 259
pp. Biblio., notes.
    A history of the various efforts to colo-
nize Santo Tomás on the Guatemalan Caribbean
coast, from Colonial times to the end of the
nineteenth century, with the focus on the
latter era. The volume, based on secondary
works and documentary research in the Archivo
General de Centroamérica, traces in considerable detail the efforts at colonization by the
Spaniards, British, and Belgians. It also
analyzes the role of the area as a port and
transportation center for the nation, and the
efforts to link it effectively with the heart-
land of the plateau. DLC LNHT BNG

1066 La personalidad del general Don Jorge Ubico:
algunos de sus rasgos biográficos con dos
pasajes anecdóticos y génesis del Partido
Progresista. Guatemala: n.p., 1931. xxvii,
124 pp.
    A reedition of Gustavo Schwartz's Columnas
del progresismo. A brief vitalike listing of
Ubico's career, a statement by him, and several short endorsements by others comprise the
initial twenty-seven pages. The contents have
little relation to the title. DLC LNHT

1067 Pevtsov, IUriĭ Aleksandrovich. Migel' Ankhel'
Asturias: biobibliograficheskii ukazatel'
[Miguel Ángel Asturias: A biobibliographical
index]. Moscow: Vsesoiuznyi kn. palata,
1960. 26 pp.
    A listing and brief synopsis of Asturias's
works, with emphasis on their condemnation of
capitalism and imperialism. DLC

1068 Piedra Santa Arandi, Rafael. Introducción a
los problemas económicos de Guatemala.
Guatemala: Editorial Universitaria, 1971.
210 pp. Notes, illus., tables. 2d ed.
Guatemala: Ediciones Superiores, 1977. 227
pp. Notes, illus., tables.
    A basic text for the university level.
Details the economic history of the nation and
the principal economic sectors, with accompanying excerpts from documents and laws. The
emphasis is on the post-1944 era, though earlier eras are discussed to show the origins of
the questions and the economic patterns. LNHT
BNG

1069 Pilli, Emile R. 80 años de quina en
Guatemala: un relato histórico del cultivo de
cinchona de 1860-1942. Guatemala: Tipografía
Nacional, 1943. 67 pp. Biblio., illus.,
maps.
    A history, from Colonial days to the pres-
ent, of the cultivation of the plant from
which quinine is produced. Traces its origin
and use in Peru, its spread to Guatemala, and
the growth of production in that nation. The
study clearly reflects the efforts to promote
production during World War II, at the urging
of the United States government, to replace
supplies cut off by the conflict and to aid
troops in the Pacific. DLC

1070 Pilon, Marta. Miguel Ángel Asturias:
semblanza para el estudio de su vida y obra con
una selección de poemas y prosas. Guatemala:
Librería Proa, 1968. 398 pp. Biblio., illus.
    A seventy-page biography of the author,
with a bibliography of his works and their
various editions, followed by his speech
accepting the Nobel Prize, and an anthology of
his works. DLC LNHT

1071 _____. S.O.S., Guatemala se envenena.
Guatemala: Editorial del Ejército, 1964.
46 pp.
    An ecological pamphlet much like those
circulated in other countries, decrying the
extensive use of pesticides and the actual and
potential damage to the nation, its vegetation, and its people. DLC

1072 Pineda C., Felipe. Para la historia de
Guatemala: datos sobre el gobierno del
licenciado Manuel Estrada Cabrera. Mexico:
n.p., 1902. 56 pp.
    An attack on Estrada Cabrera, contending
that he has failed to deliver any of his
promised reforms and that his rule has been
disastrous for the country. Also discusses
his rise to power, charging chicanery. The
volume was published in exile by an opponent

who was released from prison by an amnesty
decreed by Estrada Cabrera. DLC

1073 Pineda de Mont, Manuel, ed. <u>Recopilación de</u>
<u>las leyes de Guatemala: compuesta y arreglada</u>
<u>por don Manuel Pineda de Mont, á virtud de</u>
<u>orden especial del gobierno supremo de la</u>
<u>república</u>. 3 vols. Guatemala: Imprenta de
la Paz, 1869-72.
    Volume 1 covers the years from independence
to 1871, with subsequent annual volumes for
the 1870s. Includes some explanatory footnotes and the text of the collected laws,
arranged by topic and year. Subsequent editions, by other compilers, have appeared periodically and are listed under the government,
by title, which constantly added to and
updated the earlier series, expanding the coverage to twenty-five volumes in 1924, fifty-
one volumes by 1935, and ninety-two volumes by
1970. LNHT

1074 Pineda Pivaral, Eduardo. <u>Monografía: Santa</u>
<u>Cruz Chiquimulilla</u>. Guatemala: Tipografía
Nacional, 1969. 502 pp. Illus., maps.
    A current description of the town, with
detailed discussion of its culture, legends,
and customs, and of the Indian influence.
Histories of the Canal of Chiquimulilla and of
the various municipalities are also included.
DLC LNHT BNG

1075 _____. <u>Relatos de Chiquimulilla</u>. Guatemala:
Ministerio de Educación Pública, 1977.
121 pp.
    A series of local legends and stories
relating to the author's hometown of
Chiquimulilla, and to life there. The themes
are disparate but serve to illustrate the rich
legacy of local legends in this region. BNG

1076 Piñol y Batres, José. <u>Conferencias</u>.
Guatemala: Ayestas, 1919.
    A series of nine sermons by a bishop, open-
ing with general and religious themes but
becoming increasingly more political as the
series progresses, condemning egotism, dishonesty, abuse of power, and misuse of funds,
and calling for liberty, a new moralism, and
deliverance of the nation from its present
state. Clearly part of the propaganda of the
opponents of the then-decaying regime of
Estrada Cabrera. BNG

1077 Pinto Soria, J.C. <u>Guatemala en la década de</u>
<u>la independencia</u>. Guatemala: Editorial
Universitaria, 1978. 52 pp.
    BNG

1078 Planas-Suárez, Simón. <u>Condición legal de los</u>
<u>extranjeros en Guatemala</u>. Madrid: Editorial
Reus, 1919. 62 pp.
    A brief summary of then-current Guatemalan
law regarding foreign residents of that nation, arranged by subject and detailing the
regulations regarding all phases of life and
activities. DLC

1079 Poitevin, René. <u>El proceso de</u>
<u>industrialización en Guatemala</u>. San José:
EDUCA, 1977. 321 pp. Biblio., tables.
    BNG

1080 Polanco, hijo, D., and G.A. Polanco. <u>Perfiles</u>
<u>biográficos e históricos del licenciado don</u>
<u>Manuel Estrada Cabrera</u>. Guatemala:
Tipografía Siguere, 1898. iii, 26 pp. Illus.
    A series of articles that originally
appeared in the <u>Diario de Occidente</u> of
Quezaltenango, detailing the career of Estrada
Cabrera as he entered the presidency and
praising his accomplishments. DLC

1081 Polo Sifontes, Francis. <u>Mariano Gálvez:</u>
<u>éxitos y fracaso de su gobierno</u>. Guatemala:
Instituto de Antropología e Historia, 1979.
42 pp. Biblio.
    A brief overview of the Gálvez administra-
tion, seeking to demonstrate both accomplishments and shortcomings, stressing that despite
good intentions it relied excessively on force
and imposition, and that the radical changes
it attempted destabilized the nation and an-
gered the peasants, which led to the rise of
Carrera, who received peasant support. DLC
BNG

1082 Ponce de Veliz, María Magdalena. <u>Humedad,</u>
<u>verdor y aroma: folklore de un pueblo alegre</u>.
Guatemala: Editorial Landívar, 1965. 44 pp.
Illus.
    A collection of poetry and short stories
based on the folklore of Cobán in Alta
Verapaz, seeking to capture the spirit and
lore of the author's native region. Includes
laudatory tracts, description, and accounts of
customs, dances, and celebrations. DLC LNHT

1083 Ponciano, Juan Francisco. <u>El látigo</u>.
Guatemala: Editorial Landívar, 1962. 399 pp.
Illus.
    A collection of popular Guatemalan jokes
and humorous tales that provide a glimpse of
Guatemalan humor and outlook. The stories
make maximum use of local idioms and terminology. BNG

1084 Popenoe, Dorothy Hughes. <u>Santiago de los</u>
<u>Caballeros de Guatemala</u>. Cambridge, Mass.:
Harvard University Press, 1933. xiv, 74 pp.
Illus., maps. 2d ed. Cambridge, Mass.:
Harvard University Press, 1940. 74 pp.
Index, illus.
    A history of Antigua Guatemala, designed
for tourists, seeking to provide them with
background; accompanied by drawings by the
author, who resided in Guatemala for several
years. DLC LNHT BNG

1085 Poppe, K.H. <u>Der Bananenkrieg</u>. Reinbek,
Germany: Rowohtt, 1960. 288 pp.
    An account of the 1954 conflict in
Guatemala, sympathizing with the revolutionary
regimes and portraying the incident as a case
of the United Fruit Company financing a revolt
to regain control of its lands, thereby preserving what was in effect its own empire, as
well as Yankee dominance. NN

1086   Prado Solares, Miguel. La ley fuga. 2 vols.
Guatemala: Unión Tipográfica, 1947-49. 133,
79 pp.

A compilation of rulings by the Supreme
Court, under the presidency of the author,
acting under the authority of the Revolutionary government's decree authorizing the court
to review all cases from the days of the Ubico
regime. Details the cases considered and the
actions removing charges against the victims
and freeing those still in prison, but focuses
principally on those subjected to the ley
fuga, clearing their records and calling for
review of the circumstances of their deaths.
LNHT

1087   Protestas que los pueblos de la república
hicieron contra la Asamblea Legislativa de
1886. Guatemala: Imprenta de El Progreso,
1887. vii, 401 pp.

A collection of petitions from the various
towns of Guatemala to President General Manuel
L. Barillas that were orchestrated by the
government and used by it as evidence of a
mass movement to provide the basis for the
dissolution in 1877 of the legislature, which
had opposed the executive, and the convocation
of a Constituent Assembly to write a new constitution. DLC

1088   Puydt, Remi de. Colonisation: rapport
officiel. Brussels: n.p., n.d. 203 pp.
Maps.

A report to the Belgian Colonization Company regarding Central America, Guatemala in
particular, tracing the history of colonization there, providing contemporary data about
the country, its economy, and its future prospects, and urging colonization of the region.
DLC LNHT

1089   Quezaltenango: álbum de cincuentenario.
Guatemala: n.p., 1952. 68 pp. Illus.

A publication commemorating the fiftieth
anniversary of the earthquake that destroyed
the city in 1902, with photos and commentary
discussing the damage and the reconstruction
that followed. BNG

1090   Quezaltenango, Corporación Municipal de.
Homenaje al alcalde mártir Dr. Roberto Molina.
Quezaltenango: Talleres Tipográficos, 1963.

A brief account of the life of José Roberto
Molina, who served as mayor of Quezaltenango
in 1840, with a passionate account of his
death at the hands of Carrera when the Conservatives seized control of the nation, particularly of the western region, during the collapse of the Federation and the suppression of
the state of Los Altos.

1091   Quien: diccionario biográfico Guatemala
(Libro de oro). Guatemala: n.p., 200 pp.
Illus.

Brief biographical sketches, in the style
of Who's Who, providing basic information
about current figures in the country. Only
this one volume was published. DLC LNHT

1092   Quiñónes, Alfredo. Anécdotas históricas del
caudillo unionisa general Justo Rufino
Barrios, reformador de Guatemala. Guatemala:
Tipografía Marroquín Hnos., 1921. 40 pp.

A collection of anecdotes, previously published in the Guatemalan press, about the
career and public life of Justo Rufino
Barrios, designed to show him as a person and
viewing his actions sympathetically. LNHT

1093   Quiñónez, José A. Directorio general de
la República de Guatemala. Guatemala:
Tipografía Nacional, 1929. 561 pp. Index,
illus.

A compilation of general information about
the nation, its history, geography, and economy, as well as tourist facilities, places to
see, and similar items. DLC

1094   Quintana, Roberto R. Apuntes sobre el
desarrollo monetario de Guatemala. Guatemala:
Banco de Guatemala, 1971. xv, 808 pp.

A detailed history of Guatemalan monetary
and financial policy from pre-Columbian times
to the present, emphasizing the role of such
policy in the nation's economic development,
with consideration of the nation's various
financial crises. DLC

1095   Quintana Díaz, Víctor. Inversiones
extranjeras en Guatemala. Guatemala:
Universidad de San Carlos, 1973. 346 pp.
Biblio., tables.

An extensive compilation of data and statistics about foreign investment in Guatemala,
focusing on the years since 1950, though with
some historical background. Includes lists of
all Guatemalan companies with foreign capital,
percentages, identification of parent companies, and figures regarding the significance
of particular companies in the various economic sectors and productive fields, as well
as breakdowns by province. The author seeks
to detail the role of foreign capital and the
predominance of Yankee capital, noting that
the government has done little to keep track
of, much less regulate, such investment. He
contends that each new constitution granted
further concessions to foreign capital, that
there are few restrictions on such investment
and that such investment tends to dominate the
economic sector or activity in which it is
engaged. While the implication of the study
is that regulation is needed, it offers no
specific recommendations. LNHT

1096   Quintana Rodas, J. Epaminodas. El agro
ubérrimo pasional y trágico. Guatemala:
Tipografía Nacional, 1968. 237 pp. Illus.

A novel of violence and rural life in
Guatemala, focusing on the trials and tribulations of the campesinos. Although the story
is set in the German-owned coffee fincas of
the 1930s and there is mention of the alle-
giance of the landowners to the Nazi movement,
the focus is on local events, the lot of the
peasants, and their mistreatment by the dominant landowners. The plot includes an unsuccessful attempt to organize the laborers,
which serves to relate the frustration and the

(Quintana Rodas, J. Epaminodas)
lack of redress of grievances that ultimately
lead to violence. DLC LNHT BNG

1097 _____. Historia de la generación de 1920.
Guatemala: Tipografía Nacional, 1971. 749
pp. Illus.
A eulogistic account of a generation of
literary and political leaders who studied
together at the University of San Carlos, by
one of its members, tracing their accomplishments and extolling their collective impact on
the nation. The emphasis is on their foundation of the University Students' Association
and the student journal Stadium, their initial
role in the overthrow of the Estrada Cabrera
regime in 1920, and particularly their role in
providing much of the leadership for the 1944
revolution and the succeeding reformist governments. There is also consideration of
their political involvement during the turbulent 1920s and 1930s and their opposition to
the Ubico regime, as well as consideration of
the journalistic, scientific, and literary
accomplishments of the various individuals.
Includes brief biographical sketches of the
individuals involved as well as discussion of
their collective activities. DLC LNHT

1098 Radford, Luis N. Las cartas de la Meches.
Guatemala: Editorial San Antonio, 1965. 90
pp. Illus.
This novel is written in the form of a
series of letters from a young peasant girl to
her sister, in which she records impressions
of her first visit to contemporary Guatemala
City; this enables the author to comment on
the life-style and customs of the capital, as
well as on the differences between the lives
of members of the urban middle class and those
of the rural peons. DLC LNHT BNG

1099 _____. Rancho do Manaco. Guatemala:
Imprenta San Antonio, 1965. 241 pp. Illus.
2d ed. Guatemala: Ministerio de Educación
Pública, 1966. 241 pp.
A novel describing life in the Guatemalan
countryside, extolling the virtues of the
farmers and their relation to nature, as well
as the beauties of the country. DLC LNHT
BNG

1100 _____. Tinaja de cuentos. Guatemala:
Editorial Tiempo, 1960. 112 pp. Illus.
The first volume by a well-known Guatemalan
radio commentator and producer, this collection of short stories focuses on typically
Guatemalan folktales and expressions, capturing the varying regional traditions and the
local life-style, and using colloquial terminology appropriate to the regions of the
nation. Combines tales of the peculiarities
and typicalness of local life-styles with a
folkloric tradition and legends. DLC

1101 Raine, Alice. Eagle of Guatemala: Justo
Rufino Barrios, 1835-1885. New York:
Harcourt, Brace, 1947. ix, 229 pp.

A vividly written "fictionalized biography"
designed to acquaint the general reader with
Guatemala through the individual the author
considers its most outstanding hero. The
author claims that the book is "accurate in
its broad implications"; and hails Barrios
while comparing him to Abraham Lincoln. The
incidents and details are not necessarily
real, and there is no documentation, footnoting, or bibliography. DLC LNHT

1102 Ramírez, Ricardo. Lettres de Front
Guatémaltèque. Paris: François Maspero,
1970. 232 pp.
The viewpoint of the Marxist guerrillas
fighting in Guatemala during the presidency of
Mendez Montenegro, in the form of a series of
letters. Included are descriptions of combat,
discussion of the guerrillas, and their view
of the political situation. DLC

1103 Ramírez Colóm, José M. Reseña biográfica del
ilustrísimo y reverendísimo señor arzobispo de
Santiago de Guatemala don Ricardo Casanova y
Estrada. Guatemala: Sánchez & de Guise,
1896. 95 pp. Notes, illus.
A brief biography of a Guatemalan archbishop who served throughout much of the
Liberal reform and early twentieth century,
resulting in conflicts with the government and
a lengthy period of exile. The account, written by his secretary, provides the church
version of the events but focuses principally
on the individual, his service to the church,
and highlights of his career. Details his
activities in exile and provides information
about relations of the Guatemalan church with
Rome and the other Central American churches,
as well as with the local government. LNHT

1104 Ramírez Gutiérrez, Gustavo. Cinco aspectos de
la revolución del 20 de octubre 1944.
Guatemala: Imprenta del Servicio de
Comunicaciones, 1945. 31 pp. Illus.
A series of officially sponsored radio
programs over the government station, extolling the revolution. TxU

1105 Ramos, Plinio de Abreu. Foster Dulles e a
invasão da Guatemala. São Paulo: Editora
Fulogr, 1958. 157 pp.
A critique of the Yankee intervention in
Guatemala in 1954, extolling the reform efforts of the revolutionary regimes and condemning Yankee imperialism, seeing the entire
episode as indicative of capitalism's determination to dominate the Third World and prevent
Guatemala from joining the Afro-Asian bloc.
WU

1106 Raygada, Jorge. Democracia en Guatemala: 20
de octubre de 1944-15 de marzo de 1951.
Guatemala: Imprenta Hispania, 1951. 130 pp.
Illus.
A series of newspaper articles about the
Revolution of 1944 and the governments that
followed, through 1951. The original dates
and papers of publication are not indicated.
LNHT BNG

1107 Recinos, Adrián. Monografía del departamento de Huehuetenango. Guatemala: Tipografía Nacional, 1913. 269 pp. 2d ed. Guatemala: Ministerio de Educación Pública, 1954. xvi, 518 pp. Biblio., illus., maps, tables.

An excellent example of local history by a well-known Guatemalan scholar, political figure, and diplomat, this volume provides a detailed and well-researched account of the northwesternmost province of the nation. It recounts the history of the state as a whole and of each of the various municipalities in it, providing historical information and description of the current situation, population, and services. Includes topical treatment of items of general interest, and full description of physical features, as well as of flora and fauna. The second edition, revised, enlarged, and updated, retains the historical aspects. DLC LNHT BNG

1108 Reina, Rubén E. Continuidad de la cultura indígena en una comunidad guatemalteca. Guatemala: Ministerio de Educación Pública, 1959. 28 pp. Chinautla, a Guatemalan Indian Community: A Study in the Relationship of the Community Culture and National Change. New Orleans: MARI, 1960. 130 pp. Illus., maps.

A short essay, originally published in the Revista de Ciencias Sociales of Puerto Rico, discussing the impact of recent political events on an Indian town, Chinautla. It reveals the standard stereotypical image of Ubico, the revolution, and Castillo Armas, discussing only the benefits of the revolution and the faults of the other two, with little concrete evidence. DLC LNHT

1109 _____. The Law of the Saints: A Pokomam Pueblo and its Community Culture. Indianapolis: Bobbs-Merrill, 1966. xx, 338 pp. Index, biblio., illus., maps, tables. La ley de los Santos: un pueblo Pokomam y su cultura de comunidad. Guatemala: Ministerio de Educación Pública, 1973. 435 pp. Biblio., tables, appendixes.

An anthropological study of the Pokoman community of Chinautla, near Guatemala City, based on fieldwork conducted during 1953 and 1962. It details the life of a community of potters who live near the capital, sell their goods there and use its services, yet retain their Indian traditions at home and speak their own language as their first idiom. The discussion of the organizations of the Saints constitutes only one facet of a broad study of the values, customs, and life-styles of the people of this area, although the author concludes that the Law of the Saints is central to the preservation of their culture. DLC LNHT BNG

1110 _____. Urbanismo sin ciudad: orientación urbana en Flores, Petén. Guatemala: Ministerio de Educación Pública, 1967. 53 pp. Notes.

Considerations regarding the effect of the growth of Flores, Petén, and the introduction of patterns more typical of a city into an area with no real metropolis, in which the impact is confined to a small community. The author concludes that the mentality is indeed urban, although the life-style and physical setting are not. Originally published in Human Organization in 1964. DLC LNHT BNG

1111 Réti, Ervin. Háború a banánok földjén [War in the land of bananas]. Budapest: n.p., 1954. 39 pp.

A condemnation of the Yankee intervention in Guatemala in 1954.

1112 Revilla, Benedicto. Guatemala: el terremoto de los pobres. Madrid: Sedmay Ediciones, 1976. 257 pp. Biblio., illus.

A description of the 1976 Guatemalan earthquakes, indicating the location of the tremors and detailing the damage and the rescue efforts. DLC BNG

1113 Rey Soto, Antonio. Estampas guatemaltecas. Guatemala: Tipografía Nacional, 1929. 86 pp. Illus.

Descriptive essays in travelogue style, accompanied by lavish illustrations of contemporary Guatemala. Assembled for an exposition in Sevilla, it is designed to present an attractive image of Guatemala to the European. Includes a brief essay on notable Guatemalan writers. DLC LNHT BNG

1114 Reyes C., Consuelo. Recuerdos de Guatemala. San José: Imprenta Nacional, 1941. 44 pp. Illus.

A series of descriptive essays regarding a visit to Guatemala during 1940. Hails its progress, modernity, and the various public buildings, and discusses various tourist sites; extensively illustrated. DLC-LDS-903 BNCR

1115 Reyes Cardona, Julio Antonio. Organización de los Tribunales de Trabajo y Previsión Social de Guatemala: frente a los sistemas de México y Chile. Guatemala: Magistratura de Coordinación de Trabajo y Previsión Social, 1951. 74 pp.

A description of the newly formed labor courts that reflect the legislation of the revolutionary governments, with comparisons to the prevailing systems in Mexico and Chile. DLC

1116 Reyes Monroy, José Luís. Apuntes para una monografía de la Sociedad Económica de Amigos del País. Guatemala: Ministerio de Educación Pública, 1964. 297 pp. Illus.

An account of and collection of documents about the society, which flourished from 1794 through 1881, supplemented by a list of its published works. Most of the volume consists of excerpts of documents from the society and its meetings, reflecting its economic and social efforts and its inevitable involvement in the politics of the era. The society directed its efforts at promoting economic development through a wide range of efforts that included railroad proposals, aid to artisans,

(Reyes Monroy, José Luís)
and arrangement of exhibitions of Guatemalan products abroad. DLC LNHT BNG

1117 _____. Bibliografía de la imprenta en Guatemala. Guatemala: Ministerio de Educación Pública, 1969. 143 pp.
A chronological listing of 650 works published in Guatemala between 1769 and 1900 that the author feels were omitted from existing bibliographic studies. The list includes books, papers, and journals, with full publication information. DLC LNHT BNG

1118 _____. Bibliografía de los estudios geográficos de la República de Guatemala desde 1574 hasta nuestros días. Guatemala: Ministerio de Educación Pública, 1960. 70 pp.
An alphabetical listing, by author, with complete bibliographic information for some 500 items. Although focused on geography, it encompasses travelogues, archeological entries, and other items in fields related to geography, though the listings in these areas are somewhat arbitrary and there is no explanation of the basis for selection. Encompasses both books and periodical articles. DLC LNHT

1119 _____. Datos curiosos sobre la demarcación política de Guatemala. Guatemala: Tipografía Nacional, 1951. 189 pp.
A catalog of legislation relating to the fixing of the provincial and municipal boundaries within Guatemala, arranged chronologically, with narration and explanations to supplement the legal determinations. DLC LNHT

1120 _____. Laureles a la memorita del licenciado en derecho don Adrián Recinos. Guatemala: Tipografía Nacional, 1969. 117 pp. Illus.
A collection of speeches and newspaper commentaries eulogizing the contributions of a Guatemalan scholar, diplomat, and Liberal political figure, prepared on the occasion of his death in 1962. His career, which spanned the years from 1910 through 1962, included a lengthy tenure as his nation's representative in Washington during the 1920s, 1930s, and early 1940s. DLC LNHT BNG

1121 _____, ed. Origen y destino de "El Malacate" del año 1871. Guatemala: Ministerio de Educación Pública, 1971. 296 pp. Biblio.
This volume republished, in their entirety, the twenty-five issues of the newspaper El Malacate of San Marcos. The paper, edited by General Andrés Téllez, lasted from 26 August through 28 October 1871 and provides an account of the politics and struggles of the Liberal revolution in its efforts to seize power, seen through the eyes of a provincial supporter of Justo Rufino Barrios. DLC LNHT BNG

1122 Reyes Morales, Mario Roberto. La imprenta en Guatemala. Guatemala: Ministerio de Educación Pública, 1960. 78 pp. Illus.

A brief history of the principal printing houses and publishers in Guatemala, with biographical sketches of the individuals who played important roles in their development. Includes a chronological listing of printing houses, and a brief résumé of the principal periodicals. DLC LNHT BNG

1123 Reyes Narciso, Francisco O. Tupuy de cuentos. Guatemala: Editorial del Ejército, 1964. 124 pp. Illus.
A collection of short stories from Alta Verapaz, set in that area and using its modisms to preserve the local culture, drawing upon the legends and traditions of its folklore. The author, a native of the region, has won prizes in local competitions for his stories. The current collection is published with the endorsement of the Asociación Regional Altaverapacense, which seeks to preserve the local heritage and transmit it to the region's youth. Includes pieces dealing with all aspects of life, as well as religious tales and traditions based on the Indian heritage. DLC LNHT

1124 Reyes Ovalle, Nicolas. Uno, entre varios otros. Guatemala: Unión Tipográfica, 1947. 109 pp.
A political tract that warns of the dangers of communism, contending that it does not help the working class and advocating Christian values and cooperation as the key to the future. DLC BNG

1125 Rincón de Townson, Sonia. El destino sonríe. Guatemala: Ministerio de Educación Pública, 1961. 173 pp.
A novel based on the experiences of a tourist in Guatemala and her contacts with local citizens. BNG

1126 Rincón Menegazzo de MacDonald, Sonia. El silencio de las horas: la vida íntima de una primera dama. Guatemala: Ministerio de Educación Pública, 1975. 388 pp. Illus.
A biographical novel tracing the life of the wife of Colonel Carlos Castillo Armas and her role in his efforts to oppose the leftist revolutionary governments of the 1950s. Although the story is fictionalized, the names and places correspond to the actual exiles, arrests, political movements, unsuccessful uprisings, and the final success. BNG

1127 Ríos, Efraín de los. Ombres contra hombres: drama de la vida real. 2 vols. Mexico: El Libro Perfecto, 1945. 342 pp. Illus. 3d ed. Guatemala: Imprenta del Gobierno, 1962. 529 pp. Illus.
A sometime staff member who spent much of the Ubico regime in prison draws on his experiences to provide a highly critical account of the regime, and also furnishes a detailed description of the living hell inside the caudillo's prisons. Emphasis is placed on the brutality and pervasiveness of the security apparatus. DLC LNHT BNG

1128 Rivas, Valerio Ignacio. Vindicación que hace Valerio Ignacio Rivas sobre la impostura que el C. Marcario Rodas le suscitó en el departamento de Quezaltenango: infracciones cometidas por el juez de primera instancia de aquella ciudad, y avances de poder cometidos en su persona e intereses el que se dice gobierno provisorio de Los Altos. Guatemala: Imprenta del Gobierno, 1838. 30 pp.
A surveyor's commentary on his work in Los Altos. Denounces the local landowners for placing pressure on him during the survey, as part of their efforts to take over control of Indian communal land in that district. DLC

1129 Rivera Porres, Arnulfo. Semblanzas del pasado: Eliseo Martínez Zelada, radiotelegrafista, diplomática, escritor. Mexico: B. Costa-Amic, 1975. 217 pp. Illus.
A biography of a Guatemalan telegrafist who later served in the diplomatic service under the revolutionary regimes, designed to indicate the development of the Guatemalan telegraph service and the subject's role in the revolution. BNG

1130 Roberts, Bryan R. La educación y la ciudad en Guatemala. Guatemala: Ministerio de Educación Pública, 1971. 75 pp.
A preliminary study, part of the author's later larger works, describing the educational system in the capital, its limits, and the problems of reaching into the poor neighborhoods. BNG

1131 _____. Organizing Strangers: Poor Families in Guatemala City. Austin: University of Texas Press, 1973. xviii, 360 pp. Index, biblio., notes, tables.
A sociological and anthropological analysis of two poor barrios in Guatemala City, based on extensive field research and surveys conducted between 1966 and 1968 as part of a University of Texas program under the direction of Richard Adams. This study focuses on the plight of the poor migrants from the rural areas into the capital and the problems they face, studying their adaptations and reactions to the city. Included are details regarding slum housing, the search for jobs, the struggle for existence, neighborhood problems and organization, and the difficulties of arranging cooperative action among the slum residents. The author concludes that such individuals are worse off if they are integrated into the life of the capital, as this emphasizes their problems and enables them to be more effectively exploited by others. DLC LNHT

1132 _____. El protestantismo en dos barrios marginales de Guatemala. Guatemala: Ministerio de Educación Pública, 1967. 22 pp.
A brief study of two poor sections of the capital to examine the impact of Protestantism, using these areas as a sample. The author emphasizes the importance of the evangelical denominations in the growth of Protestantism, and examines the reasons for their success. DLC LNHT BNG

1133 Roca, José Antonio de la, and Efraín Arriola Porres. Los que fueron de viris illustribus urbis: biografías mínimas de varones ilustres, 1777-1951. 6 vols. Quezaltenango: Tipografía Occidental, 1953-. Pages unnumbered.
The initial volume consisted of thirty-one brief biographical sketches of illustrious citizens of Quezaltenango, encompassing the individuals installed in the "Hall of Honor" of Guatemala's second-largest city. Subsequent volumes continue the list. Those described come from different backgrounds and fields, and the arrangement is neither chronological nor alphabetical. The essays do provide basic data on significant figures in Guatemalan history, some well known and others more obscure. DLC

1134 Roca, Julio César de la. Biografía de un pueblo: síntesis monográfica de Quezaltenango; interpretación de su destino. Guatemala: Ministerio de Educación Pública, 1966. 431 pp. Index, notes, illus.
A history of the department of Quezaltenango, with a description of the background and development of the department and each of its towns and cities. Chapters consider geography and demography on the departmental level, while the résumé of each city summarizes its history, demography, economy, culture, architecture, urban plans, and services. DLC LNHT BNG

1135 _____. Biografías ilustres: compilación de los veintidós Botones de Oro (1961-1966) conferidos por la municipalidad de la ciudad de Quezaltenango. Guatemala: Editorial Casa de la Cultura de Occidente, 1967. 156 pp. Biblio., illus.
A collection of biographies of twenty-one individuals selected for the annual award by the Casa de la Cultura de Occidente in Xelajú in recognition of their contributions to the region's culture and its study. The brief biographical sketches are usually a few pages in length, with photographs. DLC LNHT

1136 _____. Tierranueva de Guatemala. Guatemala: Tipografía Nacional, 1965. 80 pp. Biblio., illus.
A description of the author's adventures in the Petén, including poems inspired by his visit, and some historical background. Mainly devoted to the physical attributes, climate, and future development possibilities. DLC LNHT BNG

1137 Rodas Barrios, Abelardo. Corazón adentro. Guatemala: Ediciones Revista de Guatemala, 1959. 46 pp. Index.
A collection of poetry with one portion emphasizing love poems and the other reflecting the author's social revolutionary orientation, emphasizing the exploitation of the workers and peasants and the need for reform. The author was a participant in the 1944 revolution and an affiliate of the Saker-Ti group. DLC

1138 Rodas Corzo, Ovidio. En el corazón de Zacapa: reportaje de un recorrido. Guatemala: El Imparcial, 1936. 45 pp. Illus.

A collection of articles, with illustrations, describing the impressions of a Guatemalan journalist who traveled through the region in 1936. He describes its then-current state and illustrates the changes brought by the Ubico regime and the improved facilities now available to the city. DLC LNHT

1139 Rodas Cruz, Manuel. El cooperativismo: el movimiento cooperativo en Guatemala y su legislación. Guatemala: Tipografía Nacional, 1954. 98 pp. Biblio.

Originally a thesis at the University of San Carlos, this volume discusses the cooperative movement theoretically, with comparisons to other nations, and then traces the history of the movement in Guatemala, with emphasis on the current law and presently existing cooperatives. DLC

1140 Rodas N., Favio, and Ovidio Rodas Corzo. Simbolismos (Maya Quichés) de Guatemala. Guatemala: Tipografía Nacional, 1938. 148 pp. Illus.
Chichicastenango: The Kiche Indians. Their History and Culture; Sacred Symbols of their Dress and Textiles. Guatemala: Unión Tipográfica, 1940. 155 pp.

A discussion of the typical clothing, weaving, and designs of Santo Tomás Chichicastenango that emphsizes the symbolic and traditional meaning of present-day designs. The English edition is updated and lists as third author Laurence F. Hawkins. DLC LNHT

1141 Rodman, Selden. The Guatemala Traveler: A Concise History and Guide. New York: Meredith Press, 1967. xv, 127 pp. Index, notes, illus., maps.

An account by an experienced travel-book author, providing a brief overview of the nation's history and an account of what to see and do, including a brief commentary on Belize. The emphasis is on the Indian traditions and Colonial past; there is also rich description of the physical setting. Includes extensive illustrations. DLC LNHT

1142 Rodríguez, Guillermo. Guatemala en 1919. Guatemala: Sánchez & de Guise, 1920. 191 pp. Index.

An account of the regime of Manuel Estrada Cabrera and his fall, discussing his policies and methods and the state in which he left Guatemala. DLC

1143 ____. Guatemala Libertada. Guatemala: Sánchez & de Guise, 1920. 98 pp. Illus.

A poetic contemporary account, with pro-unionist overtones, of the uprising that overthrew the Estrada Cabrera regime in 1920. The various maneuvers, demonstrations, and battles are described in verse, with appropriate photos. DLC LNHT BNG

1144 Rodríguez Beteta, Virgilio. El Partido Liberal unificado ante la tumba de Barrios: discurso pronunciado el 2 de abril de 1930. Guatemala: Tipografía Nacional, 1930. 22 pp.

A speech advocating a platform for the Liberal party and citing Barrios as the example for appropriate policy. DLC

1145 Rodríguez Cabal, Juan. La Virgen del Rosario de Guatemala. Guatemala: Sánchez & de Guise, 1934. 44 pp. Illus.

An album, written by a priest, commemorating the ceremonies honoring the Virgin in the Church of Santo Domingo in Guatemala City, which took place in 1934, detailing the history of the devotion to the statue, its coronation, and its place in Guatemalan religious beliefs, with accounts of the original ceremony and the inspiration for it. TxU

1146 Rodríguez Cabal, Juan and L.M. Estrada Paetau. La Santísima Virgen del Rosario de Guatemala y su basílica menor. Guatemala: n.p., 1970. 65 pp. Illus.

A further account of the devotion to the Virgin, providing details on its origin, practice, ceremonies, and the miracles attributed to it. BNG

1147 Rodríguez Castillejo, Juan Francisco. Mi escapada en tiempo de Cabrera: aventuras de la emigración. Guatemala: Sánchez & de Guise, 1921. 51 pp.

The memoirs of an individual arrested by the Estrada Cabrera regime, recounting in detail the story of his escape to Mexico and the perils and problems of fleeing from the dictatorship and its numerous spies and controls. Includes an account of his later travels abroad, though the focus is on the escape and the regime's harshness. LNHT

1148 Rodríguez Cerna, José, ed. Colección de tratados de Guatemala. 3 vols. Guatemala: Tipografía Nacional, 1939-43. 499, 637, 722 pp.

An official compilation of Guatemalan treaties, with accords with other Central American nations in the first volume, those with other hemispheric nations in the second, and general bilateral and Pan American Conference agreements in the third, providing the full text of each treaty. DLC LNHT

1149 Rodríguez Cerna, José. Entre escombros. Guatemala: Tipografía Marroquín, 1918. 113 pp. Illus.

A detailed account of the four earthquakes that devastated Guatemala City in December 1917 and January 1918, with description of the damage and effects. LNHT

1150 ____. Interiores: semblanzas y paisajes. Guatemala: Tipografía Nacional, 1942. 246 pp. 2d ed. Guatemala: Ministerio de Educación Pública, 1965. 278 pp.

A series of essays dealing principally with episodes and figures of Guatemalan history, though with other Latin American themes mixed in. DLC LNHT BNG

(Rodríguez Cerna, José)

1151 _____. Itinerario. Guatemala: Tipografía
Nacional, 1943. 230 pp.
    The travel commentaries and observations of
a well-known Guatemalan writer, which include
cultural and historical essays as well as
descriptions. While most of the volume deals
with Europe, an initial portion focuses on El
Salvador, and some of the European commentaries relate to continental influences in
Guatemala. DLC LNHT BNG

1152 _____. El libro de las crónicas. Guatemala:
Tipografía El Jardín, 1914. 275 pp.
    A series of short articles originally writ-
ten for the Guatemalan press. They deal with
a variety of Guatemalan themes, including
description of the various cities and regions,
discussion of political, economic, religious,
and social questions, world events, and miscellaneous other subjects. LNHT BNG

1153 _____. Nuestro derecho internacional:
sinopsis de tratados y anotaciones históricas,
1821-1937. Guatemala: Tipografía Nacional,
1938. 816 pp. Index, biblio.
    Despite its title, this volume is not a
treatise but rather a compilation of excerpts
from treaties and appropriate constitutions to
which Guatemala was a party, with synopses,
quotations of key portions, and linking narration and commentary to provide context; covers
the years 1821 through 1937. DLC LNHT BNG

1154 _____. Un pueblo en marcha: Guatemala.
Madrid: Editorial Artes Gráficas, 1931. 251
pp. Biblio., illus.
    Intended for the Spanish general reader to
combat the lack of knowledge about Guatemala
in Europe. About half this volume is devoted
to a physical geography of the republic; the
remaining portion describes the economy in the
1920s, provides a historical capsule, comments
on population, culture, and recent progress,
and provides hints for the tourist and summaries of legislation regarding trade and
investment. The emphasis is on the nation's
stability and rapid economic progress. DLC
LNHT BNG

1155 _____. Los terremotos de Guatemala, 1917-
1918. Guatemala: Tipografía Nacional, 1918.
20 pp.
    A brief preliminary account of the four
quakes that rocked the capital in December
1917 and January 1918. Later superceded by
the author's more detailed Entre escumbos.
DPU

1156 _____. Tierra de sol y de montaña.
Barcelona: B. Bauzá, 1930. iii, 251 pp.
Latest ed. Guatemala: Ministerio de
Educación Pública, 1969.
    A description of travel in the country,
with accounts of the various regions; pub-
lished under government sponsorship. DLC
LNHT BNG

1157 Rodríguez Cerna, José, and Eduardo Aguirre
Velásquez. Refutación, febrero de 1922:

carta abierta sobre los últimos sucesos de
Guatemala. Guatemala: Tipografía Nacional,
1922. 36 pp.
    Two Guatemalan scholars reply to a series
of essays by a Venezuelan writer, Jacinto
López, whose commentaries in the journal La
Reforma Social attacked the regime of General
José María Orellana. The Guatemalans defend
the regime, hailing the general and replying
point by point to the charges. DPU

1158 Rodríguez Chávez, Elisa. Oro de cobre.
Guatemala: Editorial San Antonio, 1965.
210 pp.
    A novel based on student life at the Uni-
versity of San Carlos. Seeks to portray
through the eyes of the students the university, its problems, and the forces buffeting
it during the present era. DLC LNHT BNG

1159 Rodríguez de Lemus, Guillerma. Despertar de
un gigante: Petén ante mis ojos, 1955-1965.
Guatemala: Editorial San Antonio, 1967. 289
pp. Illus.
    A reporter for La Hora and ten-year resi-
dent of the Petén describes her reactions to
the area, focusing on its development during
the 1950s and 1960s. Includes descriptions of
the terrain and towns, as well as of archeological zones. DLC LNHT BNG

1160 Rodríguez Herrera, J. Humberto. Guía
geográfica postal. Guatemala: Ministerio de
Educación Pública, 1961. 304 pp. Maps,
tables.
    The chief of information of the postal
service of Guatemala provides a guide to the
country for postal purposes. The initial
pages list each department, ennumerating their
principal cities, the distances between them,
and the types of postal and telegraph and
telephone services available. The bulk of the
volume consists of an alphabetical listing of
all the towns and barrios of the nation, providing for each its category, municipio, department, and department capital. A page for
Belize is included. DLC LNHT BNG

1161 Rodríguez Macal, Virgilio. Carazamba.
Guatemala: Editorial Norte, 1953. 157 pp.
2d ed. Guatemala: Editorial Tiempo, 1956.
157 pp.
    An attempt to capture the personality,
soul, and psychology of the women of the eastern jungle region of Guatemala, this work
continues the author's well-known description
of natural setting but combines it with the
local folklore and employs the focus on its
title figure to explore both the local ambience and the romantic fantasies of the region.
DLC LNHT

1162 _____. Guayacán. Guatemala: Ministerio de
Educación Pública, 1962. 560 pp.
    A novel about life in the rugged Petén
region that constitutes the Guatemalan frontier and the hope for the future, written in
1953 but not published until 1962. The focus
is on the trials and tribulations of life on

(Rodríguez Macal, Virgilio)
the plantations of this remote area, and on
the arduous conditions under which both landowners and laborers work. DLC LNHT BNG

1163 _____. *Jinayá*. Guatemala: Centro Editorial,
1956. 252 pp.
A novel set in Alta Verapaz that focuses on
the problems of the peasants, the discrimination against them imposed by the class structure, the privileges granted to the upper
class, and the resulting social tensions. The
rich naturalistic description for which the
author is noted is retained as he seeks to
portray the social problems by focusing on the
experiences of an individual who runs afoul of
the law and is imprisoned during a long judicial proceeding, demonstrating the slowness
with which the official apparatus moves when
dealing with the lower classes. LNHT

1164 _____. *La mansión del pájaro serpiente*. 2
vols. Guatemala: Ministerio de Educación
Pública, 1951. 188 pp. Illus. 3d ed.
Guatemala: Ministerio de Educación Pública,
1965. 235 pp. Illus.
A collection of short stories recounting
regional folklore of Guatemala, with emphasis
on stories of Indian origin. Among the
author's earliest and best-known works. The
stories focus on the lives of various animals
and are noted for their excellent and vivid
description of the animals and their setting
in the eastern jungles of Guatemala. The
descriptive portions have been compared to the
works of some of the great naturalistic writers. These animals, however, have some mystical qualities, reflecting the local
folklore. The works also employ the local
idioms of the region, with a glossary of
lengthy explanations at the end. Volume 2
bears the title *El mundo del misterio verde*,
with a subtitle identifying it as volume 2 of
the main title. DLC LNHT

1165 _____. *Sangre y clorofila: cuentos*.
Guatemala: Ministerio de Educación Pública,
1956. 157 pp.
A series of short stories vividly depicting
life on the cattle ranches of Guatemala and
Central America, focusing on the color and
violence of jungle life. DLC LNHT BNG

1166 Rodríguez Mojón, María Luisa, ed. *Poesía
revolucionaria guatemalteca*. Madrid: M.
Luisa Rodríguez Mojón, 1971. 187 pp.
An anthology of the so-called revolutionary
school of Guatemalan poetry, designed to introduce the European audience to its writing,
focusing on the Saker-Ti group that was formed
during the Arévalo administration in the 1940s
and whose poetry focuses on social problems
and political oppression. The selections
include poems depicting the hardships of peasant life, political abuses, and the impact of
the United Fruit Company and other foreign
enterprises. Includes a brief history of the
group and short biographical sketches of principal poets, as well as some poetry by predecessors not associated with the group. DLC
LNHT

1167 Rodríguez Rossignon, Mariano [Darío Guzmán
Riore, pseud.]. *Cuentos chapines*. Guatemala:
Centro Editorial, 1932. 269 pp.
A collection of short stories originally
published in *Nuestro Diario* that deal with
Guatemalan folklore and localities. Emphasizes the Guatemalan spirit and mentality,
focusing particularly on regional folktales;
encompasses a wide range of subjects, individuals, and situations that are judged typical of Guatemalan life. DLC LNHT BNG

1168 _____. *Nuevos cuentos chapines*. Guatemala:
Tipografía El Santuario, 1935. 117 pp.
A continuation of the author's previous
volume of short stories, with similar themes.
Most of the works were previously published in
newspapers. DLC

1169 Rodríguez Solís, Manuel. *Organización
y legislación militar de Guatemala:
contribución al curso de organización militar:
estudios calcados en la ley constitutivo del
Ejército*. Guatemala: Tipografía Nacional,
1936. 179 pp. 2d ed. Guatemala: Tipografía
Nacional, 1941. 301 pp.
A general military manual, with Guatemalan
military law included. DLC LNHT

1170 Rodríguez Solís, Manuel, and José Solís
Morales. *Deontología militar*. Guatemala:
Editorial del Ejército, 1964. 145 pp.
A series of essays by two Guatemalan army
officers, father and son, discussing the duties, responsibilities, and concepts of soldiers and military officers. The volume
discusses such themes as professionalism,
discipline, loyalty, spirit, bravery, and
other tactical aspects, as well as the mission
of the army, its social function, and the
relation of military and citizens. It
stresses institutionalization and the responsibilities of the army to the nation at large,
though also contending that military officers
on active duty should abstain from politics.
BNG

1171 Rojas Lima, Flavio. *Consideraciones generales
sobre la sociedad guatemalteca*. Guatemala:
Ministerio de Educación Pública, 1967. 47 pp.
Notes.
Based on census data from 1950 through
1964, this study seeks to identify the principal changes in Guatemala during this period.
It emphasizes that despite the increasingly
dominant role of the ladino in the national
culture, Indians remain the largest segment of
the population. DLC LNHT BNG

1172 Rölz Bennett, José, et al. *Pensamiento
universitario*. Guatemala: Universidad de San
Carlos, 1978. 311 pp. Illus.

1173 Romero Rodas, Francisco. *Historias que tejió
la realidad*. Guatemala: Ministerio de
Educación Pública, 1977. 224 pp.
A series of folktales and typical stories,
compiled by a Guatemalan army officer during
his service in many different parts of the
country, intended to preserve the lore,

modisms, and idioms of the interior. The author states that all are either stories he heard or incidents he saw, though he makes no attempt to identify them with particular regions. BNG

1174 Rosada, Héctor Roberto. Problemas socio-económicos de Guatemala. Guatemala: Editorial Piedra Santa, 1979. 243 pp. Maps, tables.
BNG

1175 Rösch, Adrián. Allerlei aus dem Alta Verapaz: Bilder aus dem deutschen Leben in Guatemala, 1868-1930. Stuttgart: Ausland & Heimat Verlag, 1934. 106 pp. Maps.
An account of the German community in Alta Verapaz, actually ending with World War I despite the dates in the title. Combines geography and description of the area and the Indians for the German audience with summaries of the activities of some of the German settlers and their principal businesses and projects, though there is no attempt at completeness or of chronological treatment of the entire settlement and community. Provides considerable information on the activities of the Germans, though certainly not a comprehensive history of the settlement. DLC LNHT

1176 Rosenthal, Mario. Guatemala. New York: Twayne, 1962. 327 pp. Index, biblio., notes, illus.
A Guatemalan journalist's overview of his nation's history, emphasizing the recent era and focusing particularly on the struggle against communism, which the author regards as at the heart of his nation's development. The volume assails the reformist revolutionary regimes and hails the National Liberation Movement, while casting the regime of General Miguel Ydígoras Fuentes in a particularly favorable light, perhaps reflecting his collaboration in the later publication of Ydígoras's memoirs. DLC LNHT BNG

1177 Rossignon, Julio. Porvenir de la Verapaz en la República de Guatemala, 1861. Guatemala: Imprenta de la Luna, 1861. 37 pp.
A paean to Verapaz, describing its situation and possibilities, emphasizing description of its flora and fauna, while lavishing praise on its beauty and hailing its potential. Also offers some suggestions for its development. DLC

1178 Rothery, Agnes Edwards. Images of Earth: Guatemala. New York: Viking, 1934. x, 206 pp. Illus.
The impressions of a well-known travel author during a visit to Guatemala in the 1930s. The descriptions are those of an experienced observer providing clear indications of the physical setting and the culture, particularly of life in the rural areas. If compared to appropriate sections of her other books dealing with the isthmus as a whole, each written in different decades, the three provide insights into the changes in the nation. DLC LNHT

1179 Rubio, Casimiro D. Biografía del general Justo Rufino Barrios: reformador de Guatemala, recopilación histórica y documentada. Guatemala: Tipografía Nacional, 1935. xv, 665 pp. Illus.
A biography extolling Barrios's contributions to the nation and citing him as an example for its citizens. Written under the patronage of the regime of Jorge Ubico, who regarded Barrios as his model, and of the National Police, honoring Barrios as their founder, published to commemorate the centennial of Barrios's birth. Recounts his many projects and the military campaigns of his unionist effort, reprinting extensive correspondence, government decrees, newspaper reportage, and other documents from that period. The cover title is Barrios a través de la historia; the title page bears the full title as indicated in the citation. DLC LNHT BNG

1180 _____. Cinco cartas: documentos para la historia. Guatemala: Tipográficos San Antonio, 1931. 17 pp.
A collection of assorted letters exchanged with various correspondents by a former supporter of Estrada Cabrera, relating to Jorge Ubico's separation from that regime and seeking to demonstrate that Ubico was not involved in the revolts against the regime of General Lázaro Chacón. The accounts are vague, deal with widely separated subjects, and are at times based on hearsay. LNHT

1181 Rubio, J. Francisco [Domingo El Paseador, pseud.]. Estampas de mi vida en la capital. Guatemala: Editorial Luz, 1965. 68 pp.
A series of humorous essays describing life in Guatemala City as seen by someone from rural Guatemala, providing an indication of the Guatemalan style of jokes and tales, as well as of the capital. LNHT BNG

1182 Rubio, Julio Alberto. Álbum de Guatemala. Guatemala: Talleres Gutenberg, 1937. Pages unnumbered. Illus. 3d ed. Guatemala: Imprenta Electra, 1938. Pages unnumbered. Illus.
A photo essay. DLC LNHT

1183 Ruíz Franco, Arcadio. Hambre y miseria: fermentos de lucha. Guatemala: Tipografía Nacional, 1950. 226 pp.
An account of the role of the labor movement in the 1944 revolution, written in memoir style by a leader of the printers' union at the printing plant of El Imparcial. Defends the actions of labor and the revolutionary government while condemning the Ubico regime, emphasizing repression and the existence of hunger, which the author contends is Guatemala's basic problem. This supersedes political ideology, he contends, and hence communism is merely one among possible solutions. The emphasis is on the central role of labor in the revolt and the new regime, but the narration also serves to illustrate the confusion of the 1944 maneuvers. DLC LNHT BNG

1184 Ruiz García, Enrique. <u>Historia de la</u> <u>Escuela Politécnica</u>. Guatemala: Editorial del Ejército, 1973. 296 pp.
   The official commemorative volume of the centennial of the Guatemalan military academy, sponsored by the national commission in charge of the event and prepared by a Guatemalan army colonel. The volume includes a brief history of the army in Guatemala, and a listing and brief description of the various military academies of the Latin American nations. The major portion is devoted to the reproduction of the decrees founding the academy in 1873, and various press commentaries about it, plus the commentaries occasioned by the centennial celebration. Some excerpts from books referring to the academy are included. BNG

1185 Ruiz Paniagua, Javier. <u>La educación normal en</u> <u>Guatemala</u>. Guatemala: Instituto de Investigaciones y Mejoramiento Educativo, 1964. 59 pp.
   A commentary on the Normal School of the nation, its curriculum, and its position in the nation's educational system. Criticizes the narrowness of the curriculum and notes that among the students are those individuals who attend only because of the shortage of space in other schools and have no intention of pursuing a teaching career but are merely seeking a degree. The author contends that a broader curriculum would more accurately reflect the Guatemalan needs. LNHT

1186 Sáenz, Jimena. <u>Genio y figura de Miguel Ángel</u> <u>Asturias</u>. Buenos Aires: Editorial Universitaria, 1975. 263 pp. Biblio., illus.
   A biography of the Guatemalan prize-winning author, tracing his life and relating his experience to his works, seeking to trace the influences upon his writing. The emphasis is on biography, but quotations from his works are employed to show the degree to which his novels reflected his experiences. BNG

1187 Sáenz de Tajada, Federico. <u>Guatemala</u>. Guatemala: Tipografía Central, 1908. 64 pp.
   A compilation of current data emphasizing the economy and its potential, designed to promote trade and investment. TxU

1188 Sáenz Poggio, José. <u>Historia de la música</u> <u>guatemalteca: desde la monarquía española,</u> <u>hasta fines del año de 1877</u>. Guatemala: Imprenta de la Aurora, 1878. 80 pp. 2d ed. Guatemala: Tipografía Nacional, 1948, 59 pp.
   A compendium of the history of music in Guatemala from pre-Colonial times to the present, with emphasis on instruments and their development but including lists of and brief comments on everything from composers and bands to theatrical music and the National Theater. DLC

1189 Saker-Ti, Grupo. <u>El artista y los problemas</u> <u>de nuestro tiempo</u>. Guatemala: Ediciones Saker-Ti, 1950. 29 pp.
   A panel discussion sponsored by this group of revolutionary poets, with presentations by Huberto Alvarado, Luís Cardoza y Aragón, Raúl Leiva, Otto-Raúl Gonzalez, and Guillermo Noriega Morales. The presentations are idealistic, speaking of the artist and literary figure as the vanguard of the future new man; they portray reality and speak for the masses to raise consciousness and promote revolutionary change in society. LNHT

1190 _____. <u>Cuentos de Guatemala: 1952</u>. Guatemala: Ediciones Saker-Ti, 1953. 47 pp. Illus.
   The prize-winning short stories from a 1952 competition conducted by the group of revolutionary poets. Includes works by Augusto Monterroso Bonilla, Lola Villacorta de Vidaurre, and Rubén Barreda Avila, all reflecting the group's concern with themes of social unrest and oppression, particularly in rural areas. DLC

1191 _____. <u>Enrique Muñoz Meany</u>. Guatemala: Tipografía Nacional, 1952. 87 pp. Illus.
   A series of laudatory essays about Muñoz Meany, his literary efforts and service to the nation, on the occasion of his death. Included are essays tracing his early life and hailing his diplomatic efforts on behalf of the revolutionary governments. DLC LNHT BNG

1192 Salazar, Carlos. <u>Memoria de los servicios</u> <u>prestados a la nación, 1908-1944:</u> <u>justificación y defensa</u>. Guatemala: Sánchez & de Guise, 1945. 335 pp.
   The memoirs of a leading diplomat and lawyer who represented the nation in the numerous arbitration efforts regarding the Guatemala-Honduras boundary dispute that ultimately produced a decision favoring Guatemala, and who later served as foreign minister during much of the Ubico regime. He details his experiences and viewpoints while explaining his actions. TxU

1193 _____. <u>La muerte del general Regalado: la</u> <u>campaña de 1906</u>. Guatemala: Ministerio de Educación Pública, 1956. 109 pp.
   A description of the 1906 border war with El Salvador, written by the <u>auditor de guerra</u> of one of the Guatemalan units in that region. Describes the actions of the revolutionaries that resulted in the combat, and the campaigns of his unit. Provides a valuable firsthand account, in considerable detail, of the Guatemalan actions and viewpoint. DLC LNHT BNG

1194 Salazar, Mélinton, ed. <u>Cuentos verapacenses</u>. Guatemala: Asociación Regional de Alta Verapaz, 1968. 108 pp.
   A collection of short stories about Alta Verapaz, by various authors, including representation of the nation's best-known short-story writers. The tales are set in the region and reflect its traditions and folklore, and life on its coffee fincas. DLC

1195 Salazar, Ramón Antonio. <u>Conflictos</u>. Guatemala: Tipografía Nacional, 1898. 270 pp.
   A novel set at a hacienda in the Guatemalan interior. It focuses more on life and its

(Salazar, Ramón Antonio)
problems than on national themes, but serves
to depict the life-style and customs of the
landowning class during the nineteenth century. BNG

1196 _____. El tiempo viejo: recuerdos de mi
juventud. Guatemala: Tipografía Nacional,
1896. 234 pp. 2d ed. Guatemala: Ministerio
de Educación Pública, 1957. 185 pp.
Though characterized as memoirs, the term
memories might be more appropriate because
this account of Guatemala in the mid-
nineteenth century includes extensive description of the city and its facilities in
addition to an account of the politics of the
1840-71 period. The atmosphere in the capital, the various uprisings and executions, and
the dictatorships of these turbulent years are
considered, as are social customs, dress,
social events, and the Liberal-Conservative
clash. A detailed description of the "Baile
del venado," regarded as one of the most accurate available, is also included. DLC LNHT

1197 _____. Historia de veintiún años: la
independencia de Guatemala. 2 vols.
Guatemala: Tipografía Nacional, 1928. 267,
260 pp. 2d ed. Guatemala: Ministerio de
Educación Pública, 1956. 141, 293 pp. Illus.
A history of the years 1800 through 1821 in
Guatemala, describing the conditions of the
country and the struggle for independence, and
emphasizing its origins and early phases.
Notable for its vivid descriptions of
Guatemala and its physical, economic, social,
and political setting in the late Colonial
era. LNHT BNG

1198 Salazar, Ramón Antonio, and Federico Sáenz
de Tejada, eds. Colección de tratados de
Guatemala. 3 vols. Guatemala: Tipografía
Nacional, 1892-1919. 624, 512, 478 pp.
A compilation of the complete texts of the
nation's various treaties, with the initial
volumes arranged by topic and the final one by
region. Central America occupies separate
sections in the first and third volumes. DLC

1199 Saler, Benson. Nagual, brujo y hechicero en
un pueblo Quiché. Guatemala: Ministerio de
Educación Pública, 1969. 53 pp. Biblio.,
notes, tables.
An essay, based on on-the-scene interviews, demonstrating the variations of these
three concepts in Quiché society, noting their
prevalence, the various meanings, and relating
them to present-day practices. DLC BNG

1200 Salguero, Álvaro Hugo. La brama. Guatemala:
Tipografía Nacional, 1950. 244 pp. Index.
A novel, originally written in 1943, consisting of a remembrance of the eastern portions of Guatemala and a narration designed to
preserve its traditions and folklore. DLC
LNHT

1201 Samayoa, José María, and José Tomás Larraondo.
Exposición presentada al supremo gobierno de
la república por los señores . . . sobre el

nuevo arrendamiento de los estancos de
aguardiente. Guatemala: Imprenta Nueva de
Luna, 1848. 28 pp. Appendixes.
While this item is a successful petition by
the authors for renewal of their national
aguardiente monopoly, which of course presents
their company in a favorable light, it provides useful data on the industry and the
operation of the monopoly. TxU

1202 Samayoa, Julio. Apuntes para mejorar la
economía de Guatemala. 2 vols. Guatemala:
Sánchez & de Guise, 1939. 96, 89 pp.
A survey of Guatemala and its economy that
details what the author considers its present
state, problems, and future prospects. Criticizing the coffee monoculture, it calls for
greater government activity to promote the
diversification of agriculture by providing
facilities, credit, and transportation. DLC

1203 _____. Ensayos sobre problemas de lo porvenir.
Guatemala: Sánchez & de Guise, 1944. Pages
not consecutively numbered.
A series of essays on what the author
conceives to be the pressing problems of
Guatemala and Latin America. They deal with
constitutional revision in Guatemala, including a brief historical overview and a complete
proposed constitution. Advocates the unification of Central America and also of all of
Latin America, and termination of the influence of foreign companies and external impacts
in the local economy. DLC

1204 Samayoa Chinchilla, Carlos. Chapines de ayer.
Guatemala: Tipografía Nacional, 1957. 144
pp. Illus. 2d ed. Guatemala: Ministerio de
Educación Pública, 1961. 206 pp. Illus.
A series of brief descriptive character-
izations of typical figures of everyday
Guatemalan life who, though remaining anonymous, are evident on all sides. Presents
people from all walks of life, including military officers, police, cooks, store owners,
etc. Provides a glimpse of typical aspects of
daily life that are omnipresent yet often
ignored and unrecorded. LNHT BNG

1205 _____. Cuatro suertes: cuentos y leyendas.
Guatemala: Tipografía Nacional, 1936.
220 pp.
A collection of legends from the rural
areas, drawing heavily upon the Indian traditions and deities. Though the locations are
not indicated, a glossary is provided that
defines the terms and serves to place some of
the legends. DLC LNHT BNG

1206 _____. El dictador y yo: verídico relato
sobre la vida de general Ubico. Guatemala:
Editorial Iberia, 1950. 181 pp. Illus. 2d
ed. Guatemala: Ministerio de Educación
Pública, 1967. 259 pp.
A well-known, unflattering portrait of
Ubico, written by a member of Ubico's presidential secretariet, recounting his observations of the caudillo, and including many
incidents and fables about him. DLC LNHT
BNG

(Samayoa Chinchilla, Carlos)

1207 _____. Estampas de la costa grande.
Guatemala: Ministerio de Educación Pública,
1954. 152 pp. Illus. 2d ed. Guatemala:
Ministerio de Educación Pública, 1957. 94 pp.
    A series of short folktales dealing with a
wide range of subjects, indicating Indian and
creole influences. DLC LNHT BNG

1208 _____. Historia de la Virgen del Socorro de
Guatemala. Guatemala: Centro Editorial,
1947. 26 pp.
    A very brief history of the shrine, focus-
ing on its Colonial origins. DLC LNHT

1209 _____. Madre milpa. Guatemala: Tipografía
Nacional, 1934. 203 pp. Illus. 2d ed.
Guatemala: Tipografía Nacional, 1950.
462 pp.
    A collection of short stories based on the
regional folklore of Guatemala. The stories
indicate Spanish, Indian, and modern influences and cover a broad range of themes, but
unfortunately are not identified as to origin,
location, or time. DLC LNHT BNG

1210 _____. El quetzal no es rojo. Guatemala:
Arana Hermanos, 1956. 268 pp.
    An account of the Guatemalan revolution by
a journalist, scholar, and government functionary, written in the wake of the overthrow
of the Arbenz government by the National Liberation Movement. Places the era in the context of Guatemalan history and denounces the
drift toward communism. The author, who
worked with and later opposed both the Ubico
regime and the revolutionary governments,
represents the disaffection of the moderates
who opposed the old regime, favored reform,
but bitterly opposed communism. Argues that
the nation sought reform, but that Marxism was
outside the national tradition; denounces the
leftward shift of the revolution as a political plot that amounted to an internal coup
taking over the movement. DLC LNHT BNG

1211 Samayoa Coronado, Francisco A. La Escuela
Politécnica a través de su historia. 2 vols.
Guatemala: Tipografía Nacional, 1964. 346,
389 pp. Biblio., illus., appendixes.
    One of many centennial histories of the
Guatemalan Military Academy, this work, by a
Guatemalan army colonel, includes a detailed,
year-by-year account of the Academy since its
creation, a list of all classes, chapters
dealing with the antecedents of the Academy
and the political efforts attendant to its
foundation, brief résumés of each year's activities and notable events, accounts of all
command and faculty changes, and a discussion
of curricular changes. Also appended is a
list of Academy graduates who have served as
president of the republic, in each of the
various cabinet ministeries, and in the diplomatic corps, with years of their service in
each position. DLC LNHT

1212 Samayoa Guevara, Héctor Humberto. Ensayos
sobre la independencia de Centroamérica.

Guatemala: Ministerio de Educación Pública,
1972. 303 pp. Notes, illus.
    Originally a series of essays that appeared
over a span of several years in the Revista
del Instituto de Antropología e Historia de
Guatemala, these pieces include a commentary
on independence as well as essays dealing with
the influences of significant personages of
this era, such as Alejandro Ramírez, Fray
Matías de Córdova, and Augustín Vilches.
Based on research in the Archivo General de
Centroamérica and in secondary works. LNHT
BNG

1213 _____. La enseñanza de la historia en
Guatemala desde 1832 hasta 1852. Guatemala:
Imprenta Universitaria, 1959. 148 pp.
Biblio., notes.
    The focus is on the educational reforms of
the Mariano Gálvez administration, the establishment of the various historical chairs,
particularly at the University of San Carlos,
and the pedagogical methods employed. DLC
LNHT BNG

1214 _____. La presencia de Luís Aury en Centro
América. Guatemala: Ministerio de Educación
Pública, 1965. 95 pp. Biblio., notes.
    A brief history of a French pirate who
raided Spanish ports in and around the
Caribbean in the 1820s. Documents his
incursions along the Central American coast
and details their effects. Includes description of the cities of the region in this era.
Based on archival research. DLC LNHT

1215 Sánchez, Luís Alberto. La tierra del quetzal.
Santiago: Ediciones Ercilla, 1950. 217 pp.
    A series of essays discussing famous fig-
ures from Guatemalan history and literature.
Though most are from the Colonial era, the
volume includes essays on Antonio José
Irisarri, Pepe Batres, José Milla y Vidaurre,
Enrique Gómez Carrillo, and Rafael Arévalo
Martínez. DLC LNHT BNG

1216 Sánchez Morales, Juan Rafael. Origen y
evolución de la canción patriótica: historia
y didáctica del himno nacional de Guatemala.
Guatemala: Ministerio de Educación Pública,
1969. 201 pp. Biblio., illus.
    A history and analysis of the origins,
details, and establishment of the Guatemalan
national anthem. The initial half of the
volume deals with the history of national
anthems in general, tracing them back to Greek
and Roman days. The second portion deals with
the Guatemalan case, tracing the original
efforts to find a suitable song, beginning in
1879, through the establishment of the anthem
in 1896 during the regime of José María Reyna
Barrios. It includes an analysis of the
themes and topics, and brief biographies of
José Joaquín Palma, who wrote the words, and
Rafael Álvarez Ovalle, who wrote the music.
DLC

1217 Sandoval, Francisco Ernesto. Mis memorias:
páginas íntimas (viñeta). Guatemala: Sánchez
& de Guise, 1926. 110 pp.

The memoirs of a Guatemalan writer and Liberal political figure whose activities span several of the Central American republics during the latter half of the nineteenth century. His accounts are episodical and indicate contact with numerous presidents from the region. BNG

1218 Sandoval, Lisandro. *Semántica guatemalense o diccionario de guatemaltequismos.* 2 vols. Guatemala: Tipografía Nacional, 1942. 771, 697 pp. Biblio.

A dictionary of Guatemalan idioms and local modisms that reflect the Indian traditions; arranged alphabetically, with definitions and explanations of the derivations of the terms. DLC

1219 Sandoval, Victor O. *Pequeña monografía de San Luís Jilotepeque.* Guatemala: Ministerio de Educación Pública, 1965. 189 pp. Illus., maps.

A narration of the history and ethnographic and demographic characteristics of the town, with description of its current facilities, services, economy, and customs. DLC LNHT BNG

1220 Sandoval Vásquez, Carlos Alberto. *Leifugados: crímenes del ubiquismo.* Mexico: n.p., 1946. 398 pp. Illus.

A denunciation of the Ubico regime and a catalog of its "crimes," containing accounts of the individuals arrested and executed, and denunciations of various tortures. The attack on the caudillo is particularly vicious, denouncing his family origin and impugning his honor, with a "psychological profile" characterizing him as paranoid and crazy, contending that imbecility runs in the family and ascribing various diseases to him. The author was compelled to flee into exile during the regime, and this volume constitutes his answer. BNG

1221 Sands, William F. *Our Jungle Diplomacy.* Chapel Hill: University of North Carolina Press, 1944. 250 pp.

The memoirs of a U.S. diplomat who served in many posts in Latin America, including a detailed chapter dealing with his experience in Guatemala during the regime of Estrada Cabrera that sheds light on several of the efforts to overthrow the dictator and indicates that the Yankees were behind some of the plots. The account includes filibusterers, politicians, and businessmen, and accounts of various scandals. DLC

1222 Santos, Manuel Antonio. *Una experiencia con los test A.B.C.* Guatemala: Ministerio de Educación Pública, 1950. 78 pp. Illus. 2d ed. Guatemala: Ministerio de Educación Pública, 1952. 86 pp. Illus.

A brief report summarizing the results of administering the ABC standardized test to 167 first-graders in Guatemala. The test is used to determine readiness for learning reading and writing, and hence to group classes by ability. DLC LNHT

1223 Sapia Martino, Raúl. *Guatemala: Mayaland of Eternal Spring.* 3d ed. Guatemala and Buenos Aires: River Plate, 1963. lvi, 104 pp. Illus., maps. 5th ed. Guatemala: River Plate, 1973. xcvi, 119 pp. Illus., maps.

A bilingual (Spanish and English) compendium of general and tourist information, including brief background and historical sketches. DLC LNHT

1224 Sapper, Karl Theodor. *Das Heidentum unter den chrislichen Indianern Guatemalas.* Gotha: Petermanns Mitteilungen, 1921. 69 pp.

Focuses on religious practices, considering the mixture of pagan and Christian practices among converts to Christianity in Alta Verapaz.

1225 _____. *Sobre la geografía física, la población y la producción de la República de Guatemala.* Guatemala: Tipografía Nacional, 1897. 88 pp. Tables. 2d ed. Guatemala: Ministerio de Educación Pública, 1958. 127 pp. Illus.

A description of population and economic characteristics and their distribution in Guatemala, as well as of its physical landforms. Originally designed as narrations to accompany maps showing these features, prepared for the 1897 Central American Exposition; unfortunately, the publication does not include the maps. It does include climatic tables and discussion of the influence of climate on the distribution of population and the types of agriculture, as well as economic data. DLC LNHT

1226 Scanlon, A. Clark. *Hope in the Ruins.* Nashville: Boardman Press, 1978. 175 pp. Illus.

A Baptist missionary recounts his experiences during and after the 1976 Guatemalan earthquake and the response of his mission board to the tragedy. He emphasizes, in vivid and moving terms, the assistance furnished through him to the survivors, always seeing the hand of God in the effort and hope for the future in the ties that resulted. DLC

1227 Schlesinger, Alfredo. *Comentarios alrededor de la constitución de 1956.* Guatemala: Talleres Gutenberg, 1956. 24 pp.

A series of essays, some previously published in the Guatemalan press, defending the 1956 constitution and reflecting the political polemic characteristic of the nation at that time. Argues that the new constitution offers more freedom than that of 1945, consistently citing the 1945 document as the basis for the actions of 1956, thereby using the revolutionary constitution against the leftist critics of that of 1956. Noting that all previous Guatemalan constitutions were born of revolution, particularly that of 1945, it rejects the leftist charges that the new document is illegal since it violates the previous one, an argument that would also have nullified the 1945 document as a violation of its predecessor. LNHT

(Schlesinger, Alfredo)

1228 _____. Comentarios alrededor de la ley de liquidación de asuntos de guerra. Guatemala: Unión Tipográfica, 1955. 78 pp.

A series of essays denouncing the confiscation of German-owned property in Guatemala, contending that this measure was illegal and detrimental to the economy, and that it reflected Yankee pressure. The commentaries were previously published as a series in the Guatemalan newspaper La Hora. TxU

1229 _____. Locura racial. Guatemala: Centro Editorial, 1938. 68 pp. Biblio., illus.

A denunciation of the racism of Nazi doctrine, containing a detailed description of the official ideology of the German National Socialist party, with liberal excerpts from its leaders and their texts and statements. The author contends that he seeks not to analyze but merely to explain the doctrine so that all can judge for themselves, and to contribute to a more general knowledge of Nazi objectives. One of the earliest Guatemalan attacks on fascism, it drew an official German protest at the time of its publication. BNG

1230 _____. Marxismo, antimarxismo y antisemitismo. Guatemala: Unión Tipografía, 1936.

Reflecting the wartime dilemma of Guatemala, caught between its large German community and economic ties to Germany and its geographic proximity to the United States, this work deftly renounces Nazi propaganda by combining the denunciation of anti-Semitism with an attack on Marxism, ever the parriah of the Nazis, enabling the author to reject all foreign ideologies and proclaim that true Guatemalan patriots will never tolerate any foreign doctrine in their land. The comment also reflects the author's ties to the Ubico regime and his functioning as a semiofficial spokesman in matters regarding Nazi efforts to organize the local German community, always through indirect comments such as this one. TxU

1231 _____. La paridad del quetzal con el dólar y su relación con el desequilibrio económico de Guatemala. Guatemala: Unión Tipografía, 1931. 28 pp.

A brief pamphlet, part of the debate regarding means of alleviating the problems caused by the depression, advocating the introduction of a new national currency at parity with the dollar, and commenting on the fluctuations in value of the current bills and the resulting problems. LNHT

1232 _____. La verdad sobre el comunismo. Guatemala: Tipografía Nacional, 1932. 104 pp. Biblio., appendixes.

A condemnation of communism, attacking both its doctrine and practice in the Soviet Union. These essays originally appeared in the official newspaper of the government party, El Liberal Progresista, and then were reprinted by the Government Printing Office, hence indicating clearly that the statement provided the rationale for the attitudes of the Ubico regime. The fear of communism in Central America at the time reflected a reaction to the 1931 uprising in El Salvador, which included the participation of some communist elements, and hence made the threat real throughout the region. DLC LNHT BNG

1233 _____. Voz de alerta a los jefes y oficiales del Ejército Nacional. Guatemala: n.p., 1956. 23 pp.

A hymn of praise for the actions of the Guatemalan armed forces in ousting the regime of Jacobo Arbenz Guzmán, thereby saving Guatemala from communism, enslavement, and a planned Red massacre. Contends that this patriotic action shows that the Guatemalan army, as always, performed its patriotic duty in protecting the national interests.

1234 Schmid, Lester. El papel de la mano de obra migratoria en el desarrollo económico de Guatemala. Guatemala: Universidad de San Carlos, 1973. xxix, 454 pp. Biblio., notes, tables.

A detailed examination of the role of migratory labor in Guatemalan agriculture, and of the conditions of the laborers. Originally a doctoral thesis in agricultural economics, the study is sympathetic to the laborers. Employs official reports for statistics and extensive interviews with migratory laborers to obtain data regarding their condition and views. BNG

1235 Schneider, Ronald M. Communism in Guatemala, 1944-1954. New York: Praeger, 1958. xxi, 350 pp. Index, biblio., notes. Comunismo en Latino América: el caso de Guatemala. Buenos Aires: Editorial Agora, 1959. 217 pp. Index, biblio., notes.

An important account of the leftward drift of the Guatemalan revolutionary movement, based on extensive research in the documents of the Guatemalan Labor party, interviews with participants, and other documentation to which the author had access, detailing the role of communism in the movement and the gradual takeover of the revolution. The author traces the activities of the various communist leaders and organizations in meticulous detail, arguing that they succeeded owing to their organization and the political vacuum caused by the vague positions of the other revolutionary leaders and the lack of political experience on the part of the population in general. Includes detailed consideration of the use of labor and peasant organizations to gain control and manipulate the government, as well as of other front organizations. The discussion of the fall of Arbenz avoids the issue of Yankee intervention. DLC LNHT

1236 Schultze-Jena, Leonhard Sigmund. La vida y las creencias de los indígenas Quichés de Guatemala. Guatemala: Ministerio de Educación Pública, 1947. xii, 85 pp. Biblio. 2d ed. Guatemala: Ministerio de Educación Pública, 1954. 133 pp. Biblio., illus.

A study of the Quiché Indians and their society and beliefs, based on fieldwork in Chichicastenango and Momostenango conducted in 1929-31 by a German scholar. The work was originally published in German as one volume of the author's Indiana (See item CA853) and initially appeared in Spanish in the Anales de la Sociedad de Geografía e Historia during 1945. The initial portion describes the society, social customs, and institutions, while the second part consists of an analysis of religious beliefs and their impact on the lives of the individuals. DLC LNHT

1237   Schwartz, Gustavo. Columnas del progresismo y reseña histórica del génesis del Partido Progresista. Guatemala: n.p., 1931. 124 pp.
     A brief history of the origins of the Progressive party and its early efforts during the 1920s, followed by a series of brief biographical sketches of the principal figures in the party, though with several notable omissions. The author was a party member and avows his admiration for the party's program. BNG

1238   Schwartz, Norman B. A Milpero of Petén, Guatemala: Autobiography and Cultural Analysis. Newark: University of Delaware Press, 1977. ii, 141 pp. Biblio., illus., maps, tables.
     The life-story of a peasant in the Petén region of Guatemala, with the full text of his narration, background material, and analysis of the dominant elements and cultural patterns involved. Draws on existing anthropological literature, and includes the results of various psychological tests administered to the subject, providing insights into his outlook and values. DLC

1239   Schwauss, Maria. Tropenspiegel: Tagebuch einer deutschen Frau in Guatemala. Leipzig: A.H. Payne, 1940. 191 pp. Illus. 2d ed. Halle: Mitteldeutsche Druckerei und Verlagsanstalt, 1949. 174 pp. Illus.
     A travelogue that recounts the observations and adventures of a German woman in Guatemala. Includes comments on the physical setting, culture, and Indians. DLC

1240   Selser, Gregorio, ed. Guatemala: tu nombre inmortal. Quito: Ediciones Revista de Guatemala, auspiciada por la Universidad Central de Quito, 1956.
     A collection of revolutionary poetry from Guatemala denouncing the upper class and the Yankee imperialists, and accenting the plight of the rural peasants. The latest edition bears the title Poemas para la batalla de Guatemala. DLC

1241   _____. El guatemalazo: la primera guerra sucia. Buenos Aires: Ediciones Iguazú, 1961. 188 pp. Index.
     A prolific and well-known leftist journalist provides an account of the events of 1954, denouncing the role of the Yankees and the United Fruit Company in the overthrow of the Guatemalan revolution, while praising the revolution and its accomplishments as a voice that was heard and respected throughout Latin America. Includes passages from the Memoirs of Anthony Eden to indicate the Yankee involvement and substantiate his charges. Also appended are various declarations of the revolutionary government. DLC LNHT

1242   Seminario de Integración Social Guatemalteca. Congreso Indigenista Interamericano, IV, Guatemala, 1959. Guatemala: Ministerio de Educación Pública, 1959. 449 pp.
     Summaries of papers presented at the conference, with commentaries; they deal with Guatemalan society, its structure, and changes. DLC

1243   _____. Problemas de la urbanización en Guatemala. Guatemala: Ministerio de Educación Pública, 1965. 290 pp. Biblio., tables, appendixes.
     Papers presented at the first conference on Guatemalan urbanization, sponsored by the seminar, including the final recommendations of the conference. The studies cover the many problems associated with urbanization and internal migration, from services to public health. Includes a theory of urbanization by Leonard Reissman as an appendix. DLC LNHT BNG

1244   _____. Los pueblos del Lago de Atitlán. Guatemala: Tipografía Nacional, 1968. 340 pp. Tables.
     An anthropological study focusing on the changes in the last thirty years in the villages around Lake Atitlán. The team was headed by Sol Tax and used his previously published study of thirty years earlier as the basis for comparison to the data gathered during 1966. Concludes that ladinization has accelerated, particularly in the economic sense, as reflected in dress and other customs, noting that the villages have access to more facilities now. Emphasizes the role of the Catholic Action Movement in promoting new methods in the communities. A valuable source for the study of the effects of modernization on the Indians when used with the earlier Tax study. DLC BNG

1245   Serra G., Ramón. Boctecas históricos de Retalhuleu. Guatemala: Tipografía Nacional, 1970. 523 pp.
     Another in the series of departmental monographs, this one providing a detailed history of the state, focusing on its place in national history, and covering the entire period from colonization to the present. Includes discussion of regional festivals and customs, their background and the origin of the state names. DLC LNHT

1246   Serrano Muñoz, Mariano. Datos geográficos e históricos del departamento de Chimaltenango. Guatemala: Imprenta Marroquín, 1917. 52 pp.
     A brief collection of then-current data about each of the municipios in the department, compiled by the jefe político, with due references to the leadership of the nation's

president, General Manuel Estrada Cabrera, and
a description of the government projects in
the department, all of which are attributed to
his leadership. BNG

1247 Sexton, James D. <u>Education and Innovation in
a Guatemalan Community</u>: <u>San Juan La Laguna</u>.
Los Angeles: University of California Press,
1973. vii, 72 pp. Biblio., tables,
appendixes.
     A study applying anthropological methods,
surveys, and statistical analysis to the study
of education in a rural Indian town. Concludes that the six grades available in the
village are handled adequately, but laments
the absence of further educational opportunity. The author tests a number of other hypotheses and suggests that Protestants are
poorer than Catholics but more favorably in-
clined toward education, and proposes further
study of this aspect. DLC LNHT

1248 Shaw, Mary. <u>According to Our Ancestors</u>: <u>Folk
Texts from Guatemala and Honduras</u>. Norman:
University of Oklahoma Press, 1971. 510 pp.
Biblio., illus., maps.
     <u>Según nuestros antepasados</u>: <u>textos
folklóricos de Guatemala y Honduras</u>.
Guatemala: Instituto Lingüístico del Verano
en Centro América, 1972. 502 pp. Biblio.,
illus., maps.
     A collection of folktales from all parts of
the republic, as well as Honduras, gathered by
trained investigators from the region and
recorded here in their original languages,
with translations. A brief introduction to
each region and a comparative introduction
discussing common traits are also included.
Unifying themes cited include the moralistic
nature of the tales, the relationship of man
and nature, and social mores. DLC LNHT BNG

1249 Sieckavizza A., Luís. <u>Leyendas de tierra
adentro</u>. Guatemala: Ministerio de Educación
Pública, 1966. 182 pp.
     A series of legends and memoirs repre-
senting the author's recollections of his
native region in the interior of Guatemala
during the 1930s, but written in semimemoir
and seminovelistic form. Designed to preserve
the traditions of the era and reflect the life
of those days and its trials and tribulations,
particularly the problems with the authorities
and the dictatorial rule. DLC LNHT

1250 Sierra Franco, Aurora. <u>Miguel Ángel Asturias
en la literatura</u>. Guatemala: Editorial
Istmo, 1969. 129 pp. Biblio.
     A series of brief summaries of the plots of
Asturias's novels and poems, with some excerpts and analysis. The author emphasizes
Asturias's strong Indian ties and social criticism, and hails his techniques, concluding
that he is an innovator in Latin American
literary style. A brief biography of Asturias
and a list of his works is included. DLC
LNHT BNG

1251 Sierra Roldán, Tomás. <u>Diálogos con el coronel
Monzón</u>: <u>historia viva de la revolución</u>

guatemalteca, 1944-1954. Guatemala:
Tipografía San Antonio, 1958. 153 pp.
     The memoirs of a Guatemalan army officer,
political figure, congressional deputy, and
junta member, tracing his role in the 1944
uprising, the Arévalo regime, his alienation
from Arbenz, and his service in the National
Liberation Movement and the 1954 revolution.
The author was one of the original revolutionaries, but was alienated by the leftward
shift of the movement and the assassination of
Colonel Arana. The volume details his view of
and reactions to the events of the era, as
well as his participation. LNHT BNG

1252 Silva Girón, César Augusto. <u>La batalla de
Gualán</u>: <u>junio de 1954</u>. Guatemala: Imprenta
Eros, 1977. 163 pp. Illus., maps.
     A Guatemalan army officer details a battle
in the 1954 revolution in which he commanded
the Arbenz government troops defending the
town of Gualán near the Honduran frontier.
BNG

1253 Silvert, Kalman H. <u>A Study in Government</u>:
<u>Guatemala</u>. New Orleans: MARI, 1954. xi, 100
pp. Index, biblio., notes, illus. 2d ed.
New Orleans: MARI, 1954. xi, 239 pp. Index,
biblio., notes, illus.
     <u>Un estudio de gobierno</u>: <u>Guatemala</u>.
Guatemala: Ministerio de Educación Pública,
1969. 267 pp. Biblio., notes, tables.
     A detailed study of the governmental system
during the revolutionary era, based on the
1945 constitution, examining its structure and
operation at the national, department, and
local level. The second edition includes
English translations of the nation's various
constitutions. DLC LNHT BNG

1254 Skinner-Klée, Jorge. <u>Consideraciones en torno
a la clase media emergente en Guatemala</u>.
Guatemala: Ministerio de Educación Pública,
1965. 25 pp.
     A brief discussion of the "silent revolu-
tion" entailed in the emergence of a middle
class and the resulting changes in Guatemalan
society. The author emphasizes that this is
part of a global phenomenon, but that the
local situation renders it more important: as
the interaction of the indigenous culture with
that of the ladino and the latter with the
rest of the world increases, the outlook of
all and hence the culture of the nation are
changed. DLC LNHT BNG

1255 _____. <u>Legislación indigenista de Guatemala</u>.
Mexico: Instituto Indigenista Interamericano,
1954. 135 pp.
     A compilation of the clauses of the 1945
constitution that affect the Indian, with full
text of each and commentary. DLC

1256 _____. <u>Revolución y derecho</u>. Guatemala:
Ministerio de Educación Pública, 1971. 184
pp. Notes.
     A leading Guatemalan scholar, lawyer, and
political figure examines the juridical aspects of revolution, using the Guatemalan
revolution of 1871 as a model. Drawing upon

the writings of leading legal scholars and philosophers throughout history, he concludes that revolution, although not a juridical concept, brings great changes in the law, adding that revolution can be studied from many different points of view and disciplines because it is a complex phenomenon. LNHT BNG

1257   Smith, Waldeman R. The Fiesta System and Economic Change. New York: Columbia University Press, 1977. viii, 194 pp. Index, biblio., notes.

An anthropological study focusing on the folk-Catholic fiestas of the Maya Indians and their role in village life, based on fieldwork in San Marcos in 1968 through 1970. The author concludes that economic change has modified the fiesta system, reducing its importance and causing consolidations, and that the fiesta system is associated primarily with isolated Indian villages rather than with those towns that are effectively part of the national economy. DLC LNHT

1258   Snee, Carole A. Current Types of Peasant-Agricultural Worker Conditions and Their Historical Development in Guatemala. Cuernavaca, Mexico: Centro Intercultural de Documentación, 1969. viii, 129 pp. Biblio., maps, tables, appendixes.

An analysis of the formation of social organizations, cooperatives, and labor unions among peasants. DLC

1259   Solano Guzmán, Gustavo. Guatemala a través de mi lente. Guatemala: Sánchez & de Guise, n.d. [1930]. 96 pp.

A traveler's description of Guatemala during 1930, focusing on its institutions and educational system, though including his impressions of physical aspects and society, as well as of the incumbent regime of Lázaro Chacón. Intended as part of a series of travelogues on all of Hispanic America. LNHT BNG

1260   _____. La sangre: crímenes de Manuel Estrada Cabrera. San Salvador: Tipografía La Unión, 1920. 108 pp. 2d ed. Guatemala: n.p., 1921. 52 pp.

A play denouncing the abuses of the regime of Manuel Estrada Cabrera. BNG

1261   Sólis, César G. Los ferrocarriles en Guatemala. Guatemala: Tipografía Nacional, 1952. 534 pp.

The secretary general of the presidency during the Arbenz regime prepared this official compilation of Guatemalan laws regulating railroads and the various governmental acuerdos involved in the original concessions, from the late nineteenth century to the present. BNG

1262   Solombrino Orozco, Vicenzo. El Ministerio de Gobernación de Guatemala. Guatemala: Tipografía Nacional, 1977. 376 pp. Index, notes, illus., maps.

A history of the ministry and its role in Guatemalan government, consisting of a compilation of the appropriate decrees and

regulations defining its functions through the years. Includes a brief history of the republic, a compilation of the budgets of the ministry, and photos of the various individuals who headed it and of public buildings relevant to its activities. BNG

1263   Solórzano Fernández, Valentín. Historia de la evolución económica de Guatemala. Mexico: UNAM, 1947. 370 pp. Biblio., appendixes. 4th ed. Guatemala: Ministerio de Educación Pública, 1977. 413 pp. Biblio.

A general economic history of Guatemala from Colonial times to 1930, focusing on the Colonial era and the nineteenth century. Originally prepared as a thesis, it stresses agricultural development and the impact of economic problems on the nation's history, citing economic factors that encouraged independence and promoted the Liberal revolution, as well as the economic impact of the Liberal reform era. The chapters deal with chronological eras and include excerpts from appropriate decrees and legislation. Emphasizes the private-property aspect of the Liberal movement and its importance for the development of export agriculture that was essential to this era, while noting the corresponding reduction of communal lands. DLC LNHT BNG

1264   Somoza Vivas, Fernando. El crimen de 20 y el pueblo guatemalteco. Guatemala: Imprenta de La Mañana, 1908. 272 pp.

A pro-Liberal account of the 20 April 1908 attempt on Estrada Cabrera's life and the response to it. Reprints the newspaper's original reports, the comments of other papers, and the ensuing actas and manifestoes of loyalty to the president, all designed to show that the Guatemalan people support the caudillo and that the attempt on his life was a vicious crime by a few isolated malcontents who do not represent popular feeling. DLC

1265   Soto de León, Carlos Enrique. Familia Soto y sus descendientes. Guatemala: Privately published, 1977. 144 pp. Illus.

A family history with photos, that lists the dates of birth and traces the family trees of all the descendants of a Colonial family. BNG

1266   Soto-Hall, Máximo. Biografía del presidente Estrada Cabrera al alcance de los niños. Guatemala: Imprenta Marroquín, 1908.

A laudatory biography of the current president, written for children. DPU

1267   _____. La deuda inglesa de Guatemala, su origen y su historia. Guatemala: Imprenta Marroquín, 1917. 99 pp.

An account of a controversial Guatemalan debt to England, stemming from an 1895 loan with a pledge of coffee-tax revenue. Details the problems caused and the resulting dispute on the eve of World War I when the British put pressure on the Estrada Cabrera regime, which had defaulted. DPU

(Soto-Hall, Máximo)

1268 _____. La independencia y sus hombres: lecturas para los niños de mi patria. Guatemala: Tipografía Nacional, 1911. 35 pp.
    A series of brief, basic biographical sketches of the leaders of the independence movement, intended for the general reader and for use in the schools. DLC

1269 _____. La niña de Guatemala: el idilio trágico de José Martí. Guatemala: Tipografía Nacional, 1942. 164 pp. Illus. 2d ed. Guatemala: Ministerio de Educación Pública, 1966. 193 pp.
    A description of Guatemala during the 1880s, when Martí spent some time in the country. Seeks to recapture the milieu of the time and contends that Martí's Guatemalan stay during the Liberal era exerted a great influence on him. Includes excerpts from his poetry and his memoirs regarding Guatemala. DLC BNG

1270 Soza, José María. Monografía del departamento de El Petén. 2 vols. Guatemala: Ministerio de Educación Pública, 1970. v, 666 pp. Biblio., illus., maps.
    A highly detailed history of the Petén since the Conquest and a detailed résumé of the various traditions and fiestas that reflect the region's Indian heritage. Various aspects of culture, society, and economy are also considered. Although the emphasis is on description, there is also some analysis, and the historical background is indicated. Although technically a second edition of the author's previous work, this volume, at nearly twice the length, provides much additional information. DLC LNHT BNG

1271 _____. Pequeña monografía del departamento de El Petén. Guatemala: Ministerio de Educación Pública, 1957. 332 pp. Biblio., illus., maps.
    One of the series of departmental monographs, this volume deals with the physical attributes of the state of Petén, including its flora and fauna, resources, and history, also providing a historical summary of each of its municipalities. Includes a discussion of the Maya culture and the archeological zones of the area, as well as lists of officeholders and governors during its existence. DLC LNHT

1272 Sperlich, Norbert, and Elizabeth Katz Sperlich. Guatemalan Backstrap Weaving. Norman: University of Oklahoma Press, 1980. 200 pp. Illus.
    A detailed description of Guatemalan weaving, with instructions on how to make many articles of traditional native dress, by two weavers and photographers who lived in the region to study the methods. Includes details regarding the techniques, design, style, etc., with illustrations and complete instructions. DLC LNHT

1273 Spielmann, Hans O. Ursachen, Merkmale und Bedeutung der Bevölkerungsverschiebungen in Guatemala. Hamburg: Verlag Ferdinand Hirt, 1973. 76 pp. Biblio., maps, tables.
    An overview of immigration to and within Guatemala and among its various regions, focusing on the years 1950 to 1964, though including broad historical data from the 1890s as well. DLC LNHT

1274 Steffan, Alice Jacqueline (Kennedy) [Jack Steffan, pseud.]. Fire of Freedom: The Story of Col. Carlos Castillo Armas. New York: Hawthorn Books, 1963. 185 pp. Index, illus.
    A laudatory biography by a Yankee writer, aimed at the teenage audience, part of a series of biographies of outstanding Catholic figures for the high school audience by a church-related press. DLC

1275 Stephan, Charles H. Le Guatemala économique. Paris: Librarie P. Dugourc, 1907. iii, 263 pp. Index, tables.
    A basic description of Guatemala and its economy at the time, written by the Guatemalan consul in Paris to provide information to European businessmen to encourage investment in and trade with Guatemala. Includes descriptive data, figures regarding population, economic conditions, and samples of appropriate consular forms. DLC BNG

1276 Stöll, Otto. Guatemala: Reisen und Schilderungen aus den Jahren 1878-1883. Leipzig: Brockhaus, 1886. xii, 518 pp. Illus., maps.
    A geographic description in the form of a travelogue, by a well-known German geographer. Provides detailed descriptions of land, physical features, people, customs, and lifestyles of western and southern Guatemala during the years indicated. DLC LNHT

1277 _____. Zur Ethnographie der Republik Guatemala. Zurich: Orell Füssli, 1884. ix, 175 pp. Maps. Ethnografía de la República de Guatemala. Guatemala: Sánchez & de Guise, 1938. xxxiv, 196 pp. Biblio., illus., maps. 2d ed. Guatemala: Ministerio de Educación Pública, 1958. 258 pp. Illus., maps.
    A well-known ethnographic survey of Guatemala in the late nineteenth century. DLC LNHT BNG

1278 Stowell, Ellery Cory. The Magee Incident. Washington, D.C.: John Byran, 1920. 13 pp. Notes.
    Describes an incident in 1874 involving the mistreatment of the British Consul at San José, Guatemala, and the action of the British government in dispatching a squadron of warships to enforce a demand for reparation. By implication, the pamphlet suggests that the United States pattern its actions on this incident. DLC

1279 Suarez, Alberto. La lucha del pueblo de Guatemala contra el imperialismo yanqui. Montevideo: Imprenta Adelante, 1954. 24 pp.
    A denunciation of the intervention of 1954 as a continuation of Yankee imperialism, blaming the entire affair on the gringos. CSt-H

1280 Sum Sacalxot, Maria Amalia. El matrimonio
indígena de Quezaltenango. Guatemala:
Ministerio de Educación Pública, 1965. 86 pp.
Biblio.
A thesis that discusses the regional forms
and customs associated with marriage, with a
general description of the processes involved
and the traditions associated with them. DLC

1281 Suslow, Leo A. Aspects of Social Reforms in
Guatemala, 1944-1949: Problems of Planned
Social Change in an Underdeveloped Country.
Hamilton, N.Y.: Colgate University Press,
1949. vii, 133 pp. Biblio., notes, illus.,
maps.
Originally a master's thesis, this volume
sympathetically summarizes the social-reform
program of the Arévalo administration, drawing
from contemporary publications and newspapers.
Chapters are devoted to education, land tenure, agricultural labor, rural health, and
social security, all optimistically following
the line of the new regime and accepting its
propagandistic view of the past. In the process, a coherent summary of the program is
provided, subject to the limits of then-
published material and offered quite uncrit-
ically. DLC LNHT

1282 Taracena Flores, Arturo. Los terremotos de
Guatemala, álbum gráfico conmemorativo del
cincuentenario (1917/1918-1968). Guatemala:
Tipografía Nacional, 1970. 238 pp. Illus.
A collection of vivid photos showing the
damage suffered by the capital in the 1917-18
quakes, with some before-and-after shots to
identify the damage. LNHT

1283 Taube, Evert. Guatemala. Stockholm:
Bonniers Folkbibliotek, 1961. 187 pp.
A travelogue, with particular attention on
the Indians and their culture, along with the
legends involved. DLC

1284 Tax, Sol. Los municipios del altiplano
mesaoccidental de Guatemala. Guatemala:
Ministerio de Educación Pública, 1965. 36 pp.
Notes, maps, tables.
An important study, originally published in
English as an article in American Anthropologist in 1937. It was among the first works
to argue that each municipality must be studied in depth as a separate cultural entity
rather than by efforts to identify broad patterns. DLC LNHT BNG

1285 _____. Penny Capitalism: A Guatemalan Indian
Economy. Washington, D.C.: GPO, 1953. x,
230 pp. Index, biblio., maps, charts. 3d ed.
New York: Octagon, 1972. 230 pp. Index,
biblio., maps, charts.
El capitalismo del centavo: una economía
indígena de Guatemala. 2 vols. Guatemala:
Ministerio de Educación Pública, 1964. 579
pp. Biblio., illus., maps, tables.
A pioneering work providing a detailed
study of the economy of the municipality of
Panajachel, an Indian village, describing and
analyzing land use, work patterns, agricultural methods, production, consumption, cost

of living, and other economic factors. The
expanded Spanish edition includes additional
data. DLC LNHT BNG

1286 Teletor, Celso Narciso. Apuntes para una
monografía de Rabinal (Baja Verapaz) y algo de
nuestro folklore. Guatemala: Tipografía
Nacional, 1955. 242 pp. Index, illus.
Commentaries on the department of Rabinal,
Guatemala, with emphasis on description of the
contemporary setting and culture, and on the
Indian influence. DLC LNHT BNG

1287 _____. Síntesis biográfica del clero de
Guatemala. Guatemala: Tipografía Nacional,
1966. 303 pp. Illus.
A collection of brief briographical
sketches of over 150 Guatemalan clergy,
providing basic data regarding their families,
education, and church positions. Includes
bishops, political figures, and lesser-known
parish priests. Unfortunately, the cleric who
prepared this volume did not provide any indication of the basis of selection or of the
order of arrangement; the individuals are
listed neither alphabetically nor chronologically. DLC LNHT

1288 Tellez Garcia, Rafael Armando. La función
pública: necesidad de una ley de servicio
civil en Guatemala. Guatemala: Tipografía
Nacional, 1965. 312 pp. Biblio., illus.
A commentary on the staffing of the
Guatemalan public-service agencies, arguing
the necessity for professionalization through
civil-service legislation.

1289 Tempsky, Gustav Ferdinand von. Mitla, a
Narrative of Incidents and Personal Adventures
on a Journey in Mexico, Guatemala, and
Salvador in the Years 1853 to 1855, with
Observations on the Modes of Life in those
Countries. London: Longman, Brown, Green,
Longmans, & Roberts, 1858. xvi, 436 pp.
Illus., maps, appendixes.
While the bulk of the volume is devoted to
Mexico, the author includes extensive comments
on his travels in the Indian towns of western
Guatemala and El Salvador, providing descrip-
tions of the life and culture there in the
1850s. His background information is less
useful, reflecting the stereotypes of the era
and his reliance on the explanations offered
him. DLC LNHT

1290 Termer, Franz. Apuntes sobre geografía y
etnografía de la Costa Sur de Guatemala.
Guatemala: Tipografía Nacional, 1939. 17 pp.
A brief study, following the pattern of the
author's larger works, dealing with the landforms and climate of a small segment of the
nation.

1291 _____. Zur Ethnologie und Ethnographie das
nördlichen Mittelamerika. Berlin:
F. Dummlers Verlag, 1930. 492 pp. Illus.
Etnología y etnografía de Guatemala.
Guatemala: Ministerio de Educación Pública,
1957. 299 pp. Illus.

(Termer, Franz)
    The original was a pioneering anthropolog-
ical study based on fieldwork in Guatemala
during 1925-29 when the author traveled extensively throughout northeastern Guatemala,
principally on foot. The work, which is primarily descriptive, is based on his observations of the life and life-style of the local
Indians during the 1920s. It considers the
work, nutrition, religious beliefs, social
customs, regional conceptions, historical traditions, and astronomical knowledge of the
Indians he observed and talked with. Stresses
the modernization of the region, concluding
that the Indian cultures will be ultimately
destroyed and that only the Indian's resistance to change is delaying the inevitable.
DLC LNHT BNG

1292 ____. Zur Geographie der Republik Guatemala.
2 vols. Hamburg: Kommissions-Verlag
Friederichsen, De Gruyter & Co., 1936-41.
180, 262 pp. Index, illus., maps.
    A basic geographic summary and description
of the landforms of Guatemala, including consideration of climate and hydrology, with
appropriate maps. Devotes considerable space
to the various Indian groups, describing their
cultures in detail; includes discussion of the
Colonial era Indian policy. DLC LNHT BNG

1293 Thompson, George Alexander. Narrative of an
Official Visit to Guatemala from Mexico.
London: John Murray, 1829. xxi, vi, 528 pp.
Maps, appendixes.
Narración de una visita oficial a Guatemala
viniendo de México. Guatemala: Tipografía
Nacional, 1927. vii, 167 pp. Latest ed. San
Salvador: Ministerio de Educación, 1971. 231
pp. Maps, tables.
    The detailed observation of a British agent
sent to scout the country as a possible location for colonization. He furnished an extensive account that is particularly strong
regarding customs and the daily lives of the
various individuals he met. His book also
provides data regarding the country at that
time, including the government and officials,
the economy, and transportation facilities, as
well as his assessment of the future prospects. DLC LNHT BNG BNCR

1294 Thompson, Nora Belle. Delfino Sánchez:
Guatemalan Statesman. N.p.: Published by the
Author, 1977. ix, 105 pp.
    Originally a doctoral dissertation, the
published version omits the footnotes and
bibliography, but is based on documentary
research and the available secondary sources.
It details the career of the Guatemalan political figure and diplomat who was associated
with the Liberal regimes of the 1870s and
1880s. DLC LNHT

1295 ____. Land of Eternal Spring (Guatemala).
Philadelphia: Dorrance, 1974. 172 pp.
Illus.
    A travelogue recounting the experiences of
the author over a ten-year period of trips to
Guatemala, focusing on people, life-style, and

customs. The author was associated with the
Pan American Society of Philadelphia, and
wrote with some understanding of the region,
selecting typical events and significant
fiestas. DLC

1296 Tobar Cruz, Pedro. La enseñanza de la
historia en los tres movimientos educacionales
de Guatemala en el siglo XIX. Guatemala:
Imprenta Universitaria, 1953. 29 pp.
    A discussion of the evolution of the
nation's educational system and the use of
history within it during the Liberal and Conservative regimes of the nineteenth-century
period of confrontation between these forces,
noting the changes each made. BNG

1297 ____. Los montañeses: la facción de los
Lucíos y otros acontecimientos históricos de
1846 a 1851. Guatemala: Ministerio de
Educación Pública, 1959. 175 pp. Biblio.,
notes, illus. Latest ed. Guatemala:
Editorial Universitaria, 1971. 442 pp.
Biblio., notes.
    A history of the eastern regions of
Guatemala, especially of Japala, and their
role in the politics of the independence era
from 1829 to 1840, emphasizing the area's role
in the 1838 revolt of Rafael Carrera against
Mariano Gálvez, and opposing Morazán and the
Federation. Drawn from a theses based on
published works; the 1971 edition is much
longer, with added excerpts from documentation. DLC LNHT BNG

1298 Toledo, Salvador. Un mentís al folleto de
Barbaroux titulado "El 9 de febrero de 1898"
en lo que se relaciona con Salvador Toledo.
Guatemala: Sánchez & de Guise, 1899. 50 pp.
    A response to the folio entitled El 9
febrero de 1898 by Barbaraux (pseudonym of
Felipe Estrada Paniagua), by a functionary of
the Reyna Barrios and Estrada Cabrera regimes
who disputes the details of the account and
the accusations against various officers,
defending the role of Estrada Cabrera. LNHT

1299 Toness, Odin Alf, Jr. Relaciones del poder en
un barrio marginal de centroamérica.
Guatemala: Ministerio de Educación Pública,
1969. 79 pp. Biblio., notes, illus., tables.
    Originally a master's thesis in anthropol-
ogy, this pamphlet examines a dispute regarding land ownership involving squatter settlers
in the district of Las Palmas in the capital,
which had dragged on for twelve years at the
time of the author's fieldwork in 1964. The
study details the characteristics of the
neighborhood, the social and political organizations within it and their functioning,
using these data to examine the lines of power
and authority among its populace, focusing
particularly on the organizational efforts of
the government and the Social Democratic
party. DLC

1300 Torbiörnsson, Peter. Guatemala: terror i
u-land. Stockholm: Almqvist & Wiksell, 1969.
56 pp. Biblio., maps, tables.

A Swedish journalist's overview of Guatemalan society and geography, followed by a brief discussion of terrorism, communism, and multinational corporations. Concludes with references to the Common Market and to other Central American countries; condemns Yankee imperialism. DLC

1301   Toriello Garrido, Guillermo. ¿A donde va Guatemala? Mexico: Editorial América Nueva, 1956. 122 pp. Notes.

The former foreign minister of the revolutionary government and junta member denounces the National Liberation Movement and its leader, Carlos Castillo Armas, in torrid prose. Reviewing the first two years of Castillo Armas's regime, he accuses it of being a tool of imperialism, capitalism, and the multinational corporations, particularly of the United Fruit Company. The volume is part of the continuing political polemic that characterized Guatemala in the 1950s; it levels all manner of charges of atrocities, dictatorship, etc., criticizing the new regime for following different policies from those with which the author was associated. DLC LNHT

1302   _____. La batalla de Guatemala. Mexico: Ediciones Cuadernos Americanos, 1955. 349 pp. Biblio., notes. 3d ed. Buenos Aires: Ediciones Pueblos de América, 1956. 326 pp. Bitva za Gvatemalu. Moscow: Izdatel'stvo inostrannoi literatury, 1956. 300 pp.

An emotional account of the Guatemalan revolutionary governments and the 1944 revolution, by one of the leaders of the movement who served it as junta member and foreign minister. He defends its record and bitterly denounces the 1954 counterrevolution, assailing it as a case of pure Yankee imperialism and denouncing the capitalist imperialists, foreign investors, the U.S. government, and the National Liberation Movement. While the denunciations reflect the emotion of the moment, the volume provides a useful view of the revolution as seen by the revolutionaries, the rationale for their programs, and their view of the world. DLC LNHT BNG

1303   _____. Guatemala: mas de 20 años de traición, 1954-1979. Guatemala: Editorial Universitaria, 1979. 310 pp. Index, biblio., notes, tables.

Another in a continuing series of works denouncing Yankee imperialism, which overthrew the revolutionary governments in which the author served, tracing the development of Guatemala since 1954 and hence constituting what amounts to a sequel to the author's La batalla de Guatemala. The revolutionary and guerrilla movements of the 1960s and 1970s are stressed, with appropriate excoriation of the CIA and Yankee-inspired countermeasures, which are viewed as institutionalizing terrorism and violence. Toriello contends that the Mano Blanco is the real power in control of Guatemala, though the volume also castigates the CIA, military, local bourgeoisie, and transnational corporations to prove that the

nation is under the thumb of foreign imperialists at the expense of its own masses. DLC LNHT

1304   _____. Tras la cortina de banano. Mexico: Fondo de Cultura Económica, 1976. 277 pp.

Yet another denunciation of the impact of imperialism on Guatemala, this one focusing on the role of the United Fruit Company and its subsidiaries, excoriating their control of the Guatemalan economy, and charging that they exploit the populace to make excessive profits. Includes discussion of the role of the company in the overthrow of the revolutionary governments in which the author served, with details of the conflict regarding expropriation of the company-owned lands during the regime of Jacabo Arbenz Guzmán. BNG

1305   Torres, Edelberto. Enrique Gómez Carrillo: el cronista errante. Guatemala: Librería Escolar, 1956. 384 pp. Biblio., illus.

A biography of one of Guatemala's best-known writers, tracing his life, trips, thoughts, and exiles, based on research in the press and government documents. It is a biography rather than literary criticism, focusing on the events of the author's life, though in the process it provides insights into his outlook and the events that influenced him. DLC LNHT BNG

1306   Torres, Lorenzo M. Crónicas de las manifestaciones públicas que en honor al benemérito de la patria, licenciado Manuel Estrada Cabrera, presidente de la República, se llevaron a cabo en la cabecera departamental de Escuintla, durante los días comprendidos del 13 al 17 de marzo de 1911, con motivo de su exaltación al poder para un nuevo período presidencial. Guatemala: Sánchez & de Guise, 1911. 36 pp.

An official account of the ceremonies hailing the dictator on the occasion of his inauguration for another term.

1307   Torres Rivas, Edelberto. Las clases sociales en Guatemala. Guatemala: Universidad de San Carlos de Guatemala, 1962. 115 pp. Biblio., notes.

A thesis defining in Marxist terms the characteristics and origins of the various classes in Guatemala, emphasizing the fragmentation in the society, the gaps between the groups, and the rural/urban dichotomies. Based on secondary works, principally theoretical Marxist tracts. TxU

1308   Totonicapán, Department of. Monografía del departamento de Totonicapán. Guatemala: n.p., n.d. 77 pp. Illus.

A compilation of basic data about the department, including tables of distances, descriptions and brief histories of its towns, descriptions and photos of its facilities, and essays regarding its culture and economy. Though undated, this locally sponsored and lavishly illustrated endeavor was clearly published in the late 1930s or early 1940s, during the Ubico administration. DLC

1309 Townsend Ezcurra, Andrés. <u>José Toribio</u>
<u>Medina</u>: <u>síntesis bio-bibliográfica</u>.
Guatemala: Ministerio de Educación Pública,
1952. 18 pp. Illus.
      A brief biographical sketch hailing the
work of this Chilean-born scholar who spent
much of his life in Guatemala, and his contribution to the nation's scholarship, particularly through bibliographical compilations.
DLC

1310 Travis, Helen Simon, and A.B. Magil. <u>The</u>
<u>Truth</u> <u>about</u> <u>Guatemala</u>. New York: New Century
Publishers, 1954. 23 pp.
      An attack on the Castillo Armas regime,
part of the polemics of that era. The
authors, who are associated with a Marxist
publishing house, visited Guatemala during the
1950s. TxU

1311 ____. <u>What</u> <u>Happened</u> <u>in</u> <u>Guatemala</u>. New York:
New Century Publishers, 1954. 23 pp.
      A defense of the Guatemalan revolutionary
regimes and an attack on the Castillo Armas
regime, which the authors characterize as
fascist. DLC

1312 Tumin, Melvin M. <u>San Luís Jilotepeque</u>: <u>A</u>
<u>Study in Social Relations</u>. Evanston, Ill.:
Northwestern University Press, 1944. 4th ed.
Westport, Conn.: Greenwood Press, 1975.
xiii, 300 pp. Index, biblio.
      A study of San Luís Jilotepeque, based on
fieldwork conducted during the early 1940s.
The author states that the work is designed to
compliment that of John Gillin about the same
community, but curiously makes no mention of
his own earlier work dealing with the town.
Includes a general description of the town and
its society, though the heart of the study
focuses on intergroup relations and kinship
patterns, as affected by caste and class; uses
observation and survey material, combining
perceptions with actuality and data on inter-
marriage, godparent linkages, and familial
ties. The title varies, with the latest edi-
tions employing <u>Cast</u> <u>and</u> <u>Class</u> <u>in</u> <u>a</u> <u>Peasant</u>
<u>Society</u>. DLC LNHT

1313 <u>Turcios Lima</u>: <u>biografía</u> <u>y</u> <u>documentos</u>.
Montevideo: Ediciones de la Banda Oriental,
1969. 155 pp.
      The collected writings of a Guatemalan
guerrilla leader of the 1960s, with a brief
biography extolling his efforts and contributions to the nation. DLC

1314 Ubico, Emilio. <u>El licenciado Estrada Cabrera</u>:
[<u>breve</u> <u>reseña</u> <u>de</u> <u>lo</u> <u>realizado</u> <u>en</u> <u>el</u> <u>primer</u>
<u>año del segundo período constitucional</u>].
Guatemala: n.p., 1906. 78 pp. Illus.
      A list and description of the projects
completed or begun during the first term of
Estrada Cabrera, originally published in the
newspaper <u>El Cronista</u>. The projects are
listed province by province, with description
and photos, but with little other comment.
DLC

1315 Unión Patriótica Guatemalteca. <u>Guatemala</u>
<u>contra el imperialismo, 1954-1964</u>: <u>las luchas</u>

populares <u>y</u> <u>la</u> <u>acción</u> <u>armada</u>. Havana:
Editorial EIR, 1964. 76 pp.
      The communist version of recent Guatemalan
history, defending the accomplishments of the
revolution despite their "limits," denouncing
the Yankee imperialism that defeated it in
1954, and decrying the return of the imperialist corporations, while hailing the rebellion
against Ydígoras Fuentes and the new guerrilla
movements as the wave of the future and calling for renewed struggle by the entire populace. DLC LNHT

1316 U.S., Congress. House. Committee on Foreign
Affairs. <u>Report of the Special Study Mission</u>
<u>to Guatemala</u>. 85th Cong., 1st sess., H. Rept.
207. Washington, D.C.: GPO, 1957. v, 19 pp.
Maps.
      Report of a congressional committee prais-
ing the policies of the Castillo Armas regime
regarding economic development and social
services. DLC

1317 ____. Committee on International Relations,
Subcommittee on International Resources, Food
and Energy. <u>Managing International Disasters</u>:
<u>Guatemala</u>: <u>Hearings and Markup before . . .</u>
<u>H.R. 12046 to Provide for Relief and Rehabili-</u>
<u>tation Assistance to the Victims of the Earth-</u>
<u>quakes in Guatemala, and for Other Purposes,</u>
<u>February 18 and March 4, 1976</u>. 94th Cong., 2d
sess. Washington, D.C.: GPO, 1976. iv, 92
pp. Tables.
      Hearings on the earthquake relief in
Guatemala in 1976, offering a wealth of statistics about the damage and relief efforts.
DLC

1318 ____. Select Committee on Communist Aggression. <u>Communist Aggression in Latin America,</u>
<u>Ninth Interim Report of Hearings before the</u>
<u>Subcommittee on Latin America of the Select</u>
<u>Committee on Communist Aggression</u>. 83d Cong.,
2d sess. Washington, D.C.: GPO, 1954. iii,
295 pp. Illus.
      The hearings of a subcommittee, including
testimony of Ambassador John E. Peurifoy and
President Castillo Armas, as well as other
individuals, recounting the role of communism
in the Arbenz regime and detailing its transgressions. Includes photos of bodies of victims, and alleged communist party papers and
documents. DLC

1319 ____. <u>Report of the Subcommittee to Investi-</u>
<u>gate Communist Aggression in Latin America to</u>
<u>the Select Committee on Communist Aggression</u>.
83d Cong., 2d sess. Washington, D.C.: GPO,
1954. ii, 18 pp.
      A report of a subcommittee investigation,
including visits to Guatemala, concluding that
the Arbenz regime was completely communist-
controlled. DLC

1320 U.S., Congress. Senate. Committee on Foreign
Relations, Subcommittee on Western Hemisphere
Affairs. <u>Guatemala Earthquake</u>: <u>Hearing . . .</u>
<u>on Impact of and Relief Efforts for Guatemala</u>
<u>Earthquake, February 16, 1976</u>. 94th Cong.,

2d sess. Washington, D.C.: GPO, 1976. iii, 64 pp.

The Senate counterpart to the House hearing, though not as comprehensive as the House effort. DLC

1321 U.S., Gov't of. Department of State. A Case History of Communist Penetration in Guatemala. Washington, D.C.: GPO, 1957. xi, 73 pp. Illus., maps.

A restatement of the official U.S. view of the penetration of communism into the Arévalo and Arbenz administrations, with lists of "front" organizations and details of the propaganda and organizational effort, as well as a comment on the nation's rejection of communism through the victory of the National Liberation Movement, which is viewed as a popular uprising against tyranny. DLC LNHT

1322 ____. Guatemala: Volcanic but Peaceful. Washington, D.C.: Coordinator of Inter-American Affairs, 1943. Pages unnumbered.

A brief pamphlet of general information for the layman, emphasizing interaction and trade between Guatemala and the U.S. DLC

1323 ____. Intervention of International Communism in Guatemala. Washington, D.C.: GPO, 1954. iii, 96 pp.

A so-called blue book offering a detailed collection of information that constituted the case against the Guatemalan revolution, including speeches, official statements, press briefings, and a chronology purporting to show the growth of the power of the Communist party. Includes major statements by Secretary of State John Foster Dulles and U.S. representative to the U.N. Henry Cabot Lodge. DLC LNHT

1324 ____. Penetration of the Political Institutions of Guatemala by the International Communist Movement: Threat to the Peace and Security of America and to the Sovereignty and Political Independence of Guatemala: Information Submitted by the Delegation of the United States to the Fifth Meeting of Consultation of Ministers of Foreign Affairs of the American Republics, Serving as an Organ of Consultation. Washington, D.C.: GPO, 1954. 56 pp. Penetración del movimiento comunista internacional en las instituciones políticas de Guatemala: amenaza a la paz y la seguridad de América y la soberanía e independencia política de Guatemala. Washington, D.C.: GPO, 1954. 72 pp.

An official statement of the U.S. view, attacking the role of communism in the government of Arbenz; compiled in preparation for the foreign ministers' meeting that was to have convened on 7 July 1954 but which was postponed when the Arbenz government was overthrown. Includes documents, tabulations of armament, and other supporting papers. DLC LNHT

1325 ____. Shufeldt Claim: Claim of the United States of America on behalf of P.W. Shufeldt vs. the Republic of Guatemala before the

Honorable Sir Hubert Sisnett. Washington, D.C.: GPO, 1932. 882 pp. Maps.

The complete documents of the arbitration, including the U.S. and Guatemalan cases and replies; voluminous annexes; and the decision of the arbitor, the chief justice of British Honduras, awarding damages. The case involves the 1928 cancellation of a 1922 chicle exploitation contract in the Petén in which Shufeldt had an interest. LNHT

1326 Urrutia, Miguel Ángel, ed. Índice de las leyes emitidas por el gobierno democrático de la República de Guatemala, desde el 3 de junio de 1871, hasta el 30 de junio de 1881. Guatemala: Tipografía El Progreso, 1882. 102 pp.

An index to the initial three volumes of the Standard Guatemalan law compilation, which was published with the series. See item GU570. LNHT

1327 Urrutia Aparicio, Carlos. Páginas internacionales de la vida democrática de Guatemala. Guatemala: Ministerio de Educación Pública, 1961. 148 pp.

A series of speeches and circular notes by the author written during his service as Guatemalan ambassador to the Organization of American States during the administration of General Miguel Ydígoras Fuentes. DLC BNG

1328 Valdés Oliva, Arturo. Fundación de la Escuela Politécnica. Guatemala: Ministerio de Educación Pública, 1971. 173 pp. Biblio., notes, illus.

A well-known Guatemalan historian provides an account of the foundation of the Guatemalan military academy, tracing its antecedents back to Colonial days and the training of militia officers, but focusing on its foundation in 1873 and the regulations involved. It includes a discussion of curriculum and corps size as well as reproductions of important decrees in its development. The focus is on the late nineteenth-century formative years of the academy. BNG

1329 ____. El hombre. Antigua: Tipografía Azmitia, 1935. 123 pp.

A brief history of the rise to power of Justo Rufino Barrios, focusing on his image and actions during the 1870 revolt against the government of Vicente Cerna, and on his actions from 1870 to 1874. The volume hails the contributions of Barrios and depicts him as a man of decision and action, which the republic needed to carry out reforms; attributes the criticism and false images of his early years to church propaganda. BNG

1330 ____. Lenguas indígenas de Guatemala. Guatemala: Ministerio de Educación Pública, 1965. 26 pp. Maps.

A discussion of the principal languages and their geographical distribution, focusing on the northern portions of the nation; with maps. BNG

1331 Valdes Sandoval, Elias. <u>Tizubín</u>. Guatemala:
      Ministerio de Educación Pública, 1974.
      197 pp.
          A novel set in the tropical lowlands of
      northeastern Guatemala, emphasizing the beauty
      of the country and the miserable conditions in
      which the peasants live. The author is a
      journalist who was active in the 1944 revolu-
      tion. DLC BNG

1332 Váldez Illescas, Raquel Yolanda. <u>Bibliografía</u>
      <u>sobre el recurso agua en Guatemala</u>.
      Guatemala: Universidad de San Carlos, 1974.
      321 pp. Biblio.
          An annotated bibliography of studies deal-
      ing with the nation's water resources. DLC

1333 Valenti, Walda. <u>Lumbre penumbra</u>. Guatemala:
      Tipografía Nacional, 1967. 92 pp.
          A collection of short stories, some set in
      Guatemala, dealing with disparate themes;
      includes several depicting rural problems, the
      peasants' clashes with the authorities, and
      the impact of the guerrilla movements of the
      1960s. DLC

1334 Valenzuela, Gilberto. <u>Biografía de don</u>
      <u>Ignacio Solís F.</u>. Guatemala: Unión
      Tipográfica, 1962. 63 pp. Illus.
          A brief sketch of the life of a late
      nineteenth-century Guatemalan intellectual
      active in economic development and study of
      the indigenous population, who was a proponent
      and organizer of many projects well in advance
      of his time; hails his contributions on the
      occasion of the fiftieth anniversary of his
      death. DLC LNHT BNG

1335 _____. <u>Guatemala y sus gobernantes, 1821-</u>
      <u>1958: recopilación</u>. Guatemala: Ministerio
      de Educación Pública, 1959. 128 pp. Illus.
          Brief single-paragraph biographical data,
      with photos, on each of the individuals who
      headed Guatemala, including Colonial captain
      generals, heads of the Central American Fed-
      eration, presidents of the republic, and junta
      members for the period in question. Provides
      only basic information, but is a handy source
      for this. DLC BNG

1336 Valenzuela, Gilberto, and Gilberto Valenzuela
      Reyna, eds. <u>Bibliografía guatemalteca y</u>
      <u>catálogo general de libros, folletos,</u>
      <u>periódicos, revistas, etc., 1861-1900</u>. 10
      vols. Guatemala: Tipografía Nacional, 1960-
      64. Illus.
          A multivolume series listing all works
      published in Guatemala, including some from
      other countries dealing with Guatemala.
      Entries are arranged chronologically by year
      and alphabetically by author, though in many
      of the volumes publications by governmental
      agencies are listed separately. Books, news-
      papers, and journal and newspaper articles are
      intermixed, and the distinction is not always
      clear. Most entries have "annotations" con-
      sisting of the table of contents, excerpts
      from the preface, or a commentary. Some are
      based on comments, the compilers never having
      seen the volume. Completeness of information

for the entries is variable and uneven. A
monumental compilation, but one that must be
used cautiously. DLC LNHT BNG

1337 Valenzuela Oliva, Wilfredo. <u>Las dos goteras,</u>
      <u>y otros cuentos</u>. Guatemala: Ministerio de
      Educación Pública, 1962. 120 pp. Illus.
          A series of short stories focusing on rural
      life in the humid Guatemalan coastal region,
      emphasizing description of the colorful land,
      the problems of farming in the region, and
      social conditions. BNG

1338 Valiente Rodríguez, Oscar. <u>La historia de un</u>
      <u>lustrador</u>. Guatemala: Tipografía Nacional,
      1968. 150 pp. Illus.
          A view of the life of the marginally em-
      ployed through the eyes of a shoeshine boy,
      which also uses his vantagepoint to look at
      Guatemalan society. The emphasis, however, is
      on the shoeshine boy's experiences and inter-
      action with his friends and customers. DLC
      LNHT

1339 Valladares, León A. <u>El hombre y el maíz:</u>
      <u>etnografía y etnopsicología de Colotenango</u>.
      Guatemala: Universidad de San Carlos, 1937.
      2d ed. Mexico: B. Costa-Amic, 1958. 299 pp.
      Biblio.
          An ethnographical and psychological study--
      originally a thesis--of the Indian municipio
      of Colotenango. Provides physical description
      and analysis of customs, life-styles, and
      institutions. DLC LNHT

1340 Valladares Rubio, Manuel [Frences Redish,
      pseud.]. <u>Estudios históricos</u>. Guatemala:
      Editorial Universitaria, 1962. 508 pp.
      Index, illus.
          A series of historical studies by a noted
      Guatemalan scholar and diplomat who repre-
      sented his country in many European capitals
      and at the League of Nations throughout the
      early twentieth century. Although he wrote
      under his own name in Guatemala, his publica-
      tions outside the country employed the pseudo-
      nym Dr. Frences Redish. This volume contains
      only his historical works, not his literary
      efforts, and includes studies ranging from
      independence to the era of Estrada Cabrera,
      including biographies of such figures as
      Antonio Larrazábal, José Matías Delgado,
      Manuel José de Arce, Mariano Gálvez, Justo
      Rufino Barrios, and others. DLC BNG

1341 _____. <u>Letras de oro</u>. Guatemala: Imprenta
      Galindo, 1969. xiii, 392 pp. Illus.
          A collection of writings by one of
      Guatemala's best-known literary and political
      figures of the turn of the century, containing
      mainly excerpts from his <u>Estudios históricos</u>.
      DLC BNG

1342 Valle, José. <u>Guatemala para el turista:</u>
      <u>crónicas de viaje</u>. Guatemala: Tipografía
      Nacional, 1929. 18 pp. Illus.
          A descriptive account, published under
      government auspices, of the author's extensive
      travels in Guatemala during his journalism
      career. They contain accounts of virtually

all important or sizeable cities, as well as
descriptions of transport and accounts of
conversations and events associated with the
trips. DLC BNG

1343 Valle, Rafael Heliodoro. La alegría de
producir. Segovia: Tipografía "El Adelanto,"
n.d. [1924]. 253 pp.
      A series of short stories, though grouped
in subdivisions, reflecting Guatemalan life
during the era of Manuel Estrada Cabrera.
They deal with a broad range of themes reflecting the oppression and the fear in which
the peasants lived. BNG

1344 Valle Matheu, Jorge del. Guía sociogeográfica
de Guatemala: con referencias a las
condiciones de vida, lugares de atractivo
turístico y necesidades de los municipos de la
república. Guatemala: Tipografía Nacional,
1956. 371 pp. Index, illus., maps, tables.
      A general survey of Guatemala, providing
basic geographical data, designed to orient
future sociological studies. The initial
portion deals with the present state of the
republic, providing useful statistics, maps,
and charts regarding the distribution of population and various types of production, particularly agricultural; the second portion
includes brief synopses of similar geographical and statistical data for each of the 322
municipios of the nation. DLC LNHT BNG

1345 _____. Un pueblo que se redime. Guatemala:
Tipografía Nacional, 1954. 75 pp.
      A series of essays written in support of
the National Liberation Movement, reflecting
the political passion of that era. They seek
to define liberty and democracy while rejecting Marxist and radical solutions, emphasizing
the MLN as the heir of the Guatemalan traditional values. The work was published posthumously. DLC

1346 _____. Sociología guatemalteca: manual
introductorio. Guatemala: Editorial
Universitaria, 1950. 254 pp. Illus., maps,
tables.
      Intended as a university text, most of the
volume consists of a synopsis of general sociological principles and a discussion of
sociological methods, but it also includes
essays summarizing the Guatemalan social scene
and the changes in Guatemalan society. Though
these duplicate the author's other works, they
are provided here in concise summary form for
classroom use. DLC LNHT

1347 _____. La verdad sobre el "caso de
Guatemala." Guatemala: Imprenta Moderna,
1956. 173 pp.
      Originally prepared as a series of news-
paper articles, this volume is part of the
propaganda duel that characterized the ideological clash in Guatemala during the 1950s.
The author, a former cabinet minister in the
government of Carlos Castillo Armas, provides
an account of Guatemala during the Arbenz
years; he condemns the communism, catalogs
charges of abuse, corruption, and leftism, and

depicts Castillo Armas as the rescuer of
Guatemala from a foreign imposition by the
communists. DLC LNHT

1348 Valois, Alfred de. Mexique, Havanne et
Guatemala: notes de voyage par Alfred de
Valois. Paris: E. Dentu, 1861. 446 pp.
      A travelogue describing a French consular
officer's visits, including comments on the
government and economy and historical background. Guatemala occupies two-thirds of the
volume. Includes discussion of the Belgian
colony at Santo Tomás, and a brief reference
to Belize. The focus is narration of the
author's experiences and discussions with
individuals he met, including rebel leader
Vicente Cruz, though he uses these episodes to
examine the culture and life-style, as well as
the economy and political setting. He is
critical of the Carrera regime. DLC LNHT

1349 Vargas Robles, José Armando. Las inversiones
públicas en el desarrollo económico de
Guatemala. Guatemala: Ministerio de
Educación Pública, 1961. 119 pp. Biblio.,
tables.
      Originally a thesis at the University of
San Carlos, this volume offers a brief survey
of government investment policies and their
effects, covering the years 1945-1960. Includes statistical tables of government budgets and allocations of funds by ministry. It
traces the patterns of the various regimes of
the period, noting the percentage of the national budget devoted to public works, and the
ranges involved, as well as the types of projects. He recommends more rational planning of
investments in the long run, and a greater
government involvement in the economy, with
increased taxes to provide financing. LNHT

1350 Vásquez, José Valentín. El mujer en el hogar.
Guatemala: Tipografía Nacional, 1929. 219
pp. Illus.
      A discussion of the role of women in na-
tional life and the education necessary and
appropriate for their role. Emphasizes that
the place of the woman is in the home, and
extols motherhood as the highest aspiration
for women. Proposes reforms in education and
appropriate courses to prepare primary-school
girls for their future role. DLC BNG

1351 _____. Rebeldías. Guatemala: Imprenta
Marroquín Hermanos, 1921. 116 pp. Index,
illus.
      An impassioned personal credo denouncing
the attitudes and institutions of the isthmus.
Contends that new leadership is needed to
transform the nations into representative
democracies and instill more positive attitudes among their people to emphasize reform
and eliminate corruption and cynicism. LNHT

1352 Vásquez A., Rafael. Historia de la música en
Guatemala, 1950. Guatemala: Tipografía
Nacional, 1950. 346 pp. Illus.

A series of essays regarding music in Guatemala, describing musical types and themes, composers, and organizations involved in its development. Includes discussion of nationalism in Guatemalan music and the society in which it evolved. The short pieces principally describe the work of the individuals and institutions, with analysis confined only to the thematic considerations. DLC BNG

1353 Vásquez Martínez, Edmundo. El cheque en el nuevo código de comercio. Guatemala: Editorial Universitaria, 1971. 127 pp. Biblio., appendixes.
Intended for the general public, this volume explains the new legal stipulations regarding the use of checks and their status, and reproduces the appropriate legislation. BNG

1354 _____. La universidad y la constitución. Guatemala: Editorial Universitaria, 1966. 46 pp.
Two speeches by the rector of the University of San Carlos, in which he analyzes the function of the university and its legal position under the 1945 constitution and discusses its rights and duties and the limits of its powers. DLC LNHT

1355 Vázquez, Miguel Ángel. El fuego enterrado. Guatemala: Editorial Landívar, n.d. [197?].
A sequel to La semilla del fuego, continuing the fictionalized portrayal of the abuses and hardships of dictatorship; emphasizes the use of violence, the prevalence of corruption, and the oppression of the campesinos. BNG

1356 _____. La semilla del fuego. Guatemala: Editorial Landívar, 1976. 355 pp.
A novel dealing with the oppressiveness and brutality of dictatorship, emphasizing the arbitrariness of such regimes and the hardship they cause those under their power. The author characterizes the work as a "contemporary history" of any or all of the countries of Latin America, but emphasizes that it is purely fictional and not patterned after any particular regime; his intention, he says, is rather to portray human emotions in such situations. Yet the volume ends with a reference to 20 October 1944, the date of the revolution that overthrew the Ponce regime, and the revolt described in the final chapter parallels the events of that time, even in its references to streets in Guatemala City. Although several of the items mentioned correspond to the Ubico era, the regime portrayed is, in style, that of Estrada Cabrera rather than that of Ubico, as is the case with most literary portraits of that regime. BNG

1357 Vega Barberena, José Luís. Justo Rufino Barrios y su obra. Santa Ana: Imprenta Funes y Ungo, 1935. 72 pp.
A brief résumé of the works of the Barrios administration, focusing on the beneficial results of his efforts and acclaiming his accomplishments. The author emphasizes the expansion of the Tipografía Nacional, the foundation of the Biblioteca Nacional, and the expansion of scholarship during his years in power. DLC LNHT

1358 Vela, David. La Academia Guatemalteca, correspondiente de la Española: sus actividades y la obra personal de sus miembros. Guatemala: Unión Tipográfica, 1951. 60 pp. Notes, appendixes.
A brief history of the activities of the academy from its foundation in 1888. About half the volume is devoted to brief sketches of the prominent members of the academy, providing biographical details and a list of their principal works. KU

1359 _____. Barrundia ante el espejo de su tiempo. 2 vols. Guatemala: Editorial Universitaria, 1956-57. 309, 400 pp. Notes, illus.
A detailed biography and study of the life and works of José Francisco Barrundia, whose political and literary career spans the initial half of the nineteenth century. The first volume analyzes the Liberal statesman's role in the independence movement, his opposition to Mexican annexation, his role as Senate president, and his support of the Federation. The second volume deals with his political polemics with Vicente Filísola, Manuel José de Arce, and Mariano Gálvez, and with an analysis of his literary and scholarly works. Throughout, the author's intention, in addition to biography, is to show Barrundia's actions as a reflection of the turbulence of the independence era. The author, himself a Liberal editor of El Imparcial, understandably stresses Barrundia's literary and journalistic activities. Based upon research in the newspapers of the era, the memoirs of participants, and appropriate secondary works, as well as the writings of the title character, with extensive quotations. DLC LNHT BNG

1360 _____. Martí en Guatemala. Havana: Comisión Nacional Organizadora del Centenario y del Monumento de Martí, 1953. 486 pp. Biblio. 2d ed. Guatemala: Ministerio de Educación Pública, 1954. 366 pp. Biblio.
Originally a series of articles published in the author's newspaper, El Imparcial, commemorating the centennial of the birth of Martí, the volume constitutes a history of Martí's stay in Guatemala during a period of exile. It quotes liberally from his writings and publications to present his impressions and thoughts, and recounts his itinerary. Provides some insights into Cuban-Guatemalan ties in the nineteenth century. DLC LNHT BNG

1361 _____. Temas cívicos. Guatemala: Ministerio de Educación Pública, 1962. 151 pp.
A series of essays regarding patriotism and brief histories of the national symbols, such as the flag, the national seal, and the quetzal, followed by brief minibiographies of Indian leaders who remain heroes of Guatemalan folklore. Some of the essays are in dialogue

(Vela, David)
        form, suitable for primary-school classroom
        use to introduce the figures. DLC LNHT BNG

1362   ____. Un personaje sin novela. Mexico: B.
        Costa-Amic, 1958. 175 pp.
            A novel by a well-known newspaper editor,
        written in the form of the autobiography of a
        ficticious character. Using a Guatemalan
        setting and focusing on the Guatemalan life-
        style, it carefully uses the language of the
        common people, seeking to preserve their dia-
        lect and viewpoint. DLC BNG

1363   Vela, Francisco. Datos de la República de
        Guatemala, recopilados por el ingeniero
        Francisco Vela. Guatemala: Artes Gráficas
        "Electra," 1908. 100 pp. Tables.
            A listing of basic data on mountains,
        rivers, lakes, roads, etc., with a table of
        distances between towns. BNG

1364   Venin, V.N. Gvatemala [Guatemala]. Moscow:
        Gosudarstvennoe izdatel'stvo geograficheskoi
        literatury, 1954. 91 pp. Illus.
        Guatemala. Leipzig: Veb Bibliographisches
        Institut, 1955. 78 pp. Notes, illus.
            A geographical and anthropological study
        emphasizing physical setting, transport, econ-
        omy, and Indian cultures, and concluding with
        an account of the U.S. role in the 1954 coup.
        DLC

1365   La verdad sobre la "última" conspiración del
        comunismo. Guatemala: Tipografía Nacional,
        1957. 71 pp. Illus., appendixes.
            An official account of the conspiracy that
        was discovered 23 June 1957, which is de-
        scribed as part of a continuing series of
        efforts by the world communist movement to
        undo the revolution of 1954. Condemns the
        naiveté of what it characterizes as "oppo-
        sitionists" who were used by the communists in
        their effort, listing in this category nearly
        all the leaders of the Guatemalan revolution-
        ary movement that was ousted from power in
        1954. Appropriate documents and press ac-
        counts are appended. BNG

1366   La verdadera fisonomía política del gobierno
        de Guatemala: carta dirigida a los delegados
        de las naciones americanas en la Conferencia
        de Río de Janeiro. Mexico: n.p., 1947.
        16 pp.
            An attack on the Arévalo government, sent
        to the Río conference from exile, charging
        restriction of freedoms, repression, and com-
        munism. DLC

1367   Véritas. Progresivo desarrollo económico y
        social de Guatemala desde el año de 1838.
        Guatemala: Imprenta de José Azurdia, 1886.
        15 pp.
            A brief summary of the economic and social
        progress of Guatemala from independence to the
        time of publication, hailing the programs of
        the Liberal regimes and their impact on the
        nation. TxU

1368   Vidaurre, Adrián. La constitución de
        Guatemala como obra de transformación política

y social. Guatemala: Tipografía Nacional,
1935. 224 pp.
    An analysis of the constitution of 1879 and
the various treaties and laws that amplified
it, reproducing the texts of its various
clauses and emphasizing the reforms of the
Liberal document and their beneficial impact
on the nation. DLC LNHT BNG

1369   ____. Memorias. 2 vols. Havana: Imprenta
        Sainz Arca, 1921-22. 172, 245 pp. Illus.
            A personal political memoir recounting his
        experiences in Guatemalan politics from the
        government of Reyna Barrios to that of Estrada
        Cabrera. Contains excerpts from correspond-
        ence and speeches, providing a glimpse of the
        political maneuvers of the day, including the
        flavor of the polemics. The author was a
        political associate and friend of both Reyna
        Barrios and Estrada Cabrera, and a sometime
        functionary of their regimes. The second
        volume, added later, details the overthrow of
        Estrada Cabrera and the events of 1920-21,
        during the government of Carlos Herrera,
        through the installation of José María
        Orellana. It is critical of the Conserva-
        tives, reflecting the author's ties to the
        Liberal regimes that were ousted. LNHT BNG

1370   ____. Paralelo entre dos administraciones:
        apuntes para la historia. Guatemala: Sánchez
        & de Guise, 1907. 47 pp. Illus.
            A comparison of the regimes of Manuel
        Estrada Cabrera and José María Reyna Barrios
        by a Liberal politician who served in both,
        constituting a precursor to his later more
        lengthy memoirs. TxU

1371   Villacorta Calderón, José Antonio.
        Bibliografía guatemalteca: según los
        catálogos de las exposiciones abiertas en el
        salón de historia y bellas artes del Museo
        Nacional, en los meses de deciembre de 1939,
        1940, 1941 y 1942. Guatemala: Tipografía
        Nacional, 1944. 638 pp. Index, illus.,
        tables.
            An extensive catalog of the national expo-
        sition in honor of the anniversary of printing
        in Guatemala during 1939-42. Contains a com-
        plete listing of bibliographic information for
        all volumes exhibited, as well as reproduc-
        tions of the title pages of key works and
        photographs of significant authors. The vari-
        ous sections cover books, periodicals, and
        engravings, with chronological breakdowns.
        Information is complete though entries are
        unannotated. The listings for various edi-
        tions are fully duplicated, as are the long
        lists of honors, degrees, and titles of the
        authors. This duplication and the resulting
        length of the entries renders the work awkward
        to use, but at least these problems stem from
        completeness. DLC LNHT

1372   ____. Historia de la República de Guatemala,
        1821-1921. Guatemala: Tipografía Nacional,
        1960. 590 pp. Biblio., illus.
            A detailed survey of Guatemala to 1885,
        based on extensive research in secondary and

(Villacorta Calderón, José Antonio)
archival sources and including photos of leading figures. A major portion of the volume is
given to topical treatment of social and cultural questions. DLC LNHT BNG

1373 ____, ed. J. Antonio Villacorta C. en las
ciencias y letras americanistas, juzgado por
sus contemporáneos. Guatemala: Centro
Editorial, 1949. 105 pp. Illus.
A kind of detailed curriculum vitae by the
author, a distinguished scholar, listing his
various publications, with appended excerpts
from various commentaries about them, along
with press commentaries about the various
addresses he gave during his career and a list
of his personal awards. LNHT BNG

1374 Villacorta Calderón, José Antonio. Monografía
del departamento de Guatemala. Guatemala:
Tipografía Nacional, 1926. xii, 378 pp.
Illus., maps, tables.
A detailed history of the central department of the republic, by a well-known writer.
Treats its development, physical setting,
flora, fauna, and geology. Includes general
chapters on the state and detailed discussions
of the individual municipalities and the capital, showing their development and current
situation; numerous maps and statistical
tables. DLC LNHT

1375 Villacorta Escobar, Manuel. Apuntes de
economía agrícola. Guatemala: Editorial
Universitaria, 1973. 146 pp. Biblio.,
tables.
A general explanation of agriculture in
Guatemala, stressing its importance to the
national economy and arguing that economic
development in the nation is impossible without modernization of the agricultural sector
and its coordination with that of the rest of
the economy. Includes discussion of all the
various factors needed, such as land distribution, credit, labor, and technology; cites the
current state of Guatemala and previous
efforts at improvement; briefly summarizes
programs in other nations. The statistics
cover the 1960s. DLC LNHT

1376 ____. Recursos económicos de Guatemala.
Guatemala: Editorial Universitaria, 1976.
153 pp. Notes, maps, tables.
A geographic manual intended for use in the
schools. Provides basic descriptive data
about the nation and its setting, focusing on
resources, both natural and human. Considers
themes such as energy, industry, and land
tenure, as well as the physical aspects of the
nation. LNHT

1377 Villacorta Vidaurre, Lola. Hierba mora.
Guatemala: Tipografía San Antonio, 1965. 100
pp. Illus.
A series of short stories about life in
Cobán, Verapaz, drawing upon local legends and
the author's own experiences. DLC LNHT BNG

1378 Villacorta Vidaurre, Lola, et al. Cuentos
verapacenses. Guatemala: Editorial Istmo,
1968. 108 pp.

A collection of short stories by a number
of authors from the Verapaz region of
Guatemala, seeking to preserve its unique
traditions and emphasize its natural setting.
Includes a brief biography of each of the
contributors. DLC LNHT

1379 Villagrán Kramer, Francisco. El régimen de
legalidad: ensayo sociopolítico. Guatemala:
Círculo de Estudios Constitucionales, 1963.
24 pp. Notes.
A legal-political tract reviewing the question of the constitutionality of the various
Guatemalan governments. Skirts the issue by
denouncing "rigidity" in regard to the constitutions; contends that the issue is not one of
returning to a past constitution but of installing a regime of laws; implies that a new
constitution to fit the times and correct the
errors in those of 1945 and 1956 would be
preferable. LNHT

1380 Villagrán Kramer, Francisco, et al. Bases
para el desarrollo económico y social de
Guatemala. Mexico: B. Costa-Amic, 1966. 157
pp. Tables.
A plan drawn by a commission of the Unidad
Revolucionaria Democrática (URD) party to
explain its stands. This "democratic-leftist"
party emphasizes the utility of economic planning as the rational way to make decisions for
the future. The program encompasses agriculture, public health, education, electrification, and cooperation with the Common Market,
emphasizing pluralism of methods. BNG

1381 Villegas Rodas, Miguel. Mi lucha por el café
de Guatemala. Guatemala: Tipografía
Nacional, 1965. 389 pp. Illus., tables.
A collection of speeches and articles dealing with various aspects of coffee culture in
Guatemala by a longtime functionary of the
Ministry of Agriculture and editor of the
coffee bulletins. Includes commentaries on
cultivation techniques and on particular estates, and speeches on commemorative days
suggesting and defending the nation's coffee
policy and proposing means to improve and
promote cultivation, production, and sales.
DLC LNHT

1382 Visita de Mr. Knox a Guatemala: homenaje de
la prensa. Guatemala: n.p., 1912. 31 pp.
Illus.
A pamphlet collecting the newspaper edi-
torials and reportage of the visit to
Guatemala during March 1912 of United States
Secretary of State Philander C. Knox, all
acclaiming his visit and career. DLC

1383 Vivas R., César. Biografías sintéticas.
Managua: Editorial Atlántida, 1958. 61 pp.
Illus.
A collection of brief biographies, most one
or two pages long, of various individuals,
with photographs. Though written with passion
and picturesque language that apparently seeks
to capture their personalities and spirit, the
essays provide little of the usual information

expected in biographies. The selection criteria are not indicated, and the individuals appear to come from disparate fields and backgrounds. Chapter titles do not contain the subjects' names, making it impossible to find a particular entry without scanning the volume. In sum, this is more of a literary tour de force than a reference book. DLC

1384 Vollmberg, Max. Quetzales und Vulkane: ein Maler reist durchs Mayaland. Berlin: Sibyllen-Verlag Johanne Kempfe, 1932. 173 pp. Illus., maps.
     A travelogue recounting the author's experiences and observations in Guatemala, focusing on conversations with the people he met. The emphasis is on agriculture, Indians, the physical setting, and volcanoes. LNHT

1385 Wagley, Charles. Economics of a Guatemalan Village. Menasha, Wis.: American Anthropological Association, 1941. 87 pp. Biblio., illus., maps.
     A well-known anthropologist's analysis of the economy of the rural Indian village of Santiago Chimaltenango, based on fieldwork in 1937. Concludes that the area is basically devoted to maize culture and subsistence agriculture, and that while most of the villagers own some land, its uneven distribution means that many are unable to support their families from their plots, so most rely on seasonal labor on the nearby coffee estates to augment their income. DLC LNHT

1386 _____. The Social and Religious Life of a Guatemalan Village. Menasha, Wis.: American Anthropological Association, 1949. 150 pp. Index, biblio., notes, illus.
Santiago Chimaltenango: estudio antropológico-social de una comunidad indígena de Huehuetenango. Guatemala: Ministerio de Educación Pública, 1957. 339 pp. Biblio., notes.
     Part 2 of this significant study of a Mam-speaking community in northwest Guatemala; focuses on the political, social, and religious life and on the local loyalties and culture. Based on extensive fieldwork and interviews conducted in 1937. The Spanish edition includes research notes. DLC LNHT BNG

1387 Warren, Kay B. The Symbolism of Subordination: Indian Identity in a Guatemalan Town. Austin: University of Texas Press, 1978. 209 pp.
     An anthropological study of Indian-ladino relations in the town of San Andres Semetabaj, focusing specifically on the role of religion in promoting attitudes among the Indians. Examines the belief systems and symbols of the Indian societies, shedding light on the Indians' viewpoint on Guatemalan society. The study contrasts the traditional beliefs in subordination, through the promotion of a separate Indian society and community obligations, with the upward mobility of Catholic Action members, who focus on improving

themselves and their position in the larger community. DLC LNHT

1388 Welch, Edward H. Manuel Estrada Cabrera's Place in History. San Francisco: José M. Torres, 1916. 31 pp. Illus.
     A pro-Estrada Cabrera tract hailing his projects and the progress and stability he brought to the republic, which the author sees as an indication of future prospects under his enlightened rule. DLC

1389 Whetten, Nathan L. Guatemala: The Land and the People. New Haven, Conn.: Yale University Press, 1961. 399 pp. Biblio., illus., maps, tables. Reprint. Westport, Conn.: Greenwood Press, 1974. xvi, 399 pp. Biblio., illus., maps, tables.
     A detailed rural sociological study emphasizing the agricultural sector and the problems and characteristics of the rural areas. Based heavily on the 1950 census and on field-work during the late 1940s and early 1950s. Includes rich description and statistical data, with extensive tables and maps. Details the economic and social scene, treating such topics as agricultural production, diet, marketing of goods, ethnographical considerations, population distribution and characteristics, housing, clothing, land ownership, social classes, social institutions, and governmental services. The political comments are sympathetic to the programs of the revolutionary regimes. DLC LNHT

1390 Whitman, Edmund S. How an American Company, through Advertising and Public Relations, has Combatted Communism in Latin America. New York: n.p., 1955. 20 pp.
     A publication of the United Fruit Company narrating its opposition to the Guatemalan land-reform program and efforts to expropriate company land. NN

1391 Wilhelm, Prince of Sweden. Mallan två kintonenter: anteckningar från en resa i Centralamerika. Stockholm: P.A. Norstedt, 1920. 282 pp. Illus., maps. 2d ed. Stockholm: Norstedt, 1931. 282 pp. Illus., maps.
Between Two Continents: Notes from a Journey in Central America, 1920. London: Nash & Grayson, 1922. xvii, 246 pp. Biblio., illus., maps.
Zwischen zwei Kontinenten: Reiseschilderung aus dem heutigen Mittelamerika. Lübeck: Otto Quitzow Verlag, 1925. 296 pp. Illus., maps.
     A Swedish prince describes his adventures in Central America during 1920, in a book composed of his uncorrected notes from his trip and designed to familiarize Swedes with the isthmus and provide basic information. There is a good deal of description and extensive discussion of explorations of archeological zones, the latter including a brief history of the Maya as the author learned it. The descriptions, comments, and comparisons mirror the European prejudices and outlook, as distinct from those of the Yankees. Most valuable to historians is the account of the

1920 revolt that deposed Estrada Cabrera, in
which the author was caught; he provides an
account of the confusion and events as seen by
a disinterested party. DLC LNHT

1392 Wilson, James. A Brief Memoir of the Life of
James Wilson (Late of Edinburgh), with Ex-
tracts from his Journal and Correspondence,
Written Chiefly during a Residence in
Guatemala, the Capital of Central America.
London: Panton, 1829. iv, 165 pp.
    An account of the author's travel in
Guatemala during 1825, focusing on life-
styles, customs, and culture, and exhibiting
the European prejudices and cultural aloofness
that was characteristic of this age. DLC
LNHT

1393 Winter, Nevin Otto. Guatemala and Her People
of Today: Being an Account of the Land, its
History and Development; the People; Their
Customs and Characteristics; to which are
Added Chapters on British Honduras and the
Republic of Honduras, with References to the
Other Countries of Central America, Salvador,
Nicaragua, and Costa Rica. Boston: L.C.
Page, 1909. xii, 307 pp. Index, biblio.,
illus., maps.
    A travelogue combined with historical back-
ground but focusing on description of the
economy and life-style of then-contemporary
Guatemala, by an experienced travel-book
author. The volume is aimed at the general
reader and seeks to stimulate interest in
Guatemala. Despite the title, the book also
includes several chapters on Honduras, though
the majority of the volume focuses on
Guatemala. DLC LNHT

1394 Wisdom, Charles. The Chorti Indians of
Guatemala. Chicago: University of Chicago
Press, 1940. xiv, 490 pp. Biblio., illus.,
maps. 2d ed. Chicago: University of Chicago
Press, 1974. xiv, 490 pp. Biblio., illus.,
maps.
Los chortis de Guatemala. Guatemala:
Ministerio de Educación Pública, 1961. 541
pp. Biblio., illus., maps.
    An early regional ethnographic study of
Guatemala, based on field research in 1931-33
in the department of Chiquimula, in La Unión,
and in Honduras. A detailed discussion of the
customs, life-style, traditions, religion, and
economy of the Chorti, based on prolonged
residence, observation, and interviews. Considers all aspects of life, including nutrition, agriculture, health and treatment,
political organization, and social traditions.
DLC LNHT BNG

1395 Wong Galdamez, Enrique, and Oscar Guillermo
Sáenz Archila. La educación rural en
Guatemala en los años 1975-1980. Guatemala:
Ministerio de Educación Pública, 1973. 17 pp.
Tables.
    A plan for the expansion of rural educa-
tion, focusing on the problems involved, defining the needs, and providing numerous
tables of statistics to support the proposals.
Emphasizes the need for expansion and the
necessity of convincing parents and students
of the importance of education. BNG

1396 Wood, Josephine, and Lilly de Jongh Osborne.
Indian Costumes of Guatemala. Graz, Austria:
Akademische Druck u. Verlagsanstalt, 1966. x,
154 pp. Biblio., illus., maps.
    Presents the typical regional costumes,
with descriptive information, discussion of
textiles and weaving, and photos. Also deals
with women's tasks, such as making clothes.
DLC LNHT

1397 Woods, Clyde M., and Theodore D. Graves. The
Process of Medical Change in a Highland
Guatemalan Town. Los Angeles: University of
California Press, 1973. 61 pp. Biblio.,
tables.
    A study of medical services and change in
San Lucas Tolimán, Guatemala, on Lake Atitlán,
based on fieldwork during 1965-66. Emphasizes
the replacement of native healers with modern
medical services and the interaction of folk-
medicine of both Indian and ladino origin with
modern knowledge, enunciating a model for the
process. Includes a discussion of change in
the community in nonmedical fields. DLC LNHT

1398 Woodward, Ralph Lee, Jr. Class Privilege and
Economic Development: The Consulado de
Comercio of Guatemala, 1793-1871. Chapel
Hill: University of North Carolina Press,
1966. xviii, 155 pp. Index, biblio., notes,
appendixes.
    A well-documented history of the society
through which the nation's elite sought to
promote its own wealth as well as to develop
the nation's economy. Traces its methods
during the late Colonial and early independence eras, particularly during the Carrera
regime, when it was influential. The author
concludes that although the organization was
an instrument of the oligarchy, it nonetheless
promoted development of the nation while so-
lidifying the dominant position of its members
and expanding their personal wealth, and hence
that the effort benefitted both the elite and
the nation at large. DLC

1399 Wright, Hamilton Mercer. Through the Marvel-
ous Highlands of Guatemala. Washington, D.C.:
GPO, 1917. 16 pp. Illus.
    A glowing description of the beauties of
nature and of the region's transportation
facilities, by a travel-book author; originally published in the Bulletin of the PAU.
DLC

1400 Wug de León, Emperatriz. Patrón de desarrollo
psicomotor y adaptativo en niños del medio
rural de Guatemala. Guatemala: Universidad
de Guatemala, 1968. 79 pp. Biblio., illus.,
maps.
    An analysis of tests given to Guatemalan
children. DLC

1401 Wyld Ospina, Carlos. El autócrata: ensayo
político-social. Guatemala: Sánchez & de
Guise, 1929. 272 pp. 2d ed. Guatemala:

(Wyld Ospina, Carlos)
Ministerio de Educación Pública, 1967.
242 pp.

A well-known Guatemalan writer comments on the phenomenon of dictatorship in that nation, explaining in the preface that he intended to write a criticism of the regime of General Manuel Estrada Cabrera but realized that to put the regime in its proper perspective it was necessary to recognize that the form was used by many Guatemalan leaders. Traces the history of authoritarian regimes from Colonial times to the 1920s, focusing particularly on those of Estrada Cabrera and Justo Rufino Barrios, criticizing their use of force but considering the factors in the society and culture that promote dictatorship. Calls for a change to more democratic government, recognizing that this requires cultural changes. Concludes that capitalism and caciquismo are inseparable allies that create a system of feudalism in both economics and politics, and that lust for power, with its resulting continuismo, is also a major contributing factor. An influential work by a prominent intellectual of his era. DLC LNHT BNG

1402   _____. La gringa. Guatemala: Tipografía Nacional, 1935. 332 pp. Pranke und Schwinge: ein Kieolifcher roman. Leipzig: A.H. Payne, 1940. 281 pp.

A novel set in a tropical hacienda, concerning a romance between a Guatemalan woman and a Yankee, with overtones of the conflict between civilization and the violence of the tropics; provides rich description of the tropical setting and life on the nation's coffee estates. DLC LNHT

1403   _____. Los lares apagados. Guatemala: Editorial Universitaria, 1958. 273 pp.

A novel recounting the life and traditions of the Quiché region of Guatemala, based on the author's observations in Alta Verapaz. Seeks to preserve the folklore and heritage of the Indian cultures of that area. DLC LNHT BNG

1404   _____. El solar de los gonzagas: la novela de la ciudad pequeña. Guatemala: Tipografía Nacional, 1924. 93 pp.

A novel describing the author's life in a barrio of Quezaltenango during his youth. Focuses on the regional customs and lifestyle, and on the roles of the various classes and their contrasting lives. BNG

1405   _____. La tierra de las Nahuyacas: la mala hembra-el manuscripto las palomas-de dura cerviz-Felipe Esquipulas Cuentos. Guatemala: Tipografía Nacional, 1933. 303 pp. 2d ed. Guatemala: Ministerio de Educación Pública, 1957. 208 pp.

A series of folktales from the Cobán region of Verapaz, based on its Quiché Indian legends but including modern stories that show the mixture of cultures. The author seeks to preserve the local folklore through this collection, which deals with a broad range of themes and different fiestas and aspects of life. LNHT BNG

1406   Ydígoras Fuentes, Carmen. Compendio de la historia de la literatura y artes de Guatemala. Guatemala: Ministerio de Educación Pública, 1959. 267 pp.

Though intended as a literary textbook, this volume provides a useful overview of the Guatemalan literary trends and leading figures. Includes commentary on their works and on the factors most influencing the course of the nation's literary schools. Brief essays provide biographical information and bibliographies for each author, with some excerpts from their works (though these are intermittent and unpredictable), arranging them in classes according to theme and type of writing. DLC LNHT

1407   _____. Compendio de literatura guatemalteca. Guatemala: Imprenta La República, 1948. 264 pp.

Brief biographical sketches of leading Guatemalan literary figures, including descriptions of their principal works. The volume deals mainly with the Colonial era, though there is some coverage of the nineteenth century. Poetry and journalism are included. The introductory chapters provide some overall classification of Guatemalan literature by theme and era, but the volume deals with only a few of these categories. BNG

1408   Ydígoras Fuentes, Miguel. Cartas a Hernández de León. Guatemala: Tipografía Nacional, 1955. 52 pp. 2d ed. Guatemala: Editorial Luz, 1959. 52 pp.

A series of letters from Ydígoras Fuentes to the newspaperman Federico Hernández de León, dated from 1931 to 1943 (with one additional letter dated 1955), in which Ydígoras comments on various subjects and reports on his work in diverse positions. The compilation, published during Ydígoras's tenure as president, is offered as evidence of his work and as a statment of his political credo and his dedication to providing services for the populace; it is also intended to rebut charges of dictatorial actions during his service as jefe político in various provinces. No replies from the newspaperman are printed. BNG

1409   Ydígoras Fuentes, Miguel, and Mario Rosenthal. My War with Communism. Englewood Cliffs, N.J.: Prentice-Hall, 1963. 238 pp. Illus.

The memoirs of a leading figure of postwar Guatemala, focusing on his years as president from 1958 through 1963. Written from exile after his overthrow by a military coup, they provide his view of the events of this era. He emphasizes the leftist threat, charging direct Cuban and Soviet involvement in the terrorism and virtual civil war that gripped his nation during these turbulent years, which constituted a continuation of the confrontation of the mid-1950s. Includes details of the various uprisings, plots, and terrorist acts, as well as an account of his policies as president, providing considerable detail regarding its events. The volume was written with the aid of a Guatemalan journalist. DLC LNHT

1410 Zamora Castellanos, Pedro. Episodios nacionales: el grito de independencia. Guatemala: Tipografía Nacional, 1935. 179 pp. Biblio., notes, illus.
An official publication in honor of the dedication of a monument to the precursors of independence. Provides historical background on the figures included in the monument and on the events it portrays. Recounts the independence movement, with emphasis on the role of the Liberal party. Includes excerpts from documents of the period. Based on research in secondary sources. DLC LNHT BNG BNCR

1411 _____. Nuestros cuarteles. Guatemala: Tipografía La Unión, 1887. 98 pp. Latest ed. Guatemala: Tipografía Nacional, 1932. 419 pp. Illus.
A history of the various forts and garrisons in the nation, providing a military history of Guatemala as seen through its various units. Details the establishment and expansion of the different commands and their duties, covering specialized detachments, the various branches of the army, the military academy, all important posts, the command structure and its evolution. Includes brief biographical sketches of important military figures. DLC LNHT BNG

1412 Zapata C., Adrián. Forjando vidas; memorias de Adrián Zapata C. 2 vols. Guatemala: Tipografía Nacional; Mexico: Imprenta de F.F. Franco, 1949-50. 219, 268 pp. Illus.
The memoirs of a Guatemalan professor, spanning the 1930s and 1940s, describing his experiences and his view of the events and commenting favorably on the Revolution of 1944. DLC BNG

1413 Zárate, Alvan O. Principales patrones de migración interna en Guatemala, 1964. Guatemala: Ministerio de Educación Pública, 1967. 54 pp. Notes, maps, tables.
An analysis of migration within the republic, based on the 1964 census. The trends indicate that the predominant pattern is movement to the capital, and that ladinos, being more mobile than the Indians, comprise the majority of the migrants. The folio also contains a study by Jorge Arias B. entitled "Migración interna en Guatemala," previously published in Estadística; it is based on the 1950 census. DLC LNHT BNG

1414 Zarco, T.B., ed. El pensamiento vivo de Isidoro Zarco. Guatemala: Ministerio de Educación Pública, 1973. 605 pp. Index, illus.
A collection of commentaries by a journalist who was assassinated in 1970, a victim of the continuing terrorism and guerrilla strife in the nation. BNG

1415 Zavala, Pablo A. A Glimpse of Beautiful Guatemala. Guatemala: El Imparcial, 1925. 332 pp. Illus.

A series of essays and reports compiled by a writer for the newspaper El Imparcial, designed to promote Yankee investment in Guatemala. The passages include lavish illustrations; description of the principal cities; discussion of the nation's development, progress, economy, and transportation facilities; commentaries about investment laws, mining codes, tariffs, and similar information useful to investors; and articles extolling the nation's potential mineral wealth. Includes comments on import-export firms, health facilities, and leading businesses and businessmen. LNHT BNG

1416 Zea Ruano, Rafael. Las barbas de don Rafay. Guatemala: Ministerio de Educación Pública, 1960. 140 pp.
A short costumbrista novel based on the folklore of the Guatemalan countryside, in which this well-known writer of folkloric short stories offers a more extended example of these traditions, mixing the mythical and the real. LNHT

1417 _____. Cactos: estampas del oriente. Guatemala: Tipografía Nacional, 1943. 92 pp. 3d ed. Guatemala: Ministerio de Educación Pública, 1966. 98 pp. Illus.
A series of stories, folktales, and remembrances of Chiquimula and the eastern section of Guatemala, designed to preserve the local lore and provide a view of the area and its life-style and culture. DLC LNHT BNG

1418 _____. Donde la niña hermilia. Guatemala: Ministerio de Educación Pública, 1962. 104 pp.
A brief novel describing rural life in Guatemala and the trials and tribulations of the campesinos of a small village. DLC LNHT BNG

1419 _____. Luto: novela guatemalteca. Guatemala: Tipografía San Antonio, 1963. 122 pp.
A novel about life in Guatemala, written in the form of the recollections of an old man regarding his life, problems, and friends. DLC

1420 _____. Ñor Julián. Mexico: B. Costa-Amic, 1959. 130 pp.
A short folkloric novel set in the Guatemalan countryside and based on its traditions and legends, mixing the mythical with the real world as such folklore often does. LNHT

1421 _____. Tierra nuestra. Guatemala: Tipografía Nacional, 1952. 75 pp.
A novel of rural peasant life, describing the love of the land and the kinship between campesino and nature in his native region. DLC LNHT BNG

1422 Zeceña, Mariano. La revolución de 1871 y sus caudillos: estudios políticos. Guatemala: Ministerio de Educación Pública, 1871.

133 pp. 3d ed. Guatemala: Ministerio de
Educación Pública, 1957. 121 pp.
    A discussion of the Liberal revolution that
determined the future orientation of
Guatemala, written by a Guatemalan scholar
during the period of Liberal ascendency near
the turn of the century. Although he hails
the revolution as the movement that brought
Guatemala into the modern world and condemns
the Conservatives, Zeceña finds the revolution's efforts limited. He condemns the despotism of Justo Rufino Barrios, concluding
with a call for further reforms and the
appearance of new political parties to give
fresh impetus to the process of modernization
and to promote further change in society,
especially in political rights and education,
which he feels are the nation's greatest
needs. Includes a friendly discussion of the
Liberal platform, intermingled with the
author's own views. DLC LNHT BNG

1423 Zeceña Beteta, Manuel, ed. Índice alfabético
del código civil de Guatemala. Guatemala:
Sánchez & de Guise, 1916. 151 pp.
    An index to the current law, which was the
code of 1877 with modifications and amendments
passed since then.

1424 Zeissig, Leopoldo W. Descripción de las
principales carreteras de Guatemala.
Guatemala: Tipografía Nacional, 1938. 71 pp.
    A description of the highways of Guatemala
at the time of publication, reflecting the
construction efforts of the Ubico regime and
the emphasis it placed on roads. TxU

1425 _____. Guatemala: paraíso perdido.
Guatemala: Editorial Hispania, 1946. 96 pp.
    The secretary of the Department of Rural
Economy in the Arévalo government provides a
descriptive account of the current situation
of the republic, including a brief historical
overview; designed to indicate its current
resources, with emphasis on agriculture and
its future prospects. DLC LNHT

1426 Zelada Carrillo, Ramón. Estampas del
suroriente. Guatemala: Ministerio de
Educación Pública, 1972. 145 pp.
    A series of short stories about the life
and people of the departments of Jutiapa and
Santa Rosa, written by a native of the region,
that seeks to provide an image of the region
and its customs and to discuss its problems.
BNG

1427 Zirión, Grace H. de. Datos biográficos
de general e ingeniero don Miguel Ydígoras
Fuentes. Guatemala: Ministerio de Educación
Pública, 1961. 140 pp. Illus.
    A brief outline sketch of the career of a
leading military figure and president of the
republic, written in English and Spanish, with
numerous photos. Supplemented by lists of his
posts, accomplishments, decorations, writings,
etc. DLC LNHT BNG

1428 Zúñiga Huete, Ángel. Carta abierta al doctor
don Juan José Arévalo, presidente

constitucional de Guatemala. Mexico:
Impresores Unidos, 1945. 87 pp.
    The author of this letter, the leader of
the Honduran Liberal party, was expelled from
Guatemala by the Arévalo government in 1945,
when he sought the support of that regime.
This letter is a protest against that expulsion and a defense of his political career and
his previous association with the Ubico regime, noting his later opposition to it. It
is also an attack on the doctrines of Arévalo.
DLC LNHT

1429 Zúñiga Montúfar, Gerardo. Impresiones de
Guatemala. San José: Imprenta Lehmann, 1933.
32 pp. Illus.
    A descriptive narrative of some selected
points in the nation, written by a former
classmate of President Jorge Ubico, describing
a visit with him and hailing his accomplishments. TxU

Honduras

1 Acosta Zeledón, Oscar. Rafael Heliodoro Valle: vida y obra; biografía, estudiocrítico, bibliografía y antología de un intelectual hondureño. Tegucigalpa: Universidad Nacional Autónoma de Honduras, 1964. 166 pp. Biblio., illus. 2d ed. Tegucigalpa: Editorial Nuevo Continente, 1973. 203 pp. Biblio., notes.

The biography of the Honduran writer and philosopher, based on his publications and secondary works, occupies about half this volume. Includes extensive quotation from his writings to provide his impressions, with connecting narration outlining his life, writing, work, positions, and travels. A bibliography of his works and an anthology of selections from them are appended. DLC LNHT

2 Agüero, Juan Ramón. Semblanzas hondureñas. Trujillo, Honduras: n.p., 1952. xii, 182 pp. Illus.

Brief biographical sketches of notable Honduran figures that emphasize the literary and intellectual fields. Unfortunately, there is no pattern to their arrangement and no alphabetical index, only a general table of contents. Most of the essays are one to three pages long, providing descriptions of the author's view of their major work and viewpoints, rather than vita data. DLC LNHT

3 Aguilar Paz, Jesús, and Rafael Bardales Bueso. El alfabetismo en Honduras: estudio presentado al seminario de alfabetización y educación de adultos. Tegucigalpa: Ministerio de Educación Pública, 1949. 56 pp. Tables.

A study of the problem and extent of illiteracy among the adult population, with statistical data and calls for efforts to deal with the problem. DLC

4 Aguirre, José M. Honduras: The Reply of Colonel José M. Aguirre to Some Unjust Strictures Published Against that Republic by the "New York Times." New York: G.F. Ilsley, 1884. 54 pp.

A reply by a resident of Trujillo, Honduras, to an article he happened to see in the New York Times, in which a voyager on a boat that called at that city described his recollections of it in condescending terms that reflected Yankee biases and a lack of familiarity with the region. The reply refutes the article point for point and offers a more accurate description of the city, its people, facilities, and customs. DLC

5 Álbum cronológico de los presidentes de Honduras. Tegucigalpa: Promociones Culturales, 1970. 40 pp. Illus.

A collection of photos of the nation's chief executives, without comment beyond their names, birth and death dates, and years in office.

6 Alcohólicos Anónimos de Honduras. Alcohólicos Anónimos: su filosofía y su historia en Honduras. Comayagüela: Imprenta Bulnes, 1967. 58 pp.

A brief summary of this organization's work in Honduras, emphasizing its objectives, the future of its program, and the national need for such efforts.

7 Alduvín, Ricardo Diego. Una Senda. Mexico: n.p., 1946. 94 pp.

A series of letters and addresses by the author, written in exile from his native Honduras. Combines praise for the independence movement and discussion of its heroes with attacks on Honduran dictator Tiburcio Carías Andino, calling for revolution to return the nation to its democratic tradition. Also includes an educational plan for Honduras and comments regarding education. DLC

8 Alfaro Arriaga, Alejandro. El sabio hondureño: D. José Cecilio del Valle en la Novena Conferencia Internacional Americana. Tegucigalpa: Talleres Tipo-Litográficos, 1954. 24 pp. Illus.

A brief pamphlet, intended for the delegates to the Inter-American Conference; quotes some of Valle's thoughts on Inter-American cooperation, and contends that he was the first to call for a Pan American Conference. DLC BNCR

9 Alvarado, Néstor Enrique. El día que rugió la tierra. Tegucigalpa: Imprenta Bulnes, 1969. 97 pp. Illus.

(Alvarado, Néstor Enrique)
　　　A denunciation of the 1968 elections in Honduras, contending that the Nationalist party and the military used armed terror to intimidate voters and fix the outcome. Contains descriptions of terrorism in various locations, and provacative drawings portraying the alleged events. DLC LNHT

10　　____. Morazán: político y maestro: desarrollo del programa oficial de la "Catedra Morazánica." Tegucigalpa: Imprenta Bulnes, 1968. 161 pp.
　　　A brief review of Morazán's life, based on secondary works. Stresses his unionist ideals and his initiatives in the field of education. Includes several manifestos and letters by him. LNHT

11　　____. La revolución del 19. Tegucigalpa: Imprenta Bulnes, 1967. 196 pp.
　　　An account of the Honduran revolution of 1919 in which Rafael López Gutiérrez and Vicente Tosta defeated Francisco Bertrand. Contends that contrary to previous historical accounts, it was not merely another coup but in fact a real revolution, which the author defines as a genuine popular uprising, against an attempt to seize the presidency, resulting in a short-lived victory for the popular forces. The author attributes previous interpretations to reliance on the propaganda of the era rather than historical research to investigate it, and characterizes the creole power that opposed and eventually ousted the revolutionaries as the basis of the national problems. DLC LNHT

12　Alvarado García, Ernesto, ed. Reincorporación de las Islas de la Bahía a la sobernía hondureña. Tegucigalpa: Ministerio de Educación Pública, 1961. 79 pp.
　　　A collection of articles and documents regarding the mid-nineteenth-century dispute between Great Britain and Honduras involving the Bay Islands. Traces the dispute, the agreements involved, and the 1861 actions of the regime of General Santos Guardiola in reasserting Honduran control. Included are the agreements, official exchanges, excerpts from annual ministry reports, Honduran laws relating to the islands, and selections from the press and various secondary works. LNHT

13　Alvarado Rodríguez, Martín. Cantarranas, personajes pintorescos, tradiciones, leyendas. Tegucigalpa: Talleres Tipográficos Nacionales, 1951. 109 pp. Illus. 2d ed. Honduras: Imprenta López y Cía, 1973. 211 pp. Illus.
　　　A collection of folklore and legends from and about the title city, more commonly known as San Juan de Flores, a Honduran mining town of Colonial origin whose economy is now principally agricultural. DLC LNHT

14　　____. Doctor Antonio R. Vallejo: biografía. Tegucigalpa: Imprenta La República, 1963. 28 pp.

　　　Biographical data about a leading Honduran intellectual of the nineteenth century who also held numerous government posts. Consists principally of a listing of his publications, with descriptions. LNHT

15　　____. La enseñanza de la historia en Honduras. Mexico: PAIGH, 1951. 54 pp. Index, biblio.
　　　Part of a series sponsored by the Pan American Institute of Geography and History, this brief work provides a summary of the place of history in the Honduran school curriculum, noting the levels at which the subject is taught and its general scope. DLC

16　Alvaro Contreras: gran tribuno centroamericano. Tegucigalpa: Imprenta Soto, 1953. 50 pp. Illus.
　　　A brief biographical sketch and several essays about the title character and his contribution to educational reform and intellectual development in Honduras in the early twentieth century, with reproductions of some of his speeches and commentaries. DLC LNHT

17　Amador V., Valentín. Los males que afligen el pueblo hondureño y sus remedios. León: Tipografía "La Patria," 1946. 36 pp.
　　　A denunciation of the Carías dictatorship by an exile who contends that dictatorship is the principal problem of Honduras. He calls for the ouster of the current regime, rejection of personalistic caudillos, and a commitment to democracy, offering a program of government for a new regime. DLC

18　Amaya Amador, Ramón. Destacamento rojo. Tegucigalpa: Honduran Communist Party, 1962.
　　　A fictionalized presentation of the evolution of the Honduran Communist party by a longtime member who was among its early adherents. Portrays its trials and tribulations under successive dictatorships that sought to stamp it out, and the frustration of its early efforts to lead strikes in the banana zone. DLC

19　　____. El Indio Sánchez: síntesis biográfica de un revolucionario centroamericano. San José: Imprenta Borrasé, 1948. 31 pp. Illus.
　　　A brief biographical sketch of Francisco Sánchez Reyes, a student leader of the 1944 Honduran rebellion against the regime of Tiburcio Carías Andino, eulogizing his role. Contains numerous jibes at the various Central American dictatorships of that era, advocating revolution against them. LNHT BNCR

20　　____. Prisión verde. Tegucigalpa: Editorial Ramón Amaya Amador, 1950. 244 pp. 4th ed. Tegucigalpa: Editorial Ramón Amaya Amador, 1974. 367 pp. Illus.
　　　The initial and best-known work of a Honduran social novelist who was a native of the northern region of Honduras and who worked in the banana plantations during his youth in the 1940s. This volume is based on his experiences as a participant in one of the initial, and unsuccessful, strikes in the

Honduran banana zone. The author considers himself a "war correspondent" reporting the struggle of the oppressed peasants and Honduran nationalists against the cruel exploitation of the foreign companies and the dictatorship of Tiburcio Carías Andino. He vividly relates the worst episodes of his stay, such as the assassination of the strike leader. Sympathetic to the peasants and written from their point of view, his presentation reflects his own membership in the Honduran Communist party, clearly going beyond social justice to advocate outright class warfare. The author was a party militant who regarded his novels as his most effective contribution to the party's struggle and dedicated his life to such writing, much of it in exile in Guatemala, Argentina, Mexico, and Eastern Europe. DLC LNHT

21 American-Honduras Company. Honduras and the Perry Land Grant: A New Field for the Farmer, Stockman, Lumberman and Laborer. Chicago: American-Honduras Co., 1888. 55 pp. Notes, tables.

An account of the land grant on the south Caribbean coast of Honduras, which the Honduran government sold to the company, authorizing settlement and immigration. The bulk of the volume, which is designed to encourage immigration, is a series of glowing comments on the unlimited agricultural potential of the region and the crops that could be grown there. The grant clearly lies in the region of the disputed border with Nicaragua. DLC

22 _____. Spanish Honduras, Its Rivers, Lagoons, Savannas, Mountains, Minerals, Forests, Fish, Game, Agriculture, Products, Fruits, Transportation and Natives. New York: W.R. Gillespie, 1906. 183 pp. Illus.

A glowing description of the development possibilities in Honduras, particularly in the areas of the company's concessions. Focuses on economic conditions and prospects, resources, and transportation potential, particularly regarding railroad and port facilities that the company proposes to build. Includes engineering reports, as well as general description and data on the economy. DLC LNHT

23 Los Amigos de la Verdad. Causas de las recientes revoluciones: evolución verificada por el Gral. Vásquez, su presidencia y medidas necesarias para conseguir la completa pacificación del país. Tegucigalpa: Tipografía Nacional, 1893. 15 pp.

The statement of the incumbent regime regarding the revolt in favor of Policarpo Bonilla that eventually ousted General Domingo Vásquez. Presents the regime's version of the events and its stand, casting it as the defender of the nation and its constitution. DLC

24 Amilcar Raudales, Luís. Baturrillo histórico. Tegucigalpa: Tipografía Nacional, 1953. 104 pp. 2d ed. Tegucigalpa: Tipografía Nacional, 1958. 95 pp.

Short essays on a wide range of Honduran historical themes, most relating to the nineteenth century. LNHT

25 Antúñez Castillo, Rubén. Biografía del matrimonio Bográn-Morejón. 2 vols. Tegucigalpa: Editorial Nacional, 1967. 291, 154 pp. Biblio., illus., appendixes.

The first volume is a biography tracing the political career of General Luís Bográn Barahona, which spanned the early and mid-nineteenth century. Financed by the family, the volume defends him against all charges, which are numerous because of his role in the military conflicts of the period, his support of the unionist efforts of Justo Rufino Barrios of Guatemala, and his role in executing several other prominent figures. He is characterized as a sincere unionist defending his legitimate government against rebellions. Includes reproductions of numerous documents, such as the act of Barrios's unionist Congress declaring him "Benemérito de la Patria Centroamericana," and sections relating to his tomb, monuments immortalizing him, and the celebration of his memory. Provides a detailed account of his many activities and military campaigns, complete with proclamations, etc., though always as seen by his partisans. The second volume is a biography of his wife, who outlived him by many years, which consists principally of reprints of her writings, poetry, and plays; it is titled Vida y obra literaria de doña Teresa Morejón de Bográn. DLC LNHT

26 Antúñez Castillo, Rubén, ed. Monografía del departamento de Yoro. Tegucigalpa: Talleres Tipográficos Nacionales, 1937. 187 pp. Tables.

Part of the geographic series of the National Society of Geography and History, this monograph includes topical essays for the entire department, covering social and physical setting and service facilities; includes a twenty-page history, as well as descriptions for each of the department's municipalities, focused on physical setting, flora, and fauna. DLC LNHT

27 Antúñez Castillo, Rubén. Rasgos biográficos del presbítero Manuel de Jesús Subirana. Tegucigalpa: Ministerio de Educación Pública, 1964. 59 pp.

A brief sketch of the life and work of a missionary priest who worked with the rural Indians in the interior of Honduras during the nineteenth century, extolling his efforts to protect and Christianize them.

28 _____. Retazo de la historia cultural de San Pedro Sula. San Pedro Sula: Imprenta Antúñez, 1966. 227 pp.

A chronology of printing, a dictionary of the newspapers, and a dictionary of authors from San Pedro Sula, with brief single-paragraph biographical outlines of the writers and descriptions of the newspapers, their leadership, and their years of existence, arranged alphabetically. These constitute the entire book, with no separate history of the city or its culture. DLC LNHT

29 Ardón, Juan Ramón. Al filo de un guarizama. Tegucigalpa: Imprenta Calderón, 1971. 411 pp. Illus.
A novel, based on the author's experiences and the stories told to him, of life in the banana-producing region of the Honduran north coast. Vivid description and narration trace the daily lives of the peasants and their exploitation by the foreign companies. Clearly sympathetic to the oppressed peasants and their travails in struggling with the forces of nature, corrupt officials, and the foreigners. DLC LNHT

30 _____. ¡Una democracia en peligro! Tegucigalpa: Tipografía Ariston, 1959. 43 pp.
A collection of speeches, declarations, and material relating to the efforts to overthrow the Honduran government in 1954. Denounces the antidemocratic stance of the dictatorships of Anastacio Somoza and Rafael Trujillo; accuses them of supporting the invasion, which the volume characterizes as a threat to Honduras and to democracy in the Americas, mounted by mercenary forces. Includes declarations by some of the participants in the resulting political polemics. WU

31 _____. Días de infamia. Tegucigalpa: Ministerio de Relaciones Públicas, 1970. 252 pp. Illus. 2d ed. Tegucigalpa: Imprenta Calderón, 1970. 252 pp. Illus.
A denunciation of Salvadoran migration into Honduras, viewing it as a plot. Writing in a manner that depicts Honduras as the citadel of civilization attempting to stem the tide of the barbarian hordes from Salvador, the author invokes parallels with Rome and classical civilizations. He extols the heroism of the Honduran army and makes allegations of Salvadoran atrocities and massacres in the occupied territory, with corresponding photos. LNHT

32 _____. Honduras: objectivo rojo en Centro América; el comunismo esgrime la reforma agraria para demoler la sociedad actual y para preparar el camino de la revolución hacia el poder. Honduras: n.p., 1976. 136 pp.
A denunciation of the communist threat, mixing general discussion of communist doctrine with narration of the tactics of the party in Honduras, detailing its beliefs and programs, and warning of the communist efforts to utilize agrarian reform and similar issues to promote their cause. DLC

33 _____. Monografía geográfica e histórica del municipio de Comayagüela. Tegucigalpa: Talleres Tipográficos Nacionales, 1937. 144 pp.
A description of the current facilities of the town, followed by a brief account of its development and role in Honduran history.

Includes discussion of the local lore and superstitions. DLC LNHT

34 Ardón, Victor Figueroa. Datos para la historia de la educación en Honduras. Tegucigalpa: Imprenta La República, 1957. 228 pp. Biblio., tables.
A chronological compilation of summaries of all the significant national legislation relating to education, including outlines of the programs of study and legislation relating to working conditions of teachers, benefits, etc. LNHT

35 Arellano Bonilla, Roberto. ¡Basta . . . ; para los hondureños únicamente!. Tegucigalpa: Published by the author, 1970. 92 pp. Maps, appendixes.
An emotional statement of the Honduran position in the 1969 war with El Salvador, appealing to patriotism and nationalism. Combines narration with reproduction of other comments, intending to show Salvadoran designs on Honduran territory. Indicts Salvador for plotting to take over parts of Honduras and condemns what it views as a Salvadoran propaganda campaign to influence world opinion. DLC LNHT

36 _____. Ramón Ernesto Cruz, o el presidente que merece y necesita Honduras. Tegucigalpa: n.p., 1971. 111 pp. Illus.
A campaign biography of Cruz that traces his career, extols his activities and preparation, and indicates his stance on various national questions. Considerable stress is laid on the preservation of the special measures designed to protect the Honduran economy from the full impact of the Common Market, to whose maintenance Cruz was committed but which his opponent proposed to abolish. LNHT

37 Argueta, Ernesto. Address on Honduras. Washington, D.C.: Sun Book, 1930. 23 pp. Illus.
An official description of the state of the nation, by the Honduran minister to the United States. Prepared for a CBS radio broadcast on 7 December 1930. DLC

38 _____. Conferencia sobre Honduras. Tegucigalpa: Ministerio de Relaciones Exteriores, 1930. 23 pp. Illus.
See item HO36.

39 _____. Conflicto cívico entre la dictadura y el pueblo: mi contribución por la liberación de Honduras. Tegucigalpa: Imprenta La Razón, 1949. 65 pp.
A reproduction of various exchanges, letters, interviews, and radio speeches by a Liberal leader who opposed the Carías regime from exile. They exhort Hondurans to put aside their individual differences and unite to oppose dictatorship and promote the good of the nation. Many of the pieces focus on charges the author made against the regime and his denial of its countercharges against him, though the items to which he is replying are not reproduced. DLC LNHT

40 Armas, Alejandro Enriquez. Pequeña monografía del municipio de Coatepeque. Coatepeque: n.p., 1963. 70 pp. Illus., maps.
A description of the current facilities of the city, with geographical detail, statistics, and a brief historical overview.

41 Ávila, Gustavo R. Proyección de la población de Honduras por sexo y edad, 1950-1980. Santiago: U.N., 1964. 39 pp. Illus.
A thirty-year population projection based on the 1950 census data and fecundity statistics. Attemps to portray Honduran society in 1980 and characterize the social groups and the changes they will have undergone, as well as changes in the number of people and age distribution. DLC

42 Baciu, Stefan. Ramón Villeda Morales, ciudadaño de América. San José: Imprenta Lehmann, 1970. 214 pp. Biblio.
A journalist's sympathetic biography of the Liberal president of Honduras during 1957-63, tracing his political career and particularly hailing his initiatives on behalf of isthmian unification and broader cooperation among the Latin American nations, acclaiming him as a future spokesman for the region and the Third World. The reformist nature of his regime and his stances in opposition to dictatorships are stressed. LNHT

43 Bähr, Eduardo. Fotografía del peñasco: cuentos. Tegucigalpa: Tipografía Ariston, 1969. 65 pp.
A series of extremely short stories, most only one to three pages, offering a view of the oppression and misery of the Honduran peasants and denouncing dictatorship and Yankee imperialism. The brevity of the works suggests a rapid series of photographs that provide glimpses of the author's perspective on a different world. DLC

44 Bardales Bueso, Rafael. La educación en Honduras. Madrid: Editorial Cultura Hispánica, 1953. 55 pp.
A brief summary of the current state of education in Honduras, indicating the objectives, programs, and enrollment statistics of all levels. DLC

45 Barrera Aceves, Joaquín. La Virgen de Suyapa: patrona de Honduras. Tegucigalpa: Imprenta Calderón, 1941. 18 pp.
An account of the shrine, its origin and history.

46 Barrientos, Alfonso Enrique. Rafael Heliodoro Valle: o el neohumanismo americano. Guatemala: Tipografía Nacional, 1963. 199 pp. Biblio., notes.
A biography and study of the works and ideas of a well-known Honduran writer and philosopher whose publications span the fields of history, literature, philosophy, and many others. The author contends that Rafael Heliodoro Valle adapted the classic humanist movement to America, creating a purely American style and approach appropriate to this hemisphere, and especially to Latin America, thus making an important contribution to the shaping of the region's outlook and thought. He also characterizes Enrique Gómez Carrillo as the most important influence on Valle's work. DLC LNHT BNG

47 Becerra, Longino. Honduras. Havana: Casa de las Américas, 1966.
Part of a Cuban series designed for Cuban schools, this volume provides general data and a brief historical overview, all within a Marxist interpretation stressing the role of the bourgeois capitalists in oppressing the nation's lower classes. DLC

48 ____. El problema agrario en Honduras. Havana: Casa de las Américas, 1964. 103 pp.
An ideological treatment of the Honduran agrarian problems, written by the union of Hondurans residing in Castro's Cuba. Surveys the rural scene, castigates the latifundia and the Yankee fruit companies as the cause of the problems, condemns the moderate agrarian-reform efforts of previous governments as too timid, and calls for the complete expropriation of all large holdings, especially those of the fruit companies. DLC LNHT

49 Belot, Gustave de. La vérité sur le Honduras: étude historique, géographique, politique et commerciale sur l'Amérique Centrale. Paris: Bureau du Journal des Consultes, 1869. 95 pp. Maps.
A description of Honduras, arguing that France needs to become more active in this area and selecting Honduras as the ideal location for an interoceanic railway, citing the benefits to commerce and the advantages of French participation in the project. Proposes that Honduran neutrality be guaranteed by France, England, and the United States to facilitate the project; advocates French investment in any such interoceanic railway. DLC LNHT

50 Belot, Gustave de, and Charles Lindemann. Amérique Centrale: la République du Honduras et son chemin interocéanique. Paris: Dentu, 1867. 72 pp.
One of the many propaganda pieces promoting the proposed Honduran railroad connecting the Atlantic and Pacific. Extols the virtues of Honduras and its advantages over other potential locations, discussing the nation's trade and prospects; presents data relating to the advantages for the Yankee and European economies. The book clearly seeks to promote French interest in the project. LNHT

51 Bermúdez, Néstor. Escritores de Honduras: perfiles fugaces. 2 vols. Havana: Editorial Francisco Verdugo, 1939-41. 217, 204 pp. Index, illus.
A collection of miscellaneously arranged brief commentaries on over fifty Honduran writers. Some provide biographical information but most discuss the themes of their

writings in very general terms. The author does not explain either his arrangement or his selection criteria. DLC LNHT

52 Bermúdez Meza, Antonio. La casación en lo civil: estudio del recurso en el derecho procesal de la República de Honduras. Tegucigalpa: Imprenta Calderón, 1940. 251 pp. Biblio.
    A legal treatise reviewing the Honduran law regarding the right of appeal, with a casebook of examples and brief comparison to the use of appeals in other nations, compiled by a prominent member of the Honduran Supreme Court. DLC LNHT BNCR

53 _____. Prismas. Tegucigalpa: Imprenta Calderón, 1938. 190 pp. Illus.
    A collection of essays and speeches of a leading Honduran intellectual and political figure who served as his nation's foreign minister and held high academic positions. Contains commentaries on a wide variety of subjects, encompassing both domestic and foreign affairs but consisting principally of observations on significant figures or events in Honduran history. Includes comments on contemporaries and on Spain, as well as on historical figures and on such themes as press duels and propaganda. DLC

54 Besso, Henry V. A Guide to the Official Publications of the Other American Republics. Vol. 13, Honduras. Washington, D.C.: Library of Congress, 1947. 31 pp.
    See item CR94. DLC

55 Blanco, Francisco J., ed. La mujer ante la legislación hondureña. Tegucigalpa: Tipografía Ariston, 1955. xi, 203 pp.
    A series of questions and answers combined with quotations from the statutes to indicate the basic laws of the nation as they apply to the family and to women, but also including general aspects regarding citizenship, duties of citizens, force of the law, labor and police codes, legalizing transactions, etc., for the general reader. DLC LNHT

56 Blutstein, Howard. Area Handbook for Honduras. Washington, D.C.: GPO, 1971. xiv, 225 pp. Biblio., maps. 2d ed. Washington, D.C.: GPO, 1979. 226 pp. Biblio., maps.
    See item CR102. DLC LNHT

57 Bobadilla, Perfecto Hernández. Monografía del departamento de Cortés. Tegucigalpa: Talleres Tipográficos Nacionales, 1944. 452 pp. Illus. 2d ed. Tegucigalpa: Sociedad de Geografía e Historia de Honduras, 1944. 454 pp. Illus.
    A profusely illustrated compendium of data about the department, emphasizing geography and description of current facilities. Presents also a brief historical synopsis and some excerpts from the writings of its citizens. LNHT

58 _____. Monografía geográfica e histórica de San Pedro Sula, IV centenario de su fundación.

San Pedro Sula: "Compañia Editora de Honduras," 1936. 236 pp. Illus., maps.
    A treatment of this city following the format of item HO57. DLC LNHT

59 A Bondholder. Honduras: Its Present Difficulties and Future Prospects. London: Spottiswoode & Co., 1872. 25 pp.
    A brief tract arguing in favor of pursuing the Honduras Inter-Oceanic Railway with all possible speed. Contends that political disturbances in that nation are normal and minor and that the railroad would be highly profitable when completed, and hence that bondholders should be patient and support further investment to rush the project to completion, ignoring temporary setbacks. The author contends that construction of a canal elsewhere in the isthmus is unlikely and would not in any event have much effect on the profitability of the railroad. DLC

60 Bonilla, Marcelina. Diccionario histórico-geográfico de las poblaciones de Honduras. Tegucigalpa: Tipografía Ariston, 1945. 256 pp. Biblio. 2d ed. Tegucigalpa: Imprenta Calderón, 1952. 310 pp. Illus.
    Brief, single-sentence entries, alphabetically arranged, for each of the municipalities and towns of the nation, giving location, municipality (for smaller units), department, and sometimes population. DLC

61 Bonilla, Policarpo. Wilson Doctrine: How the Speech of President Wilson at Mobile, Alabama, Has Been Interpreted by the Latin-American Countries. New York: n.p., 1914. 42 pp.
    A response to Woodrow Wilson's address of October 1913, in which he publicly stated his intention to oppose foreign (i.e., European) intervention in the hemisphere in the name of democracy. In this statement the president of Honduras summarizes Latin American reaction and speaks for the region, noting that Latins fear Yankee intervention more than they do the European efforts, owing to proximity and Wilson's policies. DLC

62 Bourgeot, Alexandre. Les états de l'Amérique Centrale: le Honduras, son passé et son avenir. Paris: Imprimerie de L'oeuvre de Saint-Paul, 1878. vii, 46 pp. Tables.
    A general description of contemporary conditions in Honduras, with emphasis on commercial possibilities; designed to encourage greater French involvement, principally through trade. DLC

63 Brooks, William Alexander. Honduras and the Interoceanic Railway: Report on the Line and Its Prospects, Being the Result of Recent Personal Visits. London: Pottle & Son, 1874. 24 pp.
    A report on the prospects and plans for the railroad, written by a supporter of the scheme, who hails its potential. LNHT

64 Bueso Arias, Juan Ángel. ¡La rosa del trapiche! Novela corta. San Pedro Sula: Editorial Antúñez, 1964. 57 pp.

A collection of short stories by a medical doctor, based on the folklore of rural Honduras and set on a hacienda. Designed to preserve the region's traditions, they include references to local celebrations and to religious and Indian themes. DLC

65 Bulnes Hernández, Edmundo. El verdadero origen de la muerte del Gral. Gregorio Ferrera. Tegucigalpa: Imprenta Calderón, 1933. 16 pp. Illus.
A political tract by a follower of Ferrera, condemning the Liberals and particularly Dr. Vicente Mejía Colindres as the implacable enemy of Ferrera and the intellectual author of his death, though there is no discussion of the actual death. A series of telegrams is included that indicates an energetic effort to track him down, but says nothing about plotting an assassination. DLC LNHT

66 Bülow, Hernán von. Los modernos nerones: horrorosos desafueros cometidos por las autoridades de la República de Honduras. Havana: Imprenta Montserrat, 1925. 24 pp.
A Costa Rican homeopathic doctor's protest against the Honduran authorities, whose crime was to summarily deport him from San Pedro Sula where he had been practicing his profession. The volume consists of a collection of letters and communications attendant to his deportation, with his protests as a few brief linking narrations. DLC-LDS-366

67 Bustamante, César. Compilación sinóptica de las leyes y disposiciones de los poderes legislativo y ejecutivo de la república, durante el período comprendido del año de 1903 al de 1928: reformas, adiciones, supresiones tomadas del periódico oficial "La Gaceta." Tegucigalpa: Tipografía Nacional, 1929.

68 Bustillo Reina, Guillermo. El libro de Honduras: directorio y guía general de la República, una obra de consulta y propaganda; The Book of Honduras: Directory and General Guide of the Country, a Book of Reference and Propaganda. Tegucigalpa: Tipografía Nacional, 1957. 143 pp. Illus.
Offers a compendium of abbreviated information, including a brief history, geographical description, tour guide, commentaries about the nation's boundary disputes and previous arbitral awards, and essays on disparate topics such as the nation's music, art, literature, etc., with emphasis on the national heroes and with accompanying photos. Includes a description of the military junta, the nation's return to democracy and the newly elected president, hailing this transition and the junta. In Spanish and English in parallel columns. DLC LNHT

69 Cáceres Lara, Víctor. Efemérides nacionales. Tegucigalpa: Editorial Nuevo Continente, 1973. 312 pp. Biblio.
A series of brief essays, most of about one page, regarding significant historical events of each day and their importance in Honduran development; arranged day by day in sequence from January through December. There is only a single event for each day, hence the listings jump from year to year; selection criteria are not indicated. Covers the entire calendar, though with different events than in the author's earlier work (see next item), and with no reference to it, which casts doubt on the importance of the events and the selection criteria for both. DLC LNHT

70 _____. Fechas de la historia de Honduras. Tegucigalpa: Tipografía Nacional, 1964. 403 pp. Biblio.
A series of short essays, each several pages in length, dealing with important historical events in Honduran history, arranged by day rather than by year, and hence providing an historical calendar of the nation. The range is wide, though the focus is on the nineteenth century through 1920, with some entries for the Colonial period. The essays are descriptive, with extensive quotations from secondary sources and published documents. DLC LNHT

71 _____. Gobernantes de Honduras en el Siglo 19. Tegucigalpa: Banco Central de Honduras, 1978. 390 pp. Notes.
A series of five- to twenty-page essays outlining the principal events during the tenure of each of the individuals who served as head of the Honduran state during the nineteenth century, by a well-known scholar. The few footnotes cite published speeches by the individuals. DLC

72 _____. Humus. Comayagüela: Imprenta Libertad, 1952. 144 pp.
A collection of vividly written short stories of life in the Honduran countryside, using the local settings, traditions, and idioms and stressing the problems of the peasants, their exploitation, and the violence in their lives. DLC LNHT

73 _____. Tierra ardiente. Tegucigalpa: n.p., 1969. 329 pp. Illus., appendixes.
A reedition of many of the author's short stories. Including the entire collection published in Humus and other tales in a similar vein of vivid accounts of human emotion and suffering that employ Honduran settings, traditions, and vocabulary. Includes a glossary of local modisms. DLC LNHT

74 Carías, Marco Virgilio. Esbozo de una política agraria para Honduras. Tegucigalpa: Universidad Nacional Autónoma de Honduras, 1967.
A detailed survey of the Honduran economy and agricultural scene from 1945 to 1960, with an analysis of its problems and proposals for policies to promote development, as well as extensive statistical tables. Prepared by the University Institute and originally issued in mimeographed form. KU

75 Carías Andino, Tiburcio. Mensajes presidenciales del doctor y general Tiburcio

Carías Andino, 1933-1945. Tegucigalpa:
Tipografía Ariston, 1946.
  A compilation of the presidential messages
sent to Congress, including the annual reports
and special communications. DLC

76 Carías Reyes, Marcos. Artículos y discursos.
Tegucigalpa: Tipografía Ariston, 1943.
131 pp.
  A series of short speeches and articles on
various subjects; many of them deal with
Francisco Morazán, a frequent theme of the
author, who is a student of that Central American independence leader. DLC

77 _____. Cuentos de lobos. Tegucigalpa:
Imprenta Calderón, 1941. 179 pp. Illus.
  A collection of political short stories,
divided into cuentos of lobos, perros, and
gatos. It seeks to show the useless nature of
Honduran politico-military struggles, the suffering they engender, and the dictatorships
they support. Brief, vivid narrations (usually in the form of flashbacks) of various
battles, confrontations, and maneuvers are
used to denounce dictatorship and combat. The
figures are human and real despite the title
and classification. The privileged aristo-
crats seeking subtle advantage are categorized
as gatos; the politically ambitious seeking
power and fame, as lobos; and those innocently
involved, as perros. DLC

78 _____. La heredad. Tegucigalpa: Talleres
Tipográficos Nacionales, 1931. 196 pp. 2d
ed. Tegucigalpa: Tipografía Ariston, 1945.
238 pp.
  A novel of revolution and political turmoil
in Honduras, involving a struggle for power
among a caudillo, a foreign capitalist, and a
peasant leader. Makes extensive use of
Honduran modisms, locales, and customs; draws
upon the episodes of that nation's turbulent
political scene of the late nineteenth and
early twentieth centuries, in which politics
and armed struggle were linked and success in
business and the protection of privileges were
tied to political and military fortunes. DLC
LNHT

79 _____. Hombres de pensamiento. Tegucigalpa:
Imprenta Calderón, 1947. 170 pp. Illus.
  Commentaries and excerpts from the works of
six historically prominent political and literary figures of Honduras. Includes brief
biographical material, commentary on their
principal works, and excerpts from their writings or speeches; these excerpts account for
most of the space. Figures included are José
Cecilio del Valle, Ramón Rosa, Juan Ramón
Molina, Luís Andrés Zúñiga, and Arturo
Martínez Galindo. No selection criteria are
given. BNCR

80 _____. La paz nacional: consideraciones
sobre aspectos históricos y sociales de
Honduras. Tegucigalpa: Imprenta Calderón,
1942. 23 pp. 2d ed. Tegucigalpa: Imprenta
Calderón, 1946. 23 pp.
  A brief essay emphasizing the civil warfare
that has characterized Honduran history,

contending that it reflected social backwardness and the lack of political institutionalization, while emphasizing that present
conditions offer the prospect of social transformation that should terminate this discord.
The author argues that the nation must stabilize and then use this stability as an opportunity to build for the future to alleviate
the problems of internal dissension. LNHT

81 _____. Trópico. Tegucigalpa: Universidad
Nacional Autónoma de Honduras, 1971. 158 pp.
  A novel set in the banana-producing region
of the Honduran Caribbean coast, focusing on
the problems and exploitation of the region
and its dominance by the large foreign companies. The work was written in 1948 shortly
after the initial banana strike in the region
during an era of change in the Honduran political scene, but was published posthumously.
It focuses on the tensions in the region and
the problems of the banana workers, viewing
their plight sympathetically, and is considered among the most overt of the author's
works in its political outlook and identification with the lower class. DLC

82 Casteñeda, Hilda de. Beautiful Honduras:
Experiences in a Small Town on the Caribbean.
London: Stockwell, 1934. 47 pp. Illus.,
maps.
  A collection of well-written essays portraying the life-style of the Caribbean coastal
tropical zone, focusing on description of the
setting and the everyday lives of the
populace. NN

83 Casteñeda Suazo, Gustavo A. Una ciudad de
Honduras: la sultana de occidente. San Pedro
Sula: Compañia Editora de Honduras, 1946.
122 pp. Illus., appendixes.
  A local schoolteacher's collection of commentaries on various aspects of the history of
Santa Rosa de Copán, tracing the development
and origin of its principal institutions,
commenting on important historical milestones
in its development, noting its existing facilities, and extolling its people and setting.
BNCR

84 _____. El general Domingo Vásquez y su
tiempo: ensayo histórico. Tegucigalpa:
Imprenta Calderón, 1934. 119 pp. Appendixes.
  A defense of the role of Vásquez in the
Honduran political scene during the turbulence
of the 1890s, contending that he is a statesman who reflected his time but has been presented falsely in Liberal-oriented and
Liberal-written histories, which denied him
his rightful place because of his alignment
against the incipient Liberal party. Includes
an account of the various governmental changes
of that decade, emphasizing the role of
Vásquez. DPU

85 _____. La revuelta de las traiciones. San
Pedro Sula: Sociedad de Geografía e Historia
de Honduras, 1937. 131 pp.
  A partisan account of the election of 1932
and the subsequent Liberal revolt. Written

from the viewpoint of the Conservatives, it
seeks to portray Liberal candidate Ángel
Zúñiga Huete as a militarist and the Liberals
as traitors who could not accept the election
results. The focus is on the tension and
combat between the election and the inauguration, with Conservative candidate General
Tiburcio Carías Andino hailed as the savior of
the republic. The author indicates that his
working title was El carnival de los
traidores. DLC LNHT

86 Castellanos García, J. Efraín. El diario de
una patria: agenda histórica y turística de
Honduras. Tegucigalpa: Ministerio de
Educación Pública, 1974. 410 pp. Illus.,
maps, tables.
     A datebook for the year, with space for
writing in personal appointments and notes.
Provides brief résumés of the significant
events in Honduran history for each day, as
well as general data of interest to the
tourist. IU

87 Castillo Flores, Arturo. Historia de la
moneda de Honduras. Tegucigalpa: Banco
Central de Honduras, 1974. 233 pp. Biblio.,
illus.
     A profusely illustrated history of coinage
and money in Honduras from discovery to the
present. While aimed principally at numis-
matists, it offers historical data on the
background of the various changes in coinage,
detailing the reorganizations of the financial
and banking systems. DLC

88 Castro, José Rafael, José García Bauer, and
Rafael Heliodoro Valle. El origen de la
tiranía en América y las nuevas orientaciones
de Honduras. Guatemala: Unión Tipografía,
1945. 35 pp.
     The text of a radio program in which three
prominent Central American intellectuals denounced the Carías regime as the epitomy of
backward dictatorship. The program was broadcast over the Guatemalan national radio during
the days of the Revolutionary regime in that
nation, under the sponsorship of a Honduran
exile organization.

89 Castro Díaz, Alejandro. Cartas al terruño.
Tegucigalpa: Banco Nacional de Fomento, 1975.
334 pp.
     A collection of 110 "letters" written by
the author as a column in his Revista
Tegucigalpa between 1917 and 1934. Using the
format of letters to a friend, he commented
freely and colloquially on a wide range of
subjects affecting his life in the capital,
including political affairs, celebrations,
services, social customs, and folklore, providing an indication of the concerns of the
citizens of the capital and life in it during
this era. LNHT

90 Castro Serrano, Catarino. Honduras en la
primera centuria: nuestra vida política,
diplomática, militar y cultural de los
primeros cien años, 1821-1921. Tegucigalpa:

Tipografía Nacional, 1921. 129 pp. Index,
notes, illus., appendixes.
     Despite its title this volume is not a
history of the nation but an analysis of its
contemporary problems, viewed in the light of
history in an effort to identify their historical antecedents. The author is optimistic, contending that Honduras has encountered
no fundamental problems during its initial
century, but does severely critize the various
governments and national institutions for
their limitations. The focus is on the 1919
election and civil war, tracing the antecedents topically to the previous decade, with
the 1907 Washington Pact and the Liberal regimes viewed as the basis of the 1919 activities. Includes excerpts from press reports
and political statements from the 1919 election and conflict, and detailed description of
the combats and troop movements. DLC BNCR

91 Centro Latinoamericano de Demografía (CELADE).
Encuesta demográfica nacional de Honduras. 7
vols. San José: CELADE, 1975-76. Maps,
tables.
     A detailed analysis of the data gathered
during the 1970 census, with separate analysis
of such items as births, deaths, marriages,
fertility, migration, and similar factors, all
detailed by age category and region, with
extensive tables and statistics. LNHT

92 Cerrato Valenzuela, Armando. Homenaje al
padre Reyes. Tegucigalpa: Tipografía
Nacional, 1941. 29 pp. Illus.
     A brief collection of documents relating to
the life of the founder of the University of
Honduras. DPU

93 _____. Monografía de los valores morales de
Comayagüela. Comayagüela: Tipografía Colón,
1948. 57 pp. Illus.
     Brief commentaries about significant per-
sons and events in the city's history, including discussion of its churches and
institutions. The focus is on its significant
residents who went on to national prominence
or served the city. DLC

94 Cevallos, Fernando P. Folklore hondureño:
tradiciones, leyendas, relatos y cuentos
populares de la ciudad de Comayagua.
Tegucigalpa: Tipografía Nacional, 1930. 39
pp. 4th ed. Tegucigalpa: Imprenta Calderón,
1951. 126 pp.
     A compendium of the traditional lore and
popular stories of the city of Comayagua.
Includes folktales, poetry, and legends about
or set in the city. Sources and selection
criteria are not indicated, and the items are
reprinted without comment. There is no explanation of why the second edition (1947) is
about three times the size of the initial one,
though the length in subsequent reprints has
remained stable. The title varies slightly in
the various editions. DLC

95 _____. Reseña histórica de las islas de la
Bahía. Tegucigalpa: Tipografía Nacional,

1916. 89 pp. Illus. 2d ed. Tegucigalpa: Tipografía Nacional, 1919. 89 pp. Illus.

A brief history of the Bay Islands, noting their stormy past, tracing the various occupations by the British, Walker, and the various other claimants, always supporting the Honduran title. DLC LNHT

96 Charles, Cecil. <u>Honduras: The Land of Great Depths</u>. Chicago and New York: Rand–McNally, 1890. 216 pp. Index, illus., maps, tables.

A travel account by an observant Yankee, designed for the benefit of Yankees who may wish to seek their fortune in Honduras and filled with helpful hints of what to take and expect. Provides impressions of the nation and its remoteness, particularly of travel modes and difficulties, as well as descriptions of its physical setting, people, living conditions, food, clothing, and housing, in addition to discussion of the economy. Offers more information about people and life-styles than is usual in such accounts, although it reflects the author's biases and his difficulties in becoming acclimated to the customs and conditions. DLC LNHT BNCR

97 Checchi, Vincent, and Associates. <u>Honduras: A Problem in Economic Development</u>. New York: Twentieth Century Fund, 1959. 172 pp. Biblio., maps, tables.

An economic survey of the republic, conducted in 1958 by a consulting firm. Details the present state of the economy and its future prospects with considerable enthusiasm, recommending a program for development that calls for greater government action focusing on transportation and communications construction, efforts to attract investment from abroad, promotion of education, and a more active government role in obtaining loans and aid and using funds from international agencies to aid in development. DLC LNHT

98 Coello, Augusto C., ed. <u>El digesto constitucional de Honduras, 1824-1921</u>. Tegucigalpa: Tipografía Nacional, 1923. 272 pp.

A collection of the texts of the various constitutions of the republic for the years in question. DLC LNHT BNCR

99 Coello, Augusto C., and Rómulo Ernesto Durón y Gamero. <u>Las Islas del Cisne</u>. Tegucigalpa: Ministerio de Relaciones Exteriores, 1926. 135 pp. 2d ed. Tegucigalpa: Talleres Tipográficos Nacionales, 1938.

A study of the title to the islands from their discovery until 1922. Supports the Honduran claims and disputes those of the United States, detailing the Spanish title and its passage to Honduras. Based on appropriate documents and published proclamations. WU

100 Collart Valle, Ángel Antonio. <u>Introducción al estudio del desarrollo integral del Valle de Cuyamel</u>. Tegucigalpa: Banco Nacional de Fomento, 1954. 80 pp. Illus., maps, tables.

A description, with statistical tables, of current conditions in the valley and a review of previous government programs. Includes consideration of such subjects as population, facilities, land ownership, climate, social services, and schools, as well as recommendations for future development, the most poignant of which is a call for more consistency in the government programs for the region. DLC

101 Colonia Hondureña en Guatemala. <u>Lecturas para el pueblo de Honduras: Policarpo Bonilla al desnudo</u>. Guatemala: Sánchez & de Guise, 1922. 23 pp.

A collection of excerpts from newspaper articles from other Central American nations, folios, and other publications attacking Bonilla. Gathered by the exile community seeking to expose his faults to the nation, it characterizes him as the nation's worst enemy. Part of the political polemics of the era. DLC

102 Comité Liberal Demócrata de Honduras en México. <u>Homenaje a las víctimas de San Pedro Sula, masacaradas el seis de julio de 1944, por mandatos del dictador Tiburcio Carías Andino y de su ministro de la guerra, Juan Manuel Gálvez</u>. Mexico: n.p., 1945. 112 pp.

A propaganda folio published in exile by the Honduran Liberals. Provides details of an incident in which a demonstration in San Pedro Sula was suppressed by troops, and of the commemoration held by the exiles in Mexico, followed by various charges against the regime. The incident reflected the turbulence that swept Central America in 1944 and the regime's efforts to demonstrate its willingness to use force to prevent a revolution in Honduras similar to that which had occurred in El Salvador and which was impending in Guatemala. DLC

103 Contreras, Carlos A. <u>Entre el marasmo: análisis de la crisis del Partido Liberal de Honduras, 1933-1970</u>. Tegucigalpa: n.p., 1970. 89 pp. Biblio.

A Liberal's analysis of his party during the previous generation, contending that its problems stem from a lack of ideology, leadership, and organization. Drawing comparisons from other nations, particularly Guatemala, he indicates the limitations within which it must work, calling for a firm commitment but for something short of socialism. He views most of the party's leaders as caudillos themselves, particularly emphasizing this in reference to Ángel Zúñiga Huete, but cautions that in view of their lack of education and experience Hondurans tend to prefer strong leaders, and hence will often choose a caudillo rather than a democrat. DLC LNHT

104 Council of Foreign Bondholders, London. <u>External Debt of Honduras</u>. London: Council of Foreign Bondholders, 1903. Pages unnumbered.
DLC

105 Cruz, Ramón Ernesto. <u>Discursos del presidente</u> <u>Cruz: año de 1971</u>. Tegucigalpa: Oficina de Relaciones Públicas de la Presidencia, 1972. 110 pp. Illus.

A collection of the major speeches of President Cruz, arranged chronologically, with indications of the date and occasion on which they were delivered, and the complete texts. DLC LNHT

106 _____. <u>Discursos del presidente Cruz:</u> <u>primer semestre, 1972</u>. Tegucigalpa: Oficina de Relaciones Públicas de la Presidencia, 1972. 175 pp. Illus.

A continuation of the previous item. DLC LNHT

107 _____. <u>Historia Constitucional e</u> <u>institucional de Honduras: derecho interno y</u> <u>derecho internacional</u>. Tegucigalpa: Imprenta López, 1964. 38 pp. Notes.

A brief overview of Honduran constitutional and legal history, indicating the dates of the various codifications. Originally published in <u>El Cronista</u> of Tegucigalpa, it was prepared by one of the nation's leading legal scholars and political figures. The account is very brief and hence highly general. LNHT

108 _____. <u>Somero análisis de algunos problemas</u> <u>sociales de Honduras</u>. Tegucigalpa: Talleres Tipográficos Nacionales, 1948. 78 pp. Biblio.

A collection of previously published articles, selected by the author, focusing on national problems of Honduras and particularly on his efforts to promote the statistical study of population and a uniform statistical system for the nation. These reflect the author's work during his academic career prior to his tenure in the presidency. The studies focus on the 1945-51 era and deal particularly with population and education. DLC LNHT

109 Cruz, René. <u>Dinero y banca en Honduras:</u> <u>reseña histórica y análisis de la situación</u> <u>originada por la legislación de 1950 y la</u> <u>creación del Banco Central de Honduras</u>. Tegucigalpa: Imprenta Soto, 1954. 58 pp. Biblio., tables.

An analysis of the banking and monetary system of Honduras focusing on the creation of the Central Bank in 1950, its causes and implications, with an extensive discussion of the new legislation and its impact on the financial system. Includes a historical sketch of banking and finance in the nation since Colonial times, and statistics regarding the current financial state of the nation. DLC

110 Cruz Cáceres, Francisco. <u>En las selvas</u> <u>hondureñas: episodios tragicómicos de nuestra</u> <u>vida turbulenta; bellezas y peligros de la</u> <u>selva y la tierra de los bananas en cifras</u>. Tegucigalpa: Tipografía Nacional, 1955. 134 pp. Illus., tables.

A combination of description and historical synopsis of the Caribbean coast provinces of Honduras, followed by data regarding the population and economy, with comparative statistics from 1910 and 1950. DLC LNHT

111 CSUCA. <u>El sistema educativo en Honduras:</u> <u>situación actual y perspectivas</u>. San José: CSUCA, 1965. 119 pp. Tables, illus.

See item CR335. DLC LNHT BNCR

112 <u>4 aproximaciones a Ramón Rosa</u>. Tegucigalpa: Secretaría de Cultura, Turismo e Información, 1976. 65 pp.

Published as part of the centennial of the 1876 Liberal movement, this small volume reprints four short commentaries about Rosa by Rafael Heliodoro Valle, Medardo Mejía, Pompeto del Valle, and Ramón Uquelí, all hailing Rosa's role in the nineteenth-century reform movement. DLC

113 Custódio, Ramón A. <u>Mosquitia adentro: tierro</u> <u>de lagos, ríos y hondureños</u>. Tegucigalpa: Federación de Estudiantes Universitarios de Honduras, 1956. 32 pp. Illus.

Observations during a visit to the Mosquito Indian area, citing the poor conditions of the inhabitants and calling in impassioned and patriotic terms for action to improve their status and integrate them into the nation. LNHT

114 Daniel, J.B. <u>The New El Dorado: A Short</u> <u>Sketch of Honduras, C.A., Its People, Climate,</u> <u>Natural Resources, and Vast Mineral Wealth</u>. Philadelphia: Dunlap & Clarke, 1888. 60 pp. Illus., maps.

A brief description designed for the Yankee audience, seeking to familiarize the readers with Honduras and convince them that it is a civilized and cultured nation with vast resources, to encourage settlement and investment there. Includes a report of the mineral deposits by Harvey Beckworth, identified as a mining expert. LNHT

115 Davidson, William Van. <u>Historical Geography</u> <u>of the Bay Islands, Honduras: Anglo-Hispanic</u> <u>Conflict in the Western Caribbean</u>. Birmingham, Ala.: Southern University Press, 1974. 199 pp. Index, biblio., notes, illus., maps, tables.

A detailed study of these remote islands, viewing them as a culturally isolated area that developed on its own with influences from the intrusions of various groups. Focuses especially on the geography, with extensive maps and diagrams of the individual towns and dwelling patterns, as well as maps and climatic diagrams of the islands and their location. Emphasizes Colonial times, when the various groups visited and landed, but includes a description of the present culture, with the intervening period covered generally. DLC LNHT

116 Davis, Richard Harding. <u>Captain Macklin: His</u> <u>Memoirs</u>. New York: Scribner's, 1902. 328 pp. 3d ed. New York: Scribner's, 1920. viii, 329 pp. Illus.

A vivid novel, in the form of the memoirs of a twenty-three-year-old former West Point

cadet, of filibustering and adventure in
Honduras, exhibiting the usual Yankee stereotypes of that era. DLC

117 Delgado, Luís Humberto. <u>Vicente Tosta:</u>
<u>evocando una revolución</u>. Lima: American
Express, 1929. 156 pp.
    A tiny volume (literally, it measures about
5 by 4 inches) briefly recounting and praising
the career of Vicente Tosta, a Honduran
caudillo, and comparing him favorably to
Peruvian caudillo Augusto Leguía. The real
purpose of the volume is clearly to hail
Leguía, with Tosta simply serving as a vehicle
to praise his programs, which are similar to
those of Leguía. DLC

118 Deutsch, Hermann B. <u>The Incredible Yanqui:</u>
<u>The Career of Lee Christmas</u>. London and New
York: Longmans, Green, 1931. 242 pp. Illus.,
maps, appendix.
    A detailed account of the Yankee fili-
busterer who became the power broker and military commander of Honduras from 1894 through
1924. Picturesquely written, it seeks to
combine vivid portrayal of his actions with
the myth that surrounded him; the appendix
reproduces many of the legends about him. The
author relied heavily on the recollections of
Christmas's associate, Colonel Guy R. Morgan.
DLC LNHT

119 Díaz Chávez, Filander. <u>Análisis crítico de</u>
<u>las condiciones técnicas de los Ferrocarriles</u>
<u>de la Standard Fruit Company</u>. Tegucigalpa:
Ediciones Liberación Nacional, 1973. 72 pp.
Maps, tables.
    A brief survey of the contracts and conces-
sions to the Standard Fruit Company authorizing it to operate railroads in the regions of
its banana plantations, followed by a critical
description of the current conditions of the
railroads. Concludes that the company has not
complied with the contractual stipulations,
since it has not provided passenger service,
and that its maintenance procedures are inadequate, resulting in substandard service even
for freight. The study contends that there is
ample basis for government action to demand
compliance with the concessions, implying the
right to terminate them, though refraining
from stating this openly. LNHT

120 _____. <u>El bote agujereado: por que salí de</u>
<u>la Dirección General de Obras Públicas</u>.
Tegucigalpa: n.p., 1959. 49 pp. Appendix.
    The author's explanation of his conduct
while serving as director of the Public Works
Department and the reasons for his resigna-
tion, detailing the controversies in which he
was involved, with appended documents referring to the events. LNHT

121 _____. <u>Las raíces del hambre y de la rebeldía</u>
<u>a la explotación: un ensayo sobre la pereza</u>.
Tegucigalpa: Imprenta Calderón, 1962. xv,
141 pp. Biblio., notes, illus.
    An analysis of social problems in Honduras,
contending that all can be traced to the
questions of hunger, agriculture, and land

ownership, and calling for land reform as the
nation's basic need. Includes discussion of
the characteristics of agriculture and the
local diet, with emphasis on hunger and what
the author calls the various levels of misery
within the nation; he also refers to other
social ills, such as alcoholism, but always
returns to the need for land distribution to
allow the peasants to produce their own food.
KU

122 _____. <u>Sociología de la desintegración</u>
<u>regional</u>. Tegucigalpa: Universidad Nacional
Autónoma de Honduras, 1972. 593 pp. Illus.,
maps, tables.
    A lengthy discussion of social theory as
applied to Central America and particularly
Honduras, written in the aftermath of the 1969
war by a Honduran scholar who calls the regional integration movement an imperialist
device that cannot benefit the underdeveloped
economies, particularly that of Honduras, and
one that helps only the oligarchies, such as
El Salvador. He contends that the region will
not be ready for unification until it throws
off the yoke of imperialism and undertakes a
program of social development to end the societal gaps within it. DLC LNHT

123 Díaz Lozano, Argentina. <u>Peregrinaje</u>.
Santiago: Zig-Zag, 1944. 277 pp. Illus. 2d
ed. Guatemala: Ministerio de Educación
Pública, 1955. 286 pp. Illus.
<u>Enriqueta and I</u>. New York: Farrar &
Rinehart, 1944. 217 pp. Illus.
    The only Central American novel to win the
Concurso Literario para la América Latina,
sponsored by the Pan American Union and Farrar
and Rinehart, this autobiographical novel took
the prize in 1943. Set in the tropics of
Honduras, it depicts the life of a widowed
rural schoolteacher and her daughter, the
author, offering vivid description of the
terrain and the details of life, including
dress, meals, customs, etc., of the region,
while dealing with the psychological aspects
of adolescence. Also included are the daily
struggles of life in the tropics, such as
natural disasters and illnesses. DLC LNHT
BNG

124 Durón, Francisco José. <u>Las Islas del Cisne</u>
<u>(Swan Island) en la cartografía de los siglos</u>
<u>XVI al XX</u>. <u>Reseña histórica</u>. London:
Published by the Author, 1962. 117 pp.
Illus., maps.
    A legal defense of the Honduran claim,
citing numerous maps supporting it. DLC LNHT

125 Durón, Jorge Fidel. <u>La battala de Washington</u>.
Tegucigalpa: Imprenta López and Cía, 1969.
30 pp. 2d ed. Tegucigalpa: Imprenta
Calderón, 1969. 30 pp.
    Originally a series of newspaper articles
reporting on the author's efforts as part of
the Honduran delegation in Washington during
the OAS meetings dealing with the 1969 war,
these essays charge that El Salvador mounted a
press campaign against Honduras and that the
Yankee press, falling victim to this effort,

(Durón, Jorge Fidel)
was hostile to Honduras. Recounts the
Honduran delegation's efforts to tell the
Honduran side of the story. Also contains
some comments about the behind-the-scenes
maneuvering, written in a bitter vein reflecting the frustration of the intense effort and
the Honduran delegation's view that it was the
victim of misunderstanding. DLC

126 _____. Cosas de tiempos pasados.
Tegucigalpa: Tipografía Ariston, 1966. 37
pp.
Reminiscences of the author's youth in
Tegucigalpa, aided by historical research (he
uses citations from secondary works to describe the era and supplement his own recollections), showing the changes that took place
in the city with the coming of modern elements
such as cars and electricity. The emphasis is
on the good-old-days type of narration of
life-styles and facilities, with no dates.
DLC LNHT

127 _____. Índice de la bibliografía hondureña.
Tegucigalpa: Imprenta Calderón, 1946. viii,
211 pp.
A listing of 3,000 items, most with publication information, and some with data such as
page count and size, without annotation. Although arranged by author's last name, entries
within letters are not in alphabetical order,
and many but not all entries are listed under
title as well as author. This combination
renders the work difficult to use. The list
emphasizes books, but also includes some articles, mimeographed items, and even journals
listed only by title, with separate listings
for each year rather than a single listing
indicating years of publication. Useful because of its comprehensiveness, but limited by
the unevenness of data and arrangement.
Clearly superceeded by Miguel Ángel García's
series. DLC LNHT

128 _____. Repertorio bibliográfico hondureño.
Tegucigalpa: Imprenta Calderón, 1943. viii,
68 pp. Index.
A bibliography of the books exhibited in a
national book fair. The author states that
the compilation was rushed and is admittedly
partial, but will provide a start in the process of developing a national bibliography.
Listings are by country, with authors arranged
alphabetically within nations. Reasonably
complete citings are provided, and there is an
author index. DLC LNHT

129 Durón y Gamero, Rómulo Ernesto. Biografía de
don Juan Nepomuceno Fernández Lindo.
Tegucigalpa: Tipografía Nacional, 1932. 122
pp. 2d ed. Tegucigalpa: Ministerio de
Educación Pública, 1937. 118 pp. Appendixes.
A brief biography of one of the Honduran
independence leaders who participated in many
of the early congresses and later served as
president of Honduras from 1847 to 1852, defending his place in history. Fernández Lindo
is hailed as a defender of Honduran sovereignty against the pretensions of Great

Britain and Guatemala. Based on documents
from the National Archives and including extensive excerpts and reproductions, this work
won a prize for the best biography of the
subject. DLC LNHT

130 _____. Biografía del doctor Marco Aurelio
Soto. Tegucigalpa: Talleres Tipográficos
Nacionales, 1944. vi, 215 pp. Illus. 2d ed.
Tegucigalpa: Talleres Tipográficos
Nacionales, 1949. 215 pp. Appendixes.
A defense of the title character, who
served as president of Honduras in 1876, seeking to restore him to his rightful place in
Honduran history. The author contends that he
was one of the few able presidents of the
nation in the late nineteenth century, and
hails his vision for the future and his intellectual ability, contending that all his opponents and critics were less able and honest
than he. The documentary reproductions, principally of public statements and addresses,
comprise most of the volume. DLC LNHT

131 _____. Biografía del presbíterio don
Francisco Antonio Márquez. Tegucigalpa:
Tipografía Nacional, 1915. 28 pp.
A brief essay tracing the career of a
priest who was active in the independence
movement, having served in most of the congresses of the 1820s and 1830s that prepared
constitutions and directed the separation from
Spain, and at one point as administrator of
the Honduran diocese. DLC LNHT

132 _____. Bosquejo histórico de Honduras. San
Pedro Sula: Tipografía del Comercio, 1927.
x, 216 pp. 3d ed. Tegucigalpa: Ministerio
de Educación Pública, 1956. v, 324 pp.
An overview of Honduran history by one of
its well-known scholars, with the emphasis on
the Colonial and independence eras. The post-
1839 era occupies only fifty pages. A broad
and succinct narrative that summarizes the
principal events of each era. DLC LNHT

133 _____, ed. Colección de escritos del Dr. don
Policarpo Bonilla. 3 vols. Tegucigalpa:
Tipografía Nacional, 1899. xxvii, 464, 357,
367 pp. Tables.
A collection of the writings of this important late-nineteenth century Honduran political leader, edited by Rómulo E. Durón. The
initial two volumes include private letters
and items published in the Honduran press
(principally the latter), providing a complete
collection. Volume 3 includes his official
messages during his years as president and
reports of the various years, proclamations,
addresses to Congress, etc. DLC LNHT BNCR

134 Durón y Gamero, Rómulo Ernesto. Historia de
Honduras, desde la independencia hasta
nuestros días. Tegucigalpa: Ministerio de
Educación Pública, 1956. 270 pp. Notes.
Written in 1903 by one of Honduras's most
prolific turn-of-the-century scholars, this
work was originally intended as the initial
volume in a lengthy history of the nation. It
covers the years 1822 to 1829, with extensive

(Durón y Gamero, Rómulo Ernesto)
excerpts from documents and some references to
secondary works, focusing on Honduran resistance to Mexican annexation, the formation of
the Federation of Central America, and the
Organization of the Honduran state. DLC LNHT

135 _____. José Justo Milla, estudio biográfico.
Tegucigalpa: Talleres Tipográficos
Nacionales, 1940. 93 pp. Notes.
A brief biographical sketch of one of the
military figures of the independence and
Federation era, consisting principally of
reproductions of documents and previous commentaries, with narration. The author concludes that while Milla was an effective
military officer, he was politically an
ambitious opportunist without firm loyalties
or political convictions. DLC LNHT

136 Durón y Gamero, Rómulo Ernesto, and Augusto C.
Coello. Las islas del Cisne: estudio hecho
en virtud del decreto legislativo número 57,
de 23 de febrero de 1922. Tegucigalpa:
Talleres Tipográficos Nacionales, 1926. 135
pp. 2d ed. Tegucigalpa: Talleres
Tipográficos Nacionales, 1938. 135 pp.
A history of the Swan Islands and jurisdiction over them from Colonial times to 1922,
written under the sponsorship of the Honduran
government and designed to support the
Honduran claims to them. DPU

137 Durón y Gamero, Rómulo Ernesto, et al. El
General Domingo Vásquez. San José: Imprenta
Soley y Valverde, 1941. 32 pp.
A series of essays by various scholars and
political figures discussing the military and
political careers of General Domingo Vásquez
and his role in Honduran and isthmian politics
during the late nineteenth century, dealing
with diverse episodes of his life offering
divergent viewpoints. BNCR

138 ECLA. Agricultural Credit in Honduras. New
York: U.N., 1950. 38 pp.
A study of the current credit situation,
with recommendations for the improvement of
financing available to agriculture. DLC

139 _____. Análisis y proyecciones del desarrollo
económico, XI; el desarrollo económico de
Honduras. Mexico: U.N., 1960. ix, 222 pp.
Illus., tables.
A detailed survey of the Honduran economy
in two parts, the first covering the years
1945 to 1959, and the second covering 1959-68,
bound together. Includes consideration of
products, production and export figures, consumption, price changes, labor and similar
factors, with extensive statistical tables and
data. WU

140 La Época (Tegucigalpa). Oposición sin Dios ni
ley: apuntes y extractos sobre el libertinaje
en Honduras. 2 vols. Tegucigalpa: La Época,
1946-47. 94, 84 pp.
A defense of the incumbent regime against
charges that it is antidemocratic, replying
particularly and passionately to the attacks

of El Norte written by Manuel F. Barahona, who
is condemned as a traitor to his nation. The
defense consists of innumerable excerpts from
the commentaries of various individuals about
the incumbent Gálvez regime and its predecessor, the Carías regime. DLC

141 _____. El Progreso de Honduras durante los
años que ha gobernado el doctor y general don
Tiburcio Carías Andino, reformador glorioso y
benemérito de la patria. Tegucigalpa:
Talleres Tipográficos Nacionales, 1942.
96 pp.
A listing, by department and municipality,
of the public works projects of the Carías
regime; compiled by the newspaper, which hails
them as the products of an era of peace and
progress. The listings are brief and not
particularly descriptive, often settling for
statements like "pavement of new streets,"
with no indication of location, or extent.
The pamphlet does, however, indicate the major
projects. DLC

142 _____. Sobre la ruta: divulgaciones de "La
Época." Tegucigalpa: Talleres Tipográficos
Nacionales, 1937. 121 pp.
A volume hailing the accomplishments of the
Conservative party and the regime of General
Tiburcio Carías Andino, which the newspaper,
the party organ, characterizes as the construction of a new Honduras through "national
renovation." Its principal purpose is to
explain the regime's continuismo, cataloging
its works and the extraordinary character of
its leader, and quoting extensively from his
declarations in launching his new term and the
new era. DLC

143 _____. La verdadera situación de Honduras.
Tegucigalpa: La Época, 1936. 77 pp. Illus.
A defense of the Carías regime by the Conservative party newspaper, hailing its efforts
to stabilize the nation and combat the effects
of the global depression. DLC

144 Escoto, Julio. Los guerreros de Hibueras.
Tegucigalpa: Escuela Superior del
Profesorado, 1967. 78 pp.
A novel set in a small town in the interior
taken by revolutionary guerrillas. Recounts
the trials and tribulations of the various
combats and episodes, emphasizing the hardships imposed on the guerrillas and the inhabitants. The setting is clearly Honduras, and
the focus is on the effect of such conflicts
on local lives; the time, the regime, and the
contending forces are not specified. DLC
LNHT

145 Esquivel, Rogelio. La Honduras de hoy bajo el
régimen admirable del presidente Carías
Andino. Tegucigalpa: Talleres Tipográficos
Nacionales, 1942. 62 pp. Illus.
A summary of the works of the Carías
regime, hailing their effects. DPU

146 Fernández, Juan José. La revolución
de Oriente: apuntes para la historia
contemporánea nacional. Tegucigalpa:
Tipografía Nacional, 1919. 62 pp. 2d ed.

Tegucigalpa: Tipografía Nacional, 1920. 64 pp.

A brief account of the military revolt of 1919 that installed General Rafael López Gutiérrez in power in Honduras, focusing on the movements and victories of the conquering rebel forces. LNHT

147 Fernández Mira, Ricardo M. Un precursor de la enseñanza. Buenos Aires: Editorial Cervantes, 1935. 103 pp.

A brief biography of José Trinidad Reyes, the Honduran priest who founded the National University in 1847, with selections from his poetry and religious dramas. DLC

148 Ferrari de Hartling, Guadalupe. Recuerdos de mi vieja Tegucigalpa. Comayagüela: Tipografía Libertad, 1953. 140 pp. Illus.

A rambling collection of the author's memories of growing up in Tegucigalpa and what the city was like in her youth. Recounts the location of various buildings, their significance, and stories about events associated with them, while indicating some of the changes that have taken place in recent years. Includes numerous photos of the old buildings. DLC

149 Ferrera, Fausta. Cuentos regionales. San Pedro Sula: Compañía Editora de Honduras, 1938. 106 pp.

A collection of short stories dealing with life in the Honduran countryside, employing local idioms and folklore, seeking to portray the nation's traditions and inspire patriotism. The stories deal with a broad range of themes, and some contain details of location, though there is no effort to identify all with a specific region. Accounts of real events, fiction, folklore, and children's stories are included. DLC

150 Ferro, Carlos A. El caso de las Islas Santanilla. Tegucigalpa: Ministerio de Educación Pública, 1969. 147 pp. Biblio., appendixes. 2d ed. Tegucigalpa: Presidencia de Honduras, Oficina de Relaciones Públicas, 1972. 160 pp. Biblio., appendixes.

The Argentine ambassador to Honduras provides a history of the Santanilla or, as they are more commonly known, the Cisne or Swan Islands, defending the Honduran claims against those of Nicaragua and the United States on the basis of research in the Archivo General de Centro América in Guatemala City. He argues that these islands were always Honduran, tracing them back to Columbus and through the various disputes and rulings about their ownership. His purpose is revealed in his frequent comparisons of this issue with the Argentine-British dispute regarding the Malvinas, which he contends is a parallel case. The Honduran government published his study supporting their claim. Pertinent documents are appended. DLC LNHT

151 Fiallos, Ernesto. Bosquejo biográfico del excelentísimo y reverendísimo, monseñor Dr. Fray Juan de Jesús Zepeda y Zepeda.

Tegucigalpa: Imprenta Calderón, 1938. 73 pp. Illus.

A brief biographical sketch of the career of a late-nineteenth-century bishop of Comayagua, who was a native Honduran and whose career reflected the turbulence of the era and the Liberal-Conservative conflict involving church and state. Includes excerpts from his letters, sermons, and statements. DLC

152 Figueroa, Fernando F. Monografía del departmento de Olancho. Tegucigalpa: Tipografía Nacional, 1935. 116 pp. Illus., tables.

Part of the National Society of Geography and History series for each of the departments of Honduras. Designed to emphasize the geographic aspects, it focuses principally on description of features and climate, though there is a brief paragraph on history. Contains similar data for each of the department's municipalities. DLC LNHT

153 Fitz-Roy, Robert. Report of Capt. Robert Fitz-Roy, Royal Navy, to the Earl of Clarendon, on the Proposed Honduras Interoceanic Railway. London: Chiswick Press, 1856. 15 pp.

A brief statement of the case for the feasibility and profitability of the Honduras railroad, rating it superior to other projects and locations. LNHT

154 Flamenco, José. Álbum gráfico: homenaje al doctor y general Tiburcio Carías Andino. Tegucigalpa: Secretaría Privada de la Presidencia, 1946. 44 pp. Illus.

An officially sponsored collection of photos of the regime's public-works projects.

155 Funes, Matías. Levando anclas: crónicas de viajes. Tegucigalpa: Litografía Suárez Romero, 1963. 259 pp.

While consisting mainly of a travelogue, this work by a Honduran poet and sailor includes a brief description of his native land and an emotional commentary on its participation in World War II, as well as his memoirs of various trips throughout the world. The articles were originally published in El Cronista of Tegucigalpa. DLC LNHT

156 _____. Oro y miseria, o las minas de Rosario. Tegucigalpa: Imprenta López y Cía, 1966. 237 pp. Illus.

A novel about the life of the miners working in the remote Honduran gold mines, focusing on the harshness of their existence, their exploitation, and the violence in their lives, emphasizing their poor status despite their contribution to the wealth of others. Includes the peasants from the surrounding countryside, and portrays the entire scene in dramatic and vivid terms. DLC

157 _____. El serio: novela de humorismo y crítica. Tegucigalpa: Imprenta Calderón, 1969. 178 pp.

A parody of Honduran life, customs, and politics. Though the characters and situations are fictional, they clearly reflect the realities of contemporary life in Central America and its problems and peculiarities. DLC

158 Galindo y Galindo, Bernardo. *Monografía del departamento de Choluteca.* Tegucigalpa: Tipografía Nacional, 1933. 101 pp. Illus., tables.

Another of the provincial geographic monographs, with essays regarding the geography and setting of each of the municipalities, focusing on physical and climatic descriptions and a catalog of existing services, though including a brief historical outline. DLC LNHT

159 _____. *Monografía del departamento de Valle.* Tegucigalpa: Talleres Tipográficos Nacionales, 1934. 49 pp. Illus.
See item HO158. DLC LNHT

160 Galo, Hernán Isias. *Bibliografías agrícolas de América Central: Honduras.* Turrialba, Costa Rica: Instituto Interamericana de Ciencias Agrícolas, 1974. 134 pp. Index.

A bibliography of articles and books relating to Honduran agriculture, emphasizing domestically published items and following the format of the other works in this series.

161 Gálvez, Carlos Alberto. *Temas laborales.* Tegucigalpa: Universidad Nacional Autónoma de Honduras, 1970. 347 pp. Biblio.

A listing, by subject, of the current Honduran labor statutes, with brief summary or quotation from the text, samples of documents required or forms prescribed to render transactions legal, and questions and answers regarding their application, designed to explain the laws to the nonlawyer. LNHT

162 Gálvez, Juan Manuel. *Breves relatos sobre algunas obras administrativas y viajes presidenciales del doctor Juan Manuel Gálvez, desde el 9 de marzo de 1949 hasta el 8 de mayo de 1952.* Tegucigalpa: Tipografía Ariston, 1952. 318 pp. Illus., maps.

A compendium of descriptions of the public works of the regime, covering the years 1949–52, including press commentaries and descriptions of the projects and their inaugurations. Presidential trips and the personal involvement of the chief executive are emphasized, with official statements and press commentary, all hailing the regime. Rounds of dedications each January constitute the focus of the organization of the volume. DLC

163 _____. *Ideario de una democracia: declaraciones.* Tegucigalpa: Tipografía Ariston, 1951. 83 pp. Illus.

A collection of short quotations from the various speeches of President Gálvez during his initial two years as head of the Honduran state, providing a guide to the thoughts of the president and those comments that the regime considers most representative of its outlook. The brief single-paragraph excerpts covering a wide range of themes are divided by

subject matter, and the source of each is identified. DLC LNHT

164 _____. *La obra del doctor Juan Manuel Gálvez en su adminstración, 1949–1954.* Tegucigalpa: Talleres Tipográficos Nacionales, 1955. 533 pp. Illus., maps, tables.

A detailed account of the numerous public works of the Gálvez regime during the indicated years, with photos of the projects and the key individuals of the administration. The volume is divided by ministries and dependencies, such as railroads, roads, and agriculture. All projects from major works to the purchase of office equipment, are listed, along with the texts of laws and production statistics. DLC

165 _____. *Obra material del gobierno del doctor Gálvez.* Tegucigalpa: OHCI, 1951. 150 pp. Illus.

Another illustrated listing of the regime's major projects.

166 Gamero de Medina, Lucila. *Aída: novela regional.* Tegucigalpa: Tipografía Nacional, 1912. 2d ed. Tegucigalpa: Danlí, 1948. 428 pp.

A novel of life in the Honduran countryside and its problems, written in the form of the memoirs of an Indian girl as recorded in her diary begun at the age of eighteen and tracing her early life. TxU

167 García, Miguel Ángel, ed. *Bibliografía hondureña, 1920–1970.* Tegucigalpa: Banco Central de Honduras, 1971. 3 vols. 203, 489, 512 pp.

A monumental compilation of items published in Honduras, arranged alphabetically within years, though in later years the government publications are separated. Includes annotation usually consisting of a summation of the table of contents. While valuable as the most complete listing of Honduran publications available, the work unfortunately contains considerable inaccuracies, the alphabetical order is not always strict, items are listed based on reports of them, some periodical articles or series are mixed in without indication, and the year-by-year listing makes entries hard to locate. DLC LNHT

168 Girón Escobar, Juan Ramón, ed. *Interpretaciones, reformas por decretos legislativos y autos acordados por la honorable Corte Suprema, a leyes de Honduras.* Tegucigalpa: Imprenta La Democracia, 1933. 384 pp. Illus., tables.

A compilation of excerpts from rulings by the Honduran Supreme Court, arranged by subject though without index, covering the nineteenth and early twentieth centuries. DLC

169 González y Contreras, Gilberto. *Un pueblo y un hombre: Honduras y el general Carías.* Tegucigalpa: Imprenta La Democracia, 1934. 40 pp.

A brief review of the regime of Carías, hailing his reconstruction of the nation and reviewing the terrible conditions of the

(González y Contreras, Gilberto)
country upon his ascension to power, noting
his various development programs. DLC

170 _____ . El último caudillo: ensayo
biográfico. Mexico: B. Costa-Amic, 1946.
233 pp. Illus.
A sympathetic view of Tiburcio Carías
Andino; seeks to portray the man and his concerns, though in the process emphasizing his
inscrutability and defensiveness. The author
traces the life of the caudillo and his early
years, also surveying the regimes that immediately preceded his. Contends that his actions
were dictated by conditions and by the nation's tradition of civil war and caudillismo;
views him as the pacifier of the nation, who
brought stability that would enable development and transformation. Carías is portrayed
as a quiet, calm, patient, pragmatic realist
who moved slowly and dealt with the situation
as he found it, while supporting traditional
values. DLC LNHT

171 Granados Garay, Rigoberto, and Fernando Danza
Sandoval. Guía para investigadores de
Honduras. Mexico: PAIGH, 1977. 45 pp.
Maps.
This pamphlet, like others in the series,
consists of a list of maps and a bibliography
of locally published works dealing with the
nation's geography. DLC

172 Grimaldi, Antonio. Biografía del Dr. Céleo
Arias. Tegucigalpa: Tipografía Nacional,
1931. 89 pp. Illus.
Originally published in the newspaper El
Bien Público of Quezaltenango in 1890 on the
occasion of the death of its subject, this
volume offers a sympathetic account of the
career of the longtime leader of the Honduran
Liberal party during the confusing era of
1860-90, when Honduran politics was characterized by frequent civil wars and constant
political and military confrontations, and
traces his stands. DLC LNHT

173 Guardiola Cubas, Esteban. Biografía del Dr.
Rafael Alvarado Manzano. Tegucigalpa:
Talleres Tipográficos Nacionales, 1934. 27
pp. 2d ed. Tegucigalpa: Talleres
Tipográficos Nacionales, 1939. 170 pp.
Illus.
A biography of a Honduran educator and
political figure who served in the cabinet or
the Congress almost continuously from 1876
through his death in 1923, held positions of
importance in various schools, including that
of rector of the National University, and
served as a judge in various courts, including
the Honduran Supreme Court. The biography
occupies the initial forty-eight pages of the
volume; it is followed by a vita and excerpts
from the works of the subject. DLC LNHT

174 _____ . Don Francisco Antonio Xavier Botelo.
Tegucigalpa: Talleres Tipográficos
Nacionales, 1942. 39 pp. Biblio., illus.
A brief biography of a Honduran Supreme
Court justice and vice-rector of the National

University during the mid-nineteenth century,
who served on the court from 1856 through
1873, and at the university during 1873 (he
had been a member of its faculty, teaching
Latin, prior to his administrative post).
Contains quotations from his official appointments and some documents relevant to his tenures. Based on research in the National
Archives and interviews with friends of the
title figure. DLC LNHT

175 _____ . Historia de la Universidad de
Honduras: centenario del Padre Reyes.
Tegucigalpa: Talleres Tipográficos
Nacionales, 1952. 207 pp.
An account of the university from its foundation in 1845 to 1930, focusing particularly
on its founder but also tracing its growth and
changes, with lengthy quotations from the
appropriate legislation and speeches at key
events. The latter half of the volume consists of lyric poems by the first rector,
which are analyzed and compared. DLC LNHT

176 _____ . Vida y escritos de don Dionisio de
Herrera. Tegucigalpa: Sociedad de Geografía
e Historia de Honduras, 1950. 153 pp.
A biography of a Honduran head of state
during the Federation period in the immediate
post-independence era, with excerpts from his
writings.

177 _____ . Vida y hechos del general Santos
Guardiola: biografía. Tegucigalpa:
Ministerio de Educación Pública, 1932. 2d ed.
Tegucigalpa: Talleres Tipográficos
Nacionales, 1953. 236 pp. Illus.
A sympathetic biography of the general who
headed the Honduran state and participated
actively in the wars that split the region
from 1845 to 1862, tracing his actions and
contending that he was defending Honduran
sovereignty in resisting the unionist pretensions of Gerrardo Barrios and others. Includes extensive quotation from the documents
of the era, accounts of the various military
campaigns, and a collection of excerpts from
Guardiola's presidential messages. DLC LNHT

178 Harris, Walter D., et al. Housing in
Honduras; La vivienda en Honduras.
Washington, D.C.: PAU, 1964. 316, 295 pp.
Illus., maps, tables.
A detailed study of the characteristics of
existing Honduran housing, prepared by a survey team under the auspices of the Alliance
for Progress. Describes and analyzes types,
plans, construction materials, availability,
cost, construction methods, etc. Includes
recommendations for future needs and appropriate types, as well as details about the
existing structures and considerations about
the best and most suitable types and means of
construction. TU

179 Helbig, Karl Martin. Die Landschaften von
Nordost-Honduras: Auf Grund einer
geographischen Studienreise im Jahre 1953.
Hamburg: Hermann Haack, 1959. 270 pp.
Biblio., illus., maps, tables.

Áreas y paisajes del nordeste de Honduras.
Tegucigalpa: Banco Central de Honduras, 1965.
287 pp. Illus., maps, tables.
   A geographical study of northeastern
Honduras, focusing on physical forms, climate,
and resources, to fill what the author considers a gap in the study of Central America.
The fieldwork was conducted in 1953. Contains
useful maps and statistical tables. DLC LNHT

180 Hernández, Ángel G. Nuestra reforma
educacional. Tegucigalpa: Tipografía
Nacional, 1931. iii, 325 pp.
   An inspector of schools offers his personal
views of the Honduran educational system and
his personal plan for improving it, including
educational philosophy, content, and organization of schools. He seeks a more effective,
far-reaching, and dynamic educational system
that is more central to the life of the
citizens. DLC LNHT

181 _____. Problemas de la educación primaria.
Tegucigalpa: Talleres Tipográficos
Nacionales, 1950. 303 pp. Index, tables.
   A survey of the current state of the
Honduran educational system and its problems,
describing its organization, methods, objectives, official syllabi, and required subjects. Includes discussion of changes and
policies during the 1940s, and some historical
background. The author, a former minister of
education with extensive experience in various
educational posts in the nation's schools,
concludes with recommendations for the educational focus of the nation, advocating that
the system emphasize democracy, nationalism,
hemispheric and isthmian unity, and peace.
DLC

182 _____. Problemas de la educación
universitaria: libros estimulantes para la
juventud. Tegucigalpa: Ministerio de
Educación Pública, 1956. 165 pp.
   A history of the University of Honduras,
with an emphasis on its present organization
and the years since 1923. Discusses the role
the institution has played in the nation and
its political and intellectual development,
and comments on its potential for influencing
future development and attitudes in the
nation. DLC

183 Hernández, Daniel. La justificación histórica
de la actual prolongación en el poder.
Tegucigalpa: Talleres Tipográficos
Nacionales, 1940. 39 pp.
   An officially sponsored account of the
rationale for extending the term of Tiburcio
Carías Andino in 1939, noting the special
needs of the nation during the depression and
hailing his accomplishments and efforts to
stabilize the nation after an era of turbulent
politics. DLC

184 _____. La tributación en Honduras.
Tegucigalpa: Tipografía Ariston, 1947. 285
pp. Tables.
   A study of the nation's tax system and its
evolution, with appropriate statistics. DLC

185 Hernández C., Miguel Ángel. El problema de la
lepra en Honduras. Tegucigalpa: Imprenta
Calderón, 1935. 63 pp.
   A survey of the extent of leprosy in
Honduras and the efforts to treat and combat
the disease.

186 Hernández Carvajal, Alvaro. El problema del
tugurio en Tegucigalpa. Tegucigalpa:
Instituto de la Vivienda, 1967. 27 pp.
Illus., maps, tables.
   A discussion of the problem of overpopulation and the housing shortage in the Honduran
capital, with statistical data as well as
proposals for improving the living conditions
in the slums and areas of temporary housing to
which the poor are relegated. LNHT

187 Herrán, Víctor. Le chemin de fer
interocéanique du Honduras: étude sur
l'avenir commercial et industriel de
l'Amérique Centrale. Paris: V. Goupy, 1868.
39 pp. Maps.
NN

188 _____. Documentos oficiales sobre los
empréstitos de Honduras. Paris: Goupy &
Jordan, 1884. 112 pp.
   A collection of documents drawn from the
Foreign Ministry of Honduras, consisting of
the exchanges and agreements involved in the
various foreign loan negotiations of that
nation, covering the years 1870-77 but focusing on the latter year. The author participated in the negotiations in Europe as
Honduran minister to France. The communications illustrate the complexity of the
loans, the problems of obtaining funds, and
the difficulties of payment because of internal political turmoil and the resulting complications. DLC

189 Herrera Cáceres, H. Roberto. Honduras y la
problemática del derecho internacional público
del mar. Tegucigalpa: Universidad Nacional
Autónoma de Honduras, 1975. 264 pp. Biblio.,
notes, appendixes.
   A legal statement of the Honduran position
claiming a 200-mile jurisdiction over adjoin-
ing waters, emphasizing its claims to the Gulf
of Fonseca and the continental shelf. The
differentiation in its claims regarding sovereignty and a zone of economic control receive emphasis. Includes quotations from the
appropriate legislation and other formal declarations on which these claims are based, to
provide a legal justification for the Honduran
stance at international conferences dealing
with this question. DLC

190 Hidalgo h., Carlos F. De estructura económica
y Banca Central; la experiencia de Honduras.
Madrid: Gráficas Ibarra, 1963. 133 pp.
Biblio., notes, tables.

(Hidalgo h., Carlos F.)
Originally a thesis, this work surveys the economic development of Honduras since 1950, when the Central Bank was created, and examines the role of the bank. Though hailing its activities, the author concludes that given the situation of the nation, a policy of channeling credit into industry is needed to stimulate an expansion of industry based on import substitution, which he sees as the only viable means of diversifying the economy. He calls for the bank to promote such industry by expanding the money supply and credit, and through more venturesome policies that favor such industry. DLC LNHT

191 _____. Highlights of Honduras: A Short Synopsis of Present Day Honduras. Washington, D.C.: Published by the Author, 1959. 24 pp. Biblio., illus.
General description and travel data. DLC

192 Hill, George W., and Marion T. Loftin. Characteristics of Rural Life and the Agrarian Reform in Honduras. Tegucigalpa: OEA Misión de Asistencia Técnica, 1961. 206 pp.
A study of rural development and land tenure in Honduras, emphasizing the needs of the peasants and their poor living conditions. Calls for accelerated land reform, citing the desperate needs and the urgency of the situation. DPU

193 Honduras, Comité Central Pro-Soriano. El problema electoral de Honduras ante el mundo civilizado. Tegucigalpa: Tipografía Nacional, 1919. 47 pp. Illus.
The political manifesto and platform of Dr. Nazario Soriano, candidate of the National party for the presidency of Honduras for the 1920-24 term, along with various statements of support, as well as a response to the accusations of Alberto Membreño in the New York Globe against the incumbent regime of Francisco Bertrand. Part of the political polemics of the era, with each calling the other a dictator and himself the true democrat. DLC

194 Honduras, Constitution. Colección de las constituciones políticas que la República de Honduras se ha decretado en los cincuenta y seis años que lleva de independencia, comenzando por la federal emitida el 22 de noviembre de 1824. New York: Chamberlin Whitmore, 1878. vi, 203 pp.
A collection of the texts of the various Honduran constitutions for the years in question. The volume omits, however, the 1831 document, which is contained in the collection edited later by Auguto C. Coello. DLC LNHT

195 Honduras, Estudiantes Universitarios de. Testamento y memorias del general Francisco Morazán: discursos y artículos relativos al héreo. Tegucigalpa: Talleres Tipográficos Nacionales, 1942. 60 pp. Illus.
The hero's last will and memoirs, with some articles acclaiming his contributions to the independence movement. DLC LNHT

196 Honduras, Gov't of. La deuda externa de Honduras en 1923: arreglo con los tenedores de bonos extranjeros de Londres. Tegucigalpa: Tipografía Nacional, 1928. 110 pp.
An official summary and compilation of the outstanding debt, detailing the various loans and listing the payment due dates and amounts. DLC

197 _____. Documentos justificativos de la conducto observado en las negociaciones de paz con el de Guatemala: habidas últimamente bajo la intervención amistosa del Salvador. Comayagua: Imprenta del Gobierno, 1855. 39 pp.
A collection of exchanges, proclamations, and declarations relating to the talks incident to the conflict between the Guatemalan regime of Carrera and the government of Trinidad Cabañas in 1855, including exchanges between the two regimes and statements supporting the Honduran position. DLC

198 _____. Archivos Nacionales. Índice de los documentos y expedientes que se custodian en el Archivo Nacional: creados desde 1580 al 30 de julio de 1927. Comayagua: Imprenta El Sol, 1927. 291 pp.
A listing of documents in the Honduran National Archives, with brief summary data and date, arranged alphabetically by title within departments. Covers the years from the 1500s through the 1920s; most of the entries emphasize land tenure and registry of titles of ownership. Provides considerable information about landownership in the nation and in each department, since the listing contains the name of the individual and extent of the holding, although the order of listing is by title of the holding, not the owner's name. LNHT

199 _____. _____. Nuevo índice del Archivo de Tierras custodiado en el Archivo Nacional: comprende los expedientes creados desde 1580 a 1901. Tegucigalpa: Imprenta del Gobierno, 1883. 64 pp. 2d ed. Tegucigalpa: Tipografía Nacional, 1901. 347 pp.
An index of more than 2,000 land titles awarded in Honduras from 1580 to 1901, arranged alphabetically by department. The second edition contains many more citations owing to new discoveries as well as additional grants. Unfortunately, it is necessary to know the name of the land parcel to find it, but the listing indicates extent, location, and owner. DLC LNHT

200 _____. Banco Central. Balances de liquidaciones presupuestarios del gobierno central 1924/25-1951/52. Tegucigalpa: Banco Central de Honduras, 1953. 19 pp. Tables.
A collection of statistics providing final figures on the overall governmental budget, by category, for the years indicated. DLC

201 _____. _____. Índice de precios al por menor para familias de ingresos moderados en Tegucigalpa, D.C., 1948=100. Tegucigalpa: Banco Central de Honduras, 1955. 51 pp. Tables.
DLC

(Honduras, Gov't of)

202 _____. _____. La nueva política bananera de
Honduras, 1903-1975. Tegucigalpa: Secretaría
de Cultura, Turismo e Información, 1975.
182 pp.
    A collection of documents relating to the
Honduran operations of the Standard Fruit
Company and the Tela Railroad, compiling the
government concessions to and legislation
regarding these two companies from the initial
concession in 1903 to 1975. DLC

203 _____. _____. Producto e ingreso nacional,
1960-72. Tegucigalpa: n.p., 1974. 38 pp.
Tables.
    A supplement to item HO435.

204 _____. Banco Nacional de Fomento. Honduras:
corazón de las Américas. Comayagua: División
de Desarrollo Industrial, 1965. 28 pp.
    A summary of current information about the
nation, focusing in glowing terms on its economic prospects and progress.

205 _____. Biblioteca Nacional. Catálogo
metódico de la Biblioteca Nacional, seguido de
un índice alfabético de autores y otro de
materias. Tegucigalpa: Tipografía Nacional,
1915. 293 pp. Index.
    An alphabetical listing, within subject
categories, of books in the National Library.
The overwhelming majority of the entries deal
with general subjects rather than Central
America, with few local publications included.
Entries provide incomplete bibliographical
information and are inconsistent as to form.
There are no annotations. DLC

206 _____. Comisión Revisora de Arancel. El
sistema tributario en Honduras. Tegucigalpa:
Published by the Commission, 1959. 177 pp.
Illus., tables.
    A summary of all existing Honduran taxes
and fees, prepared under the auspices of the
International Cooperation Administration by
two Honduran technicians. The emphasis is on
summary and description rather than analysis.
DLC LNHT

207 _____. Congreso. Homenaje tributado por el
pueblo hondureño por medio del soberano
Congreso Nacional al excelentísimo señor
presidente constitucional de la república,
doctor y general Tiburcio Carías Andino.
Tegucigalpa: Talleres Tipográficos
Nacionales, 1945. 287 pp. Illus.
    An official volume containing the decrees
of the Congress declaring Carías "Fundador y
Defensor de la Paz de Honduras y Benemérito de
la Patria" and declaring his birthday a "Día
de la Paz y de dar Gracias a Dios," both
during 1945. Complete with the full texts,
the debates of the sessions, hymns of praise
written by each of the members of Congress,
and numerous congratulatory messages in support from individuals throughout the nation.
DLC LNHT

208 _____. Consejo del Distrito Central. Cinco
años de labor administrativo: homenaje en
esta gloriosa efemérides al doctor y general

don Tiburcio Carías Andino, ilustre presidente
de la república y benemérito de la patria.
Tegucigalpa: Imprenta Calderón, 1943. 121
pp. Illus., tables.
    A commemorative volume hailing the public-
works projects of the Carías regime, particularly its creation of the Central District,
which combined the government of the entire
metropolitan area into a single entity encompassing Tegucigalpa and Comayagüela. Includes
statistics and photos of numerous projects
such as street paving and building construction, as well as statistics regarding population, births, schools, etc. DLC

209 _____. Dirección General de Censos y
Estadísticas. Encuesta de ingresos y gastos
familiares, 1967-1968. Tegucigalpa:
Dirección General de Censos y Estadísticas,
1970. xxv, 178 pp. Tables.
    A compilation of statistical data regarding
income and expenditure patterns in Honduras,
with separate categories for the capital, San
Pedro Sula, and other urban and rural areas;
based on interviews and government statistics.
DLC LNHT

210 _____. Dirreción General de Estadística.
Estadísticas demográficas, 1926-1951.
Tegucigalpa: Dirección General de Censos y
Estadísticas, 1953. 20 pp. Tables.
    A collection of data, based on census fig-
ures and including estimates where appropriate, about the Honduran population for the
years indicated, categorized by sex, age, and
location, including births and deaths. A
useful guide to indicate the trends and
change, though it must be used with caution
owing to the estimates that are included. DLC

211 _____. _____. La República de Honduras:
breve reseña para la exposición de San Luís,
Missouri. Tegucigalpa: Tipografía Nacional,
1903. 60 pp. Biblio.
    A brief official description of the current
state of the nation prepared for Yankee audiences at the St. Louis exposition. DLC

212 _____. Junta Militar de Gobierno. Retorno a
la constitucionalidad. Tegucigalpa: Oficina
de Relaciones Públicas del Gobierno, 1957. 32
pp. Illus.
    TxU

213 _____. Ministerio de Agricultura.
Estadísticas de producción agrícola, pecuaria,
forestal, de la caza y la pesca, 1925-1952.
Tegucigalpa: Ministerio de Agricultura, 1953.
Tables.
    A statistical compilation for the years in
question, providing official figures in comparable form for production and exports. DNAL

214 _____. Ministerio de Economía y Hacienda.
Honduras un país propicio para la inversión
privada extranjera. Tegucigalpa: Ministerio
de Economía y Hacienda, 1961. 24 pp.
    An official pamphlet designed to encourage
foreign investment. Stresses the economic
growth, situation, and prospects of Honduras,

(Honduras, Gov't of)
and hails its political stability, legal
structure, and prospective growth.

215 _____. Ministerio de Educación Pública.
Estado actual de la educación primaria en
Honduras. Tegucigalpa: Ministerio de
Educación Pública, 1956. 26 pp. Illus.
　　An official summary of the state of
Honduran primary education, prepared by a
government official for a hemispheric con-
ference; focuses on the present situation and
draws on statistics from the years 1954-55.
DPU

216 _____. Ministerio de Gobernación, Justicia,
Sanidad y Beneficiencia. Breve noticia del
empadronamiento general de casas y habitantes
de la República de Honduras practicado el 18
de diciembre de 1910. Tegucigalpa:
Tipografía Nacional, 1911. 28 pp. Tables.
　　Although focused on 1910, this volume includes summary population tables of Honduras
for all previous official censuses beginning
in 1791 and covering the entire nineteenth
century plus three counts in the early 1900s.

217 _____. Ministerio de Hacienda. Compilación
de las leyes de hacienda de la República de
Honduras de 1866 a 1902. Tegucigalpa:
Tipografía Nacional, 1902. 1,097 pp. Index.
　　A chronological compilation of the financial laws of Honduras, with full texts, including a subject index. DLC LNHT

218 _____. Ministerio de Hacienda, Crédito
Público y Comercio. Labor económico-
hacendaria de la actual administración pública
de Honduras: período presidencial del doctor
Miguel Paz Baraona, 1925-1929. Tegucigalpa:
Tipografía Nacional, 1928. 17 pp. Tables.
　　An official summary of the economic policy
of the Paz Baraona regime, hailing its accomplishments, providing economic statistics for
the years in question, and detailing efforts
to stabilize the nation's financial system
after the chaos of the post-World War I era.
DLC

219 _____. Ministerio de Relaciones Exteriores.
Creación del departamento de Gracias a Dios:
sus antecedentes. Laudo de su majestad el rey
de España don Alfonso XIII, algunos documentos
sobre su fuerza y validez. Tegucigalpa:
Tipografía Ariston, 1957. 113 pp.
　　A collection of documents tracing the origins of the Honduran department in question,
which encompasses the disputed border region
with Nicaragua. Designed to serve as a restatement of the Honduran claims and to emphasize that Honduras exercised jurisdiction over
the area since Colonial times. DLC

220 _____. _____. Incidente de "La Masica":
arbitramento, ante su majestad católica el rey
de España, contestación del gobierno de
Honduras al memorial del gobierno de su
majestad británica: español-inglés.
Tegucigalpa: Ministerio de Relaciones
Exteriores, 1914. xiii, 397 pp.

The Honduran case, in English and Spanish,
in an arbitration involving the killing by
Honduran troops of one British citizen and the
wounding of two others on 16 June 1910 during
a disturbance in La Masica. LNHT

221 _____. _____. Incidente de "La Masica" entre
Honduras y la Gran Bretaña: reclamación por
la muerte de un súbdito inglés y por lesiones
a otros dos. Tegucigalpa: Tipografía
Nacional, 1913. 164 pp.
　　A briefer summary of the case and the incident, indicating both the British and Honduran
positions. DLC

222 _____. _____. Índice de los tratados
celebrados por Honduras. Tegucigalpa:
Tipografía Nacional, 1935. 18 pp.
　　A list of the treaties in force at the time
of publication. CtY-L

223 _____. _____. Tratados internacionales:
período Colonial, República Federal de Centro
América y tratados bilaterales con Costa Rica.
Tegucigalpa: Tipografía Nacional, 1954.
515 pp.
　　Intended as the initial volume of a series
compiling all treaties to which Honduras sub-
scribed throughout its history, this work
focuses mainly on the Colonial era but also
contains the accords of the Federation of
Central America until its collapse in 1843, as
well as agreements with Costa Rica through
1903. Includes the full text of each. DLC

224 _____. _____. Tratados vigentes de la
República de Honduras. 2 vols. Tegucigalpa:
Tipografía Nacional, 1913-14. 514 pp.
　　A compilation of the treaties then in
force, with full text. DLC

225 _____. _____. Tratados vigentes entre la
República de Honduras y las demas repúblicas
de Centro América. Tegucigalpa: Ministerio
de Relaciones Exteriores, 1905. 171 pp.
　　An early compilation, containing only
accords then in force with other Central
American nations.

226 _____. Ministerio de Trabajo y Previsión
Social. Estudio de la industria de comercio.
Tegucigalpa: Ministerio de Trabajo y
Previsión Social, 1970. 178 pp. Tables.
　　A summary of reported data regarding
Honduran industry for 1964-65, with figures on
various aspects of operation, such as salaries
and sales, arranged by zones dividing the
nation into thirds. DLC

227 _____. Oficina de Cooperación Intelectual.
Embajada cultural de Honduras a Guatemala.
Tegucigalpa: Oficina de Cooperación
Intelectual, 1950. 91 pp. Illus.
　　An account of the visit of sixteen Honduran
intellectuals to Guatemala in 1950, detailing
the functions and ceremonies. DLC

228 _____. _____. Misión cultural de Washington
en Honduras. Tegucigalpa: Oficina de

(Honduras, Gov't of)
Cooperación Intelectual, 1951. 162 pp.
Illus.
A bilingual account of a visit, detailing
the functions and ceremonies with photos,
speeches, and press reports. DLC

229 _____. _____. Obra material del gobierno del
Dr. Gálvez: 2 años y medio de administración
pública. Tegucigalpa: Tipografía Ariston,
1951. 150 pp. Illus.
A detailed listing of all the public-works
projects of the regime, with specific locations, extent, and illustrations. The chapters each deal with a different ministry, with
the projects organized within each by the
political departments of the nation. DLC

230 _____. _____. La sucesión presidencial en
Honduras. Tegucigalpa: Tipografía Ariston,
1949. 226 pp. Illus.
A collection of commentaries, speeches, and
official acts attendant to the Honduran presidential inauguration of 1949, in which Juan
Manuel Gálvez took power. DLC

231 _____. Oficina de Relaciones Públicas del
Gobierno de la República. Misión al Sur:
relatos del viaje del presidente de la
República de Honduras, Dr. Ramón Villeda
Morales por la América del Sur. Tegucigalpa:
Oficina de Relaciones Públicas del Gobierno,
1958. 240 pp. Illus.
An official compilation of speeches and
ceremonies, with photos.

232 Honduras: The New Eldorado. New Orleans:
J.G. Hauser, 1909. 24 pp.
A brief and glowing description of the
nation's resources and development, stressing
its prospects and the high returns to investors. The focus is on gold-mining prospects, but copper is also discussed. DLC

233 Houlson, Jane Harvey. Blue Blaze: Danger and
Delight in Strange Islands of Honduras.
Indianapolis: Bobbs-Merrill, 1934. 305 pp.
Illus., maps.
The adventures of a small group touring the
islands off Honduras in 1932, searching for
pirate treasure and engaging in trade while
fighting off the hardships of nature and dodg-
ing revolutions. The volume meanders through
physical description and details of individuals met, focusing particularly on yarns,
adventure, and folklore, reproducing a good
deal of conversation. DLC LNHT

234 Huston, R.G. Journey in Honduras and Jottings
By the Way. Cincinnati: Robert Clarke,
1875. 39 pp. Maps.
An account of a railroad surveying mission,
emphasizing physical description of the tropical jungle. CU-B

235 Ilías Plata, José María. Reseña histórica y
geográfica del naciente pueblo del Paraíso.
El Paraíso, Honduras: Tipografía Martínez,
1960. 43 pp. Illus.

An account of the foundation of the town,
originally written in 1877 at the time of its
becoming a separate entity. The focus is on
its physical situation and future prospects.
DLC

236 Instituto de Nutrición de Centro América y
Panamá. Evaluación nutricional de la
población de Centro América y Panamá:
Honduras. Guatemala: Ministerio de
Salubridad Pública, 1969. Various pagings.
Illus., tables.
A detailed survey of the rural populace, in
accordance with the series pattern. See item
CR608.

237 Inter-American Institute of Agricultural
Sciences. Organización administrativa del
sector agropecuario de Honduras. 2 vols.
Tegucigalpa: Secretaría de Recursos
Naturales, 1968.
A descriptive survey of the present state
of Honduran agriculture and its facilities,
focusing on the various agencies and organizations serving it and their efforts and objectives; also provides statistical data.

238 Istituto Italo-Latino Americano. Honduras.
Rome: Istituto Italo-Latino Americano, 1971.
47 pp. Biblio.
See item CR610. DLC

239 Izaguirre V., Carlos. Bajo el chubasco. 2
vols. Tegucigalpa: Tipografía Nacional,
1945. 653, 611 pp. Appendixes.
A massive novel of social protest, written
during the tumultuous 1940s, which seeks to
capture the nation's reality in vivid scenes
designed to provoke a response and raise consciousness. Focuses on the problems of the
peasants in the banana regions and the initial, unsuccessful strikes there, as well as
on the sterility of local politics, which fail
to deal with these issues. Characters representing the major political parties' leaders
and the peasants are employed, with a detached
observer who serves as narrator and commentator when necessary providing continuity. The
emphasis is on vivid prose, confrontation,
shock, and irony. Strangely, the novel is
dedicated to the incumbent dictator, Tiburcio
Carías Andino. DLC

240 _____. Honduras y sus problemas de educación.
Tegucigalpa: Tipografía Nacional, 1935.
197 pp.
A collection of articles written in 1926
for the Honduran press during a visit to the
United States to study the Yankee educational
system and seek ways to adapt it to Honduras
to create what the author calls a more responsible citizenry and hence save the nation from
chaos. He recommends a practical focus on the
problems and means of education rather than
discussion of its ideals, and selects those
portions of the North American approach that
he considers appropriate to his nation; he
emphasizes Honduran history, culture, and
traditions as the basis and the Yankee methods
as the means. DLC LNHT

(Izaguirre V., Carlos)

241 _____. Ideario político administrativo del Partido Nacional. Tegucigalpa: Imprenta Soto, 1954. 40 pp.
DLC

242 _____. Readaptaciones y cambios. Tegucigalpa: Imprenta Calderón, 1936. ii, 205 pp.
A series of essays, originally published in El Cronista of Tegucigalpa during 1935, analyzing the nation's social problems and concluding that peace and stability are essential to their solution. Endorses the administrative reforms by which the Carías regime centralized power, contending that they are the preliminaries to dealing with the national problems that exist because of the effort previously expended in civil war and political maneuvering. The author also hails the lengthening of the presidential term. DLC LNHT

243 Jalhay, Henri. Notice sur les mines d'or et d'argent de la République de Honduras. Anvers, Belgium: Imprimerie Veuve de Backer, 1904. 48 pp. Biblio.
A brief survey, by department, of the mineral wealth of Honduras, clearly designed to promote investment. Emphasizes precious metals but includes all minerals. DLC LNHT

244 _____. La République de Honduras: notice historique, geógraphique & statisique. Anvers, Belgium: Imprimerie Veuve de Backer, 1898. 43 pp. Notes.
A brief description of the nation, its economy, resources, current situation, and prospects, designed to interest the European audience in the nation. DLC

245 Jérez Alvarado, Rafael. Defendamos el Golfo de Fonseca. Tegucigalpa: Tipografía Nacional, 1971. 92 pp.
Reflecting a national debate within Honduras about the possible construction of a new Pacific port, the author defends the role and suitability of Amapala and cites the recent conflict with El Salvador as a potential threat to Honduran rights in the gulf, arguing for modernization of Amapala and suggesting the need for a strong defense force in the region. DLC LNHT

246 _____. La educación de la mujer en Honduras. Tegucigalpa: Ministerio de Educación Pública, 1957. 250 pp.
A study of the education of Honduran women and their preparation for their role in society, including consideration of school curriculum, careers available, family and societal values, and role models. DLC

247 Jirón, Yanuario. Apuntamientos biográficos del señor presbítero doctor don José Trinidad Reyes. Tegucigalpa: Universidad Nacional Autónoma de Honduras, 1968. 121 pp.
A laudatory biography of the Franciscan friar who founded the University of Honduras in the mid-nineteenth century, extolling his role as an educator and his contribution to the nation. The author was a student of the friar, and the original manuscript was written in 1877. DLC

248 Johannessen, Carl L. The Geography of the Savannas of Interior Honduras. Berkeley: University of California Press, 1959. 283 pp. Biblio., notes, illus., maps. Latest ed. Berkeley: University of California Press, 1963. v, 173 pp. Biblio., notes, illus, maps, tables, appendixes.
A preliminary report on the region, based on fieldwork in 1954-56. Designed to emphasize the impact of human activity, it provides detailed reports on the vegetation, water, and economy. Contains appropriate maps and tables. Discusses all aspects of agriculture, including native vegetation and cultivated plants, and their impact. DLC

249 Komor, Hugo F. Apuntes de viaje por los departamentos de El Paraíso, Olancho y Yoro. Tegucigalpa: Tipografía Nacional, 1930. 152 pp. Illus.
An enthusiastic description of the region based on an official government mission to assess these then-remote departments and provide suggestions for promoting immigration to them. The account hails the resources, climate, and prospects for various crops, while narrating the author's travel experiences and emphasizing the towns and terrain. DLC LNHT

250 Lagos, César. Ensayo sobre la historia contemporánea de Honduras. San Salvador: Tipografía La Unión, 1908. 177 pp. Appendixes.
A history of the turbulent years 1876-93, focusing principally on the civil war and battles but including the political maneuvering. The volume concludes with an essay on the values of liberty. DLC LNHT

251 Laínez, Vitelia Castro de. Ensayo monográfico de las ciudades gemelas de Tegucigalpa y Comayagüela. Comayagüela: Imprenta Cultura, 1971. 104 pp.
A general overview of the development of the two cities and their rivalry, focusing on the municipal and local elements rather than national politics. Spans the era from their foundation to the time of writing.

252 Lainfiesta, Margot. Cámara lenta. Tegucigalpa: Talleres Tipográficos Nacionales, 1935. 103 pp. Illus., tables.
A series of brief biographical sketches of the leading figures of the regime of General Tiburcio Carías Andino of Honduras, hailing their contributions to the nation, followed by essays extolling the regime's programs, projects, and goals. Supplemented with illustrations of the individuals and projects, and with current economic statistics. DLC LNHT

253 _____. Honduras comienza hoy. Tegucigalpa: Talleres Tipográficos Nacionales, 1937. 113 pp. Illus.

(Lainfiesta, Margot)

Hails the work of President Carías, placing it in the context of Honduran history; calls him a new kind of caudillo who is laying the basis for a new Honduras that will be totally different from the heritage of turmoil, with ample stability and economic development to improve the lives of all. The focus is on the road-building efforts and land-distribution program, which the author claims will eventually result in all Hondurans owning land. DLC LNHT

254 _____. El renacimiento de una nación. Tegucigalpa: Talleres Tipográficos Nacionales, 1936. 59 pp. Illus.

A glowing description of the Carías regime, hailing the dictator as a divinely ordained leader sent at the moment of national crisis to save the republic, who possesses just the right talents to transform it. His rise is characterized as a "political miracle," and the stabilization under his regime is viewed as the key to the future. Includes description of public works projects, and financial and economic data for 1934-35. DLC

255 Lara Cerrato, Fausto. Aspectos culturales de Honduras. Tegucigalpa: Tipografía Nacional, 1951. v, 484 pp. Illus.

An illustrated collection of brief biographical sketches of significant cultural figures in Honduran history, emphasizing writers and educators but including political leaders. Most of the items are by the author, though a few are excerpted from the writings of others. DLC

256 Latorre Salamanca, Gonzalo. Educación nueva en Honduras. Tegucigalpa: Imprenta Calderón, 1951. 262 pp. Tables.

A discussion of recent educational theories and their applications to and implications for the educational system of Honduras. Contains summaries of the theories, chapters examining their relation to the existing system, proposals for change, and discussions of methodological and curricular implications. DLC

257 Lecturas sobre realidad nacional. Tegucigalpa: Universidad Nacional Autónoma de Honduras, 1977. 145 pp. Notes, tables.

A series of separate lectures delivered by local and foreign scholars in a sociology symposium at the university, dealing with underdevelopment, the United Fruit Company, land tenure, social classes, industry, and foreign investment in present-day Honduras, through the perspective of dependency. Contributors include Mario Posas, Rafael del Cid, Elizabeth E. Eldredge, Denis R. Rydjeski, and Antonio Murga Frassinetti. DLC

258 Leíva Vivas, Rafael. Honduras: fuerzas armadas, dependencia o desarrollo. Tegucigalpa: Editorial Nuevo Continente, 1973. 163 pp. Notes, tables.

A survey of Honduran development at the moment the armed forces assumed power. Calls on them to apply the doctrine of national security and use their opportunity to solve the problems the politicians had failed to deal with by bringing about reform and promoting development, though it is vague on just what that would entail. DLC LNHT

259 _____. Un país en Honduras. Tegucigalpa: Imprenta Calderón, 1969. 146 pp.

A denunciation of the Honduran scene, criticizing the divisions in the society and the exploitation of the workers. Hails the labor unions as the most progressive new force in the nation and denounces the role of the military, examining events from the military coup that ousted Ramón Villeda Morales in 1962 through the war with El Salvador. The author focuses on the disunity of the masses and on the unsuccessful 1968 strikes. While calling for increased popular consciousness and denouncing the oligarchy, he nonetheless advocates national unity in the face of the Salvadoran threat. DLC

260 _____. Tratados internacionales de Honduras. Tegucigalpa: Universidad Nacional Autónoma de Honduras, 1971. 84 pp.

A chronological listing of all the treaties signed by Honduras since independence. Arranged by type of pact, with separate chronologies for multilateral and bilateral pacts, each divided into Central American, inter-American, and general agreements. DLC LNHT

261 _____. Vacío político, crisis general y alternativas al desarrollo. Santo Domingo: Editorial Panamericana, 1975. 159 pp. Appendixes.

An essay on the current Honduran scene, continuing the author's volume on the armed forces and analyzing the problems of the nation and the recent military coup attendant to the "bananagate" scandal. Contends that political, social, and economic problems are linked and must be approached together; advocates a return to constitutional government, alleging that the military is compromised by the scandal and hence linked to multinational corporations. Although criticizing such companies and advocating agrarian reform, he rejects dependency theory as too rigid and abstract to solve the practical problems. DLC

262 Lemus, Manuel, and Henry G. Bourgeois. Breve noticia sobre Honduras: datos geográficos, estadísticos e informaciones prácticas. Tegucigalpa: Tipografía Nacional, 1897. 46 pp. Biblio. 2d ed. Tegucigalpa: Tipografía Nacional, 1906. 46 pp. Biblio.

A compilation of contemporary data, with emphasis on economics, finance, and resources. Designed for the European audience to encourage interest in investment in and trade with Honduras. Includes detailed current statistics. DLC LNHT

263 León Gómez, Alfredo. El escándalo del ferrocarril. Tegucigalpa: Imprenta Soto, 1978. 198 pp. Biblio.

An exposé-type account tracing the financial problems of the efforts to construct the

Honduras Interoceanic Railway during the nine-teenth century, and the attendant European loans under terms so onerous that only a small portion of the face value ever reached Honduras. Denounces these transactions and criticizes the Honduran officials involved, assessing responsibility to particular indi-viduals, especially the representatives in Europe. The author hopes that the narration will serve as a warning to current genera-tions. Based on secondary sources and pub-lished documents; deals only with the Interoceanic Railway, omitting the United Fruit Company lines on the north coast. DLC

264 Lester, Mary [Maria Soltera, pseud.]. A Lady's Ride across Spanish Honduras. Edinburgh and London: Blackwood, 1884. 319 pp. Illus. Reprint. Gainesville: Univer-sity of Florida Press, 1964. xii, 319 pp. Index, illus.
Un viaje por Honduras. San José: EDUCA, 1971. 233 pp. Illus.
The vivid observations of an upper-class English lady who rode across Honduras on mule-back, taken from her diary of the trip. In-cludes her thoughts, her reactions to situations, and background based on the explanations she received. The emphasis is on physical description of the countryside and people, the difficulty of the journey, and the chaos in the nation. The comments are colored by her biases, background, and lack of knowl-edge of Spanish, and reflect some instances in which these factors were taken advantage of by local residents. DLC LNHT

265 Leyton Rodríguez, Rubén. Honduras ilustrada. Tegucigalpa: Imprenta La Razón, 1951. 224 pp. Illus.
An illustrated tour of Honduras, with brief explanatory text and advertising. DLC

266 Lombard, Thomas R. The New Honduras: Its Situation, Resources, Opportunities, and Pros-pects. Chicago and New York: Brentano's, 1887. 102 pp. Illus.
An account of the present state of the nation emphasizing its new peace and stability and its prospects for the future, in contrast to the past. Brief historical outlines pre-cede the current description, which is based on the author's observations. Subjects con-sidered include climate, agriculture, mining, and politics. DLC LNHT

267 López Pineda, Julián. Algunos escritos de Julián López Pineda. Tegucigalpa: Imprenta Calderón, 1956. 335 pp. Illus.
Excerpts from the publications and news-paper commentaries of a Conservative commenta-tor and scholar of the 1920s and 1930s.

268 _____. Democracia y redentorismo. Managua: Tipografía "Guardián," 1942. 142 pp.
A study of recent and contemporary Honduran politics. Written by a friend of the incum-bent president, it makes a strong case for the Carías regime by citing the chaos that pre-ceded it and noting the progress made toward the institutionalization of political parties during its tenure. The economic situation, needs, and reality of Honduras are also stressed to argue that the regime is pursuing a pragmatic policy to improve the nation. DLC

269 _____. La reforma constitucional de Honduras. Paris: Ediciones Estrella, 1936. 155 pp.
A study of constitutionalism and constitu-tional theory written to make recommendations to the forthcoming Constituent Assembly, which had been called to amend the Honduran consti-tution of 1924. The author surveys constitu-tional development through the ages, then discusses key concepts for potential reform on the basis of what he considers the trends of constitutional law. He touches on a broad range of themes from proportional representa-tion to women's rights, pausing to attack socialism as a myth. Includes the text of the 1924 constitution. DLC LNHT

270 López Villamil, Humberto. El caso de las Islas del Cisne. Tegucigalpa: Imprenta Calderón, 1961. 46 pp. Illus., maps.
An historical account of the jurisdictional question involving the islands and a summary of the Honduran basis for claim, tracing both the dispute with England and the dispute with the United States involving the Isla de Tigre. DLC LNHT

271 Lozano, Julio. La industria minera en Honduras protegida por el estado: beneficio que recibe el país en relación a las utilidades que obtiene el capital extranjero. Washington, D.C.: W.F. Roberts, 1937. 33 pp. Tables.
An analysis of taxes and regulations af-fecting the Honduran mining industry, with statistics regarding income from the various taxes during the twentieth century. Criti-cizes changes made in the laws in the 1930s, and offers alternative proposals. The author contends that concessions by the Tiburcio Carías Andino regime to the Honduras Rosario Mining Company were excessive and detrimental to the nation. DLC

272 Lunardi, Federico. Choluteca, ensayo histórico-etnográfico. Tegucigalpa: Tipografía Nacional, 1945. 48 pp.
Part of a series, this brief résumé of the principal events of the history of this Honduran department by a cleric gives particu-lar emphasis to the foundation of churches and the role of the religious orders.

273 _____. El Valle de Comayagua, documentos para la historia. Tegucigalpa: Tipografía Nacional, 1945. 42 pp.
An account of the town, focusing on churches and monestaries, with documentary citations regarding their foundation and de-velopment. DLC

274 Mariñas Otero, Luís, ed. Las constituciones de Honduras. Madrid: Ediciones Cultura Hispánica, 1962. xi, 466 pp.

The full texts of all the Honduran constitutions, with a brief introduction. LNHT

275 Mariñas Otero, Luís. <u>Honduras</u>. Madrid:
Ediciones Cultura Hispánica, 1963. 399 pp.
Notes, illus.
A general geographic, physical, and cultural description, with topical essays on
social structure, economy, and religion serve
as an introduction, which is followed by a
history of the nation, written from secondary
sources and emphasizing the general trends.
The focus is on the Colonial era and early
nineteenth century. Though the volume does
come to the present, the period since the
1870s is covered in about fifty pages, and the
years since 1933 in three pages. DLC LNHT

276 Martínez, José Francisco. <u>Honduras histórica</u>.
Tegucigalpa: Imprenta Calderón, 1973. 499
pp. Biblio., illus.
A volume consisting of several distinct
parts, including a brief overview of Honduran
history, mainly by the author but with some
excerpts from previous works; an extensive
section of brief biographies of the principal
figures of Honduran history; brief summaries
of each of the many constitutions of Honduras;
and an essay on Honduran economic history.
The minibiographies comprise the major, and
most valuable, portion of the volume, though
they vary from two to twenty pages in length,
no selection criteria are indicated, and the
order of arrangement is unidentifiable. DLC
LNHT

277 Martínez B., Juan Ramón. <u>Historia del
movimiento cooperativo</u>. Tegucigalpa:
Instituto de Formación e Investigación
Cooperativista, n.d. [197?]. 90 pp. Biblio.
The initial half of this volume consists of
a brief sketch of the history of the world
cooperative movement, while the latter portion
surveys the movement in Honduras, with due
emphasis on the role of the National University in launching it in 1974, and praise for
its spread and prospects. DLC

278 Martínez López, Eduardo. <u>Honduras geológica-
etnológica</u>. Tegucigalpa: Tipografía
Nacional, 1923. 148 pp.
A series of essays, most geological descriptions but some dealing with ethnology,
covering various parts of the republic, written between 1921 and 1923. LNHT

279 Martínez Rivera, Sebastián. <u>Cane de ayer
a hoy: folklore</u>. Tegucigalpa: Imprenta
Gutenberg, 1927. 104 pp. 2d ed.
Tegucigalpa: Imprenta Cultura, 1957. 139 pp.
A monograph of the history of the town of
Cane in the Honduran department of La Paz,
providing a history of its development and of
its institutions, as well as the vitae of its
leading citizens through the years, though
selection criteria are not indicated. DLC

280 _____. <u>El folklore en la tierra de los piños</u>.
Tegucigalpa: Imprenta Cultura, 1963. 110 pp.
Illus.

A collection of disparate Honduran folklore, with an essay on its definition and
references to various other countries. The
bulk of the volume consists of narrations,
poems, songs, dances, children's tales, and
virtually every other possible form of folklore, some with illustrations. Collected from
throughout the nation and arranged by theme
rather than region. DLC LNHT

281 Matamoros y Lucha, Ernesto. <u>Yo acuso (al
tirano Tiburcio Carías Andino)</u>. Havana:
Comité Cubano pro Liberación de Honduras,
1946. 22 pp. Illus.
A brief series of charges against the longtime Honduran strongman, followed by a list of
"victims" of the dictatorship, arranged alphabetically by department but without explanation or comment. LNHT

282 Mayes Huete, Guillermo. <u>Honduras en la
independencia de Centro América y anexión a
México</u>. Tegucigalpa: Tipografía Nacional,
1956. 131 pp. Biblio., appendix.
Originally a thesis at the University of
San Carlos in Guatemala, this work was published by the Honduran government principally
because of its documentary appendix, which
publishes for the first time a series of documents regarding Honduran independence drawn
from the Archivo General de Centro América in
Guatemala City during the author's internship
there. The thesis argues that Honduran leaders were active in the independence movement,
but that the populace was not yet ready for
independence, contending that this explains
the Mexican role in the movement. The documents include the acts of the various
ayuntamientos throughout Honduras supporting
independence, and correspondence among the
leaders. DLC LNHT

283 Medina Planas, Héctor. <u>El general Vásquez:
ex-presidente de Honduras</u>. San José:
Imprenta Borrasé, 1942. 24 pp.
An attack on Vásquez, condemning his tyr-
anny and hailing the Liberal revolution led by
Dr. Policarpo Bonilla, which overthrew him.
Recounts the revolutionary campaign and
Vásquez's subsequent exile in Costa Rica,
while defending the Bonilla regime. BNCR

284 _____. <u>Hermandad del liberalismo honduro-
nicaragüense</u>. Managua: Talleres Gráficos
Pérez, 1939. 23 pp.
An essay briefly describing the numerous
occasions when the Liberal parties of Honduras
and Nicaragua cooperated, and denouncing the
Conservative government of Tiburcio Carías
Andino, then in power in Honduras, alleging
that he seeks to press Honduran claims along
the Nicaraguan frontier. The clear implication is that the Liberal Nicaraguan government
has a duty to aid its brethren in Honduras in
ousting Carías. DLC LNHT

285 Mejía, Medardo. <u>Capítulos provisionales sobre
Paulino Valladares</u>. Tegucigalpa: Imprenta
Calderón, 1959. 38 pp.

(Mejía, Medardo)
A brief biographical sketch of this Honduran journalist and leader of the Conservative party, who edited the party's newspaper El Cronista for many years. Elaborates the party doctrine and covers his career, which spans the initial decades of the twentieth century until his death in 1926, tracing his political activities and his stances on the various issues of the day while demonstrating his role in the development of the positions of the Conservative party. The study was previously published in the Revista de Guatemala in 1946. DLC LNHT

286 _____. Don Juan Lindo: el Frente Nacional y al anticolonialismo. Tegucigalpa: Imprenta La Democracia, 1959. 249 pp. Appendixes.
An account of the principal aspects of the career of Juan Nepomuceno Fernández Lindo y Zelaya, a political figure of the early nineteenth century who showed extraordinary pliability, serving successively the monarchy, the independence movement, the Mexican annexationists, the Federation, the separatists, the Liberals, the Conservatives, and other groups while serving as chief of state of El Salvador and president of Honduras. Much of his effort was dedicated to opposing the British plans for hegemony launched by Frederick Chatfield, and it is this portion of his career that the author emphasizes. The last hundred pages consist of a collection of Lindo's speeches and writings. LNHT

287 _____. Trinidad Cabañas: soldado de la República Federal. Tegucigalpa: Instituto Morazánico, 1971. 233 pp. Biblio.
A collection of articles and material about General José Trinidad Cabañas, one of the principal military leaders of the Federation of Central America, who fought at the side of Francisco Morazán to defend the Federation and later against William Walker. The articles are self-described as "polemical" and were originally published in Ariel and El Día before being collected here by the institute dedicated to eulogizing Morazán, in honor of the centennial of Cabañas. The initial section traces the background of and other writings about Cabañas, and the latter two portions reproduce documents and various commentaries about him. DLC LNHT

288 Mejía, Romualdo Elpidio. La obra patriótica del Congreso Nacional: el ideal continuista y el esfuerzo reivindicador. Tegucigalpa: Talleres Tipográficos Nacionales, 1941. 231 pp.
The bulk of this volume consists of the documents of the Congress that extended the term of General Tiburcio Carías Andino in 1939. Reprinted are the official decrees, complete debates of the session, and the numerous petitions supporting the continuismo received from citizens throughout the republic. The initial portion contains a brief summary of the regime and its "Great Reformer," hailing his work in saving the nation from the abyss of chaos, his construction

projects, and his stabilization of the nation in its most difficult time in history. Includes a brief discussion of the era that preceded his tenure, in which he emerges as the central figure in the nation's politics. DLC

289 _____. La vida y la obra de un estadista. Tegucigalpa: Talleres Tipográficos Nacionales, 1942. 85 pp. Illus.
An official biography of General Tiburcio Carías Andino, hailing his tenure as the longest period of peace and constructive action in Honduran history, and contending that continuismo benefited the nation by preventing the political turmoil and convulsions that previously occurred every four years. Notes the beneficial experience of other nations that allow reelection, and concludes that the Honduran people genuinely wanted Carías to continue in office. Includes various statements of support for the caudillo, as well as discussion of his early career and the works of his regime, which is said to have restored progress and international prestige to the nation as a result of his era of peace and stability. DLC LNHT

290 Mejía Colindres, Vicente. Recuerdos del camino. Tegucigalpa: Imprenta Calderón, 1933. 426 pp. 3d ed. Comayagüela: Imprenta Soto, 1961. 212 pp.
A collection of speeches, commentaries, and letters from throughout the life of a Honduran Liberal leader and president of the republic, consisting principally of political speeches and commentaries from the 1909–33 period, though also including essays and commentaries on various Honduran and foreign figures, including Theodore Roosevelt and Woodrow Wilson. Although the selection is unpredictable, it offers some of the author's significant political statements, as well as some miscellaneous items. DLC LNHT

291 Mejía Deras, Ismael. La deuda externa de Honduras en 1923. Tegucigalpa: Imprenta Barahona, 1923. 110 pp.
TxU

292 _____. Iris (páginas escritas a la diabla). Tegucigalpa: Tipografía Nacional, 1930. 176 pp.
A diagnosis of the problems of Honduras, written during the 1924 siege of the capital and indicating a mixture of despair and hope. The author identifies what he considers the sources of the nation's problems, ranging from illiteracy, militarism, and political instability to religion, women's rights, capitalism, and Central American unionism. He concludes that the nation's political instability reflects its freedom, which encourages fragmentation, as well as other factors that aggravate the possibilities for conflict, and offers as a solution a more vigorous, unifying national government that would centralize all authority and power to overcome the historic divisions. This he calls "avantismo." It includes totalitarian government that would

control the economy and all aspects of life, prevent other movements, build a new man who would adhere to the national creed and values, and hence unify the country in a manner suggestive of vanguardism or semifascism. DLC

293 Mejía Deras, Ismael [Aro Sanso, pseud.], Ricardo D. Alduvín, and Rafael Heliodoro Valle. Policarpo Bonilla, algunos apuntes biográficos por Aro Sanso: un estudio del Dr. Ricardo D. Alduvín, y esquema para una biografía por Rafael H. Valle. Mexico: Imprenta Mundial, 1936. xlv, 558 pp. Biblio., illus., appendixes.
   A detailed and sympathetic biography of this turn-of-the-century Honduran leader, narrating, with extensive excerpts from his correspondence, his service as a journalist, diplomat, political figure, and president, with a bibliography of his writings and an appendix containing commentaries about him and some of his writings. Based on research in Bonilla's papers. DLC LNHT

294 Mejía Moreno, Luís. El calvario de los demagogos o el gobierno para el pueblo. Tegucigalpa: Talleres Tipográficos Nacionales, 1939. 74 pp.
   An extension of the author's previous work, El calvario de un pueblo, continuing his arguments in favor of the continuismo of General Tiburcio Carías Andino, hailing the peace and stability he brought to Honduras, and responding to criticism. Includes letters hailing the series, and both favorable and adverse commentaries, with some replies. DLC LNHT

295 _____. El calvario de un pueblo o un doble error constitucional. Tegucigalpa: Tipografía Nacional, 1937. 241 pp.
   Part of the propaganda that accompanied the extension of the term of office of General Tiburcio Carías Andino, this series of essays by an aging Honduran general, originally published in El Cronista of Tegucigalpa during 1936 and 1937, reviews Honduran history, contending that the instability and civil wars of which he is a veteran have destroyed the nation. He places the blame on the Liberals and condemns the two previous constitutions as inadequate, hailing the pacification under the Carías regime and its constitution as the most beneficial events in the republic's history and therefore calling for Carías's continuation in office. DLC LNHT

296 Melick, Edith Moulton. Seed Sowing in Honduras. St. Louis: Eden Publishing House, 1927. 166 pp. Illus., maps.
   A former missionary's description of the evangelical missions in Honduras, particularly those in San Pedro Sula, providing details on the activities and facilities, as well as on the needs as she sees them. The work was prepared for use by evangelical congregations in the U.S. to encourage support of the missions. DLC LNHT

297 Membreño, Alberto. Hondurenismos: vocabulario de los provincialismos de

Honduras. Tegucigalpa: Tipografía Nacional, 1895. xii, 122 pp. 4th ed. Mexico: Müller Hermanos, 1921. 176 pp.
   A dictionary of Honduran idioms, with definition and explanation of the origins of each term, and indication of its regional variations. TxU

298 _____. Nombres geográficos indígenas de la República de Honduras. Tegucigalpa: Tipografía Nacional, 1901. xxix, 118 pp.
   Alphabetically arranged list of Indian names, with a brief paragraph of identification providing history and location if known. DLC LNHT

299 Membreño, Jesús B. Monografía del departamento de Copán. Tegucigalpa: Talleres Tipográficos Nacionales, 1942. vi, 118 pp. Tables. 2d ed. Tegucigalpa: Talleres Tipográficos Nacionales, 1949. vi, 150 pp. Illus., maps.
   A geographical description focusing on physical setting, climate, and economy, with brief descriptions of each of the municipalities in the department. DLC LNHT

300 Méndez Guillén, Napoleón. El desarrollo de la comunidad. Tegucigalpa: Imprenta Calderón, 1966. 142 pp. Biblio., illus., tables. 2d ed. Tegucigalpa: Méndez Guillén, 1969. 265 pp. Biblio., illus.
   A sociological analysis of the current situation in Honduras prepared by a professor of community education. Based on government statistics and survey data, it considers such topics as population, employment, living standards, transportation, agriculture, land tenure, health, etc., and is designed to describe the current reality and indicate the types of change occurring. The volume was later adopted for use in the schools. DLC LNHT

301 Meyer, Harvey Kessler. Historical Dictionary of Honduras. Metuchen, N.J.: Scarecrow Press, 1976. xiv, 399 pp. Biblio., illus., maps, tables.
   An alphabetical listing of people, places, and events in Honduran history, with brief definitions and identifications. Far more extensive and hence comprehensive than the comparable volumes on countries such as Guatemala, El Salvador, and Costa Rica, it is therefore much more helpful to the researcher in view of the smaller amount of existing scholarship about Honduras. Like other volumes in the series, it is subject to the limitations of space: the commentaries are excessively brief, and there is a tendency to ignore maternal names and genealogical information. DLC LNHT

302 Moe, Alfred Keane, ed. Honduras: Geographical Sketch, Natural Resources, Laws, Economic Conditions, Actual Development, Prospects of Future Growth. Washington, D.C.: GPO, 1904. 252 pp.
   A geographic study emphasizing current conditions. Focuses on the economy, the

resources, and the physical landforms, and stresses the prospects for future growth. DLC

303 Molina, Juan Ramón. *Antología, verso y prosa*. San Salvador: Ministerio de Cultura, 1959. 238 pp. 2d ed. Tegucigalpa: Tipografía Nacional, 1972. 231 pp.

An anthology of poetry by a Honduran modernist of the late nineteenth and early twentieth centuries. The introduction by Miguel Ángel Asturias characterizes Molina as a neglected figure who parallels Rubén Darío. DLC LNHT

304 _____. *Prosas*. Guatemala: Tipografía Nacional, 1947. 333 pp.

A collection of essays by this well-known Honduran, who is better known for his poetry. Themes are disparate and include general subjects as well as patriotic and national issues. While most of the essays are general, a number deal with significant historical or national anniversaries, some discuss subjects such as Honduran rights in the Gulf of Fonseca, and other treat historical figures such as Francisco Morazán and Justo Rufino Barrios. DLC LNHT

305 Molina Chocano, Guillermo. *Estado liberal y desarrollo capitalista en Honduras*. Tegucigalpa: Banco Central de Honduras, 1976. 122 pp. Biblio., notes, illus.

A brief survey of the Honduran Liberal era in the latter half of the nineteenth century, focusing on its reforms and economic programs. Notes the results of the development of an export-driven economy based on agriculture and foreign investment, as well as the failure of the efforts to develop an internal transportation system, which left the nation owing a large debt for an expensive and only partially completed railroad. LNHT

306 Moncada, José María. *Deuda del Ferrocarril de Honduras*. Tegucigalpa: Tipografía Nacional, 1904. 101 pp. Tables.

A government-sponsored work by a well-known Central American historian, providing details, based on Honduran records, of the various railway loans attendant to the efforts to use government credit to finance the Inter-Oceanic Railway proposed by Squirer after it became evident that European and Yankee capitalists were not interested; the plan ran afoul of the same skepticism and of the onerous terms imposed on the then-turbulent nation for a project considered risky. Details the loans, particularly those of 1867 and 1869, and the terms that assured that little of the face amount ever reached Honduras. Includes tables regarding the terms, and liberal quotations from the pertinent decrees and diplomatic exchanges. DLC

307 _____. *La inocencia del doctor Policarpo Bonilla*. Tegucigalpa: Tipografía Nacional, 1905. 75 pp.

A detailed discussion in which the Nicaraguan leader supports his Honduran colleague and longtime friend against charges that led to his arrest and conviction, as a means of protesting his jailing by the regime of General Manuel Bonilla in 1905. DLC

308 Montes, Arturo Humberto. *Reformas constitucionales*. Tegucigalpa: Talleres Tipográficos Nacionales, 1954. 61 pp. Illus.

A series of essays noting speculation about a possible reform of the Honduran constitution. Cites various international accords, such as the Charter of the United Nations and the Declaration of Human Rights, contending that it is time that any new Honduran constitution extend legal and civil rights in accord with these documents. LNHT

309 Morlan, Albert E. *A Hoosier in Honduras*. Indianapolis: El Dorado Publishing Co., 1897. 215 pp. Illus.

The observations of a trader and traveler from Indiana on a voyage that took him to Belize, Honduras, and Nicaragua. The bulk of the volume deals with Honduras. The emphasis is on description in spicy style, with the author recounting personal observations of physical setting, flora and fauna, and particularly of the towns he visited and the people with whom he dealt. Entertaining reading, but the information is disorganized and must be extracted carefully. The author later served as U.S. consul in Belize. Illustrated with drawings. DLC

310 Muñoz Pineda, Plutarco. *El pacto de los diputados*. Tegucigalpa: Imprenta La Democracia, 1931. xii, 86 pp. Illus.

Originally published as a series of articles in the newspaper *El Cronista*, these essays constitute part of the polemic that characterized the political maneuvering in Honduras during the 1920s and 1930s. They focus on accusations of fraud in the 1930 congressional elections and charge that the deputies of both parties agreed to seat the contested victors of each party and to ignore the widespread protests and allegations. Includes numerous petitions, letters, telegrams, newspaper comments, accusations, and similar exchanges, as well as reproductions of decrees and legislation. DPU

311 Murga Franssinetti, Antonio, et al. *Lecturas sobre la realidad nacional*. Tegucigalpa: Universidad Nacional Autónoma de Honduras, 1977. 145 pp. Tables.

A collection of essays by local and foreign scholars examining the socioeconomic characteristics of contemporary Honduras, emphasizing linkages to the world economy and dependency. DLC

312 Murillo Soto, Céleo. *Un hondureño y una actitud política: en busca de la concordia*. Tegucigalpa: Talleres Tipográficos Nacionales, 1948. 100 pp.

A series of essays defending the action of longtime Liberal scholar Rafael Heliodoro Valle in supporting the presidential candidacy of Conservative Juan Manuel Gálvez despite his earlier opposition to Gálvez's tutor, Tiburcio

Carías Andino. Many of the articles were previously published in various Honduran newspapers, some under Morillo Soto's pseudonym, Alfonso Garrido. Valle accepted Gálvez's call to national unity, essentially arguing that it was better to negotiate with the dominant Conservatives and influence their policy than to continue in futile opposition. In a prologue, Valle characterizes his earlier support of Ángel Zúñiga Huete against Carías as "the greatest error of my life." The items in the book are a miscellany that includes newspaper articles and reproductions of letters exchanged by Valle with newspaper editors from neighboring countries and with Honduran compatriots. DLC

313 Napky, Marina O. de, and Victor M. Rheinboldt. Deuda pública de Honduras, 1951-1964. Tegucigalpa: Banco Central de Honduras, 1965. Illus., tables, appendixes.
An outline of the debt, the various loans, and transactions during these years, covering both the internal and external debts, with extensive graphs and tables detailing the annual changes in the nation's fiscal standing and balance sheet. TxLt

314 Navas Miralda, Paca. Barro. Guatemala: Ministerio de Educación Pública, 1951. 276 pp.
A novel describing life in the Honduran Caribbean coastal region, especially in the area of Trujillo and La Ceiba, focusing on the peasant farmers. It emphasizes description and the conditions of life. DLC LNHT BNG

315 New York and Honduras Rosario Mining Company. Facts Relating to the Rosario Mine. New York: N.F. Seeback, 1882. 20 pp.
Extracts from reports regarding the company's silver mine, seeking to promote investment. LNHT

316 New York Navigation and Colonization Company. Olancho: An Account of the Resources of the State of Honduras in Central America, Especially of the Department of Olancho. New York: Wynkoop & Hallenbeck, 1865. 65 pp. Appendixes.
A description of the company's 1859 concession to send settlers to the region, a glowing account of its physical features, resources, and potential, data about Honduran products, and regulations regarding immigration, all designed to interest potential colonists. DLC

317 Neymarck, Alfred. Le Honduras, son chemin de fer, son avenir industriel et comerical. Paris: Dentu, 1872. 72 pp. Maps.
A brief work extolling the future of the nation and the importance of its proposed interoceanic railroad, seeking to encourage investment. NN

318 Nuñez Chinchilla, Jesús. El panorama indigenista de la República de Honduras, Centro América. Tegucigalpa: Ministerio de Educación Pública, 1960. 20 pp.

A brief proposal, which was adopted, for the creation of a Honduran National Indian Institute. Includes a draft decree and a discussion of the services that such an entity could provide. DLC

319 OAS. Informe de la misión de asistencia técnica de la OEA a la República de Honduras en materia electoral. Washington, D.C.: OAS, 1963. x, 66 pp.
A summary of the political institutions and electoral laws and practices in Honduras, with recommendations for further legislation for the 1963 campaign. Considers a wide range of technical problems as well as theoretical aspects, ranging from conducting electoral registration to changes in the political system. LNHT

320 _____. Informe oficial de la misión 105 de asistencia técnica directa a Honduras sobre reforma agraria y desarrollo agrícola. 3 vols. Washington, D.C.: PAU, 1962-64. 234 pp. Illus.
A comprehensive survey of the current state of Honduran agriculture and its characteristics, with extensive statistics, covering such aspects as land ownership, use, crops, traditions, and agricultural practices. Includes a detailed proposal for a colonization effort in the Aguán River valley, an area previously used by banana companies but now unexploited, specifying the projects and facilities required to develop 70,000 hectares in the region. NhD

321 El Observador (Tegucigalpa). La administración del general Manuel Bonilla, 1903-1907: colección de artículos publicados en el diario "El Observador." Tegucigalpa: Tipografía Nacional, 1911. 62 pp.
A series of articles defending the regime and hailing its accomplishments, particularly its public-works efforts and economic development. DLC

322 _____. "El negocio Valentine": el Ferrocarril Nacional de Honduras y el muelle y faro de Puerto Cortés. Tegucigalpa: Tipografía Nacional, 1911. 184 pp.
A collection of newspaper articles about a troubled plan to build a railroad in Honduras, involving a concession in 1892 to American businessman Washington S. Valentine. The concession was revoked by the Honduran government in 1911 and sparked an incident in which U.S. troops supported Valentine. These commentaries from the Honduran press tell the Honduran side of the story, alleging abuses and nonfulfillment of his contract by Valentine. DLC

323 Ochoa Alcántara, Antonio. Comentarios políticos: el Partido Liberal de Honduras no existe, epístola a Clemente Marroquín Rojas. Tegucigalpa: Tipografía Ariston, 1946. 56 pp. 2d ed. Tegucigalpa: Honduras Nueva, 1947. 79 pp.

(Ochoa Alcántara, Antonio)

324 _____. La nueva Honduras (hacia un verdadero nacionalismo). Tegucigalpa: Talleres Tipográficos Nacionales, 1934. 48 pp.

A call for a new nationalism in Honduras, to consist of a focus on national unity and a new consciousness designed to assure that economic development favors nationals rather than foreigners. Emphasizes agricultural development and calls for nationalization of foreign property and regulation of the role of foreigners in the economy, as well as for a new impulse to spur Hondurans to develop their nation and its resources. DLC

325 Oquelí, Arturo. El brujo de talgua. Tegucigalpa: Imprenta Calderón, 1950. 181 pp.

A folkloric novel combining local lore and superstition with an account of the problems of life in the countryside and the political turmoil of rural Honduras. Seeks to preserve the local tradition and demonstrate how it is used to explain conditions that exist and justify them. DLC LNHT

326 _____. El cultivo de la pereza. Tegucigalpa: Tipografía Ariston, 1948. 182 pp. Illus.

A collection of short stories drawing on Honduran folklore and emphasizing peculiar local Honduran customs and values, designed to present the Honduran ambience and explain "some facets of our idiosyncrasy." The stories, set in the countryside, emphasize values and behavior, and employ the local idioms. DLC

327 _____. El gringo Lenca. Tegucigalpa: Imprenta Calderón, 1947. 193 pp. 2d ed. Tegucigalpa: Imprenta López y Cía, 1952. 202 pp.

A novel that combines regional tradition with the problems of dealing with the issues of the present era. The central character, who spans the traditional and the modern worlds by virtue of a mixed parentage that makes him the transmitter and guardian of the traditions of the Guajiquiro Indian civilization of previous eras, who speaks English and has traveled widely in the outside world, particularly in the United States. Throughout the novel he dispenses wisdom to the local Honduran residents of Guajiquiro descent, using his knowledge of both worlds to provide an economic impulse within the local cultural and attitudinal traditions. DLC LNHT

328 _____. Lo que dijo don Fausto: aporte a la biografía de Juan Ramón Molina. Tegucigalpa: Imprenta López y Cía, 1948. 191 pp.

A collection of material about Juan Ramón Molina, including commentaries by several individuals, the author's recollection of his contact with him, and excerpts from his poetry. DLC LNHT

329 _____. Silbando al viento: novela hondureña. Tegucigalpa: Oficina Central de Información de SECTIN, 1976. iii, 140 pp. Illus.

Set in rural Honduras, this novel, written in the 1950s but not published until the 1970s, follows the life and experiences of a rural schoolteacher, in the process examining conditions among the peasants and their problems. DLC

330 Oquelí, Ramón, ed. Paulino Valladares: el pensador y su mundo. Tegucigalpa: Editorial Nueva Continente, 1972. 212 pp.

A selection of commentaries by a Honduran journalist whose career spanned the early years of the twentieth century and whom the editor characterizes as the most significant Honduran commentator save Ramón Rosa. The selections provide his observations on all the leading political figures of Honduran history, particularly those of the 1900-1923 era, as well as references to significant individuals from Central American history and general commentaries about politics and society in the region. LNHT

331 Oquelí, Ramón, and Irma Leticia de Oyuela, eds. Notas sobre Ramón Rosa. Tegucigalpa: Universidad Nacional Autónoma de Honduras, 1968. 137 pp. Illus.

A brief biographical sketch of this Honduran scholar, with a collection of commentaries by various Honduran scholars regarding his contributions and significance. Published on the occasion of the seventy-fifth anniversary of his death. DLC LNHT

332 Oquelí Bustillo, Miguel. Informe presentado por el señor agente confidencial Dr. don Miguel Oquelí Bustillo al señor presidente de la república. Tegucigalpa: Tipografía Nacional, 1908. 52 pp. Appendixes.

Bustillo visited El Salvador and Nicaragua to reiterate Honduran neutrality regarding their differences and to reaffirm the recently held Washington Conference. The volume contains his official report, address to the Honduran Congress, and pertinent correspondence during his mission. DLC

333 Ortega, Pompilio. Patrios lares: leyendas, tradiciones, consejas. Tegucigalpa: Imprenta Calderón, 1946. iv, 124 pp. 2d ed. Tegucigalpa: Imprenta Calderón, 1951. 191 pp. Illus.

A collection of miscellaneous folklore from Honduras, arranged by theme. Includes short stories, poetry, legends, traditions, and music. DLC LNHT

334 Ortiz García, Edgard. Estudio analítico del problema cafetalero en Honduras. Tegucigalpa: Banco Nacional de Fomento, 1953. 106 pp. Illus., maps, tables, appendixes.

Specific descriptions of the current plantations and facilities of each of the nation's coffee-growing districts, with proposals for their improvement, description of the facilities needed, and the government's plans for encouraging production. Includes a very brief summary of the development of coffee production and its role in the nation's economy. DLC

335 Osorio Pavón, Jorge. <u>Mercado de dinero y</u>
<u>posibilidades de un mercado de valores en la</u>
<u>República de Honduras</u>. Mexico: Tipografía
Ortega, 1955. 129 pp. Illus.
   DLC

336 Pagoaga, Raúl Arturo. <u>Carlos Izaguirre y su</u>
<u>múltiple actividad mental</u>. Tegucigalpa:
Imprenta Soto, 1947. 44 pp.
   TxU

337 _____. <u>José Antonio Domínguez, su vida y sus</u>
<u>obras</u>. Tegucigalpa: Imprenta Soto, 1947.
57 pp.
   A brief biography of a nineteenth-century
Honduran intellectual who worked as a journalist and wrote essays but is best known for
his lyric poetry, summarizing his career and
commenting on the characteristics of his literary works, with a few sample poems included.
DLC LNHT

338 _____. <u>Rumbos nuevos: hacia donde va</u>
<u>Honduras</u>. Tegucigalpa: Talleres Tipográficos
Nacionales, 1940. 44 pp. Appendixes.
   A commentary on the economic development
and modernization of Honduras, hailing the
programs and accomplishments of the Carías
regime. DPU

339 Pan American Institute of Geography and History. <u>Honduras: guía de los documentos</u>
<u>microfotografiados por la unidad móvil de</u>
<u>microfilm de la UNESCO</u>. Mexico: PAIGH, 1967.
iii, 245 pp.
   A chronological list of the microfilmed
archival holdings, with brief, cataloglike
descriptions. Most relate to the Colonial
era. DLC

340 Paredes, Juan E. <u>El contrato Morgan, sus</u>
<u>antecedentes</u>. New Orleans: L. Graham, 1911.
56 pp.
   A much-shortened Spanish version of the
author's more detailed publication in English,
without some of the documents supporting his
charges. See item HO341. NN

341 _____. <u>The Morgan-Honduras Loan, 1908-1911</u>.
3 vols. New Orleans: Published by the
Author, 1911-12. 204, 135, 198 pp. Tables.
   An account of the Honduran debt situation,
denouncing the government of President Miguel
Davila and the arrangement with Morgan, which
was adopted owing to a conflict of claims that
arose when British bondholders demanded custody of the railroad because of nonpayment of
outstanding loans, and the government signed
agreements granting custody to the British
while simultaneously granting a concession
giving an American control of the same line,
resulting in an Anglo-American clash. At the
suggestion of Washington a new funding loan
was worked out with Morgan and Co., involving
a financial receivership, which the author
denounces as a violation of the nation's sovereignty. The volumes consist of collections
of the pertinent correspondence, agreements,
and other documents, with some narration. DLC
LNHT

342 Paredes, Lucas. <u>Biografía del Dr. y Gral.</u>
<u>Tiburcio Carías Andino</u>. Tegucigalpa:
Tipografía Ariston, 1938. xiii, 343 pp.
   A biography of the Honduran caudillo,
tracing his career in detail. Includes his
years in Congress and as Conservative leader,
his polemics with Ángel Zúñiga Huete, and his
presidency. Hails his contributions to the
nation and his statesmanship, while criticizing his opponents. The work emphasizes his
stabilization of the nation and the resulting
peace, to which it attributes his popularity
and the reelection campaign. Zúñiga Huete is
depicted as an incipient caudillo, making
Carías the defender of democracy against his
protagonist. Contains considerable information about Carías's life despite its pro-
regime biases. The cover bears the title
<u>Biografía de un hombre</u>, though the title page
uses the title cited. DLC

343 _____. <u>Los culpables: ensayo biográfico</u>.
Tegucigalpa: Imprenta Honduras, 1970. 271
pp. Illus.
   An account of the interim presidency of
Julio Lozano Díaz, who succeeded Juan Manuel
Gálvez in 1954 and retained power until he was
ousted in 1956. Traces, from the viewpoint of
Lozano Díaz, the complex maneuvering of this
era and the various coups and countercoups,
condemning the actions of his Liberal opponents. The names of the prominent political
figures of the era, including several future
presidents, dance through the pages, indicating their involvement in the various plots and
the extent to which Honduran politics revolved
around demonstrations and coups. DLC LNHT

344 _____. <u>Drama político de Honduras</u>. Mexico:
Editorial Latino-Americano, 1959. 668 pp.
Illus., appendixes.
   A review of Honduran political history by a
Conservative spokesman, castigating its principal leaders as selfish individuals seeking
their own good rather than that of the nation,
and contending that the nation is dominated by
such caudillos because of the economic and
intellectual poverty of its people. The principal focus is on the regime of Policarpo
Bonilla and on Ángel Zúñiga Huete, both of
whom are condemned for using the Liberal name
and ideology for their own ends and hence
misleading the public. The author clearly
regards the Liberals as the main villains of
the nation's history because they failed to
live up to their ideology, and contends that
their leaders are simply caudillos just as
their opponents are. DLC LNHT

345 _____. <u>El hombre del puro: ¿Por qué Carías</u>
<u>escogió a Gálvez?</u> Tegucigalpa: Imprenta
Honduras, 1973. 141 pp. Illus.
   A discussion of the reasons General
Tiburcio Carías Andino left power and of the
selection of his successor, emphasizing the
revolutionary situation in Central America
that rendered further continuismo impossible.
Explains the speculation and maneuvering among
the associates of Carías regarding his successor; notes that they feared Vice-President

(Paredes, Lucas)

Abraham Williams because he was not really part of the inner circle of the regime and that they considered several other possibilities, and explains the attractiveness of Gálvez as successor. Although the initial portion of the volume is somewhat condescending in regard to Gálvez, the latter portion, which provides biographical information, is quite sympathetic to him. The volume concludes with several of Gálvez's speeches. LNHT

346 _____. Liberalismo y nacionalismo: transfugismo político. Tegucigalpa: Imprenta Honduras, 1963. 399 pp. Illus.

Originally a series of articles in El Día of Tegucigalpa under the title "Transfiguración político," this critique of the Honduran Liberal party and of the political scene in general covers the late nineteenth to the mid-twentieth centuries. Contends that few of the nation's leaders had clean hands and attacks the Liberals for oscillating between succumbing to caudillismo and taking a doctrinaire position that bordered on anarchy. The author concludes that the problems of liberalism and the resulting splits in the party explain its failures, while contending that Carías was a personalista leader rather than an ideologue. DLC LNHT

347 _____. Quién es y cómo es Ángel Zúñiga Huete. Tegucigalpa: Tipografía Ariston, 1947. 50 pp.

An attack on the Liberal leader by a Conservative party spokesman.

348 Partido Nacional de Honduras. Un gobierno y una patria. Tegucigalpa: Partido Nacional, 1948. viii, 219 pp. Illus.

An official summary of the benefits of the Carías regime, emphasizing its public-works projects. Published as part of the preparation for the transition to his heir, it presents a view of the governing party as it wished to be remembered.

349 _____. El Partido Nacional y la legislación laboral en Honduras. Tegucigalpa: Partido Nacional, 1970. 423 pp. Illus.

An official compilation of laws, with some narration, by the governing Conservative party, detailing its legislation regarding labor during its long tenure in power. Most of the legislation reproduced dates from 1949 through 1956, though there are also some laws from the 1960s and some references to the earlier leaders of the party. LNHT BNCR

350 _____. Comité Central. Elecciones municipales: estilo "Partido Liberal," 1968. Tegucigalpa: n.p., 1968. 41 pp.

An attack on the 1968 municipal elections, published by the opponents of the victorious Liberal party, charging it with numerous abuses and detailing alleged illegal actions. DLC

351 Partido Nacional Hondureño. El Congreso Nacional de 1936 y su patriótica determinación de convocar una Asamblea Nacional Constituyente con vista de la petición unánime de las municipalidades de la república. Tegucigalpa: Imprenta Calderón, 1936. 183 pp. Illus.

An official publication of the Conservative party seeking to demonstrate the national unanimity in favor of amending the constitution to extend the tenure of General Tiburcio Carías Andino, with extensive reproductions of the petitions requesting this action. DLC

352 _____. Libro de oro del Partido Nacional hondureño, 1939-1940. Tegucigalpa: Talleres Tipográficos Nacionales, 1939. 246 pp. Illus.

A collection of articles and petitions acclaiming the regime of General Tiburcio Carías Andino, compiled by his party. Contains flattering commentary and laudatory statements regarding his work and proclaims him the "reformer" of the nation and the "only caudillo" of Honduras. Most of the volume consists of the official declarations of the various municipalities, at their obligatory celebrations, asking Congress to extend Carías's term; the remaining portions, each numbered separately, contain private letters and telegrams urging the same extension and a series of photos and reports of the nationwide demonstrations petitioning for the extension of his term. DLC LNHT

353 Pascua, Hernán. En el centenario del Ferrocarril Nacional, en la Carátula: reseña histórica-administrativa del Ferrocarril Nacional de Honduras de 1957. Tegucigalpa: Imprenta López, 1970. 107 pp.

An account of the construction and growth of the Honduran National Railroad, with photos of its facilities, published on the occasion of its centennial and hailing its contributions to the nation's economy.

354 Paz Barnica, Edgardo. Las garantías y los principios sociales en la constitución de Honduras de 1957. Tegucigalpa: Tipografía Ariston, 1963. viii, 487 pp. Biblio., notes.

Originally a doctoral dissertation, this volume describes in detail the social portions of the Honduran constitution of 1957, examining the sections dealing with the family, education, labor, individual rights, etc. The initial portions include doctrinal considerations and provisions from other nations' constitutions for comparative purposes. The constitution is discussed clause by clause, with description, summary, explanation of antecedents, and comparison with other constitutions. The analysis is argumentative, theoretical, and legalistic. DLC

355 Pector, Désiré. Artículos sobre la Mosquitia por la dirección y condiciones económicos de la República de Honduras. Tegucigalpa: Tipografía Nacional, 1908. 109 pp.

A description of Honduras's Mosquito Coast region, emphasizing resources and people, followed by an account of the state of the Honduran economy and an optimistic assessment of its future prospects. Written by the Honduran consul in Paris, it is clearly designed to interest Europeans in investment or settlement in Honduras and particularly in its Caribbean coast. LNHT

356 Pérez Brignoli, Héctor, et al. De la sociedad colonial a la crisis de los años 30. Tegucigalpa: Editorial Nuevo Continente, 1973. 597 pp. Illus., maps.

A reading book designed for university students in social sciences, consisting of brief excerpts from documents, principally from historical and scholarly works. Deals with general concepts and historical eras, focusing on Central America and Honduras but encompassing all of Latin America. The emphasis is primarily on the pre-1870 period. DLC

357 Pérez Cadalso, Eliseo. Achiote de la comarca. Guatemala: Ministerio de Educación Pública, 1959. 117 pp.

A series of short stories set in Honduras, centering around the life of the campesinos, the violence of life, and the turbulent and violent politics of that nation. Deals with several different regions and includes a glossary of regionalisms employed. Themes include government oppressiveness, violence, election campaigns, and other similarly political subjects. DLC BNG

358 _____. El habitante de la osa: vida y pasión de Juan Ramón Molina. Tegucigalpa: CENSA, 1966. 176 pp. Biblio.

Provides an account of the life of Juan Ramón Molina by arranging his writings about the various places he visited and the episodes in his life, connecting them with narration to detail his travels and the stages of his life. Includes extensive excerpts from his poetry and prose to furnish the description. DLC LNHT

359 _____. Puntos y comas de la diplomacia. Tegucigalpa: Tipografía Ariston, 1971. 177 pp.

A semimemoir discussing Honduras's diplomacy and the evolution of its diplomatic corps; focuses on the mid-twentieth century but includes a capsule summary of the early phases and the initial statutes that regulated representation abroad in 1906. Includes comment on diplomatic methods and the establishment of a suitable university degree, as well as a series of commentaries by the author dealing with a wide range of pending questions involving Honduras in the international scene, most of which have previously appeared in that nation's newspapers or been given as addresses. The span reflects the author's extensive career in his nation's diplomatic service. DLC

360 Pérez Estrada, Tito. Medina y Soto: rectificación histórica. San Pedro Sula: Editora Nacional, 1958. 155 pp. Illus.

A study defending the reputations of two late-nineteenth-century Honduran political leaders, General José María Medina and Marco A. Soto, against all the various accusations leveled by their enemies, attributing all charges to the turbulent politics of the reform era and hailing their contributions to the nation. Includes reproductions of numerous letters and documents, as well as quotations from secondary works and newspapers. DLC LNHT

361 Pérez Estrada, Tito, and Héctor Alvaro, eds. Homenaje a la Ciudad de Gracias a Dios en el CD aniversario de su fundación, 1536-1936. 2 vols. San Pedro Sula: Tipografía Pérez Estrada, 1936. 167, 178 pp. Illus.

A compendium of information about the city and its leading citizens. Although the historical portions focus principally on the Colonial era, there are commentaries regarding citizens of more recent times. The second portion, numbered separately but printed in the same volume, consists of excerpts from the writings of prominent residents through the ages. Includes poetry, literature, history, etc. Most of the historical commentaries are compiled from previously written works. DLC LNHT

362 Perry, Edward Wilkin. Honduras. New York: Duffield, 1923. 395 pp.

A general description of Honduras, including historical commentary but focusing on physical features, agriculture, and mineral wealth, and noting conditions in 1921. Considerable attention is devoted to personal experience, inconveniences, and pests. DLC

363 Pincus, Joseph. Breve historia del arancel de aduanas de Honduras. Tegucigalpa: Ministerio de Economía y Hacienda, 1959. 163 pp.

A series of brief descriptions of the various Honduran tariffs, indicating the laws and terms, followed by a discussion of the objectives involved and a general analysis of the impact of the legislation on the development of various economic sectors in the nation since 1868. The earlier period is not included in the analysis because of the absence of data. The study notes that specific tariffs have not always worked as well as ad valorem levies, but that these can hurt the economy; recommends as the most effective prospect for the future a mixed system more carefully designed by experts. DLC LNHT

364 Pinel Moncada, Emilio. Relaciones comerciales entre Cuba y Honduras: causas determinantes, observaciones para intensificarlas. Havana: Consulate General of Honduras, 1934. 36 pp. Tables.

An officially sponsored brief summary of the trade between the two nations, extolling its potential for expansion. Written by the Honduran consul general in Havana, it is clearly designed to promote contacts between the two nations and encourage local businessmen to invest and engage in export. DLC

365 Pinto Mejía, Edmundo. Así es Honduras. Tegucigalpa: Imprenta Soto, 1973. 418 pp. Tables.

A geographic description of the nation, followed by tables of data about weather and lists of the municipalities in each department. LNHT

366 Ponce de Avalos, Reynaldo. La United Fruit Company y la Segunda República. Comayagüela: Imprenta Bulnes, 1960. 79 pp.

An essay by a Nicaraguan exile living in Honduras, inspired by the coup that ousted Ramón Villeda Morales from the presidency in 1959 and by the inaction of the army. Reviews recent Honduran history, condemning the regimes of Carías and Gálvez, criticizing the autonomy of the army, and assigning culpability to United Fruit because of its position as the nation's largest landowner and its alliance with the local landowning class. Most of the essay criticizes the army, and little evidence is provided for the charges that UFCO is linked to the army and to the regimes of Carías and Gálvez. Ends with a passionate call for the ouster of UFCO from all of Central America. DLC LNHT

367 Ramírez, Asdrúbal. Línea general política del PCH. Tegucigalpa: Ediciones El Militante, 1975. 65 pp. Notes, illus.

The official stance of the Honduran Communist party, outlining its position and its proposed actions, commenting on Honduran developments and the present situation, with appropriate quotations from Marx and Lenin, and calling the faithful to constant struggle and alertness against the bourgeois capitalists who presently dominate the nation. DLC LNHT

368 _____. El maoismo en Honduras. Tegucigalpa: Ediciones Compol, 1974. 140 pp.

A leader of the Honduran Communist party, which is pro-Soviet, denounces the appearance of Maoist elements in that nation and laboriously traces the various sectarian and ideological disputes within the party that led to its split and the appearance of the new group. LNHT

369 _____. Los militares patriotas y la revolución hondureña. Tegucigalpa: Ediciones Compol, 1972. 63 pp.

A Honduran Communist party leader's version of present-day Honduras, contending that the 1969 war with El Salvador showed the inadequacy of the nation's political and military institutions and hence sharpened class conflicts. Calls for progressive elements of the military to join the proletarian revolution; rejecting all compromises, including a revolution by the military on the Peruvian model, which he charges is a new form of anticommunism in which the military alleviates some of the abuses of capitalism while preserving the rest of the system and keeping themselves in power. LNHT

370 Ramírez y Fernández Fontecha, Antonio Abad. La deuda exterior de Honduras: los empréstitos extranjeros y el ferrocarril interoceánico de la República de Honduras. Tegucigalpa: Tipografía Nacional, 1913. vi, 332 pp. Appendix.

A brief narration of the earliest Honduran loans, covering the British loans through 1867, followed by an extensive collection of documentary material relating to the loans and their payment, extending through 1911. The narrative portion comprises only the initial fifty-five pages, and it includes extensive figures and quotations. The valuable portion of the work is the appendix, with its extensive documentation. The author intended this as the initial volume of a series to deal with all portions of the Honduran debt. LNHT

371 Ramos, Miguel Ángel. Divulgaciones militares. Tegucigalpa: Tipografía Nacional, 1929. 208 pp.

A topical history of military law in Honduras. Traces the history of each of the services and their special units while explaining the changes in the military code, the military sanitary code, etc., focusing on the recent reforms. The articles dealing with the current law are written in conversational form aimed at the average citizen or conscript, summarizing the complex legal phraseology in simple language. DLC LNHT

372 _____. La reconstrucción nacional: estudios etnológicos y etnográficos. Tegucigalpa: Imprenta Barahona, 1923. 108 pp.

The author's call for a new revitalization of Honduras, his diagnosis of its problems, and his program for their correction. He blames political passion and the lack of national integration, calling for strong measures to refocus the national energies on truly national projects. DLC LNHT

373 Ramos, Miguel Ángel, Fernando Figueroa, and Zacarías Álvarez G., eds. Conociendo a Olancho. Tegucigalpa: Imprenta Calderón, 1947. 162 pp. Illus.

A collection of material about the Honduran department of Olancho, focusing particularly on the centennial of the church of Juticalpa. Consists of numerous short works on varying subjects; includes some historical studies, as well as data on prominent citizens from the region, excerpts from the works of writers from the area, and sections dealing with folklore, society, economy, etc. DLC LNHT

374 Raudales, Ángel. Fundación, desarrollo y porvenir de San Pedro Sula. San Pedro Sula: Editorial Coello, 1950. 72 pp. Illus.

The title essay, which won the prize in a contest sponsored by the city, occupies only a small portion of the volume. The rest consists of general description, photos, and rhetoric hailing the city, offering disparate information about its history and current situation, with the emphasis on the latter. The title essay is principally Colonial. DLC

375 Reina Valenzuela, José. Biografía del Dr. Antonio R. Vallejo. Tegucigalpa: Ministerio de Educación Pública, 1969. 314 pp.
    A biography of a Honduran statesman of the late nineteenth century, which was awarded a prize in a competition commemorating the 112th anniversary of Vallejo's death. It traces his career from his early days as a priest through his political posts after leaving the order, crediting him with many of the reforms of the Liberal regimes in which he served in the latter half of the nineteenth century. He is credited with founding the National Archives and the National Office of Statistics, organizing the nation's first complete census, successfully protecting the Honduran claims to the Bay Islands, and negotiating boundary questions with El Salvador, Guatemala, and Nicaragua. Includes copious excerpts from his correspondence and writings, and a bibliography of his publications. DLC LNHT

376 _____. Bosquejo histórico de la farmacia y la medicina en Honduras. Tegucigalpa: Tipografía Ariston, 1947. 233 pp. Illus.
    A history of pharmacy and medical practices of Honduras, based on research in the National Archives. Covers the nation from the Colonial era to the 1930s, though the length of the chapters decreases from 1871 through the 1930s. Includes discussion of epidemics, of important figures in these fields, and of significant events, such as the formation of professional societies, the foundation of the university, and the creation of the appropriate faculties. Combines narration and extensive quotation from documents, laws, and decrees. DLC LNHT

377 _____. Doctor Rómulo E. Durón: estudio biográfico, promoción 1965. Tegucigalpa: Ministerio de Educación Pública, 1965. 113 pp.
    A biography of a Honduran scholar, lawyer, justice, and diplomat of the late nineteenth and early twentieth centuries, detailing his career as a judge, teacher, member of the Supreme Court, member and president of the National Congress, diplomat representing his nation at numerous conclaves, and minister of foreign affairs.

378 _____. Don Francisco Cruz y la botica del pueblo: bosquejo biográfico. Tegucigalpa: Talleres Tipográficos Nacionales, 1942. 229 pp.
    A sympathetic biography of a leading Honduran figure of the mid-nineteenth century, emphasizing his foresight in promoting development in various government posts. Includes negotiations with British envoy Chatfield, the National Railroad, the defense of the nation's sovereignty in disputes regarding the Bay Islands and the border dispute with El Salvador, his role in creating the nation's Dirección General de Estadística, and his service as president in 1869. DLC LNHT

379 _____. Tegucigalpa: síntesis histórica. Comayagüela: Imprenta Atenea, 1957. 45 pp. Illus.
    A brief summary of the history of Tegucigalpa and Comayagüela, focusing on the Colonial era but including some more recent references and a section of photos showing its current situation. LNHT

380 La República de Honduras en la América Central. Tegucigalpa: Imprenta Calderón, 1937. 40 pp.
    A bilingual volume, in Spanish and English, designed to promote investment and extolling the resources and prospects of Honduras. MH

381 Reseña histórica-administrativo del Ferrocarril Nacional de Honduras. Tegucigalpa: Imprenta López y Cía, 1970. 107 pp. Illus.
    A volume commemorating the centennial of the Honduran National Railroad, with brief résumés of its origin and the debt questions resulting from the loans needed to construct it, extensive photos of its current facilities, and financial reports for the 1960s extolling its prospects for the future. LNHT

382 La revolución de 1903 y el golpe de estado del 8 de febrero de 1904. Tegucigalpa: Tipografía Nacional, 1904. 59 pp.
    A series of articles describing a turbulent period in Honduras and the confrontation between generals Terencio Sierra and Manuel Bonilla, in which the latter seized power after a disputed election. Written anonymously by the subsecretary of the Ministry of Gobernación of the Bonilla regime, who strives to present the complex maneuvers from Bonilla's viewpoint, using some quotations from speeches and statements; he also justifies accusations regarding the previous regime, the election, and the actions of the various political figures. LNHT

383 Reyes, Felipe. Honduras y las compañías ferroviarias: Choluteca, abril de 1929. Tegucigalpa: Tipografía Nacional, 1930. 26 pp.
    A discussion of the railroad question, with excerpts from legislation and discussion of the disputes regarding fulfillment of contracts. CU-B

384 Reyes, Ramón. Biografía del general don Luís Bográn. Managua: n.p., 1886. 23 pp.
    A brief summary of the career of an individual who dominated the nation during the years 1883-91, serving either as president or a member of the Council of Ministers throughout those years. NN

385 Ribera Suazo, Marcial. El cortejo de muerte: diccionario biográfica del carísmo. San Salvador: Talleres Gráficos Cisneros, 1927. vi, 56 pp. Index.
    Compiled by exiled Liberals, this volume offers a catalog of the "crimes" of the supporters of Tiburcio Carías Andino. It consists of an alphabetical list of individuals associated with his party, noting the charges against each; these range from petty offences to abuses of political power to assassination,

often with several individuals listed as participating in the same incident. LNHT

386 Rivas, Pedro. Agua, fuerza y luz.
Tegucigalpa: Imprenta Calderón, 1945. 180
pp. Illus., tables.
    A volume commemorating the establishment of waterworks and electric service in Tegucigalpa by the administration of Tiburcio Carías Andino. Traces the history of the efforts to obtain them and provides an extensive description of the newly established facilities and the services they can provide, contrasting them with the inadequacy of earlier projects. Includes figures, tables, and extensive illustrations. DLC

387 _____. Monografía geográfica e histórica de la Isla del Tigre y Puerto de Ampala.
Tegucigalpa: Talleres Tipográficos Nacionales, 1934. 213 pp. Index, illus., maps.
    The initial seventy-five pages consist of a geographic description, with excellent maps; the remainder offers a historical résumé of the islands, based on secondary sources, covering the period from Colonial days to the early years of the twentieth century. Includes brief paragraphs regarding the principal events and the numerous disputes about the ownership of the islands, as well as details regarding economic development, transportation and communication, facilities, and leading citizens. Contains far more data than most of the existing departmental monographs.
DLC LNHT

388 _____. Monografía histórica de la batalla de la Trinidad. Tegucigalpa: Talleres Tipográficos Nacionales, 1927. 282 pp. Illus., maps, appendix.
    This study, by a Honduran army colonel, was awarded the prize in a contest sponsored by the Honduran Ministry of War to commemorate the centennial of this pivotal confrontation in which Morazán recaptured Honduras from the secessionists. Includes a detailed history of the battle and background chapters. Based on research in the Honduran Archives, private papers, interviews, and a visit by the author to the battlefield; contains an appendix of "Documentos justificados." Views the battle as the birth of the Honduran army, and emphasizes tactics, with Morazán and the Liberals clearly the heroes. DLC LNHT

389 Rivera Hernández, Alejandro. Un toque de suspenso. Mexico: Editorial Latino Americana, 1963. xvi, 621 pp.
    A Honduran diplomat's memoirs presenting his impressions of the places he visited, but also including comments about the Honduran position at some of the international conferences at which he represented his nation, as well as comments on the people he met and on a broad range of general themes and historical figures. CSt

390 Rivera y Morillo, Humberto, ed. Juan Ramón Molina. 2 vols. San Pedro Sula: Imprenta La Cultura, 1966. 268 pp. Illus.
    A collection of material about Molina, including his autobiography, excerpts from his works telling the story of various eras of his life, and a series of commentaries about his works by members of the Honduran intellectual community. DLC LNHT

391 La Rocha, Pedro Francisco de. De la educación obligatoria: medios de establecerla en la República de Honduras por el Dr. P.F. de la Rocha, ex-ministro de instrucción pública y antiguo diputado al Congreso Nacional Extraordinario instalado en Tegucigalpa en 1852. Tegucigalpa: Imprenta Nacional, 1852. 28 pp.
    An official description of Honduran laws regarding education and the plans of the Ministry to expand and develop the system.

392 Rodríguez Ayestas, Julio, ed. Adolfo Zúñiga: el progreso democrático. Tegucigalpa: Imprenta Soto, 1968. 225 pp. Illus.
    A collection of writings by and about this Honduran journalist of the late nineteenth century who edited the newspaper La Paz, in which many of the works included were published. Includes a brief biography, a selection of articles from the newspaper commenting on all aspects of Honduran life, particularly on political figures, some of his letters and speeches, and eulogies delivered upon his death. LNHT

393 Rosa, Marco Antonio. Los brujos. Tegucigalpa: Imprenta Calderón, 1969. 166 pp.
    A novelized account of the Honduran civil wars attendant to the rise of the nineteenth century Liberal reformist regimes, focusing on Marco Aurelio Soto and Ramón Rosa. TxU

394 _____. Embalsamando recuerdos. Tegucigalpa: Imprenta Soto, 1973. 117 pp.
    A collection of short stories set in and dealing with historical events in the Honduran capital, recounting incidents of the late nineteenth and early twentieth centuries and placing the events in the perspective of observers and contemporaries. DLC LNHT

395 _____. Honduras de Honduras. Tegucigalpa: Tipografía Ariston, 1962. 84 pp. Illus. 2d ed. Mexico: Editorial Latinamericana, 1963. 74 pp.
    A brief volume combining emotional and patriotic passages with a description of contemporary Honduras that emphasizes its beauty and the friendliness of its people while tracing its historical outline; includes quotations from published works. LNHT

396 _____. Jueves jacarandosos. Tegucigalpa: Imprenta Calderón, 1972. 170 pp.
    A collection of short stories set in Tegucigalpa at various points in its history. The author is known as the "chronicler of Tegucigalpa," since many of his works are set

(Rosa, Marco Antonio)
in the city and focus on its events. These
stories originally appeared in the newspaper
El Día. LNHT

397 _____. Ramón Rosa: biografía novelada.
Tegucigalpa: Editora Honduras Industrial,
1976. 247 pp. Notes.
A novelized biography of the leading intellectual of the Honduran Liberal movement in
the latter part of the nineteenth century, who
also aided the Liberals in Guatemala. Based
on secondary sources and documents from the
archives, but written in the form of a novel
to allow the author to emphasize his subject's
personality and attitudes through fictional
incidents as well as real events. Portrays
Rosa as the dominant intellectual force in the
nation, emphasizing his authorship of some of
the reforms enacted by the regime of his
nephew and protégé, Marco Aurelio Soto. LNHT

398 _____. Tegucigalpa: ciudad de remembranzas.
Comayagüela: Imprenta Bulnes, 1969. 139 pp.
A series of short stories based on the
author's youth in the Honduran capital. AzU

399 _____. La Tegucigalpa de mis primeros años.
Tegucigalpa: Imprenta Calderón, 1967.
215 pp.
A fictionalized account of the events in
Tegucigalpa during the initial decade of the
twentieth century, with references to the
author's youth and his remembrances of these
events. Though dealing with actual events and
arranged year by year, the accounts are expanded and seek to portray the viewpoint of
the citizens and the impact of the nation's
political developments on the capital. LNHT

400 _____. Tío Margarito. Tegucigalpa: Imprenta
Calderón, 1953. 187 pp. 5th ed.
Tegucigalpa: Imprenta Calderón, 1972. 120
pp. Biblio.
A novel dealing with life and its problems,
employing local folkore and traditions. DLC
LNHT

401 Rosa, Ramón. Biografía de José Trinidad
Reyes. Tegucigalpa: La Prensa Popular, 1891.
vi, 86 pp. 4th ed. Tegucigalpa: Tipografía
Ariston, 1955. 110 pp.
A biography of the Honduran priest, polit-
ical activist, and poet who founded the Na-
tional University and served as bishop of
Honduras. Some editions use the title
Biografía del padre Reyes. DLC

402 Rosa, Rubén Ángel. Monografía del municipio
de Llama. Llama: n.p., 1940. 44 pp. Illus.
2d ed. Tegucigalpa: Tipografía Nacional,
1945.
A brief monograph of this Honduran town in
the department of Santa Barbara, with a brief
history and dicussion of its current situation
and facilities. The emphasis is on the historical narrative, the church, and various
historical figures of the town. DLC LNHT

403 _____. Tradiciones hondureñas: tradiciones,
creencias, costumbres y curiosidades.
Comayagüela: Imprenta Bulnes, 1952. 120 pp.
Notes, illus.
A collection of folktales and legends concerning a broad range of themes, gathered by
the author and others; often includes details
of the location in which each story is popular. TxU

404 Ross, Delmer G. Visionaries and Swindlers:
The Development of the Railways of Honduras.
Mobile, Ala.: Institute for Research in Latin
America, 1975. 134 pp. Index, notes, maps.
A small volume tracing the rise and fall of
various railway schemes in Honduras and the
frustrations experienced by the nation in
attempting to promote development by remedying
its lack of railroads. The principal problem
was financing, with neither Yankees nor Europeans prepared to invest in the interoceanic
railroad scheme, and with several national
government loans yielding insufficient revenue
because of onerous terms and government diversion of the proceeds. Ultimately, feeder
lines to the banana plantations came to constitute virtually the only lines in the nation, all on the north coast. Based on
published sources and some United Fruit
Company documents. DLC

405 Rubio Melhado, Adolfo, and Mariano Castro
Morán. Geografía general de la República de
Honduras. Tegucigalpa: Imprenta Calderón,
1953. 267 pp. Biblio., maps, tables.
A geographic study of the nation, which
includes general concepts and description as
well as specific information about physical
features, flora and fauna, population, political divisions, economy, trade, finances, etc.
Contains numerous detailed tables of statistics, some current but many extending from
1926 through 1950, and excellent maps. DLC

406 Ruiz, José T., and Rogelio Trimino. Apuntes
biográficos hondureños e informaciones para el
turista. Tegucigalpa: Imprenta Hernández,
1943. 372 pp. Illus.
A collection of brief biographical sketches
of present-day Honduran officials and historical figures, with basic tourist information
about facilities, transportation, and things
to see. DPU

407 Saaverdra, David. Bananas, Gold, and Silver:
Oro y Plata. Tegucigalpa: Talleres
Tipográficos Nacionales, 1955. xvii, 436 pp.
Index, illus., maps.
A survey of contemporary Honduras, replete
with extensive statistics from the 1920-35
period. Includes discussion of all economic
and financial aspects, with tables, graphs,
and maps, as well as brief biographies of the
members of the current Carías regime, with
photos. A handy compendium of scarce data,
though the accuracy varies and the items are
viewed through the eyes of the regime, which
seeks to accent the positive and the recent
development impact of its actions. DLC LNHT

408 Sánchez, Roberto M. Significado de la Escuela
Nacional de Bellas Artes de Honduras, 1940-
1953. Tegucigalpa: Talleres Tipográficos
Nacionales, 1953. 22 pp.
A listing of the accomplishments of the
Honduran national school of fine arts during
its initial thirteen years of existence. DLC

409 Sánchez G. Ángel Porfirio. Senderos: relatos
regionales hondureños. Comayagüela: Imprenta
Libertad, 1952. 85 pp.
A collection of short stories set in various parts of the interior of Honduras, embrac-
ing the local folklore of the nation's regions
and portraying life in the countryside. DLC
LNHT

410 Sandoval, José María. Explicaciones sobre
practica forense hondureña en materia civil.
2 vols. Tegucigalpa: Tipografía Nacional,
1929-32.
A general legal treatise on civil law, with
emphasis on and examples drawn from Honduras.
DLC LNHT

411 Santamaría, Ramón. Ángel Zúñiga Huete: líder
en descomposición. Tegucigalpa: Tipografía
Ariston, 1943. 33 pp.
A political polemic denouncing Zúñiga Huete
and hailing General Tiburcio Carías Andino.
Stresses the constitutionality of the latter's
regime, ridicules the charges of the exiled
leader, and quotes extensively from Zúñiga
Huete's statements to show that he contradicts
himself, charging that he is careless with the
truth. DPU

412 Seminario para el Estudio de la Educación
Integral en Honduras. Tegucigalpa:
Universidad Nacional Autónoma de Honduras,
1960. 45 pp.
The formal resolutions of an educational
conference sponsored by the university to
review the national educational program. They
call for broader participation in educational
planning and more effective planning in the
future, offering a set of proposals for consideration as the basis of reform. DLC LNHT

413 Sequeiros, Gonzalo S. Vidas ilustres.
Tegucigalpa: Imprenta Calderón, 1954. 48 pp.
Brief biographies of Mariano Vásquez, Pedro
H. Bonilla, Rómulo E. Durón, and Esteban
Guardiola, providing a short overview of their
lives in about ten pages each. DLC

414 Silva Ferro, Ramón de. Relación histórica de
los contratiempos que ha sufrido la
construcción de un ferrocarril á través de la
República de Honduras, fracasos de los
empréstitos pedidos al público para llevar á
cabo esa empresa y principales dificultades
que han sobrevenido á cada nueva combinación
intentada, para terminar la línea. London:
Imprenta Clayton, 1875. 94 pp.
Historical Account of the Mischances in Regard
to the Construction of a Railway across the
Republic of Honduras. London: C.F. Hodgson,
1875. 146 pp. Illus.

An account of the problems involved in a
scheme to construct a triple-track railway
across Honduras to allow specially constructed
cars to carry entire sailing vessels across
the isthmus, one of the precursors of the
efforts to construct a canal, detailing the
problems, financial failures, etc. The enterprise failed to attract sufficient funding
from understandably skeptical investors, and
this work is clearly designed to seek funds in
Europe. Includes diagrams, financial estimates, and appropriate correspondence. The
Honduran government was officially promoting
this project. LNHT

415 Solís Da Costa Gómez, Marcial. El
cooperativismo, el cambio y el desarrollo.
Tegucigalpa: Imprenta Calderón, 1969. 156
pp. Biblio., appendixes.
A theoretical defense of cooperatives and a
justification of their place in Honduran society, arguing that they are not part of any
particular economic system but rather a highly
adaptable human institution for meeting human
needs that is compatible with various economic
systems. The author emphasizes that they
promote democracy and affect the attitudes and
social aspirations of the lower classes, but
seeks to dispel the notions of those who see
the formation of cooperatives as threatening
to existing political systems. In the process, he discusses the various types of cooperatives, their organization and functions,
and offers suggestions regarding government
policies to promote them. The author has
played a prominent role in the drafting of
Honduran statutes regarding cooperatives and
has held senior government positions in banks
and government offices charged with overseeing
their formation and growth. DLC

416 Somoza Vivas, Fernando. Guía de Honduras.
Tegucigalpa: Tipografía Nacional, 1905. xx,
359 pp. Illus.
A detailed description of each of the provinces and their facilities, and a compilation
of information regarding the state of the
republic in 1903 and 1904, including statistics and an explanation of the current laws
governing the country and its economy. Subjects covered include the church, agriculture,
mining, transportation, communications, and
immigration. DLC

417 _____. El Liberalismo: su reorganización en
Honduras. Tegucigalpa: Tipografía Nacional,
1906. 144 pp.
A series of essays, originally published in
the Diario de Honduras, reviewing the role of
the Liberal regimes of the 1890s in Honduran
development and commenting on the party credo,
with particular emphasis on various liberties,
including the role of women in society and
politics, and discussion of the family. Calls
for the rejuvenation of the Liberal party at
the grassroots level throughout the nation.
DLC LNHT

418 _____. Reivindicación: historia de la guerra
legitimista de Honduras en el año de 1903.

Tegucigalpa: Tipografía Nacional, 1903. 538
pp. Illus., maps.
A partisan account of the Honduran civil
war of 1903 following the disputed election of
1902, in which the forces of General Manuel
Bonilla defeated those of Dr. Juan Ángel
Arias. This account, originally published in
El Republicano of Tegucigalpa by the
Bonillistas shortly after their victory, pictures the struggle as one in which the people
of Honduras rose against a usurper who had
connived with his predecessor to seize control. Most of the volume consists of reproductions of letters and reports from the
participants written during the election, the
political maneuvering, and the combat, with
the latter including the commander's reports
of the engagements. DLC LNHT

419 Soto, Marco Aurelio, and Justo Rufino Barrios.
Letter Addressed by Doctor Marco A. Soto to
President General Justo Rufino Barrios and
Answer to It. New York: Las Novedades, 1883.
48 pp.
This exchange of letters in Spanish and
English between the presidents of Guatemala
and Honduras during 1883 offers an example of
the polemicism and political turbulence of the
isthmus during this era. It reflects their
mutual recriminations and accusations, with
each claiming the other is about to seek to
intervene in his country. The letters are
accompanied by a series of newspaper articles
that constitute part of the violent verbiage
that characterized their relations. BNG

420 Squier, Ephraim George. Honduras: Descriptive, Historical, and Statistical. New York:
Harper, 1858. Latest ed. New York: AMS
Press, 1970. 278 pp. Map.
Honduras: descripción histórica, geográfica y
estadística de esta República de la América
Central. Tegucigalpa: Tipografía Nacional,
1908. 446 pp.
A rewritten and somewhat expanded version
of the Honduran section from the author's
earlier The States of Central America, with
more supplemental material from secondary
works to add to his own observations. DLC
LNHT

421 _____. Honduras Interoceanic Railway Company,
Limited. Prospectus, Preliminary Report. New
York: Tubbs, 1854. 63 pp. 2d ed. London:
Charles Whittingham, 1857. xvi, 100 pp.
Maps, appendixes.
Chemin de fer Inter-océanique de Honduras,
Amérique Centrale. Paris: Matthias, 1855.
51 pp. Maps.
A detailed survey of the proposed railway
and its route, with discussion of the engineering aspects and the terrain, stressing its
feasibility and prospects. The author was a
promoter of the project, and this work was one
of his major efforts to secure investment for
its completion. DLC LNHT

422 _____. Notes on Central America: Particularly the States of Honduras and San [sic]
Salvador: Their Geography, Topography,

Climate, Population, Resources, Productions,
Etc., and the Proposed Honduras Interoceanic
Railway. New York: Harper & Brothers, 1855.
397 pp. Latest ed. New York: AMS Press,
1971. 397 pp. Index, biblio., illus., maps,
tables.
Apuntamientos sobre Centro-América,
particularmente sobre los estados de Honduras
y El Salvador: su geografía, topografía,
clima, población, riqueza, producciones,
etc., y el propuesto camino de hierro de
Honduras. Paris: Imprenta de Gustavo
Gratiot, 1856. xii, 384 pp. Illus., maps.
Notes sur les états de Honduras et de San
Salvador, dans l'Amérique Centrale. Paris:
L. Martinet, 1855. 366 pp. Maps.
Die Staaten von Central Amerika, insbesondere
Honduras, San Salvador und die Moskitoküste.
Leipzig: Carl B. Forck, 1856. 275 pp.
Illus.
Despite its title, this descriptive volume
by the U.S. chargé deals mainly with Honduras,
providing detailed descriptions of the phys-
ical features, climate, resources, economy,
society, and people, and offering accurate
data on the conditions of the region in the
mid-nineteenth century. Includes comment on
the Inter-Oceanic Railway, of which he was one
of the promoters. The portions dealing with
El Salvador are quite limited, offering far
less detail. DLC

423 _____. Report to the Directors of the
Honduras Interoceanic Railway Company.
London: n.p., 1858. 102 pp. Maps.
An official report designed to encourage
investment in this project, paralleling the
author's earlier efforts, with the usual rich
description and emphasis on the feasibility of
its construction. CU-BANC

424 Stokes, William Sylvane. Honduras: An Area
Study in Government. Madison: University of
Wisconsin Press, 1950. xii, 351 pp. Index,
biblio., illus., maps, appendixes. Reprint.
Westport, Conn.: Greenwood Press, 1974. 351
pp. Index, biblio., illus., maps, appendixes.
An effective summary of Honduran politics,
with detailed examination of the country's
various constitutions, focusing on the evolution of its political structure. The emphasis
on the development of the system takes the
volume well beyond a contemporary political
survey, though it stresses contemporary institutions, with chapters on political parties,
the courts, and the various arms of government, each described in detail and shown in
historical perspective. DLC

425 Suckau, Henri de. Une voie nouvelle à travers
l'Amérique Centrale: étude géographique,
ethnographique, et statistique sur le
Honduras. Paris: Librairie Centrale, 1866.
48 pp. Maps, tables.
Despite its title, this volume consists of
a geographical description of Honduras, preceded by a discussion of writings by early
travelers to the region. It is designed to
introduce basic data about the nation to the
French public, to encourage interest in construction of a transisthmian railroad there.

The description of flora, fauna, and resources
is rich and glowing. DLC

426 Tegucigalpa, Hospital General, 1880-sovenir-
1927. Tegucigalpa: Tipografía Nacional,
1927. 86 pp. Illus.
    A lavishly illustrated volume commemorating
the hospital's anniversary and narrating its
work, facilities, and staff. DLC

427 Thompson, Maury Weldon. Education in
Honduras. Washington, D.C.: GPO, 1955. vi,
33 pp. Biblio., notes, illus., maps, tables.
    A general description, with current
programs. DLC

428 Tosco, Manuel. Análisis monetario relacionado
con el ingreso, modelos global y por sectores:
un estudio teórico con referencia a economías
insuficientemente desarrolladas y con
aplicación experimental a Honduras, C.A.
Tegucigalpa: Banco Central de Honduras, 1958.
71 pp. Biblio., illus., tables.
    A general theoretical paper prepared for an
international economic conference, with specific consideration of its application to
Honduras. DLC

429 ____. Estadísticas del producto e ingreso
nacional, 1925-1952: según una sistema de
contabilidad económica. Tegucigalpa: Banco
Central de Honduras, 1954. 109 pp. Tables.
    A detailed statistical survey by the newly
formed Central Bank. In view of the recently
enacted income tax, focuses on governmental
revenues and accounting. Includes valuable
tables of statistics relating particularly to
government revenues at the national and local
level, covering the period 1925-52; based on
official records and new accounting procedures
that enable filling the gaps. Includes government expenses and foreign-trade statistics,
as well as GDP figures. DLC

430 Tosco, Manuel, Marino O. de Napky, and
Guillermo Bueso. Capital existente de
Honduras, 1925-1955. Tegucigalpa: Banco
Central de Honduras, 1957. 14 pp. Tables.
    Another in the bank's series of statistical
compilations, providing the perspective of
figures for a twenty-five year period and
focusing on the availability of domestic
capital. DLC

431 ____. Cuentas de estado: series revisadas
años fiscales 1924/25-1954/55. Tegucigalpa:
Banco Central de Honduras, 1956. 47 pp.
Tables.
    Statistics regarding the national budget,
indicating trends over the three decades in
question. Compiled by officials of the
newly formed Banco Central, it constitutes
part of its series of statistical publications
providing official data on the economy, which
is often the only source for such figures.

432 Tosco, Manuel, R. Cabañas, and J.A. Bobadilla.
Estadísticas de producción agrícola, pecuaria,
forestal, de la caza y la pesca, 1925-1952.

Tegucigalpa: Ministerio de Agricultura, 1953.
46 pp. Notes, tables. Mimeographed.
    Detailed figures regarding agricultural
production, forestry, and fishing over twenty-
five years. Contains extensive statistics
that are unavailable elsewhere.

433 Tosco, Manuel, et al. Análisis dinámico y
económico-social de la población de Honduras.
Tegucigalpa: Tipografía Ariston, 1952.
56 pp.
    Detailed statistics on the Honduran popula-
tion, based on the latest census. DLC

434 ____. Deuda pública de Honduras, 1924/25-
1950/51. Tegucigalpa: Banco Central de
Honduras, 1952. 23 pp. Illus.
    A compilation of figures regarding the
national debt, detailing the loans, payments,
and balances over an extensive period.

435 ____. Ingresos del gobierno central y
establecimientos gubernamentales, 1924-1925-
1951-1952. Tegucigalpa: Banco Central de
Honduras, 1953. 206 pp.
    A detailed twenty-five-year compilation,
combining figures used in several of the
bank's earlier studies. Focuses on national
income but provides extensive data on the
economy during the years in question. Represents part of the newly formed bank's effort
to systemize planning and provide data to form
a basis for that process. DLC

436 Trejo Castillo, Alfredo. El señor don Samuel
Zemurray y la soberanía de Honduras.
Tegucigalpa: Tipografía La Prensa Libre,
1926. 33 pp.
    A discussion of an incident in which
Zemurray and his Cuyamel Fruit Company had
obtained a concession from Nicaragua in the
disputed border region claimed by both
Nicaragua and Honduras. Notes that Zemurray
had cited an earlier instance involving a
similar problem with his Louisiana Nicaragua
Lumber Company, in which both nations had
validated his concession in return for his
pledge to accept the boundary awards and not
participate in the dispute. The documentation
is reprinted, with the recommendation that
Honduras reject such a proposal in the present
case. LNHT

437 Trinidad del Cid, María. La vida ejemplar de
doña María Guadalupe Reyes de Carías.
Tegucigalpa: Tipografía Ariston, 1944. iii,
158 pp. Illus.
    A volume hailing the public-service proj-
ects of the wife of President Tiburcio Carías
Andino. TxU

438 Tróchez, Raúl Gilberto. Imágenes: ensayos.
Tegucigalpa: Tipografía Ariston, 1973.
281 pp.
    A series of essays that deals with a wide
variety of themes but focuses mainly on the
national heroes and literary figures, hailing
their work. The comments are pro-unionist and
sympathetic to Morazán. The author was director of the National Library. DLC

439 Turcios Ramírez, Salvador. <u>Apuntes</u>
<u>biográficos: la personalidad de Paulino</u>
<u>Valladares a través de los años</u>. Tegucigalpa:
Tipografía Nacional, 1926. 50 pp. Illus.
DLC

440 _____. <u>Comayagüela en la historia nacional</u>.
Tegucigalpa: Imprenta La Democracia, 1959.
Pages unnumbered.

441 _____. <u>Conociendo la historia patria</u>.
Tegucigalpa: Imprenta Calderón, 1942. 193
pp. Illus.
     The initial portion of this volume consists
of a biography of Francisco Morazán that discusses his role in Central American independence; the latter portion is a series of essays
dealing with various aspects of his life and
career, which are curiously interspersed with
essays on other independence heroes of South
America. DLC

442 Ulloa, José Ángel. <u>La frutera en Honduras:</u>
<u>el extraño casa de su defensor en Guatemala,</u>
<u>Clemente Marroquín Rojas</u>. Guatemala:
Ministerio de Economía y Trabajo, 1949.
30 pp.
     A pamphlet attacking the United Fruit Com-
pany and criticizing both its activities in
Honduras and the concessions granted to it by
the Honduran government. The introduction
notes that Ulloa prepared this study in 1947
at the suggestion of Clemente Marroquín Rojas,
then Guatemalan minister of economy, and then
in 1949 Marroquín Rojas was defending the
United Fruit Company in Congress against attacks by reformers. DLC LNHT BNG

443 Urtecho Jeamborde, Andrés. <u>Problema social</u>
<u>del alcoholismo en Honduras</u>. Tegucigalpa:
Imprenta La República, 1971. 18 pp.
     An anti-alcohol tract providing estimates
of the extent of the problem in Honduras.

444 Valladares, José María. <u>La insurrección de</u>
<u>Amapala: sus causas y fines, 31 de octubre de</u>
<u>1910</u>. San José: Imprenta Alsina, 1911.
89 pp.
     A self-justifying account by the port com-
mander who rebelled, contending that all his
problems resulted from the activities of local
Germans who controlled the port's commerce and
used their positions as honorary consuls to
protect their operations and prevent reforms.
He portrays himself as the defender of
Honduran honor and interests against rapacious
foreigners, and condemns the Liberal regime of
General Miguel Dávila as weak and yielding to
foreign pressures. Includes numerous letters
and telegrams exchanged with the president and
the commanders of foreign ships sent to protect foreign interests. DLC DLC-LDS-482

445 _____. <u>Política hondureña: hechos y</u>
<u>deducciones</u>. San José: Imprenta Alsina,
1911. 60 pp.
     A continuation of the author's <u>La</u>
<u>insurrección de Amapala</u>. Attacks the Liberal
revolution of 1892-94 and the resulting administrations of generals Manuel Bonilla and

Miguel R. Dávila, contending that events have
borne out the author's prognostications in the
earlier work that the Liberals would establish
a dictatorship and that both leaders were
under and subject to Yankee influence. Includes excerpts from press comment and diplomatic and official correspondence to support
his contentions, as well as clause-by-clause
comparison of the constitutions of 1894 and
1904 to indicate the strengthening of the
powers of the government. DLC

446 Valladares, Paulino. <u>Asamblea Constituyente</u>
<u>1908: porqué se opusieron 19 diputados a que</u>
<u>se ratificar sin reforma la constitución de</u>
<u>1894</u>. Tegucigalpa: Tipografía Nacional,
1908. 22 pp.
     A protest by a minority that opposed reten-
tion of the existing constitution. DLC LNHT

447 _____. <u>Hondureños ilustres en la pluma</u>
<u>de. . . .</u>. Tegucigalpa: Presidencia, Oficina
de Relaciones Públicas, 1972. 240 pp.
     An alphabetically arranged collection of
brief biographical sketches of significant
figures in Honduran development, including
political, religious, literary, and scholarly
figures from throughout the nineteenth and
twentieth centuries, often with accounts of
the author's personal contacts with them. The
sketches, most a page or two in length, were
previously published in the Honduran press as
separate articles. DLC LNHT

448 Valladares B., Abel Arturo. <u>Monografía del</u>
<u>departamento de las Islas de la Bahía</u>.
Tegucigalpa: Talleres Tipográficos
Nacionales, 1939. 180 pp. Illus., tables.
     Part of the series of departmental mono-
graphs sponsored by the Society of Geography
and History, this work emphasizes geography,
with most of its space devoted to a detailed
island-by-island physical description. The
historical portion deals only with the Colonial period, but a number of appended brief
commentaries and excerpts from the works of
others, dealing with various significant historical dates and events, extend coverage into
the nineteenth century. LNHT

449 Valladares Rodríguez, Juan Bautista. <u>La</u>
<u>Virgen de Suyapa: historia documentada</u>.
Tegucigalpa: Tipografía Ariston, 1946. x,
269 pp. Biblio., illus., index.
     A collection of documents relating to the
patroness of Tegucigalpa and the shrine dedicated to her, tracing its development from
Colonial times to 1944. Provides insights
into many aspects of Honduran church history.
LNHT

450 Valle, Rafael Helidoro. <u>Imágenes de Honduras</u>.
Tegucigalpa: Talleres Gráficos de la Nación,
1949. Pages unnumbered. Illus.
     A collection of photographs showing
Honduras and its facilities on the occasion of
the inauguration of the Gálvez regime in 1949.
Includes archeological zones and the countryside, but emphasizes the capital and the government buildings, many built by the Carías
regime. LNHT

451 Vallecillo, Carlos A. Árbol genealógico del padre José Trinidad Reyes: año del centenario de su muerte, 1855-1955: sus pensamientos y juicios sobre su personalidad. Tegucigalpa: Imprenta Bulnes, 1955. 44 pp. Illus., tables.
    A brief pamphlet extolling the contributions of the founder of the University of Honduras, with excerpts from his writings and a tracing of his genealogy. DLC

452 Vallejo, Antonio Ramón, ed. Colección de las constituciones políticas que en la República de Honduras se han decretado en los cincuenta y seis años que lleva de independencia, comenzando por la Federal, emitida el 22 de noviembre de 1824. New York: Chamberlain, Whitmore, 1878. iv, 203 pp.
    The full texts of the various Honduran constitutions through that of 1873. DLC LNHT

453 _____. Guía de agriménsures o sea recopilación de leyes agrarias. Tegucigalpa: Tipografía Nacional, 1911. 300 pp.
    A collection of the complete texts of all the laws and decrees relating to agriculture in Honduras from 1538 to 1911, arranged chronologically and without comment. DLC LNHT

454 _____. Necrología del presbítero don Miguel Ángel Bustillo. Tegucigalpa: Tipografía Nacional, 1893. 194 pp. 2d ed. Comayagüela: n.p., 1966. 70 pp.
    CU-B

455 Vallejo Armijo, Antonio. Gobernantes de Honduras, 1824-1957. Tegucigalpa: Tipografía Nacional, 1957. 81 pp.
    A series of very brief biographical sketches or vitae of the various individuals who have headed Honduras since independence. LNHT

456 _____. Honduras, la paz y un hombre: consideraciones sobre la labor del General Tiburcio Carías Andino. Tegucigalpa: Imprenta López, 1947. 34 pp. Illus.
    A brief pamphlet lauding the contributions of the Carías regime, emphasizing its stabilization of the national political scene and what this implies for development, as well as extolling its public-works programs.

457 Vásquez, José Valentín. Álbum cívico hondureño. Progreso: Tipografía Atenea, 1952. 177 pp. Illus. 2d ed. Comayagüela: Imprenta Gómez, 1970. 249 pp.
    Though not expressly an approved text, this volume is written like a text and is designed to encourage Hondurans to become more familiar with the essentials of their nation's history. It includes geographical information, a collection of historical documents important in the nation's development, essays on the national symbols, and a series of brief biographical sketches of important figures in Honduran history. DLC LNHT

458 _____. Datos biográficos del profesor de estado y licenciado don Luís Landa.

Tegucigalpa: Sociedad de Geografía e Historia, 1965. 15 pp.
    One of a series of pamphlets by a Honduran educator detailing the lives and hailing the contributions of professors important in the development of the nation's educational system.

459 _____. Pedro Nufio: datos biográficos del venerable maestro. Tegucigalpa: Ministerio de Educación Pública, 1966. 38 pp.
    See item HO458.

460 _____. Los problemas vitales de los maestros hondureños. Tegucigalpa: Imprenta La República, 1953. 31 pp.
    A Honduran professor's comments regarding the problems and difficulties facing his cohorts and the nation's educational system.

461 _____. Rasgos biográficos del abogado y maestro don Esteban Guardiola Cubas. Tegucigalpa: Ministerio de Educación Pública, 1960. 42 pp.
    See item HO458.

462 Vela, David. Metidos en Honduras. Guatemala: Unión Tipográfica, 1946. 24 pp. Illus.
    A commentary by the editor of El Imparcial, written during a visit to Honduras and originally published in his newspaper as a series of articles. Criticizes the Carías dictatorship and compares it to that of Jorge Ubico in Guatemala, denouncing its continuismo, repression, and the participation of foreign interests in its development, while calling for democracy in Honduras on the model of the Guatemalan revolution. LNHT

463 Velásquez Cerrato, Armando. Un pensamiento dinámico al servicio de Honduras. Tegucigalpa: n.p., 1958. 84 pp.
    A collection of letters written between 1941 and 1956 by a Honduran army colonel who was one of the leaders of the 1956 coup. Expounds his views about the importance of the armed services as the guarantors of peace and stability; condemns the bankruptcy of civilian continuismo but calls for democracy, arguing that the mission of the military is normally to serve the populace. The emphasis clearly is on the primary role of the new military that was institutionalizing during these years, endowing it with a mission of its own that superseded that of the government. All the letters are identified as to date and place of writing and initial publication. LNHT

464 Velásquez Díaz, Max. Reorganización Liberal: nuevas bases para el partido. Tegucigalpa: Imprenta Calderón, 1972. 140 pp.
    A brief historical sketch of the Honduran Liberal party, followed by a call for its reorganization and reinvigoration; includes a proposed new charter and program. The author contends that the party has atrophied and needs a complete restructuring and a recommitment to its ideology, indicating that such a

change is essential to the future of the party and the nation. DLC LNHT

465 Vera, Robustiano. <u>Apuntes para la historia de Honduras</u>. Santiago: Imprenta de El Correo, 1899. x, 316 pp. Illus.

A general narration constituting one of the earliest efforts to provide a history of this republic, which, though extending to the then current regime, focuses on the Colonial era and early nineteenth century, with only very brief comment on the post-1865 era. Some of the chapters resemble chronological listings, as each event is treated in a single-sentence paragraph. DLC LNHT

466 _____. <u>Geografía descriptiva e historia política de la República de Honduras</u>. Santiago: Tipografía Valparaíso de Federico T. Lathrop; Tegucigalpa: Tipografía Nacional, 1904. 115 pp.

An updated and condensed version of the author's earlier effort, this one with more emphasis on geography.

467 Villacorta Cisneros, Abel. <u>Reseña histórica del Partido Nacional de Honduras</u>. Tegucigalpa: Imprenta Gómez, 1962. 18 pp.

An official summary of the development of the National (Conservative) party and its accomplishments. LNHT

468 Villeda Morales, José Ramón. <u>La defensa de la democracia frente a la amenaza comunista, mensaje del ciudadano presidente de la República, Dr. Ramón Villeda Morales, al pueblo hondureño, 21 de julio de 1962</u>. Tegucigalpa: Tipografía Nacional, 1962. 66 pp.

A speech warning of the communist threat, calling for constant vigilance, condemning the activities of Cuba, and hailing the Alliance for Progress, accompanied by other statements by officials of his regime. Reflects the Yankee pressures against Cuba within the OAS at the time. The president clearly couples his warning with an appeal for further aid under the Alliance to prevent the spread of communism. DLC

469 _____. <u>Mensaje al pueblo hondureño al cumplirse el quinto año de su gestión administrativa</u>. Tegucigalpa: Tipografía Nacional, 1962. 64 pp.

An official summary of the regime's accomplishments and future plans.

470 _____. <u>Mitos y realidades históricas: Honduras ante el Mercado Común, 1970</u>. Tegucigalpa: n.p., 1970. 18 pp.

A brief survey of the problems experienced by Honduras in the Common Market. Notes the unfavorable balance of payments and comments that Honduras could not sustain this for too long a period, contending therefore that in the short term special measures were necessary to protect Honduras from its neighbors' economic efforts, to finance its deficit, and to provide limits on some items of trade. The ex-president adds that in the long run

Honduras will need to promote its own internal economic integration, for the lack of it is one of the causes of the problem. LNHT

471 _____. <u>El pensamiento vivo de Villeda Morales</u>. Tegucigalpa: Tipografía Ariston, 1963. 96 pp. Illus.

A collection of brief, topically arranged excerpts from the speeches of the Honduran president, representing his views on a wide range of subjects. The original speeches from which they were extracted are not identified. Emphasis is placed on his liberalism, but subjects include the army, Central American integration, the Cuban question, the communist menace, various internal political questions, and many more. DLC

472 _____. <u>El problema social de la medicina en Honduras</u>. Tegucigalpa: Colegio Médico, 1953. 18 pp.

A discussion of the availability of medical services in the nation, noting their concentration in the cities and scarcity in the rural areas.

473 Villela Vidal, Jesús. <u>Los fundadores de la Antigua Ocotepeque</u>. Tegucigalpa: Tipografía Ariston, 1963. 146 pp. Illus.

A series of essays, most of which focus on the principal families of the city, dealing with their role in its foundation in the mid-nineteenth century and its becoming the seat of a department in the early twentieth century. Rather than a history, however, it is a discussion of the leading families, with numerous photos and data about interfamily marriages, including some reminiscences. Also includes some general essays on patriotic themes and on the celebration of various events in the city. DLC

474 Von Hagen, Victor Wolfgang. <u>The Jicaque (Torrupan) Indians of Honduras</u>. New York: Museum of the American Indian, 1943. ix, 112 pp. Biblio., notes, illus., maps.

A description of the life-style of the last remaining portion of this tribe to maintain its ancient customs, in the interior of Honduras. Provides details of all aspects of life, economy, and society. Includes historical background. DLC LNHT

475 _____. <u>Jungle in the Clouds: A Naturalist's Explorations in the Republic of Honduras</u>. New York: Duell, Sloan, & Pearce, 1940. x, 260 pp. Index, biblio., illus., maps, appendixes.

An early effort by this anthropologist, this is a travelogue, for the general audience, of an expedition to trap and tame the Quetzal bird in the highland jungles of Honduras. It emphasizes adventure and description, providing data on travel and living conditions, tribes encountered, and zones visited. The trip includes a look at the archeological zone of Copán. DLC

476 <u>La voz de los emigrados descontentos</u>. Tegucigalpa: Tipografía Nacional, 1908. 41 pp.

An article by Honduran exiles, originally printed in El Correo Español of Mexico City on 12 October 1908, containing a broad range of charges against the government of Miguel R. Dávila and his predecessor, Policarpo Bonilla, accusing them of corruption and tyranny and alleging that the Honduran people were seething with revolt. The article was reprinted by the government for circulation within the nation so that the citizens could see the charges, which the regime regarded as no cause for concern and purely the product of political discontent by the losers. DLC

477 Walz, Thomas Harold. Favorite Idioms and Expressions Used in Honduras Compiled. Tegucigalpa: n.p., [196?]. 141 pp. Biblio.
    An alphabetically arranged compilation of idioms, with definitions of their background. MnU

478 Weddle, Ken. Honduras in Pictures. New York: Sterling, 1972. 64 pp. Index, illus., maps. 2d ed. New York; Sterling, 1976. 64 pp. Index, illus.
    Illustrations, with brief commentary, designed to introduce the novice to the land and its people. DLC LNHT

479 Wells, William Vincent. Explorations and Adventures in Honduras: Comprising Sketches of Travel in the Gold Regions of Olancho, and a Review of the History and General Resources of Central America. New York: Harper & Brothers, 1857. 588 pp. Index, illus., maps. Exploraciones y aventuras en Honduras. Tegucigalpa: Banco Central de Honduras, 1960. viii, 580 pp.
    A rich description of a trip across Honduras in 1854 by an observant traveler whose jottings take in everything from physical setting and people to social customs, dress, and flora and fauna. Particular emphasis is placed on social customs and life-styles, as well as on transportation difficulties experienced by the author and the trials and tribulations of his journey. DLC LNHT

480 Winn, Wilkins B. Pioneer Protestant Missionaries in Honduras. Cuernavaca: CIDOC, 1973. Pages not consecutively numbered. Biblio., maps.
    Brief summary of the work of A.E. Bishop and J.G. Cassel in the department of Copán, Honduras. Covers their service there from 1896-1901, then reproduces their diaries recounting their experiences in cryptic entries emphasizing their travels and the hardships they endured. DLC LNHT

481 Young, Arthur N., et al. Historia finaciera de Honduras: informes de las misiones Arthur N. Young 1920-1921; Bernstein 1943 y del Fondo Monetario Internacional 1949 y estudio sobre la economía de Honduras. Tegucigalpa: Banco Central de Honduras, 1957. vi, 204 pp. Maps, tables.
    A volume sponsored by the Banco Central de Honduras, combining the report of the Young financial mission of 1921, which focused on financial stabilization and repayment of foreign debts, and lectured the government on the evils of deficit spending; the report by E.M. Bernstein in 1943, which also sought financial stabilization and proposed the formation of the Central Bank to control the financial scene; and a study in 1950 by a mission from the International Monetary Fund, headed by Javier Márquez, which assisted in drafting the legislation creating the bank. Each provides a survey of the economy at the time of their visit, and collectively they offer valuable data regarding the nation's continuing financial problems and its economic development. LNHT

482 Ypsilanti de Moldavía, Jorge. Monografía de Comayagua, 1537-1937. Tegucigalpa: Talleres Tipográficos Nacionales, 1937. 55 pp. Illus.
    Most of the historical portions of this work refer to Colonial days, with the post-independence portions consisting of current description. Also contains a list of the bishops of Honduras from 1527 through 1937, and the history of the national diocese, which is based in the city. DLC LNHT

483 Zaldívar Guzmán, Raúl. Liberalismo en Honduras. Tegucigalpa: Imprenta Bulnes, 1964. 104 pp. Biblio.
    An official history of the Honduran Liberal party, originally published in the party newspaper El Pueblo, this series of essays seeks to define liberalism and equate it with basic human aspirations. Outlines the history of the movement in Honduras, acclaiming all of its heroes and denouncing its opponents as dictators. DLC LNHT

484 Zelaya, Manuel A. Apuntes de la historia de la moneda de Honduras. Tegucigalpa: Imprenta Calderón, 1958. 60 pp.
The History and Coins of Honduras. Tegucigalpa: n.p., 1965. 34 pp. Illus.
    A history and description of Honduran coinage, with details of the various issues and background information; designed for the collector. DLC

485 Zelaya Lozano, Cecilio. Discursos pronunciados por el señor rector de la Universidad Nacional Autónoma de Honduras. Tegucigalpa: Imprenta López, 1971. 54 pp. Illus.
    A collection of addresses by the university rector hailing the role of the university, emphasizing its autonomy, and calling for it to serve as the center of reformist thought to help liberate the third world. LNHT

486 Zerón h., José. Roosevelt y Carías Andino. Tegucigalpa: Tipografía Nacional, 1942. 119 pp.
    An official compilation stressing Honduran cooperation with the United States during World War II and focusing on the two presidents; includes official exchanges pledging friendship. DLC

487 Zúñiga, Luís Andrés. Los conspiradores. Tegucigalpa: Atenea de Honduras, 1915. 3d

ed. Tegucigalpa: Ministerio de Educación
Pública, 1954. 183 pp.
   A play written in 1915, based on the life
of Francisco Morazán. Stresses his honesty
and morality, extolling his memory in a manner
that contributes to his legendary status as
the idealist of the region and the principal
promoter of unity among its states. DLC LNHT

488 Zúñiga, Melba. La familia campesina.
Tegucigalpa: Instituto de Investigaciones
Socio-Económicas, 1975. 60 pp. Notes.
   A sociological study of peasant values,
outlooks, social organization, and life-styles
in Honduras, focusing on relations within the
family. Apparently based on interviews and/or
familiarity with the peasants, as well as on
secondary works, though only the latter are
footnoted. DLC LNHT

489 Zúñiga Figueroa, Carlos [Mario Vásquez,
pseud.]. Recopilación de escritos publicados
en la sección "Un Poco" del diario "La Época."
2 vols. Tegucigalpa: Talleres Tipográficos
Nacionales, 1950-51. 353 pp. Index, illus.
   A collection of over a hundred newspaper
commentaries published in La Época of
Tegucigalpa under the author's pseudonym in
the years 1949 and 1950. They deal with a
wide range of diverse themes, most of them in
general terms, but with some commentaries
about specific contemporary Honduran political
issues. DLC LNHT

490 Zúñiga Huete, Ángel. Autobiografía.
Comayagüela: Imprenta Bulnes, 1970. 68 pp.
   The autobiography of a leader of the
Honduran Liberal party, who spent much of his
life in exile during the Conservative rule in
the mid-twentieth century.

491 ____. Un cacicazgo centro-americano. Mexico:
Imprenta Victoria, 1938. 79 pp. Maps, tables.
   A bitter and sweeping assault on the regime
of General Tiburcio Carías Andino by his longtime opponent, written from exile, leveling a
long list of charges including fraud in his
initial election, illegal extension of his
term, corruption, dishonesty, failure to defend the national patrimony by acceptance of
an arbitral ruling in the boundary dispute
with Guatemala, nepotism, use of force, and
everything else imaginable. DLC

492 ____. Cartas: una actitud y una senda,
veleidades de un veleta. Mexico: n.p., 1949.
73 pp.
   A series of letters and statements written
in exile by the Honduran Liberal leader and
continuing his polemic, now against the government of Juan Manuel Gálvez. He contends
that the Liberals are the majority party,
demands free elections, and accuses the government of various crimes. DLC

493 ____. El desastre de una dictadura.
Jamaica: Times Publishing Co., 1937. 41 pp.
   The defeated Honduran Liberal candidate
bitterly attacks the regime of General
Tiburcio Carías Andino, charging all sorts of

irregularities and atrocities in a tract written from exile. DLC

494 ____. Ídolo desnudo. Mexico: Acción
Moderna Mercantil, 1939. 113 pp.
   Another in the Liberal leader's continuing
series of political polemics attacking Carías,
this time replying to Lucas Paredes's biography of the Honduran Conservative president,
charging that it portrays Zúñiga Huete un-
favorably through misquotation, alleging that
the clash between the two men is the focal
point of Honduran politics, and debunking the
caudillo's image by replying point for point
to the items discussed by Paredes. DLC

495 ____. Recordatorio del general Florencio
Xatruch, militar centroamericana de los
ejércitos nacionalistas unidos contra el
filibusterismo de William Walker en Nicaragua.
Comayagüela: Imprenta Gómez, 1953. 2d ed.
Comayagüela: Imprenta Gómez, 1956. 32 pp.
   Two essays extolling the heroism of the
Honduran general who fought against Walker.
LNHT

496 ____. Regalos del exilio: ¿Por qué es
inconstitucional el gobierno de Tiburcio
Carías Andino, dictador de Honduras? Mexico:
n.p., 1943. 39 pp.
   Another broadside by the exiled and defeated Liberal party leader attacking the
regime of General Tiburcio Carías Andino and
his continuismo, continuing their previous
political polemics and replying to a statement
by the regime. Carías is condemned as a ty-
rant who seized office by force, extended his
term illegally, and brutalized his nation.
The author, of course, emerges as the embodi-
ment of Honduran democracy and the nation's
great hope for the future. DLC

497 Zúñiga Huete, Manuel Guillermo. Datos
biográficos del general Terencio Sierra.
Tegucigalpa: n.p., 1949. 32 pp. 2d ed.
Tegucigalpa: Imprenta Gómez, 1950. 56 pp.
   A brief biography hailing the accomplish-
ments of a general who served as president of
Honduras from 1899 to 1903. TxU

Nicaragua

1 Abaúnza Salinas, Ramiro. Un general sin estrellas. León: Imprenta Hospicio, 1974. 238 pp. Illus.

A novel of coup and countercoup, detailing the maneuvers in a small Pacific coast nation, focusing not on the politics but on their impact on those involved. The emphasis is on confusion, futility, and tragedy. Clearly a masked treatment of the contemporary Nicaraguan scene. DLC

2 Abert, Silvanus Thayer. Is a Ship Canal Practicable? Notes, Historical and Statistical, upon the Projected Routes for an Interoceanic Ship Canal between the Atlantic and Pacific Oceans. Cincinnati: R.W. Carroll, 1870. 87 pp. Illus., maps, tables. 2d ed. Cincinnati: R.W. Carroll, 1872. 88 pp. Illus., maps.

Data regarding the various canal routes and comparison with Suez and other canals, with discussion of the terrain, people, nations, and commerce, as well as of the potential of the canal and the resources of the region. Includes brief references to earlier canal schemes. DLC

3 Aburto Juan. Narraciones. León: Universidad Nacional Autónoma de Nicaragua, 1969, 94 pp.

Ten short stories about life in Managua, most written in the first person and drawing on the author's experience as a youth growing up in that city. Also includes his recollection of the United Nations. IaU

4 Actualidad centroamericana: Tratado Chamorro-Bryan. San José: Imprenta Falco & Borrasé, 1917. 220 pp.

A study by the Honduran Law Association and a commentary by Salvador Rodríguez González examining the Bryan-Chamorro Treaty and detailing the ways in which it violates Honduran sovereignty. Recommends that the government take the issue to the Central American Court of Justice and provides the basis of the arguments that would comprise its case. DLC DLC-LDS-270

5 Acuña Escobar, Francisco. Biografía del Gral. Rigoberto Cabezas. Masaya: Imprenta "El Espectador," 1940. 147 pp.

A favorable view of the general's contributions, emphasizing his efforts to bring about the reincorporation of the Mosquito Territory into Nicaragua while skirting his 1893 rebellion against the government of Roberto Sacasa. DLC

6 Adan, Émile. Conference sur le passage interocéanique. Brussels: Imprimerie A. Cnophs Fils, 1879. 28 pp.

A summary of a conference conducted by the Belgian Institute of Military Cartography, under the auspices of the Ministry of War, to discuss the feasibility of a Central American canal and the various proposals for it. The large number of engineers in attendance concluded that the Panama and Tehuantepec routes were not feasible. Although the conference refrained from directly endorsing the Nicaraguan route, the fact that it alone was not rejected outright clearly left it the one they judged most propitious, despite overall skepticism arising from the scale of the undertaking and the differing levels of the oceans. LNHT

7 Aguilar, Arturo. Reseña histórica de la diócesis de Nicaragua. León: Tipografía Hospicio, 1929. 308 pp.

An outline, based on published materials, of the development of the city of León and its churches. DLC BNCR

8 Aguilar Cortes, Jeronimo. Memorias de los yanquis a Sandino. San Salvador: Talleres Gráficos del I.T. Ricaldone, 1972. 124 pp. Illus.

A novel in the form of the supposed memoirs of a soldier who fought with Sandino against the Yankees. Recounting his experiences with the guerilla forces, it indicates his dislike for the Americans and idolizes Sandino as the representative of the true will of the people. DLC

9 Alcover y Beltrán, Antonio Miguel. La República de Nicaragua: descripción geografía del país, algo de historia origen y causa del actual conflicto, etc. Havana: n.p., n.d. 26 pp. Illus.

A geographical description of Nicaragua, followed by comments on the then-current political situation and the revolution against José Santos Zelaya, condemning the "crimes" of the dictator and extolling the revolutionaries as true patriots who represented the desire of the Nicaraguan people to reclaim their nation's honor. DPU

10 Alemán Bolaños, Gustavo. Cartas concluyentes . . . octubre de 1928. Guatemala: Sánchez & de Guise, 1928. 156 pp.
A well-known Nicaraguan journalist's comments on contemporary Central American politics, particularly denouncing Yankee intervention in his country. He calls the book the second volume of his work El país de los irredentos. DLC LNHT

11 _____, ed. Centenario de la guerra nacional de Nicaragua contra Walker: Costa Rica, Guatemala, El Salvador, y Honduras en la contienda. Guatemala: Tipográfica Nacional, 1956. 117 pp.
A Nicaraguan reporter's summation of the campaigns against the Yankee filibuster, with emphasis on the battlefield and the cooperation of the various Central American republics in rallying to the defense of Nicaragua. Contains excerpts from existing studies of the era in addition to his own commentary. DLC LNHT BNG BNCR

12 Alemán Bolaños, Gustavo. Comó ganó Nicaragua su segunda independencia. Managua: Editorial Atlántida, 1944. 79 pp.
An emotional, patriotic, semi-official account of the campaign against Walker, emphasizing the Nicaraguan aspects of the combats. Intended for use in the Nicaraguan schools. DLC

13 _____. La fauna conservadora de Nicaragua y otras yerbas. Guatemala: Editorial Argos, 1956. 48 pp.
A series of disparate press articles commenting upon Nicaraguan politics since the 1850s, focusing on the nineteenth century, and drawing heavily upon the author's previous publications. The author denounces the failure of the political parties and of dictatorship, focusing on the Chamorro regime and the Conservative party, though also working in some linkage to the contemporary Somoza regime, in accordance with his well-known opposition to it. BNG

14 _____. Lo impostergable en Nicaragua: educación pública integral. Managua: Talleres Gráficos Pérez, 1936. 64 pp.
TxU

15 _____. La juventud de Rubén Darío, 1890-1893. Guatemala: Sánchez & de Guise, 1923. 220 pp. 2d ed. Guatemala: Editorial Universitaria, 1958. 204 pp.
This volume traces the youth of Rubén Darío and his early years as a writer. Details his travels and comments on his experiences, drawing extensively from the writings of his

acquaintances during these years; also prints excerpts from his initial poems. The 1958 edition, although it covers the same subject, is completely rewritten. DLC LNHT BNG BNCR

16 _____. Un lombrosiano: Somoza, 1939-1944. Guatemala: Editorial Hispania, 1945. 208 pp.
A series of heated and bitter commentaries condemning the Somoza regime as a dictatorship and denouncing its activities, by a Nicaraguan journalist who mixes anecdotes, personal experience, and narration with quotations from the press. The author has indicated that he considers his later work Los pobres diablos a "second volume" to this book, continuing its themes. DLC LNHT BNG

17 _____. Memorias de un periodista. Guatemala: Imprenta Sansur, 1948. 60 pp.
Rambling reminiscenes of a Nicaraguan journalist recounting his life in exile, covering episodes from the years 1914-48, though focusing on the earlier period. Combines narration of his journalistic works and assignments with condemnations of the Somoza regime, dictatorship, and Yankee intervention in the region. DLC

18 _____. La novela de un prisionero. Managua: Tipografía La Prensa, 1935. 55 pp.
A novel in the form of the memoirs of a prisoner who relates his experiences in jail and during questioning. Emphasizes his situation and mistreatment, reflecting on how he got there and providing the rest of the story through flashbacks. DLC LNHT

19 _____. A ojos vistas: hechos y personajes de mayor y menor cuantía. Guatemala: Editorial Norte, 1954. 102 pp.
A series of essays covering a wide range of subjects, recording the author's thoughts on his travels and on his meetings and correspondence with well-known Central American and Nicaraguan political and literary luminaries. Many significant figures of Nicaraguan history cross his pages, though in no particular order. Includes numerous references to contemporary dictatorships the author opposes, particularly the Somoza regime in his native Nicaragua. DLC LNHT BNG

20 _____. El país de los irredentos. Guatemala: Sánchez & de Guise, 1927. 244 pp.
Yet another propaganda tract denouncing the role of the United States and its intervention in Nicaragua during the 1920s. Includes an account of the political events and figures of those years that criticizes those who comported with the Yankees and hails those who resisted. The author considers his later Cartas concluyentes a continuation of this work. DLC BNCR

21 _____. Periodismo y periodistas. San Salvador: Imprenta "La Salvadoreña," 1926. 152 pp. Biblio. 2d ed. Guatemala: n.p., 1958. 140 pp.

(Alemán Bolaños, Gustavo)
Commentaries on contemporary journalists of
the 1920s that focus on his native Nicaragua.
DLC BNG BNCR

22   _____. Los pobres diablos. Guatemala:
Editorial Hispania, 1947. 113 pp.
A denunciation of the Somoza regime and its
actions, cataloguing its alleged abuses. Although published under a different title, the
author calls it the "second volume" of his Un
lombrosiano, since it continues his diatribe
against the Somoza regime. LNHT BNG

23   _____. El "Presidente" de Nicaragua. New
York: n.p., 1916. 19 pp. 2d ed. San José:
n.p., 1919. 19 pp.
An attack on Yankee intervention in
Nicaragua, criticizing the pacts of 1921 and
the Bryan-Chamorro Treaty with more passion
than information, employing items from the
Yankee press that the author mistakes for
official statements. DLC-LDS-689

24   _____. El pueblo de Nicaragua y Los Estados
Unidos: el pasado, el presente y el porvenir
de la colectividad en relación con el Gran País.
New York: Tipografía Alemana, 1920. 56 pp.
2d ed. Managua: Tipografía Alemana, 1923.
Another in the author's series of polemics
denouncing Yankee intervention in Nicaragua.
But he also discusses the broader problems
that bring it about, criticizing Nicaragua's
disunity and contending that the greatest need
is for an educational program that reaches the
populace and imbues it with sufficient nationalism to enable a unified effort and attitude
that could terminate the political civil wars
and enable unified action, which in turn would
decrease the opportunities for Yankee mis-
chief. DLC LNHT BNCR

25   _____. Sandino el libertador: la epopeya, la
paz, el invasor, la muerte. Mexico:
Ediciones del Caribe, 1952. 247 pp. Illus.
A eulogistic biography of Sandino that
recounts the role of the Yankees in pacifying
Nicaragua, Sandino's plans and guerrilla campaigns, and, ultimately, his death at the
hands of Somoza, which the author characterizes as a "transfiguration." DLC BNG

26   _____. ¡Sandino! estudio completo del héroe
de las Segovias. Mexico: Imprenta La
República, 1932. 82 pp.
A sympathetic account of Sandino's struggle
from 1926 through 1932. Includes extensive
excerpts from his letters and statements,
which had been smuggled out of the country and
were in the hands of the author at the time.
Throughout, Sandino is hailed as a hero struggling against dictatorship and imperialism.
This is one of the earliest accounts of this
era, and one of the most favorable to Sandino.
DLC LNHT

27 Alexander, Alfonso. Sandino: relato de la
revolución en Nicaragua. Santiago: Ediciones
Ercilla, 1937. 252 pp.

A sympathetic account of Sandino's exploits, characterizing him as a national hero
and hailing his struggle for liberation from
Yankee imperialism. DLC

28 Alfaro, Olmedo. El filibustero Walker en
Nicaragua. Panamá: Editorial La Moderna,
1932. 89 pp. Illus., maps.
An anti-Yankee tract advocating the
Hispanidad movement promoted by Spain during
the 1930s. It cites the Walker episode, along
with the Sandino affair and the Panama Canal
question, with brief narrations of each, to
establish the Yankee threat, complete with
photos of Yankee troops in the Canal Zone.
Notes that Spain has offered to "protect" the
Latin American nations from the vicious gringos, provided they all combine in a defensive
alliance. Includes tirades against United
Fruit and Yankee racism. DLC BNCR

29 Allen, Cyril. France in Central America:
Félix Belly and the Nicaraguan Canal. New
York: Pageant Press, 1966. 163 pp. Biblio.,
notes.
An account of French activities in the
isthmus from the 1770s to the 1870s, detailing
their interests and the activities of the
various individuals who led the French effort
and sought to promote a greater French role in
the proposed isthmian canal, particularly
Félix Belly. Based on extensive research in
published documents and secondary works. DLC
LNHT

30 Allen, Merritt Parmelee. William Walker:
Filibuster. New York: Harper, 1932. v, 177
pp. Biblio., maps.
A highly sympathetic account that views
Walker as a man of destiny and the American
Phalanx as "the finest fighting unit in the
world," bubbling with similar enthusiasm
through the description of the heroic exploits
of this small band against overwhelming
hordes, and even arguing that they had extensive popular support in the region. The work
is based on Walker's memoirs and those of
several participants. DLC LNHT

31 Alvarado García, Ernesto. La base naval
en el Golfo de Fonseca ante el derecho
internacional. Tegucigalpa: Tipografía
Minerva, 1931. 51 pp. Biblio., illus., maps.
A history of the Bryan-Chamorro Treaty and
the U.S. efforts to secure a naval base in the
Gulf of Fonseca, originally written as a
thesis. Defends the Honduran rights and position and criticizes Yankee imperialism. Contains extensive excerpts from the relevant
treaties and accords, as well as the legal
arguments involved in the resultant cases
before the Central American Court of Justice.
DLC LNHT BNG BNCR

32 Alvarado Martínez, Enrique. El pensamiento
político nicaragüense de los últimos años.
Managua: Editorial Artes Gráficas, 1968. 97
pp. Illus.
A survey of Nicaraguan political parties
and trends since 1950 that discusses all the

various groups, their leadership, and their political platforms, commenting also on the political role of the press. The author concludes that there is little organizational or doctrinal difference among the various Nicaraguan parties. He gives particular attention to the Conservative party, contending that the Liberals have become a personal vehicle of the Somoza family, and looks hopefully at some of the new groups, though without finding much to encourage political discussion. The latest platforms of the principal parties are also included. DLC LNHT

33 Alvarado Sarria, Rafael. Breve historia hospitalaria de Nicaragua. León: Editorial Hospicio, 1969. 148 pp. Biblio.
     Brief histories of all the hospitals of Nicaragua, indicating the dates of their foundation and other significant developments in their existence, sometimes with documents relating to their creation. DLC LNHT

34 Álvarez, Miguel Ángel. De cómo perdimos las provincias de Nicoya y Guanacaste. Granada: Escuela Tipografía Salesiana, 1942. 104 pp. Illus., maps.
     An account of the decision of these two provinces to abandon Nicaraguan jurisdiction and affiliate with Costa Rica during the early post-independence era under the Federation. DLC

35 _____. Los filibusteros en Nicaragua, 1855-1856-1857. Granada: Editorial La Prensa, 1944. 114 pp. Illus., maps.
     A Nicaraguan perspective of the Walker episode. Emphasizes nationalistic themes and the patriotism of the citizens who rallied to fight the Yankee imperialist and his pretensions in the region, and details the various combats from existing secondary works. DLC

36 Álvarez Lejarza, Emilio, ed. Las constituciones de Nicaragua, exposición crítica y textos. Madrid: Ediciones Cultura Hispánica, 1958. xiii, 1004 pp. Index.
     The complete texts of all the constitutions of the nation through 1955, with a brief introductory summary of each, providing an overview of the constitutional history and serving to highlight the key changes. DLC LNHT

37 _____. Ensayo biográfico del prócer José León Sandoval. Managua: Editorial Atlántida, 1947. 65 pp.
     A brief biography of one of the leaders of the independence movement in Nicaragua, designed to restore his rightful place in history. Includes a narration of fragments of his career, with quotations from official proclamations and communications, providing an overview of his early life; an account of his actions during the independence movement; and details of his service as head of the state of Nicaragua during the mid-1840s. FU

38 _____. Ensayo histórico sobre el derecho constitucional de Nicaragua. Managua:

Editorial La Prensa, 1936. xiii, 410 pp. Maps.
     A legal history of Nicaragua and its political institutions. The first third consists of brief overviews of the various eras in the nation's development; the rest consists of single-paragraph summaries of each article of the nation's constitutions and basic laws throughout its history. DLC LNHT BNCR

39 Álvarez Lejarza, Emilio, Andrés Vega Bolaños, and Gustavo Alemán Bolaños. Cómo reincorporó Nicaragua su costa oriental. Managua: Editorial Atlántida, 1944. 95 pp.
     This self-characterized "patriotic text" consists of a collection of documents about the 1894 episode involving what the Nicaraguans considered a British-backed secessionist movement in the Mosquito Territory, and the resulting diplomatic disputes and military campaigns. Published on the fiftieth anniversary of the reincorporation decree that initiated the controversy, it includes a brief historical synopsis of the affair and some linking narrative passages. DLC LNHT

40 Álvarez Lejarza, Marcario. Impresiones y recuerdos de la revolución de 1901 a 1910. Granada: Escuela Tipografía Salesiana, 1941. vi, 401 pp.
     An account of the fall of the Zelaya dictatorship in Nicaragua, contending that the Battle of Recreo was the key to the campaign. DLC

41 American Association for the Advancement of Science. Nicaragua Canal: Discussion before the American Association for the Advancement of Science, Thirty-Sixth Meeting, Held in New York, August, 1887. 104 pp. Maps.
     A series of papers presented to this meeting of the society by various naval officers and engineers, all endorsing the concept of a Nicaragua Canal, concluding that it was feasible, that Nicaragua offered the most propitious location, and that control by the United States was essential. Includes presentations by several known advocates of the Nicaragua route on general questions, specific engineering aspects, and climatic and geological data. Included are Commander Taylor and J.W. Miller. DLC LNHT

42 American Atlantic and Pacific Ship Canal Company. Nicaragua Canal: An Open Letter to the President of the United States of America Protesting against the Proposed Bill to Incorporate the Maritime Canal Company of Nicaragua. New York: n.p., 1888. 55 pp.
     A statement of the case of one of the companies disputing the right to construct a canal in Nicaragua. Objects to the formation of a government corporation to handle the matter, arguing that this proposal was perpetrated by a rival who lacks a clear title to the route, while contending that the protestors have a clearer title and the means to carry out the construction by private enterprise. DLC LNHT

43 Ammen, Daniel. <u>American Interoceanic Ship Canal Question</u>. Philadelphia: L.R. Hamersly, 1880. 102 pp.

An American admiral who conducted many of the navy's surveys of potential canal routes provides a summary of the various surveys conducted between 1870 and 1876, including a visit to France to confer with De Lesseps, and several expeditions to Central America. Originally a paper presented to the American Geographic Society. It includes references to examinations of all the potential canal routes and stresses the importance of United States control of such a canal, given its potential significance to American commerce. Records the early efforts to promote American interest and gain the ear of the Grant administration, indicating that Secretary of State William Seward was receptive to the idea. DLC

44 _____. <u>The Certainty of the Nicaraguan Canal Contrasted with the Uncertainties of the Eads-Ship Railway</u>. Washington, D.C.: J. Shillington, 1886. 36 pp. Illus., maps.

Part of the long-standing dispute about potential canal routes, this is a pamphlet in which a U.S. Navy admiral who testified before the various congressional committees of the era defends the Nicaraguan canal route and attacks a bill promoting a Tehuantepec railway to transport entire ships by rail across the isthmus, contending that such a scheme would be unworkable and impractical, and that the natural harbors in Nicaragua are far more promising. DLC LNHT

45 _____. <u>The Errors and Fallacies of the Inter-Oceanic Transit Question: To Whom do They Belong?</u> New York: Brentano Brothers, 1886. ii, 68 pp. Maps, tables.

Part of the propaganda battle regarding the location of the isthmian canal, this work by a supporter of the Nicaragua route cites the engineering reports and contends that the advocates of a Tehuantepec railroad that would carry ships across the mountains have not been honest in their presentations. He assails the Tehuantepec scheme as impractical and argues for the practicability of the Nicaragua route. DLC LNHT

46 _____. <u>The Proposed Inter-Oceanic Ship Canal across the American Isthmus between Greytown and Brito, via Nicaragua: Its Feasibility as a Commercial Question, and Its Advantages as Compared with Other Proposed Routes</u>. New York: Published by the Author, 1878. 22 pp. Maps.

A statement supporting the construction of a canal in Nicaragua, arguing the technical feasibility of this route and contending that it would best fill U.S. needs. Published as part of the continuing debate regarding the canal location, it constitutes an early statement of the position of a staunch supporter of the Nicaragua route. DLC

47 Anderson, Chandler P. <u>The Disturbing Influence in Central America of the Nicaragua Canal Treaty with the U.S. of America</u>. Washington, D.C.: Gibson Brothers, 1917. 50 pp.

A former official of the State Department comments on the Central American Court of Justice's ruling on the Bryan-Chamorro Treaty and on its implications for the other states. Concludes that only action by the United States can preserve the court and calm the conflict, arguing for the necessity of accepting the ruling and making appropriate arrangements with the other Central American nations involved. Of course this was not the policy of the Wilson administration, which failed to heed the protest of this Republican diplomat and ignored the court, thereby destroying it. BNCR

48 Aquino, Enrique. <u>La intervención en Nicaragua: colección de artículos publicados en la prensa sobre el problema americanista nicaragüense</u>. Managua: Talleres Gráficos Pérez, 1928. 34 pp. Illus.

A collection of articles originally published in <u>El Comercio</u> denouncing the Yankee intervention in Nicaragua. DLC

49 _____. <u>La personalidad política del general José Santos Zelaya</u>. Managua: Talleres Gráficos Pérez, 1944. 121 pp. Illus. 2d ed. Managua: Talleres Gráficos Pérez, 1945.

A sympathetic biography of the turn-of-the-century Nicaraguan Liberal dictator, providing details of his career and including excerpts from legislation, official statements, and comments about him by other scholars and contemporaries. The cover title is <u>Zelaya: el libro de su vida</u>; the title page bears the correct title used herein. DLC

50 Arana, César, ed. <u>Compilación de contratos celebrados con los banqueros de New York, con el Ethelburga Syndicate de Landres y con el Banco Nacional de Nicaragua, Inc. Leyes relativas a los mismos contratos; 1911-1928</u>. 3 vols. Managua: Tipografía Nacional & Tipografía Progreso, 1929.

A documentary collection detailing foreign loans to Nicaragua over the indicated years, a period of financial crisis throughout the isthmus during which external funding constituted the only source of capital and the only hope for stabilization. Includes the various laws implementing the agreements, as well as the contracts. DLC

51 Arcano, Iván. <u>Sandino redivivo: sangramos a la hiena</u>. San Francisco: Imprenta La Latina, 1976. 125 pp.

A novel recounting the Sandinista guerrilla raid of 27 December 1974, when the group seized the house of a government official in Managua and held numerous diplomats hostage, exchanging them for imprisoned companions. Written from the guerrillas' perspective and extolling the memory of Sandino, it condemns the Somoza regime while seeking to demonstrate the regime's methods and its growing rejection by the populace. Hails the guerrillas of the Sandinasta Liberation Front as conquering heroes who constitute the wave of the future and offer the prospect of freedom from the cruel despotism. DLC

52 Arce, Guillermo E. <u>Si yo fuera dictador</u>. Managua: Tipografía Atenas, 1959. 69 pp. Illus.

A young Nicaraguan journalist's account of how he would run the country if he had the chance, discussing its principal economic, social, and political problems and his proposals for their solution. He emphasizes that dictatorship does not necessarily mean tyranny and that such a government can be progressive, contending that a strong dictatorship is essential in the case of a nation as politically and economically underdeveloped as his own and in need of imposed change to transform itself and improve the standard of living of its citizens. DLC LNHT

53 Arellano, Jorge Eduardo, ed. <u>Escritos literarios y documentos desconocidos</u>. Managua: Ministerio de Cultura, 1980. 98 pp. Biblio.

A collection of writings about and by Augusto César Sandino, published by the new revolutionary regime for the purpose of "promoting knowledge of Sandino." Includes some contemporary press commentaries about and interviews with the hero, several of his proclamations announcing the program of his movement, and a collection of his letters to various correspondents. DLC

54 Arellano, Jorge Eduardo. <u>Historia de la Universidad de León</u>. 2 vols. León: Editorial Universitaria, 1973-74. 305, 208 pp. Biblio., notes, illus., appendixes.

An administrative history of the National University of Nicaragua, noting the key rulings, the changes in program, and the formation of new faculties, with quotations from relevant documents. The initial volume deals with the Colonial era, and the second with the post-independence period through 1947, with the focus on the nineteenth century. Includes a documentary appendix and a chronology of the university. DLC LNHT BNCR

55 _____. <u>Historias nicaragüenses; 1969-1973</u>. Managua: Ediciones Nacionales, 1974. 28 pp. LNHT BNCR

56 _____. <u>El movimiento de vanguardia de Nicaragua, 1927-1932</u>. Managua: Imprenta Novedades, 1969. 73 pp. Biblio., notes, illus.

A history of the so-called vanguardist poetry movement in Nicaragua, discussing its origins and its principal writers, focusing on the years 1927-50. Includes data on its various writers and periodicals, as well as on their works. DLC

57 _____. <u>Panorama de la literatura nicaragüense: época anterior a Darío (1503-1881)</u>. Managua: Editorial Alemana, 1967. 69 pp. Biblio.

A general survey of Nicaraguan literature for the period in question, indicating general trends and principal writers, with brief descriptions of the work of each. The last chapter deals with the nineteenth century. DLC LNHT

58 _____, ed. <u>Sandino en la poesía: 50 poemas sobre el general de hombres libres</u>. Managua: n.p., 1972. 24 pp.

A collection of poems hailing Sandino and extolling his exploits.

59 Arellano, Jorge Eduardo, and Eduardo Pérez Valle, eds. <u>Sandino</u>. Managua: Banco Central de Nicaragua, 1979. 83 pp. Illus.

A collection of stories about Sandino and his exploits, presenting him in a favorable light as the defender of the nation against the imperialistic Yankees and demonstrating the extent to which he has become an almost mystical folk hero.

60 Argüello, Agenor. <u>Los precursores de la poesía nueva en Nicaragua</u>. Managua: Club del Libro Nicaragüense, 1963. 269 pp. Illus.

A series of brief essays about the Nicaraguan poets of the late nineteenth and early twentieth centuries, with excerpts from their works. The essays summarize their approaches and subjects, and categorize their works. DLC

61 Argüello, Leonardo. <u>Monografía política: el caso Nicaragua, conflicto entre la fuerza y el derecho de las naciones</u>. León: n.p., 1917. 80 pp. Notes, illus.

A denunciation of the Bryan-Chamorro Treaty and Yankee intervention in Nicaragua, by a local political figure who also criticizes the internal civil warfare of his nation. DLC

62 _____. <u>Por el honor de un partido: réplica a la Comisión mixta de reclamaciones de Nicaragua</u>. León: Talleres Tipográficos de J.C. Gurdián, 1914. 32 pp.

A defense of the 1912 uprising by Liberal revolutionaries in León against the Conservative regime of Adolfo Díaz, written by the leader of the movement in that portion of Nicaragua. Replies to the conclusions of the claims commission that ruled in favor of various claimants; the author objects principally to what he regards as slurs on the nation by a commission composed of two Yankees and one Nicaraguan, whose conclusions cite the role of U.S. forces in preventing further chaos, bloodshed, and damage. He appends his own account of the uprising, presenting the Liberal view of the events. DLC

63 Argüello, Rosendo, Salvador Lejarza, and Carlos Martínez L. <u>Public Appeal of Nicaragua to the Congress and People of the United States</u>. New Orleans: Costa & Frichter, 1914. 189 pp.

A collection of memorials by Nicaraguan Liberal exiles from the Díaz regime gathered in New Orleans, protesting against the Yankee intervention in support of the regime and seeking to lobby to reverse American policy

through the press and the Congress by providing their version of the events that led to
Díaz's rise. Includes a collection of protests, commentaries, speeches, memorials,
etc., by Nicaraguans and Yankees objecting to
the Yankee actions. LNHT

64 Argüello Hurtado, Roberto. La propiedad
horizontal. León: Universidad Nacional,
1955. 65 pp.
    A legal treatise discussing Nicaraguan
codes regarding land ownership, noting that
joint or cooperative ownership is not allowed,
though it can be accomplished indirectly.
Includes discussion of how to utilize the
current law and suggestions for reforms of the
existing code. DLC

65 Arrien, Juan B., and Rafael Kauffmann.
Nicaragua en la educación: aproximación a la
realidad. Managua: Ediciones Universidad
Centroamericana, 1977. 423 pp. Biblio.,
notes, tables.
    A detailed but rambling description of the
Nicaraguan educational system. Contends that
it is inadequate to the needs of the populace
because it reflects the society; the author
feels that the university needs instead to
become the basis of societal reform by producing educators who will teach the populace
how to promote change. LNHT

66 Atkins, Thomas Benjamin. The Interoceanic
Canal across Nicaragua and the Attitude toward
It of the Government of the United States.
New York: New York Printing Co., 1890.
54 pp.
    A collection of various statements of in-
terest in a Nicaraguan canal, ranging from
1502 to 1890. Consists principally of U.S.
congressional resolutions and statements by
presidents and other prominent citizens.
Seeks to demonstrate the continuing Yankee
interest in the canal from the earliest days
of the republic to the present. The editor is
the secretary of the canal company. This is
the title on the title page. The cover of the
pamphlet contains a different title:
Nicaragua Canal: An Account of the Explorations and Surveys for This Canal from 1502 to
the Present Time, and a Statement Showing the
Relations thereto of the Government of the
United States. DLC LNHT

67 _____. A Refutation of "The Proposed
Nicaragua Canal: An Impracticable Project" by
Joseph Nimmo, Jr., LL.D. New York: Evening
Post, 1898. 29 pp.
    A response to Nimmo's pamphlet, disputing
his figures on the likely traffic in such a
canal, and hence those on its potential impact
on United States commerce and on its financing. Provides his own estimates and figures
and cites estimates by others, arguing that
Nimmo's methods are questionable and his
figures erroneous. DLC LNHT

68 _____. Report on the Tonnage of Traffic
within the Zone of Attraction of the Maritime
Canal of Nicaragua in 1890 and as Estimated

for 1897. New York: New York Printing Co.,
1890. 27 pp. Tables.
    A company report extolling the possibili-
ties of the canal, its traffic potential, and
hence its revenue prospects, designed to encourage the effort. LNHT

69 Baily, John. Memoir on the Lake of Granada,
the River San Juan and the Isthmus between the
Lake and Pacific Ocean in Nicaragua. London:
n.p., 1837. 2d ed. London: n.p., 1843.
Apuntamientos sobre el lago de Nicaragua del
río de San Juan y del Istmo situado entre el
lago y el oceano Pacífico en el Estado de
Nicaragua, uno de los que componen la
confederación de Centro América. Guatemala:
Imprenta de la Paz, 1838. 23 pp.
    A British naval engineer's description of
the potential Nicaraguan canal route, the
product of a longtime residence in Central
America. The work is clearly designed to
stimulate British interest in the region and
in canal construction, reflecting the British
presence on the eastern approaches of the
route in the Mosquito Territory.

70 Bales, William Leslie. The Nicaraguan Canal.
Quantico, Va.: U.S. Marine Corps, 1930. 51
pp. Biblio.
    A brief survey of the diplomacy involved,
originally written as a master's thesis from
published works. DLC

71 Banco de América. La guerra en Nicaragua
según Frank Leslie's Illustrated Newspaper
(Edición bilingüe). Managua: Banco de
América, 1976. 238 pp.
    A bilingual reproduction of a contemporary
account of the Walker episode, drawn from the
pages of a North American magazine, with text
in English and Spanish.

72 _____. La guerra en Nicaragua según Harper's
Weekly (Edición bilingüe). Managua: Banco de
América, 1976. 182 pp.
    A bilingual reproduction of a contemporary
journalistic account of the Walker intervention in Nicaragua and the resulting conflict,
drawn from the pages of a popular Yankee magazine of that era and printed in English and
Spanish.

73 Barahona, Amaru. El problema agrario en
Nicaragua. Managua: Editorial José Martí,
1971. 45 pp.
    A brief analysis of the agrarian problem in
Nicaragua, consisting principally of a denunciation of the limits of the present program
and contending that drastic land redistribution is indispensable to the nation's
development. VTU

74 Barahona López, Ernesto. Realidades de la
vida nicaragüense: comentarios de problemas
nacionales que necesitan solución. Managua:
Tipografía Excelsior, 1943. 111 pp.
    An examination of present-day Nicaragua and
its problems in the light of social-welfare
doctrines, noting the need for more democracy
as the basis for a national effort to confront

its needs and promote national involvement.
DLC

75 Barberena Pérez, Alejandro. El héroe
nacional: biografía de José Dolores Estrada.
Managua: Librería Cultural Nicaragüense,
1971. 36 pp. Illus.
    A laudatory account of the heroics of a
Nicaraguan general who led the force that
repulsed an attack by a detachment of Walker's
troops at Tipitapa, which constituted the
first defeat of the filibuster by local troops
and guaranteed Estrada's immortality.

76 Barcenas Meneses, José. Las conferencias del
"Denver": actas auténticas de las sesiones
con introducción y ligeros comentarios.
Managua: Tipografía Nacional, 1926.
    The minutes of the Denver conference at
which the United States unsuccessfully
attempted to mediate between the Liberal
forces of Dr. Juan B. Sacasa and the Conservative government of General Emiliano
Chamorro, which constituted part of the maneuvering that eventually led to the installation
of the Yankee-supported regime of Adolfo Díaz.

77 Barquero, Sara Luisa. Centros de interés de
la República de Nicaragua: Managua, León y
Granada. Managua: Talleres Nacionales, 1939.
112 pp.
    A listing and brief discussion of the rea-
sons each of the three cities is a "center of
interest" in Nicaragua, explaining the historic role of each in its region and the
nation. DLC

78 _____. Gobernantes de Nicaragua, 1825-1947.
Managua: Tipografía Cordillo, 1937. 112 pp.
2d ed. Managua: Ministerio de Instrucción
Pública, 1945. 248 pp. Biblio., illus.
    Brief biographical essays, ranging from two
to over twenty pages and arranged chronologically, of each of the individuals who governed Nicaragua during the years in question.
Provides basic data regarding the men and
their regimes, with quotations from secondary
works. DLC LNHT

79 _____. Managua: centro de interés. Managua:
n.p., 1939. 2d ed. Managua: Imprenta
Democrática, 1946. 98 pp. Illus.
    A discussion of the reasons Managua is the
"center of interest" of the republic, citing,
for instance, its function as the governmental
and business center of the nation. DLC

80 Barreto, Mariano. Recuerdos históricos de
Chichigalpa, Corinto, Chinandega y León.
León: Tipografía de La Patria, 1921. 210 pp.
    Brief historical accounts of these four
Nicaraguan cities, beginning with pre-Colonial
times but focusing on the nineteenth and early
twentieth centuries. Includes quotations from
pertinent documents and references to events
of particular significance in the growth of
the city, to its participation in various
national political movements, and to its best-
known citizens. DLC LNHT BNCR

81 Barreto, Pablo Emilio. 44 años de dictadura
somocista. Managua: Talleres Gráficos La
Prensa, 1979. 117 pp. Illus.
    An account of the destruction caused by the
Nicaraguan civil war, by a reporter for the
opposition newspaper La Prensa. A brief text
leaves the emphasis on photos of starving
children and the devastation resulting from
the combat. Contains also a critical account
of the Somoza regime that reflects the charges
made by the revolutionary leaders.

82 Barruel-Beauvert, Philippe Auguste de.
Bombardement et entière destruction de Greytown [sic]: 2 lettre du délégué de la
population française de Grey-town [Nicaragua].
2 vols. Paris: Typographie A. Lebon, 1856.
42, 41 pp.
    A French resident of Greytown, Nicaragua
(San Juan del Norte), provides a sensational-
istic account, in the form of two lengthy
letters, of the United States bombardment of
the city in 1854. The first letter describes
the incident; the second details the losses
suffered by French residents and demands redress from the United States, requesting the
French government to press their claims. DLC
LNHT

83 Bass, John Meredith. William Walker. N.p.,
n.d. [Nashville, 1898]. 16 pp.
    A pro-Walker tract, based on secondary
sources, lamenting his lack of fame in the
United States and the actions of the government in opposing him. TxU

84 Baus, Ruth, and Emily Harvin. Who's Running
this Expedition! New York: Coward-McCann,
1959. 256 pp. Illus., maps.
    A humorous travelogue account of the auth-
ors' adventures exploring jungles and virgin
rivers while struggling with the local customs
in the remote interior of Nicaragua during the
1950s. Combines accounts of their travel
problems with discussion of the customs encountered and the problems they caused. The
emphasis is on picturesque description, exotica, and adventure. DLC

85 Bayo Giroud, Alberto. Tempestad en el Caribé.
Mexico: n.p., 1950. 209 pp. Notes.
    A Spanish military officer reports his
experiences serving with the Caribbean Legion,
explains his hatred of dictatorships, and
recounts his participation in the campaigns
of the group in Nicaragua and the Dominican
Republic. The bulk of the volume is devoted
to the 1948-49 campaign against the Somoza
regime. DLC BNCR

86 Beals, Carlton. Con Sandino en Nicaragua.
San José: Imprenta Alsina, 1928. 75 pp.
    A series of articles by a Yankee reporter,
originally written for the Nation, a liberal
muckraking journal. Reports on a visit with
the Nicaraguan guerrilla and on his travels
with the rebels during engagements with U.S.
forces. This series emphasizes the aspirations of Sandino and the evils of Yankee imperialism, a stance characteristic of the

Nation, and offers a parallel to the later role of the Yankee press in the Castro revolution in Cuba, though in this case Sandino never quite "caught on" in the U.S. This edition was reprinted by the Costa Rican pro-Sandino Committee and shows the efforts to use the reporting to popularize Sandino in Latin America, again paralleling the Castro episode. DLC-LDS-780 BNCR

87 Belausteguigoitia, Ramón de. <u>Con Sandino en Nicaragua: la hora de la paz</u>. Madrid: Espasa-Calpe, 1934. 244 pp.

A sympathetic account of Sandino's revolt, hailing his "moral" impulse and defense of his nation's rights. Consists principally of an account of the author's travels into the interior of Nicaragua to meet with the guerrilla leader and the resulting series of interviews with Sandino and his lieutenants, as well as enthusiastic descriptions of his forces and their spirit. The account seeks to extend his fame outside his nation by familiarizing others with his stands and with the degree of support he enjoyed among the rural populace. DLC LNHT

88 Bell, Charles Napier. <u>Tangweera: Life and Adventures among Gentle Savages</u>. London: Edward Arnold, 1899. xi, 318 pp. Index, illus., appendixes.

An account of an Englishman's boyhood, spent in the Mosquito region at Bluefields. Recounts in vivid detail and rich description the flora and fauna, the life and customs of the inhabitants, living conditions, and his adventures, with emphasis on the latter. Includes descriptions of the places he visited and the people he saw. The volume was written forty years later, based on notes taken at the time; hence the era covered is that of the late 1840s. DLC LNHT

89 Belly, Félix. <u>À travers l'Amérique Centrale: le Nicaragua et le canal interocéanique</u>. 2 vols. Paris: Libraire de la Suisse Romande, 1867. ix, 430 pp. Maps, appendixes. 2d ed. Paris: Librairie de Joel Cherbuliez, 1870. Maps. <u>A través de la América Central: Nicaragua y el canal interocéanico</u>. San José: Imprenta Gutenberg, 1929.

Although focused on the canal, this study is also a detailed geographical description of the entire isthmus and a review of the nineteenth-century history of the various countries. Considers the various canal routes but discusses in detail the Nicaragua route and its prospects. Includes technical information regarding engineering and financing. The author clearly considers the Nicaragua route the best and notes that in view of Suez, France can hardly doubt the feasibility of its construction. DLC LNHT BNCR

90 ____, ed. <u>Carte d'étude pour le tracé et le profil du canal de Nicaragua par M. Thomé de Gammond, précédée de documents publiés sur cette question</u>. Paris: Dalmont et Dunot, 1858. 90 pp. Maps.

A collection of documents relating to the Nicaragua canal, including the Anglo-American treaties, followed by a brief description of the route and necessary works, with a huge detailed map. Argues for the feasibility of the Nicaragua route. DLC

91 Belly, Félix. <u>Percement de l'isthme de Panama par le canal de Nicaragua: exposé de la question</u>. Paris: Aux Bureaux de la Direction du Canal, 1858. 177 pp. Biblio., maps. 2d ed. Paris: Bureaux de la Direction du Canal, et Librairie Novelle, 1859. 113 pp. Maps. <u>Apertura del Istmo Americano--Canal de Nicaragua</u>. Paris: En las Oficinas de la Dirección del Canal, 1859. 114 pp. Maps. <u>Durchbruch der Amerikanischen Landenge. Kanal von Nicaragua</u>. Übersetzt von Karl Schöbel. Paris: Bei der Direcktion der Kanals, 1859. 103 pp. Maps.

Another review of the canal question favoring the Nicaragua route. Written by a French scholar it extols the Convention of Rivas signed by him in 1858, whereby both Costa Rica and Nicaragua gave a French company rights to the San Juan River route. Includes details of the accord, arguments favoring the Nicaragua route and French construction of that route, data regarding the significance of the canal, a defense of European involvement, a rejection of the applicability of the Monroe Doctrine, and an endorsement by Louis Napoleon. The first edition praises the stability and potential of both Nicaragua and Costa Rica, and reproduces some pertinent government decrees; the second edition eliminates some of the Nicaraguan material. The Spanish and German translations are based on the second edition. DLC BNCR

92 Belt, Thomas. <u>The Naturalist in Nicaragua: A Narrative of a Residence at the Gold Mines of Chontales: Journeys in the Savannahs and Forests</u>. London: John Murray, 1874. xvi, 403 pp. Index, illus., maps. Latest ed. New York: Dutton, 1928. <u>El naturalista en Nicaragua</u>. Managua: Banco Central de Nicaragua, 1976. 318 pp. Index, illus., maps.

A classic descriptive account written in 1873 by a British geologist, detailing his observations during his residence in Nicaragua during the early 1870s. Flora and fauna in virgin terrain are described in extensive detail, with numerous photographs, drawings, and maps. DLC LNHT

93 Benard, Emilio. <u>Nicaragua and the Interoceanic Canal</u>. Washington, D.C.: n.p., 1874. 19 pp. <u>Nicaragua y el canal interocéanico</u>. Managua: Imprenta Nacional, 1874. 26 pp.

A former Nicaraguan minister in Washington extols the Nicaragua canal route, stressing its advantages over others and arguing for its selection by the United States. DLC DLC-LDS-804

94 Bermúdez, Alejandro. <u>Conclusión e inaguración del Ferrocarril Central</u>. Managua: Tipografía Nacional, 1902. 166 pp.

A volume commemorating the inauguration of the Nicaraguan railroad. BNCR

95 Bizemont, Henri Louis Gabriel de. L'Amérique Centrale et le Canal de Panama. Paris: Librairie de la Société Bibliographique, 1881. iii, 164 pp. Maps. 2d ed. Paris: Tequi, 1895. 164 pp. Maps.
The avowed purpose of this volume is to bring basic facts about Central America to the attention of the European public, but in fact it is an argument for the construction of an isthmian canal, with half the volume devoted to a discussion of the particulars, alternate routes, and the advantages to European commerce. The first half of the book does survey the isthmus, with emphasis on geography and economics. The historical chapter deals mainly with the Colonial era. DLC

96 Black, George. The Nicaraguan Revolution. London: Zed Press, 1980.

97 Black, George, and John Bevan. Loss of Fear: Education in Nicaragua before and after the Revolution. London: World University Service, 1980. 80 pp.

98 Blais, Valeria. Nicaragua: condizioni naturali ed economiche. Rome: Fratelli Treves, 1927. 119 pp. Biblio., illus., maps, tables.
A discussion of the current economy of Nicaragua designed to encourage Italian trade. NN

99 Blanchet, Aristide Paul D'Henrichemont. Canal interocéanico maritimo de Nicaragua. Paris: Imprimerie Sire, 1879. 64 pp.
Basically a Spanish edition of the author's 1876 work in French, though with some modifications. Stresses the author's own construction scheme, which he argues will reduce costs. DLC

100 _____. Project d'un canal interocéanique maritime, à grande section à travers le grand isthme américain, par le Nicaragua. Paris: Imprimerie Sire, 1876.
A proposal for a specific plan for an interoceanic canal in Nicaragua, advocating the creation of artificial lakes that would submerge entire valleys to bring the passage by lake as close to the ocean as possible, thus minimizing the canal portions, though locks would still be required. The author argues that such methods would reduce construction costs and minimize maintenance problems. Includes a letter of support from the Costa Rican legation in France. DLC

101 _____. Transit interocéanique par le Nicaragua, de Corinto, sur le Pacifique, à San Juan del Norte (Greytown) sur l'Atlantique. Paris: Imprimerie Sire, 1882.
A flier advocating the Nicaragua canal route. DLC

102 Blanco de Gómez, Margarita, ed. Bibliografías agrícolas de América Central: Nicaragua.

Turrialba: Instituto Interamericano de Ciencas Agrícolas, 1972. 135 pp.
A listing of books and articles relating to agriculture; emphasizes items published locally. DPU

103 Blanco Fombona, Horacio. Crímenes del imperialismo norteamericano. Mexico: Ediciones "Churubusco," 1927. 144 pp. Index.
A series of articles, originally published in the Mexican newspaper Excelsior, providing a ringing denunciation of the Yankee intervention in Nicaragua. Includes separate essays on the alleged "crimes" of the Yankees, detailing oppression, as well as thematic essays tracing the policy behind the intervention and denouncing it as a threat to all Latin America, citing comment from the hemispheric press. DLC

104 Board of Trade of San Francisco. Report of Special Committee on Inter-Oceanic Canal. San Francisco: Dempster Bros., 1880. 33 pp.
See item NI418.

105 Body, John E. The Inter-Oceanic Canal via Nicaragua. New York: Slote & Janes, 1870. 23 pp.
An address to the stockholders of the American Atlantic and Pacific Ship Canal Company and several other canal groups, delivered on 24 June 1870 by the president of the Central American Transit Company. He stresses the value and feasibility of a Nicaraguan canal and extols its prospects, calling for continued efforts to bring the project to completion through Yankee private enterprise. DLC LNHT

106 Bolaños Álvarez, Pio. Obras de don Pio Bolaños. 2 vols. Managua: Banco de América, 1976-77. 714, 345 pp. Illus.
A collection of the works of this Conservative political figure, journalist, and diplomat of the early twentieth century. The initial volume includes his books, reprinting his La ciudad trágica: monografía de Granada, a history of his native city from independence through the 1890s; his Memorias, which emphasizes his career, foreign travels and service abroad; and his La situación económica de Nicaragua, which deals with the Yankee intervention in the Díaz regime and the debts of the nation. The second volume reproduces various essays and articles written for the press, in which he comments on a wide range of subjects including cultural factors, leading Nicaraguan political figures of the day, and historical figures from throughout the hemisphere. LNHT BNCR

107 Bolaños Geyer, Alejandro. El filibustero Clinton Rollins. Masaya: Editorial San José, 1976. 147 pp. Notes, illus.
An interesting study of the role of Clinton Rollins in the Walker episode and its history, demonstrating that Rollins was not among the group and that his series of articles in the

(Bolaños Geyer, Alejandro)
   San Francisco Chronicle, later published in
   book form in Spanish and purporting to be the
   memoirs of a participant, were in fact based
   heavily on and at times plagiarized from
   Walker's memoirs. Rollins's true identity was
   determined through the copyright of the original series, revealing him as Henry Clinton
   Parkhurst, a Civil War veteran and writer.
   Includes details of Parkhurst's life,
   paragraph-by-paragraph comparisons of his
   articles with Walker's memoirs, and other
   pertinent documents. See item NI508. LNHT

108 _____, ed. *El testimonio de Scott*. Managua:
   Banco de América, 1975. 363 pp. Index,
   notes.
   An annotated translation of the testimony
   of one Captain Joseph N. Scott in a New York
   court case in 1861 involving Cornelius
   Vanderbuilt. Describes his years of service
   as representative of Vanderbuilt's company in
   Nicaragua, including rich detail on the efforts to control the transit route and San
   Juan del Norte, his link to William Walker,
   and details about conditions on the then remote and virtually independent Atlantic Coast
   of Nicaragua. The editor obtained the court
   records from the U.S. National Archives and
   translated them, providing explanatory annotations. LNHT

109 Bonaparte, Louis Napoleon. *Canal of
   Nicaragua, or a Project to Connect the
   Atlantic and Pacific Oceans by Means of a
   Canal*. London: Mills & Son, 1846. 70 pp.
   Maps.
   A plan for a Nicaraguan canal, focusing on
   its financing and practicality. Based on a
   plan drawn by the Nicaraguan envoy in Europe,
   Francisco de Castellón, who sought to obtain
   European financing for the construction of a
   canal and in particular offered the plan to
   the French prince as a means of countering
   British actions on the Mosquito Coast, in
   effect proposing a French protectorate over
   Nicaragua and control of the canal in return
   for ousting the British from the eastern
   coast. The plan later collapsed when Louis
   Napoleon lost interest. LNHT

110 Bone, Roberto C., ed. *El gobierno liberal de
   Nicaragua: documentos, 1893-1908*. Managua:
   Tipografía Internacional, 1909. 698 pp.
   An official compilation of decrees, laws,
   proclamations, etc., from the years in question, indicating the principal activities of
   the Zelaya regime. DLC BNCR

111 Bonilla, José María, ed. *Colección
   de tratados internacionales de Nicaragua*.
   Managua: Tipografía Internacional, 1909.
   viii, 564 pp. Illus.
   A complete collection of the full texts of
   all treaties signed by Nicaragua with the
   other Central American republics from independence to the date of publication, including
   the general and federal pacts and those with
   each nation, arranged chronologically by nation. DLC BNCR

112 Bonilla, T.G. *El matrimonio o sea el código
   de la familia y sus efectos civiles, en
   conformidad a las leyes vigentes en la
   República examinadas y comentadas*. Managua:
   Tipografía Nacional, 1894. iii, 243 pp.
   Notes.
   A description and analysis of the civil
   code promulgated in 1894 in Nicaragua to regulate marriage and define family rights. Discusses chapter by chapter its provisions,
   tracing their origins in Roman and Spanish law
   and explaining the rationale of the legal
   strictures. DLC

113 Booth, John A. *The End and the Beginning:
   The Nicaraguan Revolution*. Boulder, Colo.:
   n.p., 1981. 225 pp. Index, notes, illus.,
   maps, tables.
   An examination of the origins and nature of
   the 1978-79 civil war, focusing on the uniqueness of the Sandinista revolution and its
   relation to other liberation movements of the
   world. Includes a brief capsule of Nicaraguan
   history to trace the origins of the conflict.
   The final portion summarizes the junta's initial efforts and the social and economic
   changes the Sandinistas were seeking to
   promote. DLC

114 Borgen, José María. *Una incursión por la
   Costa Atlántica*. Managua: Tipografía
   Nacional, 1924. 49 pp. Maps. 2d ed.
   Managua: Tipografía Nacional, 1925. 74 pp.
   Maps.
   A brief travel account of the author's
   voyages and visits in 1923 to San Juan,
   Bluefields, and other points along the
   Nicaraguan and Costa Rican Caribbean coast,
   with emphasis on the towns. Includes some
   account of the area's history as he under-
   stands it. DLC

115 Borring, Majken. *Oprørsdage i Nicaragua:
   En kvindelig dansk Mediciners Oplevelser*.
   Copenhagen: Reitzel, 1930. 202 pp.
   An account of the turbulent politics of
   Nicaragua during the 1920s, written by a
   Danish doctor who worked in that nation during
   those years; focuses on the armed conflict and
   the maneuvers of the various leaders. Includes comments on the contemporary figures,
   the social milieu, and the health services of
   the nation, and provides an informed outsider's view of its politics and of the role
   of the Yankees. LNHT

116 Bravo, Fermín A. *Revolución de 1903:
   pedestal de gloria del general don Emiliano
   Chamorro Vargas*. Managua: Editorial San
   Rafael, 1971. 37 pp. Illus.
   A pro-Conservative summary of the 1903
   Nicaraguan rebellion that sought unsuccess-
   fully to unseat the regime of José Santos
   Zelaya, hailing the leadership of General
   Emilio Chamorro. DLC

117 Briceño, Henry. *Un ejército dentro de un
   ejército*. San José: Imprenta Borrasé, 1979.
   100 pp. Illus.
   Denounces the Somoza regime, its use of the
   Guardia Nacional and particularly the Basic

Infantry Training School, while hailing the efforts of the Sandinistas, with numerous photos of "martyrs," Sandinista leaders, and the destruction caused by the civil war. FU

118 Brindeau, Auguste. Histoire de la Mission Morave à la Côte des Mosquitos (Nicaragua) de 1849 à 1921. Strasbourg: Imprimerie Centrale Ch. Hiller, 1922. 138 pp. Illus.
An account of the development and activities of the Moravian missions on the eastern coast of Nicaragua through World War I, with details of the various posts, description of the terrain and culture of the Mosquito Indians, and comments about their principal vices as viewed by the missionaries, exhibiting the usual European attitudes. The study notes that after World War I the control of the missions in this region was transferred to the Moravian Church's branch in the United States, whereas they had been supervised from Europe until that time. DLC

119 British Central American Land Company. The New British Colony, Province of Victoria, in Central America. London: J. Cunningham, 1840. 16 pp. Maps.
A pamphlet extolling the virtues of the planned colony of the British Central American Land Company on the Mosquito Coast, emphasizing its potential but avoiding any hint of the Nicaraguan claims to the area and the resulting questions regarding the legitimacy of the British actions. Reflects one of several British efforts to colonize the Mosquito region. DLC

120 Brown, Robert David, Jr., P.L. Ward, and George Plafker. Geologic and Seismologic Aspects of the Managua, Nicaragua, Earthquake of December 23, 1972. Washington, D.C.: GPO, 1973. vi, 34 pp. Biblio., illus.
A detailed analysis of the quake, noting that it was centered directly under Managua and attributing the devastation to this factor and to the poor construction of buildings, as well as to the number of geological faults under the city. Includes scientific descriptions of the characteristics of the quake. DLC

121 Brownlee, Roland Holt. Cooperación económica de Los Estados Unidos con Nicaragua. Managua: Imprenta Democrática, 1945. 39 pp.
A brief survey of Nicaraguan-American economic cooperation during World War II, noting joint efforts to produce items and U.S. supply of Nicaraguan needs, with a concluding chapter about postwar prospects for expansion of the economic linkage. DLC LNHT

122 Buitrago Matus, Nicolás. León: la sombra de pedrarias: monografía historica. Managua: n.p., 1966. 343 pp. Illus.
A history of León from 1524 through 1882, originally published as a series of articles in the Revista Conservadora. Includes chapters on the railroads and on conflicts, revolutions, and other significant events that indicate the role of the city in the nation's

development, including extensive quotations from documents. DLC

123 Bülow, Alexander von. Der Freistaat Nicaragua in Mittel-Amerika und seine Wichtigkeit für den Welthandel den Ackerbau and die Colonisation: nach eigener Anschauung und mit besonderer Bezugnahme auf die Berliner Colonisations-Gesellschaft für Central-Amerika dargestellt von Freiherrn A. von Bülow. viii, 139 pp. Maps, tables.
A description of Nicaragua in the midnineteenth century, its economy, physical setting, resources, and prospects, and of the concession for the formation of a German colony; clearly designed to encourage potential settlers. DLC LNHT

124 Bunau Varilla, Philippe Jean. Nicaragua or Panama: The Substance of a Series of Conferences made before the Commercial Club of Cincinnati . . . before the Princeton University in New Jersey, etc., and of a Formal Address to the Chamber of Commerce of the State of New York. New York: Knickerbocker Press, 1901. 32 pp.
The case for the Panama route as expounded by the French Company's lawyer and principal lobbyist in the U.S. Emphasizes the work of the French Company and the greater ease of construction in Panama owing to the shorter route, as against the problems posed by the Nicaragua route. DLC LNHT

125 Bustillo U., Acisclo J. Consideraciones políticas: paralelo entre dos gobernantes centroamericanos. San José: Tipografía La Tiqueterhi, 1910. 13 pp.
An attack on the government of Zelaya in Nicaragua, using a comparison to the regime of Estrada Cabrera in Guatemala and contending that the political evils vastly outweigh any economic benefits to the nation, written by an individual who supported the rebellion against the Zelaya regime. DLC DLC-LDS-480

126 Butterworth, Hezekiah. Lost in Nicaragua . . . or, Among Coffee Farms and Banana Lands in the Countries of the Great Canal. Boston and Chicago: W.A. Wilde, 1898. 294 pp. Illus.
A rambling and colorful travelogue by an experienced travel-book writer, who describes his adventures in Nicaragua. The focus is on the picturesque and adventurous, despite the contention that the volume is designed to describe the resources and potential of the region. DLC LNHT

127 Cabrales, Luís Alberto. Sinopsis de la República de Nicaragua. Managua: Talleres Nacionales, 1937. 46 pp.
A summary of the state of Nicaraguan development at the time of writing, including geographic description and an outline of the political system. LNHT

128 Calabrese, Elisa, ed. Ernesto Cardenal: poeta de la liberación latinoamericana.

Buenos Aires: Editorial Fernando García
Cambeiro, 1975. 190 pp. Notes.
 A collection of critical essays about
Cardenal's works, all hailing his antidictatorial pro-social justice content and acclaiming him as the voice of Latin America, whose
message has a significance for the entire
continent. DLC

129 Calatayud Bernabeu, José. Manolo Cuadra: el
yo y las circunstancias. Managua: Editorial
Hospicio, 1968. 175 pp. Biblio., appendixes.
 A biographical and literary study of this
Nicaraguan poet, tracing his life and the
influences upon him of his generation and its
literary trends; includes the national political and economic circumstances and traces the
leftward swing in his works. Provides analysis of his use of personal experience and
various themes and forms, a chronology of his
life, a bibliography of his works, and selections from some of them. Originally a thesis.
DLC

130 Calderón Ramírez, Salvador. Alrededor de
Walker. San Salvador: Ministerio de
Instrucción Pública, 1929. 171 pp. Biblio.
 An account of the Walker expeditions in
Nicaragua and the resulting combats, emphasiz-
ing the filibuster's ambitions to dominate the
entire isthmus, characterizing him as a
caudillo. Based on secondary sources and
accounts by a survivor of the expedition.
DLC-LDS-762 BNCR

131 _____. Últimos días de Sandino. Mexico:
Ediciones Bota, 1934. 163 pp. Illus.
 An account of the last days of Sandino,
based on published accounts, viewing him sympathetically but without passion, and providing a sketch of the times and his activities
as well as of his assassination by General
Somoza. DLC LNHT BNCR

132 Calero Orozco, Adolfo. Así es Nicaragua:
cuentos. Madrid: Editorial Orytec, 1976.
238 pp.
 A collection of short stories by a well-
known Nicaraguan writer using the local setting and seeking to capture the spirit and
attitudes of the nation. LNHT

133 _____. Cuentos nicaragüenses. Managua:
Academia Nicaragüense de la Lengua, 1957. 176
pp. 2d ed. Madrid: Editorial Magisterio
Español, 1970. 154 pp.
 Short stories of life on the Nicaraguan
Atlantic Coast, using local customs, settings,
and idioms. DLC LNHT

134 _____. Cuentos pinoleros y otros cuentos.
Managua: Editorial Nuevos Horizontes, 1944.
134 pp.
 A collection of short stories which, though
they deal with general themes, are set in
Nicaragua and seek to convey the local concerns and ambience. The volume was selected
by the Ministry of Education as one of the
nation's most important literary works. DLC
BNCR

135 _____. Sangre santa. Managua: Editorial
Atlántida, 1940. 186 pp. 4th ed. Madrid:
Editorial Paránifo, 1973. 283 pp.
 A semiautobiographical novel based on the
Liberal-Conservative civil war in Nicaragua
during the 1920s and early 1930s. Uses real
individuals, places, and events, but mixes
them with fictional characters and employs
literary license to fill in events during the
campaign. The story focuses on the guerrillas
in the north and their plans, actions, and
problems, dramatizing them and seeking to
capture their emotion and life-style in the
field. DLC LNHT

136 Caligaris, Ángel. La Costa Atlántica de
Nicaragua y su porvenir económico. Managua:
Tipografía Nacional, 1901. 12 pp.
 Despite the title this is a pamphlet justi-
fying the soundness of the Banco Atlántico
Americano, which operated on the Nicaraguan
Atlantic Coast, citing the bank's balance
sheet and extolling the potential of the re-
gion in which it operates. DLC

137 _____. El gobierno de Nicaragua, el
empréstito Europeo y la compañía de
aguardiente. Managua: Tipografía Moderna,
1910. 126 pp.
 A collection of documents, with a brief
introduction, stating the Nicaraguan case in a
loan dispute; involves the legality of accords
and the guarantees provided through assignment
of the incomes of certain state monopolies,
which were later suppressed by subsequent
governments for internal political reasons.
Contains the loan agreement as well as pertinent legislative decrees and diplomatic exchanges. DLC

138 Camejo, Pedro, and Fred Murphy, eds. The
Nicaraguan Revolution. New York: Pathfinder
Press, 1979. Illus.
 A collection of broadsides, statements, and
documents relating to the Sandinista revolution and its official stance, explaining its
plans. DLC

139 Cameron, Arnold Guyot. America's Opportunity
in Nicaragua. New York: National Financial
News, 1925. 27 pp. Illus., maps.
 A brief exposition by the editor of the
National Financial News, who argues that
the United States needs a second canal in
Nicaragua in addition to the existing Panama
route, contending that World War I showed the
danger of relying on a single such canal that
could fall into enemy hands. He stresses the
advantages of Nicaragua, especially its location and potential importance, dismissing and
rebutting previous objections to that route,
and emphasizing the political ties between
Nicaragua and the United States. DLC

140 Campos Meléndez, Silvio. Un pueblo y su
conductor: terremoto de Nicaragua 1972.
Managua: Editorial San José, 1973. 151 pp.
Illus., maps.
 A brief account of the 1972 earthquake in
Managua, with photos of the destruction and

(Campos Meléndez, Silvio)
discussion of the reconstruction plans and the
agencies involved. DLC

141 _____. *Somoza ante la historia*. Managua:
Editorial San José, 1972. 363 pp. Biblio.,
illus., tables.

142 Campos Ponce, Xavier. *Los Yanquis y Sandino*.
Mexico: Ediciones X.C.P., 1962. 278 pp.
Index, illus.
A sympathetic account of Sandino and his
efforts, written in journalistic fashion by a
Mexican reporter. Includes a series of fif-
teen articles based on his interviews with
Sandino in Veracruz in 1929, originally pub-
lished in that year in the Mexican newspaper
La Prensa, and a series of essays detailing
Sandino's later campaigns and death, which
consist principally of excerpts from his press
statements, letters, comments, and press
accounts of his death. WU

143 *Canal Maritime Interoceanique de Nicaragua*.
Paris: Imprimerie A. Jolliet, 1877. 34 pp.
A collection of correspondence, conces-
sions, and summaries of canal plans. DLC

144 Cannabrava, Paulo. *Tras los pasos de Sandino:
Nicaragua 1978*. Madrid: Ediciones Encuentro,
1978. 174 pp.
A sympathetic history of Sandino and his
fight against the U.S. Marines. DLC

145 Canton, Alfredo. *¡A sangre y fuego!* San
José: Imprenta Lehmann, 1935. 500 pp.
Illus.
A rambling novel acclaiming the guerrilla
hero General Augusto César Sandino while condemning General Anastacio Somoza García and
the Yankee imperialists. Employs flashbacks
and visions of Indian deities and caciques,
and hence entails the narration of real and
supposed episodes that range through
Nicaraguan history from pre-Columbian times
to the 1930s. The emphasis is always on
caudillos, corrupt politics, and Yankee imperialism. The final vision of the Indian deity
shows Sandino being welcomed to heaven in the
hall of heroes by Bolívar, Martí, San Martín,
Washington, and others, while Somoza is being
welcomed to Hell by the Devil, Cain, and similar figures. DLC   DLC-LDS-795

146 Cardenal, Ernesto. *Antología*. Buenos Aires:
Ediciones Carlos Lohlé, 1971. 214 pp. 3d ed.
San José: EDUCA, 1975. 225 pp.
An anthology compiled by the author, who is
a representative of that nation's generation
of 1940. He has studied in the United States,
participated in the 1954 rebellion in his
native land, and has been a novice in a seminary in the Northern Colossus and later in
another in Mexico. Considered one of his
nation's outstanding poets, his works include
historical themes such as the war against the
Walker intervention, the poetry of rebellion
and political activism, descriptions of his
life in the monasteries, and poems dealing
with the idyllic life of the pre-Columbian

Indian civilizations of Central America, as
well as some dealing with more general themes
or with Yankee and European subjects. LNHT
BNCR

147 _____. *Canto nacional*. Buenos Aires:
Ediciones Carlos Lohlé, 1973. 58 pp.
A narrative poem deploring present conditions in Nicaragua and calling for its liberation from the Somoza regime, denouncing it as
an oppressor and invoking the spirit of
Sandino while extolling the efforts of the
guerrillas. DLC

148 _____. *Nueva antología poética*. Mexico:
Siglo XXI, 1979. 302 pp.
Another anthology of the works of this
modern poet, reproducing his more recent
works. It reflects his increasing politicization and his denunciation of the Somoza regime, as well as his laudatory views of the
Sandinista revolution, with which he came to
be associated. DLC

149 _____. *Oráculo sobre Managua*. Buenos Aires:
Ediciones Carlos Lohlé, 1973. 72 pp. 2d ed.
N.p.: Agermanament, 1975. 69 pp.
A revolutionary priest-poet writes a cry
for the liberation of Nicaragua, combining
biblical citations with poetry invoking figures from Darío to Marx in parallel columns
hailing the Sandinistas and stressing the need
for armed struggle. DLC LNHT

150 Cardenal Argüello, Luís G. *Mi rebelión: la
dictadura de los Somoza*. Mexico: Ediciones
Patria y Libertad, 1961. 397 pp.
A memoir of the author's rebellion against
the Somoza regime in Nicaragua covering the
years 1954-59. Includes accounts of his period as a guerrilla in the jungle, his capture, torture, imprisonment, and escape,
focusing particularly on 1958. Also provides
accounts of earlier activities and propaganda
efforts against the regime, including contacts
with its leading figures and the Yankee ambassador. LNHT

151 Carmichael, John. *A Letter to Lord Palmerston
on the Destruction of Greytown, by the United
States Corvette "Cyane" on 13th July, 1854*.
Liverpool: Albion Office, 1856. 22 pp. Map.
A British account of the U.S. bombardment
of San Juan, reflecting British attitudes and
claims. CU-B

152 Carr, Albert H.Z. *The World and William
Walker*. New York: Harper & Row, 1963. viii,
289 pp. Index, biblio., illus., maps.
A well-written popular account of the career of Walker, viewing him as a knight-errant
fighting for his ideals; designed for the
general reader of adventure stories. Emphasizes that Walker was not a supporter of slavery and probes his childhood and sex life for
clues to his energy and character through
posthumous psychoanalysis. The image of
Nicaragua comports with the attitudes of
Walker, his cohorts, and contemporaries, and

little is said about the local context. DLC
LNHT BNCR

153 Castejón Fiallos, Michel. Le traité Bryan-
Chamorro et les conflits qu'il a provoqués en
Amérique Centrale. Paris: Association des
Etudiants de Doctorat, 1925. 168 pp. Biblio.
A Nicaraguan jurist's legal defense of the
treaty. CtY

154 Castellón, Francisco. Documentos relativos a
la cuestión de Mosquitos, según la consideran
los estados de Nicaragua, Honduras y El
Salvador. San Salvador: Llevano, 1852.
30 pp.
A brief statement of the official
Nicaraguan claim in its dispute with England
over the Mosquito Territory, by the envoy
representing Nicaragua and Honduras in their
negotiations with the British government.
Includes diplomatic notes stating the claims
of both nations. CU

155 ____. Documentos relativos a la legación de
los estados de Nicaragua y Honduras cerca del
gabinete británico sobre el territorio de
Mosquitos y Puerto de San Juan del Norte.
Granada: Imprenta del Orden, 1851. 124 pp.
The correspondence of the envoy of Honduras
and Nicaragua in negotiations during 1848
regarding the British occupation of San Juan
del Norte, and his efforts to secure British
withdrawal and assert the jurisdictional
rights of the Central American states. Includes his exchanges with the British, supporting documentation, and his reports. The
diplomatic correspondence is in French or
English, with documents and reports in
Spanish. DLC

156 Castellón, Hildebrando A. Diccionario de
nicaraguanismos. Managua: Talleres
Nacionales, 1939. 148 pp. Biblio., illus.
A collection of local idioms, terms, and
place names employed in Nicaragua, arranged in
dictionary form with definitions and explanations of their origins, often tracing them to
the various Indian dialects of the area. DLC
BNCR

157 Castilla Urbina, Miguel de. Educación para la
modernización en Nicaragua. Buenos Aires:
Editorial Paidos, 1972. 162 pp. Biblio.
A topical survey of Nicaraguan education,
providing a brief historical résumé and a
description of the situation since 1961, focusing on the present, detailing the evolution
of the schools, national legislation, population trends, funding, etc. Concludes that the
nation needs a major expansion of its educational system; recommends a substantial budgetary increase to meet the needs of the
population, decentralization of the educational system, and a major effort to prepare
adequate and updated textbooks and furnish
them to all schools. LNHT

158 Castillo, Juan del. American Intervention in
Nicaragua: Dr. Manuel E. Araujo before the
[sic] History: Attitude of the Government of
El Salvador; Intervención Americana en

Nicaragua: actitud del gobierno de la
República de El Salvador: El Dr. Manuel E.
Araujo ante la historia. New Orleans: n.p.,
1912. 20 pp.
A brief folio reprinting the messages and
proclamations of Araujo and his exchanges with
Nicaraguans and the United States in seeking
to prevent the Yankee intervention in
Nicaragua. The texts are provided in both
Spanish and English, the latter exhibiting
some translation problems. LNHT

159 Castillo Ibarra, Carlos. Los Judas de
Sandino, 11 aniversario del asesinato del
libertador Gral. Augusto César Sandino.
Mexico: n.p., 1945. 47 pp.
An emotional review of the events surrounding Sandino's assassination, written on its
eleventh anniversary to keep his memory alive
and continue to condemn the Somoza regime and
encourage opposition to it. DLC

160 Castrillo Gámez, Manuel. Estudios históricos
de Nicaragua. Managua: Editorial Asel, 1947.
xxv, 170 pp. Illus.
An account of the war against William
Walker. Written to focus on the role of a
member of the author's family, Salvador
Castrillo Medina, and win his place in history, it also deals with a broader question of
the fight against the filibustering expedition
as a unifying force for Nicaragua and also for
the rest of Central America. The articles
were originally published in the journal Orbe,
but are expanded here. Most of the data is
drawn from previously published works on the
era, though there are some broader comparisons
to the general concepts of history as enunciated by the Greeks. DLC LNHT

161 ____. Próceres nicaragüenses y artículos
históricos. Managua: Talleres Nacionales,
1961. 322 pp. Illus.
A series of essays dealing with important
figures and significant events in the nation's
history. The biographies offer useful overviews of the selected individuals, although
the list is disparate and no selection criteria are indicated. Includes figures from
both the Colonial and modern eras, with some
documentary quotations. DLC LNHT

162 ____. Reseña histórica de Nicaragua:
comprende desde el año 1887 hasta fines de
1895. Managua: Talleres Nacionales, 1963.
580 pp.
An account of Nicaraguan history covering
the years 1887-95 in considerable detail, with
extensive reproductions from the documents.
Traces in narrative form the political maneuvers and constant civil warfare, beginning and
ending abruptly. LNHT

163 ____. Vocabulario de voces nicaragüenses y
artículos históricos. Managua: Imprenta
Nacional, 1966. 238 pp. Illus.
A hundred-page-long dictionary of
Nicaraguan words and idioms, followed by a
collection of historical commentaries on a
wide range of events in the nation's history

and disparate general themes. Includes observations regarding boundary disputes and various political movements and rebellions of the
nineteenth century, as well as Colonial
themes, intermixing them with such general
items as a commentary on the Sermon on the
Mount. WU

164 Castro Silva, Juan María. Catástro de miñas
del distrito de Puerto Cabezas. Managua:
Talleres Nacionales, 1944. 174 pp. Maps.
A listing, alphabetically by name, of all
the mines operating in this region, with brief
entries providing the date initiated, the
mineral mined, the location, and ownership;
based on tax records. DLC LNHT

165 _____. Nicaragua económica. Managua:
Ministerio de la Gobernación, 1949. 115 pp.
A factual résumé of the state of the
Nicaraguan economy in 1949, covering all as-
pects, with appropriate statistics. DLC

166 Central American Court of Justice. Decision
and Opinion of the Court on the Complaint of
the Republic of Costa Rica against the Republic of Nicaragua, Growing out of a Convention
Entered into by the Republic of Nicaragua with
the United States of America for the Sale of
the San Juan River and Other Matters (September 30, 1916). Washington, D.C.: Gibson
Brothers, 1916. 60 pp.
The text of the decision ruling that the
Bryan-Chamorro Treaty violates the existing
boundary accord governing Costa Rican navigation rights on the San Juan River, with full
legal reasoning. DLC DLC-LDS-682

167 _____. Sentencia pronunciada en el juicio
promovido por el gobierno de la República de El
Salvador contra el gobierno de la República de
Nicaragua por la celebración del Tratado
Bryan-Chamorro. 9 de marzo de 1917. San
José: Sociedad Editora Nacional, 1917.
75 pp.
The Republic of El Salvador Against the Republic of Nicaragua: Opinion and Decision of the
Court. Washington, D.C.: Gibson Brothers,
1917. 83 pp.
The official text of the decision ruling
against the validity of the Bryan-Chamorro
Treaty on the basis that it violates existing
accords and the Salvadoran rights to the Bay
of Fonseca. This position was rejected by
Nicaragua and the Woodrow Wilson administration in the United States, who together
ignored the court's ruling, thereby demonstrating its impotence and leading to its
demise. DLC DLC-LDS-682 BNCR

168 Cerutti, Franco, ed. Los editoriales de "La
Prensa." Managua: Banco de América, 1977.
459 pp. Index, notes.
A collection of editorials from the newspaper La Prensa, edited and published by
Enrique Guzmán Selva in 1878, reflecting the
political campaign of that year for the election to replace Pedro Joaquín Chamorro as
president. In addition to its valuable political commentaries, it also offers insights

into Nicaraguan life and daily concerns at
that time, and includes bitter exchanges with
other Nicaraguan papers. All are identified
by date, with references to other papers and
explanations of the events involved by the
editor. DLC LNHT

169 _____. Los pequeñeces cuiscomenas de Antón
Colorado. Managua: Banco de América, 1974.
170 pp. Index.
A collection from a political column that
Guzmán Selva wrote during 1893-1906 under this
title and pseudonym for the newspaper El
Tiempo, commenting in letter form on a wide
range of events, focusing on the political
scene but also discussing social events and
replying to commentaries in other newspapers.
The articles included are all from 1896. References to places and people and to other
newspapers are annotated by the editor. LNHT

170 Chamorro, Diego Manuel. Discursos de 1907 a
1921. Managua: Tipografía Nacional, 1923.
xii, 201 pp.
A collection of speeches by a leading
Nicaraguan Conservative political figure,
offering insights into the political issues,
disputes, and polemicism of the era. TxU

171 _____. El panterismo nicaragüense. N.p.:
Imprenta Pujol, 1898. 45 pp.
A defense of the politics of the Nicaraguan
Conservative party by one of its leaders,
attacking the Zelaya regime and replying to
propaganda critical of the Conservative efforts while detailing what he calls the crimes
of Zelaya. DLC BNCR

172 Chamorro, Fruto. La ruidosa quiebra.
Granada: Tipografía de El Centro-Americano,
1898. 31 pp.
MH-L

173 Chamorro, Pedro Joaquín. Entre dos filos:
novela nicaragüense. Managua: Tipografía
Nacional, 1927. 422 pp.
A novel by a prominent political figure,
set in Granada, Nicaragua. Details life in
that region and the problems of local politics, using the local settings, traditions,
and idioms. NN

174 _____, ed. Obras históricas completas del
Lic. Jerónimo Pérez, impresas por disposición
del excelentísimo señor presidente de la
República, don Adolfo Díaz. Managua:
Imprenta Nacional, 1928. ix, 854 pp. Index,
notes, illus., appendixes. 2d ed. Managua:
Banco de América, 1975. 875 pp.
A collection of historical commentaries by
a Conservative writer and political figure,
with lengthy narrations of the political
maneuvers and civil wars of the 1850s, including the campaign against the Walker expedition, all written from a Conservative
viewpoint. Includes extensive quotations from
contemporary proclamations and announcements.
The volume also provides several separate
biographies of Nicaraguan political figures,
including Manuel Antonio de la Cerda, Juan

Argüello, Tomás Martínez, and Crisanto Sacasa.
DLC LNHT BNCR

175 Chamorro, Pedro Joaquín. <u>Los pies descalzos
de Nicaragua, 1892-1970</u>. Managua: Imprenta
La Prensa, 1971. 38 pp. Illus., maps.
    A series of articles originally published
in <u>La Prensa</u>, dealing with the current economic development and state of the San Juan
River valley along the southern Nicaragua
border; hails recent progress but notes additional needs. LNHT

176 _____. <u>El último filibustero (William
Walker)</u>. Managua: Tipografía Alemana, 1933.
iv, 537 pp.
    An historical novel reconstructing the
Walker adventure in Nicaragua from the local
point of view, using literary license to fill
in details and provide drama and vividness.
DLC LNHT

177 Chamorro Cardenal, Pedro Joaquín. <u>5 p.m.</u>
Managua: Editorial Unión, 1967. 221 pp.
    A collection of editorials from <u>La Prensa</u>,
commenting on current problems and reflecting
the author's opposition to the Somoza regime.
DLC LNHT

178 _____. <u>El derecho del trabajo en Nicaragua</u>.
Mexico: Imprenta Franco, 1948. 110 pp.
Biblio.
    Originally written as a thesis, this early
work by a prominent journalist and Conservative party official examines Nicaraguan labor
law, based on the 1933 code, considering both
individual and collective rights. DLC

179 _____. <u>Diario de un preso</u>. Managua:
Editorial Nuevos Horizontes, 1963. 232 pp.
Illus.
    A Nicaraguan journalist's notes from jail
during one of his periodic incarcerations,
this one a trial for complicity in a 1959
revolutionary effort. A scathing attack on
the Somoza regime, its arbitrariness, and its
use of anticommunism, with criticism of the
inability of the OAS to affect the military
trials in Nicaragua. DLC LNHT

180 _____. <u>Estirpe sangrienta: los Somoza</u>.
Mexico: Patria y Libertad, 1957. 366 pp.
4th ed. Mexico: Editorial Diógenes, 1979.
283 pp.
    A ringing denunciation of the Somoza regime
and an exposé of its methods, in the form of
the memoirs of the author's experience in
prison after his fifth arrest, this time in
connection with a plot against the regime of
General Anastacio Somoza García in 1956. Recounts his experiences and those of others he
encountered in jail, detailing their tortures
and in some cases their deaths. Includes
commentary about the regime and the transition
to the dictator's son, and the complicity of
the United States in supporting the dynasty.
DLC LNHT

181 Chamorro Zelaya, Pedro Joaquín. <u>Don Sofonías
Salvatierra y su "Comentario polémico."</u>
Managua: Editorial La Prensa, 1950. viii,
267 pp. Illus., maps.
    Responding to a response to a previous
book, this work extends the Liberal-
Conservative political battle to the pages of
the history books, continuing the confrontation between Máximo Jérez and Fruto Chamorro.
Jérez was a Liberal hero whom the author criticized in his biography, to which Salvatierra
replied with his own work. In the present
volume Chamorro responds point for point,
contending his opponent produced no new material and said nothing to alter Chamorro's debunking of the status of Jérez, but adds an
entire new volume in reply just in case and
reviews the history of the era yet again.
Includes an essay hailing Fruto Chamorro by
Carlos Cuadra Pasos, another Conservative
Scholar. LNHT

182 _____. <u>Enrique Guzmán y su tiempo</u>. Managua:
Editorial Artes Gráficas, 1965. 422 pp.
Biblio., notes.
    A biography of a well-known Nicaraguan
journalist whose career spanned the years
1878-1911. Traces his shift from Liberalism
to Conservatism in his early years, his later
exile after the Zelaya regime restricted the
press, and his subsequent opposition to that
regime. Includes extensive quotations from
his editorials, letters, and diary. DLC LNHT

183 _____. <u>Fruto Chamorro</u>. Managua: Editorial
Unión, 1960. 425 pp. Biblio., illus., maps.
    A posthumously published volume by this
Nicaraguan Conservative scholar and statesman,
continuing his version of the Liberal-
Conservative civil wars that wracked Nicaragua
during the nineteenth century, as always from
the Conservative viewpoint. Having previously
sought to debunk the standing of the Liberal
heroes, he now presents Fruto Chamorro as the
figure who stabilized the nation and brought
order out of chaos, while consolidating Conservative control. Includes accounts of his
efforts to solve the boundary dispute with
Costa Rica and his involvement in the Walker
campaign, which coincided with his tenure in
office. The subject is a member of the same
family as the author. DLC LNHT

184 _____. <u>Máximo Jérez y sus contemporáneos</u>.
Managua: Editorial La Prensa, 1937. 436 pp.
Biblio. 2d ed. Managua: Editorial La
Prensa, 1948. 436 pp. Biblio.
    A Conservative version of the early history
of Nicaragua, part of the continuing Liberal-
Conservative polemic in the realm of historiography. Criticizes the role of the Liberal
leader Jérez, contending that the independence
movement reflected a reaction against the
chaos of the French Revolution rather than
following its example; supports the efforts of
Fruto Chamorro, an early Conservative leader
of the author's family. The author condemns
the role of Jérez in bringing Walker's troops
to Nicaragua to aid the Liberals in a civil
war. DLC LNHT BNCR

185 Chávez Alfaro, Lizandro. <u>Los monos de San
Telmo</u>. Havana: Casa de las Américas, 1963.
164 pp. Index. 2d ed. Guatemala: EDUCA,
1971. 175 pp.
    A collection of short stories reflecting
themes of social justice, set in the author's
native Nicaragua and evoking strong emotion
about the condition of the poor. Includes
some general and purely fictional themes,
though most have a political message. DLC

186 _____. <u>Trágame tierra</u>. Mexico: Editorial
Diógenes, 1969. 282 pp. 2d ed. Havana:
Casa de las Américas, 1971. 422 pp.
    A novel of the new left by a young
Nicaraguan writer, set in his native land and
conveying a clear political message. Details
a generation gap in which the older generation, having seen political chaos, accepts
limited improvement in economic conditions at
the expense of becoming submissive to the
patriarchs, while the younger generation rejects this attitude, crying out for a more
honorable stand of protest against the marginal improvement and a more drastic change to
launch a new era. DLC LNHT

187 Chávez Zelaya, Máximo Enrique. <u>Bibliografía
de William Walker y el desarrollo de la guerra
nacional contra los filibusteros en Nicaragua
y Costa Rica en 1856-1857</u>. Guatemala:
Publicaciones del Comité General Pro-
Celebración del Centenario de la Campaña de
1856, 1956. 16 pp.
    A brief bibliography listing the principal
Central American works dealing with the Walker
episode, prepared as part of the celebration
of its centennial. BNG

188 Childs, Orville Whitemore. <u>Map and Profile
of the Route for the Construction of a Ship
Canal from the Atlantic to the Pacific Oceans,
across the Isthmus in the State of Nicaragua,
Central America, Surveyed for the American
Atlantic and Pacific Ship Canal Company</u>. New
York: William C. Bryant, 1852. Pages unnumbered. Maps.
    The detailed maps and sketches of the route
survey, without comment, showing construction
details and location. LNHT

189 _____. <u>Report of the Survey and Estimates of
the Cost of Constructing the Inter-Oceanic
Ship Canal, from the Harbor of San Juan del
Norte on the Atlantic, to the Harbor of Brito
on the Pacific, in the State of Nicaragua,
Central America, Made for the Atlantic and
Pacific Ship Canal Co., in the Years 1850-
1851</u>. New York: William C. Bryant, 1852.
ii, 153 pp. Illus., maps, tables.
    A detailed report including the location,
dimensions, and costs of the construction
required for the prospective Nicaraguan canal,
the result of a survey of the terrain. Includes details of the necessary harbors,
locks, types of materials available, specifications of construction, etc. DLC BNCR

190 Cole Chamorro, Alejandro. <u>Desde Sandino hasta
los Somozas</u>. Granada: Editorial El Mundo,
1971. 306 pp. Illus.
    A series of brief items narrating or repro-
ducing comments or documents related to the
various events of Nicaragua's turbulent political scene between 1920 and 1947, tracing the
rebellion of Augusto César Sandino, his death,
the rise of Somoza, his heirs, and the
Liberal-Conservative pact of 1971. While a
disjointed "scissors and paste" volume, it
does provide useful data about some of the
episodes as well as an indication of the important events, even though in many cases it
merely reproduces published statements or
journalistic accounts. CU-B

191 Colindres, Juan. <u>Anastasio Somoza: fin de
una estirpe de ladrones y asesinos</u>. Mexico:
Editorial Posada, 1979. 154 pp. Illus.
    A pro-Sandinista account of the final days
of the Somoza regime. The first half is a
brief overview of the rule of the Somoza family denouncing their actions, leveling charges
of all types of atrocities, and holding the
Yankees responsible. The second half offers
an account of the final Sandinista campaign,
focusing on the seizure of the National Palace; it seeks to demonstrate the popular support of the movement, the bloody conflict that
was necessary, and the inhumanity of the regime. Contains extensive photos illustrating
the rebels, the dead, and the popular manifestations that accompanied the Sandinista victory. DLC LNHT

192 Colquhoun, Archibald Ross. <u>The Key of the
Pacific: The Nicaragua Canal</u>. London:
Constable, 1895. xvii, 443 pp. Index,
illus., maps. 2d ed. New York: Longmans &
Green, 1895. xvii, 443 pp. Illus., map.
    A detailed discussion of the proposed
Nicaraguan canal and its implications for
Yankee commerce. Much of the volume considers
these implications, the importance of Asian
trade, the competition with England, the necessity of fortifying the canal, and details
of Nicaragua, its situation and people. The
major focus is on a technical discussion of
the route and the construction and facilities
needed, with details of a scheme to divert the
San Juan River to improve the harbor at Greytown, offsetting a Spanish diversion completed
in 1670. Includes detailed maps and drawings
of the works, with illustrations of the terrain. Offers considerable information about
Nicaragua in 1895 as well as about the canal.
DLC LNHT

193 Comando Juan José Quezada. <u>Frente Sandinista:
diciembre victorioso</u>. Mexico: Editorial
Diógenes, 1976. 112 pp. Biblio., illus.
    An account by the Sandinista force, calling
itself the Juan José Quezada command, of the
events involved in its seizure on 27 December
1974 of a group of diplomats it held hostage,
followed by the text of the communiqués it
issued during the seizure and insisted be
published as part of the arrangement to release the prisoners. The diarylike account of

the episode, which is awkwardly interspersed with a Sandinista view of recent Nicaraguan history, rambles about condemning the Yankee imperialists, the actions of Somoza, and particularly the profiteering after the 1972 earthquake. Accompanying photos are just as disorganized, ranging from views of the kidnapping, to scenes from the earthquake, to government posters after the quake, to photos of Sandino and his forces. DLC LNHT

194 Comité Cristiano de Solidaridad con el Pueblo de Nicaragua. <u>Monimbo</u>: <u>Tragedia y símbolo de liberación</u>. Managua: n.p., 1979. 127 pp. Illus., tables.

A pro-Sandinista account of the civil war, consisting principally of lists of individuals killed and wounded and photos of the destruction caused by the conflict.

195 Un Conservador de 30 años. <u>En desagravio del Partido Conservador y del señor presidente Díaz</u>. Managua: Tipografía Gutenburg, 1916. 134 pp.

Part of the political polemic that follwed the fall of the dictatorship of José Santos Zelaya, this volume responds, point for point, to the pamphlet by "Un Nicaragüense" entitled <u>La situación económica de Nicaragua</u>, seeking to refute all its contentions. The author defends the record of the Conservative party and attacks the Liberal Zelaya dictatorship, contending that the first pamphlet overlooked the entire civil war and charging gross financial abuses throughout the Zelaya regime, which he contends bankrupted the nation and left it with a large debt. He carefully avoids discussion of the uses to which the regime put the funds. LNHT

196 Conzemius, Eduard. <u>Ethnographical Survey of the Miskito and Sumu Indians of Honduras and Nicaragua</u>. Washington, D.C.: Smithsonian Institution, 1932. vii, 191 pp. Index, biblio., illus.

An extensive collection of data and detailed description based on fieldwork in the region, although there is no indication of the dates when it was conducted. Includes physical description of the territory and inhabitants, information on the economy, description of households, tools, habits, folklore, religious beliefs, hygiene, amusements, and much more. A valuable source about the Indians' life in a region that was still remote and isolated in the early twentieth century. DLC

197 Cordero Reyes, Manuel, C.A. Castro W., and Carlos Pasos. <u>Nicaragua under Somoza</u>: <u>To the Governments and People of America</u>; <u>Nicaragua bajo el régimen de Somoza</u>: <u>a los gobiernos y pueblos de América</u>. San Salvador: Imprenta Funes, 1944. 38 pp.

A denunciation, in Spanish and English, of the political and economic control of the Somoza dictatorship. It was written during the turbulent era when revolts had shaken several of the other dictatorships in the isthmus. The authors, several exiles seeking support from other Latin American nations and

the U.S. for an effort to oust the regime, clearly hoped to utilize the momentum to extend the effort into Nicaragua. DLC

198 Córdoba Boniche, José. <u>Aspectos fundamentales de la reforma agraria en Nicaragua</u>. Mexico: B. Costa-Amic, 1963. 190 pp. Biblio., notes, tables, appendixes.

A denunciation of the Somoza agrarian-reform program generated under pressure from the Alliance for Progress, criticizing the role of the Yankees and contending that the program is inadequate and will benefit the large owners and foreign companies. The author is critical of exporting agricultural products while basic foods are imported, contending that the focus should be on self-sufficiency in food. The commentary is semi-Marxist, with many of the items in the bibliography pertaining to Cuba. DLC LNHT

199 Coronel Matus, Manuel. <u>Mi panterismo en evidencia</u>. Managua: Tipografía Nacional, 1898. 204 pp.

A response to Diego Manuel Chamorro's <u>El panterismo nicaragüense</u>. Like that volume, it details the events of the Liberal uprising of 1897 against the Zelaya regime. The author, a former aide to Zelaya, was accused by Chamorro of arranging the execution of Liberal prisoners. He denies these charges and condemns the rebellion as illegal and criminal, charging Liberal atrocities. Compares quotations from Chamorro's version of events with other published versions, documents, and press accounts, adding commentary pointing up the differences and contending that the other items disprove Chamorro's account and show that it is purely partisan propaganda. DLC LNHT

200 Coronel Urtecho, José. <u>Reflexiones sobre la historia de Nicaragua</u>: <u>de Gaínza a Somoza</u>. 2 vols. León: Instituto Histórico Centroamericano, 1962. 233, 282 pp.

The author seeks to produce a dispassionate narration of Nicaraguan history in broad overview, stating that all Nicaraguan history since independence is that of a continuing civil war. Since the participants, through polemics defending their actions, were virtually the only contributors to the region's historiography, the region's history is part of that civil war, with differing Liberal and Conservative versions that have little in common. The initial volume deals with the Colonial and independence eras, through 1821; it contains extensive discussion of the various societal classes prior to independence and the conditions that made the region ripe for civil conflict. The second volume, principally a narrative of the 1824 conflict and the early Federation period, includes also lengthy quotations from the various laws, proclamations, and speeches. LNHT

201 Cortés Castellón, José Rosalío. <u>El departamento de Chinandega</u>. Managua:

461

Tipografía Nacional, 1928. 39 pp. Illus., map.

A descriptive departmental monograph that compiles current information regarding facilities. NN

202   Corthell, Elmer Lawrence. Exposition of the Errors and Fallacies in the Rear Admiral Ammen's Pamphlet, "The Certainty of the Nicaragua Canal Contrasted with the Uncertainties of the Eads Ship Railway." Washington, D.C.: Gibson Brothers, 1886. 52 pp.

The writer is a backer of the Tehuantepec railway scheme to transport entire ships by rail and refloat them on the other side, which offered cheaper construction than a canal. This pamphlet responds to the admiral's work backing a Nicaragua canal, contending that the admiral altered the facts or made errors in his calculations in his efforts to demonstrate the feasibility of a Nicaragua canal and the impraticality of a Tehuantepec railway. He disputes the admiral on all points, including the levels of the oceans and the appropriateness of the harbors, arguing that a Nicaragua canal is impractical and would be far more difficult to construct than was the Suez Canal. DLC LNHT

203   Costa Rica, Gov't of. Concessions and Decrees of the Republic of Costa Rica to the Nicaragua Canal Association of New York. New York: n.p., 1888. 28 pp.

The accord between Pérez Zeledón and Menocal, with the supplemental decrees of the Costa Rican Congress approving them and furnishing the enabling legislation. DLC

204   _____. Ministerio de Fomento. Contrato sobre canal interoceánico celebrado en San José de Costa Rica el 30 de julio de 1888 por Pedro Peréz Zeledón, secretarío de estado en el despacho de fomento y Aniceto G. Menocal, represante de la asociación respectiva. San José: Tipografía Nacional, 1888. 30 pp.

A Costa Rican effort to promote canalization of the San Juan River by granting the Maritime Canal Company of Nicaragua rights in Costa Rica and the river. DLC DLC-LDS-261 LNHT BNCR

205   _____. Ministerio de Obras Públicas. Proyecto preliminar de canalización: lagunas del Atlántico. San José: Published by the Ministry, 1961. 198 pp. Illus., maps.

A study of the possibility of constructing a canal along the San Juan River, reflecting the dreams and charges regarding the potential of such an effort, the alleged foreign interests opposing it, and its implications for Nicaragua and Costa Rica, as well as technical studies of the feasibility and proposals for appropriate methods. The study concludes that such a canal is clearly feasible, and emphasizes Costa Rica's rights in any such effort. BNCR

206   _____. Ministerio de Relaciones Exteriores. Demanda de la República de Costa Rica contra la de Nicaragua, ante la Corte de Justicia Centroamericana, con motivo de una convención firmada por la segunda con la República de Los Estados Unidos de América, para la venta del Río San Juan y otros objetos. 2 vols. San José: Imprenta Nacional, 1916. Pages unnumbered. Complaint of the Republic of Costa Rica before the Central American Court of Justice Growing Out of a Convention Entered into by the Republic of Nicaragua with the Republic of the United States for the Sale of the San Juan River and Other Matters. Washington, D.C.: Gibson Brothers, 1916. 122, 69 pp.

The formal Costa Rican complaint about the Bryan-Chamorro Treaty, contending that since Costa Rica has navigational rights on the San Juan River, which would be part of the proposed canal route, it must be a party to any accords regarding the canal, with a volume of documents relating to navigation of the waterway. DLC-LDS-797 LNHT BNCR

207   Cox, Isaac Joslin. Nicaragua and the United States, 1909-1927. Boston: World Peace Foundation, 1927. 187 pp. Maps.

An account of the U.S. intervention and involvement in domestic Nicaraguan politics during the 1920s through 1927. Though based on careful research in newspapers and the published exchanges between the governments, it is limited by the problems of contemporary history and the availability of sources at the time. DLC LNHT

208   Craig, Hugh. The Nicaragua Canal: The Gateway between the Oceans. San Francisco: Chamber of Commerce of San Francisco, 1898. 25 pp. Illus., maps, tables.

A statement of the case for the building of a canal, by the president of the San Francisco Chamber of Commerce speaking for the Chamber. Assumes the location is Nicaragua, cites the voyage of the Oregon during the Spanish-American War and the potential impact of the canal on the West Coast. Includes details of the construction of the canal and rhetoric about its necessity for U.S. development, as well as its impact on world trade; tables show how dramatically travel distances would be reduced using a canal as against rounding South America. DLC

209   Cramer, Floyd. Our Neighbor, Nicaragua. New York: Frederick A. Stokes, 1929. 243 pp. Index, illus., maps.

A brief descriptive history of Nicaragua and American influence in it, focusing on the Yankee interventions through 1927 and picturing the Yankees as heroic saviors engaged in a Quijote-like quest for stability against hopeless odds among a people who simply cannot accept peace. Recounts the initial rebellion of Sandino as that of a dissatisfied youth and troublemaker who could have lived happily if he had stayed at home and behaved. The resulting misinterpretation of Nicaragua reflects a prevalent Yankee view of that era. DLC LNHT

210 Crawford, Mattie. <u>On Mule Back Through</u>
<u>Central America with the Gospel</u>.
Indianapolis: Privately published, 1922. 224
pp. Illus.
   A missionary recounts her adventures and
efforts, emphasizing her religious conviction
and the "needs" of the area, focusing primarily on Nicaragua but also describing her
travels en route. DLC

211 Crawley, Eduardo. <u>Dictators Never Die</u>.
London: n.p., 1979. 180 pp. Index, biblio.
<u>Los Dictadores nunca mueren: retrato de</u>
<u>Nicaragua y los Somoza</u>. Caracas: El Diario
de Caracas, 1980. 188 pp. Index, biblio.,
maps.
   An overview of Nicaraguan development seeking to show the antecedents of the current
crisis. Written for the general reader by an
Argentine reporter, it surveys Nicaraguan
history in journalistic fashion, emphasizing
the exploitation and foreign intervention
cited by the Sandinistas, the heroics of
Sandino, and the corrpution of the Somoza
dynasty. Ends in 1978 with the regime on the
verge of collapse. DLC LNHT

212 CSUCA. <u>El sistema educativo en Nicaragua:</u>
<u>situación actual y perspectivas</u>. San José:
CSUCA, 1965. xxiv, 115 pp. Illus., tables.
   See item CR335. DLC LNHT BNCR

213 Cuadra, Abelardo. <u>Hombre del Caribé:</u>
<u>memorias</u>. San José: EDUCA, 1977. 270 pp.
   The memoirs of a controversial figure whose
career has placed him on various sides of the
Nicaraguan political scene. He was one of the
earliest officer trainees of the newly formed
Guardia Nacional and became the lieutenant who
loyally served Somoza and led troops against
Sandino. Later he participated in two revolts
against Somoza from within the Guardia, and
served in the Caribbean Legion. Much of his
life was spent in prison or exile. This volume consists of his handwritten diaries
(though some are more in the form of memoirs
than that of diaries) recounting his version
of the events and his rationale. The introduction by Sergio Ramírez notes the contradictions in Cuadra's career and describes the era
as one when the old political forces, the
Liberal and Conservative parties, were replaced by new ones, namely, the Sandinistas
and the Guardia; it points to the disaffection
of the junior officers in the Guardia as an
indication of the politicization of the force
by Somoza. The diaries are apparently offered
in full, without comment, though the title
page bears a reference to their being
"presentadas y pasadas en limpio" by Ramírez,
a phrase that is never defined. LNHT

214 Cuadra, Manolo. <u>Almidón</u>. Managua: Editorial
Nuevos Horizontes, 1945. 164 pp.
   A poignant, vivid prison diary satirizing
life in present-day Nicaragua. Highly critical of the Somoza dictatorship, it describes
the plight of the poor in their own terms.
The language is that of the street, which
resulted in the work being banned for a time
as pornographic. LNHT

215 _____. <u>Contra Sandino en la montaña</u>.
Managua: Editorial Nuevos Horizontes, 1942.
141 pp. Illus.
   A collection of short stories and poems
based on the author's experience while serving
as a radio operator in the Nicaraguan Guardia
Nacional during the campaign against Sandino
in the 1930s. The account provides little
information about the campaign, focusing instead on the human emotions involved and the
life-and-death experiences of the men in the
jungle. DLC

216 Cuadra Cardenal, Pablo Antonio. <u>Brevario</u>
<u>imperial</u>. Madrid: Editorial Española, 1940.
209 pp.
   A work of the new Hispanista tradition,
following the line of the Spanish government
of Generalissimo Francisco Franco in seeking
to revive Spanish ties with Latin America by
emphasizing their common heritage and values
as well as the positive aspects of the Colonial heritage. The volume invokes concepts
such as religion and the adventurism of the
conquistadores. DLC

217 _____. <u>Los cuentos de tío coyote y tío</u>
<u>conejo</u>. Managua: Academia Nicaragüense de la
Lengua, 1957. 87 pp.
   A collection of short stories based on
Nicaraguan folklore. DLC

218 _____. <u>El nicaragüense</u>. Managua: Ediciones
Populares de Bolsillo, 1967. 168 pp. Illus.
7th ed. San José: Editorial Universitaria,
1976. 282 pp. Illus.
   A series of essays selected from the
author's regular column in <u>La Prensa</u> of
Managua, dealing with various facets of
Nicaraguan life and diverse parts of the
country. The articles, originally published
between 1959 and 1961, most under the column
title "Escritos a Máquina," seek to identify
the character and uniqueness of Nicaraguan
nationality, culture, and customs by narrating
in poetry and essay form everyday events and
vignettes that indicate prevalent local customs and practices. DLC LNHT

219 _____. <u>Por los caminos van los campesinos</u>.
Managua: n.p., 1958. 162 pp. 3d ed.
Granada: El Pez y la Serpiente, 1972. 108
pp.
   A play describing a peasant rebellion
against the oppressive regime, calling in
emotional terms for resistance and struggle
for liberation. The work was written in 1937
but not published until 1957. DLC

220 _____. <u>Tierra que habla: antología de cantos</u>
<u>nicaragüenses</u>. San José: EDUCA, 1974. 181
pp. Biblio.
   An anthology of the works of this
Nicaraguan poet of the mid-twentieth century
whose works focus on the beauties, settings,
people, and customs of his native land. DLC
LNHT BNCR

221 Cuadra Cardenal, Pablo Antonio, and Francisco
Pérez Estrada. <u>Muestrario del folklore</u>

nicaragüense. Managua: Banco de América,
1978. xiii, 460 pp. Illus.
A collection of poems and short stories
embodying local folkloric traditions.

222 Cuadra Chamorro, Pedro Joaquín. La conversión
monetaria de Nicaragua. Washington, D.C.:
Gibson Brothers, 1914. 25 pp.
A discussion of the financial problems of
the nation, which led to Yankee involvement
and intervention. DPU

223 ____. Motivos sobre el Tratado Chamorro-
Bryan. Managua: Fondo del Grupo Conservador
Tradicionalista, 1950. 37 pp.
A collection of editorials from the newspaper El Diario Nicaragüense discussing the
significance of the treaty and its implications for the political struggles that then
wracked Nicaragua. DLC

224 ____. La reincorporación de la Mosquitia:
estudio de interpretación histórica. Granada:
Imprenta El Centroamericano, 1944. vii, 205
pp. Illus. 2d ed. León: Editorial
Hospicio, 1964. viii, 207 pp. Index.
A series of essays originally published in
El Diario Nicaragüense during 1940, commemorating the 1894 accord that returned jurisdiction over Mosquitia to Nicaragua and
describing the previous disputes and negotiations involving England, the United States,
and Nicaragua. Quoting liberally from the
documents, it details the events of 1894, the
negotiations, and the rebellion at Bluefields,
seeking to separate myth from reality. DLC
LNHT

225 Cuadra Downing, Orlando, ed. Documentos
Diplomáticos de William Carey Jones. Managua:
Banco de América, 1974. 157 pp.
A series of diplomatic dispatches consisting of the reports of William Carey Jones, a
special envoy to Nicaragua and Costa Rica
during 1857-58 who promptly became embroiled
with the local governments because of his
overzealous efforts to protect the remnants of
the filibustering expedition. The exchanges
show the different viewpoints of the Central
Americans and the Yankees, the envoy's failure
to appreciate the local context, and his lack
of diplomatic experience. The documents,
which are located in the United States National Archives, are printed verbatim, without
comment. DLC

226 Cuadra Downing, Orlando. Seudónimos y apodos
nicaragüenses. Managua: Editorial Alemana,
1967. 341 pp. Biblio., notes.
An alphabetical listing of pseudonyms used
throughout Nicaraguan history, with identification of the author's real name and an explanation of the origin of the pseudonym. DLC

227 Cuadra Pasos, Carlos. Historia de medio
siglo. Managua: Editorial Unión, 1964. 173
pp. Illus.
This memoir, by a leading journalist associated with La Prensa and the Conservative
party, consists of a summary of the principal

events of Nicaraguan politics from 1900
through 1936. Although written in the fashion
of newspaper reporting, it emphasizes the
author's own role and observations and includes analysis reflecting his political activism. Despite the title, the work ends with
the assassination of Sandino and avoids commenting on the Somoza regime, reflecting the
continuing power of its heirs in 1950, when
the articles were written. The series was
originally published in the journal Semana in
1950 under the title "50 años de historia de
Nicaragua." It provides a conservative eye
view of the complex maneuvering and civil
warfare of the era, with comments on U.S.
intervention. DLC LNHT

228 ____. Obras. 2 vols. Managua: Banco de
América, 1976-77. 701, 769 pp. Index,
biblio., illus.
The collected writings of this Conservative
political leader, scholar, historian, and
journalist. The initial volume contains his
personal works, memoirs, family history, and
general historical works, while the second
volume contains historical speeches. The
overwhelming portion of the items deal with
various aspects of Nicaraguan history and the
contemporary scene, as the author's career
spanned the entire first half of the twentieth
century. LNHT

229 ____. Recognition of Governments: Case of
Nicaragua. Washington, D.C.: Judd &
Detweiler, 1926. 24 pp.
A memorandum by a Nicaraguan senator justifying the ascension to the Nicaraguan presidency of Emiliano Chamorro, which was opposed
by the United States under the terms of the
1923 Washington Treaty, which pledged the
signatories to oppose governments coming to
power by revolution. The senator argues that
Chamorro was installed by vote of the Senate
in accordance with constitutional procedures,
and that his rise therefore was not a coup
regardless of the processes involved in the
removal of his predecessor, adding that the
real coup was perpetrated by the ousted
regime. LNHT

230 Cumberland, William Wilson. Nicaragua: An
Economic and Financial Survey. Washington,
D.C.: GPO, 1928. 178 pp. Tables.
A detailed economic summary of Nicaragua in
1915, prepared by an expert furnished by the
State Department. Surveys the nation's resources and its various economic sectors and
recommends a specific financial plan that
emphasizes transportation facilities and financial infrastructure to promote development.
DLC LNHT

231 Cummins, Lejeune. Quijote on a Burro:
Sandino and the Marines: A Study in the
Formulation of Foreign Policy. Mexico: La
Impresora Azteca, 1958. 206 pp. Index,
biblio., notes, illus., maps.
A brief account of the Sandino revolt and
the involvement of the U.S. Marines, including
the author's father. Seeks to call attention

to the episode in the United States and presents Sandino and his quest in a favorable light; includes chapters about foreign criticism of the U.S. action and the anti-imperialist debate within the U.S. during the 1920s, while condemning Somoza's assassination of Sandino. The volume provides only a broad narration of basic events that are now well known. DLC LNHT

232 Danforth, Sister María del Rey. *Prospero Strikes it Rich: The Growth of a Gold Town*. New York: Harper & Row, 1968. 182 pp. Illus.
A Maryknoll nun's memoirs of her mission as part of a group that worked in the Nicaraguan gold-mining town of Prospero beginning in December 1944, with vivid description of the problems of the village, its conditions, and people. LNHT

233 Darío, Rubén. *La vida de Rubén Darío escrita por el mismo*. Many editions. Barcelona: Editorial Maucci, 1915. 287 pp.
The autobiography of this Nicaraguan intellectual, written in later life. The emphasis is on his travels, diplomatic career, and everyday life rather than on his writings. Includes commentaries about and reactions to the countries he visited in Latin America, Europe, and the United States, and his residences in Costa Rica, Guatemala, and Mexico. The accounts of his diplomatic missions are general, with the emphasis on the formal events rather than the behind-the-scenes activity. Later editions are simply entitled *Autobiografía*. DLC LNHT BNG

234 _____. *Obras completas*. 31 vols. Many editions. Madrid: Editorial "Mundo Latino," 1917-22.
The complete Rubén Darío, including all the known works of the Nicaraguan poet and essayist, covering a wide range of themes and settings, many reflecting Central America. Of particular interest to social scientists are volume 11, containing Darío's autobiography; volume 14 dealing with Nicaragua and containing his commentaries regarding his native land; and volume 31, containing commentaries by scholars on the occasion of his death. DLC LNHT BNG

235 Dauzats, V. *Note comparative entre la Canal de Suez et les divers traces proposés pour le Canal Interocéanique*. Paris: Libraire Cochet, 1879. 24 pp.
A comparison of the terrain and the construction problems posed by the proposed Central American canals with those of Suez. Concludes that some of the problems are larger, but that Suez shows that they can be solved; advocates moving ahead with construction plans in the isthmus. DLC

236 Davis, Charles H. *Report on Interoceanic Canals and Railroads between the Atlantic and Pacific Oceans*. 39th Cong., 1st. sess., 1866. S. Doc. 62. Washington, D.C.: GPO, 1867. 28 pp. Maps, tables.

The admiral in charge of the U.S. Naval Observatory summarizes canal and railroad routes in Central America, with maps and tables. DLC LNHT

237 Debayle, León. *La cooperación financiera de los Estados Unidos en Nicaragua*. Managua: Tipografía Gurdián, 1943. 16 pp.
The Nicaraguan ambassador to the U.S. provides an account of wartime loans, covering 1937-43, and lauds Yankee financial aid. DLC

238 _____. *Les emprunts extérieurs et la réforme monétaire de la République de Nicaragua*. Paris: Librarié Générale de Droit et de Jurisprudence, 1927. 146 pp. Biblio., notes, tables.
A Nicaraguan view of the U.S. financial intervention in that nation, its economic and financial problems, and the effects of the new monetary system on the nation. Originally prepared as a doctoral thesis, it covers the years 1912-24, drawing on published works and official government reports from the period. DLC

239 Debayle, Luís Henri. *Al correr de la vida: discursos, conferencias y juicios*. Managua: Imprenta Nacional, 1935. iii, 415 pp.
A collection of writings and speeches by a prominent Nicaraguan physician, poet, intellectual, and Liberal political figure, covering a wide range of themes and reflecting his longtime residence in Europe and the United States. DLC

240 De Kalb, Courtenay, et al. *The Nicaragua Canal: Its Political Relations and Commercial Advantages*. St. Louis: E.J. Schuster, 1895. 27 pp.
NN

241 Dénain, Adolphe. *Considérations sur les intérêts politiques et commerciaux que se rattachent a l'isthme de Panama et aux différents isthmes de l'Amérique Centrale*. Paris: Marchands de Nouveautés, 1845. 253 pp.
A rambling survey of the canal question that stresses the importance of such a waterway in Central America and the European-Yankee competition regarding its control, and advocates a stronger role by France. Cites the economic implications for each nation, the French effort at Suez, and actions of the British, Germans, Belgians, and Yankees in Central America. DLC

242 Denny, Harold Norman. *Dollars for Bullets: The Story of American Rule in Nicaragua*. New York: Dial Press, 1929. 411 pp. Biblio., illus., maps.
A Yankee newspaper reporter's account of the U.S. intervention in Nicaragua in the 1920s, based on published sources, official statements, press comments, and a visit to that nation. He seeks to present both rationale and criticism, and though he is sympathetic to the official statements of justification and reflects the prevailing

Yankee attitudes, he notes the limits of intervention and the problems of cultural diversity. DLC LNHT

243 Díaz Lozano, Argentina. Fuego en la ciudad. Guatemala: Ministerio de Educación Pública, 1966. 201 pp. 3d ed. Guatemala: Ministerio de Educación Pública, 1972. 212 pp.
An historical novel dealing with the fire that destroyed parts of Granada, Nicaragua, in 1856. Describes the experiences of various residents of the city, using the event as a background for a commentary on Central American life in those times. DLC BNG

244 Doña, William Henry. El espíritu de Managua: managuadas. Mexico: Editora Ibero-Mexicana, 1956. 245 pp.
A collection of short stories about and set in Managua that reflect the local traditions and folklore. DLC

245 Doubleday, Charles William. Reminiscences of the "Filibuster" War in Nicaragua. New York and London: Putnam's, 1886. ix, 225 pp. Illus., maps.
The detailed memoirs of a member of Walker's forces, who recounts his experiences down to the last shot and evasive movement. Provides an account of the force and its military activity from November 1856 to April 1857, and rich description of the scenery and the various contending forces. Throughout, he retains his adulation for Walker and his conviction that the effort was proper and the opponents unscrupulous. DLC LNHT

246 Drouillet, León. Les isthmes américains: projet d'une exploration géographique internationale des terrains qui semblent présenter le plus de facilités pour le percement d'un canal maritime interocéanique. Paris: Aux Bureau de L'Explorateur, 1876. iii, 21 pp. Maps.
A brief survey of all the possible routes, prepared by a French engineer as a report to the Commission de Géographie Commerciale of Paris, with the author's map detailing twenty-three potential locations. Concludes that Panama and Nicaragua offer the only real choices, and picks the Darien route as the most promising for further study. DLC

247 Duarte, José Antonio. La situación legal de la mujer casada en Nicaragua. León: Artes Gráficas Puschendorf, 1947. 48 pp. Biblio.
A summary of the legal rights of wives under current Nicaraguan law. DLC

248 Dueñas van Severén, J. Ricardo [Justo Nonualco, pseud.]. La invasión filibustera de Nicaragua y la guerra nacional. San José: Imprenta Nacional, 1958. 3d ed. San Salvador: Ministerio de Educación, 1962. 146 pp. Biblio., notes.
A description of several aspects of the Walker intervention and an analysis of the resulting combat. Emphasizes the military confrontation and Central American cooperation before the common enemy, while criticizing

Walker's actions. Based on existing secondary works. DLC LNHT BNCR

249 Du Lamercier, pseud. Corinto a través de la historia, 1514-1933. Corinto: Tipografía Saballos, 1933. 212 pp.
This volume seeks to demonstrate the importance of the isthmus and its linkage with nearby cities. It is organized by chapters with titles and initial paragraphs describing the geographic distances to nearby cities, within which various disparate historical elements about Corinto and the city under discussion are considered. The result is a good deal of jumping about in terms of chronology, and a list of chapter titles that is not particularly revealing of the contents. Most of the material relates to travels in Colonial times, though there are references to the nineteenth and early twentieth centuries. DLC LNHT

250 Durand, René L.F. La négritude dans l'oeuvre politique de Rubén Darío. Dakar: Universitaire de Dakar, 1970. 38 pp.
An analysis of the theme of négritude in Darío's works, contending that the Nicaraguan poet used blacks and black themes to enrich his works, and hence was one of the earliest exponents of portraying the black experience and viewing it as a positive element in the region's culture. DLC

251 DuVal, Miles Percy. Cadiz to Cathay: The Story of the Long Struggle for a Waterway across the American Isthmus. London: Oxford University Press, 1940. 554 pp. Maps. Latest ed. New York: Greenwood Press, 1968. xix, 548 pp. Illus., maps.
A former naval captain's patriotic account of the U.S. efforts to secure canal rights and construct the waterway. Includes consideration of the Nicaragua-Panama debate, but focuses mainly on relations with Panama and the maneuvering involved in gaining the rights in that nation; the Nicaragua-Panama aspect occupies one hundred pages. The title changed in the second edition to Cadiz to Cathay: The Story of the Long Diplomatic Struggle for the Panama Canal.

252 Ealy, Lawrence O. Yanqui Politics and the Isthmian Canal. University Park: Pennsylvania State University Press, 1971. 192 pp. Index, biblio., notes.
An analysis of the canal question viewed as an issue in domestic Yankee politics. While focusing principally on Panama, it does include a narration of the disputes with England and a chapter providing an overview of the Panama versus Nicaragua debate. Based on secondary works. DLC LNHT

253 Ebaugh, Cameron Duncan. Education in Nicaragua. Washington, D.C.: GPO, 1947. iv, 56 pp. Biblio.
See item GU395. DLC

254 El Salvador, Gov't of. Ministerio de Relaciones Exteriores. Alegato verbal del Dr.

(El Salvador, Gov't of)
Alfonso Reyes Guerrera como abogado del gobierno de El Salvador en la vista del juicio promovido contra de gobierno de Nicaragua. San José: Sociedad Editora Nacional, 1917. 69 pp.
A comment by the Salvadoran attorney regarding the court's decision against Nicaragua. DLC

255 _____. _____. Demanda presentada por el gobierno de El Salvador contra el de Nicaragua ante la Corte de Justicia Centroamericana con motivo de la celebración del Tratado Bryan-Chamorro. San José: Imprenta Moderna, 1916. 79 pp. Maps.
The Republic of El Salvador against the Republic of Nicaragua: Complaint of the Republic of El Salvador. Washington, D.C.: Gibson Bros., 1917. 83 pp. Maps.
The formal Salvadoran complaint alleging that the Bryan-Chamorro Treaty granting canal rights to the United States violated Salvadoran rights in the Gulf of Fonseca, and hence was invalid unless also signed by that republic. Notes that the canal would terminate in the Gulf, while the treaty awarded the United States a naval base there despite the fact that the Gulf was international waters because three republics front on it. DLC LNHT BNCR

256 _____. _____. Libro Rosado de El Salvador: Demanda del gobierno de El Salvador contra el gobierno de Nicaragua ante la Corte de Justicia Centroamericana. San Salvador: Tipografía La Unión, 1916. 58 pp. Maps.
The Salvadoran case as presented to the Central American Court of Justice, protesting the Bryan-Chamorro Treaty in the proceedings that led to the court decision that the pact violated the rights of Salvador and Honduras. DLC

257 Encuentro Pastoral, I, Managua, 1969: De cara al futuro de la iglesia en Nicaragua. N.p.: Ediciones Fichero Pastoral, 1969. 263 pp. Index, biblio., tables.
The position papers and speeches presented at the 1969 conference of the Nicaraguan clergy, focusing mainly on internal church and general doctrinal questions but including some comments that relate to the contemporary situation in the nation. DLC

258 Escóbar, Darío. Recuerdos parlamentarios nicaragüenses: constituyente de 1938-1939. Managua: Talleres Nacionales, 1939. 58 pp. Illus.
Memoirs of the Constituent Assembly and its deliberations. DLC

259 Escóbar, Esteban. Biografía del general don Pedro Joaquín Chamorro, 1818-1890. Managua: Tipografía La Prensa, 1935. ii, 398 pp.
A sympathetic account of the career of a prominent nineteenth-century Conservative party leader and president. Provides a brief biographical sketch that is somewhat episodical; contains reproductions of various letters and correspondence from the family archives. DLC LNHT

260 Escobar, José Benito. Rigoberto López Pérez: el principio del fin. Managua: Secretaría Nacional de Propaganda y Educación Política del FSLN, n.d. [197?]. 50 pp. Illus.
An account of the experiences of an anti-Somoza guerrilla, hailing his idealism and aspirations.

261 Escobar, Manuel. Derecho constitucional nicaragüense. Granada: n.p., 1943. iv, 160 pp. 2d ed. Masaya: Tipografía El Espectador, 1951. 160 pp.
A text combining general legal principles, a history of law in Nicaragua, and discussion of the current legislation. DLC

262 Escuela Pedro Murillo Pérez, Barba. Los héroes de la campaña nacional (1856-1857): Coronel Nicolas Aguilar Murillo. San José: Imprenta Nacional, 1934. 42 pp. Illus.
A collection of decrees, letters, and legislation that led to the observance in the town of Barba of the centennial of the death of its military hero, yet another in the list of those honored from among the participants in the campaign against Walker. DLC-LDS-784

263 Espinosa Estrada, Jorge. Nicaragua Cradle of America/Nicaragua cuna de América. Managua: Tipografía Alemana, 1969. 62 pp. Biblio., notes, illus., maps.
A brief essay, published in English and Spanish, arguing that the name America originated in Nicaragua, where it was applied to a mountain range. DLC

264 Espinosa R., Rodolfo, and Julián Irías. Nicaraguan Affairs: Memorial to the Senate of the U.S.A. from the Land of Exile to Nicaraguans. San José: Imprenta Alsina, 1912. 24 pp.
A protest against the Castrillo-Knox Convention by the Liberal exiles, who charge that it is a plot by the Conservatives to place their nation under the control of Yankee capitalists through a foreign loan and the accord, which in their view will give official United States protection to the loan; they contend that the Conservatives are in power illegally and do not represent the will of the nation. DLC DLC-LDS-104 BNCR

265 Espinosa Sotomayor, Enrique. Partidos Políticos. Managua: Tipografía Progresso, 1940. 120 pp. DLC

266 Estrada Uribe, Gabriel. Managua antisísmica: su ruina y su reconstrucción. Bogotá: Universidad Nacional de Colombia, 1973. xviii, 230 pp. Biblio., illus.
A detailed account, with extensive photos, of the destruction of the 1972 earthquake. Includes discussion of reconstruction plans and relief efforts. DLC LNHT

267 Estudio comparativo de los dos partidos
     políticos de Nicaragua. Managua: Tipografía
     Gutenberg, 1923. 200 pp. Tables.
         Part of the heated political polemics of
     the turbulent Nicaraguan politics of the early
     twentieth century, this work is a defense of
     the Conservative party, yet it reflects splits
     in that movement. It defends the regime of
     Adolfo Díaz while criticizing that of José
     Santos Zelaya. Most of the space is devoted
     to quoting previously published criticisms of
     these regimes and providing counterevidence,
     replete with derisive terminology. DPU

268 Eugarrios, Manuel. Dos . . . uno . . . cero
     comandante. San José: Imprenta Lehmann,
     1979. 128 pp. Illus.
         An emotional narration of the guerrilla
     seizure of the National Palace and the
     Nicaraguan Chamber of Deputies during August
     1978, one of the key factors in the success of
     the Sandinista movement. Emphasizes the hero
     of the operation, Eden Pastora, known as Com-
     mander Zero, the first deputy minister of
     defense in the initial Sandinista government.
     The author was the La Prensa correspondent
     covering the Congress and hence one of those
     held prisoner. His account emphasizes the
     terror and emotion, but is sympathetic to the
     guerrillas. Includes photos and the proclama-
     tions and press statements of the guerrillas
     during the episode. TxU

269 Fallas S., Carlos Luís. El canal de Nicaragua
     y nuestra soberanía. San José: Publicaciones
     de la Unión de Mujeres Carmen Lyra, 1950.
         A defense of Costa Rican rights in the San
     Juan River, noting that since the proposed
     canal route runs along the border, both na-
     tions need to be involved in the negotiations
     with the Yankees.

270 FAO. Report of the FAO mission for Nicaragua.
     Washington, D.C.: FAO, 1950. 200 pp.
     Biblio., illus., maps.
         A compilation of detailed information and
     statistics regarding the contemporary state of
     agriculture, livestock raising, and forestry
     in the nation, and the development problems
     faced by each of these sectors, with recommen-
     dations for promoting growth. DLC

271 Fellechner, A., Dr. Müller, and C.L.C. Hesse.
     Bericht über die im höchsten Auftrage Seiner
     Königlichen Hoheit des Prinzen Carl von
     Preufsen und Sr. Durchlaucht des Herrn Fürsten
     von Schoenburg-Waldenburg bewirkte
     Untersuchung einiger Teile des
     Mosquitolandes. Berlin: Verlag von Alexander
     Drucker, 1845. 274 pp. Index, biblio.,
     illus., maps, appendixes.
         A collection of material about the Mosquito
     Territory, including a bibliography, physical
     description of the features, flora, fauna, and
     agriculture, with appended documents and ex-
     tracts of articles about the region. DLC

272 Ferro, Carlos A. Historia de la bandera de
     Nicaragua. Managua: Ministerio de Educación
     Pública, 1969. 76 pp. Appendixes.

     A patriotic explanation of the evolution of
     the flag and its significance. DLC

273 Fiallos Gil, Mariano. León de Nicaragua:
     compañario de Rubén. León: Imprenta
     Hospicio, 1958. 135 pp.
         A series of essays about various aspects of
     the history of the city, followed by essays on
     some of its leading intellectual figures.
     These articles originally appeared in news-
     papers of the city over a period of years and
     deal with separate subjects; they are not
     arranged in any particular order, and are
     united only by the fact that they all relate
     to León. DLC

274 _____. A la libertad por la universidad.
     León: Imprenta Hospicio, 1960. 143 pp.
         A collection of various articles and
     speeches by the rector of the National Uni-
     versity of Nicaragua, written between 1957 and
     1959, dealing with the university, its prob-
     lems and administration, and its place in the
     nation and politics. Includes consideration
     of budget, proposals for change, comparison
     with other Latin American universities, and
     other aspects reflecting a period of turmoil,
     problems, and self-examination by the institu-
     tion. DLC LNHT

275 Flachat, Jules. Notes sur le fleuve de Darien
     et sur les diférents projets de canaux
     interocéanique de Centre Amérique. Paris:
     Eugene Lacroiz, 1866. 133 pp. Maps, tables.
         This volume surveys the entire Central
     American region, providing general data about
     all the prospective canal routes, considering
     geography, climate, currents, health, weather,
     future prospects, costs, and construction
     methods. Subjects are treated topically in
     comparative fashion rather than by route. DLC

276 Fletes Bolaños, Anselmo. Hechos: la curación
     del general don Frutos Bolaños Chamorro, el
     hombre leyenda. Granada: Tipografía
     Salesiana, 1924. 116 pp.
         An account of the illness and "miraculous"
     curing of this Nicaraguan general, detailing
     the religious activities and devotion to which
     he attributes this cure. DPU

277 _____. Recuerdos de los treinta años.
     Managua: Tipografía Nacional, 1914. vii, 125
     pp.
         NN

278 _____. Regionales. Managua: Tipografía
     Nacional, 1922. 105 pp. Illus.
         A collection of short stories and folksongs
     recounting the regional lore of Nicaragua.
     DLC

279 Fogelquist, Donald F., ed. The Literary Col-
     laboration and the Personal Correspondence of
     Rubén Darío and Juan Ramón Jiménez. Coral
     Gables: University of Miami Press, 1956. 46
     pp. Biblio., notes, illus.
         The texts of thirty letters exchanged be-
     tween Darío and Spanish poet Juan Ramón
     Jiménez, with an accompanying bibliography and

an introduction placing each of the authors in the context of contemporary literary movements and explaining their personal inter-actions. The missives are quite brief and include discussion of literary trends, their own works, and other authors. DLC

280 Folkmann, David I., Jr. The Nicaragua Route. Salt Lake City: University of Utah Press, 1972. 173 pp. Index, notes, illus., maps, appendixes.
La ruta de Nicaragua (El tránsito a través de Nicaragua). Managua: Banco de América, 1976. 236 pp. Tables.
   A scholarly and effective survey of the Nicaragua canal and transit prospects from 1848 through the 1860s, tracing the rise of the rail and steamship route and the growing prospects of a canal through their collapse after the Walker episode. Drawing from sec-ondary sources and newspapers as well as State Department microfilms, the author demonstrates the impact of events in the United States, the competition between the steamship lines, the filibustering intervention, and the resulting domestic political turmoil in Nicaragua. DLC LNHT

281 Fonseca Amador, Carlos, ed. Ideario político de Augusto César Sandino. Managua: Frente Sandinista de Liberación Nacional, 1980. 37 pp.
   A compilation of excerpts from the writ-ings, proclamations, and broadsides of the Nicaraguan guerrilla leader and hero of the new revolutionary movement, prepared under official auspices for popular use to famil-iarize the public with his political stances and their implications for the course of the present government.

282 ____. Un Nicaragüense en Moscu. Managua: Frente Sandinista de Liberación Nacional, 1980. 78 pp. Illus.

283 ____. Sandino: guerrillero proletario. León: Ediciones Taller, 1979. 34 pp.

284 Frente Sandinista de Liberación Nacional. La revolución a través de nuestra dirección nacional. Managua: Frente Sandinista de Liberación Nacional, 1980. 95 pp. Illus.

285 Frente Unitario Nicaragüense. Intervención sangrienta: Nicaragua y su pueblo. Caracas: n.p., 1961. 75 pp.
   NIC

286 Galarza Zavala, Jaime. Nicaragua: tiempo de fusiles. Cuenca, Ecuador: n.p., 1978
   An account of the civil war that brought about Somoza's fall, criticizing the govern-ment for brutality and blaming it for the death and destruction.

287 Gallegos, Paco. Nicaragua, tierra de maravillas. Managua: Editorial San José, 1964. 373 pp. Illus., maps, tables.

A lavishly illustrated guide to the current state of the republic, sponsored by the Cham-ber of Commerce. Emphasizes facilities, folk-lore, economy, industry, etc. DLC LNHT

288 Gámez, José Dolores. Apuntamientos para la biografía de Máximo Jérez. Managua: Tipografía Nacional, 1893. 158 pp. 2d ed. Managua: n.p., 1910. 191 pp. Illus.
   A sympathetic account of this nineteenth-century Liberal and his role in the events of the mid-century. Includes several poems acclaiming his contribution to the nation. The historical account justifies his actions against the regime of Fruto Chamorro with extensive quotations from proclamations, mani-festos, and speeches; it constitutes part of the continuing Liberal-Conservative battle in the history books, where the civil war still rages. LNHT

289 ____, ed. Archivo histórica de la República de Nicaragua. Managua: Tipografía Nacional, 1896. vi, 369 pp.
   Noting the destruction of the National Archives during the war against Walker, the author states his intention to locate, com-pile, and publish all documents relevant to the history of Central America. He intended this to be the initial volume, covering the years 1821-26, though no others ever appeared. The items are arranged chronologically, but the absence of a table of contents or index renders their use difficult. They include the decrees and manifestos of the various conven-tions as well as accounts by participants, and the various political manifestos of the era, along with the acts of independence, though the contents for each year vary considerably. The locations in which he found the documents are not indicated. DLC LNHT

290 Gámez, José Dolores. Historia de la Costa de Mosquitos hasta 1894, en relación con la conquista española, los piratas y corsarios en las costas centro-americanas, los avances y protectorado del gobierno inglés en la misma costa y la famosa cuestión inglesa con Nicaragua, Honduras y El Salvador. Managua: Talleres Nacionales, 1939. 346 pp.
   A general history of the Mosquito Terri-tory, focusing on the jurisdictional disputes involving Spain, England, and the various Central American nations. It is about equally divided between the Colonial era and the first half of the nineteenth century; the years after 1855 are summarized in a single brief chapter. Published posthumously, the work is narrative, with quotations from documents, newspapers, and secondary works, though cita-tions are in the text. DLC LNHT

291 ____. Historia de Nicaragua: desde los tiempos prehistóricos hasta 1860, en sus relaciones con España, México y Centro-América. Managua: Tipografía de "El País," 1889. 885 pp. Latest ed. Managua: Banco de América, 1975. 758 pp.
   A Liberal historian and former foreign minister of Nicaragua under the government of

José Santos Zelaya provides an account of
Nicaraguan history from independence to 1854.
Inevitably, a major portion of the volume is
devoted to a sympathetic account of the struggles against foreign intervention, including
the Mexican efforts at the time of independence and those of the Federation, the British,
and the Yankees during the middle portions of
the century. The most recent edition employed
the title *Historia moderna de Nicaragua*. DLC
LNHT

292 García Márquez, Gabriel, et al. *Los
Sandinistas*. Bogotá: La Oveja Negra, 1979.
288 pp.
A collection of accounts, interviews, and
reports by Sandinistas. Provides their views
on the movement, the Somoza regime, and conditions in Nicaragua, as well as eyewitness
accounts by participants in the various combats and uprisings. Includes comments by
Gabriel García Márquez and interviews he conducted with members of the movement. WU

293 García Peña, Angelita, ed. *Documentos para la
historia de la guerra nacional contra los
filibusteros en Nicaragua*. San Salvador:
Editorial Ahora, 1958. iv, 234 pp. Illus.
A compendium of materials relating to the
struggle against the filibusters, consisting
primarily of descriptions of the various battles but including official reports, proclamations, speeches, and press reports from that
period. The items are rather miscellaneous,
with no introductions, but do contain considerable information. LNHT

294 Gilly, Adolfo. *La nueva Nicaragua: anti-
imperialismo y lucha de clases*. Mexico:
Nueva Imagen, 1980. 142 pp.
A sympathetic account of the Sandinista
revolution, based on interviews with participants and reports from the Mexican press.
Traces the principal events of the revolution
and discusses its significance and future.
The emphasis is on anti-imperialism, nationalism, and the pivotal role of the working
class. Comparing the Nicaraguan revolution
with those of other Latin American countries,
the author argues that Nicaragua, because of
the involvement of the bourgeoisie and the
role of the laboring class, is a unique case
that can set a new example. Contends that
mass organizations are the key and that the
movement shows that a popular front can work
without theoretical Marxism. Particular emphasis is placed on solidarity with other
revolutionary nations and the fact that
Nicaragua can count on assistance from Cuba
and the Communist bloc in resisting the efforts of the Yankees to isolate the new government. DLC

295 Godio, Julio, et al. *Sandanismo [sic]:
teoría e historia*. Caracas: Ateneo de
Caracas, 1980. 112 pp.

296 Göetz Dieter, Freiherr von. *Los Alemanes en
Nicaragua*. Managua: Banco de América, 1975.
479 pp. Biblio., notes, illus.

A major account of the role of Germans in
the development of Nicaragua, with chapters
considering the early explorers, the travel
writers who visited the region, the colonization efforts and settlers, and the various
institutions formed by the Germans who settled
in the nation, as well as their intellectual,
economic, and political contribution to the
country from the early nineteenth century to
the present. Based on careful research in
secondary and primary sources. Includes mention of all figures of any prominence. DLC

297 Goldwert, Marvin. *The Constabulary in the
Dominican Republic and Nicaragua: Progeny and
Legacy of the United States Intervention*.
Gainesville: University of Florida Press,
1962. vii, 55 pp. Biblio., notes.
A study of the U.S. intervention and its
idealistic effort to provide domestic tranquillity and promote democracy by dissolving
the local military establishment and creating
a new force in the Yankee image through U.S.
Marine Corps training of a new National Guard.
Details the rationale and effects of the two
efforts, both of which produced not democracy
but a new set of leaders who used the instrument to seize control of their respective
nations. The focus is on the creation of the
forces, their training, their leaders, and
their rise to power. DLC

298 Gómez Espinosa, Margarita. *Así es Nicaragua*.
Madrid: Paraninfo, 1973. 170 pp. Biblio.
Descriptive essays on each of the principal
cities of the republic, listing their origin,
leading figures, and institutions, followed by
a series of disparate items that consist
mainly of selections from documents and from
Nicaraguan writers dealing with various
themes. DLC LNHT

299 Gonionskii, Semen Aleksandrovich. *Sandino*.
Moscow: Izdatelvstvo ULKCM Molodaia Guardia,
1965. 155 pp. Illus., maps.
A Marxist biography of Sandino, extolling
his role as a hero of the people in the struggle against the capitalist imperialists and
the Yankee interventionists. Designed as a
text for Soviet schoolchildren, it provides a
glimpse of what they are taught about Latin
America. DLC

300 González-Balado, José Luís. *Ernesto Cardenal,
poeta revolucionario y monje*. Salamanca:
Ediciones Sígueme, 1978. 216 pp. Illus.
A biography of Ernesto Cardenal, the
Nicaraguan priest and poet of social protest,
that mixes an account of his life with excerpts from his writings, providing the background for many of the works. It refers to
him as a revolutionary priest, includes his
commentary supporting Liberation theology, and
quotes him as declaring himself a Marxist.
Argues that his religion made him a Marxist
and that Catholicism and Marxism are compatible and indeed complementary. The narration
follows his early life in his homeland, study
abroad, participation in an anti-Somoza rebellion, and later travels in Europe and Latin

America, indicating the key turning points in his life that shaped his convictions, and showing how they were reflected in his poetry. DLC

301 Great Britain, Gov't of. <u>Correspondence Respecting the Mosquito Territory</u>. London: HMSO, 1843. ix, 133 pp. Maps.
Continuing exchanges regarding this jurisdiction.

302 _____. Foreign Office. <u>Papers Relating to the Arbitration of His Imperial Majesty, the Emperor of Austria, in the Differences between the Government of Her Britannic Majesty and the Government of the Republic of Nicaragua Respecting the Interpretation of Certain Articles of the Treaty of Managua</u>. London: Harrison & Sons, 1881.
Documents regarding an arbitral effort to settle jurisdiction over the Mosquito Territory.

303 Greene, Laurence. <u>The Filibuster: The Career of William Walker</u>. Indianapolis: Bobbs-Merrill, 1937. 350 pp. Index, biblio., illus., maps.
A vivid and picturesque journalistic-style account of the Walker episode, drawn from published works. Idealizes Walker and his efforts, employing sensationalism to focus attention on him as a dramatic man of action seeking to expand the United States, a man whose efforts could have changed the course of history. It is even claimed that the success of his efforts in Central America could have prevented the U.S. Civil War. DLC LNHT

304 Guardia de Alfaro, Gloria. <u>Estudio sobre el pensamiento poético de Pablo Antonio Cuadra</u>. Madrid: Editorial Gredos, 1971. 259 pp. Biblio., notes.
A detailed study of Cuadra's poetry and his place in the so-called generation of 1929, focusing on his use of Christ, mysticism, and naturalism, as well as the evolution of his style during his early career. Also provides biographical data. DLC LNHT

305 Guerrero Castillo, Julián N., and Lola Soriano de Guerrero. <u>Boaco</u>. Managua: Editorial Artes Gráficas, 1964. 50 pp. Illus., maps.
Consists primarily of description of the department's present situation and facilities. Includes a concise general history of the department and each of its towns, emphasizing development, leading citizens, and notable events. DLC LNHT

306 _____. <u>Carazo</u>. Managua: Editorial Artes Gráficas, 1964. 125 pp. Illus., maps.
See item NI305. DLC LNHT

307 _____. <u>Chinandega</u>. Managua: Editorial Artes Gráficas, 1964. 220 pp. Illus., maps.
See item NI305. DLC LNHT

308 _____. <u>Chontales</u>. Managua: Editorial Artes Gráficas, 1969. 259 pp. Illus., maps.
See item NI305. DLC LNHT

309 _____. <u>Esteli</u>. Managua: Editorial Artes Gráficas, 1967. 215 pp. Illus., maps.
See item NI305. DLC LNHT

310 _____. <u>Jinotega</u>. Managua: Editorial Artes Gráficas, 1966. 190 pp. Illus., maps.
See item NI305. DLC LNHT

311 _____. <u>León</u>. Managua: Editorial Artes Gráficas, 1969. 332 pp. Illus., maps.
See item NI305. DLC LNHT

312 _____. <u>Managua</u>. Managua: Editorial Artes Gráficas, 1964. 284 pp. Illus., maps.
See item NI305. DLC LNHT

313 _____. <u>Masaya</u>. Managua: Editorial Artes Gráficas, 1965. 241 pp. Illus., maps.
See item NI305. DLC LNHT

314 _____. <u>Matagalpa</u>. Managua: Editorial Artes Gráficas, 1967. 290 pp. Illus., maps.
See item NI305. DLC LNHT

315 _____. <u>Nueva Segovia</u>. Managua: Editorial Artes Gráficas, 1969. 311 pp. Illus., maps.
See item NI305. DLC LNHT

316 _____. <u>Rivas</u>. Managua: Editorial Artes Gráficas, 1966. 293 pp. Illus., maps.
See item NI305. DLC LNHT

317 Guido, Clemente. <u>¡Escucha Cristo!</u> Managua: Ediciones Nicarao, 1970. 158 pp.
A series of short stories and a novelette dealing with the civil wars that characterized Nicaraguan politics during the nineteenth and early twentieth centuries, continuing the themes treated in item NI319. DLC LNHT

318 _____. <u>Noches de torturas</u>. Managua: n.p., 1956. 72 pp. 2d ed. Managua: Editorial Artes Gráficas, 1963. 93 pp. Illus.
A Nicaraguan Conservative leader's account of his sufferings while a political prisoner during 1956. DLC LNHT

319 _____. <u>Prosa roja</u>. Managua: Ediciones Nicarao, 1965. 198 pp.
A collection of short stories and a novelette dealing with the political civil warfare that characterized Nicaragua during much of its history. Draws upon events from diverse eras to portray the impact of the conflict on the individuals involved and the resultant personal tragedies. DLC LNHT

320 _____. <u>Sangre y fuego</u>. Managua: Ediciones Nicarao, 1971. 133 pp. Illus.
A novelette dealing with the 1854 siege of Granada by the forces of Máximo Jérez and three short stories recounting the experiences of more modern guerrillas, all emphasizing the horrors of war and the futility of such political conflicts. DLC LNHT

321 Guier Sáenz, Enrique. <u>William Walker</u>. San José: Imprenta Lehmann, 1971. 353 pp. Biblio.

A biography of Walker, though the narration of the campaign in Central America focuses more on the reaction of the isthmian nations. Drawn principally from existing studies, with extensive quotation from these secondary works and from published memoirs. DLC LNHT

322   Gunn, Otis Berthoude. The Nicaragua Canal. Leavenworth, Kans.: Leavenworth Post, 1892. 20 pp.

A brief and forceful statement of the case for the Nicaragua canal, originally delivered as a speech in Kansas. Cites the success of the Suez Canal, acclaims the superiority of the Nicaragua route over that of Panama, and asserts the importance of United States construction of such a canal. DLC LNHT

323   Gutiérrez, Pedro Rafael. Una ciudad para Lena. Managua: Editorial San José, 1973. 151 pp. 2d ed. Managua: Editorial San José, 1974. 151 pp.

Memoirs of the December 1972 earthquake in Managua, reflecting the destruction and chaos of the tragedy. Combines the author's experiences and those of others with accounts of the relief efforts, capturing the emotional and personal impact of the event on the city's populace. DLC

324   _____. Réquiem a una ciudad muerta. Many editions, all in the same year. Managua: Banco Central de Nicaragua, 1973. 61 pp. Illus.

A photo essay and poetic description of the aftermath of the 1972 earthquake that destroyed Managua. DLC

325   Guzmán Selva, Enrique, ed. Las gacetilla, 1878-1894. Managua: Banco de América, 1976. 206 pp.

A collection of articles by this prolific Nicaraguan journalist, spanning his career in the late nineteenth century. The commentaries, which cover a wide range of domestic and isthmian political issues, represent the portion of his career during which he was a partisan of the Liberals, prior to his conversion to Conservatism.

326   _____. Huellas de su pensamiento, política, literatura, historia, religión. Granada: Talleres Tipográficos el Centro-Americano, 1943. viii, 351 pp. Illus.

A collection of writings from a prolific Nicaraguan intellectual and journalist whose career spanned the years 1878-1911 and included contributions to several Nicaraguan newspapers. An active political commentator, he began his career as a Liberal and then underwent a metamorphosis in 1896-97, emerging as a Conservative. This collection includes pieces from both eras. It contains commentaries on all the major domestic political events, ranging from the expulsion of the Jesuits to constituent assemblies; general themes, such as autocracy in the nation; personal accounts of his own activities, travels, and diplomatic service; and comments about

various historical events that affected the nation. DLC LNHT

327   Halftermeyer, Gratus. Apéndice a la historia de Managua. Managua: Editorial Recalde, 1954. 80 pp.

A continuation of the author's miscellanea about the city. Contains extracts from poetry, essays, and commentaries dealing with events, places, and people of the city, arranged in no particular order. DLC

328   _____. Complemento de la historia de Managua. León: Editorial Hospicio, 1946. 188 pp. Biblio.

A continuation of the author's previous series of works on the history of Managua, this volume consists of disparate essays, among them discussions of particular churches, collections of legends, and essays on the founders of the city. The focus is on the 1890s but coverage ranges from Colonial times to the 1930s. DLC

329   _____. Diccionario biográfico-histórico de Managua. León: Editorial Hospicio, 1945. 167 pp. Illus., appendixes.

Alphabetically arranged entries for leading citizens of Managua through the ages, with brief vita-type entries, usually a paragraph for each. Some are accompanied by photos. The individuals are from the nineteenth and twentieth centuries, predominantly the latter. DLC

330   _____. Historia de Managua, data desde el siglo XVIII hasta hoy. Managua: n.p., n.d. [1950]. 256 pp. Illus. 4th ed. Managua: Talleres Nacionales, 1965. 415 pp. Illus.

A collection of miscellanea relating to the city of Managua, with disparate essays and excerpts from documents, poetry, publications, etc. Includes historical essays, descriptions of particular buildings or districts, accounts of significant events, and a listing of single-paragraph vitae of important citizens that is arranged neither chronologically nor alphabetically. Pertains mostly to the nineteenth century, though the Colonial era and twentieth century are also included. DLC LNHT

331   _____. Managua a través de la historiá, 1846-1946. León: Editorial Hospicio, 1943. 173 pp. Illus.

A history of Managua that provides brief summaries of its development and extensive quotations from documents, sometimes mixing national affairs and international questions with local developments in the city. The emphasis is on events prior to 1930. DLC LNHT

332   _____. Del sabor de la tierruca. León: Editorial Hospicio, n.d. 77 pp.

A collection of short stories set in the various regions of Nicaragua and reflecting regional folklore and traditions. DLC

(Halftermeyer, Gratus)
333 _____. El viejo Managua. León: Editorial
Hospicio, 1944. 99 pp.
    Billed as a continuation of the author's
Managua a través de la historia, this volume
includes topical essays about varying themes.
The essays are presented in no particular
order and range from important families of the
city to various buildings and events.   DLC

334 Hamilton, Kenneth Gardiner. Meet Nicaragua.
Bethlehem, Pa.: Comenius Press, 1939. 66 pp.
Illus., maps.
    A concise compendium of basic information,
designed for prospective missionaries. Summarizes the local mores and conditions and
describes the work of the Moravian church in
the area, emphasizing the need for empathy
with the local populace and an understanding
of their customs and traditions.   DLC

335 Harrison, Francis Capel, and Charles A.
Conant. Monetary Reform for Nicaragua:
Report Presenting a Plan of Monetary Reform
for Nicaragua. New York: W.R. Fricke, 1912.
iii, 130 pp. Tables.
    Discussion of the financial problems of
Nicaragua and of the monetary reform put into
effect in 1922 as a condition for a loan from
Brown Brothers and J. and W. Seligman and Co.
Describes the problem and details the procedure by which new bills will be substituted
for the old to effect a stabilization of the
currency, a reduction of the amount of money
in circulation, and a fixed gold value. Prepared by the consultants who drew up the plan.
DLC LNHT

336 Hart, Albert Bushnell. Extracts from Official
Papers Relating to the Isthmian Canal, 1515-
1909. New York: Simmons, 1910. 31 pp.
    Excerpts from various documents, state-
ments, and correspondence relating to efforts
to promote a canal, including items relating
to both Nicaragua and Panama. There is no
other narration or explanation.   DLC

337 Harvey, Charles Thompson. Special Report
on Data Relating to the Maritime Canal of
Nicaragua, and the Regions Tributary Thereto.
New York: Maritime Canal Co., 1890. 53 pp.
Illus., maps, tables.
    A report for the company, examining the
feasibility of a Nicaragua canal and providing
a detailed plan, with maps and drawings. The
report stresses that the locks needed would be
similar in size and type to those in the Lake
Superior ship canal; contends that the fact
that they have never failed in three decades
of service indicates the soundness of the
project. Includes a geographical survey and
details of the technical and engineering aspects of construction and operation, as well
as discussion of the impact of such a canal on
the U.S.   DLC

338 Hatfield, Chester, and E.P. Lull. Reports of
Explorations and Surveys for the Location of a
Ship-Canal between the Atlantic and Pacific
Oceans through Nicaragua, 1872-73, Under the
Direction of the Hon. George M. Robeson,
Secretary of the Navy. 43d Cong., 1st sess.,
1874. S. Doc. 57. Washington, D.C.: GPO,
1874. 143 pp. Index, illus., maps, tables.
    Reports on a series of surveys and engi-
neering studies conducted by the Navy. They
examine in detail the proposed Nicaragua
routes and provide technical details and extensive maps. The initial portion of the
mission was headed by Commander Alexander F.
Crosman, who drowned during the work and was
succeeded by Commander Chester Hatfield; the
final year's work was conducted under the
direction of Commander Edward P. Lull. The
reports affirm the feasibility of constructing
the canal in Nicaragua.   DLC

339 Heine, Peter Bernhard Wilhelm. Wanderbilder
aus Central Amerika: Skizzen eines deutschen
Malers. Leipzig: Otto Purfürst, 1853. xvi,
264 pp. 2d ed. Leipzig: Otto Purfürst,
1857. xvi, 264 pp.
    A German traveler's account of his adven-
tures in Nicaragua during 1851 and 1852, when
he spent a year in that nation visiting all
the principal cities. Includes description of
the people and life-styles, accounts of meetings, events, etc., as well as physical description and discussion of the current state
of the nation.   DLC

340 Helms, Mary W. Asang: Adaptations to Culture
Contact in a Miskito Community. Gainesville:
University of Florida Press, 1971. viii, 268
pp. Index, biblio., illus., maps, tables,
appendixes.
    A detailed anthropological study of a
Mosquito town, based on historical research
and fieldwork. Provides a careful description
of the society and its interaction with the
outside world, focusing particularly on its
ability to adapt to outside pressures while
preserving its cultural identity. The author
contends that the Mosquito do not precisely
fit the category of peasants, and suggests the
alternative term "purchase society" to encompass the combination of agriculture, hunting
and gathering, and barter. As this suggests,
she focuses on the economics of the society,
though social framework and political development are also studied. The volume also contains considerable data about the Moravian
missions that are particularly active among
the Mosquito.   DLC LNHT

341 Hernández Somoza, Jesús. Curso de derecho
constitucional nicaragüense. Managua:
Tipografía Nacional, 1896. 545 pp.
    A combination of theoretical constitutional
law with a survey of Nicaragua's laws and
constitutions, originally designed as a law-
school text. The focus is on the development
of the various codes and powers in Nicaragua,
particularly under the constitution then in
force.   DLC

342 Hill, Roscoe R. Fiscal Intervention in
Nicaragua. New York: Columbia University
Press, 1933. 117 pp. Biblio., tables,
appendixes.

A sympathetic account of the Yankee efforts to stabilize Nicaraguan finances through fiscal intervention, written by a member of the high commission appointed by the United States to act in that country. Details its operation and future plans, extolling the benefits to the Nicaraguans; reiterates the usual condescending comments about the local officials and system. DLC

343 Hooker, Roberto Montgomery. La reincorporación de la Mosquitia desde el punto de vista del derecho internacional y patrio. Managua: Talleres Gráficos Pérez, 1945. 86 pp.
    Originally a legal thesis, this volume focuses on the Nicaraguan-British dispute regarding the Mosquito Territory and the 1859 treaty, recounting the background that led to the accord, the previous claims and counterclaims, and the significance of the accord for Nicaraguan sovereignty over the region. DLC

344 Hopf, Albert. Die deutschen Auswanderer auf der Mosquitoküste. Charlottenburg: n.p., 1846. 24 pp.
    Observations made during a visit to the east coast of Nicaragua during the 1850s, with brief descriptions of the Indians. CU

345 Hort, Dora. Via Nicaragua: A Sketch of Travel. London: Remington, 1887. 267 pp.
    An account of a journey from New York to San Francisco via the Nicaragua land transit during the 1880s, emphasizing the terrible conditions and the experiences and misadventures of the traveler. Several chapters are devoted to the Nicaraguan passage. DLC

346 Huberich, Charles Henry. The Trans-Isthmian Canal: A Study in American Diplomatic History (1825-1904). Austin: University of Texas Press, 1904. 31 pp. Notes.
    A brief survey of negotiations regarding canal construction, covering the years 1825 to 1904 and drawing on published documents and presidential messages. Includes consideration of U.S.-British negotiations and a summary of U.S. negotiations with Colombia and Nicaragua. DLC

347 Huezo, Efraim. En la selva: Costa Atlántica. Managua: Tipografía Hueberger, 1952. 233 pp.
    The memoirs of the author's experiences in the Nicaraguan jungles during 1943 as an employee of the Rubber Development Corporation, which was seeking to establish plantations as part of the war effort. Emphasizes the problems of the terrain and climate, as well as the undeveloped and pristine nature of the area. Includes numerous anecdotes that are not arranged chronologically. DLC LNHT

348 Huntington, Collis Potter. The Nicaragua Canal: Would it Pay the United States to Construct It? Galveston, Texas: n.p., 1900. 16 pp.
    An emotional speech to the Galveston Chamber of Commerce, pitched at the local audience and hailing the future prospects of Galveston

as a commercial center. Argues against the Nicaragua canal project, contending that it would hurt southern commerce and industrial possibilities; notes that since it would be accessible to all nations, it would threaten U.S. security rather than enhance it. DLC LNHT

349 Hurtado Chamorro, Alejandro. William Walker: ideales y propósitos. Granada: Editorial Unión, 1965. 300 pp. Biblio., illus., maps.
    A relatively objective account of the Walker episode. Focuses on the man and his views, drawing on existing secondary sources and Walker's own account of the episode to conclude that Walker, despite his excesses, was not the ogre sometimes portrayed in Nicaragua but was an extraordinary man who often acted on his own ideals rather than on any capitalist or southern imperialist plan and whose ideas were not always consistent. The narration of the events seeks to view them through Walker's eyes, though with an understanding of the Central American perspective, and the effort provides some balance to the account. DLC LNHT

350 Ibarra, Felipe Bartolomé. Memorias y episodios del coronel F. Bartolomé Ibarra, comprendida desde los primeros años de su vida hasta 1944. Managua: Editorial Atlántida, n.d. [1944]. 173 pp. Illus.
    The autobiography of a military officer, providing his view of the past fifty years and his recollections of his actions. DLC

351 Ibarra Grijalva, Domingo. The Last Night of General Augusto C. Sandino. New York: Vantage Press, 1973. 256 pp. Illus.
    A Nicaraguan exile's dramatized account of the Somoza-Sandino confrontation. The author was an officer of the Guardia who served in that force until the 1946 presidential election and the subsequent coup, after which he went into exile. His well-written and dramatic account, which reflects his journalistic career, views Sandino sympathetically and condemns the excesses of Somoza, detailing his maneuvers against Sacasa while implying that Sandino was also accumulating arms for his own purposes. Somoza clearly emerges as the villain. Includes various letters and documents obtained by the author owing to his service in the Guardia. DLC LNHT

352 Imberg, Kurt Eduard. Der Nikaraguakanal: eine historisch-diplomatische Studie. Berlin: Theodor Lissner Verlag, 1920. 111 pp. Biblio., notes.
    A survey of diplomacy regarding the canal, from a European perspective. Focuses on the Anglo-American clash between 1850 and the end of the century, drawing on published sources and quoting extensively from the statements and treaties. A scholarly outline of the dispute, it emphasizes British distractions in other parts of the world and the degree to which the ambitious Yankees took advantage of such events. Also serves to indicate the

European reaction to the expanding power of the United States. DLC

353   Incer Barquero, Jaime. Geografía ilustrada de Nicaragua: con un apéndice sobre el reciente terremoto de Nicaragua. Managua: Editorial Recalde, 1973. 255 pp. Illus., maps, tables.
     A detailed elementary geography of the nation, revising and updating the author's earlier Nueva geografía. It adds numerous illustrations and is written in more basic form to allow its use by teachers and students, though it is not designed expressly as a text. Includes data about the 1972 quake, added in production, with photos, useful diagrams, and aerial photos. DLC LNHT

354   _____. Nueva geografía de Nicaragua. Managua: Editorial Recalde, 1970. xx, 582 pp. Biblio., illus., maps, tables.
     A detailed, well-illustrated, and up-to-date treatment of the geography and geology of Nicaragua, by a Nicaraguan geographer. Deals with each region, with topical chapters on agriculture and statistics on land tenure, population, and economy. DLC LNHT

355   Instituto de Nutrición de Centro América y Panamá. Evaluación nutricional de la población de Centro América y Panamá: Nicaragua. Guatemala: Ministerio de Salubridad Pública, 1969. Various pagings. Illus., tables.
     Provides detailed information about the rural populace and its nutrition, following the series pattern. See item CR608.

356   International Bank for Reconstruction and Development. The Economic Development of Nicaragua. Baltimore: Johns Hopkins University Press, 1953. xxxi, 424 pp. Index, maps, tables.
     A detailed survey of the Nicaraguan economy and its five-year development plan, resulting from a study mission in that nation during 1951-52. Includes general considerations such as the resources and present state of the economy, a detailed review of the five-year plan, each of the various economic sectors and principal industries, and discussion of the particular problems faced, with recommendations. DLC

357   International Bureau of the American Republics. Nicaragua: A Handbook. Washington, D.C.: GPO, 1893. 183 pp. Biblio., illus., maps.
     Part of the bureau's series providing general data, particularly regarding the economy. See item GU729. DLC

358   Interoceanic Canal Congress, Paris. Documents Congrès international d'études du canal interocéanique réuni à Paris le 15 mai 1879: rapport de la Commission Technique. Paris: Imprimerie Emile Martinet, 1879. 68 pp. Maps, tables.
     The Congress met in 1879 and heard detailed presentations regarding the various potential routes, as well as specific proposals by

interested parties and companies from various nations. It resolved that the Panama route was the most propitious from a technical standpoint. DLC

359   Irias, Julián and Rodolfo Espinosa R. Nicaraguan Affairs: Memorial to the Senate of the United States of America, from the Land of Exile to Nicaraguans. San José: Imprenta Alsina, 1912. 24 pp.
     See item NI264.

360   Istituto Italo-Latino Americano. Nicaragua. Rome: Istituto Italo-Latino Americano, 1971. 74 pp. Biblio.
     See item CR610. DLC

361   Ivanovich, Vladimir Ivanovich. Pochemu Soedinennye Shtaty voiuiut s Nikaragua [Why the United States is fighting with Nicaragua]. Moscow: Moskovskii rabochii, 1927. 32 pp.

362   Jaime, Jorge. Diriamba. Managua: Tipografía Heuberger, 1954. 83 pp. Illus.
     A selection of poetry and commentary about this Nicaraguan city, followed by single-paragraph biographical sketches of its leading citizens at home and abroad. DLC LNHT

363   Jamison, James Carson. With Walker in Nicaragua, or, Reminiscences of an Officer of the American Phalanx. Columbia, Mo.: E.W. Stephens, 1909. 181 pp. Illus. Con Walker en Nicaragua. Bogota: n.p., 1909. 2d ed. Masaya: Bolaños Geyer, 1977. 316 pp. Illus.
     An officer in Walker's forces presents their view of the situation in Nicaragua and provides a stirring and vivid account of their campaign, in which Walker emerges as a tremendous leader and military tactician and his men as heroes, fighting in a strange land against bloodthirsty hordes and triumphing despite overwhelming odds in their efforts to bring civilization to these poor wretches. Their jaundiced view of the people and country is maintained throughout, and the involvement of Yankee firms and shipping interests is never mentioned. The political situation in Nicaragua is not discussed except to identify the individuals who led the various forces involved in the battles and give their affiliations. The Yankees remain the heroes and the only decent fighting force. Useful for the viewpoint of the Walker contingent, but should be read with Central American accounts. DLC LNHT

364   Jinesta, Ricardo. El Canal de Nicaragua: su historia, base internacional y participación de Costa Rica. San José: Imprenta Nacional, 1958. 92 pp.
     A Costa Rican scholar's brief history of the efforts to construct a Nicaragua canal. Focuses on the latest discussions during the 1930s, emphasizing Costa Rican rights in the San Juan River and the necessity of the involvement of all the Central American republics in any such talks and efforts. DLC

(Jinesta, Ricardo)

365   _____. <u>El Canal de Nicaragua y los intereses de Costa Rica en la magna obra</u>. San José: Imprenta Borrasé, 1964. 94 pp. Biblio.

A discussion of the canal possibilities of the San Juan River–Nicaragua route and the controversies regarding it. Defends the Costa Rican interests and contends that the nation must be careful to be sure that its rights are preserved. The study is critical of the so-called minicanal project of 1939, contending that such an effort might forfeit rights in a future major canal, which is more important. LNHT BNCR

366   _____. <u>Los derechos de Costa Rica en el Canal de Nicaragua</u>. San José: Imprenta Juan Arias, 1936. 46 pp. Biblio. 2d ed. San José: Imprenta Falcó, 1937. 84 pp. Biblio.

A brief statement of the Costa Rican case, reviewing the history of Costa Rican claims to the San Juan River, the boundary accords, the arbitral decisions, and the ruling of the Central American Court of Justice. Contends that Costa Rica must be involved in any negotiations or plans to use this route and that the United States expression of willingness to negotiate in the 1920s in the wake of the Court decision had implicitly recognized Costa Rica's rights. Includes discussion of the potential Nicaragua routes and their prospects. DLC DLC-LDS-844 LNHT

367   Johnson, Emory R. <u>Report on the Industrial and Commercial Value of the Isthmian Canal</u>. Washington, D.C.: GPO, 1911. vi, 157 pp. Notes, maps, tables.

Originally prepared in 1901, this report was initially published as part of the report of the Isthmian Canal Commission and later issued separately. A major portion of it reviews the potential impact of the canal on the industry of each state, arranged in sections that clearly indicate an effort to generate support for the project in Congress by demonstrating that it would affect all parts of the U.S. There are also broader discussions of types of cargo and ships likely to use the canal, and its impact on U.S. trade with various countries of the world. The author was a professor of commerce and transportation. DLC

368   Kamman, William. <u>A Search for Stability: United States Diplomacy toward Nicaragua, 1925–1933</u>. Notre Dame, Ind.: University of Notre Dame Press, 1968. xiii, 263 pp. Index, biblio., maps.

A meticulous study of U.S. policy in Nicaragua during the intervention, covering the years 1925 through 1933, based principally on State Department documents and secondary works. The volume focuses on U.S. policy in Nicaragua rather than on Nicaraguan politics during this era, though there is some consideration of both; the emphasis is on the Yankee viewpoint and objectives. Seeks to identify the rationale for policy and the errors involved, with an assessment of the results and the realistic alternatives. DLC LNHT

369   Keasbey, Lindley Miller. <u>The Early Diplomatic History of the Nicaragua Canal</u>. Newark, N.J.: Holbrook Printing, 1890. viii, 130 pp. Notes, maps.

Originally a doctoral dissertation in political science, this brief volume provides an overview of the early diplomatic exchanges with the Central American nations and England. Covers the first half of the nineteenth century, employing published documents, secondary works, the <u>Congressional Record</u>, and British Parliamentary Papers. DLC

370   _____. <u>Der Nicaragua-Kanal: Geschichte und Beurteilung des Projekts</u>. Strassburg: Verlag Von Karl J. Trübner, 1893. xii, 109 pp. Notes, maps.

A survey of the various canal projects proposed throughout the nineteenth century, providing an overview of their rise and fall and the reasons for their failure, as well as a review of each of the proposed routes, concluding that the Nicaragua route offered the best prospects. Based on published documents and secondary works. DLC

371   _____. <u>The Nicaraguan Canal and the Monroe Doctrine: A Political History of Isthmus Transit with Special Reference to the Nicaragua Canal Project and the Attitude of the United States Government Thereto</u>. New York: Putnam, 1896. xvi, 622 pp. Index, notes, illus., maps, tables.

A scholarly survey of Central America and canal projects, including geographic background and proposals throughout the Colonial era and the nineteenth century, and of the diplomatic clashes between England and Spain as well as between the United States and England regarding control of the region. Includes excerpts from the notes exchanged, drawn from published documents; discussion of Central American internal developments; and the diplomatic objectives of the United States. Incorporates portions of the author's earlier works but adds much material. About half the volume deals with the Anglo-American disputes. DLC LNHT

372   Keenagh, Peter. <u>Mosquito Coast: An Account of a Journey through the Jungles of Honduras</u>. London: Chatto & Windus, 1937. xi, 286 pp. Illus., maps. 2d ed. Boston: Houghton Mifflin, 1938. xi, 286 pp. Illus., maps.

A travelogue describing the author's wanderings in the Mosquito region, which was then still partly unexplored. The trip was largely one of adventure and the author had no prior knowledge to draw on, hence his report consists merely of his impressions and what he heard. Includes hearsay history such as accounts of the career of Lee Christmas, but consists mainly of description and adventure. Contains photos of the region, mainly of individuals and housing. DLC LNHT

373   Keller, François Antoine Édouard. <u>Canal de Nicaragua: notice sur la navigation transatlantique des paquebots interocéaniques, ou, Recherches sur les plus court trajet</u>

d'Europe à Saint-Jean de Nicaragua et retour,
et sur le régime des courants, des vents et
des tempêtes dans l'océan Atlantique
septentrionale. Paris: Dalmont & Dunod,
1859. 222 pp. Maps, tables.

Rather than being a discussion of the canal
itself, this volume presumes its construction
and examines in great detail the best shipping
routes to Nicaragua; the emphasis is on routes
from Europe and France, but considerations of
Pacific sailing are included as well. Discusses all the proposed routes between the
Caribbean Islands, considering currents, wind,
climate, harbors, special sailing techniques
necessary, advantages to sailing and steam
ships, and similar factors. DLC LNHT

374 Kendall, John Smith. A Midsummer Trip to
Nicaragua. New Orleans: Picayune, 1905. 22
pp. Illus.

A glowing description of Bluefields and
Cabo de Gracias a Dios and their delights for
the traveler, encouraging prospective visitors
while hailing President Zelaya. DLC

375 Klette, Immanuel J. From Atlantic to Pacific:
A New Inter-ocean Canal. New York: Harper &
Row, 1967. x, 143 pp. Index, Biblio., notes,
maps.

A summary of the issues involved in the
proposed construction of a new sea-level
canal, focusing on the broad questions of
financing, construction methods, utility,
feasibility, and so on rather than on the
details of location. DLC

376 Kretzschmar, W. Das Deutsche Kolonisierungs-
Projekt an der Mosquito-Küste, unter Angabe
des Hauptinhalts des betreffenden preussischen
Untersuchungs berichtes beleuchtet.
Königsberg: Theodor Theile, 1845. 36 pp.
Maps.

A brief account of the settlement project
seeking to extend German influence to the
region, with detailed description of the precise location and extent of the concession.
DLC

377 Laínez, Francisco. Terremoto '72: elites y
pueblo. Managua: Editorial Unión de Cardoza,
1977. 258 pp.

A critical commentary on the reconstruction
effort that followed the quake, focusing not
on the usual charges of corruption but on the
conception and utility of the effort. Contends that the plan selected was designed to
serve the elite while neglecting the needs of
the poor by spreading the city outward without
providing additional services such as public
transit, water, telephone, and electric service in sufficient amounts in the dispersed
outlying districts, with the result that the
new arrangement benefitted only the wealthy
with the money to pay for services. LNHT

378 Latin American Bureau. Nicaragua: Dictatorship and Revolution. London: Latin American
Bureau, 1979. 52 pp.

A journalistic summary of the fall of the
Somoza dictatorship in terms sympathetic to
the Sandinistas, with a pro-rebel account of
the fighting and a denunciation of the old
regime, cataloging its abuses, noting revolutionary charges against it, condemning the
Yankee support for Somoza over the years, and
echoing the Sandinista complaints regarding
the U.S. stand during the final months of the
civil war. DLC

379 Letts, John M. California Illustrated:
Including a Description of the Panama and
Nicaragua Routes. New York: William
Holdredge, 1852. 224 pp. Illus.

An account of the author's adventures in
California during the Gold Rush, with extensive chapters detailing his trips to and from
that region via Central America, providing
descriptions of what he observed and of his
adventures in Nicaragua and Panama. Reflecting the prevailing Yankee stereotypes and
attitudes, they focus on the trials and tribulations of the passage, the absence of facilities, what the author considers exotica, and
descriptions of people met and places visited,
all emphasizing the differences from Yankee
practices. DLC

380 Lévy, Pablo. Notas geográficas y económicas
sobre la República de Nicaragua, y una
exposición completa de la cuestión del canal
interoceánico y la de inmigración con una
lista bibliográfica, la más completa hasta el
día de todos los libros y mapas relativos a la
América Central en general y a Nicaragua en
particular. Paris: E. Denne Schmitz, 1873.
xvi, 628 pp. Biblio., maps. Latest ed.
Managua: Banco de América, 1976. xxv, 548
pp. Biblio., maps, tables.

A detailed study of Nicaragua, written
during 1871 and published with a subvention by
the government of Nicaragua. The author is an
engineer, and his focus is on physical geography, flora, and fauna, though he also includes
chapters on history and political organization, as well as on economy and immigration,
the latter clearly being the reason for the
support by the government, which viewed dissemination of the information as an inducement
to investment and immigration. The descriptive portions dealing with geography, flora,
and fauna are particularly valuable for their
time. Title varies slightly in the later
editions. DLC

381 Lewis, Oscar. Sea Routes to the Gold Fields:
The Migration by Water to California in 1849-
1852. New York: Knopf, 1949. xiv, 286 pp.
Index, biblio., illus., maps.

A composite view of the trials and tribulations of the Gold Rush travelers to California, written from the journals of several
travelers. Includes chapters on the Nicaragua
and Panama passages, which, though they emphasize the travelers and facilities for them,
provide their impressions of the region, generally viewing it as a pestilence-ridden ob-
stacle to be passed. The commentaries provide
an indication of the lack of development of
the region, its seaports and towns at the

time, as well as of the impact of the flood of travelers. DLC

382 Leyton Rodríguez, Ruebén. El salario mínimo. Managua: Tipografía Barreto, 1946. 28 pp.
An examination of the Nicaraguan labor code of 1945, with arguments for the necessity of a national minimum wage. DLC

383 Linares, Julio. Letras nicaragüenses. Managua: Editorial San José, 1966. 85 pp. Illus.
A survey of Nicaraguan literature that treats the authors by generation and by school of thought. Lists the nation's principal writers and their works, with brief descriptions of their main characteristics. Though brief, the entries provide an overview of the trends in Nicaraguan literature and a brief scheme for classifying those who contributed to it. DLC LNHT

384 Liot, W.B. Panama, Nicaragua, and Tehuantepec: Or Considerations upon the Questions of Communication between the Atlantic and Pacific Oceans. London: Simpkin & Marshall, 1849. iv, 63 pp. Illus., appendixes.
A survey of the pros and cons of the proposed canal routes, concluding that all have their limits but that Panama is the most feasible. Includes engineering calculations relative to the Panama route. The author was a British naval captain who had visited Panama several times. DLC

385 Loos, Eduardo. Homenaje a SS. EE. los presidentes y ministros de los dos supremos gobiernos y los señores miembros del congreso de los dos repúblicas sobernas de Nicaragua y Costa-Rica [sic]. N.p., n.p., n.d. [1863]. 48 pp.
The request by the managing director of the Atlantic and Pacific International Ship-Canal Company for confirmation of the company's rights as successor to Félix Belly, with attached contracts, justifications, and discussion of the project and its potential benefits, directed to both governments, referring mainly to Nicaragua. DLC-LDS

386 López C., Julio, et al. La caída del somocismo y la lucha Sandinista en Nicaragua. San José: EDUCA, 1979. 325 pp.
A compilation of statements and proclamations by the FSLN movement, presenting its analysis of Nicaraguan society and its inequities. The items represent the official position of the Sandinistas during the years 1977-79, covering the key years of their struggle for power, and indicate their view of the political, social, and economic condition of the nation and their condemnation of the inequities of the Somoza regime. DLC

387 Lorio, Juan. Nuestra cuestión agraria. Managua: Editora la Nación, 1963. 39 pp.
A denunciation of the current agrarian policy of the Somoza government and a call for vigorous organization of the peasant leagues to press for reform.

388 ____. Relatos nicaragüenses. Managua: n.p., 1967. 102 pp.
A collection of short stories by a manual laborer recounting, with some grammatical flaws, the perspective of his fellow workers and their everyday activities. Includes stories of conflict with the Guardia Nacional, arrest, and hassles with government regulations, emphasizing frustration. Conveys the impression of a regime of all-pervasive force that merely annoys the populace by imposing barriers, a regime under which the people are constantly compelled to find ways to outsmart or avoid the law, government, and army. DLC LNHT

389 Lorio, Juan, and Armando Amador. Unión nacional en Nicaragua; ubicación de los trabajadores frente a la dictadura de Somoza. Guatemala: Imprenta La República, 1946. 28 pp.
An anti-Somoza tract written by two Nicaraguan exiles, consisting of two separate and unrelated essays, one by each of the coauthors.

390 Lucas, Daniel Bedinger. Nicaragua: War of the Filibusters. Richmond, Va.: B.F. Johnson, 1896. 216 pp. Illus., maps.
A sympathetic account of Walker's efforts to gain control of Nicaragua, providing a brief narration in which Walker emerges as a hero who is still well regarded in Central America, though not quite as vividly or picturesquely as in some accounts. This is followed by a discussion of the Nicaraguan canal question by W.A. MacCorkle and an essay on the Monroe Doctrine by J. Fairfax McLaughlin, both arguing for construction of the canal and stressing the importance of naval power to the United States. The accounts are philosophical in nature and add little new information, though they represent the thinking of their time. DLC LNHT

391 Macaulay, Neill Webster. The Sandino Affair. Chicago: Quadrangle, 1967. 319 pp. Index, biblio., notes, illus., maps.
Sandino. San José: EDUCA, 1970. 346 pp. Index, biblio., notes, illus., maps.
A detailed military history of the guerrilla warfare in Nicaragua during the years 1927-33, when Augusto César Sandino challenged the U.S. Marines. Traces the battlefield exploits that made him a hero for defying the Yankee intervention, through his assassination by Anastacio Somoza and the Guardia Nacional. The focus is on the military conflict rather than the political situation. Based on U.S. military records and secondary works. DLC LNHT BNCR

392 MacGregor, Gregor. Plan of a Constitution for the Inhabitants of the Indian Coast in Central America, Commonly Called the Mosquito Shore. Edinburgh: Balfour & Jack, 1836. 35 pp.

A proposed constitution for a separate state of Mosquitia, which would, of course, be under British protection. Reflects the British efforts in the region and the designs of the English settlers there. LNHT

393 Madriz, José. Informes sobre la cuestión de la Mosquitia. 2 vols. Managua: Tipografía Nacional, 1894-95. 273 pp.

A collection of reports, decrees, declarations, and supporting documents relative to the Nicaraguan claim to the Mosquito Territory and in opposition to that of Great Britain. Includes documents relating to the United States position, such as the Clayton-Bulwer Treaty and Dallas-Calderón convention. DLC LNHT

394 _____. Por Nicaragua. San José: Imprenta Alsina, 1905. 62 pp.

A series of letters to the Nicaraguan minister of foreign relations, Adolfo Altamirano, responding to and taking issue with various statements and publications of the minister and attacking his actions. Part of the political polemic of this era, the commentaries depict the regime of José Santos Zelaya as a brutal dictatorship based on force and characterized by corruption. The letters were written from exile in San Salvador during 1904. BNCR

395 Manson, Nathaniel J. The Nicaragua Canal: Corporate Construction and Control against the Policy and Business Interests of the United States. San Francisco: P.J. Thomas, 1892. 27 pp.

An argument against the Maritime Canal Company, contending that the government, rather than giving monopoly control to a private entity, should excercise such control itself and operate the canal directly to guarantee the interests of all. Cites precedents of government operation of domestic locks and canals. DLC

396 Mántica, Carlos. El habla nicaragüense; estudio morfológico y semántico. San José: EDUCA, 1973. 429 pp. Biblio.

An analysis of the influence of the Nicaraguan Indian cultures and languages on the nation's speech, followed by a dictionary of Nahuatalisms, a dictionary of Toponimias in use in that nation, and a comparative dictionary of the Indian languages of the nation. The dictionaries are all arranged alphabetically, with definitions and explanations of the origins of the terms. BNCR

397 Maraboto, Emigdio E. Sandino ante El Coloso: un atentado internacional de Los Estados Unidos. Veracruz, Mexico: n.p., 1929. 36 pp.

A pro-Sandino account by a Mexican reporter who met the Nicaraguan leader during a period of exile in Veracruz. Combines some narrative with excerpts from various proclamations, protests, and public statements, all attacking Yankee imperialism and hailing Sandino's efforts to preserve Nicaraguan sovereignty. NcU

398 Marcoleta, José de. Documentos diplomáticos para servir a la historia de Nicaragua. Paris: Imprenta Hispano-América, 1869. 58 pp. 2d ed. Managua: Banco de América, 1976. 84 pp.

A collection of documents relative to the efforts of a nineteenth-century Nicaraguan diplomat who represented his nation in Washington and Europe several times during a long career. The items in this collection relate to his mission of 1854 and include his protests against the bombardment of Greytown (San Juan del Norte) and subsequent military expeditions in the Nicaraguan Atlantic Coast, which he charged reflected Yankee ambitions in the area. They include his exchanges with the State Department and with the Nicaraguan Foreign Ministry. The second edition employs the title Documentos diplomáticos de don José de Marcoleta, ministro de Nicaragua en los Estados Unidos, 1854. LNHT

399 Maritime Canal Company and the Nicaraguan Canal Construction Co. The Maritime Ship Canal of Nicaragua. New York: Published by the Company, 1890. 17 pp. Illus., maps, tables, appendixes.

A brief pamphlet extolling the Nicaragua route and the company's plans to exploit it, designed to encourage investors and promote this route in the continuing dispute about the location of the canal. LNHT

400 Maritime Canal Company of Nicaragua. Nicaragua: The Gateway to the Pacific. New York: J. Bien, 1889. 20 pp. Illus., maps.

A brief statement in support of the feasibility of the Nicaraguan canal. Prepared by the company for the 1889 Universal Exposition in Paris, it has text in English, Spanish, French, and German, and maps of the route and its location in terms of the world's trade routes. DLC DLC-LDS-261 LNHT

401 Marure, Alejandro. Memoria histórica sobre el canal de Nicaragua. Guatemala: Imprenta de la Paz, 1845. 47 pp. Notes, maps, appendix.

A discussion of the possibilities of a canal in Nicaragua, with a narration of early efforts to promote one. Deals with the period from 1800 through 1844, discussing the practicality of such an effort, the canal's potential location, and its importance to Central America. Excerpts from a report by John Baily regarding the Nicaraguan route are appended. DLC DLC-LDS-438 LNHT BNG

402 Masís Rojas, Teresa. Breve introducción para el estudio de la guerra contra los filibusteros, 1856-57. San José: Imprenta Lehmann, 1956. 79 pp. Index, biblio., illus., maps.

A day-by-day outline listing the events of 1853 through 1857 relating to the Walker intervention in Central America. The emphasis is on the Costa Rican role, but the important actions of other isthmian nations and those of Walker are included. DLC LNHT BNCR

403 Matamoro J., T. La República de Nicaragua. Managua: Tipografía Internacional, 1907. 146 pp. Illus., maps.
    DLC

404 Matus, Ramon Ignacio. Estudio crítico sobre dos órdenes de fusilación durante la guerra de 1912, atribuidas al general don Emiliano Chamorro. Managua: Tipografía Gutenberg, 1916. 51 pp. Illus.
    DLC

405 _____. Rectificación histórica a "El caso Nicaragua" del Dr. Leonardo Argüello. Managua: n.p., 1918. 144 pp.
    A response to the indicated title, constituting part of the political polemic about the Bryan-Chamorro Treaty and the role of the Yankees in Nicaragua.

406 Mayes Huete, Guillermo. Campaña nacional centroamericana contra los filibusteros en Nicaragua, 1856-1956. Tegucigalpa: Ministerio de Educación Pública, 1956. 59 pp. Biblio., illus., appendixes.
    A brief, patriotic account of the campaign against Walker, written to commemorate its centennial. DPU

407 Medina, Alberto. Efemérides nicaragüenses, 1502-1941. Managua: La Nueva Prensa, 1945. 278 pp. Biblio.
    A series of short essays discussing significant events in Nicaraguan history, arranged in calendar form by month and day, but with the years varying so that the most significant event of each day is discussed regardless of era. Dates are covered selectively, with only a few from each month represented. The essays, drawn from secondary sources, are basically descriptive and patriotic. DLC LNHT

408 Medina, Crisanto. Le Nicaragua en 1900. Paris: L'imprimerie Kugelmann, 1900. 54 pp. Illus., maps.
    A compendium of basic information about Nicaragua and the other Central American nations, prepared for the Central American Exposition in Paris in 1900. Contains the constitution then in force and other documents. DLC

409 Mejía Sánchez, Ernesto. Romances y corridos nicaragüenses. Mexico: Imprenta Universitaria, 1946. 122 pp. Notes, illus., maps. Latest ed. Managua: Banco de América, 1976. 122 pp. Notes, illus., maps.
    A collection of the lyrics of popular Nicaraguan folksongs, particularly corridos, with music. Includes source citations that provide an indication of the region of the country in which the author heard the song. The introduction provides a general context and discusses the various currents in Nicaraguan folksongs and the origins of different types. DLC LNHT

410 Melville, George Wallace. Views of Commodore George W. Melville, Chief Engineer of the Navy, as to the Strategic and Commercial Value of the Nicaraguan Canal, the Future Control of the Pacific Ocean, the Strategic Value of Hawaii, and its Annexation to the United States. Washington, D.C.: GPO, 1898. 33 pp.
    A statement by the chief engineer of the U.S. Navy, reflecting the doctrines of Admiral Mahan and the new U.S. position in the Pacific resulting from the Spanish-American War. Focuses on the importance of access to and control of the Pacific to the future of the United States, with brief remarks about the canal. CU-B

411 Mendieta Alfaro, Roger. El último marine: 1979 año de la Liberación. Managua: Editorial Unión Cardoza, 1979. 314 pp. Illus.

412 Mendoza, Juan Manuel. Historia de Diriamba (ciudad del Departamento de Carazo, República de Nicaragua). Guatemala: Imprenta Electra, 1920. 530 pp. Illus. 2d ed. Guatemala: Imprenta Electra, 1933. 532 pp. Illus.
    Though it provides a capsule history of the city's early background, this monograph focuses principally on the initial years of the twentieth century and the author's reminiscences of his native city. Contains a good deal regarding social life, customs, and folklore, and is highly critical of misrule by Conservatives, contending that the problems of this city are symptomatic of those throughout the isthmus. DLC LNHT BNG

413 Meneses, J. Barcenas. Las conferences del "Denver." Managua: Tipografía Nacional, 1926. 79 pp. Illus.
    The official minutes and agreements of the conference aboard the U.S.S. Denver, at which the United States mediated between the Liberal and Conservative parties, with commentaries about the sessions. The author was the secretary of the Conservative party delegation representing the incumbent regime of Emiliano Chamorro. LNHT

414 Menocal, Aniceto García. The Nicaragua Canal. Boston: Damrell & Upham, 1893. 38 pp.
    A continuation of the author's propaganda in favor of the Nicaragua route, reflecting his convictions and his association with a group holding part of the rights to that route. DPU

415 _____. The Nicaragua Canal: Its Design, Final Location, and Work Accomplished, 1890. New York: New York Printing Co., 1890. 29 pp.
    A brief statement of the prospects of the Nicaraguan route and progress toward securing the rights to it, written, as part of the propaganda regarding the location of the canal, by a civil engineer who served with the U.S. Nicaragua Surveying Party. By the time he wrote this, Menocal was serving with the Nicaraguan Canal Association and had negotiated an agreement with Costa Rica in 1888 granting the association rights to the portion of the route involving that nation. NN

(Menocal, Aniceto García)
416   ____. Report of the U.S. Nicaragua Surveying
Party--1885. 49th Cong., 1st sess. S. Doc.
99. Washington, D.C.: GPO, 1886. 55 pp.
Illus., maps.
    A civil engineer's survey of the potential
Nicaraguan routes for the proposed canal, with
appropriate maps and technical data. Details
the party's exploration trip and the resulting
data, concluding that the Nicaragua route is
feasible. Includes cost estimates and full
descriptions of the locks and facilities
needed, and their location. DLC LNHT

417 Merry, William Lawrence. The Nicaragua Canal,
the Gateway between the Oceans. San
Francisco: Commercial Publishing Co., 1895.
46 pp. Illus.
    A brief description of the proposed canal
and its advantages to the West Coast, extolling its practicality and arguing that such a
canal is essential to national development.
DLC

418   ____. Report of the Special Committee on
Interoceanic Canal "The Key to the Pacific" of
the Board of Trade of San Francisco. San
Francisco: Dempster Bros., 1880. 33 pp.
    A brief committee report and a memorial to
Congress by the Board of Trade. Succinctly
summarizes the relative advantages of the
Nicaragua and Panama routes, arguing that only
the Nicaragua route is feasible and that rapid
construction and control by the U.S. is essential to the growth of San Francisco and the
Pacific states. DLC

419 Meyer, Harvey Kessler. Historical Dictionary
of Nicaragua. Metuchen, N.J.: Scarecrow
Press, 1972. xiii, 503 pp. Biblio., illus.,
maps.
    The most extensive and complete of the
Central American volumes of this series, with
its usual characteristics and limitations.
Particularly strong on the definition of terms
and place names; offers some lengthy essays,
thus providing much more satisfactory information about some of the nation's key figures
and events than other volumes in the series.
DLC LNHT

420 Miller, Hugh Gordon. The Isthmian Highway:
A Review of the Political Problems of the
Caribbean. New York: Macmillan, 1929. xiv,
327 pp. Index, illus., appendixes. Reprint.
New York: Arno Press, 1970. xiv, 327 pp.
Index, illus., appendixes.
    A survey of the canal question and of
American interests in the Caribbean since the
Monroe Doctrine, describing the existing
Panama Canal and proposing an additional one
in Nicaragua, all from the viewpoint of their
significance for Yankee naval power and commerce. Includes discussion of rights under
contemporary maritime law, and the texts of
the various treaties relating to the canal
questions. DLC

421 Miller, Jacob William. Where to Build the
Isthmian Canal. New York: Wynkoop,
Hallenbeck & Crawford, 1902. 16 pp.

    A defense of the Nicaragua route written by
a retired navy commander serving as president
of the Nicaragua Canal Company, contending
that nothing has changed since the Walker
Commission report. He cites greater engineering difficulties in Panama and the greater
economic potential of Nicaragua. DLC LNHT

422 Millett, Richard. Guardians of the Dynasty:
A History of the U.S.-Created Guardia Nacional
de Nicaragua and the Somoza Family.
Maryknoll, N.Y.: Orbis Books, 1977. 284 pp.
Index, biblio., notes, illus.
Guardianes de la Dinastía. San José: EDUCA,
1979.
    A scathing indictment of the Somoza dynasty
and the Nicaraguan National Guard, based on
research in U.S. documents and appropriate
secondary sources. The portions tracing the
rise of Somoza and the formation of the
Guardia are more balanced than the discussion
of the regime of Anastacio Somoza Debayle.
The account is critical of U.S. support for
Somoza, indicating the failure of this policy
and the false premises on which it was based.
The introduction, written by a Maryknoll mis-
sioner who was one of the leaders of the
Sandinista revolution and who became the new
regime's foreign minister, reflects the revolutionary viewpoint of the Somoza years. Provides an overview of the dictatorship and the
role of the military, demonstrating the grievances that ultimately led to the civil war.
DLC LNHT

423 Miner, William Harvey. Bananas: The Story of
a Trip to the Great Plantations of Nicaragua,
Central America. Sioux Falls, S.Dak.: Sioux
Plantation Company, 1915. 59 pp.
    A description of the author's impressions
during a sojourn in Nicaragua, focusing on his
experiences and observations. He emphasizes
what he regards as valuable commercial possibilities of interest to the United States.
Commentary on crops and potential crops, such
as the banana, is included, but the work encompasses narration of experiences, description of facilities encountered and discussion
of the conditions and possibilities of the
region. LNHT

424 Molina Argüello, Carlos. La enseñanza de la
historia de Nicaragua. Mexico: PAIGH, 1953.
222 pp. Index, appendixes.
    A general description of the present state
of instruction in Nicaragua, written as part
of a series covering many of the Latin American states. Contains descriptions of the
programs, methods, and materials employed in
teaching history at the elementary and inter-
mediate levels, and notes the various types of
schools that provide instruction. The latter
portion consists of an appendix containing
existing laws relating to education and outlines of the official history programs. It is
clear that the curriculum focuses on general
history and the Colonial period, with brief
consideration of the nineteenth century. The
latter stresses Central American ties that

(Molina Argüello, Carlos)
link the entire isthmus. Coverage of the
twentieth century is minimal. DLC LNHT

425 _____. Misiones nicaragüenses en archivos
Europeos. Mexico: PAIGH, 1957. 163 pp.
Notes.
Part of a series by the Institute, this
volume lists the various Nicaraguan diplomatic
missions to Europe, providing a brief résumé
of each diplomat and his objectives, followed
by an unannotated list of documents that refer
to his mission in the various European archives. The majority of the volume consists
of a list of citations from Colonial times,
though the portion referring to the diplomatic
efforts does focus on the independence era.
DLC

426 Moncada, José María. Estados Unidos en
Nicaragua. Managua: Tipografía Atenas, 1942.
206 pp. Illus.
The Nicaraguan Liberal leader's account of
the U.S. mediation that led to the 1926 elections and the substitution of Yankee-
supervised elections for civil warfare.
Stresses the positive impact of the Yankee
efforts and the resulting peace, and defends
his own participation in the mediation. Provides a Nicaraguan counterpart to the Stimson
memoirs of the same episode. DLC

427 _____. El ideal ciudadano: obra declarada de
texto por el presidente de la república para
la clase de lectura en las escuelas
elementales, en el cuarto o quinto grades.
Managua: Tipografía Alemana, 1929. xv,
252 pp.
A patriotic text indicating what one
Nicaraguan political figure felt the nation's
youth should be taught. It includes discussions of the family and of the citizen, a
brief historical outline of the nation, and
patriotic passages about the national anthem
and flag. DLC DLC-LDS LNHT

428 _____. Imperialism and the Monroe Doctrine:
Their Influence in Central America. New York:
Gahan, 1911. 55 pp.
A commentary seeking to define the Monroe
Doctrine and imperialism in ways that separate
beneficial intervention from imperialism, investment from property ownership, and protection from conquest, all with an eye to the
author's role in Nicaraguan politics and his
links to the Northern Colossus. Treads a fine
line that justifies some types of intervention
in cases of great wrongdoing (such as those of
the author's political opponents) while limiting intervention to the special cases and
emphasizing cooperation as the norm. DLC

429 _____. Lo porvenir. Managua: Tipografía
Alemana, 1929. 207 pp. 3d ed. Managua:
Tipografía Nacional, 1930.
The autobiography of a Nicaraguan political
leader, written from exile to detail his efforts on behalf of the nation and his ambitions for it, recounting the early portion of
his life, prior to his service as president.

The emphasis is on his participation in political coups and revolutions rather than on his
program, though the broad objectives he seeks
are woven into the account. LNHT

430 _____. La revolución de 1903 y el golpe de
estado del 8 de febrero de 1904. Tegucigalpa:
Tipografía Nacional, 1904. 59 pp.

431 Montalvan, José H. Apuntes para la historia
de la Universidad de León. León: Imprenta La
Patria, 1943. 101 pp.
A brief overview of the University of
Nicaragua from its foundation in Colonial days
to the present. Consists principally of brief
paragraphs on each of its rectors but also
includes essays on the university's role in
the intellectual life of Central America and
in its administrative evolution. DLC LNHT

432 _____. Breves apuntes para la historia del
periodismo nicaragüense. León: Universidad
Nacional de Nicaragua, 1958. 89 pp.
A compilation of information about the
various newspapers and journals published in
Nicaragua since independence, providing data
on their style, content, outlook, political
affiliation, and editors. DLC

433 _____. Vida universitaria de Nicaragua.
Managua: Talleres Nacionales, 1950. 106 pp.
A brief history of the University of
Nicaragua, with emphasis on its rectors and
including quotations from the documents, followed by an account of the celebration of its
centennial in 1914 and the records of the
meetings of its alumni since 1944. Published
as a companion piece to the author's Apuntes
para la historia de la Universidad de León.
DLC

434 Montiel Argüello, Alejandro. La Corte Suprema
y el derecho internacional. Managua:
Editorial Aurora, 1967. 124 pp.
A compilation of the rulings of the
Nicaraguan Supreme Court relating to questions
of international law, with brief summaries of
each case. The chronological arrangement of
cases under various topics is intended to
enable international lawyers to consult them
easily in the absence of any published index
to the rulings of the court. The subjects
covered include consuls, diplomats, nationality, treaties, rights of foreigners, etc.
LNHT

435 _____. Incidentes diplomáticos. Managua:
Editorial San Enrique, 1955. 16 pp.
A series of essays by the Nicaraguan vice-
minister of foreign relations dealing with
disparate episodes of the nineteenth century,
principally focusing on the Walker intervention but referring also to Squier and his
mission. BNCR

436 Montúfar y River Maestre, Lorenzo. Walker en
Centro-América. 2 vols. Guatemala:
Tipografía "La Unión," 1887. 1062 pp. 2d ed.
New York: Lenox Hill, 1972.

An account of the Walker intervention and the Central American reaction to it, by a prolific Guatemalan polemicist and Liberal writer who is, naturally, sympathetic to the Central American viewpoint. The abundant detail clearly indicates that the work is based on considerable research, despite the absence of a bibliography and footnotes. Contains copious excerpts from documents and secondary works, which are identified in the text, and traces the entire episode, the background to it, as well as the responses in all the Central American republics. DLC LNHT BNCR

437   Morrison, George Austin, ed. <u>Compilation of Executive Documents and Diplomatic Correspondence Relative to a Trans-Isthmian Canal in Central America</u>. 3 vols. New York: Evening Post, 1899.
      NN

438   Morrison, Hugh A., ed. <u>List of Books and of Articles in Periodicals Relating to the Interoceanic Canal and Railroad Routes (Nicaragua; Panama, Darien, and the Valley of the Atrato; Tehuantepec and Honduras; Suez Canal)</u> . . . <u>with an Appendix: Bibliography of United States Public Documents</u>. 56th Cong., 1st sess. S. Doc. 59. Washington, D.C.: GPO, 1900. 174 pp.
      Published as a congressional document, this compilation contains an extensive list of over 800 pamphlets, books, and government reports and documents, with brief descriptive annotations indicating their content. Although the listing is general, the index allows consultation of items relative to Nicaragua. DLC LNHT

439   Moser, René. <u>Adorable Nicaragua</u>. Paris: Éditions Delroisse, n.d. 180 pp. Illus.
      A photo essay on contemporary Nicaragua, with a brief historical synopsis and narrative by Raymond Pons, former French ambassador to Nicaragua. Emphasizes beauty and exotica and presents a glowing image of the nation in living color. DLC

440   Mueller, Karl A. <u>Among Creoles, Miskitos, and Sumos: Eastern Nicaragua and Its Moravian Missions</u>. Bethlehem, Pa.: Comenias Press, 1932. 156 pp. Illus., maps.
      A history of the Moravian missions in eastern Nicaragua, from their initiation in the mid-nineteenth century. Based on mission reports and a visit by the author in 1928, it includes description of the terrain, climate, and similar factors. Focuses particularly on the Indians, discussing their customs, language, skills, adaptability, and similar aspects; reflects the educational efforts of the missions in preparing them to enter the modern world. CU

441   Murillo, Andrés. <u>Sufragio libre en Nicaragua</u>. Managua: Tipografía Nacional, 1924. 114 pp.
      An essay extolling the electoral reform in Nicaragua, contending the era of the imposition of official candidates through electoral manipulation had passed. Hails those involved in the effort and details the elections of 1924, acclaiming the result. Includes a collection of statements and commentaries by many individuals regarding the new system and its functioning. DLC

442   Murillo Valladares, Gilberto. <u>Transición</u>. Managua: Editora Nacional, 1963. 214 pp. Illus.
      An official Liberal party account of the government of Luís Somoza Debayle, viewing it as a historic and stabilizing bridge between the regime of his assassinated father, General Anastacio Somoza García, and that of Dr. René Schick Gutiérrez. Contends that this was an era in which the Liberal party renewed and restructured itself to a more democratic and civilian rule under the leadership of the two Somoza brothers, upon whom it heaps lavish praise. Half the volume consists of an account of the accomplishments of the regime of Luís Somoza Debayle, and the other half offers data regarding Schick, including his vita, an account of the campaign, and various attacks on the Conservative party and its efforts to oppose the Liberal machine. LNHT

443   Narváez Rosales, Reynaldo. <u>En las tierras del laudo</u>. Tegucigalpa: Editorial Paulino Valladares, 1963. 55 pp.
      An account of the author's travels, observations, and experiences in the Mosquito Territory, seeking to promote interest in the eastern coast of Nicaragua. The compilation includes description, collected folklore, and proposals for the economic development of the region and its more effective integration into the nation. IEdS

444   Navas y Barraza, Juan M. <u>La educación sexual: estudio de la sexualidad en Nicaragua, en Centroamérica, y en Rubén Darío</u>. Managua: n.p., 1967. 299 pp. Biblio., illus.
      A collection of material, commentaries, and statistics on all aspects of sex and sex education in Nicaraguan society, including several surveys taken in Managua. DLC

445   Navas Zepeda, Máximo. <u>Los cancilleres de Nicaragua, 1838-1936</u>. Managua: PINSA, 1976. 279 pp. Index, biblio., illus.
      A collection of brief biographical sketches of each of the individuals who held the post of foreign minister of Nicaragua from 1838 to 1936, providing for each an outline of his background, a summary of his political career, and a summary of his principal actions as foreign minister. The articles originally appeared separately in the newspaper <u>La Nación</u>. LNHT

446   Nicaise, Auguste. <u>Les filibustiers américains: Walker et l'Amérique Centrale. Le tuerie de jaguars</u>. Paris: n.p., 1861. 172 pp. Reprint. New York: Lenox Hill, 1972.
      A balanced summary of the Walker episode. DLC

447   Nicaragua Canal Construction Company. <u>The Inter-Oceanic Canal of Nicaragua: Its</u>

(Nicaragua Canal Construction Company)
History, Physical Condition, Plans, and
Prospects. New York: Nicaragua Canal
Construction Company, 1892. 88 pp. Illus.,
maps, tables, appendixes.
   A statement of the advantages of the
Nicaragua route and its history, including
previous plans and efforts, with a collection
of pertinent documents regarding the company
and its rights, detailing its concessions.
Clearly designed to encourage investment, it
provides details as to the proposed construction and its costs, as well as optimistic
estimates of traffic. DLC LNHT

448   _____. The Nicaragua Canal: With the Compli-
       ments of the Nicaraguan Canal Construction
       Company. New York: Republic Press, 1893. 21
       pp. Maps.
          DLC

449   Nicaragua Canal Convention. Proceedings of
       the Nicaragua Canal Convention Held at St.
       Louis, Mo., in the Exposition Music Hall on
       the 2nd and 3rd Days of June, 1892. St.
       Louis: n.p., 1892. 75 pp. Tables.
          The proceedings of a meeting held to pro-
       mote the construction of a canal in Nicaragua,
       with speeches and correspondence emphasizing
       its potential and importance for the economic
       growth of the United States. Also presents
       details regarding the present situation in
       Nicaragua and the concessions then available.
       LNHT

450   Nicaragua Canal: Description of Route, Esti-
       mated Cost and Business. Washington, D.C.:
       Thomas McGill, 1885. 20 pp. Maps, tables.
          A pamphlet for the general public, designed
       to demonstrate the feasibility of the canal by
       indicating potential revenue. DLC LNHT

451   The Nicaragua Canal: Expected Earnings--A
       Study of Its Commercial Geography, Its Effect
       on Ocean Routes--New Trade Advantages for the
       U.S. New York: Evening Post, 1888. 15 pp.
          A series of articles published in the New
       York Evening Post in 1888 advocating construc-
       tion of the Nicaraguan canal and discussing
       its potential and significance for the U.S.
       DLC LNHT

452   Nicaragua, Comité Pro. Nicaragua Intervenida
       ante el pueblo centroamericano. La emigración
       nicaragüense en Guatemala, anota el folleto
       conservador editado en Nicaragua. Guatemala:
       Sánchez & de Guise, 1923. 63 pp.
          Part of a political polemic in which a
       group of exiles reply to an official govern-
       ment publication. DLC

453   Nicaragua, Universidad Nacional de.
       Universidad Nacional de Nicaragua:
       Sesquicentenario 1812-1962. León:
       Universidad Nacional de Nicaragua, 1962. 171
       pp. Illus.
          A commemorative volume issued on the occa-
       sion of the 150th anniversary of the univer-
       sity. Contains documentation regarding its
       foundation but consists mainly of the

speeches and congratulatory telegrams of
the occasion. DLC

454   Nicaragua, Universidad Nacional Autónoma de.
       El terremoto de Managua y sus consecuencias.
       León: Universidad Nacional Autónoma de
       Nicaragua, 1973. 148 pp. Illus., maps.
          Several essays on the impact of the earth-
       quake on Managua, covering the geological
       event and its effects on urban planning, the
       national economy, and the university. DLC

455   Nicaragua, Gov't of. Convenciones
       internacionales de Nicaragua. Managua:
       Tipografía de Matamoros J., 1913. 286 pp.
          A collection of the texts of the various
       agreements signed by the nation. DLC

456   _____. Índice alfabético del código civil de
       la república. Managua: Tipografía Nacional,
       1883. 37 pp.

457   _____. Índice cronológico por materias
       de leyes y disposiciones generales de la
       República de Nicaragua, hasta junio 30 de
       1945. Managua: Editorial La Nueva Prensa,
       1946. 264 pp.
          An index to Nicaraguan legislation,
       arranged by topic and date. DLC

458   _____. La República de Nicaragua. Managua:
       Tipografía Nacional, 1907. viii, 146 pp.
       Illus., maps.
          An official publication of the José Santos
       Zelaya regime, produced at the request of
       Nicaraguan diplomatic representatives abroad
       to provide an official compilation of data
       about the country, its economy, and its pres-
       ent state and to help acquaint foreigners with
       the nation and its economic prospects. It
       focuses on the present situation, with exten-
       sive photographs of public buildings, facto-
       ries, and transportation facilities, many of
       which no longer exist, having fallen victim to
       the various earthquakes that have wracked this
       nation. DLC LNHT

459   _____. Banco Central. Aspectos históricos de
       la moneda en Nicaragua. 2 vols. Managua:
       Editorial San Enrique, 1963. 150, 183 pp.
       Biblio., notes, illus., tables.
          A collection of documents relating to
       Nicaraguan monetary legislation from Colonial
       to present times, with some connecting narra-
       tion, illustrations of coins, and tables re-
       lating to equivalencies and government
       finances. Arranged chronologically, with each
       decade receiving about equal space. DLC LNHT
       BNG

460   _____. Biblioteca Nacional, Managua.
       Catálogo general de los libros de que consta
       la Biblioteca Nacional de la República de
       Nicaragua. Managua: Tipografía de Managua,
       1882. 90 pp.
          A list of the holdings of the National
       Library at that time. DLC

461   _____. Consulate General in Paris. Le
       Nicaragua: L'émigration française, le canal

(Nicaragua, Gov't of)
inter-océanique; documents publiés par le
Consulat Général de Nicaragua à Paris. Paris:
Consulat Général de Nicaragua, 1875. 22 pp.
   A series of documents, designed to encourage French immigration to Nicaragua by providing the letters of settlers and communications
regarding the proposed canal. DLC

462 _____. Dirección General de Estadística.
Monografía de Managua. Managua: Dirección
General de Estadística, 1948. 55 pp. Illus.,
maps.
   A compilation of demographic and economic
data about the province, compiled by a government agency. DLC

463 _____. Dirección General de Estadística y
Censos. El café en Nicaragua, 1951-1961.
Managua: Dirección General de Estadística y
Censos, 1961. 50 pp. Maps, tables.
   A summary of data from the 1957-58 coffee
census, but with projections and data drawn
from other sources to cover a ten-year period.
The final table provides export and price
figures for the entire century. DLC LNHT

464 _____. Instituto Geográfico Nacional. Guía
de recursos básicos contemporáneos para
estudios de desarrollo en Nicaragua. Managua:
PAIGH, 1977. ii, 86 pp. Biblio., maps,
tables.
   Following the pattern established by the
Institute, this brief booklet consists principally of a bibliography of locally published
books, articles, and maps dealing principally
with the nation's geography.

465 _____. Ministerio de Fomento y Obras
Públicas. Índice del catálogo de los
contratos, expedientes, planos, dibujos y
croquis del Archivo del Ministerio de Fomento
y Obras Públicas arreglado según las
instrucciones dadas por el señor ministro de
fomento y obras públicas don José María Siero
G. Managua: Tipografía Nacional, 1927.
172 pp.
   A listing of the agreements of the
Nicaraguan government, providing an indication
of dealings with foreign enterprises as well
as of the official plans and programs for all
public-works projects. Intended as an aid to
enable consultation of the texts, which were
then in the ministry. DLC

466 _____. Ministerio de Hacienda y Crédito
Público. Trabajo histórico de los empréstitos
fiscales de Nicaragua del año de 1851 hasta el
de 1905, desde el punto de vista de sus
conceptos legales. Managua: Tipografía
Nacional, 1906. 267 pp.
   A brief summary statement, arranged chronologically, describing each of the many loans
made by the various governments and stating
their terms and purposes. There are no data
regarding repayment. DLC

467 _____. Ministerio de Relaciones Exteriores.
Derecho de gentes positivo de la República de
Nicaragua. Managua: Ministerio de Relaciones
Exteriores, 1885. 267 pp.
   A collection of all the treaties signed by
Nicaragua between 1850 and 1878, including
accords with other Central American states and
European nations, plus the Federation pact of
1825, arranged chronologically. DLC

468 _____. _____. Documentos oficiales
referentes a la guerra entre Nicaragua y
Honduras de 1907, y a la participación de El
Salvador. Managua: Tipografía
Internacional, 1907. xxii, 228 pp.
   Documents and exchanges relating to the
dispute and the conflict, reflecting the efforts of José Santos Zelaya to establish hegemony over the isthmus and impose union by
military force. Includes the propaganda exchanges and charges, as well as communications
with the other Central American states. DLC

469 _____. _____. Documents and Correspondence
between the Republic of Nicaragua and the
Representatives of the German Empire, the
United States and England, in Regard to the
Eisenstück Affair, during the Years 1876, '77,
and '78. New York: Jones, 1878. iv, 120 pp.
   A series of exchanges involving one of the
many incidents stemming from the dispute regarding title to the Mosquito Territory. DLC

470 _____. _____. Documents Relating to the
Affairs in Bluefields, Republic of Nicaragua,
in 1894. Washington, D.C.: W.F. Roberts,
1895. xxiv, 64 pp.
   The Nicaraguan government's version of the
turmoil resulting from its 1894 war with
Honduras and the rebellion in Bluefields
during July 1894, designed to justify its
actions in seizing for investigation those
involved, which resulted in a dispute with
England since several British subjects were
involved. Includes the proceedings of the
investigation. DLC LNHT

471 _____. _____. Exposé par le gouvernement de
Nicaragua des faits relatifs aux points en
discussion avec le gouvernement de Sa Majesté
Britannique. Paris: Typographe Georges
Chamerot, 1879. 64 pp.
   The correspondence regarding one of the
many Anglo-Nicaraguan disputes over the
Mosquito Territory and its affairs, involving
financial claims and sovereignty. Includes a
full statement of the history of British involvement on the coast and the basis of their
rights, according to the Nicaraguan government. DLC

472 _____. _____. El gobierno de la República de
Nicaragua, por medio de su abogado el Dr. don
Manuel Pasos Arana, evacua el translado que la
Excma. Corte de Justicia Centroamericana le
concedio de la demanda promovida por el
gobierno de la República de El Salvador con
motivo del Tratado Chamorro-Bryan. San José:
Imprenta Lehmann, 1917. 62 pp.
   The Nicaraguan response to the Salvadoran
charges, defending its right to its canal
route and contending that it could not admit

(Nicaragua, Gov't of)
the right of other nations to interfere. DLC-
LDS-797 BNCR

473 _____. _____. Nueva discusión entre el
ajente [sic] de S.M.B. y el gobierno supremo
de Nicaragua sobre los derechos territoriales
de este estado en su Costa del Norte, llamada
de Mosquitos. León: Imprenta de Minerva,
1849. 44 pp.
An exchange of notes regarding the Mosquito
Territory, with the full text of the communications between Frederick Chatfield and
Nicaraguan foriegn minister Pablo Buitrago
restating the positions of their respective
governments. LNHT

474 _____. _____. Perfil de Nicaragua. Managua:
Talleres Nacionales, 1965. 171 pp. Illus.
Designed to provide the outsider with an
introduction to Nicaragua, this volume ranges
from brief historical outlines to essays on
folklore, with liberal samples from the poetry
of Rubén Darío, statistics regarding the geographical situation of the various parts of
the nation and current production, and vitae
of some of its officials. While it is a
miscellany, some of the statistics are useful,
as are the lists of consuls abroad and of the
individuals who held the post of foreign minister throughout Nicaraguan history. DLC
LNHT

475 _____. _____. Realidad política de
Nicaragua. Managua: Tipografía Nacional,
1948. 143 pp.
The official government account of the
political maneuverings of 1947 that led to a
constituent assembly and a temporary presidency. Presents a collection of the documents
and proclamations involved, including the pact
between General Somoza and Carlos Cuadra Pasos
on behalf of a faction of the Conservative
party, which established the basis for future
political change and elections. Prepared by
the Foreign Ministry as part of the recognition campaign. DLC

476 _____. _____. Síntesis informativa de
Nicaragua. Managua: Talleres Nacionales,
1963. 76 pp. Illus.
An official summary of the state of the
nation and its resources. Provides basic
information for the foreigner in the hope of
increasing trade, but also indicates the regime's view of itself and its programs. DLC

477 Nicaragua, ein Volk im Familienbesitz.
Hamburg: Rowohlt, 1979. 164 pp. Illus.
A denunciation of the Somoza dictatorship.
DLC

478 Nicaragua: el pueblo frente a la dinastía.
Spain: IEPALA, 1978. 100 pp.

479 Un Nicaragüense. La situación económica de
Nicaragua. San José: Imprenta Lehmann, 1915.
52 pp.
A denunciation of Yankee imperialism and
intervention in Nicaragua, which it traces to
the loans and concessions and the resulting

guarantees. Emphasis is on the economic
causes and the role of the bankers. DLC-LDS
BNCR

480 Niederlein, Gustavo. The State of Nicaragua
of the Greater Republic of Central America.
Philadelphia: Philadelphia Commercial Museum,
1898. 93 pp. Tables.
A brief but comprehensive description of
Nicaragua, based on visits and research during
1897 and 1898, emphasizing physical description, resources, and economy, with appropriate
statistics. Also treats population distribution, political organization, race, and other
themes. Some of the historical data are
flawed due to the author's misunderstanding of
accounts he received. DLC LNHT

481 Nietschmann, Bernard Q. Between Land and
Water: The Subsistence Ecology of the Miskito
Indians, Eastern Nicaragua. New York:
Seminar Press, 1973. xiv, 279 pp. Index,
biblio., notes, illus., maps, tables,
appendixes.
A detailed geographical and ethnological
survey of the Mosquito Indians, based on
fieldwork from 1968 to 1971. Includes discussion and analysis of economy, climate,
landforms, food resources and distribution,
and population, with tables and charts. DLC
LNHT

482 Nimmo, Joseph, Jr. The Nicaragua Canal:
Investigate before Investing. Washington,
D.C.: Rufus H. Daroy, 1898. vi, 44 pp.
Another in the author's series of anti-
canal statements arguing that a canal is
unnecessary and impractical. Cites the bankruptcy of previous canal companies as evidence
and contends that the Suez route will always
be cheaper and more convenient, that an isthmian canal would therefore lose money and have
little impact on trade patterns. He argues
that a railroad across Panama would be cheaper
and just as effective, and calls for a detailed congressional investigation of these
factors. The author, who served as chief of
the Bureau of Statistics of the Treasury
Department, was an indefatigable propagandist
against the canal, writing frequent letters to
the press, speaking before various groups, and
always marshalling commercial statistics
against the effort. DLC

483 _____. The Proposed American Inter-Oceanic
Canal in Its Commercial Aspects. Washington,
D.C.: GPO, 1880. 136 pp. Tables,
appendixes.
An analysis of the prospective commercial
traffic through an isthmian canal, by a
Treasury Department official who opposed
proposals to construct the canal. Repeats his
contentions, based on calculations assuming
little change in existing world trading patterns would result from such a waterway, that
the traffic would be well below the anticipated amount and insufficient to maintain the
canal, and that the Suez Canal would be more
convenient and cheaper for most of the world's
shipping. Includes detailed statistical tables regarding commerce on the U.S. east and

(Nimmo, Joseph, Jr.)
west coasts, world commercial traffic, shipping patterns, movement of products, commercial fleets, etc. DLC

484 _____. The Proposed Nicaragua Canal, an
Impracticable Project. Huntington, N.Y.:
n.p., 1895. 40 pp. Tables.
An anti-canal tract arguing that present
and anticipated shipping between the two
coasts of the United States does not justify
the huge expense involved in constructing a
canal and that ample harbors exist elsewhere
to serve the world's trade. Originally written in 1895 as a memorial to the Nicaragua
Canal Board and published separately, it later
appeared as an article in the March 1896 issue
of the Forum. DLC

485 Nogales y Mendez, Rafael del. The Looting of
Nicaragua. New York: McBride, 1928. x, 304
pp. Biblio., illus., maps. Reprint. New
York: Arno Press, 1970. x, 304 pp. Biblio.,
illus., maps.
A denunciation of Yankee imperialism, written in passionate prose by an experienced
author who is a native of Venezuela and has
traveled widely during his career, which included service as inspector general of the
Turkish Cavalry. Explains the differences
between Latin and Yankee culture, contending,
among other things, that in hot climates men
of stature who have social demands on their
time cannot labor, such work being confined
only to peons who have no other demands on
them. Includes a denunciation of the Conservative party, which is allied to the Yankees;
a travelogue description of the author's experience in the country; and a compilation of
denunciations of the Yankee exploitation and a
catalog of their sins, both Nicaraguan, and
foreign. DLC LNHT

486 Núñez Téllez, Carlos. Un pueblo en armas.
Managua: Frente Sandinista de Liberación
Nacional, 1980. 140 pp. Illus.

487 Obando Bravo, Miguel, et al. Educación y
dependencia: el caso de Nicaragua. Managua:
Editorial el Pez y la Serpiente, 1977. 477
pp. Biblio.
A collective work by a group of Nicaraguan
scholars critical of Somoza. Published immediately after the state of siege and accompanying press censorship were lifted, it
contains a collection of essays analyzing
various facets of the Nicaraguan educational
system. All agree that the present facilities
are inadequate and are corrupted by the state
to teach the values of capitalism. They call
for a new educational focus, designed to alert
the populace to its condition, emphasize class
struggle, and stress the problems of dependency, to produce a new type of citizen who
will help transform the nation. The university is viewed as the vanguard of this new
effort. Some of the essays include considerations of future needs in view of population
growth. LNHT

488 Obando Bravo, Miguel. Golpe Sandinista.
Managua: n.p., 1975.
The memoirs of the archbishop of Managua,
relating his role as mediator in the negotiations resulting from the Sandinista seizure of
a group of diplomats and government officials
attending a party during December 1974. Details the negotiations between the guerrillas
and the government--the demands, the concessions, and the process--and provides insights
into the positions and desires of both sides.

489 Obando Somarriba, Francisco. Doña Angélica
Balladares de Argüello, la primera dama del
liberalismo: su vida, sus hechos, episodios
de la historia de Nicaragua. Managua:
Tipografía Comercial, 1969. 96 pp. Illus.
A tribute to the wife of a longtime Liberal
leader, referred to as the "First Lady of
Liberalism" by a party member, tracing and
acclaiming her life and role in the nation's
politics. DLC LNHT

490 Ocón Murillo, Armando. El desterrado:
apuntes para la historia de Nicaragua.
Managua: Imprenta Novedades, 1963. 27 pp.
Illus.
A pro-Liberal account of the 1912 civil
war, tracing the reasons for the Liberal defeat and the activities of its leaders in
exile, focusing particularly on a relative of
the author, General Abraham Ocón Acevedo. DLC
LNHT

491 An Officer in the Service of Walker. The
Destiny of Nicaragua: Central America as It
Was, Is, and May Be . . . By an Officer in the
Service of Walker. Boston: S.A. Bent, 1856.
72 pp. Illus.
An idealistic commentary by a member of the
Walker expeditions, rich in detail regarding
the early efforts, the participants, supporters in the United States, and similar details.
Offers optimistic comments on the potential of
Central America and its role as a route to the
California gold fields. Includes some letters
and correspondence from the expedition, and a
catalog of the ships transiting Nicaragua in
1853, with a precise record of the treasure
they were returning from the California gold
fields. DLC

492 Oliphant, Laurence. Patriots and Filibusters;
or, Incidents of Political and Exploratory
Travel. London and Edinburgh: Blackwood,
1860. viii, 242 pp.
A wide-ranging travelogue describing the
author's many adventures in various parts of
the world, including several chapters regarding his experiences while fighting with the
forces of William Walker in Nicaragua. Provides a vivid but brief account of the events
as he saw them, and his observations about the
terrain and nation. DLC

493 Oliver, Samuel Pasfield. Off Duty: Rambles
of a Gunner Through Nicaragua, January to
June, 1867. London: Taylor & Francis, 1879.
xxvii, 78 pp. Illus.

An account of the author's travels across Nicaragua along much of the proposed canal route, published to provide description of the terrain, along with a discussion of proposed canal routes in Central America. Written in diary form, the comments are principally about sailing connections, the terrain, and travel difficulties. Includes various correspondence and documents relative to the canal projects. DLC

494   Operations and Policy Research, Inc. Nicaragua: Election Factbook, February 5, 1967. Washington, D.C.: Operations and Policy Research, 1967. 39 pp. Maps, tables.
    A brief summary of the election, parties, candidates, and issues, with data from previous elections for comparison. DLC LNHT

495   Ordoñez Argüello, Alberto. Ebano. San Salvador: Ministerio de Cultura, 1954. 310 pp. Illus.
    An anti-imperialistic and nationalistic novel set in Bluefields, Nicaragua, during 1929 and the early 1930s. Evokes the sympathy of the populace for Sandino and his guerrillas and its opposition to the Yankee marines, showing the effect the intervention and the struggle had on this port city caught between pressures from both sides. The entire story takes place in the port and includes local figures, the fruit companies, and resident Yankees who oppose the intervention. The focus is on the actions of the townspeople and their debates rather than on the battlefield; Sandino remains a figure in the background. DLC LNHT

496   Organización Iberoamericana de Seguridad Social. Los seguros sociales en Nicaragua. Madrid: Organización Iberoamericana de Seguridad Social, 1961. 36 pp.
    Another in the series, providing a basic overview of the nation's social-security system and the pertinent laws. DLC

497   Ortega Arancibia, Francisco. Nicaragua en los primeros años de su emancipación política. Paris: Librería de Garnier, 1894. 171 pp. 3d ed. Managua: Banco de América, 1975. 510 pp. Index, illus.
    An account of the initial forty years of Nicaragua as an independent nation after the collapse of the Federation. Covering the years 1838-78, it was written at an advanced age in 1911 by a participant and consists of his recollections of the events. They provide a valuable firsthand account despite some errors that reflect his faulty memory of events long past. There are extensive excerpts from documents of the era, as well as commentaries about all the leading figures of the era, many of whom were known personally to the author, which provide glimpses of the individuals and their public actions. The title for each subsequent edition has been different, but they all include the phrase employed in the latest edition, Cuarenta años (1838-1878) de historia de Nicaragua, though the order and subtitles vary. LNHT

498   Ortega Saavedra, Humberto. Cincuenta años de lucha sandinista. Mexico: Editorial Diogenes, 1976. 139 pp. Notes, illus. 2d ed. Medellin: Ediciones Hombre Nuevo, 1979. 139 pp. Notes, illus.
    A history of the Sandinista movement from its precursor groups of 1956, through its formal constitution in 1960, to its efforts of 1975 and 1976. Emphasizes its military and political actions, platforms, and propaganda but also provides limited data on the various groups affiliated with the movement and rudimentary data on its leaders. DLC

499   Ortiz España, Alberto, ed. Parnaso nicaragüense: antología completa de sus mejores poetas. Barcelona: Editorial Maucci, 1912. 253 pp. Illus. 2d ed. Barcelona: Editorial Maucci, 1978. 253 pp. Illus.
    An anthology of Nicaraguan poetry, with no comment or annotations. DLC LNHT

500   Ory, Eduardo de. Rubén Darío. Cádiz: España y América, 1917. 174 pp. Notes, illus.
    A collection of commentaries and anecdotes seeking to illuminate details of Darío's life and outlook, accompanied by excerpts from other commentaries about him and selections from his poetry. IU

501   Osorno Fonseca, Humberto. El aristócrata de Solentiname. Managua: Editorial Atlántida, 1960. 116 pp.
    A novel set in Nicaragua in the mid-nineteenth century, viewing the political struggles through the eyes of an aristocrat living on an island in Lake Nicaragua, who by virtue of his position is somewhat detached from the mainstream yet inevitably becomes involved as the conflict affects the future of his island. The characters are the historical political leaders of the time, and the novel portrays the Liberal-Conservative struggle and its effects on the inhabitants. DLC

502   _____. Las delicias de Estelí y otras impresiones. Estelí: Tipografía Estelí, 1963. 95 pp.
    An account of the author's experiences in Estelí, lovingly describing the details of the city, its people and terrain, with two additional essays regarding visits to Nindri and a discussion of the sociopolitical situation of Costa Rica. DLC

503   _____. Un famoso líder de mi tierra. Managua: Editorial Atlántida, 1945. 83 pp.
    A novel tracing the efforts and adventures of a Nicaraguan labor leader. Follows his life and his problems with the government, extolling his efforts to improve the lot of his followers. LNHT

504   _____. La revolución Liberal constitucionalista de 1926. Managua: Editorial Atlántida, 1958. 71 pp. Illus.
    A partisan Liberal account of the party's resistance to the U.S.-supported regime of Adolfo Díaz. Based on the recollections of Colonel Leonidas Mayorga Carrera, who fought

in the Liberal army, as told to the author
some thirty years later. DLC

505 Páiz Castillo, Ricardo. <u>Misceláneas
históricas</u>. Managua: Editorial Unión, 1971.
154 pp.
   A collection of miscellaneous essays and
"mini biographies" spanning the entire range
of Central American history. Includes a brief
sympathetic history of the Nicaraguan Conservative party, which is the volume's largest
and most significant work. DLC LNHT

506 Palma Martínez, Ildefonso. <u>La guerra
nacional; sus antecedentes y subsecuentes
tentativas de invasión: síntesis de los
sucesos principales</u>. Managua: Imprenta
Aldina, 1956. 645 pp. Biblio., illus.
   A detailed account of the struggle against
the Walker intervention. Based on secondary
works and published documents, it quotes liberally from the sources but the citations are
in the text. The detail is useful, as are the
many documents printed in whole or in part,
many of which are drawn from newspapers and
previously published documentary collections.
DLC LNHT BNCR

507 Palmer, Mervyn George. <u>Through Unknown
Nicaragua</u>. London and New York: Jarrolds,
1945. 150 pp. Index, illus., maps, tables.
   An account of the author's trip through the
eastern jungles of Nicaragua to hunt specimens
for the British Museum of Natural History,
with numerous photographs. Contains extensive
data about the Mosquito region as noted by a
trained observer, and details the geography,
geology, flora, fauna, archeology, society,
and local customs, describing also the difficulties of travel and the lack of facilities.
DLC LNHT

508 Parkhurst, Henry Clinton [Clinton Rollins,
pseud.]. <u>William Walker</u>. Managua: Editorial
Nuevos Horizontes, 1945. 160 pp. Illus.
   A translation of the memoirs of a member of
Walker's army, originally published in English
in 1906 in the <u>San Francisco Chronicle</u>. It
narrates his experiences during the campaign
and the battles, providing vivid accounts of
some of the confrontations and demonstrating
Walker's men's perspective on him and on the
conditions they encountered. Scholars later
determined that the memoirs were a fraud,
written by Parkhurst under a pseudonym and
plagiarized from Walker's own memoirs. See
item NI107. DLC LNHT BNCR

509 Partido Liberal de Nicaragua. <u>Un hombre de
estado ante la historia: datos biográficos
del general Anastasio Somoza</u>. Managua:
Talleres Nacionales de Imprenta, 1944.
104 pp.
   A volume extolling the accomplishments and
popularity of the Somoza regime. Provides a
brief biography praising his heroism in organizing the military and bringing order out of
chaos by terminating the endless rebellions
prior to his ascension. Includes various
speeches and manifestations attendant to his

rise, the constitutional reforms that enabled
the extension of his term, and various professions of loyalty to his regime. DLC LNHT

510 Partido Liberal Nacionalista. <u>Recuerdos de un
pasado que siempre es de actualidad</u>. Managua:
Editorial "La Hora," 1962. 203 pp.
   The official Liberal version of Nicaraguan
history, charging that the Conservatives connived with Guatemalan Convervatives and Yankee
imperialists, committing all manner of abuses
of power. Contends that these conditions made
it necessary that the Liberals come to power,
and that only the period of Liberal ascendancy
enabled the development of the nation. The
volume focuses on the twentieth century and
includes extensive quotations from contemporary speeches, laws, manifestos, and press
commentary, as well as from various historical
studies that have continued the Liberal-
Conservative confrontation in the history
books. LNHT

511 Pataky, László. <u>Llegaron los que no estaban
invitados</u>. Managua: Editorial Pereira, 1975.
   An account of the Sandinista seizure of a
group of diplomats and guests at an official
reception in December 1974 and the resulting
siege and negotiations. The author, a former
officer in the French Foreign Legion and in
the Israeli army and a friend of President
Anastacio Somoza García, was one of the
hostages. LNHT

512 _____. <u>Nicaragua desconocida</u>. Managua:
Editorial Universal, 1956. 83 pp. Illus.,
maps. 2d ed. Managua: Editorial Universal,
1957. xv, 87 pp. Illus.
   A description, with illustrations, of trips
taken through the most remote parts of
Nicaragua at various times during the author's
residence in that nation. Provides basic
descriptive data and information designed for
the general reader. DLC LNHT

513 Pector, Désiré. <u>Étude économique sur la
République de Nicaragua</u>. Neûchatel: Société
neuchâteloise d'imprimerie, 1893. 167 pp.
Illus., maps, tables.
   Despite its title, the majority of this
volume consists of a gazetteer of place names
in Nicaragua, with brief explanations and
details regarding the location of the place
and the origin of the name. The initial portion does contain a summary of the economy,
with statistics and maps including data regarding steamship service and trade figures.
DLC LNHT

514 Peña Hernández, Enrique. <u>Bajo el malinche</u>.
León: Editorial Hospicio, 1961. 100 pp.
   A collection of folkloric short stories
recounting the rural traditions of Nicaragua.
DLC LNHT

515 _____. <u>Folklore de Nicaragua</u>. Masaya:
Editorial Unión, 1968. 410 pp. Index,
biblio., illus., maps, appendixes.
   A compendium of Nicaraguan folklore recording legends, describing local customs,

carnivals, and fiestas, and reproducing the lyrics of typical songs, divided according to theme and including identification of the region and location from which each is drawn. Includes a calendar of folk celebrations in the nation. DPU

516 Peralta, Manuel María de. El canal interoceánico de Nicaragua y Costa Rica en 1620 y en 1887: relaciones de Deigo de Mercado y Thos. C. Reynolds. Brussels: Imprenta Mertens, 1887. 86 pp.
A reprint of reports on the canalization possibilities of the San Juan River–Nicaragua route prepared by two early visitors in 1620 and 1887, with other documentation regarding the prospects and potential, including Yankee reports and presidential statements and some data regarding the boundary controversey with Nicaragua, all carefully defending the Costa Rican rights. DLC DLC-LDS-44 LNHT BNCR

517 Pérez, Jerónimo. Biografía del coronel Crisanto Sacasa. Masaya: n.p., 1875. iii, 18 pp.
A brief biography of a Liberal political and intellectual figure who served as the first rector of the National University and as minister of public education. CtY

518 ____. Biografía del general don Tomás Martínez. Masaya: n.p., 1879. 93 pp.
A brief biography of the general who served as president of the republic from 1859 to 1867. CtY

519 ____. Memorias para la historia de la revolución de Nicaragua y de la guerra nacional contra los filibusteros, 1854 a 1857. Managua: Imprenta del Gobierno, 1865–73. 2 vols. 854 pp.
A Conservative view of the civil wars of the 1850s, followed by an account of the campaign against Walker. Both provide effective overviews of the confusing events of that era. DLC LNHT

520 Pérez Estrada, Francisco. José Dolores Estrada: héroe nacional de Nicaragua. Managua: Tipografía Asel, n.d. [1970]. 98 pp. Illus.
A brief narration and a collection of material about the Nicaraguan commander at the Battle of San Jacinto, one of the encounters in the campaign against William Walker which, though relatively minor, represented one of the initial defeats for the filibusters. Recounts the battle and the life of the hero, and reproduces various contemporary and historical commentaries about him. DLC LNHT

521 Pérez Valle, Eduardo. Larreynaga: su tiempo y su obra. Managua: Editorial Nicaragüense, 1965. 59 pp. Biblio.
A brief biography of a Nicaraguan who served as a Spanish Colonial official and then participated in the independence movement and the Constituent Assembly that created the Federation. Based on secondary works and the

family archives, though lacking citations. DLC LNHT

522 Perry, Edward Wilkin. Nicaragua: A Rich New Field. Philadelphia: Nicaragua Co., 1898. 48 pp. Illus.
A description of the Perry land grant in Cabo Gracias a Dios, Nicaragua, designed to encourage potential settlers, whose attraction was a condition of the grant. Describes glowingly the climate and the economic possibilities, provides current data about living conditions, and appends a number of supporting letters attesting to its veracity. The author notes that he is correcting errors about the nation, and that to save time and space, rather than cite sources he offers free land in the area to anyone who can disprove his statements. The photos do provide an indication of conditions, and the text has some data about climate, etc. DLC

523 Petrov, Vladimir. A Study in Diplomacy: The Story of Arthur Bliss Lane. Chicago: H. Regnery, 1971. 302 pp. Index, notes.
A biography of an American diplomat that includes a chapter on his service in Nicaragua from 1933 to 1936. Based on his private papers and on State Department documents, it quotes liberally from his official communications. DLC

524 Picado Michalski, Teodoro. Antecedentes de la guerra nacional, apuntes para nuestra historia diplomática. San José: Imprenta Alsina, 1922. 35 pp. 2d ed. San José: Imprenta Nacional, 1968. 32 pp.
Originally a thesis, this volume by a future president of Costa Rica provides a brief overview of some of the diplomatic exchanges associated with the Walker intervention in Nicaragua, drawn from secondary sources and published documents. BNCR

525 Pijoan, Michel. The Health and Customs of the Miskito Indians of Northern Nicaragua: Interrelationships in a Medical Program. Mexico: Instituto Indígenista Interamericano, 1946. 53 pp. Biblio., notes, illus., tables.
Data gathered in a two-month medical survey in the Mosquito Indian region, providing information on diet, health, and diseases, as well as background regarding beliefs and customs. DPU

526 Pim, Bedford Clapperton Travelyan. The Gate of the Pacific. London: Lovell, Reeve, 1863. xiii, 432 pp. Index, illus., maps.
A British naval commander's account of the significance of development of the Mosquito Territory for the British Empire, including analysis of the various canal and railroad schemes in the isthmus and denunciation of the British government for failure to stand up to the Yankee bullies who seek to control the region. He demonstrates the importance of a canal to world commerce and particularly to the British empire, depicting the Mosquito Territory as the key to retaining partial control of a canal, and the importance of an

isthmian canal as an alternative to Suez in the event of trouble in the Middle East. DLC

527 Pim, Bedford Clapperton Travelyan, and Berthold Carl Seemann. Dottings on the Roadside in Panama, Nicaragua, and Mosquito. London: Chapman & Hall, 1869. xvi, 468 pp. Biblio., illus., maps.

A narration of the authors' various travels throughout Central America, particularly Panama and Nicaragua, with emphasis on the Mosquito Coast. Rich in description and observation of people and customs, as well as in relation of local lore, folktales, and the history of the region. Includes the contracts and details of efforts to construct a railway across the isthmus in Nicaragua in the 1850s and 1860s with the support of the British government. DLC LNHT

528 Pineda Erdocia, Empar. La revolución nicaragüense. Madrid: Editorial Revolución, 1980. 180 pp.

529 Pitman, Robert Birks. A Succinct View and Analysis of Authentic Information Extant in Original Works, on the Practicability of Joining the Atlantic and Pacific Ocean by a Ship Canal across the Isthmus of America. London: J.M. Richardson & J. Hatchard & Son, 1825. viii, 229 pp. Maps.

An early analysis providing a summary of existing knowledge about the isthmus. Considers its climate, topography, weather, health, and other factors, and provides details on the known possible routes in Nicaragua, Panama, and Tehuantepec. DLC

530 Poesía revolucionaria nicaragüense. Managua: Ediciones Patria y Libertad, 1968. 110 pp.

A collection of brief revolutionary pieces critical of living conditions and of the Somoza regime, exhorting the populace to rebellion. Written by various authors, it includes several pieces by Darío that allegedly predict the social turmoil of the nation, which serve to show that he can be cited by the advocates of any cause in the nation. DLC LNHT

531 Porras, Belisario. Memorias de la campaña del Istmo, 1900. Panamá: Imprenta Nacional, 1922. xi, 380 pp.

The memoirs of a Panamanian president and political leader. Includes an account of his years in exile in Nicaragua that details his relations with political figures of that nation. DLC

532 Possamay, Luciana, and Ettore Peirri. Nicaragua: la dramática lucha de un pueblo por su libertad. Mexico: Mexicanos Unidos, 1979. 174 pp. Index, illus.

An anti-Somoza tract detailing the abuses of the dictatorship and hailing the Sandinista guerrillas.

533 Pouchet, James, and Gustave Sautereau. Canal interocéanique maritime de Nicaragua: notes et documents. Paris: Librarie Espagnole et Américaine, 1879. 65 pp. Maps, tables.

A brief report to the Suez Canal Company by two engineers who recommend that it consider construction of a canal in Central America and indicate a preference for the Nicaragua route. Includes discussion of the two possible routes, in Panama and Nicaragua, and data regarding potential traffic and effects on world commerce. DLC

534 _____. Examen comparatif des divers projets de canaux interocéaniques par l'isthme de Darien et le lac de Nicaragua. Bourges: A. Jollet, 1876. 32 pp.

A summary and analysis of various canal schemes, comparing their advantages and disadvantages. Although it does not recommend a particular scheme, it stresses the importance of such a canal and of European involvement in its construction. DLC

535 Provisional Interoceanic Canal Society. Concession Granted by the Republic of Nicaragua to the Provisional Interoceanic Canal Society for a Ship-Canal across That Country, Confirmed May 22, 1880. Washington, D.C.: Gibson Brothers, 1880. 20 pp.

The text of the concession signed by Adam Cárdenas, Nicaraguan minister for public instruction and public works, and A.G. Menocal, the company representative, in May of 1880. DLC LNHT

536 _____. Nicaragua Ship-Canal: Report of the Executive Committee. Washington, D.C.: Gibson Brothers, 1880. 16 pp.

A positive report on the prospects for a canal, and for sufficient traffic to render it an economically feasible venture, to the society that had just obtained a concession from the Nicaraguan government. DLC LNHT

537 Quezada, Juan José. Frente Sandinista diciembre victorioso. Mexico: Editorial Diogenes, 1979. 112 pp. Biblio.

538 Quijano, Carlos. Nicaragua: ensayo sobre el imperialismo de los Estados Unidos. Paris: Agencia Mundial Liberia, 1928. 148 pp. Biblio., notes. 3d ed. Mexico: Pueblo Nuevo, 1978. 141 pp. Biblio., notes, illus.

A review and denunciation of the Yankee intervention in Nicaragua, which the author divides into three eras: the first, from 1909 to 1912, during which the focus was on stabilizing the nation, ousting the Zelaya dictatorship, and securing financial control of Nicaragua through the customs collector; the second, from 1913 to 1917, when control of the canal route was secured through the Bryan-Chamorro Treaty; and the third, starting in 1917, when the nation converted into a complete satellite through budgetary control. The author attributes all these actions to the need to secure the canal route and to the necessities of imperialism, which require investment and markets. He adds that Nicaragua's status as satellite suits the Northern Collosus's purposes far better than

outright annexation, which would cause international protest. The detailed narration
focuses on the financial transactions involved
in the various foreign loans and describes the
Bryan-Chamorro Treaty as a case of selling the
national terrain to pay off previous loans.
The 1978 edition bears the title Nicaragua:
un pueblo, una revolución: ensayo sobre el
imperialismo de los Estados Unidos.

539 Radcliff, William. Considerations on the
Subject of a Communication between the
Atlantic and Pacific Oceans. Georgetown
(i.e., Washington, D.C.): Metropolitan
Office, 1835. 28 pp. Maps.
    An early call for the construction of a
canal, by an American consular officer who
emphasizes the need for one and its prospects.
Discusses both the Nicaragua and Panama
routes, comparing them to existing European
canals, but does not take a position in favor
of either since at this stage the author was
merely promoting the idea of a canal somewhere
in Central America. DLC

540 Ramírez Brown, Gerónimo. Nicaragua renueva
sus instituciones con vista al porvenir.
Managua: Talleres Nacionales, 1939. 96 pp.
    An official account of the legal measures
leading to the Constitutional Convention of
1938. Employs earlier statements and decrees
to indicate that there was a perceived need,
shared by all parties, for such revision of
the nation's basic document, and reprints the
full texts of the necessary decrees calling
for the elections to the Constituent Assembly.
The care taken to justify the call indicates
the controversy involved in what was the initial effort to prepare the way for Somoza's
continuance in office even though he had just
acceded to power in 1936. DLC LNHT

541 Ramírez Delgado, Rafael. Narraciones
históricas y cuatro novelas cortas. Mexico:
B. Costa-Amic, 1963. 210 pp.
    A series of dramatic but realistic narra-
tives in the form of historical novelettes
depicting the Nicaraguan civil war of 1909-10
and the siege of León and Chinandega in 1912;
a commentary defending the Nicaraguan position
in its border dispute with Honduras, with
references to the arbitral ruling of the king
of Spain; and a series of short stories. DLC

542 Ramírez Mercado, Sergio, ed. Augusto César
Sandino. San José: Imprenta Nacional, 1978.
408 pp. Illus.
    A collection of the political writings of
Sandino, with a lengthy introduction by the
editor, a scholar and member of the Sandinista
junta, who recounts the Sandinista version of
Nicaraguan history and their case against
Somoza and Yankee intervention. The selections from Sandino's commentaries and manifestos are designed to provide the flavor and
an overview of his political stance as the
defender of the nation against foreign intervention and of his condemnation of Somoza and
the Liberal leaders who made peace under Yankee pressure. They come primarily from

already published materials. The introduction,
though highly biased, constitutes the most
sophisticated statement to date of the
Sandinista view of Nicaraguan history and
their indictment of the Yankees as the source
of all problems, as well as of their view of
traditional upper-class politicians. DLC

543 Ramírez Mercado, Sergio. Charles Atlas
también muere. Mexico: Editorial Joaquín
Mortiz, 1976. 119 pp.
    A collection of short stories denouncing
Yankee cultural imperialism in Central America
and the degree to which Yankee images, figures, and events dominate the region's media
and engage the attention of its populace.
Also includes comments denouncing the local
bourgeoisie for the plight of the peasants.
DLC

544 _____. Mariano Fiallos: biografía. León:
Universidad Nacional Autónoma de Nicaragua,
1971. 203 pp. Index, biblio., illus.
    An account of the life of a Nicaraguan
scholar who served as rector of the National
University from 1957 through 1963 and largely
shaped the institution, by one of his cohorts
and disciples. Emphasizes his fight for university autonomy, his efforts on behalf of the
university and its students, and his political
positions in opposition to the regime of General Anastacio Somoza García, reflecting his
dedication to forging a generation of concerned individuals aware of national problems
and able to think about them freely. DLC
LNHT

545 _____. Nuevos cuentos. León: Universidad
Nacional Autónoma de Nicaragua, 1969. 81 pp.
    A collection of short stories by a future
member of the Sandinista junta, many reflecting the political situation in Nicaragua and
commenting on the trends and national problems
indirectly through fiction. DLC

546 _____. El pensamiento vivo de Sandino. San
José: EDUCA, 1974. 342 pp. 3d ed. San
José: EDUCA, 1977. 342 pp.
    A collection of statements and writings by
Augusto César Sandino, drawn principally from
published sources. Includes his letters,
press statements, interviews with journalists,
manifestos, and diplomatic communications,
arranged chronologically and identified as to
source but offered without comment. LNHT

547 _____. Tiempo de fulgor. Guatemala:
Editorial Universitaria, 1970. 248 pp. 2d
ed. Managua: Ediciones el Pez y la
Serpiente, 1975. 248 pp.
    A novel set in turn-of-the-century
Nicaragua, focusing on the civil warfare and
turmoil of that era and its effect on the
lives of the populace. Uses a nun as the
observer and narrator to provide a view from
the "oustide." DLC LNHT

548 _____. De tropeles y tropelias. San
Salvador: Editorial Universitaria de El
Salvador, 1972. 96 pp. Illus. 2d ed.

(Ramírez Mercado, Sergio)

Managua: Ediciones el Pez y la Serpiente,
1976. 108 pp. Illus.

A collection of very short stories, each
two pages long, awarded a Venezuelan prize for
imagery in 1971. Depicts life under a harsh
dictatorship in vivid but humorous terms,
comparing the behavior of its officials to the
characteristics of various animals. The image
is based on a composite of many Latin American
dictators, with aspects of nineteenth- and
twentieth-century figures from several countries evident, all woven into a composite
representing the stereotype of dictatorship.
The work concludes with a lengthy piece covering thirty-five pages, written with tongue
in cheek and entitled "Suprema ley por la que
se regula el bien general de las personas, se
premian sus acciones nobles y se castigan sus
malos actos y habitos, dictada en XIV
paragrafos." DLC LNHT

549 Ramírez Morales, José. José de Marcoleta:
padre de la diplomacia nicaragüense. Managua:
Imprenta Nacional, 1975. 101 pp. Notes.

A brief sketch of the career of this
Nicaraguan diplomat who represented his nation
in the United States and Europe for many years
during the mid-nineteenth century and established some of the positions and traditions of
that nation's diplomacy. Consists principally
of excerpts from his notes and press commentaries of the era, with connecting narration. Although many of the items come from La
Gaceta de Nicaragua and the Revista del
Archivo General de la Nación, the result does
serve to provide an overview of the career of
Marcoleta by indicating the events in which he
was involved, and his general stances. LNHT

550 Ramos, Miguel Ángel. Reseña histórica de
Nicaragua desde el descubrimiento hasta la
invasión de Walker. Tegucigalpa: Imprenta
Calderón, 1956. 113 pp. Illus., maps,
appendixes.

A brief account of the Walker intervention
emphasizing the military aspects, with a
thirty-page introduction tracing the history
of Nicaragua up to that point. DLC LNHT

551 Raudales Soto, Julio. Cinco ejércitos y un
objetivo común. Tegucigalpa: Imprenta
Calderón, 1976. 102 pp. Biblio., appendixes.

A brief essay hailing the cooperation among
the Central American forces in the campaign
against the Walker expedition. The appendixes
reproduce letters exchanged among the various
commanders, as well as Walker's defense in his
subsequent trial. DLC

552 Recinos, Luís Felipe, and Rubén Hernández.
Sandino, hazañas del héroe. San José: n.p.,
1934. 45 pp. Illus. 2d ed. Managua: n.p.,
1965. 45 pp. Illus.

A highly laudatory account of Sandino's
opposition to the Yankee imperialists. InU

553 Reflections upon the Nicaragua Treaty: Is It
Constitutional? Is It Expedient?. N.p., n.d.
[188?]. 42 pp.

A brief anonymous piece questioning the
authority of the United States to annex territory abroad for a canal, noting differences
with previous annexations and anticipating
problems that might arise with England regarding previous accords. DLC LNHT

554 Reichardt, C.F. Nicaragua: Nach eigener
Anschauung im Jahre, 1852: Und mit besonderer
Beziehung auf die Auswanderung nach den
heissen Zonen Amerikas beschrieben.
Braunschweig: F. Vieweg, 1854. xxvi, 296 pp.
Maps.

A description of the experiences of Germans
who have emigrated to Nicaragua, with data on
their location, activities, and success, as
well as excerpts from letters describing their
experiences. Designed to encourage more
German immigration. DLC

555 Resolutions of the Legislatures of Louisiana,
California, and Oregon and of the Great Com-
mercial Bodies of New York, Philadelphia,
Chicago, Boston, St. Louis, Cincinnati,
Portland (Oregon), and San Diego, in Favor of
the Nicaragua Canal, Together with Opinions of
Leading Newspapers. New York: Ketcham, 1888.
39 pp.

A compendium of endorsements of the
Nicaraguan route and rapid construction of a
canal, including acts of state legislatures,
resolutions of chambers of commerce, and newspaper editorials drawn from throughout the
country in an effort to influence Congress to
act on the resolution. DLC LNHT

556 Revolución en Nicaragua: derrocamiento del
gobierno constitucional del Dr. Juan Bautista
Sacasa y ascenso del régimen militar del
general Anastacio Somoza García. León:
Editorial Centroamericano, n.d. 126 pp.
Illus.

A collection of documents translated from
U.S. diplomatic reports previously published
by the State Department dealing with the rise
of Somoza in 1936. Provides data on the U.S.
involvement and reaction to the events; includes diplomatic reports by the envoys on the
scene, instructions from Washington, and protests and memorials from the Nicaraguan political figures, published without comment but
with photos of the participants. The items
bear the State Department numbers and apparently were selected from the appropriate volumes of the Foreign Relations series. LNHT

557 Rivas, Anselmo Hilario. Nicaragua: su
pasado, ojeada retrospectiva: edición
dirigida por el Dr. Pedro Joaquín Chamorro,
con estudio sobre Anselmo H. Rivas por el Dr.
Carlos Cuadra Pasos. Managua: Ediciones de
La Prensa, 1936. xxv, 280 pp. Illus.

A Conservative history of Nicaragua from
1838 through 1869 but focusing on the turbulent 1850s and 1860s, originally published
in the Conservative newspaper El Diario
Nicaragüense during 1895 and 1896 by a former
Cabinet member of the Conservative regime of
Fruto Chamorro, which governed during part of
the era. Includes an account of the regime,

the Liberal rebellions, and the actions of the
Yankee filibusters. A brief biography of Rivas
by Carlos Cuadra Pasos is included. DLC LNHT

558 Rizzo Baratta, Domingo. Pasión y muerte
en Nicaragua. Buenos Aires: Editorial
Goyanarte, 1958. 167 pp.
     A novel set among the poor mestizos of rural
Nicaragua that, in focusing principally on
romance, the problems of growing up, and human
emotions, also serves to illustrate the problems of the peasants. The story emphasizes
the mixed cultural and racial heritages of the
region. DLC

559 Robleto, Hernán. Cárcel criolla: biografía
política. N.p., n.p., n.d. [1955]. 304 pp.
     The rambling memoirs from exile and jail
of a Nicaraguan who ran afoul of the Somoza
regime and took refuge in the Costa Rican
embassy in Managua after imprisonment, describing his experiences and thoughts and
denouncing the Somoza regime and Yankee support for it. DLC BNCR

560 _____. Cuentos de perros. Managua:
Editorial Nuevos Horizontes, 1943. 86 pp.
     A series of unrelated short stories by a
Nicaraguan newspaper reporter and politician.
They deal with a wide variety of incidents,
often focusing on life and death and in many
cases touching on the nation's political
struggles, sometimes directly, sometimes
obliquely. Throughout, the effects of struggle, turmoil, combat, and political maneuvering are evident. DLC

561 _____. Don Otto y la niña Margarita.
Managua: Imprenta Democrática, 1944. 188 pp.
     Another novel set in the Nicaraguan coun-
tryside, this one focusing on the owner of an
estate and detailing his experiences. This
novel mirrors a certain cynicism about the
futility of revolution and combat, perhaps
born of the author's long exile and participation in numerous civil conflicts during his
early career. The title figure dwells to a
considerable extent on the power of guns, the
commonplace nature of the revolutions, their
futility in terms of political impact, and the
horror of the carnage they cause. DLC

562 _____. Los estrangulados: el imperialismo
yanqui en Nicaragua. Madrid: Editorial
Cenit, 1933. 231 pp.
Ein Bauernschicksal aus Nicaragua. Leipzig:
Hans Müller Verlag, 1935. 282 pp.
     A ringing denunciation of Yankee imperial-
ism and capitalist exploitation and their evil
effects on Central America, by a Nicaraguan
Liberal politician writing in exile in Mexico
after the Yankees helped overthrow the Sacasa
regime, of which he was an official. Unlike
his semiautobiographical novels, this work
deals not with the guerrilla struggle but with
the debilitating effects of Yankee control; it
denounces exploitation by the banana companies, dominance by the financial institutions,
and the effects of these forces on the local
citizens. DLC LNHT

563 _____. Una mujer en al selva. Santiago:
Ediciones Ercilla, 1936. 164 pp.
     A novel of life in the Nicaraguan jungles,
written by a well-known journalist and Liberal
political figure whose works are in the revolutionary tradition. Features vivid descriptions of the terrain, portrayals of human
emotions, and use of the local lore and idiom,
drawing on the author's own experience. DLC

564 _____. Nido de memorias: poesía y tragedia
en el Caribe. Mexico: Libro-Mex, 1960.
331 pp.
     The memoirs of a Nicaraguan journalist and
Liberal political figure, tracing his early
life through 1912 and focusing particularly on
the Liberal-Conservative struggle, the civil
war of 1911-12, and the Yankee role in it.
DLC

565 _____. Sangre en el trópico: la novela de la
intervención yanqui en Nicaragua. Madrid:
Editorial Cenit, 1930. 278 pp.
Es lebe die Freiheit: mittelamerikanischer
Abenteuerroman. Berlin: Leuchtkugel Verlag,
1933. 238 pp.
     A novel portraying the Nicaraguan civil war
of the 1920s from the Liberal viewpoint of the
subsecretary of public instruction in the
government of Juan Bautista Sacasa, written in
exile in Mexico after Adolfo Díaz, with Yankee
support, led the Conservatives to victory over
Sacasa. The novel portrays the conflict in
dramatic terms, condemning the role of the
gringos in the nation and their exploitation
of the peasants, criticizing the Conservative
landed elite, and emphasizing the impact of
the local setting and the tropical terrain,
which frustrated efforts of the various columns to combine under General Sandino. DLC
LNHT

566 _____. Tres dramas (La cruz de ceniza, La
niña Soledad y Muñecos de barro). Managua:
Imprenta Democrática, 1946. 177 pp.
     A series of plays about life in the
Nicaraguan countryside, focusing on tragedy
and human emotion and reflecting the conditions and problems of the tumultuous times of
the political civil wars. TxU

567 Robleto Siles, J.A. Yo deserté de la Guardia
Nacional de Nicaragua. San José: n.p., 1979.
     The memoirs of a former member of the
Nicaraguan National Guard who repudiated
Somoza and joined the revolution against his
regime, in which he describes the abuses of
the Guardia. BNCR

568 Rocha, Jesús de la, ed. Código de la
legislación de la República de Nicaragua en
Centro-América, formada por el señor doctor
i maestro licenciado don Jesús de la Rocha, a
virtud de comisión del señor senador
presidente don Nicacio del Castillo,
refrendada por el señor ministro de interior
don Eduardo Castillo. 3 vols. Managua:
Imprenta de El Centro-Americano, 1871-74.
     An official compilation of Nicaraguan
legislation continuing the author's earlier

(Rocha, Jesús de la)
volume and bringing it up to date by covering
the 1860s and 1870s. See following item. DLC
LNHT

569 _____. Recopilación de las leyes,
decretos y acuerdos ejecutivos de la República
de Nicaragua, en Centro-América, formada por
el señor doctor y maestro licenciado don Jesús
de la Rocha, a virtud de comisión del señor
senador presidente don Fernando Guzmán,
refrendada por el señor ministro de interior
doctor don Rosalio Cortez. Granada: Imprenta
del Gobierno, 1867. 461 pp.
An official compilation of Nicaraguan laws,
covering the initial years of independence and
the early nineteenth century. DLC

570 Roche, James Jeffrey. The Story of the
Filibuster. New York: Macmillan; London: T.
Fisher Unwin, 1891. xiii, 373 pp. Illus.,
maps. 2d ed. Boston: Small, Maynard, 1901.
xii, 251 pp. Illus., maps.
Historia de los filibusteros. San José:
Imprenta Nacional, 1908. xvii, 249 pp.
Notes, illus., maps.
An account of the Walker expedition to
Nicaragua, portraying the adventurers as the
heroic precursors of American expansionism.
The introductory chapters trace the history of
filibustering, citing such precedents as the
Vikings, the British pirates, and the heroes
of the American westward movement, linking
Walker to them as one whose individual initiative, in advance of public opinion and the
government, blazes the way to the settlement
and eventual annexation of new territory. The
author exhibits the normal Yankee prejudices
and stereotypes of the era, seeming surprised,
for example, when isthmian troops fight well.
The preface to the Spanish edition, by Ricardo
Fernández Guardia, indicates, as can be expected, that the Central Americans find this
portrayal offensive yet illustrative of Yankee
thinking. The preface notes several errors,
emphasizing the complimentary references to
Costa Rican troops, who had opposed Walker,
and notes the passion and prejudices evident
in the book. The later English edition used
the title By-Ways of War: The Story of the
Filibusters. DLC DLC-LDS-33 LNHT BNCR

571 Rodríguez Beteta, Virgilio. Transcendencia
nacional e internacional de la guerra de
Centro América contra Walker y sus
filibusteros. Guatemala: Editorial del
Ejército, 1960. 122 pp. Biblio., illus. 2d
ed. Guatemala: Editorial del Ejército, 1965.
215 pp. Biblio., illus., maps.
A study of the Walker intervention in
Nicaragua, originally prepared as a series of
lectures for the 1956 centennial and previously published in various Central American
newspapers. Emphasizes the diplomatic aspects, particularly the attitudes of the
United States and England. The stances of
France and Mexico are also considered. Concludes that Walker misunderstood and under-
estimated Central America and that, whatever

else, Walker inadvertently contributed to the
failure of the British efforts to dominate the
area. BNCR BNG

572 Rodríguez González, Salvador, ed. El Golfo de
Fonseca en el derecho público centroamericana:
La Doctrina Meléndez. San Salvador: Imprenta
Nacional, 1917. xiv, 363 pp.
A compendium of commentaries and opinions
from the Central American press, including
scholarly and legal views, denouncing the
Bryan-Chamorro Treaty and challenging its
legal status. An introductory study by an
official of the Salvadoran foreign ministry
states its position. Designed as a supplement
to his documentary compilation (see the following item). DLC LNHT

573 _____. El Golfo de Fonseca y el tratado
Bryan-Chamorro, celebrado entre Los Estados
Unidos de Norte América y Nicaragua (Doctrina
Meléndez). San Salvador: Imprenta Nacional,
1917. xxii, 458 pp. Illus., maps.
An official publication of the Salvadoran
Foreign Ministry. Consists of a collection of
documents that include the treaty, related
accords, and the voluminous correspondence
relating to it among the Central American
governments and also between them and the
United States. Designed to support the
Salvadoran position defending that nation's
rights to the Gulf of Fonseca. The rulings of
the Central American Court are included. DLC
LNHT

574 Rodríguez Serrano, Felipe. El canal por
Nicaragua: estudio de la negociación canalera
y su proyección en la historia de Nicaragua.
Managua: Tipografía Alemana, 1968. 292 pp.
A history, from the Nicaraguan perspective,
of the canal treaty negotiations with the
Woodrow Wilson administration, covering the
Chamorro-Weitzel and Chamorro-Bryan treaties
and continuing through the discussions that
revived the nation's hopes in the 1930s.
Drawn principally from published materials,
with extensive excerpts from the accords,
press, and testimony. DLC LNHT

575 _____. Estudios sobre la convención Chamorro-
Bryan. Managua: Editorial La Hora, 1965. 60
pp. Appendixes.
A discussion of the legal implications of
the Bryan-Chamorro Treaty during the present
era, designed to support President Anastacio
Somoza García's postwar promotion of
Nicaraguan aspirations to a canal. Seeks to
demonstrate that the old treaty could constitute the basis for a new accord, but also
alleges that the Yankees negotiated the original treaty specifically to prevent construction of a canal that would rival the Yankee
route in Panama. The author hails Somoza's
efforts to persuade the U.S. to construct a
second waterway in Nicaragua. DLC

576 Rojas, Blanca. Los verdaderos días. Managua:
Ediciones Presencia, n.d. [196?]. 168 pp.
A first-person narration of the author's
arrest and imprisonment on suspicion of

involvement in an assassination, which principally provides an emotional account of the
degradations of prison life and the horrible
conditions in the jails and detention centers
of her native Nicaragua. DLC

577 Rojas Corrales, Ramón. El tratado Chamorro-
Weitzel ante Centro-América y ante el derecho
internacional. San José: Imprenta Moderna,
1914. 98 pp.
    An attack on the Bryan-Chamorro Treaty and
its precursor, citing it by the name of a U.S.
negotiator rather than the secretary of state.
Charges that Chamorro sold the sovereignty of
Nicaragua for a few million pieces of gold and
placed all of Central America in danger. Reprints the treaty and various commentaries
regarding the rights of the other states in
the Gulf of Fonseca and the San Juan River.
DLC DLC-LDS-140 LNHT

578 Román, José. Cosmapa. Managua: Editorial
Nuevos Horizontes, 1944. 276 pp. Appendixes.
    A social-protest novel set in the Pacific
Coast banana plantations of Nicaragua, portraying the life of the peasants and denouncing their exploitation by the foreign
companies and the local oligarchy. The work
combines dramatic presentation of social conditions with equally vivid descriptions of the
tropical terrain, effectively employing local
folklore and idiom. Includes commentary on
the national politics that permit such abuses.
DLC

579 Romero, Ramón. Somoza, asesino de Sandino.
Mexico: Editorial Patria y Libertad, 1959.
206 pp. Illus.
    A highly critical account of the life and
regime of General Anastacio Somoza García,
emphasizing his thirst for power, the brutality of his regime, and the ambitions of his
family. Includes an account of the execution
of Augusto César Sandino, the guerrilla hero
of the resistance to the U.S. Marines. DLC
LNHT

580 Rosales, Hernán. Nicaragua, película de una
vida. Mexico: Gráficos Guananjuato, 1950.
262 pp.
    The memoirs of a Nicaraguan journalist,
covering the years 1893 to 1910, written in
exile in Mexico. DLC

581 Rosales, Nicasio. Apuntes históricos del
Hospital de San Juan de Dios. Granada:
Tipografía Nacional, 1927. 77 pp. Illus.
    A history of the principal hospital of
Granada, recounting its growth and development
since its foundation in Colonial times, with
brief biographical sketches of its principal
doctors throughout its existence. LNHT

582 Rosengarten, Frederic, Jr. Freebooters Must
Die: The Life and Death of William Walker,
the Most Notorious Filibuster of the Nineteenth Century. Wayne, Pa.: Haverford House,
1976. xi, 226 pp. Index, biblio., illus.,
maps.

Yet another account of the Walker episode,
this one by a Yankee landowner-industrialist
living in Guatemala. Provides a picturesque
and vivid account of the campaign, with a
large collection of drawings, paintings, photographs, and maps that illustrate the era and
its image in the conception of artists. DLC
LNHT

583 Rothschuh Villanueva, Guillermo, and Eddy
Matute Ruíz. Notas sobre acumulación de
capital, control natal y desarrollo del estado
de Nicaragua. Managua: UCA, 1977. 124 pp.
Biblio., tables.

584 Ruíz y Ruíz, Frutos. La conversión monetaria
de la República de Nicaragua. Granada:
Tipografía de El Correo, 1918. vi, 93 pp.
    An account of the monetary conversion re-
sulting from the inflation of the 1912-18
period, emphasizing the changes, value of the
various currency issues, amount of currency in
circulation, technicalities of the adjustment,
and their implications for the cost of living.
Contains considerable statistical information
and includes general theoretical comments
regarding money, its value, and the national
capacity. FU

585 Ryan, John Morris, et al. Area Handbook for
Nicaragua. Washington, D.C.: GPO, 1970.
xvi, 393 pp. Biblio., illus., maps.
    A compendium of information on Nicaragua,
emphasizing the present but including a brief
historical overview. Like most of the works
in this series, it provides a handy digest of
available information for the generalist or
novice, but is subject to the usual problems
of condensation and reliance on secondary and
published material. DLC LNHT BNCR

586 Sacasa, Juan Bautista. Cómo y por qué caí del
poder, julio de 1936. San Salvador: Talleres
Gráficos Cisneros, 1936. 106 pp. 2d ed.
León: n.p., 1946. Appendix.
    A brief exposition by the former president
of Nicaragua leveling charges against General
Anastacio Somoza García, who deposed him, and
citing the illegal actions of the Guardia
Nacional to force him from power; with ap-
pended documents supporting his claims. DLC
LNHT

587 Sáenz, Vicente. El canal de Nicaragua.
Mexico: Talleres Gráficos Michoacán, 1929.
33 pp.
    A series of conferences by this prolific
writer and Yankee critic, raising a cry of
alarm about the Bryan-Chamorro Treaty and the
implications of a Yankee-dominated Nicaragua
canal. Calls on Central America to unite to
defend its very existence against the Yankee
threat, which the author contends will result
in the annexation of the entire region if
carried out. DLC DLC-LDS-732 LNHT BNCR

588 _____. Nuestras vías interoceánicas:
Tehuantepec, Nicaragua, Panamá: a propósito
del canal de Suez. Mexico: Editorial América
Nueva, 1957. 217 pp. Biblio.

An analysis of the possibility of a canal in Central America and of the various routes. Condemns the avarice of the great powers and particularly that of the Yankees, noting that Yankee intervention in the isthmus is related to the canal. The author characterizes Mexico's elimination from consideration for a canal route and the decision not to dig in Tehuantepec as a victory for Mexico. Includes a brief discussion of canal problems in other parts of the world and a collection of documents and treaties pertaining to canal routes in the isthmus. DLC LNHT BNCR

589 Salvatierra, Sofonías. Hechos e ideas. Managua: Tipografía Progreso, 1948. iv, 199 pp.

A collection of essays dealing with various themes from Nicaraguan history and emphasizing patriotism and nationalism. All are written from a Liberal viewpoint, reflecting the author's political career, and emphasize the problems facing the nation, many associated with foreign intervention and influence. The questions discussed include various aspects of economic development, transportation facilities, intellectual disputes, and intellectual institutions. DLC

590 _____. Máximo Jérez inmortal; comentario polémico. Managua: Tipografía Progreso, 1950. xliv, 340 pp. Illus.

Part of the Liberal-Conservative clash that continues in the history books, this work, written as a reply to Padro Joaquín Chamorro Zelaya's Máximo Jérez y sus contemporáneos, defends the Liberal cause and leader against the Conservative assault. The author ridicules Chamorro's views regarding the independence era, contending that it was the Conservatives who retarded the nation's progress and caused its civil wars. Makes numerous charges against Fruto Chamorro, one of Jérez's adversaries. Contends that only federalism would have enabled the region to defend itself against Yankee intervention and blames the Conservatives for its demise, while extolling the cooperation of the era against Walker's forces. The work is avowedly polemical and is entirely pro-Liberal. Includes extensive reprints of letters and documents from the era. DLC LNHT

591 _____. Obrerismo y nacionalidad. Managua: Tipografía Progreso, 1928. 207 pp.

A discussion of the plans and proposals of a Nicaraguan labor organization, written under its sponsorship to explain its goals and rationale. Stresses credit unions and the establishment of schools to educate union leaders. DLC

592 _____. Sandino: o la tragedia de un pueblo. Madrid: Editorial Europa, 1934. 291 pp. Illus.

A memoir and collection of documents focusing on the period from 1932 to 1933, during which the author functioned as an intermediary between Sandino and the Sacasa faction of the Liberal party. Reprints many of his letters to both groups and explains their exchanges regarding the peace negotiations. The account is sympathetic to Sandino, though at times it takes a position between the two groups. Includes a Liberal perspective on Nicaraguan history since the Walker intervention and ends on a strident pro-Sandino note denouncing his assassination and Somoza. DLC

593 Sánchez, Antonio. Nicaragua, año cero: la caída de la dinastía Somoza. Mexico: Editorial Diana, 1979. 165 pp. Biblio., illus., maps.

594 Sánchez, Milton. Nicaragua. Havana: Casa de las Américas, 1967. 52 pp. Biblio., illus., maps.

Part of the Cuban series designed to familiarize Cubans with other Latin American countries, this volume provides a brief compilation of current data, geographical information, and an historical overview in Marxist terms, emphasizing Yankee exploitation, the feudalism of the capitalist system headed by the upper class, and the heroic struggle of the people under Augusto César Sandino to try to throw off the yoke of imperialist oppression. Seeks to emphasize that the nation is ripe for revolution. DLC

595 Sánchez, Rodrigo. Panorama político de Nicaragua, 1821-1940. Managua: Talleres Gráficos Pérez, 1940. 22 pp.

A brief overview of Nicaraguan history mentioning each regime that governed the nation, its tenure, and in some cases its principal characteristics. DLC LNHT

596 Sandino, Augusto César. Manifiesto a los pueblos de la tierra y en particular la de Nicaragua. Managua: Tipografía La Prensa, 1933. 24 pp. 3d ed. Managua: n.p., 1979. 24 pp.

A proclamation advocating an alliance of all Latin American nations, calling for unity before external menaces such as the Yankee desire to construct additional canals in the isthmus.

597 Sandoval Valdivia, Elba. Costumbres y folklore del pueblo miskito. Rio Coco, Nicaragua: Ministerio de Educación Pública, 1958. 100 pp. Biblio., illus.

An account of the folklore, traditions, practices, and customs of the Mosquito Indians of Nicaragua. The focus is on contemporary practice, but a brief account of their historical origins is included. FU

598 Schmidt, George. Souvenir de Nicaragua. Matagalpa and San Francisco: G. Schmidt, 1903. 30 pp. Illus.

A photo album providing a view of Nicaragua at the turn of the century. Includes the capital, principal cities, and some rural scenes; shows roads, agriculture, and principal buildings. DLC

599 Schmidt, Otto. El chubasco: cuentos, leyendas estampas nicaragüenses. Chinandega:

Editorial Prensa Latinoamericana, 1956.
200 pp.
    A collection of short stories set in the
interior of Chinandega, with rich description
of the tropical jungle and the problems of
peasant life. DPU

600 Scroggs, William O. Filibusters and Finan-
ciers: The Story of William Walker and His
Associates. New York: Macmillan, 1916. 408
pp. Illus., maps. Reprint. New York:
Russell & Russell, 1969. ix, 408 pp.
Filbusteros y financieros: la historia de
William Walker y sus asociados. Managua:
Banco de América, 1975. 413 pp.
    A classic, picturesque yet detailed and
well-researched study of the Walker episode,
viewed from the vantagepoint of the United
States, focusing particularly on Walker and
his ambitions. Based on secondary works,
documents, and extensive use of Yankee newspapers. Includes discussion of the urge to
filibustering in general, Walker's ambitions
regarding Cuba, the involvement of Yankee
financiers, etc., as well as tracing the details of battles and individual heroism. The
view is sympathetic to the adventurers, whose
audacity the author admires. DLC LNHT

601 Selser, Gregorio. Los marines:
intervenciones norteamericanas en América
Latina. Buenos Aires: Editorial del
Noroeste, 1974. 79 pp. Illus.
    A brief denunciation of Yankee military
interventions in Latin America, by an
Argentine journalist. The majority of the
volume is devoted to a chronological listing,
with brief single-paragraph descriptions of
U.S. military actions in the region. Several
of the episodes are discussed in the opening
chapters. DLC

602 _____. El pequeño ejército loco: operación
México-Nicaragua. Buenos Aires: Editorial
Triángulo, 1958. 399 pp. Latest ed.
Managua: Tipografía ASEL, 1966. 387 pp.
    Another in the author's series of condemna-
tions of Yankee imperialism, written as a
sequel to his earlier Sandino: general de
hombres libres. The initial half deals with
the U.S.-Mexican dispute, and the second provides an account of Sandino's exploits, hailing his stance against the capitalist invaders
and his heroism in defending his nation. The
author contends that the Yankee military action in Nicaragua is part of a grand plot to
annex the entire region, or at least to establish friendly regimes in Central America and
use it as a base to unseat the Mexican Revolutionary government. LNHT

603 _____. Sandino: general de hombres libres.
Buenos Aires: Ediciones Pueblos de América,
1955. 300 pp. Biblio. 4th ed. San José:
EDUCA, 1974. 349 pp. Biblio., notes.
Sandino. New York: Monthly Review Press,
1981. 256 pp. Index, biblio., notes.
    A denunciation of Yankee imperialism and
actions in Nicaragua, hailing Sandino as a

hero of the struggle against Yankee domination. Details Yankee actions in Nicaragua
during the initial portions of the twentieth
century, criticizing the economic domination
while condemning the dispatch of Marines to
pursue Sandino. Based on secondary works and
citing various anti-gringo tracts, the work
provides an effective statement of the anti-
Yankee viewpoint, the leftists' image of
Sandino, and the basis of his present popularity and status as a symbol. LNHT BNCR

604 Selva, Adán. En defensa del pueblo y contra
la dinastía. Managua: Juventud Liberal
Independiente, 1961. 64 pp.
    An attack on the regime of Luís Somoza
Debayle, belittling his reforms by noting the
limited reach of the social-security program
and the land-reform effort. Discusses the
stance of the so-called Independent Liberal
party, warning against any deals with the
Somoza dynasty. Contends that agreement on a
single candidate or even on alternation in
power would be fatal and cites the example of
the Argüello regime, which was deposed in a
matter of days. Implies that the Conservative
party should combine with the Independent
Liberals to oust Somoza and insure a return to
free elections, which is possible only after
the Somozas are removed. LNHT

605 _____. ¿Hacia donde vamos? Managua:
Tipografía ASEL, 1968. 257 pp. Illus.
    The continued commentaries of a Nicaraguan
polemicist, condemning the Somoza regime and
its excesses and endorsing the leftist guerrillas that oppose it. Provides wide-ranging
commentaries and transcripts of press conferences attacking foreign loans, the regime, and
its excesses, while praising Che Guevara and
the concept of guerrilla movements. Offers
his opinions on a wide range of national and
Latin American affairs and problems. DLC
LNHT

606 _____. Lodo y cienza de una política que
ha podrido las raices de la nacionalidad
nicaragüense. Managua: Editorial ASEL, 1960.
297 pp.
    A review of the Bryan-Chamorro Treaty con-
tending that it forfeited Nicaraguan sovereignty and placed the nation at the mercy of
the Yankees; denounces the Yankee imperialists
in florid prose. Includes a commentary on the
1960 rebellion against the Somoza regime,
denouncing the government but contending that
the so-called movement of Olama and Los
Mollejones failed because of poor leadership
by the Conservatives. LNHT

607 _____. Política y verdad. Managua:
Tipografía ASEL, 1962. 24 pp.
    Yet another of the author's continuing
polemics against the Somoza regime, this one
calling for an "authentic" revolution, the
restoration of the Liberal party to its former
vigor, and its separation from Somoza control.
Offered in the form of a speech stating the
position of the so-called Juventud Liberal
Independiente, it criticizes the actions of

the Somoza dynasty and particularly the regime of Luís Somoza Debayle. LNHT

608 Selva, Carlos. *Un poco de historia: últimos días de la administración del doctor Roberto Sacasa y principios del gobierno del general José Santos Zelaya.* Guatemala: Tipografía Nacional, 1948. xci, 154 pp.

A Nicaraguan newspaperman and polemicist of Liberal ideology who nevertheless supported some Conservative regimes, wrote these essays for the Costa Rican press in 1896, seeking to chronicle the revolution that overthrew the regime of Roberto Sacasa and installed José Santos Zelaya. A useful account of the rise of Zelaya. A prologue by Pedro Joaquín Chamorro provides background regarding the author. DLC

609 Selva, Mauricio de la. *Nicaragua: ensayo biográfico-político sobre Sandino.* Mexico: n.p., 1954. 34 pp.

A brief résumé of Sandino's guerrilla campaign, hailing him as a national hero and the defender of national honor. LNHT

610 Selva, Silvio. *The United States and Central America.* N.p., n.p., 1913. 60 pp.

A justification of the Yankee role and its intervention in Nicaragua, consisting principally of an anti-Zelaya tract that portrays the Nicaraguan dictator as having invaded all his neighbors and kept the region in turmoil, and arguing that only action by the United States could save the other nations. Includes a broad survey of the Monroe Doctrine justifying Yankee actions "protecting" the Latin American nations. The English leaves something to be desired. DLC LNHT

611 Serrano Gutiérrez, Leopoldo. *Folklore nicaragüense: crónica folklórica de las festividades de San Sebastián de Diriamba.* Diriamba: Paco Alemán e Hijos, 1960. 48 pp.

An illustrated account of the traditional celebrations connected with the festival of San Sebastián in the town of Diriamba, which preserves much of the Indian lore, combined with Colonial elements. Focuses principally on the dances. DLC LNHT

612 Sevilla Sacasa, Guillermo. *La mujer nicaragüense ante el derecho de sufragar: porqué me opuse a que se le concediera; la verdad sobre mi actitud en la Constituyente.* Managua: Talleres Gráficos Pérez, 1939. 14 pp.

A Nicaraguan political figure defends himself against press attacks resulting from a speech he gave in opposition to granting women the right to vote, which some interpreted as an attack on the clergy and on women. He contends this entails a misinterpretation of his remarks, though he repeats his contention that women are too easily influenced and susceptible to religious dogmatism. DLC

613 Sevilla Sacasa, Oscar. *Estado actual de la minería en Nicaragua: informe.* Managua: Talleres Nacionales, 1941. 46 pp. Illus., maps, tables.

An official summary of the gold-mining operations that were furnishing 60% of Nicaragua's export revenue in 1940. Details their growth, operation, location, and ownership. DLC

614 Seymour (Captain). *The Isthmian Routes, a Brief Description of Each Projected Route, and of Those Now Existing, Showing the Capacity of Their Harbors, the Comparative Advantages of Each, and the Distance by Each from New York to San Francisco; from the Best Sources of Information, and from Personal Observation and Survey over Each, In the Years from 1856 to 1861.* New York: Hall, Clayton & Medole, 1863. 27 pp.

Brief descriptions of five different prospective canal routes, including those in Honduras and Nicaragua. The author advocates the Chiriqui route because it has what he considers the best natural harbors at its termini, because it would be easier to construct, and because of the health advantages it offers. The discussion is confined to the comparison of the routes, with no data regarding the nation. DLC

615 Sheldon, Henry Isaac. *Notes on the Nicaragua Canal.* Chicago: A.C. McClurg, 1897. 214 pp. Illus., maps. 3d ed. Chicago: A.C. McClurg, 1902. 250 pp. Illus., maps.

An account of the suitability of Nicaragua for the canal and its potential impact on the U.S. economy, stressing the benefits for West Coast agriculture. The author visited Nicaragua during 1895 to survey the route and later visited existing canals for comparative purposes. The bulk of the volume focuses on the prospects and on details of construction and the necessary arrangements, but it includes description of Nicaragua and the physical setting of the region through which the canal would be built. DLC LNHT

616 Silva, Federico. *Jacinta: novela verídica que parace cuento.* Managua: Tipografía Pérez, 1927. 176 pp. Illus.

A novel recounting the experiences of several Nicaraguans during the 1920s, focusing principally on human emotions and everyday events but including discussion of the impact of the Yankee monetary intervention and the resulting currency and banking reforms; the Yankees appear as the villains in several of the episodes. DLC

617 Silva, Fernando. *El comandante.* Managua: Editorial Unión, 1969. 213 pp.

A novel set in the author's native river town of El Castillo in Nicaragua. Focuses on the life of the local military commander who, despite his lack of ability and his slovenly habits, wields considerable power; but he has little to do because the town is calm, quiet, and remote. The novel consists principally of dialogue, focusing on the emotions of life and portraying the commander as being just like

(Silva, Fernando)
everyone else in his daily life and activities, despite his title. DLC LNHT

618 ____. Otros 4 cuentos. León: Universidad Nacional Autónoma de Nicaragua, 1969. 93 pp.
A collection of short stories, all previously published in the press, focusing on the lives of the peasants and the poor of the author's native town of El Castillo on the San Juan River in Nicaragua. DLC

619 ____. De tierra y agua. Managua: Editorial Unión, 1969. 161 pp.
Another collection of short stories, written from the perspective of the peasants, laborers, and fishermen of the San Juan River region of Nicaragua. The author draws on the firsthand experiences of his own youth to describe their concerns in vivid and emotional terms, employing the local idioms and modisms. DLC LNHT

620 Simmons, William E. Uncle Sam's New Waterway. New York: F.T. Neely, 1899. iv, 285 pp. Illus. 2d ed. New York: Harper, 1900. 334 pp. Illus.
Part of the propaganda attendant to the canal debate, this volume was designed to familiarize the general reader with the canal project and urge the suitability of Nicaragua for such an endeavor. There is no discussion of Panama. The focus is on description of Nicaragua, its geography, people, history, and economic prospects. The second edition, published under the title The Nicaragua Canal, is updated to reflect the signing and defeat of the first Hay-Pauncefoote Treaty; it also contains a new map identifying the different locations proposed by the Maritime Canal Company and the Nicaragua Canal Commission. DLC

621 Smith, John Lawrence. Inter-Oceanic Canal: Practicability of the Different Routes, and Questionable Nature of the Interest of the United States in a Canal. Louisville, Ky.: Bradley & Gilbert, 1880. 22 pp.
A brief summary of the then-current state of thinking on the canal question, based on the author's participation in a conference on the subject in Paris. He focuses on the Nicaragua and Panama routes, noting problems in each and reserving judgment between them. The author feels that steamships are far in the future and the canal therefore must be planned for sailing vessels; he says this was the view of the conferees. DLC

622 Smutko, Gregorio. Pastoral indigenista: experiencia entre los miskitos. Bogotá: Ediciones Paulinas, 1975. 106 pp. Biblio., illus.
A Catholic missionary's account of the missions among the Mosquito Indians during the 1960s and 1970s, written for the Conference of Latin American Bishops meeting in Bogota. Clearly advocates liberation theology and its political activism which has become a cause célèbre in the Latin American church and

throughout the hemisphere, stressing base communities that push for the rights of the local inhabitants. DLC

623 Sobalvarro Arauz, Manuel. Gratos recuerdos en demolición; Sweet Memories in Demolition. Managua: n.p., 1973. Pages unnumbered. Illus.
An account of the 1972 Managua earthquake and its aftermath. LNHT

624 Solórzano Ocón, Ildefonso [Ildo Sol, pseud.]. Vaniloquio reaccionario. Managua: Editorial Alemana, 1962. 38 pp.
A propaganda piece aimed at the working class, calling for a conservative revolution of the so-called Reactionary Revolutionary Vanguard. DLC

625 Solow, Antole A. Planificación de facilidades físicas y terrenos para industrias y el establecimiento de un parque industrial. Managua: Ministerio de Fomento y Obras Públicas. 133 pp. Biblio., illus., maps, tables.
A report assessing the prospects, costs, and necessary facilities and potential benefits of the establishment of an industrial park in Nicaragua. DLC

626 Somoza García, Anastasio. El verdadero Sandino, o el calvario de las Segovias. Managua: Tipografía Robelo, 1936. 566 pp. Illus.
An account by the Commander of the Guardia about his principal antagonist, providing his view of the revolutionary leader. Emphasizes Sandino's irresponsibility, catalogs his atrocities, and details his Marxist connections, offering the case against him to offset what the author views as the bias of the media and the intellectuals in construing Sandino as a hero by ignoring his transgressions. The emphasis is on Sandino's refusal of peace agreements acceptable to all other participants, and on his use of terror. The volume catalogs such episodes and provides photographs, but avoids discussion of Sandino's assassination. DLC

627 Sonnenstern, Maximilian von. Report on the Nicaragua Route for an Interoceanic Ship-Canal, with a Review of the Proposed Routes. Washington, D.C.: GPO, 1874. 22 pp. Maps.
A brief report originally prepared for the Nicaraguan government. Surveys the proposed routes through that country, provides specifications and details, and calls for the construction of such a canal. DLC

628 Soto, Pedro. Acusación ante la historia: Los EE. UU. y la Campaña Nacional, 1856-1857. San José: n.p., 1956. 67 pp.
A denunciation of the gringo threat, focusing on the Walker intervention in Nicaragua but mentioning the war with Mexico, the various Caribbean and Central American interventions, and the American role in Cuba to provide background for charges that the filibusters were merely agents of imperialism who

were cheered on by the Yankees. The substantive portion of the volume focuses on the degree to which American public opinion supported Walker. BNCR

629 Soto-Hall, Máximo. <u>Nicaragua y el imperialismo norteamericano y la vergonzosa tolerancia de los gobiernos de América Latina</u>. Buenos Aires: Artes y Letras Editorial, 1928. 163 pp.

An impassioned denunciation of Yankee intervention in Nicaragua during the 1920s, assailing not only the occupation but also the Latin American nations that supported or failed to protest the Yankee actions. The author views the intervention as part of an imperialist policy in all of Central America, and denounces the Yankee domination, economic control, and political and military intervention, as well as its acceptance by governmental leaders throughout the isthmus. DLC BNG

630 _____. <u>La sombra de la casa blanca: libro de emoción, de pasión, de verdad y de justicia</u>. Buenos Aires: El Ateneo, 1927. 316 pp.

A novel dealing with the Nicaraguan Liberal situation in the face of the United States intervention. The focus is on a young Nicaraguan Liberal who visits the United States seeking to influence, or at least to determine the basis of Yankee policy, and on his impressions of that nation and its people. Emphasizes their lack of knowledge of Central American politics and the contradictions between Yankee ideals and intervention. Its passionate criticism of materialism provides an indication of the Latin American view of the U.S. DLC LNHT

631 Soto Valenzuela, Marco Antonio. <u>Guerra Nacional de Centroamérica</u>. Guatemala: Ministerio de Educación Pública, 1957. 118 pp. 2d ed. Guatemala: Ministerio de Educación Pública, 1975. 126 pp. Maps, tables.

A military officer's detailed history of the military campaigns of the wars against the filibuster William Walker in Nicaragua from 1854 through 1857. Discusses the cooperation among the Central American republics to repulse the invaders, but the emphasis is on the battlefield rather than on the politics of the era; includes maps of the troop movements. LNHT BNG BNCR

632 Squier, Ephraim George, ed. [Samuel A. Bard, pseud.]. <u>Documents officiels échangés entre les États-Unis et l'Angleterre au sujet de l'Amérique Centrale et du Traité Clayton-Bulwer</u>. Paris: Librarie de Stassin et Xavier, 1856. 225 pp. Maps.

Reproduction and translation into French of a series of exchanges dating from the Clayton-Bulwer Treaty of 1850 through 1856, and the Dallas-Calderon exchanges (though not the eventual agreement they reached). The preface indicates that these are of interest to Europe because the continent has a strong interest in

the neutralization of important commercial routes. DLC

633 _____. <u>Nicaragua: Its People, Scenery, Monuments, Resources, Conditions, and Proposed Interoceanic Canal; with One Hundred Original Maps and Illustrations</u>. 2 vols. New York: Appleton, 1851. 424, 452 pp. Illus., maps. Latest ed. New York: AMS Press, 1969-73. 691 pp. Illus., maps. <u>Der Zentralamerikanische Staat Nicaragua in Bezug auf sein Volk, seine Natur und seine Denkmaeler: Nebst einer aus führlichen Abhandlung über den projectirten interoceanischen Kanal</u>. Leipzig: Deutsch, 1854. xviii, 570 pp. Illus., maps. <u>Nicaragua, sus gentes y paisajes</u>. León: n.p., 1851. 2d ed. San José: EDUCA, 1970. 570 pp. Illus., maps.

A detailed description of the nation based on Squier's years as U.S. chargé in Central America, reflecting his trained eye and attention to detail as well as the prevailing Yankee attitudes. Includes detailed consideration, based on personal observation, of the Nicaragua canal route, and one of the best descriptions of Puerto San Juan available. The author was an advocate of the Nicaragua canal project. Also offers rich description of the life in the region at mid-century, as well as information on archeological zones, which were then largely unknown. Some editions use the title <u>Travels in Central America, Particularly Nicaragua: With a Description of Its Aboriginal Monuments, Scenery, and People, Their Languages, Institutions, Religion, etc</u>. DLC LNHT BNCR

634 _____. <u>The Volcanoes of Central America, and the Geographical and Topographical Features of Nicaragua, as Connected with the Proposed Inter-Oceanic Canal</u>. New York: n.p., 1850. 20 pp.

Written in the form of the minutes of an oral presentation and the succeeding discussion, this volume is directed at a general but educated audience. It deals specifically with the feasibility and means of constructing a canal over the Nicaragua route. DLC

635 _____. <u>Waikna; or, Adventures on the Mosquito Shore</u>. London: Low; New York: Harper & Bros., 1855. 366 pp. Illus., maps. Latest ed. Gainesville: University of Florida Press, 1965. xxxvii, 366 pp. Index, illus., maps, appendixes.

A classic work, by the United States chargé in Central America writing under the pseudonym Samuel Bard, this is a semi-autobiographical historical novel. Squier resided for many years in San Juan del Norte, Nicaragua, beginning in 1848, and traveled throughout the region. The story, about a shipwrecked individual off the Nicaraguan coast and his wanderings and adventures, is clearly a vehicle for the author's observations and descriptions of the physical terrain and jungle, the Indians of the region, and the sea captains and others who lived and worked there. It provides considerable information about life

in the area during the late 1840s and early
1850s. DLC LNHT

636 Stewart, William Frank. Last of the Filibusters; or, Recollections of the Siege of
Rivas. Sacramento: H. Shipley, 1857. 85 pp.
Appendixes.
An account of the Walker expedition and the
key battle of the resulting war. Contends
that it is unfair to call Walker a filibuster
because he was, in fact, an adventurer seeking
to help the Central Americans rather than
conquer them. The emphasis is therefore on
the actions of Walker and his followers, their
arrival, their plans, their movements, and
other details of the expedition and the problems it encountered rather than on the warfare. NN

637 Stimson, Henry Lewis. American Policy in
Nicaragua. New York: Scribner's 1927. 129
pp. Reprint. New York: Arno Press, 1970.
129 pp.
A memoir of the author's role, as part of
the U.S. intervention of the 1920s, in mediating the civil war between the Nicaraguan Liberal and Conservative parties. Focuses on the
tortuous negotiations that led to the 1927
Pact of Tipitapa, recounting in detail the
meetings and problems. The work includes a
justification of the U.S. program and provides
an inside view of the talks as well as an
official view of the policy and objectives,
with illuminating insights into the personalities of the Nicaraguan leaders who participated. DLC LNHT

638 _____. La política de los Estados Unidos en
Nicaragua. Washington, D.C.: GPO, 1928.
46 pp.
A Spanish translation of an article that
originally appeared in the Saturday Evening
Post summarizing the U.S. efforts in 1927 to
mediate the civil war. Provides a brief overview of some of the items later covered in his
book-length study in English. DLC

639 Stout, Peter F. Nicaragua: Past, Present,
and Future: A Description of Its Inhabitants,
Customs, Mines, Minerals, Early History,
Modern Filibusterism, Proposed Inter-Oceanic
Canal and Manifest Destiny. Philadelphia:
John E. Potter, 1859. 372 pp. Maps.
A combination memoir, travelogue, and gos-
sipy compendium of history and essays on various topics, which the author describes as a
current history of and travel guide to
Nicaragua based on his own experiences in that
nation. The bulk is an account of his travels, observations, conversations, etc., but it
also includes geographical information, some
disparate chapters on history ranging throughout Central America and Mexico that have little relation to the rest of the volume, and
several chapters dealing with the proposed
Nicaraguan canal and the future economic prospects of the nation. Hints that the United
States should fulfil its destiny and annex the
entire region. DLC LNHT

640 Strangeways, Thomas. Sketches of the Mosquito
Shore, Including the Territory of the Poyais.
Edinburgh: William Blackwood, 1822. viii,
355 pp. Illus., maps.
A detailed description of the region and
its potential, designed to encourge British
colonization in the area. Includes physical
description of each of the various towns and
rivers, and chapters on flora, fauna, and
resources. DLC LNHT

641 Stuckle, Henry. Interoceanic Canals: An Essay
on the Question of Location for a Ship Canal
across the American Continent. New York: Van
Nostrand, 1870. iv, 137 pp. Biblio., maps.
A review of the various canal schemes and
routes, comparing them with Suez. Concludes
that the most feasible route is that closest
to the United States, namely, the Isthmus of
Tehuantepec. Most of the pamphlet consists of
analysis and discussion of this route. DLC
LNHT

642 Suárez López, Gerardo, ed. Somoza: el líder
de Nicaragua. Managua: Litografía San José,
1971. 100 pp. Illus.
A compilation of commentaries extolling
Anastacio Somoza García and his work. Includes essays on his leadership in various
fields, summaries of the accomplishments of
his regime, and extensive illustrations designed to demonstrate his popularity and his
association with other hemispheric presidents.
DLC LNHT

643 Suárez López, Gerardo. Son. Managua:
Imprenta Nacional, 1968. 136 pp. Illus.
A collection of short stories focusing on
the lives and aspirations of the peasants,
written by a radio commentator and peasant
political leader. Stresses that the peasants
are the heart of the nation and agriculture
the base of its economy, calling the peasants
the motive force in the republic. The stories
deal with such themes as land seizures, assassinations, and politics rather than the struggles of daily life, and are forcefully and
emotionally written from the peasant viewpoint. DLC LNHT

644 Suárez Zambrana, Guillermo. Los Yanquis en
Nicaragua. San José: Editorial Texto, 1978.
310 pp. Illus.

645 Sullivan, John T. Report of Historical and
Technical Information Relating to the Problem
of Interoceanic Communication by Way of the
American Isthmus. 47th Cong., 2d sess. Doc.
107. Washington, D.C.: GPO, 1883. 219 pp.
Biblio., notes, illus., maps, tables.
The report of a U.S. naval survey team sent
to the isthmus at the request of Congress,
consisting of a detailed summary of the canal
question. Contains technical surveys of the
proposed routes and lists the pros and cons of
each from a technical viewpoint. Includes
maps, routes, and construction and cost information, as well as material regarding the
harbors at the termini and distances to the
United States. DLC LNHT

646 Taylor, B.W. <u>Ecological Land Use Surveys in Nicaragua</u>. Managua: Ministerio de Economía, 1959. 338 pp. Maps, tables. <u>Estudios ecológicos para el aprovechamiento de la tierra en Nicaragua</u>. Managua: Ministerio de Economía, 1959. 338 pp. Maps, tables.
    The results of a survey undertaken by the United Nations Food and Agricultural Organization at the request of the Nicaraguan government, the fieldwork for which was conducted between 1956 and 1958. Each chapter is printed first in Spanish and then in English, with pages numbered consecutively throughout the volume. Provides a detailed description of land use, soil types, climate, water availability, and agriculture, with charts and extensive statistics, all for the current year. Covers the regions of Cabezas-Río Coco, Matagalpa-Esteli-Ocotal, and Boaco-Santo Tomás; others are still in preparation. DLC

647 Taylor, Henry Clay. <u>The Nicaragua Canal</u>. New York: American Geographical Society, 1886. 32 pp. Maps.
    An address by a U.S. Navy commander comparing all the proposed canal routes and concluding that Nicaragua offers the best prospects. DLC LNHT

648 Téfel Vélez, Reinaldo Antonio. <u>Socialización en la libertad</u>. Managua: Editorial Nicaragüense, 1964. 74 pp. Illus.
    A call not for class struggle but for a revolution in behalf of the people of the isthmus, one that would end dictatorship and instill new Christian social values based on human dignity. Written in general terms, it cites Catholic doctrine and reformist approaches. Includes a discussion of Nicaragua, references to the brotherhood of all Central Americans, and endorsement of the Common Market. DLC LNHT

649 Terán, Francisco, and Jaime Incer Barquero. <u>Geografía de Nicaragua</u>. Managua: Banco Central de Nicaragua, 1964. 266 pp. Index, biblio., illus., maps, tables. 2d ed. Managua: Librería y Editorial Recalde, 1969. 258 pp. Index, biblio., illus., maps, tables.
    A detailed and well-illustrated general geography of the nation. Covers physical features, climate, geology, flora and fauna, economy, etc., with appropriate tables, statistics, illustrations, and maps, as well as a discussion of the nation's boundaries that is designed to support the national claims in the various disputes. Terán is a UNESCO expert sent to Nicaragua; his coauthor is a well-known Nicaraguan geographer and official of the Ministry of Public Education. DLC LNHT

650 Thomé de Gamond, Aimé de. <u>Carte d'étude pour le tracé et le profil du canal de Nicaragua, précédée de documents publiés sur cette question par Félix Belly</u>. Paris: Dalmont et Dunot, 1858. 90 pp. Maps.
    Part of the literature regarding the location and type of canal for the isthmus, this study outlines a plan for the Nicaragua route that calls for damming the rivers and flooding the entire region of the San Juan estuary between Lake Nicaragua and the Atlantic coast, thereby reducing the amount of digging required. Needless to say, the technical details of the method make the feasibility of the scheme somewhat dubious. DLC LNHT

651 Tijerino, Gustavo. <u>El terremoto mas bárbaro de la historia</u>. 2 vols. Managua: n.p., n.d. [1973-75]. 114, 188 pp. Illus.
    An account of the 1972 Managua earthquake. The first volume recounts the history of earthquakes in the capital and describes the latest; the second consists of photographs of Managua showing the damage of the various quakes, with some supplemental description. DLC LNHT

652 _____. <u>Las víctimas y los victimarios</u>. Managua: Talleres Gráficas Pérez, 1939. 142 pp. Illus.
    A collection of short stories, many of which deal with regional historical episodes from the various parts of Nicaragua and make references to the nineteenth century and the Walker incursion; others deal with general literary themes. DLC

653 Tijerino, Toribio. <u>El Tratado Chamorro-Bryan y sus proyecciones en la América Central</u>. Managua: Tipografía La Prensa, 1935. 67 pp.
    A Nicaraguan Conservative political figure defends the Chamorro regime, the party, and the treaty, arguing that the Bryan-Chamorro Treaty is simply an option extended to the United States, and that when the Yankees are ready to build the canal new negotiations will take place regarding the details. Denies charges that the pact infringes on the sovereignty of the other Central American nations or places Nicaragua excessively in the Yankee orbit, noting that the accord was a recognition of the reality of the Yankee predominance and determination to build a canal, and that the funds received in payment will enable Nicaragua to develop. DLC DLC-LDS-886 LNHT

654 Tijerino Molina, Bayardo. <u>El incendio</u>. Valencia: Ediciones Prometeo, 1970. 266 pp.
    A symbolic novel of Yankee exploitation in Nicaragua during the intervention of the 1930s. Focuses on the ambassador and his entourage and his interaction with government officials, who always defer to him as a privileged character. Sandino appears as a figure in the background. The exploits of the ambassador are the focus, though his movements and actions also show the role of government officials and their alienation from the populace; the limited world of the diplomats and officials is seen as sharply distinct from that of the people. DLC LNHT

655 _____. <u>La máquina de papel</u>. Valencia: Editorial Prometeo, 1974. 181 pp.
    A novel seeking to demonstrate the decadence of the Nicaraguan upper class, which is portrayed as living in its own world apart from that of the populace and having abandoned traditional values in favor of a life-style

that values wealth, power, and personal indul-
gence, and is motivated only by personal plea-
sure and ambition. The principal figures are
surrounded by sycophants who cater to their
every whim. The gap between this group and
the bulk of the populace is stressed. DLC
LNHT

656 Toledo de Aguerri, Josefa. Anhelos y
esfuerzos. Managua: Imprenta Nacional, 1935.
x, 205 pp.
    General essays and speeches regarding
numerous aspects of the role of women in
Nicaraguan culture and society, previously
published in the Revista Feminina Ilustrada:
Mujer Nicaragüense, which the author edited.
DLC

657 _____. Cultura literaria y científica. Vol.
2 Managua: Imprenta Nacional, 1932. vi, 443
pp. Illus.
    A collection of miscellaneous data about
the nation. Only volume 2 was published, the
manuscript of the first volume having been
destroyed in the 1931 earthquake. TxU

658 _____. Personificación de la historia de
Managua. Managua: Talleres Nacionales, 1942.
47 pp. Illus.
    A series of essays tracing the development
of Managua, with a chapter on each presidential administration from 1529 to the present.
DLC

659 _____. Puntos críticos sobre enseñanza
nicaragüense. Managua: Imprenta Nacional,
1933. xiv, 368 pp. Illus.
    A collection of articles on various aspects
of Nicaraguan education written for the
Managua press between 1907 and 1928, which
provide an indication of the issues debated
during that era. The articles are arranged by
date; most deal with elementary education,
covering programatic questions, content, disciplines, urban versus rural education, and
other themes. DLC

660 Toledo Ortiz, Alberto. Grandes reportajes
históricos de Nicaragua: los que occurió hace
40, 30, 20, 10, y 5 años. Managua: Editorial
Alemana, 1972. 174 pp. Illus.
    A collection of articles written during the
author's many years as a journalist for the
newspaper El Centroamericano of León. They
focus on the Guardia Nacional, its campaigns
against Sandino, and internal rebellions and
problems, concluding with the assassination of
Anastacio Somoza García. DLC LNHT

661 Torre Villar, Ernesto de la, ed. La batalla
de San Jacinto, Nicaragua, 1856. Mexico:
PAIGH, 1957. 61 pp. Notes.
    A collection of reports about and documents
relating to one of the battles against Walker
and his filibusters. Includes the speeches
delivered on the occasion of the centennial
of the combat, hailing the patriotism of
Nicaraguans and Central Americans. DLC

662 Torres, Edelberto, et al. Mensaje sobre
Nicaragua, 1950 (unos hombres han muerto
. . .). Guatemala: Imprenta Iberia, 1950.
24 pp.
    An anti-Somoza tract written by exiles
appealing to the journalists of the continent
to recognize their protest.

663 El Tratado Castrillo-Knox y los contratos con
los banqueros de Wall Street. Managua:
Tipografía El Pacífico, 1923. xiii, 53 pp.
    A collection of commentaries about the loan
arrangements for financial stabilization in
1917-18. Some were written under the pseudonym "Historiográfico" in 1917; the rest were
published in the newspaper El Heraldo in 1918
and also comment on apsects of the U.S. Senate
debate over the Bryan-Chamorro Treaty and
respond to criticisms of the Nicaraguan accord
by Panamanians. All reflect the political
polemics of the day and criticize the ambitions of the financiers and the imperialism of
the Yankees, while defending the national
honor. LNHT

664 Travis, Ira Dudley. British Rule in Central
America; or, a Sketch of Mosquito History.
Ann Arbor, Mich.: Argus Printing, 1895. 36
pp. Biblio., notes.
    A very brief summary of the British effort
to control the Mosquito Territory and the
place of the Indians' rights in the canal
controversy. Based on published congressional
documents and secondary works. DLC LNHT

665 _____. The History of the Clayton-Bulwer
Treaty. Ann Arbor: University of Michican
Press, 1900. ix, 312 pp. Biblio., notes,
maps.
    An examination of the treaty, based on
published materials and reports, dating from a
time when it was under attack and the subject
of considerable political dispute. Surveys
its origins and concludes that it was realistic at the time it was signed, that it is
still valuable, and that the United States
does not need sole control of a canal for its
security; advocates preservation of the
treaty. Written as a debunking study, it
devotes much of its space to listing public
charges and countercharges from the then-
raging debate, and seeking to examine their
basis. In the process it does capture the
flavor of the dispute. DLC

666 Tunnermann Bernheim, Carlos. Dar a la
república la universidad que merece. León:
Universidad de Nicaragua, 1964. 19 pp.
    A listing of objectives by the rector of
the National University, which explains concerns common to education throughout the region and reflects his experience as an
administrator, as well as indicating his
goals. FU

667 Tweedy, Maureen. This is Nicaragua. Ipswich,
England: East Anglian Magazine, 1953. 116
pp. Illus., maps.
    A descriptive travelogue focusing on the
author's observations of the principal cities,

though intermixed with background. Includes chapters dealing with the Colonial era and the Walker episode for background, as well as discussion of agriculture. Designed for the general reader. DLC

668 U.S. Congress. House. Report of Historical and Technical Information Relating to the Problem of Interoceanic Communication by Way of the American Isthmus, 1883. 47th Cong., 2d sess., 1882-83. H. Doc. 107. Washington, D.C.: GPO, 1883. 219 pp. Biblio., illus., maps.
    One of many studies made during this era; this one contains summaries of the various isthmian canal projects, with particularly complete data about the Nicaragua route. DLC

669 _____. Committee on Foreign Affairs. Conditions in Nicaragua and Mexico: Hearings. 69th Cong., 2d sess. Washington, D.C.: GPO, 1927. ii, 85 pp.
    Hearings regarding the U.S. intervention in Nicaragua and the efforts to negotiate a peace ending the civil war, and future plans for stabilization, including the establishment of the National Guard. DLC

670 _____. Select Committee on a Canal or Railroad between the Atlantic and Pacific Oceans. Report of the Select Committee Authorized to Investigate Certain Routes for a Canal or Railroad between the Atlantic and Pacific Oceans. 30th Cong., 2d sess., 1848-49. H. Rept. 145. Washington, D.C.: GPO, 1849. 679 pp.
    Includes various survey reports of each of the potential routes, as well as other pertinent reports, including railroad plans, sailing times between the coasts and the canals, etc. DLC

671 _____. Select Committee on Interoceanic Ship Canal. Testimony. 46th Cong., 3d sess., 1881. H. Doc. 16. Washington, D.C.: GPO, 1881. 129 pp.
    The committee heard a large number of witnesses presenting a wide range of viewpoints and arguments. DLC

672 U.S., Congress. Senate. Documents Relating to Interoceanic Canals. 57th Cong., 1st sess., 1901-2. Washington, D.C.: GPO, 1902. 68 pp.
    DLC

673 _____. Committee on Foreign Relations. Hearing before the Committee on Foreign Relations, U.S. Senate, 63rd Congress, 2nd Session, on the Convention between the U.S. and Nicaragua. Washington, D.C.: GPO, 1914. 518 pp.
    Detailed hearings regarding the negotiations and terms of the Bryan-Chamorro Treaty, showing the degree of controversy and the focus of interest in the canal question within the United States. Interestingly, much of the debate related to the financial provisions of the treaty and the economic stability of Nicaragua rather than to the canal rights,

which become the focus of dispute in Central America, thereby demonstrating the different focus of the Yankees and the residents of the region. DLC

674 _____. _____. Nicaraguan Affairs: Hearings before a Subcommittee of the Committee on Foreign Rela-tions, United States Senate, Sixty-Second Congress, Second Session . . . to Investigate as to the Alleged Invasion of Nicaragua by Armed Sailors and Marines of the United States (El Paso, Texas, Oct. 8, 1912). 62d Cong., 2d sess. Washington, D.C.: GPO, 1913. 92 pp.
    A hearing held to record the testimony of Juan Leets concerning charges that the United States consul and U.S. Navy personnel aided a revolt against the government of José Madriz in 1910, during the maneuvering that followed the fall of the long-standing regime of José Santos Zelaya. DLC

675 _____. _____. Use of the United States Navy in Nicaragua: Hearings before the Committee on Foreign Relations, United States Senate, Seventieth Congress, First Session Pursuant to S. Res. 137. 70th Cong., 1st sess., 1928. Washington, D.C.: GPO, 1928. iii, 72 pp. Tables.
    Hearing before the Senate Foreign Relations Committee summarizing the use of Marines against General Sandino and the intervention efforts. Includes questioning of Secretary of the Navy Curtis D. Wilbur, Rear Admiral Julian L. Latimer, and Major General John A. Lejeune, with exchanges with the committee and a summary of U.S. military activities in Nicaragua. DLC

676 _____. Committee on Interoceanic Canals. Interoceanic Canals: Additional Report. 56th Cong., 2d sess. S. Rept. 1337. Washington, D.C.: GPO, 1900. 384 pp.
    Further documentation and additional testimony to supplement the Walker Commission report; recommends construction of a canal in Nicaragua as rapidly as possible. DLC

677 _____. _____. Interoceanic Canals: Additional Views of the Minority Favoring the Panama Route of the Committee on Interoceanic Canals. 57th Cong., 1st sess., 1900-1901. S. Rept. 1663. Washington, D.C.: GPO, 1902.
    Supplemental statements to the minority report, favoring the Panama route. DLC

678 _____. _____. Isthmian Canal: Views of the Minority of the Committee on Interoceanic Canals, May 31, 1902. 57th Cong., 1st sess., 1900-1901. Washington, D.C.: GPO, 1902. 140 pp. Appendixes.
    The minority report favoring the Panama route. DLC

679 _____. _____. Report of the Committee on Inter-oceanic Canals. 56th Cong., 1st sess., 1900. S. Rept. 1337. Washington, D.C.: GPO, 1900. 144 pp. Tables.
    The committee, chaired by Senator John Morgan, reported a bill providing for the construction of a canal in Nicaragua as soon

(U.S., Congress. Senate)
as possible. The report summarizes the arguments for and against Panama and Nicaragua. Includes detailed correspondence regarding the routes and construction requirements, as well as excerpts from the testimony of Admiral John G. Walker. DLC

680   _____. _____. Report of the Senate Committee on Interoceanic Canals on the Proposed Ship Canals through the American Isthmus Connecting the Continents of North and South America. 57th Cong., 1st sess. S. Rept. 1. Washington, D.C.: GPO, 1901. 551 pp. Illus.
        A massive tome providing a brief survey of Anglo-American relations, the history of canals, the route controversy in Central America, and the proposed impact of the canal on United States Commerce. Emphasizes the Nicaragua and Panama routes and American relations with both countries. Contends that the British had sought to control and then to delay Yankee action; concludes that a canal in Central America is essential to the economic growth of the United States. Most of the volume consists of the texts of the appropriate documents, treaties, and canal agreements, the reports of the various companies and commissions, and excerpts from the testimony in some of the hearings. DLC

681   _____. Committee on Interstate and Foreign Commerce. Hearings before the Committee on Interstate and Foreign Commerce . . . on the New Panama Canal Company, the Maritime Company and the Nicaragua Canal Company (Grace-Eyre-Craigan Syndicate). 56th Cong., 1st sess. S. Doc. 50. Washington, D.C.: GPO, 1899.
        The statements by and questioning of the representatives of the two rival companies regarding the advantages of the respective routes. The Panama Company's chief representative was William Nelson Cromwell, while the Maritime Canal Company's chief spokesman was Alexander T. Mason. Both brought aides who also testified. DLC

682   U.S., Gov't of. Nicaragua Canal: Appendix to the Report of the Board of Engineers for the Purpose of Ascertaining the Feasibility, Permanence, and Cost of Construction and Completion of the Nicaraguan Canal by the Route Contemplated and Provided for by the Act of January 28, 1895. Washington, D.C.: GPO, 1896.
        Yet another report supporting the Nicaragua route. ICJ

683   _____. Department of State. A Brief History of the Relations between the United States and Nicaragua, 1909-1928. Washington, D.C.: GPO, 1928. iv, 77 pp. Notes.
        A survey of the U.S. involvement in Nicaragua, stressing the events of the 1920s and providing the official view of the actions and their objectives. Includes the electoral missions and financial stabilizations, as well as the Stimson mission. DLC LNHT

684   _____. _____. Correspondence and Other Papers Relating to the Proposed Interoceanic Ship Canal, etc. Washington, D.C.: GPO, 1900. 203 pp.
        DLC

685   _____. _____. Documents Relative to Central American Affairs and the Enlistment Questions. Washington, D.C.: GPO, 1856. 485 pp. Maps.
        The first half of this volume is comprised of exchanges between the United States and Great Britain and some of the Central American governments regarding British rights in the isthmus and existing treaties, relating particularly to the Mosquito Coast, sent to Congress by the president in his annual message of 1856. Congress added correspondence regarding some other cases. DLC

686   _____. _____. The United States and Nicaragua: A Survey of the Relations from 1909-1932. Washington, D.C.: GPO, 1932. iv. 134 pp. Notes, appendixes.
        A brief summary of the situation in Nicaragua focusing on United States involvement in the period since World War I, providing an official account of the efforts and of Yankee investment in the area. Includes brief historical background and the full texts of U.S. agreements regarding canal construction. DLC LNHT

687   _____. _____. United States Marines in Nicaragua: Message from the President of the United States. 71st Cong., 3d sess. S. Doc. 288. Washington, D.C.: GPO, 1931. 34 pp. Tables.
        An official statement explaining the military intervention in Nicaragua. DLC

688   _____. Isthmian Canal Commission. Isthmian Canal Commission Circulars. 2 vols. Washington, D.C.: GPO, 1912. Pages not numbered consecutively.
        A collection of separately published circulars containing the legislation establishing, staffing, and directing the commission. Volume 1 covers the years 1904-6, and volume 2, 1906-12. DLC

689   _____. _____. Report of the Isthmian Canal Commis-sion, 1899-1901. 2 vols. 57th Cong., 1st sess. S. Doc. 54. Washington, D.C.: GPO, 1901-2. 263, 533 pp. Illus., maps, tables.
        Massive preliminary and final reports from the Walker Commission, the last of the many investigative efforts to select the appropriate canal route, headed by Admiral John G. Walker. Includes details of on-site surveys of the potential routes in Nicaragua and Panama, with engineering specifics of construction and details of financing. It recommends the Nicaragua route and was the basis of the Morgan bills that provoked the final confrontation between the supporters of Panama and Nicaragua. Contains a wealth of data including extensive statistical tables, geographical surveys, and commerce figures. The second report came from an expanded committee that rechecked the surveys of the initial

(U.S., Gov't of)
group, which had consisted exclusively of military engineers. Extensive maps are included in both. DLC LNHT

690 _____. Nicaragua Canal Commission. <u>Report of the Nicaragua Canal Commission, 1897-1899</u>. Baltimore: Friedenwald, 1899. xii, 502 pp. Index, illus., maps, tables.
An account of the activities of the Walker Commission, with the data compiled by the military survey teams. DLC LNHT

691 Urcuyo Maliaño, Francisco. <u>Solos: las últimas 43 horas en el bunker de Somoza</u>. Guatemala: EDITA, 1979. 209 pp. Illus., maps, tables, appendixes.
The memoirs of Somoza's designated successor, detailing the end of the civil war and the victory of the Sandinistas as seen from inside the command post. Includes comments on the negotiations with the Sandinistas.

692 Urruela, Rafael J. <u>The Nicaragua Canal: America's First Line of Defense</u>. New Orleans: Inter-American News Association, 1948. 29 pp. Illus., maps.
A brief statement of the case for building a second canal in Nicaragua, arguing that the expense would not be that high on a per capita basis, that the investment is worthwhile in terms of defense benefits for the U.S., and that Nicaragua would be a more hospitable site than Panama and would provide a superior route. LNHT

693 Valencia Robleto, Gilberto. <u>Un mensajero de la cultura en la hermana República de Nicaragua</u>. San Salvador: Imprenta Argentina, 1957. 281 pp. Illus., maps.
A Salvadoran professor's account of his visit to Nicaragua in 1949 as part of a cultural mission to study the nation and its educational system, along with essays on various aspects of Nicaraguan history, geography, and culture that represent the result of his mission and of his studies during his stay, all designed to familiarize Salvadorans with their neighbors. LNHT

694 Valenciano Rivera, Rosendo de Jesús. <u>Glorioso centenario de la campaña nacional contra William Walker y sus filibusteros en 1856</u>. San José: Imprenta Atenea, 1956. 23 pp. Illus.
A hymn of praise for the patriots and heroes, written on the occasion of the centennial of the invasion.

695 Valladares, Víctor Manuel. <u>León romántico e inmortal</u>. León: Editorial Los Hechos, 1954. 228 pp. Illus.
A series of passionate essays and folktales about León, hailing the city and discussing various events in its development, with a series of brief descriptions of the lives of some of its leading intellectual figures. DLC

696 Valle, Alfonso. <u>Diccionario del habla nicaragüense</u>. Managua: Editorial La Nueva Prensa, 1948. iv, 326 pp. Biblio., illus.

A dictionary of Nicaraguan terms and idioms, with definitions and explanations of their origins. DLC LNHT

697 _____. <u>Filología nicaragüense: puntos y puntas, cógidos en el diccionario de nicaraguanismos</u>. Managua: Editorial Nuevos Horizontes, 1943. 82 pp. Illus.
An alphabetical listing of Nicaraguan place names, with brief explanations of their meaning and origin. Emphasizes terms of Indian derivation. DLC LNHT

698 _____, ed. <u>Interpretación de nombres geográficos indígenas de Nicaragua</u>. Managua: Talleres Gráficos Pérez, 1944. x, 185 pp. Biblio., illus., maps.
An alphabetical listing of Indian place names from the nine Indian dialects of Nicaragua, identifying each in terms of meaning, location, and modern name. DLC

699 Valle Martínez, Marco Antonio. <u>La dictadura somocista</u>. Managua: Comité Político Universitario, 1980. 31 pp.
A Sandinista view of Nicaraguan history, blaming all the nation's problems on the Yankee imperialists and characterizing the Guardia as a substitute form of imperialism. Most of the work deals with the pre-Somoza years and his rise; the regime and the revolution are covered in only ten pages. DLC

700 Vega Bolaños, Andrés. <u>Los acontecimientos de 1851, notas y documentos</u>. Managua: Editorial ASEL, 1945. vii, 232 pp.
A collection of documents, printed in full, relating to the Liberal rebellion of 1851 and the outbreak of civil war that eventually involved the entire isthmus and led to the presence of William Walker and his adventurers. Includes government decrees, rebel proclamations, intergovernmental agreements, and various accounts, including the reports of the United States chargé. The author contends that he assembled this volume to partially replace the material lost in the destruction of the National Archives, and provides a list of documents that he was unable to locate. DLC LNHT

701 _____. <u>Los atentados del superintendente de Belice, 1840-1842</u>. Managua: Imprenta Nacional, 1971. 374 pp. Index, tables.
A collection of documents relating the efforts of British officials in Belize to secure control of the Mosquito Coast, consisting primarily of reports by British representatives in this region expounding their contention that their actions were based on agreements with the Mosquito king. Includes exchanges between England, Nicaragua, and other Central American governments. Most items are drawn from newspapers and official publications of the day. Each is identified as to source and date, but there is no comment. InU

702 _____. <u>Gobernantes de Nicaragua: notas y documentos</u>. Managua: Tipografía Rodríguez, 1944. xvi, 225 pp.

(Vega Bolaños, Andrés)
A collection of material about each of the individuals who headed the state of Nicaragua through 1858, with a brief single-paragraph biographical sketch and excerpts from their various statements and proclamations. Emphasizes constitutions and legislation dealing with the political structure of the nation, which the author states is his primary focus. LNHT

703 _____, ed. 1854: bombardeo y destrucción del Puerto de San Juan del Norte de Nicaragua. Managua: Banco de América, 1970. 294 pp. Index.
A collection of accounts of and documents about the bombardment by a U.S. warship of San Juan del Norte, or Greytown, on 13 July 1854 drawn from various newspapers and official diplomatic reports from both the U.S. and Nicaragua. Includes diplomatic and popular protests, as well as reports of debates in the United States about the incident and its causes. LNHT

704 Velez Barcenas, Jacinto. Dr. Pedro Joaquín Chamorro Cardenal Asesinado. Managua: Editorial Trejos, 1979. 546 pp. Illus.
An emotional denunciation of the assassination of the editor of the newspaper La Prensa of Managua, with details of his opposition to the Somoza regime. Demonstrates the role this event played as a catalyst for opposition to the government, and its use by the Sandinistas.

705 Vigil, Francisco. Muñoz en 1855: guerra civil de 17 meses, del 15 de mayo de 1854 al 23 de octubre de 1855. Granada: Imprenta del Gobierno, 1935. 72 pp.
An account of the action of the forces opposing William Walker at the Battle of Rivas and the cooperation of the Liberal and Conservative Nicaraguan forces against him, focusing on the efforts of General J. Trinidad Muñoz, who commanded the Nicaraguan troops. The volume recounts the battle and the arrangements for cooperation between the various factions of the Nicaraguan civil war against Walker. LNHT

706 Vivas Rojas, César. Anecdotario nicaragüense. 2 vols. Managua: Tipografía Comercial & Imprenta Nacional, 1971-73. 51, 192 pp.
A collection of humorous anecdotes recounting various incidents of the late nineteenth century and continuing through the 1920s. They shed light on Nicaragua, its people and customs, and even political events, serving to indicate the life-style and ambience of the nation in those times. DLC LNHT

707 Vose, Edward Neville. Nicaragua. New York: Dunn's International Review, 1914. 48 pp. Biblio., illus., maps, tables.
A brief summary of the Nicaraguan economy and its prospects, designed for the Yankee manufacturer or exporter. Includes description of crops and products, potential, and trade statistics, with illustrations. The booklet is an expanded version of an article that originally appeared in Dunn's International Review in March 1914. DLC

708 Walker, James, and Edward Aldrich. Ship Canal between the Atlantic and Pacific Oceans. New York: William C. Bryant, 1852. 12 pp.
A report by two British engineers reviewing the Childs report on the feasibility of a Nicaragua canal without visiting Nicaragua. They suggest ways in which the proposals could be strengthened and construction improved, finding the scheme generally acceptable with minor adjustments. There is no discussion of other canal routes, or even of the suitability of the route selected. DLC

709 Walker, James Wilson Grimes. Ocean to Ocean: An Account, Personal and Historical, of Nicaragua and Its People. Chicago: A.G. McClurg, 1902. 309 pp. Index, illus., maps, appendixes.
A U.S. naval officer's account of his year in Nicaragua during 1898, surveying potential canal routes for the Nicaragua Canal Commission. Includes physical description of the route surveyed and an account of his travels and experiences during the survey, as well as chapters on the Anglo-American rivalry over the canal and brief historical accounts, such as a sympathetic discussion of William Walker's efforts. The author argues in favor of the Nicaragua route, citing shorter transit time, reduced maintenance costs, better sanitary conditions, and contends that the region offers better prospects for commercial development that would benefit the U.S. than does the Panama route. DLC LNHT

710 Walker, Thomas W. The Christian Democratic Movement in Nicaragua. Tucson: University of Arizona Press, 1970. 71 pp. Biblio.
A summary of the Christian Democratic movement and of the party since its formation in 1957, outlining its general stance and position within the Nicaraguan political system, and discussing its leadership, based principally on interviews with prominent Nicaraguans and party leaders. The youth of the leadership is accented, along with the ways in which the party differs from other Latin American Christian Democratic parties, principally in not being an offshoot of existing parties and in being less paternalistic. Includes prognostications that note that everything depends on the actions of the Somoza dictatorship. DLC LNHT

711 Walker, William. Mexico and Central America: The Problem and Its Solution. New Orleans: n.p., 1858. 32 pp.
Walker's view of the region's needs, emphasizing the need for civilizing the wilderness with Yankee values to uplift the natives. CU-B

712 _____. The War in Nicaragua. Mobile, Ala.: S.H. Goetzel, 1860. xii, 431 pp. Notes, maps. Latest ed. Detroit: Blaine Ethridge, 1971. 431 pp. Illus.

The memoirs of the famous filibuster, describing his efforts to gain control of Nicaragua and the resulting wars, justifying his actions and detailing his ambitions. Indicates his view of the region and its needs as well as his objectives, though it focuses principally on narrating the combats in great detail. Naturally the Yankee phalanx is portrayed as confronting masses of barbarians. Fundamental to an understanding of this important event that did so much to shape Central American attitudes toward the Yankees. DLC DLC-LDS-318 LNHT BNG BNCR

713 Wallace, Edward S. *Destiny and Glory.* New York: Coward-McCann, 1957. 320 pp. Index, biblio., notes, maps.
A dramatic account of the history of filibustering in the mid-nineteenth century. Focuses on Walker and Nicaragua, but includes treatment of other lesser-known episodes, stressing the filibusters' recklessness, daring, adventure, and bravery, as well as the perils they faced. DLC

714 Weitzel, George T. *American Policy in Nicaragua: Memorandum on the Convention between the U.S. and Nicaragua Relative to an Interoceanic Canal and Naval Station in the Gulf of Fonseca, Signed at Managua, in Nicaragua, on Feb. 8, 1913.* 64th Cong., 1st sess. S. Doc. 334. Washington, D.C.: GPO, 1916. 33 pp.
La Política Americana en Nicaragua. Granada: El Centroamericano, 1916. 43 pp.
An official summary and defense of U.S. policy in Nicaragua from 1909 to 1915, including the various signed agreements, by a former U.S. minister responsible for much of it. DLC

715 _____. *Nicaragua and the Bryan-Chamorro Canal Treaty.* Washington, D.C.: GPO, 1927. 13 pp.
A statement by the former U.S. minister in Nicaragua defending the Wilson administration's arrangements to secure canal rights through that nation. DLC

716 Wells, William Vincent. *Walker's Expedition to Nicaragua: A History of the Central American War and the Sonora and Kinney Expeditions.* New York: Stringer & Townsend, 1856. vi, 316 pp. Illus., maps, appendixes. *Walker's Expedition nach Nicaragua und der Central-Amerikanische Krieg nebst der vollständigen diplomatischen Correspondenz (Aus dem Englischen).* Braunschweig: Verlag der Schulbuch Handlung, 1857. x, 217 pp. Illus., maps.
A hastily assembled volume by a previous explorer of the region and friend of Walker. Detailing the expedition, which is hailed as the new thrust of Manifest Destiny, it unabashedly speaks of Nicaragua as the next star in the Yankee flag, or alternatively the first star of a new group of Anglo-Saxon democratic states in the Caribbean, mirroring all the sensationalism and expansionism that then characterized the United States. Walker emerges as a hero bringing civilization and

democracy to a backward region and people, and his efforts are clearly viewed as marking out the new direction for the continuation of Yankee expansion, now that the Pacific has been reached in the north. Includes some of Walker's letters and decrees, as well as the U.S. diplomatic and official correspondence relating to the events. Implies that opposition to Walker is encouraged by the European powers who seek to control the canal routes to impede the development of the U.S. DLC BNCR

717 Wessing, Koen. *Nicaragua '78.* Amsterdam: Van Gennep, n.d. Pages unnumbered. Illus.
A collection of photos of the Nicaraguan civil war and its victims.

718 Wheeler, John Hill. *Diario de John Hill Wheeler, ministro de los Estados Unidos en Nicaragua, 1854-1857.* Managua: Banco de América, 1974. 171 pp. Index. 3d ed. Managua: Banco de América, 1976. 171 pp.
A translation of a previously unpublished diary by the American minister covering a turbulent era during the Walker expeditions in Nicaragua. The entries are somewhat cryptic but present a summary of the activities of the Yankee representative and reflect his support of Walker and the resulting disputes with the Department of State, for he acted contrary to his instructions in recognizing Walker's regime. Includes commentary on U.S.-British rivalry in the isthmus and on the commercial accords negotiated with the Nicaraguan government prior to Walker's appearance. The original manuscript of the diary is in the United States National Archives. The translation and a brief introduction were prepared by Orlando Cuadra Downing. LNHT

719 Wheelock Román, Jaime. *Frente Sandinista: Hacia la ofensiva final.* Havana: Editorial de Ciencias Sociales, 1980. vi, 117 pp. Biblio., illus.
An explanation of the combat in the Nicaraguan civil war by one of the key Sandinista leaders, explaining the rebel strategy and their objectives.

720 _____. *Imperialismo y dictadura.* Mexico: Siglo XXI, 1975.
A Marxist interpretation of Nicaraguan history, stressing the condition of the peasants and the existence of class conflict in the agrarian sector. The author, a leading member of the left-wing of the Sandinista movement, served as the revolutionary regime's director of agrarian reform. Reflects the Sandinista view of the problems of Nicaragua, as well as the basis for its later agrarian policy. Includes the usual denunciation of Yankee intervention, which is blamed for many of Nicaragua's problems, and the role of the capitalists, particularly the local elite. Condemns the concentration of land ownership, the export-oriented agriculture, and the rise of the coffee barons, as well as the prominence of coffee in the economy. There are also extensive passages condemning the Somoza dictatorship and detailing its methods, control, corruption, and use of force. DLC LNHT

(Wheelock Román, Jaime)

721 _____. Raíces indígenas de la lucha anti-
colonialista en Nicaragua de Gil González a
Joaquín Zavala (1523 a 1881). Mexico: n.p.,
1974. 119 pp.
    InU

722 Wheelock Román, Jaime, and Luís Carrión.
Apuntes sobre el desarrollo económico y social
de Nicaragua. Managua: Frente Sandinista de
Liberación Nacional, n.d. 103 pp.

723 Williams, Alfred. The Inter-Oceanic Canal and
the Monroe Doctrine. New York: Putnam's,
1880. 118 pp.
    An overview of the canal question stressing
the desirability of a canal and arguing that
it is vital that the United States build and
control such a waterway to keep it out of
European clutches, focusing particularly on
the dangers of the French effort at Panama.
The various efforts to initiate construction
and the alternative locations are discussed,
but the focus is on general considerations and
the canal's value to the United States. PST

724 Wright, John. Memoir on the Mosquito Territory. London: J. Hatchard, 1808. 32 pp.
    A tract urging British development and
settlement of the region, with information
about the concessions granted to England by
the Indians and information for prospective
settlers. DLC

725 Ycaza Tigerino, Julio César. Discursos
parlamentarios. Mexico: Editorial Tradición,
1975. 347 pp.
    A collection of speeches by a Conservative
party Nicaraguan congressman; covers service
in the Chamber of Deputies from 1957 to 1967,
the Constituent Assembly of 1972 to 1974, and
the Senate in 1974 to 1975. Included are
commentaries on all the major issues of these
years. LNHT

726 _____. La poesía y los poetas de Nicaragua.
Managua: Editorial Artes Gráficas, 1958.
149 pp.
    A prize-winning survey of the trends in
Nicaraguan poetry, with emphasis on the
Vanguardista school and recent writers,
including Coronel Urtecho, Cabrales, Manolo
Cuadra, Pablo Antonio Cuadra, and Juan Pasos.
DLC

727 Young, Thomas. Narrative of a Residence on
the Mosquito Shore: With an Account of
Truxillo, [sic] and the Adjacent Islands of
Bonacca and Roatan; and a Vocabulary of the
Mosquitian Language. London: Smith, Elder,
1842. iv, 172 pp. Illus., appendixes.
Latest ed. New York: Kraus, 1971.
    An Englishman's account of his adventures
in the Mosquito Territory during the years
1838-41. Designed to provide information
about the region to prospective travelers,
which he says he sought in vain prior to his
own departure. The focus is on description of
setting and people, through the form of a
picturesque narration of the author's own

adventures and travels, though with some historical background. DLC LNHT

728 Zelaya, José Santos. Refutation of the Statement of President Taft. Paris: Imprenta
Waltener, 1911. 15 pp.
    The Nicaraguan Liberal president's reply to
statements justifying the U.S. intervention
against his regime. DLC

729 _____. The Revolution of Nicaragua and the
United States. Madrid: Imprenta Rodríguez,
1910. 174 pp.
La revolución de Nicaragua y los Estados
Unidos. Madrid: Imprenta de B. Rodríguez,
1910. 174 pp.
    The fallen Liberal dictator's version of
his overthrow, written from exile in Europe,
blaming the United States for forcing him from
power. Much of the volume consists of publications of exchanges with his diplomatic representatives abroad and acts of loyalty to him
by the various Liberal clubs in each of the
cities of the nation. It also includes his
account of the events, particularly his responses, paragraph for paragraph, to the notes
of U.S. Secretary of State Philander Knox, as
well as documents relating to the Conservative
opposition, with appropriate charges against
them. DLC LNHT

730 Zelaya Goodman, Chester José. Nicaragua en la
independencia. San José: EDUCA, 1971. 349
pp. Index, biblio., notes, maps.
    A well-researched history of the role of
Nicaragua in the Central American independence
movement and during that era, covering the
years from 1810 to the formation of the Federation in 1824. Includes a sketch of the
context, considering social and economic as
well as political factors, with discussion of
the Nicaraguan reaction to the revolution and
the part it played in securing isthmian independence. Based on published documents from
the Archivo General de Centroamérica and the
Archivo General de Costa Rica. DLC LNHT BNCR

731 Zelaya U., José M. De los sistemas
hegemónicos. New York: Hispanic Printing,
1974. 153 pp. Biblio., notes, maps.
    Intended as part of a series of proposed
volumes enunciating a nationalistic view of
governmental responsibility for managing its
national patrimony, this work by a Nicaraguan
diplomat is in fact a defense of the
Nicaraguan claims in the dispute regarding
some small Caribbean islands also claimed by
Colombia. The author seeks to assert
Nicaraguan rights to the continental shelf and
its resources, contending that the 1928
Bárcenas Meneses-Esguerra Treaty was signed
under pressure by the U.S., which was interested only in protecting its canal rights
under the Bryan-Chamorro Treaty, and hence was
not in Nicaragua's interest and is invalid
because of this outside pressure. DLC LNHT

732 Zúñiga Huete, José Ángel. Para la historia:
Managua, 1929. Comayagüela: Imprenta El Sol,
1929. 18 pp.
    DLC

Author Index

Abadie Santos, Aníbal Raúl, CR1
Abascal, Valentín, GU1-2
Abaunza Salinas, Ramiro, NI1
Abd-al-Majïd, Muhammed Fäyïd, CA1
Abert, Silvanua Thayer, NI2
Abreu Ramos, Plinio de. See Ramos, Plinio de Abreu
Abril, Mateo, pseud. See Andino, Manuel
Aburto, Juan, NI3
Aceña Durán, Ramón, GU3
Aceña I., Ramón, GU4
Acosta, José María, CR2-3
Acosta, Luís Ferrero. See Ferrero Acosta, Luís
Acosta Valverde, Adán, CR4
Acosta Zeledón, Oscar, HO1
Acuña de Chacón, Angela, CR5
Acuña Escobar, Francisco, NI5
Acuña G., Augusto, GU5
Acuña Valerio, Miguel Ángel, CR6-7
Adamic, Louis, GU6
Adams, Frederick Upham, CA2
Adams, Richard Newbold, CA3-4; GU7-11
Adan, Émile, NI6
Adis Castro, Gonzalo, CR8
Adler, John Hans, ES408; GU12
Agüero, Arturo, CR9
Agüero, Juan Ramón, HO2
Agüero, Raúl, GU13-14
Águilar, Arturo, CA5; NI7
Aguilar, Juan J., ES1
Aguilar, Octavio, GU15
Aguilar Bulgarelli, Oscar, CR10-16
Aguilar Chávez, Manuel, ES2
Aguilar Cortes, Jerónimo, NI8
Aguilar J., Emanuel, CR17-18
Aguilar Machado, Alejandro, CR19-20
Aguilar Meza, Ricardo, CR21
Aguilar P., J. Humberto, GU16
Aguilar Paz, Jesús, HO3
Aguilar Peláez, Víctor, GU17
Aguilera, Julio Fausto, GU18
Aguilera, León, GU19-20
Aguilera de León, Carlos, GU21
Aguilera Peralta, Gabriel Edgardo, GU22
Aguirre, José Ignacio, CA6
Aguirre, José M., HO4
Aguirre Beltrán, Gonzalo, GU23
Aguirre Cardona, Francisco Osmán, ES3
Aguirre Cinta, Rafael, GU24
Aguirre Godoy, Mario, GU25
Aguirre Matheu, Lily, GU26
Aguirre Velásquez, Eduardo, GU1157
Aizcorbe, David, GU907

Alajuela, Instituto de, CR22
Alarmvogel, pseud. See Picado Soto, Francisco
Albayeros-Soso, Fernando, ES4
Albertazzi Avendaño, José, CR23-25
Albizúrez Palma, Francisco, GU27
Alcohólicos Anónimos de Honduras, HO6
Alcover y Beltrán, Antonio Miguel, NI9
Aldana H., Alfredo, GU86
Aldef, pseud. See Falconio, Leda
Alder, John Hans, ES406
Alderman, Ralph H., BE146
Aldrich, Edward, NI708
Alduvín, Ricardo Diego, HO7, 293
Alegría, Claribel, ES168
Alemán, Hugo Gilberto, CA7-8
Alemán, Vicente, CA9
Alemán Bolaños, Gustavo, CA10-13; ES5; GU30; NI10-27, 39
Alens Z., Alex A., ES6
Alexander, Alfonso, NI27
Alfaro, Gregorio, CR593-594
Alfaro, Olmedo, CA14; NI28
Alfaro, Ricardo Joaquín, CA15-16
Alfaro Arguedas, Gregorio, CR26
Alfaro Arriaga, Alejandro, HO8
Alianza de la Juventud Democrática Guatemalteca, GU31
Alleger, Daniel E., CR27
Allen, Cyril, NI29
Allen, Merritt Parmelee, NI30
Allwood Paredes, Juan, CA17-18
Alonso, Antonio, GU32
Alonso, Isidro, CA19
Alonso Chica, L., BE1
Alonso de Rodríguez, Josefina, GU33
Altagumea, Hilarión de, pseud. See Irisarri, Antonio José de
Altamirano, Napoleón Viera. See Viera Altamirano, Napoleón
Altos, Los, Government of, GU34
Altuve, Arturo, GU35
Alvarado, Gabriel, GU679
Alvarado, Gregorio, GU36
Alvarado, Gustavo, ES7
Alvarado, José Antonio, CA20-21
Alvarado, Miguel Antonio, CA22
Alvarado, Miguel T., GU37
Alvarado, Néstor Enrique, CA23; HO9-11
Alvarado, Rafael, BE2
Alvarado, Ricardo E., BE3
Alvarado Arellano, Huberto, GU38-40

Alvarado Fajardo, Federico, GU41-43
Alvarado García, Ernesto, CA24; HO12; NI31
Alvarado h., Hermogenes, ES8
Alvarado Martínez, Enrique, NI32
Alvarado Pinetta, Rony S., GU44
Alvarado Pinto, Carlos Román, GU45
Alvarado Quirós, Alejandro, CR28-31
Alvarado Rodríguez, Martín, HO13-15
Alvarado Rubio, Mario, GU46
Alvarado Sarria, Rafael, NI33
Alvarenga, Ivo P., ES9
Alvarenga, Jorge Arturo, ES10
Álvarez, Emilio, CA702
Álvarez, Juan, GU47
Álvarez, Miguel Ángel, NI34-35
Álvarez Cañas, Alberto, CR32
Álvarez Elizondo, Pedro, GU48
Álvarez G., Zacarías, HO373
Álvarez Lejarza, Emilio, NI36-40
Álvarez Lejarza, Marcario, NI40
Alvarez Melgar, Mariano, CR33
Alvaro, Héctor, HO361
Alvaro Menéndez, Leal, CA25-26
Alvear, Alfredo, CA544
Amador, Alberto, CA27
Amador, Armando, NI389
Amador, Francisco de Paula, CR34
Amador Guevara, José, CR35
Amador V., Valentín, HO17
Amaro, Nelson, GU49
Amaya Amador, Ramón, CA28; GU50-51; HO18-20
Amaya Leclair, Manuel, CA29
Ambrogi, Arturo, ES11-16
American Association for the Advancement of Science,
    NI41
American Atlantic and Pacific Ship Canal Company,
    NI42
American-Honduras Company, HO21-22
American University, Special Operations Research
    Office. See LaCharité, Norman
Ameringer, Charles D., CR36-37
Amighetti, Francisco, CR38
Los Amigos de la Verdad, HO23
Amilcar Raudales, Luís, HO24
Ammen, Daniel, NI43-46
Amurrio González, Jesús Julián, GU52
Anderson, A.H., BE4
Anderson, Chandler P., CA30-31; NI47
Anderson, Marylyn, GU53
Anderson, Thomas P., ES17
Anderson, Young, GU54
Anderson Morúa, Luís, CA32-35; BE5; CR420; ES18
Andino, Manuel, ES19-22
Andino, Raúl, ES21-22
ANFE (Associación Nacional de Fomento Económico de
    Costa Rica). See Fernández, Guido
Angüello, Alberto Ondóñez. See Ordóñez
    Angüello, Alberto
Angulo Novoa, Alejandro, CR39
Anino C., Juan, GU55
Antúñez Castillo, Rubén, HO25-28
Aparicio y Aparicio, Edgar Juan, GU56
Applebaum, Richard P., GU57
Apstein, Theodore, CA36
Aquino, Enrique, NI48-49
Arana, César, NI50
Arana Osorio, Carlos, GU58-59
Aranda, José, GU60
Arango, Jacinto P., CR41
Araya Incera, Manuel E., CR42
Araya Pochet, Carlos, CA27, 43-45

Araya Rojas, José Rafael, CR46
Arbingast, Stanley A., CA38
Arcano, Iván, NI51
Arce, Francisco de, GU61
Arce, Guillermo E., NI52
Arce, José M., CR47
Arce, Manuel A., CA39-40
Arce, Manuel José, CA41-43
Arce C., Jorge, CR48
Arce Vargas, Mariano, CR49
Arce y Valladares, Manuel José, GU62-63
Archila Lemus, José, GU64
Architects Collaborative, CR50
Archivo General de Centro América, Guatemala, GU65
Ardón, Juan Ramón, HO29-33
Ardón, Victor Figueroa, HO34
Ardón, Victor M., CA44-45
Ardón F., José Enrique, CA46; GU66-68
Arellano, Jorge Eduardo, NI53-59
Arellano Bonilla, Roberto, HO35-36
Arenales, Ricardo, pseud. See Osorio, Miguel Ángel
Arenys de Mar, Zenon de, CR51
Arévalo, Adrian Meléndez, ES23
Arévalo, Teresa, GU69
Arévalo Bermejo, Juan José, GU70-86
Arévalo Martínez, Rafael, GU87-100
Arévalo Morales, Rafael, GU101
Arévalo Zelaya, Rubén, GU102
Argüello, Agenor, NI60
Argüello, Leonardo, NI61-62
Argüello, Rosendo, CR52-53; NI63
Argüello, Santiago, CA47-48; GU103
Argüello Hurtado, Roberto, NI64
Argüello Mora, Manuel, CR54-60
Argueta, Ernesto, HO37-39
Argueta, Manlio, ES24
Argueta Ruiz, José Dolores, BE6
Arias, Arturo, GU104
Arias, Tomás, CR61
Arias de Blois, Jorge, CA49
Arias Gómez, Jorge, ES25
Arias Sánchez, Oscar, CR62-64
d'Arlach, H. de T., CA50
Armas, Alejandro Enriquez, HO40
Armas, Daniel, GU105
Armas Lara, Marcial, GU106-8
Armijo, Roberto, CR65
Armijo Lozano, Modesto, CA51
Armstrong, Patrick R., CR153
Arredondo, Alberto, CA52
Arrien, Juan B., NI65
Arrieta Gallegos, Benjamín, ES26
Arrieta Quesada, Santiago, CR66
Arrieta Rossi, Reyes, CA132
Arriola, Jorge Luís, CA53; GU106-16
Arriola, Osmundo, GU117
Arriola Porres, Efraín, GU1133
Arrocha, Angela Delli Sante, GU118
Arroyo Soto, Victor Manuel, CR67-68
Arthur, Henry B., CA54
Arzú, José, GU119-20
Ashcraft, Norman, BE7
Asociación de Maestros de la República de Panama,
    CR69
Asta-Buruaga y Cienfuegos, Francisco Solano, CA55
Asturias, Francisco, BE8; GU121-23
Asturias, Miguel Ángel, CA56; GU124-37
Asturias, Montenegro R., GU138
Atkins, Thomas Benjamin, NI66-68

Aube, Théophile, CA57
Aubrun, Charles V., CA58
Augelli, John P., CA990
Ávila, Gustavo R., HO41
Ávila, Julio Enrique, ES28
Avilés, Orontes, CA59
Aybar, José M. de Soto, GU139
Aycinena, Juan José de, CA60
Aycinena Salazar, Luís, BE9
Azofeifa, Isaac Felipe, CR70-72

Babson, Roger Ward, CA61
Baciu, Stefan, HO42
Backer, James, CR73
Badescu, S., GU140
Baeza Flores, Alberto, CR74-75
Baglaĭ, Marat Viktorovich, GU141
Bahiana, Henrique Paulo, GU142
Bähr, Eduardo, HO43
Bailey, Bernadine Freeman, NI69
Baily, John, CA62; NI69
Bales, William Leslie, NI70
Balsells Rivera, Alfredo, GU143
Banco Centroamericano de Integración Económica,
   CA63-64
Banco de América, NI71-72
Bancroft, Hubert Howe, CA65
Bank of London & Montreal, Ltd., CA66
Barahona, Amaru, NI73
Barahona Israel, Rodrigo, CR971
Barahona Jiménez, Luís, CR76-79
Barahona López, Ernesto, NI74
Barahona Streber, Oscar, CR80-81; GU144
Baranda Quijano, Joaquín, BE10
Barba-Jacob, Profirio, pseud. See Osorio, Miguel
   Ángel
Barba Salinas, Manuel, ES29
Barbaroux, pseud. See Estrada Paniagua, Felipe
Barberena, Santiago Ignacio, ES30-34
Barberena Pérez, Alejandro, NI75
Barcarel, Ángel Horacio, GU145
Bárcenas Barreto, Jesús M., CR969
Barcenas Meneses, José, NI76
Bard, Samuel A., pseud. See Squier, Ephraim George
Bardeles Bueso, Rafael, HO3, 44
Bardini, Roberto, BE11
Barillas, Manuel L., GU146
Barnoya Gálvez, Francisco, GU147-50
Barón Castro, Rodolfo, ES35-36
Barón Ferrufino, José René, ES37-38
Barquero, Antonio, GU151
Barquero, Sara Luisa, NI77-79
Barrantes Ferrero, Mario, CA67; CR82-83
Barreda, Pedro Froilán, GU152-54
Barreda Avila, Rubén, GU155-56
Barrera, Claudio, pseud. See Alémán, Vicente
Barrera Aceves, Joaquín, HO45
Barrera Túnchez, J. Antonio, GU157
Barreto, Mariano, GU158; NI80
Barreto, Pablo Emilio, NI81
Barrientos, Alfonso Enrique, CA68; BE12; GU159-60;
   HO46
Barrington and Company, Inc., New York, GU161
Barrios, Justo Rufino, GU162; HO419
Barrios Castro, Carlos, CA69
Barruel-Beauvert, Philippe Auguste de, NI82
Barton, Edwin, GU163
Baruch, Bernardo, CR84
Basauri, Daniel, ES39
Bascom Jones, J., GU164

Bass, John Meredith, NI83
Bateson, J.H., BE13
Batista y Pereyra, Eugenio, CA70
Batres, Luís, CA71; GU165
Batres Jáuregui, Antonio, GU166-70
Batres y Montúfar, José, GU171
Batson, Alfred, CA72
Battelle Memorial Institute, Columbus Laboratories,
   CA73
Baudez, Claude F., CA74
Bauer Paíz, Alfonso, GU172-76
Baus, Ruth, NI84
Bayo Giroud, Alberto, NI85
Beals, Carlton, CA75; GU177; NI86
Becerra, Longino, HO47-48
Beckford, George L., CA54
Béeche Argüero, Octavio, CR85
Belausteguigoitia, Ramón de, NI87
Belize, Gov't of, BE14
-Information Service, BE15-16
-Ministry of Education, BE17
Bell, Charles Napier, NI88
Bell, John Patrick, CR86
Bellini, Giuseppe, GU179
Bello, Leoncio N., CR87
Bello Codecido, Emilio, CA76
Belly, Félix, CA77; NI89-91
Belot, Gustave de, ES40; HO49-50
Belt, Thomas, NI92
Beltrán y Rózpide, Ricardo, CA78
Beltrand, Manuel, ES41
Beltranena Sinibaldi, Luís, GU180-81
Benard, Emilio, NI93
Benavides, Enrique, CR88
Benavides, Héctor, CR89
Benavides Robles, Rafael, CR90
Benavides Sánchez, Manuel, CR91
Benefeldt Rojas, Lourdes, GU227
Beneš, Vlastislav, CA79
Benharis, Ruma, CR92
Benítes, Tulio, GU182
Benítez Porta, Oscar Rodolfo, GU183
Benton, Stuart H., CR717
Beresford, Marcus, CA80
Berggren, Karl, CR93
Berghe, Pierre L. van den, GU307
Bermúdez, Alejandro, CA81; ES42; NI94
Bermúdez, Néstor, HO51
Bermúdez Meza, Antonio, CA82; HO52-53
Bert, Zdeněk, CA83
Besso, Henry V., CR94; GU184; HO54
Beteta, José Antonio, CA84; GU185-86
Bevan, John, NI97
Bianchi, William J., BE18
Bianconi, F., GU187
Biesanz, John Berry, CR95
Biesanz, Karen, CR96
Biesanz, Mavis, CR95-96
Biesanz, Richard, CR96
Bílak, León, GU188
Billig, Otto, GU189
Binckum, J. Vandenberghe de, GU190
Biolley, Paul, CR97-98
Bitter, Wilhelm Frederick, CA85
Bizemont, Henri Louis Gabriel de, NI95
Bjerregaard, Lena, GU191
Black, George, NI96-97
Blaffer, Sarah C., GU192
Blais, Valeria, NI98
Blanchet, Aristide Paul D'Henrichemont, NI99-101
Blanco, Francisco J., HO55

Blanco, Ovidio Soto. See Soto Blanco, Ovidio
Blanco de Gómez, Margarita, NI102
Blanco Fombona, Horacio, NI103
Blanco Segura, Ricardo, CR99-101
Blaney, Henry Robertson, CA86
Blondeel van Cuelebrouch, Édouard, GU193-95
Bloomfield, Louis M., BE20
Blutstein, Howard, CR102; ES43; HO56
Board of Trade of San Francisco, NI104
Bobadilla, José Ángel, CA87; HO432
Bobadilla, Perfecto Hernández, HO57-58
Bacanegra Gutiérrez, Mario, GU196
Boddam-Whetham, John, GU197
Bodenheimer, Susanne Jonas, CA88; GU198
Body, John E., NI105
Boesch, Hans Heinrich, CA89
Bolaños Álvarez, Pío., NI106
Bolaños Geyer, Alejandro, NI107-8
Bolland, O. Nigel, BE21-22
Bologna, Alfredo Bruno, CA90
Bonaparte, Louis Napoleon, NI109
A Bondholder, HO59
Bone, Roberto C., NI110
Bonilla, Harold H., CR103-4
Bonilla, José María, NI111
Bonilla, Marcelina, HO60
Bonilla, Policarpo, CA91-93; HO61
Bonilla, T.G., NI112
Bonilla, Tiburcio P., ES44
Bonilla Aquino, Daniel, GU199
Bonilla Baldares, Abelardo, CA94; CR105-7
Bonilla Ruano, José María, CA95; GU200-201
Bonis, Samuel B., GU202
Booth, John A., NI113
Borda, Francisco de P., CA96-97
Bordas, P.H., GU203
Borge C., Carlos, CR108
Borgen, José María, NI114
Borges Pérez, Fernando, CR109
Borring, Majken, NI115
Bosch, José María, GU204
Bosch, Juan, CR110
Bourgeois, Henry G., HO262
Bourgeot, Alexandre, HO62
Bowden, George F., CR825
Bower, Reuben Edward, GU205
Bowman, W.A.J., BE23
Boyle, Frederick, CA98
Boza McKellar, Amadeo, CR111
Bozzolli de Wille, María Eugenia, CR112
Bradley, Leo H., BE24-25
Bran Azmitia, Rigoberto, GU206-9
Brañas, César, GU210-12
Brandel, Marc, pseud. See Beresford, Marcus
Brannon, Max P., ES45
Brannon de Samayoa, Carmen, ES46
Bravo, Fermín A., NI116
Brenes, Rafael, CR114
Brenes Córdoba, Alberto, CR115
Briceño, Henry, NI117
Briceño Baltodano, Leonidas, CR116
Brigham, William Tufts, GU214
Brindeau, Auguste, NI118
Brindley, J.B., BE26
Brine, Lindesay, GU215
Bristowe, Lindsay W., BE27
British Central American Land Company, NI119
British Honduras, Citizens of, BE28
British Honduras Company, Ltd., BE29
British Honduras, Gov't of, BE30

-Education Department, BE31
-Information Service, BE32
-Lands and Survey Dept., BE33
-Medical Department, BE34
Brooks, William Alexander, HO63
Brown, Robert David, Jr., NI120
Browning, David, ES47
Brownlee, Roland Holt, NI121
Bruño, Pedro, Pseud., CR117
Bryce, William Gordon, BE35
Buckingham, James Silk, CR118
Buell, Raymond Leslie, CA99
Buenaventura de Cogollos-Vega, GU216
Bueso, Guillermo, HO430-31
Bueso Arias, Juan Ángel, HO64
Buhler, Richard O., BE36
Buitrago Matus, Nicolás, NI122
Bula, Clotilde A., CR119
Bulnes Hernández, Edmundo, HO65
Bülow, Alexander von, CA100; NI123
Bülow, Hernán von, HO66
Bumgartner, Louis E., CA101
Bunau Varilla, Philippe Jean, NI124
Bunzel, Ruth, GU217
Burbank, Addison, GU218
Burch, Conde de, CR120
Burdon, John Alder, BE37-38
Burgess, Paul, GU219
Bury, Herbert, BE39
Busey, James L., CR121
Bush, Archer C., GU220
Business International Corporation, New York, CA102
Bustamante, César, HO67
Bustamante Maceo, Gregorio, ES48
Bustamante y Sirvén, Antonio Sánchez de, CA103
Bustillo, Miguel Oqueli. See Oqueli Bustillo, Miguel
Bustillo Reina, Guillermo, HO68
Bustillo U., Acisclo J., NI125
Butterworth, Hezekiah, NI126
Byam, George, CA104
Byers, Douglas, GU766

Cabañas, R., HO432
Cabrales, Luís Alberto, NI127
Cabrera, Manuel Estrada. See Estrada Cabrera, Manuel
Cabrera, Roberto, GU221
Cabrera, Victor Manuel, CR122
Cáceres, Eduardo, GU222
Cáceres, Zoila Aurora, GU223
Cáceres Lara, Víctor, HO69-73
CACTO, pseud. See Contreras Vélez, Álvaro
Cagliero, Giovanni (Juan), CA105
Cagliero, Juan. See Cagliero, Giovanni (Juan)
Caiger, Stephen Langrish, BE40-41
Caille, Alexis, GU224
Cain, Ernest E., BE42-44
Cain, Henry Edney Conrad, BE142
Caivano, Tommaso, GU225
Cajina Uriarte, José León, CA106
Calabrese, Elisa, NI128
Calatayud Bernabeu, José, NI129
Calder, Bruce Johnson, GU226
Calderón, José Tomás, CA107; BE45; CR123; ES49
Calderón, Julio César, ES50
Calderón, Próspero, CR124
Calderón de Muitoz, Alba Rose, GU227
Calderón Guardia, Rafael Ángel, CR125
Calderón Quijano, José Antonio, BE45

Calderón Ramírez, Salvador, NI130-31
Calderón Salazar, José, GU228
Calero Orozco, Adolfo, NI132-35
Caligaris, Ángel, NI136-37
Callan, Richard J., GU436
Calvo, Francisco, CR126
Calvo Mora, Joaquín Bernardo, CR127-31
Calzada Bolandi, Jorge, CR132
Camacho, Daniel, CA108
Camacho, Viriato, CR133
Cambranes, J.C., GU229
Cambronero Salazar, Miguel Ángel, GU230
Camejo, Pedro, NI138
Camejo Farfán, Hugo, CA109; BE46
Cameron, Arnold Guyot, NI139
Camisa, Zulma C., CR134; GU231-32
Campos, Camilo, ES51
Campos Jiménez, Carlos María, CR135-36; GU233
Campos Meléndez, Silvio, NI140-41
Campos Ponce, Xavier, NI142
Canales, José María, ES52
Canales Salazar, Félix, CA110-12; BE47
Cañas, Victor Manuel, CR137
Cañas Escalante, Alberto F., CR138-41
Canella, Francisco, GU234
Cannabrava, Paulo, NI144
Canton, Alfredo, NI145
Canton, Wilberto L., GU235
Capella, Jacinto, GU236
Caplow, Theodore, GU237
Carbajo, Deodato, CA113
Cardenal, Ernesto, CA114; NI146-49
Cardenal, Rodolfo, ES53
Cardenal Argüello, Luís G., NI150
Cárdenas, Joaquín E., ES54
Cardona, Jorge, CR142; ES55
Cardona, Rafael, GU238-39
Cardona-Hine, Alvaro, CR143
Cardona Lazo, Antonio, ES56-57
Cardona Peña, Alfredo, CR144
Cardona y Valverde, Jenaro, CR145-46
Cardoso, Ciro Flamarion Santana, CA115
Cardoza y Aragón, Luís, GU240-41
Carey Jones, N.S., BE48
Carías, Marco Virgilio, CA116-17, 871; HO74
Carías Andino, Tiburcio, HO75
Carías Reyes, Marcos, CA118; HO76-81
Carlomagno, CR147
Carmen Pineda, José del, CA763
Carmichael, John, NI151
Carmona, José Daniel, CR148
Carnero Checa, Genaro, CA119
Carpenter, Frank George, CA120
Carpenter, Rhys, CA121
Carpio Nicholle, Roberto, BE49
Carr, Albert H.Z., NI152
Carr, David, BE50
Carranza, Jesús Enríquez, GU242-44
Carranza Cervantes, Francisco Javier, GU245
Carrera, Sotero, GU246
Carrillo, Alfonso, BE51; GU247
Carrillo Meza, Raúl, GU881
Carrillo Ramírez, Alfredo, GU248
Carrillo Ramírez, Salomón, GU249
Carrillo y Ancona, Crescencio, BE52
Carrión, Luís, NI722
Carro Zúñiga, Alfonso, CR1023
Carruthers, Ben F., CA36
Carter, Dorothy Sharp, CA122
Carter, William E., CR149; GU250
Carvajal, Manuel J., CR150-53

Carvajal Herrera, Mario, CR154
Carvajal, Maria Isabel, CR689-91
Casa de la Cultura de Occidente, GU251
Casal Viuda de Quirós, Sara, CR155
Casariego, Mario, GU252
Casasola Saavedra, Carlos Egberto, GU253
Casasola y Casasola, Oliverio, GU254
Casolla, J.R., CR156
Castañeda, Francisco, ES59-60; GU255-56
Castañeda, Gabriel Ángel, BE53; GU257-59
Castañeda, Hilda de, HO82
Castañeda, Ricardo C., GU260-62
Castañeda de Machado, Elvia, CA124
Castañeda Suazo, Gustavo A., HO83-85
Castaño, Camilo, GU263
Castejón Fiallos, Michel, NI153
Castellón, Francisco, NI154-55
Castellón, Hildebrando A., NI156
Castellanos, Francisco Xavier, BE54
Castellanos García, J. Efraín, HO86
Castellanos Sánchez, Miguel, BE55
Castelló, Julio, GU264
Castellón, Francisco, NI154-55
Castellón, Hildebrando A., NI156
Castelpoggi, Atilio Jorge, GU265
Castilla Urbina, Miguel de, NI157
Castillo, Carlos M., CA125
Castillo, Daniel de J., ES61-62
Castillo, Efrén, GU266-69
Castillo, Juan del, NI158
Castillo, Otto René, GU270
Castillo Armas, Carlos, GU271-73. See also Najera
  Farfán, Mario Efraín
Castillo Cordero, Clemente, GU274
Castillo Flores, Arturo, HO87
Castillo Ibarra, Carlos, NI159
Castillo Prado, Emilia, GU275
Castillo Ricas, Donald, CA126
Castrillo, Salvador, CA127
Castrillo Gámez, Manuel, NI160-63
Castrillo Zeledón, Mario, CA128
Castro, José Rafael, GU276-77; HO88
Castro, Julio, GU278
Castro, Rodolfo Barón. See Barón Castro, Rodolfo
Castro, Salomón, CR157
Castro, Zenón, CR158
Castro Carazo, Miguel Ángel, CR159
Castro Cartin, José Enrique, CR160
Castro de Mindez, Margarita. See Castro Rawson,
  Margarita
Castro Díaz, Alejandro, HO89
Castro Esquivel, Arturo, CR161-63
Castro Fernández, Héctor Alfredo, CR164
Castro Lujan, V.M., CA129
Castro Morán, Mariano, HO405
Castro Ramírez, Manuel, CA130-33; ES63-64
Castro Rawson, Margarita, CR165
Castro Rivera, Victor M., CR166
Castro Saborío, Luís, CR167-70
Castro Saborió, Octavio, CR171-73
Castro Serrano, Catarino, HO90
Castro Silva, Juan María, NI164-65
Castro W., C.A., NI197
Cauca Prada, Antonio, CA134
Cayetano, El Padre, GU279
Cea, José Roberto, ES65
CEDAL (Centro de Estudios Democráticos de América
  Latina), CA135-37; CR174-77; GU280
C.E.I., CA138
Centeno Cordon, Carlos Enrique, GU281

Central America, Presidents, CA139
Central American Conferences, CA141-55
Central American Court of Justice, CA156-58; NI166-67
Un Centro-Americano. See Aycinena, Juan José de; Dardón, Andrés
Centro Latinoamericano de Demografía (CELADE), HO91
Unos Centroamericanos, CA159
CEPAL. See ECLA
Cerdas Cruz, Rudolfo, CR179-80
Cerezo Dardón, Hugo, GU282-83
Cerna, Ismael, GU284
Cerrato Valenzuela, Armando, HO92-93
Cerna, Girón, GU994
Cerna, José Rodríguez. See Rodríguez Cerna, José
Cerna, Rosales, GU994
Cersosimo, Gaetano, CR181
Cerutti, Franco, NI168-69
Céspedes Marín, Armando, CR182, 440
Céspedes Solano, Victor Hugo, CR183
Cevallos, Fernando P., HO94-95
Cevallos, José Antonio, ES66
Chacón, Enrique, ES67
Chacón, Lucas Raúl, CR184-86
Chacón Chaverri, Tranquilino, CR187-88
Chacón Pacheco, Nelson, CR189
Chacón Trejos, Gonzalo, CR190-93
Chamberlain, Robert Stoner, CA160
Chamorro, Alejandro Cole. See Cole Chamorro, Alejandro
Chamorro, Diego Manuel, CA161-63; CR667; NI170-72
Chamorro, Fruto, NI172
Chamorro, Pedro Joaquín, NI173-76
Chamorro Cardenal, Pedro Joaquín, NI177-80
Chamorro Zelaya, Pedro Joaquín, CA164-66; GU285; NI181-84
Chantecler, pseud. See Trullás y Anlet, Ignacio
Chanto Méndez, Marcos, CR194
Charles, Cecil, HO96
Charter, Cecil Frederick, BE56
Chase, Alfonso, CR195-98
Chavarría, Lisímaco, CR199-200
Chavarría F., Rafael A., CR201
Chavarría Flores, Manuel, GU286-89
Chaves Vargas, Luís Fernando, CR202
Chávez Alfaro, Lizandro, NI185-86
Chávez Zelaya, Enrique, GU290
Chávez Zelaya, Máximo Enrique, NI187
Checchi, Vincent, and Associates, HO97
Cheron, Luís, CA167
Chica, Luís Alfonso, BE57
Childs, James Bennett, CA168
Childs, Orville Whitmore, NI188-89
Chinchilla Águilar, Ernesto, CA169-70; GU291-94
Choussy, Félix, ES68-69
Choza, Arcadio, GU295
Chumakova, Marina L'vovna, CA171
Church, George Earl, CR203
Churchill, Anthony, CA172
Cid Fernández, Enrique del, BE58; GU296-301
Cifuentes, Edwin, GU303-5
Cifuentes Díaz, Carlos, CA173
Citizen of New York. See Radcliff, William
Clark, David S., CR205
Clayton, G., BE59
Clegern, Wayne M., BE60-61
Cleghorn, Robert, BE62
Cleveland, Grover, CA174
Cline, William R., CA175

Club Estudiantil Unionista Francisco Morazán de Tegucigalpa, CA176
Cobos Batres, Manuel, GU306
Cochrane, James D., CA177
Coello, Augusto C., CA178; HO98-99, 136
Coen, Elliot, CR206
Cohen Orantes, Isaac, CA179
Colby, Benjamin, GU307
Cole Chamorro, Alejandro, NI190
Colegio Superior de Señoritas de Costa Rica, CR207
Colindres, Eduardo, ES70
Colindres, Juan, NI191
Colindres, Rafael B., ES71
Collar, Grant H., Jr., BE63
Collar, Jerry D., BE63
Collart Valle, Ángel Antonio, HO100
Collet, Wilfred, BE64
Colón y Gómez Carrillo, Julio, GU308
Colonia Hondureña en Guatemala, HO101
Colquhoun, Archibald Ross, NI192
Colvin, Gerard, CA180
Comando Juan José Quezada, NI193
Comisión de Festivos, Centenario de la Villa de Barba, CR208
Comité Coordinador Anticomunista, GU309
Comité Cristiano de Solidaridad con el Pueblo de Nicaragua, NI194
Comité de Investigaciones del Folklore Nacional y Arte Típico Salvadoreño, ES72
Comité Interamericano de Desarrollo Agrícola, GU310
Comité Liberal Demócrata de Honduras en Mexico, HO102
Comité Organizador de la Conmemoración del Sesquicentenario de la Independendia de Centroamérica, GU311
Comité Salvadoreño de Liberación Nacional, ES73-74
Comité Unionista Centroamericana, CA181
Committee for Economic Development, CA182
Compagnie Belge de Colonisation, GU312-19
Conant, Charles A., NI335
Conard, Louis, CR209
Conejo Guevara, Adina, CR210
Confederación de Trabajadores Centroamericanos (CTCA-ORIT), CA183
Conferencia Regional Centroamericana de la Sociedad Internacional para el Desarrollo (SID), CA184
Conferencia sobre la familia, la infancia, y la juventud de Centroamerica y Panama, CA185
Congreso Centroamericano de Economistas, Contadores Públicos y Auditores, CA186
Congreso Centroamericano de Estudientes de Derecho, CA187
Congreso Centroamericano de Historia Demográfica, Económica y Social, CR211
Congreso Indígenista Interamericano. See Seminario de Integración Social Guatemalteca
Un Conservador de 30 años, NI195
Constandse, Anton L., CA188
Consuegra, Sfelino, GU320
Consultécnica, Ltd. San José, Costa Rica, CR212
Conte, Josefa, CR213
Contreras, Agustín, CA189
Contreras, Carlos A., HO103
Contreras, Gregorio, GU321
Contreras, Ricardo, CA190
Contreras Castro, Julio, ES75
Contreras Reinoso, José Daniel, GU322-23
Contreras Vélez, Álvaro, GU324-35

Conway, Hobart McKinley, CR214
Conzemius, Eduard, NI196
Cooper, Enrique, CR215
Cordero R., Oscar, CR216
Cordero Reyes, Manuel, NI197
Cordero Solano, José Abdulio, CR217
Córdoba, Alberto Brenes. See Brenes Córdoba,
    Alberto
Córdoba, Julio, CR218
Córdoba, Horacio de, GU326-27
Córdoba Boniche, José, NI198
Córdoba González, Jacinto, GU328
Córdoba Zeledón, Alberto, CR219
Cordón de Franco, Aída, GU329
Córdova, Alejandro, GU330
Córdova, Enrique, CA132
Córdova de Roja, Sara, GU331
Coronado Aguilar, Manuel, CA191; GU332-34
Coronado Lira, Luís, GU335
Coronado P., J. Adrián, GU336
Coronado y Pacheco, Ángel B., GU337
Coronel Matus, Manuel, NI199
Coronel Urtecho, José, NI200
Corpeño, José Dolores, CA192-93
Corrales Briceño, Juan Bautista, CR220
Corrales de Chavarría, Rosa. See Chavarría,
    Lisímaco
Correa, Gustavo, GU338
Corro, Alejandro del, GU339
Cortés, Emiliano, ES76
Cortés Castellón, José Rosalío, NI201
Cortés Castro, Claudio, CR221
Cortés Chacón, Rafael, CR222-23
Corthell, Elmer Lawrence, NI202
Cosenza S., Roberto, GU340
Cospín, Miguel Ángel, GU341
Costa Rica, Academia de Geografía e Historia, CR224
Costa Rica, Centro Para El Estudio de los Problemas
    Nacionales, CR225-27
Costa Rica, Cooperativa Bananera Costarricense,
    CR228
Costa Rica, Ferrocarril de, CR229
Costa Rica, Oil Corporation, CR230
Costa Rica, Pacific Railroad, CR231
Costa Rica, Sociedad de Geografía e Historia, CA194
Costa Rica, Universidad de, CR232-37
Costa Rica, Gov't of, CR238-54; NI203
-Archivo Nacional, CR255-61
-Asamblea Constituyente de 1949, CR262
-Banco Central, CR263-65
-Banco Nacional, CR266-68
-Banco Nacional de Seguros, CR262
-Caja Costarricense de Seguro Social, CR269
-Centro de Promoción de Exportaciones e
    Inversiones, GU270
-Comisión de Investigación Histórica de la
    Compañia de 1856-1857, CR271-77
-Comisión Nacional del Sesquincentenario de la
    Independencia de Centro America, CR278-79
-Consejo Superior de Educación, CR280
-Dirección General de Artes y Letras, CR281
-Dirección General de Estadística, CR282-83
-Instituto Costarricense de Turismo, CR284
-Instituto de Tierras y Colonización, CR285-86
-Instituto Geográfico, CR287-90
-Ministerio de Cultura, Juventud y Deportes, CR291
-Ministerio de Economic y Hacienda, CR292
-Secretaría de Educación Pública, CR293-96
-Ministerio de Fomento, CR297-99; NI204
-Ministerio de Gobernación, CR300
-Ministerio de Hacienda, CR301

-Ministerio de Hacienda y Comercio, CR302
-Ministerio de Obras Públicas, CR303-4; NI205
-Ministerio de Relaciones Exteriores, CA195-206;
    CR305-13; NI206
-Ministerio de Seguridad Pública, CR314-20
-Ministerio de Transportes, CR321
-Oficina de Planeamiento y Coordinación, CR322
-Oficina de Planificación, CR323
-Oficina Nacional de Censo, CR324-25
-Patronato Nacional de la Infancia, CR326
-Presidencia, Secretaría de Información, CR327-29
-Servicio Nacional de Electricidad, CR330
-Sociedad Económica de Amigos del País, CR331
Costales Samaniego, Alfredo, CA52, 207
Cotero Aragón, Manolo, GU342
Coto Conde, José Luís, CR333
Coto Romero, Rafael, CA208
Council of Foreign Bondholders, London, HO104
Covell, Frank E., CA209
Cox, Isaac Joslin, NI207
Craig, Hugh, NI208
Cramer, Floyd, NI209
Crane, Alfred Victor, BE65
Crane, John, CA210
Cravioto, Adrián, BE66
Crawford, Mattie, NI210
Crawley, Eduardo, NI211
Creedman, Theodore, S., CR334
Crespi, Panchita, CA211
Crosbie, A.J., BE88
Crosby, Elisha Oscar, GU343
Crowe, Frederick, BE67
Crowther, Samuel, CA212
Cruz, Ernesto, CA213
Cruz, Fernando, CA214; GU344
Cruz, Pedro Tobar. See Tobar Cruz, Pedro
Cruz, Ramón Ernesto, CA215-16, 366; HO105-8
Cruz, René, HO109
Cruz Cáceres, Francisco, HO110
Cruz Torres, Mario Enrique de la, GU345-47
CSUCA, CA217-21; CR335; ES77; GU348; HO111; NI212
Cuadra, Abelardo, NI213
Cuadra, Manolo, NI214-15
Cuadra Cardenal, Pablo Antonio, NI216-21
Cuadra Chamorro, Pedro Joaquín, CA222; NI222-24
Cuadra Downing, Orlando, NI225-26
Cuadra Pasos, Carlos, CR877; NI227-29
Cuenca, Abel, ES78
Cueva, Napoleon, CA871
Cumberland, William Wilson, NI230
Cummins, Lejeune, NI231
Cunningham, Eugene, CA223
Curtis, William Elroy, NI337
Custódio, Ramón A., HO113
Cuzán, Alfred G., CA224

Dada Hirezi, Héctor, ES79
Dalton, Roque, ES80-82
Dane, Hendrik, CA225
Danforth, Sister María del Rey, NI232
Daniel, J.B., HO114
Dárdano, Marietta, ES83
Dardón, Andrés, CA226
Dardón Córdova, Gonzalo, GU349-50
Dardón R., Félix, GU351
Darío, Rubén, CR338-39; NI233-34
Dauzats, V., NI235
Davidson, William Van, HO115
Dávila, Fernando Antonio, GU352
Davion, L., GU353

Davis, Charles H., NI236
Davis, Richard Harding, CA227; HO116
Deambrosis Martins, Carlos, GU354
Debayle, León, NI237-38
Debayle, Luís Henri, NI239
Deger, Erwin Conradin, ES84; GU355
De Kalb, Courtenay, NI240
De León, J. Romeo. See León, J. Romeo De.
Déleón, Manfredo L., GU356
Delgado, Enrique, CA175
Delgado, Luís Humberto, HO117
Delgado, Rafael, GU357
Delgado Aguilera, Ulises, CR343
Delli Sante-Arrocha, Angela, GU358
Del Valle Matheu, Jorge. See Valle Matheu, Jorge
    del
Dénain, Adolphe, NI241
Dengo, Gabriel, CA228; CR344-45
Dengo, Omar, CR346
Dengo de Vargas, María Eugenia, CR347-48
Denny, Harold Norman, NI242
Denton, Charles F., CR349
Desamparados, Comisión del Centenario, CR350
Descamps, Emilio, GU359
Deutsch, Hermann B., HO118
Deutschmann, Paul John, GU360
De Witt, R. Peter, Jr., CR351
Diario de Costa Rica (San José), CA229
Díaz, Eliseo J., GU361
Díaz, Francisco, CA230
Díaz, Hugo, CR352
Díaz, Rafael, CA531
Díaz, Víctor Miguel, CA231; GU362-68
Díaz Castillo, Roberto, GU369
Díaz Chávez, Filander, CA232-33; HO119-22
Díaz Durán, Enrique, GU370
Díaz Laparra, Marco, GU372
Díaz Lozano, Argentina, GU373-76; HO123; NI243
Díaz O., José Lizardo. See Lizardo Díaz O., José
Díaz Ordaz, Gustavo, CA234
Díaz Rozzotto, Jaime, GU377
Díaz Vasconcelos, Luís Antonio, GU378-80
Diez de Arriba, Luís, GU381
Dillon, A. Barrow, BE68
Dimas, Lemus, GU382
Dimitrov, T., GU383
Dion, Marie Berthe, GU384
Un Diputado, CR353-54
Dittel, J. Walter, GU144, 385
Dixon, C.G., BE69-70
Dobles, Fabián, CR355-64
Dobles, Segreda, Gonzalo, CR365
Dobles Segreda, Luís, CR366-76
Dobson, Narda A., BE71
Dodge, David, GU386
Dollfus, Auguste, CA237
Dombrowski, John, GU387
Domingo El Paseador, pseud. See Rubio, J. Francisco
Domínguez Sosa, Julio Alberto, ES85
Domville-Fife, Charles William, CA238
Doña, William Henry, NI244
Dondoli B., César, CR378
Donis Kestler, Agustín, GU388
Donohoe, William Arlington, BE72
Donoso, Ricardo, GU389
Dos Jóvenes Colombianos, CR379
Dotti, Victor, GU390
Doubleday, Charles William, NI245
Downie, Jack, BE73

Dozier, Craig Lanier, CA239
Drouillet, León, NI246
Duarte, José Antonio, NI247
Ducoff, Louis Joseph, CA240
Dueñas C., J. Armando, ES299
Dueñas van Severén, J. Ricardo, CA241; NI248
Du Lamercier, pseud., NI249
Duncan Moodie, Quince, CR380-83, 741
Dunlop, Robert Glasgow, GU391
Dunlop, Walter Ronald, BE74
Dunn, Henry, GU392
Durán, Miguel Ángel, ES86-88
Durán Ayanegui, Fernando, CR384
Durán Escalante, Santiago, CR385
Durand, René L.F., NI250
Durham, William H., CA242
Durlak, Jerome A., CR1097
Durón, Francisco José, HO124
Durón, Jorge Fidel, CA243; HO125-28
Durón y Gamero, Rómulo Ernesto, CA244-46; HO99,
    129-37
Durston, John W., GU393
DuVal, Miles Percy, NI251

Ealy, Lawrence O., NI252
Eastern Coast of Central America Commercial and
    Agricultural Company, GU394
Ebaugh, Cameron Duncan, ES89; GU395; NI253
Echánove Trujillo, Carlos Alberto, BE75
Echavarría Campos, Trino, CR386
Echeverría, Aquileo J., CR387-89
Echeverría, Carlos Francisco, CR390
Echeverría Jiménez, Luís, CR391
Echeverría S., Buenaventura, GU396
Echevers, Malín d', GU397
ECLA, CA247-55; ES90-91; GU398; HO138-39
Econométrica Ltda., CA256
Edmond, Charles John, BE76
Ehkdosis Diethnous Emboriku Ehpēmeh-lētēriou, CA257
Ehrhardt, Lucien André, ES92
Elizondo Arce, Hernán, CR393-95
Elizondo Mora, Víctor Manuel, CR396-98
Elliot, Elisabeth, CR399
Elliott, Lilian Elivyn, CA258
El Salvador, Academia Salvadoreña de la Historia,
    ES93-94
El Salvador, Asociación Salvadoreña del Café,
    ES95
El Salvador, Centro Nacional de Información, ES96
El Salvador, Cooperativa de Abogados, ES98
El Salvador-Guatemala Joint Boundary Commission,
    CA259
El Salvador, Universidad de, ES99-103
El Salvador, Gov't of, ES104-6
-Archivo General de la Nación, ES107
-Asamblea Legislativa, ES108
-Asamblea Nacional Constituente, 1950, ES109
-Banco Hipotecario, ES110
-Banco Salvadoreño, ES111
-Biblioteca Nacional, ES112-16
-Comisión Organizadora de las Celebraciones de
    Septiembre, ES117
-Comité pro-centenario José Matías Delgado, ES118
-Consejo de Gobierno Revolucionario, ES119
-Consejo Nacional de Planificación y Coordinación
    Económica, ES120
-Consulate of El Salvador, New York, ES120a
-Dirección General de Caminos, ES121
-Dirección General de Estadística y Censos, ES122-
    24

(El Salvador, Gov't of)
-Instituto Geográfico Nacional, ES125
-Ministerio de Defensa, CA260; ES126
-Ministerio de Economía, CA261-62; ES127-28
-Ministerio de Educación, ES129-33
-Ministerio de Hacienda, ES134
-Ministerio de Hacienda y Crédito Público, ES135
-Ministerio de Instruccion Pública, ES136
-Ministerio del Interior, ES144
-Ministerio de Obras Públicas, ES137
-Ministerio de Relaciones Exteriores, CA263-69;
    ES138-42; NI254-56
-Ministerio de Trabajo y Previsión Social, ES143
-Ministerio del Interior, ES144
-Poder Ejecutivo, ES145
-Presidencia, Secretaría de Información y
    Relaciones Públicas, CA270-71; ES146-56; GU400
Emery, Gennet Maxon, GU401
Emery-Waterhouse, Frances, CA272
Empresa Alsina, CR400
Empresa Eléctrica de Guatemala, S.A., GU402
English, Burt H., CR401
La Época (Tegucigalpa), CA273; HO140-43
Erba, Adolfo, CR402
Erdozain, Placido, ES157
Ermolaev, Vasilii Ivanovich, CA274
ESAPAC (Escuela Superior de Administración Pública
    de América Central), CA275-81; CR403
Escamilla, Miguel, CA282
Escóbar, Darío, NI258
Escóbar, Esteban, NI259
Escóbar, Francisco, CR404
Escobar, José Benito, NI260
Escobar, Juan Ramón Girón. See Girón Escobar, Juan
    Ramón
Escobar, Manuel, NI261
Escobar Galindo, David, CA283
Escobar P., Alfredo, CA284
Escobar Pérez, Francisco, GU404
Escoto, Julio, HO144
Escoto León, Claudio, CA285
Escuela Normal de Maestras "España," ES158
Escuela Pedro Murillo Pérez, Barba, NI262
Esguerre, Manuel, CA286
Espinel, Juan de, pseud. See Marín Cañas, José
Espino, Miguel Ángel, BE77; ES161
Espinosa, Antonio, BE78
Espinosa, Francisco, ES159-60
Espinosa, Luís, CA287
Espinosa Altamirano, Horacio, GU405
Espinosa Estrada, Jorge, NI263
Espinosa R., Rodolfo, NI264, 359
Espinosa Sotomayor, Enrique, NI265
Espinoza, Francisco, CA288
Esquivel, Rogelio, HO145
Esser, Klaus, CA289
Estrada, Hugo, GU406
Estrada, Rafael, CR406-7
Estrada Cabrera, Manuel, GU407
Estrada de la Hoz, Julio, BE79
Estrada H., Ricardo, GU408
Estrada Molina, Ligia, CR408
Estrada Monroy, Agustín, GU409-10
Estrada Paetau, L.M., GU1146
Estrada Paniagua, Felipe, GU411-12
Estrada Uribe, Gabriel, NI266
Estrella de Centroamérica, GU413
Un estudiante de derecho, CR409
Etchison, Don L., CA291
Eugarrios, Manuel, NI268
Evangelina, pseud. See Cáceres, Zoila Aurora

Evans, Geoffrey, BE80
Ewald, Robert Harold, GU414

F., J.E. See Fernández Ferraz, Juan
Fabela, Isidro, BE81
Fabrega, José Isaac, GU416
Fabri, Joseph, GU417
Facio, Justo A., CR411
Facio Brenes, Rodrigo, CA292-93; CR412-15
Facio Segreda, Gonzalo J., CR416-18
Faerron, Francisco, CR419-20
Fagan, Stuart I., CA294
Fairweather, D.N.A., BE82
Fairweather, Henry Clifton, BE83
Fajardo Cadena, Hector, GU418
Falconio, Leda de, ES163
Falla, Ricardo, GU419
Falla, Salvador, CA295
Fallas Monge, Carlos Luís, CR421
Fallas S., Carlos Luís, CR422-30; NI269
Fanjil, Vivian, GU420
FAO (Food and Agriculture Organization of the United
    Nations), NI270
Federación de Cajas de Crédito de El Salvador,
    ES164
Fellechner, A., NI271
Fergusson, Erna, GU421
Fernández, Guido, CA296; CR431
Fernández, J.E., pseud. See Fernández Ferraz, Juan
Fernández, Juan José, HO146
Fernández, Julio Fausto, ES164
Fernández, Manuel, ES165
Fernández, Orlando, GU422
Fernández Arias, Mario E., CR432
Fernández Bonilla, León, CA297; CR433-34
Fernández Cruz, Soledad, CA298
Fernández Durán, Gerardo, CR435-36
Fernández Durán, Roberto, CR436
Fernández Ferraz, Juan, CR437-39, 937
Fernández Guardia, León, CR440
Fernández Guardia, Ricardo, CA299; CR434, 441-53
Fernández Güell, Rogelio, CR454
Fernández Güell, Victor, CR455
Fernández Marroquín, Vitalino, GU423
Fernández Mira, Ricardo M., CR456; HO147
Fernández Montúfar, Joaquín, CR457-58
Fernández Mora, Carlos, CR459-61
Fernández Shaw, Felix Guillermo, CA300-301
Ferrari de Hartling, Guadalupe, HO148
Ferraz, Juan Fernández. See Fernández Ferraz,
    Juan
Ferrera, Fausta, HO149
Ferrero Acosta, Luís, CR462-69
Ferreto, Arnoldo, CR430
Ferro, Carlos A., CA302-4; HO150; NI272
Ferrús Roig, Francisco, GU424, 550
Fiallos, Ernesto, HO151
Fiallos Gil, Mariano, CA305; NI273-73
FIAT Delegatión para la América Latina, CA306
Figeac, José Flores, CA307; ES166-67
Figueres Ferrer, José María, CR470-79
Figueroa, Fernando F., HO152, 373
Figueroa Ibarra, Carlos, GU425
Filio, Carlos, CA308
Filísola, Vicente, CA309-10
First National City Bank, Foreign Information
    Service, CA311-12
Fitz-Roy, Robert, HO153
Flachat, Jules, NI275
Flakoll, Darwin J., ES168

Flamenco, José, GU426; HO154
Flemion, Philip F., ES169
Fletcher, Lehman B., GU427, 559
Fletes Bolaños, Anselmo, NI276-78
Florencia Calderón, Juan, GU428
Flores, Alfredo González. See González Flores, Alfredo
Flores, Marco Antonio, GU429-30
Flores, Saúl, ES170
Flores Avendaño, Guillermo, GU431
Flores Avendaño, Humberto, GU432-33
Flores M., Rosa, GU434
Flores Ochoa, Santiago, CA313
Florida, University of, GU435, 568
Flynn, Gerard, GU436
Fogelquist, Donald F., NI279
Folkmann, David I., Jr., NI280
Fonseca, Jaime M., CR480
Fonseca, Pedro S., CA314; ES34, 171-72
Fonseca, Roberto Peragibe, da, BE84
Fonseca, Virginia S., de, CR481
Fonseca Amador, Carlos, NI281-83
Fonseca Corrales, Elizabeth, CR482
Fonseca Tortos, Eugenio, CR483
Fontecha, Antonio Abad Ramírez y Fernández. See Ramírez y Fernández Fontecha, Antonio Abad
Foote, Mrs. Henry Grant, CA315
Forero, Juan F., CA316
Forss, Elis, CA317
Fortín Magaña, Romeo, ES173-75
Fortuny, José Manuel, GU437
Foster, Harry La Tourette, CA318
Fotografía Industrial, S.A., GU438
Fowler, Henry, BE85
Fox, John W., GU439
Fox, Robert W., CA319
Fradín, Elisio P., CR484-87
Franck, Harry Alverson, CA320-31
Franco, Justo, pseud. See Cevallos, José Antonio
Frantzuis, Alexander von, CR488
Freemasons of Costa Rica, Grand Lodge, CR489
Freisen, John D., BE86
Frente Popular Libertador de Guatemala, GU440
Frente Sandinista de Liberación Nacional, NI284
Frente Unitario Nicaragüense, NI285
Frey, Martin, GU441, 575
Frias y Soto, Hilarion, CA322
Friedman, Burton Dean, CA323
Frison, Bruno, GU442
Fröbel, Karl Ferdinand Julius, CA324
Frýd, Norbert, GU443
Fuensanta, Emirio, pseud. See Fuentes, Mariano
Fuentes, Mariano, GU444
Fuentes Castillo, Alberto, GU445
Fuentes Franco, Andrés, GU864
Fuentes Mohr, Alberto, CA325; GU446
Fumero Paez, Alejo, CR490
Funes, José Alberto, GU447
Funes, Matías, HO155-57
Furbay, John Harvey, CR491
Furley, Peter A., BE87-88

Gabb, William M., CR492
Gadsby, Walter J., BE89
Gagini Chavarria, Carlos, CR493-98
Gagnere, J.P., GU203
Gaimusho Keizaikyoku Raten Amerikaka, CA326-27
Gaitán, Héctor, GU420, 448
Gaitán, Luís, GU449

Galagarza Cabalceta, Camilo, pseud. See Vargas Coto, Joaquín
Galarza Zavala, Jaime, NI286
Galdames, Luís, CR499
Galdames Armas, Juan, ES176
Galeano, Eduardo H., GU450-51
Galeotti Torres, Rodolfo, GU46
Galich, Luís Fernando, GU452
Galich, Manuel, GU453-62
Galindo, Juan, CA328
Galindo y Galindo, Bernardo, HO158-59
Galinier, Hector, CA329
Gall, Francis, BE90-91; GU294, 463-65
Gallardo, Miguel Ángel, ES177-78
Gallardo, Ricardo, CA330; ES79
Gallardo Volio, Claudio, CR1037
Gallegos, Anibal, BE92
Gallegos, Paco, NI287
Gallegos Salazar, Demetrio, CR500
Gallegos Valdés, Luís, ES180-81
Galo, Hernán Isias, HO160
Gálvez, Carlos Alberto, HO161
Gálvez, Juan Manuel, HO1672-65
Gálvez, Samuel J., GU60
Gálvez Castro, Armando, GU675
Gálvez Estrada, Héctor, GU466
Gálvez García, María Albertina, GU467-68
Gamboa, Elisa María, CR501
Gamboa Alvarado, Emma, CA331; CR502-3
Gamboa Alvarado, Gerardo, CR504
Gamboa Alvarado, José, CR505
Gamboa G., Francisco, CR588
Gamboa Guzmán, Francisco, CR506-87
Gamero de Medina, Lucila, HO166
Gámez, José Dolores, CA332-33; ES182; GU469; NI288-91
Gamio de Alba, Ana Margarita, CA334
Gandarias, León de, GU470-71
Gann, Thomas William Francis, CA335-37
Garavito, Humberto, GU472
Garcés Pachano, Wilson, ES183
García, A.V., GU473
García, Ernesto Alvardo. See Alvarado García, Ernesto
García, Joaquín, ES184
García, Miguel Ángel, CA338-40; ES185-87; HO167
García, Serafín, pseud. See Zúñiga Heute, Angel
García Aceituna, José Luís, GU474-77
García Bauer, Carlos, BE93; GU478-80
García Bauer, José, GU481-84; HO88
García Carrillo, Eugenio, CR509
García Goyena, Rafael, GU485
García Granados, Jorge, GU486-87
García Granados, Miguel, GU488
García L., Graciela, CA341
García Laguardia, Jorge Mario, CA342; GU489-92
García Márquez, Gabriel, NI292
García Mejía, René, GU493
García Monge, Joaquín, CR510-14
García Peláez, Francisco de Paula, CA343
García Peña, Angelita, NI293
García Salas, José María, GU494
García Solano, Arturo, CR515
García Trejo, G., GU138
Gardner, Mary A., GU495
Garner, W.D., BE59
Garnier, José Fabio, CR516
Garrido, Gines, CA19
Garrik José, pseud. See Ramírez Peña, Abraham
Garro, Joaquín, CR517-18

Garzona S., Fernando, ES188
Gavidia, Francisco Antonio, ES189-91
Gay-Calbó, Enrique, CA344
Gehlert Mata, Carlos, CA345-36
Geiger, Theodore, GU497
Geisert, Harold L., CA346
Geithman, David T., CR153
Geoffroy Rivas, Pedro, ES192
Gereda Asturias, Ramiro, GU498-99
Giacomán, Helmy F., GU500
Gibbs, Archibald Robertson, BE94
Gierloff-Emden, Hans Günter, ES193
Giesecke, Helmut, CA347
Gil, Salomé, pseud. See Milla y Vidaurre, José
Gil Pacheco, Rufino, CR519
Gillin, John Phillip, GU189, 501
Gilly, Adolfo, NI294
Girón Escobar, Juan Ramón, HO168
Godio, Julio, NI295
Göetz Dieter, Freiherr von, NI296
Gölcher, Federico, CR520
Goldrich, Daniel, CR521
Goldwert, Marvin, NI297
Gollas Quintero, Manuel, CR593-94
Gómez, Carlos Jiménez. See Jiménez Gómez, Carlos
Gómez, Ignacio, GU502
Gómez Barrantes, Miguel, CR522
Gómez Campos, José, ES194
Gómez Carrillo, Agustín, CA348-51; GU503
Gómez Carrillo, Enrique, GU504-9
Gómez Espinosa, Margarita, NI298
Gómez Miralles, Manuel, CR523
Gómez Naranjo, Pedro Alejandro, CA352
Gómez Urbina, Carmen Lila, CR524-28
Góngora Herrera, Federico, CR529
Gonionskii, Semen Aleksandrovich, NI299
González, Darío, ES195
González, Nancie L. Solien, CA353
González, Nicolás Augusto, GU510-11
González, Otto-Raúl, GU512
González-Balado, José Luís, NI300
Gonzalez-Blanco, Pedro, BE95
González Campo, Enrique, GU513
González Campo, Federico, CR530; GU514
González Davidson, Fernando, BE96
Gonzalez Dubon, Cristina Idalia, CA354
González Flores, Alfredo, CR531-33
González Flores, Luís Felipe, CR534-43
González Galván, Manuel, CA355
González Montalvo, Ramón, ES196-97
González Orellana, Carlos, GU515
Gonzalez Quezada, Carlos Alfonso, GU516
González R., Mario Gilberto, GU517-19
González Ramírez, Baltasar, BE97
González Ramos, José Luís, CR544
González Ruíz, Ricardo, ES198; GU520
González Saravia, Antonio, GU521
González Sibrián, José Luís, CA356
González Sol, Rafael, ES199-200
González Truque, Guillermo, CR545-46
González Vega, Claudeo, CR1093
González Víquez, Cleto, CA357; CR547-57
González y Contreras, Gilberto, ES201; HO169-70
González y González, Ricardo, CR558
González Zeledón, Manuel, CR559-60
Goodman, Roland A., GU522
Gottschalk, Kurt P., BE98
Goubaud Carrera, Antonio, GU523-24
Gracias, Domingo, GU525
Gramajo, José Ramón, CA358-59; GU526-28

Granados, Jenny, GU529
Granados Garay, Rigoberto, HO171
Grant, Cedric Hilburn, BE99
Grant, H., Jr., BE63
Grases G. José, CA360
Graves, Theodore D., GU1397
Great Britain, Gov't of, CA361-62; NI301
-Central Office of Information, BE100
-Foreign Office, GU530; NI302
Greene, Laurence, NI303
Gregg, Algar Robert, BE101
Grieb, Kenneth, J., GU436, 531
Griffith, William Joyce, GU532-33
Grijalva, Domingo Ibarra. See Ibarra Grijalva, Domingo
Grimaldi, Antonio, HO172
Gropp, Arthur E., CA363
Grubb, Kenneth George, CA364
Guandique, José Salvador, ES202-4, 355
Guardia, Manuel César de la, GU534
Guardia de Alfaro, Gloria, NI304
Guardia Quirós, Víctor, CR561
Guardiola Cubas, Esteban, CA365-67; HO173-77
Guatemala, Academia Guatemalteca, GU535
Guatemala, Arbispado de, GU536
Guatemala, Asociación Nacional de Constructores de Viviendas de, GU537
Guatemala, Ayuntamiento de, GU538
Guatemala, Comité Central pro-Centenario de la Revolución de 1871, GU539-42
Guatemala, Comité de Estudiantes Universitarios Anticomunistas de, GU543-45
Guatemala, Comité guatemalteco de Defensa de los Derechos Humanos, GU546
Guatemala, Congreso Nacional de Economistas, Contadores Públicos y Auditores, GU547
Guatemala, Geographical and Historical Society, GU548
Guatemala-Honduras Joint Boundary Commission, CA368-75
Guatemala-Mexico Joint Boundary Commission, CA376
Guatemala, Universidad de San Carlos de, GU549-53
Guatemala, Gov't of, GU554-71
-Asamblea Constituyente, GU572-74
-Banco de Guatemala, GU575
-Congreso Regional de Economía, GU576
-Consejo de Bienestar Social, GU577
-Consejo de Economía, GU578
-Consejo Nacional de Planificación Económica, CA377
-Consulado General en Barcelona, GU579
-Consulat General en Paris, GU580
-Crédito Hipotecario Nacional, GU581
-Department of Public Works, GU582
-Dirección General de Asuntos Agrarios, GU583
-Dirección General de Caminos, GU584
-Dirección General de Cartografía, GU585-87
-Dirección General de Cultura y Belles Artes, GU588
-Dirección General de Desarrollo Socioeducativo Rural, GU589
-Dirección General de Estadística, GU590-92
-Dirección General de Obras Públicas, GU593-94
-FYDEP, GU595
-Instituto Guatemalteca de Seguridad Social, GU596-97
-Instituto Indígenista Nacional de Guatemala, GU598-607
-Instituto Nacional de Electrificación, GU608
-Instituto Nacional de Geografía, GU609-10
-Ministerio de Defensa Nacional, GU611-12

(Guatemala, Gov't of)
-Ministerio de Defensa Nacional, Estado Mayor del Ejército, GU613
-Ministerio de Economía y Trabajo, GU614
-Ministerio de Educación Pública, GU615-21
-Ministerio de Fomento, GU622-24
-Ministerio de Hacienda y Crédito Público, GU625
-Ministerio de Relaciones Exteriores, CA378-86; BE102-9; GU626-31
-Poder Judicial, GU632
-Presidencia, Secretaría de Información, BE110; GU633-61
-Sociedad Protectora del Niño, GU662
-Tipografía Nacional, GU663-64
Unos Guatemaltecos, CA388
Gudmundson Kristjanson, Lowell, CR563
Güell, Cipriano, CR564
Güell, Tomás Soley, pseud. See Soley Güell, Tomás
Guerra, Tomás, ES205
Guerra Borges, Alfredo, GU668-69
Guerrero, Francisco José, ES206
Guerrero, José, CR566
Guerrero Castillo, Julián N., CA389; NI305-16
Guevara, Héctor Humberto Samayoa. See Samayoa Guevara, Héctor Humberto
Guevara Fallas, Manuel, CA390
Guevara Paniagua, Arturo, GU670
Guevara Solano de Pérez, Raquel, CR567
Guido, Clemente, NI317-20
Guidos Véjar, Rafael, ES207
Guier Esquivel, Fernando, CA391
Guier Sáenz, Enrique, CA392; NI321
Guillén, Fedro, GU671-72
Guillén, Flavio, CA393; GU673
Guillén, Juan Ramón, GU674
Guillén Castanon, Flavio, GU675
Guinea, Gerardo, GU676
Guinther, Mercedes, GU677
Guiteras Holmes, Calixta, GU678
Gullick, C.J.M.R., BE110
Gunn, Otis Berthoude, NI322
Gut, Ellen, CA36
Gutiérrez, Claudio, CR1023
Gutiérrez, J. Antonio, ES188
Gutiérrez, Joaquín, CR568-71
Gutiérrez, Pedro Rafael, NI323-24
Gutiérrez, Rodrigo, CA394
Gutiérrez B., Federico, CR572
Gutiérrez Braun, Federico, CR573
Gutiérrez Carranza, Claudio, CR574
Gutiérrez G., Víctor Manuel, GU679-80
Gutiérrez Gutiérrez, Carlos José, CA395; CR575
Gutiérrez Jiménez, Mario, CR576
Gutiérrez Pimentel, Rodolfo, CA396
Guzmán, David Joaquín, ES208
Guzmán, Enrique, GU469
Guzmán, Horacio, CA397
Guzmán, Mauricio, CA398; ES209
Guzmán, Virgilio A., CA399
Guzmán Anléu, Mario Alfonso, GU681
Guzmán-Böckler, Carlos, GU682
Guzmán Riorc, Dario, pseud. See Rodríguez Russignon Mariano
Guzmán Selva, Enrique, GU683; NI325-26

Hadel, Richard E., BE111
Haefkens, Jacob, GU684-86
Haines, Peter G., CA400
Hale, John, CA401
Halftermeyer, Gratus, NI327-33
Hall, Carolyn, CR577

Hall, I.H.S., BE13
Halle, Louis Joseph, CA402
Hamilton, Kenneth Gardiner, NI334
Hammock, John C., CR544
Hancock, Ralph, CA403; CR578
Hansen, Roger D., CA404
Hanzelka, Jiří, CA405
Harris, Garrard, CA406
Harris, Walter D., HO178
Harrison, Francis Capel, NI335
Hart, Albert Bushnell, NI336
Hartwell, Charles H., BE116
Harvey, Charles Thompson, NI337
Harvin, Emily, NI84
Hatfield, Chester, NI338
Haverstock, Nathan A., ES210
Hecht, Rudolf S., CR579
Hegel, Carlos Augustin Enrique, GU687
Heine, Peter Bernhard Wilhelm, NI339
Helbig, Karl Martin, CA407-9; HO179
Helfritz, Hans, CA410-11
Helms, Mary W., CA412-13; NI340
Henderson, George, BE112
Henriques, Cyril George Xavier, BE113
Henry, O. See Porter, William Sydney
Herbert, Jean-Loup, GU682
Herbster de Gusmo, Oswaldo, CR580
Heredia, Manuel de, GU688
Hereford, Karl Thomas, CA414; GU689, 1001
Hernández, Ángel G., HO180-82
Hernández, Daniel, CA415; HO183-84
Hernández, Francisco, CR587
Hernández, Rubén, CR582; NI552
Hernández Aguirre, Mario, ES211
Hernández Andrino, Félix, CA331
Hernández C., Miguel Ángel, HO185
Hernández Cardona, Romeo Manuel, GU690
Hernández Carvajal, Alvaro, HO186
Hernández Carvajal, Efraín, CR583
Hernández Cobos, Humberto, GU691
Hernández de Jaen, Mireya, CR584
Hernández de León, Federico, GU692-97
Hernández h., Hermogenes, CR585
Hernández Linares, Tadeo, GU698
Hernández Mendez, Jorge Hegberto, CA416
Hernández Poveda, Rubén, CR586
Hernández Segura, Roberto Emilio, ES212
Hernández Sifontes, Julio, GU699
Hernández Somoza, Jesús, NI341
Herradora Alcántara, María Luisa, ES213
Herrán, Víctor, HO187-88
Herrarte, Alberto, CA417-20
Herrera, Flavio, GU700-701
Herrera, Francisco, GU702
Herrera, Marta Josefina, GU703
Herrera Cáceres, H. Roberto, CA421; HO189
Herrera García, Adolfo, CR587-88
Herrera Muñoz, Francisco, GU704
Herrera Vega, Adolfo, ES214
Herrera Velado, Francisco, ES215
Herrick, Bruce, CR589
Herrick, Thomas R., GU705
Hersey, Jean, GU706
Hershey, Samuel, BE114
Herzfeld, Anita, CR590
Herzog, William, GU360
Hess Estrada, Raúl, CA520; CR591
Hidalgo, Alfredo, CR592
Hidalgo, J., GU707
Hidalgo h., Carlos F., HO190-91

Hidalgo N., J., GU708
Un Hijo del Salvador y Ciudadano de Centro
    América, CA422
Hill, David O., BE115
Hill, George W., CR593-94; HO192
Hill, Roscoe R., NI342
Hilton, Ronald, CA423
Hinshaw, Robert E., GU709
Holbik, Karel, CA424
Holleran, Mary P., GU711
Honduras, Comité Central Pro-Soriano, HO193
Honduras, Estudiantes Universitarios de, HO195
Honduras, Sociedad de Abogados de, CA425
Honduras, Universidad Nacional Autónoma de, GU712
Honduras, Gov't of, CA426, HO196-97
-Archivo Nacional, HO198-99
-Banco Central, HO200-203. See also Napky,
    Marina O. de; Tosco, Manuel; Young, Arthur N.
-Banco Nacional de Fomento, HO204
-Biblioteca Nacional, HO205
-(Central District), Consejo, HO208
-Comisión Revisora del Arancel, HO206
-Congress, HO207
-Dirección General de Estadística y Censos, HO209-
    11
-Junta Militar de Gobierno, HO212
-Ministerio de Agricultura, HO213
-Ministerio de Economía y Hacienda, HO214
-Ministerio de Educación Pública, HO215
-Ministerio de Gobernación, Justicia, Sanidad y
    Beneficiencia, HO216
-Ministerio de Hacienda, HO217
-Ministerio de Hacienda, Crédito Público y
    Comercio, HO218
-Ministerio de Instrucción Pública, CA427
-Ministerio de Relaciones Exteriores, CA428-43;
    HO219-25
-Ministerio de Trabajo y Previsión Social, HO226
-Oficina de Cooperación Intelectual, HO227-30
-Oficina de Relaciones Públicas de Gobierno de la
    República, HO231
Hooker, Roberto Montgomery, NI343
Hoover, John P., ES210
Hopf, Albert, NI344
Hoppenot, Hélène, GU713
Hornik, Robert, ES294
Hort, Dora, NI345
Hoselitz, Berthold Frank, ES216
Hossé, Hans A., HO178
Houck, James P., CA54
Houlson, Jane Harvey, HO233
Howard, Michael C., BE116
Hubbe, Joaquín, BE117
Huberich, Charles Henry, NI346
Huck, Eugene R., CA444
Hudson, Barclay, CR589
Huezo, Efraim, NI347
Huezo Selva, Rafael, ES217-18
Huffman, Maxine Fish, CR596
Huguet, Jerrold W., CA319
Humboldt, Alexander von, CA445
Humphreys, Robert Arthur, BE118
Huntington, Collis Potter, NI348
Hurtado Aguilar, Luís Alberto, BE119; GU714-17
Hurtado Chamorro, Alejandro, NI349
Hurtado Espinosa, Alfonso, GU718
Huston, R.G., HO234
Huxley, Aldous Leonard, CA446-47
Hyde, Evan X., BE120

Iaroshevskiĭ, Boris Gfimovich, CA448
Ibarra, Cristóbal Humberto, ES219
Ibarra, Felipe Bartolomé, NI350
Ibarra Bejarano, Georgina, CR597-98
Ibarra Grijalva, Domingo, NI351
Ibarra Mayorga, Francisco, CR598
Idell, Albert Edward, GU719
Iglesias, Francisco María de, CA449-601; CR937
Iglesias, Luís, ES220
Iglesias, Rafael, pseud. See Yglesias Castro,
    Rafael
Iglesias Hogan, Rubén, CR602-4
Ignotus, pseud., CR605
Ilías Plata, José María, HO235
Imberg, Kurt Eduard, NI352
El Imparcial (Guatemala), GU720
El Imparcial (San José), CR606
Incer Barquero, Jaime, NI353-54, 648
Inman, Samuel Guy, GU721
Inoati, Andras, CA453
Instituto Centroamericano de Administración
    Pública (ICAP), CA454-56
Instituto Centroamericano de Investigación y
    Tecnología Industrial, CA457
Instituto Centroamericano de Población y Familia
    (ICAPF), GU7222-23
Instituto de Nutrición de Centro América y
    Panamá, CR608; ES221; GU724; HO236; NI355
Instituto Guatemalteco Americano, GU725
Instituto Nacional de Informare si Documentare
    Stiintifica si tehnica, ES222
Instituto para el Desarrollo Económico y Social de
    América Central, GU726
Instituto Universitario Centroamericano de
    Investigaciones Sociales y Económicas, CA458
Inter-American Institute of Agricultural Sciences,
    HO237
Inter-American Institute of International Legal
    Studies, CA459-60
Inter-American Peace Committee, GU727
Intercontinental Railway Commission, CA461
International Bank for Reconstruction and
    Development, GU728; NI356
International Bureau of the American Republics,
    CR609; GU729; NI357
International Court of Justice, CA462; GU730
International Railways of Central America, GU731
International Union of Students, GU732
Interoceanic Canal Congress, Paris, 1879, NI358
Ireland, Gordon, CA463
Irías, Julián, NI264, 359
Irisarri, Antonio José de, GU733-34
Irungaray, Ezequiel C., GU735
Isthmian Canal Commission. See U.S. Congress,
    Senate
Istituto Italo-Latino Americano, CA464; CR610;
    ES223, GU736; HO238; NI360
Istituto Nazionale per il Commèrcia Estèro, CA465
Ivanovich, Vladimir Ivanovich, NI361
Izaguirre V., Carlos, HO239-42

Jackson, Joseph Henry, GU737
Jacob, Jeffrey C., GU738
Jaime, Jorge, NI362
Jaksch, Hans Jürgen, CR611
Jalhay, Henri, HO243-44
James, Daniel, GU739
Jamison, James Carson, NI363
Jenness, Aylette, GU740
Jensen, Amy Elizabeth, GU741, 944
Jérez Alvarado, Rafael, CA466; HO245-46

Jesús, Felipe de, GU742
Jiménez, Carlos María, CR612
Jiménez, Eddy E., CA467
Jiménez, Enrique, CR613
Jiménez, Gerardo, CR613
Jiménez, Lilian, ES224
Jiménez, Lorenzo, pseud. See Chacón Trejos,
    Gonzalo
Jiménez, Manuel de Jesús, CR614-16
Jiménez, Salvador, CR617
Jiménez, Tomás Fidias, ES225
Jiménez Castro, Wilburg, CA468; CR618-21
Jiménez España, Julio Ernesto, GU743
Jiménez G., Ernesto Bienvenido, GU744
Jiménez Gómez, Carlos, ES226
Jiménez Gutiérrez, Carlos María, CR622-23
Jiménez Oreamuno, Ricardo, CR624-27
Jiménez Ortiz, Manuel Francisco, CR628-30
Jiménez Quesada, Mario Alberto, CR631-32
Jiménez Quirós, Otto, CR633
Jiménez S., Emel, CR1000
Jiménez Solís, José Jorge, CA469
Jinesta, Carlos, CR634-44, 649
Jinesta, Ricardo, CR645-49; NI364-66
Jirón, Yanuario, HO247
Johannessen, Carl L., HO248
Johnson, Emory R., NI367
Johnson, George B., GU745
Johnson, Kenneth F., GU746
Jones, Chester Lloyd, CR650; GU747
Jones, J. Bascom, GU748
Jones Vargas, Fernando, CA470
Jordan, William F., CA471
Jore, Emile, CR651
Joy, Charles Rhind, CA472
Juárez Muñoz, J. Fernando, CA473; GU749-50
Juárez y Aragón, José Fernando, GU751-54
Juncadella G., Salvador, CA474
Junoy, Ramón, CR653

Kaigai Keizai Kyoryoku Kikin Chosabu, CA475
Kalijarvi, Thorsten Waino Valentine, CA476
Kalnins, Arvids, CR654
Kamman, William, NI368
Kantor, Harry, CR655-56
Kapp, Kit S., CA477
Kapuściński, Ryszard, GU755
Karen, Ruth, CA478; GU756
Karnes, Thomas L., CA479-80
Karsen, Sonja, CR657
Kauffmann, Rafael, NI65
Keasbey, Lindley Miller, NI369-71
Keenagh, Peter, NI372
Keith, Minor C., CR658
Keith Alvarado, Henry M., CR659
Kelam, T.P., CA481
Keller, François Antoine Édouard, NI373
Kelsey, Vera, GU757
Kendall, John Smith, NI374
Kendrick, John William, GU758
Kennedy, Paul Patrick, CA482
Kepner, Charles David, Jr., CA483-84
Kestler Farnés, Maximiliano, GU759
Key, Helmer, CA485
King, Arden R., GU760
King, Emory, BE121
Kint de Roodenbeek, Auguste T', GU761
Klette, Immanuel J., NI375
Knight, C. Foster, CA970
Koberg Bolando, Max, CR660-61
Koebel, William Henry, CA486

Kohli, Jutendra, BE116
Komor, Hugo F., HO249
Koninklijk Instituut voor de Tropen, CR662
Korea, Embassy of Mexico, CA487
Krehm, William, CA488
Kretzschmar, W., NI376
Krieg, P., CA665
Kroeber, Lisa W., GU740
Kuhlenkamp-Schenck, E., CA489
Kumamoto Daigaku, CA490
Kümpel, Juan, CR663
Kurtze, Francisco, CR664
Kusch, Eugen, GU762

L., F., GU763-63a
Lacayo Fernández, Eliseo, CA491
LaCharité, Norman A., GU764
La Farge, Oliver, GU765-66
Laferrière, Joseph, GU767
Lafond de Lurcy, Gabriel, CR665
Lagos, César, HO250
Laínez, Francisco, NI377
Laínez, Vitelia Castro de, HO251
Lainfiesta, Eduardo, GU768
Lainfiesta, Francisco, GU769
Lainfiesta, Margot, HO252-54
Lamarre, Clovis, CA492
Lamb, Dean Ivan, CA493
Lambert de Sainte-Croix, Alexandre, CA494
Landarech, Alfonso María, CA495
Landenberger, Emil, CA496
Landini, Piero, GU770
Lanks, Herbert C., CA321
Lanning, John Tate, GU771
Lansing, Marion Florence, CA497
Laporte, Gilbert, CR666
Lara, Gerardo, CR667
Lara Cerrato, Fausto, HO255
Lara F., Celso A., GU772-73
Lardé, Jorge, ES228-30
Lardé y Larín, Jorge, CA498-500; ES231-36
Larraínzar, Federico, GU774-75
Larraínzar, Manuel, CA501-502
Larraondo, José Tomás, GU1201
Lars, Claudia, pseud. See Brannon de Samayoa,
    Carmen
Láscaris Comneno, Constantino, CA503; CR668-70
Latin American Bureau, BE122; ES237-38; NI378
Latorre Salamanca, Gonzalo, HO256
Lavine, Harold, CA504
Leal, Héctor Alfonso, GU776
Lehmann, Walter, CA505
Leistenschneider, Maria, ES239
Leiva, Raúl, GU777
Leiva Quirós, Elias, CA506; CR671-72
Leiva Vivas, Rafael, CA507; HO258-61
Lejarza, Salvador, NI63
Lemale, Carlos, GU778
Lemke, Donald A., CA40
Lemus, José María, ES241-46
Lemus, Manuel, GU779; HO262
Lemus Mendoza, Bernardo, GU780
Lentz, Joseph, GU781
León, F. de, CA508
León, J. Romeo De, GU782
León, Jorge, CR673-74
León, Juan María de, GU783
León Aragón, Oscar de, GU784-85
León Gómez, Alfredo, HO263
Leon Hill, Eladia, GU786

León Porras, Fernando de, GU787
León Sánchez, José, CR675-84
León Schlotter, René de, GU788
León Villalobos, Edwin, CR685
Leonov, Nikolai Sergeevich, CA509-10
Lester, Mary, HO264
Leticia de Oyuela, Irma, HO331
Letts, John M., NI379
Lever, Edward A., CA511
Lévy, Pablo, NI380
Lewis, A.B., GU789
Lewis, D. Gareth, BE123
Lewis, Oscar, NI381
Leysbeth, Nicolas, GU790
Leytón Rodríguez, Rubén, CA512-13; BE124-26;
    ES247; GU791-92; HO265; NI382
Liano, Andres, CA514
Liga de la Defensa Nacional Centro-Americana, CA515
Liga Espiritual de Profesionales Católicos, CR686
Linares, Julio, NI383
Lindemann, Charles, HO50
Lindo, Hugo, CA516; ES248-50
Lines, Jorge A., CR687
Lino Paniagua Alvarado, Rafael, CR688
Liot, W.B., NI384
Lira, Carmen, pseud. See Carvajal, Maria Isabel
Lizano Fait, Eduardo, CA517-20; CR692-94
Lizano Hernández, Victor, CR695
Lizardo Díaz O., José, GU793-95
Llanas Sánchez, Enrique, BE127
Lockley, Lawrence C., CA521
Lockwood, Belva A., CA522
Loftin, Marion T., HO192
Lombard, Thomas R., HO266
Lombardo, Heraclio A., CR696
Long, William Rodney, CA523
Lonteen, Joseph Anthony, GU796
Loomis, Charles P., CR697
Loos, Eduardo, NI385
López, Francisco Marcos, CA524-25; BE128-29; GU797
López, Jacinto, CR698
López, Matilde Elena, ES251
López Alvarez, Luís, GU798
López Barahona, Sotero, CA526
López C., Julio, NI386
López Guzmán, Leyla, CR699
López Jiménez, Ramón, CA527-31; BE130; ES252
López L., Roger, GU799
López Larrave, Mario, GU800
López Mayorical, Mariano, BE131
López Pineda, Julián, CA532; HO267-69
López Rivera, Lionel Fernando, GU801
López Trejo, Roberto, ES253-56
López Valdizón, José María, GU802-4
López Vallecillos, Italo, ES257-58
López Villamil, Humberto, HO270
López Villatoro, Mario, GU805-6
Lorand de Olazagasti, Adelaida, GU807
Lorang, Mary Corde, GU808
Loretz, C., GU353
Lorio, Juan, NI387-89
Lovato, Judith, ES1
Loveland, Franklin O., CA413
Lovo Castelar, Luís, CA533
Lozano, Julio, HO271
Lucas, Daniel Bedinger, NI390
Lucientes, Francisco, ES259
Luján, Herman D., GU809
Luján Muñoz, Jorge, CA534; GU810

Luján Muñoz, Luís, GU811-13
Lull, E.P., NI338
Lumen, Enrique, GU814
Luna, David, ES260-61
Lunardi, Federico, HO272-73
Lundberg, Donald E., CR700
Lynch, David, CR701
Lyra, Carmen, pseud. See Carvajal, Maria Isabel

McAnany, Emile G., ES293
Mac Amour, Roberto A., CA535
McArthur, Harry S., GU815
Macaulay, Neill Webster, NI391
McCall, Louis A., CA536
McCamant, John F., CA537
McCann, Thomas P., CA538
Maccio, Guillermo A., CR702
McClellan, Albert, CA539
McClelland, Donald H., CA540
MacDonald, Mary B., CR703
MacGregor, Gregor, NI392
Machado, Antonio, GU344
Machado, J. Tible, GU816
Machón Vilanova, Francisco, ES262
Macías del Real, A., GU817
McLaughlin, Dwight H., CR703
McLellan, Donna L., CA568
McVicker Roy H., CA541
Madrigal G., Rodolfo, CR704
Madrigal J., Abraham, CR705
Madriz, Federico, CR706
Madriz, José, NI393-94
Maestre Alfonso, Juan, GU818, 1057
Magaña Menéndez, Enrique, ES263, 265
Magaña Menéndez, Gustavo, ES264-65
Magil, A.B., GU1310-11
Magliano, Roberto, CA542
Magón, pseud. See González Zeledón, Manuel
Maher, John, BE132
Malaina, Santiago, ES266-67
Malavassi Vargas, Guillermo, CR670, 707
Maldonado Koerdell, Manuel, CA543
Maldonado Robles, Manuel, GU819
Mallagaray, CR708
Malugani, María Dolores, CA544
Maluquer y Salvador, José, CR709
Mancilla, A., GU820
Manson, Anne, GU821
Manson, Nathaniel J., NI395
Mántica, Carlos, NI396
Mantovani, Juan, GU822-23
Maraboto, Emigdio E., NI397
Marañón Richi, Luís, CA545
Marcoleta, José de, NI398
Marconte, pseud. See Saravia, Mario
Marín, Rufino, BE133
Marín Cañas, José, CR710-13
Mariñas Otero, Luís, GU824; HO274-75
Marinello Vidaurreta, Juan, GU825
Mariscal, Ignacio, BE134
Maritime Canal Company and the Nicaragua Canal
    Construction Co., NI399
Maritime Canal Company of Nicaragua, NI400
Markman, Sidney David, CA546
Márquez, Adolfo de Jesús, ES268
Marr, Friedrich Wilhelm Adolf, CA547
Marroquín, Alejandro Dagoberto, ES269-71
Marroquín A., J. Emilio, GU826-27
Marroquín Rojas, Clemente, BE135; GU828-42

Marsden, Howard J., CR714
Martén, Alberto, CR715
Martí y Pérez, José Julián, GU843-44
Martin, Percy Falcke, ES272
Martín Carranza, Ernesto, CA548-50; CR716-17
Martínez, Fernando, CR718
Martínez, José Francisco, HO276
Martínez, Juan P., CR719
Martínez, Miguel, CA551
Martínez, Modesto, CR720
Martínez, Sebastián, CA552
Martínez Alomía, Santiago, BE136
Martínez Aybar, Juan Vicente, CA553
Martínez B., Juan Ramón, HO277
Martínez Durán, Carlos, GU845-49
Martínez Ferraté, Rodolfo, GU850
Martínez-Holgado, Arturo C., GU851
Martínez L., Carlos, NI63
Martínez López, Eduardo, CA554-56; HO278
Martínez Morales, Antonio, GU852
Martínez Nolasco, Gustavo, GU853
Martínez Palafox, Luís, BE137
Martínez Rivera, Sebastián, HO279-80
Martínez Sobral, Enrique, GU854-57
Martínez Suarez, Francisco, CA557
Martínez Vargas, Isidro, ES273
Martini Orozco, Margarita, GU858
Martz, John D., GU859-61
Martz, Mary Jeanne Reid, CA558
Marure, Alejandro, CA559-60; GU862-64; NI401
Marx, Paul, GU865
Masferrer, Alberto, CR721; ES274-88
Masferrer C., Manuel, ES289-90
Masferrer de Miranda, Teresa, CA561
Masís Rojas, Teresa, NI402
Mata Gamboa, Jesús, CR722-23
Mata Gavidia, José, CA562-63; ES291-92
Mata Oreamuno, Alberto, CR724
Matamoro J., T., NI403
Matamoros, Luís, CA564
Matamoros y Lucha, Ernesto, HO281
Matta Retana, Rafael, GU866
Matus, Ramón Ignacio, CA565-66; NI404-5
Matute Ruíz, Eddy, NI583
Maudslay, Alfred Percival, GU867
Maudslay, Ann Cary, GU867
May, Charles Paul, CA567
May, Jacques M., CA568
May, Stacey, CA569; CR725
Mayes Huete, Guillermo, HO282; NI406
Mayo, John K., ES293
Mayora, Eduardo, CA570
Mayora C., Manuel, ES294
Mayorga, Juan de Dios, CA571
Maza, Emilio, CA572
Mazariegos, Alfonso A., GU868
Meagher, Thomas Francis, CR726
Meany, Jorge, GU869
Mechin, T.P., pseud. See Peralta Lagos, José María
Medina, Alberto, NI407
Medina, Crisanto, GU187; NI408
Medina Planas, Héctor, HO283-84
Medina Ruiz, Fernando, GU870-71
Mejía, José Víctor, GU872-74
Mejía, Medardo, CA573; GU875-76; HO285-87
Mejía, Rumoaldo Elpidio, HO288-89
Mejía Colindres, Vicente, HO290
Mejía Deras, Ismael, HO291-93
Mejía Moreno, Luís, HO294-95
Mejía Nieto, Arturo, CA574

Mejía Sánchez, Ernesto, NI409
Meléndez, Carlos, ES295-96
Meléndez Chaverri, Carlos, CA575-77; CR727-41
Meléndez Ibarra, José, CR742
Meléndez Palacios, Roberto D., ES297
Melgar Callejas, José María, ES298
Melick, Edith Moulton, HO296
Melville, George Wallace, NI410
Melville, Marjorie, GU877-78
Melville, Thomas, GU877-78
Membreño, Alberto, CA578; ES299; HO297-98
Membreño, Jesús B., HO299
Membreño, María B. de, CA579
Mena, Alberto, ES300
Mencos Franco, Agustín, CA580; GU879
Mendelson, E. Michael, GU880
Méndez, Alfredo, GU360
Méndez, Francisco, GU881
Méndez, Joaquín, GU882-84
Méndez, Joaquín, h., ES301
Méndez, José María, ES302-3
Méndez, Rosendo P., GU885
Méndez Cifuentes, Arturo, GU886
Méndez Domínguez, Alfredo, GU887
Méndez Guillén, Napoleón, HO300
Méndez Hidalgo, Julián, GU888
Méndez I., Jorge, CA581
Méndez Montenegro, Julio César, GU889
Mendieta, Salvador, CA582-89; BE138
Mendieta Alfaro, Roger, NI411
Mendoza, José Luís, BE139-40; GU890
Mendoza, Juan Manuel, CA590-92; NI412
Menen Desleal, Alvaro, pseud. See Alvaro Menéndez, Leal
Menéndez, Isidro, ES304
Menéndez Rodríguez, Mario, ES305
Meneses, J. Barcenas, NI413
Menjívar, Rafael, ES306-8; GU893. See also Bodenheimer, Susanne Jonas
Menocal, Aniceto García, NI414-16
El Mensajero de Centro América, CA592
Menton, Seymour, CR743; GU894
Merin, Boris Moiseevich, CA593
Merlos, Salvador R., CA594-96; CR744
Merry, William Lawrence, NI417-18
Merz, Karl Franz, CR745-50
Mestas, Alberto de, ES309
Metzgen, Monrad Sigfrid, BE141
Mexico, Gov't of, BE-142; GU895
-Congreso Cámara de Diputados, CA597
-Ministerio de Relaciones Exteriores, CA598-99; BE143-44
Meyer, Harvey Kessler, HO301; NI419
Meza, César, GU896
Meza, Rafael, GU897
Mezzera, Baltasar Luís, GU898
Michaud, Madame, CR752
Middeldyk, Rudolph Adams van, GU899
Middle American Information Bureau, CA600
Milla y Vidaurre, José, GU900-905
Miller, Hubert J., GU906
Miller, Hugh Gordon, NI420
Miller, Jacob William, NI421
Millett, Richard, NI422
Miner, William Harvey, NI423
Minkel, Clarence W., BE145
Miolan, Ángel, GU907
Miranao, Juan, CR753
Miranda Ruano, Francisco, ES310
Mitchell, Willard H., CA601

Moe, Alfred Keane, HO302
Molina, Arturo Armando, ES311-12
Molina, Cayteano Antonio, CA602
Molina, Felipe, CA603-4; CR754-55
Molina, José Lino, ES313-14
Molina, Juan Ramón, HO303-4
Molina, Pedro, CA605
Molina Argüello, Carlos, NI424-25
Molina Chocano, Guillermo, CA606; HO305
Molina Sierra, Beatriz, GU908
Molina y Mata, Marcelo, GU909-910
Molina y Morales, Roberto, ES315-16
Moncada, José María, CA607-11; HO306-7; NI426-30
Moncado G., Arturo, CR756
Moncarz, Raúl, CA610
Monedero, Oscar Manuel, ES317
Monge, Luís Alberto, CR757; GU912
Monge Alfaro, Carlos, CR758-61
Montalván, José H., NI431-33
Monteforte Toledo, Mario, CA611; GU913-23
Monteiro, Palmyra V.M., CA612
Montero Barrantes, Francisco, CR763-66
Montero Umaña, Lilia, CR767
Montero Vega, Arturo, CR768
Monterrey, Francisco J., ES318
Monterrosa, Carlos, ES396
Montes, Arturo Humberto, CA613; HO308
Montes, Luís, CA614
Montes, Segundo, ES319-20
Montes de Oca Ramirez, Faustino, CR769
Montessus de Ballore, Fernand J.B. Comte de, CA615
Montgomery, George Washington, GU924
Montiel Argüello, Alejandro, NI434-35
Montoya R., J.F., CR936
Mont-Serrat, E. de, CA237
Montúfar, Lorenzo. See Montúfar y Rivera Maestre, Lorenz
Montúfar, José Batres. See Batres y Montúfar, José
Montúfar, Rafael, CA616-17; GU925-31
Montúfar y Coronado Manuel, CA618-19; GU932
Montúfar y Rivera Maestre, Lorenzo, CA214, 620-23;
    GU933-39; NI436
Moore, G. Alexander, GU940
Moore, John Bassett, CA624-25
Moore, Richard E., GU941
Mora, Eduardo, CR430
Mora, Federico, CR770
Mora, Nini de, CR771-73
Mora Barrantes, Carlos, CR774
Mora V., Enrique, CR588
Mora Valenzuela, Arturo, CR775
Mora Valverde, Manuel, CR776-79
Mora Velardo, Eduardo, CA626
Morales, Baltasar, GU942
Morales Molina, Manuel, CA627
Morales Urrutia, Mateo, GU943
Morán, Francisco, ES321
Morán, Chinchilla, Sarbelio, GU944
Morazán, Francisco, CA628-29
Morazán, Miguel, CA630
Morelet, Arthur, GU945
Moreno, José Vicente, CA631
Moreno, Laudelino, CA632-33; GU946
Moret y Prendergast, Segismundo, CA634
Morgan Guaranty Trust Company, CA635
Morlan, Albert E., HO309
Mörne, Hakan, CA636
Morren, F.W., GU947
Morrill, Gulian Lansing, CA637
Morris, Daniel, BE146
Morrison, George Austin, NI437

Morrison, Hugh A., NI438
Morton, Friedrich, GU948
Mory, Warren H., Jr., CA638
Moseley, Edward H., CA444
Moser, Don, CA639
Moser, René, CR1067; NI439
Mosquera Aguilar, Antonio, GU949
Movimiento Revolucionario 13 de Noviembre, GU950
Moya Posas, Emma, GU951
Müller, Adrian, GU952
Müller, Dr., NI271
Mueller, Karl A., NI440
Muguerza y Sáenz, Simeón, ES322
Müllerried, Friedrich Karl Gustav, CA640
Muñoz, Joaquín, GU953-54
Muñoz Fonseca, Enrique, CR780
Muñoz Meany, Enrique, GU955-57
Muñoz Pineda, Plutarco, HO310
Muñoz Q., Hugo Alfonso, CR781
Munro, Dana Gardner, CA641-44
Munson, Donn, GU958
Murchie, Anita Gregorio, CR782
Murga Franssinetti, Antonio, HO311
Murillo, Andrés, NI441
Murillo Soto, Céleo, HO312
Murillo Valladares, Gilberto, NI442
Murphy, Fred, NI138
Murray, Renato, pseud. See Uriarte, Juan Ramón

Nach, James, GU959
NACLA. See Bodenheimer, Suzanne Jonas
Nájera Cabrera, Antonio, GU960
Nájera Farfán, Mario Efraín, GU961-96
Napky, Marina O. de, HO313, 430-31
Naranjo Cote, Carmen, CR783-88
Narávez López, Carlos, CA645; BE147
Narisco, Vicente A., GU967
Narváez García, Emilio, ES323
Narváez Rosalez, Reynaldo, NI443
Nash, Manning, GU969-70
Nathan, Robert R. Associates, Inc., ES324
Navarrete, Sarbelio, CA646
Navarro, Carlos S., CR789
Navarro Bolandi, Hugo, CR790-91
Navas Miralda, Paca, HO314
Navas y Barraza, Juan M., NI444
Navas Zepeda, Máximo, NI445
Netherlands, Gov't of, GU971
−Economische Voorlichtingsdienst, CA647
Neutze de Rugg, Carmen, GU972
New York and Honduras Rosario Mining Company, HO315
New York Navigation and Colonization Company, HO316
Newbold, Stokes, pseud., GU973
Neymarck, Alfred, HO317
Nicaise, Auguste, NI446
Nicaragua Canal Construction Co., NI447-48
Nicaragua Canal Convention, NI449
Nicaragua, Comité Pro, NI452
Nicaragua, Elections. See Operations and Policy
    Research, Inc.
Nicaragua, Universidad Nacional de, NI453
Nicaragua, Universidad Nacional Autónoma de, NI454
Nicaragua, Gov't of, NI455-58
−Banco Central, NI459
−Biblioteca Nacional, Managua, NI460
−Consulado, Paris, NI461
−Dirección General de Estadística, NI462-63
−Instituto Geográfico Nacional, NI464
−Ministerio de Fomento y Obras Públicas, NI465
−Ministerio de Fomento y Obras Públicas, Oficina
    Nacional de Urbanismo. See Solow, Anatole A.

(Nicaragua, Gov't of)
-Ministerio de Hacienda y Crédito Público, NI466
-Ministerio de Relaciones Exteriores, CA648-61;
    NI467-76
Un Nicaragüense, NI479
Nicholas, Francis Child, CA662
Nicholson, Thomas Herbert, CR792
Nicolle, Roberto Carpio, BE149
Niederlein, Gustavo, CR793; GU974; NI480
Nietschmann, Bernard Q., NI481
Nimmo, Joseph, Jr., NI482-84
Nitoburg, Eduard L'vovich, ES325
Nogales y Mendez, Rafael del, NI485
Noguera, María Leal de, CR794
Nonualco, Justo, pseud. See Dueñas van Severén,
    J. Ricardo
Noriega, Félix F., CR795
Noval, Joaquín, GU975-77
Nuestro Diario (Guatemala City), GU978-80
Nugent, Jeffrey B., CA664
Nuhn, H., CA665; CR796, 993
Nuñez Chinchilla, Jesús, HO318
Núñez de Rodas, Edna Isabel, GU981
Núñez Monge, Francisco María, CA666; CR797-810
Núñez Téllez, Carlos, NI486
Nunley, Robert E., CR811
Nye, Joseph S., CA667

O., S.L., GU982
Oakes, Maud van Cortlandt, GU983-84
OAS, CA668-72; GU985; HO319-20
Obando Bravo, Miguel, NI487-88
Obando Sánchez, Antonio, GU986
Obando Somarriba, Francisco, NI489
Obert, L.H.C., GU987
Obregón Loría, Edgar A., CR814
Obregón Loría, Rafael, CR815-25; GU988
El Observador (Tegucigalpa), HO321-22
Ocaña, Canuto, pseud. See Marroquín Rojas,
    Clemente
Ochoa Alcántara, Antonio, HO323-24
Ocho-Ji-Kiros, pseud. See Jímenez Quirós, Otto
Ocón Murillo, Armando, NI490
ODECA (Organizacion de los estados
    Centroamericanos), CA673-77
Oduber Quirós, Daniel, CR826-27
Oehler, Klaus, GU989
An Officer in the Service of Walker, NI491
Oficina Internacional Centro-Americana, CA678; CR828
Oficina Internacional del Trabajo, CR829
Ohara, Yoshinori, CA679
Oliphant, Laurence, NI492
Oliver, Samuel Pasfield, NI493
Olivera, Otto, GU990
Olivier, Martel, GU203
Oliveros, Augusto César, GU991
Olson, Ernest C., GU12
O'Neale, Lila Morris, GU992
Operations & Policy Research, Inc., CR830; ES326;
    GU993; NI494
Oquelí, Arturo, HO325-29
Oquelí, Ramón, HO330-31
Oquelí Bustillo, Miguel, HO332
Ordóñez, López R., GU994
Ordóñez Argüello, Alberto, GU995-96; NI495
Ordoñez Jonama, Ramiro, GU997
Oreamuno, José Rafael, CR831
Oreamuno Quirós, Alfredo, CR832-33
Orellana, Carlos, CA345
Orellana González, René Arturo, GU998
Organización del Tratado General de Integración
    Económica Centroamericana, CA689

Organización Iberoamericana de Seguridad Social,
    CR834; ES327; NI496
ORIT, CR835
Orozco, Rafael, CR836
Orozco Castro, Jorge, CR837
Orr, Paul G., GU1001
Ørsted, Anders Sandøe, CA681
Ortega, Ernesto, CR838
Ortega, Pompilio, HO333
Ortega Arancibia, Francisco, NI497
Ortega Saavedra, Humberto, NI498
Ortez Colindres, Enrique, CA682-83
Ortiz, Santiago, CA684
Ortiz, Víctor, CR905
Ortiz Cartin, Bienvenido, CR839
Ortiz España, Alberto, NI499
Ortiz García, Edgard, HO334
Ortiz Passarelli, Miguel, GU1002
Ortiz Urruela, Manuel, CA685
Ortuño Sobrado, Fernando, CR840
Ory, Eduardo de, NI500
Osborne, Lilly de Jongh, ES328; GU757, 1003-6, 1396
Osegueda, Raúl, GU1007-8
Osorio, Miguel Ángel, ES329
Osorio García, Miguel, GU1009
Osorio Pavón, Jorge, HO335
Osorio S., J. Adalberto, GU1010
Osorno Fonseca, Humberto, NI501-4
Ovalle, Néstor K., GU1011
Ovalle Samayoa, Oscar, GU1012
Ovidio Rodas, Héctor, GU1013
Oviedo, Matías, GU1014
Ower, Leslie Hamilton, BE149

Pacheco, León, CR841
Pacheco, Leonidas, CR842-44
Pacheco Cooper, Federico, CR845
Padilla, José Augusto, CA686
Padilla Castro, Guillermo, CR846-47
Padilla Castro, Noé, CR848
Paetau, Estrada L.M., GU1147
Pagoaga, Raúl Arturo, HO336-38
Páiz Castillo, Ricardo, NI505
Palacios, Julio E., GU1016
Palencia, Oscar Arturo, GU1017-18
Pallottine Missionary Sisters, BE150
Palma Martínez, Ildefonso, NI506
Palma Sandoval, Alvaro Enrique, GU1019-22
Palma y Palma, César Augusto, GU1023
Palmer, Bradley Webster, CA687
Palmer, Frederick, CA688
Palmer, Mervyn George, NI507
Palmerlee, Albert Earl, CR849
Palmieri, José Alfredo, GU1024
Palomo, J. Antonio, GU1025
Pan American Institute of Geography and History,
    HO339
Pan American Union, Division of Labor and Social
    Information, ES330
Pan American Union, Division of Philosophy and
    Letters, CA694
Panama, Gov't of, Ministerio de Relaciones
    Exteriores, CA689-93
Paniagua Alvarado, Rafael Lino. See Lino Paniagua
    Alvarado, Rafael
Paniagua Santizo, Benjamin, GU1026
Parada, Alfredo, CA695; ES331
Pardo Gallardo, José Joaquín, CA696; GU1027-28
Pardo Ruiz, German, BE151
Paredes, Jacinto, ES332

Paredes, Jacinto Rodríguez, ES333
Paredes, Juan E., HO340-41
Paredes, Lucas, GU1029; HO342-47
Paredes, Victoriano de Diego, CA697
Paredes Moreira, José Luís, GU1030-31
Paret-Limardo de Vela, Lise, GU1032
Parker, Franklin Dallas, CA698-700
Parkhurst, Henry Clinton, NI508
Parra Pradenas, Ortelio, ES334
Partido Araujista, ES335
Partido Guatemalteco del Trabajo (Guatemala),
    GU1033-35
Partido Liberación Nacional (Costa Rica), CR850-51
Partido Liberal (Guatemala), GU1036
Partido Liberal de Nicaragua, NI509
Partido Liberal Nacionalista, NI510
Partido Liberal Progresista (Guatemala), GU1037-43
Partido Nacional de Honduras, CA701; HO348-49
Partido Nacional de Honduras, Comité Central,
    HO350-51
Partido Nacional de Trabajadores, GU1044
Partido Nacional Hondureño, HO352
Partido Revolucionario, GU1045
Partido Vanguardia Popular de Costa Rica, CR852
Pascua, Hernán, HO353
El Paseador, Domingo, pseud. See Rubio, J.
    Francisco
Pasos, Carlos, NI197
Pasos, Gabriel, BE152
Pasos Arana, Manuel, CA702
Pataky, László, NI511-12
Pater, Julius, pseud. See Méndez Hidalgo, Julián
Paul, Benjamin David, GU1046-47
Paul, Lois, GU1047
Payne, Walter, GU1048
Paz Barnica, Edgardo, CA703; HO354
Paz Salinas, María Emilia, BE153
Paz Solórzano, Juan, GU1049
Paz y Paz, L. Alberto, BE154; GU1050
Paz y Paz, Roberto, GU1051
Paz y Paz G., Leonor, GU1052
Peccorini Letona, Francisco, ES336
Peck, Anne Merriman, CA704
Pector, Désiré, CA705-6; HO335; NI513
Pellecer, Carlos Manuel, GU1053-57
Peloso, Vincent C., CA786
Peña, José María S., CA707
Peña Hernández, Enrique, NI514-15
Peña Kampy, Alberto, ES337
People's United Party (Belize), BE155
Pepper, Charles Melville, GU1058
Pepper B., José Vincente, GU1059
Peralta, José F. de, CR853
Peralta, Manuel María de, CA708-16; CR854-55; NI516
Peralta Lagos, José María, ES338-41
Peralta Méndez, Carlos Enrique, GU1060
Peralta Quirós, Hernán G., CR856-65
Pereira, Ricardo S., CA717
Pereira Pinto, Juan Carlos, CA718
Pereyra, Carlos, CA719
Pérez, J.P., GU1061
Pérez, Jerónimo, NI517-19
Pérez, Rafael, CA720
Pérez Brignoli, Héctor, CA115; HO356
Pérez Cabrera, Ricardo, CR866
Pérez Cadalso, Eliseo, CA721-22; HO357-59
Pérez Estrada, Francisco, NI221, 520
Pérez Estrada, Tito, HO360-61
Pérez Maldonado, Raúl, GU1062-64
Pérez Marchant, Braulio, ES342

Pérez Pancorbo, Humberto, CR867
Pérez Q., S., CR796
Pérez Trejo, Gustavo A., BE156
Pérez Valenzuela, Pedro, GU1065
Pérez Valle, Eduardo, CA723; NI59, 521
Pérez Zeledón, Pedro, CA724-25; CR557, 868-71
Périgny, Maurice C. de, CA726; CR872
Perry, Edward Wilkin, HO362; NI522
Peterson, Arthur W., CR873
Peterwerth, Reinhard, CA727
Petrov, Vladimir, NI523
Pevtsov, IUriĭ Aleksandrovich, GU1067
Peyroutet, H., CR874
Phelps, S.L. See Provisional Interoceanic Canal
    Society
Picado Chacón, Manuel, CR875
Picado Michalski, Teodoro, CA728; CR876-77; NI524
Picado Soto, Francisco, CR878-82
Piedra Santa Arandi, Rafael, GU1068
Pierri, Ettore, NI532
Pijoan, Michel, NI525
Pilli, Emile R., GU1069
Pilon, Marta, GU1070-71
Pim, Bedford Clapperton Trevelyan, NI526-27
Pinaud, José María, CR883-84
Pincus, Joseph, CA729-30; HO363
Pineda C., Felipe, GU1072
Pineda de Mont, Manuel, GU1073
Pineda Erdocia, Empar, NI528
Pineda M., Leónidas, CA731
Pineda Madrid, Pedro, CA732
Pineda Pivaral, Eduardo, GU1074-75
Pinel Moncada, Emilio, HO364
Piñol y Batres, José, GU1076
Pinto, Julieta, CR885-88
Pinto Mejía, Edmundo, HO365
Pinto Soria, J.C., GU1077
Pitman, Robert Birks, NI529
Pittier de Fábrega, Henri François, CR889-96
Pittman, Marvin S., CR897
Piza, Rodolfo E., CR898
Plafker, George, NI120
Planas-Suárez, Simón, GU1078
Plaza Lasso, Galo, CA569
Pohl, Carlos, ES343
Poincaré, Raymond, CA733-35
Poitevin, René, GU1079
Polanco, G.A., GU1080
Polanco, hijo, D., GU1080
Polanco R., Raúl, BE157
Poliakov, Mikhail Il'ich, CA736
Pollan, Arthur Aclair, CA737
Polo Sifontes, Francis, GU1081
Ponce de Avalos, Reynaldo, HO366
Ponce de Veliz, María Magdalena, GU1082
Ponciano, Juan Francisco, GU1083
Pons, Gabriel, ES344
Popenoe, Dorothy Hughes, GU1084
Poppe, K.H., GU1085
Porras, Belisario, CA738-39; NI531
Porras Mendieta, Nemesio, ES345
Porter, William Sydney (O. Henry), CA740
Portocarrero, José D., CA741
Posnett, N.W., BE158
Possamay, Luciana, NI532
Pouchet, James, NI533-39
Pougin, Edouard, CR899
Pozuelo A., José, CA742
Prado, Eladio, CR900-905
Prado Quexada, Alcides, CR906
Prado Solares, Miguel, GU1086

Prats y Beltrán, Alardo, BE159
PRELAC (Programa Regional del Empleo para América
    Latina y el Caribé), ES346
Prem, Marcial, CA743
La Prensa (Managua), CA744
Prieto Tugores, Emilia, CR907
Protti Martinelli, Eduardo, CR908
Provisional Interoceanic Canal Society, NI535-36
Pucci, Enrique, CR909
Pupo Pérez, Carlos, CR910
Putnam, George Palmer, CA745
Puydt, Remi de, GU1088

Quesada, Octavio, CR911-14
Quesada H., Fenelon, CR915
Quesada Picado, Máximo, CR916
Quesada Vargas, Octavio, CR917
Quezada, Juan José, NI537
Quezaltenango, Corporación Municipal de, GU1089-90
Quijano, Aníbal, CR918
Quijano, Carlos, NI538
Quijano Hernández, Manuel, ES347-48
Quijano Quesada, Alberto, CR919-20
Quiñónes, Alfredo, CA746; GU1092
Quiñónez, José A., GU1093
Quiñónez, Lucio, ES349
Quintana, Emilio, CR921
Quintana, Roberto R., GU1094
Quintana Díaz, Víctor, GU1095
Quintana Rodas, J. Epaminodas, GU1096-97
Quirós, Manuel A., CR922
Quirós, Ricardo Fournier, CA728
Quirós Aguilar, Ernesto, CR923-24
Quirós Amador, Tulia, CR925

Radcliff, William, NI539
Radford, Luís N., GU1098-100
Raine, Alice, GU1101
Ramírez, Asdrúbal, HO367-69
Ramírez, Marco Antonio, CA747
Ramírez, Ricardo, GU1102
Ramírez Arias, Mariano, CR296-29
Ramírez Brown, Gerónimo, CA748; NI540
Ramírez Colóm, José M., GU1103
Ramírez Delgado, Rafael, NI541
Ramírez Fajardo, Aníbal, CR928
Ramírez Gutiérrez, Gustavo, GU1104
Ramírez Mercado, Sergio, NI542-48
Ramírez Morales, José, NI549
Ramírez Peña, Abraham, CA749-50; ES351
Ramírez y Fernández Fontecha, Antonio Abad, CA751;
    HO370
Ramos, Lilia, CR929
Ramos, Miguel Ángel, HO371-73; NI550
Ramos, Plinio de Abreu, GU1105
Ramsett, David E., CA752
Rath, Ferdinand, CA753
Rath, Fernando, CA394
Raudales, Ángel, HO374
Raudales, Luís Amilcar. See Amilcar Raudales, Luís
Raudales Soto, Julio, NI551
Raygada, Jorge, GU1106
Raynolds, David R., ES353
Rebolledo, Miguel, BE160
Recinos, Adrián, GU1107
Recinos, Luís Felipe, NI552
Recinos, Marco Augusto, BE161
Redish, Frences, pseud. See Valladares Rubio,
    Manuel
Regalado Dueñas, Miguel, CA755-56; ES354

Reichardt, C.F., CA757; NI554
Reilly, P.M., BE159
Reina, Rubén E., GU1108-10
Reina Valenzuela, José, CA758-59; HO375-79
Reni, Aníbal, CR930-31
La República (Guatemala), CA760
Retana, Marco, CR935
Réti, Ervin, GU1111
Reuss, Lawrence A., CR936
Revelo, Marco René, CA763
Revilla, Benedicto, GU1112
Rey, Francis, CA764
Rey, Julio Adolfo, CA765
Rey Soto, Antonio, GU1113
Reyes, Felipe, HO383
Reyes, Marcos Carías. See Carías Reyes, Marcos
Reyes, Rafael, CA766; ES356-58, 363
Reyes, Ramón, HO384
Reyes C., Consuelo, GU1114
Reyes Cardona, Julio Antonio, GU1115
Reyes H., Alfonso, CR939
Reyes Monroy, José Luís, GU1116-21
Reyes Morales, Mario Roberto, GU1122
Reyes Narciso, Francisco O., GU1123
Reyes Ovalle, Nicolas, GU1124
Rheinboldt, Victor M., HO313
Riba, Jorge Ricardo, CA767-68
Ribera Suazo, Marcial, HO385
Richmond, Doug, CA769
Rincón Coutiño, Valentín, CA770. See also
    Guatemala-Mexico Joint Boundary Dispute
Rincón de Townson, Sonia, GU1125
Rincón Menegazzo de Macdonald, Sonia, GU1126
Ríos, Efraín de los, GU1127
Rivas, Anselmo Hilario, NI557
Rivas, Pedro, CA771; HO386-88
Rivas, Pedro Geoffrey. See Masferrer, Alberto
Rivas, Valerio Ignacio, GU1128
Rivera, Abrahám, ES369-62
Rivera, Rubén, CA772
Rivera G., José Antonio, CA773
Rivera Hernández, Alejandro, HO389
Rivera Porres, Arnulfo, GU1129
Rivera y Morillo, Humberto, HO390
Rizzo Baratta, Domingo, NI558
Roberts, Bryan R., GU1130-32
Roberts, Morley, CA774
Roberts, Orlando W., CA775
Roberts, W. Dayton, CR940
Roberts Smith, Edward, CR941
Robleto, Hernán, CA776; NI559-66
Robleto Siles, J.A., NI567
Roca, José Antonio de La, GU1133
Roca, Julio César de La, GU1134-36
Rocha, Jesús de la, NI568-69
Rocha, Pedro Francisco de La, HO391
Rochac Alfonso, ES363
Roche, James Jeffrey, NI570
Rodas, Hector Ovidio. See Ovidio Rodas, Hector
Rodas Barrios, Abelardo, GU1137
Rodas Corzo, Ovidio, GU1138, 1140
Rodas Cruz, Manuel, GU1139
Rodas M., Joaquín, CA777-78
Rodas N., Flavio, GU1140
Rodman, Selden, CA779; GU1141
Rodríguez, Guillermo, GU1142-43
Rodríguez, José Nery, CA780
Rodríguez, Juvenal Valerio, CR942
Rodríguez, Manuel Eduardo, BE162
Rodríguez, Manuel Federico, CA781
Rodríguez, Mario, CA782-86

Rodríguez Ayestas, Julio, HO392
Rodríguez Beteta, Virgilio, CA787-90; BE165-66; GU1144; NI571
Rodríguez Cabal, Juan, GU1145-46
Rodríguez Camacho, Francisco, CR943
Rodríguez Castellejo, Juan Francisco, GU1147
Rodríguez Cerna, José, CA791; GU1148-57
Rodríguez Chávez, Elisa, GU1158
Rodríguez de Lemus, Guillerma, GU1159
Rodríguez González, Salvador, ES364; NI572-73
Rodríguez Guerrero, José, CA792
Rodríguez Herrera, J. Humberto, GU1160
Rodríguez López, Alcides, CR944
Rodríguez Macal, Virgilio, GU1161-65
Rodríguez Moján, María Luisa, GU1166
Rodríguez Porras, Armando, CR945
Rodríguez Rossignon, Mariano, GU1167-68
Rodríguez Ruíz, José Napoleón, CR65; ES365-68
Rodriguez Serrano, Felipe, NI574-75
Rodríguez Solís, Manuel, GU1169-70
Rodríguez Vega, Eugenio, CR946-47
Roemer, Hans Gustav, CA793
Rogers, Ebenezer, BE165
Rojas, Blanca, NI576
Rojas Corrales, Ramón, CR948; NI577
Rojas Lima, Flavio, GU1171
Rojas Solano, Héctor, CR949-50
Rojas Suárez, Juan Francisco, CR951
Rojas Vincenzi, Ricardo, CR952-53
Rollins, Clinton, pseud. See Parkhurst, Henry Clinton
Rölz Bennett, José, GU1172
Román, José, NI578
Romero, Mario, CR954
Romero, Matías, CA794
Romero, Ramón, NI579
Romero Pérez, Jorge Enrique, CR955-56
Romero Rodas, Francisco, GU1173
Romero Vargas, German, CA795
Romeu, José Tomás, ES369
Romney, D.H., BE166
Rosa, Marco Antonio, HO393-400
Rosa, Ramón, CA796-97; HO401
Rosa, Rubén Ángel, HO402-3
Rosa Chávez, Adolfo, CA798
Rosada, Héctor Roberto, GU1174
Rosales, Hernán, NI580
Rosales, Nicasio, NI581
Rösch, Adrián, GU1175
Rosenberg, Mark B., CR957
Rosengarten, Frederic, Jr., NI582
Rosenthal, Mario, GU1176, 1409
Ross, Delmer G., CR958; HO404
Ross, James E., CR151-52
Rossignon, Julio, GU1177
Rothery, Agnes Edwards, GU1178
Rothschuh Villanueva, Guillermo, NI583
Rovinski, Samuel, CR959
Rowles, James, CA799
Rubio, Casimiro D., GU1179-80
Rubio, J. Francisco, GU1181
Rubio, Julio Alberto, GU1182
Rubio Alpuche, Néstor, BE167
Rubio Melhado, Adolfo, CA800; ES370-71; HO405
Ruhl, Arthur Brown, CA801
Ruiz, José T., HO406
Ruíz, Franco Arcadio, GU1183
Ruiz García, Enrique, GU1184
Ruiz Paniagua, Javier, GU1185
Ruíz Solórzano, Vilma, CR960

Ruíz y Ruíz, Frutos, NI584
Rull Sabater, Alberto, CA802
Ryan, John Morris, NI585

Saavedra, David, HO407
Saborio Montenegro, Alfredo, CR961
Sacasa, Juan Bautista, NI586
Sady, Emil J., GU23
Sáenz, Alfredo, CA803; CR962-63
Sáenz, Jimena, GU1186
Sáenz, Vincente, CA804-14; CR964; NI587-88
Sáenz Archila, Oscar Guillermo, GU1395
Sáenz Cordero, Manuel, CR965
Sáenz de Tejada, Federico, GU1187, 1198
Sáenz Elizondo, Carlos Luís, CR966
Sáenz Jiménez, Lenin, CA815
Sáenz Maroto, Alberto, CR967-69
Sáenz P., Carlos, CR970
Sáenz Poggio, José, GU1188
Saker-Ti, Grupo, GU1189-91
Salarrué, pseud. See Salazar Arrué, Salvador
Salas, Teresa Cajiao, CR590
Salas Marrera, Oscar A., CA816; CR971
Salazar, Carlos, CA817-20; GU1192-93
Salazar, Eduardo, CR972
Salazar, Mélinton, GU1194
Salazar, Ramón Antonio, CA821-23; GU1195-98
Salazar Arrué, Salvador, CR973; ES372-73
Salazar García, Salomón, CR974
Salazar Mora, Jorge Mario, CR975-76
Salazar Mora, Orlando, CR977
Salazar Obando, Omar, CR978
Salazar Valiente, Mario, CA824
Saler, Benson, GU1199
Un Saleriano, CR979
Salgado, Félix, CA367
Salguero, Álvaro Hugo, GU1200
Salguero, Miguel, pseud. See Zúñiga Díaz, Miguel
Salvatierra, Sofonías, CA825; NI589-92
Samayoa, José María, GU1201
Samayoa, Julio, CA826; GU1202-3
Samayoa, R., CA826
Samayoa Chinchilla, Carlos, GU1204-10
Samayoa Coronado, Francisco A., GU1211
Samayoa Guevara, Héctor Humberto, GU1212-14
Sanabria Martínez, Víctor Manuel, CR980-85
Sanborn, Helen Josephine, CA827
Sánchez, Antonio, NI593
Sánchez, Luís Alberto, GU1215
Sánchez, Milton, NI594
Sánchez, Pedro C., CA828
Sánchez, Roberto M., HO408
Sánchez, Rodrigo, NI595
Sánchez Bonilla, Gonzalo, CR986
Sánchez, G., Ángel Porfirio, HO409
Sánchez García, Alvaro, CR987
Sánchez Hernández, Fidel, ES374
Sánchez Morales, Juan Rafael, GU1216
Sánchez Ruphuy, Rodrigo, CR988
Sánchez Sarto, Manuel, CA829
Sancho, José, CA830
Sancho, Mario, CR989-90
Sandino, Augusto César, NI596
Sandner, Gerhard, CA831-32; CR991-93
Sandoval, Fernando Danza, HO171
Sandoval, Francisco Ernesto, GU1217
Sandoval, José María, HO410
Sandoval, Lisandro, GU1218
Sandoval, Victor O., GU1219
Sandoval de Fonseca, Virginia, CR994

Sandoval Valdivia, Elba, NI597
Sandoval Vásquez, Carlos Alberto, GU1220
Sands, William F., GU1221
San Francisco Chamber of Commerce. See Craig, Hugh
Sanfuentes, Julio, CR995
San Salvador, Municipality of, ES375
Sanso, Aro, pseud. See Mejía Deras, Ismael
Sansón-Terán, José, CA833
Santamaría, Ramón, HO411
Santamaría de Paredes, Vicente, CA634
Santiso Gálvez, Gustavo, BE168-69
Santoro, Gustavo, CR996
Santos, Manuel Antonio, GU1222
Sapia Martino, Raúl, GU1223
Sapper, Karl Theodor, CA834-41; CR997; GU1224-25
Saravia, Mario, ES376
Sariola, Sakari, CR998
Sautereau, Gustave, NI533-34
Savaria, Miguel G., CA842
Scanlon, A. Clark, GU1226
Schatzschneider, Hellmut, CA843
Schaufelberger, Paul, CR999-1000
Scherzer, Karl, CA844-45; CR1096
Schiavo-Campo, Salvatore, CA846
Schiffer, Jacobo, CR1001
Schlesinger, Alfredo, CA847-48; BE170; GU1227-33
Schlesinger, Eugene R., GU12
Schlesinger, Jorge, ES377
Schlick, W., CA665
Schmid, Lester, GU1234
Schmidt, George, CA849; NI598
Schmidt, Otto, NI599
Schmitter, Philippe C., CA850
Schneider, Ronald M., GU1235
Schottelius, Herbert, CA851
Schötz, Waltrand, CA852
Schroeder, John, CR1002
Schultze-Jena, Leonhard Sigmund, CA853; GU1236
Schumacher, Karl von, CA854
Schurr, Anton, CR1003
Schwartz, Gustavo, GU1237
Schwartz, Norman B., GU1238
Schwauss, Maria, GU1239
Scoullar, William T., GU748
Scroggs, William O., NI600
Secretaría Permanente del Tratado General de Integración Económica Centroamericana, CA855-61
Seebach, Albert Ludwig Karl von, CA862
Seeman, Berthold Carl, NI527
Segarra, Joaquín Julio, CR1004
Segarra, José, CR1004
Segreda, Luís Dobles. See Dobles Segreda, Luís
Segura, Rosalía de, CR1005
Segura Paguaga, Alfonso, CR1006
Sekai, Bunkasha, CA863
Seligson, Mitchell, CR1007
Selser, Gregorio, GU1240-41; NI601-3
Selva, Adán, NI604-7
Selva, Carlos, NI608
Selva, Mauricio de la, NI609
Selva, Silvio, NI610
Seminario de Integración Social Guatemalteca, CA864; GU1242-44. See also Arriola, Jorge Luís
Seminario Latinoamericano sobre Crédito Rural, ES378
Seminario para el Estudio de la Educación Integral en Honduras, HO412
Seminario sobre Aspectos Económicos, Sociales y Políticos de la Inversión Extranjera en Centro América, CA865

Seminario sobre la Situatión Demográfica de América Central, CA866
Sequeiros, Gonzalo S., HO413
Serra G., Ramón, GU1245
Serrano, Abelino, CA867
Serrano Gutiérrez, Leopoldo, NI611
Serrano Muñoz, Mariano, GU1246
Setzekorn, William David, BE171
Sevilla Sacasa, Guillermo, NI612
Sevilla Sacasa, Oscar, NI613
Sexton, James D., GU1247
Seymour (Captain), NI614
Sharpe, Reginald, BE172
Shaw, Mary, GU1248
Shaw, R. Paul, CR1008
Shaw, Royce Q., CA868
Sheldon, Henry Isaac, NI615
Shoman, Assad, BE22
Sibaja Chacón, Luís Fernando, CA869; CR1009
Sicard, Félix, CA870
SIECA. See Secretaría Permanente del Tratado General de Integración Económica Centroamericana
Sieckavizza A., Luís, GU1249
Sierra Franco, Aurora, GU1250
Sierra Franco, Raúl, CA871
Sierra Roldán, Tomás, GU1251
Sifontes, José María, ES188
Silva, Federico, NI616
Silva, Fernando, NI617-19
Silva, José Enrique, CA305; ES379
Silva Badillo, José, BE173
Silva Ferro, Ramón de, HO414
Silva Girón, César Augusto, GU1252
Silvert, Kalman H., GU1253
Simmons, William E., NI620
Simposio y Seminario Técnico, CA873
Sivela y de Vielleuze, Francisco, CA872
Sivers, Jegór von, CA874
Skinner-Klée, Jorge, GU1254-56
Slade, William Franklin, CA875
Sladek, Jaromir, CR1010
Slutsky, Daniel, CA117
Smith, John Lawrence, NI621
Smith, Waldeman R., GU1257
Smutko, Gregorio, NI622
Snedaker, Samuel C., GU250
Snee, Carole A., GU1258
Sobalvarro Arauz, Manuel, NI623
Sol, Ildo, pseud. See Solórzano Ocón, Ildefonso
Sol, Ricardo, ES380
Solano, Juan Andres, CR1011
Solano Asta-Buruaga, Francisco. See Asta-Buruaga y Cienfuegos, Francisco Solano
Solano Guzmán, Gustavo, GU1259-60
Solera Rodríguez, Guillermo, CR1012-16
Soley Güell, Tomás, CR1017-20
Solís, César G., GU1261
Solís Da Costa Gómez, Marcial, HO415
Solís Morales, José, GU1170
Solombrino Orozco, Vicenzo, GU1262
Solórzano, Carlos, CA876
Solórzano Calvo, Fabio, CR1021
Solórzano Fernández, Valentín, GU1263
Solórzano Ocón, Ildefonso, NI624
Solow, Antole A., CR1022
Soltera, María, pseud. See Lester, Mary
Somarriba Salazar, Jaime, CA877
Somoza García, Anastasio, NI626
Somoza Vivas, Fernando, GU1264; HO416-18

Sonnenstern, Maximilian von, ES381; NI627
Soothill, Jay Henry, CA484
Soriano de Guerrero, Lola, CA389; Ni305-16
Sotela Bonilla, Rogelio, CA878
Sotela Montagne, Hiram, CR160
Soto, Enrique, CA884
Soto, Marco Aurelio, HO419
Soto, Pedro, NI628
Soto Blanco, Ovidio, CA879-80; CR1023
Soto de Avila, J. Victor, CA881-82
Soto de León, Carlos Enrique, GU1265
Soto-Hall, Máximo, CR1024; GU748, 1266-69; NI629-30
Soto Picado, Francisco. See Picado Soto, Francisco
Soto Valenzuela, Marco Antonio, NI631
Soza, José María, GU1270-71
Spain, Mildred W., CA883
Spano, Angelo F., BE187
Sperlich, Elizabeth Katz, GU1272
Sperlich, Norbert, GU1272
Spielmann, Hans O., GU1273
Spino, Stelio, pseud. See Pérez Maldonado, Raúl
Spitzler, James R., CA884
Squier, Ephraim George, CA885-86; HO420-23; NI632-35
Staudenmayer, L.R., CA887
Stavenhagen, Rodolfo, CA888
Steffan, Alice Jacqueline (Kennedy), GU1274
Steffan, Jack, pseud. See Steffan, Alice Jacqueline (Kennedy)
Stephan, Charles H., GU1275
Stephens, John Lloyd, CA889-90; CR1025
Stewart, Watt, CR1026
Stewart, William Frank, NI636
Stimson, Henry Lewis, NI637-38
Stokes, William Sylvane, HO424
Stöll, Otto, GU1276-77
Stone, Doris Zemurray, CR1027
Stone, Samuel, CR1028
Stout, Peter F., NI639
Stowell, Ellery Cory, GU1278
Strachan, R. Kenneth, CR1029
Strandnaes, Børge, CA891
Strangeways, Thomas, NI640
Straughan, Robert P.L., BE174
Stuckle, Henry, NI641
Stucky, Milo, CR1030
Suarez, Alberto, GU1279
Suárez, Belarmino, ES382
Suárez López, Gerardo, NI642-43
Suárez Zambrana, Guillermo, NI644
Suay, José E., ES383-89
Suckau, Henri de, HO425
Sue, Joseph, CA892
Sullivan, John T., NI645
Sum Sacalxot, Maria Amalia, GU1280
Suñol Leal, Julio C., CA893
Suñol, Julio, CR1031-32
Suslow, Leo A., GU1281
Sutter, Víctor Arnoldo, ES385
Swan, Michael, BE176
Swan, Philip L., CA424
Swett, Charles, BE177
Szászdi, Adam, CA894

Taft, William Howard, CR1033
Tamames Gómez, Ramón, CA895
Taplin, Glen W., CA896
Taracena Flores, Arturo, GU1282
Taube, Evert, GU1283
Tauber, Arnost, CA83
Tax, Sol, CA897; GU1284-85
Taylor, B.W., NI646

Taylor, Bayard, CA898
Taylor, Douglas MacRae, BE178
Taylor, Greer, CA966
Taylor, Henry Clay, NI647
Taylor, James Milburn, CA899
Téfel Vélez, Reinaldo Antonio, NI648
Teletor, Celso Narciso, GU1286-87
Tellez Garcia, Rafael Armando, GU1288
Tempsky, Gustav Ferdinand von, GU1289
Terán, Francisco, NI649
Tercero, Rafael Antonio, ES386-87
Termer, Franz, CA900; GU1290-92
Thiel, Bernardo Augusto, CR1034-36
Thomas Gallardo, Frank J., CR1037
Thomé de Gamond, Aimé de, NI650
Thompson, George Alexander, GU1293
Thompson, John Eric Sidney, BE179
Thompson, Maury Wheldon, HO427
Thompson, Nora Belle, GU1294-95
Thompson, Wallace, CA901
Thompson Quirós, Emmanuel, CR1038
Thorpe, John, BE50
Tijerino, Gustavo, NI651-52
Tijerino, Toribio, NI653
Tijerino Molina, Bayardo, NI654-55
Tikhomirov, V.P., CA902
Tilev, H., CA903
Tinoco, Luís Demetrio, CR1039-40
Tinoco Granados, Federico, CR1041
T'Kint de Roodenbeek, Auguste. See Kint de Roodenbeek, Auguste T'
Tobar Cruz, Pedro, CA904; GU1296-97
Toledo, Salvador, GU1298
Toledo de Aguerri, Josefa, NI656-59
Toledo Ortiz, Alberto, NI660
Toledo Palomo, Ricardo, CA905
Tonblitz, C., CA906
Toness, Odin Alf, Jr., GU1299
Torbiörnsson, Peter, GU1300
Toriello Garrido, Guillermo, GU1301-4
Torre Villar, Ernesto de la, NI661
Torres, Edelberto, GU1305; NI662
Torres, Lorenzo M., GU1306
Torres M., J. Alberto, CR378
Torres Padilla, Oscar, CR1042
Torres Rivas, Edelberto, CA907-9; GU1307
Torres Vicenzi, Fernando, CR1043
Toruño, Juan Felipe, ES389-90
Tosci, Manuel, HO428-35
Totonicapán, Department of, GU1308
Tovar, Rómulo, CR1044-45
Townsend Ezcurra, Andrés, CA910; GU1309
Toyama, Taeko, CA911
Travis, Helen Simon, GU1310-11
Travis, Ira Dudley, NI664-65
Trejo Castillo, Alfredo, HO436
Trejos, Alfonso, CA305
Trejos, José Francisco, CR1046
Trejos, Juan, CR1047
Trejos Escalante, Fernando, CR1048-49
Trejos Fernández, José Joaquín, CR1050-52
Trimino, Rogelio, HO406
Trinidad del Cid, María, HO437
Tristán Fernández, José Fidel, CR1053-54
Tróchez, Raúl Gilberto, HO438
Trullás y Anlet, Ignacio, CR1055
TSC Consortium, CA912
Tulane University, Middle American Research Institute, CA913-14
Tulio Salazar, Marco, CR1056

Tumin, Melvin M., GU1312
Tunnermann Bernheim, Carlos, CA915; NI666
Turcios Ramírez, Salvador, CA916-17; HO439-41
Turner, George P., ES391
Tweedy, Maureen, NI667

Ubico, Emilio, GU1314
Ulate Blanco, Otilio, CR1057-58
Ulloa, Cruz, ES392
Ulloa, José Ángel, HO442
Ulloa Zamora, Alfonso, CR1059
Unión Democrática Centroamericana, CA918-19
Unión Patriótica Guatemalteca, GU1315
United Fruit Company, CA920
United Nations, CA921
U.S., Congress, NI668
-House. Committee on Foreign Affairs, GU1316; NI669
--Committee on Foreign Affairs, Subcommittee on
    Inter-American Affairs. See McVicker, Roy H.
--Committee on International Relations, CA922
--Committee on International Relations, Subcommittee
    on International Resources, Food and Energy,
    GU1317
--Select Committee on a Canal or Railroad Between
    the Atlantic & Pacific Oceans, NI670
--Select Committee on Communist Aggression, GU1318-
    19
--Select Committee on Interoceanic Ship Canal, NI671
U.S., Congress. Senate, NI672
--Committee on Foreign Relations, CA923; NI673-75
--Committee on Foreign Relations, Subcommittee on
    Western Hemisphere Affairs, GU1320
--Committee on Interoceanic Canals, NI676-80
--Committee on Interstate and Foreign Commerce,
    NI681
U.S., Gov't of, NI682
-Department of State, CA926-27; GU1321-25; NI683-87
-International Cooperation Administration, CR1062
-Isthmian Canal Commission, NI688-89
-Navy, Hydrographic Office, CA924; CA925
-Nicaragua Canal Commission, NI690
Urbano, Victoria, CR1063
Urbina Castro, Cornelio, CR1064
Urcuyo Maliaño, Francisco, NI691
Ureña Morales, Gabriel, CR1065-67
Uriarte, Juan Ramón, ES393
Uriarte, Ramón, CA928
Urquidi, Víctor L., CA929
Urra Veloso, Pedro, CA930
Urruela, Rafael, J., NI692
Urrutia, Claudio, CA931
Urrutia, Miguel Ángel, GU1326
Urrutia Aparicio, Carlos, GU1327
Urrutia Flamenco, Carlos, ES394-95
Urtecho, José Andrés, CA932-33
Urtecho Jeamborde, Andrés, HO443

Valdés Oliva, Arturo, CA934-38; GU1328-30
Valdes Sandoval, Elias, GU1331
Váldez Illescas, Raquel Yolanda, GU1332
Valencia Robleto, Gilberto, NI693
Valenciano Rivera, Rosendo de Jesús, CA939; CR1068-
    69; NI694
Valenti, Walda, GU1333
Valentine, Lincoln G., CR1070
Valenzuela, Gilberto, GU1334-36
Valenzuela, José Reina, pseud. See Reina
    Valenzuela, José
Valenzuela Oliva, Wilfredo, GU1337
Valenzuela Reyna, Gilberto, GU1336

Valiente, Gilberto, ES396
Valiente Rodríguez, Oscar, GU1338
Valladares, José María, HO444-45
Valladares, León A., GU1339
Valladares, Paulino, CA940; HO446-47
Valladares, Víctor Manuel, NI695
Valladares, B., Abel Arturo, HO448
Valladares Rodríguez, Juan, HO449
Valladares Rubio, Manuel, CA941-42; GU1340-41
Vallbona, Rima de, CR1071
Valle, Alfonso, NI696-98
Valle, José, GU1342
Valle, José Cecilio del, CA943-48
Valle, Rafael Heliodoro, CA949-54; GU1343; HO88,
    293, 450
Valle Martínez, Marco Antonio, NI699
Valle Matheu, Jorge del, CA948; GU1344-47
Vallecillo, Carlos A., HO451
Vallecillos, Italo López. See López Vallecillos,
    Italo
Vallejo, Antonio Ramón, CA955-57; HO452-54
Vallejo Armijo, Antonio, HO455-56
Valois, Alfred de, GU1348
Van der Laat, J.E., CR1072
Van Sinderen, Adrian, CA958
Vanni, Manfredo, ES397
Vaquero, Francisco, ES398
Varela, Arturo, CA959
Vargas, Guillermo, CR1073
Vargas Coto, Joaquín, CR1074-75
Vargas Marín, Alvaro, CR1083
Vargas Robles, José Armando, GU1349
Varona, Esteban Antonio de, CR1076
Vásquez, Mariano, CA960-64
Vázquez, José Valentín, GU1350-51; HO457-61
Vázquez, Juan Ernesto, ES399
Vázquez, Mario, pseud. See Zúñiga Figueroa, Carlos
Vázquez A., Rafael, GU1352
Vázquez Martínez, Edmundo, GU1353-54
Vázquez, Andrés Clemente, CA965
Vázquez, Miguel Ángel, GU1355-56
Veani, pseud. See Narisco, Vicente A.
Vega, Juan Ramón, CA966
Vega Barberena, José Luís, GU1357
Vega Bolaños, Andrés, NI39, 700-703
Vega Rodríguez, Jorge, CR1077
Vela, David, BE180; GU1358-62; HO462
Vela, Francisco, GU1363
Velasco, Miguel Ángel, ES400
Velasquez, César Vicente, CA967
Velásquez, Rolando, CA968; ES401
Velásquez Cerrato, Armando, HO463
Velásquez Díaz, Max, CA969-70; HO464
Velez Barcenas, Jacinto, NI704
Veloz Goiticoa, Nicolás, ES402
Venero, Juan, CR1078
Venin, V.N., GU1364
Ventocilla, Fleodoro, ES403
Vera, Robustiano, HO465-66
Vergara Escudero, Eduardo, CA971
Véritas, GU1367
Vickers, Thomas Douglas, BE181
Vidal, Manuel, ES404
Vidaurre, Adrián, GU1368-70
Viejo del Carmen, Benque, BE182
Viera Altamirano, Napoleón, CA972-94
Vigil, Francisco, NI705
Vilanova, Santiago Ricardo, ES405
Villacorta Calderón, José Antonio, GU1371-74
Villacorta Cisneros, Abel, HO467

Villacorta Escobar, Manuel, GU1375-76
Villacorta Vidaurre, Lola, GU1377-78
Villafranca, Richard, CR1079
Villagrán Kramer, Francisco, CA975-80
Villalobos, Asdrúbal, CR1080
Villalobos, José Hilario, CR740
Villalobos, Lisandro, ES406
Villanueva, Luís Manuel, CR1081
Villar, Salvador, CR1082
Villaseñor y Villaseñor, Alejandro, BE183
Villasuso Estomba, Juan Manuel, CR1083
Villeda Morales, José Ramón, HO468-72
Villegas, Rafael, CR1084-85
Villegas, Rodas, Miguel, GU1381
Villela Vidal, Jesús, HO473
Vincenzi Pacheco, Moisés, CR1086-89; ES407
Víquez, Faustino, CR616
Víquez, Pío J., CR1090
Viteri Bertrand, Ernesto, CA979
Vivas R., César, GU1383
Vivas Rojas, César, NI704
Vives, Juan Luís, CR1091
Vives Fernández, Luís Ángel, CR969
Vivó Escoto, Jorge A., CA980
Vogel, Robert Cross, CR1093
Volio, Jorge, CR1094
Volio, Marina, CR1095
Vollmberg, Max, GU1384
Von Hagen, Victor Wolfgang, HO474-75
Vose, Edward Neville, NI707

Waddell, David Alan Gilmour, BE184
Waggoner, Barbara Ashton, CA981
Waggoner, George R., CA981
Wagley, Charles, GU1385-86
Wagner, Mortiz, CA845, 982; CR1096
Waisanen, F.B., CR1097
Walker, James, NI708
Walker, James Wilson Grimes, NI709
Walker, S.H., BE185
Walker, Thomas W., NI710
Walker, William, NI711-12
Wallace, Edward S., NI713
Wallace, James Allen, BE186
Wallace, Robert, GU391
Wallace, Robert. See Dunlop, Robert Glasgow
Wallich, Henry Christopher, ES408
Wallström, Tord Kjell Engemund, CA983
Walz, Thomas Harold, HO477
Wappäus, Johann Eduard, CA984
Ward, Anna Bell, GU954
Ward, P.L., NI120
Wardlaw, Andrew B., CA985
Warren, Kay B., GU1387
Watkin, Virginia G., CA986
Wauchope, Robert, CA987-88
Webre, Stephen, ES409
Weddle, Ken, HO478
Weffort, Francisco C., CR918
Weitzel, George T., NI714-15
Welch, Edward H., GU1388
Wells, William Vincent, HO479; NI716
Wendt, Herbert, CA989
Wessing, Koen, NI717
West, Quentin M., CR873
West, Robert Cooper, CA990
Weston, Julian A., CR578
Weyl, Richard, CA991-92
Wheeler, John Hill, NI718
Wheelock Román, Jaime, NI719-22

Whetten, Nathan L., GU1389
White, Alastair, ES410
White, Edward Douglas, CA993
Whitman, Edmund S., GU1390
Wiener, Charles, CA492
Wilgus, Alva Curtis, CA994-95
Wilhelm, Prince of Sweden, GU1391
Williams, Alfred, NI723
Williams, Mary Wilhelmine, CA996-97
Wilson, Charles Morrow, CA998-1001
Wilson, H.G., CR1098
Wilson, James, GU1392
Winiarski, Andrzej, CA1002
Winn, Wilkins B., HO480
Winter, Nevin Otto, GU1393
Wisdom, Charles, GU1394
Wolters, J., CR1099
Wong Galdamez, Enrique, GU1395
Wood, Josephine, GU1396
Woodbridge, Paul, CR1100
Woods, Clyde M., GU1397
Woodward, Ralph Lee, Jr., CA1003; BE187; GU1398
Woolrich B., M.A., BE188
Wright, Hamilton Mercer, ES412; GU1399
Wright, John, NI724
Wright, Marie Robinson, ES413
Wright, Philip B., BE27
Wug de León, Emperatriz, GU1400
Wyld Ospina, Carlos, GU1401-5
Wylie, Kathryn H., CA1005
Wynia, Gary W., CA1006

Yanes Díaz, Gonzalo, ES414
Ycaza Tigerino, Julio César, NI725-26
Ydígoras Fuentes, Carmen, GU1406-7
Ydígoras Fuentes, Miguel, BE189; GU1408-9
Ygelsias, Francisco María de. See Igelsias,
    Francisco María de
Ygelsias Castro, Rafael, CR1101-2
Ygelsias Hogan, Rubén. See Igelsias Hogan, Rubén
York, E.T., BE59
Young, Arthur N., HO481
Young, John Parke, CA1007-8
Young, Thomas, NI727
Ypsilanti de Moldavía, Jorge, HO482

Zaldívar Guzmán, Raúl, HO483
Zammit, J. Ann, BE190
Zamora, Blas, CR1103
Zamora, Ciriaco, CR1104
Zamora Castellanos, Pedro, CA1009; GU1410-11
Zamora Corletto, José H., CR1105
Zanetti, Antonio, CR1106
Zapata C., Adrían, GU1412
Zárate, Alvan O., GU1413
Zarco, T.B., GU1414
Zavala, Pablo A., GU1415
Zea Ruano, Rafael, GU1416-21
Zeceña, Mariano, GU1422
Zeceña Beteta, Manuel, GU1423
Zeissig, Leopoldo W., GU1424-25
Zelada Carrillo, Ramón, GU1426
Zelaya, José Santos, NI728-29
Zelaya, Manuel A., HO484
Zelaya C., Antonio, CA1010; CR1107-8
Zelaya Goodman, Chester José, CA1011; CR1109; NI731
Zelaya Lozano, Cecilio, HO485
Zelaya U., José M., NI731
Zelaya Villegas, Ramón, CR1112-19
Zeledón, José María, CR1120

Zeledón Matamoros, Marco Tulio, CA1012-16; CR1121-28

Zerón h., José, HO486

Zikmund, Miroslav, CA405

Zirión, Grace H. de, GU1427

Zumbado, Fernando, CR1129

Zúñiga, Francisco, CR1130

Zúñiga, Luís Andrés, HO487

Zúñiga, Melba, HO488

Zúñiga Díaz, Miguel, CR1131-33

Zúñiga, Figueroa, Carlos, HO489

Zúñiga Huete, Ángel, CA1018; GU1428; HO490-96

Zúñiga Huete, José Ángel, NI732

Zúñiga Huete, Manuel Guillermo, HO497

Zúñiga Montúfar, Gerardo, GU1429

Zúñiga Montúfar, Tobías, CR1134-38

Zúñiga, Tristan, Virginia, CR1139

Zúñiga V., Medardo, CA1019

Subject Index

ABC standardized test, GU1222
Abortion
-Costa Rica, CR1096
-Guatemala, GU865
La Academia Guatemalteca, GU1358
Academy of History of El Salvador, ES93-94
Acción Democrática (Venezuela), CR177
Acosta García, Julio, CR184, 736, 807
Admas, Richard Newbold, GU432
Adolescents, CA472, CR195, 521
AEG de Berlin, CR392
Agency for International Development, CA44, 872;
    CR151, 593, 970
Agriculture. See individual countries
Aguacatán (Guatemala), GU815
Aguán River Valley (Honduras), HO320
Aguardiente in Guatemala, GU1201
Agüero Chaves, Arturo, CR67
Aguilar, Manuel R., ES371
Aguilar Barquero, Francisco, CR663
Aguilar-Wicker Contract, CR1112
Aguirre, José M., HO4
Aguirre y Salinas, Osmín, ES58, 73-74
AID. See Agency for International Development
Alajuela, Department of (Costa Rica), CR18, 22, 90,
    182, 256, 386, 448, 504, 688, 699, 756, 804,
    878-79, 882, 912, 936, 944, 949
Alberdi, Juan, GU783
Alcoholism
-Costa Rica, CR293, 494, 832-33
-El Salvador, ES275, 284
-Honduras, HO6, 121, 443
-Nicaragua, CA396
-Panama, CA396
Alfaro, José Miguel, CA296
Alfonso XIII, 1906 ruling (Honduras-Nicaragua
    boundary dispute), CA35, 82, 111, 127, 132, 161,
    163, 245-46, 425, 438-39, 441-42, 462, 466, 565-
    66, 578, 608, 625, 645, 686, 702, 723, 751, 833,
    877, 932-33; NI541
Alianza de la Juventud Democrática Guatemalteca,
    GU31
Alliance for Progress, CA39, 893; HO468; NI198
Alsina, Avelino, CR400
Alta Verapaz, Department of Guatemala, CA851; GU54,
    205, 345-47, 441, 533, 760, 790, 1012, 1082,
    1123, 1163, 1175, 1194, 1224, 1403
Altamirano, Adolfo, NI394
Los Altos, CA165, 559; GU34, 243, 909-10, 1090, 1128
Alvarado Abella, Francisco, CR960
Alvarado Family, CR659
Alvarado Manzano, Rafael, HO173

Alvarez Ovalle, Rafael, GU1216
Amapala (Honduras), HO245, 387, 445-45
Amatitlán (Guatemala), GU293, 355
American Atlantic and Pacific Ship Canal Company,
    NI105, 188-89
American Bible Society, CA471
American Geographic Society, CR849
American Historical Exposition in Madrid, CR766
American-Honduras Company, HO21-22
American Institute of Agricultural Studies, CR697
Amighetti, Francisco, CR38, 462, 886
El Amigo de la Patria (Guatemala), CA946, 948; GU551
Amigos del País (Guatemala), GU1116
Ammen, Daniel, NI202
Anales de la Sociedad de Geografía e Historia de
    Guatemala, GU548
Anderson Morúa, Luís, CR420
Anglican Church, BE39, 41, 123
Anglo-Guatemalan Treaty of 1859 (regarding Belize),
    BE20, 106, 168-69
Anglo-Guatemalan Treaty of 1863 (regarding Belize),
    CA32; BE5, 72-73, 103, 130, 140, 152
Anglo-Mexican Treaty of 1893. See Mariscal-Spencer
    Treaty of 1893
Antigua (Guatemala), GU6, 255, 283, 719, 810, 991,
    1055, 1083
Aquino, Anastasio, ES50
Arana, Francisco Javier, GU59, 656, 917, 1251
Arana Osorio, Carlos, GU58
Araujo, Arturo, ES48, 75, 207
Araujo, Manuel Enrique, ES64, 294, 335, 340; NI158
Araujista Party (El Salvador), ES335
Arawak Indians, BE178
Arbenz Guzmán, Jacobo, GU59, 137, 155-56, 182, 228,
    240-41, 264, 309-10, 326, 390, 400, 413, 455,
    461, 497, 530, 618, 628, 630, 635, 637-41, 644,
    647, 653, 655, 659, 672, 714, 716, 718, 727,
    739, 802-803, 806, 877, 915, 996, 1024, 1031,
    1105, 1210, 1233, 1235, 1251-52, 1304, 1318-19,
    1321, 1324, 1347
Arbitration of 1906. See Alfonso XIII, 1906 ruling
    (Honduras-Nicaragua boundary dispute)
Arce, Manuel José, CA42-43, 131, 339, 576, 821-22,
    941; ES371; GU1340, 1359
Architecture, CA546
-El Salvador, CA355; ES317
-Guatemala, CA355; GU292, 362, 813
-Honduras, CA355
-Nicaragua, CA355
Archives, CA363, 546, 696
-Belize, BE37

Archivo de Tierras, HO199
Archivo General de Guatemala, GU1028
Archivo Nacional, CR256-61, 667
Arévalo, Bermejo, Juan José, CA109, 813; BE109;
    CR1031, 1058; GU48, 72, 74, 77, 112, 118, 176,
    220, 235, 241, 276-77, 335, 340, 358, 384, 437,
    440, 455, 461, 576, 640, 650, 656, 672, 721,
    802-3, 805, 831, 842, 875, 878, 917, 956, 961,
    963-64, 995-96, 1059, 1105, 1166, 1251, 1281,
    1321, 1366, 1425, 1428; HO88
Arévalo Martínez, Rafael, GU69, 87, 95, 796, 1215
Argentina, CA918
-Relations with Central America, CA302-304
-Relations with El Salvador, CA313
-Relations with Honduras, HO150
Argüello, Juan, NI174, 604
Argüello, Leonardo, NI405
Argüello, Santiago, CA550
Argüello Mora, Manuel, CR60
Arias, Céleo, HO172
Arias, Juan Ángel, HO418
Arias Madrid, Arnulfo, CA742
Art, CA191, 546, 905
-Costa Rica, CR5, 46, 281, 352, 390, 462, 464, 490,
    907, 960, 1130
-El Salvador, ES158, 328
-Guatemala, GU33, 39-40, 46, 206, 221, 292, 362,
    472, 908, 981
-Honduras, HO67, 408
Asturias, Miguel Ángel, CA56, 484; GU27, 179, 265,
    282, 436, 500, 786, 798, 807, 1067, 1070, 1186,
    1250
Atchalán (Guatemala), GU940
Atenas (Costa Rica), CR699, 936
Atitlán (Guatemala), GU2, 881
Atitlán, Lake (Guatemala), GU1046, 1244, 1397
Atlantic and Pacific International Ship-Canal
    Company, NI385
Atlantic Charter, CA919
Atlantic Railroad in Costa Rica, CR605, 942
Atrato, Valley of, NI438
Aury, Luís, CA304; GU1214
Aviation services, CA924
-Costa Rica, 321, 623
Aycinena, Juan José de, CA576
Aycinena, Mariano de, CA821, 823
Aycinena, Pedro de, GU299

Bahía, Islas de. See Bay Islands
Baja Verapaz, Department of (Guatemala), GU1286
Balladares de Argüello, Angelica, NI489
Ballard Test, GU275
Banana companies, CA85, 212, 480, 614, 671, 687,
    737, 789, 920, 930, 1000
-Costa Rica, CR356-362
-Guatemala, GU131-32, 135
Banana contracts in Costa Rica, CR605
Banana production, CA2, 54, 75, 272, 483, 538, 569,
    852
-Costa Rica, CA2; CR117, 211, 228, 240-41, 297, 331,
    381, 422-24, 427, 507, 520, 558, 658, 742, 829,
    837, 898, 909, 921, 1026, 1044, 1138
-El Salvador, CA2
-Guatemala, CA2; GU173, 175, 340, 462, 784, 1390
-Honduras, CA795; HO20, 29, 82, 119, 202, 239, 261,
    320, 436, 442
-Nicaragua, NI126, 423, 562, 578
Banana strikes,
-Costa Rica, CR423-24, 427, 520
-Honduras, HO018, 20, 81, 239

Banana taxation in Costa Rica, CR87, 117, 605
Banana workers unions, CA614
Banco Agrícola Hipotecario (Costa Rica), CR1085
Banco Anglo-Costarricense, CR666
Banco Atlantico Americano, NI136
Banco Central (Costa Rica), CR263, 840
Banco Centroamericano de Integración Económica,
    CA29, 87, 682
Banco de Costa Rica, CR868
Banco de Guatemala, GU549
Banco de la Unión (Costa Rica), CR98, 868
Banco Hipotecario (El Salvador), ES110
Banco Nacional de Costa Rica, CR391
Banco Nacional de Nicaragua, NI50
Banco Nacional de Seguros (Costa Rica), CR1120
Banking. See individual countries
Banking nationalization. See individual countries
Baptist Church, CA539; BE62, 67
Barahona, Manuel F., HO140
Barahona, Streber, Oscar, CR80
Barba (Costa Rica), CR208, 1013
Barberena, Santiago Ignacio, ES30
Barcenas Meneses-Esguerra Treaty of 1928, NI731
Barillas, Manuel Lisandro, GU146, 554, 794-95, 1088
Barnoya, Ignacio, GU147
Barnoya Family, GU149
Barrantes Family, CR83
Barrios, Gerardo, CA222, 451, 916; ES23, 67, 76,
    148, 182, 185, 257, 352; GU332, 629, 774, 933;
    HO177
Barrios, Justo Rufino, CA71, 508, 511, 621, 754,
    842, 928; ES240, 350; GU21, 24, 28, 37, 103,
    162, 165, 197, 213, 219, 242, 244, 249, 284-85,
    297, 365, 369, 417, 469, 474, 492, 510, 540,
    557, 559, 683, 705, 763a, 769, 820, 843-44, 861,
    883, 897, 982, 1013, 1092, 1101, 1121, 1144,
    1180, 1329, 1340, 1357, 1401, 1422; HO25, 419
Barroeta Family, CR659
Barrundia, José Francisco, CA338, 576; GU791, 1359
Barzuna, Miguel, CA296
Base communities, NI622
Basic foodstuffs. See individual countries
Batres, Luís, GU47
Batres, Pepe. See Batres y Montúfar, José
Batres y Montúfar, José, GU120, 344, 911, 1215
Bay Islands, BE47; HO12, 95, 115, 375, 378, 448
Beeche Argüero, Octavio, CR184
Belén conspiracy, CA784
Belgian Compagnie Commerciale et Agricole des Côtes
    Orientales de L'Amérique Centrale (Guatemala),
    GU987, 1088. See also Santo Tomás, colony of
Belgian immigration to Guatemala. See Belgian
    Compagnie Commerciale et Agricole des Côtes
    Orientales de L'Amérique Centrale (Guatemala);
    Santo Tomás, colony of
Belgium
-Relations with Costa Rica, CR899, 1099
-Relations with Guatemala, GU54, 178, 190, 193-95,
    213, 312-19, 417, 761, 790, 987, 1065, 1088
Belice: Tierra Irredenta, BE107
Belikin, BE53
Belizan Studies, BE132
Belize
-Agriculture, CA410; BE21, 40, 48, 56, 64, 74, 158,
    166, 179. See also individual crops
--Early 20th century, CA834
-Budgets, CA279
-Census data, BE111
-Citrus culture, BE23, 146
-Commission of Enquiry, BE115

-Courts. See Belize, judicial system
-Culture, CA211; BE99
-Economy, CA57, 62, 227, 410; BE4, 21, 29, 48, 59,
   67, 73-74, 80, 85, 96, 98-99, 122, 141, 146,
   153, 165-66, 171, 176, 184. See also Belize,
   industry; trade
--Early 20th century, CA834
--Mid-20th century, CA211, 227, 41
-Education, CA275; BE17, 31
--Mid-20th century, CA218
-Employment, CA7;
-Ethnic groups, BE28, 77, 116, 132, 184
-Finance, CA279
-Geography, CA62, 324, 335, 411, 494, 834; BE4, 25,
   53-54, 64, 68, 70, 74, 87-89, 94, 114, 141, 171,
   177
-Geology, BE69, 149
-Historical survey, CA169; BE25, 53, 60, 176
-Immigration to, BE29, 67, 80, 94, 113, 133, 147
-Income statistics, BE48
-Independence era, BE14, 96, 132, 135, 153
-Industry, BE179. See also Belize, economy; trade
-Labor, CA7; BE48
-Land ownership, BE22, 60
-Land use, BE22, 166
-Laws, BE30, 35, 65, 113
-Legislature, BE181
-Logging, BE21, 64, 87, 146
-Maps, BE33, 69, 182
-Mexican claims to, BE52, 54-55, 58, 75, 78, 81, 92,
   97, 117, 127, 134-37, 142, 144, 159-60, 167,
   173, 183, 187
-Military, CA227, BE82
-National Library, BE19, 24-25
-Population, CA7, 17-18, 73
--Mid-20th century, CA767-68
-Relations with United States. See United States,
   relations with Belize
-Social conditions, BE94
-Social customs, BE50, 121
-Social security system, CA7
-Society, CA227, 335, 410; BE4, 25, 50, 53, 67, 89,
   171, 177, 179, 184
--Late 19th century, CA494
--Mid 20th century, CA211
-Spanish claims to, BE45
-Taxation, CA279
-Tourism, BE64
-Trade, CA57, 834; BE64, 73, 96. See also Belize,
   economy; industry
-Transportation, CA57; BE70
--Mid-20th century, CA29
-Travel, CA211, 227, 335-37; BE50, 85, 101, 114,
   175, 177
--Late 19th century, CA494; HO309
--Mid-20th century, CA446
-Water problems in, BE70
Belize and Central American Common Market, BE96, 98
Belize Boundary Dispute, CA32, 191, 685, 790; BE1-3,
   5-6, 8-11, 18, 20, 32, 40, 45-47, 49, 51-55, 57-
   58, 60-61, 66, 72, 75, 77-79, 81, 83-84, 90-93,
   95, 97, 99, 101-11, 117-19, 122, 124-31, 133-34,
   136-40, 142, 144, 147-48, 151-54, 156-57, 159-
   64, 168-70, 172-73, 180, 184, 188-90; GU300,
   354, 531, 1160; NI685
-United States and, BE6, 166
Belize City, BE42-43, 86
Bello, Andrés, CR463
Belloso, Ramon, ES, 237
Belly, Félix, NI29, 385

Belmopan, BE15-16
Bentham, Jeremy, CA952
Bernstein, E.M., HO481
Bertrand, Francisco, CA940; HO11, 193
Betancourt, Romulo, GU84, 805
Bibliography, CA140, 168, 276, 354, 470, 477, 546,
   694, 786, 859, 950-51, 995, 998
-Belize, BE19, 24, 145, 158, 186-88
-Costa Rica, CR42, 94, 237, 287, 289-90, 368-69,
   373, 433, 669, 687, 703, 709, 743, 849, 908
-El Salvador, CA543; ES1, 112-15, 137, 291, 321
-Guatemala, GU87, 227, 339, 350, 414, 523, 610, 663,
   725, 735, 981, 1027-28, 1067, 1117-18, 1332,
   1336, 1371, 1406
-Honduras, HO54, 127-28, 160, 167, 171, 198, 205,
   339
-Nicaragua, NI102, 187, 279, 438, 460, 464
Biblioteca Nacional de El Salvador, ES112-15
Biblioteca Nacional de Guatemala, GU1357
Biblioteca Nacional de Nicaragua, NI460
Bidlack-Mallarino Treaty, NI437
El Bien Publico (Quezaltenango), HO172
Birdseye, Sidney H., CA372
Birth control. See individual countries
Birth rates. See individual countries
Bishop, A.E., HO480
Black Christ of Guatemala. See Esquipulas, Black
   Christ of
Blaine, James G., CA376
Bluefields (Nicaragua), NI88, 114, 224, 374, 470,
   495
Boaco, Department of (Nicaragua), NI305
Board of Trade of San Francisco, NI418
Bogota Conference, GU354, 957
Bógran Barahona, Luís, HO025, 384
Bolaños, Pio, NI106
Bolívar, Jose Simón, CA124, 134, 507, 513, 791;
   CR24; GU48, 842; NI145
Bolivia, BE133; GU893
Bonilla-Gámez Treaty of 1894, CA35, 82, 932
Bonilla, Manuel, CA965; HO321, 382, 418, 445
Bonilla, Pedro H., HO413
Bonilla, Policarpo, HO23, 101, 133, 283, 293, 307,
   344, 476
Boruca Indians, CR285; GU1027
Boston Fruit Company, CA1000
Botelo, Francisco Antonio Xavier, HO174
Boundary disputes in Central America, CA463. See
   individual countries involved in disputes
Boy Scouts in Guatemala, GU675
Brazil
-Belgian colonies in, GU178
-Relations with Guatemala, GU143, 234
Brenes Córdoba, Alberto, CR155
Brenes Mesén, Roberto, CR348, 465, 941
Bretton Woods Conference, CR413-14
Bribri Indians, CR889
British Central American Land Company, NI119
British Guiana, BE80
British Honduras Settlement Commission, BE80
British Immigration
-Costa Rica, CR118, 782
-Guatemala, GU532
-Nicaragua, NI640
Brito (Nicaragua), NI46, 189
Bryan-Chamorro Treaty, CA344, 617, 869; ES42; NI4,
   23, 31, 47, 61, 153, 166-67, 206, 223, 254-56,
   405, 472, 538, 572-75, 577, 587, 606, 653, 663,
   673, 714-15, 731

Budgets. See individual countries
Buitrago, Pablo, NI473
Bustillo, Miguel Ángel, NI454

Cabañas, Department of (El Salvador, ES400
Cabañas, José Trinidad, HO197, 287
Cabezas, Puerto, NI164
Cabezas, Rigoberto, NI5
Cabo de Gracias a Dios (Nicaragua), NI374, 522
Cabrera, Francisco, GU472
Cacao production, CR381
CACTO, GU325
Cádiz, Cortes of, CA330, 342, 782, 784, 942; GU490, 538
Cagliero, Giovanni (Juan), CA106
Caja de Conversion (Costa Rica), CR1018
Cakchikel Indians, GU163
Calderón Guardia, Rafael Ángel, CA742; CR7, 12, 40, 53, 86, 132, 141, 156, 219, 225, 328, 430, 460, 707, 724, 742, 778, 813, 919, 951, 975, 1011, 1043, 1081
Calvo, Francisco, CR819-823
Cambridge Expedition to Belize, BE50
Campaña Nacional. See Walker, William
Campeche (Mexico), GU945
Campos, Rafael, ES67, 359
Canada, relations with Costa Rica, CR1033
Canadian immigration to Costa Rica, CR782
Canal Location Question, CA32, 91, 167, 603, 662, 790, 814, 869, 996; CR29, 59, 118, 428, 664-65, 1100; HO49-50, 59, 63; NI2, 6, 23, 29, 31, 41-47, 66, 68-70, 89-91, 93, 95, 99-101, 104-5, 108-9, 124, 139, 143, 153, 166-67, 188-89, 192, 202-6, 208, 223, 235-36, 240-41, 246, 251-52, 254-56, 269, 275, 280, 322, 336-38, 346, 348, 352, 358, 364-67, 369-71, 373, 375, 384-85, 390, 392-93, 395, 399-401, 405, 410, 414-18, 420, 437-38, 572-75, 577, 587-88, 614-15, 620-21, 627, 632-34, 639, 641, 645, 647, 650, 654, 664-65, 668, 670-73, 676-82, 684, 688-89, 692, 708-9, 714-15, 723-24, 731
Cañas de Trujillo, Juan Manuel, CR482
Cañas Escalante, Alberto F., CR590
Cañas y Villacorta, José Simeón, CA236, 500, 530-31, 800; ES107, 145, 159
Cane (Honduras), HO279
Cane sugar production, CR268
Canesa, Roberto Edmundo, ES204
Cantarranas. See San Juan de Flores
Cantel (Guatemala), GU969
Captaincy General of Central America. See Central America, Captaincy General of
Captaincy General of Yucatán. See Yucatán, Captaincy General of
Capuchin Order, CR51, 985; GU216
Carazo, Department of (Nicaragua), NI306, 412
Carazo Odio, Rodrigo, CR88
Cardenal, Ernesto, NI128, 146, 148, 300
Cardenas, Adam, NI535
Cárdenas del Río, Lazaro, CR778
Cardona, Rafael, CR744
Cardona Peña, Alfredo, CR196
Cardoza y Aragón, Luís, GU837
Carías Andino, Tiburcio, HO7, 17, 19-20, 39, 85, 88, 102, 140-44, 154, 169-70, 183, 207-8, 239, 242, 252-54, 268, 271, 281, 284, 288-89, 294-95, 338, 342, 345-46, 348, 351-52, 366, 385-86, 407, 411, 437, 456, 462, 486, 490, 493-94, 496
Carib Indians, CA353; BE110, 179; GU9

Caribbean, CA416, 990-91, 996, 1000, 1004, 1017; CR52; NI373, 420
-Relations with United States, CA491; NI716
Caribbean coastal region, CA402
-Costa Rica, CR212, 380-82, 453, 558, 796, 1112
-Guatemala, GU36
-Honduras, HO81-82, 110
-Nicaragua, BE47; NI133, 136
Caribbean Free Trade Association (CARIFTA), BE98
Caribbean Fruit Company, CR837
Caribbean Legion, CR36, 622, 1058; NI85, 213
CARIFTA. See Caribbean Free Trade Association
Carrera, José Rafael, CA50, 71, 290, 486, 552, 628, 731, 842, 906; BE67; GU165, 169, 181, 246, 249, 279, 301, 306, 332-33, 343, 403, 469, 611, 774, 838, 909, 924, 933, 945, 1081, 1090, 1297, 1348, 1398; HO197
Carrera, Sotero, GU246
Carrillo (Costa Rica), CR584
Carrillo Colina, Braulio, CA758; CR113, 180, 448, 600, 799, 810, 1038
Carro Zúñiga, Alfonso, CR88
Cartagena (Spain), CA114
Cartago (Costa Rica), CA245, 711-12; CR108, 162, 236, 257, 278, 299, 433, 448, 468, 603, 722-23, 741, 838, 857, 901, 905, 983, 990, 1011
-Colegio de, CR624
-Earthquake of 1910, CR236, 440, 468
-Santuario de Nuestra Señora de los Ángeles, CR108, 901
Carvajal, Maria Isabel. See Lyra, Carmen
Casa de la Cultura de Occidente, GU1135
Casa H. de Sola e Hijos, ES385
Casanova y Estrada, Ricardo, GU1103
Casariego, Mario, GU252
El Caso Nicaragua, NI405
Cassel, J.G., HO480
Castellón, Francisco, NI109
Casteñeda, Ramon Blanco, GU837
El Castillo (Nicaragua), NI617-18
Castillo, Pedro Pablo, CA800
Castillo Armas, Carlos, GU137, 155-56, 228, 238, 264, 271-73, 309, 326, 447, 455, 534, 543, 545, 556, 571, 583, 589, 614, 618, 634, 637, 641, 643-44, 647, 649, 651, 655, 657-58, 661, 667, 714-15, 727, 776, 805-6, 818, 915, 951, 961-62, 966, 1108, 1274, 1301, 1310-11, 1316, 1318-19, 1347
Castrillo-Knox Convention, NI359
Castrillo Medina, Salvador, NI160
Castro, Fidel, GU264, 1056; NI86
Castro Madriz, José María, CA69; CR239, 557, 810, 818
Castro Soto, Florentino, CR1005
Catholic Action Movement, GU1244, 1387
Catholic Church, CA19, 104-6, 114, 364, 720, 763, 899, 939, 951, 966; BE36, 67, 150; CR51, 66, 73, 99-101, 108, 114, 171, 182, 438, 592, 653, 686, 705, 707, 722, 762, 804, 823-24, 863, 901-5, 976, 980-82, 984-85, 1035-36, 1066, 1068, 1103, 1114; ES53, 220, 252, 266-67, 372, 405; GU8, 147, 158, 182, 216, 226, 252, 257, 279, 352, 401, 409, 423, 442, 475, 482, 501, 536, 709, 711, 722, 754, 765-66, 877-78, 880, 906, 926, 934-38, 983-84, 1049, 1052, 1076, 1103, 1145-46, 1208, 1274, 1287, 1387; HO26, 131, 147, 151, 247, 401, 449, 451, 454; NI7, 257, 276, 300, 440, 622, 648
Catholic Union Party (Costa Rica), CR863
CEDAL, CA137

La Ceiba (Honduras), HO314
Celis, Santiago José, CA800
Census data. See individual countries
Center for the Study of National Problems, CR955
Central America. See also individual countries for
    entries pertaining to any of the specific
    nations
-Agriculture, CA54, 73, 89, 115, 125, 138, 175, 239,
    242, 316, 359, 409, 480, 483-85, 518, 538, 544,
    611, 700, 737, 852, 871, 980, 985, 1000-1001,
    1005. See also individual crops
--Late 19th century, CA329, 827
--Early 20th century, CA706, 726, 834-35
--Mid-20th century, CA185, 250, 253-54, 306, 458,
    519, 671, 747, 769, 856, 864
--Late 20th century, CA747
-Banking, CA610. See also finance
-Basic foodstuffs, CA138, 254, 256, 568, 747
-Budgets, CA279
-Captaincy General of, BE58, 61, 136
-Church-State relations, CA37, 48, 307, 452, 503,
    573, 720, 939
-Cities. See cities in Central America
-Class structure. See Central America, social
    structure
-Courts. See Central America, judicial system
-Culture, CA79, 94, 211, 305, 905, 1017
-Economy, CA20-21, 52, 61-62, 79, 88-89, 100, 102,
    108, 115, 119, 125-26, 171, 175, 179, 182, 186,
    212, 249, 257, 269, 278, 300, 314, 403, 409,
    412, 420, 453, 458, 465, 483-86, 569, 620, 852,
    854, 783, 870, 893, 901, 905, 977, 980, 984,
    994, 1000-1001, 1003. See also industry; trade
--Early 19th century, CA486, 788; CR224
--Mid-19th century, CA486, 874, 886; ES40
--Late 19th century, CA329, 461, 511, 827, 916
--Early 20th century, CA238, 406, 705-706, 726, 732,
    834-35, 916, 1007
--Mid-20th century, CA73, 138, 172, 184, 211, 248,
    250, 252, 254, 306, 311, 453, 474-75, 490, 514,
    521, 537-38, 540, 568-69, 606, 610-11, 626, 635,
    647, 664-65, 667, 671, 675, 680, 727, 737, 747,
    752, 802, 829-31, 846, 850, 855-56, 858, 864,
    866, 868, 871-72, 884, 908, 989, 1004, 1008,
    1013
--Late 20th century, CA747, 909, 1006
-Education, CA455
--Mid-20th century, CA218
--Vocational, CA136
-Employment, CA7, 109
-Ethnic groups, CA14, 89, 413
-Finance, CA306, 610, 923. See also Central
    America, banking
--Early 20th century, CA314, 705-6, 1007
--Mid-20th century, CA253, 279, 306, 858, 1008
-Flags, CA302
-Foreign corporations, CA99, 108, 119, 126, 467,
    474, 480, 509, 603, 611, 671, 807, 850, 865,
    893, 907, 920, 930
-Foreign ministers conferences, CA677
-Geography, CA62, 98, 121, 188, 258, 272, 318, 321,
    328, 371, 401-3, 445, 461, 472, 476, 489, 494,
    496, 568, 665, 678, 688, 705, 726, 745, 757,
    769, 779, 827-28, 834-37, 840, 844-45, 852, 859,
    889-90, 901-2, 982-84, 992, 994, 1001, 1004,
    1017; ES228; NI89
-Geology, CA228, 237, 314, 457, 461, 543, 836; ES228
-German trade with, CA225
-Historical survey, CA58, 65, 104, 115, 168-70, 180,
    209, 212, 282, 307, 348-50, 358, 389, 403, 420,

    472, 486, 504, 550, 562, 567, 589, 704, 719,
    726, 783, 842, 854, 886, 1003, 1009; CR31, 102
-Industry, CA125, 175, 250, 252-53, 306, 399, 424,
    453, 474, 519, 540, 611, 635, 727, 752, 769,
    871-73. See also Central America economy; trade
-Investment, CA63, 88, 119, 126
--Mid-20th century, ES127
-Labor, CA7-8, 183
-Land ownership, CA52, 125, 185, 242, 254, 453, 458,
    483, 519, 611
--Mid-20th century, CA856
-Land use, CA89, 239, 413, 665, 831
-Laws, CA213, 459, 518, 816
-Liberal Party. See Liberal Party
-Literacy, CA49, 217
-Military, CA68, 316, 535, 611, 622, 780, 1009;
    CR123, 191
-Military conflicts, CA780
-Multinational corporations. See Central America,
    foreign corporations
-Peasants, CA28, 52, 80, 254, 316, 519; CR357, ES16
-Photos, CA504, 924
-Planning, CA224, 802; CR154; GU785
-Politics, CA700, 780, 854, 994, 1003; CR191, 616.
    See also names of individual political parties
--Early 19th century, CA623, 785, 788, 842, 889-90;
    CR224; GU924
--Mid-19th century, CA452, 553, 573, 623, 842, 892
--Late 19th century, CA584, 591, 697, 623
--Early 20th century, CA359, 584-85, 590, 607, 764,
    792, 1007; CR581, ES15
--Mid-20th century, CA391, 423, 482, 510, 538, 585,
    593, 595, 611, 626, 755-56, 761-62, 809, 811-12,
    847, 850, 855, 858, 868, 908, 989, 1004, 1013;
    GU692; NI19
--Late 20th century, CA755, 930, 1006
-Population, CA7, 17-18, 49, 126, 138, 240, 242,
    346, 399, 414, 611, 921
--Early 20th century, CA314, 489, 753
--Mid-20th century, CA184, 319, 394, 672, 753, 767-
    68, 864, 866
--Late 20th century, CA394
-Public administration, CA276-77, 455, 468
-Public services, CA49, 184, 866
-Railroads, CA461, 523
-Relations with other countries. See individual
    countries
-Sex education, NI444
-Social conditions, CA121, 412, 483, 561, 827, 954,
    989
-Social customs, CA11, 61, 191, 258, 318, 402, 827,
    845, 853, 858
-Social security system, CA7
-Social structure, CA37, 116-17, 341, 359, 854, 888
-Society, CA11, 180, 399, 745, 779
--Early 19th century, CR224
--Late 19th century, CA494
--Mid-20th century, CA185, 211, 254, 864
-Statistics, CA909, 980, 985
--Early 20th century, CA835
-Taxation, CA752, 986
-Trade, CA61, 87, 100, 115, 125, 128, 175, 179, 182,
    212, 225, 248, 257, 269, 280, 294, 296, 300-
    301, 306, 329, 409, 424, 464-65, 487, 511, 518-
    19, 678, 726, 827, 829, 834, 852, 861, 907, 923,
    977, 985-86, 1005. See also Central America,
    economy; industry
--Early 20th century, CA314, 835
--Mid-20th century, CA521, 540, 727, 846, 850, 858,
    872, 884; ES127

(Central America)

-Transportation, CA41, 87, 120, 128, 464-65, 480,
    700, 769, 832, 912, 924, 1001
--Late 19th century, CA461, 827
--Early 20th century, CA726
--Mid-20th century, CA29, 172, 253, 255, 306, 321,
    402, 665, 856, 884
--Late 20th century, CA523
-Travel, CA13, 55, 61, 77, 86, 98-99, 104, 106, 120,
    211, 321, 485, 636, 700, 958, 995, 998
--Early 19th century, CA401, 445, 889-90
--Mid-19th century, CA315, 547, 844-45, 874, 892,
    898
--Late 19th century, CA494, 511, 827, 836
--Early 20th century, CA238, 258, 318, 496, 637,
    707, 745, 899, 901
--Mid-20th century, CA402, 405, 478, 545, 554, 636,
    769, 779, 891, 911, 983
-United States intervention, CA37, 56, 70, 72, 81,
    208, 344, 491, 594, 609, 632, 719, 741, 810,
    878; CR506
Central American Conference of 1910 (San Salvador),
    CA146
Central American Conference of 1911 (Guatemala),
    CA147
Central American Conference of 1913 (San Jose), CA148
Central American Conference of 1914 (Tegucigalpa),
    CA149
Central American Conference of 1934, CA47, 155; ES18
Central American Conference on the preparation of
    teachers for the middle grades, CA331
Central American Court of Justice, CA130, 156-58,
    344, 395, 434-35, 522, 548-49, 572, 750; NI4,
    31, 47, 166-67, 206, 253, 255, 366
Central American Exposition of 1897 (Guatemala),
    GU883, 1225
Central American Exposition of 1900 (Paris), NI408
Central American Free Trade Association, CA487
Central American Summit meetings, CA139, 761
Central American Transit Company, NI105
Central Bank in Costa Rica, CR413-14
Central Bank in El Salvador, ES358
Central Bank in Guatemala, GU555
Central Bank of Honduras, HO109, 190, 429, 481
Central Reserve Bank of El Salvador, ES52
Centro-América, ES60
El Centroamericano (León), NI660
Centro para el Estudio de Problemas Nacionales
    (Costa Rica), CR227, 599
CEPAL, CA325
Cerda, Manuel Antonio de la, NI174
Cerna, Ismael, GU258
Cerna, Vicente, GU539, 542, 1329
Cerron Grande Dam, CA224
Chacón, Lázaro, GU836, 853, 1009, 1014, 1179
Chacón, Juan Rafael, CR490
Chaltenango, Department of (El Salvador), ES146
Chamizal Case, CA770
Chamorro, Diego Manuel, CA366, 397; NI13, 170, 199
Chamorro, Emiliano, NI76, 116, 229, 404, 413
Chamorro, Fruto, NI181, 183-84, 276, 288, 557, 590,
    653
Chamorro, Pedro Joaquín, CA164; NI168, 259, 590, 704
Chamorro-Weitzel Treaty, NI574, 577, 714-15
Champerico (Guatemala), GU594
Chapin, Juan, GU3
Chapultepec Conference, CA918
Charter of San Salvador (1950), CA288
Chase and Sanborn Company, CA827
Chatfield, Frederick, CA785; HO286, 378; NI473
Chavarría, Lisímaco, CR744

Che Guervara, Ernesto, NI605
Chiapas (Mexico), CA159, 287, 501-2, 551, 571, 592,
    597-98, 770, 773, 794, 965; GU820, 839
Chicacao (Guatemala), GU2
Chicago Tribune, CA688
Chicago Universal Exposition, CR766
Chichicastenango (Guatemala). See Santo Tómas
    Chichicastenango
Chichigalpa (Nicaragua), NI80
Chicle production in Guatemala, GU967, 1325
Child's Report, NI708
Chile, GU452, 499, 1008, 1115
Chimaltenango, Department of (Guatemala), GU266,
    1245. See also Santiago Chimaltenango
China Kicha (Costa Rica), CR285
Chinandega, Convention of, CA721
Chinandega Department of (Nicaragua), NI80, 201,
    307, 541, 599
Chinautla (Guatemala), GU1108-9
Chingo Treaty, CA263
Chiquimula, Department of (Guatemala), GU249, 434,
    779, 852, 866, 1074, 1394, 1417
Chiquimulilla (Guatemala), GU1074-75
-Canal of, GU1074
Chiquirichaoa (Guatemala), GU815
Chiriqui canal route, NI614
Chiriqui Land Company, CR238
Choluteca, Department of (Honduras), HO158, 272
Chontales, Department of (Nicaragua), NI92, 308
Chorti indians, GU1394
Christian Democratic Party, ES164, 410; GU788, 710
Chirstmas, Lee, HO118; NI372
Chuarrancho (Guatemala), GU599
Church-State relations. See individual countries
CIA in Guatemala, GU51, 1303
Cisne, Islas de, HO099, 124, 136, 150
Cities, CA25, 120, 318, 321, 496, 832, 968
-Costa Rica, CA224, 832; CR8, 31, 49-50, 61, 82,
    124, 138-39, 150, 153, 182, 204, 208, 212, 231,
    266, 403, 483, 523, 548, 589, 726, 996, 1022
-El Salvador, CA832; ES12, 36, 56-57, 167, 198,
    200, 236, 394, 414
-Guatemala, CA832; GU151, 691, 887, 1000, 1160, 1243
-Honduras CA832; HO060
-Nicaragua, CA832; NI298
Citizenship
-Costa Rica, CR184; CR311, 667
-Honduras, HO055
Citrus culture, BE23, 146
Civil Code
-Guatemala, GU1423
-Honduras, HO410
-Nicaragua, NI112, 456
Class structure. See Social structure under
    individual countries
Clayton-Bulwer Treaty, CA362; BE164; NI90, 393, 437,
    632, 665
Cleveland, Grover, CA174, 397, 660, 869
Climate, CA237, 239, 314, 409, 489, 852, 925, 982,
    984
-Belize, BE88, 146, 185-86
-Costa Rica, CA681; CR93, 131, 206, 485, 754-55,
    793, 796, 890-93, 925, 934, 968-69, 993, 1079,
    1091
-El Salvador, CA237; ES31, 125, 208, 210, 213, 381
-Guatemala, CA237, 900; GU166, 178, 550, 884, 974,
    987, 1225, 1290, 1292
-Honduras, CA900; HO100, 179, 249, 266
-Nicaragua, CA681; NI275, 522, 646, 649
Coatepeque (El Salvador), HO40
Cobán (Guatemala), GU441, 760, 1082, 1377-78, 1405

Coco, Battle of (Guatemala), GU708
Coconut production, CR1112
Cocos Bay, CR485
Cocos Island, CR289-90, 495, 578, 647
Coffee production, CA483, 827
-Costa Rica, CR110, 128, 162, 202, 211, 422, 457,
    577, 652, 690, 712, 767, 770, 829, 869, 968,
    1072, 1079, 1093
-El Salvador, ES47, 70, 95, 100, 218, 264, 306, 349
-Guatemala, GU165, 229, 371, 399, 550, 593, 701,
    760, 947-48, 1035, 1096, 1202, 1267, 1381, 1385
-Honduras, HO334
-Nicaragua, NI126, 463, 720
Coinage, HO087, 484; NI459
Colombia, CA352, 999; CR1008; GU593; NI346, 731
-Relations with Costa Rica, CR379, 1008
-Relations with Nicaragua, NI731
Colon Free Zone, CA895
Colonial Era, CA65, 78, 89, 115, 170, 191, 282, 348-
    49, 503, 546, 696; BE4, 7, 12, 21, 28-30, 37-38,
    40, 45, 53, 58, 60, 67, 71-72, 82, 94, 101, 113,
    116, 133, 136, 147, 164, 172, 185; CR99, 108,
    211, 217, 224, 256, 368, 375, 433, 541, 550,
    601; ES36, 167; GU1, 24, 171, 322
Colorado River, CR484
Colotenango (Guatemala), GU1339
Comandante Zero. See Pastora, Eden
Comayagua, Department of (Honduras), HO94, 273, 482
Comayagüella (Honduras), HO033, 93, 208, 251, 379,
    440
El Comercio (Managua), NI48
Committee for Central America Cooperation, CA253
Common Market, CA29, 63-64, 66, 102, 108, 116-17,
    125, 128, 171, 175, 177, 179, 187, 213, 232,
    247, 249-50, 253, 261-62, 280-81, 294, 296, 300-
    301, 311-12, 325-27, 330, 347, 354, 377, 390,
    404, 418, 424, 453, 460, 467, 474, 487, 514,
    516-19, 521, 536, 540-41, 572, 606, 635, 664,
    667, 670, 675, 679-80, 682, 703, 718, 727,
    730,752, 830, 850, 855-58, 860-61, 864, 868,
    871, 873, 895, 907-8, 929, 967, 971, 975-78, 985-
    86, 1008, 1013, 1016; CR81, 479, 506; HO36, 122,
    470; NI648
-and Belize, BE96, 98
-and Costa Rica, CR81
-and El Salvador, ES78, 127, 218, 414
-and Guatemala, GU1300, 1380
Communications
-Costa Rica, CR796, 805, 996, 1019
--Early 20th century, CR229
--Mid-20th century, CR697
-El Salvador, ES128, 309, 395
-Guatemala, GU152, 154, 613, 1040
--Late 19th century, GU153
--Early 20th century, GU153, 411
--Mid-20th century, GU359, 728, 1129
-Honduras, HO97
Communism, CA28, 70, 188, 274, 341, 476, 509, 581,
    593, 613-14, 626, 807, 843, 930, 1002; CR10,
    123, 197, 364, 423-24, 427, 506-8, 588, 691,
    708, 715-16, 775-79, 826, 852; ES5, 17, 25, 37-
    38, 80-81, 156, 174, 244, 246, 251, 254-56, 261-
    62, 269, 301, 325, 337, 354, 377; GU50-51, 71,
    73, 78, 82, 90, 97, 104, 137, 182, 272, 309,
    326-27, 340, 377, 390, 425, 432-33, 437, 450-51,
    461, 471, 477, 484, 497, 544, 566, 571, 618,
    628, 630, 634, 638-39, 641, 645, 647, 651, 659-
    60, 682, 714, 716, 732, 739, 741, 755, 764, 805-
    6, 860, 907, 912, 921, 950, 957, 961-62, 964,
    968, 973, 1024, 1033-35, 1056, 1059, 1102, 1124,

1176, 1183, 1210, 1232-33, 1235, 1300, 1307,
1310, 1315, 1318-19, 1321, 1323-24, 1345, 1347,
1365-66, 1390, 1409; HO18, 20, 32, 47-48, 367-
69, 468, 471; NI98, 282, 294, 299-300, 361, 487,
594, 606, 626, 720, 722
Communist Party, CA614; CR227, 690; ES82; GU50-51;
HO18, 20, 31, 367-69
Compagnie Belge de Colonisatión (Guatemala), GU312-
19
La Compañía del Ferrocarril de Costa Rica, CR1061
Compañía Nacional de Electricidad (Costa Rica),
    CR1060
Compañía Nacional Hidroelectrica (Costa Rica),
    CR1060
Concepción (Guatemala), GU815
Conservation in El Salvador, ES324
Conservative Party
-Costa Rica, CR448
-El Salvador, ES360
-Guatemala, GU169, 181, 246, 306, 412, 469, 569,
    775, 868, 902, 1048, 1090, 1213
-Honduras, HO084-85, 142-43, 267, 285, 342, 344, 348,
    467. See also National Party
-Nicaragua, NI13, 32, 62, 76, 106, 116, 135, 170-71,
    174, 181-84, 195, 199, 213, 227-28, 259, 267,
    288, 318, 325-26, 359, 413, 442, 475, 485, 505,
    510, 557, 565, 590, 606, 637-38, 725
Constitutional Party, CR630
Constitutions, CA765; ES177
-Costa Rica, CA1014; CR11, 14-15, 121, 161, 189,
    262, 575, 858, 864, 1123, 1125, 1129
-El Salvador, CA1014; ES3, 85, 97, 109, 153, 175,
    177, 179, 198, 297, 303, 364, 366
-Guatemala, CA1014; GU396, 481, 492, 560, 569, 759,
    767, 824, 1153, 1203, 1227, 1253, 1255, 1354,
    1368
-Honduras, CA1014; HO98, 107, 194, 269, 274, 276,
    295, 308, 354, 424, 445-46, 452
-Nicaragua, CA1014; NI36-37, 341, 408
-Panama, CA1014
Consulado de Comercio de Guatemala, GU1398
Contreras, Alvaro, HO16
Cooperatives, ES98; GU281, 1139, 1258; HO277, 415
Copán, Department of (Honduras), HO299, 475, 480
Copán, Santa Rosa de (Honduras), HO83
Copper in Honduras, HO232
Córdoba, Matías de, CA393, 576; GU372, 1212
Córdova, Alejandro, GU19
Córdova, José Francisco, GU331
Corinto (Nicaragua), NI80, 249
Corinto, pact of, CR312
Corozal (Belize), BE43
El Correo Español (Mexico City), HO476
Cortés, Department of (Honduras), HO57
Cortés Castro, León, CR89, 327, 427, 718, 884, 919,
    1011
Cortés Fernandez, Otto, CR884
Cost of Living
-Costa Rica, CR91, 1083
-El Salvador, ES99, 123
-Guatemala, GU549, 592, 998-1000
-Honduras, HO201, 209
Costa Rica
-Agrarian law, CR971
-Agricultural credit, CR354, 1093
-Agriculture, CA44, 285, 410, 687; CR27, 44, 87, 93,
    179, 211, 228, 283, 286, 300, 331, 402, 412,
    505, 576, 652, 692, 712, 721, 725, 733, 750,
    796, 804, 873, 967-68, 971, 991, 1003, 1007,

(Costa Rica)
    1026, 1044, 1072, 1091, 1093. See also
    individual crops
--Early 19th century, CR772
--Mid-19th century, CR563
--Late 19th century, CR1079
--20th century, CR152, 205, 238, 928
--Early 20th century, CA803, 834; CR241, 268, 354,
    658, 672, 721, 770, 869, 898, 909, 1085, 1112,
    1138
--Mid-20th century, CA38, 306; CR151, 240, 322, 587,
    593-94, 605, 650, 662, 693-94, 696, 828, 837,
    936, 969-70, 988, 1005
-Aviation services, CR321, 623
-Annexation of Guanacaste. See Guanacaste,
    annexation to Costa Rica
-Asamblea Nacional Constituyente de 1949, CR262
-Atlantic railroad, CR605-942
-Autonomous public institutions, CR580
-Banking, CR41, 267, 301, 413-14, 476, 519-531, 546-
    47, 693, 868, 922, 1020. See also Costa Rica,
    finance
-Banking nationalization, CR12, 476, 479, 666
-Basic foodstuffs, CR91, 700, 1083
-Birth control, CR35, 39, 1097
-Boundary dispute with Nicaragua, CA174, 195, 203,
    205, 286, 397, 604, 648-51, 654, 659-61, 684,
    712, 716, 724-25, 869, 877, 1015; NI166, 183,
    516
-Boundary dispute with Panama, CA15-16, 30, 34, 67,
    96-97, 103, 194, 196-202, 204, 206, 229, 357,
    506, 564, 603, 624, 634, 687, 689-93, 697, 708-
    15, 717, 733-35, 738-39, 742, 872, 993, 1015;
    CR228, 711
-British immigration to, CR118, 782
-Budgets, CA279
-Canadian immigration to, CR782
-Catholic Union Party. See Catholic Union Party
-Census data, CR119, 282, 324, 566, 811, 1040
-Central bank, CR413-14
-Church-State relations, CA720; CR171, 336, 686,
    705, 771, 823, 863, 980-81, 984, 1035, 1068,
    1114, 1135
-Cities. See Cities, Costa Rica
-Citizenship, CR184, 311, 667
-Civil service, CR1064
-Civil War of 1834-35, CR448
-Class structure. See Costa Rica, social structure
-Colonization, CR594
-Commercial law, CR717, 1119
-Conservative Party. See Conservative Party
-Constituent Assembly of 1880, CR320
-Constituent Assembly of 1949, CR586, 591, 630
-Constitutional Party. See Constitutional Party
-Constitutions, CA1014; CR11, 14-15, 121, 161, 189,
    262, 575, 858, 864, 1123, 1125, 1129
-Countryside, CR367
-Coup of 1880, CR320
-Coup of 1882, CR314
-Coup of 1899, CR317
-Coup of 1902, CR315, 318
-Coup of 1906, CR319
-Coup of 1914, CR533
-Coup of 1917, CR698
-Coup of 1926, CR316
-Courts. See Costa Rica, judicial system
-Crime, CR396
-Cuban immigration to, CR343
-Culture, CA4, 211; CR38, 190, 291, 295, 1088
-Democracy, CR13, 15, 23, 25, 28-30, 40, 52, 62, 72,
    75, 110, 121, 147, 155, 166, 188-89, 248, 349,
    418, 437-38, 466, 474, 478, 502, 807, 1046, 1111

--Mid 20th century, CR132
-Dependency analysis of, CA909; CR44, 179, 351, 918,
    1028
-Dictatorship, CR156, 427
-Earthquakes, CR298, 440, 556, 1000, 1103
-Economy, CA57, 62, 410, 673, 775, 795; CR11-12, 14,
    26, 32-34, 41, 44, 63, 76, 81, 102, 110, 120-22,
    179, 186, 201-2, 211-12, 285-86, 321, 351, 386,
    420, 457-58, 476, 479, 494, 519, 545, 551, 558,
    576-77, 593, 610, 628, 654, 692, 700, 712, 796,
    808, 811, 925, 958, 965, 967-68, 991, 993, 1003,
    1006, 1017, 1019-20, 1022, 1026, 1028, 1047,
    1050, 1090, 1108, 1116, 1136. See also Costa
    Rica, industry; trade
--19th century, CR97
--Early 19th century, CR256-61, 563, 772, 1109
--Mid-19th century, CR256-61, 563, 754-55, 899,
    1073, 1096, 1109
--Late 19th century, CR98, 130-31, 142, 301, 609,
    766, 793, 853-54, 868, 922, 1003, 1078-79, 1102
--20th century, CR121, 150, 154, 205, 218, 226, 233,
    238, 243-44, 263-64, 284, CR291
--Early 20th century, CA317, 802, 834; CR87, 117,
    120, 124, 128, 159, 209, 213, 221, 229, 249,
    253-54, 267, 330, 385, 391, 421, 486-87, 547,
    605, 613, 619, 658, 661, 672, 721, 745-48, 750,
    770, 792, 805, 828, 870, 872, 898, 909, 922,
    933-34, 937, 962-63, 1018, 1061, 1072, 1085,
    1098-99, 1112, 1120, 1134-1138
--Mid-20th century, CA38, 211, 251, 306, 411, 865;
    CR80, 91, 151, 153, 183, 214, 231-32, 240, 267,
    270, 322-23, 327-28, 331, 349, 407, 413-14, 508,
    531, 544, 546, 589, 591, 594, 619, 621, 650,
    660, 662, 666, 693-94, 696, 701, 714, 725, 749,
    761, 780, 789, 829, 834, 837, 840, 874, 936,
    946, 955, 969-72, 988-89, 993, 1044, 1060, 1082,
    1093, 1122, 1129
--Late 20th century, CA909; CR291, 692, 702
-Education, CA275, 289; CR5, 14, 17, 30, 39, 48-49,
    69, 71-72, 112, 136-37, 280, 296, 335, 411, 447,
    466-67, 491, 496, 502, 537-38, 540-41, 552, 591,
    649, 657, 723, 804, 812, 814, 818, 824, 841,
    857, 867, 897, 904, 952, 954, 990, 1014, 1016,
    1023, 1030, 1045, 1050, 1053, 1068, 1073, 1088,
    1126
--19th century, CR17, 71, 178
--Early 19th century, CR1109
--Mid-19th century, CR1109
--Late 19th century, CR635
--20th century, CR222
--Early 20th century, CR157, 223, 324, 348, 405,
    624, 635
--Mid-20th century, CA218-19; CR619, 650, 697, 866
--Late 20th century, CR702
--Agricultural, CA44
--Primary, CR24, 280, 411, 467, 503, 866
--Rural, CR24, 174, 537, 593-94, 657
--Secondary, CA289; CR18, 280, 411, 657, 1030
--Teacher training, CR48, 223, 405, 657, 1030
--University. See Costa Rica, universities
--Vocational, CA45, 135; CR537, 657
-Educators, CR294, 333, 346-47, 468, 493, 543, 643,
    941, 1042, 1052, 1087
-Elections, CR29, 1117
--Mid-20th century, CR618, 781
--Election of 1889, CR883
--Election of 1902, CR248
--Election of 1914, CR843
--Election of 1926, CR671
--Election of 1940, CR919

--Election of 1944, CR1081
--Election of 1953, CR656
--Election of 1958, CR474, 517
--Election of 1966, CR830
--Election of 1967, CR827
-Electricity, CR253-54, 330, 406, 420, 660
-Elite, CR138, 521, 1028
-Employment, CA7, 219, 275; CR26, 119, 150, 234, 335
-Energy, CR330, 406, 420, 660, 792, 972
-Ethnic groups, CR380-83
-Extraditions, CR435
-Family, CR39
-Festivals, CR1133
-Finance, CA306; CR14, 41, 80, 98, 235, 265, 402,
    412-14, 476, 479, 519, 531, 546-47, 551, 580,
    654, 745, 828, 840, 1017, 1019-20, 1039, 1102.
    See also Costa Rica, banking
--19th century, CR551
--Late 19th century, CR301
--20th century, CR263-65
--Early 20th century, CR267, 934, 1018, 1120
--Mid-20th century, CA279, 306; CR267, 391, 666,
    693, 749, 761, 780, 1093, 1107
-Floods, CR556
-Foreign corporations, CR179, 228, 331, 385, 407,
    506, 650, 809, 1044, 1070, 1098, 1119, 1138
-Foreign loans, CR302, 353, 551, 561, 870, 977, 1033
-Foreign policy, CR19-20, 42, 861
-French immigration to, CR651
-Geography, CA38, 62, 167, 411, 472, 494, 636, 681,
    834, 841, 991, CR33, 93, 97, 122, 130, 209, 215,
    287, 295, 300, 322, 337, 356, 368, 375, 386,
    402, 485, 488, 492, 573, 646-47, 664, 674, 704,
    733, 755, 766, 793, 795, 811, 873, 890-93, 895-
    96, 925, 933-34, 942, 968, 993, 997, 999-1000,
    1003, 1047, 1067, 1079, 1082, 1086, 1096, 1133
-Geology, CR344-45, 378, 488, 492, 572, 793
-German immigration to, CA851; CR755
-Government organization, CR292, 580
-Historical survey, CA169, 472, 492, 698, 896; CR14-
    15, 31, 33, 45, 49, 78, 83, 334, 441-42, 447,
    553, 578, 735, 754, 759, 765, 800, 822, 861,
    1012, 1104
-Humor, CR352, 387, 459, 504, 559, 581, 633, 668,
    797
-Idioms, CR9, 67, 70, 105, 387, 439, 498, 585, 668,
    974, 979, 1075, 1092, 1139
-Immigration to, CR93, 243, 284, 311, 343, 383, 727,
    782, 796, 842, 855, 920, 1002, 1019
-Industry, CA306; CR39, 44, 110, 270, 792. See also
    Costa Rica, economy; trade
-Intellectual history, CR217
-Internal migration, CA832; CR119, 432, 991, 1008,
    1040
-Interoceanic railway, CR854, 958
-Investment, CA2, 687, 909; CR32, 179, 212, 218,
    228, 240, 353, 406-7, 412, 593, 609-10, 658,
    748, 792, 809, 853-54, 899, 1026, 1044, 1060,
    1070, 1107, 1112-13, 1116, 1120
--Late 19th century, CR1079
--Early 20th century, CR717, 934, 1099
--Mid-20th century, CR214, 270, 331
-Judicial system, CR396, 398, 525
-Juvenile delinquency, CR326, 948
-Labor, CA7, 275; CR26, 125, 175-76, 340, 593, 813,
    829, 835, 971
-Labor unions, CR73, 175-76, 436, 1049
-Land distribution, CA285, 594, 1008

-Land ownership, CA285; CR26, 44, 87, 112, 121, 205,
    230, 256-61, 286, 355, 363, 593-94, 612, 667,
    696, 712, 853, 970-71, 1093, 1138
--Early 19th century, CR772
--Mid-19th century, CR563
--20th century, CR928
--Early 20th century, CR721
--Mid-20th century, CR322, 697, 1005
-Land use, CR26, 286, 593, 662
-Laws, CA499; CR2-3, 85, 115, 167-70, 230, 238, 435,
    549, 575, 607, 617, 651, 738, 836, 839, 853,
    911, 916, 922, 956, 970, 1002, 1021, 1039, 1113
-Legislature, CR64, 263, 435, 501, 631-32, 781, 822,
    1016
-Liberal Party. See Liberal Party
-Life expectancy, GU157
-Literacy, CR14, 324
-Living standards, CR95-96, 679
-Maps, CA2, 38, 708, 832; CR50, 303, 371, 849
-Media, CR181, 480
-Middle class, CR64, 110, 138, 570, 785-87
-Military, CR186, 245, 252, 271-72, 315, 367, 816,
    865, 881, 900, 1084
-Multinational corporations. See Costa Rica,
    foreign corporations
-Municipal government, CR515, 654, 685, 916
-Municipal Registries, CR667
-Mythology, CR359, 361
-National anthem, CR642, 728
-National archives, CR667
-National Assembly. See Costa Rica, legistature
-National characteristics, CR181, 190, 496
-National Library, CR493, 709
-National Liquor Factory, CR201
-National Museum, CR729
-National Printing Company, CR493
-National Theater, CR1059
-National Tobacco factory, CR862
-Nationalism, CR412
-Nationalization of 1948, CR519
-Nationalization of the electric service, CR253, 420
-Northern Railroad, CR329
-Nutrition, CR608
-Oxcarts, CR670
-Pacific coast of, CR303, 485-87, 673, 739, 909
-Peasants, CR54, 77, 143, 145-46, 153, 197, 200,
    340-42, 354-65, 387, 395, 422, 424, 426, 429,
    462, 490, 494, 505, 510-14, 530, 587, 597, 676,
    679, 682, 690, 713, 720, 785, 789, 885, 888,
    921, 935, 973, 1007, 1010
-Penal institutions, CR56, 645, 680
-Petroleum, CR268, 533, 1070
-Petroleum contracts, CR230, 612, 809, 844, 1098
-Petroleum exploration, CR230, 249, 844, 1006, 1098
-Philosophy, CR65, 164, 669
-Photos, CR236, 243, 300, 458, 462
--Late 19th century, CR204, 266
--20th century, CR270
--Early 20th century, CR124, 159, 221, 266, 523
--Mid-20th century, CR270, 1076
-Planning, CA224; CR154
-Political parties, CA137; CR13, 28, 30, 36-37, 62,
    64, 68, 84, 121, 141, 147, 161, 177, 219, 227,
    248, 430, 455, 518, 781, 790, 830. See also
    individual parties and politics
-Political pressure groups, CR62
-Politics, CA896; CR15, 23, 25, 28, 33, 68, 78, 102,
    104, 181, 189, 349, 461, 554, 719, 800, 808,
    816, 821-22, 825, 858, 1003, 1005, 1012, 1017,

(Costa Rica)
      1022, 1028, 1037, 1046. See also names of
      individual political parties
--19th century, CR20, 59, 97, 185, 250-52, 1024
--Early 19th century, CA758; CR99, 258, 730, 771,
      1109
--Mid-19th century, CR60, 277, 410, 541, 553, 641,
      732, 764, 815, 818-19, 845, 911, 981, 1073,
      1109-10; NI91
--Late 19th century, CR98, 114, 130, 156, 158, 245,
      247, 252, 314, 317, 320, 402, 437-38, 455, 535,
      576, 625, 705, 769, 818, 841, 863, 868, 871,
      883, 910-11, 977, 981, 1002, 1068-69, 1078,
      1101-2, 1114, 1117
--20th century, CR6-7, 12-13, 20, 36-37, 43-44, 62,
      64, 66, 68, 74, 76, 88-89, 132, 161, 225-27,
      244, 291
--Early 20th century, CA493; CR1, 10, 19, 24, 29-30,
      40, 87, 117, 120, 123, 147, 155, 163, 166, 184,
      186, 188, 192, 230, 248-49, 315-16, 318-19, 346-
      47, 353, 385, 409, 419-21, 423, 455, 486-87,
      494, 532-33, 535, 547, 561, 567, 576, 581, 606,
      626-27, 637, 663, 671, 698, 706, 736, 747, 750,
      753, 770, 798, 807, 809, 828, 831, 843-44, 846,
      869-70, 898, 917, 932, 938, 962-64, 981, 987,
      1018, 1041, 1061, 1074, 1080, 1084-85, 1088,
      1094, 1098, 1101, 1108, 1112, 1115, 1118, 1134,
      1138
--Mid-20th century, CR10, 75, 80, 84-85, 96, 100,
      121, 132, 141, 295, 329, 349, 352, 360, 367,
      401, 407, 412, 418, 436, 460, 471-73, 475, 477-
      78, 501, 517-18, 521, 531, 544, 575, 580, 582,
      586, 588-89, 591, 595, 598-99, 604, 611, 618,
      621-22, 627, 630-32, 650, 655-56, 660, 666,
      686, 707-8, 715-16, 718, 724, 742, 757, 768,
      776-81, 786-87, 789-91, 813, 826-27, 830, 834,
      840, 850-52, 865, 876, 884, 919, 947, 951, 955,
      957, 972, 975-76, 988-89, 1031-32, 1043, 1048,
      1050-51, 1057-58, 1060, 1062, 1064, 1077, 1081,
      1095, 1107, 1111, 1122-23, 1127, 1132, 1135;
      NI502
--Late 20th century, CR291, 521, 692, 826-27, 918,
      1032
-Population, CA7, 17-18; CR35, 50, 76, 96, 119, 211,
      282-83, 285-86, 335, 403-4, 488, 566, 620, 702,
      741, 796, 808, 811, 925, 996, 1008, 1040, 1097
--Early 19th century, CR1034
--Mid-19th century, CR311, 563, 681
--Late 19th century, CR311
--Early 20th century, CR134, 311, 324-25, 747
--Mid-20th century, CR38, 219, 322, 345, 432, 522,
      608, 650, 672, 697, 767-68
--Late 20th century, CR432, 522, 702
-Ports, CA775; CR334, 270, 303, 321, 486-87, 651,
      714
-Postage stamps, CR279
-Presidents, CR313, 554, 631-32
-Public services, CA224; CR150, 796, 996
-Public works projects, CR327-28
-Railroads, CA803; CR87, 159, 203, 221, 228-29, 231,
      241-42, 383, 392, 457-58, 471, 664, 672, 748,
      805, 837, 958, 962-63, 965, 1026, 1061, 1136,
      1138
-Reformist Party. See Reformist Party
-Relations with Central America, CR42, 274, 506
-Relations with Guatemala, CR36, 158, 428, 874,
      1105; GU859
-Relations with Honduras, HO66, 223
-Relations with Nicaragua, CA658, 668-69, 684; CR36,
      52, 59, 116, 122, 220, 239, 246, 274, 277, 300,
      312, 430, 1009, 1090; NI34, 91, 203-6, 269, 364-
      66, 385, 415, 577
-Relations with Panama, CA742; CR61, 69, 962-63
-Relations with other countries. See individual
      countries
-Revolution of 1948, CA7, 668; CR6-7, 10-12, 37, 43,
      52-53, 64, 75, 86, 100, 103, 110, 141, 161, 198,
      216, 225, 262, 428, 430, 436, 473, 475-77, 479,
      530, 546, 551, 565, 580, 586, 598-99, 622, 630,
      656, 660, 666, 715, 742, 768, 790-91, 851, 876,
      1011, 1058, 1081, 1123, 1127
-Rivers, CR892, 1086
-Roads, CR244, 300, 302, 321, 327, 805, 1022, 1073
-Rural areas, CR523
-Rural society, CR54, 199-200, 356, 359, 361, 387,
      393, 445-46, 451, 544, 613-14, 652
-Social conditions, CA636; CR125, 198, 422, 521,
      530, 692, 706-7, 721, 729, 784, 789, 1051, 1095
-Social customs, CA223, 775; CR58, 95, 190, 544,
      559-60, 571, 700, 804, 1055, 1096
-Social Democratic Party. See Social Democratic
      Party
-Social life, CR804
-Social reforms, CR11-12, 44, 66, 431, 813, 1095
-Social security system, CA7; CR479, 780, 834, 957,
      1049
-Social structure, CR76, 135, 153, 163, 183, 351,
      363, 563, 697, 784, 834, 946, 989, 1010, 1028,
      1129
-Society, CA223, 410; CR4, 35, 38, 50, 61, 77, 86,
      95-97, 121, 181, 196, 198, 199-200, 202, 269,
      285, 380-82, 384, 393-94, 396, 451, 483, 494,
      596, 505, 559-60, 608, 614, 652, 785, 787-88,
      939, 946, 989, 1004, 1028, 1124, 1131-32
--19th century, CR97
--Early 19th century, CR256-61
--Mid-19th century, CR256-61, 726
--Late 19th century, CA 494; CR337, 766
--20th century, CR140, 226, 291
--Early 20th century, CA317; CR516, 613, 721
--Mid-20th century, CA211; CR144-46, 153, 214, 349,
      352, 508, 585, 589, 650, 783, 957
--Late 20th century, CR291, 692
--Rural, CR54, 199-200, 356, 359, 361, 387, 393,
      445-46, 451, 544, 613-14, 652
-Stamp tax, CR235
-Statistics, CA909; CR102, 135, 150, 153, 183, 232-
      33, 283, 335, 432, 483, 522, 628, 747
--20th century, CR264
--Early 20th century, CR651
--Mid-20th century, CR270, 725
-Students, CR574, 826
-Supreme Court, CR30, 1015, 1109
-Tariffs, CR701, 749
-Taxation, CA251, 279; CR353, 654, 749, 767, 1020
-Telephone and telegraph, CR805
-Tourism, CR379, 700, 760, 1067
--20th century, CR160
--Early 20th century, CR242
--Mid-20th century, CR939, 1133
-Trade, CA57, 306, 775, 834; CR32, 118, 179, 283,
      402, 413-14, 416, 610, 628-29, 700, 772, 899,
      925, 962-63, 1107, 1099, 1113. See also Costa
      Rica, economy; industry
--Early 19th century, CR772
--Mid-19th century, CR754
--Late 19th century, CR609, 1079
--20th century, CR265
--Early 20th century, CR128, 268, 651, 717, 747-48,
      934, 1099

--Mid-20th century, CR233, 270, 650, 701, 714, 749,
    874
-Transportation, CA57, 636, 832; CR34, 87,
    203, 212, 228, 231, 244, 286, 321, 392, 457-58,
    471, 593-94, 623, 661, 664-65, 760, 805, 811,
    958, 965, 996, 1019, 1061, 1073, 1136
--Late 19th century, CR142
--20th century, CR242, 244, 303
--Early 20th century, CR159, 221, 229, 241, 486-87,
    523, 672, 748, 872, 962-63
--Mid-20th century, CA29, 38, 306; CR270, 302, 327,
    714
-Travel, CA98, 189, 211, 223; CR61, 379,
    471, 571, 739, 752, 942
--Early 19th century, CA775; CR443-44
--Mid-19th century, CR443-44, 706a, 1025, 1096
--Late 19th century, CA494; CR148, 895-96, 997, 1036
--Early 20th century, CA317, 662; CR213, 215, 746,
    1004; NI114
--Mid-20th century, CR700, 1067, 1105
-Treaties, CR306, 309-310
-Treaty of 1858 with Nicaragua, CA724-25
-United States aid to, CR725
-United States intervention, CR428, 430, 917, 1031
-United States investment in, CR558, 1098, 1120
-Universities, CA36; CR79, 174, 217, 234-35, 237,
    414, 499, 536, 574, 591, 758, 813, 824, 910,
    928, 954, 1023, 1030, 1052
-Urbanization. See Costa Rica, cities
-War of 1921 with Panama, CA692-93; CR711
-Water resources, CR299, 613, 892
-Women, CR5, 155, 848, 966, 995, 1080
-Women voting rights, CR1080
Costa Rica Oil Corporation, CR230, 1098
Costa Rica Railway Company Ltd., CR203, 242, 558
Costa Rican Academy of History, CR171, 333
Costa Rican Banana Owners Cooperative, CR228, 1138
Costa Rican Light and Traction Company, CR792, 1060
Costa Rican National Junta Electrica, CR660
Costumbrismo, CA495; CR47, 54, 56-57, 145-46, 165,
    356, 365-66, 374, 376, 454, 512-14, 614, 986;
    ES13-14, 16, 181
Coto Brus, Valle del (Costa Rica), CR593
Coto district (Costa Rica), CR711
Cotton production, CA1005
-El Salvador, ES47, 70
Cotton States Exposition, CR1079
Courts. See Judicial system
El Crédito Hipotecario Nacional (Costa Rica), CR41
El Crédito Hipotecario Nacional (Guatemala), GU581
Creole society in Nicaragua, NI440
Cromwell, William Nelson, CA689-91; NI681
El Crónica de la Habana (Havana), GU907
El Cronista (Tegucigalpa), CA940; GU1314; HO107,
    155, 242, 285, 295, 310
Cruz, Fernando, CA616
Cruz, Francisco, HO378
Cruz, Ramón Ernesto, CA366; HO36, 105-6
Cruz, Serapio, GU297
CSUCA, CA220, 275, 601; ES365
Cuadra, Manolo, NI129
Cuadra Cardenal, Pablo Antonio, NI304
Cuadro Pasos, Carlos, NI475
Cuba, CA407, 485, 999; CR343, 416, 639, 717, 837;
    ES80; GU825, 893, 1035, 1056; NI86, 198, 294
-Relations with Costa Rica, CR36, 343, 416
-Relations with Guatemala, GU264, 477, 825, 843-44,
    1056, 1360, 1409
-Relations with Honduras, HO47-48, 364, 468

-Relations with Nicaragua, CR36; NI594
-Relations with United States, CR416
Cuban Revolution, GU825, 1056
Cuchumatán Indians, GU765
Culebra, Gulf of, CR485
Culture. See individual countries
Currie, Leonard, CR50
Customs regulations, CA284, 673
Customs union in Central America, CA830
Cutter, Victor M., CR1044
Cuyamel Fruit Company (Honduras), CA789; HO436
Cuyamel, Valley of (Honduras), HO100
Cyclone Hattie (Belize), BE42, 44
Czechoslovakia, relations with Central America, CA79

Dallas-Calderon Treaty, CA361; BE164; NI393, 632
Dance, GU108, 588
Dardano, Carlos F., ES83
Dardón, Andrés, CA794
Darien Route (Nicaragua), NI246, 438
Darío, Rubén, CR65, 338-39, 644; ES202; HO303; NI15,
    149, 233-34, 250, 279, 444, 474, 500, 530
David (Panama), CA628
Dávila, Miguel R., HO340-41, 444-45, 476
De Lesseps, Ferdinand, NI43
Delgado, José Matías, CA193, 498, 529, 557, 575-76,
    800, 917, 941; ES35, 86, 118, 186, 203; GU1340
Democracy, CA342, 550, 755, 809, 813
-Costa Rica, CR13, 15, 23, 25, 28-30, 40, 52, 62,
    72, 75, 110, 121, 147, 155, 166, 188-89, 248,
    349, 418, 437-38, 466, 474, 478, 502, 807, 1046,
    1111
--Mid-20th century, CR132
-El Salvador, ES22, 78, 96, 174-75, 245, 282, 403
-Guatemala, GU97, 965
Dengo, Omar, CR223, 346-47, 543, 643
Denver (U.S.S.) conference, NI76, 413
Department of Middle American Research, CA913-14
Dependency analysis of, CA88, 108, 116-17, 606, 611,
    868, 907-9
-Belize, BE7, 21
-Costa Rica, CA909; CR44, 179, 351, 918, 1028
-Guatemala, CA909; GU40, 78, 104, 139, 198, 780
-Honduras, CA909; HO122, 257, 311
-Nicaragua, NI487, 653
Depression (1930s), CR12, 385, 531, 754, 942; ES17,
    45, 69, 207, 358, 360-61, 363, 399, 408; GU41,
    625, 1231; HO143
Desamparados (Costa Rica), CR350, 801-2, 808, 1065-
    66
El Dia (Tegucigalpa), HO346
Dialects of Central America, CA505, 885
Diario de Centro América (Guatemala), GU589, 875
Diario de Costa Rica (San José), CR431, 543, 555,
    581, 671, 1044; ES55
Diario de Guatemala (Guatemala), GU720
Diario de Hoy (San Salvador), CA972-74
Diario de Occidente (Quezaltenango), GU1080
Diario del Pueblo (Santa Ana), CA491
Diario Latino (San Salvador), CA646
Diario Nicaragüense (Granada), GU469; NI223-24
Diario Oficial (Mexico), CA794
Diario Oficial (San Salvador), ES331
Díaz, Adolfo, NI62-63, 76, 106, 195, 267, 504, 565
Díaz, Hugo, CR352
Díaz, Porfirio, BE52, 117, 135; GU895
Díaz Ordaz, Gustavo, CA234
Dictatorship
-Central America, CA26, 56, 80, 188, 232, 238, 359,
    488, 740, 783, 809, 811, 813, 876; CR36

(Dictatorship)
--Mid-20th century, CA755, 806
--Late 20th century, CA755
-Costa Rica, CR156, 427
-El Salvador, ES20, 58, 74, 259-60, 347, 406
-Guatemala, CA238; GU43, 76-77, 89, 133, 136, 143,
     180, 324, 340, 453, 459,747, 1355-56, 1401
-Honduras, CA341; HO17, 19, 39, 43, 77-78, 88
-Nicaragua, CA238, 341; NI13, 16-17, 52, 74, 85, 548
Diéguez Flores, Manuel, CR932
Diet in Central America, CA568, 747
Dirección General de Desarrollo Socio-Educativo
     Rural (Guatemala), GU233
Dirección General de Estadística (El Salvador),
     ES34, 57
Diriamba (Nicaragua), NI362, 412, 611
Dobles, Fabián, CR67, 383
Dobles Segreda, Luís, CR67, 373, 550, 953
Dominguez, José Antonio, HO337
Dominican Republic, NI85, 297
-Relations with Costa Rica, CR110
Don Quixote, CR581
Dos Cercas. See Desamparados
Duarte, José Napoleón, ES409
Dueñas, Francisco, ES67
Dulce, Golfo, CR665
Dulles, John Foster, GU1105, 1323
Duncan Moodie, Quince, CR383
Dunn's International Review (Nicaragua), NI707
Durán Cartin, Carlos, CR409, 606, 625, 834, 909
Durón y Gamero, Rómulo Ernesto, CA164; HO377, 413

Eads Ship Canal, NI202
Earthquake of 1902 (Guatemala), GU1089
Earthquake of 1917 (El Salvador), ES330
Earthquake of 1917 (Guatemala), GU337, 368, 1282
Earthquake of 1918 (Guatemala), GU1282
Earthquake of 23 December 1972 (Nicaragua), NI120,
     140, 193, 266, 323-24, 353, 377, 454, 623, 651
Earthquake of 1976 (Guatemala), GU138, 1112, 1226,
     1317, 1320
Earthquakes
-Central America, CA231, 360, 615, 992
--Mid-20th century, CA237
-Costa Rica, CR, 298, 440, 556, 1000, 1103
-Guatemala, GU138, 368, 435, 1149, 1155
Eastern Coast Company, GU213
Eastern Coast of Central America Commercial and
     Agricultural Company, GU394, 710
Echandi, Enrique, CR467
Echandi Jiménez, Mario, CR88, 501
Echandi Montero, Alberto, CR147
Echeverría, Aquileo, CR67, 744, 751
ECLA, CA126, 179, 253-54
El Eco de Comercio (Merida), BE117
Ecology in Guatemala, GU1072
Economy. See individual countries
Ecuador, BE133
-Relations with Guatemala, GU510
Eden, Anthony, GU1241
El Editor Constitucional (Guatemala), CA605; GU551
Education. See individual countries
Educators. See individual countries
Eisenhower, Dwight D., ES149
Eisentuck Affair, NI469
El Salvador
-Agriculture, CA3, 44, 285, 410; ES1, 9, 47, 98,
     120a, 163, 262, 274, 396. See also individual
     crops
--Early 20th century, CA834; ES349, 402
--Mid-20th century, CA38, 306; ES68, 70, 84, 90, 95,
     255, 264, 308, 345-46, 376, 378, 385

-Annexation of the province of Sosonate. See
     Sosonate, Annexation to El Salvador
-Banking, ES52, 69, 110-11, 172, 358, 362, 379, 382.
     See also El Salvador, finance
-Bankruptcy laws, ES45
-Basic foodstuffs, ES70
-Birth control, ES217
-Boundary dispute with Guatemala, CA192, 259, 263, 388
-Boundary dispute with Honduras, CA111, 117-18, 156-
     58, 216, 602, 956, 967, 969-70; HO31, 33. See
     also War of 1969
-Budgets, CA279
-Census data, ES6
--Early 19th century, ES36
--Early 20th century, ES171, 308
--Late 20th century, ES346
-Christian Democratic Party. See Christian
     Democratic Party
-Church-State relations, CA720; ES240, 266-67, 405
-Churches, ES156-57, 164, 267, 317, 320, 371
-Cities. See Cities, El Salvador
-Class structure. See El Salvador, social structure
-Conservation, ES342
-Conservative Party. See Conservative Party
-Constituent Assembly of 1951, ES151
-Constitutions, CA1014; ES3, 85, 97, 109, 153, 175,
     177, 179, 198, 297, 303, 364, 366
-Coup of 1944, ES58
-Coup of 1959, ES205
-Courts. See El Salvador, judicial system
-Culture, CA210
-Defense Ministry, ES7
-Democracy, ES22, 78, 96, 174-75, 245, 282, 403
-Dictatorship, ES20, 58, 74, 259-60, 347, 406
-Economy, CA57, 62, 410; ES47, 120a, 128, 163, 172,
     396, 411, 414. See also El Salvador, industry;
     trade --Early 19th century, ES136
--Mid-19th century, ES40, 316
--Late 19th century, CA839; ES31, 131, 195, 207,
     257, 356
--Early 20th century, CA834; ES21, 26,
     30, 32, 41-42, 110-11, 121, 124, 135, 171, 213,
     272, 322, 349, 355, 382-84, 393, 397, 402, 408
--Mid-20th century, CA38, 211, 251, 306, 411,
     871; ES9, 17, 43, 45, 52, 68-70, 78-79, 88, 90-
     91, 100, 103, 110-11, 120-21, 123, 126, 134,
     143-44, 146, 173, 175, 198, 210, 212, 216, 218,
     221, 223, 226, 247, 255, 264, 270-71, 306, 308-
     09, 311-12, 323, 325, 332, 337, 344-46, 353,
     360-63, 376, 378, 391, 399, 408, 410
--Late 20th century, ES354, 379
-Education, CA275, 389; ES51, 77, 89, 132, 158, 160,
     170, 265, 279, 284, 288, 293, 313-14, 320, 365,
     539, 1087
--Early 20th century, ES51, 77, 89, 229
--Mid-20th century, CA218-19; ES129, 133, 198, 214,
     226, 270, 309
--Primary, ES129, 314
--Rural, ES129
--Teacher training, ES51
-Elections, ES96, 387
--Election of 1931, ES22, 340
--Election of 1950, ES387
--Election of 1955, ES204
--Election of 1964, ES130
--Election of 1967, ES326
--Election of 1972, ES409
-Elite, ES70
-Employment, CA7, 275; ES218, 346
-Energy, ES128

-Ethnic groups, ES17, 269
-Festivals, ES199
-Finance, CA306; ES45, 69, 90, 136-37, 163, 349,
    358, 360-61, 363, 378, 408. See also El
    Salvador, banking
--Early 19th century, ES136, 150
--Mid-19th century, ES316, 349
--Late 19th century, CA839; ES52
--Early 20th century, ES30, 42, 90, 110, 172, 358,
    382-84, 393
--Mid-20th century, CA279, 306; ES69, 92, 95, 110,
    127, 136, 324, 362-63, 399
--Late 20th century, ES379
-Flag, ES232
-Geography, CA38, 62, 237, 407, 411, 472, 482, 494,
    640, 774, 839; ES11, 31, 43, 47, 56, 122, 124-
    25, 147, 165, 193, 195, 198, 200, 208, 210, 213,
    225, 230-31, 299, 325, 381; HO422
-Geology, CA640; ES210, 228-29
-Government organization, ES8
-Guardia Nacional, CA533; ES369
-Hacienda, Ministry of, ES316
-Historical survey, CA169, 472, 492, 698, 896; ES34,
    43, 54, 57, 80, 124, 152, 167, 169, 178-79, 231-
    32, 261, 273, 309, 318, 331, 342, 404, 410
-Humor, ES194, 338-39
-Idioms, ES2, 72, 192, 215
-Indian crafts, GU1006
-Industry, CA306; ES70, 103, 216, 353. See also El
    Salvador, economy; trade
--Mid-20th century, ES216, 323, 345, 391
-Investment, CA2; ES120a, 395
--Early 20th century, ES26, 70, 124, 272
--Mid-20th century, ES127, 216
-Judicial system, ES22, 71
-Labor, CA7, 275; ES106, 308, 334, 385
-Labor unions, ES334
-Land distribution, CA285; ES9, 274, 285
-Land ownership, CA285, 467; ES70, 78, 81, 95, 196-
    97, 274, 306, 308
-Land use, ES47, 345
-Laws, CA499; ES9, 44, 61-63, 71, 95, 106, 127, 174,
    187, 209, 236, 249, 299, 304, 366, 392, 398
-Legislature, ES315, 392
-Living conditions
--Early 20th century, ES19
-Living standards
--Mid-20th century, ES2, 100, 123, 143
-Local governments, ES96
-Maps, CA2, 38, 832; ES28, 138, 344, 414
-Military, CA533, 579, 627, 824; ES7, 10, 17, 20,
    24, 48, 58, 61, 73, 153, 207, 235, 245-46, 253-
    56, 260, 301, 369-70, 377, 407
-Military Academy, CA533
-National anthem, ES233
-Nutrition, ES221
-Peasant uprising of 1931, ES25, 82, 251, 262, 281,
    301, 377
-Peasants, ES10, 13-14, 81, 156, 196-97, 219, 262,
    274-75, 348, 367-68
-Photos, CA355, 408; ES198, 355, 377
--Late 19th century, ES413
--Mid-20th century, ES210
-Place names, ES225
-Planning, CA223
-Political parties, ES326, 335, 387, 409. See also
    individual parties and politics
-Politics, CA896; ES8, 48, 93-94, 101, 169, 185,
    252, 305, 405. See also names of individual
    political parties

--Early 19th century, ES267, 315, 371; HO286
--Mid-19th century, ES23, 67, 108, 182, 266, 315-16,
    350, 352, 359
--Late 19th century, ES20, 59, 131, 175, 207, 227,
    240, 257, 265, 315, 356, 407
--Early 20th century, ES15, 20-22, 42, 49, 60, 64,
    83, 104-5, 150, 207, 227, 259, 263, 276-78, 282,
    285, 289-90, 294-96, 332, 335, 352, 358, 369,
    382-84, 393, 408
--Mid-20th century, CA627, 824, 865, 918-19; ES4, 9,
    17-18, 24-25, 29, 38, 43, 53, 58, 70, 73-74, 78,
    81-82, 96, 103, 109, 119-20, 121, 126, 130, 137-
    38, 143-44, 146, 149, 151-52, 154, 164, 173,
    175, 198, 201, 204-7, 212, 237-38, 241-46, 248,
    253-56, 260, 262-64, 280-85, 289-90, 297-98,
    301-3, 306, 309, 311-12, 320-21, 323, 325-27,
    333-34, 337, 340, 342, 346-47, 358, 360-63, 368,
    374, 377, 380, 386-88, 403, 408-9
--Late 20th century, CA922; ES155-56, 307, 354
-Population, CA7, 17-18, 117-18, 346; ES125, 133,
    217, 231, 346
--Early 20th century, ES6, 47, 56-57, 100, 143, 171,
    212
--Mid-20th century, CA38, 219, 345, 672, 767-68;
    ES125, 218, 221, 271, 319, 330, 344
-Presidents, CR313
-Provinces, ES34, 56
-Public services, CA224; ES121, 126, 243, 330, 408
-Public works, ES131
-Railroads, ES240, 350
-Rebellion of 1833, ES50
-Relations with Central America, ES206
-Relations with Costa Rica, CA266, 268, CR409; ES18
-Relations with Guatemala, CA22, 264, 415; ES23,
    154, 184, 331; GU58, 400, 448, 629, 774, 859,
    1151, 1193; HO197
-Relations with Honduras, CA264, 415, 434, 695, 701;
    ES33, 147, 206, 401; GU629; HO102, 122, 125,
    197, 245, 259, 332, 375; NI468
-Relations with Nicaragua, CA22; NI158, 167, 254-
    56, 468, 472, 549, 572-73, 577, 693
-Relations with other countries. See individual
    countries
-Revolutions, CA341; ES24, 37, 205, 237, 248
--Mid-20th century, ES238
--Late 20th century, ES155-57
--Revolution of 1930, ES75
--Revolution of 1931, ES5
--Revolution of 1944, ES73-74, 82, 175
--Revolution of 1948, ES119, 126, 144, 151
--Revolution of 1950, ES88
--Revolution of 1956, ES403
-Rivers, ES56
-Roads, ES21, 121, 343
-Social conditions, CA561; ES9, 17, 164, 183, 212,
    270, 287, 311-12, 410
-Social customs, CA223; ES2, 338
-Social reform, ES226, 251, 274-75, 277-85, 287-90,
    320-21, 346, 386, 388, 403
-Social security system, CA7; ES106, 143, 327
-Social structure, CA3; ES144, 269-71, 319
-Society, CA223, 410
--Late 19th century, CA494
--Early 20th century, ES19, 49, 272
--Mid-20th century, CA211
-Statistics, ES6, 27, 70, 231
--Late 19th century, ES31, 195
--Early 20th century, ES32, 150
--Mid-20th century, ES43, 100, 133, 143, 319
-Taxation, CA251, 279; ES100, 103, 384, 408

(El Salvador)
-Trade, CA57, 306, 387, 834; ES21, 40-41, 78, 120a,
    255, 272, 322, 397. See also El Salvador,
    economy; industry
--Early 20th century, ES26, 32, 42, 124, 150, 382
--Mid-20th century, ES100, 127, 134, 222-23, 309
-Transportation, CA57, 832; ES127, 350
--Mid-19th century, ES381
--Early 20th century, ES127, 213
--Mid-20th century, CA29, 38, 305; ES309, 323, 344
-Travel, CA120-21, 189, 211, 223; ES147, 328
--Mid-19th century, GU1289
--Late 19th century, CA494, 838; ES66, 413
--Early 20th century, CA774; ES272, 412
--Mid-20th century, CA355, 407
-Treaties, ES141-42, 351, 357
-United States intervention, ES325
-Universities, CA36, 305; ES87, 99, 101-2, 173, 187,
    320, 365
-Women, ES224
El Salvador and Central American Unionism, ES50, 67,
    76, 79, 148, 177, 182, 240, 257, 282, 350
El Salvador and the Central American Common Market,
    ES78, 127, 218, 414
El Salvador-Guatemala War, ES240, 350
Elections. See individual countries
Electric Bond and Share Company, GU174
Electric utilities in Guatemala, GU308, 608
Electricity
-Costa Rica, CR253-54, 330, 406, 420
-El Salvador, ES128
Elite. See individual countries
Employment, CA7, 109, 456, 569
-Belize, CA7, 275
-Costa Rica, CA7, 275; CR26, 119, 150, 234, 335, 347
--Mid-20th century, CA219
-El Salvador, CA7, 275; ES346
--Mid-20th century, CA219
-Guatemala, CA7, 275; GU619
--Mid-20th century, CA219
-Honduras, CA7, 275
--Mid-20th century, CA219
-Nicaragua, CA7, 275
--Mid-20th century, CA219
Empresa Eléctrica de Guatemala, S.A., GU402, 513,
    578
Empresa Guatemalteca de Electricidad Inc., GU102
Empresa Hidroeléctrica del Estado (Guatemala), GU308
Empresa Nacional de Fomento y Desarrollo Económico
    de El Petén (Guatemala), GU595
Energy, CA253, 306
-Costa Rica, CA306; CR330, 406, 420, 660, 792, 972
-El Salvador, CA306; ES129
-Guatemala, CA306; 308, 402, 578, 608, 728
-Honduras, CA306
-Nicaragua, CA306
Engraving in Guatemala, GU981
La Época (San José), CR809
La Época (Tegucigalpa), HO140, 489
ESAPAC, CA276-77
La Escuela Politécnica, GU5, 208, 388, 819, 830,
    1026, 1184, 1211, 1328
Escuintla, Department of (Guatemala), GU342, 516,
    576, 789
El Espectador (Guatemala City), GU1024
Espino, Rafael, CR50
Esquipulas (Guatemala), GU423, 475, 888, 1049
Esquipulas, Black Christ of (Guatemala), CA899;
    GU475, 754, 1049
Estelí, Department of (Nicaragua), NI502
Estrada, José Dolores, NI75, 520

Estrada Cabrera, Manuel, CA607, 688, 979; ES15, 259;
    GU14, 43, 60, 69, 89, 92, 98, 133, 136, 151,
    164, 180, 186, 224, 260, 295, 353, 361, 368,
    397, 407, 411-12, 426, 473, 505-6, 510, 521,
    525, 528, 563, 579, 622, 665, 696, 707, 768,
    793-94, 796, 798, 817, 828-30, 840, 868, 879,
    892, 925, 931, 1015, 1036, 1058, 1061, 1072,
    1076, 1080, 1097, 1142-43, 1147, 1179, 1193,
    1221, 1246, 1260, 1264, 1266-67, 1298, 1306,
    1314, 1340, 1343, 1355-56, 1369-70, 1388, 1391,
    1401; NI125
Estrada Paniagua, Felipe, GU1298
La Estrella de Panamá, BE154; GU416
Ethelburga Syndicate, NI50
Ethnic groups, CA14, 89, 413
-Belize, BE22, 77, 116, 132, 184
-Costa Rica, CR190, 380-83
-El Salvador, ES17, 269
-Guatemala, GU976, 1277
-Panama, CA14
European Common Market, CA1008
European immigration to Guatemala, GU557
Evangelical Church, CA899; CR399, 940, 1029, HO296
Excelsior (Mexico), CA813; NI103

Facio Brenes, Rodrigo, CA233; CR414, 591, 955
Falkland Islands, BE129, 170; HO150
Fallas Monge, Carlos Luís, CR67, 196, 383
Family, CA966
-Costa Rica, CR39
-El Salvador, CA3; ES227
-Guatemala, CA3; GU9, 217, 591, 1046-47, 1280
-Honduras, CA3; HO55, 354, 488
-Nicaragua, CA3; NI112, 247
-Panama, CA3; CR39
Family income in Costa Rica, CR1129
Family planning, CA185
-Costa Rica, CR39, 1097
-El Salvador, ES217
-Panama, CR39
FAO (Nicaragua), NI270
FAR (Guatemala), GU270
Federación de Trabajadores del Atlántico (Costa
    Rica), CR427
Federation of Central America, CA41, 47, 60, 84, 93,
    101, 107, 118, 124, 134, 150, 160, 165, 169,
    179, 181, 202, 230, 241, 244, 267, 290, 292-93,
    298-99, 330, 343, 350, 365, 388, 392, 422, 445,
    450, 469, 479, 499, 527-29, 532, 559-60, 580,
    586, 602, 604, 613, 666, 682-83, 699, 721, 731,
    746, 756, 758-59, 778, 781, 785, 791, 797,
    875, 889-90, 894, 904, 906, 910, 943, 950, 952,
    965, 1014; BE107; CR113, 180, 377, 415, 442,
    448, 450, 452, 524, 526-28, 600-601, 603, 634,
    640, 773, 799, 817, 820, 845, 862, 864, 1038,
    1128; ES116, 177, 195, 267; GU181, 243, 276,
    332, 363, 481, 502, 710-11, 791-92, 838-39, 909,
    924, 932, 1082, 1091, 1298; HO134-35, 176, 195,
    223, 286-87; NI34, 200, 291, 467, 497, 521, 730
Fernández, Guido, CA296
Fernández, León, CR434
Fernández, Mauro, CR71, 679, 841, 1045
Fernández, Máximo, CR932, 977
Fernández, Próspero, CR705, 981
Fernández Arias, Mario E., CR1040
Fernández Ferraz, Valeriano, CR990
Fernández Guardia, Ricardo, CR67, 333, 434
Fernández Güell, Rogelio, CR938, 964
Ferrara, Gregorio, HO65

Ferrocarril Central (Nicaragua), NI94
Ferrocarril de Costa Rica, CR229, 962-63
Ferrocarril Interoceánico de Guatemala, GU622
Ferrocarril Nacional de Honduras, HO322, 353, 381
Ferrocarril Nacional de Los Altos (Guatemala), GU117
Fiallos Gil, Mariano, CA305, NI544
Fifth Meeting of Consultation of Ministers of
    Foreign Affairs, GU1324
Figueres Ferrar, José María, CR52, 75, 86, 88, 103,
    161, 216, 263, 329, 401, 430, 470, 472-78, 655,
    751, 777, 790-91, 850, 1032, 1058, 1081, 1105
Figueroa, Fernando F., ES105, 150
Filibustering, HO116, 118; NI107, 160, 176, 280
Filísola, Vicente, CA935; ES184; GU1359
Finance. See individual countries
First National City Bank, CA311-12
Fiscal policy in Central America, CA1007
Fishing in Honduras, HO213, 432
Fishing industries in Central America, CA490
Fitz-Roy, Robert, HO153
Floods in Costa Rica, CR556
Flores (Guatemala), GU1110
Flores, Luis R., CR1056
Flores Avendaño, Guillermo, GU431
FMLN, ES156-58
Folklore, CA86, 122, 844, 893; BE179; CR55-58, 92,
    193, 359, 361, 366, 380-82, 387-88, 445-46, 451,
    459, 469, 504, 585, 596-97, 636, 668, 678, 689,
    695, 720, 794, 802, 906, 930-31, 1075; ES28, 72,
    159, 162, 199, 215, 268, 338, 343, 348, 368,
    373; GU36, 61, 106, 108, 124-25, 127, 143, 150,
    171, 179, 184, 192, 218, 293, 338, 346, 408,
    445, 476, 588, 681, 700, 706, 765-66, 772-73,
    786, 807, 870-71, 881, 900, 922, 967, 991, 1004,
    1032, 1082, 1100, 1123, 1161, 1164, 1167-68,
    1173, 1194, 1201-2, 1205, 1207, 1209, 1248-49,
    1286, 1361, 1377-78, 1403, 1405, 1416-17, 1420;
    HO13, 64, 89, 94, 149, 157, 280, 325-26, 333,
    400, 403, 409; NI196, 217, 221, 244, 287, 332,
    409, 412, 443, 474, 514-15, 578, 597, 611
Folk medicine in Guatemala, GU7
Folk music, CR272; HO333
Fonseca, Gulf of, CA91, 956; ES33; HO167, 189, 245;
    NI4, 31, 254-56, 572-73, 577
Food production. See basic foodstuffs
Foreign corporations, CA99, 108, 119, 126, 467, 474,
    480, 509, 603, 611, 671, 807, 850, 865, 893,
    907, 920, 930
-Costa Rica, CR179, 228, 331, 385, 407, 506, 650,
    809, 1044, 1070, 1098, 1119, 1138
-Guatemala, GU50, 72, 102, 173, 462, 578, 1034,
    1095, 1203, 1300-1, 1303, 1315, 1390
-Honduras, HO20, 29, 48, 81, 261
-Nicaragua, NI465, 578
Foreign influence, CA342
-Costa Rica, CR540, 920, 1040, 1088
Foreign loans
-Costa Rica, CR302, 353, 551, 561, 870, 977, 1033
-Guatemala, GU12, 693, 1007
-Honduras, HO104, 313, 370, 481
--Late 19th century, HO188
--Early 20th century, HO196
-Nicaragua, NI466
--Early 20th century, NI335, 342
Foreign Ministers Meeting of 1951 (Guatemala), GU630
Foreign policy in Honduras, HO359
Forestry, BE64, 87; HO213, 432
Forum (Nicaragua), NI484

France
-Relations with Central America, CA705-6, 892, 894;
    ES40
-Relations with Costa Rica, CA329, 726, 870; CR32,
    651, 874; NI91
-Relations with El Salvador, ES40
-Relations with Guatemala, GU187, 299, 353, 357,
    767, 816
-Relations with Honduras, HO049-50, 62, 188
-Relations with Nicaragua, CA870; NI29, 82, 89-91,
    99-100, 109, 124, 235, 241, 246, 373, 461, 533,
    571
Franciscan Order, CA114; CR903, 985; GU442; HO147,
    247
Franco, Francisco, GU276; NI216
Franco, Justo, ES66
Frank Leslie's Illustrated (Nicaragua), NI72
French immigration to
-Costa Rica, CR651
-Nicaragua, NI461
French intervention in Mexico, GU299
Frente Sandinista de Liberación Nacional, NI81, 96-
    97, 113, 117, 138, 148-49, 191, 193-94, 211,
    260, 268, 282, 286, 292, 294-95, 378, 386, 478,
    488, 498, 511, 532, 537, 542, 593, 691, 699,
    704, 717, 719-22
Frente Unido de la Revolución, CA137
Friedrich Ebert Foundation, CA136
Frontier in Central America, CA776
Fuentes, Francisco, GU444
Fuentes Mohr, Alberto, GU446

La Gaceta (Guatemala), GU542
Gagini Chavarria, Carlos, CR493-94, 497
Gaínza, Gabino, GU298
Galich, Manuel, GU440
Gallegos, Daniel, CR590
Gálvez, Juan Manuel, HO102, 140, 162-65, 229-30,
    343, 345, 366, 450, 492
Gálvez, Mariano, GU112, 167, 344, 363, 487, 532,
    1081, 1340, 1359
Gálvez, Matías de, GU612, 1297
Gangellini. See Calvo, Francisco
García Bauer, Carlos, GU479
García Goyena, Rafael, GU485
García Granados, Jorge, GU480
García Granados, Miguel, GU488, 492, 510, 540, 820,
    982
García Márquez, Gabriel, NI292
García Monge, Joaquín, CR67, 372, 466, 509, 513,
    794, 941, 952, 1056, 1121
Gasahol in Costa Rica, CR268
Gavidia, Francisco Antonio, CR65; ES191, 202, 211,
    291-92, 390
General Treaty of Economic Integration, CA279
El Genio de la Libertad (Guatemala), GU551
The Geographic Magazine, CA447
Geography. See individual countries
Geology. See individual countries
German immigration to
-Central America, CA100, 225, 757, 847-48
-Costa Rica, CA851; CR755
-Guatemala, CA851; GU441, 730, 760, 1096, 1175, 1228
-Nicaragua, NI296, 376, 554
Germany
-Relations with Central America, CA100, 136, 225,
    757, 848, 874
-Relations with Costa Rica, CA851; CR392, 727, 748,
    796, 1070, 1113

(Germany)
-Relations with Guatemala, CA851; GU102, 178, 229, 313, 441, 608, 730, 1175, 1228-30
-Relations with Honduras, HO445
-Relations with Nicaragua, CA225, 807; NI123, 296, 376, 469, 554
Guerra Nacional. See Walker, William
Gibraltar, BE129, 170
Goldmining
-Costa Rica, CR648, 677, 683
-Honduras, HO156, 232
-Nicaragua, NI232, 613
Gómez Carrillo, Enrique, ES11; GU159-60, 223, 504, 509, 891, 1215, 1305; HO46
González, Gil, NI721
González Flores, Alfredo, CR421, 532, 698, 972
González Rucavado, Claudio, CR637
González Víquez, Cleto, CR248, 368, 535, 547, 671, 1056
González Zeledón, Manuel, CR47, 67, 481, 994
Good Neighbor Policy, CA48, 106
Grace and Company, CR1119
Grace-Eyre-Craigan Syndicate, NI681
Gracias a Dios, Cabo de, CA723
Gracias a Dios, Department of (Honduras), HO219, 361
Granada, Department of (Nicaragua), NI77, 106, 173, 243, 320, 581
Granada, Lake, NI69
Grant, Ulysses S., NI43
Great Britain,
-Relations with Central America, CA32, 62, 178, 235, 238, 315, 361-62, 388, 485-86, 775, 785, 790, 852, 996; GU1007; HO286; NI369, 701
-Relations with Costa Rica, CA697, 870; CR118, 305, 310, 551, 561, 616, 792, 828
-Relations with El Salvador, CA235, 388, 697, 870; ES273
-Relations with Guatemala, CA2, 388; GU300, 394, 532, 693, 710, 1007, 1267, 1278, 1293
-Relations with Honduras, CA235; HO12, 49-50, 59, 63, 95, 129, 220-21, 270, 286, 340-41, 370, 375, 378, 491; NI154-55
-Relations with Nicaragua, CA235, 870; NI39, 69-70, 90, 109, 119, 151, 154-55, 192, 224, 241, 252, 280, 289, 291, 301-2, 343, 346, 352, 369, 371, 392-93, 469-71, 473, 526-27, 571, 632, 640, 664, 680, 701, 724, 727
-Relations with Panama, CA697
-Relations with United States, CA685; HO340-41; NI70, 151, 192, 252, 280, 343, 346, 352, 371, 393, 680, 685, 718
Grecia (Costa Rica), CR804
Greek relations with Central America, CA257
Greytown (Nicaragua), CA315; NI46, 82, 101, 151, 192, 398, 703
Greytown, United States bombardment of in 1854, NI82, 398
Grito de Delgado, CA498
Grito de Dolores, CA498
Guajiquiro Indians, HO327
Gualán (Guatemala), GU1252
Guanacaste (Nicaragua), NI34
-Annexation to Costa Rica, CA724-25, 869; CR220, 239, 300, 772, 1009
Guanacaste, Department of (Costa Rica), CR92, 116, 122, 148, 220, 239, 258, 300, 345, 395, 419, 504, 569, 604, 646, 739, 763, 794, 930-31, 1009, 1075, 1082
Guardia, Tomás, CA71; CR1078
Guardia Nacional. See individual countries
Guardiola, Santos, HO12, 177

Guardiola Cubas, Esteban, CA366; HO413, 461
Guatemala
-Abortion, GU865
-Academia de Pintura, CA905
-Agrarian legislation, GU889
-Agriculture, CA3, 44, 285, 410, 485; GU44, 164, 173, 175-76, 178, 211, 214, 218, 229, 238, 310, 316, 594, 635, 704, 747, 760, 767, 776, 784, 789, 809, 836, 878, 889, 967, 980, 987, 989, 996, 1030-31, 1069, 1139, 1162, 1165, 1194-95, 1225, 1234, 1263, 1281, 1299, 1344, 1380-81, 1385, 1389, 1402, 1425. See also individual crops
--Early 19th century, GU194-95
--Late 19th century, GU166, 399, 687, 947
--Early 20th century, CA803, 834; GU224, 371, 770, 1025, 1175, 1325
--Mid-20th century, CA38, 306; GU9, 30, 57, 182, 398, 427, 501, 583, 589, 702, 728, 893, 948, 970, 985, 1202, 1258, 1285, 1390
--Late 20th century, GU281, 550, 609, 850-51, 1375
-Banking, GU12, 196, 1353. See also Guatemala, finance
-Basic foodstuffs, GU591
-Belgian colonies, GU178, 190, 790
-Belgian immigration to, GU54, 178, 190, 790, 987, 1088
-Birth control, GU722-23, 865
-Birth rates, GU233, 496, 723
-Boundary dispute with El Salvador. See El Salvador, boundary dispute with Guatemala
-Boundary dispute with Honduras, CA76, 157-58, 295, 368-75, 378-79, 381, 383-85, 415, 431-33, 437, 440, 473, 556, 570, 743, 789, 817-20, 838, 960-64, 997, 1019; GU1192
-Boundary dispute with Mexico, CA27, 214, 266, 287, 322, 376, 382, 386, 501-2, 551, 571, 592, 597-99, 616, 754, 770, 773, 794, 838, 928, 931, 965; BE137, 300
-British immigration to, GU532
-Budgets, CA279; GU204
-Caribbean coastal region, GU36
-Censorship, GU158
-Census data, GU231, 621
--Mid-20th century, GU157, 331, 621, 1171, 1389, 1413
-Central bank, GU555
-Church-State relations, CA720; GU158, 167, 216, 279, 711, 905-6, 926, 934-38, 1103
-Cities. See Cities, Guatemala
-Civil service legislation, GU1288
-Class structure. See Guatemala, social structure
-Coat of arms, GU467, 1029
-Colonization program, GU776
-Conservative Party. See Conservative Party
-Constituent Assembly of 1876, GU928
-Constituent Assembly of 1879, GU928
-Constituent Assembly of 1945, GU832
-Constitutions of, CA1014; GU396, 481, 492, 560, 569, 759, 767, 824, 1153, 1203, 1227, 1253, 1255, 1354, 1368
-Consular service, GU946
-Cooperatives, GU281, 1139, 1258
-Coup of October 1949, GU917
-Coup of 1954, CR428, 1058
-Courts. See Guatemala, judicial system
-Culture, CA4, 211; GU142, 174, 940, 969-70, 1284
-Debt peonage, GU709
-Democracy, GU97, 965
-Departamento de, GU1374

-Dependency analysis of, CA909; GU40, 78, 104, 139, 198, 780
-Dictatorship, CA238; GU43, 76-77, 89, 133, 136, 143, 180, 324, 340, 453, 458, 747, 1355-56, 1401
-Earthquakes, GU138, 368, 435, 1149, 1155
-Ecology, GU1071
-Economy, CA38, 62, 227, 410, 485; GU109, 131-32, 135, 152, 164, 249, 382, 399, 585, 589, 598-600, 602-7, 624, 669, 676, 679, 704-5, 709, 729, 753, 767, 780, 783, 872, 884, 887, 921, 985, 987, 989, 1068, 1094, 1116, 1261, 1263, 1316, 1364, 1385, 1389, 1393, 1398, 1415, 1424. See also Guatemala, industry; trade
--19th century, GU174
--Early 19th century, GU194-95, 532, 1197
--Mid-19th century, GU165, 174, 193-95, 1201, 1348, 1398
--Late 19th century, CA839; GU21, 37, 55, 66, 146, 153, 165-66, 172, 174, 187, 214, 225, 229, 365, 369, 418, 582, 687, 763a, 816, 883-84, 889, 929, 947, 974, 1225, 1334, 1398, 1422
--Early 20th century, CA238, 317, 803, 834; GU14, 41, 151, 153, 172, 214, 256, 353, 371, 411, 505, 555, 561, 579-80, 622-23, 665, 720, 731, 748, 750, 758, 770, 854, 882, 979, 1025, 1058, 1093, 1152, 1154, 1175, 1187, 1267, 1275, 1325
--Mid-20th century, CA38, 211, 251, 306, 411, 865; GU9-10, 12, 21, 29, 44, 49, 57, 63, 67, 72, 74, 77-78, 85, 104, 110, 114, 117-18, 142, 161, 173, 175-76, 182, 196, 198, 308, 310, 359-60, 380, 382, 385, 387, 398, 402, 421, 427, 501, 531, 547, 556, 562, 567, 575, 578, 581, 583, 585-86, 589, 591, 613-14, 625, 646, 649, 668, 690, 702, 728, 730, 743, 747, 753, 760, 780, 785, 789, 887, 893, 948, 970-71, 975, 978, 985, 998, 1007, 1011, 1043, 1060, 1095, 1115, 1202-3, 1231, 1254, 1285, 1322, 1349
--Late 20th century, CA909; GU280-81, 549-50, 608, 726, 745, 785, 850-51, 944, 1079, 1174, 1353, 1375
-Education, CA275, 289, 904; GU52, 75, 79, 81-82, 84-85, 118, 167, 199, 204, 233, 245, 248, 286-88, 348, 351, 358, 363, 395, 405, 424, 428, 449, 505, 515, 613, 676, 689, 735, 738, 744, 787, 822, 847, 849, 852, 858, 940, 977, 1130-31, 1185, 1222, 1281, 1350, 1354, 1380, 1395, 1412
--Early 20th century, GU694, 779
--Mid-20th century, CA218-19; GU290, 615-17, 619-21, 703, 779, 808, 848, 1001
--Late 20th century, GU550
--Agricultural, CA44
--Medical, GU121, 449
--Primary, GU70, 86, 199, 245, 275, 279, 617, 677, 1400
--Rural, GU238, 589, 617, 744, 977, 1395, 1400
--Secondary, CA289; GU70, 230, 689, 1001
--Teacher training, GU738, 1016, 1185
--Vocational, CA45, 136
-Elections, GU746
--Election of 1957, GU1002
--Election of 1963, GU72-73
--Election of 6 March, 1966, GU746, 993
-Electricity, GU308, 608
-Elite, GU1398
-Emigration from, GU54
-Employment, CA7, 219, 275; GU619
-Energy, GU308, 402, 578, 608, 728
-Engraving, GU981
-Ethnic groups, GU976, 1277
-Family, CA3; GU9, 217, 591, 1046-47, 1280

-Federalism, GU774
-Festivals, GU106, 125, 217
-Finance, CA306; GU12, 505, 679, 693, 720, 1061, 1094. See also Guatemala, banking
--Late 19th century, CA839; GU187, 929
--Early 20th century, GU411, 555, 720, 854, 979, 1267
--Mid-20th century, CA279, 306; GU196, 380, 385, 398, 547, 575, 581, 625, 728, 730, 998, 1202, 1231, 1349
--Late 20th century, GU1353
-Flag, GU467, 1029, 1361
-Flower, GU467
-Foreign corporations, GU50, 72, 102, 173, 578, 1034, 1095, 1203, 1303, 1315
-Foreign loans, GU12, 693, 1007
-Foreign Ministry, BE61, 104-5
-Foreign policy, GU276
-Generation of 1920, GU1097
-Generation of 1940, GU512
-Geographical and Historical Society, BE90-91
-Geography, CA6, 38, 62, 237, 320, 335, 407, 411, 472, 482, 494, 640, 774, 834, 839, 900, 991; GU17, 115-16, 142, 151, 166, 178, 197, 224, 274, 356, 383, 386-87, 392, 464-65, 494, 561, 586-87, 590, 609-10, 669, 706, 737, 756, 763, 767, 770, 778, 816, 872-72, 943-45, 947, 953, 974, 987, 994, 1058, 1093, 1118-19, 1154, 1156, 1160-61, 1163, 1177, 1276, 1290, 1292, 1300, 1344, 1363-64, 1376, 1389, 1399
-Geology, CA640; GU202, 355, 781, 1290, 1292
-German immigration to, CA851; GU441, 730, 760, 1096, 1175, 1228
-Government organization, GU809
-Guerrillas, GU455, 755, 764, 877, 958, 1033, 1035, 1102, 1313, 1333
-Highway labor tax, GU145
-Historical survey, CA169, 472, 492, 698, 896; GU63, 109, 322, 410, 486, 548, 671, 674, 695, 741, 747, 752, 824, 941, 953, 1150, 1213, 1263, 1296, 1335, 1367
-Historiography, GU294
-Humor, GU136, 1083, 1181
-Idioms, GU105, 116, 136, 170, 201, 1218
-Immigration to, GU102, 178, 190, 193-95, 213, 312-19, 343, 394, 417, 463a, 533, 710, 761, 816, 884, 987, 1065, 1078, 1088, 1273, 1293
-Indian languages, GU523
-Indian traditions, GU9, 26, 124-25, 127, 184, 682
-Indigenismo, GU601
-Industry, CA306; GU55, 161, 302, 668, 728, 969, 1011, 1079. See also Guatemala, economy; trade
-Internal migration, CA832; GU10, 57, 250, 550, 1131, 1234, 1273, 1299, 1413
-Investment, CA2, 909; GU30, 55, 102, 173, 175-76, 229, 353, 463a, 693, 930, 1007, 1095, 1275
--Late 19th century, GU166, 187, 582, 816, 947
--Early 20th century, GU580, 748, 1025, 1154, 1187, 1267
--Mid-20th century, CA865; GU668, 971, 1203
--Late 20th century, GU736
-Judicial system, GU15, 261-62, 334
-Labor, CA7, 275; GU57, 220, 425, 433, 550, 690, 747, 764, 921, 1115, 1281
-Labor courts, GU1115
-Labor laws, GU172, 743, 1115
-Labor Party. See Labor Party
-Labor unions, GU176, 220, 458, 800, 912, 986, 1115, 1183, 1235, 1258

(Guatemala)

-Ladinos, CA3; GU9, 104, 189, 307, 425, 432, 501, 682, 887, 940, 976, 1171, 1244, 1387, 1413
-Land distribution, CA285; GU182, 278, 408, 413, 635, 850, 893, 980, 996, 1390
-Land ownership, CA285; GU8, 30, 281, 310, 316, 393, 408, 413, 425, 450, 550, 564-65, 567, 702, 789, 877-78, 889, 893, 985, 989, 996, 1030-31, 1096, 1128, 1281, 1285, 1299, 1376, 1385, 1388-90
-Law, GU25, 172, 262, 483, 489, 521, 541, 570, 635, 699, 885, 889, 1073, 1078, 1119, 1169, 1326, 1423
-Law of national patrimony, GU812
-Law of Probity, GU648
-Legislation, GU541, 1119
-Legislation, Indian, GU699
-Liberal Party. See Liberal Party
-Life expectancy, GU157, 231, 496
-Literacy, GU286, 351, 1222
-Living standards, GU591
-Maps, CA2, 38, 832; GU586, 593, 609, 869, 1389
-Marimba, GU107
-Middle class, GU462, 764, 1254
-Military, CA227, 416, 824; GU8, 28, 35, 68, 76-77, 133, 164, 208, 291, 351, 388, 431, 474, 499, 568, 611-12, 764, 819, 830, 873, 1026, 1051, 1169-70, 1184, 1211, 1233, 1251, 1328, 1411
-Minifundistas, GU989
-Minimum wage, GU690
-Multinational corporations. See Guatemala, foreign corporations
-Municipal government, GU943, 1160
-Mythology, GU124-25, 143, 179
-National anthem, GU200, 467, 1216
-National Police, GU1180
-National symbols, GU200, 467, 1361
-Nutrition, GU501, 724
--Mid-20th century, GU501
-Old folks home, GU577, 1039
-Parasites, GU782
-Peasants, CA320; GU8, 137, 238, 270, 304, 340, 374-76, 406, 450, 462, 512, 700, 724, 754, 776, 877, 913, 970, 999-1000, 1163, 1166, 1235, 1238, 1258, 1421
-Pensions, GU596
-Periodicals, GU990
-Petroleum, GU728
-Photos, CA355, 408; GU29, 164, 203, 420, 438, 472, 520, 639, 657, 762, 883, 994, 1038, 1182, 1282
--Late 19th century, GU811
--Mid-20th century, GU556, 713, 952, 959
-Planning, GU785
-Political parties, CA137; CR36; GU31, 42, 927. See also individual parties and politics
-Politics, CA896; GU101, 249, 291, 313, 324, 497, 552, 624, 729, 986, 1231, 1261-62. See also names of individual political parties
--19th century, GU174
--Early 19th century, CA623, 842; GU24, 92, 98, 112, 167, 178, 181, 194, 210, 243, 332, 363, 392, 452, 456, 487-88, 532, 611, 684-85, 734, 775, 864, 909-10, 924, 932, 1081, 1128, 1197, 1213, 1221, 1359
--Mid-19th century, CA623, 842, 892; GU24, 165, 169, 185, 246, 306, 332-33, 343, 391, 403, 569, 769, 774-75, 933, 945, 1048, 1090, 1196, 1201, 1213, 1340-41, 1348, 1367, 1372, 1398
--Late 19th century, CA623; GU13, 21, 24, 35, 37, 47, 52, 65-66, 103, 120, 123, 146, 162, 165, 169, 172, 197, 208, 214, 219, 242, 244, 258, 284-85, 297, 321, 344, 365, 369, 412, 418,

444, 469, 474, 491-92, 511, 526-27, 539-42, 554, 557, 559, 563, 573, 582, 683, 704, 763a, 769, 793, 820, 843-44, 855, 861, 879, 883-84, 891, 899, 906, 926-29, 934-39, 983, 1013, 1036, 1048, 1061, 1087, 1092, 1101, 1103, 1121, 1144, 1180, 1217, 1256, 1269, 1294, 1296, 1298, 1329, 1334, 1340-41, 1357, 1367-70, 1372, 1398, 1401, 1422
--Early 20th century, CA493, 777; ES15; GU14, 19, 41-43, 52, 60, 69, 81, 83, 89, 93, 120, 133, 136, 143, 151, 158, 164, 169, 172, 180, 186, 208, 256, 260, 295, 301, 334, 353, 361, 373, 407, 412, 473, 505-6, 510-11, 525, 528, 563, 572, 579-80, 622-23, 665-66, 694, 696, 707, 720, 731, 748, 750, 768, 784, 793-95, 798, 817, 828-30, 834-36, 840, 853-54, 868, 879, 882, 892, 925, 927, 930-31, 979, 1014-15, 1036, 1058, 1072, 1076, 1080, 1093, 1097, 1142-43, 1147, 1152, 1154, 1157, 1179, 1193, 1237, 1246, 1260, 1264, 1266-67, 1293, 1306, 1314, 1340-41, 1343, 1351, 1369-70, 1388, 1391, 1401; NI125
--Mid-20th century, CA813, 824, 865, 919; GU8, 10-12, 16, 18-22, 29, 31, 39-40, 44, 48-51, 58-59, 67, 71-72, 74, 76-79, 83-85, 94, 97, 103-4, 112, 118, 137, 141, 143, 155-56, 173, 175-76, 182, 196, 198, 204, 207, 220, 228, 233, 235, 239, 240-41, 247, 261, 263, 271-73, 276-78, 302-3, 308-9, 325-26, 328, 330, 335, 340-41, 351, 357-58, 373-75, 377, 379-80, 382-85, 387, 390, 400, 402, 405, 421-22, 431-33, 436-37, 440, 444, 446, 450-51, 453-55, 457-61, 466, 471, 477, 482, 484, 493, 498, 501, 515, 520, 529, 531, 534, 543-47, 556, 562, 566, 568, 571, 574, 576, 578, 581, 585, 589, 614, 618, 625, 628, 630, 632, 634, 637-42, 644-58, 660-61, 667-68, 672, 680, 682, 688, 690, 692-94, 697-99, 703, 714-18, 721, 730, 732, 739, 741, 743-44, 746-47, 753, 755, 760, 764, 776-77, 780, 784-86, 797-800, 802-3, 805-6, 809, 814, 818, 825, 831, 833-35, 837, 842, 848, 859-60, 866, 875-78, 889, 893, 907, 912, 915, 917-21, 950-51, 955-58, 960-64, 966, 973, 980, 993, 995, 1002, 1007-9, 1016-18, 1024, 1030-31, 1034, 1037-45, 1050, 1053-57, 1059-60, 1066, 1085-86, 1091, 1097, 1102, 1104-6, 1108, 1111, 1115, 1120, 1124, 1126-27, 1129, 1144, 1158, 1170, 1176, 1179-80, 1189-90, 1192, 1203, 1206, 1210, 1220, 1227, 1229, 1232-33, 1235, 1240-41, 1251-54, 1258, 1274, 1279, 1281, 1288, 1299-304, 1307, 1310-11, 1313, 1315-16, 1318-19, 1321, 1323-24, 1327, 1331, 1333, 1345, 1347, 1349, 1355-56, 1364-66, 1379-80, 1389-90, 1408-9, 1412, 1424-25, 1427-29
--Late 20th century, CA922; GU280, 425, 709, 745, 755, 785, 788, 850-51, 877-78, 921, 949, 965, 1033, 1035, 1051, 1053, 1079, 1102, 1172, 1174, 1303-4, 1380, 1414
-Population, CA7, 17-18; GU496, 747, 865, 873, 1275, 1344, 1389
--Late 19th century, GU1225
--Mid-20th century, CA38, 219, 345, 672, 767-68; GU233, 567, 586, 621, 722-23
--Late 20th century, GU233, 609, 726
-Ports, CA385; GU978
-Postage stamps, GU188, 522
-Postal services, GU152-54, 522, 1160
-Presidents, CR313
-Prisons, GU284, 997
-Progressive Party. See Progressive Party
-Public administration, GU809
-Public services, GU385, 1288, 1316

-Public works, GU14, 21, 164, 353, 365, 411, 657, 1038, 1041, 1314, 1349
--Early 20th century, GU768
--Mid 20th century, GU67, 556, 649
-Publishers, GU367, 1122, 1371-72
-Railroads, CA385; GU117, 622-24, 803, 1261
-Rebellion of 1820, GU323
-Rebellion of 1955, GU493
-Rebellion of 1960, GU477
-Relations with Central America, GU285, 299, 859
-Relations with Costa Rica, CR36, 158, 428, 874, 1105; GU859
-Relations with El Salvador, CA22, 264, 415; ES23, 154, 184, 331; GU58, 400, 448, 629, 774, 859, 1151, 1193; HO197
-Relations with Honduras, CA624, 380, 433; GU104, 629, 727, 859, 1034; HO88, 102-3, 129, 197, 227, 375, 419, 462
-Relations with Latin America, GU354
-Relations with Nicaragua, CA22, 792; CR36, 52; GU58, 727, 859; NI510
-Relations with other countries. See individual countries
-Revolt of 1897, GU526-27, 793
-Revolt of June 1956, GU18
-Revolutions, CA341; GU18, 198, 270
--Mid-20th century, GU22, 422, 429, 446, 450, 455
--Revolution of 1871, GU13, 35, 65-66, 153, 321, 539, 541-42, 563, 879, 1036, 1256, 1263, 1422
--Revolution of 1906, GU794-95
--Revolution of 1920, GU180, 186, 339, 1143, 1391
--Revolution of 1944, CA824; GU18, 50, 59, 72-74, 77, 80, 86, 102, 104, 118, 173, 175-76, 182, 220, 235, 241, 276-77, 325-26, 335, 358, 374-75, 377, 384, 402, 413, 431, 436, 440, 450, 454, 458, 461-62, 497, 512, 515, 520, 531, 543-44, 552, 576, 578, 628, 633, 672, 721, 732, 739, 744, 777, 798, 800, 802, 806, 814, 818, 825, 831, 833, 860, 866, 875-76, 889, 907, 912, 915, 919, 923, 942, 955-57, 961, 964, 973, 980, 995-96, 1008, 1016, 1018, 1024, 1030-31, 1044, 1054-55, 1057, 1059, 1085, 1097, 1104, 1106, 1108, 1115, 1126, 1129, 1137, 1166, 1176, 1183, 1189-92, 1210, 1227, 1233, 1235, 1241, 1251, 1253, 1281, 1301-4, 1311, 1315, 1318-19, 1321, 1323-24, 1331, 1347, 1355-56, 1366, 1389, 1412, 1425, 1428; HO88, 462
--Revolution of 1950, GU656
--Revolution of 1954, CA843; GU155-56, 228, 264, 271-73, 278, 309, 327, 390, 400, 431, 466, 471, 530, 534, 543-44, 566, 571, 583, 614, 618, 634, 636-37, 652, 655, 661, 667, 714-16, 718, 727, 776, 797, 805, 818, 831, 860, 866, 912, 951, 961-62, 964, 966, 973, 1008, 1024, 1030-31, 1034, 1085, 1105, 1108, 1111, 1126, 1210, 1227, 1233, 1241, 1251-52, 1274, 1279, 1302-3, 1310-11, 1315-16, 1318-19, 1321, 1323-24, 1345, 1347, 1364-65
-Revolutionary Party. See Revolutionary Party
-Roads, GU145, 217, 584, 586, 613, 1043, 1424
-Rural society, GU8, 211, 704, 738
-Social conditions, CA561; GU83, 109, 114, 360, 450, 460, 471, 489, 724, 945, 984-85, 1234, 1258, 1307, 1338
--Mid-19th century, GU945
--Mid-20th century, GU457, 459, 591-92, 713, 719, 808, 940, 948, 969-70, 975-76, 998, 1131, 1171, 1204, 1254
--Late 20th century, GU357, 549, 709, 999-1000, 1174
-Social customs, CA223; GU189, 217-18, 900, 1291

-Social Democratic Party. See Social Democratic Party
-Social life, GU217
-Social Security Institute, GU385
-Social security system, CA7; GU144, 489, 596-97, 679, 1281
-Social structure, CA3; GU9, 49, 189, 198, 682, 921, 975, 980, 1242, 1307, 1338, 1389
-Society, CA6, 223, 227, 335, 410; GU94, 111, 134, 185, 197, 381, 432, 921, 1046-47, 1346, 1389
--19th century, GU174
--Early 19th century, GU1197
--Late 19th century, CA494
--Early 20th century, CA317, 320; GU750, 1152
--Mid-20th century, CA211; GU8, 11, 57, 114, 119, 386, 501, 690, 747, 887
--Late 20th century, GU726, 745
-Spiritual socialism, GU72-73, 76-77, 82, 118
-Statistics, CA909; GU371, 427, 575, 783, 985, 999-1000, 1344, 1349, 1389
--Mid-20th century, GU233, 547, 591-92, 789, 1011
--Late 20th century, GU233
-Supreme Court, GU25, 502-3, 521, 632, 1086
-Tariffs, GU1415
-Taxation, CA251, 279; GU12, 145, 380, 575
-Telegraph, GU152-53
-Terrorism, GU654, 300, 1409
--Mid-20th century, GU546
-Textbooks, GU290
-Textiles, GU53, 191, 591, 886, 972, 992, 1005-6, 1140, 1272, 1396
-Tourism, GU26, 994
--Late 19th century, GU582
--Early 20th century, GU580, 748
--Mid-20th century, GU1223
-Trade, CA306, 385, 387, 834; GU178, 214, 229, 463a, 767, 783, 884, 1275, 1322. See also Guatemala, economy; industry
--Early 19th century, GU194-95
--Mid-19th century, GU193-95
--Late 19th century, GU55, 166, 187, 225, 399, 582, 816, 947
--Early 20th century, GU371, 411, 580, 770, 1154, 1187
--Mid-20th century, GU142, 547, 971
--Late 20th century, GU736
-Transnational corporations. See Guatemala, foreign corporations
-Transportation, CA832; GU153, 584, 613, 624, 784, 884, 1261, 1364, 1415, 1424
--Early 19th century, GU392
--Late 19th century, GU145, 187, 899
--Early 20th century, CA320; GU145, 411, 622-23, 731, 758, 770, 882, 1025
--Mid-20th century, CA29, 38, 306; 117, 359, 728, 978, 1043, 1202
-Travel, CA6, 72, 121, 189, 211, 223, 227, 335-37, 352; BE175; GU2, 142, 494
--Early 19th century, GU392, 684-85, 924, 1392
--Mid-19th century, GU391, 1289, 1348
--Late 19th century, CA494, 839; GU197, 214-15, 867, 974, 1276
--Early 20th century, CA238, 317, 320, 774; GU205, 236, 256, 1113, 1293, 1342, 1384, 1391, 1393, 1399
--Mid-20th century, CA355, 407, 446; GU26, 177, 203, 218, 235, 263, 386, 416, 421, 443, 706, 737, 757, 808, 814, 821, 898, 953-54, 1114, 1136, 1141, 1178, 1239, 1259, 1283
--Late 20th century, GU1295

(Guatemala)
-Treaties, GU229, 890, 1148, 1153, 1198
-United States entrepreneurs, GU131-32, 135
-United States filibustering, GU478
-United States imperialism, GU78, 82, 93-94, 96,
    104, 131-32, 135, 137, 198, 240, 451, 1302, 1315
-United States influence in, CA6
-United States intervention, GU82, 299, 461, 968
-United States intervention of 1954, GU51, 80, 137,
    139, 155-56, 264, 278, 1007, 1034, 1105, 1111,
    1303, 1364
-United States investment, GU1415
-Universities, CA36, 44, 49, 236, 400; GU33, 92,
    136, 227, 282, 424-25, 428, 553, 699, 735, 771,
    823, 847-48, 1016, 1097, 1158, 1172, 1354
-Water resources, GU1292, 1332
-Women, GU247, 742, 1350
Guatemala City, GU1, 237, 303, 330, 392, 420, 448,
    517, 622, 772-73, 945, 1130, 1132, 1145-46,
    1181, 1196
Guatemala-Honduras arbitration of 1933, CA375, 556
Guatemala-Mexico Treaty of 1881, BE135
Guatemalan Academy of Geography and History, BE90
Guatemalan Association of Reporters, GU207
Guatemalan Central Railroad, GU882, 899
Guatemalan Folklore Society, GU108
Guatemalan Indigenous Institute, GU524
Guatemalan National Library, GU87
Guerrero, Francisco José, ES206
Guerrilla movements of the 1960s in Guatemala, GU1333
Guerrillas in Guatemala, GU455, 755, 764, 877, 950,
    958, 1033, 1035, 1102, 1313, 1333
Guido, Clemente, NI318
Guillén, Flavio, GU673
Gutiérrez, Joaquín, CR196, CR383
Gutiérrez, Manuel María, CR642
Gutiérrez, Rafael Lopez, HO11, 147
Guzmán, Enrique, NI182

The Handbook of British Honduras, BE4, 27, 38, 141
Harding, Warren G., CA201
Harper's New Monthly Magazine, CR337, 726
Harper's Weekly (Nicaragua), NI71
Hay-Pauncefoote Treaty (Nicaragua), NI620
Health care facilities, CA17-18, 59, 185, 345, 483,
    568, 815, 845
-Belize, CA17-18, 59; BE34
-Costa Rica, CA17-18, 59, 345; CR21, 112, 149, 271,
    326, 593-94, 608, 612, 650, 723, 727, 875, 910,
    923, 1048-49, 1077
-El Salvador, CA17-18, 59, 345; ES121, 144, 352, 385
-Guatemala, CA17-18, 59, 345; GU7, 121-22, 163, 222,
    231, 371, 426, 428, 449, 489, 496, 577, 698,
    722-23, 845, 873, 1037, 1039, 1380, 1397
-Honduras, CA17-18, 59, 345; CR21; HO185, 300, 376,
    426, 472
-Nicaragua, CA17-18, 59, 345; NI33, 115, 581
-Panama, CA59, 345
Health survey in Nicaragua, NI33, 525
Hemispheric solidarity, CA809, 843
El Heraldo (Managua), NI663
El Heraldo Seráfico (Costa Rica), CR51
Heredia, Department of (Costa Rica), CR54, 90, 259,
    366-68, 373-76, 397, 448, 534, 538, 550, 583,
    684, 712, 733, 912-13, 1056, 1103
Hernández, Francisco, CR581
Hernández de León, Federico, GU966, 1408
Herrarte, Alberto, CA95
Herrera, Carlos, GU186, 334, 696, 731, 1369
Herrera, Dionisio, CA759; HO176

Herrera, Flavio, GU408, 807
Herrera García, Adolfo, CR67, 196
Herrera Sanchez, Tomás, CR881
Hershey, Samuel, BE114
Hill, Edward Bruce, CA689-91
Hispanidad movement (Nicaragua), NI28, 216
Historia de la Imprenta en Guatemala, GU468
Hoffman, Carl, CR727
Hondo, Río, BE92
Honduran Banana Corporation, HO202
Honduras
-Agrarian reform, HO32, 48
-Agriculture, CA3, 44, 285, 410, 485; HO21-22, 48,
    160, 202, 248-49, 277, 324, 363, 415, 442, 453.
    See also individual crops
--Early 19th century, HO416
--Mid-19th century, HO316
--Late 19th century, HO266, 305
--Early 20th century, CA803, 834; HO362, 436
--Mid-20th century, CA38, 306; HO74, 100, 121, 138,
    192, 213, 237, 300, 320, 334, 432
-Banking, HO87, HO109. See also Honduras, finance
-Boundary dispute with El Salvador. See El
    Salvador, boundary dispute with Honduras; War of
    1969
-Boundary dispute with Guatemala. See Guatemala,
    boundary dispute with Honduras
-Boundary dispute with Nicaragua, CA31, 35, 78, 82,
    92, 111, 113, 127, 132, 161-64, 166, 178, 215,
    245-46, 273, 332, 366-67, 425, 429-30, 436, 438-
    39, 441-43, 462, 466, 526, 565-66, 578, 608,
    625, 645, 653, 655, 686, 702, 723, 744, 748,
    751, 771, 833, 877, 932-33, 955-56, 1010; HO21,
    150, 219, 436; NI443, 541
-Budgets, CA279
-Caribbean coast, HO081-82, 110
-Census data, HO091, 210, 216, 375
-and Central American Common Market, CA424; HO35
-Central bank, HO109, 190, 429, 481
-Central District, HO208
-Church-State relations, CA720; HO151, 275, 292
-Cities. See Cities, Honduras
-Citizenship, HO55
-Class structure. See Honduras, social structure
-Coinage, HO87, 484
-Conservative Party. See Conservative Party
-Constitutions, HO98, 107, 194, 274, 276, 295, 354,
    424, 445-46, 452
-Cooperative movement, HO277, 415
-Courts. See Honduras, judicial system
-Culture, CA211
-Dependency analysis of, HO122, 257, 311
-Dictatorship, HO17, 19, 39, 43, 77-78, 88
-Economy, CA62, 227, 410; HO21, 36, 97, 104, 109,
    190, 202, 204, 218, 232, 238, 258, 275-76, 321,
    324, 338, 363, 381, 383, 404-5, 415, 442. See
    also Honduras, industry; trade
--Early 19th century, HO22, 416
--Mid-19th century, HO263, 316, 420-23
--Late 19th century, CA839; HO62, 96, 188, 244, 262-
    63, 266, 305-6, 315, 322, 414
--Early 20th century, CA317, 803, 834; HO196, 211,
    217, 232, 243, 271, 291-92, 321-22, 340, 355,
    362, 407, 481
--Mid-20th century, CA38, 211, 251, 306, 411, 865;
    HO37, 56, 74, 96, 100, 108, 110, 120-21, 139,
    141-43, 145, 154, 162, 169, 178, 184, 190, 200,
    206, 208, 213-14, 226, 237, 252, 313, 320, 324,
    334-35, 338, 348, 364, 380, 386, 407, 428-32,
    434-35, 481

--Late 20th century, CA909; HO56, 203, 257, 261, 277, 311
-Education, CA275, 289; HO3, 14-15, 34, 44, 92, 97, 111, 123, 173, 180-81, 240, 246, 255-56, 354, 377, 391, 412, 427, 459-61
--Early 20th century, HO16
--Mid-20th century, CA218-19; HO7, 108, 154, 300
--Late 20th century, HO485
--Agricultural, CA44
--Primary, HO181, 215
--Secondary, CA289
--Vocational, CA45, 135
-Educators, HO255, 458
-Elections
--Election of 1919, HO90
--Election of 1932, HO85
--Election of 1948 (municipal), HO350
--Election of 1963, HO319
--Election of 1968, HO9
-Employment, CA7
-Family, CA3; HO55, 354, 488
-Finance, CA306; HO87, 104, 109, 217-18, 340-41, 370, 381, 404, 434-35. See also Honduras, banking
--Late 19th century, CA839; HO188, 262
--Early 20th century, HO196, 217, 291, 340-41, 481
--Mid-20th century, CA279, 306; HO138, 184, 190, 200, 206, 313, 335, 428-31, 434-35, 481
--Late 20th century, HO203
-Foreign corporations, HO20, 29, 48, 81, 261
-Foreign loans, HO104, 188, 196, 313, 370, 481
-Foreign policy, HO359
-French involvement in, HO062
-Geography, CA6, 38, 62, 320, 324, 407, 411, 472, 494, 640, 774, 834, 839, 900; BE177; HO40, 67, 96, 115, 171, 179, 234, 248, 275, 298, 302, 309, 316, 362, 365, 395, 405, 407, 420, 425, 448, 457, 466
-Geology, CA640; HO278
-Government of, Dirección General de Estadística, HO378
-Government of, Escuela Nacional de Bellas Artes de, HO408
-Historical survey, CA169, 472, 492, 968, 896; HO5, 24, 47, 56, 69-70, 86, 132, 204, 275-76, 301, 312, 356, 395, 455, 457, 465
-Humor, HO157
-Idioms, HO297, 477, 480
-Immigration to, HO21, 249, 316, 355, 444
--Early 19th century, HO416
-Individual rights, HO354
-Industry, HO190, 226, 257. See also Honduras, economy; trade
-Inter-Oceanic railway, HO049-50, 59, 63, 153, 187, 263, 317, 421-23
-Investment, CA909; HO22, 49-50, 59, 63, 78, 97, 202, 214, 232, 238, 243-44, 370, 380-81, 404, 414, 423
--Mid-19th century, HO421
--Late 19th century, HO062, 114, 188, 238, 262, 305-6, 315
--Early 20th century, HO196, 291, 340-41, 355, 436
--Mid-20th century, HO313, 324
--Late 20th century, HO257, 263
-Judicial system, HO424
-Labor, CA7, 161, 275, 349; HO139, 354
-Labor unions, HO259
-Land distribution, CA31, 48, 285; HO121
-Land ownership, CA285, 467; HO100, 121, 192, 199, 257, 300, 320, 334

-Law, HO34, 52, 55, 67, 107, 161, 168, 269, 371, 391, 453
-Liberal Party. See Liberal Party
-Literacy, HO3, 292
-Maps, HO115
-Migration, CA117
-Military, CA227, 416; HO9, 77, 146, 258-59, 261, 292, 366, 369, 371, 388, 463, 471
-Multinational corporations. See Honduras, foreign corporations
-Municipal government, HO60
-National Archives, HO198-99
-National Indian Institute, HO318
-National Library, HO205
-National Office of Statistics, HO375
-National Party. See National Party
-National Railroad, HO322, 353, 381
-National Society of Geography and History, HO26
-National University. See Honduras, universities
-Nationalism, HO324
-Nutrition, HO236
-Peasants, CA320; HO20, 29, 43, 72, 192, 239, 314, 329, 488
-Perry Land Grant, HO21
-Photos, HO5, 163, 265, 353, 450, 478
-Political parties, HO424. See also individual parties and politics
-Politics, CA896; HO47-48, 196, 312, 447. See also names of individual political parties
--Early 19th century, HO71, 286, 388
--Mid-19th century, HO25, 30, 42, 71, 80, 129, 197, 263, 378, 401
--Late 19th century, HO14, 23, 62, 71, 78, 80, 112, 116, 118, 130, 133, 137, 172-74, 250, 263, 266, 283, 293, 305, 307, 344, 360, 375, 377, 384, 392-93, 397, 417, 444-45, 497
--Early 20th century, HO11, 66, 78, 80, 89-90, 101, 116, 118, 146, 173, 193, 211, 218, 267, 269, 285, 290, 292, 310, 321, 330, 340-41, 344, 372, 377, 382, 407, 417-18, 445, 476, 497
--Mid-20th century, CA627, 865, 918-19; HO7, 9, 17-20, 32, 39, 53, 56, 65, 67, 75, 77-78, 80-81, 85, 88-89, 97, 102-3, 119-22, 140-43, 145, 154, 157, 162-65, 169-70, 177, 183-84, 200, 206-8, 212, 214, 229-30, 239-40, 252-54, 268, 281, 284, 288-89, 294-95, 319, 323-24, 338, 342-52, 359, 364, 366, 385-86, 389, 406-7, 411, 424, 437, 444, 450, 456, 462-63, 467-69, 471, 483, 489-90, 492-94, 496
--Late 20th century, HO36, 56, 80, 105-6, 119, 203, 257-59, 261, 367-69, 399, 464, 485
-Population, CA7, 17-18; HO210, 216, 405
--Mid-20th century, CA38, 219, 345, 672, 767-68; HO41, 100, 108, 186, 236, 300, 433
--Late 20th century, HO91
-Ports, HO22, 322
-Presidents, CR313
-Public services, HO56, 100, 108
-Public works, HO141, 154, 162, 164-65, 208, 229, 321, 348, 386, 456
-Publishers, HO28
-Railroads, CA803; HO22, 104, 119, 234, 305-6, 317, 322, 340-41, 353, 370, 383, 404, 414, 421, 423; NI438
-Rebellion of 1910, HO444-45
-Relations with Central America, HO225, 470
-Relations with Costa Rica, HO66, 223
-Relations with El Salvador, CA624, 415, 435, 695, 701; ES33, 147, 206, 401; GU629; HO102, 122, 125, 197, 245, 259, 332, 375; NI468

(Honduras)

-Relations with Guatemala, CA264, 380, 434; GU104, 629, 727, 859, 1034; HO88, 102-3, 129, 197, 227, 375, 419, 462
-Relations with Latin America, HO42
-Relations with Nicaragua, HO284, 332, 375; NI4, 31, 154-55, 438, 468, 470
-Relations with other countries. See individual countries
-Relations with South America, HO231
-Revolutions, HO78, 144
-Revolution of 1903, HO382, 418
-Revolution of April 1907, CA434-35
-Revolution of 1919, HO11, 146
-Revolution of 1944, HO19, 102
-Revolution of 1954, HO30
-Revolution of 1956, HO463
-Revolution of 1959, HO366
-Revolution of 1972, HO258, 261
-Rural society, CA3
-Salvadoran migration to, HO31
-Social conditions, HO123, 242, 275, 354, 488
--Mid-19th century, HO422
--Late 19th century, HO096
--Early 20th century, HO330
--Mid-20th century, HO82, 121, 157, 178, 186, 201, 236, 242, 300
--Late 20th century, HO311
-Social customs, CA223; HO479
-Social security system, CA7
-Social structure, CA3; HO257
-Society, CA6, 223, 227, 410
--Late 19th century, CA494
--Early 20th century, CA317, 320
--Mid-20th century, CA211
-Statistics, CA909; HO74, 209, 213, 405, 407, 429, 431-35
--Mid-20th century, HO108, 139, 200, 237, 320
-Supreme Court, HO52, 168, 173-74, 377
-Tariffs, HO363
-Taxation, CA251, 279; HO184, 206, 271, 429
-Trade, CA306, 387, 834; HO62, 139, 213, 238, 363, 405, 429. See also Honduras, economy; industry
--Late 19th century, HO62
--Mid-20th century, HO213, 364
-Transportation, CA832; HO22, 97, 104, 119, 202, 234, 317, 353, 370, 381, 383, 404, 406, 414
--Early 19th century, HO416
--Mid-19th century, HO263, 421, 423
--Late 19th century, HO096, 234, 263, 305-6, 322
--Early 20th century, CA320, 1393; HO322
--Mid-20th century, CA29, 38, 306
-Travel, CA6, 72, 189, 211, 223, 227; BE178
--Early 19th century, HO416
--Mid-19th century, HO422, 425, 475
--Late 19th century, CA494, 838; HO096, 114, 234, 264, 309, 322
--Early 20th century, CA317, 320, 662, 774; HO233, 362
--Mid-20th century, CA355, 407, 446; HO191, 265, 479
-Treaties, HO222-24, 260
-United States influence, CA6
-United States intervention, HO43, 61, 322
-United States investment, HO48
-Universidad Nacional Autónoma de. See Honduras, universities
-Universities, CA36; HO92, 147, 173-75, 182, 277, 376, 401, 451, 485
-Uprising of 1907, CA380
-Women, HO55, 246
Honduras Rosario Mining Company, HO271
Honduras Society of Engineers and Architects, CA111

La Hora (Guatemala), GU373, 831-33, 837, 842, 1160
Hospitals
-Costa Rica, CR21
-El Salvador, ES329
Hostos, Eugenio María de, GU372
Housing, CA541, 672, 767-68
-Costa Rica, CA672, 767-68; CR50, 112, 153, 202, 256-61, 613, 996, 1022
-El Salvador, CA672, 767-68; ES183, 330, 385
-Guatemala, CA672, 767-68; GU537, 1131, 1389
-Honduras, CA672, 767-68; HO178, 186
-Nicaragua, CA672, 767-68
-Panama, CA767-68
Huehuetenango, Department of (Guatemala), GU57, 297, 1107
Hughes, Charles Evans, CA878
Huité (Guatemala), GU1020
Human rights, CA763, 922; CR775; ES237, 401
Humor
-Costa Rica, CR352, 387, 459, 504, 559, 581, 633, 668, 797
-El Salvador, ES194, 338-39
-Guatemala, GU136, 1084, 1181
-Honduras, HO157, 706
Hungary
-Relations with El Salvador, CA387
-Relations with Guatemala, CA387; GU140
-Relations with Honduras, CA387
Hurricanes in Belize, BE42-43, 86
El Husas Blanco, CR1075

Idioms, CA207, 505, 885
-Costa Rica, CR9, 67, 70, 105, 387, 439, 498, 585, 668, 974, 979, 1075, 1092, 1139
-El Salvador, ES2, 72, 192, 215
-Guatemala, GU105, 116, 136, 170, 201, 1218
-Honduras, HO297, 477, 480
-Nicaragua, NI156, 163, 696
Iglesias, Demitrio, CR315
Iglesias, Francisco María, CR1114
Iglesias, Joaquín de, CR601
Iglesias Castro, Rafael. See Yglesias Castro, Rafael
Illustration of Honduras, HO265
Immigration to
-Belize, BE29, 67, 80, 94, 112, 132, 146
-Central America, CA20-21, 542, 603
-Costa Rica, CR93, 242, 284, 311, 343, 383, 727, 782, 796, 842, 855, 920, 1002, 1019
-Guatemala, GU102, 178, 190, 193-95, 213, 312-19, 343, 394, 415, 417, 533, 710, 761, 861, 884, 987, 1065, 1078, 1088, 1273, 1293
-Honduras, HO21, 249, 316, 355, 444
--Early 19th century, HO416
-Nicaragua, NI119, 123, 522
El Imparcial (Guatemala City), CA95, 385, 790; BE163, 181; GU19-20, 209, 330, 707, 720, 854, 927, 1183, 1360, 1415, HO462
Income distribution in Central America, CA175, 519
Independence era, CA5, 23-24, 41-43, 46, 50, 84, 101, 107, 118, 124, 131, 134, 159-60, 165, 170, 192-93, 210, 226, 232-33, 236, 241, 243-44, 270, 287, 293, 297-99, 302-4, 309-10, 333, 338-40, 342-43, 348-50, 365, 392-93, 401, 427, 445, 449, 469, 497-500, 502, 507, 512-13, 527-32, 534, 551-52, 555, 557, 560, 563, 571, 574-77, 580, 582, 585, 592, 597-99, 605, 613, 616, 618-19, 621, 628-30, 633, 646, 663, 666, 682-83, 696, 699, 721-22, 724-25, 731-32, 754, 758-60, 766, 770, 775, 778, 782, 784-85, 788, 794, 796-97, 800, 821-23, 825, 878, 889-90, 894, 904-6, 917,

934-38, 941-50, 952, 959, 965, 1011-12, 1018;
    BE135; CR16, 99, 113, 116, 122, 180, 211, 215,
    217, 220, 224, 239, 255, 278, 300, 332, 343,
    377, 415, 433-34, 448-50, 452, 482, 524, 526-28,
    539, 541, 553, 557, 578, 600-601, 603, 634, 640,
    659, 731, 741, 771-73, 799, 817-18, 820, 845,
    859-60, 862, 864, 1009, 1038, 1110, 1128; ES35,
    66, 86, 101, 107, 116-18, 152, 161, 184, 189-90,
    195, 203, 267, 269, 336, 371, 375; GU34, 147,
    167-68, 181, 183, 206, 210, 234, 243, 298, 300,
    311, 322, 331-32, 363, 366, 389, 392, 396, 452,
    481, 485, 487-88, 490, 502, 518, 538, 551-52,
    558, 670, 684-85, 711, 771, 775, 791-92, 820,
    838-39, 909-10, 924, 932, 1027, 1077, 1081,
    1090, 1128, 1197, 1212, 1214, 1263, 1268, 1297,
    1359, 1410; HO7, 10, 76, 129, 131, 134-35, 176,
    195, 282, 287, 388, 441, 487; NI38, 184, 200,
    289, 291, 425, 497, 521, 730
-Mexico and, CA43, 46, 101, 159, 226, 288, 309, 527-
    29, 534, 551, 571, 592, 597-99, 616, 646, 721,
    754, 759, 770, 794, 904, 935, 937, 949, 965;
    CR817, 856, 1128; ES86, 336; GU147, 210, 331,
    366, 820, 839, 1359; HO134, 282, 286; NI291
Independent Liberal Party, NI604
Indian languages
-El Salvador, ES192
-Guatemala, GU523
-Nicaragua, NI156, 698
Indian legislation in Guatemala, GU699
Indian mythology in El Salvador, ES373
Indians, CA3, 89, 98, 334-36, 391, 407, 411, 447,
    471, 505, 788, 845, 853, 885, 891, 897, 987;
    BE116, 179; CR112, 133, 148, 285, 721, 738, 889;
    ES10, 17, 28, 50, 192, 208, 214, 328, 373; GU9,
    23, 26, 53, 61, 109, 111, 114, 116, 124-25, 127,
    134, 177, 184, 189, 192, 197, 205, 215, 217-18,
    250, 304, 338, 351, 374, 392, 408, 421, 425,
    432, 476, 487, 516, 524, 598-607, 687-82, 699-
    700, 706, 709, 713, 737, 740, 749, 757, 760,
    766, 783-84, 786, 807-8, 815, 821, 880-81, 886,
    896, 920, 922, 940, 945, 969, 972, 977, 984-5,
    989, 1003, 1005, 1046-47, 1057, 1108-9, 1128,
    1140-41, 1164, 1171, 1175, 1199, 1205, 1209,
    1224, 1244, 1247, 1250, 1255, 1257, 1272, 1280,
    1283-86, 1289, 1291-92, 1330, 1339, 1362, 1364,
    1385-87, 1396; HO27, 166, 298, 318, 475; NI196,
    396, 440
Indígenismo in Guatemala, GU601
Individual rights in Honduras, HO354
Indonesia, GU970
Industry, CA125, 175, 250, 252-53, 306, 399, 424,
    453, 474, 519, 540, 611, 635, 727, 752, 769,
    871-72
-Belize, BE179
-Costa Rica, CA306; CR39, 44, 110, 270, 792
-El Salvador, CA306; ES70, 103, 216, 353
--Mid-20th century, ES216, 324, 345, 391
-Guatemala, CA306; GU55, 161, 302, 668, 728, 969,
    1011, 1079
-Honduras, CA306; HO190, 226, 257
-Nicaragua, CA306; NI356
-Panama, CR39
Inland waterways in Costa Rica, CR212
Institute of Pan American Geography and History
    (Costa Rica), CR287
Instituto Costarricense de Turismo, CR160
El Instituto de Alajuela (Costa Rica), CR18
Instituto Geográfico Nacional, CR908
Instituto Interamericano de Ciencias Agrícolas,
    CA544

Instituto Normal para Varones de Oriente
    (Guatemala), GU866
Integration, CA182-84, 186, 250, 261-62, 294, 300-
    301, 325, 347, 354, 377, 398, 419, 459, 517,
    520, 536, 606, 611, 675, 677, 718, 729-30, 752,
    850, 857, 860-61, 864-868, 871, 976, 985-86;
    CR81, 179, 693
-Costa Rica, CA673; CR81, 619, 692
Integration Industries scheme, CA752
Intellectual history of Costa Rica, CR217
Intellectual trends in Central America, CA953
Inter-American Conference, Ninth (1948), BE104
Inter-American Development Bank, CR351
Inter-American Highway, CR302
Inter-American Legal Conference, Fifth (Lima, Peru),
    BE51
Inter-American Relations (Guatemala), GU956
Inter-American School of Public Affairs, CA454
Internal migration, CA110, 832
-Costa Rica, CA832; CR119, 432, 991, 1008, 1040
-El Salvador, CA832
-Guatemala, CA832; GU10, 57, 250, 550, 1131, 1234,
    1273, 1299, 1413
-Honduras, CA117, 832
-Nicaragua, CA832
-Panama, CA832
International Bank for Reconstruction and
    Development (Guatemala), GU728
International Cooperation Administration, ES324
International Court of Justice, CA462, 645, 655,
    723, 833
-Belize Boundary dispute and, BE20, 93
International Monetary Fund in Honduras, HO481
International Office for Central America, CA150
International Railways of Central America, GU174,
    731, 758
International Red Syndicate (Costa Rica), CR427
Interoceanic Canal, Special Committee on, NI418
Interoceanic Canal Congress, Paris (1879), NI358
Interoceanic Railway
-Costa Rica, CR854, 958
-Honduras, HO49-50, 59-63, 153, 187, 263, 306, 317,
    421-23
Investments
-Central America, CA63, 88, 119, 126, 474, 486, 511,
    514, 542, 606, 611, 635, 670-71, 678, 893, 907-
    9, 923, 977
--Mid-20th century, CA458, 521, 540, 626, 865; ES127
-Costa Rica, CA2, 687, 909; CR32, 179, 212, 218,
    228, 240
--Late 19th century, CR1079
--Early 20th century, CR717, 934
--Mid-20th century, CR214, 270, 331
-El Salvador, CA2; ES397
--Early 20th century, ES26, 70, 124, 272
--Mid-20th century, ES127, 216
-Guatemala, CA2, 909; GU30, 55, 102, 173, 175-76,
    229, 353, 415, 693, 930, 1007, 1095, 1275
--Late 19th century, GU166, 187, 582, 816, 947
--Early 20th century, GU580, 748, 1025, 1154, 1187,
    1267
--Mid-20th century, CA865; GU668, 971, 1203
--Late 20th century, GU736
-Honduras, CA909; HO22, 49-50, 59, 63, 78, 97, 114,
    202, 214, 232, 238, 243-44, 370, 380-81, 404,
    414, 423
--Mid-19th century, HO421
--Late 19th century, HO62, 114, 188, 262, 305-6, 315
--Early 20th century, HO196, 340-41, 355, 436
--Mid-20th century, CA865; HO313, 324

(Investments)
--Late 20th century, HO257, 263
-Latin America, CA670
-Nicaragua, NI50, 137, 237-38, 296, 359, 380
--Early 20th century, NI335, 342, 458, 465-66, 479, 663, 707
--Mid-20th century, NI476
-Panama, CA786
Irazú volcano, CR206, 1054
Iriarte Castro, Agustín, GU206
Irisarri, Antonio José de, GU168, 299, 389, 452, 478, 627, 933, 1215
Isla de Coco, CR289-90
Islas de Santinilla, HO150
Islas de Cisne. See Cisne, Islas de
Isle de Tigre, HO270, 387
Israel, GU479-80, 956
Isthmian Canal Commission (Nicaragua), NI367, 688-89
Italy, CA542
-Relations with Central America, CA464-65, 542
-Relations with Costa Rica, CA542; CR402, 610, 1106; HO238
-Relations with El Salvador, CA542; ES224, 398
-Relations with Guatemala, CA542; GU225, 736, 770
-Relations with Honduras, HO238
-Relations with Nicaragua, NI360
Iturbide, Agustín de, CA309, 721; CR856; ES184, GU839
Ixil Indians, GU307
Izabal, Department of (Guatemala), GU249-50, 677
Izaguirre V., Carlos, HO336

Jacalteca Indians, GU766
Jalapa, Department of (Guatemala), GU249, 841, 1297
Jamaica, CA999; BE146; CR383
Japan, relations with Central America, CA848
Jérez, Máximo, NI181, 184, 288, 320, 590
Jesuit Order, CA452, 720; CR705, 984, 1114; ES266; GU935-38; NI326
Jicaque Indians, HO474
El Jicaro (Guatemala), GU253
Jiménez, Juan Ramón, NI279
Jiménez, Manuel de Jesús, CR468, 658, 1072
Jiménez, Max, CR195, 197
Jiménez Oreamuno, Ricardo, CR87, 147, 192, 241, 455, 535, 557, 576, 606, 627, 658, 671, 747, 750, 877, 883, 898, 947, 987, 1061, 1074, 1115
Jiménez Zamora, Jesús, CR178
Jinotega, Department of (Nicaragua), NI310
John M. Amory and Son (Costa Rica), CR1033
Johnson, Lyndon B., CA762, 927
Jones, William Carey, NI225
Judicial system. See individual countries
Jutiapa, Department of (Guatemala), GU249, 393, 1022, 1426
Juticalpa (Honduras), HO373
Juvenile delinquency in Costa Rica, CR326, 948
Juventud Centro-Americana, CA589
Juventud Liberal Independiente (Nicaragua), NI607

Keith, Minor C., CR658, 828, 1026, 1116
Kekchi Indians, BE116; GU10, 250
Kennedy, John, CA893
Klee, C.F.R., CA225
Knox-Castrillo Agreement, NI663
Knox, Philander Chase, GU1382; NI729

Labor, CA7-8, 183, 185, 275, 316, 456, 458, 483, 521, 611, 858
-Belize, CA7; BE48
-Costa Rica, CA7, 275; CR26, 125, 175-76, 340, 593, 813, 829, 835, 971
-El Salvador, CA7, 275; ES106, 308, 334, 385
-Guatemala, CA7, 275; GU57, 220, 425, 433, 550, 690, 747, 764, 921, 1115, 1281
-Honduras, CA7, 161, 275, 349; HO139, 354
-Nicaragua, CA7, 275; NI178, 591
-Panama, CA14; GU800
Labor code of 1945 (Nicaragua), NI382
Labor courts in Guatemala, GU1115
Labor Laws
-Guatemala, GU172, 743
-Honduras, HO161, 349
Labor Party, GU377, 1235
Labor unions, CA483
-Costa Rica, CR73, 175-76, CR1049
-El Salvador, ES334
-Guatemala, GU176, 220, 458, 800, 912, 986, 1115, 1183, 1235, 1258
-Honduras, HO259
-Nicaragua, NI503, 591
LACSA (Costa Rica), CR623
Ladino culture, CA3, 888
Ladinos in Guatemala, CA3; GU9, 104, 189, 307, 425, 432, 501, 682, 887, 940, 976, 1171, 1244, 1387, 1413
Lafragua, José María, CA598
Lake Nicaragua, CA775
Lake Superior Ship Canal, NI337
Lamb, Dean Ivan, CA493
Land distribution. See individual countries
Land ownership. See individual countries
Land use. See individual countries
Landa, Luís, HO458
Landívar, Rafael, CA951; GU168, 518
Lane, Arthur Bliss, NI523
Laparra de Ydígoras Fuentes, María Teresa, GU529
Lara, Domingo Antonio de, CA941
Lardé y Larín, Jorge, CA646
Larrazábal, Antonio Jose de Las Mercedes, CA942; GU210, 538, 1340
Larreynaga, Miguel, CA576; GU502; NI521
Latimer, Julian L., NI675
Latin America
-Military, CR1084
-Universities, NI274
Latin American Free Trade Agreement, CA460, 670
Laws. See individual countries
League of Nations, CR846; ES140
-American (proposed), ES295
Leets, Juan, CA358; NI674
Legislature. See individual countries
Leguia, Agusto, HO117
Lejeune, John A., NI675
Lemus, María José, ES4, 149, 241-44, 403
León (Nicaragua), NI7, 77, 80, 122, 273, 305, 541, 695
León Castillo, José, GU295
León Sánchez, José, CR383, 681
Letras Patrias, CR368
Ley fuga (Guatemala), GU1086
Liberación Nacional (Costa Rica), CR43, 501
El Liberal (Guatemala), GU526-27
Liberal-Conservative Pact of 1971 (Nicaragua), NI190
Liberal Party, CA350, 559, 621, 623, 666, 785, 842, 939; CR173, 448, 705, 863, 883, 947; ES207; HO39, 42, 84, 90, 102-3, 112, 172, 283-84, 290, 293, 305, 323, 343-44, 346-47, 350, 375, 388, 393, 397, 417, 444-45, 464, 471, 483, 490, 492-93; NI32, 49, 62-63, 76, 110, 135, 181-84, 195, 199, 213, 267, 288, 325-26, 359, 413, 442, 489-

90, 504, 510, 517, 557, 589-91, 607, 630, 637-38, 729
-in Guatemala, CA623; GU21, 52, 60, 65-66, 97, 123, 153, 158, 162, 174, 219, 242, 261, 295, 321, 328, 361, 365, 382, 403, 444, 456, 469, 474, 488, 491-92, 510, 539, 541-42, 552, 563, 569, 705, 711, 769, 775, 879, 891, 897, 906, 927-28, 935-39, 982, 1036, 1121, 1144, 1217, 1329, 1359, 1367-69, 1410, 1422
El Liberal Progresista (Guatemala), GU1232
Liberal reform
-Costa Rica, CR336
-Guatemala, GU21, 123, 219, 258, 382, 711
-Honduras, HO42
Liberalism, CA583, 782, 809, 1018; CR88, 114, 1114; GU13, 35, 42, 47, 71
Liberation theology, CR976; GU878; NI300, 622, 648
Liberia, CR316, 1076
Libraries, CA363
-Costa Rica, CA36; CR17, 849
-El Salvador, CA36
-Guatemala, CA36
-Honduras, CA36
-Nicaragua, CA36
-Panama, CA36
Library of Congress, CA546
Libro Blanco, BE102, 104-5
Liceo (Costa Rica), CR72
Life expectancy
-Costa Rica, GU157
-Guatemala, GU157, 231, 496
-Panama, GU157
-United States, GU157
Life-style, CA258, 272, 901
-Guatemala, GU1393
Lima (Peru), CR578
Limón, Department of (Costa Rica), CR212, 329, 380, 382-83, 520, 568, 571, 605, 714, 740, 940
Lincoln, Abraham, GU219, 1101
Lindo y Zelaya, Juan Nepomuceno Fernandez, HO129, 286
Linguistic survey, CA505
Literacy, CA49, 217
-Costa Rica, CR14, 324
-Guatemala, GU286, 351, 1222
-Honduras, HO3, 292
Literary survey of Costa Rica, CR447
Literature
-Central America, CA94, 191, 305, 359, 495; 694, 953, 968
--Early 20th century, ES15
-Costa Rica, CR47, 67, 70, 106, 137, 145-46, 165, 195-96, 198, 356-57, 359-62, 365, 372, 380-81, 383, 387-88, 395, 424-26, 429, 445-46, 451, 454, 461, 463, 465-66, 471, 481, 509, 513-14, 562, 597, 614-15, 636, 676-79, 681-84, 689-90, 703, 710, 713, 720, 783, 785-88, 794, 800, 808, 887-88, 921, 930-31, 935, 937, 941, 952-53, 973, 1063, 1071, 1104, 1124, 1131-32, 1137
-El Salvador, ES2, 5, 10-13, 15-16, 19, 23, 29, 46, 60, 65-66, 169, 180-81, 191, 194, 196-97, 202, 215, 219, 247, 250, 268, 291, 338, 343, 367-68, 373, 389-90
--Early 20th century, ES19
--Mid-20th century, ES29
-Guatemala, GU18, 27, 62, 68-69, 88, 95, 100, 125-27, 129-32, 135, 150, 159, 168, 171, 179, 184, 223, 240, 258, 270, 282-83, 304, 344, 349, 367, 372, 375-76, 378, 406, 408, 429-30, 436, 445, 457-60, 462, 468, 500, 504, 507-9, 512, 535,

673, 700-701, 742, 754, 777, 796, 798, 803-4, 856, 870-71, 881, 891, 894, 901, 903-5, 913-16, 919-20, 922-23, 955, 990-91, 1017-18, 1048, 1051-52, 1062-64, 1070, 1082, 1096, 1098, 1100, 1123, 1137, 1162-64, 1166-68, 1189-91, 1194, 1200, 1209, 1215, 1240, 1250, 1305, 1331, 1333, 1337, 1343, 1355-56, 1377-78, 1403, 1406, 1416-17, 1420
--Early 20th century, ES15; GU694
--Mid-20th century, GU703
-Honduras, HO2, 29, 43, 46, 51, 64, 68, 72-73, 78-79, 81, 149, 156, 239, 255, 303-4, 325-26, 329, 331, 336, 357, 399-400, 409, 438, 447
-Nicaragua, NI57-58, 129, 146, 149, 185-86, 215, 217, 219, 221, 226, 239, 244, 273, 277, 320, 383, 388, 474, 514, 530, 543, 578, 643, 655, 657
-San Salvador, ES15
Living conditions
-Belize, BE94
-Costa Rica, CR95-96
-El Salvador
--Early 20th century, ES19
--Mid-20th century, ES144
-Guatemala
--Mid-20th century, GU591
Lizano Fait, Eduardo, CA296
Llama (Honduras), HO402
Llano Grande (Costa Rica), CR1081
Llorente y Lafuente, Anselmo, CR980
Local Government in El Salvador, ES96
Lodge, Henry Cabot, GU1323
Logging in Belize, BE21, 64
Lombardo, Jose Santos, CR16
Lopez, Jacinto, CR831; GU1157
López Arellano, Oswaldo, CA425
López Jiménez, Ramón, BE107
López Pérez, Rigoberto, NI260
López Pineda, Julián, HO267
López Rivera, Lionel Fernando, GU801
Loubet Award, CA15, 30, 34, 200, 206, 624, 713-15, 733, 738-39
Louisiana-Nicaragua Lumber Company, HO436
Lozano, Julio, HO343
Lubaantun, CA357
Lyra, Carmen, CR67, 691

McConnell, Herbert L., CA687
Maceo Grajales, Antonio, CR343
Madriz, José, NI674
Magdalena Milpas Atlas, GU7
The Magee Incident (Guatemala), GU1278
Magón. See González Zeledón, Manuel
Mahan, Alfred Thayer, NI410
Mahogany in Belize, BE146
El Malacate (Guatemala), GU1121
Mallagaray, CR708
Malvinas Islands. See Falkland Islands
Managua (Nicaragua), NI3, 51, 77, 79, 120, 140, 244, 266, 312, 324, 327-31, 333, 377
Mano Blanco (Guatemala), GU1303
Maps, CA2, 38, 89, 123, 255, 370, 477, 612, 831-32, 859, 924, 997
-Belize, BE33, 69, 182
-Costa Rica, CA2, 38, 708, 832; CR50, 303, 371, 849
-El Salvador, CA2, 38, 832; ES28, 137, 344, 414
-Guatemala, CA2, 38, 832; GU586, 593, 609, 869, 1389
-Honduras, CA38, 832; HO115
-Nicaragua, CA38, 832; NI92, 188
-Panama, CA832
Marañon, BE133

Marcoleta, José de, NI398, 549

Marijuana, CA173; CR149

Marín Cañas, José, CR67, 196

Mariscal, Ignacio, CA322; BE78, 134, 144, 183

Mariscal-St. John Treaty of 1893. See Mariscal-Spencer Treaty of 1893

Mariscal-Spencer Treaty of 1893. BE55, 78, 92, 97, 134-36, 143-44, 167, 173, 183

Maritime Canal Company of Nicaragua, NI42, 204, 395, 399-400, 620, 681

Mármol, Miguel, ES82

Marquez, Francisco Antonio, HO131

Marquez, Javier, HO481

Marroquín, Gutierrez, GU56

Marroquín Rojas, Clemente, CA552, 906; GU373, 795, 831, 837, 841; HO323, 442

Marsh, M.M., CR241, 331

Martí, Farabundo, ES25

Martí, José, CR639; NI145

Martí y Pérez, José Julián, GU843-44, 1269, 1360

Martín, CA303

Martínez, Tomás, NI174, 518

Martínez Galindo, Arturo, HO079

Martínez Hernández, Maximiliano, ES18, 58, 75, 121, 138-39, 201, 219, 254, 260, 323, 331, 337, 342

Martínez López, Eduardo, CA118, 268

Martínez Sobral, Enrique, GU856-57

Martínez Zelada, Eliseo, GU1129

Marure, Alejandro, GU294, 344, 569

Marx, Karl, NI149

Masaya (Nicaragua), NI313

Masferrer, Alberto, ES251, 289-90, 321, 386, 388

La Masica (Honduras), HO220-21

Mason, Alexander T., NI681

Masonic Lodges, CR489, 529, 819, 823, 855; GU988

Matagalpa (Nicaragua), NI314

Matus-Pacheco Convention of 1896, CA660

Maya Archeological zones, CA337, 889-90, 988

Maya Mountains, BE13, 69

Mayan Indians, CA335-36, 987; BE179; GU61, 124, 177, 192, 215, 250, 766, 983-84, 1140, 1257

Mayorga Carrera, Leonidas, NI504

Mazariegos, Nicolas, GU35

Mazatenango (Guatemala), GU882

Media in Costa Rica, CR181, 480

Medina, José María, HO360

Mejia Colindres, Vicente, HO65, 290

Meléndez, Carlos, ES41, 104, 295

Melville, George Wallace, NI410

Membreño, Alberto, HO193

Memorias de Jalapa, CA618-19; ES116

Méndez Montenegro, Julio César, GU546, 1045, 1053, 1102

Mendez-Williamson Contract (Guatemala), GU623

Mendieta, Salvador, CA398, 590, 638

Menéndez, Andres L., ES58

Menéndez, Francisco, ES59, 131, 265, 352, 407

Menéndez, Isidro, CA499

Menocal, Ancieto García, NI203-4, 535

El Mensajero de Centro América, CA592

El Mercurio (Santiago), CA10

Mérida (Mexico), BE58; CR751

Metapán (El Salvador), ES396

Methodist Church, BE89

Mexican Revolution, GU83, 672

Mexican Tourist Office, CR939

Mexico, GU498, 1115; NI438, 711-12

-Boundary dispute with Guatemala. See Guatemala, boundary dispute with Mexico

-Boundary Treaty of 1881 with Guatemala, CA928; BE135

-Census data, CA921

-Commercial law, CR717

-French intervention, GU299

-Geography, CA990

-Railroads, NI438

-Relations with Central America, CA234, 770

-Relations with Costa Rica, CR417, 751

-Relations with El Salvador, ES184

-Relations with Guatemala, GU300, 357, 366, 498, 531, 631, 895

-Relations with Nicaragua, NI438, 571

-Relations with United States, CA376, 770; NI602, 711-12

-Travel

--Mid-20th century, GU177

Military. See individual countries

Milla, José Justo, HO135

Milla y Vidaurre, José, CA350; GU294, 904-5, 1048, 1215

Minifundistas in Guatemala, GU989

Mining

-Costa Rica, CR300

-Guatemala, GU728, 1415

-Honduras, HO266, 271, 315, 416

-Nicaragua, NI164

Mixco (Guatemala), GU32, 1021

Mobile Address, HO061

Mocoron, CA466

Modernism, ES191, 211; HO303

Modernization of Costa Rica, CR404

Molina, Arturo Armando, ES211-12

Molina, José Roberto, GU1090

Molina, Juan Ramón, HO079, 328, 358, 390

Molina, Pedro, CA135, 576, 605, 760; GU792, 1027

Molina y Mata, Marcelo, GU910

Momostenango (Guatemala), GU1236

Moncada, José María, NI427-29

Monge, Luís Alberto, CR88, 177

Monimbo (Nicaragua), NI194

Monroe Doctrine, CA32, 85, 843, 878; BE152, 164; ES295; NI91, 370, 390, 420, 428, 610, 723

Montealegre Fernandez, José María, CR732

Monteforte Toledo, Mario, GU807, 837

Montero Madrigal, Jorge, CR67

Montúfar, Lorenzo. See Montúfar y Rivera Maestre, Lorenzo

Montúfar, Rafael, CA452; CR1114; GU403

Montúfar y Coronado, Manuel, ES116

Montúfar y Rivera Maestre, Lorenzo, CA550; CR939; GU820, 926, 935-38

Mopan Indians, BE116

Mora Fernández, Juan Rafael, CR410, 526-28, 640, 773

Mora Porras, Juan Rafael, CR59-60, 172-73, 185, 250-51, 273, 641, 732, 945, 1100

Mora Valverde, Manuel, CR88, 779-852

Morales, Eusebio A., CA689-91

Moravian Church, NI118, NI334, 340, 440

Morazán, Francisco, CA23-24, 84, 107, 118, 160, 165, 210, 230, 233, 241, 243-44, 290, 293, 298, 303, 365, 392, 427, 469, 512, 532, 552, 555, 574, 580, 613, 621, 628-30, 666, 731, 766, 778, 797, 806, 808-9, 906, 959, 1018; CR332, 452, 524, 810, 817, 845; ES375; GU332, 838, 1297; HO10, 76, 195, 287, 388, 438, 441

Morejón de Bográn, Teresa, HO25

Moret y Prendergast, Segismundo, CA206

Morgan and Company (Honduras), HO340-41

Mosquito Indians, CA996; BE112; HO113; NI118, 196, 440, 481, 507, 525, 597, 622

Mosquito Territory, CA78, 178, 235, 286, 361-62, 367, 408, 425, 429-30, 436, 438-39, 441-42, 466, 526, 565-66, 578, 608, 645, 655, 657, 686, 697, 702, 708, 712, 771, 790, 831; HO355; NI5, 39, 69, 88, 109, 119, 154-55, 224, 271, 290, 301-2, 340, 343-44, 372, 376, 392, 440, 443, 469, 471, 473, 507, 525-27, 635, 640, 664, 685, 701, 724, 727
Motagua River Valley, CA997
Movimiento de Liberación Nacional (Guatemala), GU15, 155-56, 327, 466, 534, 545, 636-37, 641, 645, 652-53, 658, 661, 676, 714, 716-18, 727, 797, 802, 951, 1176, 1210, 1251, 1301-2, 1321, 1345
Movimiento Democrático Nacional (Guatemala), GU1002
Movimiento Revolucionario 13 de Noviembre (Guatemala), GU950
Moya Murillo, Rafael, CR730
Multinational corporations. See foreign corporations
Municipal government in Costa Rica, CR515, 654, 685, 916
Muñoz, Trinidad, NI705
Muñoz Meany, Enrique, GU837, 1191
Muralists in Costa Rica, CR462
Murillo Aguilar, Nicolas, NI262
Music, CR46, 642, 906; ES158; GU107-8, 967, 1032, 1188, 1352; HO67
Muybridge, Edward, GU811

La Nación (Ciudad Trujillo), GU1059
La Nación (San José), CR1048, 1075
Nahua Indians, CR439
Napoleon III, Louis, CA870; NI91, 109
Nation (New York), NI86
National Archives
-Costa Rica, CR7, 667
-Honduras, HO199, 375
National Guard. See Guardia Nacional
National Institute of Geography (Costa Rica), CR288
National Liberation Movement (Guatemala). See Movimiento de Liberación Nacional
National Liberation Party. See Partido de Liberación Nacional
National Library
-Costa Rica, CR493, 709
-Honduras, HO205
National Liquor Factory of Costa Rica, CR201
National Museum in Costa Rica, CR133, 729
National Palace, seizure of (Nicaragua, 1979), NI191, 268
National Party in Honduras, HO9, 193, 241, 348-50, 352, 467. See also Conservative Party
National Police in Guatemala, GU1180
National Printing Company in Costa Rica, CR493
National Railroad in Honduras, HO378
National Society of Geography and History (Honduras), HO26
National Theater
-Costa Rica, CR1059
-El Salvador, ES291
National Tobacco Factory in Costa Rica, CR862
National University of
-Honduras. See Honduras, universities
-Nicaragua. See Nicaragua, universities
Nazis, CA847-48
-Guatemala, GU1229-30
Netherlands, relations with Guatemala, GU947, 971
New England Grocer, CA827
New Granada, CA717, 733
New Orleans, CA511

New Orleans Times-Democrat, CA511
New Panama Canal Company (Nicaragua), NI681
New Spain, Viceroyalty of, BE173
New York and Honduras Rosario Mining Company, HO315
New York Bond Club, CR1044
New York Globe, HO193
New York Herald, CR831, 1070
New York Herald Tribune, CA807
New York Navigation and Colonization Company, HO316
New York Times, CA482; HO4
Newspapers, CA13
-Costa Rica, CR14, 207, 564, 798, 803, 884
-El Salvador, CA495; ES29, 166, 258, 263
-Guatemala, GU19-20, 207, 209, 212, 330, 364, 373, 470, 495, 514, 635, 637, 692, 694, 696, 707, 910, 1121, 1407, 1414
-Honduras, HO28, 285, 330, 337, 392
-Nicaragua, NI21, 32, 182, 218, 228, 432
Nicaragua
-Agriculture, CA3, 44, 285, 410; NI102, 387, 720. See also individual crops
--Early 20th century, CA834; NI423
--Mid-20th century, CA38, 306; NI270, 463
--Late 20th century, NI73, 354
-Boundary dispute with Costa Rica. See Costa Rica, boundary dispute with Nicaragua
-Boundary dispute with Honduras. See Honduras, boundary dispute with Nicaragua
-Boundary dispute with Panama, CA652, 656-57
-Budgets, CA279
-Christian Democratic Party. See Christian Democratic Party
-Church-State relations, CA720; NI326
-Cities. See Cities, Nicaragua
-Civil War of 1909-10, NI541
-Civil War of 1978-79, NI194
-Class structure. See Nicaragua, social structure
-Coins, NI459
-Conservative Party. See Conservative Party
-Constituent Assembly of 1938-39, NI258
-Constituent Assembly of 1947, NI475
-Constitutional Convention of 1938, NI540
-Constitutions, NI36-37, 341, 408
-Courts. See Nicaragua, judicial system
-Culture, CA211
-Dependency analysis of, NI487, 653
-Dictatorship, NI13, 16-17, 52, 74, 85, 548
-Economy, CA57, 62, 410, 775; NI73, 106, 125, 296, 340, 459, 522, 620. See also Nicaragua, industry; trade
--Mid-19th century, NI91, 123
--Late 19th century, NI2, 192, 357, 380, 480, 513
--Early 20th century, CA238, 317, 834, 1007; NI50, 94, 98, 136-37, 222, 230, 238, 264, 335, 342, 359, 403-4, 408, 423, 458, 465-66, 479, 584, 707
--Mid-20th century, CA38, 211, 251, 306, 411; NI52, 121, 127, 165, 237, 270, 287, 356, 387, 462-63, 474, 476, 589, 613, 649
--Late 20th century, NI73, 175, 354, 360, 583, 722
-Education, CA275, 289; NI14, 24, 65, 97, 157, 212, 253, 424, 440, 487, 659, 666, 694
--Mid-20th century, CA218-19
--Agricultural, CA44
--Elementary, NI659
--Secondary, CA289
--Vocational, CA45, 136
-Elections
--Election of 1878, NI168
--Election of 1924, NI441
--Election of 1926, NI426

(Nicaragua)
--Election of 1967, NI494
-Employment, CA7
-Family, CA3; NI112, 247
-Festivals, NI611
-Finance, CA306; NI50, 459
--Early 20th century, NI136-37, 222, 230, 238, 264, 335, 342, 359, 466, 479, 584, 663
--Mid-20th century, CA279, 306; NI237
-Flag, NI272
-Foreign corporations, NI465, 578
-Foreign loans, NI466
--Early 20th century, NI335, 342
-French immigration to, NI461
-Generation of 1929, NI304
-Geography, CA62, 167, 324, 407, 411, 472, 494, 636, 681, 774, 834, 841; NI2, 9, 38, 92, 123, 127, 196, 275, 287, 298, 334, 347, 353-54, 380, 462, 464, 474, 480, 507, 529, 585, 594, 620, 635, 639-40, 646, 649
-German immigration to, NI296, 376, 554
-German trade with, CA225
-Guardia Nacional, NI117, 213, 215, 297, 351, 388, 391, 422, 567, 586, 660, 669, 699
-Historical survey, CA169, 472, 492, 698, 896; NI19, 78, 161, 163, 200, 406, 419, 425, 427, 445, 474, 505, 510, 589, 595, 658, 702
-Humor, NI706
-Idioms, NI156, 163, 696
-Immigration to, NI119, 123, 522
-Indian dialects, NI698
-Industry, NI356. See also Nicaragua, economy; trade
-Investment, NI50, 137, 237-38, 296, 359, 380
--Early 20th century, NI335, 342, 458, 465-66, 479, 663, 707
--Mid-20th century, NI476
-Labor, CA7; NI178, 591
-Labor unions, NI503, 591
-Land distribution, CA285; NI73, 198
-Land ownership, CA285; NI64, 354, 463
-Land use, NI646
-Laws, NI37, 64, 178, 247, 261, 341, 456-57, 568-69
-Liberal Party. See Liberal Party
-Maps, CA38, 832; NI92, 188
-Military, NI117, 350
-Nutrition, NI355
-Peasants, NI219, 387
-Photos, NI140, 266, 353, 439, 458, 717
--Early 20th century, NI598
-Place names, NI796-98
-Political parties, NI13, 32, 265, 267. See also individual parties and politics
-Politics, CA896; NI78, 163, 296, 445, 503. See also names of individual political parties
--Early 19th century, NI29, 38, 200, 517, 557, 590
--Mid-19th century, CR277; NI13, 29, 38, 88, 91, 174, 181, 183-84, 288, 291, 497, 501, 518-19, 557, 590, 705, 712
--Late 19th century, NI5, 9, 13, 49, 110, 162, 168-69, 171, 182, 192, 199, 259, 317, 319-20, 325-26, 480, 538, 547, 580, 608
--20th century, CR52
--Early 20th century, CA493, 582, 1007; NI10, 13, 17, 20, 23-24, 50, 61, 76, 106, 110, 115-16, 125, 135, 137, 169-70, 173, 182, 207, 209, 222, 227-30, 238-39, 242, 264, 267, 317, 319-20, 326, 350, 361, 368, 394, 403, 408, 413, 426-28, 430, 441, 452, 458, 490, 495, 504, 510, 531, 538, 541, 547, 564-65, 580, 584, 602-3, 663, 669, 675, 683, 686, 714-15, 728-29

--Mid-20th century, CA918-19; CR36; ES207; NI8, 13, 16-19, 22, 25-28, 32, 52-53, 59, 74, 85-87, 127, 131, 141-42, 146-47, 150, 159, 177-80, 185-86, 190-91, 193, 197, 211, 213-15, 218, 228, 231, 237, 258, 265, 281, 283-85, 299, 318, 350-51, 368, 387, 389, 391, 397, 422, 426-28, 442, 474-75, 489, 494, 496, 509-10, 523, 538, 540, 542, 544-46, 548, 552, 556, 559-62, 575-76, 579, 586, 589, 592, 594, 602-7, 609, 612, 617, 625-26, 642-43, 648, 654, 660-61, 699-700, 710, 725
--Late 20th century, CA922; NI1, 8, 51, 53, 55, 58-59, 73, 81, 86, 96-97, 113, 117, 128, 138, 141, 146-47, 149-50, 191, 193-94, 227, 257, 260, 268, 281-84, 286, 292, 294-95, 299-300, 411, 422, 477-78, 488, 498, 511, 528, 532, 537, 542, 545-46, 567, 583, 593-94, 691, 699, 704, 717, 719-22, 725
-Population, CA7, 17-18
--Mid-19th century, CA681
--Late 19th century, NI480
--Mid-20th century, CA38, 219, 345, 672, 767-68
--Late 20th century, NI354-55
-Presidents, CR313
-Railroads, NI438
-Rebellion of 1851, NI700
-Relations with Central America, NI577
-Relations with Costa Rica, CA658, 668-69, 684; CR36, 52, 116, 122, 220, 239, 246, 274, 277, 300, 312, 430, 1009, 1090; NI34, 203-6, 269, 364-66, 385, 415, 577
-Relations with El Salvador, CA22; NI158, 167, 254-56, 468, 472, 549, 572-73, 577, 693
-Relations with Guatemala, CA22, 792; CR36, 52; GU58, 727; NI859, 510
-Relations with Honduras, HO284, 332, 375; NI4, 438, 468, 470
-Relations with Latin America, NI596
-Relations with other countries. See individual countries
-Relations with Panama, NI438, 531
-Revolt of Los Mollejones, NI606
-Revolt of 1910, NI674
-Revolt of Olama, NI606
-Revolution of 1893, NI608
-Revolution of 1903, NI430
-Revolution of 1912, NI490
-Revolution of 1926, NI504
-Revolution of 1954, CA658
-Revolution of 1959, NI179
-Revolution of 1978-79, NI81, 96-97, 113, 117, 138, 191, 260, 268, 281-84, 286, 292, 294-95, 300, 378, 386, 411, 422, 477-78, 511, 528, 532, 537, 567, 593, 691, 699, 704, 717, 719-22
-Rural society, CA3
-Sex education, NI444, 583
-Social conditions, CA636
--Early 20th century, NI591
--Mid-20th century, NI334, 382
--Late 20th century, NI355, 583
-Social customs, CA223, 775; NI132-33, 218
-Social security system, CA7; NI496
-Social structure, CA3
-Society, CA223, 410; NI340, 656
--Late 19th century, CA494
--Early 20th century, CA317
--Mid-20th century, CA211
-Statistics, NI165
--Late 20th century, NI354
-Supreme Court, NI434

-Taxation, CA251, 279
-Trade, CA57, 306, 775, 834. See also Nicaragua,
     economy; industry
--Late 19th century, NI2
--Early 20th century, NI98, 423, 707
--Mid-20th century, NI121, 476
-Transportation, CA57, 458, 589, 636, 832; NI108
--Early 20th century, NI94, 230
--Mid-20th century, CA29, 38, 306
-Transportation facilities, NI458, 589
-Travel, CA72, 98, 189, 211, 223, 352
--Early 19th century, CA775; NI640
--Mid-19th century, NI339, 379, 381, 492, 527, 635,
     639, 727
--Late 19th century, CA494; HO309; NI345, 480, 493,
     615
--Early 20th century, CA238, 317, 662, 774; NI114,
     210, 374, 485
--Mid-20th century, CA355; NI84, 287, 372, 512, 667
--Late 20th century, NI439
-Treaties, NI111, 229, 455
--Late 19th century, NI467
-Treaty of 1858 with Costa Rica, CA660-61, 724-25
-United States intervention, CA344, 509, 594, 644,
     804, 810, 814; CR489; NI8, 10, 17, 20, 23-24,
     48, 61-63, 103, 106, 222, 231, 242, 264, 280,
     297, 299, 342, 361, 368, 391, 397, 426, 428,
     441, 452, 479, 485, 495, 508, 538, 542-43, 552,
     587-88, 590, 594, 601, 603, 616, 628-30, 637-38,
     654, 663, 668, 675, 683, 687, 699, 703, 713,
     716, 720, 728-29
-United States Marines, CA72
-Universities, CA36; NI54, 65, 274, 431, 433, 453,
     487, 544, 666
-Uprising of 1897, NI199
-Women, NI247, 612, 656
-Women's right to vote, NI612
Nicaragua and Central America Union, CA805
Nicaragua Canal. See Canal location question
Nicaragua Canal Association, NI203, 415
Nicaragua Canal Board, NI484
Nicaragua Canal Commission, NI620, 690, 709
Nicaragua Canal Construction Company, NI399, 447-48
Nicaragua Canal Convention of 1892, NI449
Nicaraguan influence in Costa Rica, CR598
Nicaragüense, Frente Unitario, NI285
Nicoya peninsula (Costa Rica), CA724-25, CR26, 122,
     300, 303, 485, 673, 772, 909, 1009; NI34
-Annexation of. See Guanacaste, annexation of
Nimmo, Joseph, Jr., NI67
Nindri (Nicaragua), NI502
Ninth Inter-American Conference, CR19
Nixon, Richard, GU647
Nonualco, Santiago, ES50
El Norte (San Pedro Sula), HO140
Northern Railway Company, CR242, 329, 962-63, 1061,
     1138
Notary law in Central America, CA816
Nottebohm Case, GU730
Novels, CA740, 776, 876, 959, 968
-Costa Rica, CR60, 107, 139, 146, 162, 355, 357,
     359-60, 365, 381, 393-94, 422, 424, 426, 495,
     505, 513, 516, 530, 568-69, 587, 602, 614-15,
     677, 680, 683, 690, 711, 713, 784, 786-88, 806,
     832, 837, 887, 921, 986, 1010, 1031, 1063, 1071,
     1121
-El Salvador, ES196-97, 219, 248, 262, 341, 347,
     368, 373
-Guatemala, GU15, 27, 89, 92-93, 96, 124, 127, 129-
     33, 135-36, 179, 184-85, 305, 324, 340, 376,

     397, 408, 429, 436, 466, 474, 500, 507, 691,
     700-701, 733-34, 742, 745, 754, 803, 855, 894,
     902, 913, 918-20, 922-23, 1048, 1052, 1062-64,
     1096, 1098-99, 1125-26, 1158, 1162-63, 1195,
     1200, 1250, 1331, 1355-56, 1362, 1402-4, 1416,
     1418-21
-Honduras, HO20, 29, 78, 81, 116, 123, 144, 156,
     166, 239, 314, 325, 327, 329, 393, 397, 400
-Nicaragua, NI1, 18, 51, 135, 145, 173, 176, 186,
     243, 320, 495, 501, 503, 541, 547, 558, 561,
     563, 565, 578, 616-17, 630, 635, 654-55
Nuestro Diario (Guatemala City), CA385; GU528, 696,
     1167
Nuestra Señora de Los Angeles, CR905
Nuestra Señora de Vjarriás, CR902
La Nueva Prensa (San José), CR186, 1120, 1122
Nueva Segovia (Nicaragua), NI315
Núñez Monge, Francisco María, CR810
Nutrition. See individual countries

OAS, CA313, 426, 558, 569, 671, 676, 683-84, 765,
     799, 843, 1013; BE18, 133; CR50; ES204, 206,
     344; GU1327; HO125, 468; NI179
Obando Bravo, Miguel, NI488
Obregón Lizano, Don Miguel, CR17-18, 294, 452, 812,
     814, 1126
Ocón Acevado, NI490
Ocotepeque (Honduras), HO473
ODECA, CA7, 17-18, 39, 53, 129, 171, 277, 288, 330,
     395, 417-18, 525, 572, 674-75, 677, 682, 815,
     971, 1016; GU113, 400, 628
Oduber Quirós, Daniel, CR74, 88, 827, 1032
Olancho, Department of (Honduras), HO152, 249, 316,
     373
Oquelí Bustillo, Miguel, HO332
Orange Walk (Belize), BE76
Oreamuno, Yolanda, CR196, 1063, 1071
Oregon (U.S.S.), NI208
Orellana, José María, GU555, 666, 1157, 1369
O.R.I.T. (Guatemala), CR835; GU912
Orotína (Costa Rica), CR49
Orozca Carranza, Moisés Evaristo, GU1009
Ortega, Juan J., GU449
Ortiz, Passarelli, Miguel, GU1002
Osejo, Rafael Francisco, CR1109-10
Osorio, Oscar, ES38, 88, 144, 154, 241, 243
Ostuncalco (Guatemala). See San Juan Ostuncalco

Pacheco, Abel, CR383
Pacheco Bertora, Luís, CR734
Pacheco Cabezas, Leonidas, CR409
Pacific Coast, CA707
-Costa Rica, CR485, 673, 739, 909
-Guatemala, CA485
Pacific port in Costa Rica, CR303, 486-87
Pacific Railroad of Costa Rica, CR142, 159, 221,
     231, 392, 486-87, 661, 1136
Pact of Santa Ana in 1946, CA973
Padilla, Alberto Sixto, ES352
Palencia (Guatemala), GU404
Pallottine Missionary Sisters, BE150
Palma, Jose Joaquín, GU1216
Las Palmas (Guatemala), GU1299
Palmerston, Lord, NI151
Palomo de Castillo, Odilia, GU534
Pan American Conferences, GU354; HO8
Pan American Exposition, ES402
Pan American Highway, CA321; CR427

Pan American Institute of Geography and History, CA640; ES137; HO15
Pan American Scientific Congress of 1908-9 (Santiago), CR672
Pan American Scientific Congress of 1924, ES228
Pan American Underwriters of New York, CR1120
Pan American Union, CA694; CR1022; GU96; HO123
Pan Americanism in Central America, CA124, 330, 507, 513
Panajachel (Guatemala), GU709, 1285
Panama, CA444, 636; NI384, 438, 482, 527
-Agriculture, CA3, 687. See also individual crops
--Early 20th century, CA834
-Boundary dispute with Costa Rica. See Costa Rica, boundary dispute with Panama
-Boundary dispute with Nicaragua. See Nicaragua, boundary dispute with Panama
-Census data
--Mid-20th century, CA921
--Late 20th century, CA921
-Church-State relations, CA720
-Class structure. See Panama, social structure
-and Common Market, CA247, 895
-Congress of, CA135, 582, 791
-Culture, CA211
-Economy, CA62, 227, 775. See also Panama, industry; trade
--Early 20th century, CA834
--Mid-20th century, CA211
-Education, CR39
--Mid-20th century, CA218
-Elite, CR521
-Ethnic groups, CA14
-Family, CA3; CR39
-Family planning, CR39
-Geography, CA3, 62, 834
-Historical survey, CA169, 896
-Industry, CR39. See also Panama, economy; trade
-Labor, CA14, GU800
-Life expectancy, GU157
-Maps, CA832
-Military, CA227
-Politics, CA896. See also names of individual political parties
-Population, CA345
--Mid-20th century, CA767-68
-Presidents, CR313
-Relations with Central America, CA301, 895
-Relations with Costa Rica, 742; CR61, 69, 962-63
-Relations with Great Britain, CA697
-Relations with Nicaragua, NI438, 531
-Relations with United States, CA643
-Social customs, CA775
-Social structure, CA3
-Society, CA227
--Mid-20th century, CA211
-Trade, CA775, 834. See also Panama, economy; industry
-Transportation, CA832
--Mid-20th century, CA29
-Travel, CA189, 211, 227
--Early 19th century, CA775
--Mid-19th century, NI379, 381
--Early 20th century, CA662
Panama Canal, CA643, 848, 895; CR872; GU1059; NI6, 28, 95, 124, 420
Panama Conference, GU210
Panama-Costa Rica War of 1921, CR711
Panchimalco (El Salvador), ES270
El Paraíso (Honduras), HO235, 249

Pardo Gallardo, José Joaquín, GU322
Paris Universal Exposition, 1889, ES356; NI400
Paris World Exposition of 1878, CA492
Parkhurst, Henry Clinton, NI107, 508
Parramos (Guatemala), GU600
Partido Acción Nacional (El Salvador), ES204
Partido Acción Renovadora (El Salvador), ES387
Partido de Conciliación Nacional (El Salvador), ES96
Partido de Liberación Nacional (Costa Rica), CA137; CR37, 53, 64, 84, 103, 141, 161, 177, 401, 418, 430, 474-75, 477, 507, 517-18, 565, 598-9, 742, 751, 790-1, 826-27, 835, 850-51, 955, 1048
Partido Nacional de Trabajadores (Guatemala), GU1044
Partido Progresista (Guatemala), GU1066, 1237
Partido Reformista (Costa Rica), CR1095
Partido Republicano Nacional (Costa Rica), CR219
Pastora, Eden, NI269
El Paterismo Nicaragüense, NI199
Patria (San Salvador), ES285
Patronato Nacional de la Infancia (Costa Rica), CR326
La Paz, Department of (Honduras), HO279, 392
Paz Baraona, Miguel, HO218
Peasant leagues in Nicaragua, NI387
Peasant organizations in Guatemala, GU1235
Peasants. See individual countries
Penal institutions
-Costa Rica, CR56, 645, 680
-Guatemala, GU284, 997
Penal law, CR168, 170, 645, 836, 847; ES63
Pensions in Guatemala, GU596
People's United Party (Belize), BE32, 155, 172
Peralta, Manuel María de, CA96, 717
Peralta Azurdia, Alfredo Enrique, GU44, 562, 646, 1060
Peralta de la Vega, José María, CR862
Peralta Lagos, José María, ES227
Pérez, Jerónimo, NI174
Pérez Zeledón, Pedro, CR155, 567, 770
Periodicals in Guatemala, GU990
Perlas River, CA113
Perry Land Grant, HO21; NI522
Personnel in Central America, CA218-19
Peru, HO369
Pestalozzi, Juan Enrique, GU822
Petén, Department of (Guatemala), CA839; BE126; GU10, 254, 281, 595, 753, 874, 945, 967, 1110, 1136, 1159, 1162, 1238, 1270-71, 1325
Petroleum contracts in Costa Rica, CR612, 809
Petroleum exploitation rights in Costa Rica, CR230, 844, 1098
Petroleum exploration in Costa Rica, CR249, 1006
Petroleum
-Central America
--Mid-20th century, CA252
-Costa Rica, CR268, 533, 1070
-Guatemala
--Mid-20th century, GU728
Peurifoy, John E., GU1318
Pharmacy, GU370, 428; HO376
Photos. See individual countries
Picado Michalski, Teodoro, CR53, 141, 408, 430, 1011
Picado Twight, Clodomiro, CR875
Pineda C., Felipe, GU892
Pinto-Greulich Accord (Costa Rica), CR249, 533, 612, 809, 844, 1098, 1134
Pinto Suárez, Antonio, CR845
Pittier de Fábrega, Henri François, CR210, 1036
Place names. See individual countries
PLN. See Partido de Liberación Nacional

Poetry
-Costa Rica, CR65, 107, 196, 198, 199-200, 387-88,
    454, 469, 644, 744, 768
-El Salvador, ES81, 211, 268, 278, 287, 291
-Guatemala, GU18, 95, 130, 171, 201, 270, 327, 430,
    485, 512, 519, 777, 911, 1013, 1017-18, 1082,
    1136-37, 1143, 1166, 1189-90, 1240, 1250, 1269,
    1407
-Honduras, HO1, 303, 328, 337, 358, 390
-Nicaragua, NI15, 56, 58, 60, 128-29, 146-49, 215,
    218, 220-21, 234, 250, 300, 304, 474, 499-500,
    530, 726
Point-Four program, CR714, 1062
Pokomam Indians, GU501, 1109
Political parties, CA137, 611; CR36
-Costa Rica, CA137; CR13, 28, 30, 36-37, 62, 64, 68,
    84, 121, 141, 147, 161, 177, 219, 227, 248, 430,
    455, 518, 781, 790, 830
-El Salvador, ES326, 335, 387, 409
-Guatemala, CA137; CR36; GU31, 42, 927
-Honduras, HO424
-Nicaragua, NI13, 32, 265, 267
Political pressure groups in Costa Rica, CR62
Politics. See individual countries
Ponce Vaidés, Federico, GU325, 440, 1009, 1355-56
Pope Leo XIII, CR1035
Popenoe, Dorothy Hughes, GU6
Population. See individual countries
Porras, Belisario, CA692-93
Ports, CA884
-Costa Rica, CA775; CR34, 270, 303, 321, 651, 714
-Guatemala, CA285; GU978
-Honduras, HO22, 322
-Nicaragua, CA775
-Panama, CA775
Positivism in Guatemala, GU52
Postage stamps
-Costa Rica, CR279
-Guatemala, GU188, 522
Postal services in Guatemala, GU152-54, 522, 1160
Poveda Acheverria, Leonidas, CR111
Prado, Eladio, CR108
La Prensa (Managua), CA723, 744; CR1122; NI81, 142,
    168, 175, 177, 218, 227, 268, 704
La Prensa (San Salvador), ES382
La Prensa Libre (Guatemala City), GU963
El Presidente Arévalo y el retorno a Bolívar, GU842
Printing in Honduras, HO28
El Progreso Nacional (Guatemala City), GU253, 321,
    435, 883
Progressive Party, GU42
Prospero (Nicaragua), NI232
Protestant Church, CA364, 444, 883, 887; GU401,
    1132; HO296, 480
Provinces. See individual countries
Provisional Interoceanic Canal Society (Nicaragua),
    NI535-36
Public services. See individual countries
Public works. See individual countries
Public works projects. See individual countries
El Pueblo (Tegucigalpa), HO483
Puerto Barrios (Guatemala), GU622
Puerto Cortés (Honduras), HO322
Puerto Livingston (Guatemala), GU612
Puerto San José (Guatemala), GU660
Puntarenas, Department of (Costa Rica), CR34, 111,
    231, 319, 486-87, 555, 714, 1136

Quepos (Costa Rica), CR231
Quesada (Costa Rica), CR915

Quetzal (Guatemala), GU200, 467, 1029, 1231, 1361
Quezada, Juan José, NI193
Quezaltenango, Department of (Guatemala), GU29, 45,
    117, 201, 251, 259, 267, 328, 352, 356, 444,
    463, 550, 593, 793, 826, 1090, 1128, 1133-35,
    1280, 1404
El Quiché, Department of (Guatemala), GU677
Quiché Indians, CA853; GU217, 323, 346, 419, 439,
    1140, 1199, 1236, 1238, 1403, 1405
Quinine in Guatemala, GU1069
Quiñónez Molina, Alfonso, ES21-22, 105, 393
Quintana Roo (Mexico), BE160
Quirce Filguera, Jose, GU988
Quirós, José Manuel, CR865
Quirós Family, CR633, 924

Rabinal (Guatemala), GU1286
Radio in Guatemala, GU514
Radio Liberación (Guatemala), GU228
Radio Vanguardia (El Salvador), ES4
Railroads. See individual countries
Ramírez, Alejandro, GU1212
Ramírez, Gregorio, José, CR741
Raoul, Nicolás, CA894
Reactionary Revolutionary Vanguard (Nicaragua),
    NI625
Recinos, Adrián, GU837, 1120
Reciprocal Trade Agreements, CR629
Recreo, battle of (Nicaragua), NI40
Red Cross
-Costa Rica, CR923
-Guatemala, GU296
Redemptorist order in El Salvador, ES220
Reformist Party, CR7
Regalado, Tomás, CA190, 772, 792; ES20, 259; GU794-
    95, 1193
Regional Integration Movement in Honduras, HO122
Religion, CA191, 700; ES277-78, 287; GU765, 1004,
    1224; NI210, 648
El Reproductor Campechano (Mexico), BE137
La República (San José), CR332, 658, 770, 791, 869
Republican Party, CR977
El Republicano (Tegucigalpa), HO418
Resources, CA20-21, 40, 416, 464-65, 521, 706, 984,
    1001
-Belize, BE13, 29, 64, 69-70, 85, 101
-Costa Rica, CA38; CR122, 230, 286, 407, 419, 725,
    854, 925, 1079
-El Salvador, CA38, 408; ES31-32, 39, 42, 344-45,
    381
-Guatemala, CA38, 408; GU214, 353, 547, 567, 594,
    609, 972, 1025, 1058, 1376, 1415
-Honduras, CA38, 408; HO22, 114, 179, 243-44, 249,
    262, 362, 380, 422, 425
-Nicaragua, CA408; NI2, 123, 230, 356, 476, 480
Retalhuleu, Department of (Guatemala), GU1245
Reuben, William, CR590
Revista de Costa Rica, CR551
Revista de la Economía Nacional (Guatemala), GU693
Revista de la Universidad de San Carlos, CA563
Revista Educación (Costa Rica), CR46
Revista Tegucigalpa, HO89
Revolutionaries of 1944, CA813
Revolutionary Party, GU446
Revolutions
-Central America, CA9, 26, 283, 812; GU82
--Mid-20th century, CA806
-Costa Rica, CR250-51, 410, 1041, 1078, 1081

(Revolutions)
-El Salvador, CA341; ES24, 37, 205, 237, 248
--Mid-20th century, ES238
--Late 20th century, ES155-57
-Guatemala, CA341; GU13, 18, 198, 270
--Mid-20th century, GU22, 422, 429, 446, 450, 455
-Honduras, HO78, 144
-Revolutions of 1944, CA488
Revue Générale de Droit International Public, CA764
Reyes, José Trinidad, HO147, 247, 401, 451
Reyes de Carías, María Guadalupe, HO437
Reyna Barrios, José María, CR158; GU412, 526-27,
    793, 1216, 1298, 1369-70
Río Conference, GU1366
Río Grande de Térraba, CR896
Río Lempara Electrification Project, ES128
Río Treaty, CA969
Rivas (Nicaragua), NI316
-Battle of, CR271, 943; NI705
-Convention of, NI91
Rivas, Anselmo Hilario, CA22; NI557
Rivas Vázquez, Alejandro, CR932
Rivera, Joaquín, CA244
Rivera, Julio, ES130
Rivera Maestre, Francisco, GU820
Rivers
-Costa Rica, CR892, 1085
-El Salvador, ES56
Rives, George L., CA174
Roads. See individual countries
ROCAP, CA39, 175, 872
Rodríguez Cerna, José, GU212
Rodríguez Zeledon, José Joaquín, CR245, 625
Rollins, Clinton, NI107, 508
Romanticism, ES191, 211
Romero, Carlos Humberto, ES205
Romero, Matías, CA754
Romero, Oscar, ES156-57, 237-38
Romero Bosque, Pío, ES22, 332
Roosevelt, Franklin D., CR629, 1012; GU626; HO486
Roosevelt, Theodore, CA609; HO290
Rorschach tests in Guatemala, GU189
Rosa, Ramón, HO79, 112, 330-31, 393, 397
Rosales, Hernán, NI580
Rosario mines (Honduras), HO156-315
Rovinski, Samuel, CR590
Rubber Development Corporation, NI347
Rumania, relations with El Salvador, ES222
Rural cooperatives in Guatemala, GU704
Rural social problems in Guatemala, GU8
Rural society
-Costa Rica, CA3; CR54, 199-200, 356, 359, 361, 387-
    88, 393, 445-46, 451, 614, 652
--Early 20th century, CR523
-El Salvador, CA3; ES12
-Guatemala, CA3; GU8, 211, 704, 738
-Honduras, CA3
-Nicaragua, CA3
-Panama, CA3
Rural towns in Costa Rica, CR544

Sacasa, Crisanto, NI174, 517
Sacasa, Juan Batista, NI76, 351, 556, 561, 565, 586,
    592
Sacasa, Roberto, NI5, 608
Sacatepéquez, Department of (Guatemala), GU246, 320,
    336, 886
Saenz, Tranquilino, CR1056
Saint Louis Exposition (Honduras), HO211
Saint Vincent, BE110, 178
Saker-Ti, Groupo, (Guatemala), CR39, 1138, 1167,
    1190

Salas, Mariano, GU260
Salazar Herrera, Carlos, CR67, 196; GU1192
Salvadoran Academy of History, ES67, 118
Salvadoran migration to Honduras, HO31
Salvatierra, Sofonías, NI181
Samayoa Chinchilla, Carlos, GU807
San Andres (Guatemala), GU191
San Andrés Islands, CA286, 652, 656-57
San Andres Semetabaj (Guatemala), GU1387
San Antonio Aguas Calientes (Guatemala), GU602
San Antonio Ilotenango (Guatemala), GU419
San Bartolome Milpas Altas (Guatemala), GU603, 896
San Carlos (Costa Rica), CR915
San Carlos (Guatemala), GU501
San Carlos River, CR484
San Francisco Chronicle, NI107
San Ildefonso Ixtahuacán (Guatemala), GU57
San Jacinto, battle of (Nicaragua), NI520, 661
San José (Costa Rica), CR8, 82, 124, 138-39, 149,
    204, 260, 266, 299, 304, 317, 332, 356, 403,
    448, 483, 548, 613, 913, 926, 929, 996, 1022,
    1055
San José (Guatemala), GU1278
San José Conference of 1906, CA142
San José Conference of 1920, CA150, 267, 805
San Juan (Costa Rica), CR304, 552
San Juan Bautista (Guatemala), GU2
San Juan de Flores (Honduras), HO13
San Juan del Norte (Nicaragua), NI82, 101, 108, 114,
    151, 155, 189, 398, 633, 703
San Juan la Laguna (Guatemala), GU1247
San Juan Ostuncalco (Guatemala), GU815
San Juan River, CA91, 112, 194, 206, 651, 659-61,
    724-25, 775; CR357, 484, 488, 815, 895, 1100;
    NI69, 91, 166, 175, 192, 204-6, 269, 364-66,
    415, 516, 577, 618-19
San Juan Sacatepéquez (Guatemala), GU604
San Lucas (Costa Rica), CR680
San Lucas Tolimán (Guatemala), GU1397
San Luís Gonzaga, Colegio de, CR857
San Luís Jilotepeque (Guatemala), GU189, 1219, 1312
San Marcos, Department of (Guatemala), GU123, 268,
    550, 827, 1257
San Martin, José de, NI145
San Miguel, Department of (El Salvador), ES54, 341
San Miguel Milpas Alpas (Guatemala), GU975
San Miguel Panán (Guatemala), GU2
San Pablo (Guatemala), GU381
San Pablo de Heredia (Costa Rica), CR685
San Pedro Chenalho (Guatemala), GU678
San Pedro La Laguna (Guatemala), GU1045-46
San Pedro Nonualco (El Salvador), ES271
San Pedro Sacatepéquez (Guatemala), GU320
San Pedro Sula (Honduras), HO28, 58, 66, 101, 209,
    296, 374
San Pío (Nicaragua), CA723
San Ramón (Costa Rica), CR386, 688, 756, 944
San Salvador
-Conference of 1890, CA141
-Department of (El Salvador), CA315; ES65, 94, 239,
    394
-Earthquake of 1854, CA315
-Treaty of 1927, CA264
San Uraco (El Salvador), ES372
-Black Christ of, ES372
San Vicente (Costa Rica), CR552
-Department of (El Salvador), ES93
Sanabria Martínez, Víctor Manuel, CR73, 100, 126,
    1135

Sánchez, Cayetano, GU708
Sánchez, Delfino, GU1294
Sánchez Hernández, Fidel, ES96, 146, 374
Sánchez Lépiz, Julio, CR652, 712
Sánchez Reyes, Francisco, HO19, 92
Sandinistas. See Frente Sandinista de Liberación
    Nacional
Sandino, Augusto César, CA75, 491; ES25; NI8, 25-28,
    53, 58-59, 86-87, 131, 142, 144-45, 147, 159,
    190, 209, 211, 215, 227, 231, 281, 283-84, 299,
    351, 391, 397, 495, 542, 546, 552, 565, 579,
    592, 594, 602-3, 609, 626, 654, 660, 675
Sandoval, Francisco Ernesto, GU1217
Sandoval, José León, NI38
Santa Ana (Costa Rica), CR914
Santa Ana (El Salvador), ES174, 176, 234
-Convention of, ES55
Santa Ana Mixtan (Guatemala), GU789
Santa Barbara, Department of (Honduras), HO402
Santa Catarina Barahona (Guatemala), GU605
Santa Catarina Mita (Guatemala), GU1010
Santa Eulalia (Guatemala), GU606, 765
Santa Lucía Cotzumalguapa (Guatemala), GU516
Santa Rosa
-Battle of, CR272, 943, 950
-Department of, GU1426
Santa Rosa de Copán (Honduras). See Copan, Santa
    Rosa de (Honduras)
Santa Tecla (El Salvador), ES178
Santamaría, Juan, CR22, 187, 252, 275, 370, 456,
    500, 638, 737, 880, 900
Santamaría de Paredes, Vicente, CA206
Santiago Chimaltenango (Guatemala), GU1385-86
Santiago de los Caballeros de Guatemala, GU517, 1084
Santin del Castillo, Miguel, ES67
Santo Domingo (Costa Rica), CR913
Santo Domingo, Church of (Guatemala), GU1145-46
Santo Domingo Xenacoj (Guatemala), GU607
Santo Tomás, colony of (Guatemala), GU54, 178, 190,
    193-95, 213, 312-19, 417, 533, 761, 790, 987,
    1088, 1348
Santo Tomás Chichicastenango (Guatemala), GU217,
    1140, 1236
Santo Tomás de Castilla (Guatemala), GU1065
Sarapiqui River, CR484
Say, Juan Bautista, CA20-21
Schick, René, NI442
Schwartz, Gustavo, GU42
Scott, Joseph N., NI108
La Semana (Guatemala City), GU542
Seminario del Integración Social (Guatemala), GU109,
    114, 524, 709
Senahú (Guatemala), GU345-46, 1012
El Señor Presidente, GU500
Sensuntepeque (El Salvador), ES400
Servicio Nacional de Electricidad (Costa Rica),
    CR253-54, 972
Servicio Técnico Interamericano de Cooperación
    Agrícola (Costa Rica), CR27
Sevilla (Guatemala), GU1113
Seward, William, NI43
The Shark and the Sardines, GU963
Short stories, CA954
-Costa Rica, CR47, 55-58, 65, 92, 140, 144-45, 193,
    196-98, 356, 361-62, 380, 384, 389, 395-96, 425,
    429, 445-46, 451, 496-97, 559-60, 604, 614-15,
    636, 675-76, 678-79, 682, 689, 710, 720, 743,
    752, 785, 794, 838, 885-86, 888, 930-31, 935,
    944, 973, 994, 1055
-El Salvador, ES181, 215, 268, 286, 302, 310, 338-
    39, 343, 367, 373, 406

-Guatemala, GU4, 90-91, 95, 98-99, 125, 128-29, 143,
    150, 304, 375, 406, 445, 507-8, 751, 802, 804,
    836, 870-71, 881, 888, 914-16, 991, 1012, 1082,
    1100, 1123, 1164-65, 1167-68, 1190, 1194, 1209,
    1333, 1337, 1343, 1377-78, 1417, 1426
-Honduras, HO43, 64, 72, 76, 149, 326, 357, 394,
    396, 398, 409
-Nicaragua, NI3, 132-34, 185, 215, 217, 221, 244,
    317, 319-20, 332, 388, 514, 543, 545, 548, 560,
    599, 618-19, 643, 652
Shufeld Claim, GU1325
Sibun River, BE92
SIECA, CA128, 175
Sierra, Terencio, CA792; HO382, 497
Silva, José Enrique, CA305
Silver mines in Honduras, HO315
Simmons Construction Corporation (Costa Rica), CR244
Singapore, CA848
Slavery, CA236, 530
-Belize, BE28, 178
-El Salvador, ES107, 161
Social conditions. See individual countries
Social customs. See individual countries
Social Democratic Party, CR226; GU942, 1299
Social life. See individual countries
Social protest literature, CA968
-Costa Rica, CR196, 340-42, 355-62, 364, 395, 423-
    26, 429, 495, 510-13, 597, 676-77, 679, 682-83,
    690-91, 710, 713, 785-88, 887-88, 921, 935, 973,
    1063, 1071
-El Salvador, ES13, 16, 24, 196-97, 219, 287, 367-68
-Guatemala, GU18, 38-40, 131-32, 135, 179, 265, 270,
    303-5, 374-76, 406, 408, 429-30, 436, 445, 457-
    60, 462, 500, 512, 700-701, 712, 742, 754, 777,
    802-4, 881, 913-16, 919-20, 922-23, 1017-18,
    1052, 1062-64, 1067, 1096, 1098, 1137, 1162-63,
    1166, 1186, 1189-90, 1240, 1250, 1331, 1333,
    1337, 1343, 1355-56
-Honduras, HO20, 29, 43, 72-73, 78, 81, 156, 239,
    329, 357
-Nicaragua, NI58, 128-29, 146, 148-50, 185-86, 219,
    300, 388, 530, 543, 578, 643, 655
Social reform. See individual countries
Social security system. See individual countries
Social structure. See individual countries
Sociedad de Abogados de Honduras, CA367
Sociedad de Geografía e Historia de Guatemala, GU548
Sociedad Protectora de Niño (Guatemala), GU662
Society. See individual countries
Soconusco (Guatemala), CA159, 501-2, 551, 592, 598,
    770, 794, 965; GU820
Soil, CA228, 859; BE13, 56, 87, 166; CR378, 796,
    968; ES26; GU550; NI646
Solentiname, CA115
Soley Güell, Tomás, CR41
Solís, Ignacio, GU1334
Sololá, Department of (Guatemala), GU550, 1046-47
Somoza Debayle, Anastasio, NI191, 193, 211, 260,
    286, 292, 386, 411, 422, 442, 478, 488, 511,
    532, 567, 691, 704, 720
Somoza Debayle, Luís, CA488; NI198, 387, 604, 606-7
Somoza García, Anastasio, CA488, 658; CR36, 52, 430;
    HO30; NI13, 16-17, 19, 22, 25, 85, 131, 145,
    159, 197, 214, 231, 351, 389, 391, 422, 442,
    475, 509, 540, 544, 556, 559, 562, 575, 579,
    586, 592, 626, 642, 660, 662, 699, 720
Somoza Regime, CR36, 52; HO30; NI32, 51, 81, 117,
    141, 147-48, 150, 177, 179-80, 190, 213, 300,
    318, 378, 386, 422, 442, 477, 530, 576, 593,
    604-5, 607, 710, 720

Sosonate
-Annexation to El Salvador, CA43
-Department of (El Salvador), CA43; ES46, 188
Soriano, Nazario, HO193
Soto, Marco Aurelio, HO130, 360, 393, 397, 419
Soto Alfaro, Bernardo, CR625, 883, 1090
Soto Family, GU1265
South America, relations with Central America, CA10
Spain, CA391, 782, 784, 918; GU479
-Exile government of, GU956
--Relations with Central America, CA191, 444, 524
--Relations with Costa Rica, CR33
--Relations with El Salvador, ES322
--Relations with Guatemala, GU236, 276, 357, 1154
--Relations with Honduras, HO220-21
--Relations with Nicaragua, NI28, 216, 290
Spanish American War, NI208, 410
Spanish exile government, relations with Guatemala, GU956
Spanish Falange, GU357
Spanish influence in Costa Rica, CR581
Spiritual socialism in Guatemala, GU72-73, 76-77, 82, 118
Squier, Ephraim George, HO306; NI435
Stadium (Guatemala), GU1097
Standard Fruit and Steamship Company, CA480
Standard Fruit Company (Honduras), HO119, 202
Standard Oil Company in Nicaragua, NI602
Stann Creek (Belize), BE23, 69
Statistics. See individual countries
Steel in Central America, CA252
Stephens, John Lloyd, CA511
Stimson, Henry Lewis, NI426, 637, 683
Stone, Doris Zemurray, CR133
Stork, Juan Gaspar, CR762
Strachan, R. Kenneth, CR399, 940, 1029
Suárez, Clementina, GU712
Subirana, Manuel Jesús, HO27
Suchiate River, CA770
Suchitán (Guatemala), GU1023
Suez Canal, BE170; NI2, 202, 235, 322, 438, 482-83, 526, 533, 588, 641
Sumu Indians, NI196, 440
Suyapa, La Virgen de, HO45, 449
Swan Islands, HO99, 124, 136, 150
Sweden
--Relations with Central America, CA636
--Relations with Costa Rica, CR93
--Relations with Guatemala, CA485; GU1391

Tacoma (U.S.S.), Agreement, CA151-54, 427
Taft, William Howard, CA609, 741; CR561; NI728-29
Talamanca (Costa Rica), CR453, 492, 572, 889, 893-94
Tariff policy in Costa Rica, CR701, 749
Tariffs, CA300, 861
-Guatemala, GU1415
-Honduras, HO363
Tarrazú (Costa Rica), CR194, 774
TASS (Soviet Union), CR506
Tax, Sol, GU709
Taxation. See individual countries
Teculután (Guatemala), GU329
Tegucigalpa (Honduras), HO89, 126, 148, 208-9, 251, 379, 386, 394, 396, 398-99, 449
-Congress of 1920, CA617
-Plan of 1953, GU545, 797
Tehuantepec (Mexico), NI6, 44-45, 202, 384, 438, 529, 588, 641
Tela Railroad (Honduras), HO202
El Telegrama (Bogotá), CA96

Telegraph in Guatemala, GU152-53
Telephone and telegraph in Costa Rica, CR805
Television in El Salvador, ES293
Téllez, Andrés, GU1121
Tenth Interamerican Conference in Caracas (Guatemala), GU544
Terrorism
-Guatemala, GU1300, 1409
--Mid-20th century, GU546
Textiles, CA399
-Guatemala, GU53, 191, 591, 886, 972, 992, 1005-6, 1140, 1272, 1396
Theater, CA573
-Costa Rica, CR65, 68, 107, 109, 431, 590, 959, 961
-El Salvador, ES291-92, 340
-Guatemala, GU453, 456-60, 462, 493, 1260
-Honduras, HO487
-Nicaragua, NI219, NI566
Thiel, Bernardo Augusto, CR171, 705, 981, 1035
El Tiempo (Bogotá), CA352
El Tiempo (Managua), NI169
El Tiempo (Mexico), BE183
Tigre, Isla de, HO270, 387
Timber in Belize, BE64
Time (magazine), CA488
Tinoco, José Joaquín, CR166
Tinoco, Luís Demetrio, CR314
Tinoco Granados, Federico, CA266; CR147, 188, 191-92, 315, 423, 532-33, 561, 626, 698, 807, 831, 917, 938, 964, 1041, 1070, 1093, 1108, 1118
Tipitapa (Nicaragua), NI75
-Pact of 1927, NI637-38
Tipografía Nacional de Guatemala, GU367, 663-64, 1357
Tivives (Costa Rica), CR478
Tobasco (Mexico), CA773
Todos Santos Cuchumatán (Guatemala), GU983-84
Toribio Medina, José, GU468, 1309
Toriello Garrido, Guillermo, GU833, 837
Torrupan Indians, HO474
Tosta, Vicente, HO11, 117
Totonicapán, Department of (Guatemala), GU243, 269, 323, 442, 550, 677, 681, 1308
Tourism
-Belize, BE64
-Central America, CA253, 314, 769
--Early 20th century, CA801
-Costa Rica, CR379, 700, 760, 1067
--20th century, CR160
--Early 20th century, CR242
--Mid-20th century, CR939, 1133
-Guatemala, GU26, 994
--Late 19th century, GU582
--Early 20th century, GU580, 748
--Mid-20th century, GU1223
Towns
-El Salvador, ES56-57
-Guatemala, GU943, 1160
Trade. See individual countries
Transnational corporations in Guatemala. See Foreign corporations in Guatemala
Transportation. See individual countries
Travel. See individual countries
Treaty of Economic Integration, CA975
Trejos, Alfonso, CA305
Trejos, Escalante, Fernando, CR88
Trejos Fernandez, José Joaquín, CR88, 1050-51, 1077
La Tribuna (San José), CR41, 117, 241, 605, 883-84
Trinidad, Battle of, HO388
Tropical Trading and Transport Company, CR229

Trujillo (Honduras), HO4, 314
Trujillo Molina, Rafael, HO30
Turcios Lima, Luís Agosto, GU422, 950, 1313
Turner, Fitzhugh, CA807
Turrialba (Costa Rica), CR796, 838, 942, 978, 998
Turrubares (Costa Rica), CR992
Tzotzil Indians, GU678
Tzul, Atanasio, GU323

UBAD (United Black Association for Development)
    (Belize), BE120
Ubico, Jorge, CA47; BE8, 106, 152; GU16, 21, 29, 67,
    75-77, 103, 217, 239, 308, 340, 351, 373, 376,
    431, 453-54, 515, 531, 556, 568, 584, 625-26,
    632, 648, 693, 697, 755, 834-35, 842, 853, 866,
    897, 913, 942, 966, 1016, 1037-43, 1050, 1054-
    55, 1067, 1087, 1098, 1109, 1128, 1180, 1184,
    1193, 1207, 1211, 1221, 1233, 1356-57, 1425,
    1429-30; HO462
Ulate, Olga Marta, CR1057
Ulate Blanco, Otilio, CR430, 503, 777, 1057-58
UNESCO, CA220; CR480, 657, 897
Unión Democrática Centroamericana, CA813, 918-19
Union of Banana Exporting Countries, CA930
Unionism, CA129, 177, 187, 330, 344, 392, 517, 558,
    562, 572, 574, 584, 591, 628-30, 683, 764, 777,
    781, 792, 798, 808, 875, 976, 1013
Unionist movement, CA10, 29, 47-48, 51-52, 69, 71,
    81, 84, 90-91, 93-95, 109, 141-42, 176, 181,
    192, 208, 222, 244, 267, 290, 298, 330, 348,
    358, 395, 398, 417-18, 420, 422, 427, 450-51,
    469, 479, 487, 508, 512, 516, 520, 524-25, 532,
    552, 555, 558, 583, 585-90, 594, 596, 605, 613,
    617, 621, 632, 638, 680, 682, 728, 746, 749,
    755-56, 765, 772, 778, 783, 787, 797-98, 802,
    805-6, 809, 826, 867, 907, 916, 940, 959, 967,
    972-75, 1008, 1016, 1018; CR113, 123, 139, 693
-El Salvador, ES50, 55, 59-60, 67, 76, 79, 148, 177,
    182, 240, 257, 282, 350
-Guatemala, GU43, 48, 76-77, 89, 103, 113, 162, 180,
    186, 219, 242, 244, 257, 328, 552, 629, 774,
    792, 840, 861, 868, 897, 1013, 1143, 1180, 1203
-Honduras, CA940; HO10, 25, 42, 177, 181, 292, 438
-Nicaragua, NI590
Unionist Pact of 1921, CA979
Unionist Party, CA582-83, 585, 588, 781, 979
United Fruit Company, CA2, 75, 85, 212, 407, 483-84,
    509, 538, 569, 611, 614, 627, 737, 789, 803,
    852, 920, 930, 998, 1000; CR21, 29, 87, 117,
    133, 230, 238, 241, 297, 331, 605, 658, 898,
    947, 958, 962-63, 1044, 1061, 1138; ES61, 679;
    GU73, 137, 173, 175-76, 264, 278, 656, 680, 721,
    784, 893, 912, 921, 968, 1030-31, 1085, 1166,
    1241, 1301, 1304, 1390; HO48, 257, 263, 366,
    404, 442; NI28
United Nations, CA248, 346, 631, 799, 843; BE2, 14,
    72-73, 148, 151; CR50, 1008; ES92, 206, 216;
    GU479, 480, 628; HO308
United States
-Export-Import Bank, CR302
-Imperialism in Guatemala, GU78, 82, 93-94, 96, 104,
    131-32, 135, 137, 198, 240, 299, 451, 461, 968,
    1302, 1315
-Influence, CA208, 359
--Guatemala, CA6
--Honduras, CA6
-Intervention, CA37, 56, 70, 72, 81, 208, 232, 344,
    491, 509, 594, 609, 632, 719, 741, 804, 810,
    812, 814, 878, 916, 1002; CR506
--Costa Rica, CR428, 430, 917, 1031
--El Salvador, ES325
--Guatemala (1954), GU51, 80, 137, 139, 155-56, 264,
    278, 1007, 1034, 1105, 1111, 1303, 1364
--Honduras, HO43, 61, 322
--Nicaragua, CA344, 509, 515, 594, 644, 804, 810,
    814; CR489; NI8, 10, 17, 20, 23-24, 48, 61-63,
    103, 106, 145, 222, 231, 238, 242, 264, 280,
    297, 299, 342, 361, 368, 391, 397, 426, 428,
    441, 452, 479, 485, 495, 508, 538, 542-43, 552,
    562, 587-88, 590, 594, 601-3, 616, 628-30, 637-
    38, 654, 663, 668, 675, 683, 687, 699, 703, 713,
    716, 720, 728-29
-Investments, CA171, 212
--Costa Rica, CR558, 1098, 1120
--Honduras, HO48
-Marine Corps in Nicaragua, NI231, 297, 391, 495
-Nicaragua Surveying Party, NI415-16
-Presidents, CR313
-Relations with Belize, BE6, 164
-Relations with Caribbean, CA491, 643-44; NI716
-Relations with Central America, CA32, 37, 48, 61,
    70, 72, 75, 81, 85, 88, 91, 106, 116-17, 119,
    171, 208, 291, 344, 361-62, 391, 428, 476, 491,
    511, 537, 541, 594, 600, 609, 611, 626, 635,
    641, 643-44, 685, 688, 726, 740, 762, 785, 790,
    793, 804, 806-7, 809-10, 812, 814, 843, 850,
    878, 893, 916, 920, 923, 927, 989, 996, 1002,
    1005; CR126-27, 129, 428, 430, 489, 495, 506-7,
    581, 629; ES18, 40, 295; GU71, 299, 627, 859,
    1007; HO61, 122; NI31, 428, 601-2, 610, 628-29,
    711-13, 716
-Relations with Colombia, NI346
-Relations with Costa Rica, CA2, 869-70; CR59, 303,
    351, 424, 427-28, 430, 489, 494-95, 506, 561,
    595, 616, 629, 700-701, 717, 725, 753, 775, 778,
    828, 837, 917, 1026, 1044, 1070, 1079, 1089,
    1098, 1100, 1108, 1112, 1116, 1119-20; NI166,
    203-4, 206, 269, 385
-Relations with Cuba, CR416
-Relations with El Salvador, CA2, 274, 922; ES18,
    25-26, 73, 138, 149, 295-96, 353; GU478; NI158,
    167
-Relations with Guatemala, CA2, 274, 376, 811, 824,
    843, 922; GU26, 51, 71, 73, 80, 102, 104, 131-
    32, 135, 137, 166, 173, 175-76, 198, 214, 240-
    41, 264, 299, 343, 379, 401, 450-51, 461-62,
    478, 498, 531, 578, 582, 626-28, 630, 643, 647,
    658, 739, 818, 859, 877-78, 893, 905, 912, 915,
    921, 957, 963, 968, 979, 1007-8, 1034, 1069,
    1085, 1105, 1111, 1120, 1221, 1228-30, 1240-41,
    1279, 1302-4, 1316-25, 1364, 1382, 1390, 1402
-Relations with Great Britain, CA685; HO340-41;
    NI70, 192, 252, 280, 343, 346, 352, 370, 393,
    680, 685, 718
-Relations with Honduras, CA274; HO4, 11, 21-22,
    37, 43, 48-50, 61, 99, 114, 116, 124-25, 202,
    211, 228, 270, 306, 322, 340-41, 366, 404, 445,
    468, 486; NI31
-Relations with Latin America, CA809, 878; CR1089;
    HO61; NI596, 601, 610, 628-29
-Relations with Mexico, CA376, 770; NI602, 711-12
-Relations with Nicaragua, CA72, 344, 594, 643,
    744, 804, 810, 814, 869-70, 878, 922; CR430,
    489, 815; GU299, 478, 680; NI4, 8, 10-12, 20,
    23-28, 30-31, 43, 47-48, 50, 59, 61-63, 66-68,
    70-72, 75-76, 82-83, 86-87, 90, 93, 103-8, 115,
    118, 121, 130, 139, 142, 144-45, 150-54, 158,
    160, 166-67, 172, 176, 180, 191-93, 198, 202-4,
    206-9, 222-25, 229, 231, 236-38, 240-42, 245,

(United States)
248, 251-52, 254-56, 264, 280, 291, 293-94, 299,
303, 321-22, 335, 337-38, 342-43, 346, 348-49,
352, 359, 361, 367-68, 371, 378, 385, 391, 393,
395, 397-400, 405, 413, 415-17, 420-21, 423,
426, 428, 435-36, 438, 441, 447-52, 469, 472,
479, 482-83, 485, 491, 495, 506, 508, 510, 519-
20, 522, 524, 526, 538, 543, 549-53, 555-56,
564-65, 570-75, 577, 579, 582, 587-88, 590, 592,
594, 596, 600, 602-3, 606, 609-10, 615-16, 620,
626, 629-30, 632-33, 637-38, 644-46, 653-54,
663, 668-88, 690, 699-700, 703, 705, 707, 709,
711, 712-16, 718, 721-22, 728-29
-Relations with Panama, CA643
-Settlers in Costa Rica, CR782
United States and Central American Union, CA805
United States Technical Cooperation Administration,
CR50
Univad Revolucionaria Democrática (URD) Party
(Guatemala), GU1380
El Universal (Mexico City), CA807; GU814, 1061
Universidad Centroamericana José Simeón Cañas. See
Universities, El Salvador
Universities, CA220-21, 601, 881-82, 915, 953, 972,
981
-Costa Rica, CA36; CR79, 174, 217, 234-35, 237, 414,
499, 536, 574, 591, 758, 813, 824, 910, 928,
954, 1023, 1030, 1052
-El Salvador, CA36, 305; ES87, 99, 101-2, 173, 187,
320, 365
-Guatemala, CA36, 44, 49, 236, 400; GU33, 92, 136,
227, 282, 424-25, 428, 553, 699, 735, 771, 823,
847-48, 1016, 1097, 1158, 1172, 1354
-Honduras, CA36; HO92, 147, 173-75, 182, 277, 376,
401, 451, 485
-Latin America, NI274
-Nicaragua, CA36; NI54, 65, 274, 431, 433, 453, 487,
544, 666
-Panama, CA36
University of Chile, CR499; ES3
University of San Carlos. See Universities,
Guatemala
University of Santo Tomás. See Universities, Costa
Rica
Upala (Costa Rica), CR286
Uprising of 1897 (Nicaragua), NI199
Urbanization of Costa Rica. See Cities, Costa Rica
Uriarte, Juan Ramón, CA598
Uruguay, relations with Guatemala, GU898
Use of the English language in Costa Rica, CR1138
USIA, CA175
USSR, GU1035, 1056, 1232
-Relations with Guatemala, GU1409

Valentine, Washington S., HO322
Valladares, Paulino, HO285, 330, 439
Valle, Department of (Honduras), HO159
Valle, José Cecilio del, CA101, 124, 507, 513, 528,
576, 580, 699, 722, 732, 796, 904, 943-48, 950,
952; HO8, 79
Valle, Rafael Heliodoro, HO1, 46
Vallejo, Antonio Ramón, HO14, 375
Valverde, Panfilo J., CR455
Vanderbuilt, Cornelius, NI108
Vanguardia Popular (Costa Rica), CR430, 506, 588,
777, 852
Vanguardista School of Poetry (Nicaragua), NI56-726
Vásquez, Domingo, HO23, 84, 137, 283
Vásquez, Mariano, HO413
Vatican II Council, GU482
Vegetation, CA98, 859, 982

-Belize, BE53, 85, 87, 146, 166, 174
-Costa Rica, CA775; CR210, 647, 727
-El Salvador, ES208
-Guatemala, GU214, 945, 974, 1177
-Honduras, HO309, 405, 425, 479
-Nicaragua, CA775; NI88, 92, 380, 507, 649
-Panama, CA775
Vela, Francisco, GU869
Venezuela, CA636; CR177
-Relations with Guatemala, GU84
Veragua, CA245
Verapaz (Guatemala), CA839; GU101, 249, 289, 394,
710, 761, 945, 1177, 1377-78, 1405
La Verdad Histórica, CA616
Verdugo Family, GU148
Vesco, Robert, CR1031-32
Viajes Presidenciales, GU966
Vicente, Filisolas, CA309
Vicente, Nicolas, ES371
Viceroyalty of New Spain. See New Spain,
Viceroyalty of
Victoria, Province of (Nicaragua), NI119
Vidaurre, Adrián, GU1369
Vietnam, GU1035
Vilches, Agustin, GU1212
Vilacorta, Juan Vicente, CA527
Villacorta Calderón, José Antonio, GU1373
Villeda Morales, José Ramón, HO42, 231, 259, 366,
468-69, 471
Vincenzi Pacheco, Moisés, CR137, 164
Víquez, Pío J., CR744
La Virgen de Los Angeles, CR108
Virgen del Rosario de Guatemala, GU1145-46
Virgen del Socorro de Guatemala, GU1208
Volcanoes, CA237, 360, 615, 828, 837, 862, 992
-Costa Rica, CA681; CR206, 345, 556, 997
-El Salvador, CA640; ES84, 230
-Guatemala, CA640; GU202, 463, 781, 948
-Honduras, CA640
-Nicaragua, CA681
Volio Jiménez, Claudio María, CR653
Volio Jiménez, Jorge, CR7, 147, 316, 331, 1095
La Voz de México, CA551

Walker, John G., NI679, 689
Walker, William, CA37, 55, 348, 914, 916; CR22, 59,
126-27, 129, 172-73, 185, 187, 246, 252, 271-77,
370, 428, 445-46, 456, 500, 614, 616, 638, 727,
734, 737, 764, 815, 880-81, 900, 943, 945, 950,
961, 966, 1054; ES235; GU299; HO95, 287, 495;
NI11-12, 28, 30, 35, 71-72, 75, 83, 107-8, 130,
146, 152, 160, 174, 176, 183-84, 187, 225, 245,
248, 262, 293, 303, 321, 349, 363, 390, 402,
406, 435-36, 446, 491-92, 506, 508, 519-20, 524,
550-51, 570-71, 582, 590, 600, 628, 631, 636,
652, 661, 694, 700, 705, 711-13, 716, 718
Walker Commission (Nicaragua), NI421, 676, 689-90
War of 1894 (Honduras and Nicaragua), NI470
War of 1906 (El Salvador and Guatemala), ES48, 240,
350; GU1194
War of 1907 (Honduras and Nicaragua), NI468
War of 1969 (El Salvador and Honduras), CA90, 110,
116-17, 133, 242, 260, 265, 271, 313, 356, 418,
421, 426, 467, 533, 535, 558, 579, 627, 695,
701, 763, 799, 967, 969-70, 1002; ES38, 206,
401; HO31, 35, 122, 125, 245, 259, 369
Wars in Central America, CA780, 1009
Washington, George, NI145

Washington Treaties of 1907, CA130, 144-45, 156-57, 266, 268, 330, 522, 632, 643, 750, 764, 926; HO90, 332
Washington Treaties of 1923, CA151-54, 330, 337, 479, 632, 643, 926; ES18, 138-39, NI23, 229
Water purification in Costa Rica, CR613
Water resources, CA859
-Belize, BE70
-Costa Rica, CR299, 892
-Guatemala, GU1332
Webster, William, CR1100
Weights and measures in Central America, CA248
Wesleyan Mission in Belize, BE26
West Indian settlement in Belize, BE80
West Indies, CA14, 852; BE48, 80-81, 99; GU767
Weyl, Richard, CA572
Wheeler, John Hill, NI718
White, Edward Douglas. See White Award
White Award, CA15, 30, 103, 195-98, 229, 689-93, 738-39, 993
White Book. See Libro Blanco
Wicker, Cyrus French, CR1112
Wilbur, Curtis D., NI675
Williams Calderón, Abraham, HO345
Wilson, Woodrow, CA594; CR489, 506, 532, 917, 1070, 1094, 1108; ES296; HO61, 290; NI47, 574, 715
Women, CA334, 966
-Costa Rica, CR5, 155, 848, 966, 995, 1080
-El Salvador, ES224
-Guatemala, GU247, 742, 1350
-Honduras, HO55, 246
-Nicaragua, NI247, 612, 656
--Mid-20th century, NI247, 612
Women voting rights
-Costa Rica, CR1080
-Nicaragua, NI612
Woodcarving, CR464, 1130
World Colombian Exposition in Chicago, CR131
World War I, CR120, 421, 713; ES276; GU1175; HO218
World War II, CA595, 847-48; BE66; CR12, 302, 595, 951; GU97, 357, 626, 730, 1069, 1096, 1228-30; HO155, 486; NI28, 121, 216, 237, 347
Wyld Ospina, Carlos, GU519, 807

Xatruch, Florencio, HO495
Xelajú (Guatemala), GU1135

Ydígoras Fuentes, Miguel, CA798; GU341, 477, 642, 680, 688, 753, 1176, 1315, 1327, 1408-9, 1427
Yglesias, Antonio, CR590
Yglesias, Francisco María. See Iglesias, Francisco María
Yglesias Castro, Rafael, CR158, 247-48, 301, 455, 606, 769, 863, 932, 1101-2
Yon Sosa, Marco Antonio, GU950
Yoro (Honduras), CA244; HO26, 249
Young, Arthur N., HO481
Young, John Parke, GU979
Yucatán, CA4, 335-36; BE54-55, 75, 78, 92, 117, 134, 144, 160, 173, 214; GU197
-Captaincy General of, BE75, 173

Zacapa, Department of (Guatemala), GU64, 249, 329, 477, 677, 958, 1019-20, 1138
Zaldívar, Rafael, ES240, 350
Zamora, Santiago, CR1056
Zapata C., Adrián, GU1412
Zaragoza (Guatemala), GU887
Zarco, Isidoro, GU1414
Zavala, Joaquín, NI721
Zavaleta, Matías, CR1066

Zea, Pedro Antonio, GU779
Zelaya, José Santos, CA190, 607, 688, 792, 1007; CR877; NI9, 40, 49, 110, 116, 125, 171, 182, 195, 199, 267, 291, 374, 394, 458, 468, 538, 608, 610, 674, 728-29
Zelaya Lozano, Cecilio, HO485
Zelaya Villegas, Ramón, CR419
Zeladón, Benjamin F., NI203-4
Zeladón, José María, CR728
Zemurray, Samuel, HO436
Zepeda y Zepeda, Juan de Jesús, HO151
Zúñiga, Adolfo, HO392
Zúñiga, Francisco, CR464, 1130
Zúñiga, Luís Andrés, HO79
Zúñiga Huete, Ángel, HO85, 103, 342, 344, 347, 411, 490, 492